FLINT
Denbigh
DENBIGH
Mari
Jones
Llangwm
Bala
Thomas
Charles
MEIRIONETH
Machynlleth
MONTGOMERY
North Wales

The CALVINISTIC METHODIST FATHERS OF WALES

VOLUME TWO

The statue at Bala of Thomas Charles

The CALVINISTIC METHODIST FATHERS OF WALES

VOLUME TWO

JOHN MORGAN JONES
AND WILLIAM MORGAN

Translated by JOHN AARON

THE BANNER OF TRUTH TRUST

THE BANNER OF TRUTH TRUST
3 Murrayfield Road, Edinburgh EH12 6EL, UK
P.O. Box 621, Carlisle, PA 17013, USA

*

Originally published in Welsh as
Y Tadau Methodistaidd, vol. 2, 1897

First Banner of Truth edition 2008

ISBN-13: 978 0 85151 976 0

*

Typeset in 10.5 / 13 pt Adobe Caslon
at the Banner of Truth Trust

Printed in the U.S.A. by
Versa Press, Inc.,
East Peoria, IL

CONTENTS

Illustrations

Illustrations from the original Welsh edition have been inserted between pp. 186–7, 377–8, and 632–3.

ABBREVIATIONS

The following abbreviations are used in the notes:

CH	*The Journal of the Historical Society of the Presbyterian Church of Wales.* CH followed by a number is used for the first sixty volumes (up to 1976); CH followed by a year, e.g. CH, 1980, is used for later volumes.
CH, MS	*Manuscript Supplements* of this *Journal*, issued in two series, (i) and (ii).
CMHO	D. E. Jenkins, *Calvinistic Methodist Holy Orders* (Caernarvon, 1911).
HHRS	Tom Beynon, *Howell Harris, Reformer and Soldier* (Caernarvon, 1958).
HHVL	Tom Beynon, *Howell Harris's Visits to London* (Aberystwyth, 1960).
HHVP	Tom Beynon, *Howell Harris's Visits to Pembrokeshire* (Aberystwyth, 1966).
HJH	Hugh J. Hughes, *Life of Howell Harris* (London, 1892).
STL, vol. 1	Gomer M. Roberts, *Selected Trevecka Letters* (1742–1747) (Caernarvon, 1956).
STL, vol. 2	Gomer M. Roberts, *Selected Trevecka Letters* (1747–1794) (Caernarvon, 1962).

21

THE BEGINNINGS OF METHODISM IN THE VARIOUS DISTRICTS OF GWYNEDD

HOWELL HARRIS'S FIRST JOURNEY TO MONTGOMERYSHIRE

As far as is known, the first sermon preached by a Methodist in north Wales was delivered by Howell Harris on 8 February 1740, in a place called Lodge in the parish of Llandinam. There is no doubt whatsoever about the date. It is given in Harris's journal and also in the letters he wrote when on this journey. These confirm that the year was 1740, and not 1739 as found in *Methodistiaeth Cymru*.[1] Howell Harris undertook the venture mainly on the instigation of the Rev. Lewis Rees, who was then a Nonconformist minister at Llanbryn-mair. As he faced the north for the first time, the Reformer knew that he was entering into dangers. The nobility of Montgomeryshire were enemies of the gospel and had sworn to imprison the first Methodist that set foot on their lands. But the Evangelist of Trefeca was not one to be stopped by threats; he considered it rather a pure pleasure to face dangers for Christ's sake. During his preparations in the previous year for the visit to Montgomery, he had received a haughty letter from the vicar of Llandinam, a John Tilsbury, warning him to keep away and comparing his behaviour when preaching without ordination to the people to that of Nadab and Abihu offering strange fire with their sacrifices. It may be inferred from the letter that many from the Llandinam neighbourhood had crossed the mountains to hear Harris when he preached in various parts of Radnorshire, and had been converted under his ministry. The clergyman wrote:

> I would leave you forever to enjoy your dearly-held opinion of yourself were it not that the responsibility which is laid upon me to safeguard the eternal welfare of the souls of my parishioners requires me to ask of you, in a peaceable manner, not to sound your trumpet in such an unwarranted way, a way contrary to the laws of God and men, in my parish from henceforth. I would ensure you that your severe manner in exhorting and pouring out the wrath of

> God on ignorant hearers in your extempore addresses, have not only enticed many in my parish and the neighbouring parishes to live in schism, and to end their days under the guilt thereof, as there is reason to fear. But further, what I cannot touch upon without horror, you have left many in a state of despair, or with only a little expectation of mercy; and if they die in this condition, to what degree you will be responsible for their eternal destruction, I leave God to judge.

John Tilsbury's letter was, no doubt, typical of the attitude of mind of the parsons of the Established Church of north Wales, even the best and most peaceable of them. They were in horror of a lay person undertaking the work of counselling men with regard to religious matters, and they considered conviction to be a form of madness leading to destruction. The above quotation raises many points of great interest:

1. It suggests that either Harris, on previous journeys to Radnorshire, had crossed the boundary into Montgomeryshire and had preached within the bounds of Llandinam parish, or, that quite a number from Montgomeryshire, living close to the boundary, had gone over to Radnorshire to hear him. The flow of the letter implies that the first is the meaning intended.

2. It suggests also that his ministry had been effective to the conviction of many of these, and that some had been so deeply convicted that they had been pressed to the brink of despair.

3. Finally, it suggests that either those who had experienced the power of the gospel had begun to meet together on their own in societies and prayer meetings, or, at the least, that they had turned their backs completely on the Church.

But as we noted, it was in February, 1740, that Harris made the first trip north. He was given a glorious service at Llandinam. Great shouting broke out; there groans ascended to the heavens and tears flowed down a hundred cheeks. He says that he was as one carried out of himself. We do not have a list of all the places that he visited, but he probably preached at Llanidloes, Trefeglwys, Llanbryn-mair, Cemais, Machynlleth, and perhaps other places. He had some notable meetings and many were saved who afterwards were at the forefront of Methodism. In all probability this is when the remarkable Lewis Evan, Llanllugan, was convicted. The noblemen of Montgomeryshire kept their word that they would persecute those that came with the gospel. At Cemais, Harris was put in prison on the authority of the magistrates, whose leader was a Mr Wynne. On providing sureties that he would appear for trial at Montgomery, he was released. At Bala, on his return from this same journey, he almost lost his life because of the work of the clergy in stirring up the anger of the mob. Almost certainly he established many societies during this trip but the number of them, and the number of their members, is not known. Howell Harris also certainly visited many places in Montgomeryshire during his second visit to Bala in 1741; he could not have reached Merionethshire without passing through parts of Montgomeryshire.

Daniel Rowland also probably visited parts of Montgomeryshire. The southern part of the county is not too far from Llangeitho and was accessible to him when he journeyed to other areas in the north. We may conclude also that William Williams entered the county from time to time, especially during the period when he was a curate at Llanwrtyd. But it is to Harris that the honour of being the main instrument for the evangelization of the county belongs. As the county borders on to Radnorshire and Breconshire, Harris's first fields of ministry and the neighbourhoods where he laboured most throughout the years of his connection with the Methodists, Montgomeryshire always had a particular share in his endeavours. Hardly a month would pass without a visit from him to some part of it. From his viewpoint, Montgomeryshire did not belong to the north. When he was making arrangements for a trip to the north, or was complaining that the north was to a considerable extent closed to the gospel, he would not have been including Montgomeryshire. The county therefore received the same religious advantages during the early years of Methodism as did the south. It contained many strong societies before any, or at least, any of real strength, had been established in Gwynedd. Harris was assisted in his labours in Montgomeryshire by many exhorters, the most notable being Richard Tibbott and Lewis Evan, Llanllugan. The names of others are known: Evan Jenkins, a cobbler from Llanidloes; Evan Morgan, Glyn-gywydd; Rheinallt Cleaton; John Thomas, a schoolmaster; and Benjamin Cadman. The latter was the cause of some considerable trouble because he could not decide whether to throw in his lot with the Methodists or with the Nonconformists. His case was discussed at many an Association; eventually he joined the Nonconformists.

Montgomeryshire was deeply stricken by the controversy between Harris and the Methodists. Richard Tibbott and Lewis Evan remained faithful to Harris at first. Harris, as we have mentioned, was the founder of most of the societies of the county and it is therefore very probable that most of them counted themselves in his party. But after his retreat into Trefeca, and Tibbott's and Evans's joining with Rowland's people, most of the Montgomeryshire societies probably followed their example. But there was very little life in the county. One exhorter, Thomas Meredith, joined forces with

Thomas Sheen, and after failing to conform to the discipline at Trefeca, they attempted to form a party of their own. In *Drych yr Amseroedd*[2] their doctrine is described as follows:

> They borrowed much from the work of Mr Cudworth, and many things from the most difficult parts to understand of the works of Mr Morgan Llwyd and of William Erbury, and in order to make their beliefs as spiritual as possible, they added a good deal of the leaven of the Quakers on top of everything else. Having brought all these ingredients together, their religion was a tramp's patched-up garment of a thing, hard to make head or tail of. They had no literal understanding of any part of the Scriptures but spiritualized it all. For example, it is not this earth that we live upon that shall be burned up, but the earth that is within man. The sun that shall be darkened is the sun of reason. The two grinding at the mill are the two natures. They had no respect for the Sabbath nor for any of the gospel ordinances.

Strangely enough, this weird religion found adherents in five counties in Wales, but was strongest of all in Montgomeryshire. Though it eventually gradually declined, its influence was very damaging to the Methodist causes. Little life prevailed until the great revival of 1762 – carried by the hymns of William Williams and spreading throughout the whole of Wales – reached Montgomeryshire. God remembered his covenant and the Sun of Righteousness shone upon hundreds that before were at ease in the valley of the shadow of death. We noted that Howell Harris considered this revival to be more spiritual and less carnal than any that accompanied his earlier ministry. Robert Jones, Rhos-lan, in *Drych yr Amseroedd*, also refers to the difference between the two periods of revival. Of the awakening at Harris's first emergence, he says:

> It was, in its method of acting, very severe and fiery; but this (the 1762 revival) was as of old, in Cornelius's house – numerous multitudes glorifying God without being able to stop, and sometimes jumping for joy, as David before the ark. Whole nights were sometimes spent in singing and praising, like a crowd on a feast-day.

Hundreds joined the societies at this time, and Methodism increased in honour and respect throughout the land.

PERSECUTION IN MONTGOMERYSHIRE

No other county offered so much persecution to the gospel than Montgomeryshire. The nobility of the county in particular were noted for their enmity and oppression. We have already referred to the awful attacks at Llanidloes and Newtown in 1744 on James Beaumont, and William Evans, the warm-hearted exhorter from Nantmel. We mentioned also how a number of Methodists of the county were summoned to the Sessions at Bangor at the beginning of the same year, and how they obtained a solicitor to defend them. No account of the trial has survived, unfortunately, but certainly the Lord would have defended his own who trusted in him, and secured for them a victory over their persecutors. To the extent that the persecution of Montgomeryshire was the fiercest in Wales, so also it continued longer than in any other county. Opposition to the preaching of the gospel was manifested at Llanidloes as late as 1819. During a feast-day fair in that year, John Elias preached from a waggon placed in the street, opposite the Lion Inn. The permission of the owner of the nearest house had been obtained. The fame of the preacher had gathered together a vast crowd; some five thousand were thought to be present. After Humphrey Gwalchmai had begun the service and a hymn had been sung, Mr Elias took John 12:32 as a text, 'And I, if I be lifted up from the earth, will draw all men unto me.' He was permitted to proceed for about half an hour, and the congregation as usual were captivated by his words. Then, a Justice of the Peace arrived and, having pushed through the crowd, he called Mr Hugh Jones, an elder of considerable standing with the Methodists of the town, to him. His message was a command for the preacher to stop speaking. Mr Jones and others pleaded that Mr Elias be allowed to continue for a little longer and they succeeded in placating the man for about another twenty minutes. But by then his patience was at an end; he climbed on to the waggon and, placing his hand on the preacher's shoulder, ordered him to stop. The crowd were greatly disturbed; many were frightened, but the vast majority were filled with indignation that a gentleman should dare to obstruct the preaching of Christ. But John Elias, turning towards him, asked him quietly if he might be allowed to dismiss the people by prayer. This was granted. It is said that the service, though cut short, was sufficient to put a complete end to the fair. Mr Elias went from there to the chapel and advised the people not to show any anger towards the gentleman in that it was clear that he had been urged on by others. As far as we know, this was the last attempt in Wales to keep the Methodists from preaching.

As already noted, Howell Harris visited some places in Merionethshire – Llanuwchllyn and Bala in particular – in 1740, the year in which he first visited Montgomeryshire. He preached at Bala the next year also and only just escaped with his life. Almost certainly also, Daniel Rowland visited parts of Merionethshire in 1740, being permitted to preach because he was ordained but preaching only in the churches. Yet, though many people were converted through the ministries of these two men, no

Methodist society was formed in Merionethshire until 1745, when eight brethren and sisters met together in Bala. Previously they had joined with the few Nonconformists meeting at the home of Edward Williams, the weaver. Amongst these first members of the Bala society was John Evans, Bala, and his wife, but John Evans had not at this time begun to preach. A persecuting spirit was still abroad at Bala and the believers only dared to meet together secretly and before daybreak. In order to be sure of waking, they would tie a string to some part of their body as they went to bed the night before the society meeting, and let the other end of the string hang outside the window. A person would then be appointed to go past all their houses plucking on the line. It is said that the most faithful in this work was Evan Moses, the blacksmith, a man from the south.

In order to strengthen the weak causes in the north, the Association appointed four brethren from the south to live in Gwynedd for four months, labouring with all might and main. These men were Dafydd William Dafydd, John Belcher, Benjamin Thomas, and Dafydd William Rhys, and it seems that they made their home in Bala. It would appear that no other society was formed in Merionethshire until after 1750, because in the October of that year, Howell Harris went about the whole of Gwynedd seeking to persuade the societies to join his party, and the only place in Merionethshire that he visited, according to his journal, was Bala. It is not certain what influence he had on the society but he was probably not successful because he wrote that he spoke severely to the believers, though he had great liberty to preach. Probably, again, it was John Evans who would not be persuaded, and his influence was sufficient to keep the other members from joining Harris.

LOWRI WILLIAMS SETTLES AT PANDY-Y-DDWYRYD, BRINGING THE GOSPEL WITH HER

The second society formed in Merionethshire was almost certainly that of Pandy-y-ddwyryd in Maentwrog, about the year 1755. This was achieved through the work of a woman called Lowri Williams. She was from Caernarvonshire and had been a member of the society at Brynengan, but because she and her husband would not leave the Methodists, even though her husband was not a believer, they had been turned out of their cottage, Pandy-chwilog. From their next home, Pandy-y-ddwyryd, they had fifteen miles to walk to Brynengan and eighteen miles to Bala, and no preaching that was acceptable to Lowri Williams was to be had anywhere nearer. Nor was there anybody else in the neighbourhood of the same mind as her and interested in religion. She therefore decided that preachers must come to her own home. Slowly, a society was gathered together – eight in number, and so they became known as 'Noah's ark's family'. Soon another five joined the eight. These members were very scattered, living many miles from one another – one in Harlech, one in Ffestiniog, another in Trawsfynydd, and another in Llanfrothen parish. These became candles, illuminating their various neighbourhoods, and under God's blessing were the means of bringing the gospel to their various localities.

Lowri Williams was not satisfied merely with having brought preaching to her area; she spoke of the gospel to all and was then diligent in prayer to heaven for a blessing upon the word that had gone forth. One man for whom her words became the means of opening his eyes to his condition, and who afterwards became useful in the work of the gospel, was Griffith Ellis, Penyrallt, near Harlech. While still a young man, he was walking one day to a feast-day fair held in the Ffestiniog area. He passed Pandy-y-ddwyryd on the way and as he had to cross a river to get to the fair, he called at Lowri Williams's house to ask the way to the crossing-point. She very willingly went with him to show him the way, and as they went, she said:

'Well, my boy, do you not ask for the way to life on the Sunday?'

'No, I don't,' he replied. 'Nor do I bother about such things.'

'Come here at such and such a time.' she said. 'There will be a man here who will show you the way to heaven.' And with these words she sent an arrow of prayer to heaven on his behalf.

'No I won't at all,' answered the careless boy and off he went, his mind full of the pleasures of the fair before him. But the arrow from Lowri Williams's bow had reached his conscience. The question, 'Do you not ask for the way to life?' sounded in his ears continually, and try as he might he could not free himself from it. He kept asking himself, 'What life did she mean? And what kind of way was it to it?' And the arrow of prayer was as a spear in his side so that he had no rest day or night. Although he had meant it when he said that he would not go to the meeting, he could not stop himself from going. There was an insistence within him to hear what the man had to say about the way to life. To the meeting he went, and his journey was not in vain. He was shown his guilty state and God's way of saving the guilty, so that he decided to leave his old practices and sinful company and give himself to the Lord's service for the rest of his life. He proved a faithful servant in his house. Griffith Ellis was of great blessing to his own locality and to neighbouring localities and is still remembered with gratitude to this day. It is said that his godliness was so evident and his words so scathing that the ungodly clergymen of the parish would fear to meet with him on the street. His concern for the cause was so great that he would, in the midst of his ploughing, leave his yoke of oxen at midday and walk twenty miles to ensure a preacher for Harlech for the coming Sunday. John Evans of Bala had a similar testimony to that of Griffith Ellis. He would relate how, before he began to preach, he would often walk, with two other brethren from Bala, to a place called Blaenlliw to hold a prayer meeting at nine o'clock on a Sunday morning; from there to Pandy-y-ddwyryd by two; and then returning home that night – a total distance of about thirty-five miles. He used to say that they would have liked to have stopped for some bread and cheese at Trawsfynydd on returning, but that they had to keep well away from that village because of persecution.

The Rev. Richard Humphreys, Dyffryn, in a series of articles, described the condition of Merionethshire, and of the Ardudwy Valley in particular, before the coming of Methodism, comparing it to the situation afterwards. He recorded a conversation that took place between himself and Lowri Williams of Penar Isaf, a shrewd and discerning believer, who remembered clearly the events and history of her native region as far back as 1750.

'What do you think of the world, Aunt Lowri?' said Richard Humphreys. 'I would be glad to have your opinion, because you remember much of its ways over eighty years. Some insist that it is going from bad to worse, for all the preaching, the Sunday Schools, and all the means made use of to improve matters. What do you think? For you have witnessed all these changes.'

'I don't really know how to answer you,' she replied, 'but if I remember correctly, the world was a wicked place then, that is when I was a young girl. The young people spent their time in evenings of entertainment, in singing to the harp, listening to interludes, playing cards, sports, and roof tennis; and the old sat and watched them. The Sundays of my earliest days were days of dancing and singing. And everyone was the same . . . there was no one who stood out as being righteous.'

'But Aunt Lowri,' said Mr Humphreys again, 'what about the state of things today? Are things better or worse?'

'It must be confessed,' said Lowri Williams, 'that there is still plenty of wild and unruly behaviour in the world, together with prejudice, anger and envy. But there appear to me to be two kinds of people at large presently. There are some who are attempting to improve the world and to remove its bad practices. You can now see both bad and good. When I was young there was only bad and worse. There are many advantages for the boys and girls of today, so many more than in my days. There was hardly anything then to restrain wickedness except poverty, the punishment of thieves and the hanging of murderers.'

No doubt this was a good description of the transformation wrought by Methodism in hundreds of regions throughout Wales as well as in Ardudwy. There were evil men, presumptuous sinners and law-breakers to be had after the rise of Methodism, but there were other men to be had also, who, as the salt of the earth, sought to counteract the evil men of this world and who endeavoured to bring them to learn of the Saviour. These did not exist previously; then, there was only bad and worse.

SEVERE PERSECUTION AT DOLGELLAU

According to John Evans, Bala, the cause at Dolgellau began about 1766. At that time a religious woman called Jane Griffith came to the town to keep a school. She had been born and bred in a place called Erwbach, near Dolbenmaen, Caernarvonshire, so most probably she had attended the society at Brynengan. This good woman would converse with whoever would listen of the evil of sin and the miserable state of mankind because of the Fall. In this way she befriended a few poor people. When Jane Griffith eventually left the area, these few who remained could no longer endure without the word of life and, soon, preachers from Caernarvonshire and Bala came to minister to them. But their lives were in great danger; the town and the whole neighbourhood were raging against the new way of exhorting people in private houses and on the highway, and were strong supporters of the sports and other corrupt practices. The brethren from Bala rented a house called Pant-y-cra, about a mile from Dolgellau, in order to preach there.

One Sunday, Mr Thomas Foulkes of Bala had promised to come to exhort. The news spread like wildfire and the population was thoroughly aroused. By the appointed hour, crowds had gathered from the town and the countryside about, vowing that if the exhorter arrived they would kill him and bury his body in a peaty pool nearby. When the brethren understood the vicious mood of the crowd they went to meet Mr Foulkes and prevented him from coming to them. The persecutors, having been disappointed, attacked the house and pulled down part of it. Then a little later, upon realizing that they had broken the law, they repaired the damage. The brethren ventured to meet for exhortation at a later date and, little by little, preaching commenced in the town.

The persecution however was not yet finished. One day, three men from the south were announced to preach at Dolgellau. Again the population was stirred to anger and decided that the three men would not escape without being beaten, if not killed. They therefore kept a close watch on the two bridges at either end of the town. But believers from Dolgellau took charge of the preachers' horses, while others of the brethren led the three exhorters on foot through the river above the bridge, so that they escaped. One of the local believers however was hit on the head by a stone and fell down. His attackers then ran away, thinking that they had killed him.

At another time, one of Howell Harris's followers visited the town, presuming to preach publicly in the market-place, but he was eventually glad enough to be able to climb on to his horse and escape in haste. His persecutors arose and demanded, in their rage and fury, that he be torn in pieces. One of them came with a poacher's trident in his hand, meaning to pierce him through. The preacher was stopped by a closed gate, but the wife of the man with the trident came and opened it for him, and so, by God's grace, he escaped. From all accounts it is clear that the early believers of Dolgellau had to suffer for many years. Not only was their persecution more heated than in other places but it also lasted far longer.

Robert Jones, Rhos-lan, wrote:

> It would take too long to recite all the troubles and sufferings endured by many of the godly pilgrims there [i.e. at Dolgellau], who are now [1820], nearly all, resting peacefully from their labours. For many years, they had to go quietly into the town at night and hold their services before daybreak. They would then slip away before dawn and before the lions awoke from their dens. A man would be appointed to keep awake all night and to go about to wake each one in order for them to be up for the service. God prospered his work remarkably there, in the face of every tempest.

On one occasion, Peter Williams preached at Esgeiriau, a cottage about a quarter of a mile from the town and close to a deep gorge known as Ceunant Stuckley. Attackers burst into the cottage, extinguished the candles, broke up the furniture and threw the pieces down the gorge, and the believers had to flee for their lives. The next morning the broken furniture and crockery were found on the gorge bottom.

We would not leave out the story of Catherine Owen, standing in the window between the preacher and his persecutors, thus demonstrating her courage as well as her godliness. Robert Jones narrates the event:

> It happened like this. The friends at Dolgellau had been dreadfully baited the previous Sunday, one of them being hit on the head by a stone so that he was a long time unconscious, though on that occasion no one was preaching. The following Sabbath, two preachers were to come to them, and it can be imagined how natural it was for them to fear the consequences. However, as they gathered together, the woman, Catherine Owen, sat herself in the window saying, 'They won't be allowed to strike you, unless they strike through me!' This considerably emboldened the preacher as he saw the steadfastness of her

trust in the Lord. And to their surprise, they were not troubled throughout that day.

The following account tells how the persecution at Dolgellau was defeated:

> Preaching took place in the house of David Owen, a glazier, the husband of the Catherine who had sat in the window. David Owen himself was not a believer, but he had great respect for religion and when a society would be meeting in the parlour of his house, he would sit on his own in the kitchen. After growing tired of being abused, he was advised to bring the law down upon the ringleaders. He agreed to do so, and the case was brought to trial at the Bala Sessions. Many preparations were made for the trial. All the nobility of the region and the lawyers were sympathetic to the rioters, but it does not appear that the believers had lawyers or any other help; they depended completely on the justice of their cause. The matter was brought before the high jurors. They behaved most scornfully towards the poor believers, asking them mockingly, 'How often do you indulge in dark prayers? When is it you put out the candles in your meetings?' and other similar nonsensical questions. They returned a verdict of '*No true bill*', judging the matter to be unworthy of any further consideration. The situation for the Methodists of Dolgellau now seemed worse than ever. They turned away from the court with heavy hearts and much weeping, and called on John Evans, pouring forth their complaints and asking for advice. They feared to go home in case the persecutors would be waiting for them who, having learnt that the law would not defend the Roundheads, would be bolder and crueller than ever. 'Don't weep,' said John Evans, 'and don't go home either. Stay in the town until morning, and we will look to see what can be done to defend you.' But the dawn broke upon them in the midst of their darkness, and in the following way. A nobleman was staying at Plasyndre, a relative of Mrs Lloyd, the mother of the Rev. Simon Lloyd. He was therefore one of the Bowens of Tyddyn, Montgomeryshire. This man was persuaded to take up the case of the Dolgellau believers. On seeing that a miscarriage had occurred, he went to the court, succeeded somehow in reopening the matter, and gave a stern lesson to the jurors for behaving as they did, contrary to their vows. He turned the tables, and a sentence was returned in favour of the plaintiffs. In this way the believers obtained a complete victory. The news was brought quickly to Dolgellau and many of the main persecutors fled. Officers of the Sheriff accompanied the believers back to the town and the town-crier was sent out announcing that the law would defend them, and that any who dared attack them further would be punished. From this time the Methodists were left in peace to worship God according to their conscience.

The Revival of 1762 reached Merionethshire and was the means of producing a new spirit in the societies in that it greatly increased the numbers of believers. As we have mentioned, the hymns of Williams, Pantycelyn, were the main means blessed to bring about the revival, which manifested itself primarily in a spirit of praise and singing. About the end of the year 1768, the Rev. Benjamin Thomas told Howell Harris that Methodism had increased greatly in Gwynedd; that there were as many as twenty-four exhorters in the county and that they met together every month and every quarter. Mr Thomas added that there were 120 members in the Bala society alone (though no doubt the Bala society at that time contained many who lived at some distance from the town). Within about eighteen months, that is in February, 1770, they felt strong enough at Bala to invite the Association to them. John Evans and Humphrey Edward, the exhorter, travelled to Fishguard, Pembrokeshire, to extend the invitation, and though Howell Harris pressed that the Association come to Trefeca, the two north-Walians won the day. Though we do not have the history of this Association, it is certain that it occurred. This was the first regular Association held at Bala, and indeed in north Wales, with the exception of Montgomery.

THE BEGINNINGS OF METHODISM IN LLEYN

The beginnings of Methodism in Caernarvonshire sprang from the visit of Howell Harris to Lleyn in 1741. We have related all we know of this journey already. He preached at Glasfryn Fawr, near Pwllheli; Ty'n Llanfihangel, near Rhyd-y-clafdy; Tywyn, not far from Tudweiliog, where he had a powerful meeting and many were convicted; Rhydolion, near Llanengan; and Porth Dinllaen. Whether he established societies at this time is not known; the probability is that he did not. But his coming stirred up the whole region; religion became a topic of general conversation and persecution of the fiercest kind was aroused. It is probable that Daniel Rowland also visited parts of Lleyn, either in 1742 or 1743. In the *Interlude* by *Morgan y Gogrwr*, the sexton of Llannor, published in 1745, there are definite references to remarks made by Rowland when preaching at Porth Dinllaen. He must have passed through the county before that date therefore. He also journeyed through Lleyn and Anglesey in 1747. At the gate of Llanmellteyrn graveyard, having been refused use of the church, he had a service to be remembered forever. The meeting broke out in general rejoicing and many were convicted. There was unity between the Nonconformists and the Methodists in Lleyn at the beginning. William Pritchard of Glasfryn Fawr received the Methodists to his house to preach, as he did also the Independent ministers. Jenkin Morgan, the schoolmaster, who kept the school in his house and went about to exhort, sympathized greatly with the Methodist movement, as was natural for one of Griffith Jones's schoolmasters, and he stood at Howell Harris's side when the latter was attacked so cruelly at Bala in 1741. It was with the Nonconformists therefore that the Methodists at Pwllheli first met, and it was there that they received communion. But when Howell Harris returned on his second visit, he rebuked them for their behaviour, telling them that it would not do to keep all the salt in one bag and that the revival should be distributed throughout Lleyn. What he meant, no doubt, was that Pwllheli should not become the gathering place of all the religion of the area, but that smaller societies should be established here and there. Though Howell Harris respected the Nonconformists and co-operated with them warmly, he was not happy that those who had been converted through the Methodists should join Nonconformist congregations. He desired them rather to remain in the Church of England in the hope that the Establishment would be leavened eventually by the revival. At the Reformer's request, the Methodists separated from the Nonconformists at Pwllheli, and were happy to do so in that the new minister there, a Richard Thomas, was not as able as his predecessor and was also considered suspect doctrinally. It is only right to note that the separation was conducted without anger or argument, but with the best of feelings on both sides.

Early in the history of the Methodism of Lleyn, a young man from the south, being a clergyman and an excellent preacher, visited the region. His name was David Jenkins. A brother of his who was also a preacher was a brother-in-law to Daniel Rowland. It does not seem that he held a curacy in the area but was rather sent by Rowland to support the revival, and it was hoped, in that he was ordained, that he would not be subjected to so much persecution. The parson of Tudweiliog promised that he could preach in his church, but when the appointed time came, he feared the wrath of the neighbouring clergy and so withdrew his promise. Mr Jenkins therefore began to preach in the graveyards, the fields, the streets, and wherever he could find listeners. When he was forbidden Tudweiliog Church, he preached from a tombstone in the church graveyard and had a notable service; as powerful, it is said, as any service held in the region previously, and many were converted. David Jenkins's ministry in Caernarvonshire was of very short duration, but in that brief season, it proved a great blessing. He was a bright and shining star but his light was soon removed. He died when only twenty-five years of age. When Daniel Rowland heard of his passing, he said, with great sorrow, 'My right arm has been cut off.'

As far as is known, the first societies of Lleyn and Eifionydd were formed in places called Brynygadfa, in Llanaelhaearn parish, and Moelderwin in the Bwlchderwin neighbourhood. Before they were established the Methodists went to the Nonconformists at Pwllheli or Capel Helyg. It is fairly certain that these societies existed by 1747. There is a probable reference to them in a letter from the old exhorter, William Richard, who wrote on 20 June, 1747:

> On Friday, after returning from Lleyn, I had an engagement in a place between Caernarvon and Pwllheli. I preached there to a number of poor and ignorant souls, and had a most sweet service. I trust that the Lord has opened a door in this place.

The place referred to is almost certainly Bryngadfa, or perhaps Helygirion. He added:

> One of the brethren asked for preaching at another spot between here and Penmorfa, but he was refused. But we found a place in a small cottage near to that house. I preached there (namely Foelderwin) to about a dozen people and we had a very happy service. I therefore returned again to Bala and stayed there until Monday; it was most glorious there.

Both these societies eventually closed, in that no chapels were built, and the Brynengan society swallowed up all the smaller causes around. When this Brynengan society was formed is not known. There was certainly a strong cause before 1755, because that was the year that Lowri Williams moved from here and took the fire with her to Merionethshire. We are inclined to believe that there was a society here in 1750 and that it was to Brynengan that Howell Harris came in the November of that year when he sought to persuade the northern societies to join his party.

Religion was brought to Brynengan in the following way. A family from Maesllech came to live in the neighbourhood. One of the boys, whose name was John Morris, became very ill. At the same time, a spinster called Catrin Rhisiart, a godly woman, moved from the Moelderwin area to the locality. When she heard of John Morris's illness she felt a desire to visit him in order to warn him of the danger of dying while still ungodly. The young man regained his health but could not shrug off the warning he had received from old Catrin, and he became the firstfruits of the Methodists of Brynengan. The whole family believed as a consequence, and Rhisiart Morris, John's brother, was an elder of the society for years. The numbers at Brynenegan increased quickly and it soon became the Jerusalem of Caernarvonshire. The reason given for its increase is that there was hardly any persecution here. The landowner, a Mr Henry Jones, although not a member himself, was very sympathetic to the believers. Their meeting place also was rather isolated and out of the way and therefore more out of reach of the persecutors. While other places in Lleyn and Eifionydd suffered terribly, as we shall see, the little flock at Brynengan were able to worship without any disturbance. In a little while a society was formed at Tymawr, in the middle of the Lleyn Peninsula, and these two places, Tymawr and Brynengan, became a Sunday circuit for very many years, though there was eighteen miles of road between them. The believers would start out from various parts of Lleyn and Eifionydd for one of these two places very early on a Sunday morning, long before sunrise. They would pass through the Eifl pass at sunrise in order to be at Tymawr or Brynengan for the ten o'clock service. Brynengan Chapel, the first Methodist chapel in Lleyn, was built in 1777, and all the work in wood was by Robert Jones, Rhos-lan.

MORGAN GRIFFITH PRESSED INTO THE NAVY

As we have already mentioned, the believers of Lleyn and Eifionydd suffered much persecution. In order to infuriate the population many false stories about the Methodist exhorters were circulated. It was said that they sold children as slaves, and that they were in league with wicked foreigners who would send a boat to a convenient port to collect and take the children away. Others swore that their purpose, after collecting a sufficient number of followers, was to raise a rebellion against the government and overthrow all the national establishments and order. The Methodists suffered at the hands of all the nobility of that part of the country. They were evicted from their cottages and pressed into the army, and many of them were sent out of the country, some dying in foreign lands. As an example of the treatment they received consider the experiences of an exhorter called Morgan Griffith, who lived in Bwlchyrhiw cottage, in Rhiw parish, Lleyn. Before his conversion he used to sing to the harp in the church and had a singing class where he taught the local young people the rudiments of music. There came suddenly into his mind the thought that such singing was not what God had commanded in his Word and was therefore not acceptable to him. As a result he began reading the Bible and, when he could, to hear sermons, and he came to experience a degree of peace in his troubled heart through the blood of Christ. It was not long before he began exhorting and counselling his fellow-sinners. This was in 1744, that is, about three years after Howell Harris's first visit to the area. He was certainly one of the earliest, if not the very first, of the exhorters of Lleyn. After only a very short time, he was apprehended near Sarn Myllteyrn when returning home after preaching. It is said that the man who arrested him was only a weak, frail creature and that Morgan Griffith, a strong, well-built man, could easily have shaken himself free from his grasp. But this he did not wish to do, as the man had a legal summons to hold him. At the time Griffith was a widower with the sole care of two young children. When he appeared before the magistrates at Pwllheli, these two children were brought to the court also by an uncle of his, in the hope that the sight of them would melt the hearts of his judges. But such was the rage of these noblemen that nothing could assuage their wrath. They placed a book before the boy, who was eight years old, to see if he could read. They did the same to his sister, who was two years younger. When they discovered that both could read they considered it a further transgression, in that it indicated that Morgan Griffith intended to raise his children in the same heresies that he himself followed.

Morgan Griffith was sent, with many of his fellow believers, to serve in the navy. He was taken first to Caernarvon, and from there to Conway, where he was lodged in the prison. It was a feast-day when they arrived at Conway and many had gathered to view the prisoners. Somehow, Morgan Griffith was able to address the gathering and he told them that he and his friends were there, not because of murder, or theft, or any other crime, but for reading the Scriptures, praying, and exhorting others with regard to their souls. He then warned them, with great solemnity, to consider their ways and to return to the Lord. It is said that he did not preach in vain, but that his arrows lodged in the hearts of two young men from the district who, afterwards, were very useful in the work of the gospel. Soon the prisoners were sent on board a warship moored at some port in England. Eventually they were all granted licences to return home. As soon as Morgan Griffith arrived back in Lleyn he returned to his favourite work of warning fellow-sinners. His licence was soon revoked. He was sent back to the warship with a letter preceding him informing the authorities that he remained of the same views as before his first banishment and was a ringleader in agitation and riot. The captain of the ship thought that he could wean him from his religious views by frightening him. He told Griffith that he would have to stop praying and exhorting and become a quiet, inactive Churchman, otherwise he would be stood at one end of the ship and be shot by the sailors. Morgan Griffith chose to be shot, adding, 'We must obey God rather than men.' He was therefore placed at the stern of the ship and shot at by the soldiers but with only powder in their rifles. He demonstrated such determination and courage that the occasion proved to be of great advantage to him; it brought him respect from many who had otherwise no sympathy at all for religion. But Morgan Griffith was not to live long. He very soon became seriously ill and died. His story was brought back to Wales by his companions. When their services ceased to be required by the navy, they returned again to their homes and were unanimous in their testimony that Morgan Griffith died in much peace.

The history of Morgan Griffith's treatment is only one example of the suffering endured by the first Methodists of Caernarvonshire. As stated in *Methodistiaeth Cymru*:

> The above story seems unbelievable. It is difficult for us who have been used to the idea of religious toleration all our lives, and seen Methodism respected throughout the land, to believe that any could behave so cruelly towards their fellow men. It is true that we have heard of the cruelty of the Papists and it would not be so hard to believe such things of them, but that Protestants should act in such a way seems unbelievable. But the evidence for these accounts is incontrovertible, though they seem so barbaric. The history was written by Hugh Thomas (another of the sufferers and a friend of Morgan Griffith) and he heard it from Griffith himself.

Robert Jones also refers briefly to the story.

METHODISM BEGINS IN ARFON

The beginnings of Methodism in the Arfon region occurred, it would seem, in Llanberis. The Hugh Thomas, a native of Lleyn, mentioned in the last paragraph above, when fleeing from home in order to avoid being pressed as a soldier, sought refuge at Cwmglas farmhouse. It is known that, even though he was in hiding, he continued to contribute to the awakening of the people of the region. The following year another exhorter, William Harry, seems to have been sent here by the Association of the south. In the minutes of the Llanddeusant Association of February, 1743, we find:

> That Brother William Harry should keep school at Carnarvonshire and exhort in the neighbourhood, to the best of his ability, between school hours.

This William Harry was strong of body and brave in heart. It needed such a man to face the perils of preaching in the north. The occasion of his arrival at Llanberis earned for him a degree of respect from the local population. On his journey he had arrived at Ysbyty Ifan and he asked a man there for the way to Llanberis. The man could not provide the information but said that Llanberis was far off in a particular direction and he waved his arm towards the rugged mountains of Snowdonia. Harry had some twenty miles to go along a most lonely and dangerous route. It could hardly be said that there was any kind of road, merely isolated paths along the slopes of the rocks, above deep ravines and wild waterfalls., and where only a step or two from the path would result in a free fall over towering cliffs to the rocks below. Worse still, night had fallen upon William Harry at the most dangerous spot, namely Bwlch-rhiw-ychain. But with God's gracious hand guiding him, he managed to reach his destination of Cwmglas, sometime before morning. When it became known that a stranger had arrived at Cwmglas, having travelled overnight and without a guide, it caused much amazement. The inhabitants considered it almost a miracle. On hearing that the stranger was to exhort at Cwmglas the following evening, many gathered to the place out of curiosity, wishing to see and hear the man who had accomplished such an unheard-of journey. Amongst them was a Pierce Williams of Gwastadnant. Under the sermon he was convicted and became a true disciple of Jesus Christ. He soon offered his house for preaching. It is said, however, that there was little further success for the gospel at Llanberis for very many years.

Another place in Arfon where a Methodist society was soon established was Waunfawr. An exhorter called Evan Dafydd of Hafodrhyg lived here until his death in 1750. It is not known how or when Evan Dafydd came to a knowledge of the truth, but tradition has it that Howell Harris preached at Hafodrhyg. Early societies were set up also at Clynnog and Llanllyfni, and it seems that some kind of Association was held at Llanllyfni in the year 1769. Many societies had been set up in various places in the surrounding neighbourhood long before a cause was begun at Caernarvon. The 1762 Revival reached Arfon also and added many members to the societies and was the means of increasing respect for the Methodists in the eyes of the people.

THE FIRST CAUSES IN DENBIGHSHIRE AND FLINTSHIRE

We have no sure account of the beginning of Methodism in Denbighshire and Flintshire. Howell Harris travelled through those counties at the end of 1747 but his journal for this period has not survived and we do not therefore know what places he visited. Probably there were Methodists there before this time. John Evans, Bala, noted that it was he himself who first brought the flame to the neighbourhood of Adwy'r Clawdd. John Evans had been born here, and he was only nine years younger than Howell Harris. He moved to Bala when young and was converted, and there is an argument for believing that, because of his concern for his parents, he did not waste much time before attempting to bring the gospel to their hearing. The first Methodist meeting in the neighbourhood of Adwy'r Clawdd seems to have been at his parents' home. John Evans wrote:

> My father and mother had opposed me for a while in my wish to bring preaching to the area, saying that the Established Church was sufficient. But on recovering from a serious illness, they were made willing to allow me to bring a preacher to hold a meeting in the house.

Many of the neighbours came to listen, and they were so ignorant and pagan that they asked, 'Was the preacher in a trance, or had he seen a vision, that he could speak of such strange things to us?' He answered, 'No, and had they not noticed that he had taken his text from the Bible?'

Howell Harris also visited the north in October, 1748, but again the relevant journal has been lost. He wrote to a Mr Boddington in that month:

> 'Tis now about nine weeks since I began to go round South and North Wales, and this week I came home from my last journey round North Wales. I have now visited in that time thirteen counties and travelled mostly 150 miles every week, and discoursed twice every day and sometimes three and four times a day; and this last journey I have not taken my clothes off for seven nights and travelled from one morning to the next evening without any rest above 100 miles. Discoursing at twelve or two in the morning on the mountain, being obliged to meet at that time by reason of persecution. One man being made, the week before I went there, to pay £20 near Wrexham, to Sir W. W. Wynne, and several of the hearers £5, and some £10 that had paid before, this being the third time. Poor people have been served thus in the neighbourhood for assembling together; and now there was only one of our brethren went to prayer with some of the neighbours in the family. Sir W. triumphed over the poor people and said we had sent for law against him but could find none. Lord, answer for thyself and appear in thine own cause.
>
> I had in another place, namely Bala, a blow on my head with violence enough to slit my head in two, but I received no hurt. Such crowds I never saw coming to hear and more glory among the people. Many hearts and doors have lately been opened, and several lately which we know of have been awakened, and the Lord seems to turn his face towards the rich. Several have been this journey to hear me, and several more talk with affection to come and hear Mr Whitefield when he comes.[3]

This journey had clearly been very successful. When Harris came again in 1750, seeking to win the support of the societies, he visited many places in Denbighshire and Flintshire, as we have noted, and it is probable therefore that quite a few societies had been formed. John Evans, Bala, says that the first Methodist chapel in north Wales was built at Adwy'r Clawdd.

The following history is given of the first rise of Methodism in the neighbourhood of Llanrwst and Trefriw. In September, 1740 (though there is some uncertainty as to the date), a feast-day fair was held at Trefriw. The great day of the feast was the Sunday. Word came that a Roundhead had been engaged to preach in a home called Brwynog, a place in the mountains about two miles to the west of Trefriw. Six young men decided to go there, leaving behind the merriment. But they went, not to listen to the strange man, but with the intention of killing him. To this end they each took a strong cudgel and they appointed the strongest and bravest of them to be the leader. They also decided that they would not attack him immediately but listen to him for a while, thinking that they would quickly hear from him some insolent remark that would justify their attack upon him. So they set out. However, as soon as they came within earshot of the ministry, a sudden fear fell upon them so that the cudgels fell from their hands. Five of them ran for their homes, as if fleeing for their lives, and the leader alone was left. He pushed to the front to listen; he was as if bound to the lips of the speaker; he felt his prejudices disappearing like a mist; and he was soundly convicted. His name, it is said, was Dafydd Thomas of Wernbwys, in the parish of Llanddoget. Before long, the other five were also converted, many of them becoming very useful in their different neighbourhoods. Two of them joined the 'family' at Trefeca, where they remained for the rest of their lives.

EDWARD PARRY

The mother-church of mid-Denbighshire was Tanyfron in the parish of Llansannan. A man called Edward Parry established the society and deserves some notice. He was convicted while listening to a sermon from the exhorter from the south, Dafydd William Rhys, at Henllan in the parish of Llanfair Talhaearn. He had agreed to go there with some ten or twelve responsible men from Llansannan. 'As soon as we went into the house,' he said, when giving an account of what happened, 'and as we listened, I felt the floor of the house shaking under my feet; I thought that the plates on the dresser were knocking against each other, and I immediately came to the decision to cleave to these people as long as I lived.' Edward Parry was a man of considerable ability and knowledge. He was an able poet, being on friendly terms with *Twm o'r Nant*,[4] and is said to have composed many poems, all of which are lost now. He worked as a carpenter and was already married when he was converted under Dafydd William Rhys's ministry. The next day, the preacher passed Edward Parry's cottage as he was on his way to Adwy'r Clawdd, the next Methodist preaching station, though there was a thirty-mile journey between them. Edward failed to pluck up courage to speak to the exhorter but he left his old companions and resolved to attend preaching whenever possible. He longed to have preaching in his own home and he succeeded in getting Dafydd William Rhys to visit. As a result, Cefnbyr, Parry's home, became a centre for the preachers of the south and the north. But in this way he drew upon himself the wrath of many, including the vicar of the parish and the landowner. The latter threatened him that unless he gave over sheltering the foreign itinerants that were travelling the country and that took it upon themselves to preach, he would turn him out of his cottage. He answered carefully, 'Your land, Sir, is only for time, but my religion is forever.' He was given warning to quit. Before the time of notice was over, he had opportunity to talk to Mr Foulkes of Wenallt, who asked him:

'Why have you been turned out of your cottage?

'For receiving preachers to the house.'

'But is that not a good work?' replied Mr Foulkes. 'I do not now have an empty cottage, but as you are a carpenter I will give you a deed for the land and you may build a house of your own.'

Edward Parry agreed to the offer and quickly raised a house which he called Tanyfron. Here was established the first society in Denbighshire, and the name is well-known to the Methodists of that county to this day.

Very soon, Edward Parry began to exhort. He seems to have begun about the year 1749, the year before the disruption between Rowland and Harris. The quarrel affected him greatly, as it did so many people. While his father supported Rowland and welcomed 'Rowland's people' to the house, Edward was sympathetic to Harris's side and gave his exhorters every welcome. His brother-in-law, Hugh Davies, became one of the 'family' at Trefeca and returned to the county to persuade others to join them there. Many went from the Llansannan district but Edward Parry was not persuaded. But he sank into a deep lethargy. He gave up preaching for a while and rejoined the Established Church. The local clergyman's joy was complete and he honoured Parry by making him a warden. But true religion burned still in his heart and he used to attend the games and sports held in the parish on a Sunday, calling on the people to gather for evensong on pain of punishment. In this way he succeeded in ending the sporting and dancing almost completely. One afternoon, as he was reading the service and leading a verse of a hymn to sing, he thought that the congregation did not understand the hymn. Its content was the passage of Israel from Egypt into Canaan. He began to explain it. He followed the history of Israel from the calling of Abram, his journey to the land of promise, the oppression of Israel in Egypt, their delivery, and their entry at last into Canaan. As he spoke, there fell upon him and upon the congregation, a sweet influence, different from anything they had experienced before. This eased his spirit. He began preaching again. He soon joined with 'Rowland's party' and his house became a home to the cause for the rest of his life.

The following story testifies to the wisdom of Edward Parry. A Robert Roberts of Gregor-Isaf joined the society and afterwards became a most useful member. His wife, however, was completely opposed to his membership, as she believed the accusation against the believers that they met for vile and filthy practices. Edward Parry had opportunity to speak to her and he asked her if it was true that she objected to her husband coming to the meetings. She acknowledged that this was true and suggested that she believed the stories that were being rumoured about the purpose of the 'prayers in the dark'. 'If that is the case,' he answered, 'come yourself. I give you my word that you may come when you wish and leave when you wish, without anyone saying anything to you or asking anything of you, and in this way you can find out for yourself what takes place.' The following Sunday the woman came to the service. At its close, Edward Parry announced a society, inviting all who wished to remain. The woman stayed with the others and so appreciated the meeting that all her prejudice disappeared and from then on she was almost more zealous than her husband.

Edward Parry, as we have already mentioned, was a man of some culture. He read a great deal, being familiar with much English religious writing, as well as Welsh, and he did his best to encourage his fellow-Welshmen to buy books and read them. He distributed very many copies of Peter Williams's Bible in the neighbourhood. His main field of labour as an exhorter was mid Denbighshire but he travelled to some extent through Anglesey, Arfon and Flintshire, and once, it is said, to London, to serve the needs of the London Welsh. Eventually the congregation became too many for the house and he became eager to build a chapel. He obtained land for the building from Mr John Foulkes, the grandson of the man who had been kind to him years before. The chapel was built in 1773, one of the first Methodist chapels in Gwynedd. The place became a meeting place for many, a venue for Associations and Monthly Meetings.

On occasions, the old persecuting spirit of the parish of Llansannan revealed itself as not being completely dead. Mr Charles of Bala came there once to preach, whether to a public meeting or a private meeting is not known, but the congregation was too many for the chapel. As a result, Mr Charles began the meeting in the street but soon the church bell began to ring for the church service. Rather than show any opposition to the church, Mr Charles went to the service and all the congegation went with him so that the church was fuller than it had ever been before. After re-emerging, Mr Charles began again, but the clergyman came to him complaining that he was too close to the churchyard wall. Rather than give offence he moved to another place about a quarter of a mile away and was allowed to proceed with the meeting. At the close of the service, the clergyman sent an invitation to Mr Charles and Edward Parry for them to dine with him the next day. It is difficult to know what motivated him. Perhaps Mr Charles's courtesy had overcome his prejudice; perhaps he wished to ingratiate himself with his parishioners; or perhaps he wished for an opportunity to argue with Mr Charles because of his attachment to the Methodists. Whatever the reason, he was politely thanked for his invitation but the two men had to refuse it as they were due to preach at other places on that day.

Edward Parry died in 1784, when 63 years old. Mr Charles came all the way from Bala to preach at his funeral and during the sermon the congregation broke out in a mixture of sorrow and rejoicing so that it was with some difficulty that matters were brought to order before proceeding to the cemetery. As they approached the church someone gave out a hymn to sing, and such singing had never before been heard in Llansannan. The large crowd stood by the church gates repeating the hymn over and over, until at last a general rejoicing prevailed. The administering clergyman lost all patience and only with great difficulty managed to obtain sufficient silence to read the service. Edward Parry's influence proved of immense help in establishing Methodism in Denbighshire.

Most of the first generation of Methodist clergy and well-known exhorters preached in Denbighshire. We have already described the cruel treatment that Peter Williams received at Trefriw. Another example, illustrating the total opposition to Methodism of the nobility and clergy of the county, is noted on the following epitaph upon a gravestone in Ysgeifiog cemetery:

> Here lie the remains of Hugh Hughes, Esq., Coed-y-brain, in hope of a glorious resurrection. He had the honour of serving his country in the office of sheriff of this county. As a man, he was faithful in the worship of the Established Church; he witnessed from the heart against the fickle new sect of Methodists, who sought to draw men away from her; and in good time, he reconciled strife between neighbours before they became enraged with one another. For such conduct he was respected in his life, and mourned for in his death. He died 7, July, 1752, when 44 years old, leaving behind an only daughter and a widow.

The intensity of opposition to the Methodists must have been particularly strong for anyone in their right mind to have carved such nonsense on a gravestone. But for all the persecution and the false misrepresentations that lying minds could devise, God prospered his work and Methodism increased in numbers and influence.

THE SLOW BEGINNINGS IN ANGLESEY

Methodism was very slow in gaining ground in Anglesey. It is not known who was the first Methodist to preach on the island. There are strong grounds for believing that Daniel Rowland visited in 1742, and that William Richards, the exhorter from Cardiganshire, was his companion. What success followed their ministry is not known. Probably some of the exhorters from the south, full of zeal for Christ, had been here before them. An old man called Robert Williams, a blacksmith by profession, used to relate to the late Rev. William Roberts, Amlwch, how he remembered the exhorter, Richard William Dafydd, preaching on the island as early as 1740. He stood to speak at Arthur's Cross in the parish of Mechell, but was not given opportunity to say much. A crowd of disturbers gathered, amongst them Robert Williams himself, who was then a youth of fifteen years of age. They rushed on to the poor preacher, beating him mercilessly. He attempted to escape but when he realized that he could not outpace them he jumped into a ditch full of water, hoping to hide behind a gorse-bush. But his torturers found him and beat him again as if he was a mad dog. Fortunately, a respected farmer arrived at the scene, the owner of Tymawr, Llanrhuddlad, who on seeing the cruelty, defended the poor victim and ensured his escape. There is no certainty that the farmer was a religious man but that he was tenderhearted and would not allow an innocent man to be so treated. Shortly after this farmer died, and at his funeral, as his body was being carried to the cemetery, a white bird settled on the bier. The accompanying crowd considered this to be a sign of heaven's approbation of him for his work in defending Richard William Dafydd.

The Rev. William Roberts obtained more details of this story, together with a confirmation of it, at Lleyn, Caernarvonshire. When on a journey there, an old respectable man came to him and asked if he knew anything of Llysdulais in Anglesey. He answered that he did so. 'Well,' said the man, 'that was the first place in Anglesey where a Nonconformist was protected.' And he related the following story. About 1740, an old Nonconformist minister visited the district around Amlwch, wherever he could find acceptance. This brought down upon him a fierce persecution. The account of his troubles reached Mr Lewis, Llysdulais, one of the forefathers of the present Lord Dinorben. He invited the squire, Mr Bulkeley, to Llysdulais, so that they might decide what to do, as they were both magistrates. After some discussion, they sent for the minister to appear before them. The whole family was gathered to the hall and the minister asked to preach to them. This he did. Having finished, the gentlemen said, 'If this is his offence, we should by all means defend him and silence his persecutors.' The good man was allowed to proceed with his work from then on in peace. It is not known for certain whether Richard William Dafydd was the man, but it could easily have been he, as the two stories relate to the same period.

About 1742, William Pritchard came to live at Plas Penmynydd, being driven there from Glasfryn Fawr by the ferocity of persecution in Arfon. We have already described how this man received Howell Harris on his first visit to Lleyn. William Pritchard was not a Methodist – he belonged to the Nonconformists – and while he lived in Anglesey he went once a month to take communion at the Nonconformist chapel at Pwllheli. At the same time he was full of the spirit of the revival and welcomed Methodist preachers to his home as warmly as Nonconformist ones. There is no doubt that his arrival in Anglesey greatly encouraged the Methodist cause there. William Pritchard lived for three years at Plas Penmynydd before he was forced to leave because of his religion, and he then moved to Modlew Fawr in the parish of Llanddaniel-fab. After five years he had to leave this place also, for the same reason. In the midst of his troubles, he took his complaint to William Bulkeley, Esq., Bryndu.

'Why are you being turned out of your cottage?' asked that gentleman. 'Is it because you are unable to pay your rent?'

'No,' said he. 'But because of my religion and the fact that I have seceded from the Established Church.'

'If so,' said William Bulkeley, ' you may have some land from me.'

The gentleman kept his word and gave him Clwchdernog on a lease, and he remained there for the rest of his life. William Pritchard was an excellent man. He was very knowledgeable and of a burning zeal. He was often in danger because of his faith but died gloriously, leaning upon his Redeemer.

During the first few years of the revival, Methodist exhorters visited Anglesey regularly. The Rev. Benjamin Thomas preached there in the year 1744. He lodged at Plas Penmynydd with William Pritchard and was to speak at Minffordd, a chapel that was built by William Pritchard and licensed according to the law as a Nonconformist place of worship. But Benjamin Thomas was not allowed to speak. A crowd of disturbers arrived. They threw a bowl of water over the preacher and began beating the worshippers with staves so that many were bleeding. We have also referred already to the visit of Peter Williams to the island in 1746.

RICHARD THOMAS: ANGLESEY'S FIRST EXHORTER

Without doubt the main instrument of blessing for the establishing of Methodism in Anglesey was Richard Thomas, the first exhorter on the island. This man deserves more recognition than we can give him here. He was an under-steward on the Plascoch estate. It seems that he appreciated luxury and lived in a style a good deal above his means. As a result he fell into debt, and had to flee from his creditors to Merthyr Tydfil in the south. In those days, Merthyr was considered a safe hiding place for every kind of ruffian and outlaw. He gave himself to hard work in the south and soon amassed considerable wealth. But also, on hearing Howell Harris preach, he was converted. He became as well-known for his religion as he had been before for his ungodliness, and he began to exhort. In 1746 he returned to Anglesey and the first thing he did was to pay back all his debts to his creditors. His honesty and integrity earned him general respect. He was allowed to preach and as he was an able speaker many gathered to hear him. A letter of his to Howell Harris, when he was on the point of returning to the north, has survived:

> 21 July, 1746. Richard Thomas, to my faithful brother in Christ, Howell Harris. My dear, kind Brother, I hope that these few words will meet you with blessing in the Lord. I am, as you saw, ill in the body but with wondrous blessing to my soul. Through Christ I am enabled to say that I see every blow as full of the love of my heavenly Father. My dear Brother, it is a comfort to my soul to think of death, judgment and eternity. I see death as a small door to be flown through to that full and eternal liberty of joy. I now, through faith, see heaven open and death as a second door that allows me entrance to my eternal city. I now hear the sound of heavenly harpists singing above, and death is the messenger come to release me to their company to sing forever amongst them. Through faith I see my crown in the kingdom of my Father, my Brother and my eternally covenanted Spouse; and death is as the boat that takes me to my inheritance. Through faith I see some of my brethren that have already been redeemed in glory, and myself travelling through the wilderness, leaning upon my Beloved; but death is my Father's servant, to take me to my brethren. O Brother, this is the sight that shows me that in this world I am merely beginning to enjoy God through the promises; for I know, if I am given longer on earth, that I will see further into the love of God, and have greater enjoyment of it.
>
> My dear Brother, I find that my faith cries out, more, more, all the time; more of a view of my privileges in Christ. After one sight, faith says, 'Another look, my Father; more wisdom to know God; more strength; more self-denial; more sorrow for my sin, and for that of my brethren, and of the world's too.' 'More again of enjoyment,' says faith, 'more virtue; more conformity to the law; more heaven upon earth.' 'Amen, amen,' says faith; and 'Amen' says my own soul also.
>
> My dear Brother, though I am so weak in body, I believe that I shall be sent by God to return to my own country to warn my people according to the

flesh, before I am removed to my Father's house above. I intend to set out on the road by the end of the month. I end my contract at Cwm Camlais on Thursday night, 28 August. From there I will go through Radnorshire and Montgomeryshire. There are men in Denbighshire that I wish to see on my way home, at Wrexham and Denbigh, where I have a cousin who is a tanner, if he is still alive. It may be God will bless me at these places on my journey. Amen. I intend to be in Anglesey by the end of harvest. Some of the brethren in the south speak of coming with me there. I think it wisest if I go some time before them amongst my people, and send for them afterwards. On hearing that I intend to go, about four or five are saying that they will come with me, and this is what tends me to think that they have not sought God's will on the matter. Therefore, O Brother, I desire your advice. For I sent a letter before me to two Justices whom I know. I was a steward looking after the farms of one of them, and my father before me. I promised in my letter that I would speak to them first before exhorting in the neighbourhood. For it is these two that have stood for liberty to the Dissenters. And if God grants me an entrance, and favour in their sight, to the blessing of their souls, well; if not, I am yet resolved, by God's help, to venture my life for Christ, to preach the gospel. I believe also that I will receive all help to break through all obstacles. Therefore, O dear Brother, pray for me, and write your thoughts, and the address for me to write to you in London. O Brother, I have for seven years been effectively receiving the gifts of the new covenant, but I conceive that I am only beginning to appreciate their value . . . All things are mine through Jesus Christ! Glory ever! Amen! This is the view which is filling my soul with evangelical zeal; zeal which cries against sin, which sorrows for sin, and cries out at the same time, 'Wretched man that I am! Who shall deliver me from the body of this death!' This is the view which works in me more of a hunger and thirsting for sanctification, to be more like God, to have God's image upon my soul, to bring more glory to God every minute of my life. Amen, and amen. As a result of this view I see the way of this world is passing, the eternal glory nearly approaching, and my soul longs for God to bring forward the day he gathers his saints together.

This letter provides ample proof of the spirituality of the first exhorters, the warmth of their zeal, and the completeness of their commitment. We see also that many of them, Richard Thomas included, were naturally gifted men, and truly scriptural in their attitudes. The writer of this letter had clearly lived many years in the south for he makes use in the letter of many words and expressions that are not in use in the north. It seems that Richard Thomas was convicted during one of Howell Harris's first journeys in Glamorganshire, because he mentions the seven years that have passed since his conversion and the letter is dated 1746. One of the two justices of peace whom he refers to was Mr Bulkeley, Bryndu, one of the forebears of

Mr Bulkeley Hughes, the late member for Arfon. The other, no doubt, was Mr Lewis, Llysdulais. There is complete confirmation here therefore of the support which these two gave to the Nonconformists. We have very little of the history of Richard Thomas after his return to Anglesey. Tradition has it that he preached throughout the island, from shore to shore, and was successful in turning many from their wayward paths.

It was for a year only that Richard Thomas had the privilege of being the only exhorter in Anglesey. Soon, Hugh Griffith of Lleyn joined him. This man had been held in Lleyn and pressed to be a soldier, but as he was fleet of foot he had escaped from his hunters and for all their hunting they had failed to run him to ground again. He obtained refuge at Modlew Fawr, the home of William Pritchard. He and Pritchard came from the same region and both had been exiled because of their religion. In time Griffith made his home in Llanddaniel and remained there for the rest of his life. He was diligent in warning his fellow-sinners to escape from the wrath to come but it is said that he might have been more useful had his temper not been so fiery.

It is certain that Howell Harris visited the island many times. One of his visits is recorded in a rhyme, recited on the island:

Howell Harris on his horse	Howell Harris ar ei horse
From Llanerchymedd to Llanygors,	O Lanerchymedd i Lanygors,
And from there to Carreglefn.	Ac oddiyno i Garreglefn.

His journal mentions a visit to Anglesey made in October, 1747. He was on the island again the next year. It is unfortunate that we do not have details of these visits, so that we do not know what success or otherwise he encountered on the island. We read of him also paying a hurried visit in 1750, when he made such an effort to draw the societies over to his side. It is said that he preached at Ysgubor Fawr and in Llanfihangel. His text in the first place was, 'In the world you shall have tribulation', and at Llanfihangel his theme was the infinite nature of Christ's sufferings. The history suggests that there were very few societies on the island in 1750. Probably the general feeling on the island amongst believers at this time was similar to that in Gwynedd – in favour of Harris rather than Rowland.

The cause prospered in Anglesey in spite of all opposition. Much persecution occurred. Many were thrown off their farms because of their attachment to Methodism. We read of eighteen small farmers being summoned to appear at Plas Lleugwy in 1768 before the steward of Lord Boston and the parish clergyman, to give an account of their religion. They were asked to promise that they would not go to hear the Methodists again. Should they promise, they could remain in their farms but if not they would have to leave. Owen Thomas Rowlands, who was something of an exhorter, sought to argue with the steward. He said that the law of the land allowed people to worship where they wished. The steward would not answer him except to say, 'That is my master's command.' At this, on being struck by the privilege of suffering for his faith, one of the eighteen, Richard Williams of Tyddyn Bach, began to clap his hands and to shout out loud, 'Glory be to God! Hosanna to the Son of David!' The steward was thoroughly frightened and the paper fell from his hand. The Methodists went out and Richard Williams shouted, 'Farewell, dear brothers. Whoever would sell a kingdom and a crown for a cottage and land, and have to pay a heavy price for it, I would not ever, as long as I am helped by the Brother born for adversity.' Some returned and gave the required promise, but they fell under general contempt. But those who stood firm were respected throughout the island and lived and died happily. There were many minor preachers in this first period in Anglesey – men such as Richard Jones, Newborough; Richard Dafydd, Amlwch; Owen Thomas Rowlands; William Roberts, Amlwch; and Michael Thomas, Llanddaniel, but for reasons of space, we cannot give their histories.

[1] *Methodistiaeth Cymru* [*Welsh Methodism*], written by John Hughes (1796–1860) and published in three volumes (1851–56), was the first full-length history of the early years of Welsh Methodism.

[2] *Drych yr Amseroedd* [*The Mirror of the Age*] is an account of the Methodist Revival in Wales, published in 1820, and written by Robert Jones, Rhoslan (1745–1829).

[3] STL, Vol. 2, pp. 20–21.

[4] Thomas Edwards (1739–1810), a famous poet and writer of interludes.

2

JOHN EVANS OF BALA

HIS UPBRINGING

John Evans of Bala was the first minister from Gwynedd to become known throughout Wales. His fame was based not so much on his preaching abilities as on his unceasing labours, his unshakeable determination, his leadership and his great store of good sense. He was born at Glanyrafon, near Wrexham, in 1723, and was therefore a boy of twelve years of age when the Methodist Revival began. When he was four his parents moved to the neighbourhood of Adwy'r Clawdd, where they owned some land on which they built a few houses. Although the family was by no means rich, they lived comfortably. The parents were not Christians but attended the Church on Sundays and lived respectable lives. They taught John to observe good morals, to keep from all lying and swearing, to observe the Sabbath and not to steal, but they had no understanding of the guilty state of sinners, nor of the great truths of the way of salvation. There had been a notable Nonconformist church at Wrexham – Morgan Llwyd of Gwynedd being the minister for some years – but by this time the church, like many of the nonconforming causes in the land, had fallen into deadness and been broken by quarrels. The parents of John Evans therefore had to depend on the Established Church for their religious education, and very little did they receive.

John had a better education than most. At ten years of age he could read his Bible fluently in Welsh or English and took great delight in its historical narratives. Not only did he know of the histories of Noah, Abraham, Joseph and the like, but he used to recite them to his neighbours; and such was the rarity of Bibles in those days, and so few could read, that the Scriptures which he related were as strange to his listeners as they would have been to the natives of Africa. But as he grew he lost his love for the Bible and began to get into bad company, taking an interest in the games and sports held on the Sunday. However much his mother rebuked him, the pull of the games drew him and all the daylight hours of God's day were given to them. Yet on his return home guilt would weigh heavily upon his conscience, a fear of death and judgment would almost overwhelm him, and his mother, as she waited for him with her rebukes, seemed the very embodiment of Sinai and the Law. In his autobiography he describes how God kept him from falling openly into sin – from adultery, drunkenness, swearing and theft – and he often sought to make a plaster of these virtues to heal his wounded conscience, 'Not yet understanding,' he wrote, 'that God's Law strikes at the very seed of these things in the heart.' He did not realize that God demands that man give an account for evil thoughts as well as evil deeds.

When about twelve years old he was bound as an apprentice to a weaver and in the next few years grew into a tall strong boy, stronger physically than any of his contemporaries. On completing his apprenticeship he made attempts at becoming a soldier, until eventually his mother's entreaties dissuaded him. Dissatisfied with a weaver's pay however, he went to work in a lead mine some distance from home. Separated from his mother's warnings he threw off all appearance of respectability and became one of the wildest youths of the area.

HIS REMOVAL TO BALA

It was now that the event that was to prove the turning point in his life occurred. In order for him to hear the gospel it was necessary that he should move from his native district. Years later he wrote, 'Even today, as I look back and remember events, I marvel at the way God took to drive me from my own neighbourhood to that where I knew neither man nor woman, namely Bala, and where I have lived the last fifty-seven years.' The change occurred when a bitter quarrel arose between the man in whose house John Evans lodged and a neighbour. So strong were the emotions aroused that the neighbour, in John Evans's hearing, threatened to kill his adversary. Evans reported this to his landlord, and he obtained a warrant against the threatener. The result was that Evans was summoned to appear as a witness before the magistrates. He wrote later:

> Now was God's finger to be seen beginning the work of fulfilling his purposes, for as I was on my way to appear before the Justices the solemn thought came to me as to how great and important a matter it was to take an oath. On taking an oath, I was bound to repeat what I had heard exactly as it was stated, correct to every syllable and letter, for otherwise the oath would be false, and a false oath would be a sin against the Holy Spirit. For such a sin there would be no forgiveness, not in this world, nor in the next. These considerations had such an effect on me that on being called I declared to the Justice that I was

> not willing to be put on oath. He replied that if I as a witness refused to go on oath he would send me to prison. With tears streaming down my cheeks I replied that I would prefer it so, and on seeing this the Justice realized that it was fear of the oath, rather than stubborness, that was the cause, and he kindly explained that all the oath required was for me to tell the truth to the best of my knowledge. So I took the oath, being careful to add the words: 'to the best of my knowledge', and the offender was bound over until the next session.

The story demonstrates a tenderness of conscience and a concern for honesty not often found, especially in an irreligious young man. But his trials were not yet over. Although he had been careful when under oath to state that his testimony was to the best of his knowledge, he was again terrified with the thought that he might have said something that was untrue, and so sinned against the Holy Spirit. His mental turmoil was great; he failed to sleep for weeks, 'And scarcely,' he wrote, 'did I escape with life and wits intact.' But relief came unexpectedly. In a neighbour's house he chanced upon a small book entitled *Seven Sermons of Mr Robert Russell.* The first sermon dealt with the sin against the Holy Ghost. He read the sermon eagerly and all his fears were removed, 'as fully as the sun soaks up all the dew of dawn'.

The next session was approaching however, and John Evans could not reconcile himself to the thought of taking the oath again. As the time drew near, so his discomfort increased, and on the Sunday before the trial he decided to escape and left his father's house without a word to anyone. He originally intended to go to Flintshire, to the lead mines there, but having started on his way he remembered having heard of the extensive lead workings in Cardiganshire and realized that to get there he would need to pass through Bala town. He retraced some of his steps therefore and arrived at Bala late in the day, having walked some thirty miles. He was tired, had little in his pocket and knew of nowhere to apply for lodging. Thinking that he might be able to earn enough money to finish his journey by weaving, he inquired and was directed to the home of a local weaver, an old man named Edward Williams. Here he was invited in and a bed offered him, but Williams would not discuss employment with him that night as it was the Sabbath.

JOHN EVANS JOINS THE METHODISTS

Thus did John Evans arrive at Bala, where Providence had arranged that he should spend the rest of his life. He came here at eighteen years of age in 1742, a year after Howell Harris had been so brutally mistreated in the town. The Methodists did not as yet have a cause here, and the few who had been convicted under Harris's ministry used to join with the Nonconformists who met at Edward Williams's home. Williams was an eminently godly man. He maintained family worship consistently, and would travel miles to hear God's Word preached. By coming to lodge at his house John Evans's lines had fallen in very pleasant places. Scarcely had he recovered from his tiredness before some religious friends began arriving and without ado the evening's duties were commenced – reading, praying and singing praises. This they did with such liveliness and warmth of spirit that the young man was astounded. He had not seen nor heard of such things and knew not what to make of them, yet as he stated later, 'I saw nothing out of place in anything that they did or said.' His own heart however was not touched. He stood, as it were, at some distance, viewing everything with a critical eye. The next morning, after the reading and praying, he agreed with Edward Williams as to his remaining there as a weaver, and he began to wonder whether God's hand was not in the matter, so easily had employment come to him and that in a place with which he was so unfamiliar. But he had not yet been changed; indeed, he was not yet convicted nor yet weaned from his old excesses. For six months after coming to Bala he continued his empty pursuits as before. One Sunday evening Edward Williams, after much effort, succeeded in persuading him to accompany himself to Gweirglodd Gilfach, near Llanuwchllyn, to hear a stranger preach. This was the first time for him to sit under a Nonconformist's ministry. But John Evans sat as a judge throughout the meeting. He marvelled to see the speaker delivering his message without a book, but nothing touched his heart. The only effect of the sermon was to give him some entertainment. This was sufficient pleasure to keep him attending at the meetings however and, if his heart was not convinced, his mind at least was enlightened, and he came to understand the doctrines of the gospel and to recognize that a sinner is justified by faith in Christ. Gradually he put aside every bad habit and maintained a respectable walk of life but as yet he did not profess faith.

In 1744 he married Margaret Morris, the daughter of Morris ap Robert, a member with the Nonconformists of the town. It has been said that she had joined the Methodists before this time, but we are doubtful whether a regular Methodist *seiat* had been established yet in Bala. Had it been, and had Margaret Morris been a member, she would not have been allowed to marry John Evans, he not professing, without being disciplined. Soon after however a *seiat* was formed which Margaret joined. The members were only eight or nine in number, with two brothers from the south, Evan and John Moses, blacksmiths by profession, being the leaders. John

Evans, although not a professing member, was a regular listener. Then, at Whitsun 1745, a remarkable service occurred at Bala. Whether it was a prayer meeting or a sermon is not known but the Holy Spirit descended there as truly as He did in Jerusalem on the Day of Pentecost. Amongst those brought to their knees in that service was John Evans. From that day onwards he ceased from being a critic and became a disciple of Christ, committing himself to serve Him, with a zeal rarely equalled, until the day of his death.

On marrying, John Evans went into business as a weaver on his own. After this he was for some time a book-binder, but for many years before his death he traded as a chandler. In a very short time he became one of the most respected men of Bala. Many factors accounted for this - a nobility in his bearing and behaviour, a tall frame, an upright walk, neatness of dress. His very appearance could not fail to make an impression. In addition, he conducted his business diligently, with commitment and thorough honesty, with the result that it was soon understood in the town that he would never willingly cause harm to anyone and that a child could be sent to him with no fear of being cheated. His store of good sense became known and thus, with no effort on his part, he became the oracle of the town, being consulted on all kinds of questions. Without doubt, John Evans's connection with the Methodists raised them in the eyes of the people, not only in Bala but throughout the surrounding areas.

The group that John Evans joined at Bala was small in number but often experienced glorious meetings. They rarely received a sermon – the preachers of the south feared to visit them because of persecution, and there were hardly any in the north who had begun in the work of exhorting. The believers met to read, pray and sing praises, and not infrequently were they made aware of the divine presence evidently among them. They would meet usually before sunrise, for fear of the persecutors. A member would tie a line to some part of his body before sleeping, letting the other end hang out through the window. An awakener would then come past, waking them up by a pull on the line. The usual awakener was Evan Moses whose exhortation from the window would be, 'Arise, brother, and come to the Lord.' It is hard not to admire the zeal and determination of these faithful believers who sacrificed so much for the privilege of worshipping together.

Evans became a leader amongst the group almost immediately because of his great energy and commitment in the work. It was twenty years after his conversion before he began to preach, but his indefatigable labours for the cause continued throughout those years in his hometown as well as the surrounding districts. It was he, in his great desire to bring his parents under the influence of the gospel, who was instrumental in introducing the first preaching to the Adwy'r Clawdd area. On Sundays, taking some of the Bala brethren with him, he would walk the thirty-five miles to Penrhyndeudraeth, to Ffestiniog, or to other areas, so as to encourage those holding prayer meetings. They had no place to rest on the way, nor any house that would offer them refreshment. None would grant them a draught of milk on the journey such was the prejudice against the Roundheads, as they were called. Some bread and cheese would sustain them, together with the water from some lonely spring on the hillside. Although close to exhaustion often, they felt it the greatest privilege to be allowed to serve the Lord Jesus.

He decided to attempt to get the main preachers of the south to visit the north again, and to that end he journeyed to the Trecastle Association in Breconshire. The date is not known but it was soon after he joined the Methodists. His path took him across the mountains and he was not familiar with any part of the journey. At Llanbryn-mair he found two others travelling to the same destination, but they were as ignorant as he as to the way. At Rhayader-on-Wye some landmarks on the mountain road were mentioned to them as signposts to look out for, but soon night fell and these could not be seen. Their anxiety increased greatly, but when they were most desperate a stranger dressed as a shepherd suddenly appeared and asked whether it was to the Trecastle Association they were bound. On their replying that it was so, he answered, 'You have lost the way; go straight between those two hills and after leaving the mountains you will find a farmhouse on the roadside. The inhabitants are of the same religion as yourselves and on calling you will receive comfortable lodging.' As they marvelled at their unexpected deliverance they turned back to view their rescuer again and to thank him for his kindness, but to their great surprise he was nowhere to be seen. All had occurred on the bare slopes of the mountain with nowhere for a man to hide. At this John Evans said, 'It was an angel, most certainly.' On they went, as directed, and found everything as stated by the shepherd. They arrived at Trecastle the next morning and discovered that Rowland, Harris and Whitefield were preaching at eleven, and that these sermons were to draw the association to a close. John Evans succeeded in his purpose, receiving promises from Rowland and Harris, and many of the other exhorters, to visit the north. We must not dismiss his idea as to the shepherd. You would not often find a man less given to imagination and superstition than he, and it may be that we do not have as yet a full enough conception of the ministry of angels.

JOHN EVANS AS A PREACHER

About the year 1765, some twenty years after coming to faith, John Evans started to preach. It is more than likely that he slipped gradually into the work. As he continued to travel far and wide, assisting at prayer meetings and *seiadau*, it would not have involved much for him to take the further step of giving some words of exhortation to the mixed company. The Monthly Meeting, which could have granted permission for this, does not seem to have existed at this time in Meirionethshire but, no doubt, the more godly and discerning of the brethren, knowing the extent of his knowledge and his depth of comprehension of the truths of the gospel, would have pressed him to the work. There were few indeed of the preachers of the time who could claim to possess such breadth of knowledge. His general grasp of history was good, his knowledge of geography excellent and he was familiar with many branches of learning not commonly studied. In particular he was a fine theologian. Having taken up the ministry, he threw himself into the work with that same commitment that characterized all that he did. He journeyed far in order to preach, particularly in the mountainous regions of Meirioneth, receiving no financial recognition. Rising with the sun on the Sabbath day, he would begin his journey, often one of ten, twenty or thirty miles; he would preach three times, then return home that same night, however stormy the weather, so as to be at his work on the Monday morning. One Sunday night, after preaching at Cwm Tirmynach, he was preparing to return. It was a dark night, with a rough road ahead and the rain falling in torrents. Friends begged him to stay, but he would not, declaring that important duties required him home on the morrow. 'Trust to Providence,' one brother told him. 'I must do my own work', was the reply. 'Providence will not melt the wax, nor form the candles. I must do it or it will not get done.' Without his diligence as to his circumstances in the week he could not have served the gospel on the Sabbath, as he did.

As might have been expected, John Evans was a solid preacher, declaring the truth in its simplicity. Many of the exhorters of the time appealed mainly to the emotions. Their purpose was to awaken the ungodly and while proclaiming the destruction awaiting an evil world they would shout and cry out, literally fulfilling the command, 'Cry aloud, spare not, lift up thy voice like a trumpet.' In many ways they met the needs of the day and were the means, under God, of convicting many. But this led some to conclude that shouting and roaring were indispensable elements of preaching. John Evans, on the other hand, sought to enlighten the mind and feed the people with knowledge; he appealed, certainly, to the emotions and feelings, but only through the understanding. He therefore spoke quietly, never in fact raising his voice. The more discerning of the people greatly enjoyed his ministry – the clarity of his style, the simple and scriptural form of his language, the solidity of his arguments and the very practical nature of all his preaching, were much appreciated by them. He preached with his natural speaking voice without any artificiality or assumed intonation. When asked why he did not shout or work up steam in the pulpit as most of his contemporaries, he replied, in the wry manner that was his, that there was no need to sweat when telling the truth. Because of his slowness of delivery, a few of his colleagues began considering his case, as to whether it would not be best for him to give up preaching. This was before the time of Mr Charles's settlement at Bala, and before the establishment of the Monthly Meeting. After much discussion, it was decided that because no real unction was to be seen on his ministry and no great excitement accompanying his preaching, it were better for him to cease. A brother was appointed to convey this message. 'Ho!' was the reply. 'Go back to those who sent you and tell them I will continue to preach until I see better preachers than myself arising.' Indeed, they fully deserved this slight, for if there was a need for dramatic preachers to thunder over the ungodly, there was just as much need for preachers of John Evans's type to nurture the people in the principles of religion and build them up in the doctrines of the gospel.

It was his habit to attend the Associations of the south as well as those of the north, walking the journey each time. From Howell Harris's diary we find that Evans and his friend Humphrey Edward were present at the Newcastle Emlyn Association of October 1764. There, a heated argument arose between Harris and some of the exhorters as to the appropriateness of continuing Harris's settlement at Trefeca. The exhorters suggested that the matter be referred to the two brothers from north Wales, Edward and Evans, for their decision. Harris would not agree to this, believing that his building of Trefeca had been under divine guidance. But the brethren's suggestion shows that, even then, John Evans – for he was foremost of the two – was not only well known in the south though he had not yet begun to preach, but his opinions well respected. He was present also at the Fishguard Association of February 14, 1770, when he and Howell Harris contested the venue of the next Association – Harris conveying an invitation from Trefeca, and Evans from Bala. Harris was slightly angered that the Bala exhorter opposed him and stated that the refusal of his invitation would not demonstrate much love towards himself. At this John Evans rebuked him for placing his own personal feelings before the spiritual needs of the north. And John Evans won the day. To withstand a man of Howell Harris's influence required great courage but Evans was well up to the task.

The Humphrey Edward mentioned above was a native of Llanllugan, Denbighshire. He was converted there, probably under Harris's preaching, and subsequently ministered at Pentyrch near Llanfair Caereinion. Another exhorter living in the Bala area at this time was William Evans of Bedwarian whose ministry was, on occasions, accompanied by an irresistible power and influence. We have already mentioned also the brothers Evan and John Moses. John Evans used to say of the first that since his conversion no one had seen him frivolous or bad tempered, nor heard him indulge in idle talking. He used to compose hymns whilst working between the fire and the anvil in the forge, in the same way as Edward Coslett composed his sermons. So as not to forget any thought or verse that came to him, he would have pen and paper ready beside him when working.

It would seem that John, his brother, was converted before him. He was one of the few who stood by Howell Harris when he was attacked so viciously in Bala. Indeed, had not John Moses and others rushed in to face the danger and place their own lives in jeopardy, he would probably have been beaten to death. When the riot passed John Moses and his mother, Catherine Edward, were arrested for giving Harris leave to preach in their house. Two others of the hearers were arrested and eventually Catherine Edward was fined twenty shillings and the other three five shillings each for meeting to hear preaching.

An episode in the life of John Moses demonstrates the kinds of stratagems which the preachers of that time resorted to in order to preach. He went once to Llanfair in the Clwyd valley. On the way his horse became lame with a loose shoe and he took it to the blacksmith to repair the damage. A mob of persecutors had already collected together intending to disturb the preaching and cover the speaker in mud. They appointed as their leader a strong, aggressive character who happened also to be very short. On his way to the forge John Moses was immediately suspected of being the preacher and the leader accosted him:

'Are you the Roundhead who was announced to preach here?'

'I don't think my head is rounder than anyone else's. Look for yourself,' replied John Moses, removing his hat and cocking his head towards him.

'I'll cut that head off if you dare to stand up and speak to the people.'

'Well, even if you did, I'd still be taller than you,' replied Moses, who was over six foot tall. The humour of his answers softened his assailant, who responded:

'Come to the tavern for a pint together', and there they repaired, for Temperance had not been born yet and alcohol was not considered so sinful, provided it was drunk in moderation. Over their glasses of beer the preacher turned to the fighter and quietly asked him:

'Seriously, what benefit will you gain from attacking an old man like myself? You won't gain any respect for beating a defenceless man, you'll only be mocked by all.'

'By the Old Nick,' was the answer, 'no one will be allowed to touch you. Preach as much as you like, you'll be left in peace.'

He kept his word and John Moses preached with much success. The remembrance of these two blacksmiths of Bala is sweet to this day.

EXAMPLES OF HIS WISE AND GODLY COMMENTS

But to return to John Evans. Not much is known of his labours in the gospel; no powerful services under his ministry are recorded. His present fame rests mainly in the popular record of his wise and sensible dictums, in which his keen discernment and his wit blend harmoniously. We give a few examples from the many at hand. His wife, who in her own way was as remarkable as himself, and who kept a copy of Caryl on Job open before her while kneading the dough, asked him once:

'Do you think, John, that we shall know one another in heaven?'

'Of course we will,' he answered. 'Do you imagine we will be greater ignoramuses there than here?' Then, after considering a moment, he added:

'But, Marged, we might be side by side for a thousand years without seeing one another, so taken will we be with the glory and wonder of the Saviour's Person.'

It would seem that Margaret enjoyed an argument and that John Evans considered her prone at times to go to extremes. One day she brought to the house a man from the neighbourhood who was of the same spirit as herself. At one point the conversation turned to the necessity of maintaining balanced, moderate opinions. Listening to their conversation, John Evans was amused in hearing them praising that virtue of which they were both so deficient, and eventually he interrupted them.

'It's true that it is best to keep to the middle of the road, but I don't believe that either of you will stay any longer at the middle than you need in crossing over from one side to the other.'

The following story shows, not only his discernment but also his gentleness of spirit. A young man, who was considered a bit simple, remained behind in the *seiat* at Bala on one occasion. His name was Abram Jones and he lived in the Ceunant on Bala Common. As one considered a bit wanting, he was allowed to remain with the fellowship on a number of occasions without any notice being taken of him. But on seeing that he continued to come, one of the elders rose and said, 'I do not know what to think of Abram here. He has been coming to us for some time now.' Before he could say anything further and possibly hurt the young man's feelings, John Evans interrupted him. 'Time will tell what Abram is made of.' The sequel proved him to be correct. 'Abram from the Ceunant' was a shining Christian for sixty years, becoming known to all the Methodists of Meirionethshire as one recognized more for his love of heart towards Jesus Christ than for any deficiency of mind, and his unblemished walk proved him to be an Israelite indeed. The night before he died, Abram Jones said, 'I have been in the house of the Man (*'Y Gŵr'*, his favourite name for the Saviour) for over sixty years, but He did not say what He intended to do with me. I did not press Him to say. I found pleasure in His service and a strength to stay with Him throughout the time, but now, during this last year, the Man has told me clearly that He will not condemn Abram Jones.'

We have another example of his gentleness of spirit. After he preached once at Llanuwchllyn a woman who had previously lived a very worldly life, presented herself to the *seiat*. On examining her she was found to be very ignorant of the plan of the gospel and they were undecided what to do with her, whether to receive her on probation or not. After many had given their opinion, with all expressing some hesitation, John Evans's view was sought. 'Well,' he replied, 'the first step towards entering the narrow way is to turn your face towards it.' And this comment proved sufficient to clear the way for the woman, who had been in great distress of mind, to remain in the fellowship of the saints.

In his old age, John Evans's hearing became very bad, and, at this time, an Association was held at Bala. Mr Charles was the Chairman and the subject to be discussed was faith. Many of the pillars were present, Jones Llan-gan, Nathaniel Rowland, and others. Many views were expressed as to the grace under consideration. Some said that true faith was an enlightening of the soul, others maintained it to be a mental persuasion to take God at His word. The last to speak was David Jones, Llan-gan, who said that faith was a commitment – the commitment of one's life to Jesus Christ for eternity. Before closing, Mr Charles turned to John Evans, who was seated under the pulpit, and asked him whether he had heard the discussion. He answered that he had not understood much.

'They are speaking of faith,' said Thomas Charles.

'Indeed,' was the reply, 'and what do they say is true faith?'

'O, there are different views of it, but the last to speak described it as a committing of the soul to Christ.'

'That is correct,' said the old patriarch. 'Faith is a committing; but remember, it is a committing with one's eyes open. Faith commits, but presumption will commit also; but before faith will act, it must have a foundation, namely God's Word.'

Many of his sayings were connected with the Rev. Thomas Charles. One Saturday, an unusually stormy day, Mr Charles was worrying about a preaching engagement for the next day in a small hamlet amongst the Meirionethshire hills. He was undecided what to do, whether to risk the journey in such weather, or not. He sent his maid to the house nearby, where John Evans lived in his old age, to ask for advice. The answer returned. 'Ask Mr Charles if he is a master or a servant. If he is a master he may do as he pleases, but if he is a servant he must obey his call.' This settled the matter and, notwithstanding the danger of the storm, the preacher fulfilled his engagement.

When Mr Charles was ill and suffering greatly in the care of physicians because of the amputation of part of a thumb, John Evans would visit him every day. One day the patient was very low. The doctor had found that the gangrene had spread further than was originally thought and the remainder of the thumb would have to be removed. He asked his old friend, with some seriousness:

'John Evans, what do you think the Lord will do with me?'

'Indeed, I don't know what He intends,' was the reply, 'but I know this, Sir, He will do you no wrong, for the Lord does not see fit to deal falsely with any man.'

This answer lodged in Thomas Charles's mind and he testified afterwards to the Rev. John Parry of Chester, of the strong consolation he received from the words when under the surgeon's knife. When calling on his sick friend John Evans would not leave without reading and praying. And, without exception, the Bible passage chosen would be some reference to the sufferings of the Lord Jesus. Mr Charles noticed this and asked him the reason;

'For I know,' he said, 'that you have some purpose in view.'

'Yes, Sir,' was the reply, 'I have a reason. No real comfort arises from anywhere, other than the sufferings of Christ; and there is nothing that helps us to endure our sufferings more patiently than a deep appreciation of His pains, who suffered such contradiction of sinners against Himself.'

Mr Charles had complete trust in his judgment. On one occasion in a Monthly Meeting, a number of young men were being examined with a view to their entering the ministry. After many had spoken, Mr Charles turned to John Evans, asking him had he anything to add.

'Yes, there is one question I would like to ask them. What is your purpose while preaching? What is your aim in every sermon?'

Mr Charles replied:

'Perhaps it would be better if you told them what to aim at; that would be profitable for all of us.'

'You should firstly,' began John Evans, 'endeavour to enlighten the minds of your hearers. No real profit will be obtained while the mind is still dark. Then, seek to awaken guilty and sleepy consciences. Aim those darts which are found in the Word at their hearts, and watch to see if it pleases God to bless such means to their awakening, causing them to cry out as the multitudes on the day of Pentecost: 'Men and brethren, what shall we do?' Next, you should strive in every sermon, to win their affections and draw them to love Christ and the treasures of the gospel. And lastly, ensure that all your sermons emphasize the need for a holy life and conversation.'

It would be a hard task indeed to find a better summary of those aims that should govern preachers of the gospel in all their work.

At another time, during the *seiat* for preachers at a Bala Association, an argument arose as to the nature of the specific qualification given by God to those He calls to preach. Is it an increased portion of that grace received in some measure or other by all Christians; or does God bestow an unique qualification, a specially ministerial grace? After many had spoken, John Evans's views were sought.

'He gives both,' was the answer. 'He gives more grace than is received by the ordinary Christian, and He provides the spirit and gift of ministry as well.'

In a south Wales Association he once even floored Jones, Llan-gan, a possessor of one of the readiest tongues ever heard in Wales. John Evans had been complaining that the preachers of the south in their itineraries had not been visiting the small and feeble flock that gathered at Y Graig, near Machynlleth. Jones, Llan-gan answered him:

'Well, John Evans, not one of the brethren there has been at any time to the Association to say Come!' 'Well, Sir,' was the reply, 'have you forgotten that you have been commanded, "Go!" ?'

Jones, for all his wit, could find no answer to this and had to sit down defeated, but with a warm smile on his face.

In another Association the topic of election was being discussed. As John Evans could not hear, he asked what subject was under attention. 'The election of grace,' he was told. It would appear that he concluded that not much profit was to be had from discussing such a deep subject and that more might be gained from a more practical topic. 'Is there anyone here who doubts the truth of election? If not, there are other things just as necessary for us to consider, things that we may experience as well as believe.' John Jones of Edern, a very able and quick-witted man and a fine preacher, rose to his feet and said:

'I am a farmer, John Evans, and should you see me in one particular field, that would not prove that I did not possess other fields as well.'

'True enough,' he replied, 'but I could safely so conclude, if I saw you in the same field all the time.' His answer suggests that the doctrine of election was very often under discussion and that he considered that other doctrines were being neglected.

His courage was equal to his quick-wittedness and remained typical of him, even to his old age. At one meeting during a Bala Association, when his speech had thickened and was difficult to understand, he had turned whilst speaking to face the preachers that were sitting under the pulpit. John Elias rose up and suggested:

'Turn your face to the people, John Evans. Speak to the people.'

With a penetrating look, John Evans considered him.

'What? And are you not one of the people?'

And that great man was happy enough to sit down, out of sight, under the pulpit.

On the road to Chester at one time he met with a Quaker, who noticing his unpretentious dress, his quiet simple manner and careful walk, concluded that he was a member of his own sect. He approached him and placing an arm on his shoulder said:

'The Spirit tells me that you are one of us.'

John Evans replied in an instant:

'If a spirit told you so, it was a lying spirit.'

The Quaker departed, having received what was to him the heaviest blow possible.

It may be that John Evans excelled more in the *seiat* than in the pulpit. His habit was to throw out a question to this one or to the other. 'How do you feel towards sin? Are you hungering and thirsting after righteousness? Do you love the Lord Jesus?' If the one answering replied that he hoped so, the response would be, 'See to it that you are correct', and he would turn to the next. He would receive quite humorous replies at times, but nothing would throw him off balance or irritate him. Roland Roberts of Pandy, a rather simple and naive old man, once told him:

'John Evans, I believe that sin does me a great deal of good.'

'What!' he replied. 'Sin do you good? Certainly not! Sin never did anyone any good.'

But old Roland persisted:

'Yes indeed, John Evans, it has done me good. It has driven me to pray many times.'

'You are greatly mistaken, Roland Roberts,' said he. 'Sin does nothing but harden. If something drives you to pray against sin, that is not due to the sin itself, rather it is from heaven.'

He was completely persuaded that religious services of great length were of no profit and consistently opposed long meetings. His advice was always, 'A little, and to the point,' often adding, 'When the people have begun to tire, worship has already ceased.' He was just as zealous for the punctual commencement of services. The inhabitants of Bala were once taught a lesson that they were not to forget in a hurry. He was to preach in the chapel one Friday night and arrived punctually, to the minute. Only two or three others were present but he began immediately and it was not long before he brought the service to a close. He then locked the doors, placing the key in his pocket. On his way home he met many on their way to the chapel, who asked him:

'Where are you going, John Evans?

'Home.'

'Aren't you coming to the meeting?'

'The meeting is over,' was the rather brusque reply.

This episode put paid to the lack of punctuality at the means of grace in Bala, at least during his lifetime.

His honesty in business was proverbial. Once he bought a horse from a neighbour. Some time afterwards a friend congratulated him on obtaining such a bargain, adding that the horse was worth a pound more than the price paid. 'If that is so,' said John Evans, 'it is only right that I should pay that extra pound,' and he sent it immediately. Another time a small boy from the countryside arrived at Bala with a load of wax for him.

'My father says that he must have such and such a pound for it,' was the message.

'Well, my boy,' said John Evans to him, 'I usually pay more than that for wax these days, so your father must have the higher price.'

It is no wonder that the people of Bala held him in such respect and that the whole locality had complete trust in him.

We have already mentioned that as far as preaching gifts were concerned he was never a popular preacher, although those who considered content more important than delivery appreciated him greatly, but as an organizer his excellence was generally acknowledged. As the Methodist revival progressed and the hearers multiplied, the urgent need for meeting places arose in many parts of the country. No plan had been put forward to begin this work of building chapels, nor was there any particular fund to draw upon. John Evans suggested that every member should contribute a halfpenny a week, that is, sixpence halfpenny a quarter, towards a general building fund. The plan was approved in an Association held in Caernarvonshire. His biographer, the Rev. Simon Lloyd, stated, 'This was the beginning of the quarterly collection.' Subsequently it became a regular feature in the north and resulted in the building of chapels in many areas that could never have managed it otherwise.

HIS LAST YEARS

John Evans was granted a long life. He lived to the age of ninety-three and was connected with the Methodists for nearly seventy-two of these years. He saw the Connection in its feeble beginnings, especially in the north, when the adherents were few in number, persecuted, and held in contempt by high and low. He saw the painful quarrel between Rowland and Harris commencing; quite probably he took part in the controversy, for his influence was too great for his opinion not to be taken into account, and almost certainly he sided with Rowland. He saw, after a long and bitter night, when true religion had almost departed the land, a dawn of revival, the first-fruits of many subsequent awakenings, breaking over Wales. This was after the publication of Williams Pantycelyn's immortal hymns. He saw the saints dancing in their joy in Bala town and in the narrow valleys of Meirionethshire; he listened to their songs and noted their praises. Usually he was not in favour of extremes of religious enthusiasm – he feared lest strange fire should be brought into God's temple – but we can be sure that the Welsh revivals, being so clearly the direct fruit of the Spirit, filled his heart with thanksgiving. He saw the disagreement amongst the Methodists during the Peter Williams affair, and as the matter was debated at a Bala Association he again could not have avoided being involved. He saw the Rev. Thomas Charles join the Methodists and in all probability, being so well acquainted with him, he advised him in his work of establishing the Sunday Schools, and in the founding of the Bible Society. He took part, no doubt, in the arguments over ordination, and we can well believe that it was his opinion that influenced Thomas Charles, bringing him to agree that the Methodist body should ordain preachers from within its own ranks to the full work of the ministry. We are sure also, because of the great respect in which he was held by the churches, that he would have been one of those set apart in that first ordination, had it not been for his age. He was eighty-four years old at the time and the ceremony would have served no purpose. He was not ordained, therefore, but he was assigned a prominent part in the ordination service, held at Bala on June 19th, 1811. The following description is given in the Confession of Faith:

> Firstly, the senior and most respected member of the Connexion, John Evans of Bala, read 1 Timothy 3, and on reading made a few relevant and simple remarks concerning the necessary qualifications for ministerial office outlined in the chapter. After reading he prayed over the work of the day, again most simply and relevantly.

The report shows the extent of the regard in which the leaders of the Connexion held him. In his long life he saw a scorned few becoming a great host, organizing their various activities and forcing their one-time persecutors to respect them, so that they became acknowledged as the strongest religious force in the country. John Evans's connection with the denomination extended to nearly half its lifetime, from its beginnings to this day. Because of this, and because of his great discernment, there was no one better than he for providing an account of the beginnings of the Methodist revival – describing the condition of the country before it broke out and the influence it had on the morals and religion of the Welsh people. We are glad that he did so much in this respect by means of a report to Mr Charles, which the latter published in *Y Drysorfa Ysbrydol* [*'The Spiritual Treasury'*] in the form of a conversation between Senex and Scrutator.

He laboured diligently in his profession until past ninety years old and when his health failed, he was supported by his Meirionethshire brethren. In his last years his hearing was so bad that he could hear nothing of what was said in the services, but was always present in the public meetings and when asked the reason replied, 'I go to the sanctuary so that I may worship the Lord.' He suffered a degree of senility in his last years which resulted in some confusion of mind at times. His religious sense prevailed to the end however. Friends visiting him on one occasion found him greatly troubled with the thought that the Lord Jesus would not receive him. One of them referred him to the Saviour's words, 'He that cometh unto me I will in no wise cast out.' John Evans took hold of those words and, with hands knit together and tears filling his eyes, said, 'What better can a poor sinner like myself do than to lay hold on such a precious promise as that?' Another time a friend asked him how he felt. He answered:

> I am fairly free from pain and derive pleasure even in my illness; yet I believe that death is near. My life however is in the Lord's hand. Certainly it is better

> with me than it was for Jesus of Nazareth. He knew many a hard day, and many nights of trouble; but I am dealt with very gently. In the days of His flesh Jesus received many bitter woes; but I, though I deserve many strokes, I receive but mercies.

He died in great peace on August 12, 1817, and was laid to rest in Llanycil cemetery on the banks of Llyn Tegid.

23

ROBERT ROBERTS OF CLYNNOG

HIS PARENTAGE AND YOUTH

Robert Roberts of Clynnog was the first preacher from amongst the Methodists of Gwynedd to be considered one of the giants of the pulpit. He was the first also to be generally recognized throughout north and south Wales as one of the most influential preachers of his time. It is doubtful whether anyone in any age has surpassed him in terms of effectiveness and power. The older generation, it is true, would not accept him as equal to Rowland but they acknowledged him as the nearest of all to Rowland. At this time the lay preachers were referred to as 'exhorters' but no one thought to call Robert Roberts by such a name. He was accepted as a preacher in the full sense of the word. His life was relatively short. His preaching life was very short – a mere fifteen years, but in that time he shook Wales to its roots. He was compared to a great volcano, pouring forth molten lava in terrible streams that set whole neighbourhoods aflame. We have often had cause to complain that the early days of so many of the Fathers lie hidden in darkness, but this is not the case for Robert Roberts. There is a limited biography written by his nephew, Michael Roberts, but it is far too brief and gives very few details of his preaching and of the many remarkable experiences that accompanied it. We are indebted, rather, to oral traditions and to the memories of old people for safeguarding what we know of such occasions. In 1844 the Rev. Griffith Parry D.D. collected together all the scattered fragments of testimony that could be found, adding to them his own excellent comments on the attributes and genius of this remarkable ministry.

Robert Roberts was born in a cottage called Ffridd-bala-deulyn in the parish of Llanllyfni, Caernarvonshire on 12 September 1762. He belonged therefore to the second generation of Methodist preachers. The first Association at Watford had been held nineteen years before his birth. Daniel Rowland was forty-nine years older than him and had been preaching destruction to a wicked world for twenty-seven years before his appearance. Robert was the son, the youngest of thirteen children, of Robert Thomas and Catherine Jones. (In north Wales it was the custom until very recently for a married woman to keep her maiden name.) When he was a baby his parents came under the influence of the gospel and joined with the few Methodists that met to worship at Buarthau in Llanllyfni parish. Dr Owen Thomas states that they soon opened their home to preaching and that services were held there for fifty-two years. The father would hold family worship regularly and the whole family would join in reading, praying and singing a psalm or hymn. At first Robert Thomas had no confidence to pray but would read from some prepared prayers of Griffith Jones, Llanddowror, but after a while he put the book aside and the worship was conducted with considerably greater liveliness. He was particularly careful over his family. At night, after the labours of the day, he would keep a school for the children, teaching them to read God's Word. A portion of each Sabbath would be spent the same way. When he was away at Sunday worship, at some distance from the home, the school would be supervised until his return by John, his eldest boy, known to us now as the Rev. John Roberts, Llangwm. On Sunday evenings he would question the family on what they had learnt in the week and would teach them the Catechism. In this way Robert Roberts learnt to read at a young age. Whether he received any further education we do not know; if he did, it was, of necessity, of very limited duration, for the circumstances of a small hill farm, with thirteen children to clothe and feed, could not stretch to much education.

Robert Roberts therefore was brought up in the midst of religious influences. When he was about seven years old his brother John, then a youth of seventeen, was converted. From that time onwards Robert became his special object of care. Robert showed much promise as a boy. He had an excellent memory and would learn his Catechism with relish. However at about fourteen years of age he lost all appetite for spiritual things and became wilder in his ways, befriending ungodly boys and following them in their vanities. Books became tedious to him and it was nearly impossible to persuade him to hear a sermon. With all his zestful energies he pursued the corrupt sports fashionable in his day. His family were greatly distressed because of him and John in particular grieved to see him so committed to excess.

HIS CONVICTION, UNDER THE PREACHING OF DAVID JONES, LLAN-GAN

Then, when he was about sixteen years old, it was learnt that Jones of Llan-gan was making a tour through areas of Caernarvonshire and would preach at Brynrodyn on a certain day and hour. His coming caused a stir.

The name of Jones, Llan-gan, held the whole of Gwynedd under its spell. After much effort John obtained a promise from Robert that he would attend the service.

When the day arrived the small chapel at Brynrodyn could not have contained a tenth of the huge congregation that had gathered from all parts and Mr Jones was obliged to preach in the open air. This was at noon, on a fine summer's day. Near to the preacher's station was a stone wall, and here the careless youth of the various neighbourhoods sat in rows, whilst the religious hearers pressed as closely as they could to the man of God. The two brothers from the Ffridd were thus separated – one on the stone wall, amongst the ungodly, and the other taking his place with the saints. According to Dr Owen Thomas it was John Roberts who began the service. Mr Jones's text was Zechariah 9:12, 'Turn you to the stronghold, ye prisoners of hope.' He had three points: the prisoners, the stronghold, and the turning to the stronghold. He began to describe the state of sin's captives, their loathsome service, their dreadful end and how if they continued onwards towards that end there would be none to visit them and invite them to the stronghold. 'But,' cried the evangelist of Llan-gan, his voice melting with tenderness, 'I am calling you to the stronghold today.' The scene by now was a terrible one. The ungodly young men were white of face, fear and trembling filling their hearts. John Roberts, glancing at his brother every now and again, saw his head drop forwards. He did not know the reason. Was it illness, or had a shaft from the preacher's bow pierced home? Mr Jones proceeded to describe Christ as the stronghold, and the immense privilege of being allowed to approach him. At this, heavenly streams descended. The godly smiled through their tears and the meeting ended in much singing and praises.

But what of the ungodly boy from the Ffridd? At the close of the sermon John went to look for him but failed to find him. Then he spotted him, striding homewards on his own. His whole demeanour was sobered, his face showed signs of much weeping and he would scarcely answer a word. His brother thought at first that some sudden illness had struck him and he inquired anxiously whether he was well. 'Yes, just as well as usual,' was the brusque reply. But after three days his conflict of soul was too much for him and, pulling John aside, he confessed the burden upon his heart. His brother advised him to turn his back forever on the devil's ways and to commit himself completely to the Lord and his people. As a consequence Robert Roberts immediately joined the *seiat*, to the great joy of his family and of the brethren. But for a long time he could find no peace for his soul. It appears that the painfulness of his thoughts was intense. He felt himself on the edge of perdition. His conscience tore like an angry bear inside him. So fearful did the task of accounting for himself before God appear to him that he would almost have preferred to have been an irrational creature so as to avoid judgment. While referring to this period, years later, as he shared his experience in an Association, he described how the tensions that filled his mind were such that he would envy the goslings that were around his father's house and he wished that he had been born a chick rather than being human. How long he remained in this state we do not know. The means by which he obtained peace of mind is also unknown. But peace he did find, the bonds were broken and he escaped as a bird from the snare of the fowler. Behold Robert Roberts, now a new creature to all eternity!

At this time he worked at a slate quarry called Cilycwm, close to his home. His family thought it better for him to leave the quarry and to work on a farm. Quite possibly they wished to break the connection with his ungodly associates at the quarry. He agreed and was engaged as a labourer at a small holding called Cefn Pencoed in Eifionydd. He became a member at Brynengan. Brynengan *Seiat* was known for its warmth. Its membership included men who were strong in mind and rich in grace and the young stranger was welcomed by them with every kindness. By now he possessed an insatiable appetite for sermons and if a preacher was announced as being engaged anywhere in the vicinity, he would be at the service. So that his master should not be a loser in any way because of this, he would rise earlier and work later in order to make up for any time lost. He would write down any sermon that he heard. It hardly requires saying that he knew no shorthand. His method was to go somewhere apart immediately after the sermon and write down everything he could remember. Having such an acute and lively memory, he would end up with almost all the sermon. He would often go with the older Brynengan believers to Llangeitho to hear Rowland and did the same with his sermons. Someone mentioned to Rowland that a youth from Caernarvonshire had a copy of his sermon, word for word. 'I don't believe it,' said the preacher. 'Nobody yet has succeeded in doing that.' 'Indeed, sir,' was the reply, 'it is very similar.' At this he called for Robert Roberts and asked him to read what he had written. This a rather bashful Robert did. When he finished, the old minister told him, 'I have known many thieves come to Llangeitho, but not one that could compete with you.'

After five years at Cefn Pencoed he moved to a farm called Cae Hir, and after a year there he was engaged as head labourer at Coed-cae-du under John Pritchard. This John Pritchard was the father of the Rev. Richard Jones of Wern. By now Robert had grown tall and strong. He stood as straight as an arrow and there were not many his equal for strength. Whether this had resulted in some arrogance in his appearance we do not know, but certainly Daniel Rowland had somehow formed an impression of him that he was proud. When he was pointed out as one who would make a preacher, Rowland replied, 'A preacher! A preacher! He will never make a preacher unless he experiences some change of condition.' In due course Rowland had to change his views. Whilst at Coed-cae-du Robert gave himself to reading. He would buy candles and stay up till the early hours with his books, his Bible in particular. When his brother John rebuked him, telling him that he would surely ruin his health, Robert's answer was, 'I have such an appetite for God's word that I could not stop for the world.'

HIS ILL-HEALTH

At this time he was struck by a very serious illness. It began as a painful and persistent cough. His employer's wife was a particularly kind woman and knowledgeable in herbalism and medicine and by means of appropriate leaves she was able to clear the cough completely. But the disease, leaving the lungs, entered the limbs as a rheumatism. He was in great pains for nine weeks. His body was wracked by aches and the doctors could do little for him. When eventually he was allowed to rise, he was a strange sight. All his limbs seemed out of place, his body was bent and he was three inches shorter than formerly. A young doctor from the Penmorfa area, who had travelled much, advised him to bathe daily in the river and to stay in the water until he felt thoroughly cold and then to dress as quickly as possible. This he did, obtaining much benefit. He was relieved of pain and strengthened in his body. But his spine had been shortened and he remained bent to the end of his days. Before his illness he had become engaged to a young girl from the neighbourhood. He was now worried about what to do and asked advice from his brother John and others. All suggested that it would be appropriate for him to break the engagement. But love is strong as death. Robert Roberts was her choice and she would not release him, bent or otherwise. So the two were married. Their first home was a house with a garden, called Ynysgaled, on John Pritchard's land. Here they lived for some years before moving to Clynnog.

When he was about twenty-four years old God visited the church and neighbourhood of Brynengan in a powerful revival. The heavenly effects accompanying the ministry were so strong that hardly a service passed without someone being saved. The vessels of the older believers were full and running over with the wine of heaven. The children and young people were equally affected so that the strains of singing and praising filled the neighbourhood night and day. One of the most active in the revival was Robert Roberts. In nearly every meeting he broke out in joyous glorying. So notable were so many of his remarks as he worshipped that the preachers would listen to him in amazement. Though he was so feeble of body, yet he would leap as a hart in the services. His employer's wife once advised him not to shout so loudly and not to exhaust himself with his leaping or his very joints would give way. 'It can't be helped, mistress,' answered Robert, ' "*Ni chollwyd gwaed y groes, Erioed am ddim i'r llawr.*" ["The blood of the cross, Was never shed in vain."]' And with this he leapt and sprang like a young lamb in the field. 'True enough,' she replied, 'but neither was it shed for anyone to kill himself with shouting.' Nevertheless, according to Richard Jones of Wern, a contributor to his biography:

> Regardless of health or counsel, the sparing of his bones, or of anything else, Robert continued to sing and shout, loudly crying out, '*Gogoniant!,* Glory!', his eyes streaming with tears.

HE BEGINS TO PREACH

It is probably the brilliance of his gifts as he rejoiced that prompted the Caernarvonshire preachers to encourage him to give himself to the work of the gospel. This occurred towards the end of 1787, when he was about twenty-five years old, with a wife and two children. We are inclined to believe that he had not had a day of school before this time. He had been taught by his father to read Welsh and by reading the daily psalm from the prayer book, on alternate days with his master John Pritchard, he had become a fluent reader. Now, on commencing the important work of preaching, he attended Mr Evan Richardson's school at Caernarvon for some time. His purpose was to learn English so as to gain access to the theological treasures available in that language. He succeeded to a considerable extent and could afterwards make reasonable use of the works of English and Scottish theologians. In order to support himself he kept a Welsh school in various parts of Eifionydd for some years, preaching on Sundays and week nights. His constitution was so weak and his health brittle, so that as the calls upon him to preach began to multiply, he gave up the school and moved to the chapel house at Clynnog. He remained here to the day of his death, committing himself fully to the ministry.

We know very little of the history of his first few years of preaching but all agree that almost immediately he became the most popular preacher in Wales. Richard Jones of Wern, who knew him from his youth, said of him:

> At the beginning of his ministry, although possessing ample natural gifts, and always preaching in an orderly fashion . . . he was yet not as profitable and tender as one might wish, as is often the case with young preachers, thoughtful and zealous in their calling.

Little more could be expected from a farmhand almost completely lacking in education and culture whatever might be his gifts and imagination. It is possible that the flow of his oratory was not fully under his control, that he occasionally exhibited lack of taste, that his illustrations could be unnatural, and his use of words rough and ready. It could hardly be otherwise. But it was not long before nature and, in particular, the Holy Spirit, taught him otherwise. He shook off the lack of good taste, he became skilful in the use of illustration, and his powerful ministry began to affect not only the ignorant and uncultured but also the experienced and thoughtful. Richard Jones adds:

> The Lord led him in his ways and in a very short time enabled him to understand the experiences of the Christian, the experiences of a church, and the spiritual experiences of a minister of the gospel, more clearly than scores who have spent their whole lives in the rich pastures of the best schools of the world.

That which other orators achieved through effort and hard study, Robert Roberts seemed to accomplish instinctively. Nature was his teacher and under its tutelage he safely scaled the highest peaks of oratory. At the same time he was too sensible to undervalue scholarship. His biographers testify of his zeal in commending education and of his frequent complaints as to the lack of it in his own early days.

The cause at Clynnog was moribund when he moved there. The *seiat* was one of the earliest formed in Caernarvonshire and the original believers noted for their warmth of spirit. But, for some reason or other, their spiritual energies were failing and little life was felt in their meetings. To this church the coming of Robert Roberts was as life from the grave. He not only preached in the chapel but in various parts of the neighbourhood, and such was the power accompanying the ministry and the conviction of his message that strong men would faint under his words. Scores joined the church having been pierced and convicted under his sermons. Nor was Clynnog alone in having the privilege of hearing him. He toured the length and breadth of Wales many times. He was as well known in the south as in the north, and was referred to colloquially as *Little Robin of the north*. Twice, for periods of some weeks, he preached to the London Welsh. He often visited the cities of Liverpool and Manchester and was present at the opening of the first Calvinistic Methodist church in Manchester at the close of 1799. Throughout this time he laboured in considerable weakness. It was as if half of him was already in another world. On seeing him climbing into a pulpit you might imagine that he was more fitted for the cemetery than for work, but as soon as he began to speak he seemed to gain strength miraculously and congregations would be quelled in his presence. He lived on the edge of Jordan, almost as if he was up to his ankles in the waters, and from that vantage point eternity seemed to open up clearly before him, its misery being seen in one direction and its glory in the other. This gave an unearthly solemnity to his message. He appeared as an ambassador from another world. On his first preaching journey to Llangeitho he struck Rowland as one who would certainly become a master of the congregation. In order not to intimidate him Rowland tried to keep out of his sight during the sermon but at its close he went up to him with a broad smile to congratulate him and to counsel him to be careful not to take any praise for himself but to give all the glory to God.

POWERS ATTENDING HIS MINISTRY

Without doubt Robert Roberts was an extraordinary preacher and the church has seen few like him since the days of the apostles. We believe that he was the means of effecting in the north that which Howell Harris achieved in the south: the ungodly were filled with fear and the country subdued to the gospel. Dr Parry described him as a great spiritual force sweeping through the land. Though feeble of frame there was yet an awe-some authority in his appearance. Mr Ebenezer Richard, Tregaron, himself one of the pillars of the Welsh pulpit, said at one of the preachers' sessions of a Bala Association:

> We do not have the authority that our fathers had. We have to make use of constables to keep some of the crowd on the field in order but one look from Roberts, Clynnog, would subdue the crowd into solemnity.

According to the Rev. Robert Jones, a Baptist minister of Llanllyfni:

> He was such an accurate portrayer and so fluent a speaker that when he used to describe the Day of Judgment some of his listeners would be convinced that they were standing before the judgment throne. Often under his ministry men would fall as dead bodies on the chapel floor. Many would be unsure as to whether they were still on earth or in eternity.

Robert Jones related many interesting anecdotes about Robert Roberts. On one occasion the latter was preaching in the Gwynfryn neighbour-hood of Meirionethshire. He was standing to preach in 'Foulkes' Pulpit', so named because a man called Foulkes had built it. A large crowd had assembled in the open air but a storm of much wind and rain arose so that to remain outside would have been impossible. As the tempest started, Robert Roberts lifted his arms to the heavens and cried out, 'O my God, grant a respite for a little while, to speak and hear of thy Son.' Within five minutes the storm had quietened and the skies cleared. An intense silence descended upon all. Before the sermon was ended many had broken out in rejoicing and a deep impression was left on all present that 'this was the finger of God.' Robert Jones provides in another account an example of the conversion under his ministry of some of the worst characters of a neighbourhood. Robert Roberts was preaching on one occasion at Llanwyddelan, Montgomeryshire. In the area, as in many other places in Wales at that time, many wild and vain sports were pursued. A leader would be appointed for a year to oversee these games, much as a steward might be appointed for a horserace today. The leader for that year, Richard Bumford, turned up at the service, whether to listen out of curiosity or in order to disrupt we do not know. He was immediately converted. He left his old ways and vanities forever and became a faithful preacher for many years. Robert Roberts's words would fall as a fiery shower upon the consciences of his hearers. Whilst preaching at Manchester in 1794 an awful solemnity possessed him, so that he cried out, 'O people! Was it necessary for me to come here from Wales in order to make you fitter for the fires of Hell!' With this shout, such an influence passed through the crowd that they feared that Hell was opening to receive them and they ran about in wild terror looking for some place to hide. When Christmas Evans was ministering in Lleyn he would not waste any opportunity to hear the seraph of Clynnog. It is not too much to state that it was Robert Roberts's influence that made him what he became. He testified that it was by listening to Roberts that he discovered his own gifts, adding that he had hardly ever heard a more powerful and effective preacher.

This account of Robert Roberts's unique skills, given by Robert Jones, is confirmed by the words of the wise and discerning elder, Mr David Jones, Dolau-bach. The latter spoke of listening to Roberts preaching at Cilpill, a small mansion about a mile below Llangeitho. Robert Roberts was standing in the porch of the house with the congregation outside facing him. He described the coming of the Judge on the clouds on the Last Day. So alive and overwhelming was the description that Mr Jones lifted up his head expecting to see Christ on the clouds; so also did the whole crowd. David Jones was a very deliberate man, slow to be excited, and the strength of that portrayal that made him forget himself so completely must have been notable indeed.

Most certainly, all the qualifications needed for the preacher were found in Robert Roberts. But his skills of oratory are not adequate to explain the influences that would accompany his ministry. For all his strength of passion, his striking metaphors, the fluent flow of his phrasing and his natural dramatic gestures, these, on their own, could not produce the overwhelming effects experienced in his services. His great influence cannot be explained without recognizing an extraordinary divine unction.

Richard Jones has written:

> The most notable of all his endowments for preaching was the divine investiture of heaven. Like Aaron's flowing garments, this covered him from head to foot, concealing any weakness within. The savour of the pomegranates and the tinkling of the golden bells proclaimed his holiness throughout Israel. Yet, never was any priest clothed upon with such adornment as the Lord laid upon this poor instrument. It enabled him to shine fervently in the firmament of the Church to the end of his days and maintained him as a fiery angel, flying through the sky, proclaiming the gospel of the kingdom in its purity and strength. His voice, at times, was as a mighty thundering against great Babylon, so that one could imagine that all the martyrs and all the saints of heaven and earth were echoing forth, 'Babylon the great is fallen; the hour of her judgment is come; double unto her double according to her works.' Most certainly, God remarkably used him to make great rents and to pull down the walls of Babylon throughout Wales and parts of England. He had no education or degree to glory in, nor any human title to boast of, only 'the Sword of the Lord and of Gideon', a sling in the hand of a shepherd, and God . . . Such floods of divine unction would, at times, attend his ministry that it was more than nature could bear and the people would cry out in their scores and hundreds, as if they were being pierced with swords, their tears flowing in streams. This was the ministry with which Wales was baptized for many years and it will be more tolerable for the inhabitants of Sodom in the day of judgment than for those who heard it and who hardened themselves against it.

The description given by his nephew, the Rev. Michael Roberts, agrees completely with the above. He writes:

> I was only about six or seven years old when Robert Roberts began to preach but I remember something of his first visits to the Llanllyfni area because of the effects that followed his doctrines and all the talk of him that resulted. I used to hear him with special delight and very early on his ministry would touch every emotion within me. When about ten or twelve I would follow him throughout the Sabbath, come wind or weather, and felt nothing of the physical effort, such was the delight to my mind . . . I cannot give a better, more concise description of him than this: he was of a naturally pleasant and friendly temperament, yet courageous, leonine and no respecter of persons.

> In prayer he was never long and verbose but lively and warm in spirit. And so directly would he lay hold on his requests and on the promises of God through the Mediator, that it would be nigh impossible for any with a spirit of prayer not to unite immediately with him . . . As for his public ministry, it is difficult to provide a description. I have often thought as I heard the old people speaking of Rowland of Llangeitho, that the nearest I would have heard to him was Robert Roberts. He would study his texts from various doctrinal branches and draw the most detailed applications from them, according to his abilities. Generally, he would speak in a systematic, orderly manner on those topics which he had previously meditated. But his uniqueness was the fiery liveliness of his spirit in the act of speaking and the unction, the lustre and the streams that would descend on himself and his hearers, and the expression upon his face, so completely appropriate to the message, so that it would be impossible for anyone not to feel some effect at these times. Dozens of times have I seen congregations weeping, with not one dry eye present. If he was thundering forth the threats and curses of the law against transgressors, then the very thunders and lightning and terrors of Sinai would be experienced; if he was proclaiming the depths of the doctrine, the mystery of the Trinity, the Person of Emmanuel, the covenant of peace and the order of salvation, the soul would be filled with amazement and rejoicing; if, with heavenly ardour, he was setting forth and praising the benevolence of the grace revealed in the gospel, often the hard heart would be as a pool of water. Sin would be sin; man's condition wretched; the world would be empty; Christ adorable; and godly living very desirable to the soul, as we listened to him. Very rarely did I ever hear him without mourning, weeping, and some degree of glorying, nor did I know of anyone else who experienced the divine unction so consistently. Yet, occasionally he also would have much more difficult services, and less blessing at some times than others.

Another portrayal of him by the Rev. Michael Roberts is available. Robert Roberts was preaching at a service held by the Congregationalists at Pwllheli on 20 October 1836:

> . . . although his body was weak, he had a clear voice, a fluent speech and an excellent memory. He understood little of the professional skills of oratory and logic yet he could make himself completely understood by all. His words were delivered as sparkling streams, his illustrations always appropriate to his purpose, particularly when the light of heaven illuminated his doctrines and the Spirit of grace put his seal on the proceedings. His countenance would exhibit an unusual liveliness and boldness. The solemnity of his gaze was completely unassumed and would give rise to considerable expectation in his hearers that great matters were to be ministered – words of reconciliation and offers of free mercy to guilty sinners. He did not depend on divine blessing alone, his words would always be ordered and structured on every occasion,

yet very rarely would he be without that heavenly unction. His sermons often included many contrasts – he was adept at bringing the furthest extremes to converge in a very natural way. He would sound an alarm in thrilling warnings, breaking into weeping and tears in the next breath. The thunderbolts of the law would be flung as fiery darts upon the consciences of men at one point, and the gracious showers of the gospel of salvation would be poured forth immediately afterwards. The very reading of his text would always be a preliminary stroke in creating expectation and the attractiveness of his opening words would always satisfy. He also possessed sufficient energy, life, and fire to press the message home to every heart. The phrases of Scripture – with all the riches of their treasures – were so dear to his heart and so free on his tongue, that they were as new upon his memory, and he would never hesitate or err when quoting them. His hearers would not be allowed to rest until they had followed him to the conclusion of his reasonings, and found their stony hearts become pools of water.

EBEN FARDD'S DESCRIPTION OF HIM

The next portrait that we offer was drawn by the skilful pen of *Eben Fardd* (pen name of Ebenezer Thomas, 1802–63, a poet and literary figure) in an essay published in *Y Traethodydd* (*The Essayist*). *Eben Fardd* had no personal knowledge of the preacher – indeed, he was only a baby of three months when Robert Roberts died – but he was a native of Eifionydd where the man of God dwelt for many years and where his talent developed, and the two of them spent their last years at Clynnog. The name of Robert Roberts was therefore a familiar name from childhood to the poet and he had opportunities to talk with many who remembered him well and who knew from experience the power of his ministry and the blessing that would attend it:

> . . . let us view him in the pulpit – an agricultural labourer, short, humpbacked, but whose discerning gaze and expression suggest a mind of the highest and most disciplined character. We imagine him reading his text in a simple, solemn and striking manner. Then, the sermon – lively, fluent and authoritative – in his loud, pleasant and melodious voice, with no confusion or darkness of content, no untidiness or difficulty of utterance, no violence or awkwardness of argument and reason, and all contributing to the evident satisfaction of his hearers.
>
> But perhaps our younger, excitable, enthusiastic and imaginative readers, with some degree of disappointment, would wish to ask further, 'Is this all there is to Robert Roberts of Clynnog? If so, he is nothing like the one we had imagined him to be, for we have plenty of other Robertses of this description in our generation.' It is true, we do have, at this time, plenty who are equal to

him in the things so far noted and far better than him in some points, but we had to portray his form to begin with before breathing into it that living breath which made him such an animated spirit in preaching. And so we arrive at his unique abilities. The following were particularly characteristic of him:

1. *His loving nature.* All who knew him were unanimous in describing him as one who was notably warm and friendly, with nothing surly, arrogant or unkind about him. To illustrate this, we note the affectionate remembrance still to be found amongst his religious brethren of his very successful manner of warning and rebuking them personally and privately. Whenever he saw a brother manifesting a degree of spiritual decline, through some empty or frivolous response, or an inappropriate or proud manner, or if he had come to learn of some unworthy behaviour or habit in any of his brethren, then, when he next met them, whilst greeting one another, he would mention the misbehaviour and in a lively, pleasant and winning way, yet with great seriousness, he would counsel them in the friendliest manner, clasping their hands and saying quietly and lovingly, 'Good brother, recently your behaviour has been more fickle than is seemly for a Christian'; or, 'Dear brother, your manner suggests more pride than is appropriate to the simplicity of Christianity'; or some other similar words. And in every case, the warning or rebuke would effect a reform without producing any coldness or rebellious response.

2. *Zeal and warmth of spirit.* This is perhaps a dangerous characteristic when met with on its own, or associated with other passions of little taste or strength. In the former case it would be like an enormous fire in an empty house, wasting itself to no purpose and, at the same time, threatening to set the house on fire. When connected with degenerative tastes it leads to public presumption, and with weak abilities it can produce foolish fanaticism. But when found with a system of strong, lively and consecrated inclinations, it exalts every ability and maximizes usefulness to an unusual degree. It is suggested in his biography that this zeal threatened to undermine his own ministry at one time . . . but that in the formation of his character it was regulated by that wisdom which is from above until it became one of the most lively and powerful elements of his popularity and usefulness.

3. *The saturation of his mind and soul in the substance of his sermon.* He would be so soaked in the matter and content of his sermon that it would be, humanly speaking, as if, at the touch of the Almighty's voice, he was squeezed like a sponge full of water and would drip, or rather pour, over the congregation that which overflowed from his own soul, until they also were filled with the same heavenly liquid. The result was that the whole service acted as a kind of spiritual electric charge, providing a fearful blow to corruption and sin, and a healthy quickening to the new nature, the effect being at the same time both awesome and glorious.

4. *The liveliness and warmth of his temperament and feelings.* He felt deeply, animatedly, and passionately, the due importance and significance of all that came under his attention. So quickened was he himself by his concentrating and meditating upon things not seen and not experienced, except in part, that he appeared as one who had fully and directly entered into them. This was true both for the sufferings of Hell and the substantial delights of Heaven. Thus, the effect of his appearance and his preaching upon his hearers – fiery and severe, as it might be, or awakening and glorious – was similar to the effect that would be felt, on the one hand, if a damned soul from hell should appear in bodily form to portray to us all the fearful pains of Gehenna and the eternal woes and curses of the Law, manifesting at the same time by his tortured visage and unearthly stare the tormented feelings occasioned by such suffering. Or, on the other hand, similar to the effect felt if a blessed spirit should descend from the third heaven to reveal to us the happy mysteries and the glorious, unspeakable bliss of the rejoicing Church above and all the unimaginable privileges of the redeemed, and all the while displaying, by his shining features and blessed, ecstatic complacency, the very experience of all that he was portraying.

5. *His quickening abilities* – by means of which, as the angel of old, he 'did wondrously'. These were assisted and amplified by some, if not all, of the features mentioned previously. Because of them he would himself be so quickened with life and energy that others were necessarily affected. This would result in scenes, the reality of which it is almost impossible to convey to the reader. We will not attempt to do so, except to note some of his most striking characteristics and give illustrative examples. Those that most affected people were:

a. His severe, awakening, authoritative and piercing look.

b. His abrupt, solemn and terrifying interjections, such as *'Bobol! Bobol!'* ['People! People!']

c. His physical postures, emphasizing the nature and content of his message.

d. Sudden and unexpected pauses in the middle of a vehement, fierce passage.

e. Together with these might be mentioned his weeping . . . One of his listeners, a neighbour of his, described how he was once listening to him and Robert Roberts's tears were falling on to his own face as if water was being sprayed on him. This is probably an exaggeration, but it illustrates the point.

The following provide a few examples. At times the very reading of his text would produce amazing results. On one occasion the text was, 'Make the heart of this people fat,' etc. So stirring was his reading and in such a fiery and awakening manner, that his hearers immediately experienced a thrill of fear and

> terror that caused their hearts to tremble within them. Another time, he read the words, 'Great is the mystery of godliness: God was manifest in the flesh.' He suddenly addressed his listeners excitedly, crying out, 'People! People! People! Here is an unfathomable ocean. With God's help I will venture into its very depths. Keep hold tightly of me, you people.' This resulted in a shock of amazement passing through the whole congregation. Another occasion is mentioned when he was preaching in his lively, fervent manner and when, in the midst of the most fluent of deliveries, he suddenly bent his head low and remained thus for a little while, without a word. Then, lifting his head, he shouted three times, 'Hush! Hush! Hush! What is the noise I hear?' This was followed by a thundering cry, 'Upon the wicked he shall rain snares, fire and brimstone, and an horrible tempest,' etc., which completely shattered his congregation. Again, he portrayed Jonah thrown to the waves and the great fish swallowing him and, with him, piercing through the depths so that the waters foamed white about them, as if proclaiming, 'Clear the way for the messenger of the King!', and Jonah, crying inside, 'A Temple! A Temple! A Temple!' (The reference is to Jonah 2:4,7.) His tender, heavenly address, his melodious, plaintive and melting voice as he repeated the words 'A Temple', produced a notable effect of excitement and delight.

But the bard from Clynnog did not judge that his picture was yet complete. He realized that not even the greatest collection of natural oratorical powers could account for the influences felt in Robert Roberts's services and so he hurried to note another element, the most important of all, namely the supernatural element that would accompany his ministry.

> He would never be satisfied in the pulpit unless his sermon was in demonstration of the Spirit and of power. Often, we are told, when there were no indications that his arguments were reaching the hearts of his hearers, he would be seen, in the middle of his sermon, standing as if stunned and would then raise his eyes to the heavens, while tear after tear streamed down his cheeks, and cry out, 'O, Lord! Rend the veil! Rend the veil!' with such solemnity that his hearers, almost unawares, responded with a great united shout of, 'Amen!' Then the preacher would recommence his sermon with a cheerful, bold and lively countenance, as one reviving after much weariness. Having obtained power with God it was easy for him afterwards to obtain authority over his congregation and so the sermon, having begun dully, would end most effectively. Some of the crowd would faint, others would rejoice, all would be in tears. Some would be pleading for mercy, others full of thanks for having received it. Robert Roberts himself, overcome by the glories of eternity, would have to pray a second time, 'O, Lord! Stop! Stop! Close the veil a little, or we shall not be able to endure.'
>
> . . . We are sure that our readers would wish to know something of the way he would prepare and deliver his sermons. It would seem that he wrote out

very little of them nor, it would appear, were his notes of any great help to him. He would have with him only a short note. It seems also that he did not make use of any long or detailed introduction or preface to his remarks. One of his hearers described him, as he took his text and formed his opening comments, as similar to a man coming quickly into a house and looking keenly and briskly at everything about him, then, from the keenness of that preliminary survey, providing an immediate and accurate selection of the most effective and useful points to be found there that would serve his immediate purpose. He would then proceed without delay to the work in hand. It is said in his biography that 'in his exercise of prayer he was never long or all-encompassing, but would proceed directly to his point'. We might perhaps conclude that his method of preaching was very similar.

OWEN THOMAS' S DESCRIPTION

Such a description, by so able a man as *Eben Fardd*, is very valuable. It shows clearly that Robert Roberts was a preacher whose like the world does not often see. The same conclusion can be drawn from the excellent description of him given by the Rev. Owen Thomas, D.D., from which we cannot refrain from quoting at some length:

> His ministry, almost immediately, drew general attention, and he very soon became the most popular preacher in Wales. There was something in him as a preacher that is impossible to describe, something of which we, who never heard him, cannot imagine. All who did hear him testify that they heard no other like him. Such fluency of delivery, such passion of feeling, such liveliness and strength of imagination, such variety of voice and such ability to give himself so completely to the matters under consideration, would result in effects on his congregations that were electric. At such times he would, himself, present a strange sight. His agitation would be considerable. Sometimes his eyes would so flash with lightning that it would be nearly impossible to look at him; at other times, they would be seen to lighten, raising a smile on every face. More often still they would be fountains of tears, producing general tears throughout the congregation. Whatever the topic under consideration his powers of communication, by the expressions on his features, by the movements of his body, by the tone of his voice, as well as by his choice of words and the formation of his sentences, would be such that his hearers would not only understand his message but experience it. In particular he had an extraordinary ability for portraying the scenes that he described so that they became alive to his hearers. At times he would so depict the Judgment that his congregation would believe that they were there and would cry out for their lives. He would raise the throne, collect the great assembly together, divide the righteous from the wicked, pronounce the sentence. With the most affectionate of looks and sweetest of voices he would invite the just into the

kingdom. The glorious gates would be seen to open, the crown placed upon the head, the kingdom inherited, and the echoes of the golden songs of the redeemed hosts sound out in the ears of the hearers. Then he would turn to those on the left hand. With great solemnity in his gaze and with a voice of awful power and authority yet deepest feeling, he would pronounce the 'Go!', so that the congregation could see the poor wretches as they went, could hear their heart-breaking groans and see the prison doors opening, could view the eternal fires burning and endless despair engulfing them for ever . . .

. . . We heard Mr John Jones, Talsarn, give an account which again illustrates Roberts's ability to portray a scene. On some Sunday, John Jones was preaching at Llanllyfni upon the words, 'He will swallow up death in victory, etc.' The following week he received a letter from an old man who had been reminded by his sermon of a sermon of Robert Roberts's and had enclosed an account of it. John Jones had dealt with Jesus Christ wrestling with death but Robert Roberts had portrayed Jesus Christ wrestling with Satan. An intense, personal battle between them had occurred after his baptism and at that time Christ had obtained a clear victory over the devil. Every one of Christ's sermons and miracles was a direct attack upon Satan and in all of them Christ was, of course, the victor. The devil could see that if matters continued in this way he would lose all his own authority and power, and so he determined to have one last, decisive encounter. He put in motion all his stratagems, he collected all his hosts together. He put it in the heart of one of his disciples to betray him. The Lord Jesus was hard pressed to the extent that we find the civil authorities condemning him, the people mocking him, his disciples deserting him, he himself is nailed onto a cross and all the powers of darkness are at their best advantage for gaining the victory over him. And at Calvary, the great battle ensues. Robert Roberts imagined himself standing at the foot of the hill, witnessing the scene and describing it as he saw it. Soon the sky grows heavy, the light fades, and darkness hides the cross and the protagonists from view. He is now in the greatest of anxieties as to the result of the battle, as he knows that the life of the world hangs in the balance. He is eager to question the Lord Jesus but he realizes that there is such an awful weight upon his spirit that, in his love for him, he cannot contemplate disturbing him. He therefore shouts to the devil:

'How goes the battle, Satan?'

'We fight', is the reply.

'Ah!' said Robert Roberts, 'Our Jesus is holding his own though all the armies of hell oppose him. Great Jesus, you will conquer; our poor sinful lives depend entirely upon it.'

He turns to Satan again, and again inquires:

'How do matters stand now, Satan?'

'We fight on,' is the answer, but in a harsh, ill-tempered voice, as impersonated by Robert Roberts.

'O! Our Jesus, praise him! maintains his ground, and I rather believe that Satan is losing. He is certainly losing his temper and that would indicate that he is being beaten.'

He continued by emphasizing the importance of the struggle and the great apprehensions felt throughout heaven; in the minds of Abel, Enoch, Noah, Abraham and Moses; in the hearts of the prophets and all the saints of the Old Testament, as to the outcome of events at Calvary, so that all his hearers were overcome by the same fears, as if they had never previously heard, or had forgotten, what had ensued. Soon, another shout:

'How goes it now, Satan?'

But there is no answer.

'Satan, Satan, It will take you less than a quarter of a minute to break off and to inform me of the state of affairs.' But again there is no noise, nor any answer.

'What?' cried Robert Roberts, in amazement and fear, 'Have those two great giants made an end of each other? Dear Jesus! We are sorry to disturb you even for a second, but are you yet alive? If you are, tell us how goes the battle.'

At that, Jesus replies, in a voice of triumph:

'It is finished! I have trodden the winepress alone; and of the people there was none with me.' Immediately, the preacher cried out in great joy:

'Glory! There is Robin's life for him!' and the whole congregation also, in an instant, erupted with him into praising and rejoicing.

Amazing powers accompanied his preaching . . . We heard a wise, old elder from Brynengan – Daniel Roberts, the son of Robert Dafydd, the preacher – say of him, 'You caused me to remember Robert Roberts in the chapel today. He was preaching here and heaven was showering upon his head and upon the congregation. But sometime towards the middle, he turned to the wall, and shouted out, 'Stop, Lord! Remember that I am only flesh. Remember that I cannot hold too much.' Then he turned towards us and shouted at the top of his voice, 'Glory for the hope of a morning when I shall be surrounded by immortality; I shall be able to be full of the Godhead without ever cracking.' Clearly, there would be times when extraordinary enlightenments would flash into his own mind, and these then through him would shine upon his hearers. This unction, together with his other abilities, seemed to raise his ministry above the merely human.

In the *Introduction* to a volume of sermons called *Lampau'r Deml* [*Temple Lights*] we mentioned one story concerning him related by the late Rev. Griffith Solomon . . . Robert Roberts was itinerating, with another brother, in Anglesey and had arrived at Brynsiencyn. The late Rev. John Parry, Caerleon, was living at that time at the Bryn, and keeping a school there. Elias Parry, his brother, then a young boy and with him at the school, was familiar from an early age with preaching and preachers. Another young boy, from the Amlwch area, was also at the school. To the latter preaching and preachers were much more foreign, and Robert Roberts completely unknown. The two boys went together to hear the sermon. A large crowd had gathered and their expectation for the preachers, or at least for one of them, was considerable. The feelings in the church ran high while the first brother was preaching. Then Robert Roberts arose. An awful seriousness was to be seen on his face. He read his text. At first he seemed rather anxious. He spoke with less detail than was usual. Gradually he became more fluent, his voice cleared, his gaze grew increasingly more serious still. As he proceeded the whole soul of the congregation was held in his grip; some fainted, some shouted, and he, with his voice as the trumpet of God, filled the place At this, or sometime during the service, the boy turned to Elias Parry and with a countenance as pale as a corpse, asked, 'Tell me, boy, is he a man or an angel?' 'But an angel, boy. Didn't you know?' 'No, I didn't. Dear me! Isn't an angel a better preacher by far than a man?' There must have been something quite indescribable in the preacher that he left such an impression on a young boy's mind.

But his shining abilities impressed more minds than those of mere young boys. The more discerning and thoughtful realised that there was an indescribable glory accompanying his ministry. We once heard our dear father-in-law (the late Rev. William Roberts, Amlwch) relate a story that reveals this clearly. On his last engagement in Cardiganshire prior to the death of Mr Ebenezer Morris, he had been accompanied by the late Mr John Jones, Bethania. They were travelling from Penmorfa to Twrgwyn, and Mr Ebenezer Morris had come to Penmorfa to meet them. 'As we travelled from one church to the other,' said Mr Roberts, 'we were talking of the preachers of old. And as we neared Twrgwyn and had descended from our horses to climb up the steep hill there, I had got a little ahead of Mr Morris. But soon, I heard him shout at me: "Do you know, William Roberts, if I had died without hearing Robert Roberts of Clynnog, I would have died without possessing that view of the glory of the ministry of the gospel which I now hold." That is the testimony of one of the greatest preachers ever to arise in Wales, one who had listened to Daniel Rowland and all the old preachers.'

We cannot add anything to this description by Dr Thomas. From it we see clearly that the main strength of Robert Roberts, excepting the supernatural powers that accompanied his preaching, was the dramatic element that characterized his ministry. By this skill – involving voice, stance and expression, and by the use of word pictures – he presented the great truths of the Bible as living realities to his congregations. The same ability was possessed to a remarkable degree by George Whitefield. It is said that Hume, the atheist, was amongst his hearers one day when he was portraying the terrible danger of the sinner as he is led, quite unconsciously, by his corruption to his destruction. He depicted him as a blind man being led by his dog near the edge of a precipice. So realistic was the picture that the congregation imagined they could see the lip of the sudden drop, the great depths below, and the blind man completely unawares following his dog towards the edge and about to fall over. Suddenly, Hume, having quite lost himself, shouted out, 'Great heavens! He is gone!' There may well be no other ability which so affects both cultured and uncultured alike and it is clear that Robert Roberts possessed it in its fullness. Dr Griffith Parry relates a story which further proves our point and which had been told to him by Mr David Davies, Llanrhaeadr, Dyffryn Clwyd. A preaching service was being held at Llanefydd, a few miles from Henllan, on Christmas Day, and Robert Roberts was to be there. As in all places the expectation for him was great, with huge numbers from all directions having come together. It was a remarkable service. In his sermon he compared eternity to a clock that had stopped – at noon in heaven, and at midnight in hell. Whilst describing the land of perdition he imagined that some of the inhabitants of earth had obtained permission to ask questions of the damned. He questioned Cain soon after his arrival there:

'What time is it there, Cain?'

He lowered his head over the edge of the pulpit as he inquired. Then, looking up, he changed his voice, uttering with a slow, dragging, mournful cry and unearthly tone, as if from the grave:

'Midnight!'

A thousand years later, another query:

'What time is it by now, Cain?'

And there came the same reply, in the same hopeless tone:

'Midnight!'

Another is questioned:

'What time is it there, Judas?'

The same answer, with the same wail of hopelessness:

'Midnight!'

And so on, many times. David Davies narrated that the effect was indescribable. It was as if the terrors of judgment and eternity had laid hold of every soul in the place. The echo of that sermon seemed to fill those neighbourhoods for a long time afterwards. It affected David Davies himself to such an extent that he could not eat or sleep that night and his health was disturbed for some weeks.

Over and above his dramatic skills, Roberts, Clynnog, possessed a certain undefinable spiritual power arising from close communion with God and from an awareness and recognition of the objects of eternity. Like the Lord Jesus, he often spent whole nights wrestling with God in prayer. The Rev. John Williams, Dolwyddelan, called on him once when passing by. They were close friends and very open with one another.

'Robert *bach*,' said Williams, 'tell me from where do you get these awesome sermons which you preach?'

Robert Roberts took him by the arm, leading him a few steps, and half-opening the door to his room and pointing with his finger, he said:

'There! There! By earnest prayers and wrestling with God, there I get them!'

Such influences would often accompany his ministry that even the most seraphic of ministers would not dare preach after him. Soon after Roberts began preaching he was engaged to speak together with David Jones, Llangan, his father in Christ, in an Association held somewhere in the South. He preached to such effect that he overcame the congregation completely. After him Mr Jones stood up, and it happened – as it so often does happen when the first sermon has had a powerful effect – that the second was comparatively heavy and ineffectual. The next morning a private meeting was held; probably the meeting for preachers on their own. The topic for discussion was 'The Self'. Whilst others discoursed on the evil and dangers of being governed by selfish principles when engaged in the Lord's work, it was noted that Mr Jones was restless, rising and sitting, and sometimes walking back and forth along the floor of the chapel. At last the presiding minister called to him:

'Now, Mr Jones, you tell us something of this Self.'

But he answered, with some agitation:

'No, I'll say nothing now. But you carry on, my dear brothers! Carry on! Keep at it! Attack it, give it no mercy, for it nearly proved the death of me last night when I saw that Robin *bach* from the north had so far exceeded me.'

There is a story of Roberts and Ebenezer Morris preaching together at a Dolgellau Association. Robert Roberts had begun preaching a year before Eben Morris but in order to show his respect for the famous stranger from the south he insisted on going first. A remarkable blessing attended the preaching; the sermon deeply affected the hearers and none more so than the preacher who was to follow. When he had finished, Mr Morris got to his feet and said, 'I would not wish to quench nor diminish the convicting effects of my dear brother's sermon. Let us pray.' And with that the meeting ended.

We have not emphasized sufficiently another of Robert Roberts's excellences as a preacher, although we have referred to it in passing, namely the distinctiveness of his voice. From what we have heard it had a tendency to shrillness; it has been compared to the voice of the late William Charles, Gwalchmai. It was notably penetrative, reaching the furthest corners of a field congregation with ease. It was very pure, completely under the control of the preacher, who could change it at will to the ferocity of thunder or to the sweetness of music. No doubt such a voice was an important element in the effectiveness of his ministry.

QUOTATIONS FROM HIS SERMONS

Many of his sermons have been published. Some, transcribed by his hearers, are comparatively full; others – the majority – are short, containing only outlines written by the preacher himself. Something of the genius of Robert Roberts can be found in parts of these, and we quote a few of them.

> Many conditions pertain to the covenant of grace and none of them will be broken. The conditions of the covenant of works were laid on the earthy shoulders of Adam, and they were all broken. But every condition of the covenant of grace was laid on the shoulders of the Godhead. 'I have made a covenant with my chosen . . . I have laid help upon one that is mighty.' The covenant of works was like a bridge, with one end on rock and the other end on earth. The earth fell and the bridge came down. But the covenant of grace is a bridge built upon the rock at both ends. God is here undergirding the whole. Christ walked in deep communion with the moral law from his birth to Calvary and he there obtained the last word, 'Christ is the end of the law.' He became its full accomplishment, in its demands and its curses. The ceremonial law had carried Christ in her womb for long – in the desert, in the tabernacle, in Solomon's temple, in Zerubbabel's temple – and whilst giving birth to him, she died. The substance became the death of his shadowy mother and I think that her grave lies beneath the Cross.

He said something similar when preaching on Revelation 3:14, 'These things saith the Amen.' He referred to the moral law as being all truth but without any grace, and the ceremonial law as being all grace but without any truth. It was a shadow of good things to come. He said that God spoke to the moral law informing her that she would have to be shut up in an Ark, otherwise she would kill his people. 'You will remain there, beloved law, with a golden mercy-seat above your head.' He then related how the ceremonial law would approach, once a year, looking for her, bringing her a present of blood:

'What have you brought?' asks the moral law.

'Blood,' replies the ceremonial law. 'Three kinds of blood: the blood of a bullock for the people, the blood of a ram for the priests and the blood of a goat for God.'

'But I demand the horns of the necks of the people,' said the moral law.

'That is true but I bring you this blood to show that it is something of this nature which will pay all your demands in full, one day.'

And when the fullness of the time was come, grace and truth met together: 'The law was given by Moses, but grace and truth came by Jesus Christ.' The ceremonial law carried Jesus Christ in her womb for many centuries and received more pain from her Son than ever Mary did.

'But,' says one, 'Mary knew pain when bringing him to birth.'

No, never; before she travailed, she was delivered of a man child.

'O! but that was Zion.'

No! For as soon as Zion travailed she brought forth her children. Truly, the ceremonial law carried Christ in her womb for hundreds of years, and in bringing him to birth, she died. Indeed, it was so; she died at the birth of her Son. 'Christ is the end of the law.' Where is she buried? At the foot of the Cross.

When preaching at Bala, in the chapel window, one Association evening, he said:

There was a time when I would have been glad to have been any other creature rather than a man. I would have preferred to have been amongst the ravens, making my nest in the rocks and trees, or with the toads in the bogs and ditches, or in the dust of the earth with the lowest worm, rather than being human. For they, when they cease to live, cease to exist, but I, poor wretch, seemed destined for the wrath of God eternally. But, by today, I have changed my mind. I would not now change my place with the highest archangel in heaven, because the glorious Mediator has a human nature like mine, and all authorities bow to him. Whatever the relationship existing between Christ and the angels, to us he is a brother. Man and Godhead are found dwelling in him.

He then raised his voice in a shout of glory, 'Hallelujah for ever, from here to the third heaven, for the privilege of being human!'

When preaching on Exodus 29:45, 'And I will dwell among the children of Israel, and will be their God,' he said:

Here is a promise with no conditions. God not looking upon you but upon himself, as if he closed his eyes and looked at nothing but himself. The Infinite One declaring, 'I will consider not what they shall be to me, but what I shall be to them.' These words were a foundation for Moses as he pleaded that God's presence might remain with them. Men's consciences are full of fiery embers and sparks of flame when they pray without a promise to support them. God said to Moses:

'My presence shall go with thee, and I will give thee rest.'

'Lord, why did you yield to Moses?'

'O, Moses had my promise!'

'Moses is too bold. Set him aside.'

'O no! He has my promise.'

Let us say, 'We will not go from here to preach, to hear, to pray unless your presence go with us.' He will proclaim, 'My presence shall go with you.' Why? Because we have his promise.

The people previously had been washing and sanctifying themselves. Then God said, 'I will dwell in your midst', and there was all the more washing in Israel. Why? Because God had commanded, 'Be ye holy, for I am holy.' Israel was no cleaner by nature than any other nation but they made considerably more use of the water. God was dwelling amongst them. Churches! If you wish God to leave you, live defiled lives. But if you wish to have God amongst you, sanctify yourselves; use the water often. The King is with you. It is as evident that God has been with us, these last few days in the Denbigh Association, as that he is the Creator. God is with us! God commands Israel, 'Be not unclean.' There were some types of fish, animals and birds that they were forbidden to eat. O Lord! You take great care of Israel, but why? 'Because I wish to dwell amongst them, and wish to keep their breath sweet.' You, believer, wherever you turn your gaze, there is danger that you be defiled. God wishes to have you clean . . .

The Church is God's dwelling place. Perhaps we have here a reference to the Tabernacle. 'I will dwell with Israel in the tabernacle.' Sinai was blackness and darkness to Israel, but there was a shining glory in his presence. I refer to the rainbow – the bow of the covenant, most probably. The fiery embers and hail have passed away because of the glory of his presence... We thought that it was the cloud that would have carried us to eternal perdition! But there was a glory in his presence. Then came, 'Set up an altar, set up the Holy Place, so that I may dwell among them.' Should they come up to the mountain, to the fire and the thunder? 'No, they dare not. But I will come to them. Set thou up a tabernacle, a Holy Place, and then I will dwell in their midst.' The Tabernacle was a shadow of Christ. The greatest wonder that I have ever seen, was to see the Tabernacle – though so small – swallowing up that great, fiery Sinai. Hallelujah!

It was the darkness of many waters that brought forth the thunders of Sinai, but having obtained the Tabernacle the waters were in the laver to wash away stains. A fearful fire crowned the mountain, but having come to the Tabernacle, the fire continually burns the sacrifices, lights the candlesticks, illuminates the golden altar and the shewbread. The ten commandments thundered so terrifyingly above Sinai, but they sleep comfortably on a pillow of wood in the ark. Blessed be God for our Christ! The Tabernacle has swallowed up Sinai and its flames! The Tabernacle accompanied them through the wilderness, with Sinai in its belly! Wonder of wonders to see God coming from heaven to live in the flesh, to join with human nature. The highest meeting with the lowest, infinity with the finite, the greatest riches and the greatest poverty betrothed together. The uniting of fire and dross! of sun and sod! If you would have any dealing with God come to the Tabernacle of the Congregation. There is water to wash, sacrifice to cancel, fire to enlighten, a golden pot full of manna; Christ is all in all. Hallelujah! Amen!

There are obviously many interconnecting clauses missing from these quotations and we do not have the preacher himself to breathe life into them yet we sense the Spirit of life present in them. We are tempted to quote a little more from his sermon on prevailing prayer, even though some of its phrases have already been mentioned in the description by *Eben Fardd:*

As you seek to approach God, my brethren, ensure at all times that the name of the Son is in your prayers. We are as men on the sea in a storm, seeking to write letters to our Father. We write a short line here and then some distraction of mind, like a shaking of the ship, hinders us from continuing. Then another short line. But with little shape to the whole thing. But because of the perfect letter written by our elder Brother, the pure prayer prayed by the Son, our poor, ragged letters are received warmly at home. Think of Jonah cast into the deep, in the midst of the sea, with the weeds wrapped about his head. But he prayed from the fish's belly, which was to him the belly of hell. 'I will look again,' he said, 'toward thy holy temple.' There goes the whale like some great mail coach, with the sea boiling around it and the fishes darting from its way, as if the whale was crying out, 'Clear the way.' What is the matter, Whale? 'I have the man of God, who needs to be taken to his destination.' And old Jonah cries from his belly, 'A temple! A temple! A temple!' What, Jonah, a temple from here?

'Yes, I will look toward the temple even from here; for there is the altar, there is the ark and the mercy-seat.' So also for ourselves, brethren, let us pray from everywhere, 'A temple! A temple! The Son! The Son!' He is our true Tabernacle. If you send some little letters, Christian, from here and there, in the midst of the storms, remember to put the name of the Son in some corner. If you cry, 'Save, Lord', remember to say, 'for the Son's sake! Forgive us; for Christ's sake! Strength to stand; for the sake of the Son!' Let all our prayers ascend in this name.

In the same sermon he speaks of being serious in prayer:

Wherever I look in the Word, I see that true prayer is a vital thing. What does it consist of? Sighing, looking up, complaining, knocking, seeking, etc., like a man enduring the sharp pains of a colic. His groans are a wonder. But of another, it may be asked, 'How is it that he has ceased from his groaning?' Well, he must have been provided with something to ease his pain so that he sleeps. O! Many a soul has been seen and heard groaning because of his lost estate and the number and extent of his sins, because of the condition of the neighbourhood, with longing for God to bless his ministers. But that shameless devil came to the churches of our country with his cursed opium, dispensing so much of it to many that they sleep soundlessly. Prayer is a serious, vital thing. Not every form and word of prayer is true prayer to God. Saul of Tarsus was a praying man from his youth. He was one of those pure Pharisees notable for their long prayers. But when God heard that cry from the roadside he said, 'Behold, he prayeth.' What, O Lord, is there no mention of all those fine prayers previously? 'No, bury them all,' says God, 'let them not be mentioned; for now he prays in earnest.'

We record some of his striking, shorter comments:

The behaviour of our Saviour towards the woman of Canaan was strange. 'He answered her not a word.' As if he had said, 'Here is one turning to me for mercy, even though the devil has possessed her daughter. I never heard such a tune in heaven. Repeat it again for me. It pleases me greatly.' But at last he said, 'Be it unto thee even as thou wilt.'

Christ did not come over to our country in order to persuade the Godhead but he went to God's country to present an atonement so that God could lawfully come over to our land with forgiveness. And as Christ went he told his weak disciples, 'Whither I go, you cannot follow me; there is a rough sea between me and my Father. But I will steer the prow of my vessel into the very face of the waves until they become still.' Hallelujah! About the sixth hour it was very dark about the cross, so also about the seventh, but on the ninth hour, behold the way was opened: IT IS FINISHED! Now we are free to follow him; and if we lost the battle in Paradise, we have regained it at the Place of the Skull!

I used to think for some time that the word 'Salvation' was some kind of motto of the Methodists. But I arrived afterwards at circumstances in my own experience when 'free salvation' became the sweetest phrase I have ever heard. Free Salvation. Eternal thanks that there should ever be such a thing!

A LETTER TO THOMAS CHARLES

Many of his letters are extant and the same vivid strain is found in them as in his sermons. We would love to include them all, but one only will suffice, the letter written by him, a year before his death, to Mr Charles of

Bala. Robert Roberts was gravely ill at the time and Mr Charles himself had lately been operated upon to amputate his thumb.[1]

Clynnog, Feb.14, 1801.

Dear Brother,

When I received the letter which your dear wife wrote to me just after you had been under the hands of the surgeon, I was then certain that I would have visited you before now, but I was disappointed. Instead of coming to Bala to visit my dear friend I was diverted to the school of affliction, where I have been these last six weeks, and the Teacher in whose hands I am has made me go over many of my old lessons, such as believing, repenting, self-denying, loving God, and loving his people, etc. It is remarkable how many disappointments I am discovering in myself! When looking at these lessons from afar I am ready to believe that I am a sufficient master of them all but on drawing near to them and engaging with them I find myself a poor creature indeed – failing to believe, failing to love, failing to deny myself. And in the light of all this failure I grieve over my poor condition and find no place for my consolation, undeserving wretch, except that there is place for a sinner to hope before a Mediator. Indeed, I find life for myself at this door. O how sweet is the word that Christ Jesus came into the world to save sinners, yes, the chiefest of sinners! When I find sufficient strength to crawl to that point, in the face of all my failures, I see everything falling into place.

What an amazing thing to be supplied for poor sinners, is a great Mediator. He is my soul's only confidence for eternal life. To know that Christ Jesus receives sinners gives me greater assurance of my salvation than if I heard men and angels proclaiming together that I am a true believer. As I hide my guilty head under the wing of my dear Jesus, I know that this work proceeds in my soul, namely, to reconcile me more and more to the plan of salvation.

Up to now I have been nothing but a troublesome pilgrim in this sad world. No sooner am I enabled to worship a little and to delight myself in the Lord, leaning as it were upon the top of my staff, than it is time to run to fulfil some duty in the wilderness. But I have been thinking lately that all my unshapely limbs are close to falling on to that bed of ivory, that glorious plan of the Trinity to save man. And when I am here given an occasional rest, all the tumult of the cares of livelihood and a diseased body disappear and I then see everything clearly and in its right place...

Well, my dear friend, I am sorry to trouble you by attempting to express my thoughts in such a disorderly way but I trust you will forgive me and accept these lines as a token of love. And how glad would I be to receive one letter from my dear Charles. If you are able, let me hear from you, because I have no hope of seeing you (if I live) for a very long time.

I am beginning to recover a little from this recent attack. I spoke in the Chapel yesterday. There were signs that the gracious Lord was amongst us as we fasted. Let us hope that we shall never see the days when the Glory has departed from our congregations. O for help to cry, 'Never leave Thy people, etc. etc.'

I expect my brother John to be with you shortly inquiring for Bibles. It will be a mercy for our neighbourhood if you are able to supply some for us. Remember me kindly to your dear wife. My own wife desires to be remembered to you. I ask to be remembered by you before the Throne of Grace.

Who am, your undeserving friend,

Robert Roberts

HIS DEATH

Mr Charles recovered so as to serve God in the nation for further years but Robert Roberts approached the gates of death. His tabernacle had suffered assault for some years and a gentle touch from death's hand was sufficient to dissolve it. He was ill with stones and suffered much pain but his mind was clear throughout. A little before he died, Mr Charles visited him and asked, 'Do you fear death, Robert *bach*?' 'Yes, Mr Charles,' he replied, 'I have a great fear of death, just as you would fear meeting an enormous snake on the road, who, although you knew its sting had been drawn, you would yet fear to take into your bosom. I am the same, knowing that all danger has been removed from death yet fearing to walk the valley of the shadow of death.' But his faith strengthened after this and his fear abated. Mr Michael Roberts said of him:

> In the last days of his illness his mind was cheerful, his faith unshaken and his confidence was steadfastly upon the rock, namely Christ, and his conversation was so spiritual that it was almost fearful to the flesh to be near him. Rarely is there seen upon earth an embodied soul so akin to the inhabitants of heaven.

A few days before he crossed the river, while discussing his ministry with a friend, he said:

> All my sermons are as nothing, nothing, in my sight now. A little word like this, 'This is a faithful saying, and worthy of all acceptation, that Christ Jesus came into the world to save sinners,' and similar simple words are the great things to me at present.

A few hours before the end came he asked his wife to leave the room. 'Elin *bach*, you must not stay in the room more than a few minutes for the clouds are about to break. But before you go I have this to say to you: I am now going into the presence of the unveiled Godhead, with no curtain or flesh between myself and him, but I go to him with no fear or trembling.' Glorious experience! So slept Robert Roberts when only forty years of age, on November 28, 1802, and he was carried, amidst the tears of many hundreds, to Clynnog cemetery, where he rests from his labours until the resurrection morning. It is doubtful whether Wales has ever experienced another preacher comparable to him – his daring imagination, vivid dramatic energy and impressive voice, together with those visitations from heaven illuminating his own mind and those of his hearers. Although over ninety years have passed since Robert Roberts was laid to rest in the grave [this was written in 1897] and although his ministry lasted for barely fifteen years, the echo of his remarkable cries are to be heard in Wales, and particularly in Gwynedd, to this day.

[1] Morgan Jones made use of a corrupt copy of the letter. The above is a translation of the original whose text is given in *Robert Roberts - Yr Angel o Glynnog* [*Robert Roberts – The Angel of Clynnog*], Emyr Roberts and E. Wyn James, (Evangelical Movement of Wales Press, 1976).

24

ROBERT JONES OF RHOS-LAN AND ROBERT DAFYDD OF BRYNENGAN

THE BIRTH AND UPBRINGING OF ROBERT JONES, RHOS-LAN

The first Calvinistic Methodist preacher of note in Eifionydd was Robert Jones, Rhos-lan. He was known not only as an able speaker and wise leader but also as a fine writer. He had a long life. His connections with the Calvinistic Methodists continued for more than sixty years. He experienced the internal controversies that disturbed the Connexion and, no doubt, took part in them himself. He witnessed the development of this body of faithful believers from being an object of persecution for all to the position of honour and popularity in which it was held at the time of his death.

He was born in 1745 at a place called Sunter, in Llanystumdwy parish, Caernarvonshire. He was therefore seventeen years older than Robert Roberts, Clynnog, and only ten years younger than David Jones, Llan-gan, by whose ministry Roberts was converted. There were very few schools in the land when Robert Jones was a boy; education was not then considered necessary for the children of the workers and six weeks of school was all that he ever received. His schoolmaster was a Thomas Gough, a religious man, who not only taught his charges to read and write but also instructed them in Griffith Jones's *Catechism*. Robert also had a good mother, who loved her Bible and read much of it, and also of the Book of Common Prayer. Her favourite work was instructing her son in the word of truth. But when he was only eleven years old his mother died, to his great distress and loss. She had however awakened a love of reading in the boy who now read every book that he came across. He could be compared to that behemoth that trusted that he could draw up Jordan into his mouth. He read until midnight, and he read during mealtimes. He had constructed a device that would hold the book for him while he ate his meal, so that no time was wasted. A scholarly youth was a rare wonder in those days. An interest in books was considered almost the beginning of lunacy, and an old woman, coming to the home and seeing him reading at the table, relieved her feelings by saying, 'Bless you, Robert! Don't you know that it was by reading when eating that so-and-so became mad?' The result of all this reading was that Robert Jones became a remarkably knowledgeable man – a fine historian, a good poet, and familiar with most branches of learning.

But he was not religious nor had any tendency to religion. We do not find that he was immoral or that he sunk into open, presumptuous sins, but he preferred the company of idlers to the fellowship of saints, and it seems that he was one of those who mocked the Methodists. However, Lewis Evan, Llanllugan, visited the neighbourhood on a preaching tour together with a companion whose name is not known. Robert Jones went to the service. Lewis Evan was completely lacking in oratorical decorations; he was rough and rustic in his expressions and very unnatural in his gestures. The irreligious young man had great delight in observing him, and intended to mimic him in front of his ungodly companions. But when the second preacher stood up he had to listen. His mind was struck by the authority of the truths declared. The terrors of eternity began to grapple with him, and he departed from the service a different man. Instead of hastening to the laughing crowd to amuse them with his mimicries, he went immediately to the *seiat* at Brynengan, the only Methodist society in that part of the country, and he presented himself to God's people. His conviction deepened and his religious knowledge increased through reading more of Griffith Jones's *Catechism*.

He had been raised a carpenter but once converted was possessed by a strong desire to see the youth and children of the area receive the advantages of education. He saw no hope of anyone in the north stirring themselves to bring this about, but he hoped that Madam Bevan, who was now carrying on Griffith Jones's educational work, would take pity on hearing of their sad condition. He decided to travel on foot to Laugharne, at the furthest point of Carmarthenshire, where Madam Bevan lived. He had over a hundred miles to walk, had to cross rugged mountains and ford deep rivers, and the way was unknown to him. But his courage did not falter and he prayed with every step. When he arrived at Laugharne he found, to his great dismay, that the noblewoman was not at home. He had to return without having argued his case. But he set down his feelings and his desire for the establishing of schools in his neighbourhood, on paper, and left it at the mansion to await her return. He had heard much of Howell Harris and of his establishment at Trefeca, and so decided to visit the place while he was in the south. This he did, and passed some time in conversation with the Reformer.

It does not appear that the letter left by Robert Jones at Madam Bevan's home received any attention. He therefore resolved to make the journey a second time. His energy must have been indefatigable and his courage unending. *Methodistiaeth Cymru* notes:

> Let the reader remember that he was only a young man of eighteen years of age; that there was no body of responsible men to send him or to promise him payment for his time and labour. What compelled him was the passionate desire of his own heart to improve his nation and country, particularly with respect to that which belonged to their eternal peace.

This second journey proved more successful. The noblewoman was at home and he had opportunity to express all that was upon his heart. Madam Bevan was not inclined to agree to his request; she had suffered much distress on account of the schools after Griffith Jones's death. Many of the teachers had been undeserving of her trust and she was on the point of giving him a complete refusal. But because of his importunity and of what she saw in him that engendered trust, she said, 'If you yourself will keep the school, you may have one.' He agreed immediately, though he had not intended being a schoolmaster before.

ONE OF MADAM BEVAN'S SCHOOLMASTERS

Robert Jones's first school was at Capel Curig, a mountainous region between Bangor and Betws-y-coed. And, like many of the schoolmasters of that time, it was not long before he started preaching. He would teach religious principles to the children, would read the Bible and pray regularly with them, and it was no great step from this to speaking a word to grown-up sinners. The first time he took this step occurred in the following way. A stranger had been announced to preach in a house at Capel Curig. A congregation had gathered, with Robert Jones among them, but the preacher did not arrive. In order not to have to turn the people away unfed, the schoolmaster was pressed to deliver a word of counsel to them. This he did and so became a preacher, and remained a preacher to the end of his days. It does not appear that a Monthly Meeting had been established in Caernarvonshire at that time. There was no authority therefore to call the young man to account or to confirm him in the step he had taken. What would decide whether he was to continue in the work was the approval of the societies throughout the neighbourhood in inviting him to speak to them, and in this he received ample confirmation.

Madam Bevan's system was one of circulating schools. It was judged that six months was sufficient time for the common people to learn to read and write Welsh; after this period the school moved on. Robert Jones's next place of work was Rhuddlan, Flintshire. This occurred through the patronage of a noblewoman, a member of the Established Church, who lived in Rhuddlan. But the vicar of Rhuddlan was very opposed. He not only led an immoral life but was a cruel and oppressive persecutor. It is said of him that he came one Sabbath day from having administered Holy Communion and paid five shillings from his purse to buy beer for the persecutors, so that their spirits might be aroused and worked up into greater fury against the Methodists. Such a man was not interested in helping the people to read. Anyone engaged in the work he considered as unnecessary busybodies and irrelevant time-wasters. That the schoolmaster was not only a Methodist but a preacher as well made the school all the more disreputable. 'And as with the priest, so with the people.' Rhuddlan, it seems, was as ungodly a place as anywhere in Wales. Every Sunday during harvest-time a meeting – a mixture of a saint's feast-day and a fair – was held. During it the reapers were hired for the week. Sickles and all the other tools needed for the harvest were also sold, so that the atmosphere was similar to that of a market day. Their hiring and purchasing completed, the people would stream to the inns to dance, sing and drink into the early hours of Monday morning, and often there would be much fighting and injury before the festivities were over. The inhabitants would not allow anyone to come there to preach. Robert Jones tells of a preacher called William Griffiths, who lived near Mold, who attempted once to speak. As no one would open a home for him, he stood up in the street. He had hardly begun before the crowd threw dung and stones at him and he was dragged away and beaten mercilessly by them.

To this pagan place came Robert Jones to keep a school. As might be expected he met with much opposition, even though he was there under the auspices of the Church. The vicar adamantly refused him the use of the church. As there was no place to hold the school in Rhuddlan, an attempt was made in the nearby parish of Cwm. The clergyman here was willing that a school be set up but he predicted that it would be a failure as the local people were so inconsiderate that they saw no benefit in anything that had any true worth. His prediction was fulfilled to the letter. Though the school was announced from one end of the neighbourhood to the other, with the promise that there would be no charge for teaching the children, only three children came to receive education. The lack of response meant that Robert Jones had to return to Rhuddlan. This time he received more of a welcome. Some local gentlemen of substance who were concerned about the ignorance of the people had decided that they would not bow to prejudice, and a school was opened in a building called Banquet House. At first the new schoolmaster was hated with perfect hate. He could not walk the street without being pointed out, sworn at, and called every bad name. He had no one who would sympathize with him and so every mid-day, after releasing the children from school, he withdrew to the old castle and there poured out his heart to God. But the school succeeded, despite all opposition. The number of scholars increased, the schoolmaster won their affection, and they praised him to their parents when they returned home for the way in which he taught and catechized them. A night school was begun, to which came not only children to be educated but adults also, and crowds gathered to listen to the catechizing. By these means the prejudice of the people was overcome. Many were made aware of their spiritual condition before God, and thus began the Methodism of the area.

As he kept his school at Banquet House, Robert Jones longed to preach, but no house was open to receive him. He then received an invitation from an old lady who lived at Diserth, about two miles from Rhuddlan and he agreed to go. On the night a large number gathered to hear the schoolmaster, most of them miners. The place was full of noise and conversation. At the appointed hour, Robert Jones rose to his feet, his Bible in his hand, and said:

'Listen, all. I am now going to read to you from God's Word.'

'What is he saying?' asked some.

'He is saying,' answered others, 'that he is going to read to us from God's Word.'

'Oh, indeed,' they replied, expecting some entertainment.

The preacher commenced. As he spoke, others crowded into the home, looking for somewhere to sit. Some sat on the dresser and one of them, unfortunately, knocked over some earthenware behind him with his elbow, so that they fell on to the floor and broke. This caused much confusion. As she saw her crockery shattered, the old lady lost her temper. She picked up the distaff of the spinning-wheel that was by her side and began striking out at all and sundry.

'You'd come here to break my dishes would you? I'll pay you back.'

All rushed out of the house, some laughing loudly and others rubbing their bruises. The preacher also left the house. Any hope of a service was gone, and it was not certain that he would escape her revenge. A farmer cried out from the crowd,

'Where is the schoolmaster? He can come to my mill to speak a word. Come, people.'

All went to the mill. A halfpenny candle was all that could be found to light the place. When Robert Jones was reading his text, the candle went out; whether by accident or by someone's mischief, is not known. This confused the meeting completely. The people went to their homes without having received a sermon, but having been considerably entertained. Very little is known of Robert Jones's subsequent history in Rhuddlan. He certainly established a small society in the town, where a few would meet to counsel one another in eternal things, but it does not appear that his stay was a means of changing the customs of the town nor of improving the ungodly character of the inhabitants.

Robert Jones's next placement was at Brynsiencyn, Anglesey. He had great success at this school. Large numbers of children came to be taught to read, and through the children the schoolmaster gained the hearts of the parents. He preached also in the homes of the neighbourhood, wherever he could obtain an entrance. This stirred up the enmity of the parish clergyman. This man had no desire for seeing the children learning to read the Scriptures, and the Methodism and preaching of the schoolmaster was a torture to him. He wrote a letter to Madam Bevan calling upon her to remove Robert Jones immediately, portraying him as a foul scoundrel, a danger to the parish, and one who sought to undermine the foundations of the Church. But the noblewoman of Laugharne had learnt not to believe all that the clergy told her. She realized that the letter was motivated by a spirit of envy, and Robert Jones had so impressed her and won her trust when he had visited her, that she would not listen to any complaint made against him. The rector did not receive a reply to his letter. After a while, he went up to Robert Jones and asked him if he had lately received any communication from Madam Bevan. He replied, 'No.' The rector's surprise was great. He could not understand why his letter should not receive attention and therefore concluded that by some mischance it had not reached its goal. He wrote a second time, but again there was no response. He again inquired of Robert Jones, and again heard there had been no communications received from Madam Bevan.

'This is strange,' he said, 'but whether you heard or not, you must leave this place. You may not remain a schoolmaster here any longer.'

The school it seems used to meet in the church. Robert Jones answered him:

'I acknowledge your authority, sir, but would you be kind enough to tell me why you are turning me away? They will ask me in Caernarvonshire why I returned home before the end of my term. Tell me the cause therefore so that I will have some answer to give my neighbours.'

'Well, you are preaching towards Bryn,' replied the churchman, 'and enticing the people after you.'

'Oh, is that what you have against me!' replied Jones. 'I do nothing except for reading a portion of God's Word, praying and singing praises to the Lord, and warning the people not to break the Sabbath or sin. I believe, sir, that that is better than playing ball along the hillside on the Lord's Day and I am very careful always to be finished well before the time of the church service.'

'I don't care about that,' said the rector. 'You must leave here.'

'Will you therefore be so kind,' said Robert Jones, 'as to provide someone who will complete the education of these children? I desire their good, and my heart is filled with pity towards them. You would do well if you could find someone who could complete what I have begun.'

'That is not for you to worry about,' was the answer. 'That is a matter for me. You must go home.'

So Robert Jones returned home and the children wept bitterly after him, but as he left he told the clergyman, 'You remember, sir, that an account must be given for this on Judgment Day.'

This is not the end of the history of this rector. According to the description given by Robert Jones in his well-known book, *Drych yr Amseroedd* (*A Mirror of the Times*), the churchman and his wife paid a visit to a Mrs Lloyd of Gesail, a noblewoman who lived at Penmorfa, Eifionydd. While he was there, he called on one of his friends and was told that a tenant of Mrs Lloyd's, living near her mansion at Hendre Howell, had for many years been receiving preachers to his house.

'And,' said the friend, 'I am afraid that no one is honest enough to tell Mrs Lloyd.'

The clergyman became enraged. He considered the reception of preachers to be equivalent to the welcoming of devils.

'Is this true?' he asked.

'O yes, it is certainly true,' was the reply.

'Very well,' he answered, 'I will not eat a thing today until I have told her.'

He rushed off towards Gesail but by the time he arrived at the mansion the muscles of his mouth had become paralysed. The maids were frightened by him and asked what had happened but he could not reply. They hurriedly called for his wife but she also could get no word from him. He had suffered a stroke and never spoke again for the remainder of his life. The preaching at Hendre Howell continued as before. 'Verily, he is a God that judgeth in the earth.'

Before leaving Anglesey, Robert Jones, together with a Methodist clergyman, went on a preaching tour through the county. The people came in great numbers to hear them. For a clergyman to preach in the open air and upon unconsecrated ground was unusual, but there was considerable prejudice against an unordained preacher. When the service was over there would be considerable discussion as to whether the ordained clergyman or the unordained Methodist was the better preacher. It seems that the popular opinion was in favour of Robert Jones. His biographer states:

> This occasion was the means of removing the prejudice of the people of Anglesey, so that they accepted that the Lord sent others to preach as well as the clergy.

Robert Jones returned to Eifionydd and kept schools at Llangybi, Brynengan and Llanbadarn. During this period he was also regularly taking a night school at Llanllyfni. It seems that he was an excellent teacher. One well-known minister, who had been at one of his schools, wrote:

> I have know Robert Jones for over fifty years, since he and I were at school together at Brynengan, when I was about six years old. I do not know anyone who had such skills as a teacher as he. Though at the time he had no great knowledge, he possessed the ability to communicate what he knew to his pupils, with cheerfulness and authority. At times he laughed and played with the children, but in the midst of play, if he saw that they were going too far, he would make a gesture that would cause them all to realize their mistake and be sobered immediately. He would always have a cane in the school, but I do not remember him using it on anyone. Though he had scores of all kinds of children in his school his hold over them was so well-ordered that I do not remember one occasion when he lost control. Some of us thought that he could almost bewitch people in that he could find out whatever mischief was afoot and discover the culprits by means of simple tricks. In this way he could keep discipline and keep us in fear, not only when we were in school but also when coming and going along the road.

Many think of the first Methodists as being miserable men who thought it sinful to smile and who were unable to enter into any kind of amusement and happiness, however innocent it might be. Their work in preaching against the feast-days and fairs is attributed to this tendency. But we find in Robert Jones a lively personality, who could laugh and play in the company of his pupils, and enjoy their vivacity and fun as long as it was natural and did not go too far. Cheerfulness of spirit is not incompatible with the most profound seriousness. And he could control himself, and thereby control the children, so that their merriment never crossed over to vain frivolity.

While keeping school at Brynengan, he married Magdalen, the daughter of Richard Griffiths, Cae'r-tyddyn, of Llangybi parish. She was a help meet to him in the full sense of the term. She was one of the most cheerful women who have ever lived. Any opportunity to be hospitable was her greatest pleasure. She would welcome preachers of all ability to her home, and as there was much itinerating in those days she had many opportunities to exercise the grace given to her. When Robert Jones was away on his own journeys, she would gather her children about her, mornings and evenings, and keep family worship without fail. At first she herself would read and pray, but when her daughter Mary was old enough, she and her mother would fulfil the duty alternately.

ROBERT JONES SETTLES AT RHOS-LAN, CAERNARVONSHIRE

Eventually Robert Jones gave up the school, and he and his wife went to live at Tirbach, Rhos-lan, in the parish of Llanystumdwy. This is why he is always known as Robert Jones, Rhos-lan. He obtained a seven-year lease on the Tirbach land and built a substantial building there. Half of it was the home and the other half a chapel. Here he preached regularly; a strong society was formed; some of the services experienced here will be remembered throughout all eternity, and many were recovered from their wanderings. But the preaching of the gospel for the salvation of souls was offensive to the gentleman who became the new owner of the land. When the lease came to an end, this man therefore explained that he was willing to renew it but only if the preaching stopped. Robert Jones refused these terms and had to leave. As a result the Rhos-lan society was scattered and there has never been a Methodist cause there since. Most of the members joined the Brynengan society, whilst others formed new branches.

The family's new home was Ty-bwlcyn, a small farm on the lower slopes of Garn Fadryn, and this remained Robert Jones home while his wife was alive. He journeyed often through the south and the north; he was faithful in all his house. His voice was weak and there was nothing particularly musical about it, but he often had powerful services. The first time he preached at an Association was at Llanfair Caereinion, Montgomeryshire, and as he was a stranger to the neighbourhood he was given a place of honour in the order of services. There was an unction upon the meeting; the heavenly dew fell sweetly upon his own spirit and upon the people. At the end of the service, his friend, David Jones, Adwy'r Clawdd, came up to him, saying:

> Robert! You have surprised us all. I always thought that you were full of

good sense, but I never felt that I should receive such a blessing under your ministry.

He travelled many times on foot, in the company of the pilgrims, to Llangeitho. His purpose was two-fold – to engage the famous preachers of the south for visits to the north, and to renew his own spirit as he listened to Daniel Rowland. They were persecuted much on these journeys back and forth. To throw stones at the Roundheads was a great entertainment for the inhabitants of many localities. Harlech, in particular, was notorious for this. Once, in that town, Robert Jones barely escaped with his life. But the sweet feasts laid before them on Llangeitho's gospel tables more than made up for all their sufferings. His biographer recalled that Robert Jones was once so taken up as he listened to Rowland expounding the love of God in the delivering up of his Son; the glory of the Person, and the sufficiency of the sacrifice; the work of the Mediator and his readiness to receive sinners, that he forgot himself completely. He did not know whether he was in the body or out of the body; he had no idea where he was. He went out of the meeting without his hat and his mind was so taken up that he did not realize its loss for some time.

As with so many of the older preachers, we do not have a complete history of Robert Jones's ministerial career. He suffered much persecution, he was wonderfully protected dozens of times when in danger, and he was the instrument for the convicting of many. But the only sources of information regarding these occasions lie in the many tales about him associated with various localities. Many of them are found in the book *Methodistiaeth Cymru*. By his own testimony he was the first to preach at Abergynolwyn, Merionethshire. He did so, standing on the main street on a Sunday afternoon, but neither the month nor the year is known. By the time he arrived, the large crowd that had gathered wore a cruel, angry look. The preacher felt a shiver pass through him as he thought of having to face them. There was hardly one amongst the mob who had ever heard preaching before, nor seen a preacher, but they believed that preaching and preachers were things that should be purged out of the land. However relief came for the preacher completely unexpectedly. Amongst the crowd was a man called John Lewis, who was sympathetic towards the gospel. This man had a stepson who was very strong and very capable with his fists. John Lewis told his stepson of the people present who intended to harm the strange preacher and to stop him from speaking, 'But,' he said, 'if you have a word with them they will be quiet enough.' The young man enjoyed the task and violently threatened the leaders. Robert Jones was given peace to preach and the service was not without considerable blessing.

It appears also that Robert Jones was the first to preach at Beddgelert and that there again he was remarkably defended, as at Abergynolwyn. It was Robert Dafydd of Brynengan who had intended to make the attempt. He was a native of Beddgelert and thought that he would return to his hometown to proclaim the word of life to his old neighbours. A Sunday was appointed and the service advertised throughout the neighbourhood. A bark-house, a rather dilapidated building where the bark of oak trees was laid out to dry, was appointed as the venue. It is not known whether this arrangement was made by friends or by enemies. During the week before the Sunday the persecutors hung heavy logs of wood above the bark-house, intending to let them fall on to the building during the service and kill both the preacher and the congregation. When the day came, Robert Dafydd failed to go, and Robert Jones went instead of him. A huge crowd gathered, fierce of face and with hearts full of cruelty. There was no hope of the preacher receiving any mercy from them. But before the service began a dreadful storm of thunder and lightning broke upon them, so that all were terrified.

The thunder was so loud it might be thought the mountains were breaking apart and the flashing bolts of lightning burst from the clouds with such ferocity that even the bravest amongst them was deathly pale. Their terror was all the greater because the storm had broken over them without warning. No one had any thought of attacking the preacher. They had all been so sobered that they were willing to listen to the gospel. With his usual skill, Robert Jones used the occasion to advantage. He called upon them to consider much more dreadful thunderings than those that presently echoed about them – the threatenings of the Bible against the ungodly; and much more dangerous lightning than that now descending from the clouds – the bolts of God's wrath. It was a powerful service. Many were returned to the Lord, and no more persecution occurred at Beddgelert.

According to the author of *Methodistiaeth Cymru*, Robert Jones was also the first, not only of the Methodists, but of any denomination, to preach at Dyffryn Ardudwy. John Hughes received this information from Robert Evans, Trefriw, the father of the Rev. Evan Evans (*Ieuan Glan Geirionydd*). For some years there had been preaching in the surrounding areas such as Harlech and Penrhyndeudraeth to the north, and Barmouth to the south, but for some reason, Dyffryn Ardudwy had been left. But Robert Jones passed by one day and preached at Morfa, near Llanddwywe. He spoke in the open air; he had no pulpit or platform but stood on a convenient mound. According to Robert Evans:

> From this green mound he spoke with great seriousness and effect from Genesis 19:17, 'Escape for thy life; look not behind thee, neither stay thou in all the plain.' And it deserves mention that there was no hint of persecution though this was the first service held in the area by any Nonconformist.

That last remark sheds a stream of light on the spirit of the times. It is clear that it was unusual at that time for any Methodist to be given peace to preach without someone disturbing and attacking him.

HIS LABOURS FOR THE GOSPEL

Robert Evans provided another story concerning Robert Jones, one that emphasizes his great conscientiousness and the divine protection that so often guarded him. He was engaged to preach at Dyffryn at two o'clock on a Sunday. On the previous Friday and Saturday a great storm had broken out; the wind blew and the rain fell in torrents. At two o'clock on the Saturday, Robert Jones was at Hendre Howell, near Tremadog, and in the evening he was to be at Penrhyndeudraeth. But to reach Penrhyn he had to cross the estuary at Traethmawr. He knew that he could not cross on foot because of the strength of the current and in all probability he would not be able to find a boat either. But as he was on God's business he would not be excused. He left his horse at Hendre Howell and continued on to the beach on foot. As he arrived, a boatman was preparing to cross in order to go to the help of another boat that was in danger of breaking up on the opposite shore because of the fury of the storm. By this boatman, God's minister was taken over, and he arrived at Penrhyn when nobody was expecting him. He preached there on the Saturday evening with much blessing.

The next morning he had arranged to speak at Harlech at nine. The people of Penrhyn insisted that he could not cross Traeth Bach, and they announced him to preach with them. But Robert Jones would not stay. He went to the edge of the beach in the hope that the Lord would grant him an open door. Following him were a crowd of Penrhyndeudraeth Methodists. It so happened that the tobacco of the sailors of a large ship anchored on the opposite shore had come to an end and they had sent over a longboat to renew their stock. In this boat, all the brethren were carried over. They hurried on to Harlech but, having arrived, found that the meeting was to be at Pen'rallt. By now it was late. The congregation that had gathered had tired of waiting and had dispersed, some returning to their homes, others having gone to the parish church. On arriving at the church however they found that the clergyman was ill and that there was to be no service there. As they returned from the church Robert Jones and his friends arrived. The house at Pen'rallt was filled with worshippers and a notable service was held. In order to be at Dyffryn by two, the preacher had to pass through Llanbedr. There was no service in the church there also because of the illness of the clergyman – he had charge of both churches. The parishioners therefore followed after Robert Jones and he preached for the first time in the house built for that purpose by Griffith Richard. When a local farmer saw the people following a Methodist preacher he rode as fast as his horse could carry him to find Mr Parry, the vicar of Llanaber. As the crowd returned to Dyffryn, at the close of the service, they met with the two men, the parson and the farmer, riding hurriedly towards them. The clergyman asked them sarcastically, 'Have you now gone after this new faith?' He was answered by one of the parishioners, 'It is as well that we follow some faith. At the church there was no faith of any kind this morning.' That evening, a service was held at both churches, though normally evensong was not observed at either place. Mr Parry, Llanaber, served at one place, and the sick clergyman, having been dragged out of his bed, was at the other. Because of the fortunate coincidences involved in all these circumstances Robert Jones gave his opinion that the Lord had a great work to accomplish at Dyffryn. We note the history here in that it provides examples of the various difficulties and dangers faced by those early preachers.

Robert Evans noted that there was no persecution during that first service at Dyffryn, but this situation was not to continue. The main troublemaker was a certain Griffith Garnetts, an idle creature who depended for subsistence upon the Corsygedol family. When the old exhorter, William Evans of Bedw-arian, was preaching on one occasion, Garnetts, together with one of the hunting servants of Corsygedol, went to the service to disrupt it. In the servant's hand was a hunting horn, and his companion shouted to him, 'Blow it in his ear, Sionyn; blow in the ear of the man with the book.' This he did, until the preacher had to give up speaking. This Garnetts would also disturb Robert Jones's meetings. Along with his many other abilities, Robert Jones was a skilful mason and was sometimes called upon by the Corsygedol family to cut epitaphs upon gravestones. Once when engaged in this work at Llanaber graveyard, Garnetts passed by and on seeing him employed in work for the Vaughans of Corsygedol, he expressed regret for disrupting his meetings. However he emphasized also that he would do the same again if Robert Jones was ever to try to preach in the locality again. Nearby was an open grave and, pointing to it, Robert Jones said, 'Do you see this grave, Mr Garnetts? There will be preaching in Dyffryn when you will be rotting in a similar grave.' The man was thoroughly frightened and never again disturbed the Methodists.

Robert Jones differed from most of the Methodist exhorters in many ways. Their ministries in general would be rousing; they considered shouting to be an indispensible element of a sermon. But he would speak quietly without noise or shouts. Because of this he would often be allowed to preach in places where others would not be tolerated. But his words would always be solemn and illuminating. He sought in every sermon to enlighten the minds of his hearers and very often he would be under evident unction. He was weak of body but very courageous. He was not frightened by dangers that would overcome the generality of men. He was also very ready with his answers and by this skill, together with his great knowledge of the Scriptures, would often close the mouths of his opposers. For a time he kept a school at Beddgelert, being allowed the use of the church. When releasing the children one day, he gave them a question for which he wanted the answer by the next day. The question was, 'Where is God's Church?' When one of the sages of Beddgelert heard of the question, he exclaimed in disgust, 'Is that the kind of master you have? Asking to know where the church is, when he is keeping school in it every day!' When this reply reached Robert Jones he mentioned that the Bible spoke of the ears of the church, and he added the further question as to what these might be. But it seems that the man belonged to that species to which Solomon refers, who even if brayed in a mortar with a pestle, their foolishness will not depart from them, for he replied, 'What a lob! What is easier to see than that the ears of a church is the belltower.'

Robert Jones was a wise leader of the Connexion in the north, and in Eifionydd especially, for many years. He would be present almost without exception in the Monthly Meetings of his county, and only rarely would he be absent from the Associations. He attended the Bala Association over fifty times. He would usually travel on foot, and because of the scarcity of Methodist preaching stations a Sunday, especially at the beginning of his ministry, would often involve preaching three sermons and a walk of thirty miles. In his biography, there is an account of him preaching at Henllan, near Denbigh, on a Saturday night; at Tanyfron Chapel near Llansannan, at nine on the Sunday morning; at Bontuchel, near Rhuthun, at two; and at Adwy'r Clawdd, Fflintshire, at six. This involved travelling considerably more than thirty miles and he would have walked every step. A friend, on hearing of his long journeys, once told him, 'Robert Jones, if you could be young again, you would look after your body much more carefully.' He answered, 'I am not so certain. I heard of a certain gentleman who wasted all his estate with his prodigality, so that for some time he was poor. Then somehow he regained his wealth, only to lose it again a second time in exactly the same way.' Here was a clear suggestion that were he to relive his life he would act in exactly the same way again. He was greatly concerned that the Association should keep the faith. We have mentioned previously the Antinomian attacks upon the Methodists in various parts of Wales. A group in Lleyn argued for permissive beliefs known as 'the Rhosddu religion'. The same heresy broke out in mid-Anglesey, where it was known as 'the religion of the middle of the county'. Robert Jones exercised all his influence to fight these wild, licentious ideas, and was certainly one of the main instruments in chasing them out of the county. There is an account of how he and his friend, John Pierce, took on the 'middle of the county' religionists in a Monthly Meeting in Anglesey. The arguments raged through the night until dawn and Robert Jones did not give up until he had completely silenced his opponents.

When nearly fifty years old and living at Ty-bwlcyn he met with a severe tribulation. An inflammation in the lungs caused him to cough up much blood. He, and many of those who visited him, believed that he would die. There were many evenings when the family thought that he would be in eternity before morning. But the churches of Lleyn and Eifionydd felt that they could not do without him and they offered up constant prayer on his behalf. He recovered almost miraculously. It was thought of almost as a rising from the dead. After his recovery he said that during his illness he had gathered up all his religion, his experiences, his sermons, his labours with the schools, etc. At first, he considered that they amounted to a considerable pile. But as he drew nearer to the fiery law, the last judgment, and eternity, this religious pile became as nothing, as nothing. Then, when it had become the end of the world for him, the Son of Man came into view, and he was glad to view him as one who was sufficient for a sinner who had nothing to pay.

Robert Jones was a notably pure and religious character. It could be said of him as of John Evans, Bala, that his uprightness was proverbial. He was godly at home with a godliness that was full of kindliness and gentleness. He spoke individually to his children about their condition, about Jesus Christ, and of the privilege of becoming members of God's Church. When his youngest son, a boy of about fourteen years old, was leaving home for Bangor, his father went with him for part of the way. Before leaving, he turned to him, saying,

> Well, my boy, you are today coming to a crossroads. When you were with us, under our wing, I tried to lead you, and counsel you, and watch over you; but

now, here you are. leaving us, and many will be looking out for you. Some will try to pull you into the ways of folly, frivolity and lightness; others to sins that would be a shame upon your name as long as you live. You remember now that you have come to the crossroads, and you must choose between God's house, his people, and his work, or instead, God's enemies and their people, the murderers of your own soul.

As might be expected, this conversation affected the boy greatly, and the words of his white-haired father were never forgotten by him.

ROBERT JONES'S LITERARY WORKS

Robert Jones was also a fine writer. The following is a list of his literary productions:

Lleferydd yr Asyn [*The Ass's Utterance*] forbidding the prophet's folly, together with the portrayal of three preachers.

A translation of the first volume of William Gurnall's *Works*.

Arweinydd i'r Anwybodus [*A Guide to the Ignorant*].

Ymmddiddan rhwng Dr Opium, Galio, a Discupulis [*A Conversation between Dr Opium, Gallio, and Discupulis*].

Drych yr Amseroedd [*A Mirror of the Age*], being a History of the Religious Revival in North Wales.

Grawnsypiau Canaan [*Clusters of Canaan's Grapes*], a Selection of the Hymns of William Williams.

The most important of these, without a doubt, is *Drych yr Amseroedd.* In it he gathered together many of the traditions and stories relating to the beginnings of Methodism in north Wales. Through his own personal knowledge and his keen discernment he was able to separate the wheat from the chaff and it is certain that much valuable information would have been lost had it not been for this book. Nearly the whole of it was used in *Methodistiaeth Cymru,* and we do not think that Mr Hughes has acknowledged sufficiently his indebtedness to Robert Jones.

Lleferydd yr Asyn is in the form of a letter to a nobleman who sent his servant to disturb the worship of the Lord's Day. It seems that this man was a clergyman and a Justice of the Peace. The following quotation from the book demonstrates Jones's writing style and also reveals something of the nature of the disturbance against which he complains:

Under a solemn consideration of these things, and the undeniable warrant of the Scriptures, together with the liberty granted and supported by the valuable government of our most gracious and generous Lord, King George III, and his high counsellors, our latest service met at Rhos-lan. And if anyone were to ask what was the purpose of our meeting, we are free to answer in the sight of heaven, that the two most important purposes were to offer due worship to God on his Holy Day and to ask his blessing; and, to seek benefit for our eternal souls. In that we had no building, we had to meet in the open air. And as we worshipped, humbly and respectfully, as is appropriate for unworthy creatures appearing before the infinite Jehovah, we first sang a psalm to the praise of the glorious God; we knelt before him in prayer; and then we read and expounded a little of his most holy Word. But before finishing the passage of Scripture, namely those most valuable words, 'Neither is there salvation in any other,' the congregation was disturbed by a rowdy stranger, who had arrived in the meantime (purely for this purpose it would seem); and in order to be the more successful in his task he had brought with him an appropriate instrument for the purpose, namely, a kind of trumpet or loud horn.

The account continues with a further description of the wretched behaviour demonstrated. This book was truly as salt to the wounds of the nobleman. It sold quickly. The sixth edition is presently before us, printed at Trefriw in 1819.

At first sight, it is strange that Robert Jones was not one of those ordained to the work of the ministry at Bala in 1811. Most certainly this was not due to any lack of respect towards him, for his praise was in all the churches. Perhaps his age was the reason, though he was only sixty-six at the time and his friend and co-worker, John Roberts, Llangwm, who was ordained, was only seven years younger. It may be that tiredness had begun to overtake him. However he was given an important role in the ordination service. The Confession of Faith includes the description:

After this, the dear brother, Robert Jones of Caernarvonshire, gave a solemn word of counsel to them, and to the Body in general, and he terminated the proceedings with a fervent prayer, appropriate to the occasion.

The man entrusted with delivering the charge to the ordained in the very first ordination service must have been held in the highest respect.

Having buried his wife Robert Jones sold Ty-bwlcyn and, as all his children had left the area, lodged with a John Williams of Felin Fadryn, who was very kind to him. He lodged for a while again with a James Jones. But at last, a house was built for him adjoining the chapel at Dinas, Lleyn, and here he remained until his death. He lived to the age of eighty-four. Many of his letters have been preserved, amongst them the following letter, sent by him to the Monthly Meeting some six years before he died:

Dinas, 31 May, 1823.

Dear Brethren and Friends

I would be glad of the privilege to be in your fellowship this time again; yet, though I am relatively healthy, I am too frail to come so far without taking a very long time. I wish to be kindly remembered to my brethren, all the Preachers and the Elders, and would remind them that the burden is too great, the load much too heavy, to pull it up such steep steps these days, without the specific aid of the Holy Spirit. There is no point expecting much help from many of our listeners at present; fewer by far than was the case in the past. In that it is not probable that I shall be present to see you ever again, I leave this as a loving warning and counsel to my brethren in the ministry, as well as the elders of the churches, that not one of us presume to say much of Jesus Christ without knowing him, and experiencing personally the covenant with God through him; daily tasting his forgiveness, and feeling the power of the Word, as it is truly the Word of God; possessing the divine nature, and being led by the Holy Spirit to live godly, and to know his leading continually in pastoring the flock, so that we might say at the end that we have been pure of the blood of all men. The last days are awful days. If we lose the harrowing of the soul and the deepest mourning for sin, then fluent oratory will do instead of the sacred fire from the altar; and some will presume to rush in with strange fire, though they will be slain in the event. It is to be hoped that we shall never see such days in Wales when it may be written above the meeting-houses, 'Here are false professors worshipping the unknown God.' I pray that the Lord may be evidently among you; and that the services throughout be under the dew of blessing so that many be called anew and that Christ's churches throughout the land be under divine protection.

Yours, while life remains,
ROBERT JONES.

The reading of this letter must surely have produced the deepest influence upon the gathered Association. In April, 1829, he caught a heavy cold, which eventually brought about his death. Throughout his life he had been in much captivity through fear of death. He would often in prayer use phrases such as, 'Do not let us, our dear Father, descend into the river in the dark'; 'May the way be clear when we approach the river'; 'Remove the clouds and fears from the conscience before we face death.' And his prayers were answered. Little could be understood of his words during his last illness because of the thickness of his voice, but one brother who watched over him one night observed a look of glory on his face and a heavenly smile upon his lips, whilst the tears fell in streams down his cheeks. He moved closer to try to catch his words, and what he heard was:

Covenant grace, strong covenant of God,	Cyfamod rhad, cyfamod cadarn Duw,
It cannot fall, 'tis certain through his blood.	Ni syfl o'i le, nid ie a nage yw.

His biographer added:

> On one o'clock, Saturday morning, 18 April, he slept quietly in Jesus, at 84 years and 3 months of age, in fair old age and full maturity.

The following Monday night, Mr Robert Owen preached at the watch-night service from John 11:24, 'I know that he shall rise again at the resurrection at the last day'; and after him Mr James Hughes, Lleyn, from Numbers 23:10, 'Let me die the death of the righteous.' It was a remarkable meeting; a heavenly blessing fell upon the congregation, and they were hardly able to stop repeating at the close, the hymn:

All my brethren have departed	Mae nghyfeillion wedi myned
In their droves ahead of me.	Draw yn lluoedd o fy mlaen.

On the day of his funeral an immense crowd gathered. It seemed as if the whole of Lleyn had come together. The Rev. Richard Lloyd, Beaumaris, preached at Dinas Chapel, from Luke 2:29, and after the sermon, the Rev. Michael Roberts spoke briefly and simply on death, judgment, and eternity. From the chapel they walked in procession to Llaniestyn graveyard. They tried to sing as they went but it was half singing, half weeping. But as they sang the words,

Soon I will leave this body,	Ymadaw wnaf â'r babell
This earthly house of clay,	'Rwy'n trigo ynddi'n awr,

many broke out in rejoicing. And to the accompaniment of a mixture of singing, rejoicing and weeping, the body of Robert Jones was laid to rest until the day dawn. This famous servant of Christ did great work in his day, and his influence was of immense help in raising religion and Methodism throughout Gwynedd, particularly in the Lleyn and Eifionydd areas.

ROBERT DAFYDD, BRYNENGAN

Robert Dafydd of Brynengan could not be compared to Robert Jones, Rhos-lan, for extent of knowledge, weight of character, ministerial position, nor ability to lead, yet the remembrance of him is alive to this day and is of a sweet savour. He was born at Cwm Bychan, near Beddgelert, in the year 1747, and so was some two years younger than Robert Jones. His father, Dafydd Pritchard, was a weaver, and he himself was raised in the same profession. Dafydd Pritchard died when Robert was only a year old and all the responsibility of his upbringing fell upon his mother. When he was thirteen he went to live with an uncle of his, his father's brother, and he was there until he grew up. He became a strong young man, six foot tall, and there were few in the region that could compete with him physically. He received no education. There were no schools in the vicinity, and even if there had been, no one would have thought of sending a poor boy, the son of a widow, to such an establishment. He grew up also completely without religion. The gospel was not preached anywhere in the neighbourhood. Beddgelert Church was nearby but the clergyman had no thought of doing anything more than reading the service for the day to the few people that would be present. Robert therefore did not know the difference, spiritually speaking, between his right hand and his left. He had no idea that he possessed a soul of any kind; as far as he knew there was no difference between himself and an animal. He gave himself to immorality; he excelled in the sports; there was not a wilder youth in the whole locality; and he had no one who could give him a word of counsel.

But God had arranged better things, things that accompany salvation, for Robert Dafydd. The first influence to sober him to some degree was a sermon from Sion Robert Lewis of Holyhead, 'the Old Almanacker'. This was when he was about twenty-one years old. About the same time, Robert Jones, Rhos-lan, came to keep a school at Beddgelert. One of the schoolmaster's responsibilities was to catechize the children using Griffith Jones's *Catechism*, and as well as asking the printed questions Robert Jones would add some of his own. The news of this catechizing spread through the neighbourhood. A large congregation would gather to listen to the exercise, and so unfamiliar were the truths of the gospel to them that the things they heard came as a revelation to them. In the crowd was Robert Dafydd, who had come for no greater reason than curiosity. But the truth took hold of his soul. He experienced the end of the world and saw nothing before him but the lake of fire. His state was so pitiful that he wished he were a demon rather than a man, in that he believed that their misery in hell would be less. On seeing the young man who had been the leader of all their sports and bawdy behaviour now having lost all appetite for such things and having turned his back on his old friends, the local inhabitants were angry with the schoolmaster, and the old women swore at him as he passed in the street.

Robert Dafydd was now a new man in Christ Jesus. His one great wish was to hear the gospel, but there was no regular Methodist preaching closer than Waunfawr, in one direction, and Brynengan, in the other. He chose the latter, though it meant a fifteen-mile walk over a rough, lonely road. If there was a sermon preached anywhere within reach, Robert Dafydd would be certain to be there. And while he remained at Beddgelert, Robert Jones informed him of every service. No doubt Robert Jones's advice and guidance was of great blessing to him, but it seems that it was a sermon by Dafydd Morris, Twrgwyn, that released his feet from the shackles. Dafydd Morris's text was, 'Bring forth the best robe, and put it on him.' As he listened, the chains that held the young weaver broke in pieces.

Robert Dafydd's eagerness to hear preachers and to befriend the Methodists was not acceptable at all to his uncle, and he was forced to leave him. He moved to Brynengan and remained there to the end of his days.

ROBERT DAFYDD AS A PREACHER

Soon after coming to Brynengan Robert Dafydd began to preach. At the time it was not thought that any great preparation was necessary before preaching. If any possessed a warm heart towards the Lord Jesus, and desired to speak of him to sinners, there was a welcome for him to exercise his gift. Most probably there was something in the young weaver that moved the godly people of Brynengan to encourage him in the work. He longed to proclaim the gospel in Beddgelert, the place of his birth. He was announced to preach there for the first time but, as we have noted, because of some circumstance he failed to go, and Robert Jones, Rhos-lan, took his place. Robert Dafydd never became a popular preacher. They did not gather to hear him from every corner of the country as was the case with Robert Roberts, Clynnog. Nor was he able to handle the doctrines of the gospel skilfully, untying knots and explaining complexities, as some of his brethren. He was therefore never considered anything more than an exhorter throughout his life. But he was very acceptable, and no congregation would ever tire of him. He was remarkably simple in his speech; he dressed all his remarks in his own original clothing. If it could not be said that there was originality in the thoughts, there was considerable originality in the style and in the illustrations by which they were conveyed. Robert Dafydd was a weaver in the pulpit. The Rev. Henry Hughes, Bryncir, in his biography of him says:

> His feet would be forever on the move in the pulpit, just like the driving of a weaver. The actions of his body as he preached would also be just like that of the weaver. If everything was proceeding happily his fingers would do little more than touch his head and scratch it a little. If the thread of the argument tangled a little, his fingers would be seen playing through his white hairs, disentangling them. If the thread broke, then with his fingers he would gather up the ends and retie them. Having done so he would play with the shuttle, smoothly and easily, until any further complication arose. And all would be so natural and easy that he would carry his congregation with him.

No one would be thought of as possessing any spiritual status in the days when Robert Dafydd began preaching if he had not been to Llangeitho to hear Daniel Rowland, and this Robert Dafydd did many times. Not only did they have a long journey to walk, over eighty miles, but it was also a dangerous journey with much mocking and persecution having to be endured as they passed through the various villages. As an example of this persecution, *Methodistiaeth Cymru* describes Robert Dafydd and John Pierce, a preacher who died while relatively young, on their way to Llangeitho:

> They were fiercely hooted at in Tanybwlch, and mocking cries followed behind them in Dolgellau, but they arrived, tired out, at Llangeitho by the time of the Saturday sermon before the communion. After only a few minutes of listening to Rowland all their tiredness had gone, all their griefs forgotten, and their vessels running over with the joy of salvation.

Another example of the dangers met with is given in the same book:

> The roads were infrequent and the inhabitants of the neighbourhoods passed through were often bad-tempered. They would sometimes meet with heavy weather of wind, rain, snow and blizzard, so that it became almost impossible to proceed. Robert Dafydd and his companion, Richard Morris, were once returning from Llangeitho and crossing at Traeth Bach, when they were caught by the tide and almost drowned. Robert Dafydd, who was quite tall, was up to his armpits in the water, while Richard Morris, who was shorter, was up to his neck. It was also a cold night of snow and ice, so that it was amazing that they escaped with their lives.

The religion of these early Methodists cost them a great deal in every way, and unless they had encouraged themselves as those seeing the invisible they would have lost heart amidst all their difficulties.

Though Robert Dafydd was not considered amongst the ablest preachers he would sometimes experience powerful services. In *Hanes Methodistiaeth Gorllewin Meirionydd*[1] an account of a remarkable service is given:

> John Elias was on a journey through this part of Merionethshire. He was announced to preach at Dyffryn on a Sunday night. That same Sunday, Robert Dafydd was at Gwynfryn, at two in the afternoon, and in the night. At the end of the afternoon's service, he encouraged all who could go to be present at Dyffryn in the evening to hear the famous preacher, rather than staying at Gwynfryn. Many however remained with him, and on that evening such rejoicing broke out at Gwynfryn that it was remembered for a very long time. Humphrey Evans, afterwards of Llanfair, and John Davies, the father of the Rev. John Davies, late of Llanelli, were youths at the time and sitting at the front of the gallery. As the rejoicing increased in strength, they jumped over

the edge and down to the reed floor below in order to join in with the congregation in their jumping and praising. Another present was the young wife of Richard Owen, afterwards of Runcorn, with her baby in her arms. She also began jumping and praising, throwing the baby into the apron of her mother, who sat nearby. The two old elders of the church, sitting under the pulpit, surveyed the scene with much pleasure. On seeing the young mother throwing the baby into her mother's apron, John Jones turned to William Richard and said, 'There, you see. There's a fulfilment of that prophecy, "Can a woman forget her sucking child, that she should not have compassion on the son of her womb? Yea, they may forget, yet will I not forget thee."'

There are other accounts of similar meetings when general rejoicing would break out under the ministry of Robert Dafydd. He preached once in a farmhouse called Brydyni in the Brynengan neighbourhood. His text was Exodus 3:3, 'I will now turn aside, and see this great sight, why this bush is not burnt.' It was during a time of revival, and a large crowd had gathered so that the house was overfull. Robert Dafydd was on the high places of the field and the congregation stirred to its depths, and at the end they broke out together in much rejoicing. Amongst them was a blacksmith called Robert Edward. He had come there immediately from work, without washing. His face was still black. Listening to the sermon, his tears began to flow, and two white channels were seen on his cheeks, down which the waters flowed. They remained singing and rejoicing for a long time. One of the hymns sung was:

See the great High Priest is standing O'er the river's darkened flood; There the brethren I will follow, For the way is clear to God.	Mae'r Offeiriad mawr yn sefyll Yn yr afon dywyll, ddu; Drwyddi af ar ôl fy mrodyr, Disglair lwybr yno sy'.

LEADING THE SOCIETY MEETINGS

But Robert Dafydd is best remembered for his prayers and especially for the way in which he would lead the society meetings. He was very blunt in this work; he would not allow any respect of persons, but would say the truth however much it cost him or others. And as it was known that he was honest, and that all he said arose from a true desire for the profit of those to whom he spoke, none took offence at him. He seems also to have possessed a discernment and skill so as to separate between the wheat and the chaff. He was always being asked to go about to lead the societies, and many good people, anxious over the state of their souls, would wish to hear his view of their condition in that they considered his judgment as being almost infallible. Once, at Four Crosses, he was conversing in the society with a very godly sister, Ellen Jones of Llandyrus. As he questioned her, he noted that she was not her usual self, and that her thoughts were distracted. He suddenly asked her, 'Has there been any unpleasantness between you and some of your neighbours lately?' She had to acknowledge that this was the case.

Another time, at Chester, he talked with a rich, important man, who was considered rather wordly and miserly. Robert Dafydd tried to draw him out and get him to share some spiritual experience, but he was not succeeding. At last he began to speak severely to the man, and to suggest fairly clearly that he did not consider him a godly man. John Parry, the minister, thought that he was going too far, and was afraid of him saying something even harsher. He therefore suggested to the old exhorter that it was time to finish. Robert Dafydd was quite at home with Mr Parry, both having been raised in the same county, and he replied, 'You finish, but this man is rotting in his sin under your care.'

One of his most useful qualifications as a leader of the society was his excellent memory. He could remember the previous experiences related by those with whom he talked, and compare these with their present contributions. He was once leading a society at Brynaerau, Clynnog, and a member was sharing his experience. Within about a year he was there again, and the same man shared the same experience. Robert Dafydd was aggrieved, and said: 'Deio *annwyl,* are you still in the same place? The shepherd does not keep the sheep always grazing on the same pasture; he moves them continually. It is time for you to move to new pastures or you will starve where you are.'

We believe that we have by now given a clear picture of Robert Dafydd. We see him as a piece of true nature, without much shaping or sophistication; completely honest in every circumstance and with a keen nose for discerning mischief. One of his greatest enemies was pride. He could not bear to see young girls with ribbons in their hair, or veils on their faces, and he could say some severe things to them and about them at times. He was zealous for discipline. He demonstrated much loving care for the purity of the house. But if it should be believed that he therefore manifested an unchristian severity and that he reproved purely for the sake of reproving and was quite insensitive to people's feelings, this would be unfair to him. A matter of discipline was once before the society at Brynengan. A thoughtless man stood up and began to list the faults of the accused man in a very unbrotherly manner. He had hardly finished speaking when Robert Dafydd got to his feet and poured oil upon the wounds of the poor man before them. 'God does not list our faults,' he said. 'He forgives them.' He said this with deep feeling, greatly emphasizing the word 'forgives'.

Another similar story is told of him. A member of the Brynengan society went to Cricieth fair to employ a labourer for the harvest. Having agreed terms, he and the labourer went to the inn and drank some beer together. This was before the days of temperance, when a visit to the inn was not considered in any way inappropriate for a believer. On leaving the inn the man realized that he had drunk more than he should have, and that he was to a degree under the influence. He quietly withdrew to a nearby field and slept for a little time. On awakening, he feared that there was still some signs of drunkenness about him, so he went home along the most unobserved of paths. He was a good man, though he had stumbled. His conscience reproved him and at the first opportunity, he went to Robert Dafydd to explain what had happened. The old exhorter listened to him quietly and thoughtfully and when he had finished his story, he said, 'God help you! Did someone see you?' 'No, nobody, I think, except for the Judge himself.' 'Yes, yes,' said Robert Dafydd, 'I know that he saw you. Well, don't tell anybody else, and I will never tell anyone. Never do it again. And pray to God, and repent.' He said the last words with great emphasis. Many years passed, and it was only on the day of Robert Dafydd's funeral that the man related the story to others.

He held a society once at Capel Uchaf, Clynnog. The cause there was in a very feeble condition, and the few that gathered were very disheartened. This was before Robert Roberts had moved to Clynnog. On seeing the members with their heads down, Robert Dafydd was agitated and he jumped to his feet, saying excitedly, 'In God's name. What is the matter with you people? Aren't you well aware that Jesus Christ was born in Bethlehem, and lived at Nazareth and Capernaum? Aren't you fully aware that he suffered in Gethsemane and bore the pains of the cross at Calvary? Don't you know that he was buried, and that he rose the third day, and that he ascended to heaven, where he now intercedes on your behalf?' He went through all the history of the Saviour in this way until he had thoroughly aroused the people. They were seen to raise their heads, to begin to weep tears of gratitude, and the service finished with much glorying.

Robert Dafydd was always ready to receive heavenly impressions if they were abroad. He would raise his sails to any wind that began to blow. It is told in *Methodistiaeth Cymru* of a remarkable meeting at Capel Uchaf, Clynnog, when something sudden and strange fell upon the congregation:

> It had been announced that Robert Dafydd, Brynengan, and William Roberts, Clynnog, would preach together there on some occasion. The time came. William Roberts preached first, from Luke 9:62, 'No man, having put his hand to the plough, and looking back, is fit for the kingdom of God.' But before he finished preaching, such heavy influences fell upon the people that the majority of them began to shout, others were weeping, and all were gripped as if by shock. There was no opportunity for the old patriarch Robert Dafydd to say a word. He stood amazed in the pulpit, his hands in his hair, as usual. He showed obvious signs that his own vessel was full, and that he also was ready to break out shouting with all his might.

THE 1831 REVIVAL

Robert Dafydd was given a long life and as it drew to its close, he longed to see a revival in the Church once more before he died. He preached often on this point, and there was one notable sermon on the text, 'But I will see you again.' He made it a matter of daily prayer in his own private prayers over a period of two years. He would withdraw into his room each day with this message in particular. He would also pray aloud over the same point in a secluded corner of his garden. He used to name the farms and cottages in his prayers, calling on God to save those who dwelt in them. 'You know,' he said, 'O Lord, that there are some houses where the worshippers that used to be in them have died, and the old altars have been pulled down. O my Father, let me see one more revival before I die; let me see my neighbours in their scores turn their faces to thy house, drawing near to thee with weeping. And if you grant my request, I will be willing to die at whatever moment you decide.'

The Lord heard his prayer. In the year 1831, God visited north Wales remarkably, the Lleyn and Eifionydd areas in particular, and many hundreds were added to the churches. This visitation is called 'the Brynengan Revival', and it continued in its strength throughout the year 1832. It began with a glorious sermon from John Elias at the Pwllheli Association of 16 September, 1831, from the words, 'Let God arise, let his enemies be scattered, let them also that hate him flee before him.' It was a discouraging time for religion; the thunders of Robert Roberts were as if they had been completely forgotten; few turned their faces to the house of the Lord, and good men had been caught up in cowardice and disappointment. John Elias's sermon came as a thunderbolt from a cloudless blue sky. When, after describing the corruptions of the land and the effrontery of the enemies of religion, he shouted forth, again and again, 'Let God arise', a fear spread throughout the crowd. Many workers of iniquity fainted, and

God's saints rejoiced. One brother from Porthmadog said, 'John Elias preached then until the whole of Caernarvonshire was trembling, and it has never collected itself back together.' The following week, John Elias preached at Brynengan. The gathering was immense, hundreds having come on horseback and in carriages from a radius of many miles. The revival spread as wildfire across Lleyn. Soon after, the Rev. Henry Rees preached at Brynengan. There was a strange solemnity about his ministry; the people felt as if the terrors of the judgment had wrapped themselves around them. In the service was a red-headed boy, full of mischief, a ring-leader amongst the more frivolous youth of the area. He worked for Dewi Wyn (a well-known poet), and at mid-day he had asked his master for permission to go to the society. The bard was surprised by his request and told him to go if he thought it would improve him – an answer that suggests that there was plenty of room for improvement. When he made his appearance at the church meeting, Robert Dafydd said, 'Here is Gad; there is a troop coming.' And his prediction became true. There were a hundred and forty added to the church at Brynengan at that time, and many of them proved by their subsequent living that the root of the matter was in them. Robert Dafydd loved talking to these converts. His main question to them was: Had they been under Sinai? And if they were not able to sound that shibboleth, he would be suspicious of them. This is when the Rev. John Owen, Ty'nllwyd, joined the society. When he was asked what was on his mind, he replied, 'Nothing in particular; but I am mindful of that promise, "And in this mountain shall the Lord of hosts make unto all people a feast of fat things, a feast of wines on the lees, of fat things full of marrow, of wines on the lees well refined." I was thinking that the feast was here. And I came to the society so that I might not miss out.' To come to the society from a mere sense of duty in this way would hardly have been very acceptable to Robert Dafydd.

But even after the old patriarch had received his request from God for a revival, he was still not happy. He would withdraw again to his room to pray, and his message now was, 'O Lord! Let me live another year that I might raise these children.' The Lord answered him in this also and he was given, not one year, but two.

Many of his remarks are still remembered to this day. He said once, when referring to God's forgiveness, 'There is no one like our God for hiding sins. He throws them behind his back. And he is so tall that there is no Saul, though he might be head and shoulders higher than the people, who can see over his shoulders. Not even Gabriel, the tallest of all the angels, can see behind God's back.'

Someone argued with him once with regard to falling from grace, saying confidently, as if he was about to close Robert Dafydd's mouth for certain, 'Where was grace when Peter was cursing and swearing and denying?' 'O!' replied the old exhorter, 'If it hadn't been for grace he would be swearing still.'

He commented in the society once, 'I was passing one of the farms this morning and saw a man putting a roof over a haystack. I asked him in surprise, 'Wil, why are you putting a roof over the haystack when the weather is so fine?' 'Oh!' replied Wil, 'Though it's fine now, a storm will come.' And indeed, you know, it was Wil who was correct. By nightfall we had a tremendous rain-storm. In the same way, someone may ask me, "What is the point of coming to the chapel like this all the time, and making such a stir with this religion?" Oh! The storm will come yet, dear friends. It will be a blessing yet to have a roof over us.'

Once, when asking a blessing before a meal, Robert Jones said, 'Thank you, O Lord, for your daily mercies to us. It is not like this in hell. There it is woe for breakfast, woe for dinner, and woe for supper.'

In a society at Brynengan, he noticed that the people had sat down scattered far from one another, and said, 'Why are you so far from one another? You are like a lot of wet peat like that; you will never fire. Come closer together and you will warm up then. If the peat is scattered, the fire will soon go out, but gather it together and it will soon light and flame.'

When anyone would return to the society after having been thrown out, if there was any indication in them of wishing to justify themselves or to suggest that they had been unfairly dealt with, Robert Dafydd would scratch his head and say rather dryly to them, 'The latch is lower than that.'

Robert Dafydd had a pony called Jack who was as remarkable amongst horses as his master was amongst men. He used to speak to the pony as if he was a man. Once as he was on his way to preach at Pennant, he crossed a small stream, at which Jack stopped to slake his thirst. Robert Dafydd told him, thinking that no one could hear him, 'There you are, Jack *bach*. You drink as much as you want. You have a hard job of it. There are two men on your back. The old man and the new man.' He lent Jack on one occasion to a young girl who was going to Pwllheli fair. The fair was held on a Friday, and on the next day, Robert Dafydd himself was setting out to ride to Clynnog. As he put on the saddle he noticed a bruise on the horse. He inspected it in some surprise at first, and then said, 'Well, Jack *bach*, that's what comes of carrying a girl. You never had a sore like that when carrying me.'

A little while before his death, he moved from his old home, Tyddyn Ruffydd, to his son Robert, who lived at the Brynengan chapel-house, and it was here that he died. He had never suffered any ill health throughout his life, and he died suddenly while sitting in a chair. He was buried in Llangybi graveyard, and his biographer noted, 'There are those alive yet who remember the remarkable singing along the way and in Llangybi village.' Carved on his gravestone is the following:

Here lies the body of
ROBERT DAFYDD
of Tyddyn Ruffydd
Who was a faithful preacher
amongst the Calvinistic Methodists
for 61 years.
He died April 17, 1834,
when 87 years old.

Nodedig ei ddawn nid ydoedd, - er hynny
Rhanai fara'r nefoedd
O'i law aur i laweroedd;
Offeryn Duw a'i ffrind oedd.[2]

If our information is correct, this *englyn* is by *Eben Fardd*. It is certain that the Lord laid his hand on Robert Dafydd on scores of occasions and he was an instrument of much good throughout his life. His style, though unpolished and rustic, was well fitted to his times. In describing his outward appearance, *Methodistiaeth Cymru* states:

> He had the look of a patriarch; his hair heavy and parted on his forehead, and in old age, as white as linen. He had a considerable number of offspring and many of these also became well-known for their religion and godliness.

[1] *The History of the Methodism of West Merionethshire*, a series of articles by Richard Humphreys (1790–1863) of Dyffryn, Merionethshire.

[2] *He was not notable for his gifts / Yet he distributed the bread of heaven / From his golden hand to many; / He was God's instrument and God's friend.*

25

JOHN ROBERTS, LLANGWM

ROBERT THOMAS, THE FATHER OF ROBERT AND JOHN ROBERTS

In the chapter on Robert Roberts, Clynnog, the younger, but more famous, brother of the Rev. John Roberts, we referred to their father, Robert Thomas. But on many accounts he deserves more attention. When his first son was born he lived with his wife Catherine at a place called Blaenygarth near Nantlle. They soon moved to Ffridd-bala-ddeulyn in the parish of Llanllyfni in order to be near the copper works. These works were very successful at the time; there were men from every county in Gwynedd working there and the wages being offered were much greater than the usual. In addition, the nearby Cilgwyn quarry also offered work opportunities. The result of commercial success at that time, as always, was an increase in every kind of ungodliness, and in particular in drunkenness. Some of the workers would attend the church early on a Sunday morning and then flock together to the various sports and games on offer. The sacred day would be brought to an end at one of the many taverns found in the neighbourhood. Many, in their drunkenness, would remain at the inn throughout the night and through the following Monday and Tuesday. No Sabbath would pass without fights breaking out. And of all these drunkards and fighters, the best known was Robert Thomas of Ffridd. He would often stay in one or another of Nantlle's taverns until the middle of the week, as drunk as beer could make him. He would often get into fights and as he was a strong man and a skilful fighter he would nearly always emerge victorious.

For all his prodigality, Robert Thomas possessed some literary skills. He enjoyed writing poetry and was skilful in writing light verse. He would buy every Welsh book of verse or songs that was published. He attended the Church faithfully, and when his children were old enough he would take them with him, instructing them to join with the sexton in the responses of the service. According to Michael Roberts, preaching, or rather the reading of a sermon, occurred three times a year at Llanllyfni Church at that time:

at Christmas, Easter, and Whitsun. The parson, it seems, only possessed three sermons, so that each one, after being read, would be put aside ready for the next year's use. The first to leave the church would be the parson and the crowd of expectant revellers would follow at his heels. Once outside, the parson would compete with his parishioners in the race to the inn, the winner being rewarded with a quart of beer from his companions. Robert Thomas saw nothing out of place in this, nor in the fair that was held in the village on God's Day. This was the common practice of the day and age and it was fully in accord with his own temperament.

However, about the year 1763, the Methodists began to preach in the Llanllyfni area. A man called William Williams heard that a preacher from the south was speaking on a Sunday night at Berth-ddu in Clynnog parish. He felt a desire to attend the meeting and having attended was so profited that he became a regular hearer. It is said that he was the first from the Llanllyfni parish to hear a Methodist. He would follow the preachers to Clynnog, Bryn-y-gadfa, Waunfawr, and other places, and would bring a companion with him. According to *Methodistiaeth Cymru*:

> These were the means by which he and three other men were saved from their vain conversation, received by tradition from their fathers, and became the first-fruits of the gospel in their neighbourhood. The names of the other three were William Dafydd, William Jones, and William Roberts. To these was soon added the sister of William Williams, who was to become the wife of the Rev. John Roberts.

It was natural for these zealous believers to look to obtain preaching in their own neighbourhood. But there was no one who would receive the gospel to their house and, were any to do so, they would have been evicted, such was the wrath of the landowner towards the Methodists. At first, therefore, preaching would occur at the roadside or in a corner of a field. About the year 1766, William Williams married a girl called Catherine Pritchard from Clynnog parish. Catherine Pritchard was a deeply religious person. She had joined the Methodists ten years before and for a time had been a member of Howell Harris's 'family' at Trefeca. She would often make the journey to Llangeitho. After marrying, the two went to live at Buarthau. For some reason the landowner's hatred of the Methodists had been tempered and he allowed them to hold preaching meetings at the house. As a result, Buarthau became a station for preachers from the north and the south. A society was formed here, and although the members at the beginning were only six in number, they were zealous in spirit. It was said of Catherine Pritchard that she was the first in Caernarvonshire to jump while rejoicing during a sermon. Strong gales of the Spirit had often fallen upon various places in the county previously, as God's Word was being expounded, with congregations being overcome by tears and breaking out into praises, but Catherine Pritchard was the first to jump. Some thought that she had become unbalanced and one person tried to hold her down, but she cried out, 'Don't hold me, for I am not ashamed of the gospel of Christ.'

We have not wandered too far from the history of Robert Thomas because he also was brought to faith and it was with the small flock at Buarthau that he then joined himself. The account of his conversion, as told by his grandson, the Rev. Michael Roberts, is worth recording:

> On Whit Monday, during the feast-day fair at Clynnog, a fight had been arranged between Clynnog and Llanllyfni parishes, and the Goliath of Llanllyfni was Robert Thomas. He set out that morning from Ffridd with a large oak staff in his hand, and his wife and children in tears behind him, fearing that if he ever returned to them alive, it would be with broken bones and injuries. 'Stop your nonsense, you fools. By the devil! I will smash half a dozen of them as cockleshells and the other half dozen will run away.' As he passed by Capel Uchaf, Clynnog, the home of Edward the tailor, as he was called, he heard singing and he entered the house. The people present then began to pray. By now his mind was so disturbed that he remained rooted to the spot without a thought of leaving. The preacher took his text, 'For the great day of his wrath is come; and who shall be able to stand?' Such power accompanied the word that Robert was converted where he stood and brought truly to God. The preacher's name was James, a man from Trefeca. Robert conferred not with flesh and blood but went straight home. His wife and John Roberts were amazed; they almost thought that they were seeing a vision when he appeared before them so soon, clothed and in his right mind. At last, having recovered herself and seeing his solemnity, his wife asked:
>
> 'Robert *bach*, are you ill?'
>
> 'O, no, Cadi *bach*,' he answered. 'I am today beginning to get better for ever.'
>
> 'What do you mean, Father?' asked John.
>
> 'I will tell you,' said he. 'About a mile from Clynnog village, I heard singing in a house and in I went. I heard one of those new people preaching there, and I had never heard such a thing before in my life. Cadi, I will never ever get drunk again, and I will never fight with anyone again, except the devil and sin.'
>
> The tears were flowing down his wife's cheeks as she answered:
>
> 'I hope that indeed will be the case, dear Robert.'
>
> 'No, never again, Cadi,' he said, 'By the help of God's grace.'

> Thus it proved. He was never drunk, nor ever fought again. He changed his clothes, took food, and went to his work until evening. After supper, he took the Bible, read a chapter and prayed with his family, and continued this practice for the rest of his life.
>
> The parishioners of Llanllyfni found themselves in serious trouble in the fair, none of them had an idea what could have happened to Robert Thomas. The thought of a battle disappeared; no one felt like fighting without their giant, and it was a mercy to many a bone in Clynnog that Robert never arrived there with his heavy oak staff.

This account may be taken to be substantially true, coming as it does from the grandson of its subject. But it differs from another account given in *Methodistiaeth Cymru*. We read there:

> Robert Thomas was told that there was a service to be held on a Sunday morning at a place called Pencoed in Eifionydd and he decided to go there, not to listen but to break up the worship and perhaps to injure the preacher. It was quite possible, so little control had he over himself when roused to a fury, that he might have ended up a murderer. Before leaving he told his wife where he was going and for what purpose. He told her that he was going to teach a bitter enough lesson to the deceiver that was travelling the country fooling and duping innocent people. In this spirit and with such a bloody purpose he set out, and his wife, knowing his temper, feared greatly for the preacher, certain that he would be badly injured or even killed. She was troubled all day, often looking out of the window to see if Robert was returning. At last, she saw him far off and hurried to meet him. On coming up to him she saw immediately that he was deeply solemn and serious, which caused her to fear even more that he had brought down much trouble upon his head. She asked him in great fear:
>
> 'Robert *bach*, have you injured the stranger?'
>
> 'No,' he replied, 'and if I have anything to do with it, no one else will injure him either.'
>
> The wife realized that her prayers had been answered and that the grace of the gospel had overcome her husband.

We do not know where Mr Hughes obtained this story. It might be an account of something that befell Robert Thomas before the occasion of his conversion and that his persecuting spirit was overcome at this point before he left his worldly ways.

Robert Thomas had found true religion. He had raised a family altar on the day of his conversion before meeting with any religious society, and though his prayer was read from Griffith Jones's book it was a sight to see this champion fighter, the ungodliest creature in the neighbourhood, on his knees before God. A new world opened up before the eyes of his family. At the first opportunity he went to the society at Buarthau, and his wife was not long in following after him. The brethren were in fear of him to begin with; they could hardly believe that the giant had been floored. But Robert Thomas gave indisputable proofs of his salvation. He lived a pure life to the day he died; his soul thirsted within him for the Word of God; he would travel far to hear itinerant preachers and eventually opened his own home to the gospel. It remained a preaching-station for the next fifty-two years.

JOHN ROBERTS AS A BOY

This chapter however has to do with the eldest son of Robert and Catherine Thomas, namely, the Rev. John Roberts, Llangwm. He was born at Blaen-y-garth, near Nantlle, in Llanddwrog parish, Caernarvonshire, on 8 August 1753. He was therefore nine years older than his brother Robert. When he was only a baby, his parents moved to Ffridd-bala-ddeulyn in Llanllyfni. John Roberts showed evidences of his abilities from a very early age. Though his father at the time lived such a wanton life, he enjoyed teaching his son to read and made sure of taking him to the church every Sunday. As a result John became an able reader when very young, and could respond as accurately as the sexton to the parson during the services. He grew up a strong young man but he was always short, reaching his fullest height before he was sixteen. He does not seem to have been touched by the corrupt ways of the neighbourhood. His temperament was cheerful, he was lively and playful, always smiling and with a witty answer to any question, but his humour never led him into any wantonness or evil company. He was noted for his skill at whatever task he undertook. In the home he helped his mother and was as neat and tidy about the domestic chores as any maid. On the farm he mowed the hay and harvested the wheat; he raised the stacks in the barn; he mended the hedges and stone walls with a skill that was admired throughout the neighbourhood. He could repair shoes as well as any cobbler, he made wooden gates, he wove baskets and cradles, and could hoop vessels as if he had been apprenticed to a cooper.

Once the younger children were old enough to help their father, John worked as a shepherd at Gelli-ffrydiau. How long he remained here is not known, but he soon proved as able in the work of shepherding as in his other skills. Though there were two thousand sheep and goats in his care, he knew them all individually. He was as fleet of foot as Asahel and could catch any lamb on the mountainside in a few minutes.

Having returned home from Gelli-ffrydiau, he experienced an amazing escape. The following is Michael Roberts's account:

> At one time, a strong ram had to be caught in order kill it, and he, together with his father and others, went to Ffridd-fawr to hunt it. The ram escaped from them by climbing Cwmsilyn rock. But John Roberts was after it, following on its heels. The ram bounded across the ridge of the rock, from crag to crag, until it came to a narrow place, with John Roberts behind him like the angel before Balaam. It was impossible to move to the left or to the right. His father and the other watchers realized his danger and shouted to him, and having been alerted and looking about him, he began to think he would not escape alive. To climb up was impossible, beneath him was a sheer fall and a fearful lake, and he and the ram were standing on a small ledge of a few feet in width and length. His father shouted at him to remain where he was while they went home to fetch ropes. They soon returned with others to help and plenty of rope. They climbed to the top of the crag and threw down the ropes to him. He caught them and tied them around himself and shouted at them to leave him where he was until he had tied up the ram also. But his father, angry with him for his daring, shouted back, 'No! Leave him to hang.' John replied, cheerfully, 'The rope is round his neck and about my waist, you can hang the two of us now together as we have been so long in the same prison.' And they were both pulled up together to safety and brought home. There, the sentence upon them both was very different. John did not receive the warmest of welcomes, but the ram's blood was flowing within a few minutes.

The story shows God's providential care of him, and also his courage and cheerfulness when in considerable danger.

His heart longed for education but two months of school at Llanfihangel-y-Pennant was all that his parents could afford for him. However, as he could already read Welsh and had a strong mind, he succeeded in these two months, by much hard work, to learn to read and write English excellently. Having left school, he gave himself to increasing his knowledge. He read every book that came within his grasp, and having been read its contents became his own. He determined to perfect himself in English and in arithmetic. He delighted also in reading and researching the historical parts of the Bible. He was a walking concordance of scriptural history long before he was converted.

HIS CONVERSION UNDER DAFYDD MORRIS'S PREACHING

Though John Roberts led a blameless life and was eager to learn, he was not yet of the faith, nor does he seem to have made much effort to hear good preaching. But one night a stranger from the south was announced to preach at Bwlch-y-Gilfin and John went as company for his father. The name of the speaker is not known and his gifts were limited; his sermon consisted mainly of reciting scriptural stories. John Roberts however much enjoyed him and believed that there was no better preacher to be had. In a little while, the same man was announced for Buarthau. He came on this occasion as the 'friend' of one of Wales's greatest preachers, Dafydd Morris, Twrgwyn. His father said to John after finishing dinner, 'Well, John, *your* preacher is at Buarthau tonight. Will you come to hear him?' 'Yes, certainly,' was the reply. A large crowd had gathered so that the house was crowded. The Rev. Michael Roberts continues the account in his own words:

> Dafydd Morris had travelled through these parts once before, his fame drawing people after him from Waunfawr, Clynnog and Bwlchderwyn. The old man (John Roberts's preacher) went through his sermon, and my father greatly enjoyed him. When he had finished, my father saw a slim, severe-looking, young man climbing on to a stool, pulling a small Bible from his pocket, and reading his text as a thunderbolt. The preacher's presence drew a kind of solemn echo throughout the crowd, and brought the fear of God upon them. His text was Luke 13:9. 'And if it bear fruit, well: and if not, then after that thou shalt cut it down.' He first of all explained the parable in a clear and interesting way. He then brought out some doctrinal points from the text and parable, namely,
>
> 1. That God Almighty had placed every man upon the earth, in differing circumstances, for the express purpose of bearing fruit to his glory.
>
> 2. That God came often and in his omniscience looked carefully as to whether men were bearing such fruit.
>
> 3. That he came often and, to many, over a long period of time – 'Behold, these three years' – over years, over the various seasons of life, childhood, youth, middle age, old age.
>
> 4. That he could say, for the vast majority, after all advantages, mercies and providential care, 'I find none.'
>
> 5. That the righteousness of God, as the Moral Ruler of his rational creatures, cries out above these, 'Cut it down; why cumbereth it the ground?'
>
> 6. That the dresser of the vineyard, the preachers of the Word, are importunate in their prayers on behalf of their barren hearers, 'Lord, let it alone this year also, till I shall dig about it, and dung it.' That is, to exercise every means of grace for bringing them to bear fruit in God. But mainly that Christ, in his effective intercession, so prays.
>
> 7. That this is the verdict, 'And if it bear fruit, well: and if not, then after that thou shalt cut it down.'

> I heard my father say many times that there was no picture or comparison that he could give to describe the state of the congregation, particularly when the preacher shouted out, 'What will be the end of the whole process? Cut it down!' The nearest thing he could think of was Israel's condition before Sinai. The preacher's face was like that of an angel; his voice like thunder. My father thought that at times the earth was shaking under him, and that he was seeing the Judge upon the clouds, the judgment-seat brought forward, the books opened, and that he was hearing the word, 'Go!' into the eternal fire. It was a literal fulfilment of the scene in Cornelius's house, 'The Holy Ghost fell on all them which heard the word.' He fell upon many to renew and revive them, upon others to save them and return them to God, and upon others to make them moral and bind them as regular hearers of the gospel for the rest of their lives. When all felt at the point of death, being torn by their feelings and at the point of despairing as to any hope of salvation, Dafydd Morris paused for a while, for him to catch his breath and for them to groan. Then the tone of his voice changed, and he shouted so as to split the rocks under which they were being crushed, 'Hallelujah! Hallelujah! Hosanna! God has a gracious plan to revive the dry trees, to break them off the old stem and to graft them on to the pure Olive Tree; he is the green fir tree; and from him as the Mediator there is fruit to be found upon the likes of us, instead of damnation in the eternal fire.' The listeners now cried out with one shout of joy, 'Hallelujah!', having seen a hope of life. My father and his parents were shouting 'Thanks be to God,' with the loudest, and Dafydd Morris was in their midst, jumping for joy.

This is a vivid account of one of the meetings of old, and it exemplifies the preaching style of the early Methodists. They used to press their hearers to the very point of damnation; they drove them to the uttermost, very like the Israelites before the Red Sea, and having kept them there for a time, bereft of any ray of hope from heaven, they threw open the door of the gospel, so that the people, amazed by the majesty and suddenness of the light that fell upon them, broke out into rejoicing and glorifying of God. We have heard this kind of preaching being condemned. Whatever may be said against it, it was the means of returning thousands who were upon the broad road, and it produced a class of believers comparable to any the Christian world has ever seen.

Two points in the account call for a comment. One is the description of Dafydd Morris as a '*slim . . . young man*'. John Roberts was seventeen years old when he joined the society, and if we assume that this occurred soon after the remarkable meeting at Buarthau, this would mean that Dafydd Morris was only twenty-six years of age and had not yet moved from Lledrod to Twrgwyn. The unnatural obesity that overtook him in later life had not yet taken hold of him. The other point is the description of Dafydd

Morris descending from his stool and joining in with the praising in the midst of the congregation. This occurred with many of the preachers of the period. Howell Harris himself would often break out to rejoice and praise God in mid-sermon. Mr Lloyd of Caeo was noted for doing so. Here, Dafydd Morris was so overcome by the truths that he proclaimed that he could not refrain from joining the congregation in their praising. The preacher and his hearers were nearer to each other in those days; there was no pulpit or big seat to divide them, and it was very little work to get down from a stool or table.

John Roberts, then, was seventeen years old when he joined the society, and was working at Cilgwyn quarry at the time. His friends thought he could do better than splitting slates and they advised him to keep a school. He worked as a schoolmaster for sixteen years, teaching in the Bryneinion, Rhos-lan, Clynnog, Llanllynfi, Brynyrodyn, and Pentre-uchaf neighbourhoods. In a note of his that has survived, he wrote:

> I had a total of 1,172 children in my care. I taught them English, grammar, arithmetic and measures. Many went from me to various branches of commerce – shopkeepers, secretaries for counting houses, sailors, and clerks for offices. I would also do a great deal of drawing up legal matters such as notes, bonds, contracts, wills, marriage contracts, and similar things, until the time it became unlawful for any but lawyers to do this.

Surely a young man who could do all this after only two months of schooling and who had been brought up in a rural area with little educational resources available, possessed remarkable abilities and unwearying determination. While John Roberts was at home, he helped his father teach and catechize the younger children. Upon him would fall the care of the school in the home whenever Robert Thomas was away, and we find that his concern for the salvation of the children was great, especially for his brother Robert, in whom he saw evidences of a good mind.

John Roberts nearly had a college education. The Moravians came to preach in the neighbourhood and one of them, Dafydd Mathias from Dyfed, became a close friend of John Roberts and of the family. The young man opened his heart to him as to his longing for education. Dafydd Mathias promised to see what he could do to get him a place in a Moravian college in England. He succeeded in the attempt and John Roberts made preparations to leave for Yorkshire and the college. But on the Sunday afternoon before the Monday when he was due to go, Dafydd Mathias came to the house. Robert Thomas was reading at the time from the book of the prophet Isaiah, and he commented:

'Isn't it strange, Mr Mathias, that the prophets, especially Isaiah, were so clear over the sufferings, death and glorious ascension of Christ, and that so many hundreds of years before his appearance.'

The Moravian answered,

'Robert *bach*, is this the extent of your knowledge of the Bible after so long? The prophets did not know of whom they spoke; they would dream and then narrate their dreams, not understanding what they saw themselves, let alone being able to explain it to others.'

'No,' said Robert Thomas, 'it was the Spirit of Christ which was in them that testified of the sufferings of Christ and the glory that should follow.'

The argument between them became heated and they both lost their tempers. Mathias particularly was very sarcastic and said to Thomas that they were very appropriately called Meth-odists, in that they *failed* [Welsh = '*methu*'] in all they did. He then left them in some anger. As he crossed the threshold, the father said to John,

'Go with him! No you won't, ever, nor with any of his breed. I would rather that I and my children were forced to beg our bread than to fellowship with those who are in such error over the Bible and its glories.'

This brought an abrupt end to any hopes the son had for a college education. No doubt this proved a great disadvantage to him, but perhaps it was of advantage to Wales. Had he gone to England he might well have stayed in England and not returned to evangelize his poor countrymen.

JOHN ROBERTS BEGINS TO PREACH

According to his own testimony, he was about twenty-eight years old when he began preaching. Many slipped from being schoolmasters to being preachers, and this was his experience. If Dr Owen Thomas is correct in saying that it was John Roberts who began the service at Brynyrodyn for Jones, Llan-gan, the night on which Robert Roberts was converted, it must be that he was thought of as one with his face towards the ministry some years before he undertook the office. He had been married for five years when he began. He had four children, three girls and a boy; the boy, the Rev. Michael Roberts, being now a familiar name throughout Wales.

We know very little of John Roberts's ministerial career. It appears that he very quickly gained a name for himself as a preacher. According to *Methodistiaeth Cymru*:

> As a preacher, he was considered in the early years of his ministry to be equal to if not better than anyone else in the north. He, and Mr Richardson of Caernarvon, who had begun to preach at the same time, were the two brightest stars of Caernarvonshire. John Roberts possessed a short but strong body. His mind was quick and lively. He possessed more knowledge and was more fluent

> than most of the preachers of his day. He journeyed much through north and south Wales, as well as to the cities of England, for over fifty years. He was an energetic worker, ready and forward with the cause of the Lord, and his ministry was the means of turning many to righteousness.

The Rev. Owen Thomas refers to him as being:

> Broad and detailed in his knowledge of the doctrines of the gospel, and one who was honoured almost always, over a long period of time, with the most privileged positions at the Associations.

He was a preacher of substance and would often be remarkably stirring. Although not depending on a passionate style, he would often have most powerful services. He would usually deal with a doctrinal theme, expounding it powerfully and with much light. He never became such a master of the congregation as his brother Robert, he did not have the fiery eloquence and dramatic strength of that remarkable seraph, but John Roberts still possessed a fullness of the ministerial gift. He spoke powerfully, illuminatingly, and convictingly, and had indubitable proofs that God was honouring his ministry.

The first Association that John Roberts attended was held at Cae-rhyg near Nefyn. He was also at the Bala Association, and in an Association held at Pwllheli, in 1777. This last was a notable meeting. Its preachers included Daniel Rowland; Williams, Pantycelyn; Dafydd Morris; and Lloyd of Caeo. This was the last time that Daniel Rowland visited Gwynedd. His companion was the religious gentleman, Mr Bowen of Waunifor, Cardiganshire, and it was in Mr Bowen's carriage they travelled. In that year, the first chapels at Llanllyfni and Brynengan were opened. Daniel Rowland preached in the latter chapel when only half its roof was in place. In the following year the Association was at Brynengan. The preaching was in the chapel but the congregation was too large and it filled the outside porch as well. This was probably a Monthly Meeting. In September, 1779, a Quarterly Meeting was held at Llanllyfni and many of the mighty men of the south were present. At ten, on the main day, Dafydd Williams, Llysyfronydd, and Jones, Llan-gan, preached. The Rev. Michael Roberts called Dafydd Williams, 'Famous Dafydd from Glamorgan, part Dissenter, part Methodist, like Mr Tibbott or Mr Gray, the old breed of the country, the best kind that Wales has yet seen.' We do not know why he described Dafydd Williams in this way for the latter lived and died a Methodist; he had no connection with the Independents except for his willingness to be ordained a minister on the solemn call of a Methodist congregation, following the advice of Daniel Rowland. But we are reminded that when Michael Roberts wrote this note, his mind was already becoming confused.

At two o'clock, the preachers were 'Mr Lewis of Anglesey', probably William Lewis, Glasinfryn, who had stood up to protect Dafydd Morris when he was attacked at Beaumaris. It is said that he had a powerful service and that his voice was heard clearly a mile away. After him came Dafydd Morris, who had a service that will ever be remembered. According to Michael Roberts:

> After half an hour every true believer present was competing as to who could jump highest, all persecutors had disappeared, and all the people were either weeping or shouting.

At the close of the service, Dafydd Williams said to Robert Jones, Rhoslan, half seriously and half in jest, 'There you are, Robin, Dafydd Morris is getting so fat that I am almost ashamed to see him on the stage. But, do you know, Robin? I am not ashamed for anyone in Wales or England, or even in hell, to hear him, once he begins to warm our souls and bodies. What brave boys, Robin! In the Lord's name, we, the old men, can now die happily whenever the Chief Shepherd calls.' We do not know who else was included in Dafydd Williams's 'brave boys'; perhaps it was William Lewis, the previous speaker.

John Roberts, together with his famous brother, Robert Roberts, and others, was a major factor in the evangelization of Gwynedd. He was one of the pioneers. In what districts he had the privilege of being the first to sound the trumpet of the gospel, we do not know; nor is there any record of the dangers he passed through or the persecutions he suffered. But they are all written in God's book. However, on the testimony of his son, it was he, together with the Rev. Evan Richardson, who was the first to preach in Caernarvon town and it is said that this occurred either in 1785 or 1786. It is strange that the Methodists were so late in targeting Caernarvon. Societies had been formed many years before in Waunfawr, Clynnog, Beddgelert, Llanrug and Llanllyfni, as well as across the Menai Straits in Anglesey, but in the town itself no regular attempts at preaching had been made. It was known that Caernarvon was deeply prejudiced against the Methodists. Williams, Pantycelyn, had offered to preach there on his way home from Anglesey. He came to the town for this purpose, but though natural wit and poetic gifts often secured a hearing for him in places where any other preacher was unacceptable, he failed completely here. Having arrived in the town quite secretly, and hearing that the persecutors had decided to stop him and humiliate him, if not indeed to kill him, he decided that the only wise course was to keep out of sight overnight and escape on his journey as early in the morning as possible. The few Methodists in the town, members at Waunfawr, were often in danger of their lives. The mob would be out often to meet them as they returned on the Llanbeblig road, and would abuse them cruelly. In order to avoid the confrontation, the believers would often pass through Llanbeblig cemetery on to the Llanberis road, or return to the town on the Morfa-y-saint path. When Richard Tibbott attempted to preach here he was imprisoned in the castle, he and his horse, overnight. His son, the Rev. Abraham Tibbott, was also badly beaten here.

But the two preachers, John Roberts and Evan Richardson, decided to mount an effective campaign to bring the gospel to the town, whatever the consequences might be. Michael Roberts has described what occurred:

> I remember well the Sunday my father went to meet Mr Richardson to offer that he preach – the first time for the Methodists to do so. I was then quite a young boy. I remember my mother bringing my father his best clothes, ready for the Sunday, only for my father to say, 'There's no point in wearing the best clothes today; they will probably be covered in filth by tonight. I had better wear some poorer clothes.' When I grew up I understood his words: that he feared he would have to suffer much in the town.

Evan Richardson came from Anglesey to meet his friend, having been preaching on the island during the Easter period. At midday, the Sunday after Easter, they went to look for a site to preach, fearing for their lives. Having compared Michael Roberts's account with what is written in *Methodistiaeth Cymru*, we believe that the following account provides the best description of the service. They were acquainted with a respectable shopkeeper in the town, Mr Owen Owens, the deacon of the Independent church that had been established in the town some years before. The Independents were much more protected by the law than the Methodists because they licensed their chapels. The two preachers told Mr Owens of their plan and of the difficulty of finding anywhere to preach. He took them to his minister, the Rev. George Lewis, afterwards Dr Lewis, the author of many excellent books, including the *Corff o Dduwinyddiaeth* [*Body of Divinity*] for which the Rev. Lewis Edwards wrote an introduction. Mr Lewis examined them as to their beliefs. John Roberts replied that they held to the doctrines of the Westminster Confession of Faith. As a result, he allowed them to speak in the loft where the Independents held their meetings. They went there by two o'clock and the Rev. George Lewis began the service. But the room could not hold a quarter of the people that had gathered. They went out to a stretch of land near the road, by the side of the chapel, with the permission of a Mrs Morgans, a shopkeeper. John Roberts began to pray, and heaven's blessing was poured down upon him. A solemn fear fell upon the crowd so that no one dared disrupt matters, whereas all the fears in the hearts of God's ambassadors vanished away. After praying, he took his text from 1 Timothy 1:15, 'This is a faithful saying and worthy of all acceptation', etc. According to Michael Roberts:

> He had not been speaking for a quarter of an hour before two were convicted and many others wounded who were not healed until they came to the Saviour.

Michael Roberts said that this was the first Methodist preaching in Caernarvon. There is some doubt whether this is accurate. According to *Methodistiaeth Cymru*, Jones, Llan-gan, was the first to succeed in preaching here. We have already given an account of this service. It is said that this was in 1786, and that John Roberts and Evan Richardson came in 1787. It is impossible to be certain who was first, but if it was Jones, Llan-gan, he certainly did not succeed in planting a cause here. The father of the society was John Roberts, and it was established in the following way. The first week after the sermon, John Roberts was in Caernarvon market and noticed a man was following him wherever he went. He began to feel uncomfortable, as the man was a stranger to him and he could not imagine his purpose. At last, he turned to him and asked, 'Do you want me for anything?' 'I am glad to speak to you,' was the reply. 'I am in great trouble. I can't get any peace of mind since you and that other man preached last Sunday.' And according to Michael Roberts:

> My father, in great amazement and joy, took the man aside to a room in the Angel Inn and was there able to speak to him and comfort his wounded spirit with the things that belonged to his peace. This was the first church meeting of the Methodists in Caernarvon town. Only two were present, but they were the earnest of a large number. And though they were so few, and the meeting-place so inappropriate, there is no doubt that greater spiritual delight was there experienced than was often obtained afterwards even in a convenient place of worship and with greater numbers.

The man's name was Richard Owen and he remained faithful to the cause throughout his life. After his death, his widow married the Rev. Evan Richardson. The second man who was convicted was William Williams, a shopkeeper in Porthmawr, who afterwards became a treasury officer. He also was faithful to the grave. From this time onwards, preaching was maintained at Caernarvon. The services were held to begin with in an area of the town called Treffynnon, but they were soon moved to Danyrallt.

SECRETARY OF THE GWYNEDD ASSOCIATION AND OF THE CAERNARVONSHIRE MONTHLY MEETING

As a measure of John Roberts's standing in the Association, it may be noted that he was invited every year to the main Association in the south, held at Llangeitho. He would usually arrive the Sunday before the Association and he had there some remarkable services. The mother of Mr Daniel Davies, Ton, who was the daughter of the witty old elder, David Jones, Dolaubach, used to speak of one of John Roberts's services at Llangeitho. He mentioned how he had once seen many old pensioners in London who had been badly wounded in the service of the king. They were a sad sight; some had lost arms and legs, and had wooden stumps in order to move about. They could render no more service, but when they heard the name of the king that they had served so faithfully, they would shout out, 'Long live the king! Long live the king!', and jump up on their wooden stumps. He then referred to himself as having been long in the service of King Jesus but now not being able to do much because of old age. 'What are you doing here in Llangeitho, therefore? Oh, I have come here like those old pensioners to shout, "Long live the King! Long live King Jesus!"' His spirit was quickened; he shouted over and over again, 'Long live King Jesus!' and jumped as a hart so that some thought he would fall from the stage. The people took up the shout and the whole congregation gave way to shouting and praising. At the time John Roberts was over eighty years old.

It is almost certain that he was the first Secretary of the Methodist Association in Gwynedd. He must therefore have had a major part in the planning and carrying out of the steps taken to possess the land. We have already referred to the collection of a halfpenny a week from every member towards building chapels, which was at one time so well-known in the north. The idea for this came from John Evans, Bala, but it was through the efforts and particular skills of John Roberts that it was successfully operated. He wrote a report on this collection which, we believe, is worth recording:

> Inasmuch as the Lord succeeded his work amongst us, and the revival progressed throughout Wales by means of our efforts to preach the gospel wherever we could, in the face of all opposition; sometimes on the streets in towns and villages, sometimes on the highway, and sometimes on common land such as the hillsides, the marshes, and the like; there was great need for houses which would be convenient and appropriate to maintain the worship of God in its various branches.
>
> The gospel was gaining respect – though by means of poor instruments, earthen vessels, that the excellency of the power might be of God – and the

congregations multiplying, but the churches generally were few in number in comparison, and unable to bear the cost of raising big enough buildings to contain the multitudes that were continually increasing and thirsting for the sincere milk of the word. In the meantime, in a Quarterly Association of Exhorters and Elders, gathered at Henllan, Denbighshire, at the end of December, 1779, it was agreed to place the following matter before all the brethren throughout all the various societies in the counties of Gwynedd; namely, that if the Body was willing, all members should contribute one half-penny only a week for a period of a year, and that the monies collected should be brought together quarterly to each Association, so that the sum collected might be known; the willingness of the Body to continue might be judged; and it might be seen whether it would answer to the purpose of building places of worship in those areas where the need is most, according to any decisions of the Association.

The matter was warmly accepted generally throughout the various counties, and the work carried out zealously and with great faithfulness. After proceeding in this way for a year, it was understood that it was likely to answer a good and honourable purpose. As far as I can remember, the first year's collection was about sixty pounds. It was agreed to continue with every care and diligence, and this arrangement remained in place for eighteen years. As the work increased, and the congregations multiplied in numbers, the collections increased until they reached about £90 a quarter. By now, it was becoming too great a work to organize during the Associations, so that a more convenient method was required in order to proceed with it.

In an Association at Bala in June, 1797, the collection was discussed and it was agreed that each county should be responsible for its own collection, according to whatever arrangement they should choose, and that they should use the money in accordance with the decision of the Body and of the Monthly Meeting in each county.

As a result, it was decided by the brethren of the Caernarvonshire Monthly Meeting to encourage ourselves in the Lord to be as faithful as possible in continuing the collection with every due care and to use it conscientiously, and to the best of our knowledge, in the fear of God, and to the purpose best fitted for his glory, in appropriate buildings for his worship. When it was so arranged for each county to proceed independently, it was agreed also that each county take responsibility for the debt remaining on the meeting-places of that county. The debt for Caernarvonshire therefore was:

Llanllechid	£2-0-0
Caernarvon	£105-0-0
Penygraig	£11-0-0
Garn, Dolbenmaen	£12-0-0
	£130-0-0

We have given the report in John Roberts's own words, though the syntax is confused in places. It is seen that the collection continued for some eighteen years as a responsibility of the Association, and that it was its success that resulted in it being afterwards referred to the counties. There was a danger that too much Association time would be taken up with financial discussion, spiritual matters being therefore neglected. The phrase, *'one halfpenny only a week'* suggests that richer members of the societies were not expected to contribute more, nor the poorer less. If this rule was kept faithfully, it may be estimated, more or less correctly, that the membership of the Methodists of Gwynedd in 1797 was over 3,300. This number gives no indication of the strength and influence of the Methodists in the country, for while the society numbers could be small, the report shows that the numbers who came to hear the preaching were great and, no doubt, many of these were not far from God's kingdom. When all the counties took responsibility for their own debts, an exception was made, from what we read later, in the case of Montgomeryshire. It seems that more of a debt remained here than in any of the other counties. Either the Montgomeryshire believers were poorer and fewer, or the building of chapels had been carried out more daringly than elsewhere. By the end of the year we find that the Caernarvonshire's Monthly Meeting, 'according to its promise', sent the sum of £29 and a few shillings to its sister in Montgomeryshire.

How far the collection was maintained in the various counties of Gwynedd once they became responsible is not known; but reports for Caernarvonshire from 1797 to 1809 are available, in John Roberts's handwriting. Throughout this time he was the Secretary of the Monthly Meeting and he continued in the office until his son, Michael Roberts, succeeded him. The collection was a halfpenny a week for about two years in Arfon, and while this continued, its total varied from £20 to £30 a quarter. During these years the land was conquered for the gospel to a great extent. Robert Roberts, Clynnog, in particular was a Son of Thunder, a terror to the ungodly, and by means of his ministry and his brother's, together with Evan Richardson, hundreds were added to the churches in Caernarvonshire and the chapels became much too small. The result was a rush of building new chapels and enlarging existing ones, and as the whole county was considered responsible, there was not the appropriate financial care applied locally in all circumstances. This placed a burden on the Caernarvonshire Methodists that very nearly overwhelmed them, and the Saviour's cause was only just saved from being brought into disgrace. John Roberts describes the steps taken at this critical time:

As the numbers of hearers multiplied particularly in these years, with our teaching bearing much fruit, and with evident indications that the Lord in his grace and goodness was blessing the Word to the conversion of many from their sins to God, and from the kingdom of Satan to the kingdom of his dear Son, and the churches continually increasing in number, the need for new buildings and for enlarging old buildings was always upon us. But the means to build in many places was absent and the helpers few. As we pressed forwards in this matter seeking to fulfil each need, we built up a considerable debt in the county so that we were very weighed down by the weight of work and sorrows. As we conferred and discussed the matter we decided that all should be made known to our brethren {the Body} throughout the county. The churches having been informed, they showed every willingness of mind to cooperate immediately in order to obtain relief from this heavy burden. It was decided to act as follows:

1. That every society should take a register of all its members.

2. That every member should consider seriously and simply, as God has prospered him in his circumstances and living, how much he could contribute to this cause.

3. That the sum which each member promised to contribute every quarter should be noted next to his name.

4. That the sums be collected from every place once a quarter.

5. That it be distributed conscientiously in the fear of the Lord, wisely, to the utmost of our ability, if the Lord wills.

6. That new arrangements be made once we have paid all debts, if the Lord should prolong our lives and privileges.

7. That every arrangement or change of arrangements be decided and brought before the decision of the Body, through its representatives in the Monthly Meeting.

8. That no meeting-place be built in any place, by any person or persons, of their own volition, but by the plan agreed by the Monthly Meeting, or any other or others to whom the Body has given responsibility for the task.

These were the steps taken by the Caernarvonshire Methodists in their Monthly Meeting at the beginning of 1801, and the rules are full of common sense. On the one hand, we see the attempt to remove the disorder that had brought about their trouble, namely, those individuals in various places who had built chapels of their own volition, without appropriate consultation, but had passed on the responsibility for any debt incurred to the Monthly Meeting. On the other hand, the members were asked to rise as one man to face the crisis, and to contribute, not now 'one halfpenny only', but whatever they could, as God had prospered them. This was the first occasion of a financial appeal amongst the Methodists. The members were not backward in responding to their responsibilities. The total collection for the Caernarvonshire Monthly Meeting in the first year was over £325. The details are provided by John Roberts for the whole period for which he served as Secretary of the Monthly Meeting. He too was the Collection Secretary and much of its success must be appropriated to his skill and activity. According to the Rev. John Jones, F.R.G.S., Bethesda:

> These are the very first statistics in our history as a Connexion, namely, the statistics for the weekly Halfpenny Collection, and following it, the quarterly collection, 'as God prospered', which was made use of by the Methodists for many years. The Rev. John Roberts, Llangwm, was the worthy statistician, and as regards ability and accuracy, he need not have feared comparison with the familiar statisticians of today.

We have, however, departed to some extent from the personal history of John Roberts, and must return to it. About the year 1788, he met with a severe trial at the death of Phoebe, his oldest daughter. She was a wise, beautiful girl, of evident abilities. She loved poetry and, above all, she was eminently godly. John Roberts's love for her was great and her death was a blow that reached his very soul. The account of the last service she attended, at Llanllyfni Chapel, is worth recording. We give it in Michael Roberts's words:

> Mr Richardson of Caernarvon, the warm-hearted evangelist, was preaching to an overflowing chapel, with the congregation in tears within a quarter of an hour of reading the text, which was, 'Even so them also which sleep in Jesus will God bring with him.' There they were for some time, he shouting, and the congregation weeping or shouting, and with scores jumping for joy. The noise carried far so that those remaining in their homes ran to see what was happening. Mr Richardson, John, and his brother Robert Roberts, were jumping and dancing in one glorious crowd, like King David of old, except that they possessed the substance and antitype of that ark before which he danced. My mother was rejoicing in the house. And Phoebe felt as if an inheritance had been given her that day.

A glorious service clearly, and the last for Phoebe Roberts. Within a month, the eighteen-year-old girl was being carried to the cemetery. But John Roberts emerged from the fiery furnace having obtained a blessing for his soul. His experience deepened, his disposition became more spiritual, and a new edge was felt in his ministry. Michael Roberts said that he would always remember the prayers of his father at this time.

JOHN ROBERTS MOVES TO LLANGWM, MERIONETHSHIRE

In November, 1806, his wife died. She was notable for her faith. She possessed all the zeal and enthusiasm of the early Methodists, and her voice was often heard in the sanctuary praising God, her spirit a flame within her. After being a widower for three years, John Roberts married again and as his new wife came from the Llangwm neighbourhood, in Merionethshire, he moved there to live. It is as 'John Roberts, Llangwm' that he has been known ever since. His departure was a great loss to Caernarvonshire. Once John Elias had gone to Anglesey there was none in the county, apart from Evan Richardson, to compare with him in his gifts and commitment. Michael Roberts wrote in his diary for 20 September 1809:

> My father remarried and moved to live at Llangwm, near Bala, which was one of the saddest occasions I ever met with. Not because he remarried, but because of his departure from the neighbourhood; to lose such a hard worker when there was such need of workers.

Caernarvonshire's loss was Merionethshire's gain. John Roberts immediately became the most important and useful man, after Thomas Charles, within the bounds of the Monthly Meeting. He threw his whole soul into the work. The Sunday Schools in particular found an able supporter in him. He possessed unique skills in catechizing, and was at his happiest in the middle of a crowd of children, questioning them and teaching them the doctrines of Scripture. A letter of his exists describing a Sunday Schools convention held at Caernarvon, a year before he left for Llangwm. This was the first held in the town, we believe. Four schools had gathered together. Some had started out before five o'clock in the morning. They had set out in the dark, as the convention was being held in the middle of November. By nine, they were all at Caernarvon. As they came through the town, the children sang appropriate hymns so that the streets echoed with their voices, and the inhabitants rushed to their windows, never having heard anything like it before. The following is an example of the kind of catechisms that the children learnt; the topic is *Regeneration*:

1. The need for regeneration.
2. Whose work is regeneration?
3. The names for regeneration.
4. The nature of regeneration.
5. The privileges of the regenerate.

John Roberts added:

> A large number of various Scriptures were recited, all most appropriate and relevant to the topics chosen, and the heavenly dew abounded during the examining; the whole crowd listening intently. The hymn '*Merch Seion*' ['Daughter of Zion'] was sung.

Many of the watching crowd remained from the six o'clock service in the morning until eleven at night. As the last hymn, '*O agor fy llygaid i weled*', was being sung, the congregation broke out in praises. According to John Roberts, 'I had not seen such an outpouring upon old people and children for very many years.' If there was some prejudice in the town against the Sunday Schools before, this convention put a complete end to it. Bread and cheese were distributed from baskets to the children between the services, but nothing like sufficient had been prepared, and they had to send round the houses for more. Hundreds of such Sunday Schools conventions were held in Wales. They proved of immense benefit; they were the means, under God, of bringing hundreds to eternal life, as well as of increasing scriptural knowledge. It is a great sadness that there are signs presently that this practice is dwindling and even disappearing.

Another proof of the respect in which John Roberts was held within the Connexion, particularly in Merionethshire, was that he was put forward to be amongst the first to be ordained at Bala in 1811. He was the only one from Merionethshire that received this honour; there were only eight from the whole of Gwynedd. The North Wales Association also manifested their trust in his judgment and knowledge in the things of the gospel when they appointed him a member of the important committee that met in Aberystwyth, according to the decisions of the two Associations, to draw up the *Confession of Faith* and the *Constitution* for the Connexion. This took place on 13, 14 March 1823. We will give an account of this important occasion again, but it is interesting to note that the Rev. John Roberts, together with his son, the Rev. Michael Roberts, sat as members of this committee, and it is very rare to find a father and a son appointed together for such important work.

John Roberts was granted a long life but the time came for him to die. The following is taken from the December 1834 issue of the *Trysorfa* [*The Treasury*]:

> On Monday, 3 November 1834, the Rev. John Roberts, Llangwm, Merionethshire, died, at 82 years of age, having been preaching the gospel for 55 years amongst the Calvinistic Methodists. He joined the society when 16 years old and was therefore a believer for 66 years. As a church member his whole life was an ornament to the religion he professed; and as a preacher his teach-

> ing was sound, scriptural, and sweet; his labours in the Lord's vineyard were indefatigable and continued up to his death; his end was peace, for he fell asleep in Jesus. When his dear son asked him, a few hours before he died, how his final battle against death was being fought, he answered, 'The battle was won long ago at Calvary.' He laboured for the last 25 years in the neighbourhood of Llangwm, establishing Sunday Schools, building chapels, planting churches, etc.; and a *Life* of this useful minister and famous saint is soon to be available as he had lately written a little of his experiences.

We do not know if this *Life* ever appeared. No doubt it was expected from his son, Michael Roberts, but it was about this time that he was overtaken by a mental confusion that would have made the task impossible. But on his recovery in the year 1837, he wrote a short memoir. However the manuscript remained hidden amongst his papers for years, and was not published until it was incorporated in the *Life of Michael Roberts* written by the Rev. John Jones, Bethesda. In the description given in the *Trysorfa* of John Roberts's life, his consistent labours and widespread usefulness is perhaps emphasized more than any preaching abilities of the highest order. Although he would often experience deeply moving services, it does not appear that he was up to the standard of the pulpit giants of his day. At the same time it would be a mistake to consider him a man of commonplace gifts. His wide general knowledge, his deep and accurate knowledge of the Scriptures, the clarity with which he expounded them, and the tenderness and sweetness that characterized his ministry almost without exception, made him very acceptable to all congregations. He consecrated all his powers to the work of the gospel; he laboured in season and out of season, and contributed much in many very different spheres of the work. The name of John Roberts, Llangwm, is a sweet savour amongst the Fathers of old to this day.

The same issue of the *Trysorfa* carried the account of his funeral:

> On Wednesday before the funeral, the Rev. John Davies, Nantglyn, preached in the chapel near his house, on 2 Tim. 4:6–8. The next day, at ten, in the same chapel, the Rev. Thomas Ellis (Independent) preached on Heb. 13:7, and John Davies on 1 Cor. 15:58. Then his mortal remains were accompanied by a large concourse to Llangwm cemetery, where they rest until the morning of the trumpet call.

26

THOMAS FOULKES OF MACHYNLLETH, DAFYDD CADWALADR, AND OTHERS

THOMAS FOULKES'S CONVERSION UNDER JOHN WESLEY'S PREACHING

Although Thomas Foulkes was not very eminent as a preacher, nor did he impress his image deeply upon the Connexion, yet, on many accounts, he deserves an honourable place amongst those who were instrumental in establishing Methodism in north Wales. He was born in 1731, and was therefore a boy of nine years old when Howell Harris first visited Bala in 1740, and he could remember the occasion and the persecution meted out to the Reformer when he returned the following year. His parents were farmers of the parish of Llandrillo-yn-Edeirnion, which lies between Corwen and Bala. It is said that they were of Norman extraction, their ancestors having come to this country with William the Conqueror, and the name Foulkes, or Faulkes, being Norman. The land was full of ignorance when Thomas Foulkes was a boy and he was brought up with no religion. He had very little secular education, just sufficient for him to read and write a little, which was the most that the children of farmers had in those days.

When he was about thirteen years old he went to Chester for work and heard John Wesley preaching. It is not known where exactly this occurred because, from his *Journal*, Wesley does not appear to have been closer to Chester than Manchester, Warrington, or Liverpool, during these years. Wesley's ministry awoke him from his spiritual sleep and caused him to see himself as a lost sinner, but he was completely ignorant of God's way of salvation through Christ. He then came to know a young man called Robert Roberts, the son of a hard-working Wesleyan minister. Robert Roberts explained the gospel to him, as best as he could, and took him with him to the Wesleyan Chapel in Chester called 'The Octagon Chapel'. Here, according to his own testimony, he was reconciled to God. This took place in June 1756. He had been in a pitiable state before this. He had tried to reform and justify himself according to the law and had failed miserably. He had failed also to give himself to the Saviour. He said:

> To believe in Jesus Christ was as hard for me as to move one of the mountains of my native land; but after importunate prayer to God for grace, I was enabled, through grace, to put all my trust in him, who works in man both to will and to do of his good pleasure.

The consequence, he said, was that, 'believing was to him as easy as breathing'. Having arrived at the glorious liberty of the gospel, he joined the Wesleyan fellowship that met at Neston, a small village a few miles from Chester.

We do not know how long he remained in England, but there arose in him a strong desire to return to his home country and he made his home in Bala. The Wesleyans had no society at Bala but there was a Calvinistic Methodist society. Though their members were few in number and poor in circumstances, Thomas Foulkes threw in his lot with them. For many reasons he preferred to be with them than with the Nonconformists in the town. Firstly, they called themselves Methodists, just as the Wesleyans; the form of ministry amongst them was itinerant; they met in private meetings to discuss spiritual experiences; they professed allegiance to the Established Church; and they did not receive communion from the hands of any that were not ordained clergymen.

It is only accurate to add that Mr Foulkes maintained some degree of connection with the Wesleyans throughout his life. The Rev. David Young states that he considered himself a member of the Wesleyan society at Chester though he worshipped and laboured amongst the Calvinists as a matter of convenience. We can hardly believe that this is true. He happily made his home amongst the Calvinistic Methodists. He seemed to approve their order and doctrines and had no desire, as we shall see later, for the Wesleyans to form their own societies in Wales. He rather feared this in case it caused arguments and disruptions. The issue of assurance of salvation troubled him for some time. The Wesleyans believe that assurance is the common privilege of every godly Christian, that no one can be in God's favour without knowing it, and therefore they encourage their members to profess an unhesitating assurance in their private societies. The Calvinistic Methodists, however, while acknowledging that a believer may rise to full assurance and should make every endeavour to secure it, also hold that it is the particular privilege of the *diligent* Christian to be able to say, 'I know whom I have believed', and therefore in their societies they tend to be more fearful and hesitating, warning their members to beware of presumption.

THOMAS CHARLES EXPLAINS THE DOCTRINE OF ASSURANCE TO HIM

Thomas Foulkes opened his heart to Thomas Charles as to all his uncertainties, and the latter took his time to read and think before answering him. The resulting reply is still in existence and it reveals the wisdom, discernment and balance for which the ecclesiastical statesman from Bala remains so famous. The essay is long and we can only quote a part of it:

> *Saving faith* is:
>
> 1. A full persuasion of the sufficiency of the righteousness and atonement of Christ worked by the Holy Spirit in the heart of the sinner, and based upon the clear testimony of the Scriptures.
>
> 2. It involves also, by the same Spirit, the agreement and commitment of the heart to it, a submission to the righteousness of God, and a giving up of all else.
>
> I believe that no more can be added than this, without destroying the nature of faith; which is, to go out of ourselves, refusing our own righteousnesses, and be received by God because of his grace only . . . If anything more than this is added to saving faith, it does not appear to be of grace. If you add assurance to it, then, inasmuch as it is something within ourselves, it would make us look there (that is, within ourselves) for acceptance; whereas faith, as defined, looks completely out of itself and towards Christ, for acceptance . . . Now, I believe that faith is not recognized in any other way than by its fruits and effects. The direct fruit of faith is love. They are bound together, and not just once, but forever. Nor can there be any divine love but that which originates from this faith. 'We believe God because he first loved us.' I understand love in the widest sense of the word, as the conforming of the soul to God, which immediately follows the act of justifying belief, as a man is sanctified through faith in Christ . . . As faith increases, our conformity to God increases correspondingly, and the fruits of the Spirit manifestly reveal themselves within us. And these increasing effects of faith give us an increasing assurance that we are true believers, or true Christians. According to my personal belief, every other delineation of assurance tends to starve and trouble the soul, or to lead to the licentiousness of the flesh. And the reason why many are troubled, comfortless, and fruitless, all the days of their lives, is, in part, I firmly believe, because they do not seek life and peace in the way of God's Scriptures, by being of a spiritual disposition, and by mortifying the deeds of the flesh through the Spirit. They live carelessly, in the grip of spiritual laziness, waiting for they know not what – some extraordinary influence that God never promised in the way that they expect. Understand me well; I do not mean by what I have said that God does not sometimes break in upon the soul in an extraordinary way, and fills the believer with joy unspeakable and glorious, and

> gives him, if you will allow me to put it like this, a directly discerned assurance that his sins have been forgiven and that Christ in all his infinite sufficiency is his possession. But this is not to be expected generally or to be depended upon, for we are to live by faith and not by sight.

It seems that Mr Charles's clear and moderate explanations quietened Mr Foulkes's mind so that he was never again troubled over assurance. After a time at Bala, Thomas Foulkes married a daughter of Griffith Sion, who, with his daughter, was a member with the Methodists. A son was born to them who was also called Thomas. His wife soon died and he was left a widower with the care of the child. He lived for a while with his father-in-law, but the old man dealt fairly harshly with him, demanding a high price for his keep and for that of the child, so that, when he left him and had paid off all his debts, he had only ten shillings to his name. The child died in infancy. About this time, Mr Foulkes began to trade in small groceries and though he had very little stock to begin with, he soon prospered. There was at Bala, at the time, a widow called Janet Jones who, with her daughter, kept a shop. Mrs Jones was comfortable in her circumstances and noted for her godliness. Mr Foulkes married this widow. He pursued his trade industriously and the two were soon considered to be quite rich. Wordly success did not cause them to forget religion. They gave themselves to serve the Lord. As well as maintaining private prayer, family worship, and attendance at the means of grace, they would also go together to pray in an empty house that stood in the fields nearby; they were well-known also for their generosity and sympathy to the poor. As for Miss Sarah Jones, Thomas Foulkes's stepdaughter, she was to become the wife of the Rev. Thomas Charles, and was therefore instrumental in bringing that famous man to the north, and to Bala.

THOMAS FOULKES BEGINS TO PREACH

After joining the Methodists, Thomas Foulkes gave all his energy to the cause and soon began to exhort. It is not known when exactly he began. As with many of the old exhorters, he probably slipped gradually into the work, almost without being aware of it. The Merionethshire Monthly Meeting had not been established, but almost certainly he was encouraged to take on the work by the fraternity at Bala, and by John Evans particularly. He had no great gift of preaching and throughout his life he considered himself as 'no more than' an exhorter. There was never anything controversial in his sermons; the grace of the gospel was always his favourite theme. He would often weep as he presented the tender truths of the Bible and particularly when he referred to the martyrs, which he did in almost every sermon. But at some times, an extraordinary influence would accompany his ministry so that all would be overcome. According to *Methodistiaeth Cymru*, he and John Evans were present at the first Monthly Meeting held in Anglesey, and both preached at the meeting. John Evans wrote:

> We all had particular help in speaking, especially Thomas Foulkes, who preached with great liberty and heavenly sweetness on the words from Genesis 40:9,10. He predicted boldly that there would be a gathering of the people to Jesus, and this is being fulfilled throughout the country from that day until now.

The service must have been of particular blessing in that John Evans was always very careful in all his statements.

Thomas Foulkes had much to do with submitting Merionethshire to the influence of the gospel. The *Traethodydd* states:

> His faithfulness was proverbial. However rough the weather it never stopped him from crossing the Welsh hills and mountains in order to fulfil his obligations in the Saviour's cause. He preached wherever he could – farmhouses, small cottages on the hillsides and the common land, barns, and very often out in the open air. He rose early – between four and five in summer, and between five and six in winter – particularly on Sunday mornings, whenever he had many miles to travel to his engagement, and he would often take bread and cheese with him in his pack when travelling to poorer parts of the country. He very rarely travelled on a Saturday night, 'so as not to burden the poor people', as he would say.

This is how those pioneer exhorters travelled: a portion of bread and cheese in their bags; water to drink from some stream along the way; poor cottages to lodge them; and no pay for their labours except what they received in their hearts from God; and often in fear because of the threats of their persecutors.

Thomas Foulkes's name weaves in and out of all the histories of the beginnings of Merionethshire Methodism. He received much persecution and abuse and encountered sufficient difficulties to have broken the heart of any ordinary man. We have already mentioned how he promised to go to Pant-y-cra, near Dolgellau, to preach, and how his persecutors planned to kill him and throw his body into a peaty bog. The brethren therefore decided to intercept him and warn him not to come near the village. On another occasion he preached at a farmhouse called Gwylan in the Maentwrog region. Halfway through his sermon, a mob arrived, and laying hands on him and on Lowri Williams of Pandy-y-ddwyryd, whom we have also mentioned before, threw them both into the river. Mr Foulkes was not hurt, but Lowri Williams was very badly injured by her fall on to the stones of the river. She went home covered in blood and was not able to rise from her bed for a long time afterwards. Rowland Jones, Lowri Williams's son, was incensed by the injury offered to his mother. He sent details of the incident to a lawyer cousin in London who then wrote a letter to the gentlewoman who was the main instigator of the persecution, threatening to punish her severely if she did not end her harrying of the believers. The letter achieved its aim. Rowland Jones was told by one of the lady's servants that the solicitor's words had produced fear and alarm in the manor house. The letter had been left on the parlour table, so that the servant had had opportunity to record its contents. It read:

> Mrs Griffiths,
> I hear that you have arisen in revolt against the government in sending your servants to stone your neighbours. The English Law does not allow the stoning of any, as you did with Thomas Foulkes and Lowri Williams, at Gwylan (at such and such a time). If I hear that you are continuing to persecute, then I will prosecute yourself, and will punish you to the limit, however great a gentlewoman you consider yourself to be. This from Rowland Jones, Solicitor.

It is said that this letter put paid to all persecution in the Maentwrog area.

Mr Foulkes was the first to preach in Llanarmon Dyffryn Ceiriog. This occurred in the following way. Two men from the region had happened to hear either Howell Harris or Daniel Rowland. This had produced in them a desire to listen again to the gospel. They heard that an Association was to be held at Bala and decided to go there. Having arrived at Bala they found that they had mistaken the time and were a week too early for the Association. Mr Foulkes came to hear of their misfortune. He invited them to his house, and welcomed and fed them. He inquired of them the situation at Llangarmon and asked them if he could come there to preach. Though they had missed the Association, the two men were cheerful as they returned over Berwyn Mountain, having obtained Foulkes's promise to preach. When it became known that one of the Methodists was to visit, the whole region was agitated. It was agreed that such a thing should not be tolerated and every preparation was made to obstruct the meeting. It was understood that to hold the meeting as first planned would be impossible. But with the gospel having been refused at Llanarmon, a place was opened for it in the nearby parish of Llansilin, at a farmhouse called Ty'n-y-fedw, where a brother-in-law of one of the two men lived. There Mr Foulkes preached and was given every opportunity to speak. According to *Methodistiaeth Cymru*, Mr Foulkes played a part in bringing the Rev. John Williams, Dolwyddelan, into the liberty of the gospel. The latter was at the time under the severest conviction of sin. He had tried to win God's favour on the basis of the law; he had attempted to forsake sin, but in every instance had failed. It was while he remained in this despairing state that Mr Foulkes came to the parish to preach. He stood on some stone steps opposite to the entrance to Ty'r-llan. The preacher's gifts were small but his words, and especially his affectionate manner, melted the hearts of his hearers, and that of John Williams in particular.

As well as his labours in exhorting and journeying, Thomas Foulkes, together with John Evans, served his nation and the cause of religion through the press. He used to read the books of Whitefield and the two Wesleys in English and longed for his fellow Welshmen to have the same privilege. With John Evans he translated two sermons of Wesley's into Welsh and they were printed at Bala. The title of one was *'Awake thou that sleepest'* and the other, *'Prepare to meet thy God, O Israel'*. These were thoroughly practical sermons, not containing any controversial matters. They also published translations of John Wesley's *Primitive Physic*, and his *Rules and Order of the United Societies, formed in London, Bristol, and other places*. The original author's name was not printed on the translations so as to by-pass any prejudice. The believers of Bala were Calvinists and the name of the two Wesleys would have been a barrier that would have kept them from drawing any spiritual good from these publications. The purpose in printing the *Rules* was, no doubt, in the hope of bringing some order to the small causes throughout Gwynedd. Perhaps the original rules drawn up by Howell Harris at the beginning of the revival were out of print, or the two preachers from Bala did not know of them.

HE MOVES TO MACHYNLLETH

Mrs Foulkes died on 26 October 1785 and Thomas was once again left a widower. His stepdaughter, Sarah, had married Thomas Charles two years previously. He loved his stepdaughter deeply. They were as close to each other as a natural father and daughter. After his wife's death he lived with Mr and Mrs Charles for some time. He then passed on the shop to them and retired to live on his savings, which he considered sufficient for himself and for enabling him to contribute generously to religious and charitable causes. Within two years he married again; this time to the daughter of Mr Simon Lloyd, Plas-yn-dref, Bala. Miss Lloyd was the granddaughter of the old exhorter Thomas Bowen of Tyddyn, near Llanidloes. Her mother had been the first to go to Trefeca as a first-fruit of Howell Harris's 'family'. The Tyddyn family were exemplary Christians who deserve more attention than has been given to them. Mrs. Bowen, Thomas

Bowen's wife, was one of the first in Montgomeryshire to embrace the gospel and was noted for her godliness. For many years her house was a home to the Methodists and as well as being a preaching-station, many Monthly Meetings were held there. She spent the last years of her life at her daughter's home in Bala. She reached a good old age. She would proceed slowly to the chapel on her two sticks, taking a cake with her so that she did not need to return home between the services. Her daughter, whom Simon Lloyd had brought to Bala from Trefeca, was also a godly woman. She was soon widowed with six children on her hands. But she strengthened herself in the grace of God and raised them all in the faith. As for Mrs Foulkes, she was not behind her mother or grandmother in godliness and beauty of character. She came under the strongest convictions when young and experienced deep despair. Though she read her Bible diligently she could no more draw a drop of comfort from it than if it had been a sealed book. She went to visit an aunt of hers who lived at Pwllheli solely in order to read an account of a Mr Hart who had experienced similar distress of mind, and the reading of the book gave her some encouragement. On Easter Sunday, William Davies, Neath, was to preach at Tymawr Chapel, Lleyn. She attended, and the sermon proved the means by which her soul was filled with light from heaven and all her chains were shattered. She there and then consecrated herself to the Lord and joined herself to him by an eternal covenant. At the time she was eighteen years old and had received a good education. For some time afterwards she lived at the home of her mother's brother in Breconshire, and there made the acquaintance of the Countess of Huntingdon and Lady Anne Erskine, as the Countess's College was at Trefeca at the time. After returning to Bala, she visited Llangeitho often to hear Daniel Rowland, saying that it would not be too much to travel to America in order to hear such a preacher. She was twenty-nine years old when she married Mr Foulkes.

They had six children. On seeing the family increasing, they realized that they had better take up a business again but they did not wish to do so at Bala where they would be in competition with Mr and Mrs Charles. They therefore decided to move to another town. They first decided on Rhuthun, understanding that an open door awaited them there, but a servant of Mr Charles, on returning from a visit to Machynlleth, emphasized the importance of that town to the Methodist cause, placed as it was between the north and the south and likely to be on the route of many preachers travelling from one region to the other. This conversation was sufficient to turn the scales in their considerations, and they moved to Machynlleth. They had no relation living in the town and were complete strangers to the area but with the hope of being able to serve the gospel they made their home there.

When the family arrived at Machynlleth the Methodist cause there was in a barren state. The meetings were being held in an empty house that was leased, and they would not have had the use of this place except for the fact that the owner had failed to sell it. But when Thomas and his wife arrived things soon changed. It was soon realized that the newcomers were people of respectable social standing. Mr Foulkes almost immediately won the respect of the town; his upright character, his honesty in business, and his continual generosity, soon ensured public favour. As a result the Methodists, the group to which he belonged, also became respected. Through his instrumentality land was obtained in Maengwyn Street upon which to build a chapel, and the older pilgrims were cheered in heart. Now at last the believers felt able to walk along the main road to their meetings. No longer did they have to creep secretly through the back of the town towards Aberhosan, or Glasbwll, as they had done for so many years. Mr Foulkes continued to evangelize as he had always done. He would visit the mountainous valleys of Montgomeryshire and Merionethshire on a Sunday morning on horseback, whenever he obtained an invitation. He would proclaim the unsearchable riches of Christ to the small congregations that would gather. If his talent was not great, his affections would always be sweet, and rarely would he speak without tears rolling down his cheeks. No place was too poor or too lonely for him and he felt most at home when amongst the people. His coming to Machynlleth was not only a spur to the Methodists of the town but the means of an awakening to the cause throughout the surrounding region. Only the last day will reveal the extent of his good work and of his service to Christ's cause in that part of Wales. Even in old age, he would often journey up to fifty or sixty miles on a Sunday, and preach three or four times, according to the demand. His only motivation, in that he had a good home and was in comfortable circumstances, was a love for the work and a desire to do good.

Providence smiled upon him with respect to his business in Machynlleth and he became one of the richest men of the town. His industry in trade was equal to his faithfulness in religion. After the hard labours of the Sunday he would be up early on the Monday, and his shop would be the first to open. There was no great talk from him when buying and selling. He would require one price, and he would give one price. So well-known was he for this that the traders in Chester and Wrexham fairs would say as they saw him approaching, 'We must give our lowest price to Mr Foulkes.' The common people had endless trust in his honesty and strict accountability.

They knew that his word was as good as his bond. Many of the local owners of smallholdings would bring their sparse savings to him to keep towards the costs of a funeral; he was their first savings bank. And whenever they came to reclaim it, it would be paid over, with the interest, without any difficulty. He was as generous as he was honest. As he left the house to journey to his engagements he would take with him a pocketful of pennies to be given to the poor, and to children as a reward for keeping from playing on a Sunday. Whenever he saw anyone on the street in ragged clothes, he would take them home and provide what was needed, even in some cases clothing them from head to foot. Every year, on a set date, he would distribute about fifty pounds worth of flannel and cloth amongst the most needy. All this was only a small part of his charitable giving. He was often deceived in that he considered all to be as honest as himself. Every trick was played to take advantage of his sympathy and pity. Ungodly creatures, who would never usually come within hearing of the gospel, would attend if Mr Foulkes was preaching, and they would wear the most wretched clothes in their possession. He, in the innocence of his spirit, would provide for them with an unstinting hand without any thought of their true situation. When he was on his charitable rounds it might be thought that all the inhabitants of Machynlleth belonged to a ragged school; all were dressed in their worst. Some would come to him under a cloak of religion, stating their claim upon him on such grounds.

'Remember me this Christmas, Mr Foulkes *bach*.'

'Who are you, woman?' he would answer.

'I am one of you,' was the answer.

'One of us?' he would ask. 'Are you of the faith?'

He was, as far as liberality of spirit is concerned, the very embodiment of the principles of the Evangelical Alliance, fifty years before that Alliance ever came into existence.

Thomas Foulkes held the Methodist Fathers, especially John Wesley – his father in the faith – in the deepest respect. In his bedroom he had many pictures of the old preachers, including one imaginary picture of John Wesley being taken up to heaven by angels. As he led visitors up to their room, he would turn into his own bedroom and point out the pictures to them, one by one, finishing with the one of John Wesley, and saying, 'He was the preacher when I was convicted.' He would be very pleased if they then gave a word of praise for the great man. On the other hand he would get very annoyed if they said anything unflattering. He once showed the picture to John Jones, Edeyrn, who was noted for his wit and speed of reply:

'What do you think they intended, John Jones, by depicting him being carried by the angels in his surplice?'

'Oh,' said John Jones, out of mischief probably, 'it is in order to show what hard work it was for the angels to get John Wesley to heaven dressed like that.'

Mr Foulkes was disappointed and his face fell. At another time, a minister who understood better the lie of the land, was asked:

'Here is Mr Wesley. What is your view of him?'

'Oh, Mr Wesley was a good, godly, hard-working man,' replied the preacher.

'What do you think was in their minds in showing him being raised to heaven dressed in his ministerial robes,' asked Mr Foulkes.

'I imagine, Mr Foulkes, that it is to show that he went to heaven in his office as a minister of Christ,' was the answer.

'Do you think so?' he replied, cheering up, his eyes filling with tears.

'Oh yes. Mr Wesley was an excellent man.'

As he bade the preacher goodnight, Mr Foulkes pressed a guinea into his hand.

Thomas Foulkes had a great affection also for the Wesleyan Connexion. He contributed much every year to the various causes of the Connexion. He would never visit Chester without paying a call to the chapel where he first came under conviction. But he had made his home with the Calvinistic Methodists, and it does not appear that he gave any thought at all to leaving their fold. He often said:

> I bless God for granting me a place in his house and amongst the people with whom I serve. It is with them that I wish to be kept to the end, and I would like my children also to make their homes amongst them.

The fact that he had become a thorough Calvinistic Methodist, both in his feelings and judgment, was no hindrance whatsoever for as unprejudiced and as loving a man as Thomas Foulkes to hold the Wesleyan body in England in great affection. But when the Wesleyan Connexion agreed in 1800 to establish a mission in Wales he was greatly perplexed. He received a letter from them informing him of their intention of setting up a Wesleyan minister in Machynlleth, believing, no doubt, that this would be very acceptable to him. He was in some considerable uncertainty for a time. He did not wish to leave the people amongst whom he had laboured for tens of years. He feared that arguments would arise, and unchristian feelings result, and that the mission would produce more harm than good. After long and hard thinking, and much spreading of the matter before the Lord, he decided not to reply to the letter. He heard no more about it until the week before his death when two of the Wesleyan ministers appointed to pioneer the cause in Wales, the Revs Owen Davies and John Hughes, called on him. On informing him of who they were, they said:

'We presume, sir, that you have heard of us.'

'I have heard nothing good of you,' he teased them, 'but come in, dear friends.'

He gave them every welcome and the two were appointed to preach the next day at the Methodist chapel. Owen Davies's text was, 'For to me to live is Christ, and to die is gain.' Before the end of the sermon, Mr Foulkes was taken ill and had to leave, leaning on his wife's arm.

'I hope that I have not arrived in order to preach your funeral sermon, sir,' said Mr Davies on his return to the house and seeing Thomas Foulkes looking so ill.

'If you have,' was the reply, 'I know whom I have believed, and to die is gain.'

He died on the following Saturday. His funeral was one of the most well-attended ever seen in Machynlleth. On the previous evening, John Evans, Bala, preached, and on the day after, Mr Thomas Charles spoke in the main street from Matthew 25:23, 'His lord said to him, Well done, good and faithful servant; thou hast been faithful over a few things, I will make thee ruler over many things: enter thou into the joy of thy lord.' And so the remains of this excellent man were laid in the earth, amidst general mourning.

We have already suggested that Thomas Foulkes was not eminently gifted, but he was warm of spirit and persevered in prayer. Very rarely would his wife or a servant go to his study and he would not be wrestling with God in prayer. In untiring effort, enduring faithfulness, and courage to overcome obstructions, he was not excelled by any of the Methodist Fathers. Only the light of the day of judgment will reveal the extent of his service for Christ in Gwynedd. According to his wish, his wife and children, and their children also, remained faithful to the Methodist Connexion, and descendants of his are to found as pillars in the church to this day.

DAFYDD CADWALADR

Dafydd Cadwaladr was a very different man from Thomas Foulkes on many accounts. He was a great traveller. There is hardly a village or hamlet in the Principality where he had not preached. He was therefore as well-known in the south as in the north. He was of the second generation of preachers, but there was still only two chapels in Merionethshire when he began his ministry. He was the son of Cadwaladr and Catherine Dafydd of Erw Ddinmael, Llangwm parish. He was born in 1752. There were only a very few Methodist societies in Gwynedd at the time and they were disorganized and divided because of the controversy between Harris and Rowland. The Revival seemed to have become paralysed – preaching was to be had in only a few places – few and far between. Like the vast majority of the neighbours, Dafydd Cadwaladr's parents were completely careless of the things that pertained to their peace. They attended the church about once a month, there would be no sermon, and after the clergyman had rushed in haste through the service they would emerge, with the rest of the congregation, confident that they had fully performed all that God required of them. He, however, received some religious impressions at a very early age – when as young as four or five years. This is the account that he gave to his daughter years later:

> One night an awful storm of thunder and lightning broke out, and my mother came into my room crying bitterly and hurriedly reciting the Lord's Prayer, the Creed, and part of the Litany: 'O God our Father in heaven: have mercy upon us miserable sinners.' And as I had never seen such a thing before, I asked her what was the matter. 'Son,' she said, 'Leave me be for me to pray to God. I'm afraid that the Judgment Day has come.' This scared me tremendously, and I began to repeat her prayers, and that is when I learnt the Lord's Prayer and the Creed. My mother stopped praying when the lightning and thunder stopped, but I continued for some weeks until at last I had to stop because my father came and whipped me. After this, I would go on my own and pray, 'O God our Father in heaven: have mercy upon us miserable sinners,' so that the neighbours thought that I had lost my senses. However, to this day I believe that the Lord then heard me, a poor creature, and had mercy upon me.

From this account we see that even as a child Dafydd Cadwaladr had a remarkable memory, in that he learnt the Lord's Prayer, the Creed, and probably parts of the Litany through listening to his mother's hurried recitations. In this the child was father of the man. It seems that he never completely freed himself from the convictions impressed upon him at this time. His soul as a child was often filled with the terrors of death and judgment. He set himself tests to decide whether he would end up in heaven or hell, such as noting a branch in a hedge: if he could hit the branch with a stone, he would be in heaven, but if he failed, he would sink to hell. According to custom, many of the neighbours would gather at his home during the winter nights to knit socks and listen to stories, and his father would often entertain the company by singing songs. Young Dafydd would be in his bed, listening to every word, and if one of the songs should refer to hell he would tremble so much that the bed would shake.

It was not the custom to educate children at that time so that Dafydd never had an hour of school. He learnt to read in a remarkable way. As a child he used to help look after his father's sheep and by observing the letters marked by pitch on the backs of the sheep he began to recognize many of the letters of the alphabet. He afterwards got hold of a copy of the Book of Common Prayer and by studying it he acquired the other letters and began to learn to read and spell. This awoke in him a passionate desire for books. Someone in the neighbourhood owned a copy of *The Pilgrim's Progress* and of *Gweledigaethau y Bardd Cwsc.*[1] Dafydd Cadwaladr borrowed the two books and learnt them by heart. We have already referred to the custom of meeting during the long winter evenings to tell stories around the fire. Dafydd would attend these evenings and astound the gathering with recitals of part of *The Vision of Hell*, or of some of Christian's adventures from *The Pilgrim's Progress*. His company was often called for. The accounts that he narrated were so strange and so different from the frivolous tales usually heard. He would give a promise in advance to those gatherings where he intended to be present, just like a preacher arranging his engagements.

HIS FIRST ACQUAINTANCE WITH THE METHODISTS

When about fourteen years old he began to serve at Garthmeilio estate and stayed there for some six years. The family were fierce persecutors of the Methodists. But Dafydd could not free himself from the fear of dying in ungodliness and the terror of judgment. On Sunday, at the close of the church service, the congregation would go as one body to a nearby field to play football and handball. Often the clergyman would be their leader and many would observe that he was more energetic in his ministering of the ball than ever he was in the ministry of the Word. But the boy, Dafydd, could not enter into the game playing and sport. He would withdraw into the wood or to some secret place in order to read some Welsh book that he had obtained. One Sunday, the clergyman, by some mishap, kicked the ball through the window of the parlour at Garthmeilio and, though he never broke any hearts in the church, the glass of the window was shattered in pieces. Fortunately for the Reverend the family were not at home at the time but early on the Monday morning Dafydd was on his way to Bala to fetch a glazier to repair the damage. Along the way he met a young girl and they began talking. Soon, the girl said:

'I went to the society last night.'

'Society?' said Dafydd Cadwaladr. 'What is that then?'

'People coming together to read, pray, and to talk about religious matters,' said the girl.

'Where is the society held?'

'At our house.'

He was amazed. He had never heard of such a meeting before. The conversation was the means of producing much sympathy in his heart towards these Methodists, who were the object of such persecution and hated by all. Such solemn thoughts were awakened in him that, there on the wild hilltop, he found a mound of peat and flung himself upon his knees to pray. He found such unusual sweetness in fulfilling this duty that he never left off praying from that day onwards. He now longed for an opportunity to hear one of the Methodist preachers. The opportunity arose, and the preacher was William Evans of Bedw-arian. He took his text from Luke's Gospel. It was strange for Dafydd Cadwaladr to hear a man take a text from Luke rather than from the Bible. He knew of no Luke other than Farmer Luke who lived nearby and he could not understand what connection there might be between him and the sermon. He had never heard nor read of Luke the Evangelist, which shows how ignorant he was of the Bible and its contents. The sermon did not have much effect upon him, yet he felt some measure of enjoyment while listening. But he did not now know how to return home. He had slipped out secretly to the service. If any of the family had learnt of his intention they would have stopped him from going. Such was his fear that he devised some lie to explain his absence. But his conscience smote him and he said to himself, 'No, I will not lie. I will tell them the truth, whatever comes of it.' So it transpired, but he did not receive as severe a rebuke as he had feared. He was at this time as if between two fires; two contrary influences pulled him in opposite directions. He feared dying without God and being thrown to hell and his conscience would often cause him great distress. On the other hand, he had not turned his back completely on immorality. The corruptions of the family with which he lived would overcome him and he would break out in swearing and cursing. To one man, alongside whom he worked, he spoke continually of sin, heaven, and hell, and with such seriousness that the man became depressed and complained that 'Deio tells me such things that make me despair, and I cannot do my work at all.'

About this time he contracted smallpox and for three months was on his back in his father's house. While convalescing he read the whole of the Bible, from Genesis to Revelation. After recovering, he refused to return to Garthmeilio, though his parents pressed him to do so; he could live no longer with a family who were so neglectful of the God of heaven.

His next place of work was Nant-y-cyrtiau, some four miles from Bala. He was soon able to hear William Evans a second time, and the text on this occasion was Galatians 3:22, 'But the Scripture hath concluded all under sin, that the promise by faith of Jesus Christ might be given to them that believe.' Dafydd Cadwaladr was now in a better state to listen, and the sermon reached his heart. The first rays of hope of being saved began to dawn upon him. Previously he had been sore broken in the place of dragons; he had feared that God had no mercy for such as he, but during this service he realized that he also could be saved, though so vile and guilty. He was amazed that those round about him could listen with such seeming unconcern. From now on he resolved to hear preaching. He went to Bala every Sunday morning and stayed there all day. Sometimes he would go without food from morning until night, or knock at the door of those whom he thought might be generous and beg some food from them. At this time also he was diligent in reading and praying. He would buy candles and spend most of the night over his books, not only his Bible but every other Welsh book he could lay his hands on. He read four or five Roman Catholic books during this time, whose contents he could still recite a few months before he died, more than sixty years after reading them.

But his reading led him into trouble. A doubt arose in his mind as to which was the greater, Mohammed or Christ; and which was the true religion, Christianity or Islam. He saw that both claimed to have come from God, and he believed that only one of them could be true. The young man decided that he would not accept any doctrine as truth unless he had studied it to the utmost of his ability, because he knew that once he had submitted to any teaching it would be difficult for him to reject it again. He lay in this state for more than six months. Sometimes his mind tended to favour Mohammed on seeing how rapidly his religion had spread and the number of great nations that had submitted to it. At other times his judgment would be for Christ. It was hard for him to share his troubles with anyone. At last he ventured to his express his feelings to a brother, and asked, 'What have we that proves the truth of Christ's doctrine rather than that of Mohammed?' The answer he received was, 'Indeed, Dafydd, you worry about things that shouldn't concern you. You read too much.' Such a response only sunk him deeper in the mire. He prayed much over the issue; he cried that he might be kept from trusting in a false prophet, whichever that might be. In order to come to a decision, he began to compare their lives, point by point, and it was not long before Mohammed began to lose ground in his judgment. He saw corruption present in him in various circumstances whereas Christ's life only shone forth the brighter the more it was investigated. The following verse came into his mind with great conviction: 'For such an high priest became us, who is holy, harmless, undefiled, separate from sinners, and made higher than the heavens.' This put an end to all argument. He decided once and for all that Jesus Christ was the true prophet and that his religion was best; indeed, the only one worth following. He now felt ashamed that he had ever doubted the glorious Lord Jesus and that he had ever compared such a blessed Person with a sinner like Mohammed.

When about nineteen years of age, Dafydd Cadwaladr moved to Bedwarian, to the old exhorter, Williams Evans, and it was not long before he joined the Methodists at Bala. On joining them, he made the following covenant with God. It was found in his handwriting on the frontispiece of the first volume of Gurnall's works. The book was published in 1775. It is certain that he intended no one to see it but God alone.

THE COVENANT

> I, Dafydd Cadwaladr, do give myself this day to be the Lord's possession forever. I give my soul to him to keep and to rule; my body as a sacrifice to him, my heart to love him, my tongue to praise him, my time to serve him, my members as servants of righteousness for him. In his Person I believe, in his blood I have washed, in his grace I strengthen myself, in his Word I will meditate, his glory I will behold, on his bosom I will lean, in his commandments I will walk, against sin I will war, under the cross I will suffer, for every man I will pray.
>
> Thus I intend to live for God, and to trust only in his goodness for strength and grace to keep my vow. And lest I ever retract my words, God the Father, the Son, and the Spirit, the heavenly angels, the demons of hell, and my own conscience shall be the witnesses of my covenant. 'One shall say, I am the Lord's; and another shall call himself by the name of Jacob,' Isaiah 44:5. 'Fight the good fight of faith, lay hold on eternal life, whereunto thou art also called, and hast professed a good profession before many witnesses,' 1 Timothy 6:12. 'I have sworn, and I will perform it, that I will keep thy righteous judgments,' Psalm 119:106.
>
> Keep me, O Lord, from every kind of presumption and error, and keep me ever close to thee. May thy blessing be upon me.

Perhaps it is not correct to call this a covenant. It is rather a vow of consecration. But it shows a great solemnity of spirit, and also a wide knowledge of the Scriptures for a lad who was not yet twenty years of age. Few, in comparison, would produce such a consecration in writing, but every godly man is called upon to sanctify himself and in his mind to present himself for the Lord's service.

DAFYDD CADWALADR'S PRAYERS

Before being converted, Dafydd Cadwaladr was a great reader. He now became a great pray-er. He was given a remarkable gift for public prayer, praying with unusual power, energy and fluency. But his secret prayers were more remarkable still. At times he completely lost all sense of time in the enjoyment of his fellowship with God, and he would spend whole nights on his knees. He himself spoke of one occasion when he was at Bedw-arian. On an evening, while his meal was cooling, he went to feed the cattle. After completing the task he thought he would pray for a few minutes. Having begun he lost all sense of time but after rising from his knees in order to have his supper before going to bed, he was surprised to find the house in darkness and the door locked. Looking towards the east, he saw that dawn was about to break. Without realizing it he had spent the whole night in prayer. The spiritual influence upon him that caused him to become unconscious of the world about him for such a long time, must have been powerful indeed. There were other occasions when he experienced the same thing. Mr Robert Ellis of Tymawr, who knew him well at this time, said of him:

> I remember how Brother Dafydd Cadwaladr, when first converted, used to pray instead of going to bed. His neighbours often heard him praying for long hours. After waiting long, they would go to their beds, leaving him still praying. I, together with my brother Thomas, and many others, can testify to hearing him do this dozens of times. He also had particular places to pray, such as the large stone on Bedw-arian field, and the old cowshed, and other places.

The Rev. Lewis Jones of Bala said that he also knew of various places at Bedw-arian where Dafydd Cadwaladr used to pray. He called those places his altars, and he loved to visit them even up to the day of his death. Not that prayer was always sweet; often he would be in great distress of soul or battling against the devil. He believed, rightly or wrongly, that the evil one sometimes stood before him in visible form. But he would almost always have the victory before rising from his knees.

Dafydd Cadwaladr was not long converted before wishing to preach, though it was not before he was twenty-eight years old that he made his first attempt. But during the years while he was waiting for an opening, he was sure that God had something for him to do for his name. When about twenty-one years old, he became ill – so ill that all, except for himself, were sure that he would die. The doctor told him so, and one old woman, while weeping beside him, said, 'Dafydd *bach*, you are surely deceiving yourself. Truly, you are soon to die.' 'Not soon, I believe,' was his answer. The belief that God had a work for him to accomplish was what gave him his assurance. He told the woman who was nursing him that he needed cold water to drink. She feared to give it to him as the doctor had specifically told her not to. But he demanded the water and began to improve from that moment.

Because he was so well-known for his praying and also as a reader, his friends pressed him to preach. On one Sunday, John Evans, Bala, was to be at Llangwm and at Cerrigydrudion, but failed to keep these engagements because of illness. He therefore encouraged Dafydd Cadwaladr and Dafydd Edwards of Bala to go instead of him and to hold prayer meetings, pressing them also to give a word of exhortation to the people, if they had anything on their minds to contribute. On the way to Llangwm, they arranged that Dafydd Cadwaladr would begin the meeting there by reading and praying, and that Dafydd Edwards should preach. Matters progressed as planned but as Dafydd Edwards was speaking, Dafydd Cadwaladr began to feel ashamed and to grieve deeply because of the poverty of his friend's message, and he imagined that if he was in his place he would do far better. From Llangwm they proceeded to Cerrigydrudion. There, Dafydd Edwards led and Dafydd Cadwaladr began to exhort. But if the message was poor at Llangwm, it was poorer still at Cerrigydrudion, and two years were to pass before Dafydd Cadwaladr volunteered again for such a duty. Yet although disappointed, he did not lose his desire to preach. The desire to help sinners burned within him and his friends continued to press him to make a fresh attempt. Then when he was about thirty-one years of age he was sent by Thomas Foulkes to Llandrillo in Edeyrnion and preached that Sunday at Llandrillo and at Llanarmon with an evident measure of liberty. And from that time to his death he was a preacher.

HIS CHARACTERISTICS AS A PREACHER

Dafydd Cadwaladr soon became a powerful preacher, and a very popular one. There were two remarkable characteristics to his ministry. Firstly, he was notable for thundering and threatening as he preached. He would threaten sinners so fearfully with hell and its fires, with the demons and their tortures, that strong men would grow pale before him. He threw his thunderbolts amongst his hearers so that they trembled with fear. At his first appearance as a preacher his only message was one of warning to the ungodly. He left others to pour oil and wine upon the wounds; his work was to wound, and he fulfilled this work remarkably effectively. Secondly, his ministry was particularly Biblical. He knew by heart appropriate verses for all occasions and would recite them without mistaking a syllable. As he warned the ungodly and scourged the workers of iniquity, it was God's own words that he used – verses of the Bible, woven together and compounded were invariably what he made use of – and this, no doubt, had much to do with his success. Very often great authority and unction would accompany his preaching. According to the Rev. Lewis Jones:

> It is believed, from the many testimonies available, that Dafydd Cadwaladr was an instrument in returning as many sinners to God as any of all the powerful ambassadors that the Lord raised in Wales during the last one hundred years.

Dafydd Cadwaladr had many remarkable points. His memory, as we have mentioned, was almost perfect. He had learnt more of the Scriptures by heart than any in his own days, and very few of any age could be compared to him in this. When fairly young he heard a rumour that Romanism would probably gain ascendancy in the land once more and that as a result all the Bibles in the land would be burned and that God's Word would not be tolerated in any house. He decided that he would place himself above any such tribulation. He therefore learnt all of the New Testament by heart and most of the Old Testament. He never wrote a word of one of his sermons, yet could remember each of them effortlessly. It was the same with his engagements; he never wrote them down in a book, but there is no mention of his ever missing a service. He would go for a month of itinerant preaching in the south with all the details in his head and, having returned, though he had walked back and forth and up and down, he would know exactly how many miles he had travelled. Very often he was the Minute Book of the Connexion. Minutes were not kept so fully in those days and sometimes doubt would arise as to what exactly had been decided. In such cases, Dafydd Cadwaladr would be the Court of Appeal and his recall of the motion carried would put an end to all argument.

He was remarkable also for his prayers. At the end of a church meeting at Bala, he so lost himself in wrestling with God that he continued for three hours, and it was nearing midnight when he drew to a close. He was asked by a young man, when he himself was old, if this was true. He replied, 'I do not know how long I was, but I do know this, that nobody left, for they were all still there when I got up from my knees.'

He was also remarkable as a walker. Many of the early exhorters excelled at walking. They travelled much on their own two feet, climbing high mountains and crossing deep valleys, often in a wet and hungry condit-ion, but it does not appear that any of them could compete with Dafydd Cadwaladr. He traversed Wales, back and forth, many times. He was as well-known in Anglesey as he was in Merionethshire; he knew the south as well as he knew the north; and all these places would have been visited on foot and, at least in his early days, in clogs. While a servant at Bedwarian, he would have been the last to lay down his scythe on a Saturday evening, at harvest time, and the first to lay hold of it on the Monday morning, and yet during the intervening Sunday he would have preached at Penrhyndeudraeth and the surrounding regions, a round journey of fifty miles, all covered on foot. As an example of his journeying, he said, 'I set off from Penrhyn on Sunday morning with my stick in my hand; I preached at Gwylan at eight; at Hendre-Wenllian at eleven; at Beddgelert at three; and at Waenfawr at seven.' This would have involved at least thirty-five miles, and he testified that he felt no tiredness at all after the journey, 'because,' he said, 'I was young and strong in those days.'

He remained an excellent walker even in old age. He arrived at Barmouth one Saturday afternoon, and the woman at whose home he was to stay, asked after his health. He replied that it was fairly good, but that he felt tired. And he added,

'I felt something today, as I was climbing Aber-amphrech hill, that I have never felt before, namely, lack of breath and a weakness inside me.'

'How old are you now, Dafydd Cadwaladr?'

'I am seventy years old.'

'And how far have you walked today?'

'Only twenty-eight miles.'

The two of them agreed that the lack of breath and weakness was the effect of old age, but both were rather surprised that a seventy-year old man should have been affected in this way.

He experienced many tribulations as he travelled about with the gospel; the roads were lonely, those sympathetic to the gospel were few and far between so that it was often very difficult for him to obtain any kind of lodging, and the persecutors were fierce. Once, when on a journey to the furthest boundaries of Merionethshire, he was still many miles from his destination when night fell. He turned aside to a house nearby, at the outskirts of Dolgellau, and asked for shelter for the night. The owner asked 'Why did you not look for shelter earlier, before it got so late?

And then, turning to his wife, he said,

'Have we any room here?'

'No,' she replied, and then turned to a servant-boy beside her, 'Unless he shares a bed with you, Sionyn.'

'I don't mind,' said the boy.

And so Dafydd Cadwaladr was invited in, and he sat on a bench near the table.

'Do you want a little milk and flummery?' asked the wife.

'Thank you,' he answered, 'I would be glad to. I am very thirsty.'

In a little while the man of the house called to the servant,

'Go to bed, Sionyn. This man is very tired.'

'I usually read a chapter of the Bible at home, before going to bed,' said the strange man. 'And then go on my knees to pray with the family. May I do that tonight?'

'Yes, certainly,' said the husband.

A Bible was brought to the table, and after reading a chapter, Dafydd Cadwaladr knelt down and poured out his soul before the Lord. The family soon understood that it was no ordinary man that had come under their roof. The servant was sent to his bed, the preacher was given the best room in the house, and the wife gladly rose the next day at four in the morning in order to prepare food for him before he continued on his journey.

The following story, which he himself related, reveals the troubles which he had to endure for the gospel's sake, and also shows something of his lack of assurance.

> I was going on a Sunday morning from Aberdovey to Llanegryn to preach. As I crossed the beach towards Towyn, I saw a man coming to meet me and, standing in front of me, he asked, 'Are you the man going to Llanegryn today?' 'Yes,' I said. 'Then you will be killed,' he replied. 'They are determined to do so, and I came particularly to warn you.' His words struck deep. My mind kept dwelling on the thought, 'What if I am a hypocrite? Then, if they kill me, I will be immediately in hell.' I stood there for a while, but having reconsidered, I decided that I was not a hypocrite, and that it would be a great privilege to die as a martyr for the name and cause of Jesus Christ. This helped me to proceed confidently. The man followed me for many miles until we came to the bridge over the Syni. He then stopped and said, 'Well, you poor creature, I see that you are determined to go to Llanegryn, and I will be very sorry that a man like you should be killed. I don't dare come any further with you or I shall receive the same treatment myself. Here are two pennies for you. Go to the inn and call for their worth of beer. If you succeed in getting the family at the inn on your side you won't be in too much danger. But truly, the people have determined to kill you. Farewell to you.' I went on my way, and did what I was told with the two pence, and when the time came to start I stood on top of something and began the service. The people looked ugly to begin with, but somehow I was soon given complete freedom to preach. When I had finished, a well-dressed man climbed up on to a ridge and said, 'Friends, I don't know anything of the Methodists, but this is a good man! He speaks the Bible. I know the Bible as well as anyone, and I know that he did not say anything that is not in the Bible. Therefore I demand that you treat him fairly.' And with that all the people went home.

The history of the sufferings of the first Methodists in Gwynedd would be a strange story, if it were possible to write it. The occasional written narrative, like the above, demonstrates the difficulties and hardness through which they passed. Such persecution was commonplace at the time. They carried their lives in their hands; it is not too much to say that they 'died daily'. But long before the death of Dafydd Cadwaladr the wheel had turned and any then who tried to persecute would have had the worst of it. We read of Dafydd Cadwaladr preaching at Machynlleth when a local squire, together with a doctor, came to the meeting to disrupt it. They imitated the preacher as he read his text; they mocked him loudly, laughing like fools; and after every sentence from the speaker, they turned on him asking, 'Who told you that?' Some in the congregation tried to get them to be quiet but they would not. But by this time, the supporters of the Methodists were in the majority; the people who had gathered wanting to hear God's Word became angry. They blew out the candles and began pressing the two men hard. The squire and doctor realized that discretion was the better part of valour and they sought the door but it was not so easy to escape. Strong men stood between them and the outside, men who had decided that they should not go unpunished for their foolish disruptions. What with the crushing of the crowd and the many stampings on their feet, they soon cried out loudly that their lives might be spared. After a while they were released and repaired immediately to hide in a nearby inn, bringing to an end any further attempts by them to disturb religious services. They received only what they fully deserved.

Dafydd Cadwaladr was notably faithful to his engagements. He would not be stopped by difficult roads or adverse weather. Having given his word, he could be depended upon. There is one account of him having arranged to exchange with the Rev. Richard Jones of Wern in order that the fellowship at Bala might receive the Lord's Supper. But the weather on the preceding Saturday was foul. A heavy fall of snow had been blown by a strong wind into immense drifts so that to leave one's home was to endanger life and limb. In order to fulfil their arrangement, the two men would have to negotiate a long journey and a high mountain. The minister of Wern stayed at home; he judged that it was completely unreasonable to cross the Mignaint in such weather. But as evening began to fall, Dafydd Cadwaladr appeared at the front door, to Richard Jones's amazement.

'Dafydd *bach*,' he said, 'how in the world did you cross the mountain today?'

'Just as usual,' was the rather dry reply.

But he confessed later that it had been hard on him at the mountain top, and that only by crawling on his hands and knees did he manage to avoid the drifts that lay across the path. It is said that he was about sixty years old at this time.

He maintained the same courage and faithfulness in fulfilling all engagements even in old age. During his last winter, as an old man of over eighty years, he was to preach one Sunday in the Tymawr circuit. On the Saturday he was prevailed upon to stay at home because of an awful storm of wind and rain. But he was most uncomfortable throughout the afternoon and evening. About three o'clock on Sunday morning he called his daughter, saying that the winds were not quite so strong and that he would attempt the journey and so wished her to prepare his breakfast. After eating and family worship, off he went. He was at Tymawr, some eight miles away, long before dawn, before any of the family were out of their beds. Rather than disturb their sleep, he went to some outhouse nearby and remained there until he saw signs of life in the house. When he related events to his daughter on returning, she asked him what he did in the outhouse while waiting. 'What did I do,' he replied, 'What would you expect me to do other than attempt to pray?' The account reveals his deep conscientiousness, and such determination of mind and body that is not often met with.

Yet, though so strong mentally in some things, he was strangely fearful, almost childishly so, in others. He could not be persuaded, by any means, to get on the back of a horse. Though often pleaded with, he could never be induced to engage himself to preach in Liverpool, because he feared crossing the Mersey. On the few occasions that he did visit the city, he arrived by foot via Warrington, thereby adding twenty-four miles to the journey rather than crossing the river by boat. No one is so brave that he does not have some weakness somewhere.

Throughout his life he was an avid reader. He decided once to read every Welsh book that had been published – though as books multiplied he had to give up his ambition – but he continued to buy new books throughout his life. And he would read each book over and over again, until all was secure in his memory: the English and the Latin, should any be present, together with the Welsh. In old age, he read Thomas Charles's *Bible Dictionary,* Thomas Jones's *Martyrology*, William Gurnall's *Works*, etc., many times. He owned many editions of the Bible and read them all in turn. He read Peter Williams's *Bible Commentary* twenty-four times while maintaining family worship in the home, and had arrived at the second chapter of 1 Peter on the twenty-fifth time. Nothing would keep him from family worship, whatever his haste; he would not leave the house without first reading and praying.

It would be gratifying if more of his history was known. We would like to know of the remarkable meetings he experienced and the powers that often accompanied his ministry so that sinners trembled, but practically all has been lost in oblivion. However, we do have one account of a meeting at a South Wales Association, soon after he began preaching. He was announced to preach quite unexpectedly, he had not thought that anyone as young as himself would ever be called upon, and when he heard of the arrangement his mind became a turmoil. He slipped away and thought of escaping home, but having reconsidered he feared that it would be a sin to do so. He could not eat or drink before going to bed, and the man who slept in the same room as him testified that he had spent the whole night in prayer. The next day, upon the field, he was clothed in heavenly power. All his terrors had been scattered; he feared not the faces of men. His ministry was crowned with unusual excellence and it fell upon his hearers with such power that hundreds were crying out for their lives. Hardened sinners such as those at Jerusalem during Pentecost were pierced through by the deepest convictions and shouted out, 'What shall we do?' No doubt he experienced many such occasions but we have no knowledge of them at all.

HIS LAST ILLNESS AND DEATH

Dafydd Cadwaladr was given eighty-two years of life and enjoyed good health up until six weeks before his death. About a fortnight before his death, when feeling quite ill, he undertook the Corwen circuit, the furthest point of which was thirteen miles from Bala. He preached three times on that Sunday, travelling the twenty-six miles on foot. His constitution must have been amazingly tough. This was the last time for him to ascend into a pulpit. He went to Talybont the following Sunday, but did not preach in that, unknown to him, another man had been arranged to speak. He was at the Bala society meeting on the Wednesday, 25 June, beginning the meeting by reading and praying, and his prayer was long remembered. He laid hold upon the all-sufficiency of God; he declared that God was sufficient for himself and his brethren for all circumstances; sufficient for life, sufficient for death, sufficient for eternity. He approached the throne with great boldness, yet with perfect respect. All felt that he had been given abundant entrance to the Most Holy place, and to the presence of the High Priest and the blood; a sense of deep submission mixed with fear fell upon all in the meeting, and when they rose from their knees they looked about them in amazement. One of the purposes of the service was the receiving of two people into full membership. Dafydd Cadwaladr spoke to them, mentioning that he had read some twenty-four essays on the Lord's

Supper by various authors and that he thought that every one of them sought to make of the ordinance what it was not. He added that he had recently read and re-read the Evangelists' accounts of the Supper and that he had to conclude that its purpose was to commemorate the death of the Lord and to be a means of fellowship amongst Christ's disciples. In the use of the ordinance believers might expect to receive those benefits that flow from the fellowship of the Saviour's sufferings.

He wanted to attend the society held in Bala on Tuesday night, 1 July. The family sought to persuade him not to as he was so weak. He said, 'I'll never have another society unless I go to this one.' They held out little hope of being able to stop him, but a believing brother called by and he and the old exhorter began conversing on spiritual things. Earth was forgotten; the society was forgotten; everything was forgotten amidst the sweetness of the converse. After the brother had left, Dafydd Cadwaladr said, '— took me to heaven and left me there, otherwise I was thinking of going to the chapel.' He added quietly, 'There is no hope of my getting to another society.' And so it proved, though he was soon to know an infinitely purer and sweeter fellowship with Jesus and the saints in the third heaven. Unknown to any, he went to the chapel on the next evening to listen to the Rev. Richard Williams, Liverpool. This threw the family into consternation, and his daughter asked him on his return, why he had gone without telling anybody.

'But I wanted to take the shilling,' he explained.

She answered that anyone would have taken the shilling for him.

'No,' he replied, 'I wanted to take the last shilling myself.'

He was referring to a collection for supporting weak causes. This was the last time he left the house.

Throughout his life he had been to some extent captive to a fear of death. Someone said to him,

'If I were you, Dafydd Cadwaladr, I would not be frightened of dying.'

'No,' he replied, 'if you were me, you would be frightened of dying.'

But as his end approached all his fears were scattered. For him, as for many others, 'it came to pass that at evening time it was light', and he was given an abundant entrance. The source of his comfort was his view of the three divine Persons co-operating in the plan of the salvation of sinners, each one fulfilling his role, and each one glorying in the work of the others. He was asked, very near to the end:

'How are you in your mind?'

The old exhorter replied:

'Oh, it is perfectly clear.'

'How did you come into possession of this glorious assurance?'

'Oh,' he said, 'not as I thought I would. I always hoped that I would be given assurance, and the way I hoped to get it was by some sweet, sweet verse, such as, 'Thy sins be forgiven thee,' or, 'I have loved thee with an everlasting love,' being impressed upon my mind. I have been waiting for some such verse to come into my mind with such power that I would be sure of being in a saved state, and I imagined that I would see heaven opened and an assurance would fill my mind that I would soon be present there. But it has not been like that. I have been taken back in my mind, way back, to infinite eternity, to gaze upon the Three Persons covenanting together to save sinners. And I was then led to see each of them in turn fulfil their part in the great salvation. I also had a view of the plan of salvation completed, that is of Zion fully built, which is what I see as 'the land that is very far off'; and I saw the way in which each one of the Three Persons, in his own contribution to salvation, glorifies the other two, and how that, by the building of Zion in this way, they will continue to glorify and praise each other to all eternity, and that is what I understand by the 'King in his beauty'. I had such a view of these things that it strengthened my soul to rest confidently in the great work. I see that there are purposes a thousand times more glorious to be fulfilled by the salvation of a sinner than the happiness of the sinner himself. It is in this way that the Persons of the Godhead fulfil their vows to one another, and glorify each other. I cannot therefore fear being lost.

'And do you therefore see the plan as being sure?' asked his friend.

'Oh, yes,' he replied. 'And feel it as more solid than brass under my soul.'

The account given by the Rev. Dafydd Rowland of Bala, a few days before Dafydd Cadwaladr died, is very similar:

> 'I have professed faith for over sixty years,' he said, 'but that is not the source of my comfort now.'
>
> 'What, then?' asked Dafydd Rowland.
>
> The dying man roused himself, though his feet were well nigh in the river. His thickness of speech cleared, and he said, with a heavenly contentedness shining in his face,
>
> 'I have been meditating today on the Holy Trinity's plan of salvation to save sinners, and I have thought at times that I was in the third heaven. The Three Persons serving one another to save sinners, and in that service, each one glorifying the other. That has been the source of my comfort today.'

'It is of those things that I have always heard you preaching,' said Dafydd Rowland.

'Yes.' he replied, 'I would have easily testified to those things at any time, but they are wondrously indisputable in my mind today as I face eternity.'

In this way, drawing sweetness from the work of the Holy Trinity co-operating in the work of salvation, Dafydd Cadwaladr descended into the valley. He said to his small grand-daughter:

Mary *fach*, don't you cry after your grandfather. You keep thinking, after I have died, that I am in a far better place than here. Remember that your grandfather will be in heaven with Jesus Christ, and with your small brother, and with all the saints.

The last words to fall from his lips were the text taken by the Rev. William Morris, Cilgerran, when he preached at the Bala Association a few months before, 'I am come that they might have life, and that they might have it more abundantly.' On 9 July 1834, between seven and eight o'clock in the morning, his soul flew to a better country.

The following is taken from the *Drysorfa* [*The Spiritual Treasury*] for August, 1834:

On Wednesday morning, 9 July, after a brief illness, died the respected patriarch, the true Christian, the diligent preacher and the fervent and faithful pray-er, Mr Dafydd Cadwaladr of Penrhiw, Bala, having reached the venerable age of eighty-two years of age; about fifty-two of which he spent in labouring for souls, exhorting them and warning them in his work as a preacher amongst the ranks of the Calvinistic Methodists; and it is true to state that he fought a good fight, he kept the faith, he has received the crown of righteousness that was laid up for him. On Friday night, the 11th, Mr Evans preached at Penrhiw from Psalm 37:37, standing at the same spot upon which Mr John Ellis, Barmouth, stood when he preached at the funeral of Dafydd Cadwaladr's wife. The following Saturday, before setting out for the interment, Mr David Rowland prayed, and Mr Richard Jones preached from Hebrews 13:7 to a serious and solemn congregation, from under the same bough as Mr Charles preached on the day of his wife's funeral. Afterwards the funeral was as follows: The singers were placed first; then the body; then the relatives; next, the preachers, in pairs; and then the elders of the region, three by three. In this way the irreproachable worker in the Lord's vineyard was conducted to the graveyard of his fathers in Llanycil cemetery, in sure and certain hope of the resurrection to eternal life. These two preachers in his funeral had visited Dafydd Cadwaladr on his bed of sickness shortly before he died and could testify that they had never before seen anyone so full of faith in dying.

JOHN JONES, BODYNOLWYN

There were many well-known and influential preachers living in Gwynedd at this time, of which we have only little knowledge. One of them was Mr John Jones, Bodynolwyn, the prince of Anglesey Methodism from the day he placed his foot upon the island until the day he slept in death. He was a native of Cardiganshire and was born in 1747. We know nothing of his parents nor of the events of his childhood and upbringing but he appears to have received a better education than was usual at the time. What is more, he had true religion, and very soon he began preaching. At the request of a noblewoman, whose name is not known, he moved to Caernarvonshire to preach and to keep a school. In 1780, when he was thirty-three years old, he went to live in Anglesey, perhaps because of his marriage. He took a farm called Henllys Fawr, near Aberffraw, in partnership with a close friend called Evan Thomas, who had been thrown out of his cottage in Lleyn because of his religion. They worked together at Henllys Fawr for about two years, then John Jones moved to Bodynolwyn where he lived until his death.

Methodism was weak in Anglesey when John Jones first arrived on the island. The chapels were few in number and all were small and nondescript. He consecrated himself to the service of the cause, throwing his whole soul into the work. He travelled throughout the island proclaiming the eternal gospel and God succeeded his efforts wonderfully. He was surely an excellent preacher, though we know nothing of the nature of his talents. Tradition has it however that there was a peculiar intonation in his voice, a kind of click at the end of each sentence, and that John Elias borrowed this click from him and it formed a notable element of the latter's oratory. Because of the coincidence of a number of circumstances, John Jones became the leader of the Monthly Meeting almost immediately, and kept this office until he died. Firstly, the pioneers of Methodism on the island were by now old men and possessed no great leadership abilities. Secondly, he was himself a man of strong common sense with abundant capacity for leading. He was also well educated and had become familiar with Daniel Rowland's methods for advancing the work before he had left Cardiganshire. It was no disadvantage to him also that he was comparatively wealthy and used to travel to his engagements in a carriage and so was looked upon as a gentleman. When John Elias came to this part of the country the old brother from Bodolwyn certainly held the reins firmly in his hands, and no one suggested that they be taken from him. He would therefore invariably be the chairman of the Monthly Meeting, whoever else happened to be present. He would take the chair without anyone proposing or seconding the point, and his word would be law on all matters, with no court of appeal.

When he first came to the island he suffered much persecution. Every kind of libel was circulated about him and his fellow believers. Often stones and dung would be flung at him, but he would take no account of it, considering his sufferings a privilege. He was instrumental in establishing many new causes and in building many chapels in Anglesey, though he was cautious on the building side, fearing to run into debt. A notable personal characteristic was his meticulousness over his engagements. He would begin a service at exactly the minute for which it had been announced. He was most conscientious in exercising church discipline, and would speak the truth to rich or poor without any respect of persons. He said to a wealthy farmer who had arrived late at the service, 'John *bach*, you need to be convicted in your conscience. You have stolen the society's time.' Another time, he spoke out fiercely against slander and idle gossiping, walking up and down with his stick in his hand and his hand at his back, and ending up in front of one of the women. He said to her, 'Annas, I fear that you are guilty of these things.'

John Jones lived for some fourteen years after John Elias arrived on the island, and they worked together happily; John Jones upon the throne, and John Elias an obedient subject. Something of a disagreement would arise at times but the venerable brother from Bodynolwyn would be victorious every time. On one occasion, John Elias was speaking at the Monthly Meeting and John Jones said that he was in error. In self-defence, Elias said, 'Burkitt agrees with me.' 'I don't care what your *barcud* says. You are wrong,' replied John Jones. (*Barcud* is Welsh for a kite – the bird, or the toy.) We have already referred to his slowness in building chapels except when this could be done without running into debt, but sometimes an individual would get the better of him. A Mr Owen Jones of Cwyrt, a man of good sense and undoubted godliness, asked for a chapel at Dwyran, where none had been built though the place had long been a preaching-station. The resulting discussion shows how the brethren of old conducted their affairs:

Owen Jones said to the chairman, namely John Jones,

'We need a chapel at Dwyran.'

'You do, Owen?' he replied. 'What would you do with it?'

'Whatever it is I will do with it, we have to have one.'

'You have to have one?'

'Yes, Mr Jones. Even if it costs me fifty pounds from my own pocket.'

'Well,' said the chairman, 'you must have one, I see.'

And that was the end of the discussion.

John Jones died in 1814 at the age of sixty-seven. The Rev. John Pritchard said of him:

> John Jones was considered to be an upright man as a leader and as a Christian. He might use the roughest word first but he was compassionate towards the poor and the oppressed. It is said that his voice when preaching was loud and melodious, and that he was very popular. This useful servant of Christ died when in the midst of his labours and before old age had begun to affect him.

EVAN EVANS, WAUNFAWR

Another notable preacher who died young was Evan Evans, Waunfawr. The history of this excellent man has never had the attention it deserves. The judgment of many of those who heard him was that in north Wales, only Robert Roberts excelled him in preaching ability and ministerial power, and others thought him equal or even greater than the seraph of Clynnog. Huge congregations would gather to hear him and almost invariably a heavenly power would accompany his ministry, so that no flesh could stand before him. According to *Methodistiaeth Cymru:*

> He shone forth brilliantly for a short season, but was soon transferred from the Church below to that glorious one above. He was a candle that burnt and shone and many thousands desired to remain in its light, but it was not granted them.

He was the son of Thomas Evans of Waenfawr, who was himself an excellent preacher and considered far more than a mere exhorter. He was a good theologian and a strong debater. Evan Evans is said to have been preaching once at Aber-bach-awyr, a place near Caernarvon. There was no chapel in the area and no house that could have contained the crowd that had gathered, so that they met in the open air. As soon as the meeting commenced the sky darkened with clouds and heavy rain poured down upon the people. At this, the preacher broke out in prayer, crying, 'O, Lord, Creator and Ruler of all things, grant a little time to exhort this people who have their faces towards eternity.' Immediately, the rain stopped.

At another time, he preached at a place called Achyb, in Llanllechid parish. It is not known whether he had preached in that neighbourhood before. The inhabitants were full of a persecuting spirit and had resolved that no Methodist would be allowed to hold a meeting there. A man called William Williams picked up a handful of mud from the road and threw it, striking the preacher. But the persecutor's wife was in the crowd, and she was sympathetic to the gospel and cried to her husband, 'Oh, Williams, be careful what you are doing. Don't you see God's holy Bible in the gentleman's hand, by which you shall be judged on the last day?' This put an end to any disturbance but one of the persecutors prayed with a very devout spirit at the end of the service, 'O Lord, save Llanllechid from such cursed men!' The 'cursed men' were the Methodists and their preachers. But consumption had taken its hold upon this remarkable preacher from Waenfawr. He was advised to go to Llanidloes for the good of his health; he lived there for about a year but died on 13 February 1797, to the great loss of Wales, and the deepest sorrow of thousands.

JOHN GRIFFITH ELLIS, LLEYN

We have already referred to John Griffith Ellis, a preacher from Lleyn, for the way in which it was said that in some things he excelled even the greatest preachers of his day. He was convicted under the ministry of Howell Harris at Tudweiliog, during the Reformer's first visit to Caernarvonshire. Remarkable influences would often accompany John Griffith Ellis's preaching. One sermon of his at a Bala Association is often mentioned. He preached from Zechariah 13:7, 'Awake, O sword, against my shepherd.' The Spirit fell upon the congregation with the effect of an overpowering cloudburst. Under the weight of the influence the preacher himself fainted. It is to be regretted that his history is now completely forgotten.

[1] '*The Visions of the Sleeping Bard*' (1703) by Ellis Wynne (1671–1734) contains three 'visions': of the Course of the World, of Death, and of Hell. It is a satirical view of the path of sinners through the world and the realm of death, to hell.

27

WILLIAM THOMAS, PYLE, AND SIENCYN THOMAS, PENHYDD

WILLIAM THOMAS, PYLE

We must return to south Wales once more for there were a number of significant men who laboured there and who, chronologically, should have been referred to already. One of these was William Thomas of Pyle. His ministerial gifts were few. He never rose above the level of an exhorter, but for many reasons he deserves an honourable position in the history of Welsh Methodism. He was born in Dyffryn Uchaf in the parish of Margam, Glamorganshire, in 1723. He was therefore twelve years old when Howell Harris began to thunder forth in Trefeca, and Daniel Rowland to agitate Llangeitho. He grew up, as did all around him, with no thought of religion but in 1739, when he was sixteen, Howell Harris came to Margam to preach and William Thomas, together with many others, was convicted. He did not then submit to the Lord Jesus. He tried to live a pure life, to fulfil all duties, and to pray much, but he received no comfort to his heart. He said himself, 'I laboured hard for four years for life through the covenant of Eden but no one gave it to me.' At last, when listening to a sermon in a place called Lime Quarries near Neath, he was enabled to throw himself completely upon the Lord Jesus. He said,

Christ Jesus is my strength and stay, On him I venture, come what may.	Iesu yw'r gwr y mentraf arno, Doed o honof yr hyn a ddelo.

It is probable that Howell Harris was the preacher. We read of him preaching often at Lime Quarries. The instrument therefore that was used to wound William Thomas was the same instrument that brought him healing. It is no wonder that he had an enduring respect for the Reformer from Trefeca. In his old age, he would be stirred and cheered up just on hearing Harris's name; the excitement of his mind would induce contortions in his body and he would say, with his eyes lighting up, 'I feel the effects of his authority and of the power of his voice in my bones still, even now.' When William Thomas was converted there was no Methodist clergyman in the whole of Glamorganshire. David Jones had not yet settled at Llan-gan and Christopher Bassett was not yet born. William would therefore walk to Llangeitho to receive communion, a round journey of some one hundred and twenty miles. Later there were periods when he would sometimes visit Llanlluan Chapel, where Howell Davies administered communion once a month.

THE GENEROSITY OF WILLIAM AND CATHERINE THOMAS

William Thomas was very fortunate in his marriage; the Lord gave him a wife, Catherine, who was completely of his own disposition. The young couple remained only a short time at Dyffryn Uchaf, they moved to a cottage near the old chapel at Dyffryn, for which Mr Thomas paid a lease. In 1760 they went to live in another cottage, called Tydraw, in the village of Pyle. Here William Thomas lived until his death and it is always as William Thomas of Pyle that he is known. There was no Methodist cause at Pyle at the time but soon, without the support of a Monthly Meeting or Association, he began visiting the homes of the poor to exhort. It need hardly be said that he received no financial help. Rather, he himself would press a shilling into the hand of the occupant as thanks for being allowed to speak in the home. The local clergy were full of enmity but this did not concern him, he gave himself to exhorting wherever he found acceptance. Gradually a society was formed. The need for a chapel arose, but none of the local landowners would give any land for the despised Methodists to build a chapel. But the stars in their courses were fighting on behalf of the truth. A strip of ground with four or five houses on it came up for sale in Pyle. Mr Thomas bought it and a chapel was built. It was named Capel Carneli and, though subsequently renovated and extended, it still stands today. Some time later, two or three other houses were raised on the land and donated freely to the service of the cause.

One of the main characteristics of both William Thomas and his wife was their endless generosity. The Rev. Edward Matthews wrote of him:

> The name of William Thomas, Pyle, was as familiar to the old preachers and the travellers to the Associations as bread and cheese. Indeed, the old man from Tydraw was the bread and cheese of hundreds. All called there and were welcomed, without much questioning as to where they had come from or where they were going. No, the welcome would be, 'Come in; make yourself at home. Help yourself and make sure you get warm.' Mr Thomas's Tydraw was like our father Jacob's well, where many drank, breaking their thirst on their journeys, they and their animals. Tydraw, Pyle, was the Bethlehem of

> Wales in those days; a house of bread for many, and with plenty to spare. William Thomas was something of a miser by nature; it was grace that made him so generous . . . One day, he saw a pauper being hauled into Cardiff prison because of a debt. He had compassion on him, paid the debt, and both bailiff and debtor returned happily to their homes. Mrs Thomas too was of the same kind-heartedness. She was generous and spent her days devising generosities. She and her maids on a summer's afternoon, after the housework was over, would make blankets and every kind of clothing in readiness for the poor who would gather around the house at winter-time, knowing of the provisions available for them. 'The blessing of him that was ready to perish came upon her: and she caused the widow's heart to sing for joy.'

The author of an elegy for the old pair bore similar testimony:

Kitchen, parlour, barn, and study, All to God's cause freely given; Bed and table, food and candle, Anything that might be bidden; Gold and silver, if required, Oats, and pasture nearby; Yet the flour never dwindled, Nor the cruse of oil ran dry.	Cegin, parlwr, cell a 'sgubor, Oedd yn rhydd at achos Duw; 'Stafell, gwely, bwrdd, canhwyllbren' Pob peth arall yn ei ryw; Arian, aur, pan fyddai galwad, Gwair, a cheirch, a phorfa fras; Eto'r blawd oedd yn y celwrn, A'r olew byth yn cadw ei flas.

'Glory be to the beloved,' said one old pagan who lived nearby. 'It amazes me, that what with the husband and the wife, Tydraw should not have dried up long ago.' But provisions multiplied as fast as they were dispersed, and the more their wealth increased the less they gave their hearts to it. In order to be so generous, Mrs Thomas was very thrifty. It is said that she carefully collected the wool left by the sheep on the hedges and the feathers cast by the geese, and when asked why she was so careful when she herself had no need to be so, she answered cheerfully, 'So that I can give all the more to those who are in need.' It is said that the two of them, while so very generous to others, were quite careless as to their own needs.

WILLIAM THOMAS AS A PREACHER

As mentioned, William Thomas was no great preacher but he always spoke with great warmth and feeling, and proved of great blessing to his generation. As with most of the Fathers, he met with much persecution. One account describes him preaching at one time at St Bride's, a small village between Bridgend and the sea. The local vicar decided to stop him. He distributed beer to the local people and they, in their drunkenness, mobbed the preacher, raining rotten eggs and dung upon him. Mr Thomas's text was, 'For their rock is not as our Rock, even our enemies themselves being judges.' Notwithstanding the showers of stones and dung, the exhorter persisted. The kingdoms of heaven and of hell were in conflict. But the gospel was victorious. Power from heaven accompanied the words; a sweet breeze blew upon the gathering, and many were saved to eternal life. Tradition has it that the main persecutor met with a fatal accident the next day.

Barren meetings would weigh down his soul greatly. He was once on a journey through parts of Wales in the company of his friend, the well-known elder, Thomas Dafydd, Llangrallo. At the beginning of the journey his services were notably dry and barren, at least they were certainly so in his own judgment. He was preaching the law, thundering forth to sinners and threatening them with the lake of fire. As there was very little indication that any were benefiting from his labours, he became very worried. He could not sleep at night and grumbled at his companion because he was blissfully enjoying his sleep. He woke him one night, saying, 'Thomas, are you sleeping, while I am fighting with demons?' The two were great friends and very frank with one another, so Thomas Dafydd answered, 'Yes, I am sleeping. And as it's night, that is what I should be doing, I think. Why aren't you sleeping, you legalistic old man? Preach Christ to the people, man, and not law. What is the use of law to those under sentence of death? Life first, law afterwards.' The next day, the old preacher changed his style and proclaimed Jesus Christ as Saviour to the chief of sinners; he experienced great help and liberty. From then on his ministry on the journey was delivered with great unction and his sleep returned to him as before.

William Thomas did not prepare much before preaching; he depended a great deal on the inspiration of the moment. If the wind was with him, a good service would result. His sails would spread in the breeze and he and his congregation would receive blessing. But if the wind was not blowing, things would go difficult for him and his hearers. Once, when returning home after having been preaching in his own locality and a heavenly light having shone upon the meeting, an old brother called James Griffiths said to him, 'We had a good service tonight, William Thomas.' 'Yes,' was the happy answer, 'Yes, we struck the vein tonight where much treasure is to be found. There is no failing when on that road.'

If William Thomas was not notable as a preacher, he was famous in the private meetings. The society was his home; he would share his own experiences, which were consistently spiritual, and would invariably succeed in drawing out contributions from the brethren and sisters. He could apply his exhortations wonderfully to every condition and situation. According to *Methodistiaeth Cymru*, 'He would feed all the family in turn; young and old would receive their appropriate portion.' But he was more famous still as a man of prayer. The Rev. Edward Matthews wrote:

> He was better known as William Thomas the pray-er than as William Thomas the preacher. His prayers would be forever hanging as clouds above his preaching. It was judged that no house in Wales had known as much prayer as Tydraw in Pyle. The house was close to the main road from Swansea to Cardiff, and it was said that it was impossible for anyone passing at the time of the morning, or evening family worship, not to stop and remain about the door while the old man of Tydraw, as he was known, was calling upon his God. By the time he had finished praying, the whole of the yard in front of the house might be full of people, many of them deeply moved spiritually. He was naturally a slow and careful speaker, but as he continued he would become more heated and increase in importunity and passion, so that the family within and the people in the yard outside would be carried up to the gates of heaven and would have to acknowledge that a true wrestling with God was taking place. During this worship, William Thomas would pray publicly for many issues, naming them and spreading them before the Lord with much mental effort. He would sometimes be heard praying for some local families, or for individuals, thus: 'Remember, O Lord, Twm, Sion, Mary, or Betsy, of such-and-such a place; they are very ungodly, or on beds of sickness, or whatever.' Sometimes, the cause in Pyle would be his theme; at other times the county, or the Monthly Meeting, and so on.

William Thomas was completely free from any envy of those more talented than himself. While he listened to his brothers preaching, he would pray diligently for them. When he was old and had become deaf, he would stand at the pulpit steps. His lips would be seen to be always moving and the congregation would conclude that he was praying for the preacher and for their salvation. If he came across some young man with indications of ability and of God's intention of making use of him, he would rejoice greatly. On one occasion a young man from Carmarthenshire came to Pyle to preach and had a fairly successful meeting. He was to sleep that evening at Tydraw. After long conversation, they retired to their beds. After a while the young man heard a murmuring from the next room. Full of curiosity, he strained to hear and discovered that William Thomas was praying for him in the next room – pleading with God to grant him success on his journey, to keep him from falling, to make him an instrument for the salvation of many. After listening a long time, the young preacher fell asleep. He awoke some time later, only to hear the old man still at the same task and with the same object in view. As might be expected, the incident greatly affected the young man. His own heart was deeply moved and he also approached the throne of grace on his own behalf.

William Thomas was granted a long life. He lived for eighty-eight years, seventy-two of which were years of service under the banner of the Lord Jesus. In the last Monthly Meeting that he attended he testified that if he were given all his days again he would commit them to the same service. According to the poet:

Many brethren still remember	Y mae'n gôf gan rai o'r brodyr,
His pronouncement, warm and clear,	Ei dystiolaeth felys, glyd,
When they gathered at Cornelly,	Ar ddydd Calan, yn Cyrneli,
Fellowshipping at New Year;	Lle'r oedd amryw'n cwrdd ynghyd:
'Three score years and twelve I've laboured,	'Deuddeg mlynedd lawn a thrigain,
Servant to the God of grace;	Ges yng ngwinllan Brenin ne',
If my life were ten times longer	Pe cawn ddeuddeng mil yn rhagor,
I would never change my place.'	Ni newidiwn ddim o'm lle.'

He witnessed many of the controversies that disturbed the Methodist Connexion. He lived through the storm produced by the disagreement between Harris and Rowland and saw the societies in the Vale of Glamorgan divide and decline as a consequence. He contributed to the revival produced by the hymns of Williams, Pantycelyn, and to the revival that arose on the coming of the Rev. David Jones to Llan-gan. There is no doubt that he would be one of the crowd that passed through Bridgend on the last Sunday of every month, journeying to receive communion from that famous man. He was acquainted with the excitement that arose over the orthodoxy of Peter Williams's views, and was still strong and healthy at the time the old commentator was expelled. In particular, he lived through the period of debate over ordination. He noted the opposition of the clergymen – amongst them, his dear friend, Jones, Llan-gan; he saw them overcome by the determination of the people; and before his death, many preachers in both north and south had been ordained to administer the sacraments. He died on 22 August 1811, and his last words were, 'There is therefore now no condemnation to them which are in Christ Jesus.'

SIENCYN THOMAS, PENHYDD

The memory of Siencyn Thomas of Penhydd has been immortalized by the amusing biography written of him by the Rev. Edward Matthews. He was born on 16 September 1752, in a farmhouse called Penhydd, and it is as *'Siencyn Penhydd'* that he has been known ever since. Penhydd stands in a valley nestling between the mountains of Glamorganshire, about seven miles to the south-east of Neath. Nothing is known of his childhood except that his first years of youth were spent shepherding the flocks upon the mountain slopes. He grew up a tall young man. He does not appear to have received any education and was coarser in his morals and rougher in his behaviour even than the generality of the farm boys of the region. His character was determined and bold; he had no sense of fear or shame. It is clear also that he possessed considerable natural honesty and was a completely unique personality. We imagine him a tall stripling, rough and rustic in looks, uncultured by any education or experience of the wider world, but possessing an original and determined mind and full of life from head to toe. Needless to say, he grew up, as did all his peers, without a shred of religion.

THE PREACHING OF *'IEFAN, TYCLAI'*

But God had devised better things for Siencyn Thomas, and things that accompany salvation. The man who was instrumental in awakening him from spiritual death was *'Iefan, Tyclai'*, one of the first Methodist exhorters of Glamorganshire. This man, who in his own way was almost as remarkable as Siencyn Thomas, deserves some attention. He lived at Tyclai, a rough cottage of earth walls and thatched roof, near Llanfynydd. It is doubtful whether this cottage, even in its best days, was ever registered in the parish books. We viewed it once, about a quarter of a century ago. Its roof was then about to fall in and we understand that it is just a ruin now. From this poor home, the Apostle of Tyclai set out, proclaiming destruction upon an unrighteous world and inviting sinners to Christ. This is the portrayal of him given by Mr Matthews:

> He was a lively looking man, wearing a grey, collarless coat of homespun cloth, a multicoloured waistcoat, corduroy knee-breeches, black woollen stockings and wooden shoes. In such priestly garb, astride his red pony whose tail and mane had never been trimmed, travelled Iefan, Tyclai, up hill and down dale, bearing the everlasting gospel.

There were no Methodist chapels in the land at the time and so the old patriarch exhorted in the barns and farmhouses. His ministry was remarkably unadorned; it is said that he rarely took a text but would stand up, his congregation gathered in a circle around him, and he would turn around as he talked, sometimes proclaiming the law and at other times the gospel.

An ash walking stick with a huge knob on its head, weighing a pound or two, would be in one hand; and the other fist would be closed and held to the heads of his congregation as if he was determined to batter his sermon into their heads and hearts.

An example of one of his sermons is given in *Methodistiaeth Cymru.* It had been heard and later transcribed by Mr Lloyd of Caeo. Its theme was repentance and Iefan answered the question, 'What is repentance?' in the following way:

> Mainly, it is *aqua fortis*, which breaks in two what was once one. Secondly, it is a jalap powder, which purges the wound. Thirdly, it is a tincture of myrrh, which heals the wound completely, and does not cover it with dead flesh.

The example proves that there was nothing refined about Iefan; but let him not be held in contempt, he answered to the rough and ready nature of the times and was the means of turning scores from the error of their ways.

Edward Matthews wrote of him coming to preach to Llangrallo, a village near Llan-gan, the home of the Rev. David Jones:

> It was an evening in the week and a crowd of people had gathered in a farmhouse for the meeting. They all sat along the walls of the house, waiting the arrival of the preacher. Once arrived, he stood in the middle of them and read and prayed in a most fiery manner. He then began to move his walking stick from one hand to the other and to preach the gospel of the kingdom to all and sundry without exception. 'Come out from among them,' he said, 'and be ye separate. Do you know what, friends, if you see a hen spending most of her time among the potato-stalks, it is there that she will probably make her nest. In the same way, if you give most of your time to this ungodly world you will probably stay there, and your nest will go up in everlasting flames. Come out, people. They tell me that if a lamb takes milk from a goat, goat's wool will grow on it. If you are feeding from this world, then probably the spirit of this world will be in you, and your constant longing will be for this world. You will neglect the religion of the Son of God and so corrupt your ways that you become perfect goats, with nothing of lambs about you at all.'

In this way, the man from Tyclai walked about the house for about half an hour, throwing out similar philosophical and theological comments and applying them skilfully to each individual. At last, the steam seemed to be dispersing, the wheels gradually slowing, and every indication suggested that the Tyclai carriage was about to come to a stop. When he came up to the chair where the Rev. David Jones sat, the clergyman, with much affection and a warm smile, turned to him and said:

'Iefan *bach*, you have been in this school for a long time now. Tell us, what have you learnt there in all this time?'

'Mr Jones,' he replied, 'I have been on the same lesson through all the years, and I can honestly tell you that I have learnt it at last.'

'What lesson is that, Iefan?'

'Well, I will tell you. I have learnt that I know nothing.'

'You have?'

'Yes, certainly.'

'Well, well. You, Iefan *bach*, are one of the foremost scholars in Jesus's school. Though I have tried hard, I have not yet come up to that standard.'

After this conversation the meeting closed with prayer and praise. All returned to their homes along their various ways, marvelling at the genius and fluency of the preacher.

SIENCYN'S CONVERSION

We will only speak further of the old exhorter from Tyclai in relating how, under God's blessing, he was the means of awakening the wild youth of Penhydd from his sleep of death. Siencyn Penhydd told the story himself. Once, while on his journeys, a young man asked him how he was first brought to religion. He replied:

> I will you tell honestly how it happened. An old exhorter, who was not known for any great ability but who was particularly effective at times, used to visit the neighbourhood to preach. I went with many of my contemporaries to hear him, not with any intention of spiritual good for ourselves, but in order to amuse ourselves with his strange ways. Once he had started by reading and praying, he began to speak to the congregation just as if he was talking to us individually. I don't remember his text, if indeed he had a text; I don't remember that he referred to, or mentioned, any particular verse but I have thought many times afterwards that his address was completely scriptural throughout. His aim at the time, I remember, was to endeavour to awaken the sinner from his sleep and cause him to see that he was in awful danger of being in hell forever. It was exactly as if he was speaking personally to some man in the congregation that he knew to be an extraordinarily wicked man. I opened my eyes and looked around and then, turning my eyes back to the preacher, I saw that his eyes were fixed earnestly upon me, as he threatened the wicked man dreadfully. I was certain that he was directing his message straight to myself. However, I had not listened long before I came to believe that I was the wicked man – the extraordinarily wicked man that the preacher was describing, and that I was the object of terrible threatenings. The noise of these threats followed me so as to fill my soul with fear and with terror of hellfire. And in that state Iefan, Tyclai, left me, without even a farewell. I went home, but not in the same condition as before. Not my home, not anything that I thought about, could help me or ease my fears. I tried many things for some time to quieten my mind, but failed to do so.

The wild youth who knew no terrors or fear was now deeply wounded. Iefan, Tyclai, left him with the arrows deep in his conscience. For some time he sought relief through the means of the flesh, giving himself to pleasure and vanity. One evening, some time later, he was throwing dice in a house called Troed-y-rhiw near Penrhiw, Margam. This was a common pastime in the locality. On a winter's night, whole families: girls, boys, and old men and women leaning on their walking sticks, would gather at some place for dicing, and there they would be, cracking nuts and drinking beer, often until dawn. On this occasion, the dice favoured Siencyn Thomas and he won two geese. He hurried home with them, one under each arm, in order to share his good luck with the family. It was midnight; the birds were not happy with their circumstances and periodically gave out unearthly screams. Siencyn felt his hold weakening and the birds managed to free their wings, with which they gave him a beating. A great fear arose within him. Probably his conscience was already at work accusing him for attending such a place of vanity. He thought he saw a bright light shining around him. Views of hell and the judgment came to his mind and he thought he was about to die. The geese escaped from his arms and flew off back to their old home. Siencyn fell on his knees and remained there for some hours, pleading for mercy. He arrived at Penhydd sometime before morning with his conscience a furnace within him. For a season he endured terrible pangs; he tried to improve his ways but failed; his struggles to escape the mire only served to sink himself deeper. He said to himself:

> I vowed not to be as before, and I struggled as much as I could to make the wicked man into a good man but, however much I tried, it could not be managed. But soon, though it felt a very long time to me after listening to the damning sermon of Iefan, Tyclai, the sound of which was still roaring in my conscience, Mr Dafydd Morris came preaching through the neighbourhood. I went to hear him and by the guidance of the light of the Holy Spirit was shown the wicked man, as Iefan, Tyclai, had rightly called me, and shown that God and his law were my enemies. At this point, when every hope of being saved had been completely taken away from me, behold, the ministry opened up for me a door of hope in the valley of destruction, and I saw that I had a right to believe and hope in Jesus Christ for my life, regardless of myself or of the whole host of devils. I have been saved, to the great glory of his grace. Thanks be to him for ever!

Dafydd Morris would never wound without an attempt, before closing, to heal. He would not leave the people, like Iefan, Tyclai, in the midst of hell's terrors, without referring them to an all-sufficient Saviour. A few drops of the heavenly oil and myrrh were poured upon the wounds of the anxious young man from Penhydd that night, and he received some degree of comfort. But he was not yet a free man. His old convictions returned upon him at times with overpowering force. Throughout this period his demeanour reflected his stunned condition. Some thought that he was suffering from an illness that had stupefied him, others believed that his mind had been affected and they talked of putting him in a straitjacket, others again believed that the new religion had damaged him. About this time, he went to St Michael's to hear the Rev. William Davies of Neath. According to Edward Matthews:

> This was the ever-to-be-remembered Sabbath morning when he was brought by the ministry of the above reverend gentleman, to the wondrous light of the gospel. An eternal light of dawn shone upon him, the sun of which is, even as we write these lines, shining upon his head in that place where night will nevermore bring an end to his glory.

It was not long after listening to William Davies that Siencyn Thomas joined the Methodists, and it is probably at the old chapel of Gyfylchi that he became a member. Very soon his fame as a remarkable man of prayer spread abroad. There were various places about the house and around his holding where he was often in communion with his Lord. But his favourite spot was the quarry behind the house. Here he would be heard in earnest wrestlings with God for the good of his soul; here also he would deal with other less important matters between himself and the Lord. So often did he resort there that it became a saying in the family, whenever he could not be found, that he was sure to be in the quarry. His brothers did not know God, and their behaviour at times was not acceptable to Siencyn. Once, for all his opposition, they insisted on driving the cattle to Llandaff Fair on a Sunday. He tried to get them to start out on the Saturday and to rest over the Sunday. They argued that this would be more costly. 'Believe me,' he said, 'there will be more of a cost if you break the Sabbath, and sin against God.' Off they went to the fair, and off to the quarry went Siencyn with his heart full of zeal for the Lord. The cattle had not travelled far from the house when one of them fell and broke a knee. Thomas, one of his brothers cried out, 'Siencyn is in the quarry praying!' This was quite correct. Thomas ran back and discovered that the prayer in the quarry and the cow's broken knee had occurred at the same time.

EXAMPLES OF HIS ECCENTRICITIES

After marrying Siencyn Thomas went to live at Aberavon, but before long moved to Goetre, in Margam parish, and remained there for the rest of his life. We have already shown something of his eccentricity. Edward Matthews states:

> He was not merely eccentric in one thing but in everything. He did not look like other men. You might think he was a lunatic; he walked so nimbly and

hurriedly that you might imagine he was being harried by hounds through the mud and grime; his eyes would flame in his head, and he looked like a man bent on fleeing from the sight of all. When on horseback he was the very representation of what we might imagine to be perpetual motion: always moving; the small whip in his hand continually driving; his long muscular legs continually spurring the horse on. His whole aspect suggested that he was in a fearful haste to arrive at his destination almost as soon as he started. It was clear to all however that he was in much greater haste than his horse, and that the movements of the rider were much faster than those of the creature that bore him. He would be the same when engaged on any particular task – he was an indefatigable worker, accomplishing more than any two normal men. He laboured diligently at his holding all his life and accumulated some wealth. He would rise hours before the rest of the family and go to the threshing floor. There he would thresh without stop, as if fiercely angry with the wheat and straw, until sweat and steam rose off him. He would then go to the 'crooked Bible' as he called it, which had become bent from being kept in some awkward spot in the barn. He would read a bit in that and perhaps pray, and soon be engaged in fearful battle with some of the chief demons of darkness, the sounds of the battle being heard afar. He would then return to thresh a little more, to read further, and to pray again, until it was time for the remainder of the family to rise. He would then go to the house, call on all, poke up the fire, and lie down full-length before it for a while. This is how, as given in his own words, he would redeem the time.

Clearly Siencyn Thomas was a man of strong constitution and fervent life – a life that sometimes expressed itself in remarkable forms. It is not known when he began to preach. Probably he slipped gradually into the work, without any permission from a Monthly Meeting or Association, by giving a word of exhortation in prayer meetings and maturing into a preacher almost unawares. Nor could he be compared to anyone else as a preacher. His appearance in the pulpit was rough and wild; he did not own a black coat or white napkin. His dress was of homespun cloth, and a hat with an enormous brim, rather like a brass pan, would be on his head.

He would, of course, remove his hat, but not immediately because he would first have to remove his greatcoat. It is believed that no drop of hair-oil ever approached his head, that he was a Nazarite from his mother's womb in this respect . . . He would pull his fingers through his hair, usually across the grain, so that it stood up in all directions like the bristles of a pig. In the heat of the moment as he preached, and quite unconsciously, both his hands would often be in his hair, pulling and brushing, so that the shock of hair standing up like a brush would give him an unearthly look . . . In old age his hair was long and white, falling to his shoulders, giving him a druidical appearance.

As far as can be gathered, his sermons were just as remarkable. His language was not refined nor his phrases ornamental; he did not preach the contents of books and his illustrations were not drawn from the sciences or the arts. Nature, in all its wildness, and the Welsh Bible, were the main if not the only fields in which he researched. Yet there are innumerable proofs that he was used to great effect.

Though rough in looks and coarse of word, he possessed considerable good sense. He had great discernment in recognizing men's characters and in knowing how to deal with them, and his comments would always be very original. In truth, he was better suited to serve his generation than might be supposed, particularly when we remember that he possessed other excellent elements, such as a pure innocence, an incorruptible honesty, a fiery zeal for God, and an unhypocritical faithfulness in serving the souls of others. It is clear that he was immensely popular in his day.

Not many of his remarks when preaching have survived, but we may conclude that his illustrations were very homely. There was a gate on the mountain-side between Penhydd and Llangynwyd called 'Brynmawr gate'. One of its hinge pins had been fitted facing upwards and the other downwards to stop the gate from being lifted up and stolen. When preaching on the covenant of grace on one occasion, he said that the covenant was the same as Brynmawr gate, one pin up, one pin down, so that neither Satan nor anybody else could throw it from its place. 'One pin is up with God,' he said. 'And the other is down with his people; so that the foundation of God standeth sure: the Lord knoweth them that are his.' When preaching on humility, he said, 'This grace grows just like a cow's tail – always downwards.'

He spoke once on the words, 'We ought to give the more earnest heed to the things which we have heard,' and encouraged his congregation to memorize the text, that at least would ensure that there was something in their minds that was pure. 'It may be that there are many here', he said, 'who complain that their memories are so bad that they cannot remember anything. Stop such lies. It is not your memory that it at fault; it is you who fill it with other things, bad, worldly and filthy things, so that there is no room in it for good things. I'll warrant that you remember how much you sold that animal for in Llandaff Fair; six or seven pounds, wasn't it? That certainly hasn't dropped out of your memory yet. You remember everything except the gospel.' One old man in the congregation could not be persuaded that some of his believing neighbours had not told the preacher everything about him.

AS A LEADER OF THE SOCIETIES

But Siencyn Thomas was known most of all for his leadership of the societies. In these meetings, a kind of inspiration would fall upon him; it was felt as if he was almost discerning spirits; very rarely would he be mistaken over the condition of those before him and he was often enabled to speak a word in season. Somehow, statements would be expected of him, and accepted from him because of his implicit honesty, that would be quite unacceptable from anyone else. A young lad came to the society for the first time and Siencyn said to him, 'My boy, make sure you have Christ in your heart; he will be as much use in your pocket as in your head.' A young woman applied for membership of the society at Pyle when he was present. William Thomas explained to Siencyn who she was, that she was the daughter of Siencyn the tiler. 'Oh,' he said. 'You are Siencyn's daughter, are you? I know your father well, girl. He has tried every religion going in the country, and has failed with every one of them. Listen, my dear girl. Make sure you have a better religion than your father's, otherwise you will be sure to fall into the devil's snares one of these days.' He once said to a man that he was just like a sponge. 'A sponge takes everything in. Whether you place it in water, or milk, or beer, or bile, or poison, it soaks it all up. You are just like that – a man for everything and everywhere. You are at home in the chapel and at home in the tavern, there is no difference wherever you are.'

He had an amazing gift for putting an end to arguments and quarrelling and to restore peace to those societies that had become a prey to disputes. One word from him would often put an end to a painful strife. A man called Will, a member of the Dyffryn society, had heard a discourse on baptism and was almost persuaded that there was no entry to heaven to any but by passing through the river. He had been disturbing his brethren and sisters for some time, so that they could not think clearly. The story was told to Siencyn Thomas. 'Ho,' he said. 'Will sees one bath in the river as a much easier way than praying, mortifying sin and crucifying the flesh with the affections and lusts.' One society evening, Will came in like a bolt, as innocent as any. Siencyn sprang to his feet, as nimble as a young deer, and called out:

'Will, what's the matter with you?'

'There's nothing the matter with me, Uncle Siencyn. What do you mean?'

'Haven't you been talking about being baptized?'

'Well, there has been some mention of that; it concerns me seriously at times.'

'Listen, have you been baptized before at any time?'

'Yes. When I was a child.'

'And do you know, Will, in whose name you were baptized then?'

'Yes, I know. The form of words is in the Book of Common Prayer.'

'Well then, in whose name does the Prayer Book say?'

' In the name of the Father, the Son, and the Holy Spirit.'

'Well listen then, Will. Having been baptized already in the name of the Holy Trinity, in what devil's name do you want to be baptized now?'

This put an end to the debate. Will was freed from his concerns over baptism and no more was heard of the matter.

There is an account of two women, members of the society at Taibach, who had quarrelled fiercely. Fires had been kindled in their hearts that had proved impossible to extinguish. Many means were adopted in attempting to reconcile them but none prevailed. The greater the effort, the more stubborn grew the women, until the whole society was in turmoil. They were called forward, one society evening, in a further attempt at reconciliation. They were given valuable counsels; the desirability of peace was demonstrated to them, its value was such that to obtain it was worth considerable sacrifice. But all such counsels were in vain. They were both roused to a fiery temper, reciting aloud the wrongs received at the hands of the other. Throughout this time, Siencyn Thomas sat in seeming unconcern, his eyes closed, as if not hearing the conversation. When matters had come to a head, one of the elders asked him:

'Siencyn Thomas, is there something that you want to say to them?'

'No, not publicly, as far as I know,' was the reply. 'But I have a word to say to them in private, on their own.'

He got to his feet and said:

'You two, come with me, for me to tell you something.'

He went outside with them and led them to the top of a small mound nearby, in front of the chapel. He then turned to them and said:

'This is the place for you, you malicious pair of gossips. Stay here until you have made your peace, and don't come anywhere near the society until your quarrel is over.'

He turned on his heel and returned to the society, locking the door behind him. It was not long before weeping and flutterings were heard at the door. The two had made up and were pleading to be received back, promising that they would never quarrel again. It is said that the medication proved completely successful.

Another severe division occurred within the society at Caerphilly. Many attempts were made to still the storm but these only succeeded in stirring up more strife. The Rev. David Jones and others of the leaders of the Connexion had visited many times but to no avail. It proved impossible to stop the tongues of the disputers when once the subject was broached. In due course the matter came before the Monthly Meeting and as a last resort it was decided to send Siencyn, Penhydd, there. After much persuading he agreed to go. Having arrived, he spoke seriously of the sinfulness of divisions and the decline and destruction that it brought to religion. But for all his seriousness, the people were aflame. All spoke at the same time and expanded on the wrongs and evils that they had suffered from each other. The old preacher therefore got to his feet and began walking up and down the chapel. At times he would look up towards the ceiling, at other moments he would strike the floor suddenly with his stick. Gradually, the people's attentions were drawn from their bickering and alerted to his strange behaviour. He, while continuing to walk, and as if conversing with an invisible listener, asked,

'Lord, is this your betrothed?'

By now, all were subdued and looking attentively at him. With an awful solemnity that caused shivers to pass through them all, he repeated the same question, over and over:

'Lord, is this your betrothed?'

After a little while, he shouted out loud:

'Put her to death!'

Then, as if someone had answered, 'I will not!':

'Sell her then!'

'I will not!'

'Deny her!'

'I will not!'

He then raised his voice and roared out:

'She cost me too much: she cost me divine blood. How could I give her up, and how could I leave her?'

He then fell upon his knees and prayed with such intensity of spirit that all the people were in tears. When he rose from his knees they were embracing one another and begging forgiveness of one another. The story demonstrates that he possessed a power and spirituality that none could withstand.

Many years before his death, a complaint came to the Monthly Meeting that the cause at a particular place was in a bad way, that it was very quickly declining, very little preaching was occurring and little effort made to obtain preachers, and the chapel would soon have to be closed unless there was a sudden transformation. After listening to the sad account, William

Thomas of Pyle stood up saying, 'Siencyn Thomas, you must go there, and all our prayers will ascend to heaven on your behalf.' He obeyed, taking a friend with him as a companion. After preaching he called the society together, and as his companion explained the situation he lay full length on a bench. At last he got up and standing, leaning upon his staff in the middle of the chapel, with an unearthly look, he cried, '*Hawyr!* What is the matter with you? The wheel is a good wheel. The water is good water. Tell me, why won't the wheel turn?' He was dumb for a while, looking here and there. 'Oh,' he said suddenly, 'I see why the wheel won't turn. The fault lies with that leaking tank. The water is being lost. It's not possible for the wheel to turn.' He then began calling the people by name, for he knew them all. He began with the elder. 'Dafydd! Dafydd the tailor, isn't it? No, Dafydd the great farmer. The great miller, indeed, selling the flour by the sack. Where is the religion? Almost forgotten.' He then turned to a gentlewoman: 'Mrs So-and-so, isn't it? The godly old gentlewoman, beloved of all. Where is she? Sinking under the cares of this world, iron ore in the ground, and many other things. And where is Miss So-and-so, the young girl faithful in her religion. Yes, that is what she was, but what is she now? She has been buried by carnal love; this one more handsome, and that one more wealthy. But what of the soul? Almost forgotten. Catrin! Catrin! Is that you?' 'Yes,' she replied. 'Yes, it is her body. But where is her soul? Drowned in covetousness, I fear.' In this way, he went through them all, commenting pointedly on them. He then suddenly raised his voice, and shouted, 'Wake up, people! The Son of God is suffering in this place because of you. Wake up by grace, before you are woken up by judgment.' He fell on his knees and prayed that the Holy Spirit might come from heaven upon all in the place, to recover the cause and revive the people.

The effect was overpowering. While Siencyn Thomas was before the throne, pleading the promises, a strange influence passed over all. Nothing could be heard from them, the men and the women, but weeping and praying. From that time on, the cause flourished. About thirty new members were soon received, and God raised the elder's son to the work of the ministry.

When leading a society at Llanarthne, Carmarthenshire, it was brought to Siencyn Thomas's attention that a woman who once had been very religious had befriended the local parson. The parson was considered to be an upright man, but one who was often overcome by drink. Sometimes, at a funeral, he would not be able to read the service without serious mistakes. The members of the society felt it deeply that such a virtuous woman was about to marry such a creature, yet they did not feel that they had any right to rebuke her, still less to expel her, because the clergyman was a professed believer and a minister of the gospel. In their confusion they decided to leave the matter in the hands of the Apostle of Penhydd. After preaching and calling a society meeting, Siencyn asked the woman to come to the front. 'Listen,' he said to her, 'what you are going to do is exactly the same as yoking together a sheep and a pig. Can you imagine an innocent lamb bound to a dirty pig, and being dragged through the mud and filth until she is almost as black as the pig. Release the lamb, or she will be killed through being dragged through the filth. He feeds on the swill of the trough; she longs for the green pasture and starves while he feeds. She will die for certain.' He then smote the floor with his stick, and shouted out loud, 'Release the lamb, or she will die with her head in the halter!' 'Do you know,' he said to the woman, 'you are voluntarily binding yourself to the devil's pig. Don't be surprised if it chokes you in the end. Consider what you are about to do and get away in time, otherwise you will be physically in Satan's possession.' The woman listened to his advice and, as appropriate for a lamb, she remained in the green field and left the pig to its dunghill.

He said some rough things at times, but they were accepted from him. A certain Mari, known for her quarrelsome nature, belonged to the society at Dyffryn. She wielded a sharp tongue in the terrace of houses where she lived and was always in some trouble or other. Siencyn had been bothered many times on her account, and a serious fracas had again occurred. On the evening of the following society meeting, in came Mari as unconcerned as ever. On seeing her, Siencyn Thomas was thoroughly agitated. He rose to his feet, closed his fist, and stamping on the floor he cried out, 'Mari! Mari! Get out of the society, you Jack-o'-lantern from hell. You are leading people astray with the way you are behaving.' The woman had no choice but to leave immediately. Belonging to the same society was a sister called Sian Cwmgwynai who would often rejoice aloud in the services. Siencyn had suspicions that it was not the gospel alone that excited the old woman but that she sometimes shouted for no reason at all. He was preaching on one occasion and Sian was rejoicing loudly. In the society afterwards, he turned to her, saying, 'You speak to us, Sian. You received much during the service and so should have a solid experience to share with us.' But Sian had little to share after all. 'Do you know what?' he replied, 'You are just like Will Herbert's hunting hound. Will shouts out loud sometimes, "Fox! Fox!" and the old hound will get thoroughly excited and bark as if the greatest hunt ever was about, while in reality there wasn't even the trail of a fly to be chased. I'm afraid, Sian, that you often shout when there is no trail about. You may shout as much as you wish when there is one, but if not, shouting is of no profit whatsoever.'

SIENCYN THOMAS AND THE DEVIL

Siencyn Thomas's history would not be complete without mentioning his efforts against the devil. Satan was no abstraction to him but a powerful and cunning creature, always engaged in the work of tempting. He would often fall out with him and pile up a list of the worst names he could think of for him, calling him 'the deceiver', 'the thief', 'rogue', and so on. If a temptation rushed into his mind from any direction, Satan would receive the blame immediately. As mentioned, Siencyn was an early riser. He would be with his cart at the lime-kiln before the lime-burner had arrived and therefore the responsibility for measuring was his. One morning, when all but he were in the arms of sleep, the temptation came upon him to fill the cart as full as possible and so obtain a little more than the agreed measure. He realized that the suggestion was from Satan. He tried to argue against it, reminding himself that this would be theft. 'No,' said Satan, 'there is no need to call it theft. Just call it a full measure.' He filled the cart to the usual extent but in case there was in it more than usual, he climbed into the cart and threw back part of the load. Then, off he went at full speed. Once on top of the hill between the kiln and his field, he pulled on the reins, placed a large stone neatly behind the wheel, and turned to prayer. In a little while he was on top of the hill, waving his hat about his head and shouting out so that the hills rang, 'Victory! Victory! Success over all the powers of darkness! "I can do all things through Christ who strengtheneth me." Hallelujah!'

When travelling to an engagement on one occasion, on a horse that was a poor, thin creature, he happened to pass an old quarry. The temptation flew into his mind, from the devil he thought, that he should force the animal over the edge to its death and pretend it had slipped. 'You will get a new horse from the brethren,' said Satan, 'when they hear of your misfortune. They have enough money.' His spirit was in some pain for a while. But, with the help of grace, he was able to overcome and the innocent horse escaped with its life intact. Once the storm had passed, he tried to think of a plan to revenge himself on the devil for such a temptation. He remembered that a saint's day fair was being held that night in the neighbourhood and he decided to attend. On drawing near to the house of festivities, he could hear the sound of singing and dancing from afar. He called out to the innkeeper asking him to take his horse to the stable, but there was no room there because of all the horses of the revellers. He frowned at the innkeeper, asking, 'Have you a licence for this house?' 'Yes,' the man replied. 'Then take my horse to the stable,' was the answer. The man was frightened and turned out another's horse in order to accommodate the stranger's horse. On entering the house, the noise of the dancing from the loft above was causing the house to shake. The old Apostle of Penhydd removed his hat, turned his ear towards the direction of the noise, pulled his hands through his hair, and with a look like thunder towards the innkeeper, who by now was possessed with a degree of terror, asked:

'Have you got the devil in this house with you?'

'Oh no, sir,' was the reply. 'It is only a dance.'

'A dance, is it? A dance! They will be dancing on their heads in the pit soon.'

The innkeeper took fright; he rushed up the stairs shouting, 'Flee! Flee! There is a wizard downstairs who says you will be on your heads in the pit unless you leave immediately. Escape as best you can.' The company were thrown into panic and the girls began to scream. Within a few minutes, all had fled for their lives, and some thought that some black monster had run alongside the hedge, following them all the way. After clearing the house, Siencyn Thomas asked the innkeeper:

'Have you bread and cheese in the house?'

'Yes,' was the reply.

'Bring them here to the table.'

When he had obeyed, he told him:

'Now you must ask a blessing over the food.'

'Me, sir? I never asked a blessing in my life.'

'Man! You never asked a blessing? How old are you?'

'Such-and-such an age.'

'And never yet asked a blessing over your food? You must ask this very minute.'

In his fright, the man cried out:

'O God, what shall I do?'

'There,' said Siencyn Thomas, 'Perhaps that will do for now. If you ask God often what you should do, perhaps he will tell you in the end.'

He then began to pray, thanking God for victory over the devil on his own ground. On leaving, he flung it in the devil's face that he had gained nothing from tempting him to put an end to his horse.

The servant of a neighbour of his was driving cattle to the fair in Neath for his mistress. Siencyn Thomas decided to take his own cattle in the same drove and off they went together. About halfway through the journey, the old patriarch's head dropped; he began to groan and look very downhearted. Before the servant had time to ask him what was the matter, he saw him turning his horse round and, giving the horse his whip and spurs, shouting, 'Do your best on the road and with the cattle, Will. I'm fleeing from the noise of the world.' Will shouted back, 'In heaven's name, what is the matter?' 'There is enough the matter, boy. Neath Fair has filled my heart before I'm halfway there.' For all the servant's arguments he sped on his way, leaving the consequences to providence.

His cup was often full and running over during the means of grace, and at such times he would be a remarkable sight. His hands would be through his hair; his eyes would be shining in his head; he would emit an occasional roar that would set the place shaking. On one occasion someone was preaching at Gyfylchi Chapel and the congregation had been deeply moved. Siencyn Thomas sat at one side to the pulpit. Under the influence of the Word he would stir in his seat; mutter to himself; shrug his shoulders. He would scratch his head until his white hair was one confused mass, and his eyes flashed like fire. At last, he sprang out of the seat and amongst the people, roaring aloud, 'Satan, take me now! You've said a hundred times that you would have me in the end. Come and get me today, you devil, if you dare! Hallelujah! you will never have me! "It is God who justifieth. Who is he that condemneth? . . . For I am persuaded, that neither death, nor life, etc., shall be able to separate us from the love of God, which is in Christ Jesus our Lord."'

EXAMPLES OF HIS WISDOM AND SPIRITUAL COMMON SENSE

It appears that Siencyn Thomas was an important member of the Glamorganshire Monthly Meeting and indeed of the Associations in the south, and many of his comments, made at these meetings, have survived. A Monthly Meeting held at Llantrisant was begun by an address by Mr Richard James, who then pressed the brethren to contribute a word. But no one was in any mood to speak. At last, a young man called out, 'Siencyn Thomas, what are we to do?' 'Nothing, it seems to me, but waste time,' was the reply. 'Why don't you ask me a question, and I will ask one of you, in order to get the meeting going?' 'No,' said Siencyn, 'I will share with you my experience. I built a reservoir of water the other day, about four foot deep and with a good flow of water into it, sufficient for the animals to drink from and for the ducks and geese to swim on it. Then I sat down and began to boast, "O, I am better than all my neighbours. My lake flows cleanly while theirs are muddy and filthy." But soon I heard a voice saying, "Is that so, Sianco?" And soon he had driven a pig through my lake so that there wasn't one clean spot to be seen in it. That put an end to my boasting and I saw that what would be best for me would be a strong flow of running water to clean out my lake and myself.' Though there might be some confusion in the metaphor, the old exhorter's point was very clear. He had been tempted to boast of his own righteousnesses, thinking himself more sanctified than others; but the law had come, revealing his best righteousnesses to be only sin, and making him realize that he needed a strong stream from Calvary's fountain to flow continually over himself and all his duties in order to keep him pure.

He said on one occasion to an elder in the Monthly Meeting, 'I understand that the drink you supply is not as tasty as it once was. What do you think is the cause? There was an old woman who used to live in Ystradfellte parish in a little cottage on the side of a road that had a lot of traffic travelling to the nearby lime-kilns. She used to brew at home and had a good name for her beer. If anyone excelled, they would be described as being as good as Auntie Bessie's drink. The young men, on the road to fetch lime, would often call for a draught, and having visited once would almost invariably call again, so good was its taste. But after a while, the old woman thought it would be much less work for herself to buy in her beer by the barrel. The young men came as before but having drunk would make a face, and on looking into the glass would say, "Auntie, this isn't your beer. I won't come here again." The old lady soon realized her mistake.' He then turned to the elder, saying, 'Brother, brew your own beer at home. Don't give to your brothers and sisters anything that you have not experienced as a blessing to your own soul. Once you start dealing in foreign drink, it won't be long before your friends start leaving.'

On another occasion, he was conversing with many elders, one of whom was complaining of his dryness and dullness and appeared to be losing ground spiritually. Siencyn broke out in a blaze, 'Jack, Jack, sharpen your scythe; sharpen your scythe, Jack. You have been the foremost reaper here for many years, and, fair play to you, you have been a good reaper too. But now there is a notch in your scythe. I advise you to take it to the stone where I was this morning. He will soon bring back its edge.' Then, with his voice raised still further, he continued, 'Jack, sharpen your scythe, otherwise the Lord of the reapers will come to turn you out of the field because you are obstructing the progress of the work.' It was said that it was impossible to describe the effect of these words upon the brother himself and upon the meeting generally. It was as if the Almighty had shaken all flesh.

There was a preacher called Thomas Price, a contemporary of Siencyn's, living in the neighbourhood of Creunant, who was said to be a strong preacher at times. He was a small man, very careful of his dress and always neat in appearance. He preached one day at a Monthly Meeting when many of the Glamorganshire brethren were present, and Siencyn Thomas among them. To begin with the meeting prospered; the wind was with the preacher, and he was sailing in its breezes as if he were one of the masters of the congregation. But suddenly, just as if by a clap of the hands, a cloud passed over the meeting. Matters only got worse from then to the end of the service so that Thomas Price had to close in utter darkness. At the end, Siencyn Thomas went up to him and said, 'Tom, do you understand what happened tonight? If you don't I will tell you. You climbed up into the pulpit trembling and praying for help. "Well, Tom Price," said the Lord, "because you are conscious of your insufficiency, I will help you." And so it was, and all went well for a while, and the people were blessed. It was God's blessing, remember, not yours. But then, some devil came past and clapped you on the back, saying, "Well done, Tom Price!" There was no harm in that; who could have stopped him? But you clapped your hands together and shouted out, "Well done, Tom Price, indeed!" "Ah," said heaven, "Tom Price, is it?" and heaven removed its blessing, leaving you to the mockery of devils, contemptible in the eyes of men, in poverty, without a scrap to cover your nakedness.' The story reveals Siencyn Thomas's keen discernment and his thorough knowledge of the human heart.

All these stories that survive about him reveal that Siencyn Thomas was a remarkably thoughtful man, in his own way. He would often appear lost in his own thoughts, and at such times it would be hard to draw any conversation from him. It is said of him that he was once accompanying a young man, a friend, on a journey one Sunday. About half way along their road a complete silence fell upon them. At last, Siencyn Thomas broke the silence by shouting out, 'Phil has died.' 'What Phil?' asked his friend, 'Which Phil do you mean?' 'Phillip Morgan, from such-and-such a place.' 'Oh, yes. I had heard that.' 'Well,' said Siencyn, 'he has escaped forever, I believe. But not because he was prettier than you or me. It was because he knew what it was to fail to live in that other place and to bring it down to this place. And so it proved to be his death.' With that, he shouted out, 'Oh, to pass through from death into life!'

He knew nothing of the fear of man, though he respected all in whom he saw signs of good. He was very concerned over his horse during one journey in Carmarthenshire. The pony seemed rather thin at the beginning of the tour, and it got even thinner as they progressed. At one stop on the journey they were received by a deacon of very neat appearance, who seemed to be a considerable gentleman. Before beginning the service,

Siencyn Thomas went quietly to the stable and found that the hay given to his horse was mouldy, so that the horse could not eat any of it. He placed a handful of the hay in the pocket of his coat and went to the chapel. After the sermon there was a society meeting. The deacon praised the preaching and called upon the brethren and sisters to contribute a word. But before any could speak, the old exhorter jumped to his feet. 'What if you were to say a word, sir,' he suggested; 'they are always contributing.' The deacon began to speak of his fears, but Siencyn Thomas interrupted his address by bringing the hay out of his pocket and shaking it over his head so that his clothes were covered. 'Listen,' he said, 'your religion is as mouldy as this hay that you gave to my horse. Here's a picture of your religion!' Only he would have dared do such a thing.

Because of his innocent simplicity and the wealth of common sense that lay beneath all his eccentricities, he was of considerable influence in his own neighbourhood. A serious argument arose between the owners of the Taibach copper works and the labour force – the latter were asking for a pay rise, and the former refusing. The result was that the men stopped working. The manager of the works had some of them arrested with the intention of making an example of them for neglecting the furnaces and thereby causing considerable losses to the owners. One young man was imprisoned at Swansea and was eventually transferred to the press-gang to be transported. The whole neighbourhood was greatly distressed. Many appeals were made to the manager to have him released but all in vain. As a last resort, Siencyn Thomas was asked to visit him and he agreed. One morning he came to the house, wild in appearance, a shepherd's crook, nine feet long, in his hand, his hair like the hair of a goat, sticking out in all directions.

Without any kind of greeting he struck the ground with the crook and said to the gentleman, 'You have done it now. Sending the lad of a neighbour from the land of his birth! What's in your mind? The sword will never leave this house; as you have done, so will be done to you.' As he finished speaking there was the sound of a fall from upstairs and the maid shrieked out that one of the children had broken its neck. Panic struck the house, but it was found that the child had suffered no great harm. Once calm had been restored, the old patriarch said, 'That is only the beginning of sorrows, except that you send the boy home,' and he walked out of the house. The manager rushed after him in his fright, shouting, 'Siencyn Thomas, the boy will come home however much it costs.' Such behaviour would not have been accepted from anyone except an eccentric, but only of an eccentric of evidently pure character.

It would be a feast for the believers of old to receive Siencyn Thomas to lead a society, in that his comments were so original and his treatment of them so honest. In one meeting, he spoke with an old brother called David Christmas. Siencyn could not draw an acceptable response from him; he suspected him of being legalistic and self-righteous. He told him he had to forsake the first Adam completely, lose his life, come without a rag to cover his nakedness to Jesus Christ for eternal life, or else be lost forever. But Dafydd remained quite stubborn. At last, Siencyn became heated. He struck his staff upon the floor and shouted, '*Deio*, do you know what you are like? Your house is leaking water everywhere; the rain is coming in all over the place. And you are moving your bed here and there, from one place to another trying to avoid the rain, but it is still getting soaked. Yet you are insisting that you will keep on living in this leaking old house.' He then roared out through the chapel, 'Your old house, *Deio*, will sink into the pit!' The response to his counsel is not known, but it was a striking illustration.

Very little has survived of the content and nature of his preaching, but he was certainly completely different from anyone else. We heard of him preaching one night in the old chapel at Creunant. This was a long building with a pulpit at one end for the clergymen to preach, and a kind of stool at the other end from which the unordained men would speak. Next to the exhorter was a length of metal knocked into the wall called 'the candlestick', with a halfpenny candle thrust into it – the only light in the room. Siencyn Thomas's text at this time was, 'Christ, the light of the world.' Some of his comments were, '"Light" is the topic, friends. Would this world be of any use to us without light, tell me? Where is light to be found, people? I can imagine some of you saying, "It is in my eye." No, the light doesn't come from your eye.' With that he turned to the candle, snuffing it with his fingers. 'There,' he said, in the pitch darkness, 'can you see now? No, you are in complete darkness now, I know.' Having provided them with such a practical lesson, he relit the candle, saying, 'You believe now that light isn't found in your own eyes. People! In Christ is light and life, and not in yourselves. When you want anything you go to the place where it is to be found. If you see reeds growing anywhere, you go to that place when you want water. If you see smoke anywhere, you go there in search of a fire; and where there is a fire, you go there for light and heat. Look for anything at the place where it is to be found, otherwise you will go without. Always come to Christ for light and life.'

If he was severe with the religion of his brothers and sisters, he was severer still with his own religion. He was often troubled by his state and in extreme distress because of the plague of his heart. Once, when on top of Aberavon mountain, a great storm arose in his mind: 'I cannot at all remember, he said to himself, 'whether I prayed this morning.' In a little while he added, 'Yes, Siencyn, you prayed and you read. I heard you with my own ears.' 'Ah yes, you talked enough. But the question is: Did heaven hear you? Did you pray, man?' Suddenly, he thought that Satan was standing in front of him and saying, 'Siencyn, you have never truly prayed in your life, let alone prayed today.' With this he stood, as if struck. He raised his staff and cried out with great strength, 'That is a lie, Satan.' It was not long before the tempter fled. This victory gave him new life, and he shouted out so that the hills were echoing, 'Satan, come back. Come back now. I am going to pray now, and you can be my witness.' With that he dropped to his knees, and having gained an open door to the Father, he rose again to his feet and shouted again, 'Let our enemies be the judges! Glory! Satan has fled! I call upon God and the holy angels to be witnesses on my behalf.' Siencyn Thomas returned from the mountain that day more than conqueror.

He was very careful with his affairs, fully believing with the apostle that he who does not provide for his own is worse than an infidel. At one time there was to be preaching at Dyffryn Chapel in the middle of a weekday. At the time, he was in trouble with his animals; they were breaking through into his wheat. He felt that he should be continuing with the work of mending his hedges rather than attending at the chapel. But he was overcome by his wish to be at the service. He pushed his gloves and billhook into some hiding place and off he went. The sermon was under evident blessing; many warm 'Amens' were heard from various parts of the chapel and he himself felt stirred to cry out an 'Amen'. But just then, the devil suggested to him that someone in passing had stolen the gloves and billhook. His spirit cooled for a time. But there was an unction upon the sermon, and the warmth of the meeting was increasing further. Again he was stirred by the knowledge that the truth was sweeter than honey, and was on the point of shouting forth 'Hallelujah', when the devil whispered to him again: 'The billhook and gloves are stolen, as certain as it is day.' He was overcome by the enemy this time again. By now, Dyffryn Chapel was almost ablaze in praises. The saints had pulled down their harps from the willows and were playing sweetly upon them. Siencyn longed to rejoice with them but again, a third time, Satan thrust the thought of the billhook into his mind. But by now his excitement was too strong for Satan to damp down, and Siencyn bellowed forth, 'The billhook, devil? What is that to do with thee? If it is stolen, what is that? It belongs to me; I have paid honestly for it. Satan, let the billhook be about thy neck to all eternity. Hallelujah! Praise be to him who bought us on the tree!' The congregation must have been baffled on hearing him, not knowing anything of gloves or billhook.

As with all the believers of old, the chief sin over which Siencyn watched and prayed most was pride. One day, he and the Rev. David Jones, Llangan, were riding together to some meeting. Mr Jones had only recently returned from one of his visits to London. Siencyn Thomas feared for him, though they were the closest of friends, in case the praises that had been showered upon him from all directions in the city should have stirred up his pride. Mr Jones was riding a few paces in front. He suddenly felt two or three light taps on the crown of his head and on turning round saw that they had been administered by the walking stick of his friend from Penhydd. 'Sianco, Sianco,' he said. 'What on earth are you doing?' 'Keeping you down, sir,' said he. 'You have been to London and received much respect from the great men; you need a few taps on the head to keep it from swelling.' Mr Jones laughed heartily, and received the advice in the same spirit as it was given.

We could add much more about Siencyn Thomas, but we believe that our readers now have a clear picture of his attributes. He was a plain and honest man; he feared God greatly and was no respecter of persons; he had the eyes of a hawk to discern the spiritual character of those before him, and great ability in adapting his words to the circumstances. His wildness, his rough looks, and the occasional coarseness of his words were appropriate for the age and for the people amongst whom he lived. He made an indelible impression upon the inhabitants of his neighbourhood. For all his physical strength, he died comparatively young, and was buried in Aberavon cemetery. Above the grave, on the tombstone, is carved the following:

In memory of Jenkin Thomas of Goetre, Margam parish,
who departed this world December 26, 1807, when 61 years old.

'Put on the whole armour of God, that ye may be able to stand
against the wiles of the devil.'

Mawr elw im' fu marwolaeth – fe nodwyd
Im' fynediad helaeth
I fuddiol etifeddiaeth,
Fel y lli' o fêl a llaeth.

Top: The Lodge, in Llandinam Parish, Montgomeryshire, where Howell Harris in 1740 preached his first sermon in North Wales
Middle: Tyddyn, in Llandinam Parish, the home of Mr and Mrs Bowen
Bottom: Bala Chapel in 1900, the site of the first Methodist Chapel in Merionethshire

Top: John Evans of Bala
Bottom: Llanycil Church and Cemetery, on the banks of Bala Lake. Many well-known Methodists are buried here: John Evans, Thomas Charles, Simon Lloyd, Lewis Edwards, John Parry, Dafydd Cadwaladr, etc.

Coffadwriaeth

— AM —

JOHN EVANS,

O DREF Y BALA,

Yr hwn a fu 60 Mlynedd

YN BREGETHWR YN MHLITH Y METHODISTIAID,

YN NGHYMRU,

Ac a fu farw 12fed o Awst, 1817, yn 96 Mlwydd oed.

— Fel Dyn —

YR OEDD

YN MEDDU AR GYNNEDDFAU CRYFION, A DEALL CYFLYM:

Fel Cymmydog

YN BARCHUS A CHYMERADWY,

GAN FOD YN GYFIAWN YN EI FASNACH FYDOL,

A DIWYD YN EI ALWEDIGAETH;

— Fel Priod —

YN WR TYNER A CHARUAIDD, AC YN GOFALU AM EI DY:

Fel Pregethwr

MYNEGODD YN FFYDDLON HOLL GYNGHOR DUW:

Fel Cristion

YN ISRAELIAD YN WIR, YN YR HWN NID OEDD DWYLL.

AM SAIL EI FFYDD,

PAN OFYNWYD IDDO YN EI ORIAU OLAF

Dywedodd:

NID OES GENYF I BWYSO ARNO

OND

IESU O NAZARETH.

In Memory

of

John Evans

of Bala

For 60 years

a preacher among the Methodists

in Wales

Who died 12th of August 1817 aged 96 years

As a man

strikingly gifted and with a quick mind;

As a neighbour

respected and well-liked,

just in his business affairs,

diligent in his calling;

As a husband

gentle, loving, caring for his household;

As a preacher

he faithfully declared the whole counsel of God;

As a Christian

an Israelite indeed, without guile.

When asked in his last hour

for the basis of his faith,

he said:

'I have no-one to depend on but

Jesus of Nazareth'.

The epitaph on John Evans's grave in Llanycil Cemetery and its English translation

Places associated with Robert Roberts, Clynnog:
1. Ffridd-bala-deulyn, where he was born 2. Ynysgaled, his wife's home 3. Capel Uchaf, Clynnog, where he was a member. It was built in 1761, the first Methodist Chapel in Caernarvonshire 4. Ebenezer Chapel, Clynnog 5. Clynnog Village. *Eben Fardd* lived in the white cottage. 6. The chapel house of Ebenezer Chapel, Clynnog, together with *Eben Fardd's* schoolhouse 7. Beuno Church and Cemetery. Robert Roberts's grave is near the white memorial 8. His grave in Beuno Church Cemetery

Top Left: Robert Jones, Rhos-lan
Top Right: Robert Dafydd, Brynengan
Middle: Tirbach
Bottom: Brynengan Chapel

Top: John Roberts, Llangwm
Middle: Llangwm Chapel
Bottom: Cefn-nanau, John Roberts's home

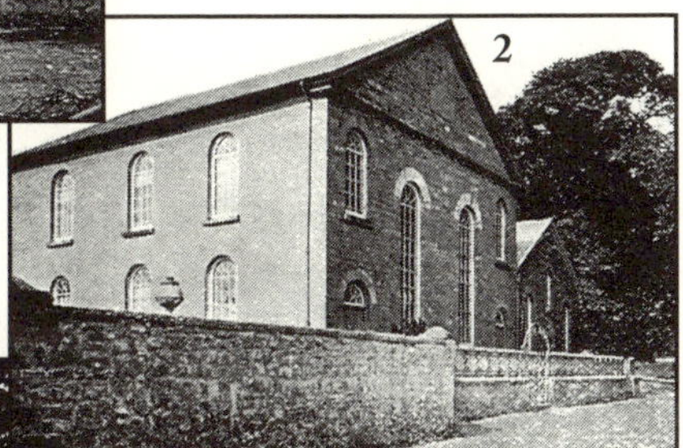

TOP: PENRHIW, NEAR BALA, THE HOME OF DAFYDD CADWALADR
1-4: PLACES ASSOCIATED WITH WILLIAM THOMAS, PYLE AND SIENCYN THOMAS, PENHYDD: 1. TYDRAW, NEAR PYLE, THE HOME OF WILLIAM THOMAS
2. PYLE CHAPEL, 1900 3. PENHYDD FARM, SIENCYN THOMAS'S BIRTHPLACE
4. CWMAFAN CHURCH AND CEMETERY, WHERE SIENCYN THOMAS IS BURIED

28

CHRISTOPHER BASSETT, THOMAS GRAY, AND EDWARD COSLET

CHRISTOPHER BASSETT

We have complained with respect to many of the Fathers of Methodism that very little of their histories were written down, and we are inclined to blame those who knew them and survived them for their carelessness. But matters are different for the Rev. Christopher Bassett because a short biography of him was written by *'Dafydd ab Ioan'* in the form of a letter to *'Ioan ab Gwilym,* the poet'. Our interest in this letter increases when we realize that its author, *'Dafydd ab Ioan'* was none less than the Rev. David Jones, Llan-gan, and the *'Ioan ab Gwilym'* to whom it was sent was the famous hymn writer and poet, John Williams of St Athan. It is true that the biography is much too short; that it leaves us with a host of matters connected with Bassett that we would wish to know more of – some knowledge of his childhood, his first religious impressions, the means used to bring him to a true knowledge of the Saviour and rest upon him for his salvation, etc. But rather than complain of that which is deficient we are thankful for what is available, and for the fact that the character of one of the godliest young men ever to arise in Glamorganshire has been kept for posterity.

BORN OF A NOBLE FAMILY

Christopher Bassett was born in the Vale of Glamorgan. His parents, Christopher and Alice Bassett, lived at Aberthaw in the parish of Penmark, within a mile of the most southerly spot in Wales. It seems they were both Methodists, having been converted most probably under Howell Harris's awakening ministry, in that he often visited the area. It is clear also that they were prosperous and enjoyed a respected position in society; indeed, they belonged to one of the noblest old families of Glamorganshire. Their son Christopher was born at a time when religion was in decline, when controversy and division had entered the societies, namely in 1735, when the sad disruption between Harris and Rowland was at its height. But it does not appear that the parents were carried away by the strong feelings that existed at the time; they clung to the cause through thick and thin. Their greatest desire was that their son might be called to the ministry. They made every effort to give him the necessary education and they prayed fervently that God would grant him the necessary gifts and godliness for the office. His own inclination lay in the same direction and his biographer commented that it was no presumption to declare that he had been called from the womb to be a servant of Jesus of Nazareth. Mr Jones added that Bassett was the only clergyman raised in Glamorganshire that century, as far as was known, who, while holding to his calling in the Church of England and to its articles of faith, had a true love and desire for the success of the gospel. Jones, Llan-gan, knew the clergy of the region well and his words are therefore an awful condemnation of their irreligious lives. When fairly young, Christopher was sent to the grammar school at Cowbridge, a school of some renown, which had been endowed through the generosity of Sir Leonine Jenkins, and was at the time under the principalship of Mr Thomas Williams. Christopher was there for some years, making great progress in the various branches of knowledge but without losing anything of his religion, nor of the seriousness of his behaviour, nor indeed of his allegiance to the Methodists. It was while he was here that he first came into contact with Mr Jones. The parish of Llan-gan was only five miles, as the crow flies, from Cowbridge and the boy, Christopher, would probably have crossed over the hill, past Pen-llin Castle, on many a Sunday, to hear that famous man preaching the gospel to the hundreds that gathered there.

Having finished his studies at Cowbridge, his father gave him the choice of either living at home or of going to Oxford. This, no doubt, the father did in order to prove him, because of his longing for his son to commit himself to the ministry. The son's reply was all that his father could wish for. 'I hope,' he said, 'that I may spend my life in the work of declaring God's truth to my fellow creatures, to the glory of Jesus and the eternal good of men.' This decided the matter. Christopher would go to Oxford, and he entered Jesus College. We know how corrupt and ungodly were the morals of Oxford at the time. Howell Harris had had to leave the place because of its ungodliness and it does not seem to have improved to any extent by the time Bassett arrived, for the Methodists that had been of some use in the University had all departed and little of their influence appears to have survived. But the purity of the young man from Aberthaw was so established and the grace of God in his heart so strong, that he returned from there without having received any harm and with his M.A. degree. The first M.A. belonging to the Methodists was either that of Christopher Bassett of the Vale of Glamorgan or that of Nathaniel Rowland, the son of the old Apostle of Llangeitho. It was probably Nathaniel, in that he was a few years older than Christopher.

CURATE TO WILLIAM ROMAINE

He was ordained by the Bishop of London and was called to be a curate of the Rev. William Romaine at St Anne's, Blackfriars. We have already referred to Mr Romaine as a notably evangelical clergyman who was on very friendly terms with many of the Welsh Methodists. The two men therefore, vicar and curate, were in complete accord. Mr Bassett gave himself fully to the work of the gospel in London; he preached with power and influence and as well as serving at St Anne's gave weekly lectures at St Ethelburga's Church. He seems however to have always been of poor health and his labours in the city proved too much for his constitution. He was soon struck by a heavy fever that brought him near to death. His parents believed that the London air was harmful to him and they persuaded him to return to Wales. He was granted a curacy at St Fagans, a beautiful village about three miles from Cardiff. According to *Methodistiaeth Cymru*, he arrived here in the year 1778, so that he would have been about twenty-five years old. The Methodists had a society in the village since 1740. Howell Harris had preached here many times. But the cause was in a poor condition when Christopher Bassett arrived. Thomas Llewelyn of Ysgubor Fawr, in whose house the preaching was held, had died two years previously and God's Ark had therefore no fixed home. Mr Bassett threw in his lot with the Methodists and his coming proved a great quickening to the religion of the area. In the village, a certain Bartholomew Williams owned a house which was licensed for dancing for the youth of the region and where the harp would often be playing until dawn. Mr Bassett rented the room and turned it into a meeting-house for the Methodists. The societies and the prayer meetings were now held here, and here the travelling exhorters, those who were not allowed to speak in the church though many were of considerable ability, preached their sermons. The curate ensured that some of the chief among the Methodists, clergymen and exhorters, visited St Fagans, and many of the meetings held in the old room will be remembered to all eternity. Edward Coslet was there scores of times and Dafydd Morris also. Later, though not when Christopher Bassett was curate, his son Ebenezer Morris also visited. Its walls echoed a hundred times to the sound of the praises and songs of the warm-hearted worshippers of old. Mr

Bassett was more of a Methodist than a Churchman, though he fulfilled all his duties in the parish most responsibly.

APPOINTED TO THE CURACY OF ST FAGANS

Whilst living in St Fagans, Christopher Bassett journeyed about to preach the gospel and like his friend, David Jones, Llan-gan, he was not concerned whether the building where he preached was episcopally consecrated to the purpose or not. We do not have the history of his travels but it is certain that he journeyed throughout Wales more than once. We find that he was once in the Clwyd Valley, accompanying either Daniel Rowland or Jones, Llan-gan, and that he had a remarkable service in Llandyrnog parish. Great rejoicing broke out. Mr Bassett was jumping as a hart as were the majority of the congregation, among whom were the daughters of Plas Llangwyfen, who had been lately converted. He was not long at St Fagans, though it does not seem that he was turned out. Many attempts were made to find him a living where he might work independently, but though many promises were given, nothing was obtained. His biographer wrote:

> The father, because of the love that many of the great men of the world professed for him, had a right to expect a promotion for his son to one of the larger parishes. But whenever the time came for their love to be proved, they kept away, using Felix's lame excuse: 'When I have a convenient season.' And when the opportunity arose, as it did on many an occasion, for him to be accepted amongst their learned doctors and to receive something of their worldly portion, they could not but reveal, at those times, the old enmity to the truth that governs the heart of every natural man, though the truth might be flowing from the lips of a Master of the Arts.

This was written by the Rev. David Jones, Llan-gan, and it may be seen that he attributes the refusal of the office of rector or vicar to Christopher Bassett, by those who had the responsibility of appointing to Church livings, to their enmity to the truth. It might be thought that there was every qualification for high office in the young man: he was of a good family; he was a learned man, having graduated at Oxford; and he was completely committed to his duties. But he possessed three great disqualifications in the eyes of the squires and bishops of the Church of England at the time: he was godly; he believed the evangelical doctrines as taught by the Articles of the Church; and he mixed with the Methodists. For such a young man there was no hope of promotion. If he were to get drunk at times and if, particularly, he were to become known as a persecutor of those religious people that were trying to save Wales from the clutches of the devil, his prospects would have been much more hopeful. But being as he was, he was never more than curate all his life.

A little before his death he moved to Porthceri, near his father's home. It seems that he had the curacy of the nearby church. At the same time he supervised the Methodist society at Aberthaw. Here he was notably successful. His biographer wrote:

> The voice of the turtledove attracted many people who were glad to be received amongst his small flock, a flock whose numbers kept on increasing up to the day of his death.

This was the time of God's right hand for the Methodists of the Vale of Glamorgan. But Christopher Bassett's bright star was unfortunately about to set. His constitution was always weak and sometime during the August of 1793, on a very hot Sunday, he preached at Cray in Breconshire. The small church was crowded and the place unbearably hot. The preacher felt his strength draining from him halfway through his sermon, and an agonizing pain in his lungs forced him to stop. He recovered after the service but did not take sufficient care after having sweated so much. As a result he caught a chill and this led to consumption. Soon a vein burst, he lost much blood, and developed a continual cough. His doctor advised him to visit the spas near Bristol. He thought there that he was regaining his strength but this is a common mistake that is often made by those afflicted with this disease. Jones, Llan-gan, loved him as Jonathan loved David and went to stay with him at Bath for a month. The description he gives of their fellowship is most touching:

> My spirit rejoiced to see him so improved. He came out to walk with me towards the fountains. As we went on together conversing, I could see that his breath was getting shorter. This melted my soul. I groaned to myself, 'We are certain to lose our friend, Bassett.' When walking in the garden in front of the house where he lodged, I had cause to fear that he would never see Wales again. When climbing a slight slope in the garden, I saw that he did not possess the two things necessary to face again the Welsh mountains – the long, free breath, and the strong knees . . . Our conversation one day revolved particularly around the nature of the land beyond the sun. I had reason to judge, in the course of the conversation, that he was no stranger to that land. He spoke to me often of the fellowship of that place, and I saw clearly that he had a surer grasp of the glorious Lord of heaven even than the consumption had of him.

On his bed of sickness his spirit was notably heavenly; one could almost imagine that the eternal Canaan had reached across to him over the Jordan. He said once:

> I see now that I can never preach again, but if God allows me to improve a little I would be happy to be a doorkeeper in his house.

He would often ask his sister to read Psalm 103 to him, but once she came to the fifth verse, 'Who satisfieth thy mouth with good things; so that thy youth is renewed as the eagle's', he would say, 'That is enough, enough, enough!' He would also draw much comfort from Matthew 18:21,22, where Jesus counsels his disciples to forgive one another until seventy times seven. No doubt he saw this as some pale shadow of God's forgiveness, and he thanked God over and over for the 'seventy times seven'. Upheld by these verses, Christopher Bassett died on 8 February 1784, in the thirty-first year of his life. These verses were those chosen by Mr Jones, Llan-gan as the text of his funeral sermon. We believe that it was in Bristol, in his sister's house, that Christopher Bassett died, but the earth of Wales was given the privilege of guarding his dust, for his body was laid to rest at St Athan, near his parents' home. The Poet of Pantycelyn testifies of his godliness, the virtues of his character, and his abilities as a preacher:

> He was a godly, learned and virtuous man; a warm and sober preacher, authoritative in the doctrines of Holy Scripture; an able leader of pilgrims through the pleasant paths of Christ's redemption; and, presently, great sorrow is felt at his loss throughout the south and the north of Wales.

As might be expected from the tenderness of his temperament, Bassett was an evangelist; it was the gentler aspects of the gospel that he most often proclaimed to his hearers. He preferred to attract them with the mercies of the promises than to frighten them with the terror of the threats. He took his stand upon Calvary. Christ's death as a sufficient sacrifice for a guilty world was the favourite theme of his ministry. On hundreds of occasions he drew forth tears of love from his Welsh congregations.

THOMAS GRAY

Thomas Gray was an Independent minister who joined himself to the Methodists and proceeded to fill a prominent place amongst them. He seems to have been born in the Morriston region and into a very poor family. His date of birth is not known. He grew up without any religion whatsoever; indeed, he was notable for his ungodliness. He was considered the greatest drunkard in the coal pit where he worked, and the coarsest of tongues, so that his name was proverbial amongst his fellow workers as an example of immoral behaviour. But God had gracious thoughts concerning the youth. One day, the manager of the coal works sent him on a message to Neath. He went, and having fulfilled his task, turned, as was his custom, to the tavern, where he proceeded to get drunk. From there he found a field where he lay down to sleep. But in the meantime an accident had occurred in the pits. The rope by which the men descended to the depths broke and all of Thomas Gray's group of workers were killed immediately. The young man was spotted sleeping by someone who knew him, who awoke him, saying, 'What? Tom Gray, is it you? I thought you had been in hell for hours.' He then told him of the tragic accident. This affected him greatly. He believed that he truly would have been in hell had it not been for the intervention of providence. He was completely sobered and began to consider his ways and to abhor them. He went to hear the gospel at Mynyddbach, Swansea, and it was not long before he joined the flock there.

He began immediately to be as active and committed to religion as he had been before to his drinking. The fraternity recognized his ministerial gifts and pressed him to begin preaching. Soon he attended the Independent Academy at Abergavenny. In a little while, Daniel Rowland passed through the neighbourhood and was announced to preach at a nearby church in the town. Rowland's name at that time was famous throughout Wales. The students felt a strong desire to hear him, such was his fame, yet their prejudice against the Church and its clergymen was a powerful obstacle. But, for all their prejudice, they attended, with Gray amongst them. Rowland was granted a powerful service; the congregation held their breath in fear as he pronounced destruction upon an unbelieving world. Whatever the effect upon the other students, Gray was completely overcome. The influence remained on his mind for weeks afterwards. He could not pursue his studies or take hold of a book; he wandered through the fields in a daze, sometimes praying and at other times meditating. He felt a deep longing that his lot would fall in such a place that he might have opportunity to hear this clergyman and he expressed his longing in fervent prayers to the Lord.

His prayer was answered. When his studies at the Academy were about to end, the church at Llwynpiod, Cardiganshire, requested the college tutor to send some young man whom he judged would prove a good minister, to them on probation. The tutor sent Thomas Gray. Thomas arrived in Llwynpiod one Saturday evening. He lodged at the home of one of the deacons, who told him that the service the next morning would be at eight o'clock in the morning, and added that the congregation was in the habit of attending the Church at Llangeitho on the last Sunday of every month to hear the clergyman, a man called Rowland. It seems that the time of the service at Llwynpiod was changed to eight in the morning as an act of self-defence. If it were held at the same time as the Llangeitho service there would be none present. Thomas Gray was amazed at his comment, nor was it very acceptable to him. At that time, most Nonconformists were bitterly opposed to the Church and its clergy. However the young man did not start an argument and, after preaching, joined the crowd that streamed towards Llangeitho. He was amazed again to see the huge numbers that were gathering from all directions; the highways were crowded, the people almost stepping on one another's toes. Gray concluded that this clergyman must be a remarkable man. On reaching Llangeitho and viewing the preacher, he realized that it was the man he had heard at Abergavenny. All his suspicions evaporated, he only felt great gratitude that he could receive such ministry again. The result of this visit of Gray's to Llwynpiod Church was that he was called to be a minister over them as a successor to Philip Pugh.

APPOINTED AS SUCCESSOR TO PHILIP PUGH

The church at Llwynpiod deserves more attention than we have so far given it. Preaching had begun in the area very early on – in the Puritan period in fact. Amongst the famous two thousand that were evicted after the passing of the Act of Uniformity there were three men from this part of Cardiganshire: Rhys Powell of Lampeter; John Harris of Tregaron; and Thomas Evans of Ystrad. Over the years, a congregation of Presbyterians had been gathered at Llwynrhys, a farmhouse between Llwynpiod and Llangeitho. The few believers usually met at night; they did not dare do so in the day for fear of being imprisoned and deprived of their possessions. The preacher who ministered to them in sacred things was Dafydd Jones, who lived at Llwynrhys. This Dafydd Jones had a son who was a soldier, from whom he had not heard a word for many years. One day the preacher saw a relatively young gentleman, of military appearance and mounted upon a horse, approaching his house. From his appearance he concluded that the man was an officer of some rank. In those days of persecution, a visit from officers of the state could only mean trouble and Dafydd Jones believed that the man had come to imprison him because he had broken the law by preaching the gospel. His wife thought the same but they decided to tell the truth whatever might be the consequences. The rider came up to the house and knocked on the door. The old lady went to receive him. 'Is this Llwynrhys?' he asked. 'Yes,' she replied, full of fear. 'Is this where Dafydd Jones lives?' The old lady thought that her worst fears were confirmed and she fell to the floor in a faint. At that, Dafydd Jones came to the door. 'Leave her alone. She is completely innocent.' The officer could not restrain himself further and he cried out, 'Father, I won't harm her. She is my mother!' And so it proved to be. Because of his bravery the young man had been promoted to officer in the cavalry, and had now come to visit his parents. By his influence he was able to keep persecution away from Llwynrhys. An extension was built to the house, where a considerable number of believers were able to meet secretly to worship God. When the Act of Toleration was passed in 1689, Llwynrhys was registered under the law and the congregation met there until a chapel was built at Llwynpiod, about a mile away. This was in the year 1700 and at a cost of thirteen pounds.

Mr Philip Pugh, Thomas Gray's predecessor, had charge of quite a few small Presbyterian or Independent churches. As well as Llwynpiod, he ministered at Abermeurig, Neuaddlwyd, Cilgwyn, and Ciliau Aeron. But by the time of Mr Gray's settlement the last two had become poisoned by the unevangelical Arminianism that was at that time spreading as a disease through many parts of the land. These two churches, together with other Nonconformist causes in Cardiganshire, gradually became Arian in their views, and by now they are completely Unitarian. Only Llwynpiod, Abermeurig and Neuaddlwyd, therefore, were left to Thomas Gray. He does not seem to have mixed much amongst the Independents after his settlement. He came under Daniel Rowland's influence and greatly desired to join the Methodists. Rowland restrained him for some time, teasing him, 'You work on that side of the mountain, and I'll work on this side, until we meet.' But Rowland would have him to preach once a month at Llangeitho. He was able to do this at the time as he had been turned out of the Church and Gwynfil Chapel had been built for him. This arrangement continued throughout their lives.

We said above that Neuaddlwyd was one of Mr Gray's churches when he first began ministering in Cardiganshire. Our authority for this statement was the late Rev. John Rees, Tregaron, a sweet preacher, who had an excellent memory. He had been raised in the neighbourhood and brought up at Mr Gray's feet. His testimony therefore may be depended on. His account is as follows:

> It is said that Mr Gray, when young, was a minister over the Independents at Neuaddlwyd. He would preach warmly, zealously and with much life, so affecting many of the young people that they would repeat the hymns after the sermon, and he would sing with them also for an hour or two. Verses like the following would be repeated many times over amidst great rejoicing:

The smallest drop of blood	Mae dafn bach o waed
Is weightier in heaven,	Yn drymach yn y nef,
Than all the guilt and shame	Na'r pechod mwyaf gaed,

That burden sinful men;	A'i holl euogrwydd ef;
The voice of Calvary's wounds prevails	Gwrandewir llais y dwyfol glwy',
O'er all their dark condemning wails.	O flaen eu damniol floeddiad hwy.

The old deacons of the cause at the time were staunch men of even temperaments, no such sounds or disorders were to be allowed amongst them. They considered the minister to be foolish. It was disruptive to good order to sing with gusto amongst the young people in this way. They therefore removed him as minister over them. One of the members, Thomas Davies of Ty'nyporth, asked one of the deacons, 'Why are you turning Mr Gray away, without informing the members?' But they were determined to remove him. 'Well, Mr Gray,' said Thomas Davies, 'though they have turned you out of Neuaddlwyd, come with me. You can preach at my house.' Mr Gray ministered there for many months, and on part of the farm tenanted by Thomas Davies another chapel was raised for him, namely Ffos-y-ffin. His preaching there was so effective that he drew hearers from thirteen parishes, and there, both pastor and people were at liberty to sing as much as they wished of the atoning blood of the cross. Two other chapels were built for him afterwards, one at Llanarth and another at Llanddewi-Aberarth. He was also the minister at Abermeurig and Llwynpiod.

Such was the report given by the Rev. John Rees, and quite apart from the fact that Mr Rees was a faithful witness and in a good position to know, his report carries with it its own evidence of its truthfulness. It is known that when the Revival broke out, and for many years afterwards, the old Nonconformists were legalistic men, cold of temper, with their religious services having become very formal and lifeless. This is the description of them given even by one of their own, namely Dr John Thomas of Liverpool. The warmth of the Revival was unbearable to them. They viewed the singing and rejoicing that filled the Methodist camps as disorder, or even as something worse. On the other hand, Llangeitho's fire had caught hold of the spirit of young Mr Gray. He bore it with him into the Nonconformist pulpits and the Independents of Neuaddlwyd could not tolerate it. Mr Rees's essay corrects another mistake into which Dr Thomas Rees and the Independents have fallen. They claim that Ffos-y-ffin Chapel was an old Nonconformist chapel and that it went over to the Methodists only with the desertion of Mr Gray. We now see that it never once belonged to the Independents but was built for Mr Gray when he was turned out of Neuaddlwyd.

As we have mentioned Ffos-y-ffin Chapel, the elders of this church deserve some attention. They appear to have been men who were, many of them, strong in the Scriptures. In religious circles they were viewed as princes, as their influence was extensive in the Monthly Meetings and even in the Associations. Their leader was undoubtedly Thomas Davies, Ty'nyporth, whom we have already mentioned. He was more a smallholder than a farmer but was brave of heart and ready with his words. He was listened to everywhere – as much in a parish council, or a Monthly Meeting, as in his society meeting at home. According to one who knew him well:

> Thomas, Ty'nyporth, had only to say to the farmers of the locality, 'You go to collect stones. You go to cut down wood,' and they would obey him without even asking why. They received his commands as the commands of a king.

He would attend the Associations in the north as well as the south, and was instrumental in getting many of the main preachers of the Connexion to come on journeys through Cardiganshire. He would always begin services for Mr Gray. On one Sunday it had rained heavily all day and his shirt was wet through. He had already begun three services and there were ten miles of road to walk before getting home that night. He began to feel angry with himself and to ask himself, 'Why do I have to walk so much more than others on a Sunday?' But as he passed a large mansion in which he could see a feast being held and hear the dancing and ungodly singing of those invited, his complaining stopped immediately and he said, 'Glory be to God; I would never yet exchange my situation with those!' His soul had been dry during the services of the day but his walk home more than compensated for all.

He had no fear of any man. A famous preacher from the north preached at Ffos-y-ffin during harvest time and a large crowd had gathered to hear him. As the people came out of the chapel at the end of the service, a gentleman of the locality happened to be passing, with three of his servants. He turned in anger to Thomas Davies and asked him, 'Tomos, what's the point of calling the people from the fields at this time?' He answered with perfect composure, 'The Day of Judgment will reveal that, sir.' The gentleman departed without a further word.

He was once called to be a witness in a court case and an arrogant lawyer, having no respect for God, began to cross-examine him:

'Well, Mr Methodist.'

'Well, Mr Prosecutor,' he replied.

'You follow your religion with old Gray, do you not?'

'I do.'

'Do you pray?'

'I do,' he answered, and then, turning to the magistrates, said, 'Sirs, I never thought that today was the Day of Judgment and that I would have to answer for my religion.'

'You should be ashamed of yourself,' said the chairing magistrate to the lawyer, 'leave this man's religion out of the matter and only ask what relates to the case.'

The other elders at Ffos-y-ffin were John Dafydd, who was also something of an exhorter, Jenkin Sion, and Ishmael Ishmael. The Rev. Ebenezer Richard used to say that he never heard doctrinal points being discussed better in the Monthly Meeting than by the elders of Ffos-y-ffin.

THOMAS GRAY'S RELATIONSHIP WITH THE METHODISTS

But to return to Mr Gray. We doubt whether he ever formally joined himself to the Methodists, but it is certain that he considered himself one of them. He never attended the conferences of the Independents and would never be present at their most important meetings, whereas he would be always present at the Associations, taking a prominent part in discussions and being asked to preach at the most popular times. *Methodistiaeth Cymru* is hardly correct in portraying him as in a similar position to Richard Tibbott. Tibbott, in the latter part of his life, was an Independent who had much sympathy for the Methodists; who received the Connexion's preachers on the same basis as those of his own denomination, and was received into the Methodist pulpits. But Mr Gray had put aside all contact with the Independents on coming to Llwynpiod, or at least very soon afterwards when he was thrown out of Neuaddlwyd. There is no subsequent history of his ever having attended any Quarterly Meeting or Assembly of theirs. He lived amongst the Methodists and with them only he mixed. Many ministers came over from the Independents in this way, the Rev. Benjamin Thomas being another example. It was hardly considered that a formal reception was necessary for them. Almost imperceptibly to themselves and to others, they slipped into their places within the Connexion.

At the same time, the congregations at Llwynpiod and Abermeurig considered themselves to be Independent causes. It is said that the minister's inclination to the Methodists and his close friendship with Rowland caused some discontent in the older members, and that he threatened to leave because of it. But as the tide of the Revival came in, making much inroads into the churches at Llwynpiod and Abermeurig as well as at Ffos-y-ffin, and bringing with it great increase in numbers, the opposition melted away. Eventually that older generation to whom the principles of Congregationalism were dear, died away, and the succeeding generation was wholly sympathetic to the Methodists. Long before the death of Mr Gray they considered themselves to be Methodists. For some years they maintained their own way of administering the Lord's Supper but gradually that practice ended and the present members hardly realize at all that there was once a connection between themselves and the Independents.

Thomas Gray's friendship with Daniel Rowland was certainly of great advantage to him as a preacher. At the outset he tended to be lacking in taste. He knew nothing of the principles of oratory and would express his message clearly and without respect of persons, but rather bluntly. Rowland therefore advised him to change his style. 'Put a shirt on the truth,' he told him. He received the counsel humbly and gained for himself a worthy position amongst the preachers of the Connexion. The prominent place given to him in the Associations shows that he was considered one of the masters of the congregation. It is said that at times he would have notable services when the influence accompanying his message would be overpowering.

The old people who remembered Mr Gray described him as a large man of rough appearance, his face scarred by the marks of smallpox. He had a strong, powerful voice and spoke warmly and with fire, just like the early Methodists. There was nothing in his style of the old Independents. Many of his sayings and portions of his sermons were remembered by the older Methodists of Cardiganshire fifty years ago, but most of them are now long forgotten. Here is an account of him preaching at Morriston, his birthplace, with Mr Charles of Bala. His theme was the relationship between justification and sanctification:

> Some place justification on the back of sanctification; but sanctification is too weak to hold it, and breaks down, broken-kneed. This, as you know, is how it was with David. But if you place sanctification on the back of justification, it can carry it nimbly all the way to heaven.

The Rev John Rees added:

> There was deep affection between himself and the church there, and such an unction and success accompanied his preaching that the whole congregation was melted.

The influence that was felt during one sermon of his at an Association held on the beach at Fishguard, not far from where the French invaders surrendered their arms, is still remembered today. This was in May 1797. His text was, 'Christ hath redeemed [Welsh = *'llwyr brynodd'*, 'fully redeemed'] us from the curse of the law, being made a curse for us.' He emphasized the '*fully* redeemed':

> Sometimes the corn is damaged by a wet harvest and the farmer must therefore sell it at sixpence the measure cheaper. The merchants at Bristol will

> sometimes receive goods from the West Indies that have been damaged on the voyage and must sell those things at a cheaper price. When these are bought at the shop, the shopkeeper must ask for less. The handkerchief will be sold for many pence cheaper. Things that are damaged must be sold at less than cost price. My dear people! We have been damaged by the great fall in Eden, but when it came to buying us the Man would not have the price dropped by a farthing; nothing less would buy us than he himself; 'Who gave himself for us.' 'Fully redeemed! Fully redeemed!'

The illustration has been used countless times in Welsh pulpits since but it belongs to Mr Gray.

Towards the end of his sermon, as he commented on the last sentence of his text, 'being made a curse for us', he shouted out with a power that not even the strongest could withstand, 'O great Jesus! Did you carry the blasphemy of the blasphemer? Yes. Did you, O great Jesus, carry the robberies of the thief? Yes. Did you bear the murders of the murderer? Yes. Fully redeemed! 'Being made a curse for us!'

It is said that he was particularly cunning when preaching after a popular preacher who had raised a congregation to a high level of excitement. He would use means to cool their heat a little before proceeding himself. In that he was an ordained minister, and by now quite old, Ebenezer Morris, Roberts, Clynnog, and others of the more remarkable preachers of that generation would never preach after him, but before him. Once, when rising after one such seraph, he was a long time finding his text. He told his listeners that he had a text and that it was in that book in which he was presently looking, and for some considerable time he waited, pretending to turn the pages backwards and forwards until gaining the complete attention of all the crowd. He then read his text and soon had a mastery over the congregation.

He used a similar stratagem during the remarkable Association held at Cardigan in 1796. Before him, Roberts, Clynnog, had preached from Revelation 10:1, 'And I saw another mighty angel come down from heaven, clothed with a cloud: and a rainbow was upon his head, and his face was as it were the sun, and his feet as pillars of fire.' It had been a notable sermon, even for Robert Roberts. The vast crowd has been raised to the highest enthusiasm. They were crying out, 'Thanks be unto God!' Mr Gray had been enjoying his brother's sermon as much as they, shouting, 'Glory!' louder than any. Once Roberts had finished, he got to his feet. 'My brother has been preaching famously,' he said. 'I wasn't allowed to speak before him, not because I am a better preacher but because I am older. I couldn't think what text to take after such a remarkable sermon, but that word came to me from Zechariah 13:1: 'A fountain opened . . . for sin and for uncleanness.' With that, he clapped his large hands together, and shouted in a most powerful voice, 'A fountain for washing us quite clean, dear people!' Accompanying the shout, a thrill ran through the whole crowd. Very soon, all preaching had to be given up, leaving the people glorying and rejoicing in the field.

Thomas Gray laboured amongst the Methodists for nearly fifty years, dying in the year 1810.

EDWARD COSLET

Edward Coslet belonged to the second generation of exhorters amongst the Methodists and was typical of many of them, possessing much natural talent and humour, zeal in abundance, a good grasp of the main truths of the gospel but very deficient in learning and without any culture. He was born in 1750 in the parish of Machen. Machen is a village on the banks of the Rhymney river, about seven miles from Newport and the same distance from Caerphilly. Its inhabitants were very few at the time of Coslet's birth and they spoke only Welsh. By today, coalmines have been opened and the area has become heavily populated, driving away all Welsh-speaking from the locality. Edward Coslet grew up with no religion at all. This was a dark time for Monmouthshire. The societies gathered together in Howell Harris's time had all been scattered during the Disruption; scores of professors had returned to their old ways and others had joined various denominations. There were Methodist societies only at Goetre, near Pontypool; at New Inn, Mynyddislwyn; and at Groes-wen. By the time Edward Coslet came of age, these societies had become half-Methodist, half-Independent, and were gradually sliding towards the Independents, though they received Methodist preachers to their pulpits. The minister at Groes-wen at the time was William Edwards, the builder, whom we have mentioned previously. He considered himself a Methodist and there was much of the Methodist spirit remaining in him. Under the influence of the inspiration produced in him by Howell Harris's ministry, he would visit the surrounding neighbourhoods to preach and on one evening he came to warn the ungodly of Machen, about four miles from Groes-wen. Among the crowd that gathered to hear him was Edward Coslet. He was by now a young man of nineteen years of age, strong of body and working as a blacksmith. An arrow from William Edward's bow penetrated his heart; he realized that he was a lost sinner before God, and a great fear rose up in him. From then on, he attended the chapel at Groes-wen regularly and, most probably, the same instrument that was used to wound him had also the privilege of pouring the balm of the gospel into his wounds. Edward gave himself to the Lord Jesus Christ forever, and joined with the church at Groes-wen.

Having been awakened to his own condition and having seen the sufficiency of the Saviour answering that condition, his heart was filled with compassion for his ignorant neighbours, who were for the most part completely irreligious. He opened his house to the gospel; he invited preachers there from far and near; and he himself paid their costs. He went also from door to door to exhort the people personally, and before leaving he would sometimes read a chapter from the Bible and pray. He never viewed this as the beginning of a path to the pulpit, it was only that God's fire burned in his spirit and he could not but warn sinners. His gift for prayer had by now become the topic of popular conversation. The Head of the Church had however purposed to entrust him with the gospel and there follows Islwyn's description of the way in which this first came about:

> Notice had been given of the engagement of a notable speaker at the home of the local blacksmith, Edward Coslet, one evening about a hundred years ago, in the village of Machen. But the speaker did not arrive in time, and for once the breaking of the engagement proved a great blessing. It was absolutely necessary for the service to proceed. Ned began the meeting, we suppose. He read with purpose and prayed for heaven's blessing upon Machen. The reading was over; the prayer was over. There was still no sign of a speaker. They went to the door and looked towards the steep slopes of Gwaren hill, but there was no one in sight. They sang one of Edmund Prys's psalms, for there were very few hymns to be had in those days, but having sung, still no preacher. They looked again towards the Gwaren: rabbits in their hundreds but no speaker. 'Well, well,' said one old brother, 'go and stand on the stool, Ned, and you give us a bit of a sermon.' Ned obeyed promptly, and preached to them with unusual power. He continued preaching for the next fifty-two years. Thanks be to that unknown speaker who broke his Machen engagement in 1776!

Thus, quite unplanned by himself, Edward Coslet found himself a preacher. He was now twenty-six years old, married for six years, and having many children. His wife is said to have been a very godly woman who proved a great help to him in the work of the gospel throughout her life. It hardly needs to be said that Coslet never attended any kind of academy. It was not usual for preachers to do so, nor even considered at all necessary in those days. Even if it had been, his domestic responsibilities were too great even for him to consider the possibility. It is doubtful whether a college education would have proved of any advantage to him, when considering the nature of his talent and the age in which he lived. According to Islwyn:

There was a college graduate in every parish of Wales at the time, but Wales was in its grave. The need at that time was for iron men, and here was a man of iron breaking forth. 'More beating,' said Ned. 'Beating the iron with one arm, and beating the devil with the other.'

It was not long after he had begun preaching that all work for a blacksmith dried up in the neighbourhood and he and his family moved to Castleton, a small village between Cardiff and Newport, in an area of great beauty. We are tempted again to quote Islwyn:

> Soon after he began exhorting, when about twenty-seven years old, we might see a wagon setting out from Machen carrying a few bits of furniture, a wife, two or three small children and, in particular, a shining anvil and weighty hammers, all on their way together to the pretty village of Castleton . . . The man at the head of the horse was strong of arm and heavily-muscled. Ned the blacksmith's vigour had often compensated for many a lame horse. But the bridge at Michaelston-y-Vedw had to be crossed and the long stretch of steep hill on the other side had to be faced, and the horse suddenly stopped as if its mind was made up. But Ned put his shoulder to the left rear wheel of the wagon, as if a steam engine had come from Rudri to help. Forward, Coslet! The move is worth the effort, you will not move again until you move to the land of your long home.

The neighbourhood of Castleton at the time Edward Coslet moved there was as dark as midnight in a religious sense. No one was concerned for his soul; no preaching was held, nor any denomination maintaining a cause for many miles. He and his wife were very troubled and they began to hunt for any who had a thought for the name of the Saviour. After much searching they found a small number of Baptists and of Independents. They succeeded in gathering these together and forming them into one church fellowship. They used to meet at Coed-y-Cernyw, a place about two miles from Castleton. A young gentlewoman, Miss Blanche Evans, would meet with them, who had been brought under religious convictions through the ministry of Jones, Llan-gan, Dafydd Morris, and others of the Methodist preachers. She was the only Methodist in fellowship at Coed-y-Cernyw, the others were considered Baptists or Independents. Many attempts were made to get Miss Evans to join one or other of these denominations but she would positively refuse. 'What objection do you have to doing so?' asked Edward Coslet, once. 'I incline towards the Methodists,' she replied, 'because it was through them I obtained relief, and I intend to request membership at Llan-gan.' 'So do I,' said Coslet. It seems that they would attend occasionally at Llan-gan before this, particularly on a communion Sunday, and on the next occasion they were received into membership there. There was some opposition to allowing Coslet preach among the Methodists as he had considered himself an Independent before, but having understood his feelings and having questioned him as to his views of the doctrines of the gospel, he was received not only as a member but also as an exhorter. It would not be inappropriate to add a few words about Miss Blanche Evans. Though she was a member of a responsible family and was wealthy in the things of this world, she spent her whole life amongst the poor Methodists, considering it a privilege to be able to wash the feet of the saints. She was notable for her charity and in her will she left between two and three thousand pounds to the Connexion. Her name remains a sweet savour in the districts of Castleton and St Mellons to this day, though there are scores of years since she was placed in her grave.

Directly after Edward Coslet and Miss Evans had joined the Methodists, a society was begun at the home of the former. It comprised of five members, Coslet and his wife, Miss Evans, and two others. But though the number was small, great glory would often attend their meetings, and 'the form of a Fourth' would be evident amongst them. The little flock would often break out in glory and praise; the sound of their singing would fill the village. This aroused opposition against them, and someone managed to persuade the owner of the house and forge to issue a warning to Coslet that he must either stop holding such meetings in the house or else leave it altogether. As a result another home had to be sought for the society, and it proved very difficult to find one. Eventually God's ark found a resting-place at St Mellons, a village about two miles from Castleton. In the long run the move proved of advantage to the gospel, in that the Castleton society became three societies: those of Castleton, St Mellons and Morfa. It could almost be said that Edward Coslet was the father of Methodism in Monmouthshire. He used to boast that he was the Connexion's best preacher in the county. 'You are remarkably egocentric,' someone told him, after hearing this remark. 'Oh no, sir,' he replied, 'because I am the only one.'

Like many of the old exhorters, Edward Coslet was a great walker. He had a strong, muscular body that enabled him to perform wonders while walking. Forty miles would be nothing to him of a Sunday afternoon, and that after a week's hard work over the anvil. He might walk on a Sabbath morning from Castleton to Merthyr Tydfil, a distance of twenty-five miles. Having preached energetically there, he would travel on foot to Llanfabon, another eight miles, by two o'clock. After again preaching powerfully, he would set out, strong in faith, towards Caerphilly, a journey of another six miles, arriving by six, and then, in the evening, the return journey home. On the morning of the following Monday, he would rise with the lark and the sound of his hammer on the anvil would be heard at five o'clock in the morning. Tradition has it that he remembered late one Friday night that he was engaged to preach the following Sunday at Llangeitho. He worked at the forge throughout the night and set out on his one hundred mile journey early on the Saturday. He had mountains to climb and deep valleys to cross, but the old exhorter was in the Llangeitho pulpit punctually before the nine o'clock service. Not only must his zeal have been great but his constitution also must have been as hard as the iron over which he worked for him to have accomplished such a journey.

EDWARD COSLET AS A PREACHER

He was a fiery preacher. The sparks would fly when he proclaimed the truth and often the ungodly would be filled with terror. 'Edward,' said Jones, Llan-gan, to him once after one very effective service, 'Where did you get that sermon?' 'In a study that you have never entered, sir,' was the reply. 'What place is that, Edward?' 'Between the fire and the anvil, sir.' But it would be a grave mistake to imagine that he only proclaimed the terrors of Sinai; often he would be full of the sweetness of the gospel and pouring out remarkable comforts. He was once preaching on the words, 'Then will I visit their transgression with the rod, and their iniquity with stripes. Nevertheless my loving kindness will I not utterly take from him, nor suffer my faithfulness to fail.' Amongst other lovely things, he said, 'There is not one hanging-tree growing anywhere on Emmanuel's land. There are plenty of beech trees where rods for chastening grow, but not one hanging-tree.' Another time, in the middle of a sermon, he came to the words, 'Lift up your heads, O ye gates; and be ye lift up, ye everlasting doors; and the King of glory shall come in.' And in his strong Gwent dialect, he said, 'See the gates with their heads lifted up; see the doors lifted up; and see the King going in. They will surely close the gates now? No, they won't. They won't close the gates until the Queen has gone in. Who is she? Oh, the bride, the betrothed of the Lamb!'

He would sometimes have unusually powerful services when God would own him wonderfully and the congregation would be as clay in his hands. A brother from Anglesey described him preaching once at an Association. Someone had preached before him rather poorly and at length, so that the people were dispirited. When this sermon came to an end, the old blacksmith was on his feet, full of a spirit of ministry. Holding on to the belt of his old-fashioned trousers and giving them a vigorous upward pull, he shouted, 'Now, boys! Hard at it for five minutes!' He *was* only five minutes, but rarely has a congregation ever experienced such a five minutes.

Within that time the narrator of the story testified that he himself was brought to eternal life.

The old people often spoke of a remarkable service when he preached at six in the morning in an Association at Caernarvon. It seems that the Rev. Evan Richardson because of his concern for a particular meeting to be held at eight that morning had asked him to be short and sweet. This request made the old exhorter very careful of not prolonging his sermon, yet his spirit was full of the joy of preaching. He soon commented, 'My brother has asked me to be short and sweet, but anyway, let me add this again.' And he added a word that fell as the dew upon the great crowd before him. A little later he repeated what was told him by Mr Richardson, 'My brother was asking me to be short and sweet, but anyway, hear this also,' and some sweeter comments still would fall upon his rapt congregation. He referred again and again to Richardson's words, but 'anyway' he had something further to say, and the thousands of people before him stood with tears shining upon faces full of love, all longing in their hearts that he would never arrive at his 'Amen'. It is especially remembered how Richardson's own smiles and tears testified to the depths of delight that he himself received on this memorable occasion.

One Sunday morning, the Rev. Shadrach Davies, a well-known Independent minister, was preaching at Maendy, a chapel near Cowbridge in Glamorganshire. There was a window behind the pulpit, as was the custom in the old chapels. Shadrach was preaching with much unction when, at the climax of his message, he turned and looked out of the window and saw outside a man that he knew. Out of the pulpit he went and through the door, without a word of explanation, with the whole congregation amazed by his behaviour. He was back in a moment, ushering in the strange man. The latter ascended to the pulpit and in a melodious voice, gave out the hymn:

Oh once again reach forth and grant Thy never-failing mercies.	O! estyn eto i barhau Dy drugareddau tirion.

A gentle dew fell upon all within the building as the hymn was announced. The man then took as a text, 'But it is good for me to draw near to God.' The divine influence came in upon them like the tide. The faithful pilgrims almost felt as if the benches on which they sat were floating away, so strong were the incoming floods. And Shadrach was shouting out, 'Glory!' at the top of his voice. At the end of the sermon they sang the verse, '*Melus fyth atgofio'r bore*', doubling and trebling the verse, again and again, in glorious rejoicing. Edward Coslet was the strange man. What brought him to Maendy that Sunday morning we do not know.

HIS BATTLES WITH SATAN

Coslet, like Siencyn Penhydd, believed firmly in the personality of the devil. Not only did he speak of him but he often spoke to him. He would address him in an angry tone, as if he were visibly before him. He once went to preach at a farmhouse in Cardiganshire. A young man who had once been an apprentice blacksmith with Coslet at Castleton, lived in the house. The young blacksmith came to welcome the old blacksmith as a companion on the way to the service. After much conversation on various matters, they approached the house and it became necessary to choose a text and sermon. 'I will preach on such-and-such a verse,' said Coslet. 'No, you won't, Ned,' said the devil, 'you have preached on that one here before.' The old exhorter felt a bit uneasy, but in a moment said, 'Well, I will preach on this one then,' naming another verse. 'No, you won't, Edward,' said the Evil One, 'You have preached that one here before also, and you will be reproached for repeating the same things so far from home.' By now, darkness was descending upon the poor preacher's mind; the house was nearby, the congregation gathering, and he without a sermon. 'Very well,' he said at last, in a much more confident voice, 'I will preach on this verse,' naming a third verse. 'No, you can't,' said Satan again, 'you have preached that one here also.' 'That's one of your lies,' cried out Coslet, 'I have only ever been here twice before. Ah, I've caught you this time, my boy!' And the father of lies had no answer before such irrefutable logic.

The old exhorter was remarkably ready with his answer; rarely would anyone defeat him in wit or humour. Indeed, it was dangerous ground for any to challenge him in this way. Someone complained against him once because of the roughness of his tongue, particularly for calling the devil, a '*diawl*' [a colloquial, and coarser, form of '*diafol*', 'devil'], as pronouncedly in the pulpit as in the forge. 'Edward,' he said, 'You should not call the Evil One by that low name which drunkards use for him. Why don't you refer to him as Satan, Beelzebub, the wicked spirit, or some such name?' 'What, my boy?' was the answer, 'you feel for him, do you? Men don't like hearing their friends being nicknamed. Is there some agreement between you and him? I only ever saw him as wicked. *Diawl* is good enough for him, and *diawl* is all he'll ever get from me.'

It is said that Coslet's coarseness of language and his use of the name *diawl* for the devil was often the means of augmenting his congregation, drawing those to hear him who would never usually darken a place of worship. He was once on a journey in Gwynedd, in the neighbourhood of the slate quarries, and one careless unbeliever said to another, as careless as himself, 'There's a strange preacher from the south at such-and-such a place. I'm going to hear him. Will you come with me?' 'No, I won't. You go on your own,' was the answer. 'No, but do come; it should be amusing. He calls the devil a *diawl* in his sermons.' 'Does he indeed? Well, off we go to hear the old rogue.' Off they went, indeed, but not to be amused. The words of the old exhorter lodged in their consciences, and the two were brought to conviction and to life. 'Boys,' he said, when preaching once. 'Do not serve the *diawl*. I served him for so many years and I never even got from him a nail to use in a horseshoe.'

Once in north Wales he preached together with a well-known minister from Gwynedd. Coslet's text was, 'The Lord God is a sun and shield.' He used his broad Gwent dialect in the pulpit, an unique dialect, as different from the usual south Wales dialect as that is from the north. We heard once that when he was at Llangeitho, which is of course in the south, the congregation could hardly understand parts of his sermon. Thus, his pronunciation of *'haul'* ['sun', pronounced as the German word *'heil'*] would be 'oil'. After the service the two preachers were at a nearby house and the northerner began to poke fun at Edward's accent, saying, 'You don't have a sun in the south then, Coslet?' 'Of course we do. As good a sun, every bit, as you've got here in the north.' 'No, no, it's some *'oil'* that you've got in the south.' 'I see,' said Coslet. 'Well, just you listen. "Come now [*"Deuwch yn awr"*], and let us reason together", was your text, but what you said for the rest of the sermon was *"Deuwch 'rwan'* " [*'yn awr'* in the northern accent is *'rwan'*]. His fellow preacher laughed heartily, having been beaten at his own game by the old blacksmith.

Very many of his witty sayings and quick answers have been remembered. He was travelling once in Pembrokeshire and it seems that the usual indication in those parts that one had had enough tea was to turn one's cup upside-down and leave it like that. Coslet either did not know of this ritual, or was too independent to follow it. In the event, he had finished his tea but not turned his cup. His kindly hostess went to pour him another cup. 'Wait,' said Edward, 'I have finished.' 'Finished?' she said. 'Then why didn't you turn your cup over? That's what we do in this part of the country.' 'That's what the pigs do in our part of the country,' said Coslet; 'they push over the troughs once they have finished eating.' He was called to London once on some commercial cause. These were the days of the stagecoach, before the steam engines began rushing up and down the land. Some Englishman, travelling with Coslet, thought he could use the old Welshman to provide some amusement for himself and his fellow travellers. 'Tell me,' he said, 'how many nanny-goats are there now in Wales?' 'Not as many as there are fools in England,' was the reply.

A lawyer, on a visit to a nobleman in the Castleton area, had heard much of the witticisms of the village's blacksmith, and that no one could get the better of him. He, like many of his brethren, possessed great faith in his own abilities and decided to test the strength of the blacksmith. He asked the nobleman to invite Coslet to his mansion. When he arrived, the lawyer greeted him in sarcastic tones,

'I hear that you go about to preach.'

'Yes, at times, I do,' was the reply.

'Do you preach in English sometimes?'

'I do.'

'How do you manage that? Do you write your sermons down in full?'

'No, I do not write a word.'

'Well, therefore, if you do not write your sermon carefully, and do not keep to a manuscript carefully, it is certain that you must make many mistakes.'

'O yes, I often make mistakes.'

'Well, when you make a mistake, do you return to correct it?'

'Yes, if it is a big mistake,' said Coslet, 'but if it is a small mistake I leave it and pass on.'

'And what would you call a small mistake?'

'Well,' said Coslet, ' if by accident I should happen to say 'liar' instead of 'lawyer', I should consider that a small mistake, and I would carry on without bothering to correct it.'

There is no need to mention that the lawyer's face fell, and that those listening were indeed much amused, but not at Edward Coslet's expense.

When on a journey through Pembrokeshire, he was asked to conduct a service throughout in English. This was not to his taste, though he was quite fluent in the English spoken in Gwent. In the end, however, after some persuasion, he was brought to agree. 'I am willing to preach in English,' he said, 'but I will not pray in English. I can speak English to you, but I have never said a word to my God in that language.' With that, they had to be content. We do not have an account of the service, but certainly more justice would have been done to the gospel than to grammar.

It seems that for all his rustic ways and his awareness of his lack of education, he possessed a very strong independent streak. The Rev. Hezekiah Jones, the godly clergyman of Monmouthshire, used to attend the Quarterly Meetings and to spend much time amongst the Methodists, as did many of the clergy of that period. For all his godliness, Mr Jones considered himself of higher station than the uneducated exhorter who travelled the country. But there was nothing servile about Coslet. When he felt he was in the right, he was as inflexible as the iron he hammered. Once Mr Jones brought a complaint against him, that he spoke too often in the Quarterly Meeting. The clergyman expected him to acknowledge his fault immediately. But the answer he received was: 'Mr Jones, the devil will have laces from the skin of your back before I'll submit to you.' But with this independent spirit he possessed much gentleness also, and to see a man in hardship would melt his heart immediately. One of the preachers in the county was once under the severest trial, with other men attaching blame to him. Coslet believed that the man had been unfortunate rather than having sinned deliberately. 'What do you, Edward Coslet, think of him?' asked the chairman of the meeting. 'I'll tell you immediately,' he replied; 'our brother is in the devil's furnace, but he will come through it as gold refined in the fire.' And so it proved. The preacher emerged from his tribulations with character brighter than ever and proved an eminently useful man for the remainder of his life.

As with many of the early exhorters, Coslet always began his services punctually to the minute, and his patience was greatly taxed by the tardiness of the people in attending the means of grace. It seems he was once preaching at a chapel in his own neighbourhood, and that he and his wife arrived there long before any others. They went to the chapel house to wait until the appointed starting time. Once that arrived, Coslet got to his feet and called on his wife to follow him to the chapel. 'But nobody else has come yet, Edward,' she replied. He sat down again but with evident impatience and discomfort. He was soon back on his feet and on his way to the chapel. When she saw that there was no way of keeping him quiet, she followed him, saying again that there was no one in the chapel. 'Don't worry about that,' he said, 'there's plenty to be said that's applicable to you, even if nobody else comes.' He began the service immediately with only himself and his wife present. Eventually others joined them and they also, together with his wife, received plenty of 'application'.

Edward Coslet suffered much persecution and was at last, like many of the Methodist preachers, forced to apply for a licence so that he might depend upon the law's protection. He attended the Quarter Sessions. One of the magistrates, seeing his rough and rustic manners, asked him sarcastically, 'You! A preacher of the gospel! God help you!' 'Amen,' said Coslet; 'his help, and your good will, sir, are all I need.' He was granted his licence with no more delay. He met with a severe providence once while travelling in Breconshire. One night, having been preaching, he visited the home of a relation, out in the country. Having arrived he found that his relation had moved to another district and in the house was a man who had just been arrested for forgery. The forger, on seeing Coslet enter, shouted out, 'Here is the man who helped me in the fraud!' As a result, he also was arrested. In his defence he argued that he was a stranger on a preaching journey through the region. The officers on hearing that they had a preacher in their gaol, amused themselves all the more by mocking him. They continued to do so throughout the night, though they had already obtained sufficient proofs that his defence was true. The next morning however, they released him. Many pressed him to bring charges against them but he would not agree; revenge had no place in his heart.

Many powerful revivals occurred during Edward Coslet's ministerial career; he partook freely of the spirit of such visitations and often his own ministry would kindle a flame of praise in his hearers' hearts. He once preached at Ty'nywlad, a farmhouse near Crickhowell. God's presence accompanied the word; the preacher was caught up in his message; the congregation was rejoicing. In the middle of the meeting, a gentleman barged in and in an angry tone shouted out, 'Keep these people quiet!' 'If these should hold their peace,' replied Coslet, 'the stones would immediately cry out.' The gentleman felt the force of his answer, bowed his head, and hurried from the place.

We have detailed much of the history of Edward Coslet because, like his contemporary, Siencyn Thomas, Penhydd, he was a good example of the class of Methodist exhorter belonging to the second generation. Their outer man was rough in appearance, their clothes rustic and their conversation possessed little culture, but they were brim full of natural ability. Humour sparkled from their lips as naturally as waters flowing from a stream; they made use of their wit quite fearlessly from the pulpit, and their style of preaching fitted the times in which they lived perfectly. If they lacked academic education and were deficient in matters of taste and style, yet their hearts flamed with love for their Saviour who died for them. Their spirits within them were stirred up as they spoke his name, and often they were instrumental in setting congregations aflame. It is impossible not to respect their memory. The extent of the good that they accomplished in their generation can never be calculated. Not the least star in this constellation was Edward Coslet. He shone in the Methodist skies throughout a long life and, just like the star of Bethlehem of long ago, he led many to 'the young child'. But death claimed him, as he claims all, in the year 1828, when he was two years short of his eightieth year, having preached the word of the kingdom for fifty-two years.

29

JOHN WILLIAMS, PANTYCELYN; JOHN EVANS, CIL-Y-CWM; AND MORGAN RHYS

JOHN WILLIAMS, PANTYCELYN

The Rev. John Williams was the second son of William Williams, the great hymn-writer of Wales. He deserves to be remembered therefore if only because of his relationship to his father, but quite apart from that he himself is worthy of consideration for a number of reasons. He was born at Pantycelyn on 23 May, 1754. He showed early signs of ability and learnt everything that was placed before him. It seemed also that he had great pleasure in the Bible, so that his father used often to say of him, in his homely way, 'Jack will be mighty in the Scriptures', and his prophecy was fulfilled to the letter. The Rev. Maurice Davies, his biographer, states that he received the principles of education from his father. As the old hymn-writer was such a restless traveller throughout his life and would often be away preaching the gospel and selling his books for weeks on end, his boys must often have had to teach themselves as best they could, or receive instruction from their mother. Jack attended a grammar school at a comparatively young age, at a place called Coed-cochion. The tutor of this school was a man, also called John Williams, who afterwards became a clergyman and rector of Llandeilo'r-fân in Breconshire. He was one of those Methodist clergymen, like Jones, Llan-gan, who travelled around preaching. John Williams, Pantycelyn, thought highly of him throughout his life and when the rector died, he wrote in a letter to his brother, the Rev. W. Williams, the vicar of Truro:

> Mr Williams, the rector of Llandeilo'r-fân, our first and best teacher, has gone the way of all flesh. He met with heavy crosses during his pilgrimage, but the Lord delivered him from them all. He died while singing, '*Ffordd newydd wnaed gan Iesu Grist,* etc.' ['A new high road by Christ was made, etc.'] He left behind him three sons, all of whom are ministers in the Established Church.

When about fifteen years old, John Williams moved to the Grammar School at Carmarthen, which was a Church School sponsored by the Bishop of St David's. He was here for about four years and such was his enthusiasm and commitment to his studies that not only did he far excel his fellow-students but he was considered equal to his tutors, and they themselves felt that there was nothing further that they could contribute to his education. From here he went to the Grammar School at Ystradmeurig, Cardiganshire, which was at the peak of its fame at this time, under the headship of Edward Richard, a very prejudiced man, but a good schoolmaster and an excellent poet. The Rev. Maurice Davies does not mention John Williams's period at Ystradmeurig but it is certain that he was there. According to the age-old custom of schoolboys he used to write on the blank pages of his textbooks, and on one he noted that he had bought it in Carmarthen in 1771. Under this note, he added, 'I came to Ystradmeurig to school, June 30th, 1773.' How long he stayed there is not known. After leaving Ystradmeurig he did not know what to do. He was too young to take Church Orders, and too eager and lively in spirit to do nothing. One afternoon, having gone for a walk to Carmarthen, he looked out of a window and saw the Bishop of St David's and his wife passing along the street. On the impulse of the moment he went out to meet them, and having bowed courteously to the bishop he asked him if he would be willing to hear a word. The bishop replied kindly that he would. 'My lord,' said the brave young man, 'your lordship knows that I have learnt all I can from this establishment, and as I do not wish to spend my time in idleness, I am at a loss what to do until I arrive at an age when I can take orders.' The bishop answered, ' You may expect an answer from me about this time tomorrow, John Williams.' He thanked the bishop respectfully, who departed with his wife, both smiling. The result of the conversation was that the young man was appointed an assistant teacher in the very school in which he himself had been such an outstanding scholar. It seems that William Williams was very pleased by his son's behaviour, for he wrote to his oldest son:

> Be brave, Billy; a preacher without courage is like a saw without teeth, like a knife without edge, or a soldier with no heart. Your brother Jacky went on his own to speak to the Bishop on the street in Carmarthen, and he was rewarded for his courage. 'The fear of man bringeth a snare.'

ORDAINED A CURATE AND THEN A PRIEST

On 17 October, 1779, a Sunday, John Williams was ordained by Bishop Warren as curate of Llanfynydd Church, Carmarthenshire. This took place at the Bishop's Palace at Abergwili. The only examination in theology that the Bishop gave him before ordaining him was the question, 'What is justification? And what is meant by "by faith alone"?' Mr Williams's response to the first question was,

> By justification I understand that a guilty sinner has a personal claim to the righteousness of Christ by faith; 'Even as David also describeth the blessedness of the man, unto whom God imputeth righteousness without works'; 'We conclude that a man is justified by faith without the deeds of the law.'

The second, he answered in the following way:

> By the phrase, 'by faith alone', I understand a spiritual principle that the Holy Spirit plants in the soul of man at regeneration, which principle teaches him to judge appropriately of God, and of himself; and enables him to rest on Christ's righteousness for acceptance with God; to trust in his blood for forgiveness and cleansing, and in his fullness for every mercy unto eternal life.

It is easy to see that the young man had fulfilled his father's prophecy by becoming 'mighty in the Scriptures'; the bishop saw no need for further questions, appreciating that the candidate before him had a good understanding of the doctrines of religion and was also a believer, and the only counsel he gave him as he departed was, 'Farewell, my son, and if you are careful to have nothing to do with the Methodists, I am sure you will be a comfort to yourself and an ornament to the Church.' It was probably the closeness of Williams's father to the Methodists that caused the bishop to give such advice. But John did not appreciate it, and as he returned home he said to himself,

> My Lord Bishop does not understand the Methodists as I understand them, otherwise he would not have advised me to keep away from them. Lord, lay not this sin to his charge. As for me, 'I will yet be more vile than this, and will be base in mine own sight: and with the maidservants' (he meant the Methodists) 'of them shall I be had in honour.'

Such thoughts show that his father's principles were rooted too deeply in him for the Bishop of St David's to succeed in uprooting them.

The young curate was less than a year in Llanfynydd. We know hardly anything of his history there, other than the strong probability that he was friendly with very many Methodists. Although Dafydd Rees, Llanfynydd, did not start preaching until two years after John Williams left the village, yet Iefan Tyclai lived there; Lloyd of Caeo, William Williams's close friend was not far away; nor was John Evans, Cil-y-cwm. It is therefore almost certain that he mixed much in the company of his father's people. Nor was his vicar, the Rev. Cornelius Cobner, though a glutton and a drunkard and completely unfit to watch over souls, at all prejudiced against the Methodists. He had great respect for the ministerial gifts of Daniel Rowland, but believed just as firmly in his own abilities, and often said that Wales had two famous clergymen, Rowland in Cardiganshire and himself in Carmarthenshire. It seems also that he had great respect for Jones, Llan-gan. During his period as vicar, the Llanfynydd friendly society would hold a service in the church every Easter Monday and pay him five shillings for leading the service. One Easter Monday, the Evangelist from Llan-gan was appointed to Llanfynydd, and some of the members of the society suggested that he might deliver the usual sermon. They took their request to Mr Cobner. 'Very well,' he replied, 'I'll speak to Mr Jones, in that I know him better than yourselves.' Mr Jones arrived on the day and Mr Cobner approached him about the sermon.

'It's the custom here on Easter Monday, Mr Jones,' he said, 'that I preach to the friendly society members here.'

'Very well,' replied Mr Jones, 'I'll go on to my next service.'

'Oh, no, Mr Jones,' said the vicar. 'You are to preach, sir. I am always here, and the people are used to me; but what I must insist is that I have the crown.'

'No, no, Mr Cobner, I will not sell my crown as cheaply as that. If you mean the five shillings, you may have that and welcome, but not the crown.'

And so the matter was arranged. It is easy to see that the curate had no need to worry of being hindered in any way in his Methodist practices by the vicar of Llanfynydd.

In September, 1780, John Williams was ordained as priest by Bishop Warren. He did not return to Llanfynydd. He remained at home at Pantycelyn for the remainder of the year, serving in the churches of the locality when they required him, and it is said that he often took services at Llanfair-ar-y-bryn, near Llandovery, the church in whose cemetery both he and his illustrious father were to be buried. At the beginning of the following year, January, 1781, he moved to Llangrallo, in the Vale of Glamorgan, to keep a school. Llangrallo is a comparatively small village, not far from Llan-gan. He went there in answer to a request from the Rev. David Jones, Llan-gan. Probably there was some connection between Mr Jones and the school. He does not seem to have held a living at this time, but ministered in the neighbouring parishes when invited. He earned for himself the respect of the clergymen of the Vale, being admired for his scholarship and the extent of his theological knowledge. A clear proof of this is seen in the following note, written in his journal for 30 May, 1781:

> Today, Bishop Barrington and I preached, one after the other, at the Monthly Meeting of the clergy of the Vale of Glamorgan; his Lordship in English and myself in Welsh.

He must have been considered a preacher of note to be appointed alongside the Bishop. The entry also suggests that the Methodists were beginning to effect an improving influence within the Church. When Howell Harris and Daniel Rowland were setting out, any attempt to gather together a meeting of clergymen to hear the gospel would have been in vain; any who suggested such a thing would have been the target of much scorn and mocking.

Mr Williams remained at Llangrallo until August 1782, when he was appointed rector of Builth Wells and Llanddewi'r-cwm. His father was on a journey somewhere in north Wales when he heard of the appointment; his muse was inspired by the news and he composed a poem, of which only the following verse has survived:

> Fly, o cuckoo; fly, swift blue bird; fly to where my kindred dwell,
> Fly away to Pantycelyn and tell Mali I am well;
> Then from there to Builth fly onward and tell Jack to keep his place,
> If on earth no more I'll see him, we'll meet in heaven, face to face.

> Hed, y gwcw, hed yn fuan, hed, aderyn glas ei liw,
> Hed oddiyma i Bantycelyn, d'wed i Mali 'mod i'n fyw;
> Hed oddiyno i Lanfair-muallt, d'wed wrth Jack am gadw'i le,
> Ac os na chaf ei weled yma, caf ei weled yn y ne'.

JOHN WILLIAMS'S CONVERSION

Though the Rev. John Williams was a learned man with a remarkable knowledge of the Scriptures, orthodox in his views and of a strong religious temperament, he was not, by his own admission, a saved man when he came to Builth Wells. Indeed he was tainted in his character, in that he would often be under the influence of alcohol. It seems that his father knew of this weakness, and that the phrase, 'Tell Jack to keep his place', was a reference to it. As far as we know, his bouts of drunkenness did not bring down upon him the discipline of the Bishop. An over-fondness for drink was not considered a matter for discipline by the judiciary of the Established Church in those days; it was deemed to be more in the nature of a gentlemanly fault. It must also be remembered that the dawn of teetotalism had not yet arisen in the land, and that beer and spirits were considered as indispensable as bread, for health and hard work. One day, at the funeral of one of his parishioners, he was more than half-drunk, and while standing at the graveside and reading the words, 'Dust to dust, ashes to ashes,' he nearly fell into the grave and would have done so had not a friend held on to him. Those present on the occasion do not seem to have paid much attention to the unseemliness and certainly did not complain of him to the authorities. They were only too familiar with such behaviour. However the episode affected John Williams greatly. He was immediately sobered; he returned to his lodgings weeping bitterly and went straight up to his room and was not seen until the following morning. Because of the depth of his grief and the extent of his despair, he almost lost his mind. The fervent prayers and confessions written by him at the time in his journal reveal the bitterness of his soul:

> I have said to corruption, Thou art my father: to the worm, Thou art my mother and my sister. My inward part is very wickedness. In me dwelleth no good thing. Unclean, unclean. It is a wonder, O Lord, that thou dost not shut me up to despair and to chains of darkness with the devil, until the Day of Judgment! I approach thee as the publican, 'God, be merciful to me a sinner' O God, who art infinite in mercy, be merciful to me. O purify, sanctify, cleanse, and grant me a new heart, O God. Thou hast granted me a change of heart many times, but I have not the new heart. How I need a new heart, even if I were to beg my bread from door to door.

We could add more, but the above is sufficient to show the bitterness of his spirit. The distinction he makes between, 'a change of heart', and, 'the new heart', suggests that he had previously experienced religious awakenings and longings for a higher life, but that he did not consider himself to have been created anew in Christ Jesus. How long he was in this agony of soul we do not know, but God revealed his mercy to him and the chains that bound him were shattered. He wrote in his journal:

> Thanks for a measure of peace from the fear of evil. O that I might never henceforth receive a spirit of bondage again to fear, but a spirit of adoption by which I might cry, 'Abba, Father'.

Here is John Williams – a new creature in Christ Jesus – finding himself in a completely new world. If the things of the world had now become empty to him, the peace of the gospel flowed as a sea into his soul. His words in his journal deserve to be written in stone forever by a pen of iron:

> O that the whole world might experience such substance and such power and consolation in religion, as I presently experience. The Lord has pardoned my sin, and has subdued my corruption. He has defeated my foes and has removed my fears. The little I have experienced here of the things of heaven has made it

> a heaven upon earth; but what of heaven itself, where the face of my Beloved is to be seen without a veil, and all his glories shine undimmed! O how great will be the feast, how wonderful the pleasure, where I will know eternal light, eternal visions, and an eternal likeness to the eternal God!

He gained a complete victory over his weakness; he felt such revulsion towards drink that it was never again a temptation for him. In a letter to his brother, dated 1784, he writes:

> To God be the thanks, I have obtained such a conquest over that sin which you know was ready to engulf me, that none of my friends doubt me; and mercifully they have no cause to do so.

TUTOR AT THE COUNTESS OF HUNTINGDON'S COLLEGE AT TREFECA

A consequence of his transformation was that he threw himself into his church duties with greater diligence, and drew much closer to the Methodists who met at Alpha Chapel. He would read the service and preach three times each Sunday at the church, and in the week would gather with those who like himself had been brought to new life. The news soon spread throughout Breconshire that the vicar of Builth, the son of the beloved hymn-writer, had found religion, and it brought forth great joy in the hearts of many. Amongst others, the Countess of Huntingdon heard of his conversion and because she was such a friend of his father's, and because she knew of his scholarship, she wrote to him asking him to take charge of her college at Trefeca for a period, in that the main tutor would often be absent for months due to other duties. This offer fitted Mr Williams's inclinations perfectly. He loved the Classics and had maintained his fluency in them, and his familiarity with his other studies, since leaving Carmarthen Grammar School. He therefore obeyed the call and was at Trefeca from the beginning of August until December 1784. It hardly needs to be said that he was successful as a tutor. Because of his loving personality, his unflagging commitment, and his support for all who were willing to labour diligently with their studies, he very soon endeared himself to the students so that it was with difficulty that some of them were persuaded to remain at the College when he left, in that they longed to follow him to Builth to continue their studies under him. The Countess also was very pleased with him and rewarded him generously when he departed.

John Williams continued his work another year at Builth but then, in January 1786, the Countess discharged Mr Phillips, the principal of her college, from his post because, contrary to the rules of the place, he had entered into theological debate with one of the students and had failed to control himself during the argument. She offered his place to Mr Williams, who accepted it. He was at Trefeca for five years during which time he worked unceasingly. It seems that he was the only tutor there; he would provide the tuition in languages and in theology; he would mark all the papers. There were about twelve students in the College at the time, some of them being excellent scholars so that it was not without great efforts that he was able to keep abreast of them. It is said that he slept no more than two hours out of every twenty-four, and would be at his work without fail by four o'clock in the morning. After labouring in this way all week, there would be no rest for him on the Sunday. He would normally preach three times that day, often with a forty-mile journey involved. In a letter to his brother, dated March 1789, he writes:

> I have now become so used to work that I need no rest or sleep, such is the pleasure I receive from the work, and the support the Lord gives me in it, but reason tells me that I shall suffer for this in the future. We have recently received a call from your county [Cornwall] from scores of congregations asking for preachers, and I have been commanded to prepare as many as I can as soon as possible. Does this not prove, my dear brother, the laziness and carelessness of you clergymen in that part of the land?

With his departure from Builth, the connection between the Rev. John Williams and the Established Church came to an end. He did not climb into their pulpits again but threw in his lot with the Methodists, his father's people, and joined the Breconshire Monthly Meeting. The religious situation in Breconshire improved considerably when he came to Trefeca; in particular, the town of Brecon was greatly blessed by his ministry. The Countess owned a church in the town, built at her own cost. It was of a similar design to some of the old Established Church chapels, with two pulpits, one for the clergyman and another for the exhorters, and with the pulpits, not one below another, but at either end of the building. This also was the arrangement at Llanlluan, Gyfylchi, and Creunant chapels, and in other places.

The purpose of the design, it seems, was to maintain as much distance as possible between the ordained clergyman and his lay brother. Usually one of the students ministered here, or Mr Williams himself, unless a visiting preacher was passing through on a journey. On one occasion, one Sunday afternoon, Mr Williams saw a crowd of ungodly young men playing in a nearby field. He immediately decided to scatter them and so rode his horse at a gallop straight at them, with the air of a man of authority. The boys fled in alarm, without waiting to see who it was who threatened them. He drew up his horse, took a notebook out of his pocket, and pretended to write their names in it. The boys thought that he was a magistrate and that they would soon be summoned before their betters. No summons arrived of course, but nor was there any more play on a Sunday on that field.

The time at Trefeca was probably the most hard-working period in the life of the Rev. John Williams and perhaps the most productive. However in April 1791, he resigned his post, to the great disappointment of the Countess of Huntingdon and of the College trustees. He gave two reasons for his resignation. The first was the death of his father and the obligation he felt to move to Pantycelyn to comfort and look after his mother in her old age. The second was his longing for greater leisure in order to pursue his favourite work of preaching the gospel. Within two months of his departure, the Countess died, and within a year or so afterwards the College moved from Trefeca to Cheshunt, Hertfordshire.

HE RETURNS TO PANTYCELYN

When John Williams moved to Pantycelyn, he joined the society at Cil-y-cwm, where his mother was a member. Though Howell Harris had visited the town scores of times, and though William Williams had lived nearby, no Methodist society had been established in Llandovery up to the time of the hymn-writer's death, if *Methodistiaeth Cymru* is correct. Some of the preachers of the Connexion called as they passed through, men like Dafydd Morris, Dafydd Rees, Llanfynydd, and Lloyd of Caeo, but there was no church in existence to welcome them. They preached in the high street or in the open-air, and they tried to arrive at the town on the day of the market or a fair. Afterwards, the Independents and the Methodists worshipped together in a home for a time, but the Methodists amongst them considered themselves members of the Cil-y-cwm society. This was the situation when John Williams joined them.

In about 1797, however, the Independents built their own chapel, and five years later, in 1802, Mr Williams, together with William Jones, Esq., Ystrad Walter, and the other brethren, decided to buy a house in which to hold their services, and after obtaining the consent of the Monthly Meeting this was done. Soon, a larger chapel was built and the membership and congregation greatly increased. From this time Mr Williams's membership was at Llandovery, but he remained a member of the Breconshire Monthly Meeting throughout his life.

He was never such a traveller as his father, confining his labours mainly to Breconshire and Carmarthenshire. Perhaps the frailty of his health was the reason for this. Yet, on many occasions, he visited all the churches of south Wales, and twice he journeyed through the north. He went there the first time in 1800, accompanied by John Prytherch, Defynnog. This is how he wrote to his brother on returning:

> I have just returned from a journey of at least 600 miles. When you wrote your last letter I was at Dolgellau in Merionethshire, in an Association. On the journey, I usually preached three times, and administered the Lord's Supper twice, every day. I travelled about fifteen miles each day. Throughout the journey I did not hear once of an awakened minister of the Established Church! How sad it is when the Lord states, 'The priests said not, Where is the Lord? And they that handle the law knew me not.' But the Lord is raising for himself pastors from amongst the farmers and craftsmen who, in his hands, are turning the world upside-down. Satan is not troubled at all by the preaching of morality and good works; it is salvation by Jesus Christ that alarms him. That is what pulls down his altars, delivers his captives, destroys the works of the devil, etc. It is no wonder the apostle says, 'I am not ashamed of the gospel of Christ.' He was not ashamed to believe it as a man, to profess it as a Christian, to proclaim it as an apostle, and to die for its sake as a martyr.

This letter shows that religion had almost completely died out in the Established Church at the time. We have no reason to believe that Mr Williams was exaggerating; he had himself been ordained a clergyman and his brother to whom he was writing was a clergyman. He was not therefore acting under any prejudice against the Church. The letter shows also that the administration of the sacrament amongst the Methodists in the north was very disorganized, and that it was very rarely that they received the privilege, otherwise it would not have been necessary for a visiting clergyman to conduct the service twice a day, as well as delivering three sermons a day.

He visited north Wales again in 1802. His friend accompanying him this time was William Bevan, Trecastle. On returning, he again wrote to his brother:

> We travelled through all the counties of north Wales and large areas of Shropshire and Cheshire. At Chester, we met the Rev. Mr Charles of Bala. I am sorry to have to say that his hand is affected by the white swelling and the doctors say that it will have to be cut off. This is as a result of catching cold when crossing one of Merionethshire's mountains. I am afraid that this faithful servant of Christ will die the death of a martyr because of his great efforts in the best cause. Though he was so weak, he read the service twice before me at Chester. When you hear that I have been on such a long journey through Gwynedd no doubt you expect me to say something of the wild mountains and the incredible scenery to be found there, but the truth is that the weight of work and the tiredness of body mortified completely all the less important

inquiries that are so natural to myself and yourself. Though there are many mountains in the north, yet there is also much good land, and the natives are tidy, hospitable people, of excellent behaviour.

HIS CHARACTERISTICS

Mr Williams exhibited many oddities. He never married and it does not seem that he ever fell in love with any girl. *Methodistiaeth Cymru* portrays him as possessing a perfect hatred towards all women, or rather that he feared them all, and that he would not on any account walk with a female to chapel. It further notes his special hatred of one old woman, who was not very sensible, who sought to push a cushion under his knee every time he prayed. We are certain that this picture is untrue or, at least, that it is highly coloured. The Rev. John Williams was a gentleman. He was on the closest terms with the Countess of Huntingdon, with Lady Jane Erskine, and with other godly women. He had such a high view of the good sense and religion of his housekeeper that he left her, in his last will and testament, all the Welsh books of his father and all his own Welsh books. This baseless tradition was probably begun by some women who had attempted unsuccessfully to ingratiate themselves. It is only natural that he felt disturbed by an unbalanced old woman who was always pushing herself upon him.

He was also very punctilious about being on time. He went once to a farmhouse near his home where he used to preach. The service had been announced for six o'clock, as usual, but when that time came nobody was present other than the owner of the house. Notwithstanding, Mr Williams stood on a chair and gave out a hymn to sing. The house-owner tried to get him to wait, saying, 'But where are the people, Mr Williams? Don't start yet.' But the preacher was determined to continue, and said, with great solemnity, 'And why is it that you yourself are not sufficient?'

Another characteristic of his was his generosity and charity. As he had received the larger part of his father's estate, and as his brother had died with no beneficiaries, Mr Williams was comparatively wealthy, and he contributed liberally of that wealth to every worthy cause. He welcomed all the travelling preachers to his home wherever they might have journeyed from, and no poor preacher set out from his house the following morning without having received a parting gift of money. All the poor of the neighbourhood had experienced his generosity. So anonymously did he perform his almsgiving that few realized the extent of his charity, but from his papers after his death it was gathered that he contributed yearly about two hundred and fifty pounds to charitable causes and to the Lord's work. The following note was found in an old book of his: 'Mary Bartlett has been many Sabbaths without bread to eat, etc.' This Mary Bartlett was probably a poor neighbour of his, and he by making inquiries had found out her needs. He often remembered the scriptural exhortation, 'It is more blessed to give than to receive.' 'Instead of sending me into the world to beg,' he said, 'the Lord has granted me sufficient for me to be able to give to any who call, as long as my wicked heart does not impede me.' In his will he left a hundred pounds each to the London Missionary Society, the Church Missionary Society, and the Sunday School Association in Ireland, and another hundred pounds for repaying the debt of Methodist chapels in Breconshire.

The Rev. John Williams was not considered a popular preacher; he did not possess sparkling oratorical skills; he had not the compassion of Jones, Llan-gan, nor the power of Ebenezer Morris. Yet his ministry was very acceptable. As regards depth of scholarship and understanding of Scriptural doctrine it is to be doubted whether any of the preachers of the Connexion excelled him. His words, also, would always be relevant, his mind clear, so that rarely did anyone leave his services without having received some new insight into the truth. Before reading his text, he would always announce, 'The Word of the Lord'; he would then read it loudly two or three times. Whenever he quoted a scriptural verse in his sermon, he would raise his voice.

When preaching, he would explain his text in detail; in order to clarify it he would draw on his knowledge of the original languages and of the customs and traditions of the countries of the East. We often read of him saying, 'Thus and thus is the rendering in the Hebrew, I was looking at it this morning before breakfast.' After explaining the verse, he commented on the doctrine contained in it, and then concluded with a few practical applications. His sermons were always short, about half an hour at the most. He abominated long sermons, and used to say that no one in Britain after the time of the Puritans possessed sufficient gifts to preach for an hour without wearying more than half the congregation. The few remarks of his that survive show that he was a clear thinker and that he could also sum up a long argument in one clear sentence. When dealing with the election of grace, he said, 'God's predestination is not like a weathercock, changing and turning about, according to the breezes of man's free will.' Again, 'You must excuse me if I believe the testimony of Christ rather than the divisive quarrels of Arminianism and rather than summoning the Almighty to be tried before the throne of our ideas – setting ourselves up as judges of the Deity.'

Amongst his papers were found sheets of short comments containing a wealth of sense and wisdom. As regards infant baptism, he says, 'Administering baptism to the children of ungodly parents is an effective way of hardening them in sin; it is a mockery of the ordinance and strengthens the arms of those who oppose infant baptism. If all who argue for baptizing infants were to keep within the confines of God's Word and refused to baptize all but the seed of the faithful, bringing them up in the nurture and admonition of the Lord, as the Apostle commands, and according to the practice of the Bohemian churches, we would, after a very few years, hear no more of rebaptizing.' Concerning presumptuous ungodliness, he wrote, 'Some men sin as if it was certain that the gates of hell will be shut before they ever arrive there.'

As he did not usually attend the Associations and was not fond of argument, he does not seem to have taken much part in the discussions prior to the ordination of ministers in 1811. But we are certain that he agreed completely with the steps taken. Nothing has survived to suggest that he was in any way opposed to the idea when it was first broached. And as to his approval, there is no need of any stronger evidence than his significant contribution during that first ordination service at Llandeilo. He wrote to his brother the following year:

> Not one clergyman from this county [Breconshire] is in fellowship with the body of Methodists except myself; the distance between ourselves and the Established Church increases every year. The young people take it for granted that the Church is nothing but some kind of state Christianity. It is true that the older people still retain a strong prejudice in favour of the Church, but it would not affect the younger element if all clergymen were exiled beyond the Ganges. Yet, none of the clergy of south Wales has published anything against us, nor do any of us, publicly or secretly, dare say anything disrespectful of the Established Church.

Though Mr Williams supported the movement for Methodist ordination, it must be added that he never lost all his affection for the Church, or his respect for its ministers. When discussing the Bible Society in a letter to his brother, he wrote:

> I am sorry to see so few of the names of clergy on the list of contributors. This shows that they have no desire to see the propagation of scriptural knowledge. And as they do not read the Bible themselves, except what they must, they do not want anybody else to do so. Forgive me for being so bold with my brethren of old, the clergymen. It is love for them and concern on their behalf that makes me write in this way. Let no one imagine that I am an enemy of my mother-church, but I am not blind to her deficiencies. You may know that

I have great respect, not only for the clergy of the Church, but also for her constitution, when I tell you that the first thing I do in the morning, every day, is to read the Psalms appointed by the Church.

It is clear that John Williams had not lost all respect for the Established Church and its officers, and this fact only strengthens his condemnation of the clergy of his day in their aversion to the Bible and apathy as regards the propagation of scriptural knowledge.

As far as his feelings for the Methodists are concerned, we quote the following:

My only friends on earth are religious people; I love these, whatever Christian party they may belong to. At the same time I feel greater affection for my Methodist brethren than for any others. Not because I think that they are more godly than others, but because I have known so much more of them and have had such proof of their faithfulness. I am so blind to my own frailties that I consider it a privilege to be part of a body of people who will tell me of my mistakes and will not tolerate sin in me.

When we remember that the Methodists were poor and comparatively uneducated on the whole, this last sentence above reveals a rare spirit of humility, particularly when we also remember that Mr Williams was a very gifted man, perhaps the most learned man in the Connexion at the time.

He does not seem to have taken any part in the framing of the Connexion's Confession of Faith. This was not because of any lack of qualification but because failing health and the weaknesses of old age were beginning to overcome him. But when the Confession of Faith was published he was delighted. He wrote:

Today I read the Calvinistic Methodists' Confession of Faith. Never before have men of such little education, and even less prejudice, taken it upon themselves to compose a confession of faith; but the weakness of God is stronger than men, and the foolishness of God is wiser than men. The *Eurgrawn Efengylaidd* [*The Evangelical Treasury*] praises it, but if it were reviewed by the hosts of heaven, I imagine that their judgment would be: 'These are God's true words.'

Mr Williams, in his loneliness at Pantycelyn, and in his inability to help his brethren in the crucial work that they had undertaken, probably felt acutely anxious with regard to the outcome of their deliberations. He knew that they possessed very little scholarship and learning as measured by the world. We are therefore certain that, when the Confession came into his possession and after he had time to study it, his spirit rejoiced within him on seeing the evident guidance given to its authors.

As has been mentioned, the Rev. John Williams spent his life after his departure from Trefeca in relative anonymity. He preached regularly in Breconshire and Carmarthenshire and laboured hard for the cause of the gospel throughout these two counties; in his quiet way he achieved much good in these areas near to his home. But because he did not journey much he did not fulfil the leading role within the Connexion, during troubled times, that might have been expected of a man of his knowledge and qualifications. To do so would not have been natural to him. The frailty of his health must also be remembered. But he fulfilled a valuable service in collecting and publishing the immortal hymns of his father, restoring them to their original state after revisers had mistreated them so shamefully. The only other literary work of his, as far as is known, was a translation from English of a work on the Trinity. Some think that something of his father's poetic gift was in him also, and this is confirmed by his flowing translation of the hymn, 'O'er the gloomy hills of darkness.' But when asked by friends why he did not write hymns of his own, he would reply, rather shortly, 'My father has sung enough.'

We hope that the reader has, by now, a clear picture of the kind of man the Rev. John Williams was – a learned man, content in his own company, but notably courteous and gentlemanlike, and very careful of the poor; a man who would withdraw from any controversy but would have a clear judgment on any debated points, and would be able to express that view unequivocally when called upon to do so; he is to be seen also as labouring with all his might and main in every form of the work of the gospel within the bounds which he had set himself.

To complete the picture, we must refer to two other characteristics of his. One was his gentleness of spirit. In the Breconshire Monthly Meeting he would contribute little, giving precedence to brethren of much lesser qualifications; but whenever he did speak, his advice would be so pertinent that all would submit to it. If anyone made some slighting reference to him, he would not be offended nor answer a word. A little before dying, he said:

> It is a comfort to me to consider that, as far as I know, I have never been a cause of hurt to anyone for one minute; no, no more than that I caused the recent eclipse of the moon; and I have not been guilty of one deceitful act throughout my life.

All who knew him agreed that there was no exaggeration in such a remark.

The second characteristic of his to be mentioned is his godliness. As well as his pure life and spiritual comments, there are many indications here and there in his journals that show that he considered himself to be completely at Christ's disposal. At the beginning of a year he wrote:

> I now have the gracious privilege of beginning a new year; whether I will see its end I do not know. But whether I am granted more time, or less, may the Lord enable me to be faithful. I need help and support, and I ask it of heaven itself, to spend the remainder of my days to the glory of that blessed Saviour, who was made a curse for a cursed world; strength to give myself completely, body, spirit, and all that is within me, to his glory. And I here promise and vow to consecrate the rest of my days to God and to his will while I continue to draw breath. I do not presume to believe that I shall accomplish these vows through trusting in my own sufficiency, but rather by praying to God that he, of his abundant and eternal grace, would strengthen me to run the race set before me; strengthen me always to fear him with a reverential fear; strengthen me to love him, and him alone, while I pass through this earthly world; and at last to enter into his eternal glory, through the Alpha and Omega, the salvation of men. As evidence of my consent to the above, I willingly set my name to this statement. JOHN WILLIAMS.

HIS LAST DAYS

As his days neared their end, it was evident that he was ripening quickly for a better world. A little before his death he wrote to a friend:

> As for my health it is only fair; I pray earnestly to God that he would make me submissive to his will, and not in any way complain at his treatment of me. What a great sin it is to be rebellious under the rod of a heavenly Father! I am quite unable to leave the house at present, but I continue to preach a little in my own house, and the neighbours gather together and fill it pretty well.

Another time, he said:

> O that my soul might be as much like heaven as my body is like the earth. The old earthly tabernacle does not fulfil any purpose these days except to act as a barometer and foretell any changes in the weather. But there is a longing in my soul towards those who have been perfected.

The following is found in one of his writing books:

> Old ___ has finished his race. He said on his death-bed, 'I remember the time when if it was said to me that only one man from the parish of ___ was bound for hell, I would have said that I was that man. But now, by grace, if it was said to me that only one man from the parish would get to heaven, I know that I am he.'

Mr Williams could probably have used for himself the words of the old man, whom he knew well.

He felt the deaths of his brethren in the ministry keenly. He grieved deeply for Mr Lloyd of Caeo, his father's, and his own, friend. In a letter to his brother, dated 14 October 1814, he writes of the death of the Rev. Thomas Charles, saying:

> The whole of Wales has received a great loss, and particularly the Body of Methodists. He was useful in so many ways. He published many excellent books. It was he, on my request, who wrote the life of our father; I gave him a skeleton and he clothed it in flesh and blood; I sent the materials and he built the building. When his usefulness amongst us is remembered, and the fact that it is now lost to us, I can only imagine having to say, 'Spare thy people, O Lord, and give not thy heritage to reproach.'

Perhaps the following extract from the same letter will be of interest to the reader:

> My health does not allow me to leave the house to preach the gospel and this is a great grief to me. I occasionally avoid the Monthly Meeting because I find I cannot refuse an appointment because of the entreaties of the brethren, yet I know that I will not be able to fulfil it. It is pointless for me to tell my dear brethren of my illness, they would but laugh thinking that it is only my hip that troubles me, for that is what they call everything that they do not understand. They do not believe there is anything wrong with the preacher except the hip, until they hear that he has died. Then they say to each other, 'Probably he was ill for a long time and we did not believe him.' When I am at home I spend most of my time reading the Bible and Dr Gill's comments. I love to follow Dr Gill wherever he leads, except down to the river . . . Whoever takes pains over the Doctor's works will be well rewarded for his trouble, and will receive as much useful knowledge, in my opinion, as if he read all the books that were ever written.

Christmas Evans had the same opinion of Dr Gill and said once to the Rev. Robert Hall, 'I wish that he had written his commentary in Welsh.' But Mr Hall's judgment was very different, and he replied, 'So do I, sir, so do I, for he then would not be such a trouble to those who read him in English. He is a continent of mud, sir.'

The Rev. John Williams died on 5 June 1828, when seventy-four years old, having been in the ministry for forty-nine years. Of these, forty-two had been in fellowship with the Calvinistic Methodists. Before his death he had arranged everything for his funeral. He wished to be buried in Llanfair-ar-y-bryn cemetery, near his parents, but, like his Saviour, in a new grave wherein was never man yet laid. To fulfil his wish an old sycamore tree nearby had to be uprooted. He had also arranged that the Revs. William Havard and Maurice Davies should preach at the funeral but as they could not be informed in time this was not possible. But he was given an honourable burial. At Pantycelyn, the Rev. John Jones, Llanddeusant, read and prayed. The Rev. Joshua Phillips, Bancyfelin then spoke, in Welsh, from Philippians 1:21, and the Rev. William Griffiths, Gower, in English, from John 10:9. A large and sorrowing crowd then conducted the coffin to the cemetery at Llanfair-ar-y-bryn. The epitaph on his gravestone reads:

Sacred to the memory of the REV. JOHN WILLIAMS, Pantycelyn, in this parish, in whom learning, piety and benevolence were united. He devoted a considerable part of his wealth to the transmission of the glorious gospel to all lands. He died June 5, 1828. Aged 74 years.

Stranger! Should'st thou approach this awful shrine,
The merits of the honoured dead to seek;
The friend, the son, the Christian, the divine,
Let those who knew him, those who loved him, speak.

A sinner saved.

It should be noted that the last phrase, 'A sinner saved', was placed on the stone according to Mr Williams's instructions. His friend and biographer, the Rev. Maurice Davies, composed an elegy to him, from which we quote the following verses:

What do you call this place of burial?
This is Llanfair-ar-y-bryn.
How silent is the air about us,
How deep the impressions felt within.
William Williams, Pantycelyn,
To think that here his body lies!
A saint who played upon the harpstrings
Like an angel from the skies.

Beth yw enw'r fynwent yma?
Mynwent Llanfair-ar-y-bryn;
O mor llonydd lle yw'r gladdfa,
Beth yw'r argraffiadau hyn?
William Williams, Pantycelyn,
Ow, ai dyma ei feddrod ef?
Sant a fedrai chwarae'i delyn
Braidd fel angel yn y nef.

* * * * *

And who else is to be found here
Under this wide slab of stone,
Side by side, under the greensward?
Read the Christian name: 'Tis John!
Yes, indeed, it is John Williams,
Son of the Sweet Singer of yore;
His soul also, now in glory,
Sings aloft for evermore.

Pwy sydd yma eto'n gorwedd,
Dan y garreg lydan hon,
Wrth dy ymyl yn y ceufedd?
Beth yw'r enw cyntaf? John!
Ie'n wir, John Williams ydyw,
Mab yr hen Ganiedydd per,
Mae ei enaid yntau heddiw
'N iach a siriol uwch y sêr.

By the Bishop's hands inducted
When a youth of twenty-five;
But a heavenly ordination
Later made his soul alive;
By the Spirit's gift from heaven
Called to be a preacher bold,
To proclaim the glorious gospel
And the testimonies of God.

Cafodd urddau llawn, esgobaidd,
Pan yn bump-ar-hugain oed;
Urddau gwell a mwy nefolaidd,
Gyda hynny iddo rhoed;
Dawn yr Ysbryd o'r uchelder
Oedd yr urdd a gafodd ef,
I draddodi mewn eglurder
Genadwri fawr y nef.

JOHN EVANS, CIL-Y-CWM

According to the unanimous testimony of an earlier generation, John Evans, Cil-y-cwm, was an excellent preacher. But because of the carelessness of the writers of his day, a carelessness that to us appears wholly inexcusable, hardly anything of his history survives. When was he born? Who were his parents? Under whose ministry was he convicted? When did he begin preaching, and when did his ministry end? None of the answers to these questions are known. But that a preacher of this name ministered in the northern parts of Carmarthenshire and was much used by God for the convicting and nurturing of many of his saints, are facts that cannot be denied. He was a contemporary of, and a co-labourer with Williams, Pantycelyn, and Lloyd of Caeo. We know that he undertook a preaching journey to the north in 1768. We may conclude therefore that he forms a connecting link between the first generation of Methodist exhorters and the second.

Cil-y-cwm is a small village of rather grey appearance, lying in the Tywi Valley about four miles from Llandovery and at the foot of the range of hills that separate Carmarthenshire from Cardiganshire. Methodism established an early foothold here, due probably to some of its inhabitants travelling to hear Daniel Rowland at Ystrad-ffin Chapel about six miles further up the valley. If the date on the front of the present chapel is correct, the first chapel was built in 1740. It is therefore the first known Methodist chapel. We have already given this title to Maesgwyn Chapel,[1] Radnorshire, but the earliest reference to the latter is in 1742. Our previous comment therefore was mistaken, and the honour of being the first community of Methodists to build a house to the Lord belongs to Cil-y-cwm. It was at this society, as already mentioned, that William Williams was a member but little is mentioned of him in connection with the cause. John Evans was the leader here, in that the hymn-writer was away so often on his travels.

Methodistiaeth Cymru states:

> As a minister, John Evans held an eminent position amongst his brethren. He journeyed much throughout the south and the north and left many indications behind him that the gospel he offered was not preached in vain. One man wrote of him as follows: 'As for John Evans, Cil-y-cwm, it is said that he possessed an exceptionally sweet gift; that there was such enchantment in his melodious voice that he could almost entice the bees from their hives. His doctrines dropped as the rain, as the small rain upon the tender herb, and as the showers upon the grass.' Mr Lloyd of Caeo used to say that his ministry was particularly effective in refreshing and comforting the saints.

We are grateful for this much information, though it is so little. From it we find that John Evans was a son of consolation; that he preferred to stand upon Gerizim rather than Ebal; he did not thunder forth curses against an evil world, but dwelt amongst the blessings of the gospel, dispensing balm to wounded, lost sinners. The sweetness of his voice is also emphasized. This was a particular characteristic of the preachers of the second generation. The voices of Jones, Llan-gan; Roberts, Clynnog; his brother, John Roberts, Llangwm; those of Dafydd Morris, and his son, Ebenezer Morris, particularly; were all full of music. John Evans also had this gift, and the sweetness of his tones was often the instrument, under God, to bring the gracious virtues of the gospel to the hearts of those on the point of death.

One account notes how the melody of his voice once brought a cruel persecution to an end. He and Mr Lloyd, Caeo, were on a journey; probably in the north. They had been announced to preach in a particular place and this had infuriated their enemies. The parish clergyman in particular was full of rage. This man gathered together the dregs and scoundrels of the people, inciting them to attack the two men. To encourage them on their way, he gave them plenty to drink. While these were drinking their beer, God's servants had arrived, and John Evans had begun to preach. Soon the persecutors rushed to the spot. They were seen by Mr Lloyd and from the hate and rage expressed on their faces he feared at least a riot and, possibly, considerable bloodshed. But to his surprise, the mob slowed down and eventually stopped. John Evans was at the height of his peroration; his voice, like a song of love, was full of enchantment and delight. As soon its sweet tones fell on the ears of their opponents, their strength failed, and without any conferring they all stopped to listen. But there was one amongst them on whom the sweetest voice would have no effect, and he was all the angrier that their assault had failed. In order to disrupt the meeting he found a brass pan from somewhere and began beating upon it. But some strong man who happened to be in the crowd, having an iron bar in his hand, went up to him and holding the bar above his head, threatened him, 'Unless you stop that noise I will hit you so hard with this that you will fall a dead man.' The persecutor took fright and the meeting proceeded peaceably.

John Evans was one of the first Methodists to preach at Mold. He spoke in the home of a Sarah Howell. When it became known that one of the 'Cradockians' had preached in the town, the curiosity of one young man was aroused. He later became well known in the Connexion as Edward Jones, Prion. He had heard much of the 'Cradockians' of the south; that they were not men but devils, and that their feet were like the feet of oxen. He developed a great longing to attend a meeting, not so much in order to hear John Evans but to see his feet. To the service he went. Very few were present, some eighteen or nineteen at most, but to his great disappointment he was not able to see the preacher's feet at all because John Evans was wearing boots. However he was a very determined young man, and so great was his desire to see oxen feet on the ends of human legs that he hung around after the service, hoping the 'Cradockian' would remove his boots. He succeeded in his plan. Through a knothole in the shutters of the window he saw John Evans's feet and behold, they were just like other men's feet. He did notice the preacher's striped stockings, and did not rest until he had obtained a pair for himself. This happened about 1768, and the story serves to illustrate the prejudice in the land against the Methodists, and the lies that were spread and believed about them.

Tradition has it that John Evans was prone to depression. Once, he and Dafydd Morris were on a journey in Anglesey and preaching at Cerrig-lleithir, the home of Sion Roland. After the service, John Evans was very uncommunicative. He sat, in a depressed slump by the fire at one end of the room, with Dafydd Morris and Sion Roland. At the other end of the room were a group of girls who started singing the following verses:

On seeing my failures and follies
I judged that I laboured in vain;
And thought that all praising and worship
Could wait until heaven was gained.

But when I can see your face shining
My soul must continually sing;
It soars from the snare of the fowlers,
And from its deep prison takes wing.

Wrth weled mor saled fy mywyd,
Meddyliais mai ofer fy ngwaith;
Bwriedais i beidio'th glodfori,
Nes myned o'r drysni maith, maith.

Pan welwyf dy wyneb yn tywynnu,
Mae'n rhaid i mi ganu bob dydd;
O garchar, a meddiant gelynion,
Daeth f'enaid yn union yn rhydd.

The singing stirred John Evans's spirit; he went to the girls and joined with them. The verses were repeated time and again, and it was not long before the singing became praising, and the depressed preacher was the loudest in his praise. Dafydd Morris turned to Sion Roland and said, 'That's Jack out of the net.'

This is all we have of the history of this famous servant of Jesus Christ. Quite certainly he laboured long and hard; he suffered much persecution; he had many impressive services in which the arm of the Lord was revealed; and he was an instrument in God's hand to turn many to righteousness. But none of these things have been chronicled in the books of men though, no doubt, they are down in heaven's books. When it was he died, and where the place of his grave, we do not know, but all is known to him who said, 'And I will raise him up at the last day.'

MORGAN RHYS

Without doubt, one of the sweetest hymn writers of the Methodist Revival in Wales was Morgan Rhys, a man who will be honoured by the Welsh people while they continue to offer praise to God in their mother tongue. It is true that William Williams is the prince of Welsh hymn writers. That is a truth that all acknowledge. But who is next to him is a matter still to be decided. We shall not attempt to do so here; we are not the ones to judge, nor would it answer any purpose, but it is worth noting that some of the best poets of the past generation and of today, have given their opinion that as a hymn writer Morgan Rhys is second only to William Williams.

It is a grief to us that so little material is at hand for any attempt at a worthy biography of this famous man. We do not know of any other of the fathers who achieved such fame, but yet with so little known of him. Morgan Rhys's way in this world is like 'the way of an eagle in the air . . . the way of a ship in the midst of the sea.' It is so hidden as to be unknown. It seems that he was born in the Llandovery neighbourhood but we have no idea where. We do not know the names of his parents, of his parish, nor of the house in which he was born. We do not know the date of his birth or any fact of his childhood and upbringing.[2] Matters do not improve when we consider his adult life, for we have failed to discover if he ever married or if there was any family to mourn him when he died. As far as we know there is no one alive who claims a relationship to him. The first place associated with Morgan Rhys is the little village of Cil-y-cwm, some four miles from Llandovery. It is said that he was converted under the ministries of Daniel Rowland and Howell Harris, and this is very probable because both these men paid early and frequent visits to Cil-y-cwm and to Ystrad-ffin, which is not far away.

If he was a native of Cil-y-cwm and was converted early in life, it is a remarkable fact that there is no mention of him in the first minute-book of that church. In the Trefeca records for 1742 is written, 'There is here a small fellowship, but it has not been put in regular order.' It is also noted that the Cil-y-cwm society, together with five other neighbouring societies, were under the care of an exhorter named James Williams; that John Thomas, one of the members, was the private exhorter, and Isaac Dafydd, the steward. We have therefore the names of the officers of the society at Cil-y-cwm, and also the names of eight of the members: Sion Thomas Sion, Ochrfforest; Richard Sion, Coed-ifan; William Lloyd, Dygoedydd; Isaac Prytherch, Dolgynon; Ifan, the furrier; Rhys Thomas Sion, the glover; Betty of Eithin-duon; and Ann James, Dolfallt. As Morgan Rhys is not named as an officer or member, it is natural to assume that he either joined the society at a later date or that he was still a young boy at the time. Williams, Pantycelyn, joined the society soon after the Watford Association of 1743, and certainly Morgan Rhys was a member at some time. For how long, and during what years, these two most famous of Welsh hymn writers were fellow members here, is very difficult to decide. Morgan Rhys lived at various other places apart from Cil-y-cwm, but Williams remained in the same neighbourhood throughout his life.

Morgan Rhys must have received some education, because it is believed that he was a master over one of Griffith Jones's Welsh circulating schools. As with all these schoolmasters, he was moved from district to district according to the calls for his service. We do not know how long he worked in these schools, nor the places where he taught. It is said that many of his books were owned until quite recently by a native of Llanfynydd and that written inside them was, 'Morgan Rhys, Llansadwrn.' But this man's house was burnt in a fire, together with all the books. If this story is true, and we have no reason to doubt it, it may be that Llansadwrn was the place of his birth and that he went from there to Cil-y-cwm, but there is no more mention of him in the early accounts of the Llansadwrn society than in that of Cil-y-cwm. Having served for years in the circulating schools, he established his own school in the Capel Isaac neighbourhood, near Llandeilo, and from there moved to Llanfynydd, where at the end of his days he lived in a small house on land belonging to Cwm-gwaun-hendy. It was in this house that he died, and he is buried in the cemetery of Llanfynydd Church. His grave is said to be to the north of the church, under the middle window, but we are ashamed at having to state that there is not even a rough stone carrying his initials to mark the spot. Surely this disgrace should be immediately attended to. In the church register of burials are found the words, 'Morgan Rhys, August 9th, 1779'. Unfortunately, this short note does not record his age so that we do not know whether he had a long life or was carried home to that better world of which he sang so sweetly, at a relatively young age.

Morgan Rhys probably lived at Llanfynydd for many years, and if we feel a need to associate him with a particular place then Llanfynydd certainly has the greatest claim. An account of the Methodist cause here is the only place in which his name is recorded. *Methodistiaeth Cymru* states that:

> ... in this church there are many men of good words and zeal of spirit, such as Morgan Rhys, the author of the hymns; William Morgan Thomas, Gallt-llan; Thomas Lewis, Pantgwineu; Thomas Lewis, Pentre-felin; Rhys Rhys, and his son, John Rhys, the father and brother of the Rev. Dafydd Rhys; Dafydd William, the carpenter; and Thomas Jones.

He seems to have been something of a poet before he came to Llanfynydd because a present elder at Llanfynydd knows a verse written by Morgan Rhys, though it is so long since it was composed that it may now be very different from the original:

I wondered at seeing the place	Rhyfeddais, pan gwelais i ble,
Where, taking my journey, I've come;	De's iddo i wneuthur fy nghartre';
Retribution must follow apace	Mae dial yn galw o rywle,
That Llanfynydd should now be my home.	Neu beth ddaeth a fi i'r fath le?

Llanfynydd must then have been a very different place from what it is now or the hymn writer could hardly have composed such a verse. It is now one of the prettiest villages of Carmarthenshire. The verse shows that Morgan Rhys was not born in Llanfynydd.

We are inclined to believe that it was at Llanfynydd that he was made an elder and an exhorter with the Methodists, and that it was here he composed the majority, if not all, of his hymns. The tradition of the church has it that he was appointed an elder there, and it is only natural to assume that it was after this that he received a commission to preach. We have reasons also for believing that it was after arriving here that his poetic muse developed. Mr Morris Davies, Bangor, in his masterly essays on hymnology in the *Traethodydd* [*The Essayist*] of 1872 states that, 'It is thought that he was born about the beginning of the eighteenth century.' This would make him older than William Williams, Pantycelyn, by about ten or twelve years, whereas it is generally believed that he was the younger man.

Be that as it may, it is almost certain that he was younger than Williams as a hymn writer. The poet from Pantycelyn published his

Alleluia in 1744, eleven years before the first of Morgan Rhys's compositions appeared. It is now also known that in the sixth issue of *Alleluia* Williams included many of the hymns of his friends, Morgan Dafydd of Caeo; J. J.; William Edward; Morgan Dafydd; and others. There is none by Morgan Rhys included however, which suggests that his muse had not yet been awakened. When he did begin to compose, we read that he used to recite his hymns to Williams in order to have his opinion. There is an account of one such occasion when Williams, after hearing a hymn, said 'Well, you've caught in that one the experiences of a good one-and-a-half Christians.' The comment suggests that the scope of the hymn was far above the experiences of ordinary believers.

Though so little is known of Morgan Rhys's history, there is enough evidence available to date the various stages of his development as a hymn writer. He flourished in his craft between the years 1755 and 1779, that is, in the last nineteen years of his life. We must add to this span the years in which he was composing the hymns in his first booklet, published in 1755. This contained only twenty-two hymns, and was sold for two pence. It is difficult to know for certain when these were written, but it may safely be said that it was in the afternoon and evening of his life that Morgan Rhys composed his sweet and heavenly hymns. Indeed, this would be our conclusion even if we had no further guidance but considered only the nature of the hymns themselves. They are not the product of youth but that of an experienced man who has long borne the labour and heat of the day.

MORGAN RHYS'S POETRY

Morgan Rhys's only publications were hymns and elegies. These were reprinted many times during his life and afterwards. The following is a list of his publications:

HYMNBOOKS

1. *A View from the Summit of Nebo of the land of promise,* 1755.
2. *A View of this Passing World, and of the eternal happiness hastening towards all of Zion's redeemed,* 1767.
3. *A View of the City of Refuge, in a collection of hymns, to entertain those pilgrims passing through the Vale of Tears towards the quiet habitation,* 1770.
4. *The Spiritual Warfare; in a collection of new hymns of various metres, by Morgan Rhys and Thomas Dafydd,* 1772.
5. *The Believer's Groans for Perfection and Incorruption, on a new metre,* 1772.

Elegies

1. *An Elegy, or a remembrance of the happy deaths of some faithful ministers of the gospel in south Wales, who lately departed this world; namely, the Rev. Howell Davies, Pembrokeshire; Mr William Richard, Cardiganshire; and Mr Sion Parry, Carmarthenshire, together with many others of the saints, who worshipped God together with some of us in this present world, but who are now healed and healthy in the eternal world.* By Morgan Rhys. Printed by J. Ross, Carmarthen, 1770.

2. *A short history of the circumspect life and happy death of Morgan Nathan*, Llandeilo, Carmarthenshire, 1775.

The author's main work is *A View from the Summit of Nebo.* The first edition came out under another name in 1755. A reprint, containing many more hymns, was published in 1764. A third edition, appearing in 1773, omitted many hymns from the first two editions, and other new hymns were added. The fourth, and last edition in the author's lifetime, was printed in 1775. In the present century the work has been published in Carmarthen in 1808; in Merthyr in 1831; and in Aberystwyth in 1841; and selections of the hymns have appeared in many booklets on various occasions. These many reprints show that Morgan Rhys's hymns came very quickly into common use, and that their strength and sweetness have continued to be appreciated down to the present day. Very many of his works are also included in every collection of hymns used by the various Welsh denominations and in some of these there are more of his hymns than of any other author, with the exception of Williams, Pantycelyn. We list below those hymns by Morgan Rhys which are sung most often in our day:

1. Pechadur wyf, O Arglwydd.
2. Wel, dyma un sy'n maddau.
3. O gariad! O gariad!
4. Cadben mawr ein hiachawdwriaeth.
5. Peraidd ganodd sêr y bore.
6. Fe welir Seion fel y wawr.
7. Mae'r bwrdd yn llawn danteithion.
8. O rhedwn bawb yr yrfa.
9. Ar fyr caf rodio'r llwybr.
10. Fyth, fyth, rhyfeddai'r cariad.
11. Fe dderfydd i mi bechu.
12. Henffych i'r bore hyfryd.
13. O gwyn eu byd y dyrfa.

14. Yna derfydd fy nghystuddiau.
15. Dyddiau blin fy mhererindod.
16. Pan sycho'r dyfroedd dyfnion, maith.
17. Dewch, hen ac ieuanc dewch.
18. Mae palldod yn naturiaeth.
19. Beth sydd i mi yn y byd.
20. Gwnes addunedau fil.
21. Y pethau darfodedig.
22. I'r Aifft daeth Iesu i'm gwared.
23. Mae gwedd ei wyneb yn iachau.
24. 'Rwy'n teimlo f'enaid nawr yn caru.
25. Fe syrth y sêr i lawr o'r nen.
26. Er gwaetha'r maen a'r gwylwyr.
27. Gwnaed concwest ar Galfaria fryn.
28. O agor fy llygaid i weled.

These listed exemplify the best of Morgan Rhys, but it would be easy to name many others of his works that are as beautiful as any hymns ever written. Mr Morris Davies, describing Rhys's work, states that:

> Their chief excellence is their originality and their sweetness. There is no paraphrasing or imitation in his work, so that it may be considered as completely Welsh in origin... His themes are scriptural, and the quality of the poetry is evangelical and experiential. He rejoices in the demonstration of the infinite love of God, the riches of his grace, the salvation of his people through the Lord Jesus. He draws his support and consolation while passing through the wilderness, and while under the oppression and persecution of the enemies of his soul, from the treasures of the promises and the Faithfulness of the Saviour; and while noting the frailty of man's life on earth, and of the passing nature of this world, he looks forward beyond time, to the great eternity; he ascends to the summit of Nebo to gaze through his telescope towards the Land of Promise, the heavenly Canaan, the inheritance of the saints beyond death. He often sings sweetly of the glorification and blessedness of the bride, the wife of the Lamb, but that which most fires his affections in glorious and victorious praises is the glory of the Person of the Saviour, as God-Man; the merit of his sacrifice; the success of his intercession within the veil; his high exaltation at the right hand of the Majesty in the heavenly places; his second coming to judge the world as the Alpha and Omega of all the divine dispensations, in Creation, providence, and the salvation of the Church.

[1] Volume 1, p. 361.

[2] It is now known that Morgan Rhys was born on 1 April 1716, at Efail-fach, Cil-y-cwm, the son of Rhys and Anne Lewis.

30

THOMAS CHARLES, B.A., BALA

THOMAS CHARLES'S PARENTS AND HIS CHILDHOOD

We come now to the history of one whose name will be forever remembered with honour; one whose influence is still felt throughout the known world though he was gathered to his fathers over eighty years ago; one who must be registered as amongst the greatest benefactors of Wales, if not indeed the greatest of them all. If it had to be decided by general ballot who were the three men to whom the Welsh nation owed most, there might possibly be disagreement over two of them, but I believe that the nation would unanimously appoint Thomas Charles as one of the three. He did not excel in one sphere but in many. He was a good preacher, very rarely do we meet his equal as an organizer, and he was an extremely effective educator through the instrumentality of the various institutions that he founded and of his published works. He was not amongst the founders of Methodism. The Revival had flourished for more than twenty years before he was born. But if he did not contribute to the laying of the foundation, he had an enormous part in the building of the superstructure. He, above all, safeguarded the fruit of the Revival in Wales so that rather than being a temporary excitement, appearing and then disappearing, it continued in its permanent influence upon our land. All of the main elements of the constitution of the Methodists may be traced back to either Howell Harris or Thomas Charles. Providentially, there is no lack of materials at hand for writing an account of his life. There are many biographies of him available and he himself kept a diary for many years until the weight of his many duties forced him to stop.

About the middle of the last century, a respectable man named Rice Charles lived at Pant-dwfn, a plain-looking farmhouse in the parish of Llanfihangel, Carmarthenshire. Pant-dwfn stands about ten miles from Carmarthen, between it and the sea. The nearest village is St Clears and the house is to be found on the left-hand side of the road from St Clears to Laugharne. The home in which Rice Charles lived has been a ruin for many years; it lay in a hollow, hence its name [*'pant dwfn'* = deep hollow], but the present farmhouse stands on higher ground nearby. We know very little of Rice Charles and not even the name of his wife, but there are indications that they were both ignorant of true religion, though possibly they attended church consistently on a Sunday. To these two were born two sons; the first was Thomas, the subject of this chapter; the second was David, namely the late Rev. David Charles, Carmarthen, whom we shall mention later.[1]

Thomas Charles was born on 14 October 1755. Little of his childhood is known other than what he noted himself in his journal, and these notes are very sketchy and have to do mainly with his spiritual condition. We may conclude from them that he was of a gentle and serious temperament, was very rarely mischievous, and avoided all fights and skirmishes. He was however a quick learner and a great lover of books. His parents therefore determined to raise him for the ministry. Full of such desires, they sent him, when he was between ten and twelve years old, to school at Llanddowror, about two miles away from Pant-dwfn. It is to be doubted whether he ever saw or heard the Rev. Griffith Jones; he was only six years old when that famous man died. But the school established in Llanddowror by Mr Jones for preparing young men to be clergymen and schoolteachers was still in existence. At this time Thomas was often troubled because of his spiritual state, though not knowing what was giving rise to such thoughts. He would go to any lengths to hear the gospel. If he heard that there was preaching at some house within a certain radius, nothing would stop him from being present, and usually he would go on his own. He was full also of desires to read the Bible and every good book that he came across. 'No time was tedious in reading good books,' he wrote. He came across a treatise by John Bunyan on the two covenants, *The Doctrine of Law and Grace Unfolded*. 'That part wherein he shows the dreadful state of those who are under the covenant of works affected me very much indeed, and made me several times to cry bitterly.'[2]

With his spirit made serious, and the desire to be acceptable to God filling his heart, he naturally longed for fellowship with those of like mind. In his journal he commented:

> I recollect I thought everybody to be religious that went pretty constant to church, but I often wondered I never heard them talk any thing about religion, especially of a Sunday. I had not one spiritual person to speak to for some time.[3]

And this, it must be remembered, is while he was in Llanddowror, the place where Griffith Jones had ministered for so many years! A great decline must have occurred in the region, and that very rapidly after the death of the old Apostle. Evidence for this is found in *Methodistiaeth Cymru*, where John Hughes writes:

> The Rev. Griffith Jones died in 1761 and we know of no effort made to scatter the darkness of the neighbourhood and to lead the inhabitants to the Saviour of mankind for thirty-five years after his death. The locality therefore fell into its primitive state, and another generation arose that had not known Griffith Jones and had not heard him preach.

But those who are like-minded have ways of finding each other, and somehow or other Thomas Charles found the fellowship of a godly old man called Rees Hugh. He was a disciple of Griffith Jones, poor in circumstances and without much talent or knowledge except in spiritual things. According to Thomas Charles:

> [He lived] a few miles off, on whom I always called once or twice a week, and his conversation was very much blessed to me. Sometimes he was filled with great joy and comfort in talking to me; and when that was the case with him, I never was unaffected. I loved him, as long as he lived, as my own soul, and always looked upon him as my Father in Christ. The remembrance of him will be pleasing to me as long as I live.[4]

It is a striking picture to imagine this youth of twelve years of age, something of a scholar, with the enchantments of the world opening up before him, talking of spiritual things with a simple old man and, as the glory of the plan of salvation shines into their minds, both being brought to rejoice. Mr Charles added:

> During this time I had but very little knowledge of the gospel scheme; my religion consisted principally in earnest longings and strong desires after something which I had not hitherto obtained; together with a determined resolution to continue to use all appointed means to find it. I made now a public profession, went to the sacrament, endeavoured to introduce religion into my father's family. I hope also my feeble attempts were not ineffectual in the end. Considering my age and my little knowledge, the authority I maintained in a family so large – generally about eighteen – was surprising. What was deficient in other things was supplied by a very great earnestness and zeal. My temper and disposition being naturally mild and soft, I was always generally beloved by all my relations; this helped me greatly in passing through many difficulties.[5]

When he was about fourteen years old, his father sent him to the Academy at Carmarthen. His heart was full of fear as he left home for the first time. Rees Hugh also feared for him. Before he left, the two of them mixed their tears with their supplications before the throne of grace, and Mr Charles attributed his safekeeping in the years following in part to the prayers of his old friend on his behalf. He was not long in Carmarthen before he became a member of the Methodist society in the town. He does not seem to have come into contact with them before, except to listen to some of their preachers when they visited the neighbourhood of Bancyfelin. He threw in his lot with them now because it was with them that he saw most signs of spiritual life. However, all is not gold that glistens:

> I soon joined a society of Methodists there, in which I met several very pious persons, whose conversation was exceedingly blessed to me, but all had been well nigh ruined by a set of careless, high spirited, jolly professors with whom I contracted too much intimacy soon after I came there, but the Lord graciously opened my eyes and delivered me out of their snare.[6]

It was while he was in Carmarthen that he arrived at a fuller understanding of the doctrines of the gospel, mainly through reading good books, in particularly the *Dialogues* of the Rev. James Hervey. By these means, together with the fellowship of godly believers, he increased in knowledge and his spiritual life was deepened.

CONVERSION WHILE LISTENING TO DANIEL ROWLAND

We come now to the turning point in his life and will allow him to tell the story in his own words:

> January 20, 1773, I went to hear Mr Rowland preach at New Chapel; his text was Hebrews 4:15. A day much to be remembered by me as long as I live. Ever since the happy day I have lived in a new heaven and a new earth. The change a blind man who receives his sight experiences does not exceed the change I at that time experienced in my mind.

Earth receded and grew fainter, Heaven's windows opened wide; Echoes of the angelic choirs Reached my ears from every side.	Ciliodd daear, aeth o'r golwg, Nef a ymagorai'n amlwg; Sain angylaidd oedd i'm clustiau, Atsain nefol bêr ganiadau.

> Then I was first convinced of the sin of unbelief or entertaining narrow, contracted and hard thoughts of the Almighty. I had such a view of Christ as our High Priest, of his love, compassion, power, and all-sufficiency, as filled my soul with astonishment – with joy unspeakable and full of glory. My mind was overwhelmed and overpowered with amazement. The truths exhibited to my view appeared too wonderfully gracious to be believed. I could not believe for very joy. The glorious scenes then opened to my eyes will abundantly satisfy my soul millions of years hence in the contemplation of them.

> I had some idea of gospel truths before floating in my head, but they never powerfully and with divine energy penetrated my heart till now. The effect of this sermon remained upon my mind above half a year, during which time I was generally in a comfortable and heavenly frame. Often in walking in the fields I looked up to heaven with joy and called that my home, at the same time ardently longing for the appearance of the glorious Saviour to take me forever to himself.[7]

This was a day forever to be remembered in Mr Charles's experience. He is to be considered before this day as one not far from the kingdom of heaven, or even indeed as one who had passed through from death to life, but he now came for the first time into the possession of the glorious liberty of the gospel, and the light that shone in his soul was so dazzling that the 'earth receded' from his sight. He gave up completely any striving to justify himself by the works of the law; he no longer laboured to weave his self-righteousnesses together in order to hide his nakedness before God; his constant cry from now on was to 'be found in him'. At the time he was a youth of eighteen years of age, but he never forgot the accents of Rowland's voice, or rather, he never forgot God's voice, heard in Rowland's sermon. In his journal and in his letters he refers to the 20th of January as a unique day in his experience. Five years later, he wrote:

> Today is a special day, to be greatly remembered. So glorious was the revelation of divine truths on this very day. By God's mercy they are to this hour as glorious and valuable as ever; they are always new, always awakening. O, may we live and feed upon them more and more!

Another time, he writes of the same day:

> O the happy return of this most beneficial day! A day to be happily remembered for on it the light of the knowledge of the glorious gospel first shone brightly in my soul in the face of Jesus Christ. On the return of this sacred day let every other thought give place to thanksgiving and praise.

The meeting with the Lord Jesus on the Damascus road formed no greater significance in the mind and heart of the Apostle than did the glory that shone in his soul during that service at the New Chapel in the mind and heart of Thomas Charles.

OXFORD AND OLNEY

In all probability he was at the Carmarthen Academy for nearly six years; that is, until he reached his twentieth year. He does not mention his scholarly progress in his journal but when we take into account the strength of his mental abilities and his diligence as a student, it must be assumed that he became a brilliant scholar before his departure. He did not now know what to do. His parents had taxed their resources heavily in maintaining him so long at Carmarthen; their circumstances did not allow them to spend any more on him. The door to ordination therefore seemed closed against him. But light dawned in the darkness. He wrote in his journal:

> In the year 1775, Providence very unexpectedly and very wonderfully opened my way to go to Oxford, what neither my parents nor myself nor any of my relations had the least idea of till just at this time, but now all obstacles were removed and it was determined I should go. The manner in which the Lord opened my way to go thither gave me great satisfaction and strong assurance that I should be kept by God's grace from being burnt in the fiery furnace.[8]

His words suggest that Oxford was considered at the time, just as it was in Howell Harris's time, a place full of immorality and therefore certain of proving a difficult test of anyone's religion. Who it was who enabled him to go there, he does not say; it may be that some rich gentleman, full of generosity and a kind nature, felt concerned for his situation. He started out in May, travelling on foot probably. There was as yet no railway and he would probably not have been able to afford to go by carriage. We may assume him to have been full of anxieties but he soon had evident indications that God was well pleased. He wrote further:

> On the road, the Lord gave me very comfortable views of himself as my Father in Christ; nay that Christ's Father was my Father and his God my God. What could I want more? Here was power sufficient and compassion enough! The following words sounded melodiously in my ears, 'I ascend unto my Father and your Father, and unto my God and your God.' I was enabled through grace to commit myself to the custody of my heavenly Father and to yield myself cheerfully and submissively to the guidance of his Spirit and Providence.[9]

It is not often that one meets with such deep piety and maturity of thought in a young man not yet twenty years old.

In May 1775, Thomas Charles arrived in Oxford and was received as a member of Jesus College. He soon came into contact with many truly religious young men in the University, who gave themselves to their devotions, who met for prayer and to discuss spiritual topics. He immediately felt at home amongst them and their company was of great comfort and profit to him. Among them were many Welshmen and with one of these, Mr Simon Lloyd of Bala, he formed a friendship that was to last throughout their lifetimes. And it was this friendship, as we shall see, that was to determine the future course of Thomas Charles's life. We have very little of his history at Oxford but we may be sure that throughout his three years there he gave himself continuously to his studies and did his best to prepare himself for the important work of the ministry. Two years into his studies, he was brought to a crisis. Quite suddenly the financial support he received from Wales was stopped. We do not know the cause; whether the benefactor who had promised to support him had died; or whether that man, as happens with men sometimes, had changed his mind, leaving the young man to fend for himself amongst strangers. For whatever reason his supplies from Wales dried up and Thomas Charles had no place to turn for relief. At the time also, he was in debt to the College to the sum of twenty pounds. For about a fortnight he was sore broken in the place of dragons, not knowing what to do. He at last decided to submit to the Lord's will, to inform the college authorities of his position, and to go to the country to seek his livelihood in whatever way that opened up to him. He could not however understand the providential arrangements that had opened the path for him to attend university in an almost miraculous way and was now closing it up as if with thorns. Throughout the experience however he had a confidence that the Lord would bring him through. Then:

> One morning as I was writing to my friends in Wales informing them of my difficulties and my consequent resolution, an intimate friend of mine called upon me to whom I immediately explained my situation and also the resolution I had formed of leaving Oxford. He answered that he did not doubt but by some means or other I should be assisted, and desired me to make myself perfectly easy about the matter. A few days after, a gentleman sent for me to dine with him; I went, and before we parted, to my great surprise, he produced the twenty pound note I wanted, and at the same time told me that I should not want during my stay at Oxford. I was much rejoiced and very thankful. The gentleman was as good as his word. This introduced me into a new connection, and considerably enlarged my sphere of acquaintance.[10]

This last sentence suggests that the benefactor was not a Welshman and indeed that he was a complete stranger to Mr Charles previously. It is clear that he did more than merely support the young man financially; he welcomed him to his house as a valued guest and introduced him to his friends and acquaintances. But it was the arrangements of Providence that Thomas Charles saw pre-eminently in the circumstances. In his journal he writes that he spent the summer vacation of 1797 in Olney with Mr Newton. John Newton was the evangelical clergyman whose name is so well known in our days as the author of very many sweet hymns and as the bosom friend of William Cowper. The closest of friendships sprang up between the young student and the old clergyman that lasted until the day of the latter's death. From Olney, Mr Charles wrote to a friend in London:

Having a Newton to be instructed by, both by edifying discourses in the pulpit, and by conversation in the closet, what place or situation can I be in, more pleasing and delightful? I had formed in my mind great ideas of him, but really he has exceeded my most sanguine expectations. Mr M[ayor] talks of your coming down. I wish you would, I am sure you would like both the shepherd and the sheep. I never pass my time with more pleasure and profit, than when I am in conversation with poor simple-hearted Christians, who pretend to know nothing but a little of their own hearts and the way of salvation through Christ. There is something pleasing and comfortable in the very sight of those with whom you hope to spend a happy eternity. That my lot may fall among them here and hereafter, is the very utmost of my wishes.

But with no small pleasure I inform you that Mr [William] Romaine stopped here two days, and gave us two very excellent sermons on Christ's glory in his person and offices, and on his preciousness to a ruined sinner, when he is enabled to lay hold upon him through faith. I was vastly delighted with his manner of preaching; which, though peculiar yet seems to me the most simple and best adapted to the capacity of the unlearned. As to the matter, it was excellent indeed, and delivered in such a feeling and pathetic strain, that even my cold, hard heart could not but be warmed a little with his fire. Had I the strongest constitution and the best advantages of human literature, yes, of all learning, both sacred and profane, yet I am perfectly convinced that all this would be much too little to make me a gospel preacher. One may speak a great deal, and that very orthodox; but unless he has a little of the unction of the Holy Spirit, he might, for aught I know, as well be silent. This is what I want in my prayers, studies, and meditations. And that God would grant you and me a great share of it, when we come to act in public capacity, will, I hope, be the fervent prayers of your affectionate friend,

THOMAS CHARLES.[11]

We have included the whole of this letter as it provides an open window that reveals the secret feelings of the writer, and his thoughts concerning ministerial qualification. Thomas Charles did not scorn human learning; he was one of the most zealous of men in his labours to attain it; but for all the enchantment that the classic writers held for him he knew that that unction from the Holy One was the main requirement for the pulpit. He returned to Oxford greatly refreshed in body and spirit. Towards the end of 1777 he wrote the following letter that again sheds considerable light on his state of mind:

I long to see Zion the glory of the whole earth, and am not very anxious about the means God shall employ for its enlargement; but I think it a very undeserved favour, though I hope I can say, it is all my desire, to be exercised in some corner in extending its borders.

> It grieves me to inform you that poor R___ , of Brazen-nose College, has had his degrees refused him by the Society on account of his Methodistical principles; which at once deprived him of the honours of the University and of the fellowship which he was sure of as soon as he had taken his degree. Perhaps he acted indiscreetly in some things; but that can never justify the rigorous severity of their persecuting spirit. By what he told me he seems to have performed what he thought to be his duty in an upright, sincere, conscientious manner; though I do not think it my duty to act as he did.[12]

Two points are clear from this letter: Firstly, that Mr Charles placed no great importance on religious denominationalism; that his spirit could ascend far above party spirit. When he stated that he was not anxious about the means used by God to enlarge the bounds of Zion, what he meant, we believe, is that it was unimportant to himself whether it was by means of the Established Church or apart from it, that the great work of the Revival be carried out. And he further suggests that it was unimportant to him whether he himself was to labour within that Church or outside it, as long as he might be about the work of the Kingdom. Secondly, that Methodism was still greatly hated at Oxford. And this is the same as saying that spiritual religion was hated there, because the main purpose of the Methodist students, that which distinguished them from the other students, was their diligence in reading their Bibles, in prayer, and in the other duties enforced by the New Testament upon every Christian. For this sin of being godly, here is one young man being refused his degree and the fellowship of his college, which, as well as being honours, would have been sources of income for him. No wonder Thomas Charles was agitated.

A CURACY AT QUEEN CAMEL, SOMERSET

Thomas Charles's time at Oxford came to an end in the summer of 1778 and as he intended entering the Church it was necessary for him to find a curacy. There is no doubt that he would have preferred to return to Wales but no door opened for him there. A place at Worcester seemed possible but nothing came of it. Eventually he accepted a curacy at Queen Camel, Somerset. The rector was a man called Newman. His feelings at the time are worth noting; the following is his entry in his journal:

> On June 14, 1778, I was ordained deacon at Oxford. Felt an earnest desire that the Lord would enable me to devote myself wholly to his service the remainder of my days on earth; was not a little impressed with a sense of the great importance of the charge I had taken upon me and of my very great inability to discharge it faithfully and in a due manner. May the Spirit of the Lord Jehovah be upon me evermore.[13]

He expressed similar views when he wrote to a friend about a fortnight after his ordination:

> I have the pleasure to inform you that I am in orders since last Trinity Sunday . . . My dear friend, this is the most awful and solemn time I have yet lived to see. My anxious thoughts about the holy function I have taken upon me, and the very weighty work I am engaged in, frequently oppress my spirits very much. That solemn exhortation and charge of St Paul, in Acts 20:28, sounds in my ears day and night. Is the Church so dear and precious to Christ that He purchased it with his most precious blood? What bowels of compassion and mercy then should I exercise towards every one, even the meanest individual, in it? How solicitous should I be about their welfare? How anxious about their salvation? May God of his infinite goodness enable me to be faithful. At the same time it comforts my heart when I reflect on God's gracious dealings with me, in making it my continual employ, my vocation, to think and speak about the astonishing scheme of salvation, and the glorious author of it. What theme more sweet and ravishing! What topic more spiritual and sublime! Let my heart and tongue, and every member I have, join with St Paul and all the angels in heaven in glorying in the cross of Christ, and be determined to know nothing else.[14]

Not often do we find a young minister beginning his work with such a high view of his office.

Mr Newman had no need of the services of his curate until Michaelmas, Mr Charles therefore accepted the invitation of his friend, Simon Lloyd, to pay him a visit at Bala. Little did he imagine, as he took his first view of Bala Lake from the hill slopes above it and of the small town lying quietly at its side, that it was here that he would fulfil his life's work; but such were the arrangements of divine Providence. The two friends were at Bala for about five weeks, taking journeys from there to various parts of north Wales. This was the time that Mr Charles first came to know Miss Sally Jones, the stepdaughter of Mr Thomas Foulkes. The two became friends immediately and their correspondence eventually developed into marriage, as we shall see. From Bala the two men travelled to the south, to Mr Charles's home. On the way they called at Llangeitho and stayed there two or three days. '[We] heard during that time,' wrote Thomas Charles, 'two sermons from Mr Rowland with inexpressible pleasure.'

On 13 August, they reached Pant-dwfn. The young curate's feelings as he arrived home are worth recording:

> I looked upon those little corners of the house, and sequestered hedges in the fields, with inexpressible pleasure, where my soul in former days had often struggled with God in prayer and obtained the blessing. I could not but view those sacred spots in which I enjoyed refreshing communion with God as

holy ground. My father's farm wore the appearance of Paradise; the memory of the various blessings at different times bestowed, filled my heart with joy and praise.[15]

Mr Charles and his friend had arrived at Pant-dwfn on a Thursday and it was arranged that he should preach the following Sunday at Llanfihangel, his father's parish church. Most probably this was his first sermon. In the congregation, having come to hear his former disciple, was the old pilgrim, Rees Hugh. Mr Charles wrote, 'I could almost have cried with joy.' The same joy must have been in Rees Hugh's heart and he could have repeated Simeon's words of old, 'Lord, now lettest thou thy servant depart in peace, according to thy word,' at seeing his young friend whose steps towards heaven he had directed so carefully, now taking his place in the pulpit as a minister of Christ, and with every indication that he had been blessed abundantly with ministerial gifts. This was the last time for these two to meet. Within about a month the soul of Rees Hugh was in heaven.

QUOTATIONS FROM HIS JOURNAL

Mr Charles began his work as curate in Queen Camel at Michaelmas, 1778. He kept a detailed journal at this time but very little, in fact hardly at all, does he record his circumstantial affairs. That which held his attention was his spiritual state before God, the pollution of his heart, and the cleansing of it found in the gospel. His comments show his complete honesty, his intense integrity, and his deep understanding of the various elements of the gospel. We would be delighted to include the journal in its entirety, but must be satisfied by a few quotations as examples:

November 8. My soul being much depressed with the sense of my inability and insufficiency for the work of the ministry, fearful lest any soul should perish through my ignorance or negligence, and lest I should bring reproach upon the glorious gospel, the Lord was pleased to apply the words in Psalm 32: 8, with great power to my soul. Help me, O Lord, to rely on thy sure word and promise and to look to thee in all things, who perfecteth strength in the weakness of thy people, and from whom alone is their sufficiency for every work.

November 15. My mind this morning dwelt with edification and comfort on the firmness and stability of the covenant of grace, and also on its suitableness in every view to the various wants of fallen sinners. 'It is well ordered in all things and sure.' In returning from my curacy my weary soul ardently longed for my Father's house, my eternal home. O when shall I be there? When shall I see him as he is and be like him? When shall I sit at the marriage-supper of the Lamb? I am weary of sin and fearful of falling into it.

November 21. My soul earnestly longs and pants after purity of heart. Nothing but the inspiration of the Holy Spirit can cleanse the thoughts of my polluted heart. There is an *acervus malorum* [a heap of evils] within, and God alone can deliver me from them. The very attempt of cleansing myself is but lost labour. But I am comforted to think, that God Jehovah hath taken the work into his own hands. 'I will cleanse them', saith He. Jeremiah 33:8; Psa. 51:7. Had I to choose the richest blessing on earth or in heaven, my soul would say, '*A pure heart,* Lord. Stamp thine image on my soul.'

November 25. 'As the hart panteth after the water brooks, so panteth my soul after thee, O God.' Help me, O Saviour, to wait patiently until thou dost see fit to lift up the light of thy countenance upon me . . . Providence at present appears dark, but thou, O Lord, art my strength and my portion. It is to thee that I must turn my sight, and thou dost always see me. In good time all will be resolved; strengthen me to watch and pray.[16]

We see the young minister deeply aware of his dependence upon God, aware also of the wickedness of his heart, but knowing also the cure to be found in the application of the gospel. Queen Camel was a rural locality. Mr Charles's time was not therefore fully engaged in the service of the parish, and he had opportunity to give himself energetically to his studies. But he certainly did not confine himself to his study and pulpit. His was an eminently practical nature and he no doubt took up the work of catechizing the children and visiting from door to door. Because of this activity and the fact that his sermons were so evangelical in tone, it was not long before he was suspected of being a Methodist, and a persecuting spirit soon arose against him. Phrases in his journal reveal this, though only briefly does he refer to his troubles. On 29 December, he noted:

It rejoices me that my name is cast out as evil for the Lord's sake. I hope I am enabled to choose to suffer affliction with the people of God rather than the pleasure of sin for a season. All my desire is that I may be enabled to fight the good fight, keep the faith and finish my course with joy and triumph.[17]

On 22 March, the following year, he wrote:

I find the Lord is graciously determined to bring me from every thing to live only upon him. I depended upon a broken reed and it has pierced me to the heart. At present I have no friend but the Lord Almighty – and is he not enough? Yes; my soul desires none beside him – he is my strength and my portion.[18]

Again, on 4 April:

Surely the fear of God is not in this place! How pleasant heaven will be, where no strife ever enters!

And on the 19th of the same month:

Lately the enemy has been permitted to attack me in every quarter – good-name, wordly-honour, and worldly-interest – all at stake, but blessed be the Lord I cheerfully and willingly part with them all and choose rather to suffer affliction with the people of God than to enjoy the pleasures of sin for a season.[19]

A comment written on 23 May is rather ambiguous:

This day, exchanged my lodging – have seen the hand of the Lord very remarkable in providing this place for me. I was much afraid and distressed having no place to go to; but all hearts are in the Lord's hands, and we shall never be disappointed if we believe and trust in him. May I be enabled to spread the savour of godliness in this family. [20]

Is he expressing his fear that he would not be received into any lodgings because of the slanders spread about him? Was the passionate preaching of the gospel in its purity such a great sin in the Church of England at that time that there was a danger that a curate who did so would be excommunicated by polite society? Such consequences were not in any way improbable.

It seems that a friend offered him another curacy but Mr Charles did not wish to turn his back in the day of battle. His letter refusing the offer contains the following:

I could never want motives to leave my present situation, while I have the prospect of living near you; yet, as the servant of another great and good master, I should divest myself of all selfish interest and have his glory alone in view in all my actions. When a person is once settled in a place, and as he thinks, by an all-wise Providence, he should, in my opinion, be very cautious in exchanging that for another, though more agreeable to flesh and blood and much more lucrative. My situation is indeed at *present* by no means desirable. I have no Christian friend to speak to within fifteen miles. Mr N[ewman]'s unexpected behaviour has produced a coolness between us. All these circumstances, together with the fair prospects your kind proposals hold out to me, strongly incline me to accept your offer. But would this be taking up the cross? Is this a proof of that undaunted fortitude which a Gospel-minister *especially* should be possessed of? Or is it not rather shaking off the cross impatiently which God in consummate wisdom has laid upon me? When Providence appears dark and mysterious, we are not to be dejected and murmur but wait patiently on the Lord, who knows best what weather is most suitable to our constitutions. I am persuaded that a few rough storms are much wanted to rouse me; though the Lord knows how weak I am to bear them. He has promised that strength shall be *proportioned* to the day; and this is my stay

> and comfort. For these reasons, I find myself, after some thought and prayer, at least some attempt to pray, disposed to decline the offer, lest influenced by selfish motives, I should dishonour God and quit the post he has assigned me. At present I am strongly persuaded that God sent me here; for what end it does not yet appear very clear.[21]

The letter reveals a heroic spirit and a degree of conscientiousness not often found. The young curate persevered with his duties through all storms, and his mind was often at peace without so much as a wave to disturb it. The following was his comment on the first day of the year in 1780:

> If thou, O Lord, hadst not been with me, I must have fallen and been brought to my end. But, blessed be thy name, underneath were the everlasting arms . . . O God, give me the privilege and happiness of living to thee. I trust I have been in thy family these seven years; *nor would I change my Master for ten thousand worlds.* His service is perfect freedom, and *the only happiness in the universe.* Astonishing the grace that first called me from the world; but more amazing, if anything can be so, is the grace, mercy and patience, which has since borne with me and pardoned my sins, and is still compassionate to my daily infirmities.

One who could think like this was far above the reach of the arrows of his Queen Camel persecutors and beyond the range of his irreligious rector's desire to harm him. It seems that Mr Newman had decided to get rid of his curate and as he was too ashamed to give him notice he had decided to starve him away and had reduced his wage from forty-five pounds to thirty pounds, a sum on which it would be impossible to live with any degree of comfort. Early in 1780, Mr Charles concluded that there was nothing to do but find another position. We should also note that he had in the January of 1779 received his degree of M.A. from Oxford University.

FOUR YEARS AT MILBORNE PORT, SOMERSET

As one door was closing, providence opened for him another, and in March he settled at Milborne Port, Somerset, as curate to a Mr Lucas. He had known Mr Lucas while at Oxford and had a high opinion of him as an evangelical clergyman. He wrote, at the time:

> Amongst our brethren, the clergy, we are looked upon as suspicious characters; but, by God's grace, I hope that we shall not fear their empty powers nor their meaningless smirks.

When we recall the mildness of Mr Charles's temper and his slowness to think the worst of anyone, we must believe that the other clergy of the district had shown very unchristian feelings towards the vicar and his curate. He describes the place as being until that time completely deprived of any evangelical ministry:

> The region in which I dwell wears the saddest of faces; sad enough to engage the sympathies of the most hard-hearted. It is a fruitful valley but, like that in Ezekiel's vision, it is full of dead bones, which are very many, and very dry. The enlivening sound of the gospel of salvation is a strange sound to the inhabitants. Religion is as something exiled for many years, and iniquity has come in as a flood, so as to cover the whole land. I hope that the Lord will enable us to raise up a banner against it, and that his Spirit will prosper us in our weak attempts at stemming the flow.

What efforts were made by him to evangelize the neighbourhood, we do not know; he is almost completely silent in his journal and letters concerning his daily labours, but we may conclude from our general knowledge of his temperament and of his later history that he would have exerted all his abilities in the work. Whether he was granted souls as a reward for his efforts is not known. Probably he was not entirely unsuccessful; the Lord does not leave his servants' labours without some degree of blessing, and Mr Charles would hardly have remained here for four years without having had some encouragement in seeing the seed sown germinating and growing. But a thick veil hides all and it is now impossible, after a hundred years, to pierce it.

Thomas Charles was received into full orders as a clergyman of the Church of England on 21 May 1780. According to Mr Hughes, Llanuwchllyn, in his biography of him: 'We do not know why he was kept as deacon for two years.' Was the unwillingness of the bishops to ordain evangelical curates the reason? His feelings immediately after his ordination are worth recording:

> This morning was ordained Priest – when I most solemnly and with my whole heart devoted myself with all I have to the service of God – time, talents and all, I hope, I have been enabled to lay down at his feet. Nor would I upon the most serious consideration, and in my most deliberate moments wish to retract one word I have spoken. I hope I can say that the constant and rooted desire of my soul is after God and his service. O Almighty God who hast given me the will, grant also power to perform the same – accomplish the work which thou hast begun in me – endow me with a double portion of thy Spirit and clothe me with power from on high – increase my love to souls – impress my mind deeply and constantly with the sense of the solemn account I one day must render unto thee of my stewardship – enable me to exercise the gifts given me – lift up my hands whenever they hang down and strengthen my feeble knees – help me to be in thy hands as the clay in the hands of the Potter, willing to

> be ruled, fashioned and employed by thy godly wisdom in the manner and for the service thou thinkest proper – I am nothing in myself – mine eyes are directed unto thee in whom the fatherless findeth mercy – O never leave me – thou art a faithful God who never failest those who depend on thee.[22]

We would like to quote extensively from his journal for the four years in which he was at Milborne Port but our limits forbid it. On the whole, his circumstances there seem to have been comfortable enough, but his heart was in Wales and his burning desire was to be of service to his own nation. Furthermore, he now longed to marry and set up home, having been corresponding for five years with the young girl that had won his heart. Through the kindness of the Rev. John Newton of Olney, who maintained a close interest in his career, he was offered a curacy in south Wales and he was on the point of accepting it. However:

> When I came to consult with dear Miss Jones – she is an only child of tender and affectionate parents. When it came to the point, I found that it would be worse than death for her to be removed, whilst they live, to any considerable distance. Indeed when I saw how their minds were affected at the thought of it, I immediately laid aside every such idea; for I would not for the world be the means of bringing their grey hairs in sorrow to the grave. Everything, therefore, must remain as it is, till I meet with a situation within a convenient distance of the place where they live in north Wales.[23]

But for all his efforts no suitable vacancy in Gwynedd could be found. More than once he thought that his wishes were being granted. A curacy became available in Oswestry and, although a distance from Bala, he was happy to accept it and his heart was happy within him as he anticipated success for his application. It was not to be however:

> But the moment the Vicar heard that I was tinctured with what they call Methodistical principles, he would have nothing more to say to me.[24]

To be a Methodist was an unforgivable sin in the sight of this clergyman. He would probably have tolerated drunkenness, or the breaking of the Sabbath, or indulgence to the flesh, but to be serious about those things that pertain to man's eternal peace, for this was the extent of Mr Charles's Methodism at the time, was an offence that could not be tolerated. A curacy at Mallwyd in Merionethshire became vacant. He trusted the matter to someone whom he had considered a friend, but the man failed to carry out his responsibility. But Mr Charles was not too agitated. He wrote:

> If I had not that moment seen the hand of God in it, I should have been very angry with Mr Jones indeed. Though I had been with him about the middle of August yet he never applied for the curacy until the 4th of October, though

I told him I should most gladly defray all expenses that a speedy application for it might incur.[25]

At last his patience failed and he decided to return to Wales. He wrote on 23 June 1783:

I left Milborne Port this morning – fully persuaded, be the consequence what it will, it was the will of the Lord I should do so.[26]

As well as his longing to return to his own country and to set up a home, it seems that he was being obstructed in his efforts to fulfil his ministerial duties for he referred to himself as being bound by chains that he could not shake off, and asked, 'What profit is it to live in the world if our lives are of no use?' Mr Charles therefore left England and the English, and returned to his own people, not to leave them again until the Lord called him to the paradise above.

HIS MARRIAGE TO MISS SALLY JONES, BALA

On 20 August 1783, he was married to Miss Sally Jones, the step-daughter of Mr Thomas Foulkes, who had settled at Bala. He obtained in his wife the very best of partners, one who was as full of desire to serve the Lord as himself and willing to bear the weight of all family responsibilities on her own shoulders so that his hands might be free to continue his great work. A few days before the wedding, Mr Charles attended the Association at Llangeitho. His main motive was to hear Daniel Rowland, whom he considered as his father in the faith. He wrote as follows:

There were, at the Association, about twenty clergymen and between sixty and eighty lay preachers, though not all belonged to the Connexion. You may imagine how glad I was to hear once more the old grey-headed Elijah proclaiming the deep things of God with that pathos, perspicuity and energy peculiar to himself. I heard him twice, and three other clergymen also, together with many lay brothers, all endowed with excellent gifts. The preaching started on Sunday and continued until ten o'clock on Wednesday morning. I will add no more except that it was good to have been there.

Mr Charles's high opinion of the Methodists, and even of their unordained preachers, is clear, even when he was still a member of the Established Church and intending to pursue his career within it.

It does not seem that any anxiety as to income disturbed the minds of Mr and Mrs Charles. They both completely trusted in God's providence that had brought them together and given the one to the other. They opened a small shop in Bala. Mrs Charles had the responsibility of it, and a small room in the house acted as her husband's study. But they were anxious that he should find somewhere to preach. And as he at the time believed that he was called to the ministry of the Church of England, he looked for a curacy. The salary accompanying was unimportant in his eyes, his great purpose was to obtain the opportunity to preach the gospel to sinners, the work to which he had been called by God. It seemed that his wish was to be granted quite quickly, but he only served two Sabbaths before a long letter was sent to him excusing him from returning again. The author of the letter, no doubt, was the vicar of the parish. He next went to help his old friend, Simon Lloyd, who was ill at the time. He was not long here again, before a storm broke over him. He described the circumstances:

> Last Sunday, the whole parish, with two or three of the principal inhabitants at their head came to me and accosted me in a rougher strain than I ever have been used to before. They insisted on my preaching no more in their church; for they added, 'You have cursed us enough already.'[27]

If Mr Charles had been of hot temper, of rough manners, and carried away by the warmth of his zeal, we might suppose that he had condemned the sins of the parish too harshly so that they had just cause for taking offence. But his moderation and natural courtesy forbids such speculation. Indeed, his own testimony confirms this:

> I took every care that nothing but the plain simple truth should give offence; nor is there anything else laid to my charge.[28]

What could not be endured in the Established Church of that time in Gwynedd was the proclamation of God's truth in an honest manner, by one of the mildest and most gentlemanly of men that ever walked this earth. It was the sin of sins to denounce wickedness and to exhort sinners, in all seriousness. For this trespass, two churches had already closed their doors against Mr Charles; no other charge could be brought against him.

For all the opposition, he was not yet willing to give up his original intention of serving within the Church of England. In a letter to a friend, dated 29 September 1783, he wrote:

> I am now waiting to see what the Lord has to do with me; making use of every means in my power to procure some employment in the established church; not for the sake of any emoluments I might have, but from a principle of conscience. I can live independent of the church; but I am a churchman on principle, and therefore shall not on any account leave it, unless I am forced to do so. But you can well conceive how disagreeable and uncomfortable it is to be doing nothing. I never felt before, in the same degree, the force of that expression, 'Woe is unto me, if I preach not the gospel.' I feel that a necessity

is laid upon me; and that my life would be perfect misery, without engaging in the work with all my powers.[29]

This letter gives rise to the following comments:

1. We would not wish to hide the fact that Mr Charles considered himself a Churchman at this time; that he felt considerable affection for the Church, and that he intended to stay within it if he possibly could. In this he stood on exactly the same ground as the first Methodist Fathers. It was not a rejection of its ecclesiology, nor any disbelief of its articles of faith, that caused them to turn their backs on the Church and to go out to the highways and hedges. Were it not for the arrogance of the bishops and the hatred of the irreligious clergy, it is not improbable that the Methodists would have remained a hard-working evangelical party within the Church right up to the present day. Mr Charles no doubt hoped that the principles of the Methodist Revival, for which he held the greatest of sympathies, would have leavened the Established Church so that he could have worked within it with a clear conscience.

2. It is as clear as the sun that he did not consider the act of leaving the Established Church as schism, if circumstances made it inevitable. The spirit of ministry was much stronger in his heart than any Church tradition, and he foresaw at this time the possibility of having to work outside its fold; indeed, that he had decided to do so rather than living a life of idleness. This is strongly suggested by the emphasis he lays on the words, 'Woe is unto me if I preach not the gospel.'

3. We see that he, or rather his wife, was succeeding in business in Bala so that there was no necessity for him to minister as a livelihood.

EFFORTS AT FINDING A CURACY

About the middle of October, he found a temporary position as a curate in Shawbury, Shropshire. The vicar of the parish, a Mr Mayor, was of evangelical views and greatly appreciated his help. Mr Charles lived at Bala, but rather than be deprived of an opportunity to distribute the Word of life he was ready to serve a church that was fifty miles away from his home. He seems to have been connected with Shawbury until the middle of the following January. The reason for his departure was his obtaining of a curacy at Llanymawddwy, a parish about fourteen miles from Bala. The road between these two places is perhaps the most mountainous and dangerous in the country (certainly this is how the section of it between Llanuwchllyn and Dinas Mawddwy is described by Thomas Pennant in his *Tours in Wales*) but Mr Charles travelled to his church in all weathers, sometimes on horseback but usually on foot. He would not be stopped however heavy the rain or deep the drifts of snow or thick the ice, even though his constitution was not particularly strong. He threw his whole soul into the work at Llanymawddwy. He not only delivered faithful sermons containing the cream of the gospel but began, on Sunday afternoons, to catechize the young in the great truths of the Bible. The Lord blessed his efforts; a stirring took place amongst the dry bones; many were brought to new life and the majority of the parish were sympathetic towards him. But others opposed fiercely. He wrote to his wife:

> I go on tolerably well; had a little of the divine presence in preaching last Sunday – the people seemed a little affected with Divine truths – and I understand most of them, though some contradict, are disposed to hear more of these things. Some threaten to behave as bad as they know how – but all is in the Lord's hands. I am much better than I expected after walking through the snow on Saturday. The Lord is very good. O, praise him.[30]

He was only suffered to serve for three months at Llanymawddwy. His opposers carried out their threats and delivered a list of complaints to the rector of the parish. We do not know the nature of these complaints but we can imagine that the Methodism of the curate was the chief complaint; malice and enmity probably succeeded also in misrepresenting matters and producing a number of lying accusations. The rector immediately, without inquiring into the truth of the accusations, nor allowing Mr Charles to defend himself, sent him notice to leave. The people who had received blessing through his ministry felt it deeply and drew up a petition to be sent to the rector requesting that the new curate be not sent away. The delivery of the petition was entrusted to one of the parishioners who, being influenced by the opposers, destroyed it instead of presenting it to the clergyman. He later confessed to this action. It was not enough for his enemies to have Mr Charles dismissed, they sought also to raise the neighbourhood against him. He wrote home to Sally:

> I understand also that Low Easter Sunday is my last here. My Quarter being out it seems the Saturday after, the gentleman who succeeds me means to be here the day after, viz, Sunday, 25 of April. Attempts have been made by the good great folks about Dinas to stir up the parishioners against me, but in general without effect. It is enough to us that the Lord ruleth. Remember also 'when father and mother forsake us the Lord will take us in'. I am happy in the Lord. Pray for me, and in the midst of everything rejoice in the Lord.[31]

It is seen from the letter that it was the gentry of the Llanymawddwy neighbourhood who were to the fore in the work of persecuting the man of God; to what extent they were encouraged in this by the local clergy, we do not know.

Mr Charles was not willing to leave the matter with the Rector of Llanymawddwy; he took it to the Bishop's Court. In the biography of him written by the Rev. W. Hughes, Vicar of Llanuwchllyn, is found the following:

> Mr Charles had every right to appeal to the Bishop, a right which, it appears, he exercised. There are references in his letters to an appeal he made about this time to Bishop Shepley, who then occupied the see of St Asaph. Every influence that Mr Charles could call upon was brought to bear on his behalf upon the Bishop. But all to no avail. There was no sympathy in the Bishop for the Welsh flock entrusted to him; nor, on the other hand, did the flock know the voice of the chief shepherd.

But Mr Hughes hurries on to attempt to release the denomination of which he belonged from any responsibility in the matter:

> However deeply we might grieve over the behaviour of the Rector of Llanymawddwy, the Church, as a body, cannot be held responsible for this unjust behaviour.

What? The Church not responsible? Here were the clergymen of Gwynedd refusing the service of a learned and valuable man because of his honesty and faithfulness to Christ; here were the few clergymen who, in ignorance, employed him as a curate, closing the doors of their churches against him as soon as they learnt that he was sympathetic to the Methodist spirit; and here is their work being confirmed by the dignitary who sat in the episcopal chair; and yet, we are told that the Church, as a body, was not responsible! If it is not, then it must be such an unsubstantial body that it cannot be held responsible for anything. If the Church is not to be found in its bishops, and in the body of its clergymen, and to such a degree as to be held responsible for their actions, we do not know where it may be found. The truth is that there is not enough water in the Jordan River to wash the Church of England clean from the guilt of its behaviour towards Mr Charles.

Having been turned out of Llanymawddwy and without any other openings for him in the Established Church, Mr Charles was in a considerable quandary as to what to do. In his perplexity he wrote to his old friend, the Rev. John Newton of Olney, asking him for his advice and prayers. In his reply, dated 19 June 1784, John Newton wrote:

> It is very possible you might obtain a curacy in some other diocese, and perhaps if you simply left it to the Lord, and waited upon him with patience, he

> might by his providence open you a way to a scene of comfort and usefulness, of his appointment, though not your own; which would indeed be much better. For it greatly animates us under the opposition and difficulties we are liable to in our ministry, to know that we are where he would have us to be. I have no objection to your leaving the Church if the Lord actually calls you to it – but I would wish you to have a better reason to give for it, than you did it, because you could not otherwise continue to live at Bala.[32]

Mr Newton's judgment was that Mr Charles should leave Bala and Wales and look for a curacy in London. He would have had no difficulty in finding one because of the influence of the Countess of Huntingdon and of others of the nation's nobility who were sympathetic to the evangelical wing of the Church. But he would not leave Wales. He often visited Mr Mayor, the vicar of Shawbury, under whom he had previously worked. On his first visit there, during May 1784, he wrote home to his wife:

> Mr Mayor would be glad to employ me as before, but I have refused, for I see clearly that I must confine myself either to Wales or to England, or I will do no good in either place. And I am strongly inclined to take Wales, as I took my wife, 'for better for worse, till death us do part'.

On another visit, in the same year, he wrote:

> There are no tidings of a church, but all friends here seem to give me up to the churches of Wales, whilst at the same time they are much satisfied with my conduct in waiting so long. All I can say is that I desire I hope sincerely to be where the Lord would have me to be . . . I cannot carry a guilty conscience any longer about me; which I must do if my days are consumed in vanity.[33]

This letter sheds a flood of light upon the state of his feelings at this time. Clearly, those friends of his who had given him up to the churches of Wales were friends from within the Established Church. It is seen therefore that even these evangelical Churchmen were convinced that Mr Charles's duty was to leave the Mother Church and throw in his lot with the Methodists, and had expressed their minds on the matter to him before he himself had made up his own mind. Yet he still remained undecided and perplexed. He wrote the following to his friend, Watts Wilkinson, on 12 June 1784:

> I am in a strait between two things; between leaving the church and continuing in it. Being turned out of three churches in this country without the prospect of another, what shall I do? In the last church I served I continued three months. There the gospel was much blessed, as to the present appearance of things. The people there are calling me with tears to feed them with the bread of life. What shall I do? Christ's words continually sound in my ears, 'Feed my lambs.' I think I feel my heart willing to engage in the work,

be the consequences what they may. But then I ought to be certain in my own mind that God calls me to preach at large. This stimulates me to try all means to continue in the church, and to wait a little longer to see what the Lord will do. I thank the Lord, I want nothing but to know his will, and to have strength to do the same.

The gospel spreads here, and thousands flock to hear it; and I believe thousands in all parts have received it in its power. I tremble lest the Lord should find me unfaithful, when I see so much work to do. I often think I hear my dear Master say to me, 'Why standest thou here idle?' This thought is still sharpened, when I consider that the night is coming on apace, when no man can work. Your own feelings will tell you that my mind must be eased one way or other. O! to be clothed with power from on high, and to be faithful unto death. Pray for me, my ever dear friend. It is the greatest kindness you can do me. I endeavour to give myself entirely to God, willing that he should dispose of me just as he pleases. Were he to give me to turn the scales, I should be afraid to throw in a straw, lest I should throw it into the wrong one.[34]

It may be seen from this important letter that matters were coming to a head. As well as the frustration which idleness always produced in Mr Charles and the fire in his soul for preaching the gospel, his words suggest that another reason was influencing him strongly. It brought him, in his desire to throw himself into the work of the ministry, whatever the consequences, to the point of an irrevocable decision. This was the powerful revival that had broken out in Bala and the surrounding neighbourhood amongst the Methodists. The whole district had arisen as one man to hear the Word, and thousands were being saved to eternal life. He did not hesitate at all as to the nature of the excitement; he saw that it was clearly from God. It is not strange therefore that his spirit was weary of being confined within the Establishment, unable to be loosed to participate in the good work.

At first sight, it is strange to see him so loyal to the Church. Both his letters and his previous behaviour show that it was not blind partisanship that kept him from leaving its communion. There are ample proofs that he was of liberal views and believed that God had flocks that were outside the circle of the Church of England. He himself had been first brought into the glorious liberty of the gospel through the instrumentality of a man who had been thrown out of his Church office. It seems to us that what kept him from taking the final step was the desire to be completely certain of God's will. He had committed himself to the ministry of the Established Church as a young man; all his hopes had been formed within this circle; this was in the forefront of his mind throughout the years at school and Oxford; and, until the doors started closing in his face, he had never doubted that this was God's will for him. Having formed a plan, it required a great deal of obstacles before he would consider giving it up. One of his strongest characteristics was his determination – cleaving to an undertaking until it became evident that it would not do. Therefore, though having failed to obtain a curacy even when he was willing to work without pay, he could not turn his back on all the hopes of his youth until he saw beyond any peradventure that this was the direction which the pillar of cloud was taking. But of one thing he was certain: that his life had to be spent in distributing the bread of life. He saw that he had been prepared for this; the Word of the Lord burnt as a flame in his soul; and in comparison with the importance of serving God in the gospel of his Son, ecclesiastical boundaries were as nothing in his eyes.

HE LEAVES THE CHURCH OF ENGLAND AND JOINS THE METHODISTS

As he thus hesitated, longing to break out, but yet fearing to do so, he served at any church which would accept him. It is said that he often filled in for another clergyman at Llanwddyn. Very little was needed at this time to turn the scales decisively in his mind, and this very little came to him in the form of a dream. In his dream he saw the Judgment Day in all its majesty and terror. On a great white throne sat the Judge of the quick and the dead, in incomparable glory. Before this Judge he saw thousands upon thousands gathered together. At the time, the judgment of the wicked and slothful servant, mentioned in Matthew 25, was in progress, and, as might be expected, the trial was going against him. At the end, the Judge pronounced the awful sentence, 'Cast the unprofitable servant into outer darkness: there shall be weeping and gnashing of teeth.' Mr Charles was filled, not only with fear but with the conviction that in the condemned man was to be found a portrayal of himself. He could almost see the Judge turn to him and say, in the words of Nathan to David, 'Thou art the man!' Once awake, he could not shake off the terror of the dream; he judged it to be more than an ordinary dream, that it contained a direct message from God to himself, and the echo of the unprofitable servant's condemnation thundered in his ears. He decided immediately that he would no longer remain idle but would throw himself into his Master's work.

The nearest thing at hand that he could undertake was the education of the young people of Bala in the principles of religion. He had enjoyed the work of catechizing when serving at Llanymawddwy and knew that he had the necessary skills for such work. He therefore invited the untaught youth to his house on Sunday afternoons, and so gentle were his methods, and so interesting his instruction, that the house soon became too small. By now the Methodists at Bala had built a chapel and as no services were held there on a Sunday afternoon, they offered its use to Mr Charles. He accepted the offer thankfully. From then on the simple building was filled every Sunday by men and women starving for religious knowledge and their respected teacher was in his element when in their midst, expounding to them the deep things of God. We can almost see this catechizing work as the root from which sprang the Sunday School movement. Mr Charles would then have more cause to be considered the father of Sunday Schools than even Mr Robert Raikes.[35] By imparting education in a building that had not received Episcopal consecration and, no doubt, through taking the additional opportunity of exhorting and warning the careless, Mr Charles had more than crossed over half-way from the Church to the Methodists. He does not seem to have joined the Methodists at Bala formally and gone about preaching in the chapels of the Connexion, until the beginning of the next year, 1785. That was when he broke the last thread that connected him with the Established Church and when he threw himself with all the energy of his soul into the work of the Lord amongst the Calvinistic Methodists.

With respect to this step that he took, it must be quite evident to the reader that it was not based on any rash decision; it was not disappointment that caused him to take a sudden leap. He had considered, hesitated, consulted friends, and, particularly, had approached God with fervent prayers, before coming to a final decision. We had almost believed that he had been slow in recognizing the hand of Providence. We do not know of any other person who has demonstrated such an obligation of duty and responsibility before God, and such freedom from selfish motive, than Mr Charles when throwing in his lot amongst the Methodists. It was not the hope of honours that motivated him, and less still did he imagine that it would bring financial profit. He knew that he was joining himself to poor people, people who were hounded by the nobility of the land, and that only scorn and weariness awaited him upon becoming a member amongst them. But through it all, he did obtain one thing – the opportunity to do his best for his Saviour and to lead his poor and ignorant compatriots to Him. Mr Charles's attachment to the Methodists was an act of prudent judgment and solemn deliberation and it was carried out under the influence of the purest motives.

It is equally certain that Mr Charles never regretted the step he took. When, in relative old age, he reviewed his life and looked back over its events, he was completely convinced that he had not been mistaken when he went over to the Methodists, but that he had been led by the pillar of cloud. In 1810, more than twenty-five years after joining the Connexion, he wrote the following to a young man who was in some perplexity:

> I feel for you in your uncertainty. But I have no doubt that if you look up simply to the Lord, that he will graciously lead you in the way in which you should go. But it is not for me to decide. I am completely persuaded that it was Providence that led me into the path in which I journey, for I never thought of it. Without being influenced by prejudice, self-profit, or the honour which comes from men, lift up your eyes unto the hills from whence comes your help, and the Lord will safely lead you, and in his own time you will see the path clearly before you. I feel very reticent when advising the servant of another. The Lord alone knows the purpose for which he has prepared and equipped you. There were many in the past who were ready to advise me; but the more forward of them were the furthest from the mark. *'Gwell pwyll nac aur'* ['Better prudence than gold'], *'Ond dan enw pwyll fe ddaw twyll'* ['But under the guise of prudence comes deceit']. These old Welsh proverbs contain much wisdom.

The context in which he writes shows that the eager advisers, those who were far from the mark, were those who had advised him to cleave to the Established Church. And the second proverb that he quotes seems to suggest that on reflection Mr Charles felt that on this point he had carried prudence too far.

A second letter written by him about the same time is clearer still. In it he stated:

> I am glad that it is in your mind to do good, and to seek, by all means possible, the salvation of the immortal souls that are destroyed around us. The *work* of the ministry is what honours us, and not its profit; and this is what should maintain all our attention. I could have received promotion in the Church; it was offered to me time and again; but I am so much gladder that I have spent the last twenty-three years of my life as I have, wandering up and down our cold and barren land, than if I had been made an archbishop. What good I have accomplished I do not know, but it is a real pleasure to have attempted it, and to have laboured without any hindrances. It was no choice of my own; Providence led me.

Nothing can be more definite and determined. These offers of ecclesiastical promotion came from England, no doubt, after he had become famous as a good man, an incomparable organiser and philanthropist. There is no evidence of Welsh Churchmen, nobility or clergy, having offered any indication of favour to him. It is clear also how he rejoices in his freedom from any ecclesiastical restraints of which he would have been inevitably aware had he remained in the Church; and how he treasures the privilege given him of being able to work out his various plans without any external authorities to hinder him.

It is only fair to mention that Mr Charles, when he began itinerating amongst the Methodists, had no intention of leaving the Church completely; he always contemplated the possibility that he would return sometime in the future. He wrote:

> When I began journeying, it was because they would not make use of me in the Church here. I intended to move to England, as soon as circumstances would permit me, without being hindered in this intention by a little itinerating. Gradually, however, I entered so fully into the work, that I could not in all conscience turn my back upon it. The way Providence has led me is no rule for others.

We see from this quotation that Mr Charles considered himself to have been led by God not only when joining the Methodists but also throughout his labours with them all his life. God's purposes for him were fulfilled, and not his own purposes. And he grew to become prouder of his situation and of the opportunities given him to work without restraint than had he been elevated an archbishop.

The addition of a man of the learning and position of Mr Charles greatly enhanced the position of the Methodists in the eyes of the country, and the best amongst them, and indeed the body as a whole, welcomed him with open arms. We saw their readiness, under the leadership of John Evans and Thomas Foulkes, in the offering to him of the use of the chapel at Bala. But some, it seems, were prejudiced against him. According to the Rev. Lewis Edwards, D. D.:

> It is natural to think that he immediately received the warmest of welcomes. But it was not so; for there were many of the Methodists who at first thought of him as proud, lacking in gifts, and not useful. But the wisest of them, of necessity, respected him.

We do not now know the authority behind Dr Edwards's statement, he probably had sufficient foundation for his words, but we can only believe that those prejudiced against him were a minority. Perhaps they were made up of two groups, namely, those who desired to rule, and who feared that this would be beyond their grasp in a society of which Mr Charles was a member; and those who reacted to learning, appropriate dress, and gentlemanly behaviour, as indications of pride. And as his language when preaching was refined and he refrained from what he considered to be undue warmth, and he did not possess the extraordinary oratorical fluency that some of the lay preachers demonstrated, it was not long before those who could never see further than the outward began to draw unfavourable comparisons between himself and these. Soon however, his humility, his compassion, together with his qualifications for the work of the gospel, were recognized.

In August 1785, he went to the Llangeitho Association. Daniel Rowland was then still alive and knew of Mr Charles's history. No doubt he felt a particular love for, and interest in him, as one who had been converted under his own ministry. Mr Charles therefore was called to preach to the thousands that had gathered. The old Apostle was greatly pleased by his sermon, he was very pleased that Charles had joined the Methodists in Gwynedd, and at the end of the service he said in his inimical way: 'Charles is the Lord's gift to North Wales.' Around September of the same year he took his first journey to Carmarthenshire and his warm, evangelical ministry was as the small rain upon the tender herb, and as the showers upon the grass, to the congregations. On this journey, he met the Rev. Thomas Jones, Denbigh, and a friendship developed that was to last while they both lived. Mr Jones noted that:

> . . . from only that much experience, he formed such an opinion of him, as to his unostentatiousness, his application, and his entire Christian bearing, together with his vivacious spirit and excellent gifts, as a preacher, that he was willingly constrained to greatly reverence and love him from that time forth.[36]

Some time after this he had a remarkable service at Lôn Fudr, Lleyn. It seems that it was not so much power that was experienced but rather a sweet and overcoming enchantment. The accompanying fragrances were so heavenly and so powerful that they filled the whole neighbourhood. At Christmas time, that same year, he preached at an Association at Pont Uchel, not far from Rhuthun. His text was Galatians 4:4, 5. He spoke on the divine Person of the Saviour and his active and passive obedience. The Rev. Thomas Jones, who was present, said that he spoke

> with such lucidity, authority, and heavenly effect, as vividly surprised and gratified, lovingly melted and stirred the congregation, to a degree seldom witnessed.[37]

Very soon all prejudice against Mr Charles disappeared as snow before the sun's rays, even from the narrowest of the Methodists. Before a year had passed, the last remains of it were vanishing and within a very short time again he was taking his place as the leader of the work in Gwynedd, to which position he was qualified by nature, learning and grace.

[1] The authors had hoped to write a third volume of *The Methodist Fathers*, but this never materialized. It would certainly have included a chapter on David Charles (1762–1834). He was 'one of the outstanding Methodist leaders in South Wales and took a prominent part in establishing the Home Mission and drawing up the *Cyffes Ffydd* (confession of faith of the denomination) . . . He was regarded as a clear thinker and an able theologian . . . His eminence as a hymn writer is assured, and his greatest hymns are to be found in all the Welsh hymnbooks.' (*Dictionary of Welsh Biography*).

[2] D. E. Jenkins, *Rev. Thomas Charles of Bala*, Vol. 1 (Denbigh, 1908), p. 21.

[3] Ibid.

[4] Ibid., p. 22.

[5] Ibid.

[6] Ibid., p. 29.

[7] Ibid., p. 35.

[8] Ibid., p. 38.

[9] Ibid., p. 39.

[10] Ibid., p. 43.

[11] Ibid., pp. 50–1. A letter written forty years later, in 1817, but relating to this period, from the above-mentioned Rev. John Mayor to his daughter-in-law, contains the following advice: 'I wish you to take out without fail McLaurin's two volumes and Dr Buchanan's *Life*. I think you would not regret it. Newton's *Cardiphonia* would be pleasant reading. Mr Charles of Bala and I copied out many of those letters for the press and can tell almost all the parties to whom they were addressed.'

[12] Ibid., pp. 59–60.

[13] Ibid., p. 80.

[14] Ibid., pp. 81–2.

[15] Ibid., pp. 86–7.

[16] Edward Morgan, *A Brief History of the Life and Labours of T. Charles* (London, 1828), pp. 37–41.

[17] D. E. Jenkins, *Rev. Thomas Charles,* Vol. 1, p. 112.

[18] Ibid., p. 118.

[19] Ibid., p. 119.

[20] Ibid., p. 126.

[21] Ibid., pp. 121–2.

[22] Ibid., pp. 185-6.

[23] Ibid., p. 246.

[24] Ibid., p. 293.

[25] Ibid., p. 377.

[26] Ibid., p. 415.

[27] Ibid., p. 426.

[28] Ibid.

[29] Ibid., p. 427.

[30] Ibid., p. 468.

[31] Ibid., p. 474.

[32] Ibid., p. 493.

[33] Ibid., p. 486.

[34] Ibid., p. 490.

[35] This suggestion is still sometimes heard in Wales but there is plenty of evidence to show that it is not true. It is certainly not a claim that Thomas Charles ever made. D. E. Jenkins in his *Life* shows that Charles had, in the words of Thomas Jones of Denbigh, 'many strong testimonies of their [Sunday Schools] utility and benefit in several places in England'.

[36] D. E. Jenkins, *Rev. Thomas Charles*, Vol. 1, p. 520–1.

[37] Ibid., p. 521.

31

THOMAS CHARLES, B.A., BALA
(CONTINUED)

THOMAS CHARLES'S LABOURS AFTER JOINING THE METHODISTS

Mr Charles was about thirty years old and had been in holy orders for some seven years when, early in 1785, he joined the Methodists. From this time on he was to labour in the cause of the gospel with unremitting commitment, up to and beyond his strength. His efforts may be divided into three types: his general labours as a minister; his efforts with various philanthropic and educational institutions; and his service by means of the press. These three categories cannot be dealt with wholly separately from each other in that they all three are to be observed woven together throughout his life. We feel however that the service he rendered in his office as minister and as a wise leader of the Connexion once it was embodied formally, has not had the attention it deserves from historians, because of the more excellent glory of those institutions he helped form and the great usefulness of all he did through the press. We also fear that we cannot now do justice to the extent of his ministerial usefulness. Bala was the headquarters of the Methodists in Gwynedd when Mr Charles joined them. We doubt if the Connexion had an exhorter or preacher in the whole of Merionethshire at the time, other than those who lived in the Bala neighbourhood. The town was the home of the wise and sensible John Evans, the noble Thomas Foulkes, the witty and memorable Dafydd Cadwaladr, the sweet evangelist William Evans, Bedwarian, together with various other exhorters such as Humphrey Edward, and the two brothers Sion and Evan Moses. The Associations held in the town were also becoming popular throughout the north; crowds gathered from every part of Gwynedd and it was in them that all important matters were decided. Mr Charles's defection to the Methodists only increased the importance of Bala to the movement.

HE TAKES RESPONSIBILITY FOR THE CAUSE AT DOLGELLAU

He does not appear to have taken any lead in the Methodist cause at Bala. The society was in the safe hands of John Evans and Thomas Foulkes, and it would have been difficult to find more able leaders. Mr Charles therefore threw himself into the general work throughout Merionethshire. He laboured to support the causes already established, to plant new ones, and to build chapels. At the time the Methodists had four chapels in Merionethshire: at Bala, Penrhyndeudraeth, Dolwyddelan and Blaenau Ffestiniog, but by his efforts many others were soon added. We might refer, for example, to Dolgellau. We have mentioned already the ferocity of the persecution there and the way in which the Methodists, like the Quakers before them, had been hounded like sheep. Dolgellau, although not the seat of the law courts, was the most important town in the county commercially and one of Mr Charles's earliest decisions was to attempt to possess the town for Christ. He made his first attempt within a year of joining the Methodists. There exists a report in which he describes his efforts at preaching in the locality. He stood up in the open air but had hardly announced his text when he saw a crowd of persecutors approaching menacingly, with their hands full of stones and clods of mud. When one of the congregation, a tall, strong man, full of courage, saw them, he jumped between them and the preacher, telling Mr Charles to continue his sermon without fear that he himself would see to the mob. So it proved, and God's messenger was allowed to continue.

At the beginning of 1786, Mr Charles succeeded in obtaining a building in Dolgellau that was licensed for preaching. The owner of the house was Dr Henry Owen, a Quaker, who lived at the time in Llwyngwril. In May of the same year, the building was bought. It included three small cottages and gardens. The price was £121-10-0; the date on the completion document is October 1786. It may be seen that Mr Charles wasted no time. He himself provided the money for the purchase; he also paid for the chapel built on the land. No one else in the town was ready to join with him in this responsibility. The names of the first trustees were Thomas Charles, Thomas Foulkes, and John Evans, all of Bala, and two young men, about twenty-five years old, from Dolgellau, Hugh Lloyd and John Lewis. Considerable financial support for the chapel was obtained from the south through the instrumentality of Jones, Llan-gan. The Northern Association also helped, for in its Minutes for 13 June 1787, there is the note, 'Paid to clear Dolgellau Chapel, £17-4-9.' The word 'clear', together with the loose change involved, suggest that all the remaining debt was being paid, either at the opening of the building or very soon afterwards. This was a most unsightly building – the floor was of earth, the walls were bare, and the only furniture inside it were benches with no backs and a simple pulpit for the preacher. But to have any kind of building was an occasion for great thanksgiving for the few poor Christians and it was not long before they obtained better seating. Later, when it became too small, they added a convenient gallery.

All the responsibility for the cause at Dolgellau rested entirely on Mr Charles. This was the case until 1793, when a young preacher was raised from amongst the fellowship, the Rev. John Griffith. From then on much of the care of the church was transferred to him. The old Methodists of Dolgellau used to say that Mr Charles was the first minister of their church. By his energetic efforts and wise organization and by the work of the Head of the Church in abundantly blessing his labours, the cause succeeded greatly. When the first collection for the London Missionary Society was made there in 1799, thirteen years after building the chapel, the sum collected was £16-12-6; proof that the congregation had grown considerably in number and in wealth. Within twenty years the chapel, even with its gallery, was again too small. The brethren looked around for a possible new site, but according to *Methodistiaeth Cymru:*

> There was not the least portion of land available in any convenient spot, and even if a possible site could be found, the hope of obtaining it for their purpose was very slight though a full price be offered.

Indirectly, Mr Charles was of some influence in obtaining the necessary land for them. Towards the end of the century there were many calls for him to be in London. He used to lodge in the city in the house of a tradesman called Mr Thomas Pugh. Often, he would take Mrs Charles with him and they would both stay for some weeks in Mr Pugh's house. Mr Charles persuaded the businessman to leave the capital and to set up trade in Dolgellau. The venture succeeded beyond all their expectations. Mr Pugh would send out a boatful of slate and receive it back with a cargo of wheat, rye and flour. As a result he became wealthy. He built a magnificent house for himself at Brynbella and mixed with the nobility of the town and neighbourhood. That such a man was associated with the Methodists gained for them a measure of respect. It was this Mr Pugh who succeeded in obtaining land for them; he did so in the following way. A notice was posted of the sale of a very suitable plot. The Methodists immediately feared that if those in authority in the neighbourhood came to know of their intentions the land would never be obtained without having to pay much more than the fair price. Mr Pugh therefore represented them at the auction, together with another very capable brother, Mr Edward Jones. They were both very anxious, and the other brethren were praying earnestly for the success of their mission. The auction was held in an inn; many gentlemen had gathered and the bids were increasing speedily. When Mr Pugh raised his bid to £250, no one immediately competed further and the auctioneer declared that should he not receive any further bids in the next ten minutes the land would be struck down to Mr Pugh. At that, two dogs began to fight. The men forgot about the auction in the entertainment of the dogfight; a quarter of an hour passed before peace was restored. Mr Pugh, who had kept an eye on his watch throughout, informed the auctioneer of the time and claimed the land according to the promise made. The auctioneer acknowledged his claim and terminated the auction. He announced, 'There's the land for the Methodists to build their chapel.' 'Had I known that,' cried out one man, 'I would have raised the bid by a hundred pounds.'

It was by Mr Charles's efforts also that the chapel at Corwen was built, though this did not occur until the beginning of the nineteenth century. The believers of Corwen at the time were few and poor and the chapel was considered much too large for so small a cause. But Mr Charles's answer to all complaints was, 'We did it in faith.' Many laughed at their faith, calling the building, 'That big house with no furniture', and many, with more wit than grace, talked of using it instead as a tithe barn. But the congregation gradually increased and Mr Charles's faith was proved to be 'a very shrewd venture', as John Evans once described it. If the original deeds of the first chapels in Gwynedd, especially those of Merionethshire, could be found, it would certainly be discovered that it was by his instrumentality that a large number of them was built.

THE MONTHLY COMMUNION SUNDAY AT BALA

It was not long after his departure from the Church of England that Thomas Charles took another step, a far-reaching one in that it gave an indication of the direction of his thoughts and of his increasing confidence as he responded to his circumstances. We are referring to the step of administering the sacraments at Bala Chapel. The ordained Methodist clergy in the south for many years had been administering communion at specific places that had not been consecrated by a bishop. They did so at New Chapel, at Woodstock, at Llangeitho Chapel, and perhaps at some other places. But nobody had yet done so in the north. Many of the Methodists travelled down to Llangeitho for the Communion Sunday there and those unable to do this would take communion at their parish churches, although to receive from the hands of ungodly clergy was painful to the consciences of many of them. As a result of the action taken by Mr Charles, the Communion Sunday at Bala became an important institution for Gwynedd Methodists. Large crowds would gather from every part of the surrounding regions, not only from Merionethshire but from much further afield. The town became a second Llangeitho as a meeting place. Not only ordinary believers would gather there for the privilege of remembering the death of their Saviour, but the exhorters would keep the 'end-of-the-month Sunday' free, in order to meet with the huge congregation that gathered around the Table. We do not know if such powerful influences were felt at Bala as those experienced in Llangeitho at the time of Daniel Rowland, but certainly the Lord caused his face to shine upon them abundantly here also. Hundreds were brought to a knowledge of the Saviour in those services when Thomas Charles was administering the bread and wine – their bonds were loosed, as evidenced by their tears and songs.

One natural consequence was the establishing of another important step. As so many exhorters were gathering at Bala on the Communion Sunday, many of the churches began to send representatives there in order to engage their services. And so, without it being planned in any way, this Sunday began to function as a kind of Monthly Meeting. For some reason, not now known, all Monthly Meetings before this time were held in the west of the county; Bala therefore became the venue of the Monthly Meeting for the eastern regions. Indeed, because of the significance of the occasion and of Mr Charles's increasing stature, it became a meeting not only for procuring engagements but for discussing important matters, and the decisions passed there were considered as important as any that were made in the Associations.

EARLY EVIDENCES OF HIS ORGANIZATIONAL ABILITIES

Very soon Mr Charles's skills as an organizer became apparent in the wise measures he took for building chapels. One of these measures concerned the deacons, or stewards. There does not seem to have been any set method in operation in Gwynedd in the choosing of deacons. The men who opened their homes to preachers would also, as a rule, be the ones who attended the Monthly Meetings to engage preachers. These also would host the societies in their homes and would act as leaders. In all fairness it must be acknowledged that many of them were excellent men, excelling not only in zeal, activity and faithfulness, but also in the knowledge of the deep things of God and in their ability to lead the fraternity into green pastures and beside still waters. But there were others, though also of excellent spirit, who, because of limited abilities, or because of being converted at a relatively old age, were comparatively ignorant and sometimes even completely illiterate. They were forced by circumstances to undertake the office in that there was no one else who would do so. Mr Charles felt deeply this lack of order; he considered it a major obstacle to the progress of the churches. At a Monthly Meeting he rose to his feet and declared that the churches had a right to a voice in the choice of their officers; that the necessary qualifications of such officers had been laid down in the New Testament; that none were appropriate as officers other than those so chosen; and that it was not those who had happened to find themselves in the office, or who had pushed themselves into it by their insolence, who should be considered elders, but only those who possessed the necessary qualifications and had been put in place by the church.

The Monthly Meeting took up the recommendation immediately and decided to act upon it. To this end they followed Mr Charles's suggestion and divided the county into classes. Preachers were then appointed to visit the churches in each class and to help them choose suitable officers. The visitors were to instruct the members as to the nature of the qualifications for eldership and to show how vital it was for the success of the work that they choose worthy men. Furthermore, they were to stress that the elders must have a clear understanding of the main truths of the gospel and that no one was to be chosen that could not, at the very least, read. With respect to those who were already officers, the instruction was that if these had proved faithful to the best of their abilities, if they loved the work and longed for its success, then, although they might be deficient in many particulars, they were not to be dismissed but others were to be appointed to assist them. All this was done; the choices in the various churches were made, with very little disturbance, and the new elders arrived at the Monthly Meeting to be examined on their scriptural knowledge, their experience, and their motivations for office. And such is still the present order amongst us.

These steps proved a great blessing in the building up of the churches and in establishing and continuing the Revival. The elders shouldered their responsibilities immediately; they gave themselves to the reading and studying of the Bible and of other religious books, and as a consequence they soon became strong men, capable of leading others. It is to be doubted whether the Church of Christ was ever blessed with more able theologians and men more capable of applying the truth for the profit and nurture of young converts, than the first Methodist elders. Some of them became key figures in the Association – able to take a prominent place in debates on doctrinal points or on matters of order and discipline. To have good elders was even more important then than now, in that the preachers, both small and great, were so often on their travels that the care of the societies and the domestic pastoring was nearly all done by the elders. And they fulfilled this trust magnificently. It is not too much to say that the success of Methodism in our country from that time until now is to a large extent to be appropriated under God to the efforts of faithful elders. This arrangement also reveals an essential difference between Mr Charles and Howell Harris as organizers. Harris, with his piercing discernment, perceived the necessity of elders to watch over the societies, and the office was established under his supervision. The name he gave for them was Stewards. His plan was to appoint these in the Associations; it was from the Associations that they received their authority. The societies do not seem to have had any say in the matter, all that was required from them was obedience. Harris's arrangement was more or less Episcopal. He depended on the authority of the Association, and, failing that, on his own authority as 'Father of the Association'. On the other hand, Mr Charles emphasized the rights of the churches. He viewed the root of authority as resting within the church, and he placed responsibility within the individual church. He did not remove the oversight of the Monthly Meeting completely in this respect, in that he saw the possibility of a church drifting off course under certain circumstances. He therefore required that the elders should attend the Monthly Meeting to be examined. But he viewed the choice of elders as the right of a church. The present order of the Calvinistic Methodist Body contains a strong element of Congregationalism, and we believe that this may be traced back to Mr Charles's influence.

The persecution at the hands of the general population had long stopped in the south of the country before Mr Charles joined the Connexion. It was also slowly disappearing in the north, with the Methodists gradually becoming regarded as respectable members of their communities. Of the little enmity that remained, very little was directed towards himself. The fact that he had received holy orders in the Established Church and was considered a learned man; the further fact that he was eminently gentlemanly in his behaviour and winning in his ways, secured peace and a hearing for him almost wherever he went. Yet even he suffered some occasions of mocking and scorn. We have already referred to the mob that threatened him at Dolgellau, but the greatest danger to life and limb that he endured was at Corwen. It proved impossible to obtain an open door to the preaching of the gospel here until the year 1790. At that time, a godly saddler called John Cadwaladr came to live in the area. He soon began to look for preachers, and engaged Mr Charles to come to his house to speak. The men of importance in the town were greatly agitated, they plotted how they could best frustrate the engagement. They eventually appointed an ungodly blacksmith called Dafydd Hughes, a man who was used to performing all kinds of dirty work for them, to raise a riot and break up the meeting. To this end the blacksmith insisted on borrowing a drum from a local mansion in order to gather a crowd and to drown the preacher's voice. The man of God arrived at his appointment punctually, and the devil's servants also gathered, led by the blacksmith. As the service began in the house a great commotion broke out in the street. The crowd was large, they swore and bellowed and their oaths were dreadful. With many blasphemies they threatened to pull down the house, and Mr Charles decided that it was best for him to leave the house and hurry away, in that there was no hope of obtaining a moment's peace to worship. He departed and a few friends accompanied him. At that, his persecutors began to throw stones. They aimed particularly at the preacher who had dared visit the town to proclaim the Word of God. They stole his cloak and one of them hit him in the face with a stone, breaking some of his teeth and causing the blood to flow. He fled, covered in blood, over the bridge and off the road into the fields, and in this way managed to escape their clutches.

But Providence caught up with his enemies. The man who struck him with the stone – a strong man, who earned his living threshing corn, soon, for no rhyme or reason, forsook his barns and wandered the countryside begging for bread. He remained a miserable beggar for the rest of his life. As for the blacksmith, a son of iniquity, the ringleader in the persecution, he added theft to his other immoralities. He was caught red-handed and having been found guilty was sent in his old age to prison. When eventually released, he was contemptible in the eyes of all. No one would employ him or befriend him and he also spent his last years a wandering beggar.

But Mr Charles was not a man to become downhearted or be defeated by obstacles. Before long, with the help of his brethren, he ventured to hold a Monthly Meeting in the Corwen neighbourhood. The private meeting was held in a farmhouse called Bodhaulog, where a good man, full of faith, named Richard White, lived. Mr Charles, Lewis Morris, and two other exhorters whose names are not known, preached. The wrath of the common people against the Methodists had by now considerably weakened; a general conviction was felt that they were God's men and that heaven's protection watched over them. Therefore for the first time at Corwen they had perfect peace to preach the gospel. But the devil's cunning was not completely exhausted. Though he could no longer make use of the common people as the instruments of his cruelty, he stirred up the gentry of the region so as to oppose the Lord's people in a different way. The consequence for Richard White of opening up his home to the Monthly Meeting was that he received notice from his landlord to vacate his home. When the time to quit arrived, he was given the choice of either leaving his farm or never allowing its use again to the Methodists. When these conditions were placed before him he answered boldly, no doubt with Christ's words echoing in his thoughts, 'Well, therefore, no more Bodhaulog for me.' As a result he bought *The Harp* in Corwen and having moved there, adapted the upper room, a large extensive area, into a meeting-place. The local believers worshipped there until a chapel was built.

Another man who sought to pour out his vial of wrath upon the head of Thomas Charles was the Bishop of St Asaph. This prelate behaved like the proverbial dog in the manger; on the one hand, he did not lift a finger in attempting to find a vacancy that would ensure Mr Charles's services for the Church of England, at a time when the latter greatly desired this; but on the other, when he saw that he had thrown in his lot with the Methodists and was becoming a man of influence amongst them and in the land, he began to snarl and show his teeth. Soon, he sent a legal warning to Mr Charles forbidding him to preach with 'the schismatics'; should he do so the bishop threatened to obtain an injunction against him to stop him. It seemed that a dead letter of a law existed by which any clergyman ordained in the Established Church could be forbidden, on pain of fine or imprisonment, to minister in connection with any other religious body. About fifty years ago this law was enforced by the Bishop of Exeter and a Mr Shore was imprisoned because of his transgressions. By now, the law has been repealed. It was this law, of which hardly anyone knew, and which no one had the heart to apply, because of its cruelty, that was threatened upon Mr Charles by the ungracious Bishop of St Asaph. Having received the warning, he travelled to London and there informed Lady Anne Erskine of his troubles. She sent the information to her brother, the Honourable Thomas Erskine, a well-known lawyer and one of the foremost barristers of the land, who afterwards became Lord Chancellor. This man wrote to the Bishop informing him that if he moved to enforce this law against Mr Charles, he himself would sponsor a motion in parliament to have it repealed. At this the bishop withdrew from the field and Mr Charles was given peace to continue his work.

HIS DEVELOPMENT AS A LEADER IN NORTH WALES

It could almost be said that it was at the instant that he joined the Methodists that Mr Charles's amazing career began. This is when the great work of his life opened up before him and when he threw himself into it. We cannot even give a synopsis of his ministerial work – we do not have the material for such a work, nor the space available were it at hand. He immediately began to journey abroad to preach the gospel. It was not long before he had visited every part of Gwynedd and was also often found in the south, especially at the Associations. The only means of transport in those days was riding or walking; the roads were rough, the hostelries uncomfortable and infrequent, and the food hard. The Methodists had only a small number of chapels, so preachers had to minister in homes, barns, or on the street. But Mr Charles was not disheartened; he was not one to be frightened by difficulties; he took no notice of the adversities which he experienced; his heart, rather, rejoiced at the freedom he had to proclaim the gospel of the kingdom to his poor countrymen. It was a small thing for him to have to ride, soaked to the skin, along remote mountainous paths; to find lodging in a tumbledown thatched cottage; to have a little bread and butter and a boiled parsnip for supper; to lie down in a small comfortless room upon a hard bed of straw; and to mix with relatively ignorant and uncouth people, who yet possessed some degree of love towards the Lord Jesus. In all his letters not a single note of complaint may be found concerning these things; indeed he does not refer to them at all; he hardly appears to be aware of them so greatly had his enthusiasm for the work possessed his soul. If indeed he did feel them, he surely rejoiced in them, in that they came his way for Jesus' sake. We could easily believe that many a poor believer living in the remote valleys of the north felt shivers of fear overcoming him as he contemplated receiving into his unadorned cottage a man of such standing and learning as Thomas Charles. But when he arrived, he was so humble and mild and so thankful for the welcome given that every fear immediately departed, being replaced by the greatest respect for him.

By his labours, the refinement and importance of his ministry, together with his particular organizational abilities, he soon came to be considered the leader of the Connexion in Gwynedd. He did not covet the position; his behaviour amongst his brethren and in all places was always humble, but his qualifications could not be hidden and he was obliged to take the highest seat. All looked up to him as a prince in Israel. The day that Thomas Charles joined the Connexion was a bright day in the firmament of Gwynedd Methodism, and indeed in the history of Welsh Methodism.

We do not wish to appear to ascribe all the success that occurred to his instrumentality; the power of the ministries of men such as Roberts, Clynnog; Jones, Edeyrn; John Elias; John Roberts; Evan Richardson and others, men who were the means of converting thousands from their unbelieving ways, must be taken into account. Yet, almost certainly, much of the fruit of the labours of these famous men would have been lost completely to the Connexion had it not been for Thomas Charles's organizational gifts. The preachers mentioned might have been ahead of him in oratorical power and in their ability to influence a congregation but he was far above them in learning, in familiarity with different theological ideas, and in wisdom. Because of this, and also because he was ordained, he became the greatest influence upon the Connexion in north Wales and was respected as the highest oracle. Nor was his influence unimportant in the south, notwithstanding the presence there of other well-known clergymen.

THOMAS CHARLES AS A PREACHER

The Rev. Roger Edwards provides a description of Mr Charles as a preacher drawn, no doubt, from a report he had received from one who had heard him:

> The Rev. Thomas Charles was preaching at a Monthly Meeting and there had been great expectation of his coming. Many Churchmen were in attendance because he was a clergyman, a brilliant scholar, and a man of such gentlemanly appearance. His text was Isaiah 28:20, 'For the bed is shorter than that a man can stretch himself on it: and the covering narrower than that he can wrap himself in it.' As an introduction he explained that the text was a proverb in Israel used in depicting the use of insufficient means for protection and safety. Then, with great ability, he applied it to reveal the hopelessness of all those things in which sinners put their trust for safety and comfort, outside of the salvation that is in Jesus Christ. He showed that the night of adversity comes to many, and the night of death to all, in which the value of a bed to lie upon and of a covering in which to wrap oneself in, is realized. He noted that men, generally, imagined that their beds and coverlets were sufficient. Some believed in the general goodness of God; others trusted in a moral life; some rested upon their devotions and religious activities; and others upon the convictions and stirring emotions that they had experienced in religious services. But with respect to these and other self-righteousnesses that he mentioned, the reverend preacher proclaimed with the utmost solemnity, 'That is a bed too short, a covering too narrow!'
>
> At the beginning of the sermon Mr Charles seemed rather hesitant and slow; the words did not flow though all he said was sensible and substantial. But long before he was half way through his sermon all hesitation had left him; his

voice was powerful and sweet; his face shone as the face of an angel; and his serious and solemn comments struck and held the consciences of every hearer. Many, at the close of the service, said that in the first part of the sermon they felt as if they had been deprived of all that they had, and that death and judgment would discover them in their nakedness. Some literally fainted such was the influence the truth had upon them. But having confined all his hearers in this way, the faithful minister opened for them the door of faith. 'Is there any here ready to say with those on the Day of Pentecost, "What shall we do? We cannot sustain ourselves; we must find something to rest on and to trust in; and you have here laid waste every bed and covering we possessed!" Listen, my dear people, I know of a bed that even a man as sinful as Manasseh could lie in without any danger of finding it too short; I know of a covering which, even if all of you came to wrap yourselves in, would be wide enough to cover you; yes, enough to shelter a world of sinners: THE ATONEMENT AND RIGHTEOUSNESS OF THE SON OF GOD!' He then led the congregation to Calvary, and as he said the words, 'It is finished', the crowd released their emotions in one great cry of thanksgiving to God, so that one might have thought that the walls of the chapel would have burst under its power.

But the preacher had not yet finished; he wished to clinch the truth, and to turn the emotion in a practical direction. He raised his hands for silence, saying, with immense tenderness and love, 'Dear friends, wait; rein in your feelings, and listen carefully. I have something more to say to you from God. Every one of you, old or young, believer or unbeliever, go, before this day ends, to some private place, in a room or in a field, and fall on your knees before God, throw yourselves upon his forgiving mercy in Christ, and pray with the Apostle Paul, "That I may be found in him!" With tears pouring down his cheeks, he added, 'It is clear, dear friends, that a mighty wind from above is blowing here today; and if you yield to the heavenly breeze I may hope to see you in the Jerusalem that is above shortly, but if you do not make good use of this precious time, 'Behold, you have sinned against the Lord, and be sure your sin will find you out.'

By now, the service had become a terrible place; all felt that they were in the presence of God. Nobody now shouted out, but all were weeping. The tears flowed in streams down every cheek. At the close, after a warm prayer, Mr Charles gave out the following hymn to sing:

O thou pure, eternal justice, Infinite in space and time! How my naked, barren spirit Cannot rest till thou art mine; Clothe me in thy shining garments, Hide my nakedness and blame, So to stand in thy bright glory With no fear of guilt or shame.	O gyfiawnder, pur, tragwyddol, O gyfiawnder maith didrai! Rhaid i'm henaid noeth, newynllyd, Gael yn fuan dy fwynhau; Rho dy wisg ddisgleirwen, olau, Cuddia'm noethni hyd y llawr, Fel nad ofnwyf mwy ymddangos Fyth o flaen dy orsedd fawr.

The precentor began one of the heavenly old hymn tunes of the Revival. The congregation sought to join in, in the midst of their tears, but the noise was a mixture of singing and weeping. Nearly everyone had their hand to their faces, their arms leaning on the seats, and the tears flowing down their faces. Some managed one line of the hymn, others contributed another, others again could only express a word of prayer or praise. Truly, the place was a Bochim, for 'the people lifted up their voice and wept'. It is said that some scores of people began to call sincerely upon God for the first time from that day. Many testified that this sermon was one of the most effective of Mr Charles's many effective sermons, and they could not describe it without breaking out anew in tears.

THOMAS CHARLES'S CIRCULATING SCHOOLS

We now proceed to describe some of the excellent institutions founded by Mr Charles. As he travelled throughout Wales he was always inquiring after the state of the people with respect to their morals, their religion, and particularly of their knowledge of the deep things of God. He soon understood that the common people were woefully ignorant, that very few could read, and that even the religious among them possessed only a very little discernment in the doctrines of the gospel. They had been broken down in the Revival and brought to believe in the Saviour, but they knew very little of him and their need of further teaching was great. His spirit was stirred within him and he resolved immediately to establish schools in order to scatter the darkness. He wrote the following in 1808, in a letter to a friend at London, describing the beginning of the circulating schools:

In my travels through different parts of North Wales about 23 years ago, I perceived that the state of the poor of the country in general was so low, with regard to religious knowledge, that not one in twenty, in many parts, was capable of reading the Scriptures; and in some districts, hardly an individual could be found who had received any instruction in reading. I found then, and still find, daily proofs of the ignorance of the poor people who cannot read, and have never been catechetically instructed, even where constant preaching is not wanting. This discovery pained me beyond what I can express, and made me think seriously of some remedy, effectual and speedy, for the redress of this grievance. I accordingly proposed to a few friends to set a subscription on foot to pay the wages of a teacher, to be moved circuitously from one place to another, to instruct the poor in reading, and in the first principles of Christianity, by catechising them. This work began in the year 1785. At first only one teacher was employed: as the funds increased, the number of teachers proportionately increased, till they amounted to 20. Some of the first teachers I was obliged to instruct myself, who afterwards instructed others sent to them to learn to be schoolmasters. The fruits of the Circulating Schools are our numerous Sunday-Schools all over the country; for without the former, we could not have obtained teachers to carry on the latter. Although, through the present general prevalence of Sunday-Schools, conducted by gratuitous teachers, the Circulating Schools are not now so much wanted as formerly, yet I still find we cannot go on without some of them. There are yet many dark places in different parts of the country, where none are found able and willing to set up Sunday-Schools. My only remedy, therefore, is to send thither the Circulating Schools, with a view, by degrees, of raising up Sunday-Schools to succeed them, and to keep on the instruction progressively after they are removed... now I constantly employ from six to ten teachers: and several more are really wanted, did our finances enable us to engage others in the work . . .

The Funds of the Schools are at present very low, and not adequate to half the expense I am under for this year. At first I hired teachers for £8 per annum, now I pay £15; so that I might keep 20 then, nearly at the expense of 10 now; and I am grieved that it is not in my power to employ more teachers, as the want of them is very evident in different parts of the country. Supposing that some friends of the gospel, who see the vast importance of instructing the poor, would willingly contribute their pecuniary aid to forward so good a work, were they acquainted with the necessity of it, I have been induced to draw up this short but true statement of the case for their information. The smallest donation, or annual subscription, will be thankfully received and faithfully applied.[1]

This letter is very interesting for many reasons. It not only sheds light on the circumstances that stirred up Mr Charles to establish the circulating schools, and on the way in which he began, but it also notes the time. It may be seen that as soon as he was aware of the need he did not allow the grass to grow under his feet; he began his venture within a year of joining the Connexion. The small wage paid to the teachers seems surprising. It is true that they were not learned men and had received few advantages, but to think that a hundred years ago schoolteachers could be found who would give all their time and labour for only eight pounds a year, seems almost incredible today. More information on the circumstances of the schools is given in the following letter written to a noblewoman in England about the year 1797:

Whatever we attempted of this nature succeeded wonderfully; till the whole country was filled with schools of one sort or another; and all were taught at once. The blessed effects were corresponding; a general concern for eternal things took place in many large districts; many hundreds were awakened to a sense of sin, and their need of Christ, and I have every reason to believe are now faithful followers of him. The schools are still carried on, and the effects the same in a greater or less degree; the number of teachers increase

> or diminish, as my finances will allow; all my income from a chapel which I serve, I devote wholly towards their support, being supported myself by the industry of my wife. I pay every teacher £12 per annum. They continue half a year, or three quarters in one place, and are then removed into another part of the country.
>
> Three quarters of a year, is found sufficient to teach our children to read their Bibles well in the Welsh tongue. I visit the schools myself, and catechize them publicly; I have the unspeakable satisfaction of seeing the general aspect of the country most amazingly changed; to see the wilderness blossom as the rose, and the thirsty land become springs of water; through the schools, and the preaching of the Gospel, the spread of divine knowledge is become universal. Bless the Lord, O my soul! I hope, dear Madam, this little account of the origin and outlines of a plan, which you have so generously supported, will prove in some degree satisfactory. As no other plan can keep our mountainous country from sinking into its former ignorance, I am determined to go on as long as the Lord enables. Assist me with your prayers. Grace and peace be multiplied to you.[2]

No originality of plan may be ascribed to Mr Charles with respect to the circulating schools; he merely followed in the footsteps of the Rev. Griffith Jones. The schools of that great man had produced immeasurable good, but by now he had been gathered to his fathers and Madam Bevan, who had assisted him in the work and continued after his death, had also died. The schools had stopped because the noblewoman's relatives had challenged her will. As far as reading was concerned therefore, the land was rapidly sinking back into its former ignorance. It was at this point that Mr Charles established a new work on the old plan. He began in the same way by teaching two or three schoolmasters himself and then sending others to them to be prepared for the same work. It must be remembered that Mr Charles had obstacles to overcome that had not existed for Griffith Jones. The latter had continued his ministry within the Church of England and it was under the auspices of parish clergymen that he had set up his schools. The mantle of the Establishment was therefore spread over him in all his undertakings and helped him in the obtaining of funds, though it must be acknowledged that he received very little from the bishops and clergy of Wales. But as for Mr Charles, he had left the Church; many religious Churchmen considered him a schismatic; all his schools were set up completely apart from the parish churches, and therefore the opposition to them was all the more fierce and the difficulty of collecting funds greater.

But his courage did not fail. If he was not the originator of the plan, he showed remarkable administrative skills in implementing it. He personally was responsible for all expense, and he does not seem to have had a wealthy noblewoman as a friend to fall back upon. It was seen in the last letter quoted that he gave the whole of the money received from the church where he ministered to the cause of the schools. He is referring to the money received at communion services in the Bala chapel. No collection for the ministry had been established at this time, but those who came to the Lord's Table contributed generously at the end of the service, and this money was recognized as being paid to the minister who administered the sacrament. This thank-offering would often produce a very honourable sum, especially when wealthy believers were present. We cannot now determine its value at Bala, but we have Mr Charles's definite testimony that not a penny of it went into his own pocket but that he donated it in its entirety to the work of the schools. As he says, the support for himself and his family rested upon Mrs Charles's labours in the shop. She was an exceptional tradeswoman, and after the death of her mother, which took place about two years after her marriage to Thomas Charles, Mr Thomas Foulkes transferred his own business to her care. Her responsibilities therefore were great and her trading extensive.

This worthy woman deserves more attention than she has received; it was only by means of her energetic efforts and her shouldering of such widespread responsibilities that her husband's hands were free for the work of the gospel. On the other hand there is evidence that Mr Charles also, or others acting in his name, undertook some commercial transactions. A company from Merionethshire took a lease on a gold mine in the Gwynfynydd neighbourhood, not far from the present area of mining. One of the company was Mr Charles, and another, Mr Pugh, the old elder of Dolgellau. Whether the venture profited them we cannot tell; most probably it proved a loss, in that so little is known of it and that it folded soon after. But if it made any money for them then, certainly, it would have been the causes of education and the gospel that would have benefited.

But we have wandered rather from the Rev. Thomas Charles and the circulating schools. His own means were not sufficient for him to carry the whole financial burden. He therefore corresponded with generous persons of his acquaintance in various parts of the kingdom, explaining the nature of the movement and appealing for support. The Lord moved some to contribute abundantly. In *The Evangelical Magazine* for March 1798, a letter of his acknowledges thankfully the donation of fifty pounds from one G. T. G. This was a remarkable and unique contribution, but he was certainly helped to a considerable degree by the generosity of Christian friends and men of good will. If it were not for this, it would have been impossible for him to maintain twenty schools at the same time in different parts of the country, at a cost of some three hundred pounds – the equivalent of fifteen thousand pounds presently [1897]. The schools blossomed for nearly twenty years; it is doubtful whether they ever completely disappeared in Mr Charles's lifetime. Two factors contributed to their decline. The first was the rise of the Sunday Schools, which to a large extent made them redundant. The second was the drying up of the generous stream upon which the schools depended. In 1808, Mr Charles wrote:

> Since the liberal collections made in Wales for the British and Foreign Bible Society, all the subscriptions and donations from England have ceased (with the single exception of two guineas annually from the Right Hon. Lord Barham) my kind friends supposing, as I presume, that there was no occasion for assistance in a country where so much money was collected, without much difficulty, for one particular purpose. But it may be necessary to observe, that this was a very particular occasion; and the minds of the people were much surprised with the novelty, as well as affected with the importance of the noble object.[3]

Mr Charles certainly considered that it was rather hard on the Welsh people that they were being punished for having contributed to the Bible Society over and above their ability, by keeping from them the support that they used to receive for the schools.

The schools were conducted through the medium of Welsh. The people were almost completely monoglot Welsh speakers, and Mr Charles was far too sensible to fall into the habit which was later established of teaching the people to read through the medium of a language which they did not understand. It would have certainly been a blessing to the Welsh people if the Welsh language had been kept in the day schools up until this day, according to Thomas Charles's method; not in order to keep out the English language but to be used in parallel with it, and held in equal status to it, as an equivalent medium of education. These schools were religious in their nature; the chief doctrines of the gospel were taught in them and the children would be catechized thoroughly in order to test their knowledge of the Scriptures. There does not appear to have been any attempt to teach them writing or arithmetic; the schools were not intended for purposes of commerce. Mr Charles intended them as means for making the common people religious and bringing them to the knowledge of the Lord by enabling them to read the Word. Out of consideration for those old enough to be at work, the schools were held at night. This meant also that none had an excuse for not attending. They were held in all kinds of buildings; in a chapel if possible, or perhaps in a home or a barn. No schoolrooms of any kind were to be found in the land at that time, except in some of the main towns. Wherever he went Mr Charles would look out for two things: a place where a school might be held, and a young man who would make a suitable schoolmaster. He showed considerable discernment and judgment of character in his choice of masters. Some of his young men, Richard Jones, Bala; John Ellis, Barmouth; Robert Evans, Llanidloes, for example, became worthy preachers in later life.

The following quotation from the papers of Lewis Williams, Llanfachreth, shed some light on the history of the circulating schools:

> The Lieutenant of the county, and the owner of much of the parish, (Sir Robert W. Vaughan of Nannau) asked me often for the history of the Methodists, and asked me how much I was receiving per quarter as a schoolmaster. He knew that the school was free to the children. I said that I received three pounds at first, but that this rose to four pounds afterwards. He used to be amazed that I could manage for food and clothing. I told him that I tried to be thrifty and that people were kind to me, one giving me half a pound or less of butter and another inviting me to his home for a meal. I would tell him that I would rather keep the school for nothing if I could than not keep one at all, such was the pleasure I received in the work. He asked me from where I received my wage, that much that I did receive. I answered that it was from Mr John Griffith of Barmouth, and that he received it from Mr Charles, and that Mr Charles had thirteen to fifteen other teachers like myself, and more sometimes, under his care. The nobleman then asked me from where Mr Charles got the money. I told him that he had many sources: that the Methodists in Merionethshire made a collection once a quarter in which they asked all to give a penny in good will; that some were wealthy and contributed more than others. He could not understand how this was sufficient for supplying our wages. I told him that the Methodists were many and that the one penny added to others soon became a large sum; that Mr Charles because of his great desire to see the poor children able to read, gave much himself; that he often visited the towns of England, and London, holding large meetings when wealthy noblemen, like yourself, sir, would be present, of the same benevolent spirit as himself; that he would place the needs of Wales, and of Merionethshire particularly, before them, and that they would often contribute generously to support him in his efforts. Sir Robert praised the work greatly and the means by which it was carried out.

There is much in this quotation that reveals how the schoolmasters were able to keep soul and body together. It is seen that they were homely men, mixing easily with the common people, and visiting them in their homes; and that they were not above receiving kindnesses from the farmers of the region in the form of butter or cheese or food. This does not seem to have diminished their influence in any way, it rather enhanced the affection and friendship of the people amongst whom they lived towards them. Lewis Williams described further the way in which he, together with other religious friends, would put an end to the corruptions of the neighbourhoods where he laboured. He writes:

> Whenever we heard of an immoral meeting, we would announce a prayer meeting to be held on the same evening and mention that some of us would attend the immoral meeting to see who would be so faithful to the evil one as to support him. We were present at a few and the result was that they stopped the meeting immediately. At other times, when we announced the prayer meeting together with the occasion for it, and the evil against which we would be praying, those who were arranging the meeting would declare that it would no longer be held. We would answer that the prayer meeting would still be held as a time of thanksgiving to God for inclining their minds to cancel the meeting. Before long all such meetings were given up.

Clearly the godly schoolmasters employed by Thomas Charles, together with the education and influence of the schools in their charge, played a large part in the purging of many of the old corrupt practices from the country. The following story related by a godly old pilgrim called Evan Roberts, who lived at Bryn-y-gath near Abergeirw, depicts the darkness of the land in Mr Charles's time and his great longing for establishing his schools:

> I remember, as clearly as anything, how Mr Charles preached outside this house on a beautiful day, one summer. His theme was Jesus Christ teaching Nicodemus about regeneration. Many had gathered together from the valleys between here and Llanfachreth and from Trawsfynydd, and they listened as they sat on the grass before the house. I was a young boy, standing behind them. And when Mr Charles said that you had to be born again, the young men said to one another, 'Do you hear, do you hear the man say that you have to be born a second time?' After the sermon, Mr Charles asked the owner of the house, 'Is there anywhere here I could send a man to keep a school?' 'I wouldn't be surprised if Bryn-y-gath Isaf would be willing,' was the answer. This was arranged at the time, and the next winter, that is, in 1790, John Ellis of Barmouth arrived. And from him, at Bryn-y-gath Isaf, the eccentric old preacher, Lewis Morris, received the only three weeks of daily schooling that he had in his life.

We have detailed much of the history of the circulating schools because they were the first of the various beneficent institutions set up by Mr Charles, and because of the extent of their influence, especially in Gwynedd, in extending the knowledge of God's Word and of religion in the country. According to the Rev. Lewis Edwards, D. D.:

> Had he done no more than his work with the day schools it would be as much as that accomplished by some that have volumes written about them in England. In this area he did as much as it was possible for him to do, and if others acted similarly there would be a different view on things in Wales today.

THOMAS CHARLES'S SUNDAY SCHOOLS

But just as the light of the stars are hidden by the brilliance of the burning sun so the fame of the circulating schools is hidden by the greater glory of the Sunday Schools. And with respect to the Sabbath Schools of Wales, we claim for Mr Charles the full honour of being the father of the movement. It was in his mind that the concept was formed; he announced it to the world; and he, with the determination and skilfulness that were so characteristic of him, implemented it and sent forth judgment unto victory. The English consider Robert Raikes as the father of the Sunday Schools, and we well know that that good man began to provide education on a Sunday for the poor children of Gloucester as early as 1782 or 1783, and was on the field therefore some four years before Mr Charles. But it was not by Mr Raikes's method that he worked, but according to his own unique vision. Dr Lewis Edwards states:

> There are Sunday Schools in England, and they began before those in Wales, and because they bear the same name, many have concluded that they are the same. But there is as much difference between them as between the dispensation of Moses and the dispensation of the New Testament. The purpose of the Sunday Schools in every other country except Wales is to teach children only; and not children either, as such, but poor children, who are unable to receive education by any other way. Neither the minister, nor the deacon, nor any respectable member of the congregation would think of sending their children there. The result is that the Sunday Schools are unknown in areas where there is a sufficiency of day schools within the reach of the poorer children, as in so much of Scotland; and as day schools become more common in England it is very likely that the Sunday Schools will disappear, unless they are established on a higher principle. Until now however a school on the Lord's Day, in which all ages meet to search the Scriptures, is unusual in all countries except Wales. It may be no exaggeration to say that this institution is the pre-eminent glory of Wales, and that this is the greatest of the works of Charles of Bala.

Truly, indeed, it is only in Wales that old men and old women are to be seen leaning on their walking sticks, their spectacles on their noses, seated as a class around the Word of God, with the intention of understanding its teaching; while nearby classes of infants and children, boys and girls of every age and status, give themselves to the same task. This is the unique element of our Sunday Schools and it grew from the mind of Thomas Charles.

As far as we can gather the Sunday Schools began in Wales about the year 1787. The longing for his countrymen to know the Scriptures had become an overwhelming passion in the Rev. Thomas Charles. Whenever he met an old man or woman as he journeyed amongst the mountains of Merionethshire or Arfon, he could not pass them without asking them whether they knew something of the Bible. He would stop a young man or girl on the road with the same question. He did this so often that he became a byword. It is reported of him that he once, far from home, met an old man, leaning on his staff, and asked him:

'You are an old man, getting close to another world.'

'I am,' was the reply, 'and I hope that I am going to heaven.'

'Do you know the way to get there? Are you familiar with God's Word?'

Instead of answering him, the old man turned to him with his own question:

'Are you Mr Charles?'

He had immediately concluded that a man who asked such questions as these must be he. The Sunday School was a natural development from the circulating schools. Without them the former would have been impossible; it could never have succeeded because of lack of teachers.

In the memoirs of that remarkable old preacher, Lewis Morris, may be found various examples of the extensive ignorance that covered the land before the foundation of the Sunday School. He once asked an old man whom he met in Anglesey:

'How old are you, uncle?'

'Eighty-two years old,' was the reply.

'Have you read much of the Bible in your lifetime?'

'I never had any education,' said the old man. 'But are you a chapel man?'

'I generally go to the chapel,' answered Lewis Morris.

'You chapel people,' said the old man, 'know the Scriptures. We church-goers know very little of them, but I have a very fine prayer and I say it every morning and evening.'

On asking him to repeat it, it turned out to be a prayer to the Virgin Mary!

'That is a Papist prayer,' said Lewis Morris, 'It won't help you at all.'

'Truly,' said the old man, 'that is the best that I possess.'

The same preacher, when once in Montgomeryshire, asked a woman of about eighty years of age:

'Have you read much of the Bible?'

'I cannot read,' she replied, 'and I never did any harm to anyone, and I have never been to anywhere other than to the parish church.'

'You are like me, aunt, a sinner who has broken God's commandments.'

'I don't know what it is to be a sinner,' she said, 'but if I am one, I am a good one.'

Many further examples could be given to show in what darkness the common people lay. It was only to a small extent in comparison that even the preaching of the gospel could scatter that darkness. Men listened but without discernment. They often felt stirred by the Word but very often their understandings were not illuminated.

Strangely enough, the Sunday Schools met with much opposition to begin with. They were condemned by the other religious denominations, and many of the Methodists also were completely opposed to this novelty. They believed that the teaching of reading, yes, even the reading of Scripture, on God's Day, was to profane the day; they considered it exactly the same as teaching any other branch of learning, such as music or painting. With respect to Mr Charles, Dr Lewis Edwards stated:

> He suffered moral martyrdom for long years, and at the hands of his friends. But on he proceeded, quietly and busily, with no fuss and bother. There was a life that would not die in the Sunday Schools.

Some ministers of other denominations joined with these prejudiced Methodists in opposition against Sunday Schools. The first school in Llanfrothen parish was held at Hafoty, directly opposite the home of the Rev. John Jones, Ramoth. He was a fierce opponent, who said many bitter things against them. He used to say that it would be just the same for him to see men go to the fields with their picks and spades on the Lord's Day, as to see them keeping a school to teach reading. There was a strong feeling in Penrhyndeudraeth against the movement. The school was not allowed to use the chapel on any account, the building was considered too sacred. The most unfounded stories were related as to the motives of the supporters of the Schools. Some would even go so far as to spread the tale that their intentions were to make all the boys into soldiers and to send them off to war. They would say, 'It is a most dangerous matter. We should rise up as a neighbourhood against it!' Even in Dolgellau, where Mr Charles's influence was almost absolute, such was the opposition of the elders and the leading members of the chapel that the school there had to be given up soon after its commencement. When Lewis Williams, Llanfachreth, came to the town in 1801 he decided to make a determined attempt to re-establish it. There was a considerable difficulty in fixing on an appropriate hour. A society was held at nine in the morning; a service in the parish church at eleven when none of the Nonconformists dared hold a meeting; and a prayer meeting or sermon at two and at six. He therefore decided to hold it at six in the morning. None of the brethren would help him; he was the supervisor and the teacher. He began the school and closed it; he gave out the hymn to be sung and also led the singing; it was he who catechized the children. The opposition increased. The society was moved from nine o'clock in the morning to six; Lewis Morris moved the school to four in the morning. Between sixty and eighty children turned up at this hour. At last, after much entreaty, Mr Charles succeeded in establishing a regular school at nine in the morning.

All opposition however gradually fell away. It was seen that the schools were conducted in a most religious way; that the teaching of reading was merely the outer court; that great emphasis was placed on prayer, praise, exhorting and warning; that the young people were learning chapters of the Bible by heart and being catechized publicly on what they read and learnt. In short, the meetings bore the hallmarks of a society as much as that of a school. Their influence was soon appreciated as young people were made serious and evil practices put away.

Lewis Williams depicts the battle at Llanfachreth between the supporters of the Sunday School and its opposers. He said:

> Those of the opposers who could do so would attend at other causes for the means (during the School time), sometimes travelling considerable distances. They did not consider the School a means of grace, nor even a means of religion. Much effort was exerted to prove this, but gradually it became clear that it was a means of providing and nurturing grace; that it included the worship of God; that it was also an advantageous means for obtaining that knowledge which is able to make one wise unto salvation, as well as supplying most effective assistance to the ministry of the gospel. This was proved by God's work in blessing it, with the result that some became more zealous for it than for any other means, and prejudice against it died away completely. Once the School had succeeded and its students were profiting from the instruction received, they would go so far as to say that those who did not attend, in that they travelled to the means elsewhere during Sunday School times, had only religion in their legs, and that those who merely stayed at home were unfruitful in their religion. The School proved of great benefit to Llanfachreth; through it corrupting customs were subdued and overcome, something which preaching on its own had not been able to do up until then.

It is doubtful whether such a moral and intellectual transformation was ever achieved so rapidly and thoroughly in any other country than that which occurred in Wales through the influence of the Sunday School. The change could be viewed as a revolution. Mr Charles, who, it is acknowledged, was always moderate in his comments, wrote in 1808:

> The spirit of learning has spread with rapidity among grown-up young people and children, in large populous districts, where hitherto it was wholly neglected among the common people; and the reformation in their morals, in most instances has been evident and satisfactory to all. Their usual mode of profaning the Sabbath, in meeting for play and amusement, or in public ale-houses for drinking and its usual concomitants of idle sports, and at last quarrels, have been forsaken; and the Sabbaths are spent together in the schools, or in some religious exercise, of either reading, or hearing the word preached, or in praying together. The attention is fixed, and the mind is engaged with such intenseness, that in some instances, which I have known, the greater parts of night after night have been spent with very little sleep, either in learning chapters out, or in searching the Scriptures on points given them to elucidate and prove by Scripture passages . . . I have known young people emerge at once, as it were, from a state of idleness, profaneness, and ignorance, to diligence, sobriety, and pleasing attention to divine things. They are delighted with the work, and you may distinguish those who are thus engaged from the idle and ignorant, by the comfort and joy manifested in the cheerful aspect of their countenances. They are profited and delighted with their new employment. I know them when I meet them on the road, though I had no previous acquaintance with them; there is kindness, affection, and joy in their very looks, which is highly gratifying.[4]

When writing to the Religious Tract Society, he provides further details:

> Thousands of young people, all over the country, have at this time their attention wholly engaged about divine things. They are learning Catechisms, and chapters out of the Bible, with wonderful facility. It has been my delightful work, since I left London in December last, every Sunday to catechize publicly, and hear them repeat chapters before thousands of people; besides preaching twice generally every Sabbath, and sometimes thrice, in different places. In order to give you some idea of the work, I would just mention some of the following particulars, which are strictly true: Whole families, young and old, the governors and the governed, learn the Catechisms together, and chapters of the Bible; they have appeared together, and repeated alternately what they have learnt. All the grown-up young people, in some of our Societies, have done the same. Boys and Girls, from eight to sixteen years old, learn whole books of the Scripture; and repeat what time will permit us to hear, such as the whole epistle to the Ephesians, Hebrews, etc; others learn select chapters to an astonishing number, such as 10, 20, 30. One little girl learnt seventy-two psalms and chapters; and another the astonishing number of ninety-two, the

> list of which I have in my possession. Now, we want to feed this fire, so happily kindled in their minds, by putting into their hands a few useful Tracts in the Welsh language. The 500 Scripture-Extracts which you sent, were nearly all disposed of in one day; and our young people are busy learning the whole out. I am just come from our chapel, where I heard two chapters of the Scripture-Extracts repeated publicly. In the course of a few weeks our children will learn the whole tract.[5]

HIS SKILL AT CATECHIZING

The rapid success of the Sunday Schools to such a degree throughout the country must be appropriated to Mr Charles's personal influence. There were many men of greater pulpit gifts than he, but once he was placed in the midst of a number of young people he would be as a king upon his throne. The lively spark in his eye, the warmth of his smile, the gentleness of his tone, and the notable skilfulness of his questioning, would draw the children and enable them to answer almost above that which they knew. It became a tradition that he would catechize at the end of every service, and many considered that this latter part was the most blessed of his services. Hundreds gathered to hear the questioning and answering, and often they sensed their hearts being warmed as well as their understandings illuminated as the truths were dealt with. This was the beginning of the tradition of *'holi'r pwnc'* ['catechizing the text'], which has proved of such benefit in Wales. Worthy successors followed Mr Charles, men such as Owen Jones, Gelli; Ebenezer Richards, and others, but no one excelled him.

We have already referred to the influence of the Sunday Schools and catechizing in overcoming corruption. Thomas Charles would sometimes compose catechisms on the evil customs of the land, showing their folly, or he would sometimes direct the questioning in that direction. One town in particular was said to be sinking ever deeper into corruption. At fair times especially the people, both young and old, would spend all their time in revelry and not even the most fiery and thunderous ministry would avail anything to moderate their behaviour. Mr Charles decided to attack the evil by other means. About two months before the fair he wrote to the teachers of the Sunday Schools directing them to ask the children to look for verses that emphasized the evil of drunkenness, prostitution, and dancing; and he promised to come and catechize them before long. The children's topic became known, and it caused considerable disturbance and discussion. The day before the fair he arrived according to his promise. The children had gathered together and a large crowd had come to hear. After singing and praying, the catechizing began. Mr Charles asked:

'Is dancing a sin, my children?'

'Yes,' said one boy, with emphasis, 'because of the dancing of Herodias's daughter, the head of John the Baptist was cut off.'

'Does Scripture condemn it?'

'Yes,' he answered, and then recited the verses, 'Woe unto them that rise up early in the morning, that they may follow strong drink; that continue until night, till wine inflame them! And the harp, and the viol, the tabret, and pipe, and wine, are in their feasts: but they regard not the work of the LORD, neither consider the operation of his hands.'

In a similar manner, various vices were discussed, one by one. Mr Charles warmed to the task of questioning; the children answered with much relevance; and soon the guilty hearers began to feel ashamed and to drop their heads. At the end, he exhorted them, with great tenderness, to leave their ways and to seek higher pleasures. The effect was overwhelming. The next day, the fair was transformed. Once their trade was over, the people returned home sober and serious; the musicians were left to themselves in the public houses, and there was no one to hear the harp. Soon, the harpists were seen leaving the place in disappointment, cursing 'the priest with the black cap' who had bewitched the people.

As a development of the Sunday School movement, Thomas Charles established the Schools Festivals, which immediately became popular and were next in influence to the Associations. It seems that he began these in 1808. He wrote of them as follows:

> We have also this year held associations of different schools meeting in some central places, to be publicly catechized together. Three meetings of this nature have been held in South Wales, and three in North Wales. A subject is given to every school, on which they are examined, and which they are to elucidate by repeating various passages from the sacred writings.[6] At the appointed time, generally a Sabbath day, the children of the different schools assemble, accompanied by their teachers. Some of the schools have walked ten miles by eight o'clock in the morning. The children being scattered in their different habitations over the country (for they do not dwell together in hamlets here as in England) they all met at an assigned place, and at the appointed hour went to prayer and sang a verse of a hymn together, and then marched cheerfully and orderly for the place of their destination, and had some refreshment before the public meeting began.
>
> As no place of worship is spacious enough to contain the immense concourse of people which attend on those occasions, we have been obliged to erect stages out of doors in the field – one, very large, for the children to stand upon, two or three schools at a time, and the other for the catechists opposite to that for the children, at fifteen or eighteen yards distance; the place between

is for the congregation assembled to stand to hear. We begin the work early in the morning, and the whole day is spent in these public examinations; every opportunity lasts three or four hours, and is generally concluded with short and appropriate addresses to the children and the congregation. In the short interval between the public opportunities, the children of each school are conducted by the teachers to a room, engaged for the purpose, to partake of a little refreshment provided for them; and at the appointed time they are orderly re-conducted again to the place of meeting. We have had on these occasions from fifteen to twenty schools assembled together. Hitherto these assemblies have been most profitable. The previous preparation give employment for months to all the youths of both sexes in large populous districts, which they engage in with great eagerness and delight; the public examinations also, we have reason to conclude, are very profitable to the hearers assembled, from their great attention and feeling on hearing the responses of the children. I have seen great meltings and tears among them. When the work of the day is over, the children are re-conducted by their teachers to their respective homes, or committed to the care of their parents. Everything has been conducted hitherto with great order and decorum in these meetings, and the utility of them, in various points of view, is ascertained beyond doubt. The schools assume publicity and importance by these public examinations of the children, which tend greatly to recommend the further spread of them; they animate both teachers and children; bring others in, who have hitherto been inattentive and negligent, and powerfully excite the setting [up] of new schools where they have been neglected.[7]

This is Thomas Charles's account of the setting up of the Schools Festivals, the memory of which is blessed in Wales to this day. They left a deep impression on the life of the nation. Next to the preaching of the gospel, and beyond it even in some areas, they proved to be the most effective means of overcoming superstitions and corruptions and bringing sinners to the Saviour of men. In every neighbourhood of Wales the day assigned for *'adrodd y pwnc'* ['reciting the topic'] was a high feast; it was looked forwards to for months beforehand. Those involved would study the various 'topics' and turn the pages of the Scriptures as they looked for relevant verses. The young girls would meet in houses in the neighbourhood in order to learn the group recitations; and in the villages the women would often practise their part of the 'topic' as they wove stockings in the light of the peat fire. Great was the competition between different schools, and between different classes of the same school, with respect to the perfection of recitation, the accuracy of accentuation, the appropriateness of the tone, and especially with respect to answering the questions. But when the day came, so often did the Spirit of God descend, that all reciting in unison would be forgotten, and all the skilful presentations would be in pieces.

On scores of occasions at these meetings, the catechizer would be seen in tears, the children exhilarated, the congregation holding their breath at the excellence and glory of the truths being considered; and often the meetings would come to an end with glorying and singing.

THE 1787-88 REVIVAL IN NORTH WALES

Soon after the establishing of the Sunday Schools, that is, at about the end of 1787, north Wales was shaken from one end to the other by a powerful revival. The Holy Spirit fell upon the services with a power as at Pentecost; unbelievers fainted in fear; hundreds cried out, 'What must we do to be saved?', and the saints of God took down their harps from upon the willows. There was hardly another topic discussed throughout all districts other than the state of the soul. This is how Thomas Charles described the revival in a letter to a friend:

> You enquire about the state of the churches in Wales. I have nothing but what is favourable to relate. We had, lately, a very comfortable association at Pwllheli; some thousands attended more than ever was seen there before. And here, in our town of Bala, for some time back, we have had a very great, powerful, and glorious out-pouring of the Spirit of our God, on the people in general, especially young people. The state and welfare of the soul is become the general concern of the country. Scores of the wildest, and most inconsiderate of the people, have been awakened. Their convictions are very clear, powerful, and, in some individuals, very deep, till brought, for a time, to the brink of despair; their consolations also, which soon follow, are equally strong...
>
> [A] spirit of conviction spread so rapidly, that there was hardly a young person in the neighbourhood but began to enquire, What will become of me? The work has continued to go on ever since with unabated power and glory, spreading from one town to another, all around this part of the country. New conquests are gained every week, and new captives brought in. A dispensation so glorious, I never beheld, nor indeed expected to see in my day. In [the] course of the eight years I [have] laboured in this country, I have had frequent opportunities of seeing, and feeling also, much of the divine presence in the Lord's work and ordinances, and great success attending the ministration of the word; but nothing to equal the present work...
>
> I am well aware, that should the *Rationalists*, in England, hear of what is going forward in this country, they would consider the whole as wild enthusiasm, and the effects of over-heated imagination; we deny not, but there may be dross mixed with the fine gold; but that this work is of God, we can no more doubt, than that light and heat proceed from the sun. We are willing to rest the credit of it upon the fruits of righteousness, which it produceth in great abundance ...

Ride on! Ride on! thou King of Glory, is the fervent cry of my soul day and night; and in this, I doubt not, but you will join me. I verily believe the Lord means soon to give the kingdom of darkness a dreadful shake; for he takes off the pillars of it. Those who were the foremost in wickedness and rebellion, are now the foremost in seeking for mercy and salvation in the blood of the Lamb. It is an easy and delightful work to preach the glorious Gospel here, in these days; for many are the fervent prayers put up by the people for the preacher; and they hear the word for eternity. Divine truths have their own infinite weight and importance in the minds of the people. Beams of divine light together with irresistible energy, accompany every truth delivered. It is delightful, indeed, to see how the stoutest heart bended, and the hardest, melted down by fire from God's altar; for the word comes in power, and in the Holy Ghost, and is made mighty, through God, to the pulling down of strong holds. I bless God for these days, and would not have been without seeing what I now see in the land – No, not for the world . . .

. . . many, under the age of twelve years, are deeply affected, astonished, and overpowered with divine truths, and their minds filled with nothing else day and night; of these things they talk when they lie down, and when they rise up.

All I relate are matters of facts, and have not exaggerated in the least degree; nor related but a small part of the whole. The Lord hath done great things for us, and to his great name be all the praise![8]

A famous minister in Scotland saw the above letter and wrote to Mr Charles asking for further information on the revival, suggesting that he would like to have proofs that God's hand was in the work. This is how the latter responded, about a year after his first letter:

That it is a work of God I am not left to doubt in the least degree: it carries along with it every scriptural satisfactory evidence that we can possibly desire; such as deep conviction of sin, of righteousness, and of judgment; great reformation of manners; great love for, and delight in, the word of God, in prayer, in spiritual conversation, and Divine ordinances. These, in *particular*, among *young* people, occupy the place and employ the time that was spent in vain diversions and amusements. No harps, but the *golden* harps which St John speaks of, have been played upon in this neighbourhood, for several months past. The *craft* is not only in *danger*, but entirely destroyed and abolished. The *little stone* has *broke* in *pieces* and *consumed* all those ensnaring hindrances. But I am far from expecting that all those who have experienced Divine influences are savingly wrought upon, and soundly converted. If that were the case, all the country would be converted; for, at one time, there were very few in it but what felt an awful impression, from the hand of God, upon their minds, producing foreboding fears respecting their future existence in another world. It was a most solemn time indeed! I never saw a livelier picture of the state

> of people's minds in the day of judgment, according to their respective conditions. That awful dispensation lasted but few weeks; but the ministration of the word is still lively and powerful; and fresh awakenings take place, though not so *numerous* as at first.[9]

The testimony of a man of such discernment, balance of mind, and equity of judgment as Mr Charles, with respect to the Welsh revivals, is of the utmost value. He judged the tree by its fruit; he studied the nature of the awakenings according to their practical outcomes. On the one hand, he was not carried away by the enthusiasm and influence; he did not imagine that everyone who was shouting had been saved; on the other hand, he was not so fastidious as to condemn a religious awakening just because there was a degree of disorder connected with it. He saw that the revival was driving the young people to their Bibles and to the throne of grace; that it caused them to turn their backs on their old pleasures and practices; that it produced in them a fear of offending the Lord, and brought eternity so close to their thoughts that the world and its affairs was distasteful to them. Because of this he judged it to be of God. And to what other conclusion could he have come? If a transformation of life and morals is not proof of divine influence, I do not know what is. Let the Welsh revivals be judged by their fruits; by their effects in overcoming immoral practices and in producing men of pure morals, full of thought, and mighty in the Scriptures; it must then be acknowledged as the direct fruit of the Spirit of God.

In his biography of the Rev. Thomas Charles, Mr Hughes, Llanuwchllyn, makes the following comment:

> While these religious awakenings were proceeding, most Welsh clergymen remained only as onlookers. This is something to be regretted. Had the clergy only taken the reins this wonder of religious enthusiasm might have been purged of its less refined elements, and kept within the borders of the Church, rather than allowing it to escape almost entirely into the channels of Nonconformity. The religious revivals produced by means of some of the missions that are now common among English Churchmen are similar awakenings to the old revivals of Wales, but with this difference, that the English revivals are less powerful and of shorter duration in their effects than the revivals in Wales.

We will not debate with Mr Hughes as to what he considers to be the less refined elements of Welsh revivals, though it would be appropriate for him to remember that the divine dispensations are never designed to meet the fastidious, pseudo-gentlemanly tastes of men. Nor do we wish to sit in judgment on whether it would have been an advantage or a disadvantage to the revival if it had been kept within the confines of the Established Church. But we would comment that that which he desires, namely, that the clergy should have been to the fore in the revival, was completely impossible. They had not been awakened themselves; the glories of the things of the gospel were completely hidden to them; they were so much more at home at the hearthside of an inn than in the pulpit; and better able to lead in the various sports of the day than in the effort of saving souls. But as for the comment that the revivals of Wales were similar to the 'missions' of the Established Church today, this is thoroughly wrong and misleading. The one was divine, and the other is human. We do not wish to condemn what are called 'missions'; insofar as they are a result of the desire to bring men to Christ they are good. But after all, they are merely human; they are characterized by efforts to effect the emotions by singing, and by thrilling addresses; they seek to bring men to a pitch of excitement. No wonder therefore that Mr Hughes describes them as short-lived influences. The excitement dies away when the means are brought to an end, just as the breeze on the threshing-floor dies with the last beat of the winnowing-sheet.

The old Methodists would have considered it an awful presumption to try to 'raise a revival' by such means. A Welsh revival was something supernatural; a strong wind blowing where it wishes, often springing up quite unexpectedly and with overpowering influences, but without the least effort by any to produce it. It was power accompanying the usual means of grace. It would break out sometimes in a prayer-meeting, at another time during the sermon of some little-known man; it would progress like wild-fire through the country, producing incomparable effects. The frivolous would be sobered, the blasphemous would become religious, the leader in wickedness would cry for his life, and the land, instead of being full of swearing and blasphemy, would be full of praise. Nothing could produce such a transformation except the direct influence of the Spirit of God.

[1] D. E. Jenkins, *Rev. Thomas Charles*, Vol. 3, pp. 193–5.

[2] Ibid., Vol. 2, pp. 163–4.

[3] Ibid., Vol. 3, p. 194.

[4] Ibid., pp. 195–6.

[5] Ibid., pp. 136–7.

[6] 'In one case of these examinations, a young girl of seventeen, in repeating the close questions put by the Saviour to St Peter – "Lovest thou me?" – when she came to the third, was overcome, burst into tears, and the bulk of the congregation wept with her; an awful silence continued for a few minutes, all solemnly waiting for the reply; at last, on recovering herself, she loudly, and with a strong voice cried out – "Thou knowest all things, thou knowest that I love thee."'

[7] D. E. Jenkins, *The Rev. Thomas Charles*, Vol. 3, pp. 196–7.

[8] Ibid., Vol. 2, pp. 88–91.

[9] Ibid., p. 97.

32
THOMAS CHARLES, B.A., BALA
(CONTINUED)

A HUNGER FOR BIBLES IN WALES

A direct result of establishing the Sunday Schools, and of the revivals that shook the land as an earthquake, was the awakening of a desire among the common people to acquaint themselves with the Scriptures. But unfortunately no Bibles in Welsh were to be had for love or money. The Rev. Griffith Jones, Llanddowror, had succeeded in persuading the Society for the Propagation of Christian Knowledge to bring out two editions of the Welsh Bible; one in 1746, and the other in 1752. These had been sold mainly in the south. There were very few Bibles to be found in Gwynedd and before the end of the century they had even become scarce in the south. Peter Williams had made valiant efforts to meet the needs, but his Bibles were too expensive for the common people and, because of the changes made by him in John Canne's Bible and the subsequent controversy between himself and the Methodists, there was a period when this edition was not bought even by those who could afford it. Mr Charles was deeply grieved because of this unmet hunger for God's Word and he looked for possible ways of overcoming it. As early as 1787 he was in correspondence with the Rev. Thomas Scott, who at the time lived in London, seeking to persuade that good man to bring out an edition of the Welsh Bible. Mr Scott failed in this attempt. As the number of circulating schools increased so the cry for Bibles became louder. Requests for copies poured in upon Mr Charles from every part of the country and his soul was pained within him that he could not find some means of help.

In the midst of his difficulties, he thought of the Society for the Propagation of Christian Knowledge. There was no point in him approaching this society personally because it was a Church of England Society and it would have been in vain for a man who had turned his back upon the Church to hope for help from that direction. He therefore wrote to the Rev. Thomas Jones of Great Creaton, Northamptonshire, a close friend. Mr

Jones was born in Cardiganshire but served as curate and rector in English churches for over fifty years. He had visited Wales at the end of 1791 and was familiar with the great need. As a result of Charles's letter, he wrote to the S.P.C.K. describing the situation in Wales and the longing of the people for Bibles. He pleaded for the Society to print ten thousand copies and offered to pay for the first four thousand himself. He received no reply from the Society at first but he continued to knock at the door. At last, on 17 July 1792, he received a letter informing him that his request had been granted. But then the committee had second thoughts and about the middle of the following year wrote to Mr Jones expressing their unbelief that the demand in Wales could be as great as he had portrayed. They were not of the opinion that such a number of copies could be sold and they seemed strongly inclined to go back on their promise. Mr Jones therefore wrote to the Bishop of Peterborough and through his influence succeeded in obtaining a printing of ten thousand Bibles and two thousand New Testaments. These were published in 1799. Within a few months not a single copy remained unsold; yet only a quarter of the need had been met; 'the joy of those who had obtained Bibles was glorious, and the sadness of those who had failed inexpressible'. A further appeal was presented to the Society, supported strongly by the Bishop of Peterborough, the Rev. Thomas Scott, Mr William Wilberforce, and other prominent men, but, after much correspondence, the Society's decision was that they would not print any further Welsh Bibles. What influenced them to act in this way we do not know, but ultimately their refusal was overruled, in that it led to the formation of the Bible Society.

MARY JONES AND HER BIBLE

The history of the beginning of the Bible Society cannot be given without providing the affecting story of Mary Jones. She was the daughter of a weaver, Jacob Jones, who lived in a cottage called Ty'nyddol at the foot of Cader Idris, in the parish of Llanfihangel-y-Pennant. She was born in 1784. Her parents were members of the Methodist society that had been established in the area. In those days children were not allowed in the society, but Mary used to accompany her mother on dark winter nights, carrying the lantern for her. As a reward for her help she was allowed to sit at her mother's side during the meeting. When she was about ten years old, John Ellis came to Abergynolwyn village to set up one of the circulating schools together with a Sunday School. Though Mary lived over two miles away and had a very stony path to travel, she was one of the most faithful members of both schools. She learnt to read in very little time and became well known for memorizing and reciting God's Word. Jacob Jones had no Bible in his home; the nearest copy known to Mary was in a farmhouse about two miles away. Fortunately she was given permission to read it, and she would walk there every week, as the hart to the water brooks, in order to read and memorize. She continued to do this for six years. But the desire to possess her own Bible became an overwhelming longing within her. Every halfpenny received from her neighbours as a reward for various services, she would place aside, in the hope that her fund would be sufficient one day to buy the treasured Pearl. After years of saving, she had collected the sum that she had heard was the price of the latest edition of the Bible. She went immediately to the old exhorter, William Hugh of Llechwedd, to ask where a Bible might be bought. He replied that there were none for sale nearer than Bala, from Mr Charles, and that he feared that every copy received by that good man had been sold.

One fair morning, in the spring of 1800, Mary Jones set out for Bala. She had over twenty-five miles of rough road ahead of her. She walked barefoot and had, over her shoulder, a wallet that she had borrowed in order to carry the Bible safely home, and which she presently used to carry her shoes. By the time she arrived at Bala it was late in the day. She put on her shoes and, as she had been advised, she asked for the home of Dafydd Edwards, the preacher. His heart melted as he listened to her story; he told her that it was too late to call on Mr Charles in that he was known to go early to bed, but that he would be in his study at the break of dawn. 'You may sleep here tonight,' said the kind old preacher, 'and I will take you to Mr Charles tomorrow morning.' Very early the next day they were at the famous man's door; he himself opened to them and invited them in. He listened to Mary's tale and asked questions to discover the extent of her knowledge of the Bible. He inquired how it was she had learnt so much and yet without a copy in the house. As Mary told him of the two mile journeys to the neighbouring farm, and the treasuring away of halfpennies in order to buy God's Word, Mr Charles's feeling nearly overcame him. With much sadness, he said, ' I am very sorry to see this poor girl having come all the way from Llanfihangel for a Bible, and I not having one to give to her. I have sold all that I had from London, apart from a few copies that I have promised to keep for friends. What I shall do for more Welsh Bibles, I do not know.'

Mr Charles's words pierced Mary's heart like a dagger The hope that she had cherished in her heart for years was shattered at a stroke. She broke out into loud weeping, with the tears running in streams down her cheeks. Her weeping overcame Mr Charles. 'My dear girl,' he said, 'I see that you must have a Bible. Though it is hard to disappoint friends, I cannot refuse you.' Mary Jones began to cry again, but now out of sheer joy, and the tears of Dafydd Edwards and Mr Charles mixed with her own. After Mr Charles had prayed earnestly for her, the girl placed the Bible in the wallet and set off immediately over the rugged mountains as one who had found great spoil. 'Dafydd Edwards,' said Thomas Charles 'isn't that a sight to melt the hardest heart – an intelligent, poor girl, walking barefoot over fifty miles, in coming and going, to obtain a Bible? I must not now rest until I find a way to fill the country with God's Word.' We are glad to be able to add that Mary Jones lived to a ripe old age; that she spent all her life in the service of her Saviour; that she was one of the most faithful supporters of the Bible Society; and that she died with the Bible obtained at Bala on the table at her side. This treasured Bible, handed to her by Mr Charles, is now kept carefully by the Bible Society in London. For many years it was kept at the Theological College at Bala, but at the request of the Society it was transferred to them.

The history of Mary Jones and her quest for a Bible does not stand entirely on its own. One evening, as he walked through the streets of Bala, Mr Charles came across a poor girl of his acquaintance. He asked her if she could recite the text on which he had preached the previous Sunday. Instead of answering him immediately as she usually did, she hung her head and was dumb. 'Can you remember the verse, my girl?' he asked again. At that, she burst into tears. Having recovered she said, 'The weather has been so bad, sir, that I could not go to read the Bible.' 'You could not go to read the Bible? What do you mean?' He soon learnt the reason. There was no copy of God's Word in the girl's house, nor in the homes of any of her friends, and usually, every week, she would walk seven miles over the mountains to read the Bible and learn the text. Mr Charles was greatly pleased, but the determination was strengthened within him of seeking to bring the Holy Scriptures into the possession of his fellow-countrymen, and he continually sought for some plan to achieve this.

THE FORMATION OF THE BRITISH AND FOREIGN BIBLE SOCIETY

In December 1802, Mr Charles went to London to serve the church at Spitalfields for a period, as he often did. By this time he had decided to place Wales's needs for Bibles before his friends in the capital and it seems that he had already formed some scheme in his mind of establishing a Bible Society in London on the same basis as the Religious Tract Society. It is fair to say that his intentions for this new scheme were that it might serve as the answer to Wales's problems. Full of this mission, he met one morning with his friend, Mr Tarn. They decided to present the matter to the R.T.S. during its annual meeting on the seventh of the month. There the matter was first presented by Mr Tarn. After him Mr Charles stood up and explained in detail the situation in Wales, portraying clearly the longing of the people for the Bible. He finished by explaining his plan for a Bible Society to be set up in London. As he spoke, his words induced deep feelings – tears were seen on many cheeks – and when he referred to a Society to meet the needs of Wales, the fire caught, and a Baptist minister, Joseph Hughes of Battersea, shouted out, 'And if for Wales, why not also for the Empire and for the world?' Thus began the British and Foreign Bible Society. The Rev. Joseph Hughes was requested to prepare a circular inviting Christians of every denomination to join together to form a society with the purpose of sending out copies of the Bible, without notes or commentary, throughout the world. The plan met with a host of objections at first; the high and mighty mocked it; the leaders of the Established Church kept away; but every obstacle was overcome and the Society was finally established on 7 March 1804 at London Tavern, Bishopsgate Street, London. The longed-for consignment of Welsh Bibles did not arrive until 1806, but great was the rejoicing when they finally came. The people surrounded the carrier that bore the Bibles like starving people pressing around a delivery of bread. Old men and women, leaning on their walking sticks, wept freely such was their joy and the young people shouted out so that valleys echoed with their cries. The following is an eye-witness description of the scene, given in the *Christian Observer* for July 1810:

> When it was known that the carrier that bore the first sacred load was in sight the people streamed out in droves to welcome it as the Israelites did the ark of old. They pulled the cart themselves into the town, and eagerly carried away the copies as quickly as they could be dispersed. The young people spent the whole night reading the Word. The labourers took it with them to the fields so that they could enjoy it during their break from work and not lose an opportunity to familiarize themselves with its sacred truths.

We believe that it is sufficiently evident that if anyone deserves the right to be called the Father of the Bible Society, it is Mr Charles. The Rev. Dr Lewis Edwards wrote:

> The only two men who have some right to be registered as the founders of the Society are Thomas Charles and Joseph Hughes. The first was the one who brought about the felt need for such a society; and not only that, but inquired; and agitated; and did not rest until he had obtained it. But in the meeting held in London as a result of Mr Charles's labours and unwearied importunity and

> in which they agreed to set up a society to meet the needs of Wales, it was the Rev. Joseph Hughes who suggested the idea of making it a general society, not only for Wales but for Britain, and not only for Britain but for the whole world. This is as it should be; and Mr Charles's own standing would not be so high had it been otherwise. Imagine that he, in the midst of the need of his own country, when the children of the Sunday Schools were crying out for Bibles and failing to obtain them, was to have gone up to London and to move the formation of a society to send out Bibles to the furthest extremes of the world. He would then have been more like those fools whose eyes scour every corner of the world. Such behaviour could hardly have arisen from a simple desire to do good; and even if it were acknowledged that it showed an exemplary feeling, it is clear that that feeling would not have been born of wisdom. But Mr Charles did that which was appropriate for himself; he laboured in that sphere in which divine providence had placed him, and in so doing, his labours became the occasion of the formation of the Bible Society. To ask whether he or Mr Hughes was the author of the Society is the same as asking who was the author of the victory at Waterloo: whether the English, who withstood the enemy throughout the day, or the Prussians, who arrived later in the day and finished the work . . .

The other pertinent comment on this matter is that there is less weight than is considered by many in the phrase 'British and Foreign'. The great purpose was to have a society that dispersed Bibles inexpensively, without notes or commentary. Not to think of it, or debate of it, but to have it. That is the great principle that forms the soul of the Society, and this principle lay at the heart of Mr Charles's suggestion.

It must be acknowledged that others such as the Revs. Joseph Hughes, Battersea, and John Owen, Fulham, laboured more extensively than Mr Charles with the Society once it had been formed; living in London, they had the better opportunity for doing so; but as for the efforts that led to the existence of the Society these must in their entirety be attributed to the Rev. Thomas Charles.

As we have mentioned previously, the first edition of Welsh Bibles from the Bible Society appeared in 1806. It comprised of twenty thousand copies, and a further five thousand separate copies of the New Testament. One of the reasons for the delay was that Mr Charles had been appointed to prepare the text for the press. He wished to make some changes in the orthography, according to the system of William Owen Pughe. This brought the wrath of the Rev. J. Roberts, Tremeirchion, down upon him, who wrote a strong letter to Dr Gaskin, the secretary of the S.P.C.K., protesting against any change even of a single letter. Dr Gaskin had shown every indifference in response to Mr Charles's previous applications, but was now very ready to hinder him and he wrote at once to the Bishop of London informing him of the matter. The issue came before the Committee. Mr Charles was asked to explain the nature and extent of his changes. 'This explanation,' writes the Rev. John Owen, 'was given clearly and satisfactorily by the Rev. Thomas Charles. The Committee was satisfied that Mr Charles had *no intention of changing the translation*, and made no attempts at this.' The words in italics prove that Mr Charles had been accused of changing the content of the Bible in order, doubtless, to make it more supportive of his own views. The Committee understood that the accusation was false, but it could make no decision as to the changes in orthography. They therefore presented these to be adjudicated by the Rev. Walter Davies (*Gwallter Mechain*), the vicar of Meifod, who decided against Mr Charles's changes. His mildness and wisdom were such however, that he took no offence at the refusal of his efforts; he displayed the same zeal with the publication of the edition as if it were his own choice of orthography that had been accepted.

Mr Charles was a faithful encourager of every form of missionary endeavour. When the London Missionary Society was established in 1795 he supported it zealously. He contributed to it generously personally and took every opportunity in the Monthly Meetings and Associations to call attention to the condition of the pagan world and the duty of Christians to send the gospel to every part of the world.

He wrote a Welsh circular describing the work of the Society and this had a wide circulation. He argued its case also in the *Drysorfa Ysprydol* [*The Spiritual Treasury*]. As a result, a deep sympathy towards the pagan was felt throughout the land. Earnest prayers were offered to heaven on his behalf, and the sums that were collected in order to send out missionaries were amazing when considering the poverty of the country. Ever since that time, Wales is ahead of every other country in the world in the amount of its giving per head of population to every kind of missionary work. Thomas Charles had a particular interest in the first missionary vessel, *The Duff*; he had opportunity to see her when he was in London, and he dined on board:

> . . . much pleased I was with the thought, that amidst all the hundreds of vessels I saw in the river, trading to different parts of the globe, carrying the perishing things of this world from one nation to another, there was one trading for heaven, engaged in conveying the everlasting gospel to benighted heathens perishing for lack of knowledge. Perhaps it is the first vessel in any age of the world that was ever solely so employed, I thought the nation highly honoured by the event, as well as the persons principally concerned.[1]

In 1806 he was invited to preach the sermon at the annual meeting of the L.M.S. in London. His text was Isaiah 10:27, 'The yoke shall be destroyed because of the anointing.' He was warmly thanked for his substantial support of the Society and for his sermon, and it was requested that it be published. Perhaps there is nothing of great portent to be read in it. He did not aim for such things, just as he did not aim for oratorical fluency, but an excellent spirit pervades every sentence.

As we have followed his various activities it has proved impossible to keep a strict chronological order. There was no end to his energies, at home or away. Because of the number of the activities in which he was either directly or indirectly engaged, his correspondence was never-ending. He spent a considerable time every year in London, serving the chapel at Spa Fields, and another chapel also belonging to the Countess of Huntingdon's Connexion. Those from Wales similarly honoured were David Jones, Llangan; David Griffiths, Nevern; and Nathaniel Rowland. His labours in this field were not without much blessing and success. In a letter to him written in April 1792 by Lady Anne Erskine, there is a reference to two who had died in great faith, and who had testified that it was under his ministry that they had been brought into the knowledge of the truth. She wrote further that there were others whose testimony was that that the Lord had blessed his sermons to their awakening, their building up, and their comfort. He did his best to establish Sunday Schools similar to the Welsh ones, in the Countess of Huntingdon's Connexion, and private societies on the Welsh model also. To some extent these efforts proved successful.

A DANGEROUS ILLNESS

The year 1799 stands out as a remarkable year in the life of Thomas Charles. We have already referred to his many travels along narrow valleys and over the cold and rugged mountains of Gwynedd, and that in all weathers. When travelling over Berwyn Mountain towards Bala on a very stormy day, he said to his companion, 'The Berwyn is not a bad mountain to be crossing on one's way home.' One night, in the winter of 1799, he was travelling home from Caernarvonshire over Migneint Mountain. The ground was covered in snow and the icy wind was cold enough to reach to the marrow of the bones, and as he tried to hold on to the reins of his horse the frost bit into the thumb of his left hand. The result was an infection that almost ended his life. After visiting many physicians, a very well known man in Oswestry among them, he had to return home and have the thumb amputated. God's people feared greatly during his illness and the prayers offered on his behalf were many and importunate.

One particular prayer meeting at Bala was especially notable. When Mr Charles's life was in the balance with the doctors shaking their heads over his case, the Bala congregation met to pray for an extension to his life. As he addressed the throne of grace, one godly old man laid hold of God's promise to Hezekiah, 'And I will add unto thy days fifteen years.' He repeated the words over and over with ever increasing life; he seemed to be taking hold of God's power. 'Fifteen, Lord; wilt Thou not give him to us for fifteen years? For my brethren's sake, this prayer is made, and for the sake of my neighbours too.' The people dispersed with an assurance that the prayers of the old saint had been heard, and that Mr Charles would not die at that time. Indeed, he improved from that day. He also lived exactly fifteen more years, and it is worth noting that these last fifteen years were the most fruitful of his life.

To some extent we have been sparing in quoting from Mr Charles's letters except for those that have shed light on his various activities, but a letter written to a friend soon after his recovery from his illness reveals so much of his nature that we feel obliged to quote freely from it. He wrote:

> I have received your two kind letters; for which I feel very thankful, and beg to acknowledge my obligations. That you and the brethren remember me before the throne of grace, is to me a cause of great joy. I consider the prayers of the church on earth to be next to the intercession of Christ in heaven. Those 'groanings that cannot be uttered'; the language and voice of the Holy Spirit in the hearts of his people, are sweet, powerful, and most effectual with God. 'The effectual prayer of a righteous man availeth much.' And there are no limits to this 'much', except 'asking amiss'. That the church is praying for me is a great honour. This cheers my mind when most dejected; though at the same time, it so fills me with shame, that I know not where to hide my worthless head. It is a pleasure to me to think that I shall have to spend a joyful eternity with my brethren, who are on earth so dear to me. All things are well; I could not wish them better.
>
> It is true the dispensations of my heavenly Father towards me, appear to me mysterious; yet while viewing them, wonder, joy, and gratitude, fill my mind. His ways are unsearchable; and yet all his works are glorious. He can, by the same means, kill and make alive; he can draw life from the dead things; and fill with joy unspeakable and full of glory a soul that is in the midst of clouds, the darkest and the most threatening; yea, he leads his people into the wilderness, for the purpose of speaking peace to their souls, in the manner most advantageous to their good. I do not think it becomes to speak much of myself, lest I should become a boaster before God; which I dread to be. There are some of God's dealings with his people, which it is not lawful for us in this world to make known, in all their circumstances. They will in the next be

> known to all, to the eternal praise of the Redeemer. Yet it is my delight and it is my duty, even while here, to bear my humble testimony, together with thousands of my brethren gone before, that God is faithful, and that nothing has failed of all that the Lord has spoken in his word – but all has come to pass. He has remembered me in my low estate and afflicting circumstances, and has given me strength according to my day. He has manifested so much of his glory, and of the glory of his salvation, through his Son, that my spirit has become submissive under his hand, with joyful serenity and calmness. I fully believe, that he who gave his life a ransom for me, cannot but do me good in the end.
>
> A believing view of Christ crucified has made me whole. He has told me again and again, 'My covenant of peace shall stand.' I have felt the stability of the 'two immutable things', (O the importance of having something immutable in the day of trouble) sufficient to support my soul, and to raise me above all my fears, enabling me in a degree to obtain a glimpse of the incorruptible inheritance that fadeth not away. Viewing these wonderful things, I felt my soul drawing nearer the heavenly city; desiring and in a measure longing, to enjoy it fully. All things below receded from my view, in a degree I never before experienced. There was but very little, I thought, between me and the full enjoyment of the purchased possession. These views, and the serenity which resulted from them, continued in a degree, without any change during all my illness. To die seemed more pleasing and more delightful to me than to live – the country beyond the grave appeared to me extremely desirable; and the company and the employment suitable to my taste. I viewed the eternal happiness of heaven, as enjoyed by the glorious hosts above, to be that of *worshipping God perfectly,* with all the heart – of worshipping him, the only worthy object of worship; and of praising him unceasingly, who had loved and washed them from their sins in his own blood.[2]

We must not continue with the quotation, though so sweet the content. Clearly, Mr Charles, when writing this letter, felt as if he was on the threshold of heaven. All his thoughts were on the things of the spiritual world rather than on those of this world. These glorious thoughts lifted his soul above fear and his body, to some degree, above pain, when he was under the cruel knives of the surgeons. He never regained his previous strength, and though he was to travel much again, he could never take a journey as he had done before. He therefore resolved to serve his fellow-Welshmen through the press.

THOMAS CHARLES AS AN AUTHOR

He enjoyed writing; he wrote in a pure, classic Welsh, much less circuitous in style than that of the Rev. Griffith Jones. He began writing and publishing books as soon as he joined the Methodists, but gave himself to it with greater energy when his health confined him more to the house. His first book published[3] was *Crynodeb o Egwyddorion Crefydd* [*A Summary of Religious Principles*] which came out in 1791. It was a short catechism for children, of some 96 pages, and in his foreword the author wrote:

> The widespread carelessness in the instruction of children, which I see amongst all categories of people, compelled me to print this short summary of religious principles, hoping that it will be of help, as well as an encouragement, to parents and others to instruct children and young people in the saving truths of the Word.

Later, he adds:

> I was bold enough to take many questions and answers from the excellent commentary of Mr Griffith Jones.

This book went through many editions, changing in form slightly each time, until at last its title was changed and it took its present form as *Hyfforddwr yn Egwyddorion y Grefydd Gristnogol* [*An Instructor in the Principles of Christian Religion*]. Mr Ashton states, 'It may be seen that it was gradually, and by means of much labour, that the Instructor came to the form in which we now have it.' The Instructor took hold of the nation immediately; the demand for it became greater than for any other Welsh book. From 1803, the year that a press was set up at Bala, to 1813, the year of Mr Charles's death, 320,000 copies were printed. How many have been printed from then until now is beyond counting.[4] It was memorized by all the pupils of the Sunday Schools. The young boys and girls of the country could recite it fluently; it was considered almost as infallible as the Bible.

In 1798, Thomas Charles published *Hanes fer o Fordaith lwyddiannus y llong Duff* [*A Short History of the Successful Voyage of the Ship* Duff], the missionary ship to which we have already referred. In 1799, he established *Y Drysorfa Ysbrydol* [*The Spiritual Treasury*] in conjunction with the Rev. Thomas Jones, Denbigh. This was a quarterly publication and six issues appeared. Mr Charles wrote much of its contents and other contributors, together with Thomas Jones, were the Revs. Thomas Jones, Creaton; Edward Morgan, Syston, and others. The publication was recommenced in 1809 with the name changed from *Y Drysorfa Ysprydol* to *Y Drysorfa*, and without the joint editorship of Thomas Jones. Twelve issues had appeared up to the final issue of November 1813. What brought it to an end, most probably, was the failing health of the editor. It was under his editorship also that the first Disciplinary Rules of the Calvinistic Methodists were published. The frontispiece of the first edition reads, in translation, '*The Rules and Objects of the Private Societies among the people called Methodists in Wales; agreed upon in an Association at Bala, June 16, 17, 1801*. Chester: Printed by W. C. Jones, 1801.' We will refer to these *Rules* again.

His next book was *The Welsh Methodists Vindicated*, written in English and published at the request of the Association. The Rev. T. E. Owen, the rector of Llandyfrydog, Anglesey, had published two essays attacking the Methodists, one in English, with the title, *Hints to Heads of Families*, and the other in Welsh with the (translated) title, *The Solemn Advice of a Rector to his Parishioners*. These essays are full of the gall of bitterness; it is doubtful if there is anything more poisonous printed in Welsh. The author suggested the most awful things about the Methodists; they were libelled as guilty of treason and of every evil, and he called upon the government to suppress their heresy. Mr Charles's defence is strong and final. Though written in a courteous tone, he has clearly thrown off the gloves and deals with his opponent in a manner that we would not have thought him capable of. As proof that the Methodists had no thought of destroying or damaging the government, he states that they privately and publicly pray for the King and all in authority; that one of their disciplinary rules was that no one would be tolerated as a member if they spoke against public authorities; and that when it had been considered that the state was in danger from any foreign power, they had often showed their loyalty by registering in their hundreds as volunteers, and by raising funds to set up defences. In a footnote he stated that he had collected one hundred and twenty pounds for this purpose in Anglesey alone. As an answer to the accusations brought against the private societies, he showed that Christians in every age, since the days of the Lord Jesus, had held such societies; that nothing occurred in them other than religious conversation; that it was a lie to claim that they met late at night; and he challenges their opponents to prove that they were a cause of disorder. He then carries the battle into the enemy camp by showing his opponent's inconsistencies and his mangling of logical reasoning:

> This gentleman may prove what he wills, for he will never be short of proofs, such as they are; he can produce them abundantly with a few strokes of his pen. He can prove with ease that sin is the same as sanctity; that loving and hating Christianity are exactly the same things; and that the followers of the Lamb are the same people as the sons of Belial.

This vindication, as well as shutting the mouth of the clergyman, changed the opinions of many with respect to the Methodists, for it was distributed widely throughout Gwynedd, and the head of every family in Anglesey received a copy.

THOMAS CHARLES'S BIBLE DICTIONARY

But Mr Charles's main literary work, by which he performed an immeasurable service to the nation, was his *Geiriadur Ysgrythyrol* [*Bible Dictionary*]. This book appeared in four octavo volumes: the first in 1805, and the others in 1808, 1810 and 1811. It does not seem that Mr Charles originally intended to write a whole dictionary himself. According to Gwilym Lleyn it is doubtful whether he had any hand at all in the writing of the first volume – the eighty-eight pages, from 'Aaron' to 'Barnu' (to judge). Gwilym Lleyn based his opinion on the 'Conditions' found on the cover of the first issue:

> I. We intend to continue the work, in method, order, and content, as closely as possible as it is in this issue.
>
> II. The work will be completed as concisely as is possible without harming the body of articles contained in it.
>
> III. We intend that all copy will pass through the editorship of Mr Charles and Mr T. Jones before it goes to the press; at least one of them, should it not be convenient for them both to edit.
>
> IV. The title page, together with the Foreword will be given in the last issue of the book.

On the basis of Condition III, Gwilym Lleyn argued, correctly we believe, that Mr Charles had very little to do with the first issue; and Mr Charles Ashton believes that the main author of this part was the Rev. John Humphreys of Caerwys. It was printed and published in Chester by W. C. Jones, an Englishman, in spite of his Welsh name. According to Mr Ashton, there were three young men, who worked as typesetters in W. C. Jones's office. They were not Welshmen but all three had learnt Welsh. One was Robert Saunderson; another Thomas Gee; and the third, Jonathan Harris, who later settled as a printer in Carmarthen. It is not known what stopped Thomas Jones and the other writers who had promised contributions from proceeding with the book, but Mr Charles was soon convinced that he would have to be more than editor if the Dictionary was to be completed, indeed, that he would have to write all of it. He therefore exerted all his energies upon it and persuaded Robert Saunderson to establish a press at Bala, and it was at the latter's office that the remainder of the book was published.

Gwilym Lleyn has brought a serious accusation against Thomas Charles by suggesting that Sion Robert Lewis had prepared a second edition of his *Dictionary*; that he had sold this book to Mr Charles for five shillings; that Mr Charles had not acknowledged this, thereby causing some of Sion Robert Lewis's family considerable dissatisfaction; and that this earlier *Dictionary* formed the core of Charles's *Dictionary*. Mr Charles Ashton has researched the matter thoroughly and impartially and has proved beyond all doubt that it is completely without foundation. According to Mr Ashton:

> We have already honoured Sion Robert Lewis for being the first to bring out a Bible Dictionary in Welsh. And the quotation we made from it will allow the reader to see that it contained only very little of the necessary material in a book as important as Charles's *Dictionary*. We are in a position also to show that Sion Robert Lewis's intended second edition was scarcely in any way more to the purpose than his first.

After quoting extensively from the second edition, he adds:

> This example from Sion Robert Lewis's revised and enlarged Dictionary is exactly as he produced it, spelling mistakes, mistakes in punctuation, and all. We have quoted it here so that the reader might compare it with the equivalent parts of Charles's *Dictionary*. If he were to do so, he would be fully satisfied that Mr Charles had little, if any, help from the writings of Sion Robert Lewis. The latter excellent work is appreciated by literary people of all denominations in Wales; and for a long time it was the only standard and scholarly work of its kind. The only service that Mr Charles sought, and obtained, we believe, from any of Sion Robert Lewis's products, were the two maps by Robert Roberts of Holyhead that illustrated the second and third volumes of the *Dictionary*.

It is only because of the sheer impossibility of completely destroying a false accusation once it has begun its course, we believe, that anyone still dares to claim that the old Holyhead Almanac compiler contributed anything to Charles's *Dictionary*.

It is impossible to appreciate the benefit derived by the Welsh nation from the *Dictionary*. Nothing similar had existed before in Welsh. On one hand, it is scholarly, tracing words back to their root meaning in Welsh, and providing synonymous words in Hebrew, Greek and Latin; on the other hand, it is written in a simple, easy to understand, style. It contains a full explanation of all the main doctrines of religion; in doing so it acts as a body of divinity; no one therefore who reads and studies it can ever be considered ignorant. Dr Lewis Edwards states:

> The specific field of the book, from cover to cover, is the Scriptures, and whatever provision is required to enable the monoglot Welshman to study the Bible thoroughly and in detail, is to be found, within what limits permit, in

> the Dictionary. If an introduction to all the books of the Old and New Testaments is needed, it is to be found in the *Dictionary*. If a book on the history of the Bible would be useful, the *Dictionary* provides it. If the geography of Bible lands is to be known, that also is in the *Dictionary*. If one enquires for an explanation of many of the difficulties encountered when reading the Bible, it would not be in vain to seek them in the *Dictionary*. And lastly, if one wished to read a Body of Divinity, though he might search the most well-equipped libraries, he would not often come across a better one than that possessed by the Welsh in Charles's *Biblical Dictionary*.

By means of this excellent book, a new world was opened up to monoglot Welshmen. To those exhorters who had no knowledge of English it became the main source of information. Scores of them familiarized themselves thoroughly with its contents, and in this way opened up their understanding of the Word of the Lord. It certainly proved very effective in raising the pulpit standards of the land. It was bought extensively, though its price was high. It has by now gone through seven editions, and for the specific purpose for which it was written, there is no finer volume to be had – not in Welsh, nor in any other language.

About the year 1808, Mr Charles wrote *Y Sillydd* [*Spelling Primer*]. As well as instructions on spelling, it contained a detailed explanation of punctuation and proved of great help to the Sunday Schools. In the same year he brought out a new edition of Morris Kyffin's Welsh translation of Bishop Jewel's *Apologia Ecclesiae Anglicanae*. At this time, the Methodists did not have a Confession of Faith, apart from the Thirty-nine Articles. They believed, as did Mr Charles, that no further declaration of their beliefs was necessary; and, to this day, if these articles are interpreted evangelically the Connexion would have no objection to them. He also composed an *Esboniad ar y Deg Gorchymyn* [*Exposition of the Ten Commandments*] in order to draw his compatriots' attention to their moral obligations, and Dr Edwards has stated that it is no honour to the Welsh nation that this book is less popular than the *Instructor*.

Thomas Charles received also the honour of performing one other important service for his fellow-Welshmen. He longed to be able to present to them an edition of the Bible that was free from faults and containing no mistakes of spelling and punctuation; and he achieved his aim with the definitive edition of the Welsh Scriptures published by Oxford University, for which he was the editor. He had a great desire to live long enough to finish this work. 'I would then,' he said, 'be happy to lay down my head and die.' His wish was granted and it is believed that the last words he ever wrote, 'It is now finished', referred to this work. It seems that he wrote a Welsh Grammar; why this was not published we do not know, nor do we know what became of it. In his last years he had begun to write a Biblical Concordance on a completely new pattern but he died before its completion.

As with all his activities, the books written by Mr Charles were eminently practical. He possessed an infallible instinct for recognizing the needs of the nation and for discerning the practical steps to be taken to meet them. It is here perhaps that his greatness is most evident. Other authors have written more scholarly books. He does not appear to have discovered any new principles or theories in any branch of knowledge; but in terms of the production of books that are effective for raising the morals of a nation and increasing their knowledge of God, Mr Charles has not been surpassed in any age or country. His works will be treasured by the common people for as long as the Welsh language endures.

In the midst of all his literary efforts, Mr Charles's care for the churches did not diminish; on the contrary, his burdens seemed to increase from one year to the next. In 1800, the responsibility for the congregations of the Rev. Philip Oliver devolved upon him. Mr Oliver was a hard-working, evangelical clergyman. Like Mr Charles, he had been turned out of the Established Church because of his labours and zeal. He subsequently ministered in Chester and the surrounding neighbourhoods, and succeeded in gathering together a number of congregations for whose care he and a number of friends were responsible. Mr Charles preached for them on many occasions while Mr Oliver was alive. These congregations did not belong to any denominational connection. They were closer in form and spirit to the Methodists than to anyone else, and when Mr Oliver died in 1800 it was discovered that in his will he had bequeathed the responsibility for the churches to Mr Charles. The latter willingly agreed to his friend's wishes and superintended these flocks for the remainder of his life. We might add that Mr Charles's successor as superintendent was the Rev. John Hughes, Wrexham, better known as John Hughes, Liverpool, the author of *Methodistiaeth Cymru*. Under the latter's leadership, these churches joined the Methodists, and they remain members of the Connexion to this day.

During his last years Mr Charles laboured under much weakness and was often ill. However, throughout this period, he sought to continue writing and travelling. In 1808 he was greatly troubled by a painful condition in his leg. It was a small matter at first and had he been able to remain at home and rest the leg it would not have amounted to much. But this he could not do and as a result the wound became infected and its condition became dangerous. In all his pain and against the instructions of his doctor and the pleas of his friends, he insisted on fulfilling a preaching engagement in Montgomeryshire. He preached and catechized the children at Llanfyllin and at other places in the county and by the time he returned to Bala his health had seriously deteriorated. For some time he was confined to his bed, not even able to write, but the moment he began to improve he set out again on his ministerial journeys throughout the land.

A JOURNEY THROUGH IRELAND

Both Scotland and Ireland benefited from Thomas Charles's labours, and his influence upon these countries is still to be seen. Having heard of his circulating schools, in which both young and old were taught to read Welsh, some of the Scottish Highland nobility wrote to him asking for information and with the intention of establishing similar schools in Scotland. As a result, one of these friends visited him at Bala. During their conversation Mr Charles learnt that English was the only language used in the Highland schools, even though the region contained over three hundred thousand inhabitants who could not understand a sermon in that language. A basic principle of Mr Charles's belief was that the common people should be taught in their own language, and that they should be provided with appropriate literature in that language. In this he was a hundred years before his time. Even today, many Welsh schoolteachers have not understood this point. His advice to his Highland correspondents was for them to establish Gaelic schools throughout those areas where Gaelic was the main language of the population. His advice was followed and the correspondence led to the formation of the Society for the Support of Gaelic Schools. This society has been of immense benefit. It has established schools throughout the Highlands and in most of the islands of Scotland. In them the people are taught to read God's Word in their own language.[5]

We have referred to Mr Charles's connections with Ireland. In 1807, he received a request from the Hibernian Society asking him to act as their representative, together with three other men, on a visit to Ireland to gather information on the nature of the population's knowledge, morals and religion, and, in particular, to decide whether it would be better to further their education through the medium of Irish or that of English. This request exactly fitted his own interests, and though hard-pressed by his many activities, he could not bring himself to refuse it. His companions were the Rev. David Bogue, an Independent minister from Gosport; the Rev. Joseph Hughes, a Baptist minister from Battersea, London; and Mr Samuel Mills, a Churchman, also of London. They departed from Holyhead on 24 July. They travelled the length and breadth of the island, mainly in pairs, for nearly a month, and landed back at Holyhead on 20 August. Their report was published and, as might have been expected, Mr Charles came down strongly for the establishing of schools in every neighbourhood, with Irish being the medium of learning wherever this was the majority language. His advice was accepted and soon many thousands were being taught to read the Bible in their mother tongue.

Mr Charles kept a detailed diary throughout this journey in which he noted his observations. The following are a few quotations from it:

> July 20, The Lord's Day. I preached at Bethesda Chapel [Dublin]. The congregation not numerous – but there was attention. The religious people seem in a great degree destitute of vigour and exertion in the cause of religion, full of disputations and dissensions; and therefore no wonder that little good is done. Dublin is supposed to contain 200,000 papists and 50,000 Protestants, but few of these hear the gospel preached.[6]

Almost certainly the 'religious people' of whom he complained of their lack of energy in religion were Protestants. The tone of his observations throughout the diary show that he discerned a hardness and indifference, and an awful spirit of strife, that had possessed the Protestant churches, and that the Catholics greatly excelled them, at least in the outward observance of worship.

Of Kilkenny, he writes:

> The Papists have a great school here, and it is the principal place of ordination. The *Irish* is *generally* spoken, though English is understood by most, and taught in the schools. Complaints everywhere of the bigotry of the Methodists. The carnal clergy oppose those that are evangelical more than they do the Popish priests.
>
> At Athy, when Mr Kelly preached in the courtyard, the Popish priest stood at the end of the lane to prevent any of his people from going to hear. Mr Bogue preached there to about two dozen people. A few good people, though very few, in all these places.
>
> Clonmel, 24 miles from Kilkenny – All the country spoke Irish, and were principally Papists. Assizes just over – nineteen tried, *mostly for murder.*
>
> August 2 – We spent the Sabbath here. Went in the morning at ten to the Quakers' meeting – all silent. At twelve, to the Popish chapel and heard an Irish sermon. The congregation very attentive and about 3,000. At one, to church. Congregation about 200; the sermon as usual. I preached a little to about forty or fifty people in an old meeting-house that belonged to the Quakers. Throughout the day the town was full, as on a market-day, and was a pitiful sight so far as religion was concerned. Ten Papists to one Protestant. They spoke *Irish* in the streets.

August 3. Went to Carrick on Suir, and nearby had our breakfast in the house of a godly Churchman, Mr Townsend. In his parish the gospel has been preached for ten years by Mr Shaw, Mr T. himself, and others, but with very little success. Mr T.'s comment was, 'They defeat us; Mr Shaw's untiring words have no effect.'

Arrived at Waterford about one after a pleasant ride through a romantic countryside. Lodged in the house of a Mr Harris, a Welshman from Newcastle Emlyn. He and his family showed much kindness. There are here nine Catholics to one Protestant. Religious people here, as everywhere else, in some degree infected with Sandemanianism. Sacrament every Sunday; administered without a minister. They spend their time in vain janglings, instead of laying themselves out in endeavours to spread the gospel and save sinners who are perishing all around them.

Fermoy, August 4 . . . The poor much neglected and very ignorant. Went into a school on the road. English only taught. Very few can read Irish, though universally spoken. The spirit of industry is not encouraged by the landowners . . .

August 9. Sabbath Day. Went to the Methodist chapel at eight, and had a very moderate sermon from an illiterate man, on John 2:1. He seemed a sincere man, but fast bound by Mr Wesley's ideas on falling from grace and perfectionism. He held Judas to have been saved, and Peter to have fallen from grace but afterwards repenting. He said that God was love, but not justice and mercy, as if it were possible for anything to be God other than God himself. He did not understand what he was about.

August 11. We travelled today through much country from Limerick to Tuam, not able to view the inhabitants except as all enveloped in darkness and superstition. On asking we found that the schools everywhere teach English. None learn Irish. The government's liberal grant for the teaching of English is woefully abused. At Athenry, only four children were being taught for ten pounds. The poor in their cabins very civil and communicative, but *ignorant of the Bible, to a man.* I turned into a few of their cabins in every place; their ignorance of the Bible, the only source of real and permanent comfort, affected me much. They have been sadly neglected! I hope that the time is drawing nigh for the Lord to show them mercy. The earth must be filled with the knowledge of the Lord, and as Ireland is a part of the earth, it must also be filled with this knowledge. This is a cheering consideration. The clergy riot in wealth and luxury, unmindful of their duty. The priests make a prey of the people, whom they keep in ignorance for that purpose. The Protestants of all denominations mind earthly things, and therefore the cause of God is neglected. Mercy or judgment must produce a change, and that speedily.[7]

The delegation evidently carried out a detailed and thorough inquiry and it provided Mr Charles with a heart-breaking view of the island, both as to its society and its religion. It may be seen that he complains not only because of the strength of Roman Catholicism and the efforts of the priests to keep the people in darkness, but also because of the indifference of the Protestants, who argued over unimportant details rather than endeavouring to save those who were being carried away to destruction. His recommendation for ensuring reformation was that the people be educated in the deep things of God – an education to be carried out in the language which they understood, namely Gaelic. For all his godly hopes, Ireland's day of salvation has not yet dawned.

As a proof of the continuation of his efforts in the preaching of the gospel even when in the midst of his literary endeavours, consider the following quotation from a letter he wrote in June 1806:

> I reached home two days ago. From London I went to Liverpool, where I preached twice in English and twice in Welsh. Thence I went to Warrington where I opened a new room for preaching among the late Mr Glazebrook's people. I wish something could be done in that dark and ungodly place. There seems to be a general disposition for hearing, if they had but a godly, active man among them. From Warrington I went to Manchester, where I preached in English and Welsh. I returned to Chester to my friend where I preached three times. Mr J. is much beloved, and the cause prospers there under his ministry. At Wrexham I preached once out of doors to about 1000 people. In Liverpool the congregations were numerous. Thousands attended every time. Among the Welsh there is a great increase. We have now two chapels there. One is large enough to contain 3000; and the other 2000; and both were full at the same time. In Liverpool, Manchester, and Chester, I catechised hundreds of children in the congregations, when at the fullest. The prospect was delightful.
>
> Since my return home I find the work among the children going on with increasing activity and vigour. The very thought of succeeding in making our young people acquainted with the *book of God*, transports me with joy. Blessed be God! Thousands of them are very busy, with great delight. What a gratifying pleasure would it be to see the whole kingdom of darkness dissolved, and not a wreck left behind. The whole world might as well be in flames this moment, and the elements be melting with fervent heat, if the *gospel* were not to prosper in it. All other designs are trifles – wholly unimportant. But the design of the gospel is grand beyond all conception, and it is sure to succeed triumphantly. God glorified and sinners saved! How important, how glorious the design! It cannot fail: all is fixed and determined. All the wheels are in motion; and he who guides the whole is infinitely wise and powerful. Whether we live, or whether we die, we shall see it with our eyes, and glory in its success.[8]

Clearly, Mr Charles was not in any way saving himself, but was taxing his body over and above what was reasonable. To preach three times a day, and to catechize a large group of children at the end of each service – during which he would no doubt exert himself even more than when preaching – was too much for him, particularly when we remember that his constitution was already beginning to fail. It may be thought that he was exaggerating when he states that the Liverpool chapels were able to hold two and three thousand. But it must be remembered that there were very few seats in the chapels at this time, the centre floor being completely empty, so that a large congregation, standing close together, could be contained in a comparatively small space.

During one of his visits to Liverpool, Mr Charles experienced a remarkable escape, one in which he believed he could clearly discern the hand of Providence. He was travelling by boat and his saddlebags had somehow been placed in a different vessel from that in which he had intended to sail. He was obliged to change boats. The first boat in which he had been seated, sank, drowning all its passengers, whereas his own reached land safely. As his biographer reminds us, God's servants are immortal until they have completed their work. Mr Charles had another engagement in Liverpool soon afterwards, and his wife was loath to let him go because of his previous narrow escape. But the night before he was due to leave, one of their children fell out of bed. Mrs Charles was frightened by the accident because at first she feared that the child had broken an arm. Eventually it was realized that there was little harm done. The occasion brought her to realize that the Lord could as easily bring affliction upon them at home as when further afield, and she told her husband, 'I give you into his hand, to do with as he wills, as you serve him on land or on sea.'

THE PETER WILLIAMS CONTROVERSY

It is necessary at this point to consider again the excommunication of Peter Williams as it relates to Mr Thomas Charles. Notwithstanding the tradition that is maintained by the descendants of Peter Williams, we believe strongly, and have previously stated our belief,[9] that Mr Charles did not take much part in the deliberations. We believe that he opposed the views expressed by Mr Williams: in a number of his articles in the *Geiriadur Ysgrythurol* [*Bible Dictionary*] there are many references to the views of the old Commentator in which it is shown that these are unscriptural. This could not have been otherwise for Mr Charles was a clear thinker, able to express his views cogently and transparently and with a particular emphasis on ensuring consistency, whereas the Commentator, to say the least, was very confused, and even when correct in his views was notably unhappy in his expressions of them. Yet for all the degree of unhappiness that there must have been in Mr Charles's mind, we are convinced that he took no leading part in the debate that resulted in Peter Williams's excommunication. Our reasons for believing this are as follows:

(1) The gentleness and tender-heartedness of his spirit. We cannot believe that he took part in the persecution of a brother in the ministry, who was a learned man and, according to Mr Charles himself, a godly man. We will not now go over the arguments as to whether the excommunication was just or unjust, but it is fairly evident that the way in which it was carried out, particularly when considering the age and position of the accused, was very unworthy, and we cannot imagine the gentle-hearted man of Bala as leading in such an unfortunate action.

(2) Mr Charles had been a member with the Methodists for not quite six years when the Llandeilo Association decided to break all connections with Peter Williams. There were in the Connexion at that time many clergymen who were highly regarded on many accounts; Jones, Llan-gan; Griffiths, Nevern; and Nathaniel Rowland, for example. It would not have been appropriate for such a comparative newcomer, and one of much lesser ministerial gifts than those mentioned, to have taken a prominent part in a debate of such importance to the Association, so much more so when it is remembered that it was a debate to do with a man whose praise was in all the churches and who had been considered one of the pillars since many years before Mr Charles was born.

(3) After the death of Peter Williams, Mr Charles published a short memoir of him in the *Drysorfa* [*The Spiritual Treasury*] in which he portrayed him as a good and godly man who turned many to righteousness. The tone of the article throughout, though so short, is remarkably respectful, and it does not contain a single reference to the excommunication nor to its cause. It is quite unbelievable to us that Mr Charles could write in this way had he taken any part at all in the affair.

(4) The testimony of the older people who were alive at the time was that it was Nathaniel Rowland who was at the root of the excommunication. We spoke once to some old elders who were young boys during the time of the Llandeilo Association and had heard of the matter from those who were present. They never referred to Thomas Charles but considered Nathaniel Rowland as the leader in the affair, and Griffiths, Nevern, as his deputy. If a man who was afterwards to become as prominent as Thomas Charles, had been involved in the unfortunate business, it is difficult to explain why

these old men did not refer to him and why his name has not been part of the stories from the period passed down amongst the Methodists.

Lately, however, a letter written by Peter Williams has come to light amongst the papers collected by Mr John Jones (*Myrddin Fardd)*, Chwilog. He wrote it to his son, the Rev. Eliezer Williams, during the period between the Associations of Llanidloes and Llandeilo, and as it is a letter of some importance we include it here:

> My dear Son
> I have the pleasure to acquaint you that we, at Gelli[lednais], in Town, Nant y Llan, etc., enjoy our health as usual! But, I must tell you, I never was in such a critical situation in the whole course of my life: I have finished Cann's Bible, but am deeply indebted to the printer, and my own *brethren* (if I may call them brethren) hinder ye sale: for they intimate through all the country that they are full of dangerous errors, that I have changed the words of scripture, and that I have put *references* in ye margin of my own devising instead of Cann's! They intend, I suppose, to revive the old dispute in ye *next association*, concerning what I wrote on the first chapter of John 20 years ago. Mr Rowland is now dead, and I have none to plead my cause! I am told that *Charles* of Bala is determined to give a *decisive* stroke, viz. to *expell* me from their connection entirely.
>
> However I should not mind their *expulsion*, the country is wide enough. But how shall I pay the printer, is the question? Peter tells me in a letter that 15 pounds are wanted to pay some debts at Oxford! Can you excuse the sum? I wish something was done for Peter, then I would be eas'd of these burdens. I hope God will deliver me out of all my trouble. I have printed a Remonstrance, by way of a letter to a friend, not to be made publick – being only a quire of paper to be put into the principal preachers' hands. I send you one; and expect your answer to a poor weather beaten Pilgrim – who am your affectionate Father,
>
> PETER WILLIAMS

The letter is dated 7 May 1791. To our mind, it leaves matters exactly as they were before. At a time of excitement many rumours fly around, some are true in part and others are wholly untrue. No doubt many things came to the ears of Peter Williams in those days, and he, in the depths of his unhappiness, was ready to accept many of them. But he himself does not state that he had heard of the intention appropriated to Mr Charles from anyone who was in any position to know: 'I am told', are the words he uses, and if anyone of importance, or who was in a position to know, had 'told' him, he would probably have given that man's name to his son. The story is just a rumour, carried about in some inexplicable way, and quite unworthy to be believed.

THOMAS CHARLES AND THE ORDINATION CONTROVERSY

Another matter of very great importance is the relationship between Mr Charles and the first ordination amongst the Methodists. We do not wish to discuss at this point the wider aspects of the ordination. The topic will require a chapter of its own later. But we need to discover Mr Charles's attitude towards it. There are two sources of evidence that help in this respect: accounts written by the Rev. Thomas Jones, Denbigh, and by Mr Robert Saunderson, Bala. Thomas Jones wrote as follows:

> At first, the aim and object were not to the mind of Mr Charles and some others. He continued to oppose for several years, but in a kind way, and admitting that it might become a necessity, by the increase of demands, and the ripeness of the time. In the Methodist Association at Bala in 1810, he made a public declaration in the midst of the preachers and elders of his satisfaction with the request and purpose; and, to the comfort and joy of those present and to the Body in general, he promised to draw up the rules agreed upon, that were to be used on the occasion.[10]

Mr Jones is a witness who can be entirely trusted. He was an able man of undoubted godliness, and a bosom friend of Thomas Charles from the day the latter joined the Methodists to the day of his death. He was also present at the Associations when the matter was discussed.

On the other hand, the Churchmen of today seek to prove that Mr Charles's opposition was fierce; that he was defeated in the Associations; that it was against his will, and purely to avoid the greater evil of a division amongst them, that he eventually agreed and prepared the rules to be followed. One of the main defenders of this theory is the Rev. William Hughes, the vicar of Llanuwchllyn, in whose partisan biography of Mr Charles many chapters are given to the topic. He portrays Mr Charles as returning excitedly to his house from an Association and crying out, 'They have defeated me! They have defeated me!' It is said that he heard this story from the daughter of Mr Robert Saunderson, who had heard it from her father who was present at Mr Charles's house on the occasion. It is quite certain that this story sprang from the imaginative mind of Mr Saunderson's daughter, who was an ardent Churchwoman. Nobody else heard Mr Saunderson mention it; it was not included in the full and detailed account of Mr Charles's relationship to the ordination which he wrote for Bishop Short; and the daughter never mentioned it to anyone while her father was alive. We can dismiss the story as quite unworthy of attention.

Mr Saunderson's account to Bishop Short is as follows:

When this new thing of ordaining lay preachers to administer the sacraments began amongst the Methodists, about three years before Mr Charles died, it was a cause of much trouble and distress for him, and he told the writer that it caused him many a sleepless night. It certainly affected his health. On seeing, however, that the main body of the Connexion was determined in its favour and intending to carry their point, he, in order to avoid unhappy divisions amongst them, yielded and drew up some rules for them to consider, which were received by them; and in June 1811, eight of their preachers were set apart to administer the ordinances. Throughout the time Mr Charles ministered amongst the Methodists, he endeavoured almost always to be at home on the first Sunday of the month in order to administer the sacrament, which he did using the form of service of the Church, and the same prayer before and after receiving the elements. It was a wonder to behold the concourse that gathered on these occasions, many of whom came from further than twelve or fourteen miles away. And it was pleasant to see on their faces the beneficial effects obtained from these solemn services.

Mr Robert Saunderson was an honest man; in addition, he was on very good terms with Mr Charles. Therefore, although he was a Churchman, and was anxious to portray his friend to Bishop Short in the best possible light as far as the prelate was concerned, we are willing to receive his testimony at its full worth. And indeed, there is no essential difference between his words and those of Thomas Jones, other than the fact that they both consider the matter from different viewpoints. On comparing their evidences, and drawing also on what we have learnt from other sources, the following points seem to be clear:

(1) That Mr Charles at first opposed ordination strongly and determinedly for some years. He opposed 'in a kind way'. His gentlemanly spirit and mildness of temper were sufficient to keep him from any display of passion, but his opposition was no less determined though his words were moderate. We can well believe that the arguments caused him much distress and disturbed his sleep. Indeed, within the context of that increasing tiredness that was coming upon him like an armed man, it is very probable that the controversy affected his health. He hated any disagreement amongst the brethren. There was also a strong conservative streak in his nature; it went completely against his nature to remove the old landmarks. There are many comments in the letters of the Revs Thomas Jones and John Elias that prove that Mr Charles stood firmly for some time against any movement in the direction of ordination. In a letter written by Thomas Jones to Mr Daniel Jones, the son of the Rev. Robert Jones, Rhoslan, who was then living in Liverpool, we find the following:

> There is no person on earth from whom I would be more unwilling to differ in spiritual matters than Mr Charles and further add may the Lord use, support and advance him more and more to the glory of his grace for many years to the end of his life and an endless eternity, and this I hope and trust he will do as he has begun a good work in him. Yet in this matter I cannot before God and his word assent to what he has expressed as his wish in conjunction with our truly reverend father Mr Jones of Llan-gan and I must now say and confess that I have at times felt myself strongly tempted to be angry with dear Mr Charles. From this or any other corruption that hell itself can display I wretched sinner am not clean. But whilst it behoves me deeply to bewail my sinfulness in this and every thing I take in hand I think I may through the infinite goodness of God declare that neither envy, prejudice nor self exaltation have had the privilence in my heart in this matter, but that I have the testimony of a good conscience towards God and all men.

We do not know the date of this letter but believe that it was written towards the end of 1809 or the beginning of 1810 when the debate over ordination was at its most heated[11] and Mr Charles's attitude was causing considerable anxiety to his brethren. There is no reason for doubting that Mr Charles was strongly opposed to the movement for many years.

(2) It is clear that bias in favour of Episcopal orders was not the reason for his objection. The doctrine of apostolic succession formed no part of his creed, nor did he look upon the ministers of the Dissenters as men who had rushed into an office to which they had no right. He co-operated warmly throughout his life with Nonconformist ministers and wrote in his journal before his own ordination that it mattered not to what part of Christ's vineyard he would be called. It was not therefore any doubt as to the right of the Methodist churches to set apart preachers to administer the sacraments that was the reason for his opposition. It never entered his mind that such ordination would repeat the history of Korah, Dathan and Abiram. What, therefore, was at the root of his aversion? Amongst other reasons, *Methodistiaeth Cymru* provides the following:

> Many also of the preachers that were highest in character and most popular as to their preaching gifts were involved in some worldly craft or business and it was difficult to shake off the feeling that craft or commerce was inappropriate to the ministry of the gospel; and that the Connexion would fall under the reproach of the religious world, from every denomination of the believing world, for calling craftsmen and businessmen to administer baptism and the Lord's Supper.

We cannot allow such an empty reason to be appropriated to Mr Charles for an instant. Were we to believe it, our respect for him would be considerably less. He knew that the most zealous of the apostles did not consider it any shame to follow his craft as tentmaker in Corinth. Mr Charles himself was associated with a business almost throughout his life as a minister. What was it then that lay behind his opposition? For one thing, he feared to take any important step unless sensible of the pillar moving before him. The same spirit moved him in this case as previously when he waited so long before leaving the Church. He felt that it was in their present form, namely in their receiving of the sacraments from those who had been ordained in the Established Church, that God had blessed the Methodists; and he feared to change their order in case they departed from the divine will. Circumspection and prudence were amongst his most characteristic features; indeed, he sometimes carried them to excess. Next, there was an immense difficulty as to the form of ordination were it to take place, and this certainly troubled Mr Charles greatly. It could not be an Episcopal ordination. For all the gifts and usefulness of John Elias, Ebenezer Morris, Ebenezer Richard, and Thomas Jones, there was not a bishop in the land who would have ordained them. Nor could it be an ordination according to the usual Nonconformist order. It is a specific congregation, assisted by various ministers, that has the right in their system for setting apart a minister; so also amongst the Presbyterians. But the Methodist preachers had no specific connection with any congregation. They undertook the care of all the churches, and they ministered wherever they felt there was a call for their labour. Mr Charles's initial idea was to ordain in an Association, for the profit of all congregations. He next considered ordaining at the Wesleyan Conference. He may also have felt something of the force of another reason given in *Methodistiaeth Cymru*, namely that it would be impossible to ordain all the brethren, old and young, gifted and not so gifted; so that he feared, once choices were made, that discontent and disappointment would arise in the minds of those passed over, and would eventually cause strife. These reasons, together, no doubt, with others of which we do not know, accounted for Mr Charles's unwillingness to move forward with ordination.

(3) Without a doubt, Mr Charles became thoroughly convinced of the appropriateness and the necessity of ordaining a certain number of the most qualified of the preachers for the administering of the sacraments. According to the Rev. Thomas Jones:

> In the Methodist Association at Bala in 1810, he made a public declaration in the midst of the preachers and elders of his satisfaction with the request and purpose.

Mr Charles was not defeated at this Association, as Mr Hughes, Llanuwchllyn, claims, nor did he rush out, disappointed and in a passion. Rather, he himself stood up amongst his brethren and declared that he had been brought to agree with them completely. It is not only Mr Thomas Jones's word that we have for this; he published the above testimony within a very few years of the event, when there were scores still alive who had been present when Mr Charles made his statement, and had his account not been entirely consistent with the truth, some would surely have hastened to correct him. It is said that it was Ebenezer Morris, with the important question that he asked him, who was the means of convincing him. He not only accepted the idea but he freely volunteered to compose the rules and to make the necessary arrangements. Whoever believes that he took such steps while at the same time being secretly convinced that the whole movement was unnecessary and unscriptural, did not know Mr Charles. It would have been hopeless for anyone to attempt to drag him against his convictions. For all his love of Methodism, he would preferred to have seen the Connexion dashed to pieces and scattered to the four winds before he would have taken part in an ordination of preachers to the full work of the ministry, which he believed to be incompatible with the teaching of the New Testament and an act of violence against the rights of the Head of the Church. Mr Hughes, Llanuwchllyn, in seeking presently to make Mr Charles a man of the Church, has belittled him as a man. Though a deeply courteous man of serene disposition, he was a man of immense integrity; there was in him the stuff of martyrs. We could imagine him dying for his principles, but not denying them in any circumstances. That he prepared for the ordaining, and took part in the service, is irrefutable evidence that he considered the step to be necessary and to be completely consistent with the teaching of the New Testament on the offices of the church, nor in any way contrary to the prerogatives of the Son of God.

We are able to corroborate our claim of Mr Charles's complete satisfaction with the ordination by means of a tale for which there is no possible doubt as to its truth. It seems that there was considerable feeling in Llangeitho and its neighbourhoods against the ordination, particularly amongst the elders of the region. They positively refused to host the August Association of 1811, even though it was at Llangeitho that this Association was always held, because it was at these meetings that the brethren who had been chosen were to be ordained. This was not the reason that they gave – their argument was that by allowing the ordination service to be conducted in their chapel they would be endangering the lease of the building – but the true reason was their opposition to ordination. So the

Association was held at Llandeilo, and Llangeitho lost the honour of being the venue of the first ordination amongst the Methodists. In the following year, 1812, Mr Charles and Mr John Roberts, Llangwm, were travelling together to an Association in Pembrokeshire and preaching in many places in Cardiganshire on the way. They were to be at Llangeitho on a Sunday morning, and a communion service was arranged after the two sermons because no such service had been held there for many months. The reason for this was as follows. It was the Rev. John Williams, Lledrod, who used to administer communion there because he had received episcopal ordination. The Rev. Ebenezer Richard was not allowed to do so though he had been ordained and was greatly loved and respected as a preacher. At this time, however, John Williams had injured his leg so that he could not leave home, and the Methodists of Llangeitho and its neighbourhoods had been deprived of communion for many months. Mr Charles was therefore eagerly awaited. The Sabbath morning arrived; the preachers had arrived early, and the people gathered at Llangeitho in their hundreds from all the surrounding regions. The preaching took place in the village square as the chapel – Daniel Rowland's old chapel – was being enlarged at the time. We do not have an account of the sermons but no doubt the vast congregation received a feast of fat things.

At the end of the sermons all who professed faith in Jesus Christ went up to the chapel. The table had been set up inside the roofless walls and those who intended to communicate sat outside. Mr Charles approached the table and gestured to Mr John Roberts to draw near to assist him. When the elders saw this they were greatly agitated; they came up to the table and refused completely to allow Mr Roberts to take part in the service. His only disqualification was that he had not received episcopal ordination. No amount of pleading or arguing could make them change their minds. When Mr Charles saw that they were determined and not to be convinced, he withdrew from the table, refusing to administer, and the nine hundred to a thousand people present who had intended to receive communion had to return to their homes disappointed. Some of them had only recently been received as members and were hoping to remember the death of their Lord in this way for the first time that morning. Amongst these was a youth called David Hughes who later became a well-known minister – the Rev. David Hughes, Carmarthenshire. He lived to a patriarchal old age, but the occasion must have made an indelible impression upon him for he referred to it a few years before his death. The Rev. Evan Evans, Nant-y-glo, was also present as a boy of eight years of age. After the people had dispersed, Mr Charles called the elders to him and after rebuking them sternly he commanded them to appear before the Association and told them that he would be present and would inform the brethren of their behaviour. This also he did and, on the expression of their repentance and the receiving of their promise that they would not behave so again, they escaped with only a slight rebuke. The account is interesting in and of itself and also as an example of how determined Mr Charles could be. But we relate it here as proof of Mr Charles's strong support for ordination and his belief that its authority amongst the Methodists was not to be denied. Had there been any degree of hesitation in his mind he would not have reacted as he did. He would not have made a scene on the occasion of the sacred ordinance had he not been convinced that the ordination was of God and that it was the duty of the Church to acknowledge it.

Another important question in this context is whether Mr Charles repented of the part he played, before he died. 'Yes,' say some Welsh Churchmen. The first to publicise this theory was Judge A. J. Johnes in his, on the whole, impartial book, *On the Causes of Dissent in Wales*. He there wrote:

> There is reason to believe, that he [Mr Charles] afterwards felt cause to regret the step he had thus taken, and that this feeling, operating on his mind naturally sensitive, combined with his incessant labours and reckless exposure to the inclement skies of the bleak hills of Gwynedd, contributed to hasten his decease, which occurred in 1814, while he was yet in the prime of life.[12]

If we are not mistaken, the first edition of Mr Johnes's book appeared in 1832 when Mr Charles had been buried for eighteen months. The paragraph drew very little attention. The literary life of Wales was in a low state at the time – the first Welsh newspaper had not yet appeared. As Dr Lewis Edwards has commented, if Mr Johnes had written that he was stating something of which he had personal knowledge, no one would dream of questioning his testimony. But in this case he was declaring something reported to him by others and his conclusions based upon what he had heard. And he would certainly have been the first to acknowledge that no one else was obliged to arrive at the same conclusions.

No more was heard of Mr Charles's 'regret' for forty-six years, until the spring of 1878, when Dr Joseph Hughes, the Bishop of St Asaph, was addressing a Diocesan Conference at Oswestry, and used the following words:

> It is a fact that Thomas Charles on his death-bed regretted that he ever left the church of his fathers, and that should God spare his life he would return to it.

His words created a stir, not only in the Conference but throughout Wales. Soon afterwards, the Rev. Joseph Hughes, vicar of Cwmdu, wrote a letter to *Goleuad Cymru* [*The Welsh Lamp*] declaring that he was responsible for the Bishop's words. He wrote:

> Sir,
>
> In your issue for May 11, the Bishop of St Asaph is blamed for stating that Charles of Bala had confessed on his death-bed that 'he regretted he had ever left the church of his fathers, and that should God spare his life he would return to it.' I am told that letters have appeared since, on the same subject, but I have not had the privilege of reading them. I wish to inform the readers of *Y Goleuad* that *I* am responsible for what the Bishop knows of the confession attributed to Mr Charles, and that it is at the request of the Bishop I am trying to make known my responsibility through the medium of your journal. The only ground I have for the story is the testimony of the late Mr Saunderson of Bala – a bosom friend of the Rev. T. Charles. About eighteen years ago, Mr S. told me personally, as he had previously told several of my neighbours, that he had heard from Mr Charles's own lips, a short time before he departed this life, words similar to the following. 'The Methodists trouble me. If God spares my life, I will return to England, and will take a curacy in the Established Church.'
>
> Yours, etc,
>
> Joseph Hughes[13]

This letter was dated 4 June 1878. We do not wish to accuse the Rev. Joseph Hughes of bearing false witness, but we have every right to ask why he kept secret such an important fact for eighteen years? And why he did not name one or more of the several, other than himself, to whom Mr Saunderson had related the story? How does he account for everyone's silence on the matter until Mr Saunderson was in his grave? We would call attention to the following facts. Mr Saunderson wrote a memoir to Mr Charles at the request of Bishop Short. This memoir is still extant, in Mr Saunderson's own handwriting. He states in the introduction that his purpose in writing the story was 'to show that Mr Charles was a true, faithful and warm friend to the Church of England.' He deals fully in the memoir with the distress felt by Mr Charles over the debate on ordaining but he makes no reference whatsoever to any regrets felt by him for taking part in the service, nor of any thought of leaving the Connexion should he be restored to health. This would have been an omission of the strongest proof possible of his statement that Mr Charles was throughout his life, 'a friend to the Church of England'.

The Rev. David Charles, D. D., Mr Charles's grandson, a truly scholarly man, who was for a time tutor at Trefeca College, has written:

> After being born and dwelling many years in the same house in which he [Mr Charles] lived and died, and seeing all his writings, most of which are presently in my possession, and having in my youth conversed with many of his friends and contemporaries at Bala, I had better occasion than most to become acquainted with the details of his history. In the first place there is no foundation whatever to the rumour spread about by some, for whatsoever purpose, to the effect that in his last hours he stated that he regretted leaving the Established Church, and that he was determined, were he to live, that he would return to it . . . Next, nothing can be further from the truth than the statement that he regretted the part he played in ordaining his lay brethren, and that this feeling had contributed to the hastening of his death. From all that I have ever learnt of him, his mind was perfectly happy with respect to what took place in 1811.

After the death of Mr Charles and of his contemporaries, it would be impossible to obtain a more credible testimony than that of his grandson.

How then are we to account for the story related by the Rev. Joseph Hughes? That it is not true in the form he relates is quite certain. He himself suggests in his letter that his memory of the conversation with Mr Saunderson is not completely clear. He says that the latter told him words *similar* to those that he relates. We believe that two things are certain. The first is that Mr Hughes, as his imagination responded over eighteen years to what he had heard, inflated Mr Saunderson's expressions and thereby gave to them a completely different meaning. And secondly, that Mr Hughes mistook the time to which Mr Saunderson was referring. He was speaking of the time when the controversy over ordination was at its most heated, and Mr Charles's mind at its most distressed. It is quite possible at that time for Mr Charles, under the influence of the moment, to have let slip something of the weariness brought upon him by some of the Methodists. But it was quite impossible for the words to express Mr Charles's fixed opinion a little time before or at any time after the ordination.

We have even stronger proofs that the story could not represent Mr Charles's feelings after the ordination. Mr Thomas Jones, Denbigh, was his closest earthly friend and spent many hours in his company on the day before he died. He wrote of him:

> On this issue [the ordination] Mr Charles was given much Christian prudence and wisdom; and, to the end of his life, it was clear to his closest friends that his mind was perfectly content and at peace as he looked back on events.

Mr Jones's testimony cannot be questioned; his integrity is beyond doubt. Furthermore, he wrote these words soon after Mr Charles's death, when many who knew him were still alive. Had there been any doubt as to the accuracy of his words, someone who knew better, Mr Saunderson in particular, would have immediately responded.[14]

On 24 June 1814, Thomas Charles wrote to a Mrs Astle, a lady in London with whom he corresponded:

> We had last week our great annual Association here. The congregation, though always large, was more numerous, by some thousands, than we have ever witnessed before. The meeting lasted part of four days. There were fourteen discourses delivered; and four private meetings held. Great harmony prevailed in the private meetings, and love which is the 'bond of perfectness'. The public discourses were edifying and powerful, and commanded the attention of between 15,000 and 20,000 people without intermission. The order and decorum, which prevailed among such a large concourse of people, was great and pleasing. No signs of intemperance or disorder, were perceived among them. Nothing but the hand of God could preserve so much order among so many corrupt sinners so long together. It was the Lord's doing; and it is marvellous, surpassing marvellous in our eyes. When I was young, the Lord brought me into his house; and goodness and mercy have followed me all my days; and I have continued, preserved by undeserved, powerful grace to see these wonders of his kingdom. Great additions have been made in general to our churches last year, about 2,000 in all. The Bible Societies, the schools and every good work set on foot, succeed among us: and we hope the kingdom of the little stone will soon fill our land. May thy kingdom come speedily, O Lord.[15]

Mr Charles wrote these words less than four months before his death. Can these in all seriousness be considered the words of a man whose spirit was wearied within him because of his brethren, and who was thinking of turning his back upon them? Do they not rather reveal a contented spirit, full of love for the Connexion, delighting in its success and looking with hope for a glorious future? If any further proof is needed it is to be found in the message he sent to the Caernarvon Association held on the last days of September, 1814, the week before his death. The following account is by the Rev. Thomas Jones:

> In the last days of September, his brethren were conferring at Caernarvon. He sent to them his friendly greetings by the hand of John Roberts, Llangwm, expressing himself as one with the preachers and elders and blessing God for inclining him to cast in his lot with them, and for the happy fellowship which he had enjoyed with them for thirty years. He promised his prayers for the blessing of heaven upon their labours, and added that he desired their prayers

on behalf of him and his household in their day of trial and suffering. The accompanying news also was that he seemed somewhat better than he had been, with sufficient signs of improvement to encourage the hope of recovery.

Mr Charles on many occasions expressed his thankfulness to God that his lot had been cast among the Methodists and with these words, his last public act amongst them, he did so again.

The Association's answer, by means of a letter from its secretary, the Rev. Cadwaladr Williams, is worth recording:

> Reverend Sir
>
> I write to inform you that Mr J. R. faithfully delivered your kindly greetings to the Association at Caernarvon; and that they were received with no little feeling and tenderness by the whole assembly: because I am sure many were weeping. All the brethren in the Association join in sincere greetings to you, and all declare their sympathy with you in your personal afflictions, and in your many family sorrows. We remembered you and your family with much solicitude in our private and public supplications, praying (if it be the Lord's will) that you may be restored to come among us again. The Lord's will be done.
>
> I am, on behalf of the Association,
>
> Yours, etc.,
>
> C. W.[16]

This last message of Mr Charles to the Caernarvon Association should put an end to all debate as to the nature of his feelings towards the Methodist Connexion towards the end of his life.

From the beginnings of Methodism there had been indications of God's satisfaction with the steps taken by his people for the progress of the kingdom in the way that he visited the Connexion with spiritual awakenings. Powerful revival had broken out with the publication of the hymns of Williams, Pantycelyn; with the expulsion of Rowland from the Church of England; and with the establishing of the Sunday Schools; and the Lord again powerfully visited his people soon after the first ordination. In 1813, Mr Charles wrote to a Miss Mary Hughes of Liverpool:

> I am happy to inform you that the prospect in our poor country is in many parts encouraging. About three hundred have been in less than a twelvemonth received into different societies in Caernarvonshire, principally from the Sunday Schools; which increase exceedingly both in number and in the progress they make in learning.[17]

In another letter he wrote:

> I have received a letter giving a pleasing account of the progress of religion in some parts of the county of Caernarvon. I will translate here a part of it: 'The Lord hath done a wonderful work in our country in less than a year. There have been added to the church in the two chapels of Clynnog, 138; in Llanllyfni, 90; in Penygraig and Tymawr, above 100; and many in other societies in the county. The Sunday Schools abound with scholars, and the teachers are diligent and faithful.' Let us praise the Lord.[18]

Again in the same year, 1813, he wrote:

> In a religious and moral point of view, the state of our peasantry is gradually and continually improving. Fresh advances are made every year. Hundreds of children and young people have this year joined our different societies. On Sept. 27, the children and young people of a whole district were publicly examined by me in our chapel, I never witnessed so affecting a scene. They could hardly make their responses, being so overcome with weeping; and the whole congregation was similarly affected. All these young people experienced religious impressions on their minds within these nine months; and a very striking change has taken place in their moral conduct. May God make the work on their minds deep and lasting. In repeating scriptures descriptive of the misery of the ungodly who die in their sins, they wept bitterly.[19]

We find, in these letters, the same commitment to the work, the same pleasure in it, and the same hope for the future of Wales through the influence of the gospel that Mr Charles displayed throughout his life.

HIS LAST YEARS

The Rev. Thomas Charles lived to see much fruit springing up from his labours, in the improved morals and increase in knowledge of the Scriptures of the common people. We hardly know of a history of any other nation that displays such a sudden increase in religion and culture than is seen in the Welsh nation at this period. As an example of how the desire for knowledge of the Bible had leavened even the most mountainous regions of the land, consider the following quotation from a letter that Mr Charles wrote to a friend in the Scottish Highlands in 1811:

> I lately visited a district between our mountains, in which a good woman, a widow, and her two children, a girl of twelve years of age, and a boy of eighteen, have been the chief instruments of teaching all the inhabitants to read well, and to understand the first principles of Christianity; and that only by Sunday and night Schools. About a week past I visited her; (she lives on her small farm) when she convened all the inhabitants together at her house: and they repeated several chapters to me with great propriety and intelligence; and I catechised them as long as time permitted, and preached to them afterwards.

She herself and her children stood up at the head of all, repeating the chapters and the catechism. My gratification, you may suppose, was of no ordinary kind on the occasion.[20]

Here is one of the secrets of Mr Charles's success. Nothing was too small or too mean for him to do. He would visit the home of a poor widow in the midst of the rugged mountains of Merionethshire, to catechize a few children and preach to a few rough mountain folk, with the same enthusiasm that he would approach an Association where the thousands would have gathered. He was as much at his ease in a labourer's cottage with a peat fire burning on the hearth, as in a gentleman's parlour. It was his personal influence and efforts in small circles that contributed to the success of his plans on a large scale. Consider the following, taken from the same letter, on the numbers of Bibles distributed throughout Wales:

Such has been the demand there, that it has been necessary to print three editions of the Bible, being more than 20,000, and seven editions of the New Testament, amounting to 45,000 copies! It is remarkable, that all these have been printed, and nearly all disposed of, in the short space of *four years*.[21]

We have the authority of the Secretary of the Bible Society for the fact that the first edition of the Welsh Bible was of 20,000; Mr Charles therefore must mean that each of the three editions were of 20,000 copies. There was therefore as many as 105,000 Bibles and New Testaments distributed in the land in four years. We have no doubt that this fact is unique in the history of nations.

By now the day of this famous servant of Christ was drawing to its end. In 1812, when journeying in Montgomeryshire, he met with a serious accident, the effects of which eventually led to his death. When struggling to open a gate he felt a severe pain in his side. Some internal rupture occurred which became inflamed and he was able to accomplish very little work after this. During the spring of the following year his friends noted with distress that his features were changed and his voice much weakened. Yet in all his weakness he struggled to go about with the gospel. In June, he journeyed extensively, preaching and resting alternately, on his way to the Holyhead Association. From there he hastened, preaching at only a few places, to Llanidloes where a meeting had been arranged to establish a branch of the Bible Society. This was the last journey of any great length that he undertook. In September 1813 he wrote to a friend in London as follows:

I have been, for these two months past and more, in a state of great body debility; supposed by the doctors to be the effect of an over-exertion of body

> and mind. I had frequent pains, and was confined to the house; and I was frequently on the bed. I was not fit for any thing that required exertion either of body or mind, and was recommended to indulge myself in rest and cessation from all work, as the most likely way to restore my strength. Through mercy I am now much better, free from pain, though still languid. I have found great support from the last words of David – the everlasting covenant, 'well-ordered in all things and sure', containing *all my salvation*. Though I was feeble, I found strong ground to stand upon, and I rejoiced in it. When heart and flesh fail, here is strength for my heart, and a portion – all my salvation. I cannot now pen on this paper what I saw in it; but I saw *enough*, and that for ever. God remembered me and showed me the best things he had – a salvation in a covenant made by himself.[22]

Not only was he weakening but his wife had been struck by a stroke and was much disabled as a result. Yet he still preached occasionally as his strength allowed. He wrote the following to his dear friend, the Rev. Thomas Jones, Denbigh:

> In answer to your kind letter, I am sorry that it is not in my power to attend the meeting at Holywell. I am to be next Sunday in Montgomeryshire, at a public meeting, to preach and catechize the children; and Whit Sunday, according to our monthly custom, is Sacrament Sunday. Besides, my strength is far from being equal to the hurry and exertion connected with our public gatherings. If the Lord permit, I intend going to the meetings at Chester and Wrexham. It pains me to have to send to you, and my dear friends in your parts, a negative answer twice; but such is the will of God in His providence towards me at present. I rejoice in your success, and grieve when I hear any unfavourable news. My strength is in some degree restored; *but I am not as I was*; and in all likelihood, *neither shall be.* Mrs C. is weak; and she can hardly endure a short journey, of three or four miles each day in the Gig: any long journey is more than she can contemplate. She and I feel very much obliged to you and Mrs J. for your kind invitations, and your efforts to exert yourselves on our behalf; but I am afraid she will never see Denbigh. We are both on the hill's descent, though our descent is easy and gradual.
>
> I am, etc.,
>
> T. Charles[23]

About the same time he wrote, 'We are both on life's descent, but she appears to be travelling faster than I am.'

In the Bala Association of June 1814, he appeared very cheerful. He was greatly pleased by the number and order of the meetings, the unity that flourished in the private meetings, and the divine power that accompanied the ministry. In the following August, the Rev. Thomas Jones met him together with his wife at Bronheulog, near Llandderfel, and saw that their health was deteriorating. But such was the gracious maturity and the heavenly spirit apparent in Mr Charles that it made a deep impression upon all.

The 1814 Association in Bala, the last Association for Mr Charles to attend, was notable on many accounts. During it, the Revs. Michael Roberts, Pwllheli; John Jones, Edeyrn; John Jones, Tremadog; John Hughes, Pontrobert; and John Parry, Chester, were ordained: mighty men, each one of them. Henry Rees was also present as a young sixteen-year-old; and this is the occasion when he, Mr Charles and John Elias met, the only time in their lives for all three to be together. The story, as related by the Rev. Owen Thomas, is very interesting:

> [Henry Rees's] main purpose in attending the Association was to obtain a copy of the *Geiriadur* [*Bible Dictionary*]. He longed to possess the book but did not have enough money. His mother told him, 'Get up early every churning day, and churn for me, and I will give you a pound of butter to put in a vat, and when it is full you may sell it to buy the *Geiriadur*.' He agreed immediately, but the vat was long in filling. And the Bala Association was drawing near. He thought of another plan, namely taking over a tenth of their land in order to earn a little money from it. But both enterprises involved waiting a long time. He decided that the best thing to do would be to visit the Association; to insist on seeing Mr Charles, and to tell him how matters stood, and ask him would he sell him a copy of the *Geiriadur* on the security of the butter and the tithe. Off he went to Bala, but he was so shy that he failed to call on Mr Charles until the day after the Association. Having entered, he announced his request, and the plans he had for paying for the book with the butter and the produce of the land, promising to bring the money before All Saints' Day. Mr Charles smiled indulgently upon him as he delivered his speech; he was certain from the boy's appearance that he was honest, and he allowed his request. At that, John Elias entered the room, having come to farewell with Mr Charles before leaving the town. Mr Charles related the boy's story, and he also smiled at Henry and gave him a few kind words to encourage him. This was the first time for Henry Rees to meet John Elias and the only time that he met Thomas Charles. It was the only time that all three met together, and that only for a few minutes.

No doubt Henry Rees paid honestly for the *Geiriadur*, but he was not able to demonstrate his honesty to Mr Charles because before All Saints' Day arrived, the latter was in his grave. Mr Charles's letter written after the Association describes the powerful influences accompanying the ministry. The following is the order of the services on the last day: At six in the morning, Michael Roberts and Richard Lloyd, Beaumaris; at ten, John

Jones, Edeyrn and Ebenezer Morris; at two, Thomas Jones, Denbigh, and John Elias; and at six, Thomas Richards, Fishguard, and Evan Richardson, Caernarvon.

Soon afterwards Thomas Charles took his wife to Barmouth, hoping that the sea air would do her good. He there preached many times and a remarkable gentleness pervaded his ministry and conversation. He said to his wife, 'Well, Sally, the fifteen years is almost at an end,' referring to the prayer of old Richard Owen of Bala on his behalf. Within a fortnight they visited Mrs Foulkes and her children at Machynlleth. On the Sunday, 4 September, Mr Charles preached twice and these were his last sermons. His text in the morning was Luke 15:7; and in the evening, 1 Corinthians 16:22. He was given a remarkable service in the evening. He spoke on the free and infinite love of God towards sinners; of love to the person of Christ; and of the great danger of refusing the love and grace that are offered in the gospel, until the hearts of the congregation were completely melted. In the pulpit his spirit was lively and fiery, though his body was weak, but by the time he reached the chapel house he was completely exhausted.

During the following week he could feel himself weakening and he longed to return to Bala. After many difficulties, he arrived home on Saturday, 10 September, in such obvious weakness as to cause considerable distress to his family and friends. To a friend who helped him to his bedroom, he said, 'I am very thankful to God for enabling me to reach home once more. Now I have nothing to do but to die.' During the next days he was often heard murmuring the verses found in 2 Kings 13:14, 'Now Elisha was fallen sick of the sickness whereof he died.' He was often in intense pain. A doctor told him he would have to be operated upon. He agreed, and after the treatment the pain was less. A few days later the doctor said that nothing much more could be done for him, that all he could do now was to rest. He answered, 'If I get better I believe I will preach Christ to perishing sinners with more diligence than ever I have done hitherto.'

During his last weeks his family had to endure many tribulations. Apart from the fact that he and his wife were, as it were, racing each other to the grave, his eldest son also was very ill and in danger of his life. His maid also, who had served them for eight years and who was very dear to them was suddenly taken ill with typhus fever, and died within nine days. 'You see that we are in the furnace,' said Mr Charles to a friend, 'but when we have suffered a little while, we shall be brought forth purified.' To one who often sat up with him, he said, 'Charles is a great sinner; just a poor and unworthy sinner. I know that there is no way for me to be saved without forgiveness.

There is forgiveness with God.' He was greatly cheered on hearing of the prospects of his son's recovery and cried out in gratitude, 'The Lord is very good – his mercy endureth forever,' repeating the last sentence again and again. He then asked for his Hebrew Psalms and turned to Psalm 136. Placing his finger on the word translated 'mercy', he spoke of its wealth of meaning and of its comfort.

We have already referred to his letter to the Association at Caernarvon held in the last week of September. The following Monday, 3 October, the Rev. Thomas Jones visited Bala on his way home. He found Mr Charles, together with his wife and a few friends, seated for a meal at the table. He seemed very cheerful and conversed warmly and animatedly with his friend. To avoid tiring him too much, Mr Jones did not stay with them but went to another house to lodge. Before he left his room the next morning, he heard that Mr Charles had been in agonising pain all night and that his life was despaired of. He hurried to his bed. At Mr Charles's request, he went on his knees to commit him and his family to God's care. Having finished praying, Mr Charles sought to converse with him, though in a voice that was very indistinct. When Mr Jones told him that he had no anxieties as to his case but that he was very concerned at the loss to the Church and to the country, Mr Charles's answer was, 'Be calm in the Lord – he is able to raise hundreds of servants more faithful and successful than I have ever been.' And so the two friends departed, never to see one another again on earth.

In the midst of all his pain his soul was cheerful. On the Tuesday morning, he woke after a brief sleep and said, 'I have been trying to imagine where heaven is, and how it is I shall find it. But no doubt the Lord will send some kind angel to show me the way.' When attempting to walk across the room, he said, 'My flesh and my heart faileth, but God is the strength of my heart and my portion forever. This is that portion that all must have or be forever miserable.' Another time, and with a glorious solemnity about him, he said, 'Lord, now lettest thou thy servant depart in peace, according to thy word: for mine eyes have seen thy salvation.' Before going to his bed on the Tuesday night, he said to his wife, 'Well, my dear, if I should die and leave you, the Lord still lives to take care of you.' He had very little sleep that night. The next day he was overcome by a trembling that lasted for nearly an hour. On seeing him sinking, Mr Saunderson drew up to the bedside and said, 'Well, Mr Charles *bach*, the day of tribulation has come.' He immediately replied, 'There is a REFUGE!' These were his last words. His breath soon became fainter and about ten o'clock on Wednesday, 5 October 1814, his soul flew to the eternal Canaan, when six days short of his fifty-ninth birthday. Within nineteen days his wife had followed him to the quiet habitation. It is doubtful whether she ever realized that she had been left a widow.

He was buried on the following Friday and though short the notice, an immense crowd had gathered. During the service, the Rev. John Roberts, Llangwm, prayed, and the Rev. Thomas Jones, Denbigh, preached from Hebrews 11:4, 'And by it he being dead yet speaketh.' While speaking of the faith of this committed servant of Jesus Christ and the excellent testimony that he had left behind him, the preacher failed to continue because of the strength of his feelings. The tears of the congregation mixed with his own so that the place became another Bochim. They walked in procession, singing appropriate hymns, from Bala to Llanycil. There was no room in the church for a tenth of the people who had gathered. Having read the service and sung a hymn, the body of Thomas Charles was laid in the ground until the day of resurrection.

GOD'S GIFT TO WALES

Mr Charles, physically, was a man of average height, not being large or small, but well-proportioned and of a very gentlemanlike appearance. The portrayal of him by John Jones, Tremadog, is as follows:

> He was of medium height and rather plump; graceful and handsome in appearance, lively in manner, and with the look of a gentleman. When his face was studied, it could be seen that he was not a cruel lion, nor a mild old woman, but a man full of thought, sense, and prudence. My daughter used to say when a child that she thought him the man who looked most like Jesus Christ. At first perhaps the sight of him might fill you with a reverential awe, but he would soon charm you to his breast with his geniality and kindness, always contributing something of true profit.

These are not the exaggerated words of a hero-worshipper but a statement of facts that were generally acknowledged. It was said that some went to hear Mr Charles purely because of the attractiveness of his features and his angelic aspect. It was not that he possessed physical beauty but rather that his kindness and tenderness of spirit, and the gospel of God that had pervaded his soul, were visible in his features and caused his face to shine. When he preached his missionary sermon in London, a well-known minister came up to him and said, 'Had you not opened your mouth, Mr Charles, you yourself are an excellent sermon to us.'

Wales has never had such a philanthropist as Thomas Charles. He had a natural tenderness; kindness was apparent in every line on his face. Had he never become religious, we believe that he would have given himself to lighten the burdens of mankind and to seek to improve the condition of his fellow-countrymen; but his conversion, and the strong hold that the gospel had upon him, gave life and strength to his natural feelings so that the salvation of souls and the bringing of them into the possession of the highest treasures that man can possess, became the overwhelming passion of his life. This is what sustained him in the face of opposition and caused him to labour above what nature could endure, as he journeyed across the wild mountains of Gwynedd in rains and storms. He knew nothing of pride. He was one of the humblest men who ever lived. He eventually wielded an immense influence amongst the Methodists; they considered him as an angel of God; almost, his word was law to them; but in all this he did not promote himself, but rather, every honour laid upon him only drove him lower in the dust. His humility was evident in his ministry. As he possessed a deep learning and a knowledge of the thoughts of all the best-known theologians in almost every aspect of theology, it would have been easy for him to exalt himself above his hearers and cause them to wonder at the extent of his abilities. But in the pulpit, he would be the simplest and easiest of all to understand. He made it a point of being so clear that the weakest amongst his hearers could follow him.

The only other men to have wielded such influence amongst the Methodists were Daniel Rowland, Howell Harris, and Williams, Pantycelyn, but Mr Charles was quite unlike any of these. It was the sacred oratory of Rowland that carried all before him. We would not suggest that he possessed no organizational abilities, but it was not in this that he excelled. It was his fame in the pulpit that accounted to a large extent to his influence outside the pulpit. Howell Harris, on the other hand, was an organizational genius. He combined oratorical skills of the highest quality with an unique ability for organizing. But he ruled by maintaining the exhorters and societies in fear of him. If he could not have his way, sometimes even in trivial matters, he could become thoroughly agitated. Unlike Mr Rowland, Mr Charles could not be listed amongst the foremost preachers of Wales. He was a good, clear, profitable, substantial preacher. In all probability he could have become a more popular preacher still had he not exerted all his natural energy in the work of the Sunday Schools and, particularly, in the work of catechizing children. But there were many in his day that excelled him in preaching skills and in the ability to move congregations. In contrast to Harris, Mr Charles brought his plans to fruition by explaining their nature and showing their necessity, and in such a winning way that all were carried with him as by the current of a river. And all his arrangements were admirably practical. He had an almost infallible instinct for identifying the country's need, and producing a plan to meet it. We could attribute the impact of his influence to his notable wisdom, his perfect courtesy, his deep humility, his never-ending commitment to the service of his Connexion and country, and above all to his sincere godliness. Because of these virtues, Mr Charles became a king amongst the Methodists without seeking the position in any way.

We would be wrong to forget his generosity. Mr Charles received very little and that very rarely as payment for his ministry. He lived on the proceeds of the business conducted by his wife. We do not know how much income he made from his books, but, on the authority of his own word, we know that this was all given for the maintenance of the schools. When poor people came to him for Bibles and other books with no money to pay, he could not resist their pleas. We believe we are correct in saying that he gave away hundreds of books freely. In his days, Bala was the Jerusalem of Wales. Vast crowds would gather there on the first Sunday of every month, the main Gwynedd Association was held there annually, and there was no end to the children's meetings and religious meetings of every kind that were held in the town. At such times his house would be full. In this respect, Mrs Charles was as generous as he. To feed strangers was a tradition she had learnt from her mother. It was said of Mrs Jones, Mrs Foulkes afterwards, that she used to feed six hundred at her house whenever the Association came to Bala. Both Mr and Mrs Charles were worthy successors to her in this, throughout their lives.

We must now leave Thomas Charles. All in all, we are certain that neither the Connexion, nor Wales, ever had such a valuable gift from God than he. As we have already mentioned, he safeguarded the fruit of the Methodist Revival. It was to his organizing, under God's hand, that the incorporation of the Connexion and its continuation in Wales as an influential body must be attributed. Nor are the effects of Mr Charles's labours confined to Methodism or to Wales; they are to be felt today throughout the world.

[1] D. E. Jenkins, *Rev. Thomas Charles*, Vol. 2, pp. 187–8.

[2] Edward Morgan, *A Brief Memoir of the Life and Labours of the Rev. Thomas Charles* (London, 1831), pp. 302–4.

[3] John Morgan Jones refers to another book as being the first written by Thomas Charles, but D. E. Jenkins (*Rev. Thomas Charles*, Vol. 1, p. 501) shows clearly that the book referred to had been wrongly attributed to T. C.

[4] By about 1888 it had reached its eightieth edition.

[5] Two of those with whom Thomas Charles corresponded, and who were the main instruments in the formation of the Society, were the Revs. John Brown. D. D., Edinburgh (1754–1832) and his brother, Ebenezer Brown, Inverkeithing (1758–1836). They were the sons of the well-known John Brown of Haddington.

[6] Edward Morgan, *Brief Memoir*, p. 344.

[7] Ibid., pp. 345–8.

[8] D. E. Jenkins, *Rev. Thomas Charles*, Vol. 3, pp. 139–40.

[9] See Volume 1, pp. 680, 688.

[10] Thomas Jones, *Cofiant y Parchedig Thomas Charles* (1816), pp. 210–2.

[11] D. E. Jenkins (*Rev. Thomas Charles*, Vol. 3, p. 245) gives the date as 29 December 1810.

[12] A. J. Johnes, *The Causes of Dissent in Wales* (1832), p. 48.

[13] D. E. Jenkins, *Rev. Thomas Charles*, Vol. 3, pp. 590–1.

[14] The clearest proof of all of Thomas Charles's agreement to ordain is provided by D. E. Jenkins (*Rev. Thomas Charles*, Vol. 3, p. 264):

'We have been fortunate enough to find his own account of the share he took . . . The June Association was held, as usual, at Bala, and the date this year was June 20 and 21. The brethren met in conference on the 20th, and the matter in dispute came forward for discussion at the afternoon sitting, and this is how Mr Charles writes about it to Mr Tarn, on July 12, 1810:

> I forgot to inform you of any particulars of importance which have taken place in the Methodist connection in Wales. I brought forward at the private meeting several propositions respecting the admittance of what is called the lay preachers, to administer the Sacraments in conjunction with the clergy which passed unanimously, to the great satisfaction of the whole body. I never had so delicate a subject under my consideration as I had prejudices of an opposite nature to combat with. However, thro' the Lord's blessing upon my endeavours, I hope I have succeeded. To pass incensured by different parties I do not expect; but I am happy that the body of Welsh Calvinistic Methodists seem to have been, by the means adopted, by all appearance more firmly compacted than ever; and by that means likely to be more extensively useful in promoting knowledge and reformation thro' the whole country.'

[15] D. E. Jenkins, *Rev. Thomas Charles*, Vol. 3, pp. 530–1.

[16] Ibid., p. 543.

[17] Ibid., p. 492.

[18] Ibid., p. 488.

[19] Edward Morgan, *A Brief History of the Life and Labours of T. Charles* (London, 1828), p. 380.

[20] Ibid., p. 370.

[21] Ibid., pp. 370–1.

[22] Ibid., pp. 373–4.

[23] D. E. Jenkins, *Rev. Thomas Charles*, Vol. 3, pp. 523.

33

FROM THE FIRST ASSOCIATION AT WATFORD TO THE ORDINATION (1743–1811)

METHODISM ESTABLISHED IN GWYNEDD

We have referred in previous chapters to the first eight years of the Methodist Revival in Gwynedd. Our main purpose in this chapter is to note some important events that cannot be appropriately discussed in connection with any one individual, and that occurred between the first Association at Watford in 1743 and the next significant step in Welsh Methodism, namely the Ordination of 1811. As the period is a long one of sixty-eight years we can only refer to a few of its main elements. It began at a time of incomparable enthusiasm; it is to be doubted whether there has ever been such rapid success in the Lord's cause during any period as occurred in Wales amongst the Methodists from 1743 to 1750. Then the storm arose because of the sad controversy between the Connexion and Howell Harris. Those dark days continued for thirteen years. The range of the Connexion is narrower and its numbers fewer to this day, because of that unhappy strife. God visited his people again in 1762 when the hymns of Williams, Pantycelyn, were published, and Howell Harris returned to his brethren. Another storm arose over Peter Williams's troubles and many bitter feelings were aroused, but the results of this controversy were nothing like as damaging as the previous one. We have discussed these topics fully when dealing with the lives of the individuals concerned, as also the rise of the Sunday Schools, and the establishing of the Bible Society. But a few things have either been omitted, or not given the attention they deserve, and we wish to concentrate on these here.

It was within this period that the land of Gwynedd was possessed. The north was a land of darkness at the time of the Watford Association. Howell Harris had journeyed through parts of the region on two occasions. Perhaps he established a few societies there but if he did so, they were few in number and few in members. A cruel spirit of opposition to the Revival pervaded all neighbourhoods and this mentality was planted and nurtured by the gentry and clergy. Exhorters from the south often visited the north and spoke wherever they could obtain an audience. The Association in the south arranged also for preachers to labour in Gwynedd and paid them their expenses. But up until twenty years from the end of the eighteenth century Methodism had only a very weak representation in the region. The societies and members were few, they were very poor in their circumstances, and they were hardly tolerated by the common people. However all this land was then possessed with exceptional speed and by the time of the Ordination, the Connexion was stronger in the north than in the south. The means that were blessed in this work of evangelization were, firstly, the visits of the men from the south: Howell Harris, and the clergymen, such as Daniel Rowland; Howell Davies; Williams, Pantycelyn; Davies, Neath; Jones, Llan-gan, together with the exhorters, in particular Dafydd Morris, Twr-gwyn. Next, exhorters native to Gwynedd arose, men like John Evans of Bala; Humphrey Evans, Bala; and Lewis Evan, Llanllugan. Thirdly, there arose in the region preachers of such abilities that have not been excelled in any period or country. We refer to Robert Roberts, Clynnog; his brother, John Roberts, Llangwm; John Jones, Bodynolwyn; John Jones, Edeyrn; John Elias; and others. These were sons of Anak; flesh could not stand before their ministry; the faces of the ungodly would grow pale and their knees would knock together in their presence. The visits of the great preachers from the south would cause great excitement that would then die down, but these latter men lived in the province, and their words would fall upon the consciences of the workers of iniquity as white-hot sparks. It was these who defeated the general persecution and opposition; these harrowed the ground and pioneered the way, and if it had not been for their preaching Mr Charles would not have been able to lay down and further his plans, however practical these may have been.

The last means blessed by God for the possessing of the north by the gospel of Christ was the coming of Thomas Charles, and particularly his joining with the Methodists. As we have already shown, by his organization and plans he safeguarded for Methodism the fruits of the great revivals that shook the land. As far as the Connexion is concerned much of the fruit in the south was wasted. Howell Harris's withdrawal brought about the loss of two whole counties, Radnorshire and Monmouthshire. For other reasons, which we shall refer to later, the Methodists of Pembrokeshire became very few in number. But in the north, Mr Charles, as well as striking out himself and taking possession of new territories, nurtured the products of the successes of the preachers. By means of the Sunday Schools, the children's conferences, the provision of good books and particularly the distribution of Bibles amongst the common people, he was continuing the influences they had received in stirring services, and it is to his wisdom, under God's blessing, that the strong hold that Methodism has on north Wales must be attributed. In his days the core of the Connexion's strength moved from south Wales to north Wales. Nor is the south itself without its great debt to Thomas Charles, but being further from him his influence was not felt to such an extent as in the region where he lived.

BUILDING CHAPELS

It was within this period that the land was filled with chapel buildings. The first chapels associated with the Methodists were Cil-y-cwm in Carmarthenshire and Maesgwyn Chapel in Radnorshire. It is not known which of the two is the oldest, as we do not have the date for the erection of Maesgwyn; practically all that we do know about it is that a Judge V___ threatened to pull it down in August 1742. Cil-y-cwm Chapel (according to the stone that remains on its wall to this day) was built in 1740. These are the only two chapels that are known certainly to have been in existence before the time of the first Watford Association. The next that we know of is Groes-wen Chapel. The land here was obtained on 2 June 1742, that is, more than six months before the Association, but we believe that the building was not erected until some time afterwards. We then find that a chapel was built, probably at Llansawel, Carmarthenshire, in 1744, according to the decision taken at the Porth-y-rhyd Association. Within three years, that is, in 1747, Alpha Chapel in Builth Wells was built. The New Inn chapel had been completed a short time previously, and in 1749, Aberthin Chapel in the Vale of Glamorgan was raised.

The above is the complete list of buildings that are known to have been built before the Disruption. There are some reasons for believing that more existed but their number could only have been very small, or there would have been some reference to them in Howell Harris's journal. It is certainly clear that the Methodists were very loath to build meeting-houses. Had they been readier to obtain houses of worship for the masses that were convicted by their preaching they would have possessed more of the land and the number of converts who became members of other denominations would have been far less. At the same time, it is easy to excuse the Methodist Fathers. There were two strong reasons for not building chapels. Firstly, all their energies were thrown into the work of evangelizing the country; they were filled with zeal for bringing souls to Christ, and it was impossible for them amongst all their travels and preaching of the gospel to appreciate the appropriateness of building chapels. Secondly, their relationship with the Established Church had not been defined; they did not know themselves the direction in which they would be led. To begin with they did not call their buildings chapels. This would have made them too much like the Dissenters. Howell Harris called them 'society houses', and later one of them was known as a 'meeting-house'. Their uncertainty as to their position in the Church of England acted upon them as a considerable restraint as far as building chapels in various parts of the country was concerned. We should have mentioned also that the Methodists before the Disruption had taken possession of many of the old chapel buildings that belonged to the Church of England and which had fallen into disuse for lack of congregations. As examples of these we could refer to the chapels at Abergorlech, Ystrad-ffin and Llanlluan, in Carmarthenshire, and Gyfylchi Chapel in Glamorganshire.

Great strides forward were taken with respect to building 'meeting-houses' during the thirteen years of Howell Harris's withdrawal and amongst the party that remained faithful to Daniel Rowland. Whether this is an indication that the Reformer from Trefeca, because of his strong allegiance to the Established Church, was the main obstacle to building, we do not know. But it is a fact that very soon after the Disruption Rowland and his followers pursued with determination the task of providing places in which to meet. In 1763, when returning from the Llansawel Association, the first that he had attended for thirteen years, Howell Harris wrote:

> Seeing so many new open'd by them [the Methodists] and none by me, and to see it an honour to go among them.

For various reasons, we believe that it was not churches or congregations that he meant by 'new', but places of worship.

It does not appear at all that the work of building chapels in the south during this period was considered a burden. The houses erected were small in size and without any decoration whatsoever: four walls and a roof, with an earth floor and a few backless benches, but with two pulpits – a large one for the man upon whom the Bishop had laid his hands, and a smaller one for the unordained preacher – and often these would be at either ends of the building. No architect would be needed to draw up the plan; we doubt whether anyone would have had a plan on paper – a decision on the number of strides for the width and length would have been sufficient guidance for the builder. The cost therefore was minimal, labour being particularly cheap in those days. Furthermore, the friends of the cause would freely quarry the stones themselves from the mountainsides and local farmers would transport them, together with the lime, slates and wood, to the site. And in nearly every neighbourhood, in the south, there were some respectable families of reasonable circumstances and position who were sympathetic to the Methodists and helped these building efforts..

Nearly half a century had passed since the beginning of the Methodist Revival before the Connexion had any number of chapels in Gwynedd. The first that was built, the first-fruits of all the Methodist chapels of the north, was Bala Chapel. We are not certain as to the date, except that it was certainly before 1777. In that year two others were built, at Brynengan and Penrhyndeudraeth. When Mr Charles joined the Methodists in 1785, the Connexion owned four chapels in Merionethshire – at Bala, Dolyddelen, Penrhyndeudraeth, and Blaenau Ffestiniog. The following year he added another, namely, the chapel at Dolgellau As a result of his labours with the circulating schools and Sunday Schools, and as the fruit of the powerful ministry of heaven-sent preachers, the congregations of Gwynedd soon multiplied, and a great cry for chapels was heard from all quarters. The end of the eighteenth century and the beginning of the nineteenth was an unprecedented period of building. And in the north this nearly brought the Connexion to ruin. In the various neighbourhoods, the members of the societies would nearly all be poor and usually small in number, though the congregations might be large. The Association therefore would have to take responsibility for very nearly all buildings erected.

This produced the result that should have been foreseen, namely, that everyone built a chapel of whatever size they desired, without taking cost into consideration. Very soon the Connexion found itself responsible for an enormous debt and at one point it was feared that it would become bankrupt. But by means of John Evans's timely leadership and his insistence that every congregation adopt the penny collection, and the ability and faithfulness of John Roberts, Llangwm, as an untiring secretary, the debt was gradually discharged. Eventually each Monthly Meeting became responsible for the finances of its region, and in order to ensure that such a situation never arose again it was decided that no congregation was to erect a building without the permission of the Monthly Meeting to which it was affiliated. By the time of the Ordination, Methodist chapels were scattered throughout Wales, from Holyhead to Cardiff, as well as in the major English cities.

RESPECTABLE FAMILIES JOINING THE METHODISTS

It was within this period that many of the gentry joined the Methodists. This was true only of the south; apart from the Tyddyn family of Montgomeryshire and Simon Lloyd's family near Bala, very few wealthy families belonged to the societies in Gwynedd. The gentry were nearly all under the influence of the clergy and were prejudiced against the Methodists. But quite early on many of the gentry of the south began to associate with them and most of these remained faithful up to the time of the Ordination. In Glamorgan we may refer to Thomas Price, Watford, and his son, Captain Price; Howell Griffith, Trefeurig; Squire Jones, Fonmon; and Bassett, Aberthaw. In Carmarthenshire, there were Mrs Griffiths, Glanyrafonddu; Mrs Walters, Pantyresgail; Squire Jones, Ysgair Walter; and Mr Jones, Pantglas. In Cardiganshire, Bowen, Gwaunifor, and his sister were members with the Methodists, together with Colonel Lloyd, Bronwydd. The last named built a chapel at his own expense and called it *Capel Drindod* [Trinity Chapel] as proof of his opposition to the Unitarians, and having completed it, he came himself to the Monthly Meeting to present it to the Connexion. It is said that his manner in so doing was sincerely humble and self-denying. This occurred in 1794. Within four years afterwards he received permission from the Association for the Lord's Supper to be administered there, and it was here that the Colonel and his wife took communion for the rest of their lives. In Pembrokeshire, Squire Bowen, Llwynygwair, joined the Methodists. It was in his house, employed as a tutor to his children, that the Rev. Ebenezer Richard lived before he moved to Tregaron. We refer to the links between these gentry families and the Connexion because it was these that made it impossible for the common people to continue their persecution. No one dared attack a Connexion with whom such respectable families were associated. The patronage of these families proved of immense advantage to the Revival; it helped obtain social respectability for the Methodists. Conversely, after the Ordination, when many of these withdrew, returning to the fold of the Established Church, there was an equivalent disadvantage.

THE WEAKENING OF THE INFLUENCE OF THE METHODIST CLERGY

It was within this period that the authority of the clergy in the Connexion was weakened. As we have shown, Methodism was a child of the Established Church and its government at first was episcopal. The first bishop was Howell Harris. It is true that this is not the name that he professed. His title, as found in the Association minutes, was *General Superintendent,* but in practice he was a bishop, and he exercised the role as autocratically as any bishop of the Church of England. When he withdrew from the Methodists no one was appointed to take his place, and no one afterwards ever had such an extensive rule amongst them. His place was still vacant when he returned a second time to the fold. At the same time, of necessity, there were some in positions of leadership and others following. After Harris's departure the mantle of leader fell upon Daniel Rowland. William Williams and Howell Davies acted as his assistants but he was certainly the leader and as he was held in such respect and had no inclination to rule with a rod of iron, all were very ready to submit to his judgment. When Rowland died the Methodist clergy believed that there should be one pre-eminent leader over the Connexion. They did not wish to call the man in this position *'Bishop'* but were ready to name him *'Father'*, and their inclination was to view the Rev. Nathaniel Rowland, the old Reformer's son, as the occupier of the position. Williams, Pantycelyn, certainly saw him in this role. He refers to him in his elegy to Daniel Rowland:

Thou, Nathaniel, heaven's servant,	Ti, Nathaniel, gwas y nefoedd,
Guard thou well thy father's fold –	Gwylia ar y gorlan glyd
Gathered by unwearied efforts,	Gasglodd Rowland, dy dad ffyddlon,
And by faithfulness untold;	Trwy ryw orchest fawr ynghyd;
Much more learned, not less gifted,	Uwch mewn dysg, nid llai mewn doniau,
Hold the torch, and point the way,	Saf fel llusern olau, clir,
That thy father's flock may never,	I helpu ei ddefaid ef i gadw
Homeward hast'ning, go astray.[1]	Yr union ffordd i'r nefoedd dir.
Be a father to the *'Sasiwn*,	Bydd yn dad i'r Assosiasiwn,
And if wanting help from man,	Ac os teimli'th fod yn wan,
Turn to one of faithful service,	Ti gei help gwir efengylwr,
Honest David of Llan-gan,	Dafydd onest o Langan;
He who melts the stones with sweetness,	Dodd y cerrig a'i ireidd-dra,
As he sows the gospel seed,	A thrwy rym ei 'fengyl fwyn,
Makes the sturdiest oak before him,	Wna i'r derw mwyaf caled
Bend as pliant as the reed.	Blygu'n ystwyth fel y brwyn.

Readers will remember that Howell Harris often gave himself the name 'father' and claimed to rule in such a capacity. It was quite clear therefore what Williams meant when he called on Nathaniel Rowland to be a father over the Association. He was asking him to sit in the position of authority and to undertake episcopal rule. This Rowland did with avid eagerness. To rule was in his nature. One of his greatest weaknesses was arrogance and love of authority. At first the Connexion was quite happy for him to hold the reins. As far as we know no decision was taken on the matter, he slid into the role by common consent; partly because he was the son of his father, and partly because he was a clergyman and full of ambition. It seems that the next to him in authority was the Rev. David Griffiths, the vicar of

Nevern. Jones, Llan-gan, had more influence over the churches but he was a son of peace, disliking argument and controversy, so that he took a back seat and allowed those who were more ambitious to push to the front.

The point being made is that the authority of the clergymen in the Association was all-powerful at first. Very rarely would any of the exhorters dare to oppose them and if one of them were to do so he would have little hope of carrying his point. There were many reasons for this: respect for the office; an awareness of the superiority of the clergymen in learning and ability; and also the greater preaching gifts were to be found amongst them. But, gradually, this influence was lost, and authority came into the hands of the unordained preachers and elders. There were two specific reasons for this: firstly, the misrule and immoral life of Nathaniel Rowland. His autocracy was intolerable. The societies groaned under the yoke that he placed upon them. He was more tyrannical in nature even than Howell Harris and without the deep spirituality and unceasing labours of the latter to support his claims. And when it became clear also that he drank to excess, and came to the Associations under the influence of drink, he lost all his authority and the Methodists stirred up sufficient courage to excommunicate him. The second reason was the appearance of unordained preachers in the Connexion possessing gifts of oratory and ministerial abilities that far surpassed even those of the clergymen: in the south, men such as Dafydd Morris, and his son, Ebenezer Morris, together with David Charles, Carmarthen, though the latter was not such a popular preacher; and in the north, Robert Roberts, John Elias, and John Jones, Edeyrn. Amongst the Methodists, from their very first days and continuing up to the present, preaching gifts will ensure for their possessors a strong influence within the conferences of the Connexion. This is the result of what appears to be a deep-seated principle within the human nature. And when those who were termed 'laymen' began to excel the clergymen in preaching and ministerial gifts, the wheel turned so as to raise them in authority also over their previous masters. In addition they possessed great solemnity of mind, fine discernment in judgment, and striking articulation as they expressed their thoughts before the Association. For all these reasons, the authority and influence within the Connexion had departed from the clergy and rested with the unordained preachers, long before the Ordination of 1811.

THE PERSECUTION OF THE METHODISTS UNDER THE CONVENTICLE ACT

It was within this period that the Methodists were compelled to resort, as Nonconformists, to the protection offered by the law. As those who considered themselves members of the Church of England, many of the Methodists believed that to leave the Church would constitute schism. And as there was so little true spirituality amongst the Nonconformists they could not bear the idea of being under the same name. Therefore, as they journeyed about and preached in dwellings, they laid themselves open to the penalties of the Conventicle Act. This law dated from the days of Charles II and prohibited the holding of a religious meeting in an unconsecrated building if more than five people were present. When found guilty of this offence the man who preached was liable to a fine of twenty pounds and so also was the owner of the house who had allowed him to preach. Each member of the congregation over sixteen years of age was liable to a six shillings fine. But in the reign of William and Mary the Act of Toleration had been passed. This gave Nonconformists the right to hold religious services in unconsecrated buildings if these had been licensed at the Bishop's Court as Nonconformist chapels, and if the preacher had taken the necessary vows and received a licence as a Nonconformist minister. The Methodists' decision to remain loyal to the Church of England and not to register their buildings or license their ministers meant that they could not claim any protection from the Toleration Act.

On consideration it might appear strange that their enemies did not make more use of the Conventicle Act against them. Perhaps at first it was not clear whether the Methodists came under the terms of the Act or not. Howell Harris claimed strongly that he could not be prosecuted by it as he was a faithful member of the Church of England, and it seems that the magistrates were in some doubt at first. It may be also that the persecutors depended predominantly on the ignorant common people as the main instruments of their wrath. At the same time, the law was not allowed to remain a dead letter. Sir Watkyn Williams Wynn ennobled himself by this means of persecution. Howell Harris wrote in 1748, when on a journey in Gwynedd, that he had to preach in lonely places on the mountain, either in the middle of the night or at the dawning of the day, in order to avoid a fine for himself or his hearers. He said further that Sir Watkyn, some time previously, had fined a man twenty pounds and many of those present, five pounds each, and that this was the third time that he had done this.

The appropriateness of licensing the exhorters and so bringing them under the protection of the Act of Toleration was discussed in the Associations quite early on. The Trefeca records include the minutes of the Blaen-y-glyn Association of 3 June 1745. Two letters were read, one from Richard Tibbott and the other from John Richards, the exhorter from Llansamlet. The two were undecided what to do, in that they feared to go to some of the places where they used to preach in case they would be pressed into the army. They asked whether it would not be better to obtain licences so as to place themselves above the reach of their enemies. But the Association could not agree to this. To obtain licences would have meant describing themselves as Nonconformists. The decision arrived at was:

> ... that taking a licence at this time would dishonour the Lord, as would also leaving the work. Most therefore of the opinion that such as are out of the power of the enemies [that is, those that had been ordained, probably] should go publicly to places of most danger and others to go more private, and so to use all innocent wisdom, as this is only a trial for a time and not to be looked on as a persecution ... and we agreed that if the persecution should become general, and the gospel wholly stopped then appeal to the legislation, and if rejected, to the bishops, and then if our liberty be wholly taken, our way will be clear to a separation.[2]

This is almost certainly Howell Harris's decision – his image is clearly upon it. Daniel Rowland was not present at the Association. It is seen that they considered the action of obtaining a licence as equivalent to separation from the Church, and they were no doubt correct in this. The brethren, under Harris's guidance, decided to appeal to the bishops, the government, and anyone else, before turning their backs on the Established Church.

It seems that it was only on occasions that the Conventicle Act was used against them, during periods when a more than usually wrathful magistrate was aroused to persecution. We have already given an account of the Dolgellau Methodists at a Bala Association. Usually the rage of the mob could be depended upon to disrupt meetings. But one of the gentry who lived in the Towyn neighbourhood decided to make thorough use of the Conventicle Act and by it pursue the Methodists out of the region. This man was Edward Corbett of Ynysmaengwyn. He was a justice of the peace and one of the greatest landowners in the land. According to the usual custom, he kept a pack of hunting dogs; also, because the country was at war with France at the time, he maintained a large number of soldiers – as many as eighty, according to Lewis Morris – in the vicinity of his mansion. He seems to have been a man of much determination, of warm temper, and of a consuming rage against the Methodists. He is also said to have been good-natured and kind-hearted, and that it was the tales of the clergy that aroused him against the societies. They were described to him as, 'the people of dark prayers', as those who held secret, immoral meetings, traitors against the government, and that no possessions or persons would be safe unless they were exiled from the land. Having been stirred up by such descriptions, Mr Corbett determined that he would defeat them.

He began the persecution in Merionethshire about the year 1789. He placed pieces of artillery before houses where services were to be held and threatened to blow into pieces whoever gathered there. Once, when the Monthly Meeting was to be held at Towyn, it had to be moved to Bryncrug. There is an account of a remarkable occasion at Pen-y-bryn, near Towyn. Mr William Jones, a young man who pastored the Congregational Church at Machynlleth, had arrived to preach. Someone ran to Mr Corbett with the news and he sent his servants with a pack of hounds to disturb the meeting. As the service began the master of the hounds blew his horn, expecting the dogs to bark and howl as usual. But the dogs took no notice of him. He blew again and again but nothing happened. He whipped the dogs cruelly but some influence had made the dogs dumb. What the dogs would not do however the servants would. They surrounded the preacher with every kind of shouting, jeering, blaspheming and swearing, and threatened to release the hounds and tear the congregation to pieces unless they departed. This soon put an end to the meeting. William Jones lived for only another two years after this event and the cruel treatment he received at Pen-y-bryn is thought to have hastened his end.

But the societies were increasing in number and the houses where God's Word was being preached were proliferating. As he saw this, Mr Corbett became enraged, and when he realized that the houses were not being registered, nor the preachers licensed, he decided to enforce the Conventicle Act immediately. By 1795 a great storm was about to break. He began at Corris by giving John Roberts, Rugog, notice to quit because his wife was a member of the society at Corris. The following is the account in *Methodistiaeth Cymru:*

> Jane Roberts and her husband were the tenants of a gentleman who lived some ten or twelve miles from them. They had eleven children. A notice to quit was sent to the cottage. The husband visited the landowner, pleading to be allowed to stay. His wish was granted provided his wife left her religion. John Roberts returned home and his wife asked him:
>
> 'Well, John *bach*, what happened with the gentleman?'
>
> 'Middling.' said John, 'It could have been worse.'
>
> 'Did you get the land back?' she asked.
>
> 'Yes,' said John, 'provided you leave those people.'
>
> 'Well, John *bach*,' said Jane, 'if you think that it is better for you and the children for me to go, then I will leave you. But I will never leave my religion!' It seems that this was said to test the wife because she never had to leave her cottage, children, or religion.

Mr Corbett's next effort had to do with Hen Gastell, the house at Corris where preaching was maintained. It stood on the land of Dafydd Humphries, a godly and determined man. We quote again from *Methodiaeth Cymru:*

> Like many of the preaching venues of those days, Hen Gastell had not been registered according to the law, and the gentleman decided to see what a new method of persecution might achieve towards stamping out this new heresy that was spreading so fearfully throughout the land. He determined to catch the owner of the house and as many as he could of those gathered there, and to fine them all under the Conventicle Act, according to the law. About ten or twelve of his armed soldiers set out towards Hen Gastell to catch them. A man who sympathized with the Methodists heard of this and ran as fast as he could to pass on the news. A second man, to whom he passed on the message, undertook the next stage of the journey. And so, from one man to another, the warning arrived at Hen Gastell long before the marching soldiers. When Dafydd Humphries heard, he hurried to carry the pulpit out of the house and to hide it under straw in the barn. He hid himself also amongst the bracken overlooking the road. 'I saw the armed band arriving and firing their weapons until Cwm Corris was full of smoke from one end to the other. One of the servants was sent to ask for me and when they were told that I was not in the house, they announced that I was to see my master the following day. They then left, without causing much damage other than wasting a good deal of gunpowder.' The next day Dafydd Humphries visited the great man and once the offender had been led into the presence of his lord, he was asked:
>
> 'Do you allow preaching in your house?'
>
> 'I do, sir,' was the reply.
>
> 'To whom do you give permission?'
>
> 'To Vaughan Jones, sir.'
>
> 'Vaughan Jones must answer to the law,' shouted the gentleman. The matter was taken to the Quarter Sessions at Bala but as Vaughan Jones was not present and as there was no lawyer willing to take up the matter, the case was dropped.

Mr Corbett was more successful with William Hugh, one of the first exhorters of Merionethshire, who lived at Llechwedd near Abergynolwyn. He had begun preaching about four or five years previously. It came to Mr Corbett's notice that he had been holding services in a house in Towyn. He sent twelve soldiers there to arrest him. Persecuting Christians was not a duty that appealed to some of the soldiers and one of them pretended to be ill on the way and excused himself. But the other eleven arrived at William Hugh's home early on a Friday morning in early summer, 1795, and caught him while he was still in his bed. Having been shown the summons he went with them immediately to the magistrate. He was then sternly rebuked for holding meetings in breach of the law and fined twenty pounds. He was imprisoned for only a few hours. Throughout the day his wife asked friends for help, and before evening the fine had been collected and the prisoner released. For a time he was afraid of going about to preach. But after a few weeks he visited friends in Dolgellau who, after rejoicing at seeing him, compelled him to address them with a few words. In his zeal, he agreed. The enemies of Methodism were busy in those days. It is said that it was a relative of William Pugh who complained of him to the magistrate but certainly, before nightfall on the day after his sermon at Dolgellau, someone had carried the news to Mr Corbett. The order went out to apprehend him a second time and had he been found this time the fine would have been forty pounds. He was told of his danger in time however and managed to escape and to remain hidden until the next County Sessions had passed.

Perhaps the most romantic of all the stories relating to this persecution was that of Lewis Morris. We must first say something of the man himself. He was born in 1760 in a house called Coed-y-Gweddill that stands on a slope above the small village of Llwyngwril, Merionethshire. He was a giant of a man – like Saul – a head and shoulders taller than his contemporaries and there was no one in the neighbourhood that could compete with him in feats of strength. He was as ungodly as he was strong. He was the chief of the local fighters and a ringleader in all their games and sports. For some reason his spirit was full of bitterness against the Methodists. One Sunday there was to be preaching at Llwyngwril with John Ellis, Barmouth, speaking, and a promise had been obtained for the use of a room at the village inn. As was his practice, Lewis Morris arrived at the inn looking forward to the usual drinking and merriment. But he was told that he and his friends could not be served with their beer until the preaching was over. This angered him greatly. He went up to the inn-keeper immediately and told him that if the inn continued to be rented out for religious meetings of this kind he would take all his various meetings and activities to another inn and thus ensure that the business would be ruined. The inn-keeper knew that he could carry out his threat, he therefore withdrew his promise and the preacher had to leave in disappointment without having spoken. About a year after this event, that is, in about 1789, a saint's day feast and a horse race were to be held at Machynlleth. Lewis Morris arrived there on the Saturday night. He wasted away the Sunday, going from tavern to tavern and enjoying the festivities. On the Monday, as he passed Maengwyn Street, having been watching the horse-racing, he heard enthusiastic singing from a small house nearby. It was the singing of a hymn at the close of a service, where Dafydd Morris, Twrgwyn, had been preaching. The thought suddenly struck Lewis Morris, 'They are at better things than you.' A dart pierced his heart. He remembered all his old sins and his work of hindering the service at Llwyngwril, and was convinced that he was an enemy of God and of all good. The bustle of the tavern and the dancing before the harp failed to heal his wound, and he told his dearest friends that he was leaving them forever. Off he went, home.

His parents were amazed to see him having returned, especially on hearing him cry out that he was a sinner. 'You, a sinner,' said his mother. 'Don't believe such nonsense. You are not an adulterer or a thief.' But the light of God's law had shone upon the soul of the giant from Coed-y-Gweddill and the world could offer nothing that would alleviate his pain. His conviction of soul was terrible. He would beat his body, and he almost lost his senses. He would go to the church on a Sunday and whenever he heard that the Methodists were preaching anywhere nearby, he would attend. At last he obtained relief. John Williams, Lledrod, was engaged to preach at Barmouth and spoke from Isaiah 32:2, 'And a man shall be as an hiding place from the wind, and a covert from the tempest; as rivers of water in a dry place, as the shadow of a great rock in a weary land.' We know nothing of the service other than that it was here that Lewis Morris first saw his Saviour. He passed from death into life and his soul escaped as a bird out of the snare of the fowlers. He joined the Methodists immediately but was still very ignorant of religious matters because he could not read. He attended the school kept by John Ellis at Bryn-y-gath, near Trawsfynydd, and it was there, at thirty years of age, that he learnt to read the Bible. Within two years he had begun to preach and soon became a very acceptable preacher who was asked to preach at Monthly Meetings and even at Associations sometimes. He spoke of himself preaching at an Association at Carmarthen. He was nervous and trembling as he climbed on to the platform and saw the size of the congregation and the learned and able men that were present. But Mr Charles of Bala turned to him, saying in his gentle way, 'Remember that it will only be sinners who will be listening to you, and that the truth that you have is greater than anybody who is here.' That kind and sensible statement lifted his spirits and he had a successful service. Lewis Morris lived to be ninety-five years of age and was buried in Dolgellau in 1855.

But to return to the period of persecution and Lewis Morris's experiences during that time. Both he and his friends knew that Mr Corbett was determined to catch him and that if he succeeded, he would either press-gang him into the army or send him to the crew of a man-of-war. The day after William Hugh was caught, soldiers were sent with a warrant to Coed-y-Gweddill. Lewis Morris however, in God's providence, had already left home for a journey through Radnorshire. On his way home he passed through Bala and by that time Mr Charles, John Evans, and others had heard that the soldiers were looking for him and were anxious as to his safety. They persuaded him not to return but to escape to Llwyngwair in Pembrokeshire, the home of Captain Bowen, a magistrate and a member with the Methodists. It seems that he was sent to Llwyngwair rather than to Bronwydd, though the latter place was so much nearer, because Mrs Lloyd of Bala, wife of the Rev. Simon Lloyd, had been born in Llwyngwair and was the sister of Captain Bowen. Probably Lewis Morris carried a letter from her to her brother. He set out for Pembrokeshire immediately. He wrote later:

> On the way from Bala, I had to pass through Llanymawddwy village. It was night-time and I had to call out the toll-keeper. The man came out in his shirt to open the gate and he asked me where I was travelling. 'Forwards,' I said. 'There is a great noise around Towyn,' he said. 'One of the gentry is persecuting the Methodist preachers and will give forty pounds to catch one of them,' (naming myself) 'and the soldiers are searching everywhere for him.'

It is surprising, on remembering his size, that no one recognized Lewis Morris, but God's protection was over him. He reached Llwyngwair safely and received every welcome from Captain Bowen. There was little danger for him there. The Captain took him to the next Quarter Sessions at Carmarthen and obtained a licence for him.

While Lewis Morris lived safely in Pembrokeshire the persecution became more and more heated in Merionethshire. Mr Corbett raged as an angry bear, searching out all who allowed preaching in their homes or who attended the sermons, in order to punish them to the furthest extent of the law. As well as fining William Hugh twenty pounds, he placed a similar fine on Griffith Owen, Llannerchgoediog; on Edward Williams, Towyn; and on a house-owner in Bryncrug. It seems also that Vaughan Jones, Corris, was warned he would have to pay twenty pounds. Scores of poor people were forced to pay five shillings because of listening to the Methodist exhorters. During the summer of 1795 the poor believers were in complete confusion. The preachers' tongues had been silenced, many of them had taken to their heels and fled, and some of those who had received them into their homes had fled with them. All were afraid of opening the door to a preacher fearing that any more heavy fines would ruin them. Anxiety and distress possessed many regions and for a season the work of the Lord amongst the Methodists had come to a stop. Most of the people could not find the fines imposed upon them by the magistrates and some of them would have had to go to prison for lengthy periods had not the Association helped them. Mr Charles stated in his *The Welsh Methodists Vindicated* that the fines had cost the Association over a hundred pounds in one year. Mr Charles and his wife also contributed much out of their private income for the support of those who suffered under the persecution.

If the prosecutors failed to find those for whom they were looking, they confiscated some of their possessions. Griffith Owen, Llannerchgoediog, had fled when he was fined. Having failed to catch him Mr Corbett sent his steward, together with a number of constables, to his cottage to take his animals to Towyn to be sold. As it was summer the cattle were grazing outside and the men went into the fields to herd them together. On seeing their purpose the believing women of the neighbourhood went to their knees, praying that they might fail in their mission. Whether the consequences were an answer to prayer or not, we do not know, but it is a fact that the officers failed to catch a single animal. The cattle, with their tails up in the heat, ran in all directions; the constables ran in their shirt-sleeves after them but for all their efforts they had to give up and return empty-handed.

It became clear that matters could not continue in this way. The Methodists were being hunted as partridges in the mountains, their farms were being taken from them, their circumstances ruined, and they were either being thrown in prison or being forced to flee the region. Many of them were scattered throughout Wales. We know of many families that had to run for refuge to Cardiganshire – men and women whose characters shone as the light. One of these was Mr Daniel Jones, who moved to Gamer Fawr near Tregaron and whose family were faithful servants of religion for many years. The believers feared to meet to pray to God. What was it that could enrage a gentleman like Mr Corbett, a man said to be of a kind nature, that he should behave so cruelly? The only credible explanation is that he believed the tales of the clergymen. The latter followed up every advantage for blackening the character of the Methodists. They portrayed them as men who gave themselves to immorality in secret, who nurtured sedition against the government, and who opposed all forms of order and authority. For the good of society therefore it was necessary that they be hounded from the land. In the midst of this persecution, the Methodists endured patiently, exhibiting much grace and forgiveness. According to *Methodistiaeth Cymru:*

> After conferring with a respectable lawyer with regard to the persecution the Methodists were suffering at the hand of a gentleman and justice of peace of the county, Mr Charles understood that Mr Corbett himself had transgressed the law when fining preachers and those who received them to their houses, by not distributing the fines amongst those who informed on them, and amongst the poor of the parish, in the presence of those fined. The lawyer offered to take up the case and exact the fullest punishment. Mr Charles would not agree to this before he had discussed matters with his brethren. On meeting with them and informing them of the situation, it was decided that it would be more Christian, and more likely to have a beneficial effect on Mr Corbett and others, if they were not to hand him over to the law.

It might be concluded that Mr Charles and his brethren were carrying forgiveness to extremes.

The Methodists were suffering in this way because of their faithfulness to the Established Church. Had they declared themselves Nonconformists their preachers might have been licensed, their meeting-houses registered, and they might have placed themselves under the protection of the Toleration Act so that no one would dare harm them. This, for a long time, they did not wish. At an Association in Bala at the beginning of the persecution, the question was raised whether it was the duty of the Connexion to place their preachers and chapels under the protection of the law immediately. Mr John Evans, Mr Charles, and others, believed that this was what should be done but they were opposed by some, by the brethren from Caernarvonshire in particular, who did not want on any account to be considered Nonconformists. But the persecution proved that they had to choose between two things – giving up the work completely, stopping the preaching, and allowing the societies to be scattered; or, acknowledging themselves to be Nonconformists and claiming the protection of the law. Having arrived at this point, they heard that others of the gentry were intending to follow Mr Corbett's example, and that the persecution which at the time was confined to Merionethshire, would very likely become widespread. At a subsequent Bala Association therefore, the decision was taken that all the preachers should be licensed, and all homes that received them be registered for preaching.

Having made this decision every effort was made to implement it but nothing could be done before the next Quarter Sessions; until that time the preachers and those who received them, would be in danger. In his autobiography, the Rev. Robert Griffith, Dolgellau, wrote:

> A letter came from Bala to Dolgellau stating, if I remember correctly, that the payment of fines for preaching in a house that had not been registered could

be avoided by taking the necessary vows within five days of receiving the legal warning, and not preaching in those places until the Quarter Sessions. Brother Hugh Lloyd, one of the Dolgellau elders, and myself went immediately to Vaughan Jones at Corris, and Griffith Owen at Llannerchgoediog, two men who had been summoned to pay a fine of twenty pounds each. That same afternoon we crossed the Mawddach River to Mr Owen at Llanenddwyn, and to Mr Parry at Hendreforion, two justices of the peace, and took the necessary vows. And so that particular storm passed.

These measures were defensive steps taken in the light of impending court cases. The two leaders preparing for these were Mr Charles and Mr John Evans. They secured the help of a lawyer who came to Bala and argued the case for those who were seeking licences. *Methodistiaeth Cymru* gives the following account:

In the meantime the Bala Quarter Sessions were approaching and preparations had been made to seek the protection of the law there, by means of a well-known lawyer from Chester (and afterwards from Cymau, near Caergwrle) who was himself a Nonconformist. The Merionethshire justices had been very unwilling to license preachers, but they had no right to deny those who came before them. When the lawyer, Mr David Francis Jones, Esq., explained to them that they had to choose between giving the law's protection to the preachers and being liable to the law themselves, they had to submit. One of the justices, the vicar of Llandderfel, said, 'Though my hand has to sign these papers, yet my heart is against it.' 'All that we want is your hand,' said Mr Jones. 'As for your heart, we are not concerned with that.' They were therefore licensed, and from then onwards all the preachers were encouraged to obtain licences as eagerly as previously they had been dissuaded. The chapels and meeting-houses also were registered. Thus, victory was obtained over this form of persecution. The method was not used while the mob could be roused to riot and bully, but once the Methodists had won over the hearts of the people, recourse had to be made to the law in attempting to subdue them. From now on this was not possible – the authority that before condemned them, now protected them. And the country, henceforth, was in quietness.

Amongst those who appeared before the justices in Bala to register his house, was Edward Williams, a tailor from Towyn. We have referred to him already as one who was fined twenty pounds, and he had been in hiding since that time. He was granted a licence. According to the Rev. Robert Owen, M. A., Pennal:

A little while ago I had the privilege of seeing this licence as it was originally written on a skin, and it was exhibited publicly to the Towyn Association of 1885. It is preserved as a valuable treasure by some of the old pilgrim's descendants ... The following is a verbatim copy:

'Meirioneth to wit – Thomas à Becket Sessions, 1795, held before Rice Anwyl and Thomas Davies, Clerks, Justices of the Peace, in and for the said county.

That a certain house called Porthgwyn, now in the occupation of Edward Williams, Taylor, situate in Towyn, in the County of Meirioneth, was this seventeenth day of July, 1795, recorded as a place of religious worship for the use of the Protestant Dissenters, according to the statute in such case made and provided,

Edward Anwyl, Deputy Clerk of the Peace.'

By now, the danger was past. The preachers returned from their exiles and the means of grace were made available in the homes. Edward Williams was to be seen in Towyn town as cheerful as a magpie after having his house registered.

Lewis Morris returned from his retreat in Pembrokeshire. He wrote in his memoirs:

The first Sabbath after my return home I went in the morning to Towyn to preach. When I arrived the soldiers were in the street, which was unusual on a Sunday, and some of my friends advised me not to hold a service for fear of them. But I said that there was no reason to yield before them any more and no need to fear any more, for I was under the shadow and protection of British Law. We therefore held the service in much peace.

Lewis Morris was perfectly correct. The little congregation must have worshipped with great joy and warmth that Sunday morning in Towyn, having the sense that their opponents had been disarmed and that the law was a shield for them from the spears of their persecutors. What occurred in Merionethshire was duplicated throughout Wales in general. The preachers hastened to obtain licences and to register the preaching stations and no one dared lay a hand on them.

As for Mr Corbett, Lewis Morris wrote:

It may be noted that this gentleman did not end his days in peace, neither in his estate nor his mind. It is said that in his last years he was in great terror of the Methodists. During the time of the riots in Manchester in 1817, he would say, 'What if the Methodists rise up? They will surely kill me.' Poor man. He did not know them and never realized that throughout their societies they nurtured a quiet and generous spirit. It was the guilt in his own mind that created his terrors.

However, long before he died, he came to realize that he had been misled in his view of the Methodists. For example, in 1817 and 1818 there was a great lack of food in the land, particularly of bread. Hoping to be of some help, Mr Corbett paid for a ship carrying a cargo of barley to arrive at

Aberdovey. The whole cargo was sold within two days. He was very surprised, not having imagined that the need of the poor was so great. With an oath, he said, 'You know, if the Methodists had done something I would have heard it all from the talebearers, but they felt no need to tell me of the sufferings of the poor.' He was clearly referring to the clergy.

Within twelve years of this persecution, that is, in 1807, the Methodists dared to convene an Association at Towyn. Many were anxious at the thought of holding it so close to the magistrate's mansion. A man who kept an inn in the town visited Mr Corbett to inform him of the meetings and to confess that, for the sake of his licence, he could not refuse entrance to the Methodists. Furthermore, he knew that of his customers, they were the most upright. Mr Corbett expressed his willingness for the man to do as he saw best. On the first day of the Association some of the talebearers went to the mansion with the news that the people had gathered and that many more again were expected the next day. They presumed that their tales would be received with interest. But the only response from him was a dry comment, 'They will greatly benefit the town.' Within a year the Association returned, and it continued to visit Towyn annually. On that second occasion the magistrate's daughter sent a request that one sermon be delivered in English. Her request was granted and the Rev. Robert Ellis, Mold, preached in English. She stood in the street and listened attentively from beginning to end. By today there are none of the descendants of the Corbetts remaining in the country.

We have described this period in detail because of its intrinsic importance: it forms a turning-point in the history of the Connexion. Up to this point the Methodists considered themselves members of the Church of England. It is true that their position was completely inconsistent. They did not attend the church on Sundays to hear the clergy, nor did they attend church for communion if they were in any way able to travel to Llangeitho, or Bala, or anywhere else where a Methodist clergyman was administering the sacrament. The bishops and clergy on their part denied that they held any connection with them; they disowned them before the world; they spread lying stories about them and stirred up the common people against them.

Even before this particular persecution, the Methodists could hardly be considered Churchmen. Their Churchmanship was entirely superficial, existing in nominal profession rather than in any practice and truth. For all this, they maintained a prejudice in favour of the Establishment; they refused to consider themselves Dissenters. But they had now been forced, through having to consider their own safety, to assume the mantle of

Nonconformity. They were pushed out of the Church in spite of themselves. They did not separate voluntarily but were evicted. Church historians argue that the Methodists remained in connection with the Established Church until the Ordination of 1811; that they would be still members today were it not for the ambition of John Elias, Ebenezer Morris, Thomas Jones, Denbigh, and the other unordained preachers; and that it was the Ordination that broke the connection. These historians are ignoring the facts when they express such views. Any remaining connections between the Methodists and the Church were broken completely eleven years before the Ordination when they were forced by the clergy to register their preaching stations as nonconformist places of worship and to ensure that all their preachers were licensed as Nonconformists. It is impossible to consider them as Churchmen after they had made solemn statements – statements that were equivalent to vows – before the magistrates, that they were Nonconformists. The only way to believe that they were still of the Church after this time is to understand that the vows were Jesuitical; that they did not mean what they said; that they wrote one thing but in their hearts meant something entirely different. No one who knows anything of their character could accept this for a moment. The Methodists must be considered as having separated completely from the Church and having formed an independent Connexion from the moment that they were forced to declare before courts of law that they were Nonconformist Protestants.

Matters had come to a head when they were forced either to leave the Church or leave the work. They did not dare turn their backs on the work because they had received the strongest possible proofs that it was of God. The Lord had descended amongst them hundreds of times as truly as he descended upon Mount Sinai. Though their meetings were often in barns and homes, they had felt the Divine Presence amongst them, filling the place with glory, as unmistakably as when he was known by Solomon at the consecration of the temple. Their efforts had been blessed to the conversion of hundreds and to the raising of the common people of Wales from the lowest depths. No, they would not dare to leave the work; they would anger God in so doing. And in that they could not be tolerated to continue with the gospel work and remain in any connection with the Church, there was nothing to do but to leave. From now on, the only link that remained of their previous history within the Church was that it was clergymen who had received Episcopal ordination who administered the sacraments to them. This situation also was so inconsistent with all their circumstances that it could not continue long.

THE RULES FOR THE ASSOCIATION

It was within this period that rules were formulated for the Association. No such rules existed at first to regulate the affairs of the Association. It was agreed that it should meet quarterly, but the time, the number of services, and other relevant matters, were decided by the circumstances. As the number of preachers and elders multiplied, and as the public meetings began to draw more and more hearers, more detailed rules became absolutely necessary. The following rules were passed at the Bala Association of 9 June 1790, and they are almost certainly the thoughtful product of Mr Charles's keen mind:

1. That those persons only who minister in the Church in holy things, that is, who labour in the doctrine or are leaders in spiritual things in the private societies, shall be members of the Association of North Wales.

2. That the Association be held quarterly at the place and time agreed to by the members themselves.

3. That the preachers meet apart at ten o'clock of the morning of the first day of the Association, to exhort, instruct, and admonish each other in the spirit of love, that union and brotherly love may abound, and that, by mutual help, they may become the light of the world and salt which has not lost its savour.

4. That all who are, by the first rule, members of the Association, meet at two o'clock in the afternoon of the same day, and at eight o'clock on the following morning. The door shall be closed at half past two and half past eight, after which none shall be admitted without the special admission of the assembly.

5. That the members assembled choose one of the brethren to preside. It will be his duty to see that all things are done decently and in order, and for edification.

6. That every member be at liberty to speak upon the subject under discussion, until the matter is decided. None shall make long speeches, unless it be at the request of the assembly on a subject of special importance.

7. That at one of these meetings spiritual subjects only be introduced. By spiritual subjects we mean the doctrines of the Gospel, together with a spiritual experience of them, religious exercises, church discipline, etc. Matters of business must be discussed and settled at the other meetings.

8. When no special subject is introduced for consideration, one of the members shall be conversed with in reference to his knowledge of the doctrines of the Gospel, his experience of them, and his fellowship of God. These things cannot be repeatedly neglected without injury to the Connexion; neither will they be neglected as long as the life of religion and the power of godliness abide among us. Or else, let a portion of the Bible be read with deliberation

and intelligence, and let a portion of the Bible or a doctrine of religion be laid down as a subject for consideration and inquiry.

9. Every disputed point shall be decided deliberately by a majority. The minority, who differ in opinion, should submit peacefully, and be kindly affectioned towards their brethren.

10. Every Monthly Meeting shall give to every one of its members, who is also a member of the Association, a printed certificate, in which his name and that of the Monthly Meeting shall be inserted. This only will give him admittance into the private meetings of the Association.

11. The Connexion in North Wales readily and affectionately invite all their brethren from South Wales, who may be present, to take part in every discussion and deliberation, inasmuch as we are anxious to keep the unity of the Connexion unimpaired throughout Wales, and thankfully to acknowledge also our obligations to them for granting us the same privileges.[3]

So read the rules drawn up by Mr Charles and passed at the Bala Association. It may be seen that they relate to the North Wales Association but it is certain that they were very soon adopted in south Wales also. They manifest a strong common sense and a deeply religious mind, and these substantially are the rules in force in the north and south Associations to this day.

METHODIST RULES OF DISCIPLINE

It was within this period that Disciplinary Rules were decided upon. As we have already noted, the Methodist Reformers drew up rules for the private societies in 1742. These had been written by Howell Harris and after being approved by Daniel Rowland were published and sent to the societies. They were concerned with the order and management of the societies. It is clear that they were not being followed even before Mr Charles's time. Indeed it may well be that they were never in operation in Gwynedd, in that John Evans, Bala, and Thomas Foulkes had translated John Wesley's rules for his societies and had distributed them for the benefit of the Welsh societies. No rules regarding conduct – rules that could have acted as a basis for church discipline – had been drawn up. Such matters were dealt with in the light of the Bible, appeals being made to the word and to the testimony. But Mr Charles and his brethren felt that the Connexion stood in need of a little simple guidance, based on Scripture, by which members could gauge their conduct and which could act as a touchstone for the membership of the societies. No doubt it was his able hand that wrote it, and it was published and approved at the Bala Association of 16 June 1801. They are identical to the *Disciplinary Rules* found in the *Confession of Faith,* except that the *Confession* omits the Introduction. As this Introduction is of such interest we include it here. It reads:

> Man, according to his original nature and instinct, is a social creature, enjoying fellowship; and from harmonious unity and society mankind draws much mutual help, protection, and support. It is true that the grace of God produces a great transformation within the soul of man, yet we must remember that this is not a transformation of his nature and instincts as a creature, but of that which he is as a sinner and a fallen creature. The one who is made a new creation possesses the same faculties as before but that these faculties, once corrupted by sin, have now been renewed in the divine image by the Holy Spirit. The man therefore gravitates towards fellowship and society as before; but in a more excellent way he now engages socially in holy exercises, and the Spirit of grace equips him for gracious fellowship.
>
> Christ's Church is a spiritual society; a society based on, and stemming from, the mutual unity of its members in their Head, the Lord Jesus Christ. All true members are members of one another in their most excellent Head; and that same spirit of love and sympathy which is in their Head is supplied by every member, so that they all by virtue of this union, bear with one another, sorrow with one another, and rejoice with one another. The Church is indeed an exalted society; its members are one in having God as their Father; and are one in having Christ as their Head and Spouse; they are one in being together in Him; and the Holy Spirit provides the seal and life of that abiding unity. It is clear that the mutual enjoyment of this unity will provide a peculiar addition to their happiness and rejoicing, both here and to all eternity. 'I in them, and thou in me,' (Christ prayed to his Father) 'that they be made perfect in one,' (John 14:23). There is not, nor ever will be, any perfecting without this most excellent unity and fellowship. 'Behold,' therefore, 'how good and how pleasant it is for brethren to dwell together in unity!' (Psalm 133:1). These considerations, together with the example of the apostles and the pre-eminent churches,[4] and the various exhortations of the Scriptures to this end, brought about the formation of private Societies by the Methodists.
>
> They are incorporated as members of Christ's Church Militant on earth, to pray for and with each other, and to instruct the one the other; to comfort the feeble-minded, warn the unruly, and support the weak; desiring to speak a word in season to erring souls. Thousands in Wales can testify confidently to the spiritual profit, consolation, and nurture that they receive from such meetings. They have been greatly slandered by scoffers and ungodly blasphemers; but the slander of such is no proof that the societies are not part of God's work. None indeed! but to the contrary; were they not of God, why should the enemies of God blaspheme them?
>
> We do not designedly dissent or look upon ourselves as dissenters from the Established Church. In doctrine we exactly agree with the articles of the Church of England; and preach no other doctrines but what are contained and

fully and clearly expressed in them. We highly approve of her excellent and most evangelical liturgy. In general the people in connection with us baptize their children in the Church, and many of them frequently receive the Sacrament of the Lord's Supper there. Our meetings also are seldom held in church hours, but in union with the Church, we desire the full enjoyment of those privileges, which the laws and happy constitution of our favoured country amply afford us, of having liberty without restraint, to use every scriptural means to spread the knowledge of the gospel of Christ among poor, ignorant and perishing sinners. Whatever appears in our proceedings as in any degree tending towards a separation from the Established Church, takes place from necessity and not from choice. Making a sect or forming a party is not the object we are aiming at – God forbid! But we think it our bounden duty and high privilege in the diligent use of all lawful means, to edify one another and to promote the knowledge of Divine truths and the power of practical godliness amongst all. The Methodists have taken refuge under the protection of the Toleration Act from necessity – they wish to cleave to the Established Church, and by no means desire to consider themselves a separate body.

We are fully aware that our behaviour is not acceptable to Churchmen on the one hand nor to Dissenters on the other. But the Righteous Judge is at the door, and on the Day of Judgment everyone, and everything, will be seen in clear and direct light. Until then, it would be well for us all to endeavour to tolerate each other in love. We testify that we desire to be at peace with all who, in simplicity and sincerity, endeavour, not to form sects and parties, but to save immortal souls – to defeat all ungodliness and immorality in our country – and to propagate the knowledge of Christ our Lord, and the necessity of that faith in him which is worked in the heart of a sinner by the Holy Ghost, and which bears fruit to God in true sanctification and a godly life. We judge that everything else is trivial in comparison to these weighty matters; therefore we do not take much notice of the ceremonies and methods that are found in the various religious groups of our country. We consider some of these to be but bells rung to attract and win adherents; and even for the best, they are but the shell about the core of true religion. But as for the weightier things of the law, namely, judgment, mercy, and faith, we would wish with all our hearts that these should be on the increase, amongst all of whatever name.

As proof of this, as we hold as a Body wholly to the same doctrines as are found in the Doctrinal Articles of the Established Church,[5] and as we do not know of more appropriate and scriptural words to express them than those laid out by the Reformers of old; we see no necessity for a published expression of our beliefs and doctrines. But to ensure right order, we find a need for brief and clear Rules and Regulations for our proceedings. We have judged that the few regulations following may all be justified from the Holy Scriptures (which is our sufficient and certain rule), and there is no free and continuing acceptance, as members of our private societies, to any without an agreement and a serious effort to conform to them.

The *Disciplinary Rules* follow, in exactly the form found in the Confession of Faith. It may be seen that the Introduction's main purpose is to prove the necessity of the private societies – the *seiadau* – notwithstanding all the calumny and misrepresentation poured upon them by their opponents. By clear arguments and appropriate phrases, the Introduction argues that deep within the human nature lies a need for such societies and that they were to be found in the New Testament Church from the first and also in all the main Churches. The Association is found protesting repeatedly that it had never intended forming a new sect. These protests seem to arise from the growing realization amongst the leaders that the Methodists eventually would have to separate, in spite of their wishes, and indeed that they were practically separate already. In all this the Association was being completely honest. They would not have left had they been allowed to continue their work within the fold. It is now clear that, at the time, they did not fully appreciate their position. They looked upon themselves as not being Churchmen or Nonconformists, and as being misunderstood by both sides. They were not of the Church in that they were licensed and registered, but they had still not yet appreciated that the steps they had taken had made them Nonconformists in spite of themselves. Their blindness to their situation was not because they were stupid or unthinking men but because they had no leisure to consider the question. To preach the Word; to fill the land with the knowledge of Christ the Lord; to bring men into possession of eternal life; these were the matters that fully engaged their minds and hearts. Compared to these goals, ecclesiastical arrangements and the minor differences between one denomination and another seemed to them to be unworthy of consideration. At the same time the distinction drawn in the Introduction between the doctrinal articles of the Church and those that have to do only with the outward governance of the Church, and the agreement declared with the former, suggest strongly that the Episcopal system with all its ecclesiastical implications had become irrelevant in the eyes of the Association. We do not wish to suggest that the Methodists at this time were completely consistent in their thinking – they would not become so until they took the step of ordaining their own ministers – but they were rapidly moving to that position which they presently occupy.

THE RISE OF WELSH WESLEYANISM

It was within this period that Wesleyanism was planted in Wales. We have already shown that the Methodist Revival in Wales occurred quite independently of the revival in England. However, both movements were of the same Spirit and the Calvinistic Methodist and the Wesleyan Methodist were fruits of the same awakening. A strong bond of friendship existed between John Wesley and the Methodists of Wales, particularly so between himself and Howell Harris, and this friendship survived the controversy between Whitefield and Wesley. Harris believed the Calvinistic doctrine. He could never receive some of John Wesley's views, particularly some of the phrases with which he clothed his beliefs, but he was generous enough to put aside the views that separated them and to acknowledge that the Wesleyans were as much in possession of the essence of the gospel as himself, and a mutual understanding prevailed between himself and Wesley's followers throughout his life. In his last years he was often present at the Wesleyan Conference and was granted an honourable position amongst them. As the Methodists and Wesleyans considered themselves brethren in the days of Harris and Wesley, they were very careful not to encroach on one another's boundaries. In a Bristol Association of 1747, to which Mr Wesley and some of his followers had been invited, it was decided that neither group would establish a society in an area where the other had already gathered believers. The minutes read:

> 'Twas fear'd that the consequence of Mr Wesley's preaching at Neath would be a Separation in the Society. Mr Wesley answer'd, I do not design to erect any Separation at Neath, or in any other Town in Wales, where there is a Society already: But to do all that in me lies to Prevent any such Separation. And we all agree wheresoever we occasionally [preach] among each other's People, we will endeavour to Strengthen, not weaken each other's Hands, in particular by labouring to prevent any Separation in the several Societies.[6]

What is meant by *'any Separation'* is any division in a society, be it Methodist or Wesleyan. Both parties kept faithfully to this agreement so that, at the beginning of the nineteenth century, the Wesleyans did not have a single Welsh-speaking congregation in Wales. They owned chapels in Cardiff, Swansea, Bridgend, Haverfordwest, Brecon, and other places, but the preaching was in English and in that the language of the common people was Welsh there was very little growth in these congregations.

The first to establish a Welsh-speaking Wesleyan cause in any part of Wales was Mr Jones, Bathafarn. Edward Jones was from the Rhuthun area. He was born in Bathafarn mansion in 1777 and received his education at Rhuthun Grammar School. His father was a wealthy man but, for reasons that are not known, Edward Jones went as a youth of seventeen to Manchester and obtained work as a cotton weaver in a factory. He was a gentle, quiet young man, courteous in manner and irreproachable in behaviour, but not knowing much about religion nor having felt anything of its saving influence in his heart. One Sunday night, about the end of

1795 or the beginning of the following year, he was led to the Wesleyan Chapel in Oldham Street. The preacher was the Rev. George Marsden, a very effective speaker. The service was a powerful one and the truth so grasped the soul of the young Welshman from the Vale of Clwyd that he emerged from the chapel that night a new man. He joined the church at Oldham Street and committed himself with great zeal and enthusiasm to every work that he was asked to do. Shortly after, his elder brother died; his parents were getting older and unable to cope with their affairs; he himself felt that the smog of Manchester was affecting his health. He saw that he would have to return to the Vale of Clwyd. This was about the end of 1799. He greatly missed the religious fellowship that he once enjoyed amongst the Wesleyans and he sorrowed over the irreligious ways of so many of his countrymen. One day he visited Chester to confer with the Rev. Thomas Hutton, the superintendent of the Wesleyan circuit in that part of the country, and he obtained a promise of help from him. While in the city he heard of another Welshman there, a zealous Wesleyan, whose name was John Bryan. Edward Jones visited him and a friendship was formed between them that lasted all their lives. At the beginning of 1800 he rented a large room in Rhuthun, owned by a carrier called John Edwards, in order to hold religious services. Soon the Rev. James Ridal, one of the ministers of Chester, came to them and preached to a large crowd. It was arranged that someone from Chester would come to them every other Sunday. On the vacant Sundays Edward Jones would hold a prayer meeting and give a short address. This was done in English but the main body of the people were monoglot Welshmen so that the service was of no profit to them. Edward Jones decided to attempt a meeting in Welsh, in which, over a period of some months, he began to choose a text and preach in Welsh. About May of the same year Mr John Bryan, who by now had been accepted as an assistant preacher, came to Rhuthun to help. Within a short time they had gathered a congregation and formed a society. This was the first Welsh-speaking congregation for the Wesleyans in Wales; it was composed of six souls. Societies were also formed at Denbigh and at other places in the Clwyd Valley.

In the Methodist Conference held in London in 1800 a request was presented by Edward Jones and John Bryan that a Wesleyan mission be established in Wales as soon as possible. It met with very little attention at first; it does not seem that anyone supported it, and when the preachers were allocated to the various circuits no provision for Wales was made. But Dr Coke arrived before the end of the Conference. His crossing from Ireland had been delayed by bad weather and so he missed the arranging of the circuits. He was a Welshman, born in Brecon, and though understanding only very little Welsh and not being able to speak it at all, his zeal for his fellow-countrymen was great. His influence in the Conference was such that he succeeded in reopening the question and it was passed that the Revs. John Hughes and Owen Davies be sent as missioners to Wales. Previously, Owen Davies was to have gone to Redruth in Cornwall, and John Hughes to Leek in Staffordshire, but these arrangements were put aside and the two travelled to Wales and lived at first in Rhuthun. They arrived there on 27 August 1800, and began the work of preaching immediately.

These two ministers deserve some attention. The Rev. Owen Davies was born in Wrexham in 1752. He knew something of the influence of the gospel when very young on hearing Mr John Gardner, an assistant preacher with the Wesleyans, but his father would not allow him to join that Connexion. It was not long before he moved to London and was there convicted and saved. He joined the society at Brentford and began preaching at Mile End. Before this time he had married a widow who kept a school at Ealing. Soon after his conversion John Wesley tried to persuade him to give himself wholly to preaching. For some time he hesitated, because he was a married man, but Mr Wesley gained the day. His first circuit was Manchester; afterwards he was superintendent at Penzance and Redruth in Cornwall; and his labours were much blessed. He could speak a mongrel Welsh but could not preach in that language, and this proved a great disadvantage to him in his work.

John Hughes was a man of considerable ability who had received more of an education than was usual. He was born in Brecon on 18 May 1776. His father was a respectable tradesman in the town and had provided the best education for his son in the hope that he would become a clergyman. But when John Hughes was thirteen, Dr Coke came to preach in Brecon. The boy went to hear him and the sermon affected him deeply. The following year he joined the Wesleyan society in the town, laying aside completely any thought of ministry in the Established Church. He started preaching amongst the Wesleyans at a very young age and in 1796 he was appointed to the Cardiff circuit. As we have seen, he was sent by Conference in 1800 as a missioner to Wales.

These are the men that were instrumental in establishing Welsh Wesleyanism – Mr Edward Jones, Bathafarn, and the Revs. John Bryan, Owen Davies, and John Hughes. Mr Jones, Bathafarn, was no more than an assistant preacher all his life, though he possessed more ability than many a minister. At first they were welcomed warmly, particularly so by the

Methodists. Methodist chapels were lent to them very willingly and they received much hospitality. We have already noted how they preached at the Methodist Chapel in Machynlleth and the kind reception they received at Mr Thomas Foulkes's house. They were also loaned the chapel at Bala for many consecutive Sundays in order for them to hold their services and to attempt to establish a Wesleyan cause in the town.

> John Hughes, in his biography of Owen Davies, speaks of Thomas Jones (afterwards of Denbigh) inviting Davies to his house during Davies' first preaching visit to Mold, and welcoming him most hospitably. At that time, and on another occasion afterwards, they had considerable satisfaction in one another's company. He mentions also that Davies and he journeyed to Anglesey, soon after their arrival in the country. Davies preached on the Sabbath in Holyhead and Hughes in Beaumaris; both of them doing so, 'in the Chapels of the Calvinists, which were freely lent to us'. Afterwards Hughes preached in Llangefni and Beaumaris, and Davies in Caernarvon, and we suppose that on these occasions also they made use of the chapels of the same people.[7]

We wish to draw attention to this point, namely that the Wesleyans had every welcome and kindness from the Methodists when they first began their activities in Wales. We are sorry to see that the Wesleyan historians have passed this by without comment, while enlarging upon the opposition that their early missionaries met with.

Very soon however, the storm broke. The Wesleyan missionaries saw that they would never establish a new Connexion in Wales only by preaching the gospel; even though it was that form of the gospel in which they believed. It was found necessary also that they attack those Connexions that were in the land already. This they proceeded to do, and they did not hesitate to ascribe to the Calvinists ideas which Calvin himself and nearly all who believed Calvinistic principles would have renounced as dangerous heresies. Dr Owen Thomas states:

> Certainly, in their preaching, [the Wesleyan missionaries] laid particular stress on the universality that, they would argue, is found in the redemption of Jesus Christ. They held that if Christ has not died for every man, in exactly the same sense, then there cannot be salvation for all, and that therefore the call of the gospel to every man is a deceit and a dishonesty; it is to call the hungry to a feast which, when they arrive, is found not to exist. They particularly preached against the Calvinistic view of election, equating it with an unconditional reprobation, and claiming that Calvinists teach that only a small number were elected to salvation and the great remainder elected to damnation, regardless of their character and conduct. The former would be saved, however much they sinned, and the latter would be lost, no matter how great their effort.[8]

We hardly need to state that this was not the creed of the Methodist Reformers and was not what they declared from their pulpits. In vain would the sermons of Daniel Rowland, the journals of Howell Harris, the writings of Charles of Bala and of Thomas Jones of Denbigh, be searched for such Antinomian doctrines as these. Rather, they excommunicated without mercy all who held to such beliefs. Without any hesitation they proclaimed the sufficiency of the atonement for all; that the Redeemer receives whoever comes to him; and that the true reason for the damnation of those who depart from this gospel world without faith is that they have refused the grace of God. It was completely unjust to ascribe to the Calvinists those ideas that others have imagined are the necessary implications of their doctrines.

Dr Thomas adds:

> They [the Wesleyan preachers again] dreadfully misrepresented also the Calvinistic view of man's natural condition, announcing that some of the Methodists preached that 'hell was paved with the heads of small children'. This was claimed, in the Press, of the Rev. John Jones, Treffynnon. That old preacher happened later to visit the town where the minister who had made this claim was living. As he was one who often in the pulpit would follow whatever path opened up to him at the time, and as he was anxious to take advantage of the situation in order to strike a blow at one who had accused him of such blasphemy, he said, while preaching on the pleasure which the Lord Jesus takes in seeing little children coming to him:
>
> 'Some creature here, in your town, has published abroad that I have said that the heads of little children are paving hell. A terrible lie. I have never said such a thing. Such a thought has never entered my head. I had never before understood, nor ever heard, that there were pavements in hell. "A bottomless pit" is what my Bible calls it. And if it had a bottom which needed paving, it seems to me much more probable that this would be done, not by the heads of sweet, innocent children, but by hard, bruised heads like his, that have spent a lifetime knocking against the election of grace.'[9]

Such an attack may hardly be considered suitable in the context of public ministry, but as far as the man who had accused a fellow-believer so rashly was concerned, he fully deserved this verbal lashing.

Owen Thomas continues:

> It was completely intolerable ... to all the moral feelings of such notably moderate men as Charles of Bala, Thomas Jones (Denbigh), John Jones (Edeyrn), Ebenezer Morris, George Lewis (Llanuwchllyn), Benjamin Jones (Pwllheli), John Roberts (Llanbryn-mair) and many others . . . to hear the distorted understandings of their beliefs, and the utterly unreasonable, unscriptural and offensive conclusions drawn from them. These supposed consequences

were presented in a most arrogant and oracular manner, as if they were the very essence of the doctrines and the truths taught plainly by these preachers to their congregations. It was particularly intolerable to them coming from inexperienced men of little ability, too young as yet to have acquainted themselves with the Divine Revelation and with the Christian Church's developing understanding throughout the centuries of the great truths taught therein . . . Furthermore, it is fairly certain that the Wesleyan brethren in their first years were considered too eager to proselytize, and too desirous of winning people over from the other denominations, from the Methodists particularly. In this their practice was incompatible with the fairness and honesty necessary to ensure peace and good neighbourliness between religious denominations. All in all, the Calvinistic denominations unquestionably felt that these newcomers to the country were dealing with them unfairly, misrepresenting their views, stealing their people and sheltering those who were disciplined by them. All this, quite apart from the fact that the Wesleyan doctrines, according to their conscientious judgment, were completely contrary to the Scriptures and dangerous to the souls of men.[10]

If it was the Wesleyans who began the war and were the first to fire, the Calvinists, with the Methodists among them, were not slow to retaliate. The Arminian Controversy spread throughout Wales. A sermon was not considered of any worth unless it was full of arguments against the Arminians; an attack upon the new ideas was considered just as necessary as an attack upon sin. At the van amongst the attackers were Christmas Evans, John Jones, Treffynnon, Thomas Jones, Denbigh, and John Elias. John Elias denounced Wesleyanism mercilessly, and in the heat of oratory occasionally went to extremes. Dr Owen Thomas quoted a witness who heard him preaching on the love of Christ in a Bala Association of 1808:

He had been given much freedom of speech, and when drawing to a close he cried out, 'One further challenge to any devil or Arminian before ceasing – "Who shall separate us from the love of Christ?" – so that the word 'Arminian' was in my mind, for many years, the nearest meaning of any to the word 'devil'.[11]

From the pulpit the debate made its way to the press. The first step in this case was probably the publication by the Wesleyans of a Welsh translation of an essay by John Wesley under the title, *The Eternal Decrees – The Scriptural Doctrines of Predestination, Election and Reprobation.* It appears that some bookseller in south Wales was the translator, and the Wesleyan preachers made a great effort to distribute it throughout the land, particularly in Denbighshire. It certainly caused much agitation. Many wrote against it and among them was Christmas Evans. We cannot follow the controversy here; it culminated in a literary duel between the Rev. Owen Davies, on one side, and the Rev. Thomas Jones, Denbigh, on the other. The Wesleyans were under the disadvantage of not being fluent in Welsh. When translating the works of John Wesley and others, they would write in such an awkward style that it was difficult to understand what they meant; indeed, they almost completely distorted the sense at times. They caused the author to state what he had never intended or ever imagined, and practically every grammatical rule was broken by them. No doubt their lack of knowledge of the language accounted for the distasteful comments found in their books and for their tendency to depend on coarse reviling. Indeed, though the Wesleyans in Wales had by now produced good thinkers and excellent preachers the standard of Welsh that they exhibited from the pulpit and in the press was completely different in character from that of any other denomination.

It is not appropriate here to discuss which of the opposing armies won the day. Both the Wesleyans and the Calvinists thought that they were victorious. But as a controversialist, the Rev. Owen Davies was not to be compared with Thomas Jones, Denbigh. Mr Jones was an excellent scholar possessed of a wide-ranging knowledge of the writings of all the main theologians, old and modern. Furthermore, his mind was exceptionally logical – he would ensure that his conclusions were correctly inferred from the basis of the facts presented. His conscience would not allow him to claim anything that he could not prove, and when quoting from the works of other authors he would give his citations in great detail. The Rev. Owen Davies was quite another type of man. Wesleyan zeal possessed him fully and to overflowing, but his knowledge of biblical doctrines, particularly in their historical development, was very deficient, and his reasoning ability small. But he made up for this by an adventurous fearlessness for expressing whatever came into his head. His proclamations would be oracular and infallible, and he had no appreciation, or at least did not care to appreciate, when it was that they had been refuted by an opponent. At the same time it must be acknowledged that this method of debating, though unfair and clothing ignorance with a mantle of infallibility, accurately reflected the low tastes of an ignorant people. In all probability therefore he was more successful in gaining followers than he would have been had he been an abler thinker and a more learned man. For a season, the Wesleyan preachers were very successful and were the means of establishing very many churches in the land. When the heat of controversy died down however, the Wesleyan chariot made little progress and their Connexion is presently the weakest of all the orthodox Welsh denominations.

We would not have referred to these controversies except that they were the means, some time later, of producing a considerable difference of opinion amongst the Methodists themselves. Any extremes will inevitably produce their opposite extremes. By maintaining a controversy against the Arminians, some of the Calvinistic ministers began preaching something akin to Hyper-Calvinism. Outside the Calvinistic Methodist camp, Christmas Evans went far into this territory, for a period at least. He defended a commercial atonement, with that atonement equivalent in worth to the merited guilt of the sins of the elect. Amongst the Methodists, some preachers concentrated almost exclusively upon the relationship between the gospel and the elect. According to the late Rev. Robert Davies, Llanwyddelen, Montgomeryshire:

> I was at this time in deep concern over my lost estate, with that question in my mind day and night, 'What shall I do to be saved?' . . . About this time the Wesleyans came to Wales and as one man the Methodists rose up to preach against that which they termed Arminianism. Those in my neighbourhood stood squarely for election, limited atonement, the inability of man and the irresistible powers of the gospel. The salvation I heard preached could not be bettered, but it was a salvation for the elect, and I could not dare to think myself a member of that happy family. I did not dare reach forth my hand to grasp that which was theirs for I could not conceive of anything prepared but for them only. I viewed these things as absolute truths, but saw no door through which to enter. I could not climb up to heaven to see if my name was in the Book of Life. When I resolved, in my affliction, to turn my face to the death of the cross for life, the first sermon I heard insisted that nothing was to be found there but for the elect, characterized as 'sheep', 'His own' or 'friends', etc. But in mercy, and that a mercy sufficient as to pay for my life, an ambassador was sent, one called John Roberts of Caernarvonshire (afterwards, Llangwm), who preached Christ crucified without the gate, his death being life, refuge and healing for the ungodly – the chiefest of sinners – who thirst. Now was opened a door of hope for my poor soul in the valley of Achor; the dawn broke on my mind, the clouds were scattered, and I, the chiefest of sinners, was enabled to offer myself to the Almighty Saviour, without worrying my head as to whether I was elect or not.[12]

Mr Davies added :

> My decided opinion is that the Methodists, by their narrow and unwise method of preaching, gave every advantage to their opposers and were instrumental in making as many, if not more, Arminians in Wales than the Arminians themselves. And not only this, but their preaching method placed the sinner convicted of his lost estate at a disadvantage, for there is no other door open by which sinners may approach Christ other than the

general and indiscriminating relationship that pertains between the gospel and sinners.[13]

Amongst those who were for a period preaching an equivalent atonement, that is, equivalent to the merited guilt of the sins of the elect, we must list John Elias. But this extreme Calvinism was a wave that engulfed the Connexion for a short season; it was not approved in any Association, and John Elias and others who had favoured it, soon renounced it completely, regretting that they had ever been led to express such limited views of the atonement of the Lord Jesus. For a description of the ways in which God rescued the Methodists from these narrow doctrines, and maintained the unity of the Spirit amongst them in the bond of peace, we must refer our readers to the biography of John Jones, Talsarn, by the Rev. Owen Thomas, D.D.

[1] Translated by D. E. Jenkins (in his *The Rev. Thomas Charles of Bala*, Vol. 2, p. 72.)

[2] CH, 50, pp. 29.

[3] *The History, Constitution, Rules of Discipline and Confession of Faith of the Calvinistic Methodists of Wales, translated from the Welsh* (Caernarvon, 1877), pp. 13–14.

[4] 'That the churches of Christ from the beginning, and occasionally their predecessors, kept private meetings (apart from the public meetings in which preaching to believers and unbelievers took place) is very evident from the beginning of the Book of Acts to the letters to the seven churches of Asia in the Book of Revelation. Consider the following, and others: Acts 1: 3–15; 2: 1, 4, 23, 21; 6: 2, 6; 11: 1, 4, 22; 12: 12; 13: 1, 2; 14: 22, 23, 27; 15: 1–6, 22, 23, 32, 40, 41; etc. Also, all the Epistles to the various churches in Rome, Corinth, Ephesus, etc., prove this; so that it is indisputable that the original Christians had their private societies.'

[5] 'We mean the following Articles, which are creedal in nature and do not relate to the ecclesiastical order of the Established Church: 1, 2, 4, 5, 6, 7, 9, 10, 11, 13, 15, 17, 18, 19, 25, 27, 28, 31, 38, 39.'

[6] CH, 50, p. 51.

[7] Owen Thomas, *The Atonement Controversy in Welsh Theological Literature and Debate*, 1707–1841, translated by John Aaron (Edinburgh: Banner of Truth, 2002), pp. 26–7.

[8] Ibid., p. 27.

[9] Ibid., pp. 27–28.

[10] Ibid., pp. 28–29.

[11] Ibid., p. 30.

[12] Ibid., p. 289.

[13] Ibid., pp. 289–90.

TOP: LLANFYNYDD, CARMARTHENSHIRE, THE HOME AND BURIAL-PLACE OF BOTH MORGAN RHYS AND DAFYDD REES
MIDDLE: THOMAS CHARLES, BALA. LEFT: A BLACK AND WHITE COPY OF THE PORTRAIT OWNED BY THE BIBLE SOCIETY RIGHT: A PORTRAIT PRINTED IN *THE EVANGELICAL MAGAZINE*, SEPTEMBER 1798
BOTTOM: THOMAS CHARLES'S HOME IN THE MAIN STREET OF BALA

Top: 'Can you recite the text, my dear?'
Bottom Left: Mary Jones on her way to Bala
Bottom Right: Mary Jones's grave in Bryn-crug Cemetery, near Towyn, Merionethshire

Top Left: Richard Owen, Bala   Top Right: Robert Saunderson, Bala
Middle: Bryn-crug Chapel, Towyn. Mary Jones's grave lies behind the chapel
Bottom: The graves of Thomas Charles and Lewis Edwards, Llanycil Cemetery, Bala

Top: Llanycil Church on the banks of Lake Bala
Bottom: These portraits appeared in *The Gospel Magazine* - that on the left in April 1799, of David Griffiths; that on the right in September 1799, of Nathaniel Rowland.

34

THE FIRST ORDINATION AND ITS CONSEQUENCES

EARLY REACTIONS AMONGST THE METHODISTS TO RECEIVING COMMUNION IN THE ESTABLISHED CHURCH

For about seventy-five years, that is from its beginnings up until 1811, the Methodist Connexion depended for the administration of the sacraments upon the clergymen of the Anglican Church. According to *Methodistiaeth Cymru:*

> At the beginning, the number of those called priests, those who had received a bishop's ordination, was sufficient to satisfy the needs of the Connexion in that they were diligent, hard-working men who in their turn visited all areas of the country. And for many years, no complaints were heard of this arrangement.

This last statement is far from the truth. Questions as to the administering of the sacraments arose at the very start of the revival. As early as 1744 many of the members of the *seiadau* expressed their unwillingness to attend communion at the Established Church. In the Trefeca Records we have the account of a Monthly Association held at Llanidloes, 3 May 1744. Noted amongst the other decisions taken is the following:

> ... having before agreed ... not to call the exhorters ministers ... and especially as the scruples of most seem to rise from their corruptions and darkness and not their grace; firstly, looking to, and stumbling at, the faults of others with them receiving, which savours much of the Pharisee pointing at the publican, and betrays too great an ignorance of themselves and want of pity to others; secondly, looking at the meanness or sinfulness of the minister, and saying, 'How can we expect a blessing or receive benefit from such a one, etc.?' which argued a weakness of faith to look through the means to God, looking and depending on the grace of the person administering instead of that in Christ.[1]

Neither Daniel Rowland nor any of the ordained men were present at this meeting. It was chaired by Howell Harris and he, without doubt, is the author of the minute for it clearly has his stamp upon it. How the question arose, whether from a direct request from some of the *seiadau* or because the exhorters reported on a tendency that they had observed, we do not know. But it is clear that a considerable dissatisfaction was present generally because of the Association's directions to the members to receive communion in the Church of England. We see also the two factors that caused the unease – the ignorance and low standard of life of many of the parish priests, and the immoral and godless lives of many of the other communicants.

HOWELL HARRIS'S OPPOSITION TO ORDINATION

In an Association held at Caeo, Carmarthenshire, in the following year, a forceful letter written in a Christian spirit was received from the Groes-wen exhorters asking that they might be ordained so as to be able to administer the sacraments. We have given this letter previously.[2] In it the exhorters explain that they had sought to raise the matter previously but had not been given permission. The Association's reply to this letter is not available – it is doubtful whether it was ever formally acknowledged – but Howell Harris's diary reveals that he was considerably disturbed by the request and considered it as evidence of spiritual pride in its authors. He wrote:

> There was a strict and long examination of the nature, evil, and symptoms of pride and self appearing in the exhorters, and I had some cutting lashes given, but not lasting . . . the Lord did indeed give me a message to deliver to the brethren, most awfulsome and cutting, about humility and poverty of spirit . . . It went mostly about the absolute danger of pride, and how abominable it was to see us [i.e. the exhorters] proud, seeing we have but little gifts, very little knowledge in anything, no learning or parts, mean and contemptible in the eyes of all; and so really, the vilest, etc. [3]

Another similar letter had been received from a society in Monmouthshire. Daniel Rowland was present in the Caeo Association but to what extent he agreed with Howell Harris's comments is not known. If he was of another opinion it does not appear that he expressed it. It is clearly evident that the problem of administering the sacraments had begun to disturb the churches in the various counties at this time. The knot was broken by the Groes-wen church when they ordained Thomas Williams and William Edwards, two of their exhorters, to administer the sacraments amongst them.

The topic appears to have been shelved to some extent for many years after this. Perhaps the main reason for this is that the dispute between Rowland and Harris, which eventually resulted in the Separation, swallowed up all other topics. Harris's peculiar views and his position as a general superintendent became matters of such heated contention and of such serious consequences to the Connexion, that all other matters, ordination included, were forgotten. Yet, not entirely; for we find that in 1751, the New Inn church, Monmouthshire, ordained Morgan John Lewis to administer the sacraments. There is a strong basis for believing that this was done through the direct influence of Daniel Rowland. It seems that the church had sent two representatives to Llangeitho to explain their circumstances: that they were far from the Methodist clergy, that the members would not communicate at the parish church because of the unruly life led by the priests, and that they did not wish to join the Nonconformists. Rowland, having considered the matter, advised them to call Morgan John Lewis as minister over them, with prayer and fasting. He added, 'The prayer of faith will do him more good than the hands of any bishop under the sun.' In a similar way Dafydd Williams was ordained at Aberthyn, that is, by the solemn call of the church and according to Daniel Rowland's guidelines. The church at Mynyddislwyn followed the example of the Groes-wen and New Inn churches.

RECEIVING COMMUNION AT UNCONSECRATED SITES

No more agitation over the ordination of preachers arose during the latter part of the lives of Rowland and Williams, Pantycelyn. The further regions of the country, namely Monmouthshire and Radnorshire, had been lost to Methodism, and no doubt there was an unwillingness to change the original arrangements while the first clergymen were still living. But progress was made on this point in a different direction, namely by administering the sacraments in houses that had not been consecrated. The English Methodists had decided, as early as 1743, that, should parish priests refuse to serve them, they would administer the sacraments in the societies, and there is some evidence that Howell Harris was party to this decision. In the earliest days he was of a more liberal spirit and less committed to the Church than we find him towards the end of his life. As far as we know, the Lord's Supper was not administered by the Welsh Methodists in an unconsecrated building until 1754, when Whitefield opened Woodstock Chapel. He preached on this occasion and, at the close, administered the sacrament. And the sacraments continued to be administered at Woodstock from then on, that is for the 56 years up to the Ordination. Howell

Davies was the man most responsible for this step, but it is certain that he would not have taken it without discussing the matter with his close friend, Daniel Rowland.

In the year 1763, two other unconsecrated sites joined Woodstock as meeting-houses where the sacraments could be received, namely New Chapel, in north Pembrokeshire, and Gwynfil Chapel, Llangeitho. Howell Davies was instrumental in the building of the first, and it was he who preached there at its opening and who first administered the sacraments there. Until the time of the Ordination, believers from the upper parts of Pembrokeshire and the lower regions of Cardiganshire came in great numbers to New Chapel to communicate. Gwynfil Chapel was the meeting-house erected for Daniel Rowland on his excommunication from the Church. After the church doors had been closed against him he administered the sacraments here until the day of his death. Thousands flocked to the chapel to him as they had done previously to Llangeitho church. And as the chapel was much larger than the church it was so much the more convenient. Rowland would often administer also at Woodstock and New Chapel. As far as we know, these are the only unconsecrated sites in the south where the sacraments were administered regularly during Daniel Rowland's lifetime. At the same time it is not improbable that he did so elsewhere, and it is almost certain that he did not refrain from doing so wherever he was encouraged to. The two communionion cups which Rowland would use at Pensarn may still be seen. In 1785 (before Rowland had died) Thomas Charles had begun to administer the sacraments at the Bala chapel, and the multitudes would gather there as they did at Llangeitho.

Soon after the death of the apostle of Llangeitho, the sacraments became available at many other places: at Aberystwyth and Twrgwyn, in Cardiganshire, about the year 1795; at Haverfordwest in Pembrokeshire, and later at Fishguard and Tre-fin. A little before the Ordination the privilege was also extended to Water Street Chapel, Carmarthen. As well as these chapels, great numbers of the Methodists would communicate at those parish churches served by Methodist clergy, such as Nevern, where the Rev. David Griffiths ministered; Llanfyrnach with the Rev. J. Griffiths; and St Dogmaels with the Rev. William Jones.

THE SECOND GENERATION METHODIST CLERGY

The establishment of every one of these unconsecrated sites for administering the sacraments was accomplished in the face of the fiercest opposition from the Methodist clergy. It is worth noting that the second generation of priests who considered themselves Methodists were much narrower in outlook than the first, and much more strongly attached to the Church. Neither Daniel Rowland, Williams Pantycelyn, Howell Davies, Peter Williams, or William Davies, ever received livings in the Church. Though their gifts were so great, not one of them was ever raised higher than a curate, and with the exception of Howell Davies they were not even allowed to remain in that office. The bond that held them to the Church was therefore very weak. But when it came to their successors, very many of them held livings. The Rev. David Jones was vicar of Llan-gan; Griffiths, vicar of Nevern; Jones of St Dogmaels; and Davies of Llanfyrnach. It is natural to assume that their position and livelihood weighed heavily upon them, and it must be confessed that many of them were more Churchmen than they were Methodists.

Of those priests who remained in the Church, the most evangelical and most liberal of spirit, by far, was the Rev. David Jones, Llan-gan. But we find that he feared for his livelihood when the subject of ordination was first raised. Because of their connection with the Established Church the men referred to, with the honourable exception of Jones, Llan-gan, would not communicate in the chapels, and so the work of administering the sacraments in the meeting-houses fell completely upon those clergy who had left the Church. The priests tried to serve two masters. They attended the Methodist Associations and undertook preaching itineraries throughout the country but at the same time they sought to please their bishops and to avoid doing anything that would bring down upon them the frowns of their superiors. Over a period of time they began to refuse to preach in the chapels, at least in the south. When they visited the north, no church door would be open to them and they were therefore obliged to preach in the open air, in homes, and in the chapels as the opportunity arose; but in the south, they eventually refused to preach in the chapels on any account.

We have the history of a Monthly Meeting held at Bwlch-y-groes, Pembrokeshire. On the first evening, Mr John Williams and Mr Evan Harris preached. None of the other unordained men were considered worthy of the honour of such a responsibility. There were present, however, many of the clergy who associated with the Methodists, and among them, Mr Davies, Nevern. They all declined to preach because the meeting was being held in a chapel, and the same two preachers had to be announced for the following morning's services. But God's blessing upon these services was very evident; gracious showers fell heavily upon the congregation and the meeting terminated in much praise and song. And in the middle of his sermon, Mr Harris declared, 'Let us pray, brethren, for the gospel to visit the priests in their churches, or for them to come out to the gospel outside the camp.'

Amongst these priests, the narrowest of them all was the Rev. Nathaniel Rowland. It is very hard to account for the strength of allegiance for the Established Church that possessed him, particularly when we consider the treatment which his father had received at the hands of the bishops. Perhaps personal wealth and social respectability had blinded him and he considered himself too great a personage to mix with the Methodists, other than when he would descend upon them as a king during their associations. Yet he was completely inconsistent. At Haverfordwest he regularly preached at an unconsecrated chapel and administered the sacraments there, and it appears that there were two other chapels under his care. But abroad on his journeys he would refuse to darken the door of any chapel. When he came to Fishguard he would not go near the chapel on any account. He would preach in the church, and after having preached he would go to the house of an old widow who was an invalid and there, in a small room that was totally inconvenient, he would administer communion. Those who were full members of the Methodists had to accompany him there, or else be deprived of the sacred ordinance. The religious amongst the people would plead with him again and again to come to the chapel, but he would refuse. If they persisted, he would lose his temper and say, in his anger, 'No, I will never come.' And in this, he kept to his word.

It was Nathaniel Rowland therefore who would oppose any request that would arise for additional places where the people might communicate. In an Association at Carmarthen, Mr David Charles, before he had begun to preach, asked for permission to administer the ordinances in that town.

'The church in this town,' he said, 'have charged me to ask on their behalf, May they be given the privilege to meet together in remembrance of the death of their Redeemer?'

Nathaniel Rowland rose up in some agitation:

'No, you may not,' he shouted loudly. 'The church at Llanlluan is near enough for you.'

This was an old Anglican church that was empty and had been taken over by the Methodists. It was out in the country, about ten miles away, and on an unfrequented road. But Nathaniel Rowland thought it acceptable to send the Carmarthen Methodists there, for all its inconvenience, because it had received episcopal consecration, rather than allow them to commune in peace in their own chapel.

But David Charles was a determined man who would not be thwarted purely on the whim of Nathaniel Rowland.

'I ask again,' he said, 'may we have this privilege? We are permitted to preach Christ, to profess him and to believe in him; may we not remember that he died for us?'

'No you may not, in this place', said Mr Rowland, no doubt with increasing ire as he sensed that his judgment was being questioned.

'I was not charged to bring this request to yourself,' said Mr Charles, 'but to the Society.'

At this, the heart of Mr Jones, Llan-gan was thoroughly overcome. It seems that it was he who was in the Chair, and he cried out, 'You may.' And in his uniquely friendly way, he turned to Mr Charles, saying,

'When do you want it, Deio *bach*? I will come to help you remember him.'

The chairman's reply drove Nathaniel Rowland into an awful temper; he fell upon him mercilessly. But for all his efforts, the communion was held at Carmarthen from then on.

Mr Griffiths, Nevern, was of the same spirit as Nathaniel Rowland. Any increase in the number of places where the sacraments could be administered was completely unacceptable to him, and he would become incensed whenever the question would arise. In a Monthly Meeting in Pembrokeshire, a request came from St David's that they might have permission to hold communion there, whenever one of the clergy might be passing on an itinerary. The request, we may be sure, was perfectly reasonable and the elder who presented it was noted for his wisdom and moderation. But to the Rev. David Griffiths the nature of his message was as a red rag to a bull.

'You do not truly desire a more frequent administration of the ordinances,' he said. 'You are wanting to join with the Dissenters.'

'Not at all, sir.' replied Mr W. Williams, who had presented the request. 'You come to administer communion to us, and there will be no ordaining in this county for as long as you live.'

This reply quietened Mr Griffiths for a while, but he soon repeated his accusation:

'I see that you insist on becoming Dissenters.'

This was the bogey that terrified the clergy, a fear that the Methodists would join the Nonconformists. Perhaps it was this that made them narrower in their outlook than they would otherwise have been, and caused them to tighten that cord (by now almost non-existent) which kept the Methodists bound to the Established Church. It is easy to see that a great gulf had opened up between them and the people. While they pulled in the direction of the Church, the people pulled in the opposite direction.

The leaders of the common people in the south were Ebenezer Morris, Ebenezer Richard and David Charles. These were men who were looked up to as teachers, and although much respect was afforded to those who had received episcopal ordination, their yoke was becoming unbearable and their influence fast disappearing.

At the beginning of the nineteenth-century, the position of the Methodists as regards the administering of the ordinances was as follows:

(1) Many communicated in the parish church and took their babies to be baptized by the parish priest. The numbers in this category were greater on average in the south than in Gwynedd. In the south a good many clergy sympathized with the Methodists and attended their Associations. Others were at least half-Methodist and respected the Revival and the Methodist members, whilst they themselves kept within the confines of their parishes. It does not appear that this latter group was to be found in the north. The three clergymen who lived there had turned their backs on the Church completely.

(2) Other members communicated only in the chapels that had been appointed to that purpose by the Society. Though many would congregate once a month at the Communion Service at Bala, we tend to believe that communion would also be administered in every society in the north, before the Ordination, whenever an ordained priest would be visiting.

It is easy to see that the whole situation was unstable and that the order, or rather the disorder, of things which then prevailed amongst the Methodists could not last for long.

RECEIVING COMMUNION IN THE CHURCH BECOMING IMPOSSIBLE

It was becoming impossible for the members to continue communicating at the parish churches. One reason for this was the immoral lives of many of the clergy. It is useless to try to deny that many of those who had received holy orders at this time were leading unworthy lives. This is presently acknowledged even by Anglican historians. It is easy to understand therefore why spiritual men, with the fear of God in their hearts, would strongly oppose the receiving of the elements from drunken creatures, more used to the wantonness of the tavern. One could easily argue with these believers, as Howell Harris did in the Associations, that such an opposition implied a lack of faith, that the blessing did not depend on the degree of grace in the man who administered at the table, but on the grace which is in Christ Jesus, and that they should look beyond the priest to the Lord Jesus. Yet the prejudice against receiving the sacrament from a man known to be immoral remained, and it must be acknowledged that it is a healthy prejudice.

It was not the officiating priest alone who was suspected of not being regenerate. At the table one met with others of the same character as he, of unclean lives, filthy language, leaders in ungodliness and licentiousness. Not without much pain could one attempt to remember the death of the glorious Redeemer in the midst of such company. In the north particularly, the priest, at whose hands the Methodists were obliged to receive the elements, would be known as their chief persecutor, who encouraged the mob to harass them. Godly parents experienced the same disinclination to take their babies to be baptized by such priests. Some would go to nearby Nonconformist ministers whilst others would neglect this sacred ordinance altogether. Clearly, continuing to communicate at the parish church was becoming out of the question for most Methodists; the practice was inevitably coming to an end.

Another reason against communicating at the church was that it made church discipline impossible. The Methodists were eager to maintain the purity of the society; they would not tolerate failure. They rebuked sharply those who fell into sin, without making any distinction between high or low; and if a sincere repentance was not forthcoming they would excommunicate the wrongdoer immediately. But the Anglican priest would take no notice whatsoever of the discipline of the societies. Indeed he could not; he was to administer the elements to all who approached 'to the altar'. The Methodists therefore, after excommunicating a man for gross immorality and declaring him unworthy of the company of the saints, might possibly have to meet him, holding his head as high as any, at the Lord's Table the following Sunday. There is a record of Mr Ebenezer Richard, Tregaron, Cardiganshire, excommunicating a man. There was no question as to the correctness of the discipline; the man had been proved guilty of public drunkenness on more than one occasion and the whole fraternity had agreed on the judgment passed upon him. On the first Sabbath after this had occurred, the elder who had brought the charge against him had to meet him at the communion table. When Mr Richard heard of this and after he had found out by careful questioning that what he had heard was perfectly true and that similar occurrences were often experienced, he was stirred to the depths and stated, with characteristic determination, 'I cannot tolerate this without attempting to change it.'

It was becoming impossible to depend upon the Methodist clergy for the administration of the ordinances. As we have already shown, the Methodists increased enormously in churches and membership at the end of the eighteenth and the beginning of the nineteenth centuries, particularly so in Gwynedd. As a result of the formation of Sunday Schools and as the fruit of the powerful revivals that had stirred up the whole country, hundreds had joined the churches that had already been formed, and many new churches had been established. The natural consequence was a need for more men to administer the sacraments. The lack of ordained men in the north was extreme. Only three clergy had there joined the Methodists: the Rev. Thomas Charles in 1785; the Rev. Simon Lloyd in 1789; and the Rev. William Lloyd, Caernarvon, in 1795. The thousands of Methodists in the north depended almost exclusively on these three men for opportunity to remember the death of the cross, and for the baptism of their babies. And what were these three among such a number? Occasionally, one of the Methodist clergy from the south would pass through the north and advantage would be taken of his presence to administer the ordinances, on weekdays as well as on the Sabbath. The Rev. John Williams, Pantycelyn, itinerated through Gwynedd in 1800 in company with John Prytherch, Defynnog. In a letter to his brother he mentions that during each day he had travelled an average of fifteen miles, preached three times, and administered communion twice.

Notwithstanding these occasions, the provision of the Lord's Table in the north was completely irregular. Months would pass, sometimes years even, without an opportunity for members to communicate, and parents would often be forced to take their children to the ministers of other denominations to be baptized. Nor was there any indication that an improvement in circumstances would arise in the future, in that no further clergymen showed any signs of throwing in their lot with the Methodists. On the contrary, unless some relief appeared from somewhere the administration of the ordinances would cease altogether amongst the Methodists in the north in some twenty years or so at most, in that the three men referred to were getting older. As far as Gwynedd was concerned the Methodists would not exist, as a distinct grouping, for more than another twenty years, unless they ordained ministers from among themselves, or were satisfied to do without the sacraments. Such a choice would of course deprive them of one of the highest privileges of religion, and also be contrary to the express commandment of the Lord Jesus.

Things were very different in the south. Here at least eleven clergymen associated to more or less of a degree with the Methodists, but only two of them had completely separated from the Church, namely, the Revs. John Williams, Pantycelyn, and John Williams, Lledrod. The others all held livings and were therefore too bound to their homes to be able to satisfy the needs of the churches throughout the country. Also, as we have shown, they were daily becoming more and more Established in their loyalties and had begun to refuse to communicate in the chapels. Yes, even in those chapels to which they had been set apart by the Association, and where Daniel Rowland, Howell Davies and Williams, Pantycelyn, had administered the sacraments in their day! In Glamorganshire, Carmarthenshire and Pembrokeshire the administration of the ordinances in unconsecrated houses fell almost completely upon Mr Jones, Llan-gan, assisted by Mr Howell Howells, Tre-hill. Nobody was available in Cardiganshire, except the Rev. John Williams, Lledrod. Nor was there any to be found that could take their place after their death. The difference between south and north was therefore only superficial. The continuance of Methodism as a separate denomination in the south, as much as in the north, depended completely on the ordaining of preachers to the full work of the ministry from within its own ranks.

THE QUESTION IS FIRST RAISED IN SOUTH CARDIGANSHIRE

The debate over Ordination appears to have begun about 1806. It arose from a pure accident. Mr Gray used to communicate monthly at Ffos-y-ffin, and although to all practical purposes he was a Methodist at the time and Ffos-y-ffin Chapel has never at any time belonged to the Independents, yet it was on the basis of Independent ordination that he administered, following the Nonconformist order of service. Many of the Methodists of Pensarn, Twrgwyn and Blaenannerch would communicate with Mr Gray. One day, quite by accident, a number of godly brethren and sisters happened to meet at the home of a sister who was a member at Pensarn. She was probably an invalid, deprived of the means of grace, and they had met together to hold a prayer meeting with her. Once the meeting was over they began to discuss various matters, including Mr Gray's communion services at Ffos-y-ffin and the irregularity of the administering of the sacraments amongst the Methodists. After a while, a woman noted for much common sense as well as grace, asked,

'Why may we not have our own preachers, whose ministry is accompanied by so much blessing, to administer the ordinances amongst us?'

The question produced complete silence; no one had any answer to give. The most eminent of the clergymen, and Mr Gray also, could hardly be compared as far as their preaching abilities were concerned with the majesty and influence of Ebenezer Morris, Ebenezer Richard, Thomas Richard or John Elias, and the respect of the people towards them was correspondingly lower. After a long silence, there came an answer, 'I do not know.' 'Nor I,' said another. And the others could only provide the same response.

The next day, or the one following, Ebenezer Morris was to preach and to lead a society meeting at Pensarn, according to his usual custom. The gathering at the invalid sister's home decided to present the same question to him. An opportunity arose at the end of the service when many others were present as well as some officer bearers.

'Why not?' said Mr Morris. 'Why not indeed? It is you, the church societies, that are to blame. You are responsible because you have not called us to the work, and settled us in proper order in it.'

As a result of his words all agreed that the matter should be raised at the next Association and that they should not rest until their aims had been achieved.

Thus the stone began to roll, and thus it would now take its course until it arrived at the valley floor. The discussion spread throughout the area and as there were so many preachers and exhorters travelling the country at that time it was not long before the topic was a matter of debate throughout the Principality. Indeed, the friends from Pensarn did no more than express feelings that were already widespread. Many before them had asked the same question in their hearts and had failed to find an answer. In his autobiography, the Rev. E. Griffiths[4] of Meifod has written:

> The brethren of old used to go to the parish church many times a year to partake of the Lord's Supper, and they would encourage other members to do so also in that they would scarcely receive communion from the ministers of the Connexion (that is from the Methodist clergymen) more than once a year. But only once could I bring myself to go with them because of the false doctrine taught, the immorality of the priest and of those with whom I would communicate. Once I stopped going, the practice was not long continued with. The loss, and the failure to receive the ordinance, weighed heavily on my mind, causing me often to cry to the Lord in secret to equip the Church with the breasts of the ordinances. But I had to live through many years of sadness, despairing of seeing it in my lifetime.

By 'equipping the Church with the breasts of the ordinances', Mr Griffiths is referring to a regular and frequent administration of the sacraments in the Methodist churches, by means of ministers ordained from among themselves. All the evidence suggests that this desire was both deep and general, but that before this time all were somehow too frightened to speak. By now also, the influence of the Rev. Nathaniel Rowland was fast disappearing and before long it would be necessary to excommunicate him.

The next objective, if the decision of the Pensarn fraternity was to be carried out, was to find someone who would present the matter clearly and fairly before the Association. Ebenezer Morris and his friends were well aware of the enormity of the responsibility that they had undertaken and of the extent of the obstacles before them. They knew that the clergymen would certainly oppose them fiercely. Not only was it natural for the clergy to be jealous of the dignity of the office to which they had been ordained, but there was also the fact that their monopoly of the administration of the ordinances to the Methodists represented a not inconsiderable source of money for them, of which they would lose a large proportion should the unordained preachers be allowed to share the responsibility. Many respectable families had joined the Methodists and these were in the habit of contributing freely of their gold and silver at the close of the Communion service. It was accepted that this offering was the property of the officiating priest. It is known that Jones, Llan-gan, and, perhaps, Griffiths, Nevern, received more from the communion offering than anything they obtained from their Anglican livings. It was natural therefore for them to oppose Ordination, and Ebenezer Morris could foresee their objections. The wealthier families also, over whom the clergy had a strong hold, would probably side with them. Consequently it was necessary that the person who was to bring the matter to the attention of the Association should understand the situation thoroughly, should be capable of arguing strongly and with much clarity, should nor shrink from the task when attacked, and should possess some measure of influence within the Connexion. Mr Morris sought long and hard for such a person but was unsuccessful. The 'people of influence' were uneasy about accepting such a charge; partly because of their own great importance and partly because it would bring upon them the frowns of the clergy and would make them the target of many a poison-tipped arrow.

EVAN DAVIES AND EBENEZER MORRIS PRESENT THE MATTER TO THE ASSOCIATION

Eventually a standard-bearer was found in the person of Evan Davies, Pensarn, or, as he was known colloquially, 'Evan Twrgwyn', the father of the Rev. Jenkin Davies, Twrgwyn, and the grandfather of Mr David Jenkin Davies, Aberystwyth. Evan Davies was an elder who, though short in body, was a deep thinker. As a rule he spoke little, but whenever he did so it was as one who had authority. It was always very quickly evident that he had mastered his topic. He possessed a truly religious spirit; his character was transparent, nobody doubted him; he was completely without fear; and, to his very great advantage, he had complete control of his temper. In every difficult matter, he was Ebenezer Morris's chief counsellor. This was the man appointed to impress upon the Llangeitho Association the appropriateness of ordaining Methodist preachers to the task of administering the ordinances.

The day of the Association dawned. Jones, Llan-gan, was in the chair. Evan Jones got to his feet and presented his case. He spoke with perfect self-possession but with due humility. He showed how irregular was the administration of the sacraments among them as a Connexion and stated that he feared that the churches were being let down. But his words were as white-hot sparks to the feelings of the clergy present – we do not know if they had been forewarned that the matter was to be brought forward – and when his intentions were fully comprehended, he was immediately interrupted by a loud shout from one of the priests:

'Who is that man who is speaking? Turn him out. It is a disgrace to tolerate such a man amongst us. Out he goes, without any more ado.'

This command to turn out the speaker is usually attributed to Mr Jones, Llan-gan, but Mr David Jones, Dolaubach, stated categorically that it was said by Griffiths, Nevern. We tend to believe that he is correct; the action is much more typical of Griffiths than of the old evangelist from Llan-gan. It may be that it is because he was in the chair that this has been attributed to Mr Jones.

Before anyone carried out the command, Mr James James, Penblaen, a powerful preacher, who feared no man, got up:

'Wait,' he said, 'It may be that the gentleman has a message for us; and it would be utterly unreasonable to turn him out before we consider the nature and content of that message.'

The moment he sat down, John Elias was on his feet:

'If our brother was presenting his case before a court of law he would receive a respectful hearing and what he had to say would receive attention. Are we, religious people, going to treat the members of Christ's Church with less respect and mercy than is received by any citizen before the magistrates.'

At this, the priests lost all self-control with many of them shouting out across one another. They presented few arguments; most of their protests were but condemnations of the 'troublers'; there was a danger that the meeting would end in uproar. But there were others, in addition to Evan Davies, who were completely self-possessed amongst the disturbance; men like Thomas Jones, Denbigh, Ebenezer Morris, and David Rees, Llanfynydd. One of these, Ebenezer Morris, rose to his feet and having obtained a measure of quiet, suggested that, in view of the fact that the matter under consideration was so important and so likely to produce serious repercussions within the Connexion in the future, it would be appropriate to set aside a day of prayer and fasting, that all might go before God on their knees in supplication for one another and for the success of the great Mediator's cause amongst them. This was enough to melt Mr Jones, Llangan, who possessed the gentlest of tempers and most religious of spirits, and with hands clasped and loud weeping, he cried out:

'For goodness' sake, dear brethren, do not pray me out of the world. I will be out of your way soon enough.'

His words, 'do not pray me out of the world', prove that, in his heart, he was convinced that it was those in favour of Ordination who were on heaven's side of the question. Furthermore, we also believe that he had already taken part in the ordinations that had occurred within Lady Huntingdon's Connexion.

Thus ended the first Association in which Ordination was discussed. One who was present said it was more like a parish vestry than a religious meeting. Yet the ferocity of the response worked in favour of the motion. It was the means of drawing much attention to the issue, and of bringing it forward as a matter of debate in many Monthly Meetings. All this occurred about the year 1806. Having set his hand to the plough, Mr Evan Davies was not one to turn back, and in an Association afterwards held at Cardigan he stood up again and raised the same question. Mr Griffiths, Nevern, who was most probably chairing this meeting, saw fit to shout out, as he did in Llangeitho:

'Turn out that man. He attends these sessions purely to cause trouble and split the cause. Out with him.'

'Mr Griffiths,' replied Mr Davies,' the great chariot proceeds forth. Take care that you do not stand in its way, lest you be trodden underfoot, as happened to the prince in the gate of Samaria.'

At that, Ebenezer Morris got to his feet. He was the most able of all the Methodists preachers of the south and the most influential. He would not have Mr Griffiths and the other clergy agitated but rather that they would prudently consider the issue and discuss it fairly in the spirit of the gospel. He added:

> I would be content and happy without this Ordination which is so much spoken of, if I could believe myself innocent on Judgment Day of being deaf to the appeals, and careless of the needs, of the churches; I would never refer to the matter again. But I am afraid of keeping silent or being careless, in case God would call me and my brethren to give an account for that carelessness.

It is said that Mr Morris's demeanour when he spoke in this way was solemn in the extreme. The priests trembled in his presence and none of them dared to question the complete accuracy and seriousness of his statement. His words recovered the equilibrium of the meeting. Opportunity was obtained to discuss the topic relatively peacefully. The clergy argued that in the New Testament it was the bishops only who had the authority to ordain; that in their present form, namely as a reformed extension of, but still in connection with the Established Church, and receiving the sacraments from the hands of the priests, God had blessed them. Changes to this old order of things might bring about the danger of displeasing God. But Ebenezer Morris was a stronger disputer than any of the clergy and mightier in the Scriptures. In addition he possessed complete self-control and he succeeded in overturning all their arguments. At the end of the Association it was felt that he had gained complete victory.

THE DEBATE CONTINUES

It is only fair to note that not all the south Wales clergy were opposed to ordination. Four of them supported it, namely the Revs John Williams, Pantycelyn; John Williams, Lledrod; Howell Howells, Tre-hill; and William Howells, Long Acre. The latter had in fact taken part in a service of ordination amongst the Methodists, though not the very first such. It does not appear that John Williams contributed in any way to the discussion. The state of his health and his recurring physical weakness prevented him from attending the Associations, but in spirit he was in complete sympathy with the movement. But as for Williams, Lledrod, he was so deeply convinced of the matter that not only did he argue for it in the conferences but he also preached on the topic. The opposing clergy did not dare to do this, and the preachers did not care to do so in case they were accused of seeking their own gain, but it seemed entirely appropriate for Mr Williams to do so. He used a variety of texts to this purpose. Once, his text was Psalm 122:6, 'Pray for the peace of Jerusalem: they shall prosper that love thee.' Mr David Jones, Dolaubach, with his wonderful memory, used to describe Mr Williams preaching on the topic from Matthew 14:24, 'But the ship was now in the midst of the sea, tossed with waves: for the wind was contrary.' From these words he drew the following comments:

1. That to meet with oppositions while undertaking any matter is not an indication of the sinfulness of the undertaking. The disciples had taken to sea in obedience to Christ's command, and yet they had encountered these cross-winds.

2. That the strength and the safety of the disciples of Jesus Christ, as they fulfilled their duties, lay in the fact that Christ was on the mountain, praying for them.

3. That the happy conclusion for all who persevere faithfully in their course, even in the face of difficulties, is that Christ will come to them and still the storm.

Mr Williams applied these comments, with great skill and much power, to the question of ordination.

It was not only in the Associations that the matter was the topic of conversation; it would be the issue discussed whenever and wherever preachers and elders happened to meet. Fierce debates upon it would often spring up in the lodging houses after services. We have already referred to the opposition of the elders of the Llangeitho district to ordination. It is only right to note that this was due to the influence upon them of local clergy such as Mr Lloyd, Cilpill, and Mr Jones, Glanmarch. These two, both very fierce opposers of the movement, were particularly influential not only because of their office but because they were powerful preachers and also owners of much local lands. The elders feared for their livelihoods if they went against these men. Mr Williams, Lledrod, would often argue with these elders, exposing their inconsistency and stubbornness. According to Mr Jones, Dolaubach:

> I heard him often arguing with the old elders who were zealous for the old order, rebuking them severely. 'I cannot imagine what would satisfy you, you foolish men', he would say, 'Regular clergymen will not do, nor nonconformist ministers either. It has to be an excommunicated clergyman for you; nothing else will please you.'

No doubt the words of the old priest of Lledrod were as salt on a wound.

The opposition to ordination was nothing like as strong in the north. Only three clergymen were associated with the Methodists in the whole region: Mr Charles, Mr Simon Lloyd, and Mr W. Lloyd, Caernarvon, and not one of these held a living in the Established Church. It appears that only Mr Charles from amongst them took part in the debate. It must be said that for many years he persisted in being a strong opposer and carried his opposition so far as to endanger the good relationship existing between himself and his brethren. We have expressed the view previously that Mr Charles was not opposed to ordination in theory. He was not prejudiced in favour of episcopal ordination, nor did he doubt the right of the Connexion to set apart men to the work of ministry. Rather, he feared division. He saw that the Methodist clergy were held in much respect in the land and that they were determined to fight against the new proposals. He therefore feared the consequences, foreseeing that Ordination would result in irreparable damage. It is certain that this was his point of view, for we have his own testimony on the matter. In a memoir of the Rev. Evan Griffiths, Meifod, part of which was written by Mr Griffiths himself, we find a note of a conversation between himself and Mr Charles on the topic. He states:

> While talking to the late Rev. Thomas Charles from Bala, many years before the first Ordination, he told me that he was greatly distressed, longing that such a thing (the setting aside of preachers to the full work of the ministry) might be a part of the work of the Body. He said that he could not see that we were ready for that at present without it causing a division or too much of a tendency to Independency, and that he therefore preferred to appear opposed to the notion, until he saw a greater maturity for it. This conversation gave me a new heart to wait and pray for the day, and many a wave passed after that before the first ordaining. And when I heard that every county was being called upon to agree to set aside some of the preachers my mind was considerably cheered.

No one can doubt the veracity of Mr Griffiths's testimony. He was well known for his honesty as well as his godliness, and was writing this account purely as a memoir of his own knowledge of the debate and with no polemical motive whatsoever. He would never have thought that any controversy on the matter would ever have arisen. We see from what he said to Mr Griffiths that not only was Mr Charles not opposed to ordination but that he desired it, that he longed for it to be brought about, and that his opposition to it over many years was due only to his judgment that the body was not then ready for a step of such importance.

THE DEBATE IN NORTH WALES

The main supporters of ordination in Gwynedd were John Elias, Robert Jones, John Evans and Thomas Jones, Denbigh. They would express their thoughts boldly on the matter; they did not fear being falsely accused of ambition and worldly presumption. They felt that faithfulness to God and the need of the churches of the land called upon them to speak out. Because of his outstanding gifts of oratory, John Elias was the most public of them in his support, yet it was perhaps Thomas Jones who was the greatest influence, and committed his thoughts to writing so clearly and prudently that it is impossible to mistake his meaning. In a letter to a friend, he wrote as follows:

> 1. The Scriptures seem to me to be quite clear and definite in commanding the practice of the two sacraments in the Church of Christ, and also of requiring the administration of the Lord's Supper more frequently, if not more regularly in timing, than is the practice amongst us.
>
> 2. I cannot remember reading of the visible church being depicted by any writer other than as a congregation of God's people possessing the Word of God being faithfully preached and the sacraments having their due place amongst them.
>
> 3. I note that baptism, in the ordinary sense of speaking, is not administered amongst us.
>
> 4. That in many of our societies there are many people who are very unwilling to have their children baptized in the Church of England and by her ministers. It appears that this unwillingness, together with the number of those who manifest it, is on the increase; and as far as communicating in the Church of England is concerned, very few indeed of our people practise it.
>
> 5. That many of our fellow-members, it is said, are undoubtedly pained in their consciences by being pressed to have their children baptized in the Church of England, by unawakened ministers, etc.
>
> 6. That many, from more than one consideration, seek the ordinance at the hands of ministers of other bodies, although with some uncertainty of mind.
>
> 7. That to encourage any of our members to seek either of the sacraments outside the circle of our own Connexion is something of which we should not be guilty. It would be contrary to God's Word and to the common practice of God's Church in every age and country.
>
> These are the considerations which strike me forcibly and which convince my mind; and ever since I have dwelt at this town, it is the last few points, by even more convincing examples, which have weighed most heavily upon my mind. I have often attempted to examine myself and to discern my motives, with prayer to the Lord to enlighten me, to restrain me and to rule me, lest I be led by any selfish or sinful tendency, and entrapped into becoming a cause of disturbance in God's church. And now, though I feel myself to be a most corrupt and sinful creature, I cannot but say that as far as I am able to judge, my aim is sincere and honest. Also, the cause is good and important. If I have in any way wandered in motivation, practice or method, may the Lord convict and reform me.

The thorough sincerity of these words is plain to see; it is evident that their author was eminently conscientious and very aware of the need for innocence of purpose. There is no date to the letter but many of its phrases – especially the last sentence, 'If I have in any way wandered…' – prove that it was written after its author had ventured to administer the sacraments before being ordained to that end by the Association. The letter reveals Mr Jones's views on the matter of the sacraments, views which he arrived at only after much research, deep deliberation and fervent prayer for divine guidance.

We note also parts of a letter which Thomas Jones wrote to Mr Daniel Jones, Liverpool, about the end of the year 1809 or the beginning of 1810. Daniel Jones was the son of the Rev. Robert Jones, Rhoslan, and a preacher with the Methodists. Thomas Jones and he were close friends. The letter reads:

> In that my dear and respected friend, Mr T. Edwards, in his last letter to me, has warned me solemnly *not to have anything to do with those given to revolutions*, to this you will perhaps say, 'Amen, and Amen'. And he (Mr T. Edwards) gives me, and others *who are notable men*, the counsel of guarding against that spirit manifested in Numbers 12:2, and appearing in Sheba, son of Bichri, in 2 Samuel 20:1. These warnings, truly, are solemn and important. I have therefore to consider that my dear friend would not attempt so to apply them to me were he not influenced by strong fears, or serious impressions of mind. Therefore, while assuring him that I am not in any way offended, I will attempt a serious and respectful reply, in sincere brotherly love. The God of Israel knows, and Israel shall know, that we do not in any way seek to foment trouble nor encourage discord and division in the churches of Christ, we rather love peace and unity when they may be found on terms of truth and sanctity. But we are raising our voices on behalf of Christ's Church, which is crying out for that which her Husband has obtained for her, and we cannot do less than be a mouthpiece for her to argue her cause.
>
> You are troubled in case I am tempted to be envious of that most respected and valuable gentleman, who, by God's mercy, was raised as a notable and powerful instrument in God's hand for north Wales for the furtherance of his kingdom and glory. These are exactly my own thoughts of him and as such I love him with my whole heart and hold him in the greatest respect possible. I can say quite sincerely that there is no other man on earth from whom I am less likely to differ over spiritual matters than Mr Charles, and I would wish to add, may the Lord use him, sustain him, and prosper him more and more to the glory of his grace for many years to come until the end of his life and then for endless ages. And all this I hope and believe he will do, in that he has begun a good work in him. Yet notwithstanding this, in the present matter I cannot, before God and before his Word, agree with that which he expressed as his wish, in accord with our respected father, Mr Jones of Llan-gan. And I must now confess that I have been tempted at times to be angry with dear Mr Charles. As a poor sinner I am not safe from this, nor any other corruption seen in hell. But while it is always appropriate for me to lament my sinfulness

in this matter as in all other matters that I undertake, I believe I may, by the infinite mercy of God, state distinctly that neither envy, prejudice, nor self-interest has had dominion in my heart but that I have the testimony of a good conscience towards God and man.

That which I, or rather, we desire is this: that some qualified person be appointed to baptize the infants *of however many desire this and ask for it in our churches;* and when there is a real need, and when there is no one of the clergy at hand at the time, to administer the other ordinance to however many of our churches as desire and ask for it. I believe that God's Word is clear on this matter, as in Matthew 28:19, together with many other verses, many of which advocate the frequent receiving of the Lord's Supper. Presently we profess to 'teach' and 'make disciples', but we allow others to 'baptize'. In addition, as far as I have been able to discover, there has never been another body of people anywhere in the world nor in any age, from the first preaching of the gospel until now, who, having received the ordinances as part of their creed, have then deprived themselves of the practice of one or both of those sacraments to the extent that we have been doing. And therefore, quite apart from the fact that some of our members are forced to bring their children before wicked clergymen for baptism, or before Nonconformists, though they might long to have them baptized by some of their own religious teachers, is not the following Scripture, although written for another, less important, purpose, applicable to us – 1 Corinthians 11:16, 'But if any man seem to be contentious, we have no such custom, neither the churches of God.' If we are presently in the right it must be that all the churches of God have been wrong over this. It is true that this is how the Methodists first arranged matters, and that the Lord has greatly prospered them. Yet, I believe that they must seek a reformation for the better, just as Whitefield and his friends did, as also the Countess of Huntingdon, etc. . . .

Furthermore, I truly believe that if you knew how much I have had to endure over this cause, you would sympathize greatly with me. With a view to this matter, may the Word of God rule above everything else in your heart, then I believe that you will not only desire that the two sacraments have their place in our churches, but you will yourself cast your vote firmly to this end. I intend to write to Mr Charles within a few days. I hope the Lord will enable me to write with the respect which is due, and with Christian love and faithfulness. If I have gone astray in any action, word or thought, may the Lord forgive, and may he also guide Mr Charles by his counsel, and apply the remedies of grace if he also has wandered to any degree. Continue to pray for the peace of Zion and for righteousness to shine forth as a burning lamp. Pray for your unworthy friend, Thomas Jones.

The *'T. Edwards'* mentioned above, was Mr Thomas Edwards, Liverpool, a well-known preacher among the Methodists. He was born in Llanelidan,

Denbighshire, but moved to Liverpool when a youth of twenty years old. He began to preach about the year 1789 and continued in the work until his death. Thomas Jones and he were contemporaries, and the closest of friends. The letter suggests many things:

1. It shows us quite clearly that Mr Thomas Edwards (and Daniel Jones also to some extent perhaps) had doubts concerning the issue of ordination and that he particularly opposed Mr Thomas Jones's action in administering the ordinances before he was ordained, judging him, like Korah, Dathan and Abiram, as having taken upon himself an office to which he had not been called by the Lord. No doubt there were many of the preachers and elders who had similar views.

2. That Mr Jones, Denbigh, was an excellent church historian, and that in forming an opinion upon any doctrinal or ecclesiastical matter, he would lay great stress on the beliefs and practice of Christ's Church from its beginnings. It was no small matter to him in this context that every branch of the Christian Church that acknowledged the sacraments, with the sole exception of the Methodists, had drawn up arrangements for the frequent administration of both ordinances. He seriously questions whether it was possible for the Methodists to be alone correct and all other churches to be in the wrong.

3. Although he was a doughty debater and capable in the heat of battle of using strong words, it can be seen that he was very successful at maintaining control of his spirit. He does not descend to vituperation in any way nor suggests anything unworthy of his opponents.

4. That his friendship with Mr Charles continued throughout. It would be most useful to discover the letters of correspondence between these two good men. Is there no hope that they may yet see the light of day? But with the evidence that we have it is as clear as the sun that their friendship continued unbroken even though they held opposing views.

We cannot follow all the details of the debate. The Methodist camp was thoroughly agitated by the affair. Heated argument took place not only in the Quarterly Meetings and Associations but also in the private societies, personally between preachers and elders, and by letter. The main supporters of ordination within the Association, as we have previously mentioned, were Thomas Jones, Denbigh, in the north and Ebenezer Morris in the south. The latter was very effectively supported by two other, very popular preachers, Ebenezer Richard and John Thomas, Cardigan. The main activity of these two was by private conversation, they were not ready to take a prominent part in the Associations and perhaps they did not possess the necessary courage. But as for Mr Morris, he feared no one. It is easy to see that all rational arguments belonged to the supporters of ordination; the priests were mainly characterized more by prejudice and uncontrolled hot tempers. As well as the pride of office and the superiority that they felt they possessed because of their ordination by bishops, they could see that their source of income was endangered. As we have noted, the administration of the sacraments resulted in much flow of money to the coffers of the clergy, and, in that many of the lay preachers were superior to them in preaching ability, they feared that if these were ordained they would receive more calls to minister communion, with a considerable loss to themselves resulting.

Mr Williams, Lledrod, confessed openly that this fear exerted a strong influence on his mind for a time, so much so that he was very near to being ensnared. He states:

> I was foolish enough to oppose the ordaining of ministers, until Christ himself came to me and asked, 'Have you ever been without anything?' And I had to reply, 'No, Lord.'

Another time, he states:

> I used to fear what would become of me if the preachers were ordained, but the Old and New Testaments so spoke to me that Doubting Castle came tumbling down. This is what the Old said to me, 'For the Lord thy God blessed thee in all the works of thy hand: he knoweth thy walking through this great wilderness: these forty years the Lord thy God hath been with thee: thou hast lacked nothing.' Thus the Old; and the New repeated the message, 'When I sent you without purse, and scrip, and shoes, lacked ye anything?' Before the testimony of both Testaments I had to cry out, 'Unbelief, be quiet.'

The reference in the verse to forty years was particularly apposite in that this was exactly the period for which Mr Williams had been in the ministry. Having been thoroughly convinced himself, he did his best both publicly and privately to support his brethren.

Dafydd Edwards, Pwllclai, an exhorter from the neighbourhood of Lledrod, used to travel as a friend with Mr Williams on his journeys. He would receive very little as acknowledgement on the way, much less than the costs of the journey, and so he could only undertake to come when his circumstances allowed him. He once said to his wife at the start of a trip, 'I have only six pounds spare, after paying the rent and everything, so I will travel on for as long as that lasts.' Off he went, and when he returned he had only sixpence remaining of the six pounds. During the troubles over ordination, Dafydd Edwards tended more and more towards the parish church.

'Deio *bach*,' said Mr Williams to him, 'I came out of the church to you. We've been a long time together. I hope that you are not going to leave me again, and go back to my old place. We had better cleave to the Connexion from now on.'

But his words had little influence on the old exhorter, who replied,

'You cleave as much as you like, but I am going.'

And so he did.

Mr Williams could use strong words at times, particularly when faced with empty arguments. He was once told by a churlish elder from near Llangeitho:

'I am surprised at you, Mr Williams, that you lend your breath to such folly.'

'I know best, man.' was the answer. 'And if you knew as much as I do, you would not oppose so much.'

Another time, to a young man from Abermeurig who was preparing for the Anglican ministry and who had spoken scornfully of ordination in his hearing, he answered, in his down-to-earth manner,

'It would be wiser for you and your type to be quiet. Why should a boy like you be talking about something of which you know nothing. Be quiet, and shame on you.'

No doubt the discerning old priest judged that the best instrument for this fool's back was the rod.

TWO SIGNIFICANT EVENTS

Sometime about the beginning of the year 1810, two events took place that brought the debate over ordination to a crisis. One was the question posed by Ebenezer Morris to Mr Charles in an Association (though we do not know exactly the time, nor indeed the place where it occurred). The argument had become quite heated, the meeting was to a degree agitated, and Mr Charles, who was in the chair, seemed completely unwilling to allow any further development. Many feared for the consequences, sensing that the meeting might end in disruption. When the discussion was at its fiercest, Ebenezer Morris rose to his feet in the big seat and leant his weight on one of the pillars supporting the pulpit. Everything about him expressed dignity, solemnity, and the air of one who had a message and was himself aware of its importance. Soon, all discussion ceased and the eyes of the whole assembly were upon him. For a moment he did not speak but remained standing, as dumb as an idol. At last, with perfect self-possession but with a masterly manner, he stated that he had a question to ask and that he wished to receive a truthful answer. The congregation anticipating that the question would be crucial, strained to hear with every eye fixed upon the questioner. Mr Morris proceeded:

'I represent many hundreds of people in this congregation and other places and I call upon Mr Charles to answer me, charging him to provide a sincere, honest answer to my query. And this is it. Which is the greater, the preaching of the gospel or the administering of the sacraments?'

The Association immediately recognized the importance of the question and the attention of all was transferred from Mr Morris to Mr Charles. After a moment's consideration he also got to his feet. The expression on his face proved that he himself realized that he had been pushed into a corner and in the midst of a profound and painful silence he replied:

'The greater work is the preaching of the gospel.'

'We are one therefore,' responded Mr Morris. 'The Devil thought he would split us as an Association today, but thank heaven, we are one.'

With these words an indescribable emotion shot through all hearts like a bolt of lightning, and all breathed freely. It does not appear that any resolution was passed on the matter there and then, but all departed with the conviction that the battle was over and that the argument for ordination had been won. The news of the meeting spread quickly throughout Wales. It was the one topic of conversation everywhere – Mr Morris's question, and Mr Charles's reply. And the hearts of the people rejoiced at the thought that they would receive a regular administration of the sacraments, and that from the hands of those fluent preachers from whose ministry they drew such benefit.

The second occurrence that was instrumental in bringing matters to a head was the step taken by Mr Thomas Jones, Denbigh, an unordained man, in baptizing a baby at the request of the church and congregation at Denbigh. We will allow Mr Jones himself to describe the circumstances:

> Many of the brethren, myself included, had already been campaigning for a year or two for the ministry of baptism amongst us as a Body and for a more frequent amd more regular administration of the holy supper. Previously our people would generally baptize at the Anglican Church, with quite a few receiving communion there also, but their numbers were decreasing. Amongst ourselves, the few churchmen that had joined the Connexion used to administer that ordinance in various places. But in that these men were few in number and the membership of the Connexion was, by God's goodness, increasing so rapidly, many of our congregations had not received communion for a year or more, and a few had never received it. As the complaints to the Connexion about this situation increased, some of the churchmen (eminent men within the Body) began to hesitate, and were unable to agree to proceed with the developments that others judged essential; namely, the ordaining of a number of the preachers to assist the churchmen and to supply the needs of the churches in relation to the two ordinances.

At this juncture, and in the following way, I was called before a number of the brethren who were of one mind and voice on this point. A baby had been born to one of the friends and he had sought the help of others of the brethren to call upon me, whom they considered the minister of the congregation, to baptize the child. He added many arguments and reasons in support of the request and in opposition to his taking the baby to some other congregation for baptism. After much consideration and much seeking of guidance from the Lord, I decided, and promised, that I would perform the ordinance if the whole body of the church, that is the congregation, would call me to it, and only after they also had pleaded to the Lord that he would lead and direct them according to his Word and will. After they had met together in my absence and considered the matter with much prayer to God, they informed me that they had all agreed, with the exception of one member who was in some degree of fear and hesitation, to call upon me so to act.

This matter had been pressing heavily upon me, day and night, before ever this request came to me. By study of God's Word and by prayer, I had been seeking leading and understanding. When a close friend had argued against me with a degree of seriousness and some passion, I became distressed of mind. Nevertheless, on considering his arguments, and with much earnest pleading before the Lord, the scales seemed to turn in the same direction as before. I realized that my thoughts were contrary, if not to the ordination and command, yet certainly to the practice of that Body to which from the heart I had joined myself, and I regretted and still do regret causing distress to any of my brethren. Indeed, one brother and father I was particularly grieved to distress, whose remembrance was and is more revered in my mind than any other with whom I have had fellowship on earth. Yet, for all these things, necessity was laid upon me to proceed, leaving the consequences in the hand of the All-knowing and All-powerful God. I had to conclude that if he had called me to preach his Word, something which I could not really doubt, then that call, together with the call upon me from a Christian congregation, as well as other circumstances, were sufficient reasons for me to proceed with administering the ordinance of baptism. Therefore, with trembling, but with some measure also of peace from the Lord, I ventured upon the work.

Mr Jones writes in full awareness of the seriousness of the step he took. We see that both he and the fellowship in Denbigh acted prudently in the matter. They both made the subject a matter of prayer and sought the Lord for enlightenment. It is clear also that he sought the counsel of others, outside the Denbigh congregation, and reflected upon their arguments most seriously. Many have blamed him completely for the step he took. They argue that he should have waited for the Association to decide on the matter and not have rushed irregularly to administer the divine ordinance before being ordained to the work. But it is certain that circumstances arise at times which require men of strong principles to proceed independently of the decisions of church councils, and to trample underfoot any oppressive minor rules and regulations that have no foundation in God's Word. His condemnation by Churchmen is particularly raucous. They judge him mercilessly for rushing into a sacred office without a call, and compare him to Korah, Dathan and Abiram. They ascribe his behaviour to ambition and lack of conscience. But whether we approve of his behaviour or not, there is not the least reason to doubt his complete conscientiousness. His whole life is a proof of the sobriety of his character; his every word demonstrates the gravity with which he approached this step; and he considered that his call to preach and the request that proceeded from the Denbigh congregation gave him sufficient authority to administer the ordinance.

The name of the baby baptized by Mr Jones, as found in the registry of baptisms, was Evan Simner. He was the brother of the late Mr Abel Simner of London. He was born on 17 February 1810, and baptized on 9 March of the same year. The discussions between Mr Jones and the Denbigh church took place therefore between the February and March of that year, that is, about three months before the agreement in the Bala Association to recommend Ordination, and about fifteen months before ordaining took place. After having broken the ice in this way through administering baptism, Mr Jones proceeded, under the strong urging of the Denbigh brethren no doubt, to administer holy communion. He would have been acting inconsistently and manifesting irresolution and lack of determination had he not done so. But it appears that before he took this second step the matter came under consideration at the Denbigh and Flint Quarterly Meeting and that this gathering gave him liberty to proceed. He states:

> Soon after this (i.e., the baptism of the baby, Evan Simner) many of the brethren, in a Quarterly Meeting, allowed or tolerated the congregation and myself to follow our own consciences with a view to the other ordinance, namely the Lord's Supper. As a consequence we received that privilege, enjoying the blessing with a measure of godly fear, peace and gratitude.

Quite certainly, Mr Thomas Jones's behaviour raised considerable agitation and was a greater influence than anything else in leading the Association to a decision on the issue. If they had not decided in favour of ordaining preachers then Mr Jones would have had to have been excommunicated, together with the Denbigh church, and indeed the Denbigh and Flint Quarterly Meeting also for giving them their freedom in this matter. But it does not appear that anybody wished to suggest such a step.

Meanwhile Mr Jones continued to administer the sacraments regularly. The Denbigh Register of Baptisms proves that he baptized twelve children of church members before he was ordained. We are not aware that he was asked to administer the Lord's Supper to any other congregation but there is ample evidence that he was called to various places to baptize infants. The register for baptisms kept at Llanrwst show that he baptized a girl called Catherine Roberts at Pwllterfyn, 10 September 1810. He also baptized a baby called Ebenezer Jones at Llandyrnog, Clwyd Valley. The following is found in the diary of Mr David Davies of Caerwys, who died at 99 years of age on 12 February 1889:

> 3 June 1811, namely Whit Monday, Thomas Anwyl and I went to St Asaph to a preaching service. Thomas Lloyd, Abergele, and Thomas Jones, Denbigh, were preaching at 10 in the morning; and Mr Jones, Denbigh, and John Humphreys, Caerwys, at 2 in the afternoon. Mr Jones took a meeting at Caerwys in the evening and he baptized a child of John Jones the stonemason. This was the first to be baptized at Caerwys chapel.

Mary Jones, the girl baptized by Mr Jones on this occasion, lived until December 1891, dying at eighty years of age. Although these are the only ones for which we have proof of their baptism by Thomas Jones, the likelihood is that there were many more but that their history has not been passed down to us.

We are assured that John Elias approved of the behaviour of his friend from Denbigh. An elder from Liverpool had written to Mr Elias in 1810, representing to him the pitiable state of the Methodists in English towns with respect to the administration of the sacraments. He showed that they were being neglected more than any other members of the Connexion. In Wales they could take their babies to the clergy of the Church of England for baptism and could attend at their parish church for communion. Whatever deficiency there might be in the service they could at least hear it in a language which they understood. But in Liverpool and other English towns they had either to go to English clergymen to whom their relations, feelings and language were all foreign, or else be deprived to a great extent of the holy sacraments, for very rarely and irregularly did the Welsh Methodist clergy visit them.

Having presented this need to Mr Elias the elder asked him, in the name of Christianity and for the sake of men's souls, how long were things to remain in that state; and what advice had he to give to those who found themselves in such circumstances. Mr Elias's answer is to hand. Having expressed his deepest sympathies with the Liverpool church in its needs, he provides the following advice:

> Write to Bala to ask Mr Charles or Mr Lloyd to come to you and administer the ordinances; and if they will not come I do not think it will be too great a sin for you to ask Mr Jones of Denbigh to do so.

These words show clearly that John Elias approved Mr Thomas Jones's actions, and no doubt Ebenezer Morris and the others who favoured Ordination were of the same mind. It was not that they approved of irregularity but that they recognized that exceptional circumstances called for extreme measures.

THE NORTH AND SOUTH ASSOCIATIONS DECIDE IN FAVOUR OF ORDINATION

At the Bala Association of 19–20 June 1810, was passed the first formal decision in favour of ordaining within the Connexion. It does not appear that there was any debate on the matter at all. Once the topic was raised, Mr Charles got to his feet and made a clear and unambiguous statement that he had been completely convinced of the necessity of such a step. He was followed by Mr Simon Lloyd, himself also an ordained clergyman held in high respect because of his office, his learning and his godliness. As the clergy had changed their position and were in favour, no one else remained, or had the courage, to oppose. A unanimous decision was taken that a certain number of the preachers would be set apart to administer the sacraments and that the choice of these brethren be made by the different counties. Furthermore, Mr Charles agreed to prepare the form and rules for implementing their purpose. The fact that he was in favour of Ordination had filled the hearts of all the brethren with such joy that they would have accepted whatever plan he proposed. The next step was to obtain a similar agreement from the Association for the South. The Rev. John Williams of Lledrod was present at Bala and he was commissioned to carry the request to the south. It seems that the task of transporting the letter proved a distressing task to Mr Williams. He knew that he would be condemned without mercy by the clergy of the south in that the majority of them had formed themselves into a kind of league, rather like a Trade Union, and had decided to excommunicate any clergyman that betrayed their league. He did not avoid the temptation of destroying the letter. But conscience and duty won the day.

'As I journeyed home,' he stated, 'with the letter in my pocket, I promised the Lord that I would cleave to the Body even if it meant that I would have to beg for bread.'

It was not without fierce battles that the motion was carried in the Association of the South, for the clergy wielded so much more influence there. Williams, Lledrod, delivered his embassage to the Llangeitho Association of the following August. The Rev. David Jones, Llan-gan, was in the chair and this was the last association that he attended before entering heaven. He argued strongly against that which he considered a novelty. He told the preachers:

'I ventured my daily bread in order to be with you, and with you have I been privileged to remain hitherto, but if you intend to tear the cause apart you must go on your own; I will no more accompany you.'

At this John Elias replied:

> Your heavenly Father will not leave you in need of bread, dear Mr Jones. Trust him yet. As for tearing the cause, we will have nothing of that, but we will proceed according to God's Word and according to the mind of the majority of the churches, and that with unceasing prayer. And let him be called a tearer who behaves in a contrary fashion.

Whether a motion in favour of Ordination was passed at Llangeitho we do not know. We believe that that was the case, or at least that the trend was strongly in that direction, but in all probability the discussion was not brought to a vote and it was understood that the matter would be raised again before proceeding to a decision. The spirit of the old evangelist from Llan-gan was not unsettled by the debate; he preached gloriously during that Association on the words, 'For my flesh is food indeed, and my blood is drink indeed.' He gloried in praising the Saviour, and the people rejoiced as they listened to him. Before dawn the following Sabbath his placid and tender-hearted spirit had escaped to that country where no argument or strife is found. And with his death was removed the last obstacle to Ordination in the south.

It was understood at Llangeitho that the final decision would be taken at the Swansea Association, the following October. The week before this Association, a Pembrokeshire Quarterly Meeting was held at St Dogmaels. Pembrokeshire was the stronghold of the clergymen. Griffiths of Nevern and Jones of Llandudoch were of that county, together with other men of some considerable dignity and all attended this meeting. Early on in the meeting, Mr Thomas Rees, Trepuet, presented a message from St David's requesting the Quarterly Meeting to petition the Swansea Association with the request that the brethren there present attend to the needs of the south, and especially of Pembrokeshire, as regards the administering of the sacraments, and to meet those needs by separating brethren from among them to administer the ordinances. A deathly silence gripped the meeting while Mr Rees presented the motion. He showed that the death of Jones, Llan-gan – the only clergyman in Pembrokeshire who was willing to communicate in the chapels – had greatly intensified their need. Once he had finished, the storm broke. The clergy first sought to belittle the messenger by asking:

'How long had he been a member of the cause?'

When he replied that he had been religious since his youth, they said:

'It is a tragedy that a man who has been so long in the work should turn out to be one of those who tear it apart.'

They then asked:

'What kind of ministers do you seek?'

'Men chosen and set apart by the Body,' he replied. 'Not having been consecrated by the hand of any bishop.'

At that the clergy lost all control of themselves and began to threaten and revile him, calling him, 'Traitor! Seceder! Troubler!', and similar names. So great was the agitation and shouting that he, poor man, was unable to put forward a word in his defence. If it were not for the fact that he was bold in spirit and confident of a clear conscience he might well have fainted on the floor. But the brother from St David's was not one to flee in the day of battle. He stood as a rock, and when opportunity arose he persevered with his task, eventually forcing the meeting to give the request an appropriate consideration. His plea was supported by Cardiganshire friends who were freer from the influence of the clergy. They in return only roared the louder:

> You are transgressing the laws of the fathers; trampling underfoot the principles of famous divines of the past – those principles that were part of the awakening from its beginnings; you are presumptuously attacking that which has been honoured by the Almighty himself with his approval, and that order which has been the means of salvation for many thousands.

To which the other brethren replied:

> We do not deny that God notably honoured the early Methodists and that a great and glorious work was performed by them. Yet, we judge that this was not achieved because of their association with the Church of England but because they were sent by God and accompanied by worthy gifts of his Spirit. It was an honouring not of the ordination of a bishop but of the anointing of the Spirit; not of human arrangements but of divine truth. Furthermore the Fathers expected, or at least, hoped for, a reformation in the Church. But as we are presently we have very little hope of this. That dream has more or less vanished by now; the thirty years that have passed have put paid to it completely.

The weight of argument was unquestionably with those who were for Ordination. They possessed the rational arguments; the clergy had only prejudice and tempers, and accusations that they could not prove. The meeting ended firmly in favour of the request from St David's. The defeat hurt the priests deeply. They had been beaten in their very stronghold and could not now hold out any further hope of stemming the tide.

A week later, in October 1810, the Association met at Swansea and the issue was brought to a conclusion. Here again the clergy defended their position with much heat, but they could not carry matters with their previous arrogance for they laboured under the conviction that they were certain of losing the day. The supporters of Ordination received help from an unexpected source in that the Rev. Rowland Hill was present at the Association and took an important part in the debate. Mr Hill was not formally associated with Lady Huntingdon's Connexion nor with any other denomination but, rather like the Rev. Philip Pugh at Chester, he had collected a number of congregations together, the main one being that which worshipped at Surrey Chapel, London, and he ministered to them to the best of his ability, assisted by other preachers. His position was very like that of the Methodists and there was frequent intercourse between them. He often preached in their chapels in Wales and some of the Methodists preachers ministered in his chapels. He therefore felt that he had a right to attend their Associations and express his opinion. He argued strongly for the appropriateness and necessity of proceeding with Ordination. One of the clergy took it upon himself to answer him but because he spoke in Welsh Mr Hill could not understand him, but he heard him use the English word 'valid'. From this Hill understood that the clergyman was denying the legality of a baptism performed by a preacher who had not received episcopal ordination. He was shocked to hear such statements and took the opportunity to address the meeting again, with much clarity and liveliness, on the nature of the sacraments of the New Testament and of those who might administer them. His arguments were so powerful and effective that not one of the clergy dared reply. Their weakness and shame was such that when the vote was taken they were unable to raise their hands in opposition. This decision of the Swansea Association put an end to all dispute on the ordaining of preachers, to the great blessing and profit of the Connexion.

The following letter from John Elias to a friend in Liverpool sheds some light on the events of the Association:

> Dear Brother,
>
> I have received a letter from Mr Ebenezer Morris since the Swansea association, giving me a cheering account of their having agreed with what was passed at Bala, with regard to increasing the privileges of the churches. That

> was done there at (at Swansea) very peacefully; the association also as a whole agreed, no one raising a hand to declare his displeasure. There has been a remarkable change of providence to have brought this about so tranquilly: it has exceeded expectation. The Rev. Rowland Hill heard of the Swansea association, and that this matter was to be dealt with there; his mind was so moved that he went from Bristol to Swansea to the association; it seems as if the Lord had sent him, and that He has greatly prospered his coming. Some of the clergy (as they are called) tried to raise some objections to granting the connexion the further privileges they desire; Mr Hill answered all their objections, and pointed out the necessity of granting the connexion what they ask for. He said that he had been brought up with a bias in favour of the Church of England; and that he had loved the ministers who preach the Gospel within its pale; but that, inasmuch as the generality of its ministers deny the doctrine to which they have once pledged themselves, pious people have been obliged to leave it, and that the children of God cannot live on chaff. He also said that the renowned Mr Whitefield had lost much, because he did not do in his day, what is now desired by our connexion; had he done so, that very likely the whole connexion would be one great body the whole kingdom over; instead of that, it had split up into many branches: and he added that our own connexion would certainly go the same way unless they were granted what they desire. So it was decided to allow the Bala association to proceed with the matter, they then to follow suit ...[5]

This letter was written by Mr Elias on 26 December, that is about a month after the Swansea Association. We have stayed a long time with the history of the Ordination because of its significance for the Connexion. The debate shook the Body to its foundations. From its beginnings no other issue had produced such agitation except perhaps the unfortunate division between Rowland and Harris. Many feared that it would be wrecked in the storm but God defended his cause. Nor was the crisis passed without some loss. Seven of the clergymen who were acknowledged as Methodists withdrew from their ranks, and as many of them were fluent preachers and of much influence in the localities where they preached they took the main body of the people in those regions with them, leaving behind a much enfeebled Methodist cause. This is the reason, to a great extent, for the weakness of Methodism in Pembrokeshire. We will return to this point again, adding here only that the greatest loss of all was that sustained by these clergymen themselves. They suffered a considerable financial loss, because they used to receive much more from the Methodists than they did from their livings. A still greater loss was their removal from so many opportunities for usefulness. Instead of being torches itinerating throughout Wales and lighting up the whole Principality from Holyhead to Cardiff, they became cornered in their own small localities. Their fame dwindled away and they died comparatively unknown. It is also quite certain that some of them bitterly regretted the step they had taken.

In conformity to the request of the two Associations, the various Monthly Meetings immediately proceeded to choose the brethren to be ordained. They did so with such wisdom that it does not appear that any envy arose in those not chosen. Some of those selected were amazed that their Quarterly Meeting had ever considered them, and having a deep sense of their unworthiness were inclined to refuse the call. One such was Mr E. Griffiths of Meifod. He said:

> It never entered my head that any would consider myself for this (the administering of the sacraments) until that moment when I was told I was among those chosen. I cannot express the thoughts with which I then considered myself, and the ordinances, so unhappy was I. Baptism being judged a mere state ceremony by most people; the children of religious people being raised outside the church; and they talk of sending me to such a work, to uphold the ordinances before the church and to administer them! I felt myself sinking to such misery that I longed to refuse the work outright. But then I received a letter from the Rev. Thomas Charles of Bala, in which he outlined the work with respect to its Owner, and stressed that the weakest instruments, in his hands, were sufficient for the greatest ends. This was the means of encouraging me to commit myself to the service of the Body, praying earnestly at the throne of grace that the will of God might prevail in me in this respect, for I was certain from my own experience that the Lord could make a man that which he was not, and qualify a man for every part of that work to which he had called him.

We have grounds for believing that many another felt the same hesitation, and that it was not without much earnest exhortation that they obeyed the call of the churches. This thoroughly disproves the accusation that these who were first ordained to the work of the ministry were men of ambition, lusting for honours and disturbing the peace of the Connexion until they were satisfied.

In the north, the choice fell upon the following brethren:

John Elias, Anglesey; Richard Lloyd, Anglesey; Evan Richardson, Caernarvon; Thomas Jones, Denbigh; John Davies, Nant-y-glyn; John Roberts, Llangwm; William Jones, Dôl-y-fonddu; and Evan Griffiths, Meifod.

In some ways it is strange that John Jones, Edeyrn, was not included. As far as gifts and qualifications for preaching were concerned he was not behind any of his brethren. At the commencement of his ministry he was as popular as John Elias, and had started to preach before him. But drink was a snare to Mr Jones, and the Connexion manifested their disapproval by waiting a further two years before ordaining him.

The brethren appointed in the south were:

> John Evans, Llwynffortun; David Rees, Llanfynydd; Arthur Evans, Cynwil; David Charles, Carmarthen; James James, Abergavenny; David Parry, Brecknockshire; Evan Evans, Ffos, Brecknockshire; Ebenezer Morris, Twrgwyn; John Thomas, Cardigan; Ebenezer Richard, Tregaron; Evan Harris, Pembrokeshire; Hopkin Bevan, Glamorgan; John Rees, Monmouthshire.

All of these had been preaching for many years, apart from David Charles, who had been preaching for only three years. But he was such an exceptional man and the churches held him in such high regard for his intellectual ability, his deep understanding of the doctrines of the Bible, his wisdom, and his godliness, that he was unanimously chosen for the work. In addition, he had been prominent as a leader for many years before he began to preach.

THE FIRST ORDINATIONS, AT BALA AND AT LLANDEILO

The first ordination took place in the north, in the Association held at Bala on 19–20 June 1811. As the time approached, Mr Charles and others of the brethren were troubled by much fear. We find that he, together with his friend, the Rev. Simon Jones, were present at Whitsun services in Liverpool a few days before the Association. In the *seiat* on the Monday morning they both referred to the approaching ordination and, as is stated in the *Life* of the Rev. John Elias, 'We were all exhorted most seriously to intercede with importunate prayer for divine guidance in this matter.' Mr Charles had also written to all those who were to be ordained asking them to gather at Bala on the Monday night, 17 June, so that they might spend the following Tuesday, the day before the Association, in prayer, 'and confer together privately'. We may be sure that all the brethren agreed.

The history of the ordination service is given in the *Confession of Faith:*

> Mr John Evans of Bala, the oldest and one of the most respected preachers in the Connexion, commenced the service by reading the third chapter of the Second Epistle to Timothy, making appropriate remarks on the qualifications which, in that chapter, are pointed out as requisite in ministers of the Gospel, and then offered prayer in a very devout and solemn manner. The Rev. Thomas Charles then read the names of the persons who had been chosen by the monthly meetings of the several counties. Having done so, he asked the representatives of the different churches, of whom about three hundred were

> present, whether they wished him to put a few questions to the brethren who were to be ordained, on the fundamental articles of the Christian religion, and if that was their desire he requested them to signify the same by raising their hands, which all immediately did.

Mr Charles then asked the questions which we have in the *Confession of Faith* and which are still used today in all ordination services.

> Having obtained their solemn and enlightened replies to these questions, he asked the representatives whether they chose these brethren to administer the ordinances of Baptism and the Lord's Supper among them; and if they did, to signify the same by holding up their hands. This was done by all present, without exception.
>
> He then asked the brethren whether they consented to the call of the Connexion, and whether they willingly yielded themselves to be faithful, laborious, and diligent, to feed the flock of God, by devoutly administering the ordinances according to the assistance which they should receive of God.
>
> They answered in a humble and serious manner, that they did, and earnestly desired the prayers of the whole Connexion in their behalf.
>
> The venerable brother, Mr Robert Jones of Caernarvonshire (Robert Jones, Rhoslan), gave them in conclusion a word of exhortation, and offered up an earnest prayer appropriate to the occasion.

It can be seen that Mr Charles did not believe in 'succession'; two men who were not themselves ordained, were responsible for the most important elements of the service.

In the August of the same year the brethren from the south were ordained in the Llandeilo Association according to the same order that was used at Bala, except that different men conducted the service. The Rev. John Williams of Lledrod began with prayer and the reading of the relevant portions of the Word, the questions were asked by the Rev. Thomas Charles, and the Rev. John Williams of Pantycelyn closed with prayer.

Some of the churches were for a while prejudiced against those preachers who had been ordained as ministers. They did not ask them to administer the sacraments but took their children to be baptized by the parish priest and received the communion also, as before, at the parish church. This occurred mainly in those localities where the serving clergy were evangelical. Not one of the ministers of the Connexion administered communion at Llanddewibrefi for many years after the Ordination, even though Mr Ebenezer Richard lived less than three miles from the village and was very acceptable and popular as a preacher. The situation at Llangeitho was similar. The elders there considered that there was no preacher equal to Mr Richard; as such they respected him as the angel of God, but they would never ask him to baptize or to serve the Lord's Table. For that, they must have Mr Williams of Lledrod. We have previously noted the history of Mr Charles refusing to serve the Lord's Table at Llangeitho and dismissing the members without communion because the elders refused to allow the Rev. John Roberts of Llangwm to assist him at the Table. We must be fair also to the Llangeitho elders. They were not moved wholly by prejudice. To a large extent they were under the thumb of the two local clergymen: the Rev. Hugh Lloyd, Cilpill, who served at Llanddewi and Llangeitho, and the Rev. John Jones of Glanmarch, (afterwards, Tregaron). As well as being clergymen, these two were landowners and one of them, if not both, were Justices of the Peace.

Furthermore Mr Lloyd was a fine preacher who greatly favoured the Methodists while they remained as a branch of the Church of England. His home was always open to those who frequented the Associations at Llangeitho, though possibly this had more to do with the influence of Mrs Lloyd, for she was a truly religious person who later, in her last years, became a member with the Methodists. As for Mr Jones, Glanmarch, he excelled even Mr Lloyd as a preacher, his gifts gaining him great popularity. An over-fondness for drink however affected him and his later career deteriorated.

These clergymen were furious that the Methodists had ordained ministers, and because of the influence and authority which they wielded the elders of the local churches feared to invite those ministers to administer the ordinances amongst them in case they offended the two men. However, respect towards the Connexion and conviction of conscience won the day. The first man invited to take communion at Llangeitho who was not an ordained clergyman was Ebenezer Richard, and such was the unction upon the meeting and so evident was the divine presence that every prejudice against the ministers of the Connexion disappeared forever. In this way all ill feelings gradually departed from the churches of the land.

THE REV. THOMAS JONES OF CREATON

But Churchmen throughout the country were greatly agitated because of the Ordination, particularly those who had looked with favour upon the Methodists previously when they were still associated with their parish churches. These Churchmen proclaimed the actions taken as sacrilegious; they denoted the ordained ministers as usurpers, rushing to the altar to serve the holy vessels in defiance of the direct commandment of God. They did all they could to blacken the character and circumstances of the Methodists, and wherever they found the slightest legal grounds they stole their chapels from them. It is only fair to mention that nearly all such occurrences took place in the south.

One of the evangelical clergy who fired the greatest broadside possible at the Methodists through the press was the Rev. Thomas Jones of Creaton, who up until this time was one of Mr Charles's closest friends. But before we consider his book we must give something of his history. He was born in the Hafod locality, Cwmystwyth, Cardiganshire, in April 1752. He received a better education than was common. About eight miles from his parents' home was Ystradmeurig, where Edward Richard kept his famous school, and Thomas was sent there when thirteen years old. Soon after entering Ystradmeurig he heard that Daniel Rowland was to preach at Pontrhydfendigaid and he went there to hear him. Rowland preached with great power; it was the manner of his address that struck the schoolboy more than its content. He left the service a new creature. Jones was to listen to Rowland many times after this, and after being ordained received the privilege of assisting the famous clergyman during the communion season at Llangeitho. He half-worshipped Rowland, believing that the world had never before seen such a preacher. A picture of him hung in his study and Mr Jones would often cast a look at it as he composed his sermons in order to draw inspiration from it. When he was twenty-two years old he was ordained to the curacy of Eglwysfach and Llangynfelin, between Aberystwyth and Machynlleth. He was here five years and succeeded in accomplishing much good during his stay. He put an end to the ungodly sports that were held in the vicinity and was the instrument, under God's blessing, of saving some souls. In 1779 he moved to a curacy in Leintwardine, Herefordshire, a village near Ludlow. What compelled him to leave Wales we do not know, but it is certain that it was not any lack of patriotism because his love for his country was always very strong, as the following *englyn* [a traditional Welsh poetic form] testifies:

Chwi, Gymry anwyl, gymeraf – i'm coel,	You, dear Welsh people, I take to cherish
I'm calon anwylaf;	In the depths of my heart;
Mi'ch cerais, fyth mi'ch caraf;	I have loved you and ever will;
Neb, neb o'ch bath, ni wnaeth Naf.	None like you God ever made.

Jones was not very happy in Herefordshire. He describes the people as being completely irreligious, almost pagan in their ignorance of God, being taken up with sports, especially on Sundays, and drunkenness. He sought to suppress the sports, and because of this, and because of the evangelical tone of his preaching which made the people suspect him of being a Methodist, he brought upon himself the anger of many in the parish. These went to the vicar to complain and as a result Jones, having been there for about eighteen months, was given a month's notice. His next curacy was at Lognor, about seven miles from Shrewsbury. The people there were more moral in behaviour but thoroughly devoid of spiritual religion. Only one godly person lived in the parish, according to Jones's estimate. He was fifteen months in this place. His seriousness earned him the title Methodist, and as a consequence he had to leave.

He moved next to Oswestry where about ten clergymen dwelt, whose livings were in the countryside nearby and who came in to the town church in the evenings. The evangelicalism of his ministry soon drew this faction upon his head. In particular, a sermon of his on regeneration offended the Rural Dean so that he was given a month's notice by the vicar, who at the same time testified that he was sorry to lose him. Mr Jones's ministry was eminently successful at Oswestry. Soon after his departure about forty of his converts joined the Wesleyans, a similar number united with the Methodists, and the Independent chapel, where Dr Williams, afterwards of Rotherham, was minister, became too small for its congregation.

After a period in Loppingham, near Wem, from where he was again forced to leave, Thomas Jones received the curacy of Creaton in Northampton. Here he spent the remainder of his days, forty-two years, as curate and then as rector. He lived to reach the great age of ninety-three years and died in peace on 7 January 1843. He was a truly godly man possessing an able mind. Furthermore he was a fine preacher, deeply evangelical, and he composed many books of a religious nature that have been of blessing to many. He was a bosom friend of Mr Charles and the two of them corresponded and planned together how to advance Wales morally and religiously. While the Methodists were in some kind of association with the Established Church, Thomas Jones favoured them strongly; he saw himself as a member of them.

But when the Connexion ordained its own ministers, setting aside the ordination of bishops, the Rev. Thomas Jones was enraged. He became one of the worst persecutors and no name was too bad for him to use against his former friends. As well as sending bitter letters to the main leaders of the Methodists, Mr Charles in particular, he wrote a book called *The Welsh Looking-Glass* whose only purpose was to condemn the ordinations. We doubt whether there is anything more full of bile to be found in the English language. The book is devoid of any rational argument but is full of every kind of misrepresentation. In order to give the reader a taste of its character we will quote a little of its contents:

> Let us consider this new ordination, lately invented, though we do so unwillingly and with displeasure. At the beginning, the Calvinistic Methodists of old would receive the sacred Supper at the parish church, and afterwards would do so, if not within consecrated walls, then at least at the hands of those who had received Episcopal ordination; and they never gave place to any belief that others, apart from legitimately ordained priests, had the right of administering the sacred sacrament. But, strange though it is to relate, and miserable the tale, some of their preachers recently have nurtured the arrogant presumption that they are priests without having received any ordination; or that some mockery of an ordination is sufficient. It seems that they have something that they call by this same name ('ordination') and, if I have been correctly informed, it was of that nature. No one was present who had himself received ordination of any kind. Though I was not witness to the ludicrous ceremony nor have received a full description of its proceedings, yet I imagine that it would have had something of the following form. After a company of lay people had gathered together, whether men or women, many or few, is of no consequence, the preachers came forward and appealed to those present to confirm them as qualified to be priests of the Lord, not only to preach the gospel but also to undertake all the offices of a priest. On hearing the appeal, the others, whether men or women, I cannot say, affirmed that John, Richard, William, and the rest, were qualified to be ministers of the gospel; and they were declared to be so without any objections. These men, by the force of powerful error, returned home after such an ordination thoroughly satisfied, I imagine, by the choice and confirmation of their brethren, and with a considerable sense of self-satisfaction. It would be little more than a waste of time to continue discussion of what is no better than a serious mockery and caricature of heavenly ordinations; what is indeed an ungodly presumption.

This is how Mr Jones, in anger of spirit, wrote against his erstwhile friends. Most certainly, this is not reasoning but an unworthy reviling; mere bitter words instead of proofs. It would be difficult to gather together more misinterpretation of facts within such a short compass:

(1) Mr Jones alleged that no one was present during the ordination of the first Methodist ministers that had themselves received ordination. This is clearly false witness. At Bala, Mr Charles took part in the service. He had received episcopal ordination – that ordination which Mr Jones himself accepted as legitimate. At Llandeilo there were three ordained clergymen present: the Revs. John Williams, Lledrod, John Williams, Pantycelyn, and Thomas Charles. To our mind the ceremony would have been completely valid without them, if the ordination was taking place according to the formal call of the church, but in that Mr Jones had laid such stress on the presence of ordained men he should have inquired

diligently before proclaiming publicly such dire untruths. He cannot be defended on the grounds that he had been misinformed, that others had passed on to him that which was untrue, because by means of but a little research it would have been easy for him to have discovered the truth of the matter. The fact is that he was willing to welcome every idle rumour about the Methodists in this connection and that those therefore who dealt with such merchandise were happy, as is their practice, to provide for him that which he desired.

(2) Jones described the first ordained ministers as pushing themselves to the front and appealing to the feelings of a mixed and ignorant congregation as to their appropriateness for being set apart to the work. This again is a false witness and an evident travesty of truth. The noble character of John Elias, Ebenezer Morris, and the others who were ordained, and the exalted view of propriety to which they held are sufficient proofs that they would prefer to suffer the cutting off of their right hands rather than forcing themselves upon the attention of the congregations. Their names were chosen by church representatives gathered at different Monthly Meetings and after due consideration and constant prayer for the Lord's guidance. The fact that some gifted and able men were passed over, in that they were not considered to be blameless in character, is proof enough of the prudence and care that was manifested. Mr Jones's suggestion that women had taken part in the ordinations is libellous.

(3) Jones suggests that the first ministers were insignificant men by alluding to them by the names John, Richard, William, etc. But he very well knew that they all were preachers whose praise was in all the churches and that God had blessed their ministries to the conversion of sinners on hundreds of occasions. Mr Jones himself could not compete with them in respect of ministerial qualification. They could have appealed to scores and, like Paul, have claimed them as the seal of their ministry.

Having separated the contents of Mr Jones's book from its untruthful allegations and its tasteless, churlish abuse, we find that its main burden is an attempt to prove that no ordination is legitimate other than that by a bishop. No matter what gifts a preacher may possess; no matter the extent that God has blessed his labours to the saving of souls; he has no right to administer the sacraments, not even if the Church of Christ calls him to that work, except that the hands of a bishop have been laid upon his head. Such virtue must belong to the hands of a bishop! This claim can certainly not be proved from the New Testament. As Daniel Rowland used to say, there is more virtue in the prayers of a godly congregation, and more assurance with respect to the legitimacy of any call proceeding from it, than is found in any action of a bishop. Mr Jones's position was unfortunate to say the least. On the one hand he acknowledged that innumerable clergymen of the Church of England were enemies of God and of his truth, and were not therefore true ministers in that they did not possess the necessary qualifications. He states:

> No more painful a scene is to be found under the sun, than to see a bishop laying careless hands on the heads of those who are slaves to diverse lusts, enemies of God and his truth and strangers to decency, and telling the same to feed the flock of God.

On the other hand Jones considered ordination by these very bishops who established enemies of God and his truth in the ministry, as being essential for the legitimate administration of the sacraments. And as they would not ordain suitable men, upon whose labours lay the evident unction of heaven, he considered that the church of the living God should remain in complete deprivation of the sacraments rather than call upon men refused by bishops but possessing every other requirement. Mr Jones, without himself knowing it, was a sacramentalist and a sacerdotalist.

We have discussed fully the reaction of the Rev. Thomas Jones of Creaton because he represented the feelings of a wide section of the Church with regard to the ordination of the Methodists. They approved of the Methodists' work in preaching the gospel, in forming *seiadau*, in building chapels, and in awakening the country; they acknowledged that it was the Methodists who had delivered the land from paganism; but they considered that the latter's behaviour in ordaining preachers to administer the sacraments was presumptuous. Mr Jones ventured to prophesy their destruction because of this behaviour:

> Mark my words. The Lord in his anger will sweep them away. Perhaps this will not take place in my lifetime, which is approaching its end, but it will come and a future generation shall see it.

He wrote these words in 1812, and although over eighty years have passed since then there is not the least possibility of the fulfilment of his prophecy. *The Welsh Looking-Glass* produced considerable excitement at the time, but it cost the author his popularity in Wales, particularly among the evangelical class. His biographer, the Rev. John Owen of Thrussington, who was also a clergyman, states that as a result of this book Mr Jones gained considerable praise from High Churchmen, but criticism from Evangelicals.

A LOSS OF CHAPELS AS A RESULT OF ORDINATION

But it was not only persecution in the press that the Methodists endured because of Ordination. Many of them suffered greatly in their temporal circumstances as we shall later show, and an unfair advantage was also taken in many places in the south to steal their chapels from them. This was more possible in those days because the leases had been drawn up in a more open-ended, unspecified manner. It must be remembered that the *Confession of Faith* had not yet been produced, nor yet the *Constitutional Deed* or the *Trust Deed*. As a result there was an inevitable difficulty in drawing up leases for buildings owned by the Connexion. The clergy argued that the Methodists, by their Ordination, had become a new denomination and had therefore lost their claim to their property. Furthermore, in many cases clergymen and Churchmen were the trustees. They had been so appointed because it was believed they were Methodists, but they broke their connection with the movement at the time of the ordinations and were not above taking an unfair advantage of their position. Lastly, the Methodists themselves were not happy in resorting to law, nor did they have sufficient means to maintain long legal battles against wealthier opponents. Because of these reasons, the Methodists lost many of their chapels and in some parts of the country they are still at a disadvantage as a result.

One of the places where a building was lost was Llanddewibrefi, though it did not occur until some years after the Ordination. A chapel had been built in the middle of the village for the Methodists soon after Rowland had been thrown out of his living. The deed stated categorically that the 'followers of Daniel Rowland' were the true owners of the building. As we have already noted, after the Ordination many years passed before the church called any of their ministers there to administer the sacraments. This was because the local parish priest, the Rev. Hugh Lloyd of Cilpyll, was held in much respect and was a very evangelical preacher and they did not wish to cause him any offence. The most faithful went to Llangeitho, about five miles away, on the first Sunday of every month, and the others would communicate with Mr Lloyd. At last however they decided that they would administer the sacraments at the chapel and by the hand of a minister of the connexion. The Churchmen, Mr Lloyd in particular, were very much disturbed, and the Methodists soon received legal notice that they would be turned out of the building. The Churchmen had prepared for the event. It seems that all the chapel's trustees had died since the Ordination, and when new ones were appointed it was ensured that they were all Churchmen. It is evident that the notice was illegal, and that the Methodists alone had the right to be called the followers of Daniel Rowland, but at the time they were weak, were averse to taking any legal actions and were naturally submissive, rightly or wrongly, to the local gentry. The poor members therefore decided to give up their chapel and to go out, like Abraham of old, not knowing whither they went. The last meeting that they held there was a thanksgiving service for the harvest. At its close, one of the elders, Jonathan Richards, locked the chapel door and took the key to the trustees. He first offered it to Dr Rogers of Abermeurig who refused to take it. He then proffered it to the Rev. Hugh Lloyd who placed it in his pocket. The pulpit and furniture were all left behind, apart from a small table and the Bible. These were placed on the road outside the chapel. According to tradition, whether true or false, the following night was particularly windy and wet, and although all the ground around was drenched, the Bible in some near miraculous way was preserved dry and undamaged. The following Sunday, those turned out had nowhere to go nor was any door open to receive them. A service was held on the open road near to the locked building with Mr Williams of Lledrod preaching. We do not know his text but it seems that his sermon was accompanied with uncommon unction. At one point in the sermon he referred to the closed chapel and locked door, crying out with irresistible effect, 'If the door of the chapel is closed, thank God the door to heaven is open. There is not one trustee living who can lock that door.' By the following Sunday an empty house nearby was rented for the means of grace and meetings were held here until a new chapel was built.

Although he took part, or rather instigated, this injustice of throwing the Methodists out of their chapel, Mr Lloyd was a tender-hearted man and it appears that his conscience troubled him because of the deed. Before long he visited Jonathan Richards offering the return of the key on certain terms. What these terms were we do not know, they possibly involved a promise that the sacraments would not be administered. In the event, they were more than the Methodists felt able to accept and they refused the offer. Probably Mr Lloyd's conscience was a good deal more comfortable after the refusal. But some time afterwards he met a godly old man, one of his farm bailiffs, called Jac Tyn-y-bedw, who told him:

'Mr Lloyd, you did something in Llanddewi that I would not for the world wish to have the responsibility of.'

'What was that?' said he.

'Locking the door of the chapel against God's people,' was the answer.

'I know,' said Mr Lloyd, 'but I offered them the key back again.'

'It may be,' said the old man in return, 'but I heard that Judas Iscariot offered back the money for which he betrayed his Lord, but he didn't atone for his sin by doing so.'

Jac Tyn-y-bedw's words went straight to the heart, and it is said that Mr Lloyd was never free from ill health from that day. It was not long before he was carried to the grave.

At the same time it was a blessing to the Methodists to lose the Llanddewibrefi chapel because it was relatively small and they did not own any land to extend it. The unworthy behaviour of the trustees excited a general sympathy towards them throughout the region even in the hearts of the irreligious. They obtained land from Mr Davies, Maesycrugiau, a native of the area, to build a new chapel, on a thousand-year lease of sixpence a year. This is how it came about. An unbeliever, David Evans of Abercarfan, went to Maesygrugiau to pay his rent. He had a letter in his pocket from Ebenezer Richard, Tregaron, to Mr Davies describing the way in which Llanddewibrefi chapel had been locked against the Methodists and asking if he would intervene by giving land for another chapel. The nobleman read the letter at his dinner table. He was completely overcome by what he read and broke out into loud weeping. Present at the dinner table were many of the local clergy. Mr Davies, with an oath, threw the letter at them, saying, 'Why cannot one of you devils write like that?' – referring to the charm of Mr Richard's style of writing. David Evans of Abercarfarn returned with the promise of part of a garden plot on which to build a chapel. He and another unconverted man, Jenkin Williams of Abercoed, were very zealous on behalf of the new chapel. They travelled to Tregaron at the time of the Monthly Meeting and waited outside the door while the discussion with respect to Mr Davies' offer was in progress. Once they understood that the offer had been accepted they returned home joyfully and the very next day their carts were at the quarry, picking up stone for the building. Both of these men died without making a profession, but it is difficult for us to believe that their deeds were not written as a remembrance before the Lord. The Churchmen turned the old chapel into a schoolroom and it was in their possession for over fifty years. But about 1872 the original trust deed was discovered which clearly showed that the Methodists were the true owners. The Church was given legal notice that its spoil should be returned. This was quickly done once the true nature of the situation was understood. Since then the old building has been in the possession of its rightful owners.

Another chapel lost was the meetinghouse at St Dogmaels, Pembrokeshire, across the river from Cardigan. The Methodist Reformers preached here regularly and, no doubt, a small society was formed in the village. A clergyman, William Jones, of evangelical spirit, came to the parish church. He was a native of Glamorganshire and like Jones of Llan-gan and Christopher Bassett was associated with the Methodists, preaching to their congregations and attending their Monthly Meetings. During his time there the Connexion built a chapel in the village and he had much to do with the planning involved. But the Rev. William Jones was a fierce opponent of Ordination and after the ceremonies in Llandeilo he withdrew from the Methodists and prevented their preachers from using the chapel. Whether the wording of the lease gave him the legal right to do so we do not know, but certainly all the trustees were Churchmen. As he was a good preacher and of much influence the bulk of the congregation stayed with him, and the small remnant that clung to the Connexion were too weak and timid to demand to see the lease and to claim their rights. The chapel has remained a kind of schoolroom belonging to the Church ever since. The Methodists did not preach in the village after this for twenty-five years. About the year 1836 a small cause was re-established and a chapel built. But the majority of the population are attached to the Established Church to the present day.

Similar events occurred in Eglwyswrw. There is an account of Howell Harris preaching there and a reference to a *seiat* in the Trefeca Minutes. We do not know if it survived the storm of the Disruption; it probably did so because of Howell Davies's influence. No chapel was built here until 1807, before then the means of grace were provided in a house adapted to the purpose. The members it seems were faithful enough but as was usual with rural people they tended to be timid and servile before the clergy. Some of them took communion in the parish church but the majority went on the last Sunday every month to Nevern where the Rev. David Griffiths ministered. It was necessary to ensure that there was no service in the meeting house at the same time as the service in the parish church, and should the fervour of the preacher extend the meeting on a Sunday morning, there would be a good deal of tumult. Once, Williams of Lledrod was present and both preacher and congregation were in such a happy frame that it was impossible to terminate. At the time the local clergyman was approaching the church. He was astounded to find that the chapel meeting had not finished. He put his head in through the door and shouted at the congregation to disperse instantly or he would present their case to the Bishop's Court. Mr Williams was well aware of the implications and he released the people immediately, urging them to follow the priest to the church. The influence of Mr Griffiths of Nevern over this region of the country was complete and when he withdrew because of the Ordination the feelings of the membership at Eglwyswrw towards the Methodists cooled. It does not appear that the chapel closed, as at St Dogmaels, but there was no one there concerned enough to take responsibility for finding preachers. For a time the occasional itinerating preacher would be allowed to use the building but in a short while Methodist services ceased completely.

Many years later some Methodists came to live in the area and began to keep a Sunday School in a home, together with the occasional preaching service. The old chapel was disused and the Methodists felt strongly that it was their property and that the wording of the lease demonstrated this clearly. They therefore made an effort to repossess it. This was about the beginning of the year 1848. Some means were obtained to enter the building one Sunday and a service held. It was also announced that Mr Williams, Cardigan, would preach there on the following Sunday. The Sabbath and the preacher arrived, but on approaching the meeting house an armed guard was found at the door, preventing all from entering. An appeal was now made to the landowner, T. O. Lloyd, Esq., of Bronwydd. He, as lord of the manor, was holding court at Newport (Pembrokeshire) and the two parties presented themselves before him there. The phrase in the deed on which the Churchmen based their case was that 'the standard of doctrine preached in the chapel should be the Articles of the Church of England.' The argument continued as follows, as given in *Methodistiaeth Cymru:*

> *Clergy:* The Methodists have no right to the meeting house; they are not the successors of those who built it in that they have never received episcopal ordination.
>
> *Methodists:* Sir, we do not profess to be their successors, but we do claim to be those who occupied the building at its opening.
>
> *Clergy:* But Sir, there is a definite reference in the lease that the teaching was to be the teachings of the Church of England.
>
> *Methodists:* The lease only refers to the *doctrinal* standards of the Church, there is no mention in it of church government.
>
> *Clergy:* The highest doctrine is Holy Communion, and according to the *Articles* the Methodists do not have the right to administer it.
>
> *Methodists:* Ordinations and church practice are not doctrines, and all that we preach is in agreement with the *Articles* of the Church of England, just as all other orthodox Protestants.
>
> *Clergy:* They (the Methodists) have left their fathers' principles. In reality, there are no more Methodists in existence. Previously they were in union with the Church and their ministers were in holy orders.
>
> *Methodists:* We were never in formal union with the Church of England; our first founder (Howell Harris) was not a priest, and if priests did minister to us

the majority of them were those who had been turned out of the Church of England. If it is a fact that a clergyman ministering to any connexion associates that connexion to the Established Church, then all the Nonconformists of the nation are Churchmen as it was the Bartholomew Act which brought them into existence. Furthermore, according to the ninth canon, the Methodist priests broke their connection with the Established Church from the moment that they held their first Association. And over and above all this, the priests are the greatest opponents of Methodists throughout Wales.

There was a clause in the deed to the effect that if there was no preaching in the chapel for a period of twelve months then the deed would be void. It was proved that there had been no preaching there for six years.

Clergy: That is not true. There is preaching there every week.

Methodists: By whom?

Clergy: By Mr P——, the parish priest.

Nobleman: Has the chapel received episcopal consecration?

Clergy: No.

Nobleman: Then Mr P—— had no right to preach there. Do you preach in the chapel, Mr P——?

Mr P——: No Sir. But in the prayer meeting I occasionally read and explain a chapter.

Methodists: The lease requires that this be done also, but we would submit that the one is not the other.

Nobleman (turning towards the Methodists): Do you wish to take advantage of that clause in order to break the lease?

Methodists: We leave the matter to you completely, Sir. We will abide by your decision, whatever it be.

Nobleman: I will therefore give my judgment. Not now, orally, but written; and I shall send a copy to the two parties.

Mr Lloyd kept to his word; his judgment is still presently available and is completely in favour of the Methodists. But in order to maintain good relationships he suggested that both Methodists and Churchmen made use of the building; the Methodists to use it on a Sunday and whenever they wished in the week, and the local vicar to be given permission to deliver a weekly address there. But the Churchmen would not receive the adjudication and in that the chapel was in their possession the Methodists could not make good their claim without taking the trustees to court. They were not willing to do this and the Connexion does not have a place of worship in Eglwyswrw to this day.

The Nevern chapel was lost also. This is where the Rev. David Griffiths ministered. He was a gifted and fluent preacher and a leader amongst the Methodists in Pembrokeshire. A large and beautiful building had been built at about the beginning of the century and here the exhorters preached and the weekly services were held. The sacraments were administered in the church and such was Mr Griffiths's fame that all the surrounding population streamed there on communion Sundays. As we have mentioned, he was the leader also of the party opposed to the Ordination and after it had taken place he broke with the Methodists completely. His abilities and influence was such that he maintained the whole of his congregation. From this time every Methodist preacher was forbidden to cross the threshold of the chapel. Whether this was consistent with the deeds of the building we do not know; it does not appear that anybody investigated the matter and in that the people were lost, the loss of the chapel was of small consequence.

The Newport (Pembs.) cause suffered in the same way. The chapel there had been opened by Mr Jones, Llan-gan, and Mr Nathaniel Rowland. An exhorter named David Evans, of considerable preaching gifts, lived in the village and was also the parish bell-ringer. There was one occasion when he and the Rev. Nathaniel Rowland were preaching together in a Monthly Meeting at Tre-fin and the exhorter's ministry received the greater blessing by far. A Christian gentleman arrived at the chapel house at the close of the service and said, in Mr Rowland's hearing, 'Brethren, I have a proposition to put before you; that the priest be made a bell-ringer, and the bell-ringer a priest.'

At the time of the Ordination, the Methodists of Newport were split. As the village is only two miles from Nevern, Mr Griffiths's influence extended here also and the majority of members cleaved to him and closed the door of the chapel to those who remained loyal to the Connexion. The owner of the land was a Churchman and it appears that there never was a lease on the building so that he had a legal right to use it as he saw fit. But Mr Bowen of Llwyngwair remained with the Methodists and gave them a piece of land on which to build a chapel and replace the one that was lost. This new building was opened in 1815.

There was a division also amongst the Methodists of Dinas, a village between Newport and Fishguard, and here again the Methodists lost a building. This was one of the oldest chapels that the Connexion owned in Pembrokeshire. It had been built in 1770, mainly by the exertions of the old exhorter, John Harris of Treamlod. About the beginning of the following century the building was enlarged as the church and congregation had increased greatly in number. At the time of the Ordination a strong cause was found here. But because of the agitation the church split into two parties of equal number. The one stayed with the Connexion, the other with the clergy. An attempt was made to steal the chapel but it failed. The stable however, which had been built to serve the cause, was not on the same land as the chapel and had a different owner, and the Church party succeeded in gaining possession of it. For a time they kept a school here, with the occasional sermon, but this soon came to an end. The stable is still in their hands presently.

All these events, with the exception of the troubles in Llanddewibrefi, occurred in Pembrokeshire, but considerable difficulties arose also in Llannon, Cardiganshire. The local clergyman, the Rev. David Herbert, was considered one of the Methodists. He was not a member with them formally, as far as we know, but he used to visit the chapel to hear their preachers and took part in the prayer meetings and *seiadau*. The Methodists on their part communicated with him at the parish church so that both chapel and church were almost considered as belonging to one people. But Mr Herbert was angry at heart because of the Ordination. Many of the members sympathized with him and were not ready to change their custom and invite ministers of the Connexion to their midst to administer communion. One of these sympathizing members was a Mr Nathaniel Williams who lived in the vicinity and was well known in the region as a preacher. Matters became completely confused. There was no peace in the church meetings; many argued for the right to enjoy the privileges of the gospel amongst the Methodists and also to continue as members in the parish church. The Rev. Ebenezer Morris was sent there to restore order. He soon realized that the situation required strong measures, namely that all be deprived of membership and only those willing to accept the arrangements of the Body be received back into membership. These steps he carried out, and as a result many were offended and turned their backs on the chapel, choosing to remain with Mr Herbert. One of the latter was Nathaniel Williams's wife, but he himself was away on a preaching tour. Mr Morris met with him on his return journey and after he had heard what had happened and that his wife was of the departing group, he said in some anger:

'Very well, Mr Morris; if that is how you treated Jane, you must do so also to me.'

And so it turned out. He left the Methodists and was never a member with them again. All acknowledged that Mr Williams was a godly man but of very stubborn temper. He did later request the brethren that he might return, but as he demanded to be received back with all the full privileges of a preacher and the fraternity at Llan-non could not see their way clear to allowing this without referring the matter to the Monthly Meeting, he withdrew his request and finished his career with the Established Church.

But to return to the building. An attempt was made by the Church party to possess it, claiming that they were the true Methodists and that the contrary party, by ordaining ministers, had forfeited all rights to the name. In their presumption they went as far as to place a lock on the door. The local magistrate, Mr Lloyd, Mabws, was held in great respect by all and considered by all to be virtually infallible. Both parties therefore agreed to appeal to him. The Church party got to him first. It seems that they had failed to find the deeds of the building but they showed the magistrate the deeds of other chapels and maintained that Llan-non Chapel was a similar case, and that they were the people described in the lease. Believing them, Mr Lloyd gave a judgment in their favour. Hot on their heels arrived the Methodists. They had with them the required deed. By some mishap it had come into the possession of Sion the Tailor, one of their members. Being an illiterate man, he had no idea that the vellum was a chapel deed and had cut a pattern out of it. Fortunately, his scissors had not cut through any crucial part of the deed and it had been successfully put together as at the first. The lawyer for the Methodists, a man called Mr Morris, showed it to Mr Lloyd and asked him if it was true that he had told the other party that they were the legal owners of the chapel.

'Yes,' said Mr Lloyd, 'They swore to me that they were the Methodists.'

'Who then are the Churchmen?' asked the lawyer.

'I did not ask them that,' replied the magistrate.

'It would have been wise to have done so,' answered the lawyer, 'for these people with me are the Methodists; the others were the Churchmen.'

'You know more about different religions than I do, Mr Morris,' replied Mr Lloyd, 'But the Methodists, whoever they are, are the true owners of that chapel.'

But because the Church party was not present when the Justice delivered his opinion, and because they claimed that they were the true Methodists, they refused to give up the building but kept the lock on the door and placed two men on guard to ensure that no one interfered with it. On the following days, the Monthly Meeting was held at Penmorfa, and the matter was raised. It happened that a lawyer, a Mr Davies, was present, who asked whether the chapel was licensed. He was informed that it was, due to the activity of some John Jones of Llanddewi Aberarth, a revenue officer, who had often turned up and disturbed the meetings.

'As the building has been licensed as a Nonconformist place of worship,' said Mr Davies, 'it belongs to the Methodists. The Churchmen can have no claim to it. But I advise you not to touch the lock, but rather to take the person who fitted it to court.'

But the Llan-non brethren were not patient enough to await the advice of the Monthly Meeting. Somehow, a fear had fallen upon the two guards set on watch by the church party, though they were two ruffians. They believed that they were drawing upon themselves the frown of the Almighty and they soon took to their heels leaving the place unguarded. The Methodists were ready for their opportunity and one of them, Dafydd Sion, broke the lock with an iron bar and let in the people. Soon, services were again being held there. The Churchmen threatened them fiercely as a result; they taunted the Methodists for their poverty and that they had no hope of going to law against the wealthy of the land. But Dafydd Sion was as blithe and carefree as a lark and answered:

'Don't you be mistaken. We have only to pay five pounds a year to an association in London and we will have all our rights defended and all our costs safeguarded.'

The warring continued for about a year. Then Mr Daniel Jenkins, the son-in-law of Daniel Rowland and a preacher with the Methodists prior to the Ordination, arrived at Llan-non to claim the Chapel for the Church. He was one of the trustees. He had hardly arrived when he was taken ill and died within a few days. A terror swept through the Church party as a result and they made no other attempts at claiming the building.

OTHER PERSECUTIONS OF THE METHODISTS

As well as being hounded in the Press and deprived of their chapels, the Methodists suffered considerably in their circumstances in many regions because of daring to cross the priests by ordaining their own ministers. Many of the clergy were landowners, and those who were not still possessed much influence over the landowners of the locality. The Methodists therefore felt the weight of their displeasure and scores of them were turned out of their houses or cottages. We can refer as an example to Mr David Jones of Dolaubach, a man noted for his good sense and discernment and considered one of the foremost elders of Llangeitho. Before the Ordination he was greatly respected by the clergymen. He was a surveyor of timber and houses and worked as a land-steward for both Mr Lloyd of Cilpyll and Mr Jones of Glanmarch. But as a result of asking the Rev.

Ebenezer Richard to baptize his child he lost those posts. Not only so, but he was driven out of his cottage, The Castle, which had been held by himself and his parents before him. If we are correctly informed, Mr Jones, Glanmarch, was the owner. He was a godly man according to the judgment of all who knew him and respected for his generosity and philanthropy but his opposition to Ordination had thoroughly embittered his spirit. Many in the Llangeitho neighbourhood were similarly treated and only through erecting one-night houses on Mynydd-bach Mountain were some of them able to find shelter.

Attacks were also made on some of the ministers who had been ordained. They were invited to receive holy orders and to turn their backs upon their brethren. In only a very few cases was this strategy successful, the vast majority stood to their principles in the face of all threats and inducements. The clergy realized that the people adhered to the preachers and that the only way to win them back to the bosom of the Church was to persuade the Methodist preachers, the masters of the congregations, to receive episcopal ordination.

Such an attempt was made upon Mr Ebenezer Richard. John Jones, Esq. of Derry Ormond was related to Mr Richard's wife and was a particularly close friend of his also. Many of the Cardiganshire clergy, including the Vicar of Llanbadarn Fawr, visited Mr Jones with the hope that he would influence Mr Richard to accept Church orders. The gentleman agreed willingly and invited Mr Richard to his mansion. He then told him that he had been conversing with many of the local clergy and that they had come to the decision to offer him a Church living where he would receive better pay and a more comfortable life than he might expect amongst the Methodists. Without any hesitation Mr Richard gave him a firm reply:

'The thing is impossible, Sir.'

Mr Jones was very surprised to hear such an answer and asked him:

'Why is that?'

He replied:

'To accept this offer would be completely against my conscience for I have departed from the Established Church on principle. Secondly, I am of the opinion that I will be of more usefulness in my present position. And thirdly, there is such union and affection between myself and my brethren that the division would be unbearable for me.'

Mr Jones could not fault these arguments but added, with a reluctant smile, that he considered him very foolish as far as his own good was concerned, in refusing such an offer.

In summing up the consequences of the Ordination it does not appear that the Methodists suffered any loss in the north because of the step they took. Only three clergymen in that region belonged to the Connexion and all three remained faithful. Very little was lost in the south also, with the exception of Pembrokeshire and parts of Cardiganshire. The influence of the clergy was greatest in Pembrokeshire; this was their tower and strong defence; and as some of them, the Rev. David Griffiths in particular, were such fluent preachers, they took the body of the people with them in many areas. This is true for all the country from Cardigan down to Fishguard. It is one of the main reasons for the weakness of Methodism in Pembrokeshire. For the Connexion as a whole however the Ordination was a means of nurture and progress and it established elements of their continuity. But the Ordination proved fatal to evangelical religion within the Established Church. At first, the clergy who used to meet with the Methodists sought to maintain similar meetings and they arranged that their best preachers would minister at them. But although these meetings prospered for a while they did not catch the imagination of the people at large. As the clergy who had been leavened with the spirit of Methodism died one by one, the meetings became less popular, less influential, and in the end disappeared completely. As for the preachers and exhorters who had turned their backs on the Connexion at the time of crisis and cast in their lot with the clergy, their popularity and usefulness soon came to an end. There was no place for them in the Established Church nor any work for them to accomplish. A few returned but the majority spent the rest of their lives apart, quite useless, and bitter of spirit.

[1] CH, 48, p. 78

[2] See Volume 1, p. 428–30.

[3] D. E. Jenkins, *Calvinistic Methodist Holy Orders* (Caernarvon, 1911), p. 107.

[4] Evan Griffiths (1778–1839). Brother-in-law to Ann Griffiths, the hymnwriter.

[5] D. E. Jenkins, *Thomas Charles*, Vol. 3, pp. 271–2.

35

THE CLERGYMEN WHO REMAINED

THE REV. JOHN WILLIAMS, LLEDROD

A total of seven clergymen threw in their lot with the Methodists during the agitation over ordination: four in the south and three in the north. In the south, the Revs John Williams, Lledrod; John Williams, Pantycelyn; Howell Howells, Trehill; and William Howells, Llangen, stood firm; in the north, the Revs. Thomas Charles; Simon Lloyd; and William Lloyd, Caernarvon. We have already discussed the histories of Thomas Charles and John Williams, Pantycelyn, and in this and the following chapter will consider the others.

We will look first at John Williams, Lledrod. He was born in 1747 at Penwernhir, a farmhouse about half a mile to the northeast of Pontrhydfendigaid in Cardiganshire. His parents were William Rees Mathias and Anne Rees Mathias, and according to the custom of the age he took his father's first name as a surname and became John Williams. He was the youngest but one of seven children. It is said in *Methodistiaeth Cymru* that both parents were religious but this was not the case. His father died when John was only four years of age and it does not seem that there was any inclination in him towards religion. Nor did his mother, nor any of the older children profess religion. But Martha his aunt, the daughter of the nearby farm, Dolfawr, and his mother's sister, was a notably godly woman. She had been convicted in all probability by the ministry of the Rev. Philip Pugh, the Presbyterian minister at Llwynpiod, and she attended regularly at Llwynpiod. But when the Methodists came to the neighbourhood and established a society at Penlan, near Swyddffynnon, Martha joined them. She was the means of bringing preaching to Pontrhydfendigaid village, and in *Methodistiaeth Cymru* it is said that she built the chapel there 'at her own cost'. After his father died, John Williams, together with his youngest sister Martha, were sent to live with this aunt and they were both raised under her wing. Martha, Dolfawr, eventually married a man called John Thomas. Nothing is known of him but they do not seem to have had any children of their own, so that all their love and care fell upon the two orphans from Penwernhir. John Williams was a very playful boy when a child; he would always be in some trouble and there was no end to his mischievousness and tricks. He was the ringleader of all the local children. But he was a ready learner and his aunt ensured that he had every opportunity to develop his talents. It is said that he excelled his peers in wrestling, football, and arithmetic. Ystradmeurig School was near at hand, where the famous Edward Richard was master. John Williams attended the school for years learning Latin and Greek and all the other knowledge that was considered essential at the time. From there he was sent to the grammar school at Carmarthen where a clergyman called Maddox was in charge. It was understood from the beginning that John Williams was to be raised for the Church. That was his aunt's ambition for him; that was also the spirit that pervaded the Ysgolmeurig school; and it was thoroughly consistent with his own inclinations, because of his love of books. There was not the slightest desire in him to save souls; indeed, he had felt no anxiety whatsoever as to his own soul. He must have heard Daniel Rowland many times when young; perhaps he went with his aunt to hear him at Pontrhydfendigaid or Hen Fynachlog; he also held the Calvinistic Methodists in considerable respect, but through it all he had never had a sight of his guilt and uncleanness as a sinner.

APPOINTED CURATE OF LLANNWNWS AND LLEDROD

He was ordained as a deacon by Dr Charles Moss, 19 August 1770, when twenty-three years old. He received the title for the curacy of Llannwnws and Lledrod from the Rev. Daniel Jones, Sunny Hill, Tregaron. This man received the livings of four parishes: Tregaron, Mynachlog, Llannwnws and Lledrod, but was now of such an age that he could not fulfil his duties, not even in the superficial and careless way in which it was done in those days, without the help of a curate. At the same time, he was afraid that the young man from Dolfawr had inclinations towards the Methodists. He had heard nothing against him in this respect but he knew of his aunt, Mrs Martha Thomas, that she was a zealous Methodist. Before providing him with a letter introducing him to the attention of the bishop, the old clergyman demanded that this matter be cleared up.

'They tell me that you are a Methodist,' he said.

'Not at all,' replied the young man, with some excitement, 'I am not one of those devils.'

This satisfied the clergyman and the young man was approved. The condition of the Church of England must indeed have been dire if its clergy would rather choose men of strong language rather than those who sorrowed for the ungodliness of the land. The letter of introduction was provided and John Williams was ordained as priest by the Bishop of St David's, on 1 September 1771.

He married Miss Anne Rosser, Llwyngronwen, in the same year, and they went to live at Ty'nddrainen, a farm near Swyddffynnon. He had some distance to travel to the churches that he served but he had a good horse and no doubt the services in both places were not long nor of a nature that would tire him unduly. He felt nothing of the importance of his office; he galloped through the services quite thoughtlessly and would then deliver something in the form of a sermon that contained nothing that might convict the careless or comfort a grieving soul. The priesthood was for him merely something that provided a living. But he was in his element with the sports. He threw himself into these with all the enthusiasm of his nature. As in the days of his youth, he would be the ringleader wherever he might be. There is an account of how, one Saturday afternoon, he played football in front of Lledrod Church. He was covered in sweat with his coat thrown aside and his sleeves rolled up. He was caught up in the game but it was getting late, and every now and then he would remember that he had not prepared the sermon for the following day. At last he picked up his coat abruptly and said to his friends,

'I can't stay longer; I'm enjoying the game but I must go home and prepare a sermon for tomorrow.'

'Don't worry,' said one of his companions, 'I've got the sermons of Rowland, Llangeitho, at home. You may borrow them and read whichever you want.'

'Excellent,' replied the curate. 'One of those will do. They are Goliath's sword; there is nothing like them.'

He therefore threw down his coat again and played on as energetically as usual until it got too dark. We do not know how he prospered with the sermon on the next day. He probably read Rowland's quickening, evangelical sermon so thoughtlessly that no one paid any heed to the truths declared.

Though the Rev. John Williams gained no great name as a preacher during this period, his fame spread abroad for another reason, namely as an exorcist of ghosts. The land was full of superstitions from coast to coast, but the parishes of Lledrod, Llangwyryfon and Llanrhystyd seemed to be more fully possessed by the fear of hobgoblins than any others. Soon after Mr Williams began to serve the church at Lledrod, two men came to the house, pale and trembling, and in the greatest excitement, asking him to help in a great tragedy that had occurred in a house at the far reaches of the parish.

'What is the matter?' he asked.

'Oh,' said one of the men, breathlessly, 'we went to collect the body of a man who had died and to raise him from the trestle in order to place him in the coffin, but he fell like an eel through our hands on to the floor, and no one now dares to touch him.'

The local knowledge was that a spell had been placed upon the man while he was alive; that under the influence of evil spirits he had wasted away and died; that these now lived in his body watching over their prey, and that the proof of this was that the body had not stiffened after death. Therefore, fearing to provoke the anger of the spirits, no one was now willing to touch him. Mr Williams himself was not completely free from the effect of this superstition, though he knew that there was no truth in it. But as a clergyman who indulged in sports, he felt that his character was already in the balance and so he went with the men, though it was night, and with every appearance of courage. 'But little did they know,' he said later, 'that I could hardly draw breath as I approached the house, and especially as I entered it. I knew well enough that there was nothing there to fear but the old impressions still had their mark of me.' However, he took hold of the body immediately and placed it in the coffin. Furthermore, in order to keep the family from fears, he remained there all night. The story of the clergyman's bravery spread throughout the neighbourhood. All believed implicitly in his authority over spirits, and were comforted in the knowledge that the curate of Lledrod stood between them and any evil from that direction. Later, again, he said, 'I do not believe that the evil spirits had any fear of me at that time, but I believe they have had something to fear since that time.' That is, since he had begun a serious assault upon the kingdom of darkness.

Though he was so thoughtless about his hearers' conditions at this time and the thought of being the means of spiritual blessing to them had never entered his head, yet it seems he was full of envy at the popularity of the Methodist preachers, and was particularly angry at the hordes that would travel to Llangeitho to listen to Rowland. Many years later, when Mr Lloyd, Cilpyll, had locked the doors of Llanddewibrefi Chapel, as mentioned in the last chapter, someone went to Mr Williams to ask his advice on the matter. His answer was, 'Let the man be; he is one to be pitied; the poor man has not had his eyes opened. I was just like him once when I was the sinful curate of Lledrod. I felt at that time, as I saw the people going in their hundreds over the mountains to Llangeitho, that I was ready to shoot every one of them; but there was a time soon afterwards when I rejoiced to go with them. His eyes have not been opened.'

HIS CONVERSION

It is not known how long John Williams ministered at Llannwnws and Lledrod before he was converted. But on one occasion, Mr Williams, the vicar of Llanfair Clydogau, known locally as 'Williams *bach*', came to Lledrod to preach. There must after all have been some tolerance in the curate's makeup: he not only permitted the use of the church but also came himself to hear the preacher. 'Williams *bach*' was a fiery preacher and it is hard to understand why there has not been more attention paid to him as one of the Methodist clergymen. He certainly travelled much in order to preach. It was in his company that the Rev. Evan Richardson went to Gwynedd for the first time. Possibly, as with so many other bright stars of whom only their names are presently known, he was taken away when still young. His sermon at Lledrod however was accompanied by very evident unction; the flashes of lightning were such that terror held sway throughout the church, and in amongst the congregation the curate trembled like an aspen leaf. And if the sermon was strange, the prayer afterwards was even stranger. Instead of using a prayer out of the Book of Common Prayer, the preacher poured out his soul on behalf of the minister and the congregation; he confessed that the one was just as bad as the other; that the hearers were goats and the minister a billy-goat. At the close of the service, they met in the church house.

'Well, Mr Williams *bach*,' said John Williams to the preacher, 'you listed many of my sins before the Almighty today.'

'And did I say too much?' was the response.

'No, no, but you left out something important.'

'What was that?'

'You forgot to ask the Lord to forgive me.'

'Oh, as far as forgiveness is concerned,' said the preacher, 'you must go and ask for that for yourself, and you may have it freely.'

The Rev. John Williams was never the same man again. That sermon in Lledrod Church lodged in his soul as a summons from God. His heart was filled with an unspeakable dread. For a while he was on the verge of insanity, and his despair was so great that his wife feared that he would put an end to his life. When he would go out to walk in the fields, his wife would ask the labourers to watch over him. They noted that he was always on his knees in the corners of the fields and in the shade of the hedgerows, and they often heard him crying out for mercy. One of the first things he did was to burn his old sermons. On seeing some papers on the fire, Mrs Williams asked him what they were.

'Only the sermons,' he replied.

'Remember,' she said, 'if any man's work shall be burned, he shall suffer loss.'

'They are all a loss,' he replied. 'They were never a help to anyone.'

Mr Williams never forgot this awful wrestling with God along the fields of Ty'nddraenen. He would always remember the 'Black Setting', as he called it, throughout his life. The 'Black Setting' were the hedges of blackthorn that were rife in the hedgerows lining the fields of Ty'nddraenen, and after which the farm was probably named [*Ty'nddraenen* = the house in the thorn bush]. In an Association, years later, he once said while counselling the preachers:

> I was for many years with no knowledge of what it was to compose a sermon, but when I was lost for a message I found it under the Black Setting. And as soon as I had found it, it proved to be too sharp for the Church people, so that I had to leave, and I have always been thankful that I could go somewhere where I could express my mind to the people.

At another time, in a Monthly Meeting, he said:

> No preacher should be without some booth, or room, where he may go for a message. I am quite sure that for all those sermons that were a profit to the people, I obtained them under the Black Setting.

The account given in *Methodistiaeth Cymru* of Mr Williams's conversion is different from the above. According to Mr Hughes:

> There is no certainty as to when or where this wild sham preacher was convicted, but the following is certain: that it was while listening to Daniel Rowland that the arrow pierced his heart.

This cannot be correct because Evan Rhys, Llan-non, states in the elegy that he wrote for John Williams, and that was published at the request of the Cardiganshire Monthly Meeting:

When listening to a Williams, from Llanfair,	Wrth wrando un Williams, o Lanfair,
He lost all assurance of life.	Y collodd pob hyder cael byw.

Evan Rhys was one of Mr John Williams's closest friends; they journeyed much together in carrying the gospel through the length and breadth of Cardiganshire and they died within three years of each other. It cannot be doubted that Mr Williams would have shared with his friend, dozens of times, the service in which Sinai's terrors pierced his soul and in which he saw himself for the first time as a guilty sinner before God. Furthermore, this elegy was published within six months of Mr Williams's death and had it contained a mistake on this issue, someone certainly would have pointed it out. At the same time there might still be an element of truth in John Hughes's statement: if it was the sermon of 'Williams *bach*' that wounded John Williams, Lledrod, it might well have been under the ministry of Daniel Rowland that the balm was poured into his wounds. There is a hint that this might have been the case to be found in his own words when he said that there came a time when he rejoiced to go to Llangeitho. 'Williams *bach*' left him trembling before a broken law, with the sound of the thunderous threats of the law filling his ears, but Rowland directed him towards the mercy-seat and the blood, and this view wrought an eternal peace in his soul.

Mr Williams was by now not only a new man but also a new preacher, full of desire for bringing sinners to the Saviour. On one of the first Sundays after his conversion he announced at the end of the service that he would be glad to meet with any one of his hearers who was distressed as to his or her spiritual state, and he announced a time and place for the meeting. In this, no doubt, he was imitating the Methodist society. The appointed time came and only three people turned up: an old man and two old women. After beginning the meeting with a reading and prayer, he spoke to them:

'What is it,' he said to one of the two women, 'that is on your mind?'

'It is a very acute pain in my side,' she said, 'so that I can't sleep, or walk, or do anything almost; and I came to you, sir, to ask if you can give me any advice.'

'Isn't the state of your soul grieving you?' he asked.

'No,' was the answer, 'I am perfectly happy as to my soul.'

Having failed to do anything for her, he turned to the second old woman, asking what it was in particular that was disturbing her.

'I came here,' she said, 'to ask your help, sir, to intercede with the overseer; he has reduced my pay from the parish and I cannot live on the little that I get now.'

By now, Mr Williams was vexed in spirit at seeing such darkness of ignorance and such perfect carelessness with regard to spiritual matters, so that he began to speak seriously to them as to their condition; that another world was approaching, and that a great, deep river lay between them and that world, the waves of which had carried many away into an eternal dead sea. The old man listened carefully to his words and as he heard of the depth of the river and its awful current, he broke out:

'I had an old mare that I swear could swim any river, but unfortunately she has been sold.'

These are examples of the gross ignorance that possessed those who attended the Church of England at this time. Their minds were not awakened; the service was an empty form; they passed through the world as thoughtlessly as animals. This was not illustrative of the whole of the country because the Methodists had by now been proclaiming destruction upon an ungodly world for almost forty years and hundreds had been brought to a knowledge of the truth. But for those who had kept away and had stayed with Mr Williams in Lledrod and Llannwnws churches, this was their dark condition. He found another example of similar darkness when visiting a sick old lady who had been a faithful attender at Llannwnws. When he asked how she was, she replied:

'I am not well; someone broke my dog's leg in the woods, yesterday morning, and I'm worried about him.'

'He was chasing rabbits, I suppose,' said Mr Williams.

'They had no business touching my dog,' said the old woman grumpily.

He tried to turn the conversation to spiritual things. He told her, very solemnly, that he saw signs of decay upon her house and that in all probability it would soon fall. But the old lady understood everything literally and said:

'I have spoken to the landowner about the old house many times, but there's not a suggestion that he will come to repair it.'

Some might be able to smile at answers that reveal such a poverty of spirit, but they will draw a tear from the eye of every thinking person.

JOHN WILLIAMS LEAVES THE CHURCH OF ENGLAND

We said that Mr Williams was by now a new preacher. He began to thunder against the sins of the land with such an awful strength that even the blockish creatures that came regularly to the Church began to fear. The story spread that some strange change had occurred to the sermons of the curate and the two churches filled so that there was no room for all the people. Before long, a powerful outpouring of the Holy Spirit was experienced, producing singing and praising, just as in Llangeitho. Lledrod and Llannwnws became the gathering places of vast numbers of the common people, both on Sundays and on other days when Mr Williams was preaching. He was often called upon to visit other churches also. When travelling together, many years later, with Mr Daniel Jones, Dolaubach, to a Monthly Meeting at Blaenannerch, and when passing Blaenporth Church, he said:

> I preached in that church many years ago. I was speaking of the meticulous demands of the law of God upon a sinner, and how the sinner has nothing with which to return an answer, and a strange influence spread through the place. It affected the curate so much that he lost his senses and was never again afterwards able to go about his duties.

But such intense seriousness as this was not to be tolerated in the Established Church; tranquillity was the accepted characteristic there. And as Mr Williams felt it a duty to warn the ungodly of their danger and then to send them to Christ for relief, somebody hurried off to the Bishop to complain of his behaviour. He was also accused of mixing with the Methodists and of attending their meetings. This was not acceptable to St David's and the curate soon received letters warning him to stop and to change his ways or else be deprived of his post. Some of his friends advised him to be more careful but he would not listen to them. He had put his hand to the plough and would not look back. He eventually learnt of a plan to stop him from preaching in the churches on the Sunday following. He was not sure what to do and journeyed to Llangeitho to ask Daniel Rowland for advice. He was told not to go any longer to the churches, so that his persecutors might not have the pleasure of throwing him out, but to come to Llangeitho the next Sunday.

This he did, and he never again preached in the Established Church. It is said, although we do not know on what basis, that he was offered the curacies of the two churches again later, and that his wife tried to persuade him to take them 'because of their swarm of children', but his answer was, 'I cannot; they are not my people; and if we had better nourishment for the body by returning, we could not have peace of conscience nor approval from God.' How long Mr Williams served in the Church is uncertain. *Methodistiaeth Cymru* states that it was for twelve years and that he departed in 1784. It says further that this was the year in which the Association was held for the first time at Aberystwyth and that Mr Williams was present, and that he obtained such a hold on God when praying at family worship in the house where he lodged that all broke out into praising. The noise was heard by the neighbours and a crowd gathered. The fire soon spread to these also, who also began to praise God. Those inside joined the crowd outside and they went together to the market-house and were there until dawn, singing and rejoicing.

When the Rev. John Williams joined the Methodists they did not have a chapel in Pontrhydfendigaid or in Swyddffynnon. The home of the cause was at Penlan, a farmhouse near Swyddffynnon. Preaching would take place there and the society met there also. The meetings were led by Sion of

Gamer, a relatively unknown exhorter from the Tregaron neighbourhood; he also was the superintendent of the cause. The brotherhood rejoiced greatly at the acquisition of the new member. His aunt, Martha, Dolfawr, had been a member here for years and been a blessing to the cause. The cup of Sion of Gamer was running over. After the society he said to some of his friends, 'We caught a good fish in the net at Penlan,' and added, 'Here's a strange state of affairs: an old exhorter like me receiving a clergyman into the society.' To the end of his life he felt that the one great work of his life was the receiving of John Williams into the fellowship of the society. The old exhorter was a companion to Mr Williams scores of times afterwards in their travels to evangelize, and sometimes he would have occasion to refer to his weaknesses but would usually add at the end that whatever his failings there was at least one great thing that he had done during his life.

We have no material from which to follow the life of Mr Williams after he joined the Methodists. In one sense his history ends as his usefulness begins. But everything points to his having worked hard all his life and his labours were blessed to the conversion of many. His break with the Church was complete; he was not half-Churchman and half-Methodist, but a thoroughly Methodist preacher, without the slightest desire to return to the Egypt from which he had departed. His contribution before the Ordination in administering the sacraments was immense. After the death of Daniel Rowland, the Methodists of the south depended primarily upon him for the ordinances. His connection with Lledrod ended when he left the Church but he was always known colloquially as 'Williams, Lledrod'. As the Rev. John Evans has said, 'It was not his going to Lledrod but his leaving Lledrod, that connected his name so inseparably with the place.' The cause throughout the whole surrounding area succeeded greatly once he had joined the Connexion. Chapels were built in Pontrhydfendigaid and in Swyddffynnon, and it was through his influence over Mr Lloyd, Mabws, that land was obtained for the latter.

JOHN WILLIAMS'S PREACHING

This is perhaps the most appropriate place to portray him as a man and as a preacher. Mr David Jones, Dolaubach, describes him thus:

> He was a strong, lively and handsome man. He was not much shorter than six feet, with a long face bearing the marks of smallpox, a high forehead, quite a large nose, and eyes that tended to be closed but that sparkled with a cheerfulness that always made his companions happy. His hair was auburn until it became white with age. His voice was clear and bell-like until middle age. He stood as upright as a staff and all his movements were brisk and lively.

This description of him from middle age onwards may be depended upon in that Mr Jones knew him well, heard him preach scores of times, and spent many hours in his company.

As to his character as a preacher, there is less agreement. When he joined the Methodists he was full of the spirit of the Revival and he maintained this for several years. At this time his voice was pleasant, his soul on fire, and his passion for obtaining the great goal of preaching was intense. But about twenty years before his death he caught a heavy fever in which he completely lost the tunefulness of his voice; from then on it was a hoarse, rough voice. The content of his sermons however was full of matter and on occasions he would have powerful services, overcoming all before him. As far as we can gather, his style was simple and his language plain and rustic, and when the power came upon him, it would be in a sudden rush, falling abruptly upon the congregation. Ebenezer Morris, Ebenezer Richard, and Thomas Richard, were more gifted than he but because he was an ordained man and older than they, it was considered appropriate that he should always preach last in the Monthly Meetings and Associations. Because of this he found himself in difficulties on many occasions. Yet often he obtained a complete mastery over a congregation notwithstanding the remarkable influences of a previous sermon.

There is an account of him at an Association at Capel Newydd, Pembrokeshire. It had been an outstanding Association. In it, Ebenezer Morris had experienced one of the greatest services of his life when preaching from the words, 'But the path of the just is as the shining light.' A local member of the gentry had promised to help the Association as much as he could if it were arranged that he could hear Mr Morris at ten o'clock. He had his wish, and heard the preacher upon his high places. At two, the Revs. Robert Griffith, Dolgellau, and John Williams, Lledrod, preached. The Rev. Robert Griffiths was well known for his wisdom and orderliness.

His sermons always had an ordered structure that was then worked out regularly and in detail; his taste was pure, and his words chaste and choice. He had a very successful service and pleased the people greatly, as he spoke on the text, 'God hath chosen you to salvation . . . whereunto he called you.' We do not know what Mr Williams's text was, but his delivery was rather leaden and slow to begin with. Before he concluded however, an influence, 'like a ball of fire', according to one witness, fell upon the congregation. What affected his hearers was his description of a man on his way to perdition. Having described his sinful life he called upon the congregation to consider him hanging over the precipice of destruction. Raising his voice to a sound of thunder and stretching his long arms down over the edge of the platform, with his whole frame manifesting his agitation, he called upon them:

'Do you see him? Do you see him? Proudly pursuing his course straight towards the edge. He knows nothing of the danger ahead of him. But here he is, on the very edge! Is anyone able to save him? But what is the point of asking? There is no one but God! Ask him, people: "According to the greatness of thy power preserve thou those that are appointed to die." He will fall at any instant, unless he finds deliverance. But God can save.'

The scene by now was indescribable. Thousands were excited to the verge of madness and were stretching upwards on their feet as if to see the man falling over the edge. At the close, Williams gave out the following hymn:

A fountain of water and blood,	Caed ffynnon o ddwr ac o waed,
Is found for the blackest to wash.	I olchi rhai duon eu lliw.

Great rejoicing broke out as they sang; the last line:

Jerusalem too shall be clean.	Jerusalem hefyd ddaw'n lân.

was repeated again and again. There were scores of people from Newcastle Emlyn at this Association and they all shared in the rejoicing. They returned home, singing all the way. As they approached the town, some changed the words and sang:

And Newcastle too shall be clean.	Castellnewydd hefyd ddaw'n lân.

John Evans, Llwynffortun, was to preach at Newcastle Emlyn that night and those who were arriving from the Association called upon the townspeople to attend the service, saying, 'It is going to be a Bethel here tonight,' Bethel was the name of the chapel, and the service became a Bethel indeed because the old evangelist from Llwynffortun flew aloft into the midst of heaven, bearing the everlasting gospel.

Mr Williams had another very effective meeting the following evening when preaching on the storm on the Sea of Galilee. Having described brilliantly the safety of the boat, he called out powerfully, 'Tell me, will you enter her? I can assure you that it is perfectly safe. I will show you one plank of it now. Here it is: "Come unto me, all ye that labour and are heavy laden, and I will give you rest." There you are, venture upon him, as you are; I guarantee you that you will never regret it.' Loud praises broke out throughout the chapel as the people rejoiced at the view given to them of the security of salvation and they remained for many hours in the chapel, worshipping and praising.

Mr Williams and the Rev. Ebenezer Richard preached at the Llanddewi Aber-arth Monthly Meeting at eleven o'clock on the last day. Great illumination accompanied the words of Mr Richard when speaking from the text, 'For him has God the Father sealed.' He said that Christ, when on earth, wore the garments of a servant but that God, when he saw that it was necessary, would raise the fringe of the curtain and reveal the seal of authority. The dew was fast falling, and the people revelling in the Word. After him, Mr Williams arose. The congregation appeared a little disappointed; they feared that the remainder of the meeting would be dry and lifeless. He took as a text, Song of Solomon 8:6, 'Set me as a seal upon thy heart.' He began slowly and without life but soon he remarked, 'My brother in his sermon said that Christ had been sealed in order to save us; and my text expresses the desire of the Church to be a seal upon Christ's heart to show that he has accomplished his purpose, just as a soldier wears a medal on his breast as an indication of victory. My brother showed Christ as one authorized to save; I wish to describe him as one who has performed his work, and the work becomes his glory, a seal upon his heart, and a seal upon his arm.' His spirit gradually warmed; his words began to take hold of his congregation, especially when he began to speak of love's coals of fire:

> The flame of love is a flame that scatters fiery coals in all directions; and as it sparks forth, ungodly men cannot stand before it. We have an old elder in Tregaron who has only to appear, and whatever the force of the devil in the place, he will be sure of clearing the pit. The sparks from a sanctified life, stemming from the heart of Christ, can defeat the worst men of the land. Do not let the enemy close you in too much; resolve at times to clear the pit.

By now, his spirit was thoroughly aroused. He threw his arms about, and shouted out powerfully:

> Oh, that some of this power might come down! Oh, for this fiery coal! It would clear the stench of the world and its ways and would give us some scope in the midst of this crooked and perverse nation.

The whole congregation was in his hand and the service concluded in much excitement. At the close the following verse was sung:

O love, O love, of such infinite depths;	O gariad, O gariad, anfeidrol ei faint;

and the people returned home after experiencing one of the most remarkable of meetings in which they had been taught to wonder and fear. The meaning of the phrase, 'to clear the pit', refers to the selling of a horse at auction with the crowd pressing around it, and the horse is set trotting around in order to extend the circle. This sermon was talked of in Cardiganshire for many years and was known as the *'Clearing the Pit' Sermon*.

A powerful service in a Monthly Meeting at Lledrod is also remembered. There had been nothing significant in the preceding sermon; Mr Richard, Tregaron, had slept through it all – he was troubled by a sleeping-sickness during the latter part of his life. But as soon as Mr Williams opened his mouth, the atmosphere changed. Soon the preacher's spirit was aflame and the sparks flying throughout the congregation. Before the sermon was half way through, the people were melted and weeping. As for Mr Richard, his whole frame was shaking as if caught in an earthquake and great tears were flowing down his cheeks. It is said that Mr Williams shouted, with upraised arms, '*Bendigedig*; I have been allowed to live to see one more springtide in Lledrod. Do not be surprised if the vessels of some of you are afloat and free before the end of the service.'

LEADING THE SOCIETIES

He once preached also at Llan-non, when his text was, 'And I will put enmity between thee and the woman.' The sermon had not been particularly fluent but he had exerted himself particularly to describe the attacks upon the head by one, and upon the heel by the other. On concluding, he was given remarkable strength in prayer and amongst other things, said, 'Pull up your heels, O Lord; the enemies are attacking; but they will not have the sport of bruising even your heel, if you will hasten to bring forth your work.'

It is clear from the above that 'Williams, Lledrod,' was an effective preacher who at times had glorious services, but, if anything, he excelled even more in the society – the '*seiat*' – than in the pulpit. Here, his thorough honesty, his homely way of speaking, his directness, and the attractiveness of his wit, opened up for him the deepest communion with the souls of those with whom he dealt, and to this day there are scores of his sayings in the societies that are remembered up and down the various neighbourhoods where he ministered. When counselling the young people once, he said that he had heard from one old woman the best explanation he knew of the deceitfulness of the devil.

> The old woman told me, 'These words came to my mind, "We are not ignorant of his devices", and I saw immediately that there was some weakness in his kingdom or he would not have to practise his devices in order to sustain it.' That old woman was absolutely right, and you be careful that you don't help to prop up a kingdom that is too weak to stand without the help of deceitful tricks.

When speaking to a brother in trouble, he said:

> It is circumstances that reveal to us what kind of religion we have. It is hard to know what is in the barrel before tapping it. Cain was tapped, and he became a murderer; Abraham was tapped, and 'he was called the Friend of God'; Joseph was tapped, and he said, 'How then can I do this great wickedness, and sin against God?' Job was tapped, and he said, 'Blessed be the name of the Lord'; but his wife was tapped, and what she said was, 'Curse God, and die'.

Once in Lledrod, a young woman had quarrelled with her mother, without much cause, and the matter came before Mr Williams in the church meeting. The mother soon came to terms, stating that she was ready to take any step and that if she had been unfair to her daughter she asked her forgiveness. But the daughter remained stubborn – she seemed as hard as adamant. 'What?' he said to her, 'Will you not forgive your own mother? The mother who laboured to carry you in her womb for many months; the mother who gave birth to you when between the living and the dead; the mother who suckled you on her breasts, and who kept you day and night from every harm and danger, when you could not lift a hand to defend yourself. Remember that she is your mother. Who should have compassion on her if not her daughter? Who is it who is bound closest to her if not her daughter?' His words went straight to the heart, and the feelings of the members of the society had long been overcome; their tears were flowing freely. But as for the girl, she remained as unfeeling as a rock, and it seems that she had to be excommunicated. That was still her situation when she died, an object of contempt to the whole neighbourhood.

He was once sent by the Monthly Meeting to help the church at Newquay to choose elders, and in order to teach the members what kind of man to elect, he told them the following parable:

> A man and his wife in our neighbourhood required a head-servant at All Hallows Day, and Evan asked Mary, 'What do you think we should do about a head-servant this year?' 'I don't know,' said Mary. 'What do you think?' 'Well,' said Evan, 'I've been thinking about Sianco, the second servant. Sianco is very careful. If there's a gap in the hedge he'll be there immediately with his pick and spade to rebuild it; if a gate is open, he will usually see it and close it; if some of the cattle break into the clover so that they are in danger of swelling up, he is sure to spot them and to hasten to find medicine. Whenever he comes home in the night, if he hears the horses kicking each other in the stable he will be sure to quiet them before he goes to bed. And if it is stormy, and the wheat and straw stacks in danger of losing their covers, Sianco will be there straight away rearranging the sheaths.' 'I am of exactly the same opinion,' said Mary. 'What if we called him up to the house?' This was done and the man said to the servant, 'Sianco, we intend to make you head-servant this year.' 'Oh, I am not fit, master,' said Sianco. 'Yes, we will raise your wages,' said Evan. 'I

> have much more than I deserve now,' answered the servant. 'Are you tired of working for us?' 'Oh no, not at all, dear master. I would be happy to serve you forever.' 'Well,' said Evan, 'will you agree to the appointment.' 'I will, if you think that I am fit for the work, but you must show me what to do.'
>
> Now, you must look for some second servant like Sianco; he will make you an excellent elder. There are many gaps in God's Church that need to be closed up and it would be good to have an observant servant to spot them. There are many diseases that must be dealt with, lest the people die in their sins.

Mr Williams used a very homely and rustic parable but the weakest of the congregation could understand his meaning, and it seems that the church succeeded in finding an elder possessing the characteristics described.

Mr Williams could express himself very bluntly and could be severe when the occasion required it. At the Swyddffynnon society, a man whom he knew well was relating a particularly spiritual experience but as his daily life did not conform to what was being said, Mr Williams doubted the truth of the experience. The man however waxed ever more eloquent, stating that he had received assurance as far as his state before God was concerned and that he had been full of glory and light ever since that time. Mr Williams could not take any more of his claims and broke out in some agitation: 'All of the head; all of the head. You must find a religion of the heart or else you will be in the flames.' But he could be very tender when he discerned evidences of repentance and he would be wonderfully skilful in treating wounds and in pouring balm upon the deeply injured. In a Pont-rhydfendigaid society once, a man was being reproved for drunkenness; he manifested a deep grief on account of his behaviour and because of the shame he had brought upon the name of Christ. When some of the elders began to deal rather harshly with him, Mr Williams got to his feet and said, with tears flowing, 'Shall we smite one whom God has smitten?' Another time, in Tregaron, when some woman's case was being considered because of some transgression, and all were rather scornful of her, Mr Williams encouraged some others to contribute. For some time no one would respond. He therefore came down from the little pulpit where he had been sitting after preaching and asked the woman if she viewed herself as a sinner. She confessed that she did; that she was a great sinner; and that she could see nowhere to turn to for help but to Jesus Christ. On questioning her about her sins and her Saviour, and on receiving such simple and honest answers, his heart melted, together with that of the congregation. 'Here we are, *pobl bach*,' he said. 'This is where we must all come. This is where I was forced to come, and where I found my life.' The woman was received back into her place amidst general satisfaction and it is said that she lived a bright Christian life from that time until her death.

He possessed a store of common sense that was often in evidence when he was leading a society and dealing with the various circumstances that came before him. In Llangeitho once, he was presiding over the case of someone who had become drunk at a mart. 'I am surprised,' he said, 'at men who become drunk in an auction of all places in the world, in that they know that it is only to fool them to bid more than the worth of the goods that they are given drink in the first place. Once drunk, a wise man will see a heap as big as a stack, and a stack as big as a hill; he'll judge the year-old calf to be a three-year-old bullock, and the three-year-old bullock to be an elephant. And according to the view will be the bid. It is a shame that believers like you should show yourselves such fools before the world.'

It would be unforgivable of us not to mention the extraordinary Association held at Llangeitho in 1819, at the beginning of one of the most powerful revivals that ever shook Wales. It began with a sermon preached on a Sunday morning by Ebenezer Richard, Tregaron, on the words, 'And these shall go away into everlasting punishment.' Powers from heaven had gripped the place that morning; sinners became pale with fright at such truths; their knees knocked together like those of Belshazzar at the feast seeing the fingers of a man's hand writing on the plaster of the wall. Mr Williams was to hold a society at Llangeitho during the following week and seventeen new faces were to be seen amongst the fellowship, all seeking a place in God's house. As he questioned them, one by one, with each one testifying that it was the fearful sermon the previous Sunday that had brought them to realize their need, Mr Williams broke out in excitement, 'Wonderful, the number shot down with one discharge!' He was much broken himself as he conversed with the converts:

'Who is this young man?' he asked of one.

'The son of Morgan.'

'Morgan's son? My dear boy, your father has been in heaven for many years, and how glad I am to see you today beginning to follow after him.'

He had some tender remark or other, of this nature, to say to each of them, so that the older members as well as the newcomers were very soon one mass of tears. This revival affected him greatly in making him more heavenly-minded and tender of spirit. Previously he had been inclined to be a strict disciplinarian, though no one was ever offended by him because of his own entire conscientiousness to the truth, but now, with the gentle south wind blowing so pleasantly upon the garden, he became almost unable to discipline. When a case calling for excommunication was placed before him, he stood dumbfounded before the church and eventually said, 'I don't know what's the matter with me. I am not so ready for this as I once was. There was a time when it did not bother me to throw out a member when I saw that justice was on my side, but now, my feelings are too broken, and I would rather be anywhere else than having to deal with this case.'

HIS LEADERSHIP IN THE CONNEXION

We have already mentioned that John Williams became a thorough Methodist. His love for the Connexion was strong; he held its traditions and the practices of the Fathers in great respect, particularly all that he had learnt from Daniel Rowland, and it was not his wish that any of the old landmarks be removed. The fact that he argued so strongly for the ordination of ministers, and at a time when the other clergymen were showing such opposition, inclines us to think that he may have heard Daniel Rowland suggest that this ultimately would have to be agreed. He was loath to accept change even in small things. The practice in Cardiganshire since the days of Rowland with regard to communion was for all the members to approach the altar – that was the name for 'the big seat' in those days – in order to participate. This was Mr Williams's practice from the beginning. But before the end of his life, he heard that the Rev. Edward Jones, Aberystwyth, had changed the form – keeping the communicants in their seats and taking the elements to them. In the next Monthly Meeting, Mr Williams got to his feet and delivered an address on the practice of the Connexion from its beginnings with respect to the administration of the communion service. 'But,' he said, 'I hear that some in these days are thoughtlessly departing from the traditions of the fathers; men of whom we shall never see their better.' Mr Jones was at the Monthly Meeting and he replied, ' It seems that I am the sinner here; I meant no harm in what I did. I only thought that this was a more appropriate method. I do not believe that you have any reason for calling the people in swarms to the altar, other than that this is the way it always has been done.' How the argument was resolved we do not know but Mr Williams did not succeed in passing any motion of rebuke on Edward Jones.

Mr Williams also shared in some measure in that prejudice held by some of the fathers against equipping ministers with the highest level of education. When the Rev. John Rees, Tregaron, was beginning in the work of the ministry at Ffos-y-ffin, he asked the Monthly Meeting for permission to attend the Countess of Huntingdon's College at Cheshunt. He had been previously at Neuadd-lwyd school with Dr Phillips and the education he had received there had created an appetite in him for more. As far as we know, all he was asking for was permission to attend the College, he had no intention of depending on the Connexion for his support. He had previously expressed his views to Ebenezer Richard, Tregaron, and had been encouraged by him to proceed. But when the matter came up before the Monthly Meeting, Mr Williams hurriedly stood up, stating authoritatively, 'You may not go, John. There are plenty of those college men to be had now; proud creatures, that are no good for anything except living lazy lives. If you want to be a great preacher, John, find the shade of some hedge and deal more in secret. If it wasn't for the Black Setting I would never compose a single sermon that would be of any help to anybody. Believe me, John, you have had enough schooling.' The Revs. Ebenezer Morris and David Evans, Aberaeron, expressed similar thoughts, and the young man had to give up any ambitions for further education. Many will remember the experience of the Rev. Lewis Edwards, D.D., many years after this, being hindered in the same way when he wished to go to university. This prejudice seems strange to us but before we rush to blame these old brethren and to condemn them for their blind narrowness, we must remember that they were all too familiar with the vast majority of the clergymen of Wales, very many of whom had received an university education and one or two of whom were scholars of genius, who were completely devoid of any of that wisdom which is from above, and completely apathetic as to their work as ministers of the Word. It was not lack of scholarship that was the reason for the land before the Methodist Revival to be sunk in paganism, but the lack of awakened ministers. It is not surprising therefore that John Williams and others feared to send the young men to the colleges in case they also were infected by a similar apathy. It may be also that the brethren felt that Cheshunt College could not make John Rees a better preacher. In the event, Mr Rees took the opposition in the best spirit and often referred, in a society or from the pulpit, to Williams, Lledrod, and his Black Setting.

John Williams, like many of his contemporaries, was something of a tyrant in the Monthly Meeting. He would usually chair the meeting if he was present and rarely, at that time, would any matter be put to a vote. Once the chairman had given his judgment, this would be considered law and further discussion would cease. There were quite a few exhorters belonging to the Cardiganshire Monthly Meeting at the time and these tended often to be absent from their homes on preaching journeys so that the churches complained that they were being burdened. It was often necessary therefore for them to be refused permission to journey, and as a rule the responsibility of issuing the denial fell upon Williams, Lledrod. The old exhorter, Isaac James, Penygarn, was a considerable sinner in this respect. On one occasion he and Edward Coslett had agreed to travel together on a journey to Gwynedd. As far as we know they were not responding to a particular invitation. But when Isaac James went to the Monthly Meeting to ask for permission, Mr Williams told him:

'You, Isaac *bach*, are a cobbler, and you should stick to your last. If you are away like this all the time you will deceive the people as to their shoes, and if the people feel that they cannot trust you as far as the boots on their feet are concerned you will undermine all you do as a preacher. The people must have shoes. If they cannot have them from you, they will go where they can find them. I'm afraid, Isaac, that you will harm your craft in this way. And worse still, I'm afraid that the unreliability of the cobbler will damage the sermon of the preacher. Stick to your craft, Isaac.'

Isaac replied:

'Let me go this once, and I will not ask again.'

Mr Williams stamped authoritatively on the floor, saying:

'Upon my word, Isaac, you shall not go.'

But Isaac was quite as agitated himself by now, and he continued:

'I shall go this time and you may do what you want with me on my return, but this shall be my last journey.'

Off he went, but because of his considerable age and because he had promised not to itinerate again, he escaped without any rebuke.

Mr Williams was a great man for detail. He was meticulous with the arrangements of his family and cottage. Every meal had to be on the table to the minute and he ensured that all went to their various tasks at the appropriate time. He was just as meticulous with the arrangements of the Monthly Meeting. He could not tolerate lack of punctuality. A friend of his said that he had a small timepiece, about the size of an ox's eye, and with that he ruled the county. It is recorded that he once began a service at Llanafan when only one old woman was present, and on another occasion at Blaenplwyf when only two others were in the chapel. He often preached at Llangeitho and the congregation would make sure that they were present on time because they knew that he would start on time, people or no people. He was engaged once at Capel Drindod when the Rev. David Griffiths was preaching in the church nearby at about the same time. Mrs Lloyd, Bronwydd, a very godly and generous member of the gentry, greatly desired to hear the two of them, Mr Williams and Mr Griffiths. She drove past Capel Drindod in her carriage and sent her servant to Mr Williams with the request that he would grant her a favour and not begin the service this once until she had returned from the church after hearing the vicar of Nevern. He replied to the servant, ' Go and tell Mrs Lloyd that I will begin the service upon the instant at which it has been announced, but that she may do as she wishes – wait here for the service or not.' The lady remained. Mr Williams's courage was all the greater in that he knew that the Bronwydd family owned all the land about; that Trinity Chapel was built on their land, and at their expense, and that they contributed fifty pounds a year to maintain the cause. He probably also remembered Mr Griffiths' behaviour during the Ordination, particularly his work of closing Nevern Chapel by virtue of his authority as a trustee. David Jones, Dolaubach, used to say that there was no evidence of John Williams ever having broken an engagement, other than when he was ill, and even this was rare in his case, in that he was granted good health throughout his life. Not rain, snow, or storm, would prevent him from preaching once he had given his word. One Sunday morning, it was snowing hard. A strong wind arose, almost certainly meaning that the roads would become blocked by drifting snow. The family judged that it would be presumptuous for him to set out for his engagement. But it was impossible to stop him; he insisted on trying, whether he succeeded or not, and succeed he did.

We have already referred to his usefulness in administering the ordinances in Cardiganshire before the Ordination. The demand for his services in this respect does not seem to have diminished after ministers were ordained. He almost certainly baptized more children than anyone else of that time. Years ago, hundreds of old people from the neighbourhoods of Llangeitho, Tregaron and Lledrod testified they had been baptized by him, and that it was at his hand that they had first received communion. Whenever a new chapel was built it was he, without exception who would be asked to conduct the first communion service. One reason for this was the fact that he was an ordained clergyman, because it was only gradually that the prejudice of many of the Methodists against the ministers of the Connexion evaporated. A large congregation would always gather for the first communion service in a new building. There is an account of the occasion at the new chapel at Pennant. Mr Williams lifted up the plate with the bread to show to the congregation, saying, 'Here it is, *bobol bach;* here is the portrayal of Christ crucified come to us as Methodists. It was long kept within the bounds of the Church, but at last the door has been opened for it to come to us, the Gentiles.' A ray of light from heaven accompanied these words and all broke out in sweet weeping. Some had opposed celebrating the ordinance in the chapel but by the close of the service all prejudice had disappeared. Such was the experience in many other places.

When Mr Williams, Lledrod, joined the Methodists they had sixteen chapels in Cardiganshire. He would preside over Monthly Meetings in many places long before a chapel was built there. There is an account of Mr Gray and himself preaching on top of a lime kiln at a Monthly Meeting in Borth, to the north of the county. In Llanarth, in a similar meeting, he preached from a horse-block; and in Soar, in the mountains between Llanddewibrefi and Llanwrtyd, from on top of the Bron-yr-helem earthwork. But the meeting-places of the county soon multiplied, particularly in the north. The credit for this belongs mainly to Ebenezer Richard, but Mr Williams certainly supported and assisted him in this work to the best of his ability. They both saw more clearly the significance of this step, and were more aware of the need of the country, than were Ebenezer Morris, to the south of the county, and Thomas Richard in Pembrokeshire. They filled the region with chapels from Lampeter up to Graig, near Machynlleth, so that any other denomination could hardly get a look in. It is to the vision and hard work of these two that the fact that the northern half of Cardiganshire is almost completely in the possession of the Methodists must be attributed.

HIS LAST DAYS

Mr Williams never once lived in Lledrod; it was his connection with the church there that caused the name of the place to be linked with his. At the beginning of his married life he lived at Ty'nddraenen, near Swyddffynnon; afterwards, he lived for some time at Tregaron, where he built himself a house, thinking to spend the rest of his days there. But long before he died, he dwelt at Pentre Padarn, a farm about two miles from Llangeitho. The farm came up for sale, he bought it, and there lived out the remainder of his days. He was given a long life, being eighty-four years old when he died. He was able to continue preaching almost right up to the time of his death. We know very little of his last illness other than that it was brief and hard. When he was confined to the house, the Rev. Ebenezer Richard visited him often. On the last visit, Mr Williams said:

'I hear the sound of the chariot coming, and it seems that it comes in haste.'

'What will we do when you are gone, Mr Williams *bach*?' asked Mr Richard.

'Oh, the ark is safe,' he replied.

And having waited a while to gather his strength, he added,

'The God of Israel is he who gives power and strength to the people.'

Mr Richard returned in sadness to his home, having parted with his old friend for the last time. On seeing him so mournful, his wife asked him how Mr Williams was. He replied, with the tears flowing down his cheeks:

'Finished, finished! O, the old dear friends! Mr Williams, Lledrod, also, is soon to meet with them.'

His words were true, for on Sunday, 29 August 1831, the spirit of the Rev. John Williams flew to the land of pure blessedness. On the following Wednesday and Thursday, before he was buried, his brethren held a Monthly Meeting at Lledrod, and their mourning was great for the one whom they all looked upon as a father. Mr Richard and others spoke with deep feeling and the chapel was full of tears.

The next day, the Friday, was the day of the funeral and an immense concourse gathered to honour him. The Rev. Ebenezer Richard preached at Pentre Padarn from the words, 'And Elisha saw it, and he cried, My father, my father, the chariot of Israel, and the horsemen thereof. And he saw him no more; and he took hold of his own clothes, and rent them in two pieces.' He noted, firstly, what Elijah was to Elisha – a father:

> I knew many in Pembrokeshire who were converted under the ministry of our dear brother at a time before I had the privilege of meeting him; I came to know others afterwards here in Cardiganshire and beyond, who had the same testimony. His ministry when he first joined the Methodists was as powerful as to cleave the rocks, and so it remained for many years afterwards.
>
> Secondly, note what Elijah was to Israel – a chariot and horsemen. Williams, Lledrod, also has been of more service to religion than a whole army of chariots and horsemen can be to a country. He was so in his holy life, his awakened ministry, his continuous assaults upon the sins of a land and a Church, his continued care of the churches, and his wise and safe leadership through many a crisis.
>
> Thirdly, his departure – 'He saw him no more.' You also will not see Mr Williams again, not in the pulpit of a chapel, nor in the big seat, warning and exhorting.
>
> Fourthly, that which Elisha proceeded to do – crying out and taking hold of his clothes. We need also today to remember whom it is we are burying. It is a great loss to lose such a man as this; may God enable us to acknowledge this. Do you know of anyone who has taken up his mantle?

A remarkable influence accompanied Mr Richard's words; he himself wept copiously as he spoke, for his own heart was deeply moved, and the people wept as they listened. They then travelled in procession towards Llanwnws cemetery. The distance was about ten miles, but though it was raining and the journey long, they did not turn back. And in the cemetery where he first began preaching they laid the remains of the Rev. John Williams to rest until the resurrection morning.

THE REV. HOWELL HOWELLS, TRE-HILL

The next Methodist clergyman whom we shall consider is the Rev. Howell Howells, Tre-hill. He could hardly be acknowledged a master of the congregation; at no time in his career was he considered a great preacher, but his spirit was warm, his life pure, and his usefulness considerable. He therefore deserves more attention from the Connexion than the brief reference given to him in *Methodistiaeth Cymru*. He was born on 12 May 1750, at Ystradgynlais, a rural area in Breconshire but on the boundary with Glamorganshire, whose commercial and religious connections are all with the latter county. Nothing is known of Howell Howells's parents but that they were probably of comfortable circumstances and that they attended, occasionally at least, at a chapel-of-ease nearby. He also went with them and when a youth of nineteen years old something which he there heard caused him to begin to consider his condition. This resulted in his joining the Methodist society that had been formed at Palleg. He received a rather cold welcome from the old brethren at first. He had not been trembling before Sinai and could not put his finger on the place and time that the great change had occurred in his case. But it soon became clear that he had met with his Saviour even though he might not be able to state where and when – as clear as that Saul met with him outside Damascus.

The young man Howell immediately took to the religious life as conducted amongst the Methodists at that time. The most faithful of the Ystradgynlais pilgrims would go to Llangeitho to take communion, and he would go with them, crossing the Black Mountain, traversing the Towy Valley and then the Teifi Valley, with no sense of weariness such was the sweetness of fellowship along the way. He soon became known for his ability in prayer. His heart was so warm and his spirit so broken, that he was pressed to begin the meetings for the preachers and soon began to travel with them on their journeys. John Evans, Cil-y-cwm, one of David's mighty men, became acquainted with him and the two journeyed together through the north. It must be remembered that Mr Howells went as the companion to the preacher and that his office extended no further than the care of the horses and the beginning of the services. But because of his gift in prayer, John Evans persuaded him to speak a word on a verse to the people. This he did, and from then on he preached throughout the journey and returned to Ystradgynlais a mature speaker. It seems that the persecution in Gwynedd was at its worst at this time; on many occasions cruel men would gather in order to mistreat the two itinerants and they often feared for their lives, but the Lord protected them from any real harm.

Mr Howells however wished to be more than an exhorter only. He decided to become a clergyman. With this purpose he went in 1778 to the grammar school at Llanddowror that had been established by the Rev. Griffith Jones. On 23 September 1781, he was ordained deacon by Dr Warren, Bishop of St David's, and within a year he was ordained priest by the same man. He was not turning his back on the Methodists nor weakening his connections with them in any way as he undertook his training for the ministry. It was clergymen of the Church of England who were considered their leaders at this time, and it was only at the hands of clergymen that the sacraments were received.

The Rev. Howell Howells's first curacy was at Glyncorrwg, a fairly remote parish amidst the mountains of Glamorganshire. How long he ministered here is not known, nor the extent of the success or otherwise of his labours. He is found next a curate at St Nicholas, a parish midway between Cowbridge and Cardiff. It soon became known that he was a Methodist; the warmth of his spirit drew hundreds to hear him, so that the church became too full. The congregation would often break into rejoicing, the walls of the church echoing with their praises, and often the clergyman would join in with them, breaking into praises in the middle of his sermon. This was not the type of priest favoured by the gentry of the Vale of Glamorgan. They desired a man who would gallop enthusiastically behind the hounds and join with them in hunting the otter; one who would attend their feasts, be first on the dance-floor, and prove himself a merry companion during the long winter nights in the taverns of Cowbridge and Cardiff. To them it was disgraceful that the man who ministered in the church on a Sunday should mix with the hotheads and become heated himself as he preached in such a way as to cause others to lose control of themselves. Some of them visited the Bishop's Palace at Llandaff to complain but, to be fair to Bishop Watson, no kinder, or rather no more indifferent prelate ever wore a mitre; and matters never became too difficult for the Methodist curate of St Nicholas, though he was summoned to appear before his bishop many times. All that the prelate required was that he should do his best not to offend the other clergy.

HIS LABOURS IN THE VALE OF GLAMORGAN

It was a wonderful period for religion in the Vale of Glamorgan at this time. Many evangelical clergymen had come to the surrounding neighbourhoods: men such as Christopher Bassett at St Fagans; Howells at St Nicholas; and David Jones at Llan-gan. The small societies were blossoming as roses as a result, and many an old pilgrim would break out into singing on finding relief for his soul. Llan-gan was considered a Jerusalem; there the tribes gathered to praise the name of the Lord. A preparatory society would be held at Salem Chapel, Pencoed, on the last Saturday of every month; believers would gather eagerly there from all directions; and the curate from St Nicholas would not fail to be among them. There, each month, they usually received a feast of fat things, a feast of wine on the lees. Often Mr Howells, with his spirit flaming within him as he spoke of the Man who died, would sing his favourite verse:

God remembered me right early,	Fe'm cofiodd Duw yn fore, fore;
Inscribed my name in letters, clearly;	Fe roes fy enw ymhlith yr achau;
Neither world, nor flesh, nor Satan,	Nis gall na byd, na chnawd, na Satan,
Can blot that name from out of heaven.	Ddim blotio fy enw innau allan.

And after finishing the hymn he would leap as a hart. He would not often return home on the Saturday night but would stay, with other godly clergymen, to assist Mr Jones with the communion the following day. 'And,' according to the Rev. Edward Mathews, 'very rarely would he not obtain relief from the merit of a slain Saviour and would not be shouting of victory on Llan-gan Common before leaving the place.' He would not be on his own – scores would join with him in glorying in the Lord.

Mr Mathews adds:

> Many a selfish little clergyman would snarl angrily because of this, and threaten that the Bishop would take them by the nape of their necks, and this would sometimes cause some difficulty. But then, the occasional breeze from Calvary would clear away all difficulties, and the sound of the world's complaints would be silenced by the shouts of the blood-bought family before the ark of God. The Venerable Jones would evangelize and pronounce peace, would declare goodness and proclaim salvation, and say to Zion, 'Thy God reigneth', until all the hindrances of earth faded away and disappeared.

One of the clergymen most opposed to Mr Howells was the Vicar of Bonvilston but his daughter, Miss Thomas, was of a very different spirit. She fellowshipped with the Methodists. She was not perhaps a member of the society but she loved to be in the company of the saints, sharing with them in the things of the kingdom. She and Mr Howells became acquainted and grew attached to one another. But when he visited her home and asked for her hand, her father became enraged. He reviled Howells for his Methodism and commanded him not to darken his door ever again. But love will laugh at all obstacles, and the young girl decided that if she could not marry with her father's blessing she would do so without it. A few days before the ceremony there was a kind of inquisition into her case. Her uncle attended, and she was called into the parlour to face him and her father. They threatened her severely; the father said that if she were to go with Mr Howells she would never again be received within the walls of his house and he added, 'That man will never come to any good; there is nothing in his head but the wish to follow the Methodists.' But for all the threatening and scolding, the two were married.

After the wedding they went to live in a cottage not far away, called Nantbrân. Mr Howells was not a great farmer and the sages predicted that it would not be long before their affairs collapsed. This prophecy, like many another, was not fulfilled. Mrs Howells was a careful and thrifty woman, knowing well how to deal with the world. Their circumstances soon prospered amazingly. God's blessing lay upon all in the house and in the field. According to Edward Mathews, 'The cottage was fruitful for him, and he was fruitful for God, and God blessed them both.' They had two children, both of whom died in infancy. Neither Mr Howells nor his wife were in any way niggardly; if they saved, it was in order that they might be able to give. Their home became a hostel for wayfarers, every wanderer knew that he would find an overnight home there. Methodist exhorters from every part of the country would direct their way there and know that they would receive a welcome. After Mrs Howells died, her husband inherited considerable wealth from her brother in England. His generosity only increased; he contributed thousands of pounds to religious causes during his life and left large sums in his will to clear the debts of chapels.

The Vicar of St Nicholas was very unhappy over the behaviour of his curate. He complained of the crowds of people that thronged the church, saying that they were causing too much noise and damaging the pews. But it seems that Mr Howells had been given a licence by the bishop and that therefore the vicar could not drive him away without coming himself to serve in his place. Eventually, this is what he did. But Mr Howells was not long out of the ministry; he was soon called to fill the vacant curacy of Llanddiddan Fach, a parish adjoining St Nicholas. His ministry there was accompanied by the same blessing as was experienced at St Nicholas. The common people gathered from all directions. It is said that on the last Sunday of the month they would come from distances of up to ten miles to receive communion. But he was not long suffered to remain at Llanddiddan Fach either. A Dr Marsh had been appointed to the see of Llandaff and he was determined to weed out all the Methodists from amongst his clergy. The prelate sent Mr Howells an ultimatum by the hand of a Mr Deere, the rector of the parish, that he must either leave the Church or else the Methodists; it had to be one or the other. He does not seem to have hesitated for an hour over the course to be taken; he turned his back on the Church of England once and for all and cast in his lot completely amongst the Methodists. This occurred in 1818, when he was sixty-eight years old.

The Rev. Howell Howells does not seem to have journeyed much. The Vale of Glamorgan was his field of labour. He was not free to travel when connected with the Church because of the care of his parish, and when he was turned out he was an old man with his health already deteriorating. As already suggested he was not a gifted preacher but the warmth of his spirit and his gift in prayer made him very acceptable to the congregations of the Vale. With respect to his ability in prayer, Edward Mathews notes:

> All would be delighted when the old pilgrim would approach the throne of grace and plead with God on his own behalf and on that of the congregation. Our late father was an incomparable intercessor with God. Often would he wrestle with his Creator; he would gain the victory over Jehovah and would emerge victorious having received the blessing.

A great affection existed between Mr Howells and his brethren. After it became impossible for him to attend the Associations he would pay particular attention to their deliberations. He would often send his best wishes to them in the warmest of letters and the reading of these would warm the hearts of the whole fraternity. He would be concerned for the ark of God and from his isolated situation would send encouragements to the preachers and elders to remain faithful. Copies of many of his letters are included in the biography of the Rev. Ebenezer Richard, the secretary of the Association for south Wales and we include one of these below as an example of the others. He writes:

> Dear and respected brethren,
>
> I trust that you will kindly receive these lines from me for your encouragement. The great cause in which you are privileged to have a part has been laid heavily upon my poor mind, and also, I hope, upon my heart, weak though that is; and I may confess how often I have greatly feared for the ark of God, namely his great cause amongst us. But I may say with a measure of hopeful trust: I believe that the cloud is still to this day upon the camp, and will remain there until the trumpets sound to cause the tribes to fight their way to the land of promise, and to bring the ark to its own land, to the land of Israel, and to Mount Zion, the city of the living God, with joy and rejoicing, singing and dancing. 'Beautiful for situation, the joy of the whole earth, is mount Zion,' the Church of God. God is known in her palaces for a refuge.
>
> Though I am deprived of the privilege of being amongst you, I believe that my soul and heart long to taste with you of the success of the cause amongst us. O dear brothers, pray for me. Be faithful over a little to the end, you will

be placed over much. Work, labour, dig at the Rock until you find its treasures. If the manna from heaven fails we shall eat of the old corn of the land, until we arrive at home, at our inheritance that fades not away, not one of whose stakes shall ever be removed.

I desire you from the bottom of my heart, and from necessity, that you impress upon the elders and the stewards of the societies in our county, and in all counties, that they be awake in the work; that they go in and out from gate to gate; that they prepare the way of the people; that they cast up the highway and gather out the stones thereof, that the banner might be raised before the people. I imagine I hear the sound of a great multitude approaching; the promises must be accomplished: 'The mountain of the Lord's house shall be established in the top of the mountains . . . and all nations shall flow unto it.' O that the Lord would illuminate us more so that we would prize and appreciate our privilege of being associated with such an excellent and glorious cause. It shall prove of endless profit to us ultimately; such as a hundredfold now in this time, and in the world to come eternal life.

This from your well-wisher, and your dear friend,

HOWELL HOWELLS

The letter clearly proceeds from a warm heart and from one who had the keenest interest in the activities of the Connexion and a heart's care for its success. We are tempted to include here Mr Richard's answer to another letter of Mr Howells's to the Association, as it reveals the great respect in which he was held by his brethren, and is also so characteristic of its author:

Tregaron, 3 September 1827,

Reverend Brother, and Father in the Gospel,

Your sweet and valuable letter to the Llangeitho Association, dated 20 July, came punctually to my hand, and was read by me in the hearing of about three hundred preachers and elders from the north and the south of Wales, gathered at the Association, at one o'clock, the 8th day. Dear sir, it is impossible for me to convey to you the feelings of the Body as they heard it read; it was heard with much tears and joy; and with the deepest feelings of glorying and longing. Glorying, as they beheld one of the oldest brethren of the Body dwelling in the neighbourhood of heaven; glorying, as they understood that he was bearing the fruits of the land of promise on staves to his neighbourhood; glorying, at sensing his heart so concerned for the ark and for the servants of the Lord in the battle along side it; and glorying also at realizing that he has not lost his interest, nor his love, towards the vessel that is our poor Body, found in the midst of many waves. And a deep longing also for seeing your face again amongst us; a longing for drinking deeply from that same spirit that is found so fully upon our dear confined brother; and longing also for that happy morning when we shall meet in one eternal assembly, with none of the family absent, and none but the family together.

The whole Body, with one voice, has commanded me to remember them to you in the most loving and kindest way, and to state that they are sincerely thankful to you for your simple, faithful and evangelical letter, at the reading of which many a weak brother found himself strengthened, and said, 'Let us go up and possess the land.' They charged me, as their poor secretary, to communicate the above decision to you, sir. But O that the duty might have been passed on to someone more appropriate! It distresses me to think of writing to a man who lives under the dew of Hermon, with myself on Gilboa; to a man on the summit of Pisgah viewing the land flowing with milk and honey, and myself in the vale of carcasses and the valley of slaughter.

Sounds of battle,	Swn y rhyfel
Still surround me all my days.	Ydyw'r fan rw'i eto'n byw.

Every part of your letter was truly profitable; but as you approached the end, with the heart of a soldier, calling upon your brethren to lift up their banners and to stand in the ranks, ensuring us that we would soon receive the command to fire, the army of our Israel was ready at an instant to go forth to battle. Continue, dear sir, and never weary of sending to us on every opportunity possible, for we truly love to hear from you. Remember us continually as a Body in your daily prayers, and do not forget the weakest of all your brethren, and your servant in the Gospel,

EBENEZER RICHARD,
Secretary.

From the letters above, and from the history we have given, we trust that a fairly full picture has been provided of the clergyman of Tre-hill – one that portrays him as warm of spirit and generous of heart, an acceptable preacher though not attempting the high and lofty peaks, careful of God's cause, and bound to his brethren though failing to be present with them. It is clear that he loved the Methodists intensely. There is no history that he took part in the battles over Ordination, controversy was not natural to him and in the Vale of Glamorgan he was somewhat removed from the fire, in that there was hardly any opposition to what was intended. But it is certain that Mr Howells approved the act of ordaining ministers from amongst the Connexion. After losing Jones, Llan-gan; the friends to whom he kept closest were Ebenezer Morris, Ebenezer Richard, and others of like spirit. He was never anything but a Methodist and when he was informed that he could no longer remain in the Church without renouncing his Methodism, he bade farewell to the Established Church with no hesitation whatsoever, so as to keep his place amongst his brethren.

He was married twice. His second wife was Miss Samuel, Cowbridge, a woman noted for her godliness and generosity. (Quite probably it was a daughter of this marriage who became the wife of the Rev. Thomas Harris, Haverfordwest.) After leaving Nantbrân, he lived at Tre-hill, a small farm a little to the north of St Nicholas. Through his instrumentality, a chapel was obtained for St Nicholas, or rather, permission was received for a dwelling place to be turned into a chapel, for there was not one landowner in the district willing to rent land for a Methodist place of worship to be built there. We remember the old meeting-house well. Its roof was thatched, its floor was earth, with undecorated, rough benches to sit on. It was rented without a lease so that the small church was completely at the mercy of the owner of the building. As recently as thirty years ago [1870], Mr Bruce, the grandfather of the present Lord Aberdare, refused the sale of the land for the church. It is no wonder that such a gulf opened up between the common people of Wales and the owners of its land.

Mr Howells was granted to live to the patriarchal age of ninety-two. Before his final illness he used to say to Edward Mathews that he could not become reconciled to his death; that a continual sorrow rested upon his mind whenever he thought of the event. 'But,' he said, 'I do not fear anything the other side of the water; I am at peace with that land for many years. It is the passage I fear, not the Judge. I fear the unravelling, not the looking upon the face of God.' The Lord was very gracious with him in this respect, for his illness was brief and he crossed over in the arms of Jesus, knowing nothing of the torrents and swelling of the Jordan. He fell asleep on 19 January 1842, and was buried in Zoar cemetery, Bonvilston. The Rev. William Evans, Tonyrefail preached a very appropriate sermon at the funeral. There, in one of the most beautiful glades in all Glamorganshire, lie the mortal remains of the Rev. Howell Howells, in sure and certain hope of the resurrection to eternal life.

36
THE CLERGYMEN WHO REMAINED
(CONTINUED)

THE REV. WILLIAM HOWELLS, LONG ACRE

We claim the Rev. William Howells, Llan-gan, or 'Howells, Long Acre', as one of the clergymen who remained with the Methodists, even though he ministered within the Established Church throughout his life. It is known that he approved of the Ordination; indeed, he participated in the ordination service in 1814. Furthermore, whenever he visited Wales, he would fellowship with the Methodists. He showed repeatedly that they were his people; his greatest pleasure was to be with them in their Associations and he considered the Rev. David Charles, Carmarthen, to be the ablest preacher he had ever heard.

William Howells was born in September 1778, in Llwynhelyg, one of the biggest and most prosperous farms in the Vale of Glamorgan. His father was Samuel Howells, a member of a worthy and much respected family of the Cowbridge area. Samuel had twelve children, of whom William was the eldest. As often happens in a family of many children, the offspring scattered all over the world, following the various directions that their different temperaments took them. William was raised for the priesthood; Jonathan joined the army, was a captain in the 73rd regiment, and after fighting desperate battles under Wellington in Portugal and Spain, ended his career in Cardiff about the year 1846; Thomas emigrated to the West Indies and superintended a plantation throughout his life; many remained at home continuing with the quieter vocation of the father; two of the girls died without marrying.

But we have to do with the eldest son, namely William. From boyhood, his was a serious disposition, preferring a book to the games of his peers, and of such a sensitive conscience that he would fail to sleep all night if he thought he had done some wrong. His parents were regular attenders at Church, taking the whole family with them. His mother was notable for her godliness and no doubt her solemn warnings and importunate prayers were strong influences in the formation of her eldest son's character. Cowbridge had an excellent reputation at the time for its schools – the town was the Athens of Glamorganshire. William Howells received his earliest education at the 'School of the Eagle' under the care of a Mr Williams, a tall, thin, one-eyed man who was left-handed and described by one humorist as 'one of the best schoolmasters that ever flourished a beech cane.' The child is father of the man, and the elements of William's character were evident while a boy in the School of the Eagle. Nothing would induce him to tell a lie. If he transgressed any rule he would confess it immediately, though he knew that a merciless punishment would result. Sometimes he was placed as an assistant teacher and though he was of the kindest temperament, neither threatening nor flattery would make him betray the trust invested in him. He learnt quickly and was a better than average scholar when he left the school at fourteen years of age.

His father first intended him to be a lawyer and placed him in a local office for training. He seems not to have questioned the boy as to his own wishes, nor to have paid enough attention to his character, otherwise he could never have come up with such an idea. William's stay at the lawyer's office was brief; he soon realized, or believed that he realized, that he could never succeed in this vocation without the use of cunning, bordering on deceit. He went home to his father and told him that he could never be a lawyer. It was understood that he was inclined to the priesthood and in order to prepare him for this calling he was placed under the care of the Rev. John Walters, the vicar of Llandough, a learned man, and the author of a well-known Welsh/English dictionary. He was four years with him, until Mr Walters died. William Howells enjoyed writing poetry and at the death of his master he composed an elegy to him that was printed in one of the Gloucestershire papers. This brought him to the attention of the famous Robert Raikes, who wrote to him suggesting that he give himself to journalism. But he was destined for better and higher things. For a while he was a pupil of Dr Williams, the master of Cowbridge Grammar School, and then, in April 1800, he went to Oxford.

William Howells had always been weak in health and frail of constitution since his boyhood and, while in Oxford, he met with the disappointment of being refused by a young girl with whom he had fallen in love. This so affected his mind that he became very ill and almost died. Having partly recovered, he found that he could not continue his studies as before but would walk the fields around Oxford, his Greek New Testament in his hand, often kneeling in some corner apart to pray to the Lord of all the earth. His condition as a sinner began to weigh heavily upon him.

Though before he was always of a religious nature, moral in behaviour and his intentions firmly on the ministry, he had never believed that he had a saving interest in the Redeemer. But now, in his distress, the Saviour was revealed to him and he was enabled to thank God for the disappointment that had befallen him. Years later, he told a friend:

> I could take you now to the glades around Oxford where I used to read and pray and wrestle with God, and where the Spirit of God strengthened me to call upon Christ as the pearl beyond price.

He used to say of Oxford, 'It was there that the Lord found me.' At this time he became acquainted with a Mr Hinton, the minister of the Baptists at Oxford, and the ministry and personal friendship of this good man were of great help to him. In his weakness he could yet forget himself when confronted with the tribulations of others. A fellow-student of his was taken ill with an infectious fever. Because of fear of infection, it proved difficult to find anyone who would nurse and watch over him. For all his weakness, Mr Howells volunteered for this duty and he stayed up with the patient night after night until he was out of danger. It is no wonder that his own health broke down completely as a result.

BEFRIENDED BY DAVID JONES, LLAN-GAN

He had to leave Oxford in 1803 without receiving a degree and with his hopes considerably dashed. On returning to his parents at Llwynhelyg, he gave himself, as much as his health would allow, to preparing for ordination. He would also visit the sick of Pen-llin village and its surroundings, reading and praying with them, and exhorting them solemnly. Once this became more widely known, a congregation would gather to hear him almost every night, so that there would be no room at the cottage where he exhorted and Mr Howells, without having put any thought to the matter, found himself a preacher. His father worried desperately that his son, on whose education he had spent so much, was degrading himself by becoming a *'pregethwr pen 'stôl'* [a 'stool-top preacher']; but he himself was not concerned that he was on top of a stool, or on top of anything else, so long as he could continue to do good to sinners on the brink of death. It was at this time that he became acquainted with Mr Jones, Llan-gan, whose parish was a few miles from his home, and the two became the warmest of friends. Mr Jones loved the young man because of his intellectual ability, his clear views of the truths of the gospel, and his determination to serve the Lord Jesus faithfully with no thought for the threatening or flattery of any. When evangelical clergymen were so rare in the land it was a continual joy for the 'silver trumpet' of Llan-gan to find a young man with an awakened spirit, aflame with the desire to save souls. Mr Howells, on the other hand, had an infinite admiration for the older clergyman. He considered that in David Jones was found the perfect union of the simplicity of a patriarch and the fiery zeal of an apostle: 'There was some kind of existence for my soul in his soul; he was to me everything that a man could be.'

We have a description of Mr Howells's experience at this time, written by himself:

> When I was stopped from following my studies by a sad dispensation of Providence, and particularly after I had been enlightened in some measure to appreciate the value of books written by learned and godly men, I was for sometime unable to understand what the Lord wished to do with me, nor what was the purpose of such a dark dispensation towards one whom, it seemed, was intended for the work of the ministry, and I was almost despairing. But now, on being enabled to continue my studies in the Holy Scriptures, I think I can see the wise and gentle hand of a Father conducting the whole matter, and I am sincerely thankful to him. He indeed enclosed me, for a season, within the folds and pages of my own heart, in order for me to read the black letters printed there by sin, so that I was struck by fear on seeing the contents, and I could say with the apostle, 'O wretched man that I am! Who shall deliver me from the body of this death?' But now, thanks be to God, because I can read the pages of the Scriptures, I am helped to understand, in a way that I never understood before, that the character of the sinner that is portrayed there corresponds completely to my own. And O! unspeakable mercy! I can also now perceive the glory, merit and priceless worth of the divine Saviour as completely appropriate for the need of such a sinner, and as exactly the kind of High Priest fitted for us.

We see in these words that the young man understood the gospel and that he was particularly mature in much of his thinking.

In June 1804, William Howells presented himself to the Bishop of Llandaff to be ordained. He passed the necessary examinations successfully but someone had tried to poison the Bishop's mind towards him, because he mixed with the Methodists. Bishop Watson was a liberal, or rather an indifferent, man. He was tolerant of Mr Jones, Llan-gan, and others at a time when the Glamorganshire clergy were bringing heavy complaints against them; he does not seem to have considered refusing Mr Howells for an instant, but he did believe that he might teach him more accurately in the truths of religion. He started questioning the young man as to his beliefs; the latter defended himself readily and ably, easily forestalling the objections of his lordship. The situation at the episcopal palace developed into a friendly argument. The bishop felt that he was being pressed to the wall, and said at the end, with a smile on his face, 'Mr Howells, we have changed places. Instead of yourself being examined by me, I find that it is myself who has been examined.' Without any further hindrance, William Howells was ordained to the curacy of Llan-gan.

The Vicar of Llan-gan and his curate were of one mind; they were both more Methodist than Anglican; they regularly attended the Monthly Meetings and Associations; and they were acknowledged as leaders within the Connexion. They preached in barns, homes, or in the open fields, as opportunity allowed, without any concerns at to whether the ground on which they stood was consecrated or not. Mr Howells soon made a mark for himself as an able theologian; his mastery of topics that were considered abstruse surprised his hearers. The vicar was considered the sweeter and more feeling preacher, but the old Glamorganshire professors inclined to the belief that the curate was able to penetrate more deeply into the principles of the gospel. Once, in an annual meeting in a part of Glamorgan, the two preached together. Mr Howells preached first, as was only fitting. His topic was the Sonship of Christ. He began humbly by referring to his youth and ignorance, and expressed the hope that his respected father in the gospel would correct any errors that he might have fallen into. He then threw himself into his sermon, and the truths that he proclaimed were so illuminating, and his whole message so masterly, that he amazed the congregation and had a most successful service. The first thing that Mr Jones did on getting up after him, was to call upon the hearers to pray for the young man who had just addressed them, that the Lord would place enough thorns in his way, that he might not be raised above himself, that after such a bright morning his sun might not set under a cloud. The remainder of Mr Howells's history proves that this prayer was fully answered.

Soon after Mr Howells was ordained, the Rev. David Jones moved from Llan-gan to Manorowen in Pembrokeshire, so that the care of the whole parish fell upon the shoulders of the curate for nearly a year. Soon he was asked to pastor two other adjoining parishes, Eglwys Fair and Llandyfodwg, to which he agreed, to the great delight of the parishioners. There was in Llandyfodwg parish a strong Unitarian element and he took immense pains, by preaching and through private personal visiting, to seek to convict those who clung to such an error. Many of these, it seems, were men of considerable ability; he used to say when he had moved to London that 'some of them were as capable disputants as Dr Priestley,' and he appropriated their controversial skills, rightly or wrongly, to the support they received from the devil. We do not know what degree of success he experienced by these efforts. However, after the departure of Mr Jones, the curate gave himself fully to the work. The characteristic tone of his ministry was evangelical. The topics on which he spoke were the two covenants; the fall of Adam as the representative of all his seed; the person of Christ as the God-man; the aweful majesty of God's perfections as revealed in the law; the all-sufficient atonement of Christ; the effective operations of the Holy Spirit; etc., etc. He spoke simply but with immense solemnity and often with a fluency that would carry all before it. One writer describes an Association in Glamorgan at which he was present when a child. On a fine summer's morning a huge crowd had gathered. The Rev. William Howells preached at six in the morning on the subject of the resurrection. Few of his comments had remained in the boy's memory but he remembered the sermon, and especially its effect upon the large congregation. Mr Howells, with the intensity of his message seen shining in his face, had compared the bodies of the saints coming up from their graves to the phoenix rising from its own ashes and with all the strength of new life powering its wings, flying aloft to delight in the radiance of the sun. Many able sermons were delivered by masters of the congregation in that Association but all those present agreed, as they returned to their homes, that none had compared in power and influence to the six o'clock morning sermon of the curate of Llan-gan.

Mr Howells was the Vicar of Llan-gan's right-hand man. Mr Jones could at times be very heated in his temperament. Sometimes this was to his advantage as a preacher – it acted as oil to the wheels. The truths of the gospel, having been warmed in his own heart, were unstoppable when hurled forth as bullets amongst the congregation. But his hot temper was no advantage when dealing with men. Fortunately his wife, his dear Sina, was a peacemaker, and when she saw that he was getting overly excited, she would say, 'Dafydd', and place her hand on his shoulder, and he would quieten immediately and become as placid as a lamb. The two were a loving pair throughout their lives and had promised each other that their dust should lie, not in some ground consecrated by a bishop, but in Salem cemetery, Pencoed. There the remains of Mrs Jones were laid. And when he died at Manorowen, over twenty strong men, remembering the promise made between them, volunteered to carry his body on their shoulders home from Pembrokeshire. A man on horseback was sent to explain the situation to his second wife but when the army was on the point of starting, or had already started out, they were met by a horseman with the news that they were forbidden the body, and that he had to be buried in Pembrokeshire in a cemetery belonging to the Established Church. To this day the inhabitants of the area regret that Mr Jones's bones do not lie in their midst, as he wished. As far as the relationship between himself and Mr Howells was concerned: it was a joy to his spirit, whenever he visited the parish, to see that the glory of Llan-gan was being maintained, that the congregations were still gathering as before, particularly on Communion Sundays, and that the gospel was being preached faithfully and effectively.

WILLIAM HOWELLS MOVES TO LONDON

But in 1819, as mentioned, Mr Jones died, and Mr Howells's curacy therefore came to an end. His request for the living was refused, solely because of his Methodism. According to the Rev. William Williams, Swansea:

> At the death of his rector, the Rev. D. Jones, Llan-gan, he requested the honourable patron that he might receive the living. His Lordship might have delighted thousands merely by granting this request. Who was more appropriate to take the place of the sweet evangelist, who had gathered together such a vast flock at Llan-gan from all the surrounding neighbourhoods, than the fiery curate from Llwynhelyg? To all those familiar with the local circumstances, this seemed the only solution for keeping the congregation from being scattered across the mountains as sheep without a shepherd. But his Lordship judged differently:
>
> 'You are a Methodist, Howells,' he said. 'You are a Methodist, and I do not choose to give the living to a Methodist; had you not been one, you would have received it immediately.'
>
> 'True, my Lord,' he replied. 'Whether it pleases your Lordship to give me the living or not, I am a Methodist.'
>
> That was the end of the matter. But let it be understood that the patron was not producing an excuse just in order to be rid of William Howells. He would have received the living had he only promised to part with his Methodism. His Lordship respected the family; there was reason enough to do so and he had shown proofs of his respect. He had placed the brother next in age to William Howells as a secretary in an old warship at Sheerness, and he had used his influence on behalf of another son who had entered the army as an officer. Neither of these had been corrupted! But William was not to have the living of Llan-gan if he was a Methodist, and William would not compromise nor deny his faith; he would not cast aside, or promise to cast aside, his Methodism for all the livings in the world. We can well imagine his strong, determined voice crying out, 'I am a Methodist.'

He felt deeply his separation from his people at Llan-gan. He was still in possession of his curacies in the other two parishes, and it seems that he was also being paid well for preparing a rich young nobleman for entering one of the famous schools, so that his financial circumstances were sound. For about a year after the death of Mr Jones he continued to serve the churches at Eglwys Fair and Llandyfodwg and to preach among the Methodists. But in the October of 1811 he turned his back upon the land of his birth and accepted a curacy in London. What induced him to take this step? It was not from any desire for popularity or praise and certainly not from any cooling on his part towards his fellow-Methodists, in that his love of them was deep. He once said:

> Had not the Methodists done more for my poor country than all the Welsh bishops, the devil would long ago have laid claim to the Principality as his own episcopate.

And his homesickness for the land of his fathers continued all his days. Years later, as a greatly respected clergyman of the capital, he said:

> I would sometimes give many worlds to be able to recall that feeling that often used to fill my breast as I passed from cottage to cottage, amongst people of the most simple of hearts, who would receive me, in the name of the Master, as an angel of God.

How can we account for the departure of the Rev. William Howells from Wales? If he had been pained by the opposition of the bishops to the gospel and by the arrogance of the patrons of the livings, why did he not take his place as an itinerant preacher amongst the Methodists, like Charles of Bala or Williams, Lledrod, and others? We believe that the answer lies in his love for Llan-gan. Had he remained in Wales, his home would naturally have been at Llwynhelyg – just a few miles from Llan-gan. To see the place that had been the Jerusalem of south Wales bereft of worshippers; its church path grassing over, so dry a stick was the present incumbent; to see this would have been too much for his feelings, and for all his love for Wales, he decided to leave the country rather than be an eye-witness to such a tragedy.

His first curacy in London was in the parishes of St Andrew and St Anne, near Blackfriars, under the rector, Mr Goode. He is depicted by his English biographer as being, at his arrival in London, an untidy man; ignorant or careless rather of the common social courtesies; having a strong Welsh accent and a form of speech that was painful to the ears of the cultured. His biographer adds that he was a great smoker, a habit that he had brought with him from Wales! We protest against such a description; it is a complete caricature. Were there no smokers to be had amongst ministers other than those from Wales? Could it be imagined for a moment that a man of Mr Howells's tender spirit, raised in one of the most respected families of Glamorgan, being familiar with the upper classes of society since his youth, educated at grammar schools and at Oxford and becoming a fine scholar; could it be imagined that he was unaware of how to behave like a gentleman in whatever company he found himself? It is true that he did not form his gentility according to the rules laid down by a Lord Chesterfield; that he was quite free from affectation and false modesty; that he did not wear rings on his fingers and was not careful that his clothes be of the best cloth; but in everything that is essential, William Howells was every inch a gentleman.

He was not long in London before his preaching drew attention. He was preaching evangelical Calvinism, declaring the truth boldly, and doing so with fluency and power, a rare thing in the capital. The talk of the remarkable curate of St Anne's spread far and wide. The stories reached his bishop. One day, Mr Goode received a letter from Dr Randolph, the Bishop of London, asking who and what was his new curate, and adding that a certain nobleman had visited the church expecting, from all he had been told, to meet with folly and eccentricity, but that the curate had far exceeded his worst fears. All that Mr Howells was guilty of, it seems, was that rather than reading a dry sermon that contained no nourishment for souls and no hooks to catch the consciences of sinners, he had proclaimed the truth of God as one who believed it and declared the gospel with an oratorical fluency that was not often heard in London churches. Mr Goode must be commended; he supported his curate and answered his bishop by declaring that Mr Howells was a young man from Wales; that he had received excellent references witnessing to his good character; and that he (Mr Goode) could find no fault in him, other than that he possessed plenty of Welsh fire to meet the needs of the cold hearts of the English. The rector did not preach much himself because of the state of his health but, having received the Bishop's letter, he paid a visit to St Anne's to see and hear for himself. To his amazement the church was overflowing, he had never seen such a congregation there before. The Welshman preached the gospel with such power that Mr Goode's heart was filled with a spirit of thanksgiving. 'There were thoughts in that sermon,' he said, 'that I would give anything to be able to remember.'

Yet although the rector was an evangelical man and very pleased with Mr Howells's service, the salary that he gave him was completely unworthy. Mr Howells's biographer says that at times he had to go without daily bread. Mr Williams, Swansea, suspects the truth of this:

> There were oddities that belonged to him, and perhaps these caused him some inconveniences, but it is another matter to be in real need because of poverty.

> We know that throughout his life, and long after, Llwynhelyg never lacked for essentials. We know also that there was always much love and support provided for Mr Howells.

All this was no doubt true, but we can also imagine that a sensitive and thoughtful man would prefer to suffer hardship rather than reveal his need to his relatives. While a curate at St Anne's he visited his homeland on two occasions, as far as we know. He was present at the Llangeitho Association of 1814, when he prayed at the close of the ordination service. It is not recorded that he preached at the Association, which is strange. Possibly, he preached in English, between two Welsh sermons, and his service was never noted. As far as we know, this is the last time that he was in Wales.

In April 1816, Mr Goode, his rector, died, and he was again without a post. He applied for the rectorship; the patronage of the living was in the hands of the parishioners, and because of Mr Howells's great popularity and the love that his hearers had for him, one would have expected that he would have been their choice. However no election was ever conducted in a more disgraceful fashion. The public houses were opened for those voting against him and there was no end to all the tricks and deceits that were resorted to. The vote went against him by a small majority. After an inquiry even this small majority disappeared almost to nothing, and Mr Howells's friends believed that if his case were brought before the Court of Chancery he would win the day. But he would not agree to this, and he turned away from the people amongst whom he had laboured for nearly five years.

For almost a year he was like Noah's dove with no place of rest for the sole of his foot. His only employment was a Sunday night lecture at St Antholin's Church in Watling Street, for which he received eighteen pounds a year! He made persistent efforts for a curacy but none of the London clergy desired his services. According to his biographer, whose testimony may be believed in this matter in that he also was a clergyman, 'Until the day of his death there were in the Established Church persons who believed that they would be committing the unpardonable sin if they ever opened their pulpit doors to Mr Howells.' And for what was he to blame? Only that he was faithful to his God, proclaiming the evangelical doctrines that are found in the Articles of the Church as well as in the Bible; and that he proclaimed them not in the usual cold manner but with warmth and conviction and in a completely different style from everyone else.

HE BUYS THE LEASE OF LONG ACRE CHAPEL

In 1817 he bought the lease of an episcopal chapel in Long Acre, where he could minister free from the authority of any bishop or rector. This venture was an important one; he made the purchase with a large sum that had been lent him by his friends. Much money had to be spent renovating the chapel before it could be used, and it held no endowments. For income Mr Howells depended entirely on the pew rents. He remained here until his death. He became popular immediately; people gathered from all parts – the nobility, members of parliament and traders, together with the poor from the Seven Dials locality. Such popularity might have swollen the heads of many and caused them to moderate the proclamation of the truth to the rich, whose carriages were drawn up in long rows along the street of the chapel, but it had no effect on William Howells. He was the same in Long Acre as when he exhorted from on top of a stool in a small cottage in Pen-llin village.

We cannot pursue his history in the capital further, but hasten to provide a description of his characteristics. Physically, he was tall and slim, with a large nose and a wide, open mouth that seemed designed for pouring forth words. It would be difficult to find two men so completely opposite in looks as he and Mr David Jones, Llan-gan. He, as thin as a rake, and Mr Jones, short, wide and full-fleshed. But during his curacy in Llan-gan the same gown had had to do for both of them and often this caused much inconvenience. The gown would slip over Mr Howells's shoulders, half-way down his arms and he would have great difficulty retrieving it time and again back on to his shoulders. But one Sunday he could not endure it any more and tore off the gown, asking rather heatedly, 'What use is such an inconvenience?' But he soon remembered that it was a disgraceful sin, condemnable by judges, to seek to address sinners in such a consecrated place without a gown. He therefore picked it up from the dust, dressed in it again, and continued with his sermon as if nothing had happened.

All knew of his generosity and kindness. The beggars of London were well acquainted with him and knew that if there was something in his pocket they would not have to depart from him empty-handed. He never believed that the Ruler of the world gave him anything in order for him to keep it. 'I was helped, and I will help the next man,' was his motto. 'Wil-liam,' his sister said to him once when he was back at Llwynhelyg, 'go to the cupboard and give a little food to that poor man at the door.' 'Gladly,' said he, and proceeded to give a whole loaf and a whole cheese to the beggar.

'Howells,' said Dr Nichol of Ryde to him, shortly before his death, 'you are getting older and likely to be poor. Why did you not put something to one side for your old age, instead of giving it all away as you do?'

'Oh, my friend,' said he. 'I have enough while I continue preaching, and when I fail, my congregation can keep me.'

That was his way of life, and the first section of his last will and testament read, 'I forgive all who are in my debt.'

Together with the gentleness of his nature, he possessed a lion-like spirit, and he would not hesitate to rebuke a transgressor, whatever his situation and without thought of any consequences. According to the Rev. William Williams, Swansea:

> He would rebuke sin, not by saying, 'There are some who do such-and-such, which is very bad, not that I am accusing you of being so.' He would not play in this way with people's faults and consciences. No, he would point out directly the sin and the sinner. 'Here is the evil,' he would say, with zeal lighting up his eyes, 'and these are the consequences, and here are the guilty.' What? Fear of man in William Howells of Long Acre? Never! He had no more fear of men than fear of grasshoppers. 'My hearers,' he said one Sabbath at Long Acre, 'my hearers! You are familiar with the character of the man who has been newly appointed Bishop of ____. The Lord gave to us a good Book of Prayer, and excellent Articles; but somehow, the appointment of bishops, up until now, remains in the devil's hands.' There were not many men in his position brave enough to declare, in the hearing of many members of the two Houses of Parliament, that the right honourable Prime Minister of His Majesty was no more than an instrument in the hands of the Evil One. But such a one was William Howells.

He understood the brotherhood of the human family thoroughly. He would help a man in any way he could, provided it was honest. He once stood on a pavement of a steep road in London; it was raining heavily at the time. He noticed a poor man trying to pull a heavy truck up the hill. The man was pulling upwards, the weight in the truck was pulling downwards, and it was the weight that was winning the battle. Mr Howells imagined that he could see in the event the fruit of the Fall. 'Sin,' he thought, 'this is one of your tricks.' With that he hurried on to the road, and with no fear of dirtying his priestly hands, he wrestled with the truck. The man also tried his best, and between them the load was brought to the top of the hill.

The Rev. William Williams again comments on his style of preaching:

> Very rarely do you find a preacher who says so much *to* his hearers as he – something to be said *to* the congregation; some message *for* them; that was always the nature of his sermon from beginning to end. When he was in the pulpit, just as when he was anywhere else, it was a case of William Howells amongst his friends and neighbours. There are some who part with themselves on the stairs to the pulpit. In the chapel house they are themselves, but the minute they close the pulpit door behind them they seem to lose their identity. The shape of their face is not the same; a great change takes place in their eyes; and as for their voice it is as unlike to what it was before as the sound of a

drum is to that of a trumpet. He has become a strange creature in an instant; a creature, one imagines, who is addressing the stars. He believes that preaching is not speaking, and he labours all his days under the effects of that unhappy understanding. It is true that William Howells possessed a fiery nature; he could become thoroughly excited; shaking his arms; striking the pulpit; and giving the occasional shout that would echo through the chapel. But it was an excitement while speaking with people; and you understood when he became excited that he was speaking about something that should be exciting yourself also. But there was never any danger that his own zeal, or any response on the part of his hearers, would ever cause him to lose the drift of his thoughts and become confused. The following story bears this out:

'There was a Scotsman living in Bridgend whose name was George Watson, who made a living carrying goods on his back throughout Glamorganshire, and, not unlike many of that profession at the time, this George feared the Lord. We do not remember seeing anyone epitomizing the expression, 'listening with all his heart', more than he whenever he was present in a service. Oh, his sweet, 'Amen, Amen'. It still echoes in our ears. The zealous old brother! He has by now, almost certainly, gone to glory. He would always be present to listen to Mr Howells at Hen Gastell, Llan-gan, Salem, etc. One Sunday, the preacher spoke of Christ redeeming men from their sorrows, and said, 'Christ, people, does not take a burden with him wherever he goes, as you find some men doing. Oh, no! Removing burdens is his work.' But suddenly he remembered that the dear man from Scotland was amongst his congregation; he paused; looked around; his eyes found the carrier, and he said, 'George Watson *bach*, don't worry; I wasn't thinking of you at all; truly it was of the Son of God that I was speaking.' This part of the sermon had a deep effect on George Watson, but the preacher merely continued with his sermon.'

It was not easy to throw William Howells off balance. He went once to hear the remarkable William Huntington preach. Huntington was a loud, strident preacher, of little or no culture, yet of remarkable natural gifts, who was blessed of God to the conversion of many. Some part of the sermon touched Mr Howells's heart; he failed to hide his feeling, but with a smile responded, 'Amen.' The preacher noted it and believing he was mocking him, stopped, and fixing him with a look, questioned him authoritatively, 'Why do you laugh, sir? If you cannot behave better, you had better leave.' This would have been enough to cause many an innocent Welshman to faint but William Howell did not consider it of any great significance. The preacher had misunderstood, that was all. A word would set everything to right. He rose to his feet and said with perfect composure, 'Sir, it was not laughter, but a smile of appreciation of your comments.' The preacher's spirits were pacified and Mr Howells listened with much satisfaction to the end.

In his process of thought, Mr Howells combined the depth of the philosopher with the flighty imagination of the poet, and there are sections of his sermons that manifest these characteristics. Consider the following comments on the miracles, for example:

> The miracles, had they not ceased, would have clouded the glory of the Old and New Testaments; men and women would neglect the Bible in their pursuit of signs and wonders; and faith, being made captive by the sensual, would nest with the wren upon earth rather than soar aloft with the eagle – with the whole family of heaven carried on its wing. The divine privilege of believers in this age, by the operation of that faith, 'the evidence of things not seen', whether in the past, in the present, or in the future, is to enjoy a fellowship more exalted and more miraculous than any miracle then performed. Once they had achieved their purpose by their remarkable and novel effects, these wonders, in God's wisdom and mercy, ceased, so that the glory of the God who performed them might continue through the inspired pages to address the immortal souls of believers rather than their senses. 'Because thou hast seen me, thou hast believed: blessed are they that have not seen, and yet have believed.' He who has pondered deeply and has felt intensely, would be very unwilling for a miracle to intrude while he, enjoying his greatest pleasure, was deep in communion with his God.'

He possessed a wealth of comparisons and he would develop them in a delightful and masterly way. Consider the following on the rainbow:

> To Noah's family it was a terrible thing to see clouds gather, together with the accompanying thunder, storm and flood; it seemed to them to be the re-accumulation of destroying forces against a guilty world. But the Lord, in his mercy and compassion, not only promised that no flood would again destroy all flesh, but as a further sign of his covenant he set his rainbow in amongst the very elements of his revenge. By this ordination these elements of his revenge reflected and projected the glory of the sun; they were required to disperse the primitive colours of light and to reveal them in their individual glories. Noah's family is commanded to set their eyes upon the bow in the cloud, so that all their fears may melt away. This reminds us of many important truths. We look to Calvary and see the bow set in all its glory against the darkest clouds of the elements of revenge; we see the glory of the Sun of Righteousness reflected in it; we see the perfections that meet in Jehovah each in its own individual beauty and glory. The exhibition of the elements of revenge, as they gather in all their wrath over the head of the Messiah, are seen by the eye of faith as the bow of divine attributes meeting and working harmoniously together for the salvation of guilty man. There mercy and truth are met together, righteousness and peace have kissed each other. It is there that the believer is always to direct the eye of faith, so that his fears may disappear, and hope and joy dwell in his heart.

The following account reveals his mastery of metaphors and the ease with which he made use of them. On the afternoon of the day in which he died, he appeared to be rapidly sinking; he was not noticing anything around him or uttering a word, and his heart was beating very faintly. His doctor, who was a good Christian, decided to attempt to rouse him by engaging his mind. He began to speak of man as one who was once a glorious mirror reflecting all the perfections of the Godhead. He continued by saying that that mirror had been shattered by the Fall, but that the remaining pieces contained some traces of the ancient glories and that to some degree, though very imperfectly, they reflected the divine attributes. The meaning of his words penetrated Mr Howells's mind, though his feet were far into the river; he gathered together all his energies that were swiftly evaporating, and said, with his eyes flashing:

> Your comparison reminds me of a story I heard of a tiger who, when pursuing its prey, leapt into a house and saw its own reflection in a mirror. Believing it was an enemy he pounced upon it, only to smash the mirror into a hundred pieces. But on seeing a tiger snarling at him from every piece, he fled for his life, terrified by the sight of himself multiplied a hundred times.

A complex metaphor coming from a man who had already entered half-way into the land of the dead, was it not? Throughout his ministry, and again by means of this metaphor, Mr Howells had taught the truth that it was not God's image but the devil's image that was reflected by a fallen sinner.

The Rev. William Howells's constitution was weak throughout his life, and in 1832 it was clear that he was drawing to the end. He delivered his last sermon in Long Acre Chapel on Sunday, 11 November, from Psalm 86:7, 'In the day of my trouble I will call upon thee: for thou wilt answer me.' The following Tuesday he was taken ill, and by the next Sunday his spirit had fled to the land of peace, in his fifty-fifth year. No cemetery was attached to Long Acre; it was a chapel-of-ease that had not received episcopal consecration. Mr Howells's body was therefore laid to rest in the cemetery of Holy Trinity Church, Cloudesley Square, Islington. Various clergymen officiated, and on the following Sunday, two funeral sermons were preached at Long Acre; one by the Rev. Mr Melvill, and the other by the Honourable Baptist Noel.

A beautiful marble tablet was placed in his memory on the wall of Holy Trinity, paid for by a few of his friends. Such was his popularity and the love felt towards him that his sudden death raised a wave of distress throughout the land.

THE REV. WILLIAM LLOYD, CAERNARVON

The next Methodist clergyman to be considered is the Rev. William Lloyd, Caernarvon. Very little of his history is available, particularly as far as his early years are concerned. He himself preferred not to speak of his youth, possibly because it may have been spent in dissipation. He was the son of Mr Robert Lloyd of Penmaes, near Nefyn, who was the chief customs officer for Porth Dinllaen. William was born in 1771. He learnt to read in some school in Porth Dinllaen and was then sent to the grammar school at Botwnnog, and from there to Oxford. He was a brilliant student with a gift for languages. It is said that he gained a complete mastery of Latin and throughout his life his chief reading was in that language. But he was thoroughly devoid of any spiritual concern. There is no evidence that his guilty condition before God ever concerned him in the slightest and he spent the days of his youth without any thought for the things that belonged to his peace. He developed rapidly while obtaining his degree at Oxford and the gentry in the neighbourhood of Nefyn were considerably interested in him.

There was no obstacle to ordination standing in the way of such an excellent student, nor to his finding a curacy. Godliness was not considered a prerequisite for ministry in the Church of England at the time, otherwise a young man such as William Lloyd would never have been allowed to serve in sacred things. Rather, the fact that he was careless towards religion and, particularly, that he was an enemy of the Methodists, was to his advantage. Furthermore he was a notably handsome young man, cheerful in temper, courteous in behaviour, and willing to participate in any sport. He was ordained by Dr Cleaver, the Bishop of Bangor, on 20 September 1801 and on 7 October was licensed to the curacy of Llanfair-yn-neubwll and Llanfihangel in Anglesey.

He shouldered his responsibilities with all the carelessness that characterized the Anglesey clergy of the time. Having, in his churches on a Sunday, thoughtlessly run through the lessons and coldly delivered something of a sermon, with nothing in it for sinners, he considered that he had fulfilled all that was required of him and was not troubled by the ungodliness and immorality of his parishioners. He seems to have spent much time in the company of the Anglesey nobility, joining with them in their corruptions. He would also often be at the Episcopal Palace in Bangor and the Bishop was very fond of him. Mr Lloyd used afterwards to say that he had no anxieties as to his calling to the ministry, that he considered that his success in pursuing the necessary preparatory steps and his ordination by a bishop whom he considered as standing in the apostolic succession, was completely sufficient proof that he had been placed in his office by the Head of the Church.

HIS STRANGE CONVERSION

How long he was in this thoughtless condition is not known exactly, but he was certainly sharply awoken from it. And the way in which this occurred proves that the Holy Spirit uses every kind of means to lead a sinner to a proper view of his state. The chief Methodist preachers often visited Anglesey and would shake the island from one end to the other with the power of their ministry. John Elias, in particular, would draw thousands after him, utterly overcoming them with the storm of his oratory. But these things never touched the Rev. William Lloyd; he would never be anywhere near a Methodist meeting; it would be a disgrace upon the dignity of a learned gentleman such as himself to mix with such a crowd of fanatics. He joined the gentry of the island in mocking them and doubtless they were often the subject of amusement and scorn for Mr Lloyd and his friends as they drank each other's health. But as he would not go to hear human preachers, God would use a dumb creature to preach to him.

Here is the story, as he himself used to relate it. He had borrowed a horse from a Mr John Williams, Lledwigan, to attend a confirmation or an Episcopal christening. It was a Sunday and a crowd of clergymen, together with many of the upper classes, had gathered for the service. When the ceremony was over, a good dinner was served and the learned priest of Llanfair was amongst those invited to the feast. Such were the charms of the wine and the allurements of the society that the time passed without him being aware and it was late in the day when he returned home. He therefore ordered his servant to take his animal to the field and to keep him there until the next day. Because of the liveliness of the horse, the servant went to put fetters on him. He succeeded in placing one end of the chain on one pastern but before he had secured the other end, the animal rushed at him. As he galloped wildly, the horse was beaten by the loose end of the metal chain, injuring himself so severely that he could not be ridden again. William Lloyd was very grieved by this accident, particularly as he had borrowed the horse. He did not know how to return it to its owner or what to say to him. We do not know what the outcome was between Mr Lloyd and John Williams, Lledwigan, but the young clergyman somehow could not shake off the effect of the incident upon his mind. He questioned himself as to whether he had somehow brought down this misfortune upon himself. He remembered that it had occurred on the Lord's Day; that under the cover of serving God, he had spent the day feasting amongst dubious company. He began to see the sinfulness of his life and the guilt of his condition, so that his mind became filled with an unbearable sorrow. He wandered the fields like a madman and was afraid of sharing his feelings with anyone. God's means of forgiveness through the death of the cross was completely unknown to him though he read the Bible every Sunday in the churches.

He made every effort to find peace by means of the flesh. He frequented the feasts and dances more often; he gave himself more completely to godlessness and prodigality. But every effort to quench the flames of a guilty conscience in this way was a failure; they only served to kindle further guilt. Every time that he visited his corrupt friends he returned with deeper wounds in his soul. In a further attempt to shake off his troubles, he visited Nefyn, his place of birth. One day, having been riding in the country, he met a woman coming towards him. He recognized her as a woman he had been friendly with in his youth, and he remembered that she was known for her wit and humour and that on many nights she and he had danced together. He cheered up on seeing her, thinking that perhaps he might receive something from her that would banish his melancholy. He dismounted in order to talk to her, but having greeted her, the woman answered him with the utmost gravity and decorum. Mr Lloyd feared that he had made a mistake, that she was not the one he had taken her for, and he asked her pardon.

'No,' said the woman, 'you are not mistaken; I am she.'

'Why is it then,' asked Mr Lloyd, 'that you are looking so serious? Has a relative of yours died?'

'No, not that,' she said, 'but I have realized that I am a great sinner and that I have rebelled against the Lord. And that we must have forgiveness for our sins, Mr Lloyd *bach*, and for our folly in attending corrupt societies and ungodly sports in the days of our youth, or we shall be lost.'

The clergyman was too shocked to answer her. He turned away in disappointment, not having received what he had hoped. In this way, 'He would fain have filled his belly with the husks that the swine did eat: and no man gave unto him.' He compared himself to a fish, pierced by a spear, diving to the depths and rising again to the surface in an attempt to escape, but with every twist and turn deepening the wound and strengthening the hold upon him, until at last he felt he would have to yield and be caught by the power that had overcome him.

He decided to speak of his troubles to someone who he thought might sympathize with him and help him reach the bank safely. He knew that it would be hopeless to attempt to pour out his fears to the Bishop of

Bangor or to any of the Anglesey clergy, but he knew a poor old man in the Rhoscolyn neighbourhood who was a member with the Methodists and was known to be godly. He overcame all his prejudices and visited the man and this was the means blessed to him to bring him to lean on Christ for the salvation of his soul. From then on, William Lloyd was a new man. He was no longer seen at the dances and feasts. He no longer joined the youth of the area in their sports of racing and jumping. He began preaching seriously in his churches and established prayer meetings in the homes. His old friends were amazed; they felt that they had lost the best ornament of their gatherings. It was not long before the authorities began to hear complaints against him, and not long before he received threatening letters from his bishop commanding him not to emulate the Methodists or else his licence would have to be taken from him. To be a serious preacher was a transgression to be punished in those days, as also was the sin of joining with the common people to hold prayer meetings; such behaviour could not be tolerated in the Bangor diocese. A greater crime still was the fact that he had sought to establish societies in which opportunities were given for all who grieved over their condition to share their feelings.

His seriousness was soon put to the test. A day of general fasting was announced because of the wars that were ravaging Europe at the time, and because of the general fear that Napoleon would invade Britain and conquer the land. The Methodists held a prayer meeting at Caerceiliog at nine in the morning, and Mr Lloyd was to minister at Llanfair Church at eleven. The meeting in the chapel was terminated punctually and the congregation moved on together to the church. By the time they arrived, the vicar, a most immoral man, was reading the lessons and prayers and the congregation felt disappointed. However, Mr Lloyd soon entered, looking very ill. When the vicar had finished reading the curate ascended the pulpit, his face grave and solemn. He grasped the Bible, refused the surplice offered him, and addressed the people as follows:

> Well, friends, we are gathered here today to fast, but I believe that our fasts in previous years have been nothing but blatant hypocrisy, for we have no evidence of any nation ever repenting sincerely and yet still continuing with the same sins, and being threatened with the same judgments. I fear that Britain is a nation that has been given up to judgment. But notwithstanding all that, I will read you a text that has in it matter enough to comfort every true Christian, whatever shall be the end of these things: 'In that day shall this song be sung in the land of Judah,' Isaiah 26:1.

The vicar looked at him in amazement and the congregation were wide-eyed, but Mr Lloyd carried on and delivered a very effective sermon.

WILLIAM LLOYD JOINS THE METHODISTS

He joined the ranks of the Methodists in the following way. A Methodist society was to meet at Caergeiliog early on Michaelmas Day. As it was a feast-day, Mr Lloyd had a service at Llanfihangel Church, but that was to be later in the day. On his way to the church therefore he went to the society and asked for membership. The cause at Caergeiliog was very weak at the time and very few had gathered together. They were all astounded on seeing the curate joining them; they were even more amazed when he asked for membership. For a moment there was only silence in the society. Eventually one person was brave enough to ask him what his views were of himself as a sinner and whether he was prepared to meet his Judge. He answered, scripturally, that he was completely miserable in and of himself and that it was through faith in Christ alone that he expected to receive eternal life. It was an interesting scene: a learned clergyman, educated at Oxford, being examined by a few poor people as to the things that belonged to his peace. All seemed willing to receive him, when an old man called David Lloyd stood up, saying that he also had a question for him.

'Mr Lloyd,' he said, 'do you intend to profess religion as we do, with all its shame and the crosses that it brings with it, or did you only call on us in passing?'

'As I believe that you call upon the Lord out of pure hearts,' he replied, 'I intend to spend my life among you.'

Such an answer satisfied all. The clergyman was received as a member of the society and he was encouraged to attend the Monthly Meeting. He continued on his journey, happy in spirit, having cast in his lot with the people of God, and he ministered in the church in Llanfihangel.

Thomas Jones of Amlwch, Rice Lloyd, Treflysg, and he, journeyed together to the Anglesey Monthly Meeting. The three of them were nervous, as they all were attending for the first time. We have no knowledge of the reception given to William Lloyd, but he was surely welcomed warmly by the fraternity were it only for the assistance that he could give to the other Methodist clergy with the ministration of the sacraments. He was present also at the next Monthly Meeting. As he was returning home from it, a friend asked him, 'There is a prayer meeting in our neighbourhood tonight.' The place was about three miles from Mr Lloyd's home but not in either of the parishes in which he served. 'O yes,' he replied, 'I will come to you and speak a few words, if I am allowed.' So it transpired, and this was the first sermon that he ever preached in a building that had not been consecrated. At the end of the meeting a man came up to him and asked if he would engage himself to preach at his home in the following week, and he consented willingly. The meeting was announced throughout the surrounding region and a very large crowd gathered; so many that the house could not have held half the number. Without a moment's hesitation, Mr Lloyd climbed on to the hedgerow outside and there, on the side of the road, he preached Christ, to great effect. From then on he never failed to evangelize whenever he had opportunity and he became a true Methodist preacher, leading the societies and attending the Monthly Meetings.

It is easy to appreciate that this behaviour of his stirred up much excitement in Anglesey, and that the narrow and prejudiced Churchmen felt betrayed. The news soon reached the Bishop's Palace at Bangor and the curate was summoned to appear before his Lordship to give an account of himself. It is said that the bishop, who had been kind to him when he was careless of the salvation of souls, now became very bitter. He condemned him as a heretic for joining the fanatics that troubled the peace of the land; but Mr Lloyd ably defended himself, stating that the Methodists were just as zealous in defence of the doctrinal articles of the Church as His Lordship himself. He was obliged to depart with the frown of his bishop upon him. As we have mentioned, the vicar under whom Mr Lloyd served was an immoral man who was completely indifferent to religious matters, but he was a gentle, humane man with a high view of what was honourable and he therefore severely condemned those who had complained and carried tales about his curate to the bishop, and condemned his bishop also for his bitterness and prejudice.

When Mr Lloyd joined the Methodists he does not seem to have intended to turn his back upon the Church. There were those, especially in the south, who held Church livings and were yet zealous Methodists. Perhaps this was the situation that he foresaw for himself. He does not seem to have been turned out of his curacy, nor does it appear that the bishop withdrew his licence. For some time he served in his two parishes and preached also as an itinerant preacher in the homes of the neighbourhood. But he soon realized that it would be impossible to continue with both activities; the ethos of the Church was now no longer compatible with the main purpose of his life.

He also began to be uneasy with respect to many of his duties as a clergyman: the duty of baptizing the children of openly ungodly men; the duty of administering holy communion to men whom he knew to be drunken and wanton – men whom he knew to be eating and drinking damnation to themselves as they took communion; and that he could not bury the greatest villains of the neighbourhood without having to declare publicly of them that they were being laid to rest 'in sure and certain hope of Resurrection to eternal life.' He saw how much Roman Catholicism still remained in the Church, such as the anointing of a baby with the sign of the cross at its christening. And he was not tolerated to cross the boundaries of his parishes to speak to his fellow-countrymen of the Saviour of sinners without being called to account. Because of these things he decided to free himself completely of the yoke of the Established Church.

Mr Lloyd left the Church about 1807. Having relinquished his curacy he had to find some means of income. A brother of his had established himself as a tanner in Caernarvon and he went to him at first, working in his apron in the tannery, completely free of any pride. The local clergymen considered that such behaviour was bringing shame upon the sacred office. They thought it a disgrace that an ordained priest should wear a leather apron. One of them said that no one had brought more dishonour upon the surplice than Mr Lloyd. But on he went, preaching on a Sunday wherever he was invited, and working with leather at the tannery in the week. After some time he moved from Caernarvon to Nefyn, to his mother and sister, and was there for some years working the little land that they possessed. He had now more time for the work of ministry and was eminently useful in his preaching and other contributions. Some time later again, he was at Brynaerau, near Clynnog, keeping a school. He was an excellent teacher and the school was very successful. In 1817 he moved back to Caernarvon where he kept a school until 1826, when he married a Miss Jane Roberts and gave up the school. His wife was fairly wealthy. More importantly she was a truly godly woman and proved of great help to him in the work of the Lord.

His return to Caernarvon caused much interest in the town. It was not every day that an ordained man who had turned his back upon the Church was to be found preaching in a Methodist chapel. Many who would never have darkened a Nonconformist door before came to hear him, along with others who would never usually have been present at any public means of grace. But having begun to attend and been impressed by what they experienced they became faithful attenders, with very many of them being accepted as members. The first time he preached there, the crowd that gathered were too many for the chapel – no such congregation had been seen at Caernarvon except during an Association. His text was Romans 2:5 and as he spoke on treasuring up wrath against the day of wrath the minds of all were filled with terror. The early years of his ministry seem to have been spent mainly on Mount Sinai's summit. His main themes were the exacting nature of the Eternal Law, the sinful condition of man by nature, and the misery of those who die without repentance. Perhaps something of the intensity of his own conviction coloured his ministry at this time. His sermons would often be overpowering. The seriousness of his own spirit and the importance of his message would grip the minds of his hearers, so that they were often filled with a solemnity that carried with it a sense of eternity. But gradually his mind was brought to meditate on the love of God, the glory of the person and offices of the Mediator, the wisdom and gracious nature of salvation, and its complete appropriateness for the worst of sinners. The style of his ministry changed, and from this time until the end of his life he was primarily a son of peace and his favourite work was to preach peace to those that were afar off and to those that were nigh.

The evidence suggests that William Lloyd was an unpredictable preacher. At times his speech would not flow and his ability would not be apparent, so that a service might prove a burden to himself and of little benefit to others. At other times the Lord would illuminate his spirit; he would rise up to the high places of the field, his words would flow with a power that would overcome all. The main reason for the deadening services that he experienced was lack of confidence. He read much in the works of the Latin Fathers; so much so that to some extent he was brought into bondage to them, fearing to say anything from the pulpit that he had not seen in their writings. He would hardly take the responsibility for uttering a comment without having a clear foundation for it in the works of these old divines whom he counted as sound in the faith. He was often therefore under heavy yokes, his natural ability being hampered by disappointment, and his sermon and its delivery falling well below the best that he could achieve. On other occasions, however, his mind would be so illuminated as to cause him to forget all Fathers and divines; the Spirit's breezes would blow upon him; he would spread his sails before the wind; and his natural ability would have free course. He experienced many remarkable meetings and his ministry was the means of salvation for scores.

His favourite study was the Letter to the Ephesians. It was here he mostly meditated, on some part of it he mostly preached, and a phrase from it would often be the foundation of his remarks in the society. When free from the bonds that hindered him when preaching, he would often make use of question and answer. He would question Paul concerning the redemption which is in Christ Jesus and the salvation which is by grace, and then Paul would answer, and explain, and glory in the method of grace, until all his hearers were entranced. But he was more of a pray-er than a preacher. There would always be striving in his prayers; his congregation would be reminded of Jacob wrestling with the angel, and refusing to let go until he blessed him. At times it was felt that he was drawing so near to the divine Presence as to be able to converse with God as naturally and amiably as a man with a friend. His godliness was proverbial. His friends used to call him 'godly and innocent Mr Lloyd'.

William Lloyd was much troubled towards the end of his life by some who endeavoured to persuade him to return to the Established Church. On the one hand they tried to frighten him by calling him a backslider, and on the other hand they promised him a good wage and a comfortable position. Furthermore, they would pour out continual criticisms of the people among whom he had cast his lot, calling them poor, ignorant and discourteous, and nicknaming their ministers as 'the men with the blue coats'. This greatly affected his mind, especially as his health was rapidly disintegrating. He said, weeping, on his deathbed:

> Complaining against those whom I love most in the world, those with whom God is so evidently present; they may be uneducated but God's face is towards them; they may wear blue coats but it is they whom God is using most to possess the land. Christ's cause will succeed, and his cause amongst the Calvinistic Methodists will succeed also.

His health began to deteriorate about a year and a half before he died. He gradually weakened until he became unable to travel and too weak to preach at home. But he did preach at Caernarvon about three weeks before he died. For some time he could not fix on a text. He told his wife that he wished to speak on the words, 'If we believe not, yet he abideth faithful.' But later he chose another text, 'My little children, these things write I to you that ye sin not.' And as a reason for the change, he said, 'I was afraid of wandering into error when speaking on the first verse, but I'm sure I will not do so when I exhort the people not to sin.' This was his last text; he does not appear to have left the house after this occasion. Throughout his sufferings he showed great patience; he did not fear eternity at all in that he knew that he and God were at peace, but for a little while he feared the pangs of death. The Lord saw fit to release him from these fears. During the last week, he sought to compose a sermon on justification and sanctification but in his weakness he could not remember the verse, he could only remember that it began with a 'therefore'. 'Is it this verse?' asked his wife, 'Therefore being justified by faith, we have peace with God.' 'Yes, that's the verse,' he said. He then, on his back in the bed, began to preach:

> There are two points in the sermon today, namely, justification and sanctification. Justification is a once and for all action, and sanctification is an action that is brought about gradually. My justification is complete for all eternity; my sanctification has not yet been completed; but it will be so in a day or two, and then I will go the way of all the earth.

When commenting on the last phrase of the verse, 'through our Lord Jesus Christ', he could not proceed, so great was his rejoicing. He could only raise his voice in praise and song, and clap his hands together.

A few friends came to visit him on the Tuesday before he died. They found him on his high places, and he described to them, in a very melting and effective manner, his latest victory over Satan:

> Satan has been berating me painfully these last few days, accusing me of being a hypocrite and of possessing a worthless religion. Jane, my wife, was emphasizing that this was all of Satan and that I should not believe it as he is the father of lies. But unfortunately, I listened to Satan rather than to my wife. By today, I see that it was Jane who was telling the truth. She was telling me that I had true religion. I would not believe her, but I see now that she was right. I do have true religion; the root of the matter is found in me.

He then broke out in rejoicing, so that his brethren felt that they were at the gates of heaven. His last words before closing his eyes in death, were, 'All is very peaceful within.' The swell of Jordan's waters rose up and passed over him; the earth faded, and eternity opened up before him. Through the mists of the valley he saw his Judge with the books open before him, but all that this Christian uttered, in possession of that peace which passeth understanding, was, 'All is very peaceful within.' The Rev. David Jones, Caernarvon, referred to this when he said:

> He must have had a sense of his conscience being under the blood of sprinkling, and that that same blood had rendered the account of his life in the Judge's book completely illegible forever. I imagined at that moment that I was seeing him as a ship under full sail, and before a strong breeze, passing into the pleasant harbour on the other side, and gazing on the thousands of saints and angels standing at the pier-head, waiting for him to join them; and that he raised up his banner in the sight of those of us left behind, and on it in clear letters, 'All is peace within.'

William Lloyd died on 16 April 1841, when seventy years old. On the following Tuesday, his body was laid in the ground in Llanbeblig cemetery where it rests in hope until the trumpet's sound. A great crowd gathered together and in the midst of scenes of much grief and sorrow his earthly remains were laid to rest. A funeral sermon was preached in the evening, from Hebrews 13:7, 8, by the Rev. John Jones, Talsarn.

THE REV. SIMON LLOYD, B.A., BALA

The last that we shall consider of the clergymen who remained faithful to the Methodists after the Ordination is the Rev. Simon Lloyd, Bala. We have already given an account of a gentleman from Bala, Mr Simon Lloyd, Plasyndref, meeting Howell Harris at Trefeca and falling in love with the beautiful girl that opened the door to him, namely, Miss Sarah Bowen from Tyddyn, so that he did not rest until he gained her for his wife (vol. 1, p. 603). The Rev. Simon Lloyd was the oldest son of this couple. He was born at Bala in 1756.

The character of his parents is proof sufficient that he was given a religious upbringing, together with every educational advantage. From all accounts he was a serious boy and his boyhood amongst the Methodists left an impression upon his mind that nothing could delete. As a youth, he was sent to the grammar school at Bath. It seems that many Welsh boys were sent there at the time and they used to hold a Welsh prayer meeting in their rooms. At times these meetings were so blessed that they broke out into rejoicing. There is a story that on one occasion the master, on hearing some considerable noise, came in to the room and found Simon Lloyd and his companions in great excitement, jumping as young roes. From Bath he was sent to Oxford. He and Mr Thomas Charles were there at the same time, and it was as Mr Lloyd's friend that Mr Charles first visited Bala. Simon Lloyd kept his religion at Oxford; he discovered young men of similar views as himself and instead of wasting their leisure hours with vanities, as most of their contemporaries did, they held meetings for prayer and for Bible study. Before leaving the University he graduated as a B.A.

Simon Lloyd was ordained a deacon by the Bishop of Gloucester and Bristol about the year 1770, and it was in the neighbourhood of Bristol that he obtained his first curacy. He was here for three years and then received full orders as a priest. But in his heart he longed for Wales. His father by now had died and his mother left a widow and alone, so he decided to return to Bala and live at Plasyndref, the home of his forefathers. He remained a minister of the Established Church for twenty years after his homecoming, serving as curate in various places. In this way he served at Llandegla, Bryneglwys, Llangwm, Llanycil, and Cerrigydrudion. No doubt the wage he received was small but it was not for the money that he remained in the ministry for he had enough wealth to live independently. Rather, his spirit was full of a desire to help his fellowmen. His stay in every one of the parishes mentioned was probably short; his solemnity, his faithfulness as a godly pastor, his efforts at catechizing the youth of the parishes, and particularly the connections he maintained with the Methodists, were insurmountable obstacles to his staying long in any place. He attended the sermons of Methodist exhorters and preachers, he visited their chapels, and thereby gave great offence to his fellow clergy. Such a man was not to be tolerated as a curate, even if he ministered without pay; complaints would soon reach the vicar who would hasten to give him notice to quit.

The following description of his eventual departure from the Church of England is provided by *Methodistiaeth Cymru:*

> Mr Lloyd was a curate at Bryneglwys, Denbighshire, and as he lived not far from Bala, Mr Charles, who by now had left the Church and joined the Methodists, went to visit him. As Mr Charles had been ordained in the Church of England, Mr Lloyd sought to have him minister in the church on that day, because he knew that clergymen in the south who had left the Church for the Methodists still preached from time to time in the churches. Mr Charles agreed and preached that Sunday in the parish church. Because Mr Lloyd lived a godlier life, and preached a more evangelical sermon, with no respect of persons, than his predecessors in Bryneglwys, and his fellow-clergy generally, many of his parishioners were already feeling resentful. His work in allowing Mr Charles to minister in the church gave these an opportunity to demonstrate their opposition. It happened also that most of those of greatest wealth and influence in the area belonged to this opposition; they hated everything that tended to promote revival. These men decided that the young curate would not be allowed to have his own way as to the direction in which he was taking the church and by the following Sunday, to his great surprise, he found the doors to the church locked. Though he pleaded his cause, he was refused entry. As he could not gain entrance he decided that he would preach in the cemetery, but having started the service, a friend came to him begging him to stop because a number of men had decided to attack him and beat him. He accepted the advice and withdrew from the cemetery and from that Church in which he had been ordained a minister.

The above account by the Rev. John Hughes is not wholly accurate; it includes many important mistakes. Mr Charles had not left the Church when he preached for Mr Lloyd at Bryneglwys. His reason for doing so was because Mr Lloyd was ill, and it seems that he ministered there for some time. Nor was it Mr Lloyd who was hindered from entering the church but Mr Charles himself. In a letter dated 7 September 1783, Thomas Charles wrote:

> However, last Sunday, the whole parish, with two or three of the principal inhabitants at their head, came to me and accosted me in a rougher strain than I had ever been used to before. They insisted on my preaching no more in their church; for they added, 'You have cursed us enough already.'

Nor is it true that Mr Lloyd, at this time, turned his back on the Established Church. He remained in communion with the Church for a further fifteen years at least, that is, until the middle of the year 1802. But very probably his work in sending Mr Charles as his substitute lost him his curacy.

A different account again is found in the *Dictionary of Eminent Welshmen*. It is there said that Sir Watkin W. Wynn appointed Simon Lloyd to the perpetual curacy of Llanuwchllyn, but that Dr Horsley, the Bishop of St Asaph, refused the appointment. He therefore had to leave the place and soon joined the Methodists. After much research, we have succeeded in obtaining the true facts. About the middle of the year 1800, the living of Llanuwchllyn became vacant at the death of the incumbent. The whole parish, by this date, through the ministrations of the Independents and the Methodists, had been almost completely won over to hearing the gospel, and the parishioners desired an evangelical curate for the living. The patron was Sir Watkin Williams Wynn and the churchwardens requested, on behalf of the parishioners, that he appoint the Rev. Simon Lloyd, B.A., to the vacant post. Because of some reasons unknown to us, Sir Watkin delayed the appointment but agreed that Mr Lloyd should minister there until he had time to consider who would be an appropriate man. Mr Lloyd therefore served at Llanuwchllyn for two years to the great satisfaction of the inhabitants of the parish. What success accompanied his ministry, we do not know. He was not a popular, nor a greatly talented preacher, but his views were evangelical and he never hesitated from declaring the truth. After a long delay, a letter arrived from Sir Watkin confirming an offer to him for the perpetual curacy of Llanuwchllyn. Nothing further was required but the consent of the Bishop to the appointment. But the Bishop instead of granting it summoned Mr Lloyd to St Asaph to answer for his misdemeanours.

On arriving at the Bishop's Palace he discovered that his lordship was in a fearful temper. 'Are you not in the habit,' said the Bishop, 'of frequenting the chapels of Schismatics?' Mr Lloyd answered gently that his parents were Methodists and that he had been brought up amongst those people from birth; that he believed that the Lord had used them for much good in Wales, and that he had therefore been used to hearing them throughout his life, but had not done so recently so as not to offend the local clergymen. The Bishop asked him further whether or not his wife and children went to hear Thomas Charles, a man who had departed from the Church of his fathers and had joined the heretics. Mr Lloyd answered that his family were in the habit of hearing Mr Charles. At this the Bishop lost all control; his eyes flashed in rage, and he cried out, 'What! You, in holy orders, and you allow your children to listen to the hotheads! You are nothing but a hothead yourself!' Mr Lloyd tried to defend himself by saying that they lived a long distance from Llanycil, the nearest church, and that it was impossible for the children to make the journey in bad weather. 'Why then do you not keep them at home,' said his lordship, 'giving them the Catechism to learn, instead of allowing them to go the Schismatics' meeting-house?' The Bishop's last question had respect to ordination: from where did it derive? He answered that it derived chiefly from Christ, who entrusted it to his Church. He himself (Mr Lloyd) favoured Episcopal ordination but he believed that other religious denominations possessed worthy and authoritative ministers. His lordship would not listen to any more; he commanded Mr Lloyd to withdraw to the next room. Shortly after, he called him to return and informed him that he had decided not only on no account to confirm his appointment to the Llanuwchllyn living, but that he must also relinquish his licence so that he could never minister again in any church within the St Asaph diocese.

This episode reveals the bad temper and prejudice of Bishop Horsley. He nurtured a stronger hate of the Methodists than of the devil, and he could not abide zeal and seriousness in his clergy in their performance of the duties of their office. Simon Lloyd's great sin was his attendance at Methodist preaching and his permitting of his wife and children to attend at Mr Charles's chapel. It does not seem that this setback had any great effect on Mr Lloyd. He had sufficient private income as to be unembarrassed by the actions of the Bishop of St Asaph. It was clear also that his heart had been given to the Methodists for many years; they were his parents' people, and it was to them that he felt bound though he had been raised and educated for the ministry of the Established Church. From 1802 until the day of his death it was with them that he laboured. As we have mentioned, he was not endowed with the greatest of gifts; he could not excite a great congregation on the Association field or melt a congregation to tears in the chapel; but his ministry was eminently profitable, and was particularly valuable in the administration of the sacraments, up to the time of the Ordination. He travelled much with the gospel and though he was a learned man, of good upbringing and possessing much of this world's goods, he would be perfectly at home in the homes of the poor people where Methodist preachers were made welcome.

Simon Lloyd was a diligent student all his life and took great pleasure in biblical studies. He wrote many good books, the most important of which is his *Amseryddiaeth Ysgrythurol* [*Scriptural Chronology*]. It is said that he spent thirty years of labour over this book and it is one of the few books that have left a deep impression upon the Welsh. He wrote also a commentary on the book of Revelation, and for two years after the death of Mr Charles he was the editor of *Y Drysorfa* [*The Treasury*]. He suffered weakness and ill-health for a long time before being called from his work to his reward, which took place on 6 November 1836, when he was eighty years old. He was buried in the family tomb at Llanycil and there, beside the quiet waters of Bala Lake, his mortal remains rest in hope.

The Rev. Simon Lloyd was a very genial man in all his relationships and one of the mildest and most humble men that ever lived. He took no part in controversies. There is no mention of him ever disagreeing with anyone on any matter, but yet he possessed strong views concerning the great truths of the gospel and could defend them ably, if there was need. He was fully in favour of the Ordination. We believe that he expressed his agreement with this step before Mr Charles did so. In the important society held in Liverpool at Whitsun 1811, he united with Mr Charles in calling for the approaching Ordination to be a subject for serious prayer on the part of all the churches. He was greatly respected by the Methodists; his amiability, his deep humility, his readiness to undertake any work that was asked of him, together with his undoubted godliness, more than made up for any lack of remarkable preaching ability. He was greatly loved by his brethren and great was their sorrow at his death.

THE USE OF THE BOOK OF COMMON PRAYER

Before we leave the clergymen who remained with the Connexion after the Ordination, we must attempt to answer one question that is often asked, namely, whether these clergymen, after leaving the Church of England, continued to use the Book of Common Prayer in their public services? Some believe that they did so, particularly as we read, for example, that Mr Charles read the lesson before the Rev. John Williams, Pantycelyn, at Chester. But it must be remembered that this service took place in the chapel of the Rev. Philip Oliver. Mr Oliver was a clergyman, even though he had left the Church; he certainly used the Book of Common Prayer throughout his life and there is some evidence that it was used for some time after his death in the various chapels connected with him. But we have the firmest foundations for declaring that the Methodist clergy did not make use of the Prayer Book, except when they were ministering in a parish church. When Jones, Llan-gan, Griffiths, Nevern, and others of those clergymen who remained in the communion of the Church throughout their lives, went on their journeys, an exhorter would usually accompany them as a friend. It would be the exhorter who would usually lead the opening parts of the service and perhaps preach briefly to begin with, then the clergyman would continue. There was no room for the Prayer Book in such situations. As for Daniel Rowland at Llangeitho, and every other place also after he had been turned out of the Church, he would never begin the service himself. Without exception, it would be some well-known exhorter renowned for his gift in prayer, and he would have ended before Mr Rowland entered the church. He would emerge through the 'small door' behind the pulpit as sudden as a ghost; he would preach as an angel from heaven, rousing the congregation to heights of glory and worship, then retreat as swiftly as he came, leaving the people singing and rejoicing. Now, exhorters were not permitted to read the Book of Common Prayer publicly in the services, nor is it likely that its reading would be the appropriate preparation that Rowland would prefer for the sermon. There is no doubt that it was never used at all. The rule was: that when the clergymen were ministering in a building that had been consecrated by a bishop they would use the Prayer Book, but when they preached in a chapel that had not been consecrated, or in the open air, the Book would not be used.

37
THE CLERGYMEN WHO WITHDREW

WHO ARE MEANT BY THE 'METHODIST CLERGY'?

It may be appropriate at this point to define whom we mean by the term 'Methodist clergy'. At first, all clergymen were considered Methodist if they walked worthily, if their doctrine was evangelical, and if they solemnly warned their parishioners to flee from the wrath to come. By the time of the Ordination, the Methodist Revival had leavened the Established Church to some extent, so that a considerable number of clergymen in different parts of the country were preaching powerfully, illuminatingly, and effectively, and the common people were flocking to hear them. But by 'Methodist clergy' is meant those clergymen who, in addition to preaching evangelical doctrine, emulated the Methodists in the manner in which they conducted their religious services: holding prayer meetings and private societies and exercising discipline; and, furthermore, who joined formally with the Methodists in carrying forward the work of revival by being present at the Monthly Meetings and Associations and taking part in their private meetings. Some of them itinerated a great deal, preaching in the north and the south, wherever they found an open door; others journeyed very little, they possessed little of the necessary gifts, and felt also, perhaps, an unwillingness to preach in unconsecrated places. But they all supported the preaching of the laymen and agreed with the general movement for evangelizing the nation. It is these clergymen, who remained within the Church of England when the Methodists decided to ordain their own ministers, with whom we presently have to do.

For all our research, we have failed to discover much about them. For many of them it is only their names that have survived to our day. How they were converted, what were the characteristics of their ministries, what persecutions they endured, and what success accompanied their labours, are questions that presently cannot be answered. The reward they received for turning their backs upon their brethren was to be forgotten completely. Surely it was no responsibility on the part of the Calvinistic Methodists to maintain the memory of their names, for they had voluntarily broken their links with the Connexion because of ecclesiastical prejudice and from a desire to secure their livings, and they did so also with much bitterness of spirit. And on the other side, the Established Church had no desire to commemorate them because their former connections with the Methodists and the reforming spirit that possessed them made them completely unpopular with the majority of the clergy. We have searched the Church records diligently in an attempt to discover the histories of these men but any references to them are few and far between. We came across tons of rubbish in the form of libel against Nonconformists and scorn of their ministers, but of those clergymen who endeavoured to make the Church a spiritual power in Wales, there is hardly a mention. It is therefore impossible to do them justice presently. They still considered themselves Methodists after the Ordination, but that they were Methodists within the Church. They continued with the activities and meetings of the Methodists, and indeed would argue that those who had departed had lost all claim to the name and that they only were the true Methodists. For a while they welcomed travelling exhorters to their schoolhouses and endeavoured to maintain Monthly Meetings and Associations but the attempts soon proved a failure. One reason for this was that all these clergymen were, on the whole, limited in their preaching gifts, though there were some honourable exceptions. And the other reason was that it was amongst those that departed that the spirit of the revival dwelt.

THE REV. NATHANIEL ROWLAND

The first of these to be considered is the Rev. Nathaniel Rowland. We acknowledge that it is not completely correct to list him among the clergymen who withdrew because, four years before the Ordination, he was excommunicated by the Methodists. But for many reasons something of his history should be recorded, and we believe that this is the best place to do so. He was the eldest son of the Rev. Daniel Rowland, Llangeitho, the famous Reformer. Tradition has it that Daniel had many sons before Nathaniel, all of whom died while still small babies. However Nathaniel prospered and indeed was granted a long life. He had the best education and graduated honourably from Oxford. His father raised him for the Church and no doubt intended him to take his place as a leader amongst the Methodists. Nor was he without foundation for his hopes for Nathaniel Rowland, as well as being a fine scholar, also possessed brilliant ministerial skills and the Methodists, quite apart from the unending respect that they held for his father, were very ready on his own account to place him in their most prominent seat. Soon after being ordained a clergyman by the

Bishop of St David's he married Miss Margaret Davies, the only child of the Rev. Howell Davies. As a result he moved to Parke in Pembrokeshire, his wife's home. By this marriage he became a very wealthy man. Not only was he the owner of Howell Davies's house at Haverfordwest and of the mansion and estate of Parke but also of considerable wealth. Nathaniel and Margaret Rowland had five children, two sons and three daughters. Nathaniel, the eldest son, lived and died at Parke and never married. John, who was raised to be a doctor, went out to India, but never returned nor had children. The daughters married young men of the locality and it is the grandchildren of one of them who presently live at Parke [1897].

As mentioned, Nathaniel Rowland possessed brilliant gifts and was a popular preacher. We have evidence for this in the elegy written by Williams, Pantycelyn, to his father:

Thou, Nathaniel, heaven's servant,	Ti, Nathaniel, gwas y nefoedd,
Be a shepherd o'er the fold	Gwylia ar y gorlan glyd
That your faithful father, Rowland,	Gasglodd Rowland, dy dad ffyddlon,
Gathered in the days of old;	Trwy ryw orchest fawr ynghyd;
With more learning, no less talent,	Uwch mewn dysg, nid llai mewn doniau,
As a guiding lantern stand,	Saf fel llusern olau, glir,
Bringing all his sheep to safety	I helpu ei ddefaid ef i gadw
Homeward to the heavenly land.	Yr union ffordd i'r nefol dir.
To the Connexion be a father,	Bydd yn dad i'r Assosiasiwn,
And when wanting help from man,	Ac os teimli'th fod yn wan,
Turn to one of faithful labour,	Ti gei help gwir efengylwr,
Honest David of Llan-gan;	Dafydd onest o Langan;

Williams knew a preacher when he heard one, and though it might be argued that it was only his great love for Rowland that can explain his comment that the son was as gifted as the father, yet it must be acknowledged that the words of the old hymn-writer are an unequivocal proof of Nathaniel's genius. The testimony of those of old who remembered Nathaniel among the Methodists was the same. They would not accept that he was his father's equal – and he surely was not – but they said that he had a strong and melodious voice that he controlled well; that he was an able and effective speaker; and that at times he would have very powerful services. By 'a father to the Association' is meant a kind of archbishop amongst the Methodists. It is a term used by Howell Harris who applied it to his own position as a general superintendent over the societies. It was hardly necessary to encourage Nathaniel Rowland to take the reins of authority into his own hands; he had done so already to some extent even before his father died. His ambition was limitless and he was encouraged in it by all the clergymen associated with the Methodists, other than Jones, Llan-gan. After the death of his father his arrogance became intolerable. Though they might disagree as to the extent to which others were involved in the excommunication of Peter Williams, yet all agree that the ringleader in the affair was Nathaniel Rowland. His motivation throughout was not zeal for doctrinal purity but the desire to remove from his path the man who, because of seniority, learning, weight of character, popularity and service, had greatest right to sit upon the throne. He was assisted in the matter by Griffiths, Nevern; and Jones, Llan-gan, was sufficiently downhearted and timid to remain quiet.

HIS PRIDE AND ARROGANCE

It was a tragedy for religion, or at least for the Methodist form of religion, that Nathaniel Rowland ever entered Pembrokeshire. His spiritual pride, arrogance, and oppression of the societies, nearly succeeded in destroying them. There is unanimous testimony to his pride. Rowland Hill said of him that he was the proudest devil he had ever seen. He assumed supreme authority over the Association and until the rise of Ebenezer Morris no one dared oppose him. He clung firmly to the Established Church notwithstanding the contempt that it had shown towards his father. Not that this was due to any love for the Church but probably that he wanted to make the most of his position as a clergyman and to emphasize the difference in honour between himself and any unordained preacher. He would not administer the sacraments in the Methodist chapels; before long, he was to refuse to preach in them. The fraternity asked him to preach in Fishguard Chapel; his constant answer was, 'No, never.' He would preach in the church and then withdraw to the home of an old lady nearby, that was much too small and thoroughly inappropriate, in order to administer communion. It was in the teeth of his most determined opposition that Jones, Llan-gan, succeeded in persuading the Association to appoint Fishguard Chapel as one of the places where the sacraments were to be administered. His attitude was the same towards Carmarthen. When Mr David Charles, before he was an elder, asked permission to remember the death of the cross at Water Street Chapel, Mr Rowland replied, 'No, you may not; Llanlluan Chapel is close enough.' And it was against his will that the request was permitted. Yet, every month, he would lead a communion service in a chapel in Haverfordwest that had not been consecrated. No wonder that men squirmed under such capriciousness and misgovernment, and that hundreds who had been convicted under the powerful ministry of the Methodist Fathers turned their backs on the Connexion and joined the Independents and the Baptists. The forty years of Nathaniel Rowland's oppression accounts for the weakness of the Methodists in Pembrokeshire to this day. Tradition has it that not only was Nathaniel Rowland proud and arrogant but also very miserly; that he tried to challenge his father's last will and testament, and that only by giving him three hundred pounds above what was his due did his family manage to quieten him.

At Haverfordwest he preached in Tabernacle Chapel, which had been built by the Methodists mainly through the instrumentality of the Rev. Howell Davies. In *Hanes Eglwysi Annibynnol Cymru* [*History of the Independent Churches of Wales*], the building of the church is attributed to Whitefield and it is suggested that an Independent element belonged to the church from the first. This is thoroughly misleading. There were Methodists in Haverfordwest long before Whitefield visited the town; they had been convicted under the preaching of Howell Harris and Howell Davies and the latter had been the main mover in the building of the chapel. Whitefield rarely had anything to do with chapel building, and it is doubtful whether he ever set foot in the Tabernacle, Haverfordwest. The following account provides the explanation of how the building became an Independent chapel.

At a time when the Rev. Nathaniel Rowland had been absent for some months and the church had been deprived of the communion service as a result, a Captain Joss was asked to lead such a service. He was one of Rowland Hill's preachers who it seems had been given permission to administer the sacraments in Rowland Hill's churches. He had been preaching at the time in the Tabernacle during Rowland's absence and when the church's request came he agreed to it. In the middle of the communion service, who should arrive but Nathaniel Rowland. He became thoroughly agitated, seeing such behaviour as an intrusion upon his domain. In a foul temper, he took over the pulpit. Having put an end to the service, he attacked the officers cruelly. He said that he was the owner of the chapel and that no one had a right to minister there without his permission and he threatened to throw them all out. As a result, the officers of the church hastened to gain possession of the trust deed of the building, which they succeeded in doing by paying the outstanding mortgage on the building. They then challenged Nathaniel Rowland to do his worst. He therefore left the fellowship, taking many with him, and after meeting for a time in the loft of a warehouse, they built a chapel in Bridge Street, calling it Rowland's Chapel. There was nothing of Independency belonging to the Tabernacle after Mr Rowland had turned his back on it. The worshippers there were Methodists but were in fellowship with Lady Huntingdon's Connexion. And the church remained associated with that Connexion until about thirty years ago. At that time, when a Mr Stamper was the minister, the Tabernacle began to be called an Independent church and the trust deed was conformed as much as was possible to the form of governance of the Independents.

NATHANIEL ROWLAND EXCOMMUNICATED BY THE METHODISTS FOR DRUNKENNESS

The trust deed of the building in Bridge Street was most probably drawn up in Mr Nathaniel Rowland's name and the building was therefore legally his property. Around the beginning of the nineteenth century the unhappy rumour concerning his character began to spread abroad: that he indulged in immoderate eating and drinking and that he would sometimes ascend to the pulpit under the influence of drink. At first this was only a whispering in the wind; no one could be found to come forward with a clear testimony. But about 1807 undeniable proofs were presented confirming the truth of the rumours, and the Association called a special meeting at Newcastle Emlyn to discuss the matter. The Rev. David Jones, Llan-gan, was in the chair. Nathaniel Rowland was proved guilty without a shadow of doubt. The clergymen who, out of respect for his father and good will towards himself, had hoped to defend him, could find nothing to say. The next question was: What kind of discipline should be exercised? Some suggested that he should be dealt with gently, that they should not proceed with the ultimate rebuke. But Mr Ebenezer Morris rose to his feet and moved that every connection between the Rev. Nathaniel Rowland and the Methodists be broken; his motion was seconded by Mr David Charles, Carmarthen. Such was the strength of their words and the deep impression made upon all by their conscientiousness, that all were convinced. The chairman requested Mr Morris to put the motion to the meeting in that he himself was overcome by his feelings. 'In the name of Jesus Christ, I will,' said he. So he did, and every hand was raised; it is said that every clergyman present raised his hand.

Nathaniel Rowland had been excommunicated from the Connexion of which his father had been the main instrument of its founding! But he was still a clergyman of the Established Church, and his bishop, His Lordship of St David's, paid no attention to his misbehaviours and had even less thought of rebuking him for his failures. He also was the owner of the Methodist Chapel in Bridge Street, Haverfordwest. He continued after his excommunication to preach and to administer the sacraments at that chapel and, no doubt, he found some who were willing to remain with him. But as for those of his congregation who were faithful to the

Connexion, they, for the third time, had to look for a place to worship. No wonder therefore that the Methodists are weak in Pembrokeshire, in that two of their buildings were stolen from them.

How long Mr Rowland continued to minister at Bridge Street Chapel after his excommunication we do not know. It seems that he was unable to gather a congregation there after the Methodists withdrew, so that he eventually became disappointed and gave the place up. Presently, 'Rowland's Chapel' is being used, if we are informed correctly, as a blacksmith's forge. Mr Rowland's history from his excommunication to his grave lies under a cloud of darkness. As far as we have been able to gather he never obtained a living in the Church of England – because of his wealth he had no need of one. The probability is that he would minister occasionally, whenever there was a call for his service, in the parishes near to his home, but that his main occupation was the care of his estate at Parke. He lived to an old age and we have heard that, long before he died, he was able to overcome that sin which had so often caused him to stumble. He died at Parke in 1831 when 82 years old and was buried at Henllan Amgoed. Many of his descendants still live in that area of Pembrokeshire.

THE REV. DAVID GRIFFITHS, NEVERN

The next to be considered is the Rev. David Griffiths, Nevern, Pembrokeshire. Of all those clergymen who withdrew from the Methodists at the time of the Ordination and who clung to the Established Church, he was the greatest without doubt – the greatest in ability and the most popular and dazzling as to his gifts. His parents are said to have come from Llandygwydd parish in south Cardiganshire but before David was born they moved to Melin Lan, near Narberth. His father's name was John Griffiths, a clothier by trade and a much-respected man in his neighbourhood. The family must have been in comfortable circumstances for they could afford to give their children a better education than was usual in those days. It seems that a vein of genius ran through the family in that John, the second son, became a minister of some fame with the Countess of Huntingdon's Connexion. David, the first child, was born in 1756 at Melin Lan in the parish of Lampeter Velfrey, Pembrokeshire. We know nothing of his early life, nor of his early spiritual experiences and conversion. Melin Lan was not far from Llanddowror where the Rev. Griffith Jones ministered, and the Rev. Josiah Thomas Jones, who was a near relation to David Griffiths, suggests in his *Geiriadur Bywgraffyddol o Enwogion Cymru* [*Biographical Dictionary of Eminent Welshmen*] that it was through the influence of Jones's preaching that the boy David first began to consider his spiritual condition. This however can scarcely be true because David Griffiths was only five years old when Griffith Jones died. It is more probable that he was convicted under the ministry of the Rev. Howell Davies, who regularly preached and administered the sacraments at Mounton Church, which is not far from Narberth. David Griffiths was fourteen when Howell Davies died. He afterwards had many opportunities to listen to Howell Harris, Daniel Rowland, and Williams, Pantycelyn, and it is hard not to believe that their awakening ministries affected him greatly and were a deep influence in the formation of his character.

As we mentioned, his parents gave him a good education and he studied the classics for some time at Pembrokeshire Grammar School. At eighteen years of age he was employed by Mr Bowen, Llwyn-gwair, as a family tutor for his sons. Mr Bowen was a member with the Methodists; it was in his house that the early preachers would stay when they came to the neighbourhood to evangelize. His purpose, most probably, was to secure a serious and religious young man as a tutor for his children. David Griffiths's appointment, while still so young, is a clear indication therefore that he had already been converted and had drawn close to the Methodists. The Rev. Ebenezer Richard, in later times, was a tutor in the home of Captain Bowen, Mr Bowen's son.

It seems that David Griffiths was a handsome young man, of princely appearance, and very gentlemanlike behaviour. It was no surprise therefore that Mr Bowen's eldest daughter fell in love with him. He also loved her, and the two were married. He felt a call to the ministry and on 17 October 1779, when he was twenty-three years old, he was ordained a deacon by Dr Warren, the Bishop of St David's. The same man ordained him priest on 3 September 1780. He immediately became a popular preacher; he was full of the spirit of the Revival and churches were filled wherever he preached. In 1783, four years after his ordination, the living of Nevern became vacant. The living was in the possession of the Lord Chancellor and through the influence of Mr Bowen, who lived in the parish and attended the church for communion, it was obtained for David Griffiths. The Llwyn-gwair estate extended almost to the cemetery wall of the church and Mr Griffiths therefore lived in his father-in-law's mansion after receiving the post. There his children were born and raised and he was known throughout the land as 'Griffiths, Llwyn-gwair'.

Up until the Ordination, Mr Griffiths fellowshipped with the Methodists. He became a personal friend of Daniel Rowland, and Rowland rejoiced at the brilliance of his gifts and the evangelical strength of his doctrine. Once, after hearing him preach, he told him, 'My son, I see that you have found the golden vein; remember to cling on to it, giving all the glory to God.' From then on, Mr Griffiths would often visit Llangeitho during Mr Rowland's life in order to assist the Reformer in administering communion to the thousands that would gather from every part of Wales. Usually, many of the Llwyn-gwair family would travel up in a carriage, but the Rev. David Griffiths, without exception, would ride like a gentleman on a fine horse and with a servant following him. It is said that he made a very dignified impression upon all who saw him. He came to know the Rev. David Jones, Llan-gan also and the two would often travel together throughout Wales, preaching the unsearchable riches of Christ. At first Mr Griffiths would refrain from preaching in places that had not been consecrated, whereas Mr Jones would preach the gospel wherever he found an opportunity, whether the place had been consecrated by a bishop or not. Gradually, Mr Griffiths also was won over by his example.

David Griffiths himself relates how he first came to preach outside the walls of the Established Church:

> Mr Jones [Llan-gan] and I were preaching in the morning in a church in Monmouthshire. Though many had gathered, we both experienced difficult services. Mr Jones had arranged to preach that afternoon at a farmhouse in the neighbourhood. I went with him to hear him, without intending to preach myself. As it was a fine, sunny afternoon, with many having gathered, he was asked to preach outside from on top of a mounting-block. The owner of the house brought out a stool for me to sit beside him. When he had finished, the owner got hold of the Bible and placed it in my hand, saying authoritatively, 'Now you must preach, sir; the congregation is waiting for you.' When I said that I would not, he lifted me in his arms and stood me on the mounting-block. There was nothing I could now do except preach or feel ashamed, and I never had a better service. I heard afterwards that many had been saved that afternoon.

Mr Griffiths had now broken the ice; from then on, throughout the journey, he would not ask whether the building in which they gathered was consecrated or not, but proceeded to speak the word of life boldly wherever opportunity was given. After this, he drew even more closely to the Methodists. A Methodist chapel was built near Nevern in which the exhorters would preach. He would always be there in the congregation, if he happened to be at home. It was in this chapel also that the societies and the prayer meetings were held, and the vicar would lead every meeting. Soon, Nevern Church became a Jerusalem for that part of Pembrokeshire. There the Methodists would gather for communion from Fishguard, Tre-fin, Newport (Pem.), Eglwyswrw, and other places in the locality.

Often, the heavenly anointing would fall heavily upon them, filling the place with its perfume; the pilgrims who had gathered there from so many different places would be found praising and glorying God.

During the first years of his ministry, the Rev. David Griffiths journeyed often throughout the length and breadth of Wales on behalf of the Methodists. 'Griffiths, Llwyn-gwair' became as familiar a name in Gwynedd as in the south. The people followed him in hordes from one place to the next, and great influence would be present in some meetings. In Gwynedd particularly he had to preach in all kinds of places: in a chapel, where one had been built; in a barn; in a farmhouse; or out in the open air. There was not one church open to him throughout Gwynedd. He would certainly administer the sacraments also in unconsecrated places, because the Methodists in north Wales before the Ordination would make use of every visit from a Methodist clergyman in order to hold a communion service. And he would not in any way refuse them. In that he was used to assisting Rowland in administering communion in Gwynfil Chapel, a building in which no bishop had ever set foot, he could give no reason for refusing. On the occasion of his first journey to north Wales, the old persecuting spirit had not completely died out; preachers were beaten mercilessly and meetings were broken up. But it does not appear that any kind of attack was ever made upon Mr Griffiths because he was an ordained clergyman and also probably because of his dignified appearance and lion-like spirit.

As a proof of his remarkable courage, consider the following. About the year 1787, during the time of the wearying wars against Buonaparte, about 1,400 Frenchmen landed in Pembrokeshire not far from Fishguard. Before they had made much damage, they were defeated and taken into prison. Mr Griffiths, together with Mr Jones, Llan-gan, who was by now married to his second wife and had moved to Manorowen, Pembrokeshire, decided to hold annual religious services on Gwdig beach to commemorate this deliverance. In the first meeting, the two clergymen preached, assisted by many well-known preachers. The meetings became popular and were well-attended for years. Because of the element of military interest that belonged to them, a number of the gentry of Pembrokeshire, Cardiganshire and Carmarthenshire would attend. Unfortunately it has to be said that their behaviour was not always appropriate, nor did their appearance afford any kind of example to the common people present. In one of these meetings the Rev. David Griffiths was speaking, and while he was preaching the word of the kingdom many of the nobility, situated at the furthermost peripheries of the crowd, were behaving completely thoughtlessly: riding back and forth along the beach, talking to one another, and sometimes breaking out into laughter. There was never any fear of man in Griffiths, Nevern. He stopped in the middle of his sermon, stretched forth his hand, and shouted at the top of his voice so that all could hear, 'You great men, who are disturbing the service, and today seem so thoughtless and unconcerned, remember that there will be no mounts to ride in hell, towards which your faces are so set!' The noblemen were struck with fear; they were ashamed of their carelessness and there was no more disturbance of the meeting from them.

A REMARKABLE PREACHER

David Griffiths was a truly remarkable preacher. Of all the clergymen associated with the Methodists it is to be doubted whether any one of them, with the single exception of Daniel Rowland, was to be compared to him for oratorical gifts. He possessed powers of voice of great sweetness and stamina. It was said of him that he could preach for two hours in the open air to the Association, with the listening thousands nailed to his every word, without being overcome by any hoarseness or discomfort. Tradition has it that at times he continued speaking for three hours. He had all the requirements of an effective speaker. He would never be at a loss for a word, he possessed a fullness of idiomatic language and vocabulary that was easily understood and flowed from his lips as smoothly as water down a hillside.

The warmth of his spirit was a great advantage to him as a speaker; the fire within his spirit would soon kindle his thoughts, and those thoughts when expressed to the congregation before him would soon set them ablaze. In addition, he was a good theologian, evangelical in his beliefs, and able to express himself clearly. All in all, he was one of the masters of the pulpit, probably even excelling his friend from Llan-gan, if not in sweetness and charm, certainly in power and authority.

It is said that there was a remarkable dignity about his appearance when addressing an Association gathering at Llangeitho. His stature was princely, authority was stamped on his face, his head would be white with the apothecary's powder, according to the custom for gentlemen of the period. His clear, melodious voice would be heard at the furthest reaches of the crowd. His piercing eyes would search out all before him. Every movement, gesture and accent would prove his oratorical mastery. The people would soon begin to respond; hundreds of 'Amens' would rise up from the hearts of aged pilgrims; 'Hosannas' would be heard, and some feet would be seen leaving the ground. The clergymen and preachers on the platform are caught up in delight at his words. So eager are they to catch his every word that they gesture the congregation to keep quiet. Silence is again maintained for a while, and the evangelist proceeds to proclaim the word of salvation, but soon some further comment fires the souls of Zion's pilgrims and enables them to throw their burdens from off their backs. Whilst heaven pours out its blessings with such abundance it is hopeless to try to keep the people quiet. The 'Amens' double in number and volume; the praises flow forth again; the meeting concludes with rejoicings and glorying echoing across the valley. From what we have heard he preferred to dwell on the gentler strains of the gospel: he would usually take his stand upon Mount Gerizim, though at times he might scale to Ebal's heights. According to his elegist:

Closer to the cross than Sinai	Nes i fryn y groes na Sinai
Stood the pulpit of his choice.	Safai ei areithfa ef.

It was said that it was worth travelling a hundred miles to see and hear him. His biographer notes that he had not had opportunity to see Mr Griffiths until he was almost forty years old, but that he never saw a more handsome, comely, and gentlemanly man. The Countess of Huntingdon had an eagle's eye for a true preacher, and she soon picked out the Vicar of Nevern and appointed him one of the four from Wales that served her chapels in London. He performed this work very acceptably for many years. The other three were Nathaniel Rowland; Jones, Llan-gan; and Thomas Charles of Bala.

The Rev. John Owen, Thrussington, has provided the following description of Mr Griffiths's gifts and style of preaching:

> His appearance in the pulpit was very respectable, his voice was sonorous, and his speech free. But that which made him remarkable were the assaults – if that is the correct word – which he made upon the congregation at times, and which were almost impossible to withstand. His voice would not often be raised; he would generally deal with his matter slowly and without excitement, yet clearly, simply, and attractively. He would begin as if eager to hold the attention and understanding of his hearers and to prepare the way for that which he wished to impress upon their minds and hearts. As he drew near to his most important point, his features would enliven, his actions would become more animated, his voice would rise pleasantly, and then he would break out in great power and energy, so that his words penetrated every heart. I have seen hundreds together thrown into profound amazement with tears rolling down many cheeks. He would not continue this powerful attack longer than was necessary, but would return to his more usual delivery. Another topic would be turned to, or a different part of his text. He would never be found without material or words, though he would often be slow when beginning to deal

with a topic. This next point perhaps might be dealt with in a different way. He would use short, serious phrases, expressing himself warmly and attractively.

Even with a conversational style and an appropriate voice, he spoke as from the heart. He had more variety of styles than any I have heard. He opened and explained his text clearly and quietly; talking gently, arguing carefully, counselling lovingly, comforting meltingly, rebuking severely yet with compassion, thundering forth dreadfully, and glorying with all his strength, yet without an inappropriate word or gesture throughout. There was never any suggestion of artifice or device in anything he said; all was natural, arising, as far as could be seen, completely instinctively from the direction of his thoughts and the inspiration of the moment and perfectly reflecting the matter being discussed. No doubt, at first, he had struggled to discover his natural voice and found it only by trial and error. He had studied deeply the nature of man, and he endeavoured to adopt that style that was most effective for opening the mind, for gaining the attention, and for affecting the heart and feelings. And such an endeavour should be given more thought by most preachers of the gospel, not so much in order to gain popularity, but in order to save souls. Nothing in Mr Griffiths's manner gave any suggestion that he had any interest in anything else. His whole purpose was, not to please the ear, but to reform the heart. He never used great swelling words, but only words of truth and seriousness. He did not proclaim man's wisdom but 'the wisdom that is from above'.

HIS DETERMINATION DETERIORATES TO OBSTINACY

We would be glad to be able to finish this history on that note, but historical accuracy demands that we refer to other characteristics that belonged to Mr Griffiths, characteristics that must be described in order to explain his relationship with his fellow-Methodists and the stance that he took at the time of the Ordination. He was naturally authoritative; nothing was more typical of him than a bold and determined courage. Over the years these characteristics of his grew beyond measure; he became domineering and dictatorial and laid a heavy yoke upon his brethren in the Monthly Meetings and Associations. His determination deteriorated into obstinacy. He would not allow any opposition on any account. It would be useless to argue with him; unless he had his way, he would rage and shout and terrify everyone other than those as determined as himself. His biographer commented that he had heard from one of the older people who knew him well that throughout his life no one had dared to suggest advice to him on any matter, and that no one could handle him, other than his heavenly Father.

The following account gives a proof of his stubbornness of mind. When living at Llwyn-gwair, a young son of his died, a particularly charming and beautiful boy. He felt the loss grievously and was angry that such a providence had befallen him. Instead of kissing the rod, he was bitter against the Almighty. For many months he confined himself to his house, refusing to serve in the church or to attend any religious meeting. But God can subdue the contumacy of stubborn men. His little girl, fifteen months old, was taken ill and very soon died. Many clergymen came to the funeral, some of whom offered to preach for him the following Sunday. He would not give a word of reply; he sat as dumb as an idol, but the lines of his face revealed the tumult and battle within. At last, his wife ventured to ask him,

'Who, my dearest, is to minister in the church next Sunday?'

He had, by now, gained the victory over his perverse spirit and answered quietly,

'I myself will serve.'

'No, no,' she said, 'it would be better if we had someone else.'

'No,' he replied, 'I have stood out long enough; it is time for me to submit; to hear the rod and who hath appointed it.'

If men did not know how to deal with him, God knew well enough how to bring him down. For many years before his death he served as a Justice of the Peace and his biographer acknowledged that he was one of the most high-handed on the bench – the strictest in his judgments and the most unfair in his administration of the law. How to reconcile the gentle and evangelical nature of his ministry with the autocratic arrogance that possessed him and with his hard-heartedness on the bench, we do not know. Man is full of inconsistencies, and the Rev. David Griffiths was dishonoured by failings that made him a hard man to work with and an impossible man to serve.

It must be remembered also that Mr Griffiths had never drawn so fully and so closely alongside the Methodists as had David Jones, Llan-gan. Mr Jones was a Methodists first and foremost; if he had ever been driven to the pinch to have had to choose whether to give up his living or cease to preach the gospel amongst the Methodists, he would have turned his back upon the Established Church without a moment's hesitation. There is no question in our mind that had he lived he would have remained with the Methodists after the Ordination. But this was not the case for the Vicar of Nevern. It was true that he was called a Methodist; that he came to their Monthly Meetings, and preached at their Associations. We agree that at times he went on long journeys to Gwynedd and parts of the south, preaching wherever he found an open door, asking nothing for conscience's sake. But in Pembrokeshire, he would not on any account preach in the open air or in a chapel that had not been consecrated. Nor would he administer the sacraments except in a church. During the last years of his association with the Methodists, he limited his service to the Connexion, at least in south Wales, to the chairing of conferences and to preaching at Associations. He was a Churchman and full of Church prejudices, contemptuous of lay preachers, even though many of them were his equal in gifts and far exceeded him in commitment and service. Even if the question of ordination had not arisen the Rev. David Griffiths could hardly have remained much longer in fellowship with the Methodists. It was not possible for men of the independency of mind and self-respect of an Ebenezer Morris or a David Charles to have submitted to his authority, but he would only be willing to be lord or nothing.

We will not relate again the history of the Ordination and the opposition of the clergy. The Vicar of Nevern was the leader of this opposition. It was he that ordered that those who raised the question should be thrown out of the Connexion; it was he who undertook to answer, as far as he could, the arguments of Ebenezer Morris and of Thomas Jones of Denbigh; and it was he who led the withdrawal of those clergymen who would not remain. It is only fair to acknowledge that financial considerations had no part in his opposition. In general the Ordination proved costly to the clergy. All monies contributed at Communion services went to the clergymen; these could at times be considerable sums, for various members of the nobility were often present and would contribute generously. Some of the clergy received more from their Methodism than from their livings. We do not believe that this was ever a factor for Mr Griffiths. He was wealthy in this world's goods. He held the richest living in Pembrokeshire and had come into considerable wealth on marrying the daughter of Llwyn-gwair. He opposed Methodist ordination for two reasons. The first was his Church of England prejudice. He could not submit to being on the same ground as those preachers upon whom he looked down from his priestly throne. The second was the domestic feud that had arisen between himself and his brother-in-law, Captain Bowen, Llwyn-gwair. Some time previously, he and his family had moved from the Llwyn-gwair mansion. Captain Bowen and he were far from being on friendly terms; and in that Captain Bowen was strongly in favour of ordaining ministers from amongst the Methodist preachers, this was sufficient reason in and of itself, quite apart from anything else, for the Rev. David Griffiths to oppose it.

His withdrawal proved very damaging for the Methodism of the upper part of Pembrokeshire – weakening the work and greatly decreasing its numbers. The society members in those parts would usually take communion at Nevern and St Dogmael's, and when they lost their chapels in

Nevern, St Dogmael's and Eglwyswrw, they had no heart for raising new ones. Most of them therefore joined the Established Church. It must be acknowledged that the brilliance of Mr Griffiths's ministerial gifts was also a factor, for his sermons possessed an almost overpowering charm and sweetness, and he remained popular to the end of his life. Quite certainly, the division was a bitter experience for him also. For a man such as himself, replete with preaching gifts and delighting in the work of addressing congregations, it must have been heart-breaking to have to keep away from the Methodist Associations where ten thousand might gather to hear the word of life. It must have been the case also, after the heat and bitterness of the controversy was passed, that his heart longed for the fellowship of his erstwhile brethren, with whom he possessed so much more affinity, for all their disagreements, than with the dry, faithless clergy all about him. But after the Ordination he confined himself exclusively to his parish.

There are however some references to a few occasions when he came into contact with his Methodist companions of previous years. At an Association in Cardigan, whose date we do not know, thousands had gathered from all parts to hear the preaching. On the platform were the main leaders of the Connexion, from both north and south Wales. Also present were many clergymen who sympathized to some degree with the Methodists though they had not left the Established Church. Amongst these was Mr Griffiths, Nevern, having failed to resist the pleasures of an Association. The main preacher of the foremost service was John Elias, who experienced one of those meetings that shall never be forgotten. As he proclaimed the word of the kingdom, his spirit was a flame, fire sparked from his eyes, his words fell like living embers into the consciences of his hearers. Very soon, every eye was nailed upon the speaker and the congregation was a flood of tears. The influences continued to increase, the waters rose, until at last they became floods in which one could swim. The crowd seemed as if transfixed by surprise and the reverend gentlemen on the platform were weeping as children. Where was the Vicar of Nevern? He had pushed to the front beside the preacher, being completely overcome, his two eyes like two fountains. At the end, Mr Griffiths and Mr Elias, the two former opponents, came face to face. One look, and the love of years past rekindled, all disagreements were forgotten, the two fell upon one another's necks, weeping freely. We would almost say that the occasion was a foretaste of heaven, of which it was so sweetly sung:

All of the brethren will be one	Bydd pawb o'r brodyr yno'n un
And every mind agreed.	Heb neb yn tynnu'n groes.

We have heard also that Mr Griffiths and Mr Ebenezer Morris met one another soon after the Ordination. The preacher removed his hat and bowed respectfully, but the clergyman passed by on the other side without taking any notice. The same thing happened on many other occasions: Mr Morris behaving with kindness and every courtesy and Mr Griffiths ignoring him rudely in return. However, the next time Ebenezer Morris saw the vicar of Nevern coming towards him, he said to himself, 'There's an end to all toleration and patience; I will repay him in the way that he repays me; I will pass by as if I had not seen him.' This he did. He had hardly gone twenty paces before he heard Mr Griffiths's voice calling, 'Ebenezer Morris.' He turned to see the vicar rushing back with his arm stretched out towards him and saying, 'Ebenezer *annwyl!* How are you? Let us shake hands and forget all the awful things that have happened and be friends until we die.' And from the heart, they forgave each other. They met scores of times afterwards and though they belonged to different camps – one a Churchman and the other a Methodist – their Christianity was greater than their sectarianism, and they considered one another as brothers in the gospel.

Another time, about two or three years before Mr Griffiths died, there was a communion Sunday at Nevern and a good congregation had gathered. On the same day, the Rev. John Evans, Llwynffortun, was preaching somewhere in the vicinity – at Newport (Pem.), probably. Mr Evans had longed to hear his friend of old once more, and as the church service began early, he was able to fulfil his wish. When he entered the church the reading of the lessons was almost over, and the Rev. David Griffiths was ascending into the pulpit. His hair was as white as snow and his face lined with the sorrows of life, but his eyes were as piercing and discerning as ever.

We do not know from what part of the Scriptures he preached, but his spirit was stirred within him on seeing 'Evans, Llwynffortun' before him. He had a most powerful service; the heavenly oil was flowing freely and the Methodist preacher was as blessed as any, contributing his 'Amens' loudly. Mr Evans remained to receive communion with the saints. We have no knowledge of the emotions within the vicar as he extended to him the elements of the Lord's Supper, but they must have been very mixed, and his mind must have been filled with memories of days long gone. At the close of the service they sang the sweet hymn:

For Zion yet shall shine with light	Fe welir Seion fel y wawr
Though now she lies bereft.	Er saled yw ei gwedd.

As for the fellowship that ensued afterwards, we can only speculate. Surely it must have been warm and deep and full of longing, in that neither could have felt that they would see each other's face again.

Long before he died, Mr Griffiths had bought a large estate called Y Berllan in the neighbourhood of Eglwyswrw. He built there a handsome mansion and there spent the rest of his days. As he was always a busy man, full of life, and as his separation from the Methodists had barred him from expending his energies in one direction, he turned his mind to farming, throwing himself into the work with all his usual enthusiasm. He bought some hundreds of acres of land and was eventually considered one of the most successful farmers in the whole of Pembrokeshire. No wheat in Haverfordwest market could compare with the wheat of the Berllan, nor such oxen sent to any fair. Because of his knowledge of animals, he bred the best horses and cattle in the land. He also was one of the trustees of Madam Bevan's will, by which that noblewoman had left ten thousand pounds for maintaining the circulating schools begun and administered by the Rev. Griffith Jones. Some of her relatives had sought to break the will and take possession of the money. The matter was sent to the Court of Chancery where it remained for thirty years. But Mr Griffiths never became downhearted, and through his hard work and energy the inheritance, that by now had increased three-fold in value, was safeguarded for the use of the children of the poor in Wales.

We are sorry that he was not allowed to see the end of his days without having to meet many sorrows. Most of his children died as infants. Only one son lived to adulthood. He was given every advantage and was sent to Oxford to finish his education. But he dashed all his father's hopes, giving himself to a life of pleasure and excess. It is thought that all the tribulations brought upon him by his son's behaviour contributed to hasten Mr Griffiths's death. On 18 September 1834, his spirit fled to the land of pure delight. On the following Tuesday his mortal remains were carried to the church where he had ministered for over fifty years. The service was taken by the Rev. Mr Thomas, Begelly, an old clergyman who had been ordained on the same day as the departed. His body was laid to rest within the walls of the church. It is said that about three thousand people gathered to pay him their last respects.

David Griffiths, Nevern, was certainly one of the most fluent preachers that ever ascended a pulpit in the Established Church in Wales. Only Rowland excelled him in oratorical powers. It is difficult to explain why William Williams, in his elegy to Rowland, when he encouraged Nathaniel Rowland to 'be a father' to the Connexion, and promising the help of 'honest David of Llan-gan', did not include a reference to the Vicar of Nevern. One reason perhaps was the age of David Jones, in that he was twenty years older than the younger man. But David Griffiths had already won considerable fame before Rowland died and was placed at the very front of the Association at Llangeitho. Had the hymn writer discerned perhaps that the vicar was not as committed to the service of the Connexion as Mr Jones and was stronger in his allegiance to the Church? We do not wish to quarrel with him any longer however. He was certainly a means of saving many souls and of binding up the wounds of many who were bruised of heart, and as he turned many to righteousness he is today amongst those who shine as the stars for ever and ever.

THE REV. WILLIAM JONES, ST DOGMAELS

We know very little of the Rev. William Jones, St Dogmaels, except that he was an evangelical clergyman and that he fellowshipped with the Methodists. It is said that he was a native of Glamorganshire. He was appointed vicar of St Dogmaels about the year 1776. Quite possibly therefore he had been leavened with the leaven of the Methodist Revival through the ministry of Mr Jones, Llan-gan. He held the livings of Llantood and Monington as well as that of St Dogmaels; it is said that he also had the charge of Mwnt Church, near Cardigan. According to *Methodistiaeth Cymru*, the Rev. William Jones was the founder of the Methodist cause at St Dogmaels. We find this hard to believe in that Howell Harris, Daniel Rowland and Howell Davies passed through the region regularly, and there are many reasons for believing that a society was formed here very early on and was under the stewardship of the old exhorter, William Richards. It may be that the small cause here was extinguished during the controversy between Howell Harris and Daniel Rowland, and that the Rev. William Jones was the means of re-establishing it. However it was certainly through his instrumentality that a chapel was obtained here. Most probably his name was the only one on the trust deed and therefore, when he withdrew after the Ordination, the Methodists lost the chapel.

Mr Jones does not appear to have been well known as a preacher. He had few gifts, but was completely evangelical and therefore drew large congregations to hear him. As well as attending the Monthly Meetings and Associations he would regularly hold society meetings and prayer meetings at St Dogmaels, taking a leading part in them himself. The lay preachers would often preach at the chapel. Mr Jones would never be absent from a service if he was at home, and without exception it was in his own house that the preachers would receive hospitality. Tradition has it that his wife was truly religious and hospitable. It seems that Mr Griffiths, Nevern, had considerable influence over him, and like Mr Griffiths, he remained with the Established Church when the Methodists decided to ordain their own ministers. The Connexion therefore lost the chapel, and not only the chapel but all the church members and the congregation also, and there were no more Methodist sermons in that place for twenty-five years. But William Jones kept up Methodist practices – the society meetings and prayer meetings – until his death. So also did Mr Griffiths, Nevern, and his followers also, namely, the late Mr Hughes, Caron, and his brother, Joshua Hughes, the Bishop of St Asaph. So also did the Rev. Henry James Vincent, his son-in-law and his successor, for almost forty years. Indeed, there is a Methodist aspect to the Established Church at St Dogmaels still to this day. They are still careful to safeguard the society and the prayer meetings. A day-school now meets in the old chapel, but it is still called 'the chapel' locally. Mr Jones died on 13 October 1825, the same year as Ebenezer Morris. A marble tablet was placed in his memory on the wall of the chancel, and inscribed on it are the words:

> Sacred to the memory of the Rev. William Jones, who for nearly 50 years was vicar of this parish, and died on the 31st October 1825, aged 76 years.

THE REV. DAVID DAVIES, CYNWIL

The Rev. David Davies, Cynwil, was another clergymen who withdrew from the Methodists after the Ordination. He was limited as a preacher, having little ability and being clumsy in speech, but he had joined the Methodists and attended their private gatherings. He, and others of the Methodist clergy who were lacking in oratorical powers, were often embarrassed at the Associations. They had to be allowed to preach, but nearly always the preacher who spoke before them would be evidently more gifted than they – the dignity of the priest's office requiring that they have the honour of preaching last. There is an account of the Rev. John Elias preaching at an Association on the very first occasion that he visited south Wales. He had a remarkably powerful service. The people were nailed to his every word, and the influence of his unique oratory had overcome all. After him arose Mr Davies, Cynwil. Poor man! What can the man do that cometh after the king? The old clergyman's ministry, with his stuttering speech, his dry delivery, his small, trifling sermon, fell as cold water upon the people, compared to the previous passionate influences. Many could not remain and turned away, completely sickened by the contrast.

We know next to nothing of the other clergy that withdrew. *Methodistiaeth Cymru* suggests the names of the Revs. J. Hughes, Sychbant; Daniel Jones; and his brother, Hezekiah Jones. Mr Hughes, Sychbant, was the grandson of Mr Gray, Abermeurig. He was raised a Methodist, and a Methodistic style remained upon his ministry, but we do not believe he continued in fellowship with the Methodists once he was ordained. He could hardly be said therefore to have 'withdrawn'. As for the Rev. Daniel Jones, he was the vicar of Radyr, near Cardiff, and belonged to the earlier period, before Griffiths, Nevern, and Jones, St Dogmaels. He had died before the question of Ordination had ever been raised amongst the Methodists. Hezekiah Jones, his brother, was of the same period and remained united to the Methodists throughout his life.

38
EBENEZER MORRIS

HIS BIRTH AND PARENTAGE

*I*t is to be doubted whether any brighter star arose in the firmament of the Welsh pulpit than the Rev. Ebenezer Morris. Although it is now over seventy years since he was called to his rest his name is still familiar in the country and his memory is blessed. When he began his ministry the leadership of the Associations was entirely in the hands of the clergy; hardly anyone dared to oppose them and the respect afforded them by the common people verged on idolatry. But by virtue of the incomparable ministerial abilities, the resolute courage of spirit, the intense seriousness, and the fullness of wisdom which he possessed, it was not long before the Rev. Ebenezer Morris rose above them in influence and grasped the sceptre from their hands almost effortlessly. Unquestionably he was the leader of the Connexion in the south after the death of Rowland. Nathaniel Rowland and Griffiths of Nevern sought for a season to lay their yoke upon the churches. But theirs was a tyranny, a government by force. Mr Morris reigned by the agreed will of the whole Body. He occupied such a place in the consciences of all, that strong men such as the Vicar of Nevern trembled in his presence.

Ebenezer Morris was the son of Dafydd Morris, who was himself an incomparable preacher. He was born in the year 1769 in a farmhouse called Henbant, near Lledrod, Cardiganshire. The house has been demolished for many years and nothing remains to mark its site. But there are those still alive who remember where it stood in a field of grass belonging to Henbant, not far from the site of the present house. In 1774, when Eben was five years old, his parents moved from the Lledrod neighbourhood to the region of Penffos, near Troed-yr-aur, south Cardiganshire. He received a good education and was for some years a pupil at a grammar school kept in Troed-yr-aur Church by a priest called Davies. It is said that he was a lively boy, quick-witted, mastering his lessons with little effort and, in addition, full of mischief and tricks. The boys of the school used to swim in the river Ceri nearby. On the river was a deep pool, Pwll-dwfn, where only the strongest swimmers ventured. One day, a boy stood near this pool facing the water. Eben Penffos came quietly behind him, giving him a sudden push so that he fell into the dangerous waters. As the boy could not swim he was in danger of drowning. As soon as school commenced the young culprit was called to account. He excused himself by saying, 'For all I knew he could swim like a fish.' It seems his ready reply and the mischievous twinkle in his eye influenced Mr Davies to the extent that he was let off with no punishment. As for Eben, he truly could swim like a fish, and if there were any in the neighbourhood who were better swimmers than average they were said to be almost as good as Eben Morris, Penffos.

His father wished him to become a preacher but when he saw him so full of frivolity and so deficient in seriousness Dafydd Morris despaired of his wish ever being fulfilled. He would sometimes sadly say:

'I only see in Ebenezer every disqualification for the pulpit. His brother Dafydd is a good boy, serious and thoughtful. He is likely to be the preacher.' But Mrs Morris had a better understanding of Eben and greater faith in him and she would sometimes tell her anxious partner:

'I believe that my prayers on Ebenezer's behalf will be heard, but I have received no satisfaction yet as far as Dafydd is concerned.'

When he was seventeen years old Ebenezer Morris moved to Trecastle, Breconshire, to keep a day school. It is not known how he received an invitation to such a far away place, perhaps his father mentioned him on hearing Trecastle people inquiring for a schoolmaster. However we can now see that God's hand was in it. When he left Cardiganshire Eben Morris had no thought of his condition and was a complete stranger to the things that belonged to his peace. He must have heard the chief preachers of his day, and heard them at their most powerful. Daniel Rowland visited Twrgwyn regularly; Williams of Pantycelyn and Jones, Llan-gan, would often pass by in their turn; the most pre-eminent preachers of Gwynedd would not neglect the place on their tours. But for all their prowess at drawing the bow, and the sharpness and edge to the arrows they drove into the consciences of sinners, not a single shaft had ever lodged in the heart of Dafydd Morris' eldest son. Indeed, he does not seem to have received any kind of wound. At the same time it would be a mistake to imagine that he was an immoral boy. Such a person would not have been tolerated as a schoolmaster amongst the Methodists of Trecastle. The testimony of one aged mother in Israel who remembered him was that he was a most cheerful and pleasant boy, full of merriment, who enjoyed hearing an eloquent preacher but who did not profess religion nor manifest any concern over his spiritual state.

HIS CONVERSION AND BEGINNINGS AS A PREACHER

But God had definite intentions for this young schoolmaster. About two years after Ebenezer's move to Trecastle a preacher called Dafydd William Rhys or, according to the Trefeca records, Dafydd Williams, passed by. He was raised in the same locality as Ebenezer Morris, namely Lledrod, and was sometimes called Dafydd Williams of Swyddffynnon. *Methodistiaeth Cymru* suggests that he was the same as David Williams of Llysyfronydd. We can hardly believe this to be true. We think rather that he was Dafydd Williams the blacksmith, father of the Rev. J. Williams, M. A., the famous old schoolmaster of Ystradmeurig, who was himself the father of Archdeacon Williams, the noted antiquarian. The blacksmith was a little known preacher who spent all his life at Swyddffynnon. We do not know what his text was at Trecastle, nor what kind of service he experienced, but one arrow from his bow sped deep into the heart of the irreligious master. The youth failed to find any remedy for his wound until he obtained the balm of Calvary. Before long he presented himself for membership of the local *seiat*. Ebenezer Morris could never do anything by halves: he immediately began praying with the children at the close of school and taking part in the public prayer meetings. It was very soon recognized that he possessed remarkable gifts. On his knees he manifested such strength, together with such an appropriateness of language and sweetness of voice, that all would be overcome. He was as noted for seriousness after his conversion as he was for frivolity before. When out of school he spent his time in deep meditation over God's Word. Because of these things he was encouraged to preach the gospel, and he soon agreed.

Thus we find Ebenezer Morris a preacher when only a youth of nineteen and only newly converted. He immediately became a remarkably powerful and popular preacher, and it was recognized that a star of the first magnitude had arisen. According to *Methodistiaeth Cymru* he preached his first sermon in the home of Llewelyn Dafydd of Llwynynn, but his biography states that the old elder Llewelyn Dafydd had died before Mr Morris ever arrived at Trecastle, and that it was at Llwyncôr, the home of one Morgan Price, that he first spoke. After beginning to preach he continued at Trecastle for about eighteen months and his preaching in the chapel and in the farmhouses of the locality was blessed in a remarkable manner. As many as twenty-five remained behind at the *seiat* on one occasion to request church membership and they all, with one exception, testified that it was through listening to Mr Morris that they were convicted. Soon he paid a visit to his parents and the brethren at Twrgwyn asked for a service. He promised that he would preach on a particular night at Troed-yr-aur farm. That morning he and his father went on an errand to Newcastle Emlyn. On their return Ebenezer turned to go to Troed-yr-aur and his father pretended to continue on his way back home, so that he would not be a distraction to him. A large congregation had gathered and the farmhouse would not have contained a half of them. The young man therefore preached in the open air, standing on the horse-block. The sermon was remarkably effective. His strong voice filled the beautiful Troed-yr-aur valley; his expressions fell with an irresistible force upon the hearts of his hearers. All felt that Ebenezer Morris was one of heaven's ambassadors, a man sent by God. Sitting on the wall listening was Dafydd Morris, who had not gone home. His feelings cannot be described, and he broke out in thanksgiving at the end of the service, crying out, 'The gospel will never die, while Eben, my son, lives.'

While he was still only twenty and having preached for little more than a year, Morris travelled to north Wales as a companion to the Rev. David Parry of Llanwrtyd. Strict rules as regards young preachers had not yet been drawn up at that time nor was permission needed then from the Monthly Meeting before undertaking a preaching tour. The field was open and the rule that prevailed was 'the survival of the fittest'. David Parry was a tender and melting preacher; he did not cause sinners to tremble but rather enticed them with the sweetness of his message. His sermons did not convey the profoundest of thoughts but they were always brimful of the gospel. There has been insufficient commemoration of the memory of this famous man. We do not know of any particular events on this journey but it is certain that the young preacher would have received much profit. The exercise of preaching many times a day is generally beneficial and added to this, no doubt, would be the instruction and advice received from David Parry. Although the 'companion' became more famous than his master, yet Mr Morris always held very high views of the gifts and character of the evangelist from Llanwrtyd. On one occasion when David Parry was preaching in an Association in Glamorganshire and heaven was smiling on his efforts, the effect on Ebenezer Morris was such that he cried out at the close, 'The Lord would seem to be obliged to bless anything said by Mr Parry.'

As mentioned, Morris remained only eighteen months at Trecastle after beginning to preach. He journeyed back to his parents' home at Twrgwyn, preaching the word of the kingdom throughout the intervening countryside. His fame as a remarkable preacher spread abroad. Daniel Rowland heard of him and was determined to have him, though still short of two years' preaching experience, to address the Llangeitho congregation on the Saturday before a Communion Sunday. Rowland himself preached at eleven as usual. Hundreds of men and women would be gathering during the day, in the village and the surrounding countryside, in readiness for the communion on the Sunday, so Rowland would usually appoint the most notable preachers for the afternoon. On this Saturday he chose the son of his old friend Dafydd Morris to speak to the multitude. Before the Sunday of the week following, Rowland had been called to his rest, and the old people would often refer to this remarkable coincidence: the greatest preacher ever seen in Wales, if not the whole world, preaching his last sermon on the Sunday, and the greatest Welsh preacher after him preaching his very first sermon at Llangeitho on the previous day. It might be thought that God did not wish to take Aaron from the earthly to the heavenly sanctuary without first presenting the Eleazar who was to succeed him. Mr Morris preached for the first time at Llangeitho on 8 August, 1790; Daniel Rowland died within the week, on 15 August.

THREE IMPORTANT EVENTS IN HIS LIFE

It was not long before three significant events took place which were to determine his thinking and deepen him in his commitment to the work of the ministry. The first was the death of his father which occurred on 17 September 1791, that is about thirteen months after the departure of Rowland. Dafydd Morris died whilst in the midst of life and not yet forty-seven years of age. Ebenezer Morris was journeying in the north on his way to the Association at Caernarvon when the news was brought to him. Needless to say, the event affected him greatly for he not only lost a kind and tender father but the Methodists of Cardiganshire lost the two greatest preachers that they possessed, and their departure necessarily made his own position so much more prominent. Apart from the young Ebenezer Morris there were only two other well known preachers attached to the Monthly Meeting after the death of Dafydd Morris, namely Mr Williams, Lledrod, and Mr Gray, Abermeurig. Although older than Ebenezer Morris, John Thomas, Cardigan, had not yet begun his ministry. So, in his twenty-second year and in only his third year as a preacher, we find Mr Morris thrust by circumstances, or rather by God's providence, into the leadership of the brethren in Cardiganshire and the leadership, soon, of all the brethren of south Wales.

The second of the three events to which we referred was his marriage to Miss Mary Jones of Dinas, a village some three miles from Twrgwyn. It is said in *Methodistiaeth Cymru* that this occurred when he was twenty years old. This is not correct. In his biography it is stated that it was in

1792, within a year of the death of his father, and when he was twenty-three years old, he entered into marriage. Mary Jones had lost her mother when she was only a girl of seven and had been raised in consequence by her uncle and aunt at Dinas. These were without children and they raised Mary as their adopted daughter. The family was wealthy and Mrs Jones, the aunt, was also noted for her good sense and religion. It was with them that Daniel Rowland, Williams, Pantycelyn, and others of the Reformers used to stay when they passed on their itineraries. From the beginning Mary Jones was a serious girl, much given to hearing the gospel and fully committed to the cause of the Revival, but she did not apply for church membership until she was eighteen. She did so eventually at Newcastle Emlyn after being encouraged by the old hymnist of Pantycelyn, who had noted the spirituality of her character and her modest behaviour. A young gentleman of the locality, the owner of much land and property, had offered her marriage and her uncle favoured the match, but she adamantly refused to be unequally yoked with an unbeliever and gave her hand to Ebenezer Morris. Her uncle was enraged; he did not consider the young exhorter of Penffos, who only owned one horse and its bridle, to be in any way worthy of the hand of his niece. She had to leave the house with nothing and in his last will she was not even referred to, all his wealth being passed on to her brother.

The subsequent history of Mr and Mrs Morris is given by the late Rev. John Rees of Twrgwyn and afterwards of Tregaron :

> After the wedding [Mrs Morris] went to live with her dear husband at Penffos, the home of her father-in-law, the eminent preacher Dafydd Morris, who had died the previous year. Her husband was only a young man who had only just begun preaching, and no doubt he and his wife encountered hard times in the first years. For all this, God did not allow Mrs Morris to go unrewarded, even in this world, for her love and zeal in refusing an earthly inheritance for the sake of God and his people. Her choice brought her good; the God of Jacob defended her and brought her success. Her husband increased notably in ministerial gifts and usefulness earning the attentions of the world and the church ... Providence smiled upon them as he received somewhat from the churches for his labours, and as she was diligent and well-ordered in domestic arrangements. After the death of her uncle at Dinas, her dear brother, David Jones, Esq., inherited all his lands and possessions and in his good will and love towards his sister he made over to her a large sum of money. This generous man was a godly and religious individual; he was an elder in Salem church from its opening in 1811 until his death in 1833, and his gentlemanlike action towards his sister is worthy of respectful remembrance. The gift enabled Mr Morris to buy a plot of land and to build on it a fine new house called Blaenywern.

It was built in 1804 and they were able to enjoy as many years of happiness together there as the number of the years of their earlier difficulties.

One expression in the Rev. John Rees's account hints at the third important circumstance which occurred to Mr Morris soon after the death of his father, namely the reference to his receiving payment from the churches. Dafydd Morris had been called as pastor over the churches of the Troed-yr-aur valley, and as far as we understand he was the very first pastor, in the sense of having a 'pastorate', amongst the Methodists. After his death his son was asked to take his place. The position required that he preach regularly to these congregations; that he chair their church meetings; visit their sick; advise those whom he perceived were departing from the gospel; superintend the cause in all its various branches; and receive some amount of remuneration for the work. Undoubtedly this worked to the advantage of the churches as well as to himself. It brought him to an awareness of his responsibility; it called forth all his spiritual efforts; it forced him to read extensively and to meditate deeply so as to ensure fresh provision for his people; and it gave him the pleasant opportunity of preaching regularly to the same congregation. According to the unanimous testimony of older people, he was one of the best pastors. He ruled over them efficiently but with every tenderness. He induced fear in transgressors and those who loved strife. It was said that merely to refer to Eben Morris in the hearing of workers of iniquity would cause them to tremble and that the peace that flourished in all the churches of his charge was due to the great respect in which he was held. No doubt his wage was very small but his people were very careful to maintain it for him. Even the serving maids contributed towards it, for it is said that when they were tempted at times to buy a ribbon or a costlier dress, they would say to each other, 'We must be careful to save our contributions for Mr Morris' pay.'

It is sufficient to mention one fact as proof of the great respect in which the whole countryside held him. He was preaching on one occasion at Blaenannerch on a weekday. It was the middle of winter and when the time came to begin the journey home the road to Twrgwyn was already covered in snow and quite impassable. It appeared to him that he must remain where he was for some time. But the local population decided to open a way for him through the snow. A brave volunteer ventured through the drifts to Twrgwyn to encourage the people there to begin the same task from their end. The two companies eventually met and the Lord's servant found an open road home, between high, white snow walls.

A DESCRIPTION OF THE MAN

Perhaps this is an appropriate place to describe the outward man. We can hardly believe that he was a short man, although that is how he is usually portrayed. We have been told on good authority that he was in fact reasonably tall but that because of his stocky build and because he put on much weight, he appeared short. His shoulders were strong and wide, his face fair and well-adapted to express the feelings of his soul, his eyes as piercing as an eagle's, his mouth wide, as befitted an orator. His lips, the lower lip in particular, expressed an unbreakable determination. His whole outlook conveyed an impression of authority and cheerfulness. He died before reaching old age, yet his hair turned white very early on and receded, so that he took to wearing a black cap in the pulpit. Because of this, and because he had to wear spectacles to read, he looked a good deal older than his age. He was once described as a pulpit-ful of a preacher and of a very reverend appearance.

Ebenezer Morris very soon became one of the princes of the Welsh pulpit and that at a time when there were giants in the earth. For most of his life he laboured amongst the second generation of Methodist clergy, men like Jones, Llan-gan, Davies, Llanfyrnach, Jones, St Dogmaels, and Griffiths, Nevern – all of them possessing reviving ministries, clear voices, evangelistic spirits and great influence. In his lifetime also arose a number of unordained preachers in Wales, the like of which has never been surpassed and only rarely equalled. We refer to Robert Roberts, Clynnog; his brother, John Roberts; John Jones, Edeyrn; John Elias; Richards, Tregaron; Richards, Fishguard; David Charles, Carmarthen; John Evans, Llwynffortun; John Thomas, Cardigan, and others. They were all mighty men of David, masters of the congregation, who could shoot an arrow within a hairsbreadth. It is no exaggeration to say that Ebenezer Morris, even before reaching his thirtieth birthday, had climbed to the first rank amongst them in popularity, influence and authority, and in some respects at least, excelled them all. He achieved this status without any conscious effort on his own part. It came to him rather as the natural legacy of the pre-eminence of his gifts, the power and influence of his ministry, his profound integrity and courage, and his purity of character. When on tour, whole neighbourhoods would gather to hear him, and rarely did he fail to overcome his hearers. That old patriarch, Siencyn Thomas of Penhydd, told him once, in his own unique way,

'You travelled the country the first time on the back of your father's strong horse, but now you have as strong a mount as he. Mind you don't fall off, lad.'

Certainly it is not as a profound thinker that Ebenezer Morris excelled, nor in any intricate composition of sermons. He had very little time to spare for the study because of the innumerable calls for his service. He would attend the Monthly Meetings of the county with constant regularity. Very rarely would his place be absent in the Associations of the south, and he would attend one or two of the Gwynedd Associations every year. It must also be remembered that it was not merely a case of going and returning, as if fetching water from the well, but that every far off Association would involve a preaching tour of some weeks. When at home, he would preach and keep a *seiat* on every day of the week, except for Mondays and Saturdays, at one or other of the churches in his care. He would preach three times every Sunday, very often administering the Lord's Supper twice also. He held services in homes, he preached at funerals, far and near, and also on board nearly every ship that went to sea from Aberaeron harbour down to Cardigan. It is easy to see that his time for reading and meditating was scarce and that it was impossible for him to compose elegant and finished sermons. But he made good use of the little time he had amongst his books. Even his great opponent, Mr Griffiths, Nevern, said of him that he knew of no one who could make the cream of a book his own in so short a time. His favourite authors were the Puritan writers, and Dr Owen in particular. Rarely would a useful comment escape without his having noted it and made it his own, pressing his own image upon it and adapting it to fit his own style of address. It is fairly certain also that though he might have very little time to read when travelling he would be in constant meditation when mounted on his horse. When crossing the lonely Welsh hills, in that deep silence, far from the busyness and noise of the world, without anything to distract them, the preachers of old would have excellent opportunities to search and meditate upon the great truths of the gospel, and to a large extent these times made up for their lack of acquaintance with books and authors. In the pulpit also, when face to face with their congregations, and all their natures stirred up, they would discover glorious views, not attainable in their studies. Ebenezer Morris made excellent use of his opportunities and men such as David Charles, Carmarthen, and others, were amazed that his sermons were so full of strong theology, and that he could form such long, balanced and self-consistent sentences. Yet, having said all, his excellence did not consist in the composition of his sermons.

HIS COURAGE

We must hurry on to note some of his characteristics. He possessed *a profound integrity and an enduring courage in maintaining his convictions.*

He did not know what it was to be cowardly and to fear man. Once he perceived the path of duty clearly, he would hasten to take it, whatever the consequences. He respected dignity and was not in any way deficient in appropriate courtesy, but when he saw men obstructing the passage of the chariot of the gospel he would not fear any rebuke but would thrust them out of the way, whatever their station in life. We have many examples of such behaviour. We have already referred to the fact that at the beginning of the Methodist revival certain religious women were given considerable freedom in the *seiadau*. They would examine experiences and, at times, would address the church. They were considered almost as deaconesses, though no one had established them in such an office. Many of these women were to be found in the southern parts of Cardiganshire, and one in particular at Blaenannerch. She would take the lead in the *seiat* even when Mr Morris was present, examining the brethren as well as the women in their experiences. He noticed that she was guilty of favouritism. She would distinguish between the wealthy and the poor, continually praising the religion of those of prosperous circumstances and only rarely approving the poor. Mr Morris tolerated this for a while, though his spirit was stirred within him. He considered his own youth and the danger of causing a rift in the church. But eventually, when keeping a *seiat* at Blaenannerch, with the deaconess having taken the lead as usual and scolding harshly a poor, humble woman, he could not contain himself. Turning his lion-like face towards her, with his eyes blazing, he said,

> Is this the way you conduct God's business? If a rich woman relates her experience, you smooth over all carefully with much praise, though it may be she is to be blamed; but if a poor woman comes forward, though she be the godliest in the country, you beat her mercilessly. Whatever happens to me, I will not tolerate such behaviour any longer.

He uttered these words with such princely authority that every one present felt there was one in their midst born to rule, and for all his youth no one dared oppose him. The old sister lost her position in the church completely, the other deaconesses also had to go. From now on they had to be content with relating their own experiences without having the right to catechize their brothers and sisters.

After the death of Howell Harris, Ebenezer Morris was the first to dare to oppose the clergy at the Associations. All used to look up to them as if they were angels, and a kind of superstitious dread was felt in their presence. When Ebenezer was young it was Nathaniel Rowland who ruled, his armour-bearer was the Vicar of Nevern, and their yoke was heavy. But Mr Morris would resist them to their face if he saw that they were departing from justice. Once, towards the end of his life, an old friend referred to his bravery in the Associations at this time and said that he was amazed at his honesty and valour. He replied:

> Every time, before I would open my mouth on some point of importance, I would make sure that I was on God's side. Then, if I fell, his name would fall also, and I believed that he would always appear to defend his glory.

An Association was held once at New Chapel, Pembrokeshire, in which Nathaniel Rowland and some other clergyman fell into such argument and quarrelling that the whole meeting became profitless and they could not proceed with any business. Every one else sat in silence whilst the two great gentlemen shouted at each other like two fractious fishwives. Mr Morris felt deeply the disgrace to the sanctity of the private *seiat*; he confidently expected that some of the older men would rebuke the quarrellers. But all were in such fear of Nathaniel Rowland that they dared not open their mouths, particularly so as New Chapel was one of his own churches. At last, tired of waiting, he stood up with an air of authority and with considerable power, stated,

> If you do not come to better order than this whilst engaged with the Lord's work, we will require that you both be disciplined.

His words carried with them a sense of awe, and the two clergymen sat down, fearing to speak another word. As they left the building, his friend, John Thomas, Cardigan, said,

> Eben, I could not have spoken the way you did to Rowland and the other for the world. I was afraid that one of them would have hit you for daring to presume to quieten them.

But Ebenezer Morris was not one to be silenced by the fear of men.

We have already referred to the part he played and the courage he displayed in the matter of the Ordination of ministers, so that we need not repeat that history. He, together with the Rev. Thomas Jones of Denbigh, was the chief instrument for bringing about the steps taken. But it is perhaps in the circumstances relating to the excommunication of Nathaniel Rowland at the Newcastle Emlyn Association of 1807 that we find the clearest example of his bravery. Mr Rowland's unacceptable behaviour had been proven beyond any doubt. It had been evidently demonstrated to the Association that he was a glutton and a drunkard. The question was, what to do with him? The gathering waited for guidance from Jones, Llangan, and Griffiths, Nevern, but neither would open his mouth. The first, because of the gentle kindliness of his nature and the respect which he had felt for the father of the accused; the other, because of the personal friendship between them. Someone half-suggested that he be gently rebuked. Amidst absolute silence Ebenezer Morris got to his feet, an expression of deepest solemnity on his face; it was clear that he was stirred to the depths. With much feeling he referred to the godliness, apostolicity and inspiring ministry of Daniel Rowland, and the respect which all had for his memory. He then mentioned the doctrine, gifts, dignified position and long service of his son, whose case was now being considered, and the disinclination they all felt to excommunicate him.

'But,' he said, 'his unruliness has been proven so clearly, and his behaviour found to be so inconsistent with the purity of the gospel that I am forced to move that every tie between himself and the Methodists be broken and that he be no longer considered a member of the Association.'

The motion was seconded by Mr David Charles, Carmarthen, who because of his learning and ability was already one of the leaders in the Association, though still only an elder. For a while there was only complete silence. Then Mr Jones, Llan-gan, who was in the chair, asked if there were any other suggestions. There were none.

'Put the motion to the meeting, Mr Jones', said Mr Morris.

'No, Eben,' he replied, with tears running down his cheeks, 'I cannot do it; you must do it.'

'Well, Mr Jones, it is your place to do it. But if you will not, then in the name of Jesus Christ, I will do so.'

Then, in sorrow but with great authority, he proclaimed,

'I therefore call upon all present at this meeting who feel for the purity of Christ's Church and the honour of the ministry of the gospel, to agree with myself and with Mr David Charles, according to the motion put before you, to break every connection with Mr Nathaniel Rowland until he shows signs of true repentance.'

Immediately all hands were raised, even those of Mr Jones, Llan-gan, and the other clergy. The meeting closed with a remarkable prayer from Mr John Evans, Llwynffortun. By his fearless courage on this occasion, Mr Morris established his reputation as the man of greatest influence in the South Association. It appears that one of his greatest admirers was Siencyn Thomas of Penhydd and that he was delighted by the disciplining of Nathaniel Rowland. Soon after the event Mr Morris was touring Glamorganshire. At some point the old patriarch met up with him and clapping him upon the back said,

'Good boy! You did well in Newcastle. All the clergymen in the world will be scared of you now.'

Then, after a minute of silence, the old man repeated the advice he had given him previously.

'Your horse's head is today above the head of every other mount in the south. Beware lest you fall. Should you do so, you would get an awful bruising.'

Mercifully he was preserved from all such falls until his arrival in heaven.

At the same time it would be a grave mistake to conclude that Ebenezer Morris was some lion of a man with no compassion and tenderness. He combined lion-like bravery with the gentleness of a lamb. We have plenty of examples that show this. He was preaching once at Llangeitho and as usual held a *seiat* after the sermon. A man called Thomas Lewis of Cilrhig was called forward to share his experience and as Mr Morris wished to learn something of his character and religion before questioning him he called upon an exhorter to begin the discussion. There were two of them present, John Williams, known as *Sion Sgubor* [John of the Barn] and Evan Evans or Evan Tanner. As the old man laboured under much fears and doubts the two exhorters did not deal too gently with him. One of them said that he did not know what to think of men who had been so many years with religion and yet had hardly anything to say as to the basis of their eternal life. Mr Morris felt for the poor man and began to question him:

'How old are you?'

'I am seventy-eight years old.'

'For how long have you been religious?'

'More than fifty years,' said the old man. 'Ever since I had the privilege of a place amongst the Lord's people.'

'Were you ever out of the church during all that time?'

'No, never; though I deserved to be thrown out many times.'

'Have you ever been under church discipline?'

Thomas Lewis began to weep, and the people wept with him, and through his tears he said,

'No, and I do not understand how I avoided it; I am such a worthless creature.'

'Fifty years without one rebuke!' said Mr Morris. 'Fifty years without rebuke! That is more than many an able man can say. How many of you others can pronounce that shibboleth?'

The sweetest of breezes passed through the meeting at that remark but the two exhorters blushed with shame, and as it happened, one of them had been under discipline on a number of occasions.

Another example of Mr Morris's tenderness, as well as of his good sense and ability, is seen in his dealings with an old elder of Blaenannerch, Michael Jones, or Michael Penuwch, as he was known locally. The Sunday Schools having started, it had become the custom for the young people to recite a chapter of the Bible publicly at the beginning of a service. Girls as well as boys would do this in their turn. Michael Penuwch considered this to be a dangerous novelty, but he dared not intervene because Mr Morris, together with the remarkable old elder, Owen Enos, approved of the custom. However, Mr Morris, on one preaching journey to the north, took Owen Enos with him as a companion. During their absence Michael took the reins and soon put an end to the practice, stopping one reciter publicly after he had got to his feet. The whole place was astir. Ebenezer Morris was sure to expel him, Michael was threatened, once he returned. The old man himself was not without a degree of fear and he prepared himself for a battle. Home came Mr Morris and soon he was at Blaenannerch, preaching and keeping a *seiat*, and the complaints against Michael's behaviour began to flow. They expected to see their pastor become heated and thunder forth the law. But Mr Morris understood his man, he knew that Michael Penuwch was one of the godliest men in the land and also that he was not one to take fright or be compelled. He turned to the old man and stood over him as if in amazement, repeating three or four times in the most affectionate manner,

'Oh! the godly old Michael. Oh! the godly old Michael.'

Michael could take a rebuke without flinching, but this unexpected gentleness overcame him completely. His heart melted to water, his eyes filled with tears, and it was evident that he was willing to accept whatever came. The members now questioned amongst themselves only as to the sentence that Mr Morris would pass.

'He will be kept back from the Lord's Table,' whispered one.

'No, he is sure to turn him out,' said another, 'and so he should, for he stopped our Peggy from saying her chapter.'

Ebenezer Morris got to his feet and pronounced his judgment.

'Michael,' he said, 'you know that I am to preach here next Sunday afternoon. You must begin the meeting for me and you must choose whoever you wish of the girls or women to recite a chapter.'

This quietened everybody and Michael accepted the sentence. And when the Sabbath came the old man was in floods of tears as he listened to the chapter recited. The story shows that Ebenezer Morris was a good judge of character and could distinguish between a wilful act and an error of judgment.

It seems that Michael Penuwch was a particularly noble character, zealous for the sanctity of God's house. He was the servant of Mrs Jones of Penarisaf, a wealthy widow and a prominent member at Blaenannerch. The widow married Mr Howells, the vicar of Maenordeifi, a man who had been disciplined for immorality. Mr Morris was troubled as to how to deal with her case. On the way to Blaenannerch he called at Esgair-ieithyn to speak to Owen Enos and, amongst other things, they wondered whose side Michael would take, in that he was usually very firm for discipline. The meeting was held and Mrs Howells's case raised. Michael stood up with a solemn look on his face.

'The mistress has to go,' he said, 'otherwise I am bound to throw my Bible on the fire. She has married one of the worst creatures on the face of the earth.'

And out she went. Soon afterwards, a Monthly Meeting was held at Blaenannerch, and although she was under discipline the woman contributed an abundance of provisions for the meeting. But when Michael heard he went immediately to the meeting and returned the food as an accursed thing. As a result his mistress joined the Established Church. We record this story in order to show what kind of man was Michael Jones, Penuwch, and to illustrate the manner in which discipline was administered in those days, without any respect of persons.

HIS VOICE

Ebenezer Morris possessed *a strong, fluent and sweet-sounding voice, as if it were made for the proclamation of the gospel.* In its combination of strength, sweetness and penetration it was unique. It possessed the fluency of the voice of Evans, Llwynffortun; the tenderness of the voices of Ebenezer or Thomas Richard; the penetration of Michael Roberts's voice, together with an overcoming power which was all its own. The old people used to say that 'Dafydd Morris had the stronger voice but that Eben's was the sweeter by far.'

'He had,' said the mother of Dr Owen Thomas to her son, 'not a chapel-ful, but a field-ful of a voice.'

It was not merely that he could carry his voice to those on the very edges of the crowd on an Assembly day, but that he could do so with ease. His comments could produce the same effects upon those on the outer fringes of a gathering as they did on those close to the stage. And over this magnificent voice he had complete control. He could raise or lower it as he wished; he varied it at will according to the nature of his message. At times it would roar forth as thunder; at other times it would sound as the sweetest notes of the harp; sometimes it would be harsh as it proclaimed the threatenings of the law, and then as gentle as the softest breeze in the tops of the trees, when dispensing gospel promises. It was an unfailing instrument for presenting his heartfelt emotions.

All who ever heard him agreed on this pre-eminence of voice.

'Do you remember Ebenezer Morris?' once asked the Rev. William Rees of Dr Owen Thomas, as they were discussing the Welsh preachers of old. And when he replied in the negative, he added,

'You never heard a voice, then.'

So also declared Mr David Jones of Dolaubach, well-known for his discerning comments:

> The most notable thing about Ebenezer Morris, over and above everybody else, was the excellence of his voice. It was melodious as well as being powerful. With some sentences of his sermons he would release all the power and fluency of that majestic voice so that he could be heard some miles away, especially if he was preaching in the open-air; and at those times the thoughts being expressed would be as weighty as the delivery. He could then return again as naturally as if he had never raised his voice. He was also particularly skilful in complementing the matter in hand by means of his facial expression, so that a deaf person even could understand from his countenance whether he was preaching on the law or the gospel.

Mr Jones's comment that Ebenezer Morris's voice could be heard some miles away is a literal fact. On one occasion, the late Rev. Evan Evans of Aberffrwd, a respected old minister from Cardiganshire who died in the year 1856, had failed to attend the services on the promenade during an Aberystwyth Association because of bodily weakness, though he was at the town and had been present at some of the meetings in the chapel. He inquired eagerly of someone who had been present. Amongst other things his informant told him that some of the congregation were complaining that they could not hear the preachers, particularly as there was a strong wind blowing.

'Yes,' answered Mr Evans, 'the great men, fit to address the thousands of an assembly are nearly all dead. When I was a young boy I was helping my father as a shepherd at Capel Seion when Ebenezer Morris was preaching on the promenade at Aberystwyth. And although the distance was some three miles, we could from there not only hear the preacher's voice but also understand an odd word every now and again.'

We have a similar testimony from the Rev. Thomas Howell Davies, the parson of Llangunllo, whose mother was a member with the Methodists at Capel Drindod:

'When he preached,' he said, 'Mr Morris would begin quietly and slowly, gradually increasing in volume as he proceeded until his voice before the end was as a silver trumpet. It was a louder, more penetrating and more melodious voice than any other I heard. When preaching on the platform in the open-air his voice could sometimes be heard for miles. I heard of an old lady in Pembrokeshire who was convicted through his ministry when she was sitting on the slope of a hill about two miles from where he was preaching. In an open-air assembly his voice would congregate the crowd and knit them together as one. All of them with their eyes wide open and their mouths half open, as if they were swallowing the weighty, glorious and eternal truths which were pouring forth from his mouth.'

We will quote one more testimony relating to the uniqueness of his voice, namely that of Dr Phillips of Hereford. He states:

> There were giants in the earth in those days, and he was one of them. Who has not heard of the eloquence of Ebenezer Morris. His person was dignified, his voice loud, clear and pleasant. His oratory was not artificial or false. He would raise his voice when the tide of feeling was rising. He could shout so that thousands heard what he had to say, and he shouted, not from habit, but from emotion, because he could not refrain from doing so. His physical and mental abilities were always controlled by the inspiration of the truths being considered. After the waters had gradually gathered together, they would break in great torrents over the heads of the listeners. And between the floods from above, the rending of emotions within the people, and the increasing eloquence of the preacher, the scene at times was indescribable.

HIS ADAPTABILITY

Ebenezer Morris possessed *a particular ability to adapt to the circumstances in which he found himself.* He preached in all kinds of places: in homes, at funerals, in nearby chapels, or in the open-air on Assembly days with thousands of hearers before him. In every place he was completely natural. He would not make use of the great volume of voice, which was as the sound of many waters when preaching in a cottage, neither would he attempt much oratory. He would speak rather in a relaxed and intimate way. Mr David Jones of Dolaubach testifies again on this point:

> I never saw a preacher who could adapt himself so appropriately to his situation. When preaching in the open-air he would be the master of the congregation; like Saul, head and shoulders above everyone else. When preaching in the kitchen of a farmhouse he would be as one conversing with the family about the hearth, and yet never descending too low. He never lost his influence over his hearers in either situation. I remember him speaking on a Sunday

> night in a farmhouse in the year 1817, or 1818, when food prices were very high. He took as a text Matthew 6:33, 'But seek ye first the kingdom of God, and his righteousness; and all these things shall be added unto you.' He commented on seeking God's kingdom in its personal gracious rule in the heart, on seeking its success on earth by prayer, and on seeking it in external circumstances by contributing to the cause of religion according to the example of the widow of Zarephath in Zidon towards Elijah, who gave the first cake to the prophet and discovered that in doing so she had ensured that the meal and oil would not fail. Then, with a most solemn look at his hearers, he added, 'And do you know friends, I believe that if we were led to seek God's kingdom in the way that I have been trying to describe, we would find a means of passing through this world with no wants; even if it became necessary for God to turn the stones of the field into bread for us.' And after a pause, as if he were giving time for the congregation to consider the point, he added, 'Indeed, that is the case. I will not withdraw the remark.' And he repeated the comment, and with such influence accompanying his words that it was clear to see from the look on their faces that all believed him thoroughly.

When travelling to an Association and preaching in the countryside on the way, he would not always reveal all his strengths. He would speak soberly and with profundity but without the irresistible force which typified his ministry on feast days. The Rev. Joseph Thomas of Carno used to say that he did not like seeing a preacher at his most intense in every service. In any case, Ebenezer Morris was not so. A special occasion would excite his nature and awaken resources that would be hidden in his everyday ministry. And to see him in his greatest glory, he would need to be heard on an Association day with the thousands before him. It is narrated of him that he travelled to a Trecastle Association with his friend Owen Enos. On the journey he preached many times on the words from Isaiah 43:7, 'For I have created him for my glory, I have formed him; yea, I have made him.' It was a good sermon, but Mr Enos did not see anything out of the ordinary in it, and it did not seem to be gripping the congregations particularly. Certainly he did not consider it an Association sermon. The main service during the Association – the ten o'clock meeting – was, as usual, given to Mr Morris, and to Mr Enos's surprise he read out the text, 'For I have created him for my glory.' The old elder was immensely disappointed and said to himself quietly, 'He won't do much this time.' But to his amazement the sermon seemed to be adorned in new glory; every sentence transfixes; every oar pulls firmly; Ebenezer Morris shakes heaven so that the vast crowd trembles in his presence. He sheds a wonderful light on the creation of the rebirth, the forming of sanctification, and the making of the finished work. His voice is as a trumpet and the look in his eye as flashes of lightning, and he cries out again and again, with that strength which was uniquely his,

'For my glory! *For my Glory*! FOR MY GLORY!'

Long before the end of the service, the atmosphere of the place was extraordinary. It was as if the sky had darkened with the clouds and the heavens had poured forth the gracious rain upon the ground, with the result that thousands were shouting and crying out just as much as the preacher. An old elder of Trecastle, a Mr Watkins, said that not one carriage passed through the town during the service without having stopped, and that all work had stopped, that idlers were running out of their houses and towards the Association field in great fear, and that no one ever knew how many of those travellers passing through or those careless men in the town or on nearby slopes, had been convicted. This one service advanced Methodism in Trecastle and scores were converted. On leaving the field, Mr Morris, rather playfully, asked Owen Enos what he thought of the sermon.

'Extraordinary,' was the answer. 'I was in fear and trembling when you announced the text, but it was wonderful how it turned out.'

'Yes,' replied Mr Morris. 'I knew that there was something glorious in the verse and I was only shaking the box on the way, but here I intended to break it open.'

A similar thing happened in an Association at Caernarvon in September, 1818, when he had an unforgettable service with Leviticus 17:11, 'It is the blood that maketh an atonement for the soul.' About the time of the Association an old elder from Bethania, Cardiganshire, called John Davies, was following his trade, journeying through the north, selling hats. When in the Tremadog area he lodged with Mr Ellis Owen, Cefn-y-meusydd, who is well known as a writer and poet. While conversing, Mr Owen told the elder that Ebenezer Morris was engaged to preach at Tremadog on the following Sunday morning and he added:

'Do you in Cardiganshire consider him a great preacher?'

'Indeed we do,' was the answer. 'One of the greatest.'

'Well I have not heard anything extraordinary from him,' said Mr Owen. 'Nothing more than I have heard from many another good preacher. There is in this area a young preacher called Moses Jones and I consider him to be just as good as Ebenezer Morris.'

'I have heard Moses Jones,' replied John Davies, 'and for a young man he is an excellent preacher. But he has a good deal of growing to do even to reach Ebenezer Morris's ankles.'

The Sunday morning arrived and the two men went to Tremadog to hear Mr Morris but Ellis Owen heard nothing to change his mind about the preacher. However, in the afternoon, they both went to hear him at Criccieth. So many people had gathered from every quarter that there was not room for a tenth of them in the chapel. God's ambassador therefore had to preach in the window and such an unction accompanied his ministry that the crowd broke out in glorying and rejoicing and the service concluded in much praise and song. As they walked home, the man from the south asked Ellis Owen,

'What do you think of Ebenezer Morris now?'

'You were correct,' was the answer, 'I have changed my mind about him completely.'

'Yes,' said the other, 'but what if you had heard him in an Assembly, clothed with power from on high?'

And this is what he, and thousands of others, did experience the following week in Caernarvon. On the last day, in the ten o'clock main meeting, the Rev. John Evans of Llwynffortun preached first. He had an excellent service; his doctrine came down as rain upon the mown grass; there was hardly a dry eye in the congregation. But while he spoke, some of the gentry of the neighbourhood who were visiting the field out of curiosity, were riding around the crowd to the great annoyance of many. But as soon as Mr Morris had announced his text, the words from Leviticus that were referred to, 'It is the blood that maketh an atonement for the soul,' he addressed the disturbers.

'Gentlemen, would you be so kind as to stand still for a while that we might hear the words of the Lord? I am to speak of the soul, and of the blood that makes atonement for it; and you have souls.'

The noblemen were ashamed and listened carefully throughout the sermon. The preacher soon gained complete authority over his hearers, they listened as if bound to his lips. He spoke of the soul of man; the guilt of the soul; all and everyone insufficient for providing an atonement for the soul; and the merit of Christ's blood as a sufficient atonement in heaven for it. And following his custom of raising his voice on some important word, repeating it over and over, he cried out so that the the rocks of Snowdonia resounded, and hearts could not hold without being shattered:

'It is the blood! *It is the Blood!* IT IS THE BLOOD!'

Hundreds were pricked in their hearts, we believe, and the service broke up in sudden glorying. Large numbers turned to religion for the first time at the various *seiadau* of Anglesey and Caernarvonshire and their unanimous testimony was that it was when hearing Ebenezer Morris preaching on 'It is the blood' that they were saved. Amongst others was an immoral woman from Caernarvon town; she had arrived on the field just as Mr

Morris was beginning his sermon; the truth shot through her heart as a fierce arrow, and her senses were confused for a little time. She evidenced a complete change and lived for many years afterwards an honour to her confession.

Michael Roberts used to discuss this sermon with Dr Owen Thomas and would refer to the seraphic smile on Mr Morris' face as he expounded the merit of the blood.

'It was that smile that would smite them,' he said.

And Michael Roberts would then add:

> The tear in the eye of Jones of Edeyrn; the weeping of my uncle, Robert Roberts; the shout and, in particular, the smile of Ebenezer Morris; and the piercing look, the silence, and the finger of John Elias; those were the things that affected me above everything.

HIS SELF-POSSESSION

Ebenezer Morris *would never at any time lose his self-possession*. It is evident that he was a man of strong emotions and that he would be moved by the truths with which he dealt in his sermons; his words often fell upon his hearers as sparks on dry straw. But he himself would be completely self-possessed even at the height of his oration. According to the late Rev. David Hughes, Ynys:

> I remember a Monthly Meeting at Swyddffynnon about the year 1822. Mr Morris was announced to preach at a farmhouse on the first night, and at ten in the chapel the next morning. I remember little of the morning meeting but remember the evening in the old farmhouse clearly. The house was over crowded, and he was stood on something in order to raise him a little above the people and he had a large candle hanging at his side. His text was 2 Samuel 23:5. After reading the text, he handed the Bible to a man standing by him and preached clearly and powerfully, holding his spectacles in his hand. After a while he mentioned that there were remarkable words that illuminated the truth under consideration in the Book of Psalms, or in Isaiah. He put on his spectacles, asked for the Bible and turned to the required words with ease, all the while continuing to preach. He then said;
>
> 'Here are the words; pay heed! Listen carefully!'
>
> He would then read them, explaining them so vividly and expounding them so gloriously that you might think you had never heard them before. He would then return the Bible to the man beside him. This would occur some five or six times during the service. I was listening and watching carefully throughout the two hours or so of the meetimg. The feelings of the hearers were such that

> many of them broke out in shouting, 'Glory! Hallelujah!' and I do not know at what hour they eventually departed.

The late Dr Owen Thomas, mainly on the basis of information he received from the Revs. William Roberts of Amlwch and Henry Rees, testified to the completeness of composure which typified Ebenezer Morris. He wrote as follows:

> Clearly he could not always have been without fears but he never showed any sign of being troubled so as to lose composure or appear confused or forget what he had intended to say. And when a required verse, needed to explain a point, did not immediately spring to mind, then in the most patient way without any agitation, he would take out his spectacles, put them in place, turning quietly to the verse and all the while referring in some way to it. Having found it, he would read it clearly, reverently and powerfully, and with a flow of simple but sacred oratory arising from the verses, so that they remained fixed forever in the minds of his hearers. In this composed way he would converse quietly with the people, and on Assembly days he might turn to the ministers behind him on the platform with some appropriate comment especially for them. Turning back again to the people, with his left hand behind his back and his right hand lifted high holding his spectacles, he would throw out his voice like a thunder clap towards the idling groups beyond the crowd or, at Bala, at careless loungers on the furthermost mounds. He would again return to discourse quietly to his listeners, with everything about him manifesting his complete pleasure in the great work which he was about, and consciously aware that he was God's messenger to the people.
>
> We heard Mr Rees mentioning often of him preaching at an Association at Bala when he had some injury to one of his fingers and a ribbon of cloth wrapped round it. When in mid-sermon the knot on the bandage loosened, and the cloth unravelled. But the preacher, who had just been at his most powerful, quietly wound it back, attempting to re-tie it but failing so that it slowly unravelled again. He would then start again to wind it on. This occurred many times during the sermon without affecting him at all or disturbing in any way his hold upon the hearers.

HIS ORATORICAL GIFTS

Ebenezer Morris possessed *all the necessary skills of the true orator*. His speech was fluent, his countenance keen and aquiline, and his appearance truly princely. In addition he possessed clarity of thought, a passionate heart, quickness of mind, and the ability to establish a personal rapport between himself and his hearers. As an orator he was second to none, except perhaps John Elias, and in some aspects he even surpassed that notable man. There is unanimous testimony to his rhetorical powers.

The Rev. John James, a minister with the Unitarians, said that Ebenezer Morris was the most fluent and able speaker that he had ever heard from any denomination. The Rev. John Rees of Tregaron would tell of an occasion when Mr Morris was preaching at an Association in Towyn, Merionethshire in 1823. He was speaking twice: on the first afternoon, and at ten the next day. After hearing him in the open-air, the Rev. Robert Griffith of Dolgellau said,

> Chrysostom was so famous as a preacher that they used to say that it would be better for them if the sun did not rise than if he failed to preach. I am prepared to say the same of Ebenezer Morris. Wales could have no greater loss than that he were to stop preaching.

The Rev. W. Hughes, when writing of a remarkable service at New Chapel, a service which we shall refer to again later, said:

> I was only a boy of about twelve years old when I first heard the Rev. Ebenezer Morris at an Association at New Chapel, Pembrokeshire. His text was Proverbs 9:18. Presently, long years afterwards, I can only say that that sermon was a torrent of Demosthenian eloquence. The effect he produced on the congregation was electric. Some were bathed in tears; others, rejoicing, were shouting out, 'Hallelujah'. I was unwilling to leave the place. It was to me as Mount Tabor was to Peter, 'It is good for us to be here.' I heard him again afterwards when I was at school in Cardigan. His appearance in the pulpit was majestic, his every action appropriate to an orator. The black velvet cap that he wore gave him the appearance of a bishop wearing a mitre. His style of preaching made me think of the courage of Luther, the acumen of Calvin and the passion of Knox. His sermons were not some *vox et praeterea nihil* (a voice and nothing else) but rather conveyed the depth of a Chalmers combined with the eloquent warmth of a Stowell. His main themes would be: God's eternal purpose and love; the lost condition of man because of sin; redemption by grace; and regeneration and sanctification by the gracious influences of the Holy Spirit. He knew how to pass strongly through the fire and smoke of Sinai, and he could carry his hearers with him, in his arms as it were, and show them the New Jerusalem. His main standing ground was Calvary, and his greatest theme was the cross of our Lord Jesus Christ.

Men who had no great sympathy with the doctrines preached by Ebenezer Morris would still testify to his powers of oratory. A gentleman, Morgan Jones, who lived at Cilwendeg on the border between Cardiganshire and Pembrokeshire, said that he heard Mr Morris once, preaching on the parable of the prodigal son, and though he, Mr Jones, had seen the best actors of the day in the main theatres of the land, he could not think of one amongst them who could portray circumstances and characters as skilfully and effectively as Mr Morris portrayed the meeting of the father and the son in that sermon. The Rev. William Evans of Tonyrefail used to speak of Mr Morris preaching in the open-air in a town in the south, when a well known lawyer and atheist was listening. The man had heard much of the preacher and had placed himself in a convenient position to hear and see him. 'I had never before heard such a speaker,' he said. 'He made me weep in spite of myself. I did not believe a word that he said, and yet I could not stop myself weeping in floods while listening to him.'

The late Dr Phillips, Hereford, used to speak of a similar occasion at a Carmarthen Association when Mr Morris preached with evident unction. Two members of the Bar were attending, namely Councillor Jones of Ystrad and Councillor Taunton, who afterwards became Lord Denman. Mr Taunton did not understand a word being said, but such was the effect of Morris's voice and eloquence upon him that he could not contain himself and throwing his hands up in the air, he turned to his friend and said, *'I have never heard anything like this.'*

We have already referred to his preparedness. He would never compose a sermon in detail. His habit was to meditate deeply over his text until he himself was electrified by it and full of it, just as the iron in the forge becomes full of fire. Then, on facing his congregation, he could throw off sparks in all directions. The following is the testimony of the Rev. John Rees of Tregaron, who was a travelling companion on many journeys:

> After Mr Morris had finished his introduction and arrived at his text he would draw the most natural heads from it. But he would not usually comment in detail on each head. Rather, he would take up the one particular theme which had most impressed his own mind and would continue with that, and the impression would increase and deepen until it powerfully affected all the listening congregation. When heard on another occasion, speaking on the same text, he might not make any comment at all on the point on which he had enlarged when expounding the words the first time, but instead he would concentrate on one or two of the other heads, as he was led at the time. Very rarely would you hear the same material from him on the same text, except for the heads. Often in the middle of a sermon, when wishing to prove from the Scriptures some point he was making, he would say:
>
> 'Have you ever noticed that verse in such-and-such a place? Only recently did I understand its significance.'
>
> In this way he would draw the attention of all his listeners to the verse, and as he expounded it, an unique illumination of it would be provided so that it became impossible ever to forget that verse again.

Because of this preparedness he could adapt his message to his hearers' condition. The late Rev. Thomas Harris, Haverfordwest, who afterwards joined the Established Church, used to mention the occasion he listened to Mr Morris preaching at a Carmarthen Association in the summer of 1817. His text was Psalm 90:1, 'Lord, thou hast been our dwelling place in all generations.' Great power accompanied the preaching.

> He did not keep the application of his message until the end of the sermon, but wove it throughout the whole. His great question was:
>
> 'Men! Do you have a dwelling place to go to when you are taken away to the eternal world?'
>
> The sound of this question echoed in my ears and in my heart for a long time, and I hope that I will be the better for it when I pass into the next world.

The late Rev. John Jones, Lampeter, remembered him preaching from the same text in a Monthly Meeting in that town. The unction accompanying his words was sufficient to overcome the whole gathering. One girl fell into a faint and was for a while half-dead; the first words she uttered when recovering was, 'Am I now in Hell?' It is believed that she experienced an eternal change through that sermon for she was a different girl from then on.

Dr Owen Thomas suggests that Ebenezer Morris was to some extent lacking in imagination. We can hardly believe that this was fully true. At the very least he had the imagination necessary in every true orator to put himself in the position of the characters he portrayed. We have proof of this in the sermon to which we have already referred, delivered by him at a New Chapel Association in 1822. But before describing it let us note something of the circumstances. It appears that it was throughout a very successful Association. On the first afternoon John Davies, Nantglyn, had delivered a notably fresh and lively sermon. After him came Ebenezer Richard, melting and pleasing, with his doctrine distilling as rain upon the mown grass. The next day, at six in the morning, the preachers were William Havard and David Evans, Aberaeron, and the cloud was still in place over the camp. The main meeting, at ten, approached, and as the weather was so warm and fair a huge congregation, not merely from Pembrokeshire but from Carmarthenshire and Cardiganshire also, had gathered. The service was begun by Richard James, a brother from Glamorganshire, noted for his importunity in prayer. The first to preach was John Evans, Llwynffortun, and the oil was in glorious flow so that all were delighted. Then came Mr David Charles, Carmarthen, who was rather brief, preaching in English.

Lastly, Ebenezer Morris came to the front, with the vast assembly before him in utmost expectation. His text was Proverbs 4:18, 'But the path of the just is as the shining light, that shineth more and more unto the perfect day.' Very soon after he began speaking it was realized that the sermon was 'in demonstration of the Spirit and of power'. For a while he described 'the just', without much raising of voice, but gaining the attention and exciting the feelings of the listeners completely. In his treatment he struck upon his favourite theme, justification by faith, and in a skilful way he used a comparison made by the Rev. John Newton when describing his own conversion. The latter had said that he had knitted and sewn a cloak for himself of which he was very proud, made from some wool and a little linen. His Master greatly disapproved of this garment and commanded him to throw it away, saying that he would give him a better one in its place. But Jack refused, thinking that no one in the land had as good or as beautiful a cloak. At last the Master called upon a strong man called Moses to come and to beat Jack, and with his rod Moses thrashed the mantle savagely with the result that so much dust arose from it that its owner thought he would be suffocated and lose his life on the spot. Meanwhile his Master stood nearby holding up the best robe ever seen. At last Jack cried out,

'I yield, Master. I don't mind what happens to the old cloak as long as I may be clothed in that one.'

So he was dressed in new clothes, and in his new robe he was called upon to the hall to dine; and not as a servant but as brother and friend was Jack accounted from that day. With power and much skill the preacher led the minds of his hearers from the parable to the words, 'And be found in him, not having mine own righteousness.'

He then turned to show the similarities between light and the path of the just. He referred to the small amount of light at its commencement, so small that one does not really know if it is the true dawn or not, but that it then brightens, shining on and through the dark clouds until it scatters them. So also is the path of the just, it proceeds in strength just as the sun. By now the preacher had complete mastery over the crowd; there was such an accord between his topic, his spirit and his voice, that the congregation were fully overcome.

'I remember,' said the Rev. John Jones, Penmorfa, 'that as I listened it was as if a great wind was blowing and the whole assembly was as a grove of trees bending before it.'

But Mr Morris had not yet reached the climax of his sermon. Before finishing he dealt powerfully with the contrasting phrase following the text, 'The way of the wicked is as darkness.' The immense voice, like the sound of many waters breaking in all its strength upon the congregation:

> What a different path! The path of the just shines, *shines*, SHINES, MORE AND MORE UNTO THE PERFECT DAY. But what of the path of the ungodly? a path that darkens, *darkens*, DARKENS, MORE AND MORE UNTIL MIDNIGHT!

This was more than flesh could bear. A cry of fear ran through the crowd. At the edges of the assembly were the carriages of the local gentry together with physicians, lawyers and clergymen. They were all stricken and weeping as babes. A number of careless youths from the Cardigan grammar school were present and they had lost all control of themselves, some weeping, some rejoicing, as if in competition with each other. The effect of this one sermon was vast. Some one hundred and twenty souls joined the churches at Cardigan and the surrounding areas, without counting the scores added to the churches of Pembrokeshire and Carmarthenshire. These comments are surely proof of a strong imagination as well as all the other requirements for an orator.

Here is another example of the same thing. One Sunday afternoon he was preaching in a farmhouse between Penmorfa and Blaenannerch. His text was Revelation 6:17, 'For the great day of his wrath is come; and who shall be able to stand?' With indescribable strength and clarity he portrayed the kings of earth, the great men, the rich men and the chief captains, hiding amongst the dens and rocks and calling upon the mountains and rocks to fall upon them. He said:

> 'Kings! who held the whole earth in terror, where are you now? Why the change in your faces? What is this hiding, instead of sitting on your proud thrones? Leaders! You who used to stand fearlessly in the fiercest battles in blood to the tops of your boots. What is the terror that holds you now? Why do you use such fearful language? Why cry for the rocks to fall upon you? Great men! Yesterday, your language was oaths and presumptuous swearing but it is very different today. You are attempting something like prayer, though it is not prayer to God! What is the matter?'

> 'Alas! the Man whom we refused and scorned has appeared on the clouds! He whom we scorned has appeared to judge us! His face is awful to us! We would prefer to be crushed and killed and dashed to pieces under mountains than to stand a minute in his presence!'

Then Mr Morris lowered his voice to a conversational level and in the most solemn tones asked the congregation;

> 'People! Have you any means of standing on that day?

And every heart trembled. That service proved to be the onset of a powerful revival which spread over all the surrounding areas. About thirty went after this sermon to seek membership in the surrounding churches and many others to the local Independent church. These and many other examples that we could give prove that Ebenezer Morris possessed to a very great extent the elements of a successful orator.

THE GLORY OF HIS PREACHING

Ebenezer Morris possessed *an incomparable ability of presenting the simple truths of the gospel to his hearers in the most wonderful and glorious way.* It can hardly be said that there was any great novelty in his thoughts, but his way of presenting them was completely new. He would not plunge into the depths, as his friend Mr David Charles, Carmarthen, and bring up from the deep handfuls of the brightest pearls, holding them before the congregation so that they were well nigh dazzled by their glory. He was not an adventurer, crossing seas and mountains to find the diamond fields and discovering the most priceless of stones. He would rather take hold of a rough stone, one that hardly appeared to hold any beauty. He would then work on it and polish it until its glory shone forth for even the dullest eye to see. In this way, his sermons were nearly always consistent and yet glorious. And all was further perfected by his delivery. He would often shout out one word over and over again, but each time in a different key, and the effect would deepen with every repetition. We will provide testimonies from those who knew him well to prove the point.

The late Rev. David Jones of Caernarvon wrote:

> I had heard much of the Rev. Ebenezer Morris and had the privilege of hearing him preach at a Bala Association in June 1820. I was quite young at the time, only fifteen years old. I had promised myself the pleasure of attending the Bala *Sasiwn*, a pleasure second only to being at Jerusalem on the high day of the feast, and to add to the anticipation there was a rumour that Ebenezer Morris was expected. At last, the long-awaited day arrived and in much nervousness I took the long and strange road to Bala, looking forward to realizing my hopes. On the first afternoon Mr Morris spoke on the Green to a large crowd, from Romans 8:17, 'And if children, then heirs; etc.' By now (March 1867) I have very little memory of the sermon, except that for a long time he pressed the value of the relationship and the importance of being assured of it, and that such an assurance was possible in this world. He noted the characteristics of the relationship and then showed that the inheritance was certain to the children. He pictured the immensity of the inheritance most effectively. There were some gentlemen on the Bala Mound, opposite the stage on the Green, who had come to watch the proceedings and were looking quite amused as the preacher, without yet having raised his voice, was warming to his task. At last, with a piercing and authoritative shout, came the words:
>
> > 'I do not want those gentlemen there, on the mound, to think that they alone are of the nobility. All of God's children are heirs. God's children are the heirs.'
>
> He shouted these words many times, not only in Welsh but also in English, 'The children of God are the heirs,' until the gentlemen on the mound were completely subdued and listened carefully from then on.

At ten o'clock the next day, Mr Morris was preaching in the same place, on Romans 3:25, 'Whom God hath set forth to be a propitiation,' etc. He began quietly by explaining the relationship between the text and the previous verses, which show that all, Jews and Greeks, are under sin, all have actively sinned, and the Scriptures therefore have concluded all guilty before God so that there is therefore no hope for any except through believing in the Lord Jesus Christ. He then went through his text, word by word.

' "*Whom*": the Son of God, the mighty God, the everlasting Father, the Rock of Israel, the Rock of Ages, the Stone that God established in Zion. "*Whom God hath set forth*": It was God who set him forth, and there is great significance in the appointments of God. A sinner can commit himself contentedly to God's appointment. He set the sand for the bound of the sea, and it is as if the sands say: "Here the swellings of your waves are stopped. To here you will come and no further." In Egypt he set the blood on the lintel and sideposts of the door to keep away the angel of destruction, and there was sufficient power and virtue in that setting to safeguard Israel. He set the brazen serpent upon a pole to heal whoever looked at it after they had been bitten by the fiery serpents, and it did not fail to heal any of them. There is power in God's appointment. See the antitype of the brazen serpent raised here today on the pole of the gospel, in the sight of all this congregation. "As Moses lifted up the serpent in the wilderness, even so must the Son of man be lifted up: that whosoever believeth in him should not perish, but have eternal life." Lean your soul upon God's appointment. "Whom God hath set forth *to be a propitiation*": The word *propitiation* is a majestic word. The Almighty alone understands all that it involves. A propitiation for God; he owns it. It satisfies God. And why will it not satisfy yourself, Oh, my soul? As it is sufficient for God, it surely must be sufficient for the sinner.'

He then proceeded to the next part of his text,

' "*Through faith in his blood.*" "His blood": that is Christ's merit. "Through faith": through believing the witness that the Father has testified of his Son. "And this is the record, that God hath given to us eternal life, and this life is in his Son." Perhaps there are some here who ask, "What is faith?" As there is so much debate on the point, let me answer that faith is a godly nature, because a godly nature includes the essence of every grace. A godly nature as it acts on different objects gains different names for itself. Is there any difference between faith and believing? It is the same as the difference between love and loving, and between hope and hoping. "*To declare his righteousness for the remission of sins that are past, through the forbearance of God.*" Those godly men and women who have gone home to heaven, those spirits of just men made perfect; they, when they were on earth, were sinners. They repented of their sins and prayed much for forgiveness; and they were forgiven on the basis of what the Messiah would do in the time to come. But it was by the propitiation that his justice in forgiving sin was actively demonstrated. And "*to declare, I*

> *say, at this time his righteousness*": at this time, and until the end of the world. It is not said, "to declare his mercy", but "his righteousness". His mercy would certainly rejoice over the forgiveness of a sinner but it is the declaration of his righteousness, and that through forgiveness, which is a wonder to all.'
>
> The preacher then explained how the divine intervention depended on the propitiation. This was the mechanism for declaring his righteousness.
>
> From the start until now he had been speaking quickly and with authority but without raising his voice, though the crowd could hear his every word. He appeared to be warming more and more to his subject and this manifested itself in a more tender and melodious timbre to his voice. But as he spoke on the means through propitiation for forgiving sins, he gave out a tremendous shout. He cried out,
>
> 'Propitiation! *Propitiation!* PROPITIATION!'
>
> with an indescribable power and effectiveness. The word was proclaimed over and over, ten or more times in all. And each 'PROPITIATION!' was louder than the previous one. Oh, strange shout! As if it came from another world; a shout that I never heard the like before, nor ever afterwards heard anything that had such authority and effect. The great assembly was weeping and in tears, as if out of their senses; the preachers on the stage were weaving in-and-out of one other, crying and rejoicing. It is impossible to describe such an impressive scene; I think I had better not attempt it. No more powerful thunderings were ever seen, so sudden, and followed by such great rains! From the beginning it was as a sea; restless, swelling higher and higher; until it broke out in great waves upon the shore, one after another, stronger and stronger, until the whole of Bala Green was one sea, swimming with waters! This is what I saw for myself.

Perhaps it is not possible to have a better picture of Ebenezer Morris as a preacher than that given here by the Rev. David Jones. We see that he would point out with an instinctive accuracy the crucial teachings of a text; that he possessed a wealth of good doctrine; that his warmth for his message would kindle as he proceeded, until at last, with an irresistible shout, the fiery lava would stream forth such that no soul could withstand it. Having reached this point, he would make use of just the one word or phrase which he would shout out, and that word or phrase would then grapple with men's souls and lay hold upon them as a summons from above. Often, however great the sermon, it was that one phrase that was afterwards remembered. An elder from Cardiganshire told a minister from Gwynedd who was journeying through the county:

'It was in the window of this chapel that Ebenezer Morris had that amazing service when preaching from the words, "The way of life is above to the wise, that he may depart from hell beneath"; and when all outside and inside were struck dumb while listening to him.'

'Do you remember parts of the sermon?' asked the minister.

'Remember, sir?' said the old man. 'Remember? I shall always remember! Oh! no flesh was able to withstand him.'

'Yes, but what specifically did he say about the text?'

'What did he say, sir? What did he say? He said, "beneath, *beneath*, BENEATH, Friends!" he said, "Hell is beneath, *beneath*, BENEATH", until the end of the world had come for all in the meeting house and outside.'

And although all that the elder could remember was 'BENEATH!', quite certainly his mind and that of the congregation had been gradually moulded by the sermon to accept that word with all its authority when it arrived, nor must we forget that the 'still small voice' from above mingled with the preacher's shout and gave it its power and effectiveness.

It was not only this old country elder who encountered difficulty in describing the essence of Ebenezer Morris's preaching. Dr Owen Thomas mentions that he had often discussed him with the Rev. Henry Rees, who had more respect for him than for any other preacher, with the exception possibly of Mr Elias and Mr Roberts, Amlwch.

'Give me some picture of him,' said Dr Thomas to Mr Rees.

'Well,' he replied, 'what if you had heard him at an Association in Machynlleth, when he was preaching on the text, "which things the angels desire to look into". Oh, it was a wonderful time.'

'But what did he say?' asked Dr Thomas.

'Oh! "Which things! *Which things!* WHICH THINGS! WHICH THINGS!" Not "the things which" but "which things".'

'He had,' added Mr Rees, 'an amazing ability of catching hold of one word, and he would shout it forth very many times, and there would be such an illumination with the word that the thing itself would become clear to the people. I remember that he preached that same time at Machynlleth on the last morning and on those words in Acts about the sailors thinking that 'they drew near to some country'. He produced amazing effects by his shout of 'some country'. He cried out "some country, *some country*, SOME COUNTRY", very many times, until all in the place felt themselves near to eternity.'

OTHER NOTABLE SERVICES

There is a hardly a place in the country which does not have some enduring tradition of a powerful service under Ebenezer Morris's ministry. One story describes him on a journey to Monmouthshire with the Rev. John

Jones, Penmorfa, as companion. One evening they came to Llaneurwg and Mr Morris preached there on the same words that he used as a text in the Machynlleth Association to which Mr Henry Rees referred, namely, 'About midnight the shipmen deemed that they drew near to some country.' After narrating the events and providing interesting and lively comments upon them, he borrowed the words to illustrate the approach of men to one or other of the two eternal worlds, emphasizing that this was no speculative possibility but a reality.

He described the two very different worlds that await the godly and the ungodly in the world of the spirits. And as he so powerfully portrayed heaven as the final destination of the voyage of the saints, and stressed that Christ's own, for all the stormy winds that assail them, were daily drawing nearer, a Miss Blanche Evans, along with many others, was so completely taken up by the glory of the heavenly home and the hope that she herself was approaching to it, that she lost all sense of her surroundings. All the preachers, great or small, on their journeys in the region, used to lodge at Miss Evans's house and invariably she would be full of welcome. But that night she was so inattentive that Mr Morris asked her if she was unwell.

'No,' she replied, ' I am remarkably well.'

And she had to be left that evening in an almost stunned condition, with her friends worrying whether she would ever come to herself again. But by the following morning the lady had returned to her senses. She apologized profusely to Mr Morris that she had not been able to welcome him and his friend properly the previous evening, but that on hearing how glorious heaven was, she had been lost in its contemplation and for many hours had been unaware of anything or anyone around her.

The following history was received from the Rev. William Evans, Tonyrefail:

> A woman of my acquaintance having heard of an Association to be held at Llantrisant, Glamorganshire, was determined to be present in order to find out what kind of thing an Association was. She arrived for the ten o'clock service on the last day, when Ebenezer Morris was preaching on 2 Corinthians 5:20, 'Be ye reconciled to God.' After returning home, the woman could talk of nothing else but of 'that strange man – my goodness! – who preached last at ten o'clock'. On one of the following days she paid a visit to a farm-woman, one of her tenants, who was a member with the Methodists. As she crossed the threshold she broke out in cries,
>
> 'Bess! Oh, Bess! the man - the man with the black cap! Oh! He made me tremble. I cannot shake it off.'

At a Monthly Meeting at Lledrod about the year 1819, in the middle of a powerful revival, Mr Morris was preaching on Hebrews 6:18. As he expounded the words, 'Who have fled for refuge to lay hold upon the hope set before us,' he commented as follows:

> 'You, hard-hearted people of Lledrod, are ready to say, "We have seen a revival before, and we have witnessed many who, having started with religion at that time, have turned back to their old ways afterwards." But whatever might be true of those who have turned back, it will be the case that you yourselves one day will seek to turn from the state in which you are today. If you do not now flee to Christ for your life, your fleeing has still to come. Fleeing, you will attempt to flee, when it is too late, as Pharaoh and the Egyptians in the Red Sea, when God had removed the wheels from their chariots, cried out, "Let us flee!" But the sea had returned in all its strength between them and the shore, and they could not escape but were rather drowned. It must be the case that you flee! *flee!* FLEE! here today, while there is a hope set before you to lay hold upon.'

As he cried these words, there came an irresistible outpouring from heaven upon the people (not unlike that outpouring on the day of Pentecost) and some scores of hardened creatures, whom the previous excitements of the revival had not been able to touch, were jumping in the air as if in confusion. They repeatedly cried out the preacher's words, 'Let us flee! Let us flee for our lives!'

On another occasion he preached in a Monthly Meeting at Lampeter on Hebrews 8:1, 2, 'Now of the things which we have spoken this is the sum: We have such an high priest, who is set on the right hand of the throne of the Majesty in the heavens; a minister of the sanctuary.' Amongst other things, he referred to Aaron's work of lighting the lamps in the sanctuary and the priests' duty of continually maintaining the sacred flame. And in this context he said:

> No doubt there are some here who are ready to say, 'There was more fire to be had from the preachers of old than from yourself; and if we were to lose you again, we do not know from where to find an equal after you.' Ho! if that is what worries you, tell the Minister of the Sanctuary. It is he who guards the sacred flame, and he alone lights up the lamps for the sanctuary. It is not learning nor talent that can light up a lamp for the sanctuary.

He then gave a mighty shout:

> Our great High Priest! Let him come again to light the lamps! His is the work of maintaining the flame!

It is said that the effect was thrilling; all being quite overcome.

Very rarely did he preach at a Monthly Meeting without being clothed with power and authority. Thomas Davies, Tyn-y-porth, an old elder from Ffos-y-ffin chapel, stated,

> At some Monthly Meetings, if the sermons of the first afternoon tended to be heavy and dull, a sad and solemn expression would be seen on Ebenezer Morris' face, as if he were jealous for God and his cause. The next morning, at eleven o'clock, he himself would preach; and Oh! what a heavenly light would shine on the sermon, what a shaking there would be of the whole congregation; and how God's cause would be elevated to the highest beauty. I particularly remember, and will ever remember, his sermon in a Monthly Meeting on the words, 'And as many as walk according to this rule, peace be on them, and mercy, and upon the Israel of God.' The whole assembly was moved and brought to a spirit of worship. The Rev. Ebenezer Richard who was also present said that he was conscious of being plucked up from the depths as he listened, and that he was quite sure that there were hundreds of others experiencing the same thing.

We knew of an old Christian from Llanddewibrefi, John Jones by name and a tailor by trade, who was converted through the ministry of Ebenezer Morris. At the time he was an ungodly young man of about twenty years of age who had never given any serious consideration to his state. He happened to be at Llanwrtyd on a work-day evening and heard Ebenezer Morris preaching from the words, 'He that hath the Son hath life.' The wild boy received an awful fright. He imagined that somebody had given the whole of his history to the preacher and that every arrow had been expressly aimed at himself. He left the chapel with his conscience a fiery flame within him. But there were others there upon their high places and they remained in the chapel, rejoicing and praising, until two in the morning. John Jones remained under deep conviction for two years. He had no pleasure in his old sins but yet could not see his way to lay down his burden before the cross of the Saviour. Two years later, Ebenezer Morris journeyed through the middle of Cardiganshire again, and John Jones was a hearer at Llangeitho, Llanddewibrefi and Tregaron. At Llangeitho the sermon on 'the wild ass' was preached [Jeremiah 2:24], and when Mr Morris cried out, 'In her month they shall find her', and added, 'There is a month for the ungodly', the scene was one of devastation. Strong men, bold in their ungodliness, fainted from fear. In Llanddewibrefi, he preached powerfully on Acts 16:30, 31. But it was at Tregaron, while Mr Morris was preaching on Hebrews 1:8, 'But unto the Son he saith, Thy throne, O God, is forever and ever: a sceptre of righteousness is the sceptre of thy kingdom,' that John Jones was loosed from his fetters and began to taste the glory of the gospel in the face of Jesus Christ. Nearly fifty years had passed over John Jones when he recited this story but the events were as fresh in his memory as if they had occurred the previous day. He could not speak of them without his eyes filling with tears and his heart warming. And his pure and useful life proved that he had truly passed from death to life while listening to Ebenezer Morris.

Mr Morris was preaching once at Llangeitho at a time when the arguments over Ordination were at their warmest and when strong feelings had been evidenced on both sides. A lady from the neighbourhood, a member with the Established Church, felt very bitter towards him at the time, considering him to be the leading advocate against the views of the Church. Her prejudice was such that she spoke disparagingly of him as a preacher, avowing that he did not deserve all the respect that was given him. For all this, she could not keep from coming to the chapel to hear him. His text this time was, 'The wages of sin is death.' A power from heaven was accompanying his words; it held the whole congregation spellbound and as for the prejudiced woman, she appeared completely bewildered. Such a shock of amazement had fallen upon her that she did not know where she was. A church meeting was held after the sermon, as was usual, and who was to be seen remaining with them but this woman! No one expected to see her, of all people, remain behind. She was pointed out and was asked whether she was intending to join the church. Only then did she come to her senses. Recognizing where she was, she shook off her bewilderment and escaped the building.

It is certain that Ebenezer Morris was blessed as an instrument for the saving of many hundreds. He was sent once by the Monthly Meeting to smooth out some misunderstanding that had arisen at Aberystwyth, which he did to the satisfaction of all concerned. On this occasion he preached one of his most powerful sermons, on the words, 'Gather ye together first the tares, and bind them in bundles to burn them: but gather the wheat into my barn.' While he was describing the bundles of the ungodly being bound up, the effect on the congregation was intense. At the very next church meeting there were twenty-nine seeking admission, all of them having been convicted during that service. Another sermon of his which was blessed to the salvation of many, particularly from Denbighshire and Flintshire, was from Matthew 16:26, 'For what is a man profited, if he shall gain the whole world, and lose his own soul?' It was said that this sermon was similar in power and influence to the one by his father on the same verses. Some hundreds joined the churches in different parts of the country as a result of this sermon. Mr James Thomas, an elder at Twrgwyn chapel, used to mention the remarkable service under Mr Morris, held in his own home and with Mark 4:26–29 as the text, 'So is the kingdom of God, as if a man should cast seed into the ground,' etc. Mr Thomas was a young man at the time but all his life he remembered the profound effect on the hearers. They remained in the place until midnight singing and rejoicing, and as she left the building one woman was joyfully shouting out the verse:

He grappled with man on the earth,	Ymaflodd mewn dyn ar y llawr,
He took him and joined him to God;	Fe'i dygodd a'r Duwdod yn un;
The infinite difference in worth,	Y pellter oedd rhyngddynt oedd fawr,
Made up by the shedding of blood.	Fe'i llanwodd a'i haeddiant ei hun.

He preached another time at Twrgwyn on a Sunday morning and his text was, 'And when I see the blood, I will pass over you.' The scene was a strange one. The saints were rejoicing, unbelievers were sobered, and it is believed that a great number were saved. The arrows stuck fast in the hearts of many, and among them was one man remarkable for his ungodliness, who had become almost insane. His subsequent life showed however that this was the occasion when he had passed from death to life.

As proof of the hold that Ebenezer Morris had over the country around, consider the following narrative. He ministered at the funeral of a respected and wealthy man from Llechryd. A large congregation had gathered and because of its size the sermon was delivered in the open-air. Another minister preached first, speaking profitably and sensibly but without much effect. But as Ebenezer Morris got up after him on to the horse-block to preach, the crowd surged forward from all directions and converged as one mass before and around the preacher. An English gentleman present on seeing the people pressing together so hurriedly thought that some danger threatened, and he called nervously to a man nearby, a Mr Evans, Llwynygroes:

'What's the reason for this?'

'Nothing,' was the reply, 'except that Ebenezer Morris is to preach. It is a sign of the respect that God has placed upon him.'

Before we leave these characteristics of Ebenezer Morris's ministry, we must supply a summary of the description of him given by the late Rev. Roger Edwards. He was preaching at an Association from 2 Samuel 23:5, 'Although my house be not so with God; yet he hath made with me an everlasting covenant, ordered in all things, and sure: for this is all my salvation, and all my desire, although he make it not to grow.' Mr Morris gave a kind of running comment as he proceeded. He showed that God had made the covenant mentioned in the text with David, not so much in his capacity as a king but as a sinner believing in Christ, in the promised

Seed. When he came to the words, 'For this is all my salvation, and all my desire,' he stopped and, turning to the congregation, asked:

> How many of you can honestly say these words? Truly, says someone here, I can say that it is on the basis of the covenant that I hope for salvation, but I can't lay hold on those two letters – *my* salvation. I would much prefer to be able to say before God and his people today, 'This is all *my* salvation', than to be given the whole world. But wait, poor brother or sister, what about laying hold on this then? 'All my desire.' Does not this come close enough for you with your short arm to catch hold of? Truly, says a child of affliction and groaning, I would be betraying the goodness of God were I not to avow that. It is the desire of my soul to be part of the covenant and bound up in it. If that is so, brother or sister, if God's covenant in Christ is all your desire, then it is also all your salvation. This experience is one complete work; the covenant cannot be someone's desire without it being at the same time all his salvation. But on binding up that which was broken and strengthening that which was sick we must guard against allowing any latitude to the fat and the strong. Oh, says the Antinomian there, I can come up to that; I have a ready will for it; I also desire to be in the covenant. But let me ask you: Is it all your desire? If you had your heart's desire from God before the clock struck twelve today, is this what you would ask for? 'Oh Lord, draw me within the bounds of the covenant.'

These comments were delivered by Mr Morris in a quiet and conversational tone, hardly raising his voice, yet maintaining complete control over the ears and thoughts of his hearers. He proceeded to enlarge in a more doctrinal way on the covenant between God and the sinner in Christ. He depicted it as a covenant of peace with an enemy, as a covenant of friendship and close relationship, and as a marriage covenant, reciting the words, 'And I will betroth thee unto me forever.' His voice was now louder and more powerful and yet still melodious. He could raise and lower it in volume with the greatest of ease and appropriateness. While considering the words, 'ordered in all things, and sure,' the preacher's spirit was kindled within him and he poured forth a flow of sacred eloquence. Nature, talent and grace were manifest in him in a most beautiful combination but without anything of the contrived or the theatrical.

'To be ordered completely or in all things,' he said, 'includes all the things of God and all the things of the Christian. Within this *'all things'* is God in all the persons of the Trinity, in all the perfections of his nature, in all the riches of his grace and all the provisions of his providence. The Christian cannot imagine anything relating to himself that is not encompassed by this ordering in all things. Here is an ordering that will subdue all his sins, that will overcome all his enemies, that will sweeten all his sorrows, that will quieten all his fears, and will satisfy all his longings.'

'This word, "in all things", in our text,' he said, 'is a sweet word, a great word, an all-encompassing word. And here is another, just as good, even better than it: *"sure!"* The covenant is ordered and sure! Oh, poor people of this uncertain world, it will be health for you to come with me now and have a sight of this sure covenant between God and his saints.'

Having contrasted in this forceful way the fickleness of the things of this world with the immutability of the plan of salvation, the preacher stood up straight and cried out, more loudly:

> But we are still too far away to view fully the certainty and security of this covenant. Further on, beyond the grave and past the bounds of time, that is where we will perceive the immense value of having our souls within the folds of a sure covenant. Souls! You will see an end to this world but eternity will not see an end of you. Behold the fires of the last day licking up the oak cupboards of the wealthy, consuming fair palaces into ashes, breaking up iron chests and destroying the deeds of old inheritances that have been there kept safe for generations and generations! And see the great men of this earth left with no provenance for their title to their lands; and, for that matter, the lands themselves have disappeared forever somewhere! But what of the covenant made between God and the soul in some *Sasiwn* or service? What of the marriage covenant made between Christ and the believer? Will it hold in the fires of judgment? Will it hold? *Will it hold?* WILL IT HOLD?

With this, a godly old woman in the gallery, to the left of the preacher, could not contain herself and quite unconsciously, burst out,

> Oh, yes! It will hold! Thanks be to God! Neither shall the covenant of my peace be removed!

Her shout shook the congregation like a whirlwind; a current of excitement passed back and forth and many broke out spontaneously into praises.

In the middle of all this excitement Ebenezer Morris appeared completely self-possessed, though the bright tear drop in the corner of his eye betrayed his emotion. After a period of silence, he continued,

> Yes, I was going to recite those words. Listen all of you! 'For the mountains shall depart, and the hills be removed.' Oh, you old mountains and hills of Wales! After having stood unshakeably through all the changes of the ages, a day will come when their foundations will be broken and they will be shattered. But when the thunder of their disintegration is heard and their fragments will be darkening the skies, you, family of the covenant will have nothing to fear. 'But, *But*, BUT' – it is our God who says it, and that is sufficient – 'But my kindness shall not depart from thee!'

The tension in the place was now about to sweep everything before it. The preacher stood up, stretched out his arm, raised his voice to the highest pitch, and the great shout, yet full of fragrance, burst forth:

'NEITHER SHALL THE COVENANT OF MY PEACE BE REMOVED.'

With this the dam broke. The congregation within the building gave way to shouting, some crying out, 'Thanks be to God! Hallellujah!', and others singing that sweet hymn of Edward Jones, Maes-y-plwm, to the covenant:

This is a perfect ring, it has no break,
A sure knot, that every strain can take;
The children can no longer sell their right;
God has them in a ring, and holds them tight.

Does bwlch yn hwn, fel modrwy'n grwn y mae,
A'i glwm mor glos, heb os nac oni bai;
Ni all y plant ddim gwerthu eu meddiant mwy;
Mae gan Dduw gylch, a'u deil, o'u hamgylch hwy.

so that it was pointless for the preacher, for all his strength of voice, to continue the sermon.

He was preaching in the window and when those within boiled over in this way he turned to those outside and said,

> Many of those, here in the chapel, are ready to put their names to the contract with heaven, to receive life from the Man who died on the cross, and to spend that life in his praise. How many of you are willing to enter into the bonds of that everlasting covenant; that covenant which is ordered in all things and sure.

He then spoke a few words to them and very soon the assembly outside became possessed of the same praising spirit as those inside, and in this warmth of praise the service was closed.

We heard of him preaching once at Nantfflyniau, a farmhouse not far from the church at Mwnt, when he had an ever-to-be-remembered service. It seems that the priest who served at Mwnt kept a *seiat*, a private society, according to the fashion amongst the Methodists, and on the Sunday after Mr Morris's sermon twenty members of the church asked to be accepted as *seiat* members. The clergyman questioned each one of them as to what had influenced them and on hearing every one giving the same answer, he cried out in something of a temper,

'What? Cannot God do anything, except through Eben Morris?'

As a result of this same sermon many also joined the Methodist *seiat*, and a revival broke out in the neighbourhood. It came to be known as 'The Mwnt Revival'. The custom on a Sunday in the area previously was sports-playing, and a farm-hand would sound his horn on a hilltop to call the players together. But after Mr Morris had come to the region to preach, with his strong, melodious voice and profound solemnity, the people began to lose all taste for their games. The master of the labourer referred to above was angered by this and told him: 'Now, Edward, out you go to the hill. You'll assemble more with your horn than ever Eben Morris will with his preaching.'

But the prophecy proved to be false; it was Ebenezer Morris's preaching that overcame. The sports were forgotten. Edward the farm-hand was convicted and became an elder at Llechryd afterwards. It is said that these were the circumstances that led to the planting of the church at Blaencefn, near Cardigan.

There is a region of Cardiganshire, not far from Mr Morris's home which is possessed completely by the Unitarians. Although they did not believe the doctrines taught by him, they could not keep away from hearing him because of the excellence of his oratorical abilities and he would express his views forthrightly in their presence. Once in the course of a sermon, he came across the words, 'Who is over all, God blessed forever. Amen.' After making some excellent remarks proving that this was said of the person of the Lord Jesus and was expressive of a desire that his divine glory be revealed, he added, 'Now, Socinians, let me have your "Amen," for once.'

He preached fairly often in the farmhouse of Lloyd Jack. The farm was also the home of a well-known Arian, Dafydd Siencyn Rhys, and indeed Ebenezer Morris and he were good friends. On one occasion Dafydd Siencyn Rhys told Mr Morris that for his next sermon at the farm he must preach on something that was not a matter of controversy. The next time Mr Morris's text was, 'And without controversy great is the mystery of godliness: God was manifest in the flesh.' His first words after reading his text were:

> Here is a truth over which there is not, nor should there be, any controversy.

He then added:

> But if you continue to argue, the controversy will not be long unresolved, because the same Person is to appear a second time, 'Looking for that blessed hope, and the glorious appearing of the great God and our Saviour Jesus Christ.'

He, and a number of the leading ministers of the Methodists, would hold a preaching service annually, every Easter Monday, at Ystrad village on the banks of the river Aeron, right in the middle of Unitarian country. He often had powerful services there, deeply affecting the feelings of his hearers, but it does not appear that any lasting good was done, nor hardly any convicted of their errors. But on one occasion an English family was visiting the place. They were members of the Established Church and full of prejudice against Nonconformists. During the afternoon service they were to be seen in the window opposite the platform with the most contemptuous looks upon their faces. Mr Morris hailed them authoritatively, in English, and the power of his address, together with the influence it carried, was such that at the end of the service he received an invitation to join the family for tea. This also he did and received every respect from them. The occasion, it is said, was the means of removing the prejudice of the gentleman towards Nonconformists and the means of salvation for his wife.

One of the ablest of the Unitarian ministers once accompanied Mr Morris for some twenty miles of journey and the topic of conversation throughout the time was the Person of the Mediator. After a long but perfectly friendly argument, Ebenezer Morris asked the minister:

'What do you think of Stephen the martyr? Was he a good man or a bad man?'

The minister responded promptly:

'Oh, Stephen was a good man, certainly.'

'If so,' replied Mr Morris, 'why was it allowed him in his last minutes to commit his spirit into Jesus's hands, if Jesus is no more than a man?'

The Unitarian fell silent, then after a while, with his hand falling on Mr Morris's shoulder, he said:

'That is something I never thought of before.'

MORE DESCRIPTIONS OF SOME OF EBENEZER MORRIS'S NOTABLE SERVICES

We have already mentioned how Ebenezer Morris would sometimes speak in English during a sermon if there was need of it. Although not a scholar and living in one of the most Welsh areas of the Principality yet by effort and energy he had become able to preach fluently in English, though not without a very strong Welsh accent. About the year 1818, he and the Rev. David Charles, Carmarthen, were called to Wotton-under-Edge to take part in the ordination of Mr Theophilus Jones. Wotton-under-Edge was one of Rowland Hill's chapels. Mr Hill was not a member of any particular religious denomination but he felt a greater affinity and closeness to the Calvinistic Methodists than to any other, and Theophilus Jones was an out-and-out Methodist. Mr Hill fully acknowledged the excellence of the Welsh pulpit and looked forward to the best kind of feast from the two ministers but as he was also full of humour he promised himself some amusement from Ebenezer Morris's broad Welsh accent. The day arrived and Mr Morris was called upon to offer the 'ordination prayer'. He obtained a remarkable access in prayer. All felt that he had entered within the veil and was face-to-face with the divine presence, and before he had ended there was not a dry eye in the congregation. Then Mr Charles arose to deliver the charge to the minister. His text was Acts 20:26, 27: 'Wherefore I take you to record this day, that I am pure from the blood of all men. For I have not shunned to declare to you all the counsel of God.' He could speak as ably in English as in Welsh, and the seriousness of his tone and the grandeur and glory of the truths he declared amazed the congregation. He showed the uniqueness of 'all the counsel' as it gave glory to the entirety of God and as it was necessary for the entire man. Mr Charles had got hold of that important truth which had not yet found a place in the creed of the Methodists, namely that the minister of the gospel should not hinder himself with the affairs of this world:

'Let the pulpit be as undefiled as the marriage bed,' he said, 'consecrated to the cause of Christ and the service of the eternal souls of men and not to give place to the temporal and mutable things of this world.'

Afterwards, Mr Morris delivered the charge to the church. His text was Psalm 50:5, 'Gather my saints together unto me; those that have made a covenant with me by sacrifice.' Unfortunately, hardly any of his comments are on record, but his solemnity was profound. He laid hold upon his hearers' consciences and brought them to such a recognition of the exactness of justice that terror ruled in every heart. Again and again, in his own unique way, he cried out, 'The day of judgment,' and no one could withstand it. Some of the gentry turned pale through fright; ladies, clothed in silk, fainted in terror; and the fear of judgment possessed all. But where was Mr Hill? Behind the preacher, with the tears running in streams down his face, having completely forgotten about the Welsh accent and crying out continuously,

'Amen! Go on, my brother. Give it them well.'

The next day the two ministers went on to Rodborough where the Rev. John Rees ministered. There Mr Morris had a service forever remembered. His words were like bolts of lightning, particularly when he cried out, over and over again, the word, 'Eternity!' One lady, sitting in the gallery, had to be carried out in a faint and when she had recovered she said that the minister from Wales was too terrifying to be listened to. The memories of these services were evergreen in Wotton and Rodborough for very many years. Whenever Mr Hill preached there and found that the congregation was tending to lifelessness, he used to say, in his own way:

'We must get that fat preacher from Wales back again to awaken you.'

About twenty years after this time, the Rev. Thomas Harris, once of Haverfordwest, went as minister to Wotton and when speaking to the old people found that they clearly remembered the sermons of the two Welshmen and testified of them:

'Oh! the Welsh Apostles! They were men of God, with clear credentials.'

FURTHER EXAMPLES OF HIS CHARACTER

We have been quite unsuccessful in our description if the reader has not formed an idea of Ebenezer Morris as a man of the utmost seriousness who was often raised to remarkable heights as he preached the gospel. But as often happens with this type of person, he was sometimes prone to depths of depression when he would hardly speak a word. That eccentric old elder, Owen Enos, was particularly qualified therefore to act as a travelling companion for him. Owen Enos was a cheerful man, quick and lively as a bird, and as carefree as the cuckoo whatever his circumstances, and his wit and comic scrapes dispelled Mr Morris's melancholy on many an occasion. Once they were returning from an Association in Pembrokeshire, together with another elder called Thomas as a third companion. This man was rather too careful of his animal. They arrived at a very steep hill and Mr Morris and Mr Thomas descended from their horses to walk but as for Owen Enos he remained in the saddle. Mr Morris and Mr Thomas walked on in conversation leading their horses behind them. But as soon as they had begun to walk, Owen Enos leapt off his own horse and on to the back of that of his fellow elder. Ebenezer Morris saw the manoeuvre out of the corner of his eye but said nothing though he had difficulty hiding his laughter. When they came to the top of the hill, Thomas turned round to get back into the saddle only to see Owen Enos already there. Ebenezer Morris burst out into uncontrollable laughter and when recovered said:

'Well, well, Owen *bach*; there are some odd demons that trouble you, that most people mercifully know nothing about.'

At another time, Mr Morris and Owen Enos were travelling in Breconshire. It was winter and the weather was fearfully cold, the road also was rough and desolate. Having these circumstances to contend with, together with his own tiredness, Mr Morris had become ill of body and low in spirit.

Owen tried to lift his spirits by every means of wit and innocent teasing. At last Ebenezer Morris said:

'You are just telling funny stories, Owen, while I am near to death.'

'Please, Mr Morris *annwyl*, don't die here or there will be awful difficulties in carrying you home to be buried. I will have more trouble with you, because you are so fat, than with a basket of herring.'

This so tickled the preacher that it restored his good humour but he did take his revenge on his friend.

'Owen,' he said, 'you are still teasing, but you had better put a stop to it, for you are sure to die before Christmas.'

Owen tried to continue with his witticisms but he had experienced the fulfilling of so many of Ebenezer Morris's predictions that the word sank deep into his mind. They arrived home and as Christmas drew near Owen's fear affected him so much as to make him really ill. He was confined to his bed for some days but then, Christmas having passed and finding himself still alive, he felt strong enough to make the journey to Twrgwyn and as soon as he saw Mr Morris he cried out:

'Oh! the old prophet! Here is Christmas gone and I am still alive. What about that prophecy now?'

'Yes, yes, Owen *bach*,' replied the minister, 'but I did not say which Christmas.'

Owen saw that he had been caught, and was from then on a lot less ready with his teasing when in Mr Morris's hearing.

We have already referred to the great respect in which Ebenezer Morris was held throughout the country, even by the gentry. No doubt he lost much of the favour of the mighty because of the leading position he took with the question of ordination; certainly some of the clergy and their families never forgave him, but as he had acted completely conscientiously and with a sense of his duty before God, it did not concern him. However, as to those gentry who best knew him and were aware of his seriousness and humility, they were not long in being reconciled. They gathered to hear him when he was preaching; they called for him when in distress; and they showed their appreciation of his character in many ways. On one occasion he was called to appear at a Quarter Session in Cardigan involving some legal case. As he made his appearance a respectful silence fell upon the whole court. As the clerk handed him the Testament in order for him to take the oath, the magistrate in the chair intervened and stopped him, saying:

'Mr Morris's word is sufficient.'

He himself gave his testimony in such an unassuming and upright manner that it only deepened the impression already upon everyone's mind, that he was a man of God. He once met Mr Lewis of Llysnewydd, one of the wealthiest and most level-headed in that part of the country, who said to him,

'I am grateful to you, Mr Morris, for your valuable influence towards keeping the peace in the land; you as a countryman are of more worth than a dozen of ourselves as magistrates.'

He was as remarkable in prayer as he was as a preacher. If there was ever some melancholy Christian tempted to be downcast and ready to make use before God of those words of the prophet, 'There is none that calleth upon thy name,' there would be hundreds ready to reply:

'Yes, there is one at least, Ebenezer Morris, who does so.'

Often as he prayed, he would come across a particular verse and would then lay hold upon it until he had drawn the marrow of it, and found in it great spoil. On one occasion that faithful old preacher, Ishmael Jones of Montgomeryshire, was itinerating through Cardiganshire and met Mr Morris at Cardigan town.

'I will begin, and you must preach,' said Ishmael Jones.

'No, no,' he replied, 'you are the stranger and they are used to me as a neighbour. I will begin.'

Begin he did. And it is said that his prayer was remarkable for its effect and influence. In mid-prayer he struck upon that verse, 'Father, glorify thy Son.' He repeated it, again and again, and each repetition brought forth a different aspect of the phrase, so that many of the congregation began to pray out loud with him, some of them praising God with much rejoicing, and all under the effects of the deepest of feelings. At the close of the service there was much more being said of Eben Morris's prayer than of Ishmael Jones's sermon. Another time, at Hawen, a Congregationalist chapel near to his home village, when two famous preachers were to preach, he was asked to begin the service. He did so with such an unction as is very rarely experienced. The praying threw the preaching into the shade and the occasion was often talked about for years afterwards.

In an Association at Caernarvon, in one of the meetings of the preachers and deacons, the topic under discussion was prayer. It was a time of revival, with a pronounced liveliness attending the prayer meetings and a degree of disorder present because of the shouts of the newly converted. The Rev. John Elias took advantage of the circumstances to speak out reprovingly of shouting in prayer.

'It might be thought,' he said, 'while hearing some pray on their knees, that our God is deaf, or that, as Elijah said when mocking the god of the prophets of Baal, "He sleepeth and must be awaked."'

Ebenezer Morris was aware that he himself often raised his voice when praying and indeed sometimes shouted loudly, so, when called upon to contribute, he said:

> I do not agree with my dear brother Elias on this point. What of our great Saviour, in the days of his flesh, offering up prayers and supplications, with strong crying and tears?

'Well, yes, Mr Morris *bach*,' replied John Elias immediately, 'I am speaking against strong crying without tears. Those whose feelings are such that they are in tears, they may indeed cry out strongly.'

Mr Morris would not at any time forget that he was a minister of the gospel, and he was notable for his faithfulness in maintaining a clear conscience before Christ. When visiting a large town once, he lodged in the house of an eminent doctor whose wife was the daughter of a wealthy elder with the Methodists. After the sermon the Lord's Supper was administered. Having returned to the house Mr Morris, in a gentle and kindly way, asked the lady:

'Were you with us tonight at communion, madam?'

'No,' she replied, 'I am not a member of the *seiat*.'

'How is that?' he asked her.

She explained that she now socialized amongst a group of friends whose standing were such that it made it difficult if not impossible for her to belong to the *seiat* in the chapel. He looked at her, with both sadness and kindness in his eyes, and asked:

'And will that group of friends be of any help to you when you come to die, madam?'

The lady had no answer for him. When he and a friend were left to themselves, he said:

> I find I must always clear my conscience with those of this sort, before I take my leave of them.

At another time there was an Association at Caerphilly and Ebenezer Morris was staying at the home of a gentleman who took an avid interest in agriculture. After breakfast he asked him:

> I understand, Mr Morris, that you work on the land, just as myself. I would very much like for you to look at the cattle I have, and the way I feed them.

In the most courteous manner, Mr Morris replied:

> With every respect for you, sir, and for your kindness, but I must ask you to excuse me, because I did not leave my home to view cattle, but to do with those things that pertain to the kingdom of Jesus Christ.

Rather than being offended, the gentleman respected him deeply, and declared later:

'Surely, that is a true minister of Christ.'

His deep conscientiousness was manifest in all his dealings with the things of this world. He once bought a cow at a fair, paying for it the price asked by the seller. At the very next fair in the locality the price of cattle had risen sharply from what it was. When Mr Morris realized this, he sought out the man who had sold him the cow and said, 'According to the present price of animals, I received too much change for the cow,' and handed him a guinea, though the man was not in any way expecting it. It is no surprise that all the surrounding country esteemed him as a prince of God in their midst. He was offered as a gift, because of the respect in which he was held, the ownership of a house called Rhiwfelen. He was very grateful for the offer and the kindness that it displayed but refused it firmly, and when asked the reason, he replied:

'I could not, on any account, bear the thought that I was keeping it from the true heir.'

Even among the best men of earth, there are surely only very few who would act in such an honourable manner.

While he was always careful to observe gentlemanly behaviour towards all, he was at the same time careful of the respect that was due to himself. The late Rev. Thomas Phillips, D.D., Hereford, used to relate an anecdote that shows this:

> At an Association at Llangeitho, a strong exhortation was given to the brethren from the south to attend the next Association in the north. When Mr Morris was particularly urged, he replied firmly that it was not convenient for him to agree to the brethren's request that year. It seems that another effort was made after the meeting, in the afternoon, to persuade him to agree. The following morning, with the permission of the chairman, Mr John Roberts of Llangwm raised the matter again, and said that he understood that Mr Morris's difficulty with respect to a visit to the north was that he was at the time without a horse. He appealed for someone present to lend him a horse that he might be able to come. At that Mr Morris was on his feet and having thanked the visiting brother for his kindness, said:
>
> 'I have at home plenty of horses, but there is none of them presently fit to carry me. I do not wish to ask a favour of anyone because as soon as I hear of a horse that pleases me I can afford to buy it.'
>
> His feeling was not so much ingratitude nor pride but a proper awareness of what was due to him and his position. When Mr Roberts realized that he had inadvertently touched a sore spot in Mr Morris's feelings, he apologized in a most fraternal, courteous manner.

Ebenezer Morris was always full of sympathy towards young preachers, particularly if he saw signs that the Lord had entrusted them with the gospel. When the Rev. John Hughes, Pontrobert, made his first journey to south Wales he met, at one place, an elderly preacher, not considered famous or particularly able, who said to him:

'You be careful, young man, that you are brief with your sermon, so that you don't steal my time.'

Within a day or two he met the certainly famous preacher, Ebenezer Morris, who told him:

'Don't you hurry, my friend; prepare yourself and take your time; I only intend to preach very briefly today.'

The late Rev. John Jones, Lampeter, related how he attended an Association at Blaencefn, the first time that he had been in that part of the country, and quite unexpectedly as far as he was concerned he found himself announced to preach. This threw him into into an acute anxiety, particularly as he saw that there were many notable preachers present. Mr Morris discerned his state and with a warm smile went up to him at the side of the pulpit, saying:

'Dear brother, don't be down-hearted. Everyone here is just a sinner exactly the same as yourself, and we will all be praying for you.'

It was through Mr Morris's instrumentality that John Elias came on his first journey through the south, when he was only a comparatively young preacher. Some of the older preachers of Gwynedd were very dubious of Mr Elias and behaved coldly towards him. They suspected the severe seriousness that he displayed, believing it arose from Pharisaism, and there is also some place to fear that they were not completely free from a jealousy of his remarkable oratorical ability. But when Ebenezer Morris heard him he realized that John Elias would soon be one of the princes of the pulpit and he did not rest until he had obtained a promise from him that he would visit the south. Some predicted that the journey would be untimely; that it would be injurious to the preacher's spirit and of no great benefit to others. But the contrary proved to be the case. Mr Elias's itinerary was like the rush of a whirlwind. He was followed from chapel to chapel by hundreds of eager listeners. By the strength of his eloquence and the power of the accompanying influence he would floor the workers of iniquity and the strongest of them was not able to stand before him. No one rejoiced more at the unction attending the ministry of the young man, than Ebenezer Morris. He used to say afterwards that this journey by Mr Elias was the means under God's blessing of one of the greatest and most beneficial awakenings in the south that he could remember in his lifetime. The reports of this tour and the powers that accompanied it were soon widespread in the north and were the reasons for bringing some of the leading preachers there to think more highly of John Elias and to give to him that respect which was his due.

Ebenezer Morris's usefulness in church meetings was notable; it was almost as influential as his work in the pulpit. He did not like to see people in the *seiat* with their heads bowed down as reeds. He would often say:

> At the means of grace be like men in their element, and not as if all your heart was away at the fair.

Very rarely did he fail to reconcile any that had fallen out and there was no one like him for putting an end to quarrels. When he was once away from home, some from the Twrgwyn church began wrangling over completely unimportant details. As soon as he had returned he heard about the affair. On a week-day evening, the following week, he was as usual preaching and keeping a *seiat* at the chapel. The text of the sermon was Proverbs 17:14, 'The beginning of strife is as when one letteth out water; therefore leave off contention, before it be meddled with.' The sermon was so biting and contained such an exposure of the nature of strife and the awful consequences that follow, that the disturbance evaporated with no one daring to speak of the matter again.

He knew when to exercise severity as well as gentleness. A quarrel arose at one time in the Cil-y-cwm *seiat* between two eminently respectable ladies: Mrs Lewis, the wife of a well-known lawyer, and Mrs Jones of Henllysg. Henllysg was a handsome mansion, and Mrs Jones was the mother of David Jones, Esq., of Blaen-nos, who represented Carmarthenshire in Parliament for years. Though every effort was made, the two could not be reconciled.

As a last hope, the Association decided to send Ebenezer Morris. He would not go on any account without the agreeable old elder, Owen Enos. On the day, Ebenezer Morris began the journey to Cil-y-cwm. It is probable that he knew what day the church meeting was held. He called on Owen Enos on the way, finding him ploughing his field, and requested him to accompany him. After arriving and beginning the meeting, he asked if the two quarrelsome women were present. On being assured that they were, he called them out to the front and commanded them to leave and to refrain from returning until they were pacified.

'What, Ebenezer Morris?' said Mrs Jones, 'Is that how you would treat me after I have given hospitality to you and to your father scores of times?'

He replied, with awful authority:

In the name of that God who enabled you to provide for me and my father, I command you to leave.

There was nothing for it but to obey. But there was more grace than wickedness in the two ladies, and at the door, Mrs Jones burst into tears and said to the woman with whom she had been quarrelling:

Mrs Lewis *fach*, where on earth are we going?

And the two of them fell on each other's necks on the spot. Seeing that the treatment, though harsh, had met the purpose, Mr Morris called them back, and after giving them appropriate counsels they were received back in their places, and it is said that they were friends to the grave. The story demonstrates the greatness of Mr Morris's influence in the Connexion as well as his fearless courage.

Without doubt, Ebenezer Morris was a notable gift from God to the Methodists and to Wales, and especially so to Cardiganshire. No one was above him in the pulpit or on the field at the Association. In those days when there were giants on earth, he stood shoulder to shoulder with the tallest of them. He was, moreover, equally as famous in the private conferences. Though not ordained for the first twenty years of his preaching, he became of greater influence at the Association conferences than any of the south Wales clergy. His words accounted for much and he could well have referred Job's description of the elders to himself and his brethren, 'After my words they spake not again.' He possessed to the full all the attributes of a leader: slow and prudent, full of discernment, viewing all matters that came before him from all aspects before pronouncing upon them. It was a privilege for the Connexion to have the presence of such a powerful man in its courts and meetings.

At the same time, we would be doing both himself, and the present condition of Methodism in the lower parts of Cardiganshire, an injustice if we were to present him as a perfect man. It must be acknowledged that he could not be compared to his friend, the Rev. Ebenezer Richard, Tregaron, as an organizer of the administrative side of the cause. Rather like the Rev. Thomas Richard of Pembrokeshire, he was completely opposed to the multiplication of churches.

'We have quite enough chapels,' he would say. 'The people only want to save their bodies. If you pay too much attention to them the gospel will lose its influence in the land.'

He himself was a means of stirring up the country to hear the gospel. Great numbers would gather wherever he was announced to preach, and through his effective ministry hundreds were convicted for eternal life. But he believed that a small number of chapels was best, each one a kind of Jerusalem, where the tribes gathered. He therefore set his face as flint against every effort to obtain a chapel in a new neighbourhood. The people should come to Jerusalem. The result was that preachers who were mere grasshoppers in comparison to him, would watch his movements and build schoolhouses and chapels in those areas where he preached in the farmhouses, and would gather to those buildings the souls that were convicted under his ministry. He considered the desire to have a chapel near to the people to be a spiritual carelessness of the gospel and a lack of zeal for hearing it. He was not in any way consistent with himself. Many, many times during his life he preached at farmhouses situated far away from any chapel, but when it was said to him that there was a sufficient congregation for a chapel to be built, he steadfastly refused, saying that they should give no place to laziness. Had he been a wise organizer in this respect he could easily have safeguarded the whole of the lower part of Cardiganshire for the Methodists, from Llanarth down to Pembrokeshire, just as Ebenezer Richard did for the upper part of the county. But because of his stubbornness and his opposition to new chapels, other denominations entered into his labours and reaped for themselves the harvest that he had sown. Perhaps, had he lived to see old age, he could have vouchsafed the area to himself, but as he died so young, and as no one comparable to him in gifts and eloquence arose in that part of the country after him, his refusal to multiply chapels was the means of transferring whole regions, which should have been in possession of the Methodists to this day, to other denominations.

When we journeyed once from Llandysul to Twrgwyn, we passed, some four miles from the latter place, a small beautiful chapel belonging to the Congregationalists. Our guide told us that the whole area was once Methodist but that as Mr Morris had refused to build chapels, the Congregationalists had moved in to make up the deficiency and that presently only Congregationalists were to be found there. We are not here condemning Congregationalists but blaming Ebenezer Morris's leadership. Losing the bottom part of the county to Methodism was not his purpose, but to a large extent that was the consequence of the course he followed. And it would not have happened had he been as zealous for providing spiritual homes for the people as he was for saving them.

He was deficient also in his evaluation of the Sunday Schools and the benefits that they could impart. It is true that he laboured diligently with the Sunday School and he would agree to take part with the Rev. Ebenezer Richard in the Schools Conventions, but he considered it mainly as an institution for children. In his mind every meeting should be subservient to the sermon. He said to the adults:

> Two are enough to be with the children in the school; let all of you others come to the sermon at Blaenannerch or Twrgwyn.

In all this he was completely conscientious, this was the light that he had on the matter. The value of the Sunday School as a place for meditating upon the truth and a means for saving souls had not occurred to him. We believe that it is only fair to mention these things. They show that the wisest and most committed of men are open to making mistakes and this was also the case for Ebenezer Morris. But we promise not to find any more faults in him.

HIS LAST YEARS

Ebenezer Morris did not escape afflictions and undoubtedly one of the heaviest that befell him was the death of his eldest son, David, in 1819. He was a promising and good-natured young man who was at the time the foreman of Mrs Foulkes's factory at Machynlleth. He was on the point of marrying and many bright prospects were opening before him. But on the 18th of August he went to bathe in the river Dovey and was drowned, at the age of twenty-seven. The previous Sunday Mr Morris had been preaching at Aberystwyth in the morning and at Penllwyn chapel at two in the afternoon. At Penllwyn his text had been Acts 21:14, 'The will of the Lord be done.' He spoke solemnly and substantially but without his usual freedom, and before finishing made the comment:

> The sermon is rather heavy today, and I do not know whether the message relates to myself or to yourselves but it has been on my mind for some time.

During the days following there was an Association at Llangeitho, and it was there that the news of the sudden death of his much-loved son reached him. The news pierced to the depths of his soul, his very nature seeming as if rent apart, but even in the midst of such brokenness he managed to express the text of the previous Sunday, 'The will of the Lord be done.' He hastened to Machynlleth, from there to take his son's body to be buried in the family grave at Troed-yr-aur. The first words with which he greeted his wife on crossing the threshold were:

'I hope, Mali *fach*, that you were kept from saying anything against the Lord.'

The next Sunday he was engaged for Twrgwyn and though sorely bruised at heart he decided to fulfil the engagement and preach. He managed to control his emotions during the sermon but at the end he gave out to sing the verse:

And I won't be long before ending, Won't be long before mooring home; Every promise, every threatening, Every commandment helps me come; The depths will never be my dwelling, I know I shall arrive at last; After all the waves have washed me, To heaven's landings safely cast.	Ac ni fydda'i 'n hir cyn gorffen, Ddim yn hir cyn glanio fry; Pob addewid, pob bygythiad, Pob gorchymyn sydd o'm tu; Nid y dyfnder fydd fy nhrigfan, Gwn y deuaf yn y man; 'Nol fy ngolchi gan y tonnau, Yn ddihangol byth i'r lan.

Because of the references to 'the depths' and 'the waves' and because he himself could hardly get through the verse because of his feelings, there was an indescribable effect on the congregation. They attempted to sing but mid-way through the hymn broke out into weeping, and the remainder of the service was a mixture of singing and weeping.

Ebenezer Morris was never the same man after the death of his son David. In addition, he laboured to excess, far beyond his physical capabilities. His long journeys throughout Wales in all weather; his own excitement when preaching to vast assemblies, particularly on the Association field; and the care of the cause in all its aspects which weighed continually on his mind; all these added up to more than his constitution could bear. He was overtaken also, like his father, although not perhaps to such an extent, by an unhealthy and unnatural corpulence. Between everything, by about the year 1824, although in the prime of life as far as age is concerned, there were signs that his health was on the verge of breaking. In the February of 1825 he went to London to serve the Methodist church at Jewin Crescent. He had been twice in London previously. He had received warm invitations from the capital city many times and his brethren in the south encouraged him to accept them, but for some reason he was unwilling to go, so that he made only three visits to the capital during his entire ministerial career. He was very reluctant also to go this third time, but friends in London were very eager to welcome him. It was also the turn of the Cardiganshire Quarterly Meeting to supply; so that in the end he consented to go. When considering the journey, his mind was filled with a deep solemnity. In the churches of his care he repeatedly asked to be remembered in the prayers of the brethren and sisters, and at Blaenannerch he said:

'It is the prayers of those who do not put much value on their prayers that I desire.'

On the way to London he preached at Carmarthen. In the chapel-house before the service many friends had gathered. Mr Morris was possessed by an unusual melancholy; he said that the journey weighed heavily upon him and he then addressed them all in a very striking manner:

> Remember, friends, that an important journey lies before every one of you. That great journey to eternity.

His text in the chapel was Psalm 2:12, 'Kiss the Son, lest he be angry, and ye perish from the way.' He had a remarkable service; it was the means of the conversion of many. One of them was a young man of much respectability but no religion, drawn to the service by the fame of the preacher. Mr Morris's words caught hold of his conscience and he knew no more peace until he had turned to the Saviour of sinners. He lived the life of a zealous Christian for the rest of his days, and was for many years a commendable elder. This is what he wrote twenty years after that service:

> I will never forget the appeal made by Mr Morris for the young people to make their peace with God by kissing the Son, that is through believing in him and that without delay. He explained how terribly dangerous it was to delay, for the Son could become angry and drive them out of the way so that they perish.
>
> 'You young men,' he said, 'if you do not seek reconciliation tonight, he might become angry by the morning. Perhaps you might live afterwards for many years. But Providence might take you away to somewhere in England, and you might be carried away by temptations, as chaff before the wind, so that you forget the means of grace and keep well away from those truths which might be of benefit to you, and all that because the Lord became angry with you for your disobedience in not responding here to the gospel.'
>
> I remember that I could not sleep that night without first giving myself wholly to the Lord, for fear that by the morning I might have lost every religious feeling and been left to hardness of heart.

The old elder added that forever afterwards he had considered Ebenezer Morris his spiritual father.

Mr Morris's labours at this time in London were eminently successful and much blessed to the church. Before he left, the annual Assembly was held there, on Good Friday and Easter Sunday, as was the custom, and the Rev. John Elias joined him to minister at the Assembly and to supply his place after him in the capital city. A peculiar unction accompanied the meetings of the Assembly from the onset, the dew falling heavily in every service. But the last service, on Easter Monday evening, when both Mr Morris and Mr Elias preached will long be remembered. The church was packed with Welsh people. No seating was available for half the multitude that had gathered and all were full of expectation. Mr Elias, who was to speak first, took as a text, Psalm 1:5, 'Therefore the ungodly shall not stand in the judgment, nor sinners in the congregation of the righteous.' A remarkable power accompanied his words; many discerning men testified that they had never heard him more fluent and powerful than on this occasion; he held the immense assembly in his hand. Amongst other things, he emphasized the *congregation* of the righteous. He strikingly portrayed the difficulties for the righteous to be as one congregation on earth; they dwelt in different periods of time, for example, and in different parts of the world; they were divided by language; they belonged to different religious groupings; but, he said, they would all be in one congregation in the judgment, without one ungodly or sinful person amongst them. All hypocrites would have been shaken out, just as Paul shook off the viper from his hand. The divine radiance was so evident that men could not endure it. Ringleaders in iniquity were weeping as children.

After Mr Elias, the Rev. Ebenezer Morris arose. His bearing was princely, but a beautiful tenderness shone in his features. He took as a text, Luke 10:34, '(He) brought him to an inn, and took care of him.' Mr Morris's friends felt deeply for him, that he had to preach after such a man, and after such a sermon from that man. They feared also that his text was not a powerful enough word to enable him to catch hold of the people after having experienced such influences. But it was not long before all realized that Mr Morris too was in the Lord's hand. He began describing the value and excellence of God's Church as an inn or refuge, and the circumstances that made it necessary for all his hearers to obtain a place in that refuge, or to be forever outside with no dwelling place. He cried out, with an irresistible authority:

> 'People! The night is coming; the great torrents are about to fall! Do you have a refuge?'

He shouted forth, again and again, with such fresh power accompanying each shout:

'Refuge! *Refuge!* REFUGE!'

By now the chapel presented an amazing scene. If strong winds had been blowing upon the previous sermon, there was now a tornado blowing and no one could withstand it. The people began shouting, 'REFUGE!' as loudly as they could, so that the preacher's voice was completely drowned. Some scores of converts joined the Jewin Crescent church after this Assembly, with many backsliders among them, and they all testified that it was the 'Sermon on the Refuge' that had overcome them.

There is a sequel to this story of the 'Sermon on the Refuge.' At Easter time the following year, the Rev. William Evans, Tonyrefail, was in London, and while hunting for books he turned into the store of a bookseller called Mr Hamilton at Paternoster Row. When Mr Hamilton realized that he was a Welsh minister he told him that the previous year he had gone to hear a Welshman, an Ebenezer Morris, preaching at Surrey Chapel, the chapel of the Honourable Rowland Hill. The text was, '(He) brought him to an inn, and took care of him,' and powerful effects were experienced by all present. On understanding that Mr Morris was preaching in Welsh at Jewin Crescent on Easter Tuesday, Mr Hamilton, out of curiosity, attended there also, and although he did not understand a word of the sermon there was yet such a presence in the meeting, such communication through the features and voice of the speaker and such an influence evident upon the hearers, that the Englishman was again completely overcome, just as previously at the Surrey Chapel. Among the many other ministers and clergy present on the Easter Monday Service was the Rev. William Howells, Long Acre, who was seen to rejoice as one who had obtained much spoil.

The following Tuesday saw Ebenezer Morris deliver his farewell sermon in London, from Hebrews 12:1, and on the journey home he preached again at Carmarthen, from Psalm 119:32, 'I will run the way of thy commandments, when thou shalt enlarge my heart.' By the time he arrived home he was extremely weak, and the illness of which he was to die had already laid hold of him.

His labours in London had been arduous, the damp and cold March climate of the city had not agreed with him, and his health had already been undermined so as to make him susceptible to any passing illness. Soon after his return it was found that his lungs were affected and that he was in a dangerous condition. He was only able to preach about three or four times again. His last sermon in Twrgwyn was from Psalm 30:5, 'For his anger endureth but a moment; in his favour is life: weeping may endure for a night, but joy cometh in the morning.' He ventured forth to Newcastle Emlyn on the Sabbath, 25 June. He preached there in great weakness and before the evening service was forced to return home. This was his last sermon; its text was Psalm 65:4, 'Blessed is the man whom thou choosest, and causest to approach unto thee, that he may dwell in thy courts.' His notebook shows that he intended to preach in the night from Psalm 71:9, 'Cast me not off in the time of old age; forsake me not when my faith faileth,' a verse on which he had never previously preached.

So ended the work-day of the Rev. Ebenezer Morris. He did not leave his house after returning from Newcastle Emlyn and very shortly afterwards was confined to his bed. The news of his illness, and particularly of the unlikelihood of his recovery, threw the land into a kind of amazement.

Ebenezer Morris, whose strength was viewed as the strength of a rock; the unique preacher and man of prayer bound by ill-health; he of whom the land was so proud and who was looked up to as a judge and father. He was about to depart and they would see his face no more! The thought filled the hearts of hundreds with sadness. Crowds, of every class and degree, arrived at Blaenywern to inquire of his condition, and many friends from far and wide came to visit. While he could, he conversed lovingly with all. Those who visited grieved to see the extent of his weakness but he was enjoying the consolations of God. He repeated over and over that he did not wish to live after having finished his day's work.

'This time of suffering is a weariness,' he said, 'but it is good enough for such a sinner as myself. The only thing of real worth is to know the Lord. Here I am, approaching the end of my journey and almost landed in heaven, but I do not have the least fear or discomfort.'

At the beginning of August an Association was held in Cardigan and many brethren and friends came to visit him on their way there. He told them:

> Remember me kindly to all my brethren and ask them not to forget me. My prayer is that the trumpet shout of the Lord might be amongst you. It has been a rejoicing to my heart to hear that there were indications that this was so in recent meetings. May those indications of God's presence being enjoyed kindle further strong desires for more such experiences.

And with much seriousness he added:

> When the Lord draws near to his people, it is as if he were asking them, 'Is it your wish for me to draw nearer still?'

But of all the visitors there was none for whom he felt such love as for the Rev. David Charles of Carmarthen, the friend who had stood by his side in the conferences of the Association, leading the whole movement. It is easier to imagine than to describe the feelings of these two evangelical heroes, fellow-soldiers in so many battles, as now they took their farewells for the last time on earth. After his friend had left, Mr Morris said to his wife:

'Mary *fach*, there were many friends here by the side of the bed, but it was Dafydd who has made the bedclothes wet with his tears.'

About two days before his death, two young preachers from Penmorfa came to visit him, and as they asked him for advice and counsel, he told them:

> Direct your sermons at the consciences of your hearers. It was not their natural feelings but their consciences which was my target always, and now, now that I am about to die, that is a great comfort to me. If you two are

allowed to live long then no doubt you will see a period for religion when hardly any new convert joins the *seiat*. At that time, do not drag unexercised men into the church but wait for God, and seek him, who in his own good time will succeed the work. God gave a promise to Abraham of a son, but Sarai felt the time long and despaired that she would ever have the privilege of becoming a mother, and so she gave Hagar to Abraham, and Ishmael was born. He was not the son of the promise and this brought much sorrow to Sarai afterwards. So also, you must wait for God's promise, and not go after the flesh, until the children of the promise are found for the Church.

Churchmen, as well as Nonconformists, grieved on hearing that Ebenezer Morris was on his deathbed, and many clergymen came to pay their regards. The following was written by the Rev. H. L. Davies, then a curate at Llangrannog but afterwards the vicar of Cenarth:

I will never forget the last day I was with Mr Morris, a day or two before he obtained his eternal reward. Perhaps I was the last minister, certainly the last Church of England minister, to see him. I was struck with surprise to see him so simple and unassuming: a man whose history was the history of a whole religious denomination for the last fifty years, and that during such stirring times. He told me:

'All I did was to act according to what my conscience told me, making every effort for that which was necessary.'

He then shared his personal experience:

'As for preaching gifts, they are nothing in the hour of death, and success in the ministry is nothing. I rest completely on the merits of Christ for an acceptance before God. "And be found in Him!" Say that those were the last words of Ebenezer Morris.'

Having woken from sleep, he called for Mrs Morris and told her:

'I saw myself last night in the company of those happy brethren who have fallen asleep in Jesus these many years: Mr Lloyd of Caeo and Mr Jones of Llan-gan. And their company was so sweet. I have tasted, truly I have tasted, of the fruit of the land.'

A little later, he added:

'No one has loved his country and family more than myself, but now, after the view I have had of heavenly bliss, and after the wonderful things revealed to me, I do not feel any attachment to anything here, nor any desire to remain in the body. I had such a sight as I never saw before of that better country where I will soon be.'

Then with a glorious smile, he cried out:

'I see it now! O beautiful land! O the unspeakable delight that I experience, yes, even in the pangs of death.'

His last day arrived, when his breathlessness and thickness of speech were such that only a few of his words could be understood. But he was heard praying for the nation:

'O that the knowledge of the Lord might increase in the land!'

This was on his lips all morning. In the afternoon he was heard repeating, over and over again:

'Where is the Holy Spirit? Where is the Holy Spirit?'

After a little while, he lifted his hand, and said:

'O! Holy Spirit!'

And worshipping thus, he died, on the afternoon of Monday, 15 August 1825, when 56 years old.

He died at harvest-time, and that Monday was a fine day, so that all the people were out in the fields, busy with harvesting corn. When the news came that Ebenezer Morris had died the reapers threw their sickles away and fell to the ground weeping. Farm labourers, who did not even profess religion, wept loudly. It is no exaggeration to say that the whole country mourned. An old elder from Twrgwyn mentioned that he had never seen such a funeral nor so much weeping and crying. The interment took place on the following Thursday. Large crowds had gathered from different parts of the country and as Twrgwyn chapel could not hold anything like the numbers present, the funeral service was held in the open-air, close to the house, at eleven o'clock in the morning. The Rev. David Griffiths, Llantood, Pembrokeshire, began with prayer and the Rev. Ebenezer Richard preached from Hebrews 13:7, 'Remember them which have the rule over you, who have spoken unto you the word of God: whose faith follow, considering the end of their conversation.' The body was then carried to Troed-yr-aur cemetery, where he was buried next to the body of his famous father and those of his son and two daughters, all of which had preceded him to that predetermined home of every living creature.

From all that has been said, we see that Ebenezer Morris was a pulpit-ful of a preacher, a neighbourhood-ful of a countryman, and a Association-ful of a leader. God raised him to be a guide to the Connexion in difficult times, when not only kindly wisdom was needed, but resolute courage also. In this he did not fail nor despair. He was faithful to the convictions of his conscience, for all the frowns of the gentry and the opposition of his brethren. As a preacher he must be placed in the highest category and in the very first rank of that category. Because of the power and sweetness of his voice, the strength of his feelings and his unique solemnity, the peculiar ability he had to communicate the simple truths of the gospel, he was the master of the congregation whenever he spoke. As a preacher of the Association, addressing the thousands out of every station in society and of every grade of knowledge, there were very few that could compare with him, and we do not hesitate to state that we have not seen his like since his day. The day he was laid in his narrow bed was a dark and black day for Wales.

39
THOMAS JONES, DENBIGH

THOMAS JONES'S FAMILY

About a mile and a half to the west of Caerwys, Flintshire, stands a farmhouse called Pen Uchaf. There, about the middle of the eighteenth century, lived Edward Jones, with Jane, his wife. They were both respectable people, of good morals, well thought of by their neighbours, members of the Established Church and very zealous for the cause. They were relatively wealthy, for as well as Pen Uchaf farmhouse and its forty acres of land, for all of which they possessed the freehold, they also owned many houses in Caerwys and other plots of land in the vicinity. Altogether this amounted to a considerable estate. Three children were born to them: Thomas, Mary, and another son whose name is not known and who, in all probability, died young. Mary became well known for her godliness and lived at Pen Uchaf all her life. She was married three times; the late Mr Enoch Lewis, Mostyn Quay, was her grandson, and Mr Herbert Lewis, the honourable member for the Flint boroughs is her great-grandson. But we are concerned with the eldest son, Thomas, who is always known as Thomas Jones, Denbigh, and is generally acknowledged as one of the greatest of Welsh theologians. If we were asked to name David's three mighty men as far as the theology of the Methodist Connexion is concerned; those who planted their image heavily upon its theology and above all others gave form to its expression of the main truths of the gospel, we would refer to William Williams, Pantycelyn; Thomas Jones, Denbigh; and Lewis Edwards, Bala.

It is not the case with Thomas Jones, as with so many of the Methodist Fathers, that we are at a loss as to so much of his history. As well as the many biographies of him that have been printed, he himself published a fairly detailed autobiography. The circumstances of his doing so were as follows: In the year 1800, when he was living at Mold, the Rev. Thomas Charles wrote to him asking a number of questions, intending, no doubt, to encourage him to write something of himself. Here are some of the questions:

When and where were you born? Of what calling and circumstances were your parents? What was the nature of your upbringing from birth? When, and by what means, did the Lord visit you with convictions as to your condition as a lost sinner? How were you sustained, and by what means, while under these convictions? When, and by what means, did God reveal his Son in you? What motivations drew you to the ministry of the Word? What is the basis of your hope of eternal life in the light of death and judgment?

These examples are typical of the other questions proffered. When he received them, Thomas Jones was ill, and many feared that he was rapidly hastening to the grave. Mr Charles was anxious to ensure that much information about him would not be lost. The questions secured their purpose; Mr Jones wrote copiously of the adventures of his youth, the way in which he was brought to religion, and to the Methodists in particular, the influences and reasons that directed him in the many decisions that he had to make during his public life; and, in that he lived in troubled times and had himself an important part to play in the movements that swept through his Connexion and through Wales, the *Autobiography* is more valuable than gold that perishes.

HIS BOYHOOD AND EDUCATION

He was born in February 1756. His date of birth is not known, but according to the church register at Caerwys Church he was baptized on 20 February 1756. It seems that his parents as well as being wealthy had a better realization than most of the advantages of education, and they decided that their son would receive the best education possible. Before he was four years old he was sent to school. His teacher, most probably, was Mr Owen Thomas, Caerwys, a very different man from the majority of schoolteachers in Wales at the time in that he had been educated at St Asaph Grammar School, possessed remarkable ability, and was fluent in many languages. Owen Thomas was a small hunchbacked man of exemplary morals, an excellent theologian, and a zealous Methodist. He was afterwards an elder for many years with the Methodists at Caerwys. The boy, Thomas, soon showed that he was talented; he wrote himself that there was in him, 'a tendency and ability to learn more than was the case for children generally.' To a young boy, fond of books and delighting in knowledge and quick to take in all learning, there was only one goal to aim for, according to general opinion at the time, namely, the priesthood. Thomas Jones's parents decided to make a priest out of him; no sooner had they decided than they informed the child and he mentions in his autobiography that this was very much to his taste. It was the outward honour of the office together with the opportunity that it gave to study that probably satisfied his childish thoughts, not yet old enough to appreciate responsibility. He mentions the fact that this was 'his parents' wish' for him, and as his mother died before he was eight years old it must be that this wish was disclosed to him when he was still very young.

He was in Owen Thomas's school until 1766, that is, up to the age of ten. He was then sent to the Grammar School at Caerwys kept by the Rev. John Lloyd, the curate of the parish. Little is known of either school or schoolmaster. A fellow-student of his at this school was a boy called Edward Williams, Glanclwyd, who afterwards gained a considerable reputation as a scholar and theologian. This young boy became Dr Edward Williams, Rotherham. Though Edward Williams was more than five years older then Thomas Jones, they immediately became firm friends; they were brought up in the same society; they both possessed the same zest for acquiring knowledge; and they were not dissimilar in their ways of thinking. We might add that Dr Williams was raised as a Methodist, and remained a Methodist until adulthood. When he died, Mr Jones wrote a tribute to his memory, and when referring to the time that they were at school together, he described him as a brilliant talent, noted for his ability at story-telling and at keeping younger children amused but with little taste for the children's games that were popular at the time. It was a striking coincidence that these two friends afterwards, about the same time and from exactly the same reasons, both rejected the ministry of the Church of England.

From what we can gather, Thomas Jones, even as a child, had a very tender conscience and was a very serious boy. 'One of the first things I remember about myself as a boy', he wrote, 'was that conversations or references that I heard about heaven and hell, and sometimes dreams also, had a solemn effect upon me.' The death of his mother added to this seriousness and he mourned her death for many days. He also mentions many deliverances that he experienced when young and which left a deep impression upon his sensitive mind. He says that these formed important links in the chain that drew his soul to Jesus Christ and bound it to him. It is in this context, and not merely as interesting facts, that he relates them. He wrote:

> I had a great fear of snakes, yet, at the age of eleven, had never seen one. At mid-day when looking for a ball that we had lost while playing, I heard a hissing sound under my foot. I looked and saw a snake that had been coiled up on the ground, but could not harm me because my foot was on its head. I sprang away in fear, and my friends who were older than me killed it. Another

time, having lifted up a bundle of corn from the field, I saw a snake that had been lying under it slithering away. Again, when collecting strawberries from a hedge I saw that I had placed my hand within the coils of a large viper that was lying there. At another time, when I was at school in Holywell, when I was tired from playing in the hot sun, I lay down on a steep slope at the side of the churchyard, thinking to doze a while. But before falling completely asleep I felt something under my head, tickling my ear and in my hair. On lifting my head, I saw it was a snake that I had disturbed, that was now making for its hole.

It is rather surprising that so many of his boyhood scares were due to snakes, the very creatures of which he was so scared.

He relates three other important deliverances that occurred when he was at Holywell, sometime about the year 1771, when he was fifteen years old:

When they were rebuilding parts of the church, the lead for the roof was kept in an old Catholic chapel above a well known as Winifred's Well. This also was the schoolroom. And as the workmen had left a rope over one of the strong beams of the roof... we, the schoolboys, used it to swing back and forth. When I and another boy were on the swing, one of the old carved blocks, placed under the cross-pieces of the beams, came down suddenly . . . It fell in two very heavy pieces near to us. But by a kindly Providence we escaped without harm.

The following is his account of another escape:

We (the school children) used to climb at times to the top of the bell tower. One day, I went and stood on the high point of the battlements. And as if this was not enough, in order to exhibit more of my presumptuous foolhardiness, I climbed up on to the highest point on the ridge and stood on one foot; yes, I looked down, and all around me; I took off my hat and shouted in my empty-headed excitement. But soon, on hearing the terrified shout of an old man who was in the cemetery, frightened on my account, I also became terrified and giddy; and I hardly knew which side to take to climb down, or rather to slide. By God's goodness, I landed on the lead roof, without mishap.

The third deliverance was as follows: A group of players in the town had built a theatre of wood within an enclosed garden.

And as my longing to see the play arose more often than I had the money to pay, I set to it, together with a few companions, to scrape a hole under the lower boards of the building and so at last pushed inside. But because the benches were banked one above the other, for all our efforts, we found ourselves in an empty pit, below all the people and not able to see anything. At last, after being there some time amusing ourselves in various ways, we were

> able to whisper to some friends and persuade them to make room for us to sit amongst them. It was their timely kindness that was the means of saving our lives. Had we been underneath a few minutes – or even only one minute – later, we would have been suffocated. Because almost as soon as we sat down, the benches collapsed and fell, together with the crowd that sat upon them, down into the empty space below. All were very much frightened, but apart from numerous bruises, only two or three were badly hurt. As for myself, for some time, in fearful and solemn wonder, I acknowledged God's hand in saving my life; yes, and my soul from hell also. But Oh! I soon forgot, or lost the sense of the experience; and continued to follow empty pleasures as before.

We record these escapades, not for their own interest, but because they were the means, to some degree at least, of creating and deepening a religious influence upon the mind of Thomas Jones.

THE BEGINNINGS OF METHODISM IN CAERWYS

He does not seem to have come into contact with the Methodists until his youth. As far as we can ascertain, none of their preachers visited Caerwys apart from Dafydd Morris, Twrgwyn, who passed by during a preaching journey in 1762, when Thomas Jones was six years old. It is true that they had a small society at Berthen-gron and that a well-known preacher lived there: John Owens, 'the Father of Flintshire Methodism'. They also owned a small church the other side of Caerwys at Dyffryn, Llandyrnog, and had a preacher there also, Robert Lloyd, Plas Ashpool. But as both these places were five or six miles distance from Caerwys, the young son of Pen Uchaf knew nothing of them. In the first service held by the Methodists in Caerwys (of which an eyewitness account exists), Edward Jones of Halkyn, near Holywell, preached. He had been invited there by a weaver named John Anwyl. When Edward Jones reached the village, the weaver was out collecting those who had promised to attend. His wife knew nothing of the meeting and refused the preacher when he and two friends came to the door. They turned on their heels disappointed but in the middle of the village met John Anwyl himself, and the meeting proceeded on the spot. The preacher stood near the cross in the middle of the village, and when the weaver's wife came out she saw the preacher in the midst of a crowd of singing people, with her husband among them joining in for all he was worth. We do not know how successful this service was but Edward Jones was said to be a good preacher, of better gifts and abilities than the average exhorter. He was a society superintendent for many years.

The next preacher to visit Caerwys, as far as is known, was Richard Harrison of Llaneurgain. He was half-English, a weaver by trade and a man of very gentlemanlike appearance. He too came on John Anwyl's invitation. A conspiracy to disrupt the meeting had been discovered, so John Anwyl persuaded the two Ellis brothers, his wife's brothers, to guard the door of the house. They were well known for their strength and belligerence and were feared by all. They stood by the door with great staves in their hands, ensuring that there was no noise or disturbance, so that God's servant had complete silence in which to declare his message. The meeting was held in John Anwyl's house, near 'Twm Bills's lake', and preaching continued here, more or less regularly, up until 1772 when a larger building was rented.

But Thomas Jones, Pen Uchaf, was not of those who attended sermons at the weaver's house. His father would not have encouraged such behaviour, and he had no inclination for it himself. However when he was between ten and twelve years old, his father married a second time, to a woman from the Penycefn neighbourhood who had some sympathy for the Methodists. She took her stepson on one or two occasions to the services near 'Twm Bill's Lake'. According to the *Autobiography* these meetings left no favourable impression on his mind:

> I was a bit surprised to see some of the girls crying and to hear the preacher say at the end of the sermon that he had not known what to say at the beginning but that the Lord had given him a door of utterance, and had helped him to declare the truth. Yet, for all this, I did not think them of much account, for of those who attended I did not know one who lived a pious, godly life.

Clearly the son of Pen Uchaf was a good judge, even at this age, and almost infallible, as young men so often are, at finding faults in others. Nor should we give too much attention to what he says about the lives of the listeners; there is no knowing whether any professed faith or not. There is nothing more certain, on the other hand, than that the early Methodists were well known for the purity of their lives. He, at this time, had to a large extent given himself to the pleasures of life. He says:

> I enjoyed myself, as others of my friends, in every vain and wicked pleasure that was within the reach of someone of my age, particularly in following the sports on a Sunday, though my conscience often rebuked me, as did my father's rod at times.

Not that conscience's voice was entirely without effect at this time:

> Once, I remember, having removed some of my clothes in order to play, such a fear came upon me – it was on a Sabbath day – that I had to dress again and slip away, fearful in my mind but giving to my friends the excuse that I was ill.

EARLY SPIRITUAL CONVICTIONS

When he was about thirteen years old and having mastered all that could be taught him at the schools of Caerwys, he was sent by his father to the Grammar School at Treffynnon. He was here for three years and though still a great follower of the sports played, he kept up all his studies. He became a good scholar, becoming fluent in English and gaining an excellent knowledge of Latin and Greek. He always kept in mind his goal of applying for the ministry of the Established Church. His time at Treffynnon was a significant and fairly mixed period. On the one hand he gave himself to every frivolity, keeping evil company, swearing, playing cards, profaning the Sabbath day, as was the custom generally. On the other hand his mind was filled with the terror of dying as an ungodly person, his conscience roared as a she-bear within him whenever he gave himself to wantonness, he was disturbed by dreams at night, particularly once when he dreamt, 'that the everlasting fiery furnace opened up to receive me, and closed about me'. He tried to quieten his conscience by resolving to live a better life, and to be a faithful and zealous minister of the Church once he was ordained. Sometimes, when he heard his friends swearing, he would rebuke them sternly and run quickly to his lodgings, 'to recite something of a prayer'. It was on the basis of the law that he sought peace for his soul at this time, and there is no wonder therefore that he was so unsuccessful. This was his state during his period at Treffynnon. At times he gave himself to the wildest behaviour, and then, as a kind of reaction, he would attempt to win God's approval by his good works. At last, he says:

> A kind of hopelessness began to overcome and ruin my soul; I decided it was quite impossible for me to love godliness or to leave my sins . . . I thought also of heaven, that all its activities was completely contrary to my taste and nature; therefore there was nothing left for me but to endeavour to take my share of the pleasures and sins of this world, and to forget the punishment until the time came when I had to endure it. This was the poor, miserable remedy that Satan and my wretched heart offered me.

He was clearly, throughout this time, frequently examining the state of his soul and would often be weighed down for hours under an awful weight of conviction. We suspect also that the enemy realized that he was closer to the kingdom of heaven than he did himself, before he would suggest such desperate remedies. Having failed to get him to follow such a course, Satan now pursued a different course – tempting him to believe that no such things as God or devil, heaven or hell, existed; that all talk of responsibility and judgment was emptiness and that the breath of man within him is of no greater significance than that of an animal.

> In this way I wallowed in my blood, yet the Lord never left me, but followed me with his arguments that at times laid hold of me in gentler, more melting ways. I remember occasions when, on my own, I would be suddenly overwhelmed by sadness for my sins and by self-loathing, together with such hopeful thoughts of salvation that my heart would melt, my eyes would flow with tears, and my lips would pour forth supplications and thanksgivings. I would have been happy to have spent all my life in such a frame, and with such thoughts.

It must be remembered that he was only a youth, not yet sixteen years old, when this battle was taking place in his soul – good and evil striving for victory.

At the end of 1771 he left Treffynnon and his period of education came to an end. This was not what he had intended, for he had hoped to proceed to university; this was his father's wish also. It is clear that his convictions were deepening at this time and that the balance of the scales was turning towards religion. He had still not departed from trusting in the law however; he sought escape through works; he had still not yet seen or grasped God's method of justifying a sinner by the gospel. He says:

> I began to follow some weak desire to be godly, believing, from the fleeting fears and joys that I experienced, that this is what would make me truly happy, in this life and for eternity. I would often seek privacy, where I would read many forms of prayer – prayers for repentance; for faith; and especially for the grace of perseverance, as I feared that I would fall back, as had happened to me at other times.

He began to attend the meetings of Methodist preachers, not only at Caerwys but far and wide, wherever he saw an opportunity, and their ministry made a deep impression upon him. A sermon by Robert Llwyd, Plas Ashpool, affected him greatly. About the beginning of March 1772, his father received a request from the Methodists to rent a house that he owned at Caerwys in which they could hold meetings. Mr Edward Jones had no great sympathy for the request; he was a zealous Churchman, sharing in the prejudice of the clergy against the new party. But his eldest son was more perceptive. The sermons of the Methodist exhorters that he had heard for himself, and the effect of similar sermons upon the morals of the people, had gained his interest. He interceded on their behalf before his father and the request was granted. The building obtained was situated on a strand of ground beside the village and was called locally 'Y Capel Main' ('The Narrow Chapel').

There is an account of Thomas Jones taking his younger brother, with his stepmother's approval, to Ffynnon Beuno to hear Robert Evans, Llanrwst.

The text was Psalm 86:11, 'Teach me thy way, O Lord.' Thomas so enjoyed the service that he went there again to hear Edward Parry, Bryn Bugad.

Not only were the sermons that he heard beginning to have a deep effect upon him, but the main truths of the gospel were more and more engaging his meditations. He sought to understand them and to see how they harmonized together and with his own thoughts. He was for some time disturbed by the election of grace. He states in his *Autobiography*:

> About this time, or a little after, I was in some trouble for a few weeks with respect to God's decree, and election. Not because I doubted whether the doctrine of predestination was consistent with the Scriptures; I was convinced it was, particularly in the light of Ephesians 2 and Romans 8 and 9. My confusion had to do with how God could be just and gracious and no respecter of persons, in his work of electing some and leaving others for destruction, with the result of such eternal difference in their conditions. In seeking to break the knot by my own reasoning and understanding, I could make no headway and was only confusing myself more. But as I sought to pray for more light and help from the Lord, I realized that I, together with all of Adam's race, were poisonous creatures, serpentine in nature, and that this was not of God's doing but of our own. As a result, I said: 'I certainly deserve to be damned, and if God ordained to show forth his glory in my damnation and in that of myriads like me, he would be doing me no injustice.' By such thoughts the bitter arguments of the enemy and of my rebellious heart were quietened.

This quotation shows that even at the young age of sixteen he had arrived at a considerable maturity of thought and a good understanding of some of the basic doctrines.

THOMAS JONES JOINS THE METHODISTS

At last, he decided to apply for membership with the Methodists. He did this in the summer of 1772. As might be expected, he was given the warmest of welcomes by the few poor people that gathered together in the Narrow Chapel. Such a step on his part required considerable determination for the Methodists were objects of derision in the area, and he was from a respectable family and known to be the heir to the estate. His father also strongly disapproved of his actions and of his habit of travelling the country far and wide in order to attend religious meetings, and as he was too young to be sent to any of the universities he considered returning him to the Grammar School at Treffynnon. Thomas Jones replied that whereas he had no desire at all to oppose his father's wishes, yet to send him back to Treffynnon in order to prepare him for holy orders in the Church of England would be a vain exercise; that he had completely given up any such intention. He made this statement before he was seventeen years old. He had two reasons for refusing this course. In his own words:

> I had such an opinion of the behaviour of clergymen that I thoroughly hated and feared the thought of being one of them. I was afraid [that is, if he went back to the school] that I would forget the state of my soul, and would return to my old pleasures because of the temptations and crosses that I would meet with at the school.

As he refused to continue his preparations for the priesthood, his father dealt very severely with him. He put him to work as a common labourer on the Pen Uchaf farm. It must have been almost more than nature could endure for a young man of relatively little strength of constitution, who had known only a scholarly life since the age of four and not used to hard physical work, to have to plough, to handle mattock, bill-hook and scythe, to dig trenches, and perform the other duties of a husbandman. But he did not complain but faithfully completed all the tasks given to him. After finishing the work of the day, he would either attend at a service at the Narrow Chapel or somewhere further afield, or go to his room to read and meditate. He studied the Bible and other religious books. He says that he felt such an aversion to his schoolbooks that for a period of seven years he could not bring himself to look at them. As he had rejected the vocation of clergyman, other honourable positions were offered him, but as each offer was conditional on his giving up attendance at religious meetings and breaking his connection with the Methodists, he refused them all without hesitation. 'The Lord kept me,' he says, 'from contemplating any of these.' Gradually, his father's feelings towards him moderated, and on seeing him continue to attend meetings, often when very weak in body and after a hard day's work in the field, he bought him a horse. It seems to have been a small, unattractive horse, costing only fifty shillings, but it proved very serviceable to Thomas Jones for many years and he was very grateful for the gift.

No doubt he thought that his soul would be at peace on joining the church, but that was not the case. For a full seven years he was sore broken in the place of dragons, attacked by unbelief and knowing very little of the liberty of the gospel and of the joy that it brings. He wrote:

> My old shameless atheism returned as a flood. There was nothing of God's word, nor of his nature, his attributes, his essence, that I was not tempted to doubt, to refuse; indeed, to ignore and blaspheme.

This mental strife arose partly because, in his strict conscientiousness, he paid so much attention to every aspect of his spirit, and partly because he saw tares raising their heads, and offences and controversies breaking out, in the church fellowship. But at times, the sun would shine down upon him for a little while through the black clouds. Once, shortly after coming to religion and when his spirit was at its most troubled, he heard that Daniel Rowland, Llangeitho, was to preach at Pontuchel. He decided to go to hear him, in the hope that he would be relieved of his burden. The old apostle's text was Genesis 49:18, 'I have waited for thy salvation, O Lord.' 'But though I had some relief,' writes Thomas Jones, 'my burden remained.' Rowland was preaching the next day at Berthen-gron, much nearer to Pen Uchaf, but the young man felt too disheartened to attend. But he went that night to the church meeting at Caerwys. It proved to be a wonderful meeting. One of the sisters began to describe how the Lord had visited her, raising her soul from the depths, by means of Rowland's sermon at Berthen-gron. As he listened to her Thomas Jones told himself, 'I also am in the pit, and I know that that is where I shall remain.' Before the meeting ended the congregation had broken out in great rejoicing and glorying. He withdrew from them, thinking to himself, 'There must be more to religion than mere imagination; surely the joy that they are experiencing must come from the Lord?' He could not deny the heavenly origin of the visitation; that God truly was in the place. With that, the further thought came into his mind with overpowering force, as if the Lord was reasoning with him, 'Are you ready to believe the testimony of these, your poor fellow-creatures? And will you not believe the testimony of my word?' With the thought, light shone into his soul. He saw the Word as *God's Word:*

> My heart acknowledged that the divinity of the Scriptures is as evident as the light of the sun; my chains fell off me; I was ashamed and abhorred myself; I returned to my friends and with them I expressed my gratitude.

He mentions later that this specific temptation of doubting the divinity of the gospel was never again allowed to attack his soul with such force.

HE OBTAINS ASSURANCE OF SALVATION

But he had still not yet arrived at a constant enjoyment of the gospel; he was still in captivity. His condition weighed heavily upon him. He had no appetite for food or drink; he had glimpses on occasions of the glory of Jesus Christ but could not bring himself to believe that he was his Saviour. In the summer of 1779 he fell ill with a fever from which he nearly died. The illness only added to the fears that troubled his spirit. When in this state, the text of Romans 5:10 was impressed upon his mind, 'If, when we were enemies, we were reconciled to God through the death of his Son, etc.,' and he began to reason with himself, 'As *enemies* have been reconciled to God, there is hope for me to be saved. I am nothing worse than an enemy, though I am the blackest one this side of hell.' He added:

> In this way my soul was raised as if from the deepest dungeon. Instead of guilt and fear and the wearying striving with my corruptions, I began to experience tender thoughts of God and comforts of hope flowing into my mind, and I had some degree of strength to believe, despite all my wretchedness, that the death of the cross, the death of the Son of God, was fully sufficient to save me, to save me justly, yes, to save me forever from sin and wrath.

We have not space to follow any further the travails of his thoughts. He had many buffetings of the enemy after this but by about the end of 1779 and the beginning of 1780, when he was around twenty-four years old, the glory of the gospel had begun to shine brightly upon his soul. He says:

> God's promises and the gracious treasures of his covenant were too great for me to refuse. For all the strength of my instinctive unbelief, it was too difficult not to believe.

He soon felt a strong desire to preach to his fellow-sinners:

> Something of this desire continued with me at times throughout the previous years, for all the darkness and captivity that I felt in my soul; but at this present time it was stronger and more constant so that I had to think, 'I must pursue this great work.'

But he feared the purity of his motives. He judged them to be the fruit of a proud heart so that he prayed earnestly against them, mixing with these prayers others in which he cried to God for direction. He was again troubled by doubts. Questions like the following would come to his mind: How can a guilty man be made truly righteous by the righteousness of another? How can the death of one man provide life, eternal life, to myriads? How can one person be both God and man? But he was given strength to take his doubts to the Lord, and that verse was applied with particular force to his mind, 'Christ, the power of God and the wisdom of God.' He noted:

> I had a glorious view of the person and sufferings of Emmanuel, so that my soul was glorying within me, acknowledging that the salvation he provides is throughout the greatest of the works of Almighty and All-wise God, and provides the strongest foundation for the hope and comfort of a sinner.

But his hesitation as regards preaching continued. He was at the Bala Association of June 1782, and experienced great pleasure while listening to Mr John Pierce preaching on the bush that burnt with fire and was not consumed.

CHURCH OF ENGLAND OR METHODIST?

By Michaelmas Day of the next year he seems to have committed himself to 'the great work', but could not decide with whom to throw in his lot, whether with the Methodists or with the Established Church. He favoured the Church to some extent, for the following reasons, given in his own words:

> 1. I thought that if the Lord was calling me to preach, I might be less insufficient in a parish church than amongst the Methodists, because of my bashfulness and lack of fluency in speech.
>
> 2. I thought also that there was a greater need in the Established Church because of the vast numbers of benighted, prejudiced souls that would not come to other places to hear the Word.
>
> 3. The encouragement I received from one or two ministers.
>
> 4. When I was hesitating between this and another matter, I seemed to be led to choose Church orders in that those who offered to help seemed capable of carrying the matter through.

Everything seemed to be directing him towards the Church: this was his father's wish, his path towards it was open, and he saw there a opportunity for doing good. He testified very solemnly that the honour and financial gain associated with the Church had no place in his mind. But yet, he still hesitated. In order to obtain more light he attended the Gwynedd Quarterly Meeting held in November or December 1782, so as to confer with his brethren there. 'I met with no opposition, but rather encouragement,' he wrote.

It must be remembered that for Thomas Jones to be ordained would not of necessity separate him from the Methodists; the leaders of the Connexion in the south at the time were clergymen. There were presently no Methodist clergy anywhere in Gwynedd and the brethren probably judged that they would obtain one in the person of Thomas Jones were he to be ordained.

Yet on taking the matter before the Lord, he failed to obtain peace of mind; he remained uncertain and in the dark. He would repeatedly address the throne of grace and plead the great promise, 'I will bring the blind by a way they know not,' and gradually the light dawned in his mind. The circumstances were as follows. In January 1783, he was away from home, either making inquiries or actually preparing for the step of taking orders. That night he had a dream. He wrote later:

> I saw myself sitting in a house along with many others; I heard knocking at the door and when it was opened a pale horse entered. Behind it followed its rider, with a gun in his hand. He came straight up to me, aiming his gun at my breast. At this point I was so frightened that I woke up, but soon slept again. I then saw myself in the house as before; a man came towards me with two pistols, one in each hand, aiming them towards me. This again woke me in fright.

Thomas Jones was not superstitious in any way but he was immediately convinced that these dreams contained a message from God, and he kept to this view throughout his life. He believed that the pale horse was death and that death, or the gravest danger of death, was near at hand. He believed also that the two pistols were two great dangers assaulting him. He continued:

> Whether that was the case or not, from that night an illness took hold of me that has never fully left me, and it does not appear that I shall ever be free of it.

This was the beginning of the disease from which he suffered, to greater and lesser degrees, throughout his life. He went to his bed cold and trembling. The bedclothes were few and the weather cold, and he failed to get warm throughout the night. He was there for three days and took no further steps with respect to ordination. He returned to Pen Uchaf, sad in spirit. For eight days he was in great distress of mind and trying to pray for guidance. He said:

> Such a sense of God's absence lay upon my soul that I began to think that something of the pain of the spirits in prison was upon me... But I obtained relief in the following way: I concluded at last that God's frown was upon me, and that this storm had arisen against me, because of my intentions, and I therefore decided to throw my Jonah overboard; I did indeed do so; and the storm was quietened.

The 'Jonah' was his resolve to apply for Episcopal ordination. He continued:

> Soon I arose, determined never again to give room to such a thought, and to bear whatever crosses might come my way because of this decision. But all of these have been so much less than I expected.

We see therefore that about the end of January 1783, he had decided forever not to pursue a career in the Established Church. One more attack was made upon him; a relation of his offered him a rich living were he to accept ordination, but he was given strength to refuse this offer also.

HE BEGINS TO PREACH

About the end of August, or the beginning of September 1783, he began to preach. He was then twenty-seven years old. We would almost have blamed him for hesitating so long but we should remember that the previous years had provided an excellent preparation for the ministry. Because of his wide reading, his serious studies, his extensive and detailed knowledge of theology – historical theology in particular, because he had defeated within his own soul the difficulties that are associated with some of the main truths of the gospel, and because he had been battling for so long with the different forms of the corruption of the human heart, he had a greater maturity of thought and more discerning judgment than most candidates for the ministry. Though he had been thinking of the possibility of preaching for years, his first step in this direction was accidental. He went to Caerwys one Sunday night in order to hear a sermon, having heard two other sermons at some other place during the morning. No preacher arrived at Caerwys, and Thomas Jones was persuaded to give a word of exhortation to the people that had gathered. He rose from his chair, and read Hebrews 11. He had intended only to read and pray, but the content of the chapter struck him and he shared a few comments, to his own blessing and to the profit of those listening. We would wish to thank the preacher, whoever he was, for breaking his engagement, because this was the spur for Mr Jones to take up his life's work. The news soon spread that Pen Uchaf's heir had begun 'speaking'; calls were made upon his service from various quarters, and his friends compelled him to respond to them. The Denbighshire and Flintshire Quarterly Meeting had not yet been established (according to the Rev. Jonathan Jones it was formed before the end of 1783). It was therefore without the consent of any church court but with only the persuasion of friends and the awareness within him of his suitability for the work, that he gave himself to preach the word of the kingdom wherever a door of opportunity might be opened for him.

He would speak mainly in farmhouses and barns – only seven Methodist chapels were to be found throughout Denbighshire and Flintshire when he began. He had to travel many miles and on arrival make do with very inadequate provision, though the welcome would be of the warmest. But he took no offence at this. He did his best to itinerate as much as his health allowed him. However he soon realized that he had little physical strength. He was troubled by stones in the bladder and could not ride or walk without intense pain. When unable to travel to his engagements, he would preach at Pen Uchaf and in the barns of the neighbouring farms, as well as in Caerwys. Tradition has it that the occasion of his first sermon at Pen Uchaf was as follows. One night his father noted many people approaching the house, one after the other, and going into the barn. On asking one of the servants, he learnt that his son Thomas had promised to give a word of exhortation to the people. The father had no wish to stop proceedings though he was not at all happy with the situation. The service began. Edward Jones could not restrain his curiosity and went into an adjoining building to listen. He was so pleased with what he heard of his son's preaching that he was kindness itself to him from then on, stating that Thomas would have no need to walk any longer whilst on his journeys.

Thomas Jones lived at home with his father for twelve years after beginning preaching. His health was always fragile; he was often confined to the house. He would experiment with various medications. Some would seem to be effective for a period, and he would then throw himself energetically again into the work of the ministry, until his weak nature would inevitably give way once more. This was the case throughout these twelve years. But neither weakness nor ill health could put a stop to his studies. He read, he studied, he wrote, without interruption; he gave himself to learn the rules of poetry; to compose poetry; to translate books.

We have already mentioned how Thomas Charles joined the Methodists in 1785 and the way in which he and Mr Jones became friends and remained friends for as long as both were alive – a friendship that knew no cloud but for a very short time during the controversy over ordination. In 1788, Thomas Jones first appeared before the public as an author. He wrote and published *Marwnad ar Farwolaeth Mrs Ann Parry* [*An Elegy on the Death of Mrs Ann Parry*]. Mrs Parry lived at Brynmulan, a cottage in Llanrhaeadr parish, between Rhuthun and Denbigh. Religious services were held in her home and she seems to have been a very godly woman with a discerning knowledge of gospel truths. In 1793, Mr Jones published his first book of theology – a polemical work with the title, *Sylwadau ar Draethawd a elwir 'Undeb Crefyddol, neu Rybudd yn erbyn Schism* [*Comments on an Essay entitled 'Religious Union, or a Warning against Schism'*]. This essay had been written by a man who called himself, *'A Minister of the Church of England'*. Who he was is not known, nor is this of importance, but Mr Jones answered his filthy attacks upon the Methodists with such adroitness, and revealed such a comprehensive understanding of the views of ancient and modern theologians with respect to the issues discussed, that the *Minister of the Church of England* chose not to offer a word of reply. During these twelve years at home, Mr Jones translated the Third Part of Gurnall's *The Christian in Complete Armour*, a book of about 400 octavo pages, but this was not published for some time afterwards, probably because of lack of money. During the same time he composed many poems that did not see the light of day until after his death.

HIS FIRST MARRIAGE

In October 1795, when he was forty years of age, Thomas Jones married a Miss Elizabeth Jones. He left Pen Uchaf and went to live at his wife's home at Mold. Miss Jones was a very religious woman, a member with the Methodists, and of some wealth. He found it hard to leave the small society at Caerwys with which he had been involved for twenty-two years, but Caerwys's loss proved to be Mold's gain. The number of Methodists in the town was very small when he arrived there, and their circumstances very poor. His arrival – because of his learning, his weight of character, and his comparative wealth – served to raise the profile of the Connexion in the town. By means of his labours and commitment the cause succeeded considerably; over sixty members were added to the society, many of whom considered him their spiritual father. New causes were begun at Rhosesmor and Cilcain. But his marriage lasted only two years. In March 1797, he had to undergo surgical treatment. Mrs Jones was greatly disturbed by the sight of the doctors in the house and she feared the worst. The two of them knelt together to seek God's help, then, in tears, they parted – he, to submit to the knives of the surgeons, and she, at the mercy of her fears in another room. The operation was successful; a stone of some considerable size was removed from the sufferer's body, though he refused the surgeons' request to search for another stone because he could not endure the continuation of the operation. Mr Jones recovered his health, but the episode affected Mrs Jones in her concern for her husband to such an extent that she sickened, and on 2 November 1797, her soul fled to a better country.

Whilst very ill, towards the end of the previous year, Mr Jones had published his translation of the Third Part of Gurnall's work. No doubt his improved financial situation on marrying enabled him to do this, and also to publish the many other books that he afterwards wrote, books that were of immense value to the Welsh. The Rev. Jonathan Jones states that the First and Second Parts of Gurnall's work had been translated previously: the First Part by Robert Jones, Rhoslan, in 1773; and the Second Part by a Thomas Humphreys, Penybryn, Edeyrn, Carnarvonshire, in 1784. These translations were awkward and clumsy; so much so that it is difficult to make out the meaning of many paragraphs. But Thomas Jones was a brilliant translator. As well as being a good English scholar, his taste was pure, his style clear, and his mastery of the wealth and resources of the Welsh language was complete.

Very soon, from painful experience, Mr Jones realized that there was a second stone remaining within him yet, notwithstanding the pains he endured nor the sorrow he felt at his bereavement, there was no cessation of his labours. In 1799, Thomas Charles and he edited and published *Y Drysorfa Ysbrydol* [*The Spiritual Treasury*]. Six issues were produced between April 1799, and December 1801; its publication came to an end probably because of Mr Charles's illness. From a letter written by Mr Jones it seems also that he had something to do with the bringing out of the *Rules and Design of the Private Societies* that was published in 1801. Previously, in 1790, he had published a Welsh and English dictionary that for years was considered the standard work and reprinted many times. As well as these literary endeavours, Mr Jones was certainly assisting Mr Charles a great deal with the Circulating Schools; his letters to Thomas Charles show that this was the case; it seems that he superintended the schools and helped in the work of finding schoolmasters.

The friendship between the two men was very deep; they were very similar in temperament, very nearly the same age, and both of them suffered greatly with their health. As proof of their friendship we include one of Thomas Charles's letters to Thomas Jones, sent in answer to a note from Mr Jones, and dated 12 February 1801:

> My very dear friend,
>
> Am grieved to hear of your several complaints; especially of your old disease, which, it would seem, inclines you to go a second time under the hands of the doctors. I have no doubt that the Lord will support you through all, and direct you as to what to do. I am able to sympathize with you and to pray for you; but advise you I cannot... While I live, my desire is that the few friends I have may live with me. My mind is not ready to part with you, my dear brother, though I am fully confident that that would be a great gain to you. I expect the Lord will direct you to some means, which he will think fit to bless, to lengthen out your stay and to increase your usefulness. Yet, in this, perhaps, as well as in other things, I may be called to deny myself and to submit. As soon as I am able to travel, I hope to visit you.
>
> Yours faithfully,
> T. CHARLES

When we remember how moderate Thomas Charles always was with words, this letter reveals the depth and sincerity of feelings towards his friend.

It is seen that the letter refers to Thomas Jones's intention of 'placing himself a second time in the hands of the doctors'. This intention was carried out in April 1801, but when the surgeon arrived at the house and examined him, he was not convinced that a stone was present. It was therefore thought best not to proceed. Within a year however, that is, on 20 April 1802, the operation was performed successfully; the surgeon removing a very large stone – larger even than the previous stone – from his bladder.[1] He was in danger of losing his life for a time because the wound became infected, but through the use of a leech, the infection eventually cleared. He then quickly recovered and enjoyed better health than he had known since his childhood, he could ride and walk with complete freedom from pain. He made the most of the opportunity, travelling some hundreds of miles before the end of September, as he laboured both home and away in the work of the Lord. In September 1803 he went to London to preach to the Welsh of the city, and he stayed there for four months. He also occasionally preached to English congregations.

Sometime in the year 1783 he preached on the roadside in Llan Nanerch, near the home of a woman who respected the Methodists. Previous meetings there had been disrupted because of the plotting and arrogance of the local clergyman. When Mr Jones was mid-sermon, a gentleman of the neighbourhood passed by on his horse and stopped to ask what was happening. The preacher answered courteously that he was attempting no more than to provide a word of counsel for his fellow-sinners. 'Dear me,' said the gentleman, 'there is no doubt that if the French were to invade the country these people would immediately join them.' Off he hurried to find the local landowner, complaining that such seditious meetings were being allowed. The nobleman sent his steward to the cottagers to rebuke them. He arrived, swearing and blaspheming, and shouting aloud, 'What the devil are you doing, Tom? Allowing these hotheads to gather around the house so as to scare people? My master is determined that you will have to leave because of it, so you had better run and ask his pardon as soon as you can.' The cottager did so, and received his pardon on the condition that he would never allow such meetings again.

HIS SECOND MARRIAGE

In March 1784, after being a widower for six years, Mr Jones married again. His partner was a Miss A. Maysmor, an Englishwoman who could speak a little Welsh and who, at the time, lived not far from Rhuthun. It is said that she was a small woman, full of vitality, possessing the kindest of hearts and well-known for her godliness. Having married, Mr Jones decided to move from Mold, after living there for some eight or nine years. When this intention became known, the church at Caerwys extended to him an urgent appeal that he might consider returning to them. Mr Edwards Jones, his father, had by now died and Pen Uchaf had become his. Though appreciating their kindness, Mr Jones did not respond to their call but made his home in Rhuthun. His labours here were again most useful. The fellowship at Rhuthun and at Pont-uchel considered him as a prince of God among them. But he experienced heavy sorrows here also, because it was not long before Mrs Jones was overcome by a sickness that ended with her death on 15 August 1805, after a married life of sixteen months.

Before Thomas Jones left Mold, he and Thomas Charles had set up a printing press in Bala and appointed Mr Robert Saunderson as the manager of the office. The suggestion of purchasing a press came most probably from Mr Charles, and the office was set up mainly for his advantage, as he was producing his *Bible Dictionary* at the time. We believe that it was Mr Charles also who undertook most of the responsibility for it. But the Rev. Jonathan Jones has proved beyond any doubt that Mr Jones had much to do with the venture. The name of the company at the beginning was Jones and Co., Printing House, and there are two booklets in existence that bear this name. A letter from Thomas Jones to Mrs Charles, dated 8 September, 1804, proves that he was the 'Jones' of the Company. We do not now know why his name rather than Mr Charles's was used. Perhaps it was mainly his money that had been used to set up the press and maintain it. Thomas Jones was by now a considerably wealthy man. As well as the money that had come to him by marriage, he had now inherited Pen Uchaf and other farms from his father, and he was happy to use all for the sake of his kinsmen. Without the wealth that had come to him he would not have been able to publish so many books for they probably did not cover their cost, let alone provide a profit. However Mr Jones's connection with the Bala press did not last long. Mr Charles felt that as he himself was producing such a number of books it would be better if he had sole control of it.

HIS THIRD MARRIAGE

Mr Jones married a third time on 6 October 1806, having been a widower the second time for some fourteen months. His third wife was Miss Mary Lloyd, Tan-y-pendist, Llanrwst. She was a very able woman and known for her musical skills. There are many of her hymn-tunes scattered throughout the issues of the old *Treasury* with her name, Mary Jones, Denbigh, beside them. During these years he gave himself to literary labours. He translated the Fourth Part of Gurnall's *The Christian in Complete Armour*, and was also hard at work on his *Martyrology*, his *magnum opus*. In 1808, he set up his own press at Rhuthun. His main reason for this was, no doubt, in order to have a convenient press near at hand to bring out his own books and other profitable books that he wished to see published. But it is probable also that a disloyal action on the part of a typesetter in Mr Robert Saunderson's office at Bala influenced his decision. When Mr Jones was bringing out his book, *Religious Conversations*, this unprincipled type-setter showed the proofs to the Rev. Owen Davies, the Wesleyan minister against whose views he was arguing. Mr Davies was therefore able to publish his answer to the book almost as soon as it appeared. We cannot but condemn the Rev. Owen Davies severely for being party to such a dishonourable action. Mr Thomas Jones wrote to Chester, to Mr W. C. Jones, the printer, asking him if he knew of anyone who could manage a press. He answered positively: that there was a young man, named Thomas Gee, who had worked for him but was now in London, who could be trusted with the responsibility. A call was sent to London and the young man responded to the call, and thus Thomas Gee's well-known press at Denbigh was established.

While he lived at Rhuthun, Thomas Jones's health was comparatively strong and there was no end to his labours. As well as writing almost continually for the press and caring for the Methodist causes in the town and neighbourhood he would itinerate to preach the gospel and be present at the Monthly Meetings and the Associations. He often attended the Associations of the south as well as those of Gwynedd and was without exception asked to preach and always at one of the best-attended meetings. He was at the Llangeitho Association of 1806. Those who preached with him at that Association were: John Roberts, Llangwm; Michael Roberts, Pwllheli; John Jones, Edeyrn; John Elias, Anglesey; David Jones, Llan-gan; John Ellis, Mold; and David Parry, Llanwrtyd. These were all sons of Anak, and anyone included amongst them must also have been a giant. Again, at the Bala Association of 1809, he preached at six o'clock on the last evening, after Mr John Davies, Nantglyn. The others who had preached during the Association were John Hughes, Pontrobert; Richard Lloyd, Beaumaris; Nathaniel Williams; Watkin Williams; John Jones, Edeyrn; Evan Richardson, Caernarvon; Thomas Richards; John Elias; Robert Jones, Rhoslan; and John Roberts, Llangwm. Mr Jones's presence at Rhuthun proved of great blessing to the cause in the town; it drew the attention of the country towards them and many were added to the numbers of the members and of the congregation. But with the modesty that was typical of him, his only comment on the matter was:

> In Rhuthun I had the privilege of seeing a measure of increase in the congregation where I attended.

However, in the spring of 1809, Thomas Jones left Rhuthun, having lived there for five years, and made his home in Denbigh. He stayed there for the rest of his life, apart from a two-year period at Syrior.

[1] The two operations undergone by Thomas Jones were of course without anaesthetic. During the first, the surgeon discussed the situation with the patient, and during the second, Thomas Jones had to advise the surgeon where to find the stone. The first stone weighed one and three-quarter ounces and the second, two and a quarter ounces. Both stones were still in the possession of the family in 1956.

40

THOMAS JONES, DENBIGH (CONTINUED)

For the last fifteen years of his life, Thomas Jones was caught up in heated controversies and took a leading part in them. This was not natural to one of his temperament. He was a quiet man, mild of spirit and appreciating theological study for his own benefit, but possessing sufficient courage to enter the fray on behalf of God's truths once he realized that this was his duty. On the other hand it must be acknowledged that he was particularly well qualified for debate. He possessed an eagle-like discernment of the weakness of an opponent's position, a completely logical mind, a wealth and clarity of language for expressing his thoughts, a wide knowledge of theology, both doctrinal and historical, and plenty of sharp-edged sarcasm. The Rev. Owen Thomas states that Mr Jones was a very fair debater who would never take advantage of an opponent, other than when he was himself convinced that he possessed a true advantage. At the same time he implies some criticism of him for sometimes attributing unworthy motives to his opponents. The type of opponent with which he was dealing must be borne in mind however and, if this is done, what becomes amazing is the degree to which Mr Jones was able to control his spirit.

THE WESLEYAN CONTROVERSY

We will refer mainly to the Wesleyan controversy. As we have already noted, the Wesleyan mission in Wales began about 1800 and while their missioners were satisfied simply with the preaching of the gospel without attacking the religious bodies that already existed in the land, they were granted a ready acceptance by the Methodists. But they found that they had little hope of gaining proselytes by this method. They therefore endeavoured to undermine the foundations of the Calvinistic denominations. We would not wish on any account to misjudge the Wesleyan missioners. We are ready to acknowledge that they were thoroughly sincere. At the same time it must be said that their denominational zeal was greater than their knowledge and that they misrepresented the Calvinistic doctrines atrociously, attributing to the Calvinists beliefs that they had never entertained and would not wish to entertain. The root of the Wesleyan ministers' errors was to be found in their belief that the Calvinists held to the views that they (the Wesleyans) considered the necessary conclusions of Calvinistic doctrine. No man is responsible for the conclusions that his opponents draw from his statements. The first publications inaugurating the controversy were by Christmas Evans and Benjamin Jones, the first a Baptist and well known throughout Wales as a preacher, and the second a minister with the Congregationalists. Their works appeared in 1804.

The debate had run its course for some two to three years before Mr Jones entered the lists. About the beginning of the year 1806, he published an essay of about 72 pages defending Calvinistic doctrine and bearing the title, *Drych Athrawiaethol* [*The Doctrinal Mirror*]. In his autobiography he stated the motives that lay behind the work:

> About the end of the previous year [1805], on the occasion of the multiplying of Arminian sectaries in Wales, with some of them, by their sermons and various small pamphlets, caricaturing untruthfully the doctrines that they sometimes called Calvinism and sometimes Antinomianism, I had, being persuaded by my brethren, brought out a short essay entitled *A Doctrinal Mirror*, and had promised a further, extended essay on the same subject. In these, my goal was to portray true doctrine in its simplest form, as revealed in the Scriptures, and according to the understanding of the true Church, or that of the most correct representatives of the Church, from the apostolic age to the time of the Reformation and beyond.

For all the brevity of the essay, Owen Thomas describes it as 'a masterpiece of composition'. In it, Mr Jones shows that he was a true scholar and an able and thorough theologian. He also revealed in it his characteristic philosophy, namely the value and importance he attributed to the judgment of the Christian Church upon the doctrines of the faith, from the days of the apostles onwards. He deals cogently with the 'Five Points', showing that the essential difference underlying the differing views of Arminians and Calvinists arises from their different understandings of the nature of sin. He then proceeds to show that Arminians and Roman Catholics agree with regard to nearly all the points that separate Arminians from Calvinists; he proves that the views of Arminians – including those of Wesleyans – are the same as the heresy of the Morganites [Pelagians] that were opposed so successfully by St David and condemned by the Church. The *Mirror* is written in a very courteous style with very little of a polemical nature about it. It explains the true doctrine by means of able Scriptural exposition and by quotations from the works of the Church Fathers.

As an answer to Thomas Jones, Mr Owen Davies published a book called, *Amddiffyniad o'r Methodistiaid Wesleyaidd* [*A Defence of the Wesleyan Methodists*]. Mr Davies had only a weak grasp of the Welsh language; he therefore wrote in English. He was also unfortunate in his translator. His theological abilities also were only small; he did not understand the Calvinistic principles that he was endeavouring to oppose. And he was a very poor scholar. But he made up for all these deficiencies – at least in the eyes of the ignorant – by the liveliness of his zeal and his oracular claims. In attempting to prove that other Protestants had held to Wesleyan beliefs, he quoted extensively from a book entitled, *Necessary Doctrines and Eruditions for any Christian Man*. But Mr Jones showed that this was a Roman Catholic book: that it contained all the heresies of the Catholics, defending the belief in seven sacraments, the worshipping of idols, transubstantiation, praying to the saints, etc. Owen Davies was not man enough to acknowledge his mistake and to apologize for it. Rather, after confessing that he had never seen the book but only quotations from it, he wrote, 'Whether it be your historian, or my historian, who is closest to the truth, I do not know, nor do I care.' In all the history of controversies it would be difficult to discover a statement that betrays such lack of principle: it is nothing less than a confession that the author does not care whether the arguments he uses are true or false.

Thomas Jones suggested in *The Doctrinal Mirror* that he intended to publish a larger book dealing with the points at issue. This he fulfilled in 1807 with the appearance of, *'Ymddiddanion Crefyddol (rhwng dau gymydog), Ystyriol a Hyfforddd'*, [*'Religious Conversations, between Two Neighbours, Mindful and Instructed, in the form of historical and scriptural debate; together with a few comments on the Letter of Mr Owen Davies to the author; and a proof of the inconsistency of the late Reverend J. Wesley in many topics of doctrine.'*] This is one of Mr Jones's chief works. Though the occasion of its writing was a time of controversy and controversy was responsible for the form of the book, yet its contents convey mature ideas that are thoroughly thought out and it is evidently the product of years of study. Dr Owen Thomas says of this book:

> Not only did we not have in our language at that time anything on these topics and dealing with them in this particular form, that in any way compares with it, but nothing like it has appeared since. Nor do we know of anything in English to compare with it.

Mr Jones's purpose was to defend Calvinistic doctrines partly by means of the history of Christian doctrine, and partly by means of the light of God's Word. It is this book whose proofs Owen Davies succeeded in obtaining, in a most disreputable way, as it was passing through the press, by which he was able to bring out an answer within a month of its publication. Before leaving the *'Religious Conversations'* we must call the reader's attention to one matter which it discusses – a point which will be of considerable importance later – namely, the claim made by Thomas Jones that there exists a difference of opinion amongst Calvinists with regard to the extent of the atonement. While he explains words such as 'world', 'the whole world', 'all', 'every man', as referring to Jews and Gentiles, or all from every nation that have a heart to come to Christ, he yet says:

> ... in this I would not wish to be inflexible, nor too definite in my own mind. I believe that the whole of Adam's race is under great obligation to the second Adam, because 'by him all things consist', *Col.* 1:17. It is because of him, through him and for him that the gospel is proclaimed to all who receive the privilege of hearing it, and it is good tidings of great joy to all people, even though many refuse or misuse it, and even though God foreknew they would do so before he sent it to them. I believe also, that in order to show that all have need of Christ, that ministers of the gospel should exhort all to receive him and so to receive the forgiveness of sins and salvation, through him.

We see that there is a wideness that pertains to Mr Jones's views and that he never tended towards a narrow Hyper-Calvinism.

As mentioned, Mr Davies had his answer ready within a month. He called it, *'Ymddiddanion rhwng Hyffordd a Beread'* [*'Conversations between Two Neighbours, Instructed and Berean'*]. Of this book, Dr Thomas writes:

> ... although it provides the occasional riposte ... we yet feel sorry for Arminianism that it was not more fortunate in its defender, particularly in one that had to encounter Thomas Jones. The carelessness over historical accuracy and the readiness to make completely baseless claims, which were found in Davies' first book, are even more evident here.

However the book is full of wit and accuses Thomas Jones of every kind of libel. In 1808, Mr Jones published his answer to Mr Davies's book: *'Sylwadau ar Lyfr Mr Owen Davies'* [*'Comments on a Book by Mr Owen Davies, namely his Conversations between Instructed and Berean, together with a weighty reward offered to him on fair conditions'*]. Owen Thomas states that this is an abler composition and manifests more spirit and energy than the previous works by Thomas Jones; it also provides useful additions to the historical statements he had previously published. In his introduction to the book Mr Jones made the following comment:

> My conscience testifies before God that it is not to satisfy any selfish desire, nor out of love of controversy, that I sent this further booklet abroad, but with a measure of sincere desire to defend the cause of God and of his truth.

There is no doubt whatsoever of his honesty in this statement. At the same time it must be acknowledged that his spirit was decidedly more bitter within him because of Mr Davies's unfair behaviour and his presumptuous words in accusing his opponent. The following is a quotation from Mr Davies, typical of many others:

> In my judgment, it would not be worse for you to prove from them [that is, from Romans 9 and Ephesians 1] that there is no God, than that he is worse than the devil, which would be true if you could prove your point.

Not even the most heated spirit of controversy could excuse, let alone justify the use of such rash words, and we are not surprised that Mr Jones in his *Comments* retaliates with severe statements. At the end of the book he offers a reward of a hundred pounds to Owen Davies if he could succeed in answering as little as a third of the forty-one questions that he poses to him. It must be acknowledged that such an offer appears strange, but it was an attempt to force Owen Davies to some point, instead of pronouncing on all and sundry, and it must be remembered that these were questions relating to facts that could be easily proved or denied.

Another book by Mr Davies was soon published, bearing the title, *'Sylwadau ar Lyfryn a gyhoeddwyd yn ddiweddar gan Mr Thomas Jones' ['Comments on a pamphlet published recently by Mr Thomas Jones, late of Ruthin. In these Comments Untruths are laid bare, and truth defended'*]. Owen Thomas says of this book:

> This composition is abusive throughout. It is completely unworthy of the important and dignified position of its author as representing his denomination at the time; unworthy also of the exalted topics to which reference is made occasionally, although it can hardly be said that they are under discussion here. There is no indication of any attempt at answering Jones's book, except by means of wild and open-ended claims, without any shadow of justification.

Soon after the publication of these *Comments*, Thomas Jones brought out a reply to them. Its title was: *'Ateb Byr i Bapyrlen o Sylwadau a wnaed yn ddiweddar gan Mr Owen Davies'* [*'A Short Answer to a Pamphlet written lately by Mr Owen Davies, on a Booklet published by T. Jones, in September, 1808'*]. This Short Answer consists only of twelve pages but is full of discerning comments. Mr Davies wrote a further letter but of such an unworthy nature and so full of abuse and libel, without any attention to the points under discussion, that Mr Jones paid no attention to it.

The controversy continued throughout the remaining years of Thomas Jones's life (and for some years afterwards) but he took no further part in it. His aim was not to argue but to defend that which he considered to be the truth of the gospel, and when the debate deteriorated into abuse, and he had already explained his own views, he withdrew from the battle. We believe that his books far excel all others published at the time in their strength of argument, scholarship, depth of thought, and appreciation of scriptural truth. From one standpoint Mr Jones's great care for accuracy and his profound conscientiousness were disadvantages in debate. His opponent cared little whether his claims were true or false; having been driven out of one hole when it was shown to be a refuge of lies, he would fly quite shamelessly to another false position and continue his barking from there as if he were Sir Oracle himself. And his shamelessness and vituperation fooled the ignorant into believing that the worst argument was the best argument. But to Mr Jones, an incorrect historical claim had the effect of salt on a wound, and it was a pity in one sense that he had condescended to debate with a man of Owen Davies's nature. It is not our purpose presently to decide which of the evangelical Arminianism of the Wesleyans or the moderate Calvinism of the Methodists is closest to the Biblical truth, but rather to show that Thomas Jones presented to Welsh people the ablest books in their language on the subject, and that as far as any reasonable judgment decides such matters, he emerged from the debate as victor. We should add that in 1809 he published *'Cyfieithiad o Gatecism Eglwys Loegr'* [*'A Translation of the Church of England Catechism'*], and his purpose in this, we are sure, was to show that the theology of the Established Church is Calvinistic.

HIS COURAGEOUS LEADERSHIP WITHIN THE CONNEXION

While Mr Jones was about to end his engagement with Mr Owen Davies and the Wesleyans, he found himself caught up in the ferment of another controversy within his own Connexion. We are referring to the controversy over Ordination. We have already narrated the history of this debate and need not repeat it here. We may note however that, with the exception of the bitter separation between Harris and Rowland, this was the most critical argument that has arisen in the history of Welsh Methodism, and that the Connexion was never in greater danger of dividing than at this time. The main advocates for Ordination were Ebenezer Morris in the south and Thomas Jones in the north. Mr Jones displayed remarkable courage and strength of will; by baptizing a child in Denbigh at the request of the church and congregation when he himself had not been ordained by the Connexion to administer the sacraments, he brought matters to a head, so that the issue had to be decided one way or the other. He must have endured considerable persecution at this time, and at the hands of his own brethren; every kind of wrong motive was attributed to him and a cloud arose, to some extent, over his friendship with Thomas Charles. But neither the frowns of his opponents nor the dismay of his friends could dissuade him from the path pointed out to him by his conscience. He soon regained his former position of respect in the minds of his brethren and his relationship with Mr Charles was fully restored when the debate came to an end. The two men continued in devoted friendship, like David and Jonathan, while they both lived. We have already noted that Thomas Jones was numbered amongst those set aside to administer the sacraments in that first ordination at Bala.

While he was at Denbigh he proved himself an able statesman who was not to be terrified by every bogey raised in order to stir up the people. In 1812 the issue of Roman Catholic emancipation was agitating the country. The majority of the Methodists were firmly opposed to the measure; they feared for their religious freedom; they believed that to pass the Parliamentary Bill being debated would lead to the rekindling of the fires of Smithfield. No one was fiercer in his opposition than the Rev. John Elias. A nobleman from Denbighshire drew up a petition against the Bill and sought to obtain the signatures of all the religious congregations of the region, Dissenters and Established Church, before presenting it to the two Houses of Parliament. The petition was brought to Thomas Jones. He hesitated to sign it; and though he eventually agreed, he published a strong protest against much of its content. He insisted that he was an inveterate enemy of all the heresies of the Roman religion, that he supported the British Constitution and wished to safeguard the religious liberties of Protestants. But he also stated his firm belief that greater liberties could quite safely be granted to Roman Catholics, especially in Ireland; that clear promises had been given by the Government to Catholics; that everything that tended to promote dissatisfaction and strong feelings should be removed; and that it was in this light that he wished his signing of the petition to be understood. It is clear that he was far ahead of his time in his views on religious liberty and he had to bear the punishment that inevitably falls upon such men. He was denounced as a Papist and abused by men immeasurably smaller than himself. He would not allow himself to be troubled by them, and the storm passed without any great agitation of his feelings.

In 1813 he brought out his major literary achievement, a work over which he had been labouring for many years. This was *'Hanes y Merthyron yn Mhrydain Fawr'* [*'A History of the Martyrs of Great Britain, together with the chief Martyrs of Scotland and of Foreign Lands, and a clear and accurate proof of those religious Principles for which they fought'*]. The book contained 1,165 quarto pages, and was printed by himself at Denbigh. In his Foreword to the *'Martyrology'*, as he called the book, he states that he believed that the Welsh needed a book of this type:

> 1. That they might be better informed of the histories and principles of these famous men, the martyrs, and faithful sufferers, who laboured and were instrumental in liberating our land from the darkness and heresies of Popery.
>
> 2. In order to increase their knowledge of Church History, or the History of the Church of Christ, generally.

We are sorry that we do not have the leisure to discuss this magnificent book at length. Dr Thomas says of it:

> In its field this is, without argument, the best book ever published in our language. We doubt whether in any language there exists a more complete, or even as complete a discussion of the various topics considered.

We are able to add that the book was very well received. It immediately gained its place as a classic. It is to be found in the library of every minister and every elder who can afford to buy it. The instinctive opposition felt in Wales towards Popery, and everything else that bears its image, must be attributed to some degree at least to this book.

Early in the year 1814 Thomas Jones published *'Hymnau Newyddion ar amryw Fesurau'* [*'New Hymns on various metres, and designed for various occasions'*]. He himself was the author of these hymns. There are 97 in the book, amounting to 341 verses. They are eminently scriptural and full of a devotional spirit, and worthy to be numbered amongst the highest class of hymns. Many of them are today to be found in the collections of every orthodox denomination in the land. It is stated on the frontispiece that the book was printed by Thomas Gee. We may conclude therefore that by this time Mr Jones had sold the press to Mr Gee. During this year Thomas Charles died and Mr Jones felt his loss greatly. Upon him, of necessity, fell the responsibility of writing a biography of Mr Charles, and this book appeared in January 1816.

During these years Mr Jones's health was comparatively strong and he gave himself as much as he could to itinerating with the work of preaching. He attended the Associations in the north and was present at the Llangeitho Association of August 1814. He preached at the foremost service, that is, the ten o'clock meeting of the last day of the Association. The preachers at the other meetings were Henry Jones, Llaneurwg; John Roberts, Llangwm; Edward Watkin, Llanidloes; David Rees, Llanfynydd;

John Evans, New Inn; John Elias; John Jones, Tremadog; James Hughes, Lleyn; and John Jones, Edeyrn. The fact that he was placed first out of such a list of giants is proof of the high position he occupied amongst his brethren. During this Association two famous men were ordained: Thomas Richards, Fishguard, and David Griffiths, Llantood. This was the third ordination service held in the south by the Methodists and the first at Llangeitho. The order of the service was as follows: a reading and prayer from the Rev. Thomas Jones; the usual questions put by the Rev. John Williams, Lledrod, and the Rev. William Howells, Long Acre, concluding in prayer.

HIS OPPOSITION TO HYPER-CALVINISM

We now arrive at the most important period in Mr Jones's history and at the occasion of the priceless service that he rendered to the Methodist Body and indeed to all Wales. Had he not stood in the breach at this time and shown such courage and ability while defending the Calvinistic doctrine with regard to the greatness of Christ's atonement and the sincerity of God's call in the gospel, the likelihood is that a Hyper-Calvinism of a peculiarly narrow and barren strain might have taken possession of the land to a large extent. The Methodist Fathers were never, at first, Hyper-Calvinists, as we have previously shown. The doctrine that was undoubtedly believed among them was that of the Articles of the Established Church, and in agreement with these they preached Jesus Christ as a sufficient Saviour for the whole world, inviting all to him. One need only read the journal of Howell Harris, the sermons of Daniel Rowland, and the hymns of William Williams, to see that they laid down no limits to the value of the Saviour's sacrifice. But just as one extreme always produces the opposite, many of the Calvinists, in the warmth of their zeal against the Wesleyans, claimed that there was no universal aspect to the call of the gospel; that the elect alone were to be called; so that one old minister could declare publicly:

> If I knew who here today was predestinated to eternal life I would not say one word to the rest.

They thus turned the doctrine of election to the disadvantage of the sinner, making it a barrier against him as he sought to lay hold of eternal life, rather than its being to his advantage. Furthermore, they limited the merit of the atonement, presenting it as if it were a commercial transaction – a price for a price – claiming that it was not sufficient for any but the elect. If we were asked how it became possible that Methodist preachers could harbour ideas that were so opposed to the original beliefs of the Connexion, we would refer to two facts that offer some degree of explanation: the first, the fact that there was no *Confession of Faith* in existence as yet; and secondly, that the Rev. Thomas Charles, who was considered to be a guardian of the faith and a leader as regards doctrine, had been gathered to his fathers.

It was not only among the Methodists that Hyper-Calvinistic views were beginning to gain an acceptance and to be expressed. The Independents and the Baptists had travelled just as far in the same direction, if not indeed even further. As far as is known, the first to publicize these views in the press was the Rev. Christmas Evans. In 1812 he published a book with the title, *'Neilltuolrwydd y Prynedigaeth'* [*'The Particular Nature of Redemption sought out, taking notice of all it entails'*]. In this book he argues for a commercial, or equivalent, atonement, stating that there is no sufficiency in the sacrifice of Christ other than for those for whom he died. He wrote:

> Not something less, or something more, or something different, but the very thing that was owed, was that which Christ paid . . . The price, or the suffering, had to be equivalent to the measure of the sins, as far as number, weight and extent. Though suffering of an infinite nature were necessary to redeem only one man, even if he were guilty of only one sin, yet if Christ suffered according to the degree of sins, according to their number and weight, according to the demerit of sin, then how this expands our view of his sufferings - equivalent to that which these sins deserved, in all their number and weight, and every degree calling for infinite punishment (beyond what man could bear). Oh, such a deluge of infinite wrath did our Saviour pass through when he bore our curse, that curse which equated to the number and weight of our sins according to the most exact justice!

From the words in brackets we see that what Christmas Evans meant by the term '*infinite*' was '*beyond what man could bear*'; therefore, according to this view, one infinite thing could be greater or less than another. While these opinions, or others similar to them, were spreading amongst the Calvinistic denominations in Wales, a quiet reaction to them was also taking place. Its leaders were the Revs. John Roberts, Llanbryn-mair, and James Griffiths, St David's. In 1804 John Roberts published a small book on the topic called, *'Cynigiad Gostyngedig'* [*'A Humble Attempt at explaining what we are taught in the Scriptures concerning the general and particular purposes of the sufferings of Jesus Christ, in two letters to a friend'*]. The book contains only 24 pages. In it John Roberts defends a moderate Calvinism in which, while agreeing that there is a specific relationship between the death of Christ and the elect, and that it is only by means of the election of grace that those who are to be saved are indeed saved, yet he also states his belief that there is an universal aspect to the atonement, and that it is on the basis of that universality that all men are called to repent and that temporal blessings flow towards mankind.

Up to this point the controversy had not aroused much excitement amongst the Methodists. But about the end of the year 1814, the Rev. John Elias fell into a Hyper-Calvinistic error, expressing very narrow views as to the merit of the atonement. He believed that he had received new light on the matter, and while holding strongly that every minister of the gospel should call on all people to come to Christ because such was the commission that they had received from God, he maintained that the sacrifice of the Saviour was equivalent only to the total demerit of the sins of the elect. Having received this light, as he thought, he composed a sermon on the topic, and as with all of Mr Elias's compositions it was notably able and capable of carrying all before it. He took a short journey through Denbighshire and Flintshire preaching this 'new light'. In particular, he delivered a sermon to the Monthly Meeting at Wrexham. In this sermon he argued for an 'equivalent atonement':

> Not equivalent to the worth of the persons of the elect; nor equivalent to that which they themselves would have suffered eternally in hell; for this would suppose that the salvation provided for them, and of which they would be brought into possession, did not restrain them from sinning extensively in this world; but an atonement equivalent to the evil and dishonour of their sins against God; sufficient, eternally sufficient, on the basis of his Substitution, to satisfy justice for all those given to him by the Father.

He portrayed the atonement of Christ for the persons and sins of his people as being sufficient to balance the scales of justice – holding them in equilibrium with not a hair's-breadth of movement to one side or the other.

> We are used to singing: *'Y gair "Gorffennwyd" wnaeth i'r clorian pwysig droi'* [1] [*'The words "It is finished" caused those momentous scales to swing'*] but we shall not so sing again. No! An atonement is an atonement: sufficient to meet the need; less would have been insufficient, and more would have been unnecessary . . . The sins, all the sins, of his people were laid on Christ; the eye of the omniscient mind discerned the iniquity associated with each one and justice administered to him the punishment each deserved; and when the total wrath due to these sins had been fully poured out upon him and he had drained the last dregs of that cup of God's wrath, then was atonement accomplished and he cried out, 'It is finished.'

While proclaiming these narrow views of the worth of the atonement, he still maintained firmly the universal invitation of the gospel, and he pressed on all the danger of refusing it:

> 'But how is it that you call on everyone?' I do not call. It is God who calls. I am but an ambassador for him, speaking only in his name. 'But how is it that God calls on all, if there is no salvation for all?' What kind of salvation do you want, sinner? Do you expect both salvation and a life of sin in service to the devil? There is salvation in Christ to the greatest, vilest sinner that lives, who would receive it; but there is no salvation to any, whoever they be, who would refuse it.

Such a sermon, preached by a master of the congregation with all the power of oratory of which he was capable, could not but produce an effect. To the Hyper-Calvinists it was the sweetest of feasts to their ears. They were now confident that to bring the whole Association over to their side was only a matter of time.

During his tour John Elias came to Denbigh and the chapel was overflowing. The 'new light' sermon was delivered here also, and unusual influence attended the delivery. As the preacher warmed to his matter the effectiveness of his oratory increased, carrying the congregation with it as with the flow of a river. The people were given no time to meditate and consider the ideas presented – Mr Elias's irresistible fluency made them forget themselves. But Thomas Jones was seated below the pulpit and his soul grieved over the limitation being imposed upon the value of Christ's atonement. His mental agitation brought a physical distress upon him and he had to reach for his hat and push through the press out of the chapel before the completion of the service.

There has been no more dramatic a scene in the whole history of the Connexion, and we are quite certain that the sight of so moderate a man as Mr Thomas Jones, and one so mighty in the Scriptures, turning his back on the meeting because he disapproved of the opinions being expressed, must have checked something of the fluency of the popular preacher from Anglesey. John Elias was lodging at Thomas Jones's house that night and the content of the sermon was hotly disputed by them.

During this discussion they each held strongly to their own views, but at last Elias admitted that in limiting the worth of the atonement he had passed beyond the reach of scriptural teaching and he acknowledged that Christ's sacrifice was to be accounted infinite in a different and higher sense than the infinity of the evil of sins. Before leaving, he promised never again to describe the atonement as being 'sufficient to balance the scales of justice'.

THE RHUTHUN ASSOCIATION OF 1815 AND ITS DECLARATION OF THE INFINITE NATURE OF THE ATONEMENT

By now the Flintshire Monthly Meeting was thoroughly agitated. Mr Elias's sermon had acted as leaven in the bread. The leader of the Hyper-Calvinistic party was the Rev. Robert Ellis, Mold, a man who had once been a minister in the Countess of Huntingdon's Connexion and who had joined the Methodists in 1811. It is said of him that he was a godly man but very narrow in his views and a strong Hyper-Calvinist. Many of the ministers and elders of the Flintshire Monthly Meeting held similar opinions. These decided to bring the matter to the attention of the Association and such was their confidence in Mr Elias that they had no doubts as to the result. They intended to excommunicate those whom they called Arminians, or at least put an end to their opinions. On the other hand, there were other capable men amongst the ministers and elders of Flintshire who clung to Thomas Jones's views, maintaining the infinite sufficiency of the atonement and inviting all sinners to rest in it. Some of this latter group were from Caerwys, Thomas Jones's own home. The issue came before the Rhuthun Association of 3–4 March 1815. It seems that the Hyper-Calvinists were the aggressors and that their arrows were aimed at Mr Jones. They called him a heretic, an agitator, and an Arminian, and they attributed to him the blame for all the excitement and controversy that had arisen in the country. It seems that the bad temper they displayed and the extreme language made use of weakened their arguments and caused John Elias to be ashamed of these who professed to be his followers.

After a while Mr Jones had an opportunity to defend himself and his views. He was deeply serious and solemn. It was realized that both he and the Methodist Connexion had reached a point of crisis and that the discussion under way might produce irrevocable consequences. He argued strongly for the infinite value of the sacrifice of the glorious Mediator, he declared that this was the doctrine he had received from the Connexion, that this was what was preached by Daniel Rowland and Howell Harris, and that this truth was woven throughout all the hymns of William Williams, Pantycelyn. He further argued that the teachings of the Hyper-Calvinists were not only new to the Methodists but as far as he knew were new to the Church of Christ, and that he believed them to be a degradation of the Person of the Saviour and a distortion of the scriptural doctrine of redemption. With reference to the charge that he was an agitator, he said that he had not introduced anything that was new, but that if the views that he believed and preached were unacceptable to his brethren, he would leave quietly. With this he broke out in loud weeping, saying that if the decision of the Association was in favour of this narrow interpretation of the atonement of Christ, he would come to the next Association at Bala with the intention of resigning his office.

By now the whole Association was awash with tears and it was clear from John Elias's face that he was deeply moved. He rose to his feet and with great tenderness of expression declared that he would never wish to change the doctrine of the Association and that he could not bear the thought that Mr Jones might feel uncomfortable in the midst of his brethren, let alone that he might depart from them, and that if he (Mr Elias) had said anything to hurt his feelings he withdrew it immediately and begged him for forgiveness. He then confessed that in the sermon he had preached in Flintshire and Denbigh he had not paid sufficient attention to the words, 'He is the propitiation', 'Who gave himself as a ransom for all', and others similar. 'I now see quite clearly,' he said, 'that the atonement in and of itself is infinite; while it is as equally as clear to me that it was appointed for the Church alone'. With these words from Mr Elias, peace was restored. It was realized that there was no danger of a separation and Mr Jones, Mr Elias, and Mr John Roberts, Llangwm, were appointed to draw up a draft of the matters decided upon, for the next day's meeting.

The following is a report of that meeting, taken from the minutes of Mr Cadwaladr Williams, the secretary of the Association, as published in the *Treasury* of July 1823:

> In the 8 o'clock meeting, March 4, the proceedings of the first meeting of the previous day were read, when the doctrine of redemption had been discussed. The danger of losing the unity of the Spirit was pointed out, so as to avoid any injuring of one another because of differing views; as was the particular necessity for all to have right views of the Person of Christ and his redemption. As concerning redemption, the following was agreed :
>
> 1. That the Person of the Mediator was of immeasurable infiniteness.
> 2. That the atonement effected by him was infinite, in that 'He is the propitiation'.
> 3. That this Person was the substitute for other persons.
> 4. That the sins of these persons were accounted to this infinite Person.
> 5. That the punishment of those sins were laid on this Person.
> 6. That infinite satisfaction for sin had been wrought by this infinite Person.
> 7. That this redemption was according to the predestination and eternal covenant of God.

A warning was given to avoid using groundless and speculative phrases concerning redemption, such as that if there were to have been more persons saved, than were saved, Christ would have had to suffer more and procure a greater satisfaction than he did; or, if more worlds existed, Christ's atonement would be sufficient for those also. It was decided to put aside all arguments and all phrases that might lead to argument and, when preaching, to keep to the clear approach of the Bible.

The importance of this Rhuthun Association cannot be overstated, for in it was obtained a clear declaration, for the first time, of the infinite value and virtue that pertains to the sacrifice of the Lord Jesus, and the Connexion has never, to this day, departed in any direction from this declaration. The tables were turned completely upon the narrow party and they departed from the Association in great disappointment. Instead of being condemned as a heretic, Thomas Jones had emerged as victor. Even Mr Elias, whom they had thought of as an ally, supported him. They were humbled in the Association, the degree of feeling was too great for them to stand before it, and they had been forced to raise their hands in favour of the propositions. But on returning home the old brethren of Flintshire expressed their Hyper-Calvinistic views just as before, and if they could not do so quite as shamefacedly and publicly as previously, these views certainly coloured all their sermons. They were the basis also of their conversations in chapel houses and other places, in which they belittled Thomas Jones, calling him an Arminian and a troublemaker and so on. As a result, Mr Jones wrote a letter to the Llanrwst Association, dated 25 December 1815, in which he complained bitterly at the injury done to the truth, in his opinion, at the hands of some of the brethren, and done to himself also as he sought to defend the truth. This letter was given a kind reception and a thoughtful consideration, and the following was sent in reply to it. Dr Owen Thomas states that Mr Elias composed it and it was then signed by six people, one from every county in Gwynedd. It reads:

Llanrwst, Dec. 29, 1815.

Dear Brother,

We are sorry that your thoughts have been disturbed by that which you mention; and we deeply regret should the remarks of any of us have been the cause of your sorrow. We do not consider you as one who has erred, nor are we pleased that any should call you such. We are not unhappy that you proclaim fully the greatness and worth of the Person of the Mediator; and we believe that we could not, though we exerted ourselves to the utmost of our little abilities, declare the thousandth part of his greatness or worth. Neither do we assign any measure to his sufferings and death, for he is a completely sufficient sacrifice and atonement for all those in whose place He was appointed. And though their sins be innumerable, and the evil of their sins be infinite, yet the infinite nature of his atonement makes it sufficient. And we would not presume to say that the atonement was not sufficient for countless thousands more, should God have appointed him for them and in their place. Kind friend, we love truth and peace, and would so avoid every needless disputing. Peace be to you, brother.

Your brothers in the Gospel,
John Elias, John Roberts [Llangwm],
John Davies [Nantglyn], Robert Ellis [Mold],
John Hughes [Pontrobert], John Jones [Tremadog]

Thomas Jones's biographer states that he was very pleased with this reply in that it revealed that there was no support at all within the Association for those who accused him. In that the Rev. Robert Ellis was one of his chief opponents, it is inexplicable how his name came to be amongst those of the signatories.

At this time the Rev. Thomas Jones was preparing a book on Redemption and in order that he did not include anything that would give just cause for offence to his brethren he decided to offer it to the attention of the Denbigh Association held on 29 February and 1 March 1816. In the committee of the first day, a number of men were appointed to read the book and to report on it in one of the later meetings. During the eight o'clock meeting the next day, these men declared that it contained wholesome and acceptable doctrine and recommended it to the whole Connexion. It is a fairly small book of about 58 pages and as it is included as part of a much larger book published by Mr Jones three years later we will postpone any comments on its contents.

The controversy on the nature of the atonement continued in Gwynedd and, regardless of the decisions of the Association, the members of the 'old school' continued to misrepresent Thomas Jones's views. He therefore decided to compose a sermon on the topic and, having done so, he preached it at the Bala Association of 19 June 1816. The preachers of this Association were: Captain Williams, Chester, and Thomas Richards, Fishguard, on the first afternoon; at six the next morning, Mr Michael Roberts, Pwllheli, and Mr David Evans, Aberaeron; at ten, Mr Jones, Edeyrn, and Mr Jones, Denbigh; at two, Mr Ebenezer Richard and Mr Elias; at six in the evening, Mr Lloyd, Beaumaris, and Mr Richardson, Caernarvon, with Mr Wilks in English between them; at six on the last morning, Mr James Hughes, Lleyn, and Mr Roberts, Amlwch. It may be seen that Mr Jones was given the most honourable position of the Association, and this again shows the respect in which he was held by his brethren. When preaching on the atonement on this occasion he was given a most remarkable service. He spoke in a most glorious way of the majesty of the Person of the Mediator and of the direct connection between the Person and the atonement. The influence upon the vast crowd was considerable. It might be thought that the sight they were afforded of the Son of God giving himself as an atonement for the life of the world was so clear that no controversy as to the value of that atonement would ever again arise.

The Rev. Morris Roberts, Remsen, U.S.A., has given a description of this sermon:

> When I was a boy of about fifteen or sixteen I went to the Bala Association. At the ten o'clock meeting I saw an old, fat man of handsome features, wearing a black cap on his head, standing up to preach on the text 1 John 2:1, 2. He preached on the atonement and especially on its majesty and infinity, both stemming from the majesty of the person whom God had ordained as an atonement, '*He* is the propitiation'. He maintained this strongly and unyieldingly. He mentioned at one point, exerting with all his strength that, 'if he had a strong enough cannon he would shoot the error of an equivalent atonement (or of thinking too narrowly of it) in the forehead, a hundred miles away.' He spoke most soberly, forcibly, and with great effect. The first Sunday after the Association, many of the old members of the church nearest to my lodgings, the Old Congregational Chapel, Llanuwchllyn, spoke much together and the one topic was this remarkable sermon. I remember that all the comments were warm and appreciative, commending it highly, and rejoicing greatly in the doctrine of the infinity of the atonement.

About May 1816, because of the state of his health, Mr Jones moved from Denbigh, having lived in that town for seven years, and made his home at Syrior Goch. Syrior Goch was a mansion near Betws-yn-Rhos, about three miles from Abergele. He did not farm the land here but held a few acres only in order to keep a horse and two or three cows. He believed that the place provided a mixture of sea and mountain air, and that it was possible that he might therefore regain some of his strength there. This does not seem to have occurred; he remained poorly throughout the two years that he spent at Syrior Goch. He still committed himself to all aspects of his ministry however, and with an amazing zeal and energy, when his condition is taken into account. He continued with his literary labours as well as undertaking preaching itineraries. He also held religious meetings every week in his own house when he was at home. These meetings were not called services or sermons because the owner of the house thought foolishly that if this were done the number of people that would gather would bring down the building. But though not called so, these certainly were services, and Thomas Jones would explain the Scriptures, preach, and lead a society at the end of the service. These meetings contributed much to the spread of religion in the locality.

THOMAS JONES AND HENRY REES

Throughout the time that Thomas Jones lived at Syrior Goch he had a servant, a man who afterwards became famous throughout Wales. This was a young man from the neighbourhood of Llansannan, between eighteen and twenty years old, very rustic in his appearance and of a very serious disposition. He had been converted before leaving Llansannan and had made a name for himself amongst his religious brothers and sisters for the warmth and solemnity of his prayers. All believed that his face was set towards the pulpit; many surmised that his purpose in working as a servant for Mr Jones was in order to learn how to be a preacher and some were surprised that he had chosen someone who was not generally considered to be gifted as a teacher.

This young man was Henry Rees. He had not yet begun the great work of his life, nor did he do so until nearly a year after leaving Thomas Jones's service. Rarely did a servant have such a variety of tasks. He was the door-keeper for the religious meetings held at Syrior Goch; he was responsible for his master's favourite horse; it was expected that he make himself useful about the house; but his main responsibility was to be a 'traveller' for Mr Jones, taking invoices to book-sellers and collecting monies from them. According to Mr Rees:

> I was by now quite a great traveller, on my master's errands, sometimes carrying a considerable amount of money, and I was often very worried over its safety.

On these journeys the servant would ride his master's horse and because he was at times careless, often falling into a daydream, the horse would often stumble under him and he would be thrown into the ditch. Mercifully he suffered no harm from these dangerous falls. His time with Thomas Jones certainly proved of immense benefit to Henry Rees. His master's library was at his service and though he could not gain much from the English authors he read the Welsh books avidly, and in this way a new period in his life was begun.

A close friendship existed between Mr Jones and his servant and the former sympathized greatly with Harry's hopes for the ministry. According to Henry Rees:

> In those months, my desire to preach strengthened continually. I remember a day when I was on my own in the cowshed and meditating on some topic and when, without thinking, I began to express my thoughts out loud, and with some degree of energy. Unfortunately for me, someone overheard me, and the word got round immediately to Mr Jones that I was preaching to the cattle. When I got back to the house, he presently came through from the parlour to the kitchen, and walking back and forth as was his habit he eventually quietly asked me, his tone a mixture of the serious and the playful, whether I had had a good service in the cowshed? Had I preached well? My whole nature shrank from his questions. I blushed and said nothing. 'Well, well,' he said at last, in a not unkindly tone, 'the mind and the imagination work strongly at times, don't they, Harry?'

The story shows that master and servant were on good terms.

But we must return to the history of the Rev. Thomas Jones. In May 1817 he was called upon to deliver the annual sermon of the London Missionary Society. His text was Isaiah 52:15, 'So shall he sprinkle many nations.' The sermon was published in English by the Society at their expense; he translated it into Welsh and it was published after his death. John Elias was in London at the time and he and Mr Jones met at the home of Mr Matthew Wilks, one of the directors of the Society. Mr Jones asked Mr Wilks whether he should read the sermon or depend on his memory. Mr Wilks answered that it might be better for him to read it as it was such an important gathering. 'But remember,' he added, 'make sure that you include in it plenty of Welsh fire.' 'What?' said John Elias, 'Carry fire with paper! It cannot be done.' 'Very true,' said Mr Wilks, 'but paper is excellent material for lighting a fire.' It is not now known whether Mr Jones did read the sermon or not, but it was a substantial composition and made a deep impression on the minds of those who heard it.

Immediately on his return from London, Thomas Jones attended the Bala Association of 16–17 June 1817. There were men to be ordained at this Association – the fifth ordination service to be held at Bala. Mr William Roberts, Amlwch, and Mr Cadwaladr Williams, Anglesey, were set aside for the work of the ministry. It is not known if Mr Jones took part in the service but he was one of those who preached in the open air. The following is the order of the preaching. The first afternoon: Michael Roberts, Pwllheli, and David Griffiths, Llantood. At six on the morning of the main day: Richard Jones, Wern. At ten: John Jones, Edeyrn, and Ebenezer Morris. At two: Evan Richardson, Caernarvon, and John Elias. At six: Richard Lloyd, Beaumaris, and Thomas Jones. This was the last Bala Association that Mr Jones attended.

HYPER-CALVINISTIC VIEWS CONTINUE TO BE EXPRESSED

During the period Mr Jones lived at Syrior Goch the disagreement within the Connexion over Hyper-Calvinistic views continued. Though the proponents of such views had been defeated in the Association they did not cease to preach them and they were very bitter against Thomas Jones. In the pulpit and out of the pulpit they accused him of Arminianism, they took advantage of every opportunity to abuse him, they held him up as one who introduced novel ideas to the Body, so that many good men were persuaded to view him with suspicion. We believe that the brethren who did this were completely honest, and they probably considered that they were doing God a service. But whatever their motives, the means that they employed were unworthy. The leaders in transgression were the preachers of Flintshire, with the Rev. Robert Ellis, Mold, at the van. This man abused Henry Rees brutally on one occasion when he called at his home on an errand for Mr Jones. As soon as he had entered Mr Ellis asked him, 'What poison is your master mixing for the country presently?' The question struck Henry Rees as being so unkind and unchristian, and particularly so completely inappropriate from an older minister to a young man, that he did not know what answer to return. However, he ventured to say politely, 'I hope that my master is not in the habit of mixing any poison, nor of dealing with any who do so.' 'Mix it he does!' cried he, 'And you go about distributing it over the country.' For all the gentleness of Henry Rees's nature, he was stung by the old minister's words, and he answered back, 'If it is poison, then that poison has been recommended by the Rhuthun Association. And I do not believe that it is poisonous to anything except error.' 'Ah,' said Mr Ellis, 'I see that it has poisoned you.' Years afterwards, when Mr Rees related this story, he would say, 'Whatever we think of Mr Jones's views – and I believe that they were correct – I am quite certain that his spirit was better than Robert Ellis's.'

Because some preachers were persisting to make use of inappropriate phrases with respect to the atoning work of Christ, phrases that tended to limit and diminish its worth, Mr Jones sent a letter to the Caernarvon Association held at the beginning of October 1816, complaining of them. We are sorry that no copy of this letter has survived but the Association's reply was as follows:

Caernarvon, October 4th, 1816

Dear Brother,

We received and read your kind and mournful letter. We were sorry to hear of your impaired health, and of your troubled mind. We discussed the matter referred to in your letter very fully. Though we inquired, we failed to find any evidence that the Body is deviating in any way from the orthodox views of the infinity of the Person and atonement of the Mediator. If some have used unwise and inappropriate words in the past, yet all, in this present meeting, have bound themselves not to use any forms of expression in the future that might provoke controversy; hoping that you also will do likewise. If, from now on, you hear of any person or persons, using any inappropriate words of the Mediator's atonement do not hold it against the Body, but note that man that he may be called to account, either in the Monthly Meeting or in the Association. We most warmly wish you every success, and we would request, most respectfully, that you do not receive nor believe every tale that you hear of the brethren from those who would colour the situation more than is necessary. Time does not allow us to enlarge. We all, with one accord, wish to be remembered to you, sincerely desiring for you every success.

I remain, on behalf of the Body,

Ever your unworthy Friend,

ROBERT JONES

This letter was written by the Rev. Robert Jones, Rhoslan, and it is clearly the fruit of some considerable discussion. It suggests many interesting points:

1. That the Association, as such, had put away forever any idea of an equivalent atonement, and had taken an unalterable stand for the truth of an infinite atonement.

2. That a clear distinction was being made between the *'some'* and *'the Body'*. It is acknowledged that *'some'* have used unwise and inappropriate words – the reference is, no doubt, to the Hyper-Calvinists of Flintshire – but it is claimed that *'the Body'* is wholly free of any association with them in this. By *'the Body'* is meant the Connexion when gathered corporately in Monthly Meetings and Associations.

3. There is found here a gentle suggestion that some were carrying tales to Mr Jones and portraying events in a much darker light than was the case, and that he was too ready to believe their tales. To what extent this was true we do not know.

During this Association at Caernarvon, two men distinguished themselves. One was the Rev. Ebenezer Morris, the ablest member of the Connexion in the south, who exerted all his influence for the cause of peace. The other was the Rev. Richard Jones, Wern, who manifested for the first time his remarkable ability to quieten strife and to expound the truth. At the same time there is reason enough to judge that this Association was lacking in courage, in that they allowed those who were accusing Thomas Jones to escape without rebuke. And perhaps, had the required rebuke been administered, much of the later trouble that arose in Gwynedd might have been avoided.

These general decisions of the Association did not however put a stop to the comments of those who harboured narrow views of the atonement of Christ. They continued preaching the same doctrines, they denied that the gospel offered any call except to the elect and that the merit of the price paid was sufficient only for them, and they charged all who thought otherwise with being rank Arminians. The preachers travelled constantly in those days so that men from Gwynedd would often visit the south. The Hyper-Calvinists of the north would proclaim their views blatantly while itinerating in the south, and as these opinions had never been heard previously in the southern regions they occasioned considerable excitement and strife. The southern men felt that they were being assailed by 'another gospel', and feared that a rapid departure from the faith was occurring in the north. As a result it was decided in an Association held at Llangeitho, August 1817, to send the Revs David Rees, Llanfynydd, and Ebenezer Richard as representatives to the next Association in Gwynedd, in order to receive a final answer from the gathered brethren there on the point at issue. Their mission included the delivery of a further statement declaring that they could not see how the unity of the Body between the two provinces could be kept while some were given licence to go about, without any rebuke, preaching against the all-sufficiency and infinity of the atonement of Christ. Notice of this decision had been sent beforehand to Mr Cadwaladr Williams, the secretary of the northern Association, and such a statement, coming from the likes of David Charles, Carmarthen, Ebenezer Richard, and Thomas Richard, his brother, was certain to be received in Gwynedd as of the greatest importance.

The Association in the north thus found itself again in a critical position. It was clear that they could no longer continue to issue general statements and general calls for peace, while at the same time allowing intractable brethren to preach their narrow views with impunity, thereby trampling underfoot the decisions of the Association. The situation was judged to be so serious that, sometime before the Pwllheli Association, a meeting of the senior ministers in the north was held at Bangor to discuss the matter. Many made the journey to Bala and the Rev. Robert Jones, Rhoslan, was appointed chairman. Thomas Jones failed to be present because of bad health. All were aware of the seriousness of the occasion and therefore spoke circumspectly and with moderation. The Rev. John Elias was the man of greatest influence in north Wales at the time and it was to him that they looked for guidance during any crisis. He, however, was reluctant to speak, particularly because of the absence of Mr Thomas Jones. After some pressure, he agreed to speak a word. It was clear that he was troubled in mind and very aware of the difficulty of the situation. He was only half persuaded of the inappropriateness of using the word 'equivalent' when describing the atonement and it was against his will, as it were, that he had ceased using it. He must also have been aware that he had been responsible for stirring up much of the controversy by the sermon of his to which we have already referred. He began his address with a mild complaint against Mr Jones. He said that Mr Jones had quoted some phrases from his sermon, phrases for which he had expressed his sorrow, both to Mr Jones personally and to the fraternity at Rhuthun, and had retracted. He then attempted to prove that the idea of an equivalent atonement was not a new, strange doctrine to the Methodists but was to be found in Mr Charles's *Bible Dictionary,* and he read a long quotation out of that book as proof. He then acknowledged that the connotations of the word 'equivalent' were not to be found in Scripture, and that he therefore would not make use of it further, nor had he done so since the Rhuthun Association. He spoke moderately, for about an hour, seeking to assuage every wounded feeling and, as much as was in him, to maintain the unity of the Body

Once he had finished, the Rev. Richard Jones, Wern, who was beginning to make his mark as an able theologian and a skilful debater, stood up, and delivered a remarkably effective address. Dr Owen Thomas provides an account:

> At one point during his comments, he referred to the use made of the word 'equivalent':
>
> 'I have nothing against the word, as long as we understand to what it is 'equivalent'. Equivalent to the honour of the Eternal King; equivalent to the 'glory of God'; 'without spot to God'. Here is something infinitely greater than the whole creation, in all its immeasurable vastness, insomuch as the Creator is greater than the creature. The tragedy of man as a sinner is that he has 'come short of the glory of God'; and the perfection of the sacrifice of Calvary, which arises from the infinite majesty of that glorious Person who sacrificed himself, is that it was 'without spot to God.' Sufficient! ever sufficient! to answer all the claims of justice, and to fill the heart of the infinite Godhead.'
>
> As he continued in this vein, and before he had time to complete what he had to say, such a glorious light illuminated the truths being described that all those present began to weep, and the Chairman, the venerable Robert Jones, having lost all control, was shouting, 'My Lord and my God!' and all, with one accord, were ready to put aside all narrowness of thought and to bear the

strongest witness, in the most determined fashion, to the infinity of Christ's sacrifice.

In this manner, to the sound of weeping and praising, this important meeting at Bangor concluded. As far as we can discover, no decisions were taken at the meeting; but something much more important than a decision was obtained, namely, an unction from the Holy One to know the truth and to bind together the hearts of brethren. All arrived at the Association with rejoicing spirits, feeling that the storm was blowing over and the threatening clouds scattering. Having arrived at Pwllheli, the two brothers from the south were waiting for them; so also was a letter from Mr Thomas Jones again complaining that some of the brethren were making use of belittling language when describing the atonement of Christ and calling upon the Association to put in place effective measures to stop such behaviour. No disagreements seem to have taken place; they confirmed the decisions taken at the Bala Association of 1809. The following letter was sent to Mr Jones:

Pwllheli, October 1st, 1817.

Dear Brother,

We received your letter, which was read in the eight o'clock Committee. It was listened to, and its contents considered, with care. The greatest concern and kindness towards yourself in your tribulation, were also expressed. Much dissatisfaction was manifested towards those who use phrases such as: 'Were there *more* to be saved, then Christ would have had to *suffer* more', etc., and all similar phrases which tend to limit the INFINITY OF THE PERSON, HIS SACRIFICE, OR HIS ATONEMENT. In the ten o'clock meeting, some persons who had been guilty of using the said phrases were called to account, and they received the warning meekly, promising to put them aside from now on. Furthermore we read out, from the *Treasury*, that which we agreed upon in an Association nine years ago. It was judged that those statements on the redemption constituted a centre point or plan of the right expression of the doctrine of the redemption, when speaking on it. And in case any should hold to opinions on the matter which differ to some degree, it was ruled that no one should so express themselves in any way that might suggest that there was any disputation amongst us. Acknowledging that we are all, here, subject to much imperfection, we earnestly encouraged each other to forbear one another in love.

I am, on behalf of the Association,

Your unworthy Brother,

GABRIEL DAVIES

Dr Owen Thomas states that the decision of the Association fully satisfied the Association in the south and was a great relief to Mr Jones. In his *'Ymddiddanion ar Brynedigaeth'* [*'Conversations upon Redemption'*] which was reprinted with additions a couple of years later, Thomas Jones made the following comment in the Foreword:

> To God be the thanks that he not only gave support for the burden, as for many other burdens (notwithstanding my wretchedness and great unworthiness) but that he also provided great relief, by inclining the minds of my brethren (in an Association) against 'this flatterer and alien blasphemer', (the 'new and maligning view of Christ' to which he had referred a few lines previously). They there, with great seriousness, came to the decision: 'that the sacrifice of Christ is to be accounted truly infinite in worth'.

The 'flatterer and alien blasphemer' was the novel doctrine that limited the worth of the atonement.

In this way the infinite value of the sacrifice of Christ and its sufficiency for a world of lost sinners was established as the doctrine of the Methodists. It is a doctrine that, as far as we know, has never been questioned since in any Association, though it has not perhaps been given sufficient emphasis in the Confession of Faith. It became from this time onwards a truth that was believed without question by the Body, though some individuals remained Hyper-Calvinistic. And the honour of ensuring that this was so belongs to the Rev. Thomas Jones. He fought for it in season and out of season; he defended this truth in the pulpit and through the press with invincible force, until the mouths of all opposers were stopped. He suffered for it as far as his character and his feelings were concerned, but notwithstanding all, and while in considerable ill-health, he succeeded in obtaining from the Association a clear and definite declaration in its favour – a declaration that has not been revoked to this day. If it were only for this, Thomas Jones deserves to be listed amongst the foremost heroes of the Connexion.

It is true that he had considerable support, particularly from the Revs. Richard Jones, Wern, and Ebenezer Morris, but the greatest burden of the battle fell upon himself. It is necessary to remember also that the brethren of the south were of his mind throughout the controversy and this must have been a major encouragement to him. Some two years later, when he was publishing his second edition of *Conversations on Redemption*, he sent a letter to the Association at Llangeitho, held on 18–19 August 1819, in respect of his writings, and he received the following reply from the secretary of the Association, the Rev. Ebenezer Richard:

> Dear and Reverend Brother, we received your kind and fraternal letter at the Llangeitho Association, and it was read before all the preachers and elders. After seriously considering the contents it was agreed unanimously that all of what you have published is particularly acceptable to the Body throughout south Wales.

Mr Jones's sojourn at Syrior Goch did not bring about the recovery of health for which he had hoped and therefore, in May 1818, he returned to Denbigh to live and remained there until his death. It was a great advantage to him to be close at hand to the press but his move proved a great loss to the cause at Betws, and to Henry Rees in particular. In his support of the young man's desire to preach he had begun to give him English lessons. His valuable library was also available for the aspiring preacher. Mr Jones continued to feel an interest in Henry after his return to Denbigh, as the following story shows. In the Monthly Meeting held at Denbigh, 4–5 February 1819, Henry Rees was being received as a preacher. The Rev. John Roberts, Llangwm, happened to be present, and even though he was a member of the Merionethshire Monthly Meeting, yet because of his experience and seniority he was asked to speak to the young man. And Mr Roberts was particularly heavy-handed on young ministers. John Elias had suffered much under him at the beginning of his ministry. Unfortunately, Henry Rees had broken the rules, having preached outside the circle of the Monthly meeting at the request of Mr John Williams, Meidrim, Carmarthenshire. The old brother from Llangwm began to attack him severely. Peter Roberts, Llansannan, sought to defend him, explaining that most of the blame was due to John Williams for compelling him to preach. But John Roberts would have none of that; he continued to rebuke him mercilessly. Thomas Jones could take no more. He got to his feet in great weakness and said, with a voice full of tears, '*Harri bach*, don't you break your heart, but keep on strongly in the power of the Spirit of the Lord, no matter who opposes you, or however much you have to suffer.' Having said this, he was overcome by his emotions and had to sit down. The old brother's respect for Mr Jones was without measure, he immediately withdrew his horns and Mr Henry Rees was received as a member of the Monthly Meeting with no further opposition.

'CONVERSATIONS UPON REDEMPTION'

Towards the beginning of October 1819, Mr Jones brought out his second edition of *'Conversations upon Redemption'* in which much new material had been added to the first edition. The book also contained an Appendix, *'Sylwadau Gwahanol'* [*'Various Comments on two booklets, one tending towards a degree of Generality in the Redemption; and the other tending to the opposite, which is much worse, and setting a limit to the merit of Christ's Sacrifice!'*]. Dr Owen Thomas states:

> This book is notable in the history of the Welsh theological controversies not only because of the ability it demonstrates and the wealth of theology found in it, but particularly because of the arguments and unhappy feelings which were aroused by its publication.

The booklet *'tending towards a degree of Generality in the Redemption'* was the work of the Rev. John Roberts, Llanbryn-mair, to which we have already referred. The difference between Mr Jones and Mr Roberts was not great. Both laid considerable emphasis on the infinite worth of the Saviour's sacrifice and upon the special and particular relationship between it and the elect. They differed over the following aspects:

1. Mr Roberts held that the Lord Jesus in dying purchased temporal blessings for all mankind. In other words, that it is on the basis of the sufferings of the Lord Jesus that temporal blessings are provided for the ungodly as well as the godly and that 'the common mercies of providence proceed along the path of the blood'. Mr Jones, on the other hand, believed that the phrase 'purchasing blessings' was inappropriate; that what Jesus purchased in dying was the persons of his people. He considered the continuance of mankind after the Fall, together with the administration of sufficient temporal blessings to maintain that continuance, as the product of the original covenant between the Creator and our first parents, and the fruit of God's general goodness. But he acknowledged that it was because of the mediatorial reign of the Son of God that the world possesses such a fullness of comforts, so that ultimately the gulf between himself and Mr Roberts was not great. The argument gradually became one of phraseology: whether it was appropriate to say that the Lord when dying purchased blessings. Thomas Jones's view has been incorporated in the well-known verse written by the Rev. James Hughes, London:

> 'Twas not heaven or the blessings that Christ purchased on the cross,
> But a multitude of sinners, when He suffered pain and loss;
> He, the fount of every blessing, had no need to purchase more;
> 'Twas the elect of God he purchased when our guilt and sins he bore.
>
> Nid y nefoedd na'r bendithion, brynodd Iesu ar y groes;
> Ond fe brynodd fyrdd o ddynion, pan ddioddefodd angau loes;
> 'Roedd e'n ffynnon pob bendithion, nid oedd achos prynu rhai'n,
> Prynu wnaith yr etifeddion, pan goronwyd ef â drain.

2. Mr Roberts argued that the same relationship exists between the blood of Jesus Christ and sinners in general, as exists between the call of the gospel and sinners in general. Mr Jones, on the other hand, argued that if there is a relationship between the blood of Christ and all who hear the gospel, then he must have shed his blood in vain with respect to those who do not believe. But Mr Jones believed also, with Mr Roberts, that it was on the basis of the death of the Saviour that the gospel call is extended to all without difference. That which he condemned particularly was the use of the word 'relationship'. It does not seem that they disagreed greatly other than over the phrases used.

3. Mr Roberts would apply the widest meaning to the words *'all'*, *'every man'*, and *'the whole world'*, as used in the New Testament with respect to those objects for whom Jesus died. He did not claim that Jesus had died for all in the same sense; he acknowledged that there was particularity in his death as far as his own people were concerned – a particularity that ensured their ultimate eternal security – but that he died for all in the sense that he brought salvation within their reach, and gave them opportunity for eternal life. But Mr Jones confined these words to the Church, and showed from the Scriptures that they were often used, not for all mankind but for part of it, and that the purpose of the inspired writers in using them was to do away with the narrow Jewish understanding of the extent of Messiah's kingdom. The difference between the two is not great on this point either, and it all but disappears when considered from a practical viewpoint.

John Roberts was an excellent man, godly in temperament, honest and courteous in debate, and with strong reasoning powers, and Mr Jones was courteous and fair in reply. In that they were in such agreement with one another on so many things, differing mainly in the phrases that they used, it is a pity that they entered into debate at all. The controversy may be attributed, on both sides, to their zeal for keeping as close as possible to the truth. Within about six months of the appearance of the *Conversations*, Mr Roberts published a reply. But when it appeared, Thomas Jones was within three months of his death and so had no opportunity to comment on it.

The *'other tending to the opposite, which is much worse, and setting a limit to the merit of Christ's Sacrifice!'* to which Mr Thomas Jones refers in the Appendix to his book, was the essay by the Rev. Christmas Evans on *'Neillduolrwydd y Prynedigaeth'* [*'The Particularity of Redemption'*]. We have referred to this essay previously. In it the author argues for an equivalent atonement, that is, an atonement equivalent to that which the elect would have had to suffer were they to have been thrown into hell; if more were to be saved then the Son of God would have had to suffer more; and for some of the elect he suffered more than for others. This narrow understanding of the atonement stirred up Mr Jones's very nature in opposition to it. His distress was compounded by the knowledge that the author was one of the most popular preachers in Wales and acknowledged as the leader of the denomination to which he belonged. He therefore does not deal with these ideas as he did with those of John Roberts. Instead he writes strongly, though completely fairly, showing their unscriptural nature and their tendency to diminish the Redeemer's honour and to limit the infinite nature of his sacrifice, and before closing he calls on Christmas Evans to withdraw his words and to do so as publicly as he first sent them forth. He ends his Appendix with a sharply worded poem in which he deals very roughly with his opponent's views.

Mr Jones's book appeared at the beginning of October, as we have said. At the time, Christmas Evans was on a preaching journey through Denbighshire. On his way home, he heard of Mr Jones's intention of publishing the book and that in it Thomas Jones would criticize his essay. He therefore wrote him the following letter:

Llangollen, October 1819.

Dear Brother,

I understand that you intend to write against something that I wrote on the particularity of the atonement. I would request that you might delay your intention until you see me early next week at Denbigh. I do not now stand for that method of argument that I adopted in that book, namely, for weights and measures, that tended to place a limit upon that which is infinite – infinite in and of itself. I am reviewing the point these days, and find cause to reject completely that approach of weighing and measuring, which no doubt was what caused you grief. It is probable that we are, presently, of the same opinion, and if this is indeed the case I account it a pleasure of the highest degree. You will hear when I will be in Denbigh, at which time I promise you much delight as we speak together and as I receive your comments on my writing. Things have appeared in a new light to me, but, no doubt, this is due to my weakness and lack of attention. Great grace be with you.

I am, dear brother,

Yours,

Christmas Evans

Here was a courteous, Christian letter that gave great satisfaction to Mr Jones. Unfortunately he could not consent to the request it contained because his book had by now been selling for over two weeks already. Christmas Evans came to Rhuthun according to his promise together with a friend called Richard Foulkes, and it seems he had seen Mr Jones's book before arriving. He deeply regretted the words that he had written; he said that he had come to submit to the rebuke that he had received, like a child under a father's rod. He also produced a book on redemption that he had written and requested Mr Jones to read it and to give his opinion of it by the following week. Mr Jones did so, and the week following Christmas Evans returned to Denbigh and had a long conversation with Mr Jones with respect to the book and its contents. Mr Evans seemed to be recanting all his old views and agreeing fully, or at least to a considerable extent, with those of Mr Jones as regards the infinite value of the atonement. The whole discussion was conducted in great friendliness. According to Mr Jones:

> As for his expressions of respect (if not undue respect) towards myself, a poor worm, indeed, I do not remember anything said to me previously, even from my dearest friends, which reached such a degree of respect as these words from the mouth of C.E.

Christmas Evans left Denbigh confessing the hollowness of his previous opinions and promising to withdraw them publicly. But, poor man! Consistency was never one of his strengths! There is no doubt whatsoever as to the brilliance of his genius nor the unrivalled popularity of his preaching; he was clearly a deeply spiritual man, and as a rule was governed by pure motives. But he could never be called the most constant of men. In some things he was very childlike and open to be led astray by cunning men. It seems that this was what occurred in this case. On his way home to Anglesey he met some such men; he was persuaded that it would be an enduring disgrace if he, the foremost in his denomination and one of the chief preachers of Wales, were to withdraw his words publicly, and at the request of a minister of another Connexion! As a result, he returned home determined, not to fulfil his promise to Mr Jones, but to defend, as far as he was able, the views that he had said he had rejected and had promised to withdraw! He soon published a book entitled *'Prynedigaeth o fewn Cylch Etholedigaeth'* [*'Redemption within the Compass of Election'*]. Dr Owen Thomas's comment on it is:

> We presume that this book was written in great haste. Its plan is very awkward and its composition throughout is clumsy and untidy . . . It is clear that the author had felt keenly the whipping administered by Jones and, like someone half-crazed, not knowing what to do, he dashes back and forth from one thing to another – protesting, denying and protesting again – just like a creature caught in a snare and unable to escape, his efforts at doing so only tightening the net around him.

Mr Evans acknowledged that he had changed his viewpoint to some extent since the publication of his first book on the topic but states that the change involved was relatively unimportant. He then placed a completely unnatural meaning on some of his words in the first book in order to make them conform to his new position. Worse still, and what was quite unforgivable whatever the pressures upon him, he dared to suggest that Mr Jones's comments against Mr Roberts were insincere and had been expressed purely in order 'to throw dust into the eyes of his friends and pretend he is of the same opinion as they'. In other words, that Mr Jones was hypocritical in what he wrote. Mr Evans complained also that he had been libelled in the Foreword to Mr Jones's book as 'this flatterer and alien blasphemer', but if he had only paid sufficient attention to the syntax he would have seen that there was no reference here to himself, personally, but to the narrow view of Christ's atonement.

Thomas Jones decided that he would not debate further with Mr Evans but instead published an eight-page pamphlet describing the discussions that had taken place between them. The title of this pamphlet is, *'Llythyr oddiwrth T. Jones'* [*'A Letter from T. Jones to all who read it and especially to those ministers and members of that body of people known as Baptists, concerning a booklet written by Mr Christmas Evans'*]. This is the last of his published works and it is clear that he wrote it under considerably wounded feelings. Christmas Evans did not reply under his own name against Mr Jones and did not dare deny the accuracy of the account of their discussions, but within about three weeks an anonymous pamphlet was produced in Rhuthun with the title, *'Llythyr oddiwrth ychydig o Aelodau'* [*'A Letter from a few members in Denbighshire of that body of people known as Baptists to Mr Thomas Jones'*] This was an unpleasant piece of work as the following examples of the kind of questions it contains shows:

> (6) Is not your opinion on redemption in opposition to that of the body to which you belong? And did you not publish your book without the permission of that body by giving a false description to the Pwllheli Assembly?

> (14) Are not your present controversies within your own body, and those of the past against the Arminians, clear evidence that you are too dim-sighted and clumsy, for all your sackful of learning and stores of knowledge, to deal with such matters as these? And is not this the general belief of the most discerning men of your own denomination?

Certainly, such a letter did not deserve the slightest response. Soon, an *'Ail Lythyr'* [*'The Second Letter of Answer and Defence to Mr Thomas Jones'*] of similar content appeared, again anonymous. Thomas Jones gave it no more attention than the first. It was believed at the time that Christmas Evans himself was the author of these two letters, though he tried to distance himself from them, and by now this is quite certain. It is a shame that a man of such stature and position should have stooped so low. But it was Christmas Evans, after all, who was most wounded by this controversy. Very soon after the publication of this 'Second Letter' Thomas Jones died, and the news entered as a sword into the heart of his adversary. Mr Evans was never one to prolong a quarrel and his heart was in the right place, though at times he could lose his temper. Years later he confessed:

> Oh, what pain I endured through my controversy with Mr Jones of Denbigh! How it distressed me that he died and entered heaven, as I fully believe he did, while we were still engaged in argument!

When commenting on these words, Owen Thomas concluded:

> We have not the slightest doubt that they are now, both of them, in heaven, searching together into the wonders of the nature of the atonement, praising together for its virtues, and, it may be, wondering together at their disagreements over it, like two under-age boys, when here on earth!

We have referred to the sympathy existing between Mr Jones and the Rev. Ebenezer Morris and to their doctrinal agreement over the points at issue. This is confirmed by the following letter to Mr Jones:

> Blaenannerch, May 1820.
>
> . . . As for your book on the infinite worth of the Sacrifice of Christ, I consider it excellent, and thoroughly sound in its doctrine; and very valuable for its contents throughout; it is, to a great extent, worthy of the truth which it defends, and appropriate to that glorious Person it speaks of. I know of many of the brethren who have had great pleasure, and substantial profit, from reading it. It has produced good impressions in their minds, and I can also testify to the same.
>
> Your unworthy brother,
>
> EBENEZER MORRIS

As we conclude this description of Thomas Jones as a controversialist it is worth emphasizing again the value of his service to Welsh theology. It is impossible to underestimate our debt as a country to him in this respect. To his instrumentality, chiefly, must be attributed the wider, more moderate interpretation of Calvinism that prevailed in the country and the emphasis placed in our pulpits on the infinite worth of the sacrifice of the Redeemer. When popular preachers such as John Elias and Christmas Evans were going astray and tending to limit the call of the gospel to the elect, it was he, under God's blessing, who was the means of withstanding the flow and to maintain the necessary emphasis on that infinitely comforting truth that the atonement of the Son of God is sufficient for all and that all may safely be invited to come to him. A proof of the balance and fairness of his thought is the fact that, on the one hand, he was the main opponent of the Arminianism of the Wesleyans and, on the other hand, he also was the main debater against those who tended towards Hyper-Calvinism. To a large extent, the fact that the Welsh pulpit has kept to the narrow way and not veered on the one side to Arminianism and Pelagianism nor, on the other side, to Antinomianism, must be attributed to the influence of the Rev. Thomas Jones.

Because he was involved in so much argument and because there is such a polemical tone to many of his books, many might suppose that he enjoyed the battle and loved controversy. Such a conclusion would be a grave mistake. He was naturally a peace-loving man, sensitive in his feelings and kind in spirit; in fact, he hated argument. His first biographers, the Revs. John Humphreys, Caerwys, and John Roberts, Llangwm, provide clear evidence confirming this description, and they both knew him well and loved him deeply. A passionate zeal for what he considered to be God's truth was Mr Jones's only motive and the spur that drove him to unsheathe his sword. At the same time, as we have noted, he possessed all the necessary skills that made him into a polemicist of the first order. He was clear and discerning in his judgments and able to expose all false thinking; he possessed a wide knowledge of all areas of theology and rich reservoirs of historical knowledge; his mind also was naturally of a rational and logical bent. His weakness, in this respect, was his inability at times to restrain his strong satirical instincts. Dr Owen Thomas noted that it was not enough for him to strike an opponent down, but he had to strike him down dead. Notwithstanding this we believe that he, together with the Rev. John Roberts, Llanbryn-mair, were the fairest and most courteous of all the Welshmen who engaged in controversy, and that it was in opposition to their natures that the two of them fought their battles.

THOMAS JONES AS A PREACHER AND AUTHOR

We have said little of Thomas Jones as a preacher in that it was not in this area that he performed his greatest service to his country and his Connexion. At the same time, the honourable position in which he was always placed in the Associations shows that he was one of the ablest preachers. His biographers say that 'his voice was clear and melodious, his look piercing, solemn and winning, and his attitude sober and sincere'. They add that he 'in his treatment of the work of the Lord, was as one who felt its weight and spirituality, and not as some vain jester'. Owen Thomas, on the other hand, says of him that 'his style was heavy and his voice not too pleasant', but that 'his sermons were consistently able compositions and, if he were placed in a sufficiently public position so as to excite his feelings', then he would be instrumental in producing remarkable effects. We conclude from these testimonies that Thomas Jones was not considered a popular preacher in ordinary circumstances. In a farmhouse with a small congregation his delivery would be quiet and slow, though always expressing the marrow of sound doctrine. But when placed before a vast congregation, and dealing with an important doctrine, his soul would be stirred within him; he lost all his slowness and deadness and became truly fluent, sweeping all before him as a mighty flood. No doubt also his continual ill-health prevented him from becoming as popular a preacher as his abilities suggested.

His biographers also state that he was a famous poet, both in Welsh and in English, but especially in Welsh. By this they meant not only that he exercised a complete mastery of the rules of poetry, both *vers libre* and strict metre, but that he possessed a clear gift and could scale the heights of poetry. In addition to the poems that he published, there are to be found scattered throughout his printed sermons many beautiful sentences, full of poetry. He also composed many hymns, some of which are amongst our most popular. Examples are:

'Mi wn fod fy Mhrynwr yn fyw'
'Rhyfeddod, rhyfeddod, i Brynwr y byd'
'D'oes eisiau'n bod, nac ofn, na chlais, na chlwy'.

According to the Rev. Jonathan Jones, the following list includes nearly all of Thomas Jones's printed works:

1. *Elegy for Ann Parry.* Published 1788.

2. *Elegy in memory of the Rev. Daniel Rowland, also of the Rev. William Williams, Pantycelyn, and, lastly, of Dafydd Morrys, Twrgwyn.* Published 1791.

3. *Comments on an Essay entitled 'Religious Union, or a Warning against Schism.'* Published 1793.

4. *The Christian in Complete Armour.* A Welsh translation of Part 3 of William Gurnall's work. Published 1796.

5. *A Word in Season to the Inhabitants of Wales.* No date.

6. Many articles in *The Spiritual Treasury,* which was edited by himself and Thomas Charles.

7. *A Welsh and English Dictionary*. Published 1800.

8. *A Doctrinal Mirror.* Published 1806.

9. *Conversations between Mindful and Instructor.* Published 1807.

10. *Comments on a Book by Mr Owen Davies*. Published 1808.

11. *The Christian in Complete Armour*. Part 4 of Gurnall's work. Published in 1809.

12. *The Catechism of the Church of England*. A translation into Welsh. Published in 1809.

13. *A Brief answer to a Pamphlet*. Published 1811.

14. *A Cause for Thanksgiving.* Published 1811.

15. *Reformers, Martyrs, and Confessors, or the Martyrology.* Published 1813.

16. *New Hymns*. Published 1814.

17. *The Life of the Rev. Thomas Charles*. Published 1816.

18. *Conversations on Redemption between Two Friends, Enquirer and Oldman*. Published 1816.

19. *A Gift to a Child. The history of the deaths of some godly children.* Published 1816.

20. *A Song, or a Humble Complaint*. Published 1816.

21. *A Song of Harvest*.

22. *The Christian in Complete Armour.* Translation of Part 1. Published 1819.

23. *Conversations upon Redemption between Enquirer and Oldman, with an Appendix*. Published 1819.

24. *A Letter to the Ministers and Members of the Baptists*. Published in 1820.

In addition, he published a number of poetical works and his autobiography appeared after his death.

We must now describe the circumstances leading up to his death. He preached for the last time at Denbigh on Sunday, 28 May 1820. His text was 2 Corinthians 5:4, 'For we that are in this tabernacle do groan, being burdened: not for that we would be unclothed, but clothed upon, that mortality might be swallowed up of life.' During the sermon he expressed the conviction that he had been granted to ascend to the pulpit for the last time. The next week he was taken ill. Though he was in great pain he displayed every patience and was completely confident at the thought of crossing over to the eternal world. He was also fully assured in the truths that he had defended. He told John Roberts, Llangwm, who had visited him, referring to his book on *Redemption*:

> I am dying in peace and of the same mind completely, and without any mental worries over any of their content, except that they are very poor work.

The Bala Association was approaching and John Roberts was intending to be present. Thomas Jones asked to be remembered to the Association and desired that the divine presence might be evident. He then added, as a charge to the brethren, 'Watch over the great cause that it might not fail under you. Give yourselves to prayer. Walk in love and humility. Strive to be profitable in every place, and with every part of the work, and to be increasingly careful over the doctrine and discipline.' He also recited many hymns, and asked Mr Roberts and the others present to sing them.

His biographers have recorded many of his last words as he lay on his bed aware that he was approaching another world, but we must restrain ourselves. He said, at one point, 'And shall I, the blackest sinner, praise Thee Jesus, eternally? Oh! to love and praise Jesus eternally! O Saviour of sinners, in your hand I shall ford the river!' The last of his words that could be understood were, 'And shall I die at peace with the infinite God? O happy heaven, happy heaven!' About one o'clock on Friday, 16 June 1820, his pure spirit flew to the eternal bliss.

His funeral was held on the following Monday. The congregation that gathered was said to be more than three thousand – the greatest ever seen in a funeral in Denbigh. The Rev. Daniel Jones, the son of Robert Jones, Rhoslan, preached from Colossians 3:4, 'When Christ, who is our life, shall appear, then shall ye also appear with him in glory.' After him, the Rev. John Davies, Nantglyn, preached. He had been ordained at the same time as Mr Jones at the Bala Association. His text was Hebrews 13:7, 'Remember them which have the rule over you, who have spoken unto you the word of God.' It was on this text that Thomas Jones himself had preached at the funeral of his old friend, Thomas Charles, about six years previously. Then his remains were carried to the cemetery at Eglwys Wen, about a mile outside Denbigh, and there, amidst general grief and mourning, he was laid to rest until that morning when the trumpet sounds.[2]

[1] A line of a verse from a popular hymn

[2] We wish to acknowledge our obligation for much of the material in these chapters to the *Life of John Jones, Talsarn* by the Rev. Owen Thomas, D. D., and the *Life of the Rev. Thomas Jones, Denbigh*, by the Rev. Jonathan Jones. The relevant chapters in the first of these books have now been translated and published as Owen Thomas, *The Atonement Controversy* (Edinburgh: Banner of Truth, 2002).

1-6: Three buildings lost to the Connexion at the time of the Ordination, and the chapels that were built to replace them: Nevern Church, Pembroke (1) and the Methodist Chapel, Nevern (2); the present (3) and original (4) chapels at Newport, Pembrokeshire; the present (5) and original (6) chapels at St Dogmaels
Bottom: Llandeilo Chapel. The first Ordination Service in 1811 was held in the original building on this site

THE HOMES OF THREE WELL-KNOWN SOUTH WALES METHODISTS:
TOP: GARTH, NEAR BUILTH WELLS, THE HOME OF MARMADUKE GWYNNE
MIDDLE: MANOROWEN, NEAR FISHGUARD, HOME OF DAVID JONES, LLAN-GAN
BOTTOM: LLWYN-GWAIR, NEAR NEVERN, HOME OF JAMES BOWEN

Top: Pengwernhir, Cardiganshire, the birthplace of John Williams, Lledrod
Bottom Left: Simon Lloyd, Plas-yn-dre, Bala
Bottom Right: William Howells, Longacre, London

Top: Ebenezer Morris
Middle: Blaen-y-wern, the home of Ebenezer Morris
Bottom Left: The tomb of the Morrises in Troed-yr-aur Cemetery
Bottom Right: Troed-yr-aur Church and Cemetery

Top: Thomas Jones, Denbigh. The portrait on the left was published in 1820, the year of his death; that on the right in *The Evangelical Magazine*, November 1817
Middle: Thomas Jones (Left) and his home in Denbigh (Right)
Bottom: Plasucha, near Caerwys, Denbighshire, Thomas Jones's birthplace

1

2

3

4

Places associated with Thomas Jones:
1. Capel Mawr, Denbigh 2. Syrior Goch, near Betws-yn-rhos, Abergele 3. Abergele Chapel, 1900 4. Eglwys-wen, Denbigh, where he is buried

Portraits of John Elias:
Top Left: Painted in 1839 by William Roos.
Top Right: published in *The Evangelical Magazine* in 1820
Bottom: This engraving was published in 1847. It is based on a portrait by Hugh Jones

Places associated with John Elias: 1. Brynllwyn-bach, his birthplace 2. Ynys-y-pandy, the home of Griffith Jones 3. Llanrhuddlad Chapel 4. His home in Llangefni 5. Hendre Howell, near Penmorfa, where he became a church member 6. Llangefni Chapel 7. Y Fron, Llangefni, his home in his latter years 8. His grave in Llanfaes Cemetery, Beaumaris

Ebenezer Richard, Tregaron (Top) and places associated with him:
1. His birthplace at Tre-fin 2. Tregaron Church and Cemetery where he is buried 3. His home at Tregaron 4. His grave

41
JOHN ELIAS

HIS UPBRINGING

One tragedy with respect to the Rev. John Elias – on many accounts the greatest preacher that ever arose in Wales, if not, indeed, in the whole world – is that no worthy biography of his life has appeared to this day. Not that his memory has been wholly neglected. We know that he himself wrote down something of his history, that many memoirs of him were published after he died,[1] and that there are examples to be had of vivid descriptions of the characteristics and effectiveness of his oratory. But on the other hand, when we consider the position he gained, the remarkable influence that accompanied his ministry, the respect paid to him as a man of counsel as well as an incomparable speaker, and that his history for nearly forty years defines the history of an important religious denomination, in north Wales at least, we cannot but feel that he has not received the attention that he deserves. The disappointment is all the greater in that the one man who could have made good the deficiency, namely, the Rev. Owen Thomas, D.D., has been gathered to his fathers. Presently, we can only do our best with the materials that have been left us.

John Elias was born on 6 May 1774. His father's name was Elias Jones, a weaver by trade and something of a farmer on a small scale as well. His grandfather also was a weaver and something of a farmer, and lived at Brynllwynbach in Aber-erch parish, about four miles from Pwllheli. When his son, Elias, married a young girl from Llanaelhaiarn called Jane Roberts, the young couple came to live with him. He soon built them their own home however, near to his own dwelling. He and his son shared in the work of weaving and farming. Their circumstances were poor but they paid their way and were not without the necessities of life, and so were respectable in the eyes of their neighbours. Though the subject of this chapter is always known as 'John Elias', his real name, according to common usage, was John Jones, and this is how he was first known, whenever any surname was mentioned. We shall see later the reason for the change of name.

Elias Jones and his wife had no great inclination towards religion; they seem to have been given fully to the world and not paid any attention to the things that belonged to their peace. But the grandfather was a very circumspect man, attending the parish church every Sunday, maintaining family worship in the home, and exhibiting much higher moral standards than those of his neighbours. Soon, he and his young grandson were the best of friends. Once the young boy began to talk, the grandfather began to teach him the paths of virtue, warning him to keep from swearing and from taking God's name in vain, teaching him to avoid lying and oaths. As soon as John could walk, he would take him by the hand to the service in the church on a Sunday. He charged him solemnly to keep the Sabbath and to respect the worship of the living God. John Elias, therefore, in spite of the indifference of his parents, was raised in the midst of religious influences. When he was between four and five years old, his grandfather taught him to read Welsh. By the time he was six he could read the Bible well, and at the age of seven he had read all of the Old Testament from the beginning of Genesis to the middle of Jeremiah. Also at seven years of age he contracted smallpox and was very ill indeed and near to death. For a period of weeks, all hope of a recovery was lost. He was unconscious for many days and was blind for a fortnight. He wrote:

> I remember when I began to recover, and to open my eyes, that my grandfather came to my bedside, weeping, and addressing me thus: 'My dear boy, do you remember what your lesson is?' I answered, 'Yes', and mentioned some chapter in the book of Jeremiah. The old man rejoiced greatly when he saw that I could remember in spite of my affliction the portion of Scripture I was reading when I was taken ill, and that there were hopes that I should have the use of my eyes again to read the Bible. I was long in a low state, and often afflicted for three or four years.

On recovering, his appetite for books increased and became an unquenchable passion. For some time the Bible was the only book that he possessed himself but he devoured any other that came his way and, to the extent possible for a child of his age, he mastered their contents. It is said that he would scrape the butter from his bread in order to make reed candles so that he could read at night when the family had retired to bed. His grandfather continued to take him to church and would now stand him on a bench so as to alternate with the priest in the readings, according to the tradition of the parish. As they walked to and from the church, the old man would continue his serious counsels, warning the boy that he should keep from every kind of falsehood. Mercifully, the seed fell upon good ground and brought forth fruit a hundredfold. According to Elias, 'The Lord blessed his counsels to keep me from those things.'

From his childhood John Elias was noted for his seriousness; considerations of God, of another world, and of judgment, filled his mind. He was frightened by dreams about judgment and eternity, and terrified of being cast into hell. He gave early evidences of being very tender of conscience. Like many of those who lived on the coast, his father dealt in smuggled goods – to sell spirits for which the government had not received tax was not considered a crime at all. One Sunday, a message arrived for Elias Jones from a gentleman in the neighbourhood, asking for a flagon. The boy heard the request and shuddered at the thought of trading on God's Day. With tears filling his eyes, he pleaded with his father not to respond to the request. He, however, only mocked the boy's conscientiousness and care for the sanctity of the Sabbath, and the servant was given the flagon as instructed. The boy then withdrew, with his Bible under his arm, and when looked for some time later he was found lying full length upon a stone bench made to support beehives, with his Bible by his side, and the stones wet with his tears. His parents' disregard of the Sabbath caused considerable pain to the young boy. Often the irreligious neighbours would gather at Elias Jones's house on a Sunday and their conversations would be completely out of keeping with the sanctity of the day. They would always be talking of superstitions or wordly excitements. John Elias wrote:

> I wept much on this account. Sometimes I would remonstrate with them, but they would not hear me!

He describes one occasion when on a Sunday he was sent by his parents to the home of his mother's father, about four miles away. It pained his heart to go, but he did not dare disobey.

> On my way I saw one of the mountains before me black and smoky, after the heath had been set ablaze on Saturday night. I thought the day of judgment had come, that the earth was beginning to burn, and that I was going to judgment by breaking the Sabbath. Such was my distress and great terror that I was obliged to cry out; I endeavoured to pray that I might be spared from going to judgment in my sins.

He acknowledges however that while he prayed in this way for his sin to be forgiven he was completely ignorant of the true means of forgiveness and of God's method of justifying the ungodly.

We would be far from the truth however if we portrayed the boy from Brynllwynbach as some perfect angel, living a pure life, and not knowing or being overcome by the power of corruption. At times he experienced, as do all, the seduction of lying:

> Sometimes I was enticed by children of my own age, and some older, to follow them on Sabbath evenings as we came out of church, and to engage in what

> they called innocent play, that is, without making any noise. Sometimes, on such occasions, I was unable to say the Lord's Prayer, and could not sleep by reason of guilt and terror.

Once he went as far as to swear out loud. He heard an ungodly youth swearing and blustering forth oaths and blasphemies. In his folly he admired the boy for his verbal skills and an overpowering desire arose in him to emulate him. He therefore went to the middle of a field where no one could hear him and uttered one blasphemous word. This was the first and the last time for John Elias to swear. He was immediately struck by such fear and terror that he thought the earth would open up and swallow him down into hell immediately. For some time afterwards his spirit was deeply troubled – attempting to call on God in prayer but failing to do so. The story confirms the existence of the natural opposition to God and to his holy law, in the heart of man, even when the outward life appears beautiful and moral.

HE BEGINS TO ATTEND METHODIST MEETINGS

Up until this time he had not made the acquaintance of any Methodists. But when still young he heard that famous preachers from south Wales and from other parts of the country would periodically visit Pwllheli, Pentre Uchaf, and other places in Lleyn, and he longed to hear them. He tried to persuade his grandfather to come with him. Though the old man was a zealous Churchman he was not in any way prejudiced, and once he and his grandson had attended the parish church in the morning they would go together again in the afternoon or evening to hear a sermon. Sometimes the preacher would be late arriving and while they waited for him the thoughtless amongst the crowd would begin to gossip. This grieved the devout old weaver and to put a stop to it he would place his grandson in some prominent spot and get him to read a chapter from the Bible aloud. The people would gather around him to listen because, says John Elias, 'to hear a small boy reading well was a remarkable thing in those days'. From what we know of him afterwards we would judge that he not only read well but that his seriousness, his tone of voice, and his ability to convey the meaning as he read, contributed as much as his youth in attracting the attention of the people. He gives an account of the first time he ascended to a pulpit:

> One Sabbath, in Pentre Uchaf, we had a long wait for the preacher to appear. My grandfather approached me, saying, 'It is a pity that the people should lose their time in this manner; go to the pulpit and read a chapter to them out of the Bible.' Then he opened the door and pushed me in and shut the door

> upon me. I read a part of Christ's sermon on the mount, the people listening attentively. At length I looked over my shoulder and saw the preacher standing at the door of the pulpit; I was greatly alarmed, I closed the Bible and came down as fast as I could. I do not recollect what was my age then – it might have been from nine to twelve years. This was the first time I entered the pulpit. And neither did I nor any other person think I should have the privilege of occupying it so often afterwards.

Even at this young age his heart was full of a desire to do good. After returning from church with his grandfather on a Sunday he would, in the afternoon, gather the children of the neighbourhood together and teach them to read. This school was first held in his father's house but when that became too small it had to move into a barn. This was the first Sunday School in that part of the country. Many children of the poor first learnt to read at Brynllwynbach barn, with the cottage boy as their teacher. One old sailor who afterwards lived in Bangor for many years, used to acknowledge that John Elias was his first teacher and that without him he would never have learnt to read.

When he was twelve years old he began to work as a weaver with his father and grandfather. His desire to hear sermons was increasing. He says that he could understand only a little of what the preachers were saying, yet found endless delight in the sound of a sermon. Sometimes the heavenly breezes would blow, resulting in general rejoicing throughout the congregation. None would enjoy such visitations more than himself, yet he would confess that no great impressions were made upon him at those times, though he could see that this was the case in others. His grandfather was eventually overcome by the frailties of old age and was not able to accompany him to the services as before, but he would continue to attend the preaching of the gospel whenever he had opportunity. He had no guide or friend. He would walk to the meeting on his own in that he did not consider himself worthy of sharing the company of professing Christians, and he could not endure the frivolity and careless talk of those who had no profession. By much effort, and miles of walking, he would sometimes succeed in hearing three sermons on a Sunday.

> When a popular preacher from South Wales was expected on his rounds in this locality, I would sometimes walk over ten miles on a Sabbath morning in order to hear the first sermon. I would then follow him until nightfall, taking but little food all day.

It seems that at this time he received considerable kindness from a poor old woman who lived at Brynengan. She had noticed the young stranger who attended so often and the solemnity of his appearance as he listened to

God's Word being preached, and at the end of the service she would invite him to her house for some food. He never forgot her kindness all his life.

Alongside his longing to hear the gospel there arose in him a strong desire to read religious books but, he says, 'there were but few such in the Welsh language at that time'. He also understood no English. Whenever he heard of a book, near at hand or far away, he would try to borrow it. He discovered some good books that were the means of enlightening his mind with respect to God's method of saving sinners. Amongst these he refers to the works of the Rev. Griffith Jones, Llanddowror – his catechisms in particular; the work of Elisha Coles; and *The Marrow of Modern Divinity*.

YEARS OF SPIRITUAL CONVICTIONS

When he was fourteen years old he experienced a severe crisis. His inner corruptions were aroused; he became aware of his tendency to wildness; the charms and illicit pleasures of the broad way were often about to overcome him. At the same time the religious impressions upon his mind were diminishing in strength. His steps had well nigh slipped at this time. But the Lord kept him from being defeated by evil and he was not allowed to break out into public immorality. It was a battle that he fought within himself, unseen by any man. It needs to be noted also that, even when the battle was at its most fierce, he did not stop reading his Bible regularly nor lost his tenderness of conscience. There is an account of him at this time sitting on the bank opposite his home on a Sunday afternoon and reading his Bible. His mother came out of the house intending to visit a neighbour for a cup of tea, and she urged her son to come with her. His spirit was stirred up because of her behaviour. The tears flowed down his cheeks and in an agitated voice he said, 'O mother! Don't you know whose day it is? Don't you remember the commandment, "Remember the Sabbath day to keep it holy"?' His words, and especially his tears, overcame his mother and another woman who had called on her, so that the invitation to tea was forgotten and neither woman again accepted such an invitation for a Sunday.

By the help of God's grace, John Elias was enabled to conquer his inward corruptions and the religious impressions upon his mind strengthened. He now began, though with considerable humility, to mix with the professors of religion as they walked to and from the services. They spoke together of the sermons and of their experiences of the truth and this, together with the example of their godly behaviour, was of great help to him. He longed to join them in the fellowship of the society but viewed himself as unsuitable. He considered himself a lost sinner but feared that what he felt was not true conviction and he was terrified of backsliding and of bringing disgrace upon religion. 'I would rather die outside of the church than do that.' On the day of the society meeting he would be in a quandary between longing to attend and a sense of his unworthiness. He would go out into the fields to grieve and to try to pray, but could not break through. He was in this state for three years. During this time he was greatly troubled by the knowledge that he was not maintaining family worship:

> One evening, hearing a minister preach in allusion to this, that word from Mark 8:38 came strongly upon my mind, 'Whosoever shall be ashamed of me and of my words in this adulterous and sinful generation, of him also shall the Son of man be ashamed, when he cometh in the glory of his Father with the holy angels, etc.' I went home with a troubled heart, in tears, trying to pray. I asked the Lord to pardon me and to give me strength to avow Christ from thenceforth. When I came home my father and my mother were up. I told them my distress of mind, and I asked their permission to attempt to read and pray in the family. They allowed me, and I began that hour. I continued, every opportunity, though I had not much encouragement from my family at that time.

At the age of sixteen, John Elias longed to go to Llangeitho to hear the Rev. Daniel Rowland. He had heard much about him and of the extraordinary effects of his preaching from the older believers of Caernarvonshire, and he looked forward to receiving a particular blessing to his own soul through him. He knew that the seraph was now too old to visit the north but he promised himself that when he was older and stronger he would walk every step to Llangeitho to hear him, though the distance was some eighty miles. But:

> I went one Sabbath to Pwllheli to hear a certain preacher, but I found I was too early for the service at the Methodist chapel there. I went to hear the Rev. Benjamin Jones [an Independent minister]. He read for his text those words, 'Know ye not that a prince and a great man hath fallen today in Israel?' (*2 Sam.* 3:38). He said that the reason why he took that text was that he had heard the mournful news of the death of the Rev. Daniel Rowland, who was a prince and a great man in the church of God in Wales. I still remember my feelings when I heard that news – I wept unceasingly.

As Rowland died on Saturday, 16 October 1790, it is probably on the Sunday, 24 October, that this event occurred.

Now that he was disappointed in his purpose for visiting Llangeitho, he decided to attend the Association at Bala. In his *Autobiography*, though he writes almost fifty years after the event, he provides a vivid picture of the journey and the memory of it was still sweet:

> Sometime after this, when I was about eighteen years old, a strong desire arose in my mind to go to Bala Association, thinking I should be favoured there with something wonderful. I conversed with some religious young men in my neighbourhood on the subject, and asked them if they would allow me to go with them to Bala. They answered, I might: and it was agreed for us to meet at Pwllheli, and to start together from thence. A great number of religious young people from many places in Lleyn met: they knew of the places where we could hear sermons on the way, and we started on the journey, talking about the Bible and sermons. Occasionally we sang psalms and hymns, and sometimes we rested, and one or two would engage in prayer. Then we would proceed again on our journey, singing on the way. Very few words were uttered by any one among us all the way, except respecting the Bible, sermons, and religious subjects. Though there were many young men and women in the company, yet I do not recollect seeing any wanton looks, nor did I hear an idle word from any person all the journey. They seemed as if they well understood that they were going to the Assembly, expecting to meet God there. Oh that all young people who make a profession of religion in this age were like them! Thus, from strength to strength, we arrived at Bala. When we came there we saw parties from many places coming together, and the whole multitude appeared as persons of one mind, and engaged in the same business. Great sobriety and decorum were observable everywhere in all the streets. It was customary with the Devil in those days to bring together his crowds of reckless fools to such places. The ministry was so full of fire, and attended with such power, that the Devil dreaded to let his choice ones frequent such a place. This Association occurred in 1792, and was remarkable. The brightness of flaming fire fell upon the Assembly, life and power was in the ministry, and heavenly dew descended upon the people. After the Assembly we went to our several homes rejoicing, talking about the sermons, and singing and praying. The journey, though forty miles long, seemed to end much too soon – we all walked on foot all the way. I had such enjoyment in the fellowship of these godly people on this journey, that I determined to join them.

This is how the Methodists journeyed in days gone by on the way to the Associations, with the sound of singing and praising, as a people celebrating a feast. The conversations along the way on spiritual matters, the hearing of sermons, the singing, the prayer meetings when resting and eating a little at the sides of the clear mountain streams, were the best preparation for an Association. And if the labourers in the field were clothed with power from on high and the doctrines distilling from their lips as the dew upon Mount Hermon, the hearts of their hearers, for their part, were tender and melting and ready for an impression to be made upon them. It is good to have this lively picture of the journey to an Association and from a man who could not tolerate any kind of levity and whose testimony no one would dare question, if only in order to disprove the claims of those who portray the Associations and the journeying to them in a very different light.

John Elias's modesty kept him from describing one event that occurred on this journey and which was reported to Dr Owen Thomas by an old elder who was present:

> The old man informed him that he had never seen such seriousness of aspect in any man as appeared in John Elias on that occasion. At Ffestiniog, on the way to Bala, they held a prayer meeting. A request was made for a copy of the Bible, but apparently nobody had one. At length, the quiet serious young man who was a stranger to most of the company said that he had a copy, and he produced it from his pocket. He was asked to read a chapter. 'He did so,' said the old man, 'in such a manner as to make the chapter seem new to us all.' He was then urged to offer a prayer. 'And if the reading was wonderful,' he said, 'the prayer was far more wondrous. I never heard such praying in all my life.'

And it must be remembered that at this time John Elias had yet to be received into Christian membership.

His tendency up to this time had been to strive for a purer morality and to offer this morality to God as a basis for justification. But he now received more evangelical views of God's plan for the forgiveness of sinful men – that it was not based on anything in man himself but on the atoning obedience of Jesus Christ. One means used to correct his wrong views was a remarkable sermon from Mr Robert Roberts, Clynnog. He refers to another occasion in his *Autobiography*:

> One day – I remember it well, in a certain place on the way to Pwllheli – the words, 'the ministry of reconciliation, etc.' (*2 Cor.* 5:18,19) came to my mind with some light which was quite strange to me. My soul had such a feast in the words, that 'God was in Christ reconciling the world unto himself, not imputing their trespasses unto them'! I saw that the way to accomplish this was by imputing our sins to Christ, and imputing his righteousness unto us (verse 21). The doctrine of imputation has been, since that time, of infinite importance in my estimation.

Here is the young lad turning at last to the proper direction, estimating all his righteousnesses to be mere filthy rags and crying out with the apostle, 'That I might be found in him.' It is no wonder that the doctrine of imputation in which he here found a basis for his eternal salvation, had an emphatic place in John Elias's ministry throughout his life. He adds:

> I felt from the pleasure I experienced then in that word, that I could preach it to my countrymen everywhere. But I saw that this desire of preaching the reconciliation was unreasonable, because I myself had not been received as a member of the Church.

AN APPRENTICE TO GRIFFITH JONES

We have already seen that he had decided on the way back from the Bala Association to join the Lord's people but somehow he could not bring himself to act upon his decision. His deep self-loathing and his terror of bringing disgrace upon the holy name were as strong ropes holding him back. At last he decided that to obtain a place with his craft amongst a godly family would be of great advantage to him. He heard that a man from the Penmorfa neighbourhood, Griffith Jones, Ynys-y-Pandy, who was also a weaver, was in the habit of keeping an apprentice. As well as being a godly man, Griffith Jones was something of an exhorter. Having obtained his parents' rather reluctant permission, John Elias journeyed to Penmorfa. Though he was a complete stranger and not professing religion, he was employed by Griffith Jones and welcomed into the family. Here the lines had fallen to him in pleasant places: the family worship, the spiritual conversations, and the religious atmosphere were all his heart could wish. He said:

> I was very happy there, but I was not able to attend the Society. They would often converse with me about religion, and ask me why I stayed out; but they never pressed me to enter.

When Griffith Jones would be away from home, the young man, at the request of the wife, would read and pray instead of him, and there would be much talk in the neighbourhood that a boy who was not a member in the *seiat* was leading family worship.

Griffith Jones related the following history with regard to John Elias to the late Rev. William Roberts, Amlwch:

> His mind was very deeply exercised when he first came to our family. I found proof of this from many of his written papers that he would place in holes in the partition walls of the workshop, together with many other signs. One day, during the harvest, a strange preacher came to take a service at my house at ten in the morning, and the sermon affected John Elias greatly. At the end of the service we were to hold a society so I told John, 'Go with the maid, Jack, to make hay until I come for you.' I then closed the door behind him. When I went to them about two hours later and saw what little work had been done, I said to the maid, 'Is this all that you have done?' She answered, 'Jack has done nothing but cry, and lie in the hay, the whole time.' 'Oh yes,' I said, 'Why is that, Jack?' He answered, 'Oh my dear uncle, that word broke my heart, "And they that were ready went in with him to the marriage, and the door was shut." You shut the door today and I was out.'

Griffith Jones sought therefore to dress his wounds by directing him to the Lord Jesus and by encouraging him to join God's people.

HE IS GRANTED MEMBERSHIP IN THE SOCIETY

At last, the desire for church membership became too great for John Elias. It happened in the following way:

> It appears that Elias and the servant-maid were employed . . . in the corn-harvest, in a field belonging to their master, Griffith Jones. Elias, on account of his great uneasiness about going to the church meeting, was very strange in his movements and work. The concern of his soul and the solemnity of the world to come filled his mind so much that he was not disposed to go home for dinner, and sleep had forsaken him for some nights. The girl, not knowing what was the matter with him, told her master that the lad's conduct was very strange: that sometimes he would work with all his might, then would stand as if in deep thought; at other times he would weep much or go to the other side of the hedge with deep groans as if about to die. The master, knowing the cause, said to the girl, 'Good will come of all this.'

There was to be a society in the neighbourhood that afternoon at a place called Hendre Howell. The old exhorter from Ynys-y-pandy was too good a Calvinist to interfere in what he saw as the course of divine activity and to pressurize the boy to join the society before he himself had fully made up his mind on the matter. But on the way to the meeting he and his wife made a point of walking through the field where John Elias was working and saying, 'We are going to the Society, do you according to your mind.' After a fierce internal battle, the young man decided to follow them. He would have made a strange sight; the tears flowed down his cheeks; at times he hurried on so as to catch up with his master and mistress, at other times he lingered at the side of the hedge – a mass of hesitation and uncertainty. At last he found himself at the door of the house and with his hand upon the latch, and then in the presence of three preachers and a number of men and women. The preachers were his master, Griffith Jones, John Edwards, Ereiniog, and John Griffith Ellis, a very popular young man who was cut down in the flower of youth. John Elias continues:

> I was afraid the preachers would examine me very strictly, and that upon finding my experience so unsatisfactory, they would refuse to accept me: but they, to my great astonishment, were very kind to me. I was accepted, and had what I had longed for many years, and had often feared I should never obtain, a place in the house of God.

This took place about the end of September 1793, when he was nineteen years old.

Mr Elias has described the little church that met at Hendre Howell as made up of eminently godly men and women – humble-minded, self-denying people, full of brotherly love and kindness, with a deep reverence for the Lord Jesus and loving to talk about him. He was often amazed and thankful that he had been granted a place among them. But for a long time after joining them he was at the mercy of his fears. The enemy assured him that he would soon backslide and bring shame upon the name of Christ. He said:

> I was in this state for many weeks, wondering and thankful when the Society day came, that I was permitted to have one more meeting before backsliding; and I tried to pray earnestly that 'I might dwell in the house of the Lord all the days of my life'.

One of the first consequences of joining the society was that he was made to alternate with his master in leading the family worship. In this work he showed such familiarity with the various forms of the corruptions of the heart and with the method of grace to meet the sinfulness of his nature that the family would listen in amazement. According to Griffith Jones:

> His discernment and importunity in prayer made us all wonder greatly. In my mind I would compare his prayer to my own, imagining the situation as if we were both entering the drawing-room of some nobleman. My own prayer I thought of as if I had only said, 'There are here half a dozen pictures.' But when John prayed, it was as if he had described the whole room in detail, before he rose from his knees, so that the whole family was amazed, and ready to ask, 'From where did this simple boy receive such wisdom and power?'

JOHN ELIAS BEGINS TO EXHORT

On joining the church he was almost forcibly persuaded to take a leading and public part in the work of religion. The Sunday School, the usual field of labour for young men, had not yet been established in the neighbourhood, but a night school was maintained in the houses of the locality during the winter months. In this school John Elias was the leader; it was he, because of his familiarity with the Bible, who would catechize; it was he also, because of his gift in prayer and his ability as a reader, who would usually lead the devotional parts and often give a word of advice to the young people. In prayer meetings – of which there were many in the area – he would often be asked to begin the meeting by reading a chapter of the Bible, and many a warm-hearted old brother would call on him to give a word of exhortation from the passage read. When a preacher failed to fulfil an engagement, in order that the people might not return hungry to their homes, he would be called upon to address the congregation and give a word of warning or exhortation. Griffith Jones states:

> When he happened to be present in a congregation, before the set time for worship, he used to take the Bible, read a chapter and expound it, and warn his contemporaries, with much power and fluency.

All this, it must be remembered, took place within a few months of him joining religion. The word spread throughout the neighbourhood that the boy in Griffith Jones's house had begun to preach. This caused much talk and commotion, especially amongst those who were very zealous that all things should be proper and in order, and even more particularly amongst the preachers, to most of whom he was completely unknown. It must be acknowledged that his behaviour was irregular, but the fault was to be found with the older brethren. He says, 'In my childishness I tried to do all that was asked of me.' These men were hardly exercising the necessary caution with respect to the ministry, in pushing such a young man, a novice in the faith, to the fore in this way, and had he not been one in a million, with so much substance in his character, and grace in his heart, they might have spoilt his usefulness for the rest of his life. At the same time, they could point to the uniqueness of his gifts and his passionate zeal to do good, as excuses.

On seeing his gifts some of the older brethren approached him, asking him if he felt any compulsion to preach. He answered that he did feel strong compulsion to exhort and warn the people but that he knew he was not qualified, being too young, ignorant and inexperienced. They encouraged him to foster such feelings and to pray earnestly for guidance. He soon became acquainted with an old preacher who lived in the Llanfyllin neighbourhood. William Dafydd possessed no great gifts himself but was a discerning man and full of sympathy for young preachers. He was the first of the preachers to realize that a bright future awaited the young John Elias, should he live. On one occasion, when there were many of the local leaders in his house discussing the young man, he said to them, in great seriousness, 'Brethren, something great will come of this boy, when I am in the grave.' William Dafydd encouraged John Elias to preach whenever he could, assuring him that doing so would be the best education for his development. He would also take the young man with him at times on his journeys, asking him to lead the meetings, and generally behaved towards him with great kindness. On his last visit to Llanllyfni John Elias related to his friend, the Rev. John Jones, Tremadog, what William Dafydd had once told him, half-playfully, half-seriously. '*Sionyn bach*,' he had said, 'if you beat Robert Roberts [Clynnog] and John Roberts [his brother] at preaching I will put a guinea in your hand. They have both, long ago, got far ahead of me.' This was a friendly teasing, but it also suggests the high hopes that the old exhorter had in his mind for his young friend. Mr Parry, Chester, related another interesting story about William Dafydd, namely that the old man was once engaged in an intense struggle with God that he would send forth labourers into the harvest, and that he received such a definite answer as to be convinced that the Lord would raise four powerful men for the work in Caernarvonshire. He was so convinced of this that he proceeded to name the men, and to do so some years before the last of them had begun to preach! The four were John Elias; Richard Jones, Wern; Evan Evans, Waunfawr; and John Parry, Chester. It is a remarkable fact also that, with the exception of Michael Roberts, no great preacher arose in Caernarvonshire after these four for a considerable period of time.

HE IS RECEIVED BY THE MONTHLY MEETING

Though John Elias preached, he was not as yet approved by his denomination to do so. He was therefore encouraged by his brethren at Hendre Howell and by the elders of the local churches, particularly by one of them called John Richards, an elder at Garn, Dolbenmaen, to attend the Monthly Meeting in order to be approved formally. He agreed to go. The Monthly Meeting was to be held at Brynyrodyn on Christmas Day, 1794. He was persuaded by John Richards to stay with him on Christmas Eve on his way to the Monthly Meeting. What he also did, unknown to John Elias, was to announce him to preach at the early morning service on Christmas Day in the Garn Chapel, while on his way to a meeting to seek permission to preach! We do not know what kind of service he had, but he felt himself that his behaviour was most irregular, and he was afraid of standing before the famous preachers of Caernarvonshire, who were, in his eyes, as the angels of God. Dr Owen Thomas writes that some of these brethren were very heavy-handed in their treatment of him at the meeting; he himself notes that he was examined very seriously and in detail as to his conviction, his view of his lost estate, his thoughts on the order of salvation, and of his experience of Christ and his grace. It is said that he was so nervous that his answers were hesitant and confused, and that the main impression made on many present was that there was no great promise in him. But on the testimony of his master, Griffith Jones, and of John Richards, Garn, and others who knew him, he was accepted as a member of the Monthly Meeting, and was given permission to preach at those places for which his services were sought.

He himself wrote of this occasion:

> Christmas Day, 1794, was a day to be remembered by me. I was received a member of the Monthly Meeting, and was allowed to preach the Gospel. I was

> but twenty years and six months old, and had been only two years and a half a professor of religion, very deficient in knowledge and experience of spiritual things. So I commenced in my simplicity a work, the nature, importance and excellency of which, I very imperfectly understood. However, from the very beginning, I was not left to view the work as a human art, undertaken capriciously, nor to talk in a trifling manner about it. I was sensible that I knew too little of God in Christ to be able to speak in a clear manner of him; little of the evil of sin, and the wretched state of sinners; to address the people in a rousing manner. I saw myself very deficient in my views of the glory of Christ and experience of his love, so as to speak clearly and fervently of him to the people. But God bore with me, and supported me in a wonderful manner.

It is also said that it was in this Monthly Meeting at Brynyrodyn that he changed his name to John Elias. John Jones, Edeyrn, asked, 'What is the young man's name?' He was told it was John Jones. 'What is his father's name?' continued the preacher. 'Elias Jones,' was the reply. 'Then, in the name of goodness, let the boy be called John Elias, otherwise we shall all be John Joneses soon.' John Jones, Lleyn, John Jones, Penrhyn, and he himself from Edeyrn, were present, and possibly others also. And therefore it was as John Elias that he was known from then on.

According to Dr Owen Thomas:

> And he was very soon well-known. It was felt immediately that an incomparable preacher had arisen in the country. There was such seriousness in his approach, such relevance and originality in his matter, such passion in his feelings, such power in his delivery, such illumination upon his spirit, and in particular, such divine unction upon his word, that his ministry from its very beginning excited the whole country. Wherever he went, the surrounding neighbourhoods would gather to hear him. The calls upon him from all parts were endless, and he, without sparing himself, would accept them. He himself, in his *Autobiography*, attributes his popularity at this time to the curiosity of the people and their desire to hear a boy preaching, but the truth is that his sermons then as afterwards were a fire that consumed ungodliness, terrified the careless and presumptuous and added to the churches of the localities he visited.

It might be appropriate here to provide a description of John Elias as he was at this time when he set out on what was to be his life work. On one hand, he was no more than a youth of twenty years old, rough of dress, rustic in his manners and uneducated. He had never had a day's schooling, not even at a Sunday School; he did not know a word of English; his knowledge was poor and his range of reading was limited, even when taking into account the scarcity of literature that was available in Welsh at the time. On the other hand, he had been born with a rare genius and gift, the like of which had not been seen before in Wales; he had been blessed by nature with all the necessary qualification for an orator; and he possessed to overflowing that eloquence that nails a congregation to the lips of the speaker. In addition, his seriousness was intense and his desire to save souls burnt as a fierce fire in his bones. If he had little familiarity with literature he had at hand and at his call, in the verses of the Bible, bullets that he could fire at will into the midst of a congregation. And when we consider the state of Wales at the time, it could hardly be said that lack of refinement was any great disadvantage to him; on the contrary, it probably brought him closer to his hearers. And if his eloquence was at the beginning rough and unadorned, it was completely natural and overcame the congregations.

When noting the immediate popularity that he won, it should be remembered that there were giants dwelling in Caernarvonshire in those days. There was Robert Roberts, Clynnog, weak of body and bent of back, but who lived on the borders of the spiritual world and who would sometimes so lift the veil that his congregations would faint at the strangeness and sublimity of the views. There was John Roberts, his brother, who then lived in Llanllyfni, who was greater in knowledge than Robert and not far behind him in gifts, who was also a master of the congregation, whose services at times would overcome all. John Jones, Edeyrn, was at the height of his powers, his early radiance undiminished, thrilling the crowds with his wit and flooring them with the awful power that accompanied his sermons. Evan Richardson, again, whose doctrine distilled from his lips as dew upon the dry land and whose melting words seemed able to dissolve the hardest stone and cut down the stoutest oak. There was Robert Jones, Rhoslan, also, a man of letters and a notably scriptural preacher. And there were John Griffith Ellis and Evan Evans, Waenfawr, both of whom died just as their genius was beginning to emerge but who, in their brief lives, left an indelible impression upon Caernarvonshire congregations. These were the fiery stars that shone in the firmament of the Caernarvonshire ministry when John Elias began to preach and the fact that he, with all his disadvantages, immediately became as bright a star as any of them, if not indeed to outshine them all, is an undeniable proof of the pre-eminence of his preaching.

We have already mentioned that calls for his service showered down upon him from all parts as soon as he was received as a member of the Monthly Meeting. In consenting to these calls, he was transgressing the rules that had by then been drawn up with respect to young men beginning to preach. He states that it was in ignorance he did this; he broke the bounds, not knowing that the bounds existed, for there has been no one on earth who so respected a rule as John Elias. Of this time, he states, 'Some of the old preachers called me to account, and kindly reproved me for my irregularity.' Tradition has it that they dealt very roughly with him; that they would often scourge him mercilessly, and it is suggested that this severity found its source in their jealousy of his popularity. Before condemning these old brethren from Caernarvonshire the following points must be taken into consideration:

1. The fact that many of the legends that have come down to us dealing with John Elias's life have undoubtedly been exaggerated; in passing down from one narrator to the next they have gathered material like a rolling snowball, so that by now some of them are more untrue than true. Many of the stories told are so objectionable, betraying such ill manners and such unseemly high-handedness with respect to the ordinances of God's house, that they cannot be true. The high moral character of those accused is sufficient proof of their falsity.

2. It must be remembered that at the beginning of his ministry John Elias demonstrated much of the boldness of an ignorant young man from the country; that his roughness and corners had not been smoothed and that there were some displeasing aspects to his oratory that grieved the feelings of more refined men such as Robert Jones, Rhoslan, and John Roberts, Llangwm. He himself acknowledged that both Mr Evan Richardson and, after him, Mr Charles, helped him to recognize and remove many unhelpful aspects in his ministry.

3. The old brethren feared in case his unique popularity should spoil him. In their view the sin of sins was pride; this was the sin that they most warned against. There was no end to their watchfulness lest any shadow of it crept into the heart of a young preacher. They saw in Elias the signs of an extraordinary ability and they believed that his great danger was of becoming proud from a realization of his gifts, as well as from the frequent calls he received from various congregations. If he was therefore smitten by the righteous of Caernarvonshire, it was done in kindness and their excellent oil did not break his head.

4. There was not the slightest element of jealousy behind these rebukes. This is clearly proved by the respect that he showed these brethren throughout his life, and the homage that he paid to their memories after they had died.

At the same time he, no doubt, felt their rebukes keenly and the chastening at that present time did not seem to him to be joyous. It was not long also before some of these brethren changed their opinions of him. On one occasion he went to Bala to preach but on arriving, found that the Rev. John Roberts, Llangwm, was there before him. The old man became very surly and John Elias had to leave Bala that Sunday without doing much. The following Monday however he was to preach in some small chapel near Bala. He started towards the place much disheartened by the treatment he had received. But as it happened, Mr Roberts followed him and came quietly into the meeting without his knowing. He was enabled to lay hold of God in his very first prayer; he pleaded for guidance and for help to be kept from rushing forward in his own strength. The prayer alone was sufficient to melt John Roberts. A remarkable light shone upon the sermon that followed; power from on high accompanied the truths that were being presented so that the wicked were trembling and the ungodly melting as wax before the fire, and the old evangelist could hardly keep himself from shouting out from his hiding place. He returned to Caernarvonshire with completely different views of John Elias and he told his brethren there that the Lord was undoubtedly with the young man, and that they should support him in every way possible lest they find themselves fighting against God. From that day onwards John Elias and John Roberts were friends and fellow-labourers in Christ's vineyard.

HIS LONGING FOR EDUCATION

We have referred to Elias's lack of knowledge when he began to preach. There was no one more aware than himself of the disadvantage this was to him in his work. He heard of English authors who had written ably on theological topics but they were names only to him, he could not commune with them in their works nor enrich his mind with their treasures because of his ignorance of the language. This produced a great longing in him for a period of schooling in order to learn English. At this time the Welsh in Manchester had few preachers. John Elias came to them for a Sunday and gave them such satisfaction that they asked him to take a period of schooling in the city; they would feed and clothe him and pay for his education, on condition that he would preach to them on Sundays. The offer was just what he was looking for, and in the first Monthly Meeting afterwards he placed the suggestion before the brethren. But it received a very cold response. Not only was it not allowed but he was severely rebuked for thinking of such a thing, and informed that it was pride of heart and a desire to be a great preacher that led him to think of school and education.

We cannot at all explain this behaviour of the Caernarvonshire brethren for many of them had received a good education. Mr Richardson had been raised for Church orders and was fluent in the Classics. John Roberts, Llanllyfni, also was a fine scholar, and except for an unfortunate circumstance would have attended the Moravian college at York. Why they refused permission for John Elias to have a few English lessons is one of the mysteries that cannot be explained; it must be left to the Searcher of hearts. He however received the refusal humbly. He accepted that they saw dangers of which he was unaware, and that it was their care of him and of God's work that caused them to act as they did.

But his longing for education increased. He met often with Mr Richard Jones, afterwards of Wern, a young man who had had a good education and was of the same age as he. Richard Jones told him of the English authors, and would sometimes read him passages from their works, translating them for him. He would grieve that he had not the key for gaining an access to such treasures. Before long he asked his brethren again, in a Monthly Meeting, for permission to attend Mr Richardson's school at Caernarvon. This was granted him, and though he was not there for more than a few months he learnt English reasonably well and became largely familiar with its grammar. His teacher praised him highly for his persistence and zeal; he said that he had never before had such a scholar and that, quite apart from his commitment, he had a natural gift for learning languages. According to Elias:

> I did not learn anything to perfection, for I was but a short time there; but I was set on the way to learn many things through my own application. I was given help to work diligently day and night until I acquired in some degree a general knowledge of the things that were most necessary for me. But I am still learning, even in my sixty-seventh year, and see a greater need of knowledge.

He said further that he had determined that no congregation of his should be at a loss because he had not had the advantages of education in his youth.

Becoming acquainted with Mr Richardson proved a great advantage to John Elias in more than education alone. It seems that for all his oratorical ability, he made many theatrical and unnatural gestures while speaking and also emitted a peculiar grunt in his throat whenever he became heated in his preaching. His teacher decided to cure him of these blemishes. In the privacy of his house he impersonated John Elias, copying the unnatural stances and imitating the hoarse grunt. Elias soon saw how ridiculous these were and stopped them immediately. According to his biographers:

> Very soon after this time all aspects of his pulpit work were worthy and decorous, and a suitable model for any preacher to emulate.

And a further comment from another biographer is relevant:

> Elias appeared like a comet, in full blaze, at the beginning of his ministry. He made progress in the course of time with regard to the richness of his resources, such as elegance of speech, appropriateness of style, and all the ornaments pertaining to the craft of oratory. But in force and vigour, warmth and originality, he never surpassed the opening years of his ministry. This is why the Rev. William Roberts, Amlwch, once remarked to Dr Owen Thomas, 'You have never heard John Elias.' 'Of course,' Dr Thomas replied, 'I have heard him preaching hundreds of times.' 'No, never,' Roberts countered, 'you heard *Mr* Elias – you never heard *John* Elias!'

This is proof sufficient that there were powers accompanying the ministry of his first years that were beyond even those experienced in his most mature days. The truth is that no flesh could stand before him. One old pilgrim from Merionethshire, Mr Meredith Morgan, Maes-y-careiau, said once to Owen Thomas:

> I will tell you the first thing I heard of John Elias. Dafydd Cadwaladr passed by our house one day. 'I have been,' he said, 'to the Monthly Meeting the other side of the Barmouth estuary and am taking a journey between these two rivers, and am calling by hoping for a bite of food on my way home.' 'Good,' I answered, 'I am always glad to see you. What kind of Monthly Meeting did you have?' 'Well,' he answered, 'there was a young weaver from Caernarvonshire who has just commenced preaching, and they put him to preach in the meeting. May the Lord keep him from error, *for the people will have to believe whatever he says!*'

The following account describes his first visit to Anglesey. A Monthly Meeting was to be held at Bryndu. A man from the town went to Caernarvon to ask Mr Richardson to come there and preach. He replied that he was unable to come, but that he had a young student in the school who was an excellent preacher, better than he himself, and that he would send him. This however did not satisfy the man at all and in order to end matters Mr Richardson said that he would come if he could, but that if not he would send John Elias. The word spread throughout Anglesey that Mr Evan Richardson would be at the Monthly Meeting – the messenger never suggested that there was any doubt about the arrangement – and there was great expectation for him. It was not only the preachers and elders that gathered for the meeting but all the Methodists of the island that could come were there. But instead of Mr Richardson, the learned teacher and popular preacher, here was some tall, bony, country boy, whom no one had heard of, making his appearance. It is easy to imagine the disappointment. There was some hesitation as to whether he would be put up to preach but rather than offend Mr Richardson he was asked to say a word before an other man. It seems also that he was to begin the service. His demeanour on entering the pulpit, the solemnity impressed upon his face, the devotion that he manifested on being found in such a sacred situation, and the reverent way in which he opened the Bible, began to convict the congregation that there was something in the youth. This was confirmed as he read the chapter. His penetrating voice carried to the furthest corners of the congregation. His tone was so natural, changing according to the changes of the text, and his emphases so striking, that it seemed to all as if they were hearing the chapter for the first time and that the reading was the very best explanation of it. The prayer that followed was more wonderful still. It was felt that the young man had obtained entry to the holiest of all – that he had reached the mercy-seat and stood before the divine presence. It was soon realized that his humble and importunate pleas had gained the throne and that God was answering from his dwelling place. Before he had ended his prayer, tears were flowing on all sides. Preaching was now an easy task; all prejudice against him had disappeared as snow before the rays of the sun. What his text was we do not know, but he had a service that was long remembered; the old people would describe it, with tears in their eyes, tens of years afterwards. From that day until his death, John Elias was considered in Anglesey to be the most popular preacher. At the end of the service elders from various parts of the island gathered around him requesting services from him, and he was very ready to agree.

He was present at an Association at Llanfair Caereinion on 11–12, April 1796, where it seems that those who were to arrange the public means of grace had heard about him and had placed him to begin one of the meetings. It is said that there was more mention of the wonderful prayer of the boy from Caernarvonshire, as he was then called, than of anything else in that Association. Humphrey Gwalchmai, who was only a boy himself at the time, said that he, together with all around him, were broken down in tears. 'We were trembling,' he said, 'as if we were appearing before the judgment seat of Christ.' His fame as a preacher reached the south and many hoped that he might arrange a preaching journey there. The Rev. Ebenezer Williams, Radnorshire, relates how his father and another elder travelled to a Bala Association at this time purely in order to obtain an engagement from John Elias. The first person they met, having arrived at the town, was Mr John Roberts, Llangwm. They informed him of their purpose and asked if the Association would be willing to allow John Elias to come on a journey through south Wales. 'In heaven's name,' replied Mr Roberts, 'leave him be, in order to see what the Lord will make of him. In all probability he will rise very high or plummet to the depths. We believe that there is in him the making of a great preacher as long as he is not spoiled at the beginning.' The two brethren from the south therefore had to return home disappointed.

JOHN ELIAS'S FIRST JOURNEY THROUGH SOUTH WALES

The men of the south however would not take no for an answer. Mr Ebenezer Morris met Elias when on a journey through Anglesey; he immediately formed a high opinion of him as a preacher and managed not only to obtain a promise from him that he would visit the south if he was given permission, but also to prevail upon the Monthly Meeting to grant the required permission. Having been given his freedom, John Elias set out. On the way he preached at Mathafarn, the home of the Rev. William Jones, afterwards of Dol-y-fonddu, and a description of the service was given to Dr Owen Thomas by Mr Morgan Meredith, to whom we have already referred:

> John Elias preached outside, on the farmyard, because too many people had gathered to hear him for them to remain in the house. Indeed, a great crowd stood before him. Mrs Jones and one of the maids were inside preparing food, because many strangers were present, but they would come out alternately, every now and again, in order to hear a little of the sermon. The text was the words from John 1:29, 'Behold the Lamb of God, which taketh away the sin of the world.' He preached with a light and power and effect that we had never heard before in that part of the country. The people before him were as if you were looking at a field of wheat before a great storm of wind. Tall, strong, hard men were there crying out for their lives. Soon, he took up those words, 'And if the household be too little for the lamb,' (*Exod.* 12:4). 'What is all this itinerating between North and South, and South and North? *The household is too little for the Lamb!* What is all the excitement these days to send missionaries to the millions in darkness in India, to the black pagans of Africa and to the wild tribes of the islands of the South Sea? The household is too little for the Lamb! Why did you come here in the middle of a working day taking men from their duties at such a busy time? The household is too little for the Lamb!' 'People,' he cried, raising his voice, 'The feast is on the table. God himself has provided it. The abundance of God is here. There is a welcome, there is a call to you all to come. I am here today with the express purpose of proclaiming to you that there is room at the table – that the household is too little for the Lamb!' With that, great shouting broke out throughout the congregation. Mr Jones, Dol-y-fonddu, was to be seen shouting and jumping like a little boy. The maid, who happened to be out at the time, rushed into the house terrified, calling out, 'Mistress! Mistress! Come straight away. The Master is out of his mind!' It was the strangest sight that you might ever see. Well, we

> went after him, every soul of us as far as I know, to Machynlleth that night, so that the people of Machynlleth were frightened, thinking that we had come to take the town. There was not room in the chapel for half the people that had gathered. One of the old clergymen from the south, who used to make journeys through the north, was engaged to preach, and he thought, the poor creature! that the people were there to hear him, and he wanted to stop John Elias from preaching. It was explained to him that it was the young man who was the centre of attention, and that if he was not allowed to preach most, if not all the congregation would immediately disappear. And so he preached, standing in the window. And he met with such success that the clergyman did not offer to preach after him. And indeed, he was much wiser in not attempting to do so than he was in attempting to hinder him at the beginning. He merely closed the service with prayer.
>
> Owen Thomas adds:
>
> The above account is exactly as we heard it from the lips of the old elder himself on 12 March 1850. We have included it as we believe it would be a shame for it to be lost. As far as the old man could remember, the events occurred at about the same time as the death of the Rev. Peter Williams, and he died on 8 August 1796. If this is so, John Elias was barely twenty-two years old and had only been preaching for two years.

Although this is the only service of which we have an account, it appears that John Elias had remarkable meetings throughout this itinerary – the same powers being evident in every place. The Rev. Ebenezer Morris testified that the visit was the means of beginning one of the most powerful revivals that he ever experienced. It is no exaggeration to say that he shook south Wales from one end to the other. The roads were filled with people anxious to hear him, following him from place to place – scenes that had not been experienced since the death of Daniel Rowland. He usually preached out in the open air because of the size of the gatherings. If he was appointed to speak in a chapel he would have to stand in the window out of necessity, and the congregation outside would be greater than that inside.

The influence and illumination was indescribable. As a hurricane rips through a thick forest, leaving in its wake the shattered remains of once-strong trees, tall trees uprooted, and thick branches torn away and scattered, so was John Elias's assault, in the power of God, against the kingdom of darkness. The bravest of the brave amongst the ungodly would grow pale before him; hardened creatures would cry out in terror; drunkards in their hundreds deserted their cups; and the careless and thoughtless thronged in deep solemnity to find a place in the house of God.

It seems that only once did he experience a hard and difficult service throughout this tour, and this was the only meeting that he himself referred to. He was preaching one day at Merthyr Tydfil, at two o'clock in the afternoon, and as the meeting proved so successful and the people were eager to hear more, he was persuaded to preach again in a populous locality in the neighbourhood – Dowlais most probably – at six in the evening. Somehow, and for some reason unknown to us now, instead of making use of a familiar sermon, he ventured to take up a text on which he had not preached before, trusting in his ability and fluency, and to the help that would be given to him at the time. But he had hardly begun to preach before feeling guilty before God for presuming to preach his word to a gathering of sinners without taking those pains over the truth, and that meditation and prayer, which was necessary and appropriate. For this presumption and self-confidence he was severely chastened by his heavenly Father – thick darkness came upon him, he was thoroughly disappointed in his natural abilities, and he had to give up much sooner than he had intended.

As soon as he had finished, he went on his knees on the pulpit floor, and in the deepest grief and much tears, he cried out for forgiveness and for God in his grace to keep him from falling into such a fault ever again. He remembered this lesson for the rest of his life. With the exception of this one lifeless meeting, John Elias's first visit through south Wales was terrible in its influence, and by it he was immediately raised in the eyes of the people into the ranks of the foremost preachers of the nation. Some time later, someone inquired of Siencyn Thomas, Pen-hydd, as to the state of religion in south Wales. 'Religion,' said he, in his own unique way, 'no one there talks about religion. Everyone there talks about John Elias.' This was his peculiar way of praising the young preacher. No doubt the story of Elias's amazing success was carried rapidly to Gwynedd and put a stop forever to any prejudice against him that remained in the minds of the older brethren.

Having returned home he gave himself to unremitting labour, and wherever he went remarkable effects accompanied the word. So highly was he regarded that he was placed to preach on the last morning of the Bala Association of 1797, and Owen Thomas states that his sermon that morning was the crowning event of the whole Association. His text was Isaiah 53:11, 'He shall see of the travail of his soul, and be satisfied,' and it is said that he preached for an hour and three-quarters. This was the first time that he preached at an Association in Gwynedd. He preached at the Bala Association the next year, and every year after that until his death, with the sole exception of the year 1832 when he was still suffering from the effects of his accident of that year.

HIS MARRIAGE TO ELIZABETH BROADHEAD

The next event in his history was his marriage to Miss Elizabeth Broadhead, the eldest daughter of Mr Richard Broadhead, Tre'rgof, Llanbadrig, Anglesey, that took place on 22 February 1799. The groom's friend was Mr Richard Jones, afterwards of Wern, who was his contemporary in age and in preaching experience, and who preached that afternoon at the house to a large congregation from the text, Genesis 3:20. Richard Broadhead was a fairly prosperous landowner and Elizabeth has established herself as a trader in Llanfechell. Her father, who was a zealous Churchman, was offended by her marriage to a poverty-stricken preacher like John Elias. He gave her no dowry, nor any assistance of any kind, during their first years of marriage as they struggled to raise their children, and he threatened to cut her out completely of his will. The old man lived long enough however to change his view of his son-in-law; he came to the conviction that John Elias was a gentleman in every sense other than in terms of wealth, and in his last will Mrs Elias received as much of his estate as her other sisters.

John Elias's wife deserves individual attention. She was the eldest of six sisters and had been raised in part by an uncle who lived with his sisters at Neuadd Cemlyn, and who was a clergyman in the Church of England. He was full of prejudice against the Methodists. Once, when she was a little girl, Elizabeth went to visit her parents and on the way she turned into the home of an old elder, Edward Jones, who lived on their land and who had been harried from one place to another because of his religion. The family at the time were drinking tea, and another cup and a honey sandwich were soon found for their landlord's daughter. At the table with them sat a preacher. This man laid his hand upon the head of the young Elizabeth and said, 'It may be that she shall see one day.' Though she was not aware of what they implied, these words and the preacher's manner made an indelible impression upon her mind. It is thought that at the time the family were optimistically discussing the success of the gospel. The prejudice of her uncle and aunts at the Hall against the Roundheads was so great that for three weeks they would not speak to their niece after she had said that she had called on Edward Jones. The preacher at the table was George Griffiths from the south, a good speaker but a hunchback. He once preached gloriously at a Bala Association; after him preached Robert Roberts, Clynnog, also a hunchback, with such power that all were overcome. At the end of the service, Mr John Jones, Edeyrn, turned to the preachers around him and said, 'Brethren! Oh that we were all hunchbacks.'

But to return to Miss Elizabeth Broadhead. It seems that she received a good education; she was for some time at a school in England. It was in the house of an aunt of hers who lived at Bronddu that the truth had first taken hold of her mind, as she quite accidentally happened to hear a sermon. Fears with respect to her eternal state overwhelmed her and when her parents and relatives saw that she tended towards the Methodists, they were embittered against her so that she had to flee to the house of an uncle on her mother's side, a Shadrach Williams, where she found refuge. Her independence of spirit was sufficient to ensure that she would not be indebted to anyone, and she opened a shop on her own account in a house owned by Shadrach Williams in Llanfechell. She there met a godly young girl called Jane Thomas. The two enjoyed sweet fellowship together. 'Dear Jane, this is how my heart is tormented so much by my fears that I almost despair,' the one would say. 'It was exactly the same for me, Miss Broadhead,' the other would reply, 'but the word says such and such, and part of a sermon from So-and-so helped me.' She considered which society to join, in that the Methodists did not have one at Llanfechell. At last she decided to offer herself for membership at Llanrhuddlad as the meetings there were held in the afternoon and her parents were strongly prejudiced against evening meetings. One day, she closed the shop and started out nervously for Llanrhuddlad. She could hardly muster sufficient courage to open the door and said to herself as she put her hand on the latch, 'O Lord, will they refuse me?' The stewards were old men, leaning on their sticks and of very ordinary appearance. They were amazed on seeing this beautiful young girl, dressed in fineries, coming amongst them. One of them approached her, placing his hand on the spencer of white muslin that she wore. 'Betty Broadhead, what is this that you are wearing? If you wish for a place amongst us, you must not come dressed like this.' 'I won't, Owen Jones *annwyl*,' she replied. She was received and became very dear to the fellowship. She once shared her experience in a rather low voice. 'Who is speaking?' asked an old elder who could not see or hear well. He was told that it was Elizabeth Broadhead. 'Let her speak,' he replied, 'Every time she contributes she bears an olive leaf in her mouth.'

As a result of his marriage Mr Elias moved to Llanfechell to live, and it is with Anglesey that he was afterwards associated for the rest of his life. The young couple struggled for some years. He has noted:

> We were, the first years after marriage, in adverse and trying circumstances as to worldly matters. My mind was much distressed by fear that we could not

> pay our creditors, and thereby become guilty of injustice to men, and bring reproach on God's name and cause. It was well for me in those circumstances that I had liberty to go to the throne of grace. Many times I tried to pray earnestly that the Lord would keep me from doing an injustice to any man. I did not desire or ask for riches, but means to deal justly with every man. I can say that God, in his great mercy, heard me, and granted my desire. In a few years our business improved, and we were enabled to live comfortably, to pay our way, to bring up our children, and to give them education.

Mrs Elias was an excellent woman and a choice wife. She was as convinced as her husband of the dignity of the ministry as a high calling, of the importance of the position of a preacher as ambassador of God to sinners, and of the necessity that he should be fully prepared in every way for fulfilling the duties of the office. Therefore, as much as was possible, she took upon herself all the responsibilities of the shop. It was her name: 'Elizabeth Elias' that was upon the shop, above the door. John Elias's name was never used. Even when the children were small and the tribulations of trade and family considerable, she sought to complete all the necessary duties so that her husband was not hindered in any way from fulfilling an engagement or from setting out on a preaching journey. When he was in his study she made sure that nothing and no one disturbed him – not bills to be paid; no traveller calling for orders; no sudden messengers – unless the matter was of utmost importance. She kept the children so that they did not play or make a noise near the study, impressing upon their young minds that their father was involved in a great work. She maintained the shop, and the shop maintained the family. For all his unique popularity, the remuneration that Mr Elias received for all his labours was remarkably small – completely insufficient for a family to live upon. Let it not be thought however that hard work and commercial skills made up the sum of Mrs Elias's excellences. She was a godly woman, full of devotion and a worshipping spirit.

Whenever Mr Elias was away, which happened fairly often, she would maintain the family worship daily. Nor was there anyone as eager as she to hear sermons. So familiar were all with this desire, and so great was the respect for her amongst Anglesey farmers, that very rarely did she have to walk to Llanrhuddlad on a Sunday morning, a distance of about four miles. As soon as family worship was over, the maid would be heard calling, 'A servant from Tymawr' – or some other farm – 'is at the gate with a horse.' One of the kindest towards her in this respect was Richard Hughes, the parish clerk of Llanfechell. If she ever mentioned in his presence that she could not go to hear some new preacher that was touring the country because she had no means of transport, the sexton would close his fist with his thumb up, and say, 'Stay home, Mrs Elias? No you shan't, not if I can help it! I own Lion, and he is at your service whenever you need him.' As well as being grateful for preachers, whose equal are rarely to be found, the Methodist Connexion should also thank heaven for the wives of preachers, for without them the preachers, however great their talent, could not have accomplished the work they did. Amongst these, one of the worthiest was Mrs Elias, and only in the light of the Last Day will Wales appreciate the extent of our debt to her.

Yet, for all her courage of faith, there was one occasion when she also despaired. A ship carrying a full cargo of woollen cloth and similar goods was wrecked off the Cemaes rocks. The inhabitants of Anglesey in those days believed that they had a right to goods lost at sea and washed up on their shores. Everyone therefore hurried to the wrecked ship, looting everything that they could lay their hands on, so that there was hardly a house in the neighbourhood that had not sufficient stock of cloth and of material for clothes, for a year or two. Because of this event and of the opening of a new shop in the vicinity, nobody came to purchase cloth from Mrs Elias for a considerable time. When her husband was away, either in London or in the south, she began to despair that she would never be able to pay her creditors and she wrote him a heart-rending letter. He replied, urging her to trust in Providence and to be encouraged that the Lord was sure to watch over them and to safeguard his own name. This letter was the means of lifting her up from the deep pit into which she had sunk through unbelief.

JOHN ELIAS'S FIRST YEARS IN ANGLESEY

When Mr Elias moved to Anglesey the Methodist cause was weak on the island. There were only a few chapels and these were small and very inconvenient. Most of the members were poor and the hearers were few in number except when a popular preacher from the south came on a journey through the island. There were however fairly large congregations meeting at Amlwch and a few other places. There were only two preachers of any reputation on the island: Mr John Jones, Bodynolwyn, who was of comfortable circumstances and travelled in a gig and whose abilities ensured for him the position of leadership over the Anglesey Methodists, and Richard Lloyd, Beaumaris, to whom we shall refer later. Another famous man had been raised on the island, namely Mr John Jones, Amlwch, but he had moved to Caernarvonshire and was known everywhere as John Jones, Edeyrn. But soon after Mr Elias's arrival, many other powerful preachers emerged, men such as the Revs. William Roberts, Amlwch, Cadwaladr Williams, John Prydderch, etc.

Immediately upon arriving on the island John Elias gave himself to the work of the gospel in every possible way and with all the energy and determination that characterized him. He preached wherever he found opportunity, in farmhouses, in the open air, beside the sea, on a mountainside, or beside the highway; and his gifts and preaching abilities were such that the crowds flocked to hear him wherever he was. He very soon became the most powerful spiritual influence on the island. It is no exaggeration to say that he produced a religious revolution amongst them, and a further revolution as regards the morals of the inhabitants. His labours were almost never-ending. He read widely, and meditated deeply, in order to have sufficient material to preach to the people. He would then proceed forth as an ambassador of heaven, thundering against all ungodliness and preaching the gospel of the kingdom. There were many sinful practices that were publicly tolerated in those days, and without consulting with flesh and blood, nor being concerned with what might be said of him, he immediately attacked them.

One of the main sins of Anglesey was the desecration of the Sabbath, a transgression that John Elias could not endure. The inhabitants of Llanfair-yng-Nghornwy would gather together on a Whit-Sunday in order to set fire to a raven's nest. This nest was built every year on the crags of a steep rock called *Y Gadair.* It seems there would be chicks in the nest at the time. They would bind some gorse and heather together and having fired it would lower it on to the nest by means of a metal chain. With their nest ablaze, the chicks would be roasted. Such poor and cruel pleasure would attract a large crowd of fools. Having indulged their cruelty against the raven and her chicks the people would then gather to drink at the inn; there would be much drunkenness and disorder and often the revelry would end in bloody fights. Mr Elias decided that he would put a stop to the shameful practice. He went into the midst of the crowd preaching the sanctity of God's day and exposing the sin involved in its defilement, and his sermon was so effective that the practice came to an end that very day.

It is said that many people in the Llanrhuddlad neighbourhood had learnt an interlude, which they intended to perform on Easter Sunday. A stage had been built in the open air on which to show the performance. John Elias heard of the intention and his spirit was stirred within him. He proceeded to the place, strong in faith and in the strength of his God, and having found a conspicuous position, he took as a text Joshua 6:26, 'Cursed be the man before the Lord, that riseth up and buildeth this city Jericho.'

His words carried such influence that the whole crowd were possessed by terror; the players hid their faces for shame, hurriedly ran home and threw their books on to the fire, and there were no more performances of interludes at Llanrhuddlad from that day onwards. He preached the same sermon at an immoral gathering at Pentir with the same effect. On this occasion the players climbed on to the stage but it collapsed to the ground and the main character broke his arm. This, together with Mr Elias's sermon, put a permanent stop to the practice.

Rivers and deep streams are scarce in Anglesey and there are therefore many windmills on the island. If a breeze was blowing there were many in those days who would not hesitate to grind corn on the Sabbath day. Mr Elias felt keenly the profanity of the practice and proclaimed woe upon all who thus robbed God of his day. It was not long before all the windmills of the island enjoyed rest on the Sabbath day, whatever the need for grinding. Another very harmful practice to morality and religion that flourished in Anglesey at that time was the 'invitation-wedding'. Considerable brewing was carried out in preparation for the wedding, and people from far and wide would gather in order to drink and to provide a profit for the young couple. These weddings would, without exception, terminate in general drunkenness.

Mr Elias could not tolerate such corruption; he thundered against them with all the passion of his nature. At first he gained little support – the tradition was an old one and tolerated by the society; believers also joined in the practice, though they would not share in the excesses of others. But he would not be disappointed. He continued his fiery speeches, which no flesh could withstand, in the societies, Monthly Meetings, and out of the pulpit. He gradually succeeded in moulding public opinion, and in gaining the agreement of the Methodists that no one who attended such gatherings should be accepted as members.

He would not attack any one form of sin and immorality but sin in its entirety, in whatever form it revealed itself. Soon after he had settled on the island, the Lord visited the country with a series of wet harvests for many years running. As a result food became scarce and food prices high. The wealthiest men, taking advantage of the situation by setting extortionate prices for their corn, increased their fortunes, while labourers descended into abject poverty and starvation. John Elias sympathized deeply with their plight and composed a sermon of biting severity against miserliness and pitilessness, from Isaiah 57:17, 'For the iniquity of his covetousness was I wroth, and smote him: I hid me, and was wroth, and he went on frowardly in the way of his heart.' He preached this sermon, and others like it, up and down the island, and it produced much excitement. Some of his hearers would blame him severely; they said that he took an unfair advantage of the pulpit and interfered with matters outside his jurisdiction. But such were the powers that accompanied his words and the convictions produced in the consciences of all, that no one dared oppose him to his face. Mr Roberts, Amlwch, testified that it was his efforts that brought about relief to the poor of the island by inclining those who had much of this world's goods to have compassion upon those in trouble.

His mind was filled at this time, on observing the oppressed situation of the land, with the thought that Almighty God was about to deliver the nation to judgment, should it not immediately turn its back upon its sin. He believed that the success of Great Britain was to come to an end, unless a very deep repentance took place very soon. Mr Roberts, Amlwch, described his sermons at this time as awesome and terrible. His hearers, on listening to him preach from Hosea 9, 12, etc., felt as if the judgment of the Last Day with all its terrors was opening before them. But having driven his congregations to the edge of despair, he would show them that there was some measure of hope in the words, 'Woe also to them when I depart from them!' (Hosea 9:12). He cried out, with unimaginable effect:

> Has he abandoned our nation? No; he has not! But the glory of God has removed from the place where it was. It is not now on the mercy-seat, where it used to be; it is not now in the sanctuary; not in the sermons, as it was in the days of Harris and Rowland. I cannot tell you exactly on what spot the glory of God is now, whether on the threshold or in the middle of the city, or on the mountainside, or far away on the horizon, preparing to depart forever. I can only say that it is not now in its place. But I venture to tell you, from the meaning of this little word *when*, that it is not yet gone; and that it is still within the reach of the human voice, if you wish to cry out.

And then, in sobs and tears, he cried,

> Shall these hard-hearted people see Thee again return into Thy sanctuary? They shall, says God, if they repent for their sins.

With that, the dams broke, and the thanksgivings of the crowd burst forth in praise and worship.

The coming of John Elias to Anglesey was truly like the shaking of a strong earthquake. The inhabitants felt immediately that an immense power had come amongst them, and they rose as one man to hear this strange preacher. The fame of John the Baptist at his first appearance in the region round about Jordan, when all Jerusalem and Judaea went out to him, scarcely equalled the popularity of Mr Elias in Anglesey. The most ungodly of men could not resist coming to hear him. Once they came within reach of his addresses the terrors of the other world would break in upon them; their faces grew pale in his presence, their knees trembled, and they hardly knew if their spirits remained in them. Hundreds were convicted; multitudes were added to the churches; there were many calls for enlarging chapels and building new ones throughout the island, and the Methodists were raised from being the targets of scorn and persecution to being objects of respect and a power in the land. From this time on, John Elias was the hero of Anglesey. All revered him as a prophet from God. The nobility of the land gave him their respect, the poor and needy would bow to him, and when he was announced to preach the concourse would rejoice. No stranger from the south or any other man would be accepted as his equal as a preacher.

As one small example of the respect paid him, it is recorded that he was once travelling in some haste to an Association at Caernarvon. On arriving at the Menai Straits, which divided the two counties, he saw that the boat had already embarked for the other side and he gestured to the boatmen to return as quickly as they could. Though there were many important people on the boat at the time, the oarsmen immediately turned round, in order to pick him up. Old John Jones, Bodynolwyn, was not at all happy with this, and said, half-jesting, half-serious, 'What have we done to these boatmen, that they respect John Elias so much more than ourselves?'

Of this time John Elias has written:

> I used to travel much in those years, and afterwards also; I would go to the south every two years, and on the alternate year go to London, as well as to many of the counties of north Wales, and to Liverpool, Manchester, etc. Though large crowds used to hear me, and many appeared to receive something by hearing, the Lord kept me from conceit, although my heart was so depraved, and Satan so crafty! I frequently trembled, lest I should be tempted to pride by reason of popularity; but the Lord kept me through grace. The thought of the deficiencies and imperfections of my best sermons made me grieve when I thought of the sermons the people were praising. I was glad, many an evening, after preaching, to have the opportunity of praying that my sermons might be washed in the blood of the Lamb. Thinking of the thousands that had heard me without any profit, caused my mind to sink and lament that I was traversing the country in so useless a manner.

This is the experience of one of the most used of God of all the Welsh preachers, and there can be no question as to the honesty of his confession.

A BRIEF ACCOUNT OF ANOTHER JOURNEY THROUGH SOUTH WALES

We have the history of only a few of his preaching journeys and could not give an account of all of them because of lack of space, even if the necessary material was at hand. But we feel obliged to give a synopsis of his own description of his journey through south Wales in the year 1801. This was probably his second journey to the south and his first after settling in Anglesey. He set out from Llanfechell on Monday, 20 July, and was to preach at Waunfawr that night. The weather was very hot and he himself felt weak physically so that he was exhausted by the time he reached the place and it was long past the usual time for a service. Mr Richardson, Caernarvon, had preached while they waited for him. He felt confident as he ascended to the pulpit that he had a message from God and was not disappointed in his expectations. The next day, the 21st, he preached at Beddgelert at ten, on Ephesians 1:7, 'In whom we have redemption through his blood'; at Penrhyn at two, from Ephesians 1:19, 'And what is the exceeding greatness of his power to usward who believe'; and at Harlech in the evening, from the same text as at Beddgelert. The Lord was good to him throughout the day. On the 22nd, he spoke at Dyffryn in the morning, at Barmouth at two, and at Llwyngwril, in the evening. On the morning of the 23rd, his engagement was at Bryn-crug, and as he saw the people leaving their harvest work and gathering in their multitudes to hear him, he was troubled in his mind in case the Lord should be absent. But he was pleasantly surprised, he had a new insight of Christ as the root of the Christian, providing him with sap and vitality, and that this vitality arrives not by virtue of the drawing action of the believer but by Christ's gracious power, working upwards from the roots to the branches. By afternoon he had arrived at Pennal. His text was Mark 8:38, 'Whosoever therefore shall be ashamed of me and of my words, etc.'; and having begun to preach, the sermon came to him with a new freshness. The Lord was very close to him at Machynlleth that night, when he preached from Job 7:17, 'What is man, that thou shouldest magnify him?' He was amazed at the respect shown him here and at the kindness he received from the hands of those who were something in this world, but he felt that this was nothing compared to the honour of being about the Lord's work.

On the morning of the 24th he set foot in the south and preached at Tre'r-ddol, Cardiganshire. Few people had gathered to hear him, but the Lord did not completely hide his face. At two, he was at Llanfihangel; the text was James 1:22, and 'the doers of the word' was the theme. He had here a most effective service. In the night he preached at Penllwyn, from

Philippians 1:11, 'Being filled with the fruits of righteousness.' On Friday, he was at Cynon by ten. Being ashamed of confessing Christ was the theme and he was given much assistance in preaching. By two o'clock he was at Aberystwyth, and although it was a Saturday there was a society meeting after the sermon. The text was Ephesians 4:30, 'Grieve not the Holy Spirit of God.' The wheels of the sermon turned heavily, yet he felt that he had a message, though only a few appeared to be listening. He says that the church at Aberystwyth was at this time in a very serious condition; that drunkenness was very evident amongst the members; yes, even amongst the elders. In that society, one man was excommunicated for drunkenness and another was not received for the same reason. At the same time he was encouraged because of the efforts of the church to purify themselves. Having cleansed the house, the temple, perhaps the Shekinah would return. The next day was a Sunday and he preached twice in Aberystwyth, at nine in the morning, from Romans 3:31; and at two, from Mark 9:49. He was troubled at the expectations for this service, particularly as he had to preach after Mr Williams, Lledrod, but he was greatly helped by God, particularly in the morning, and felt that he had much cause for thanksgiving. In the night he preached at Llanilar; there was no point attempting to go to the chapel so great was the congregation. Hundreds had followed him from Aberystwyth and he had to preach in the open air at the side of the chapel. The text was Romans 8:28, 'All things work together for good to them that love God.' He had a very effective meeting; he writes that a very remarkable breeze blew upon the people there. On Monday, the 27th, he was at Llangwyryfon at ten; at Lledrod at two; and at Swyddffynnon in the evening. The Lord smiled upon him to a greater or lesser degree in the three services.

On Tuesday, 28 July, an Association commenced at Llangeitho, but Mr Elias had to be at Blaenpennal by seven in the morning to preach and there he obtained confirmations of God's presence with him. He was very anxious about the Association; he mentions that there were matters discussed at the ten o'clock meeting that could cause strife. What these matters were we do not know. The topic of Ordination had not yet arisen, but they probably had to do with some aspects of the relationship of the Connexion with the Established Church. At four, he preached in the open air after Mr Ebenezer Morris. He felt this to be a great trial. Mr Morris was the older man and famous throughout Wales, whereas Mr Elias was a young man of twenty-seven. He was enabled however to pray earnestly that Mr Morris might be helped, and he had much pleasure in listening to him. He experienced much assistance himself in speaking on the greatness of Christ's power towards those who believe. That night he preached at a farmhouse called Goetre. The next day, the 29th, was the great day of the feast. There was a meeting for the preachers and elders at nine, and as Mr Elias began with prayer he obtained remarkable access, especially as he pleaded for the Lord to keep them from worldliness. They discussed with great seriousness the dangers of elders becoming ungodly, of their weapons losing their edge, of lightness when dealing with God in secret; they talked of the necessity of their doctrine being complete and rounded in all its aspects, and the necessity for the saving activities of the Holy Spirit, and for the lives of preachers to be simple and an adornment to the gospel. This seems to have been a notable meeting. Mr Elias wrote:

> The Lord was evidently amongst us, so that my soul was full of joy and thankfulness at seeing signs that God was revisiting the brethren in the south, and rebuilding the breaches in Zion's walls. The meeting thus ended with great peace and gratitude.

He added that the public preaching was excellent. Robert Roberts, Clynnog, and Griffiths, Nevern, preached at eleven; At two, Lloyd of Caeo, and John Elias. Mr Elias's text was James 1:22 and he spoke on being doers of the word. That night he preached at Gelli. We see that Mr Elias preached twice at this Association, even though he was so young. Dr Phillips, in his introduction to the *Minutes of Old Associations in the South,* published in the *Treasury* says:

> Importunate requests (for preachers for the Associations) would be sent from one province to the other, and the news that John Elias was coming would excite the whole country, because he would engage to preach on his journeys to and from the Associations. The same people would travel to hear him for days before and after the Sessions. It was not the practice in those days for any man to preach more than once in the same Association, but there is an exception to every rule, and we conclude from these minutes that Mr Elias preached two or three sermons in three Associations over a period of nine years.

We must hasten over the remainder of his journey. On 30 July he spoke in the morning at Pennant. When preaching on Mark 8:38 at two o'clock in the afternoon at Llanrhystud, he had a remarkable meeting. Great rejoicing broke out and the people remained to praise in the chapel for a long time. They then followed him for the evening service at Llan-non, singing along the road the whole way. He passed through Aberarth and Aberaeron without preaching but then spoke on the morning of the 31st at Ffos-y-ffin, on Romans 8:29. The Lord was very gracious to him here. At two he was at Pensarn where Ebenezer Morris met him. He had a hard service here and he felt that the fear of man was a snare. In the night he was at Penmorfa; a huge crowd waited for him, it seemed as if the whole population of the region had gathered together, and he preached from Ephesians 4:30. He said:

> I do not know if I have had such help from the Spirit to speak on the Person of the Spirit, and of grieving him, as I had there.

Clearly it was a meeting that was long remembered. On 1 August he set out for Twrgwyn and crowds from the vicinity of Penmorfa journeyed with him, so that his soul was overcome on seeing them. He preached on Romans 3:31. Amongst his hearers were many preachers and three clergymen. He obtained much help here. He was driven to Capel Drindod by one o'clock; to Clos-y-graig by three; and to Newcastle Emlyn by evening. He complained of being very tired after preaching four times during the day.

The 2nd of August was a Sunday, and he crossed to Pembrokeshire, preaching in the morning at Capel Newydd. A large crowd drawn from various neighbourhoods had gathered and he was very much afraid in case he was left to himself, but the Lord graciously visited him and he had much help. By two o'clock at Llechryd the crowd was even bigger – some thousands, it is said – so that it was impossible to think of using the chapel and he had to preach in the open air. His text was Job 7:17. His soul had much pleasure while speaking and a deep seriousness possessed the people. As he travelled to Cardigan for the evening, he saw that the road was full of people and he felt convicted should they all be coming out of curiosity merely to hear him. By the time he reached the town, not only the chapel but the road also was full. He preached from the window on the text, Ezekiel 9:4, and with much unction. On the 3rd he was at St Dogmaels in the morning, and again at two, and in the evening at Newport. The next day, he spoke at Tredafydd, Dinas, and Fishguard. He stayed that night at the home of Mr Jones, Llan-gan. On the 5th he was at Trehowell, Felindre, and Carnachenwen; the next day, at Tre-fin, Caerfarchell, and St David's. On the morning of the 7th he was at Solva and had a very effective service preaching on the Lamb of God taking away the sin of the world, but at its close he had to farewell with a brother who had followed him for nineteen meetings. He had a heavy service at the Hall in the afternoon, with no divine illumination and the people sleepy, and afterwards said farewell to a sister who had followed him for fifteen meetings. God visited him in the evening at Haverfordwest. The next day he spoke at Woodstock, Bull Hook, and Bromblain near Narberth. The 8th was a Sabbath, and he was troubled to some extent by being pressed to preach in English, but he was helped and the service proceeded better than he had expected. At two, he spoke at Dolfaen, near the house of Mr and Mrs Nathaniel Rowland, but he does not say whether he met Mr Rowland. On Sunday night he preached at Llanboidy, near an inn door, opposite the house of Captain Bowen. The service had begun before he had arrived, the road being full of people, and he found himself carried by the heavenly breezes. He says that notable solemnity possessed the crowd and that many were weeping. The next day he was at Llanwnio in the morning; at Meidrim, Carmarthenshire, at two; here, Captain Bowen and his wife, who had followed him for five services, had to leave him, and they requested him to remember them before the throne.

From Meidrim he proceeded through Carmarthen, where he had a hard service, Cynwyl, Cwmdwyfran, Nantgaredig, Cross Inn, and Llanfynydd. He had an extraordinary meeting at the last place mentioned when speaking of the departure of the glory to be replaced by judgment; general shouting broke out mid-sermon, and the meeting ended amidst the shouts of the people for the glory to remain. In Llansawel, next day, the sight was marvellous as he preached on reconciliation with God, and the people broke out in singing and praising. The people seemed sleepy at Caeo; he feared for Cil-y-cwm that the glory was departing; he does not seem to have preached at Llandovery, but he met Robert Roberts, Clynnog, there and they went together to Ystradwalter mansion where the two of them, Robert Roberts in particular, had much help in speaking. A sweet service next day at Llanddeusant; nothing of note at Llangadog; but at Llansadwrn that night, though he read his text, Mark 8:38, he was not permitted to say a word on it, but was led to speak on the necessity of knowing Christ. He mentioned two things – the illuminating of the soul to know Christ, and the softening of the will to receive Christ. It seems that these were points that he was given at the time and they took hold upon the feelings of the congregation as sparks amongst dry tinder. The place became a blaze. The meeting ended amidst indescribable scenes of rejoicing and joy.

August 16th was a Sunday and his engagement was at Llandeilo at nine in the morning. By the time he arrived thousands had gathered and he had to speak in the street. Among his listeners was the parish priest who offered the use of the cemetery for the meeting but to avoid the possibility of his being criticized for his kindness, the offer was refused. There were scores of soldiers with their officers present. Mid-sermon the bugles sounded to recall the soldiers, but the clergyman mediated so that all were able to stay to the end. A glorious meeting resulted. John 1:29 was the text and as he described the Lamb of God taking away the sin of the world the people were given the privilege of feeding upon him, so that they broke out in rejoicing throughout the street. At two, at Cefnbyrach, the crowds were so large that not even his far-reaching voice could reach the further edges. Here again God's face was turned towards them, and scenes of glorying and praising were found throughout the congregation. At Bremenda that night, the heavenly breezes blew sweetly throughout a great concourse. The next morning at Llanddarog there was little evident blessing on the preaching, but the society that followed was remarkable. Many of the people had been to a horserace meeting and after being spoken with these were all excommunicated. But before doing so, Mr Elias spoke powerfully on walking the boundaries between the church and the world and making good the breaches; he then gave himself to prayer on behalf of those thrown out. There came down upon them a sense of the eternal; some wept bitterly while others fainted.

From there he travelled through Brandy Way; Llandyfaelog; Kidwelly – where there were opponents of sound doctrine; Llanelli – where the Lord was very gracious; Gopa Fach, Swansea; Llansamlet; and Neath, where a glorious feast was provided. At Penrhys a most memorable meeting took place; the Lord was not hidden from them at Dyffryn; but at Pyle that night the brightness of God's face lit up the meeting, and all gloried and jumped. The people did not break out at Bridgend but the message was received; so also at Pencoed. After receiving help in preaching at Aberthin, he came to Aberthaw and had a hard meeting, but said:

> I saw godly old Bassett at the edge of Jordan waiting for the call to his Father's house. He was saying quietly that God's hold still remained strongly upon him, and though the waves were rough they would soon throw him on to the shore before long. Oh, he was peaceful!

He had a remarkable service that night at Tre-hill – the people remaining on their horses to listen after returning from market and a strange solemnity having possessed them. On 23 August, a Sunday, he preached at Cadoxton in the morning, in the open air under the shade of an old tree, to a large gathering mainly of strangers; at two, at Dinas Powys, a wonderful sobriety fell upon the crowd; and that night, at St Fagans, seeing the host before him who had followed him all day, he longed that he might preach Christ to them, and the Lord shone upon him so that the people marvelled at the Lamb of God. A beautiful breeze was felt the next day at Pentyrch; a good meeting at Bryntirion; but at Llantrisant that night he experienced one of the most wonderful services of the whole tour; the Lord provided an evident testimony to the word of his grace and powerful outpourings fell upon the people throughout the chapel. On Tuesday, he was at Llanwynno and Merthyr Tydfil. On Wednesday, at Llanfabon; few people had gathered but the meeting was remarkable and if the chapel was empty of men, it was full of God. After that he spoke at Whitchurch and at another place (Cardiff, probably), St Mellons, Risca, Newport, and Capel Nash. In the last place the Lord shone upon them abundantly and the sound of his wind was heard amongst them.

On Sunday, 30 August, he was at Bristol, where he preached three times but found matters very disorganized. There was no great blessing on the meetings at ten and two, and he was distressed by the thought that he would have to leave without having proved God amongst them, but in the evening service he was most evidently present. On the last day of August, Mr Elias crossed back into Breconshire, preaching at Forge, Ty'n-y-wlad, Brecon and Defynnog. In the last place a clergyman publicly opposed him and the event was used by the devil to stir up strife, but the truth was proclaimed notwithstanding the opposition. This was on 2 September, about six weeks since Mr Elias began his itinerary.

The remainder of his engagements have been torn out of his journal of the journey – by whom we do not know. It is clear that his travels through the south produced great excitement and that overpowering influences often accompanied his ministry; influences so strong that great physical strength was needed to maintain such a ministry, and great grace required to keep from becoming proud. And Mr Elias had tens of similar journeys. Mr Ebenezer Richard, Tregaron, said of him:

> I sometimes almost feared to hear of his coming through the country, as there was so much talk about it, and all preparing for the opportunity to weigh him, as it were, in their scales – the evil and the well disposed. I almost feared lest he should be lowered in their esteem, and that he should not answer the expectations formed of him. I was almost sorry to see him, and to observe them coming to hear him. But when they came together, I was very glad to see the two parties there. Elias was enabled to go on most triumphantly in preaching the gospel, and all were deeply, and some, it is to be hoped, savingly impressed; even such as were not convinced of sin were greatly amazed. I never saw the cause of religion so much exalted by the preaching of any other individual.

PUTTING AN END TO RHUDDLAN FAIR

The following year, at harvest-time, 1802, he made his remarkable attack upon Rhuddlan Fair; an occasion that provides proof of his courage as well as of the influence that attended his words. It was an old practice in Rhuddlan, almost from time immemorial, to hold hiring fairs for reapers every Sabbath at harvest time. Here young men and women would gather from the surrounding districts, some looking for work and others coming for the drinking and rioting. Responsible farmers would attend also, some from distances of up to ten or twelve miles away, to hire harvesters for the following week, and the wage paid here was considered the standard wage throughout Denbighshire and Flintshire. Scythes and sickles and all kinds of harvest implements would be sold, turning the Sabbath into a market day. At the same time the taverns would be full of singing, dancing, shouting and every kind of immorality and riot. Mr Elias's spirit was oppressed by this desecration of the Sabbath and he determined to go into the midst of the fair and to attack this citadel of Satan. His intention was announced beforehand to the members of the societies in the vicinity.

When the Sunday came there were assembled some hundreds of supporters. A number of friends came with John Elias from Denbigh and St Asaph. A good man of the name of John Roberts had come with him from Denbigh, who had a very good voice and was a great singer. They arrived at the fair between two and three o'clock in the afternoon. John Elias and his party went up to the New Inn. Before the door there were two or three stone steps. He stood upon the highest of these. The place was already full, but when anything extraordinary occurs in a fair the people flock together directly from all parts. It was a strange kind of audience that crowded around John Elias on this occasion. Many of them had their sickles under, or on their arms, and their scythes glistened as they were held with their points upwards. At that moment the hum of the fair was high, the sound of the riot and the revelry, the fiddling and the dancing from the taverns was loud in their ears. But John Elias had come there on purpose to preach to this people, and he was not a man that was to be daunted by anything. It is said that there were some thousands of people before him. He looked soberly and earnestly upon them, and gave some of the words of the twenty-fourth Psalm to be sung:

> Yr Arglwydd biau'r ddaear lawr
> A'i llawnder mawr sydd eiddo;
> Yr Arglwydd biau yr holl fyd,
> A'r bobl i gyd sydd ynddo.

> 'The earth is the LORD's and the fulness thereof; the world, and they that dwell therein.' (Psalm 24:1).

He gave out the words with great authority, and the appearance of the preacher was such as to inspire all present with awe. According to one eye witness:

> I never heard more serious and impressive singing . . . The sobriety and awe in Elias's voice and manner were very impressive. Such effect was produced

> shortly on the people that not a hook or a scythe was to be seen! Nothing but opposition and persecution were expected but scarcely anything of the kind was experienced, for they all put their different implements of husbandry out of sight very soon. Elias read a chapter in the most solemn and impressive manner, then engaged in a very earnest prayer. He was most importunate with the Lord in prayer and supplication: it might remind one of Jacob's wrestling with him until he was blessed. His heart was in a very melting frame, from which his words flowed, and the tears ran profusely down his grave and serious countenance. The people by this time were seized with awe and great sobriety. He repeatedly thanked the Lord that he did not suffer the earth to open and swallow them up alive into hell. He most earnestly entreated the Almighty several times to incline the hearts of the respectable and influential men of the neighbourhood to regard the Sabbath and to prevent the evil practices that desecrated it so awfully; he prayed and entreated the Lord, with the greatest feelings of compassion, for the farmers, labourers, servants, publicans, and all men of evil practices. Amazing effects followed his words in prayer.

Elias took for his text, Exodus 34:21, 'Six days thou shalt work, but on the seventh thou shalt rest: in earing time and in harvest time thou shalt rest.' His spirit was soon stirred up within him, and the words of the Lord came with amazing force out of his lips, carrying light and conviction home to the consciences and hearts of the wicked. He took the several parts of the verse separately.

1. Six days thou shalt work.
2. On the seventh day thou shalt rest.
3. In earing time thou shalt rest.
4. In harvest thou shalt rest.

He quoted instances from Scripture to show how God visited Sabbath breakers with punishment. He mentioned also the case of the great fire in London, which commenced on the Sabbath day and which came upon the people as a visitation for their crimes, and especially for their want of reverence for the Sabbath. He enumerated some of the excuses which were possibly arising in the minds of his hearers. He made some very pertinent and homely observations in a powerful manner, suitable to his audience. 'Should we,' it was asked, 'rest on the Sabbath day if it were a fine day, the harvest being very wet and bad, and the corn much injured?' 'Yes,' he answered in a most powerful voice, 'yes, you should obey the Word of God at all times. It is said, "in earing and in harvest thou shalt rest." The Lord had rather send a legion of his angels to manage thy harvest, than that thou shouldst disregard his his holy day.' He exclaimed repeatedly to the people with all his might, the following words, with his arm lifted up, and tears flowing down his face: 'Oh robbers! Oh robbers! Oh thieves! Alas! Stealing the day of the Lord! What! Robbing my Lord of his day! Oh robbers! The most vile and abominable!'

Such terrifying words fell upon the people like the shock of an earthquake. They were caught red-handed in the act of breaking God's day, and they were filled with fear lest some of the judgments they had heard should fall upon them there and then. This sermon put an end forever to these fairs. Many said after the sermon was over that they would not for the world go there again. That single sermon of John Elias put a complete stop to it.

The late Rev. Robert Roberts, Tan-y-clawdd, used to relate how he overtook a man returning, like himself, from the fair. Mr Elias's words had had such an effect upon the man that he believed that his arm that carried his sickle was paralysed and so the tool dropped from his hand on to the road. He did not dare pick it up in case his other arm should be paralysed also. 'He lost his sickle,' said Robert Roberts, 'but he had his two arms and much more than that, he was reborn in that service; he lived for the rest of his life a shining Christian and he died in peace.'

The news of Mr Elias's sermon spread throughout the land. It reached the ears of the Bishop and some of the leading noblemen of the area. These sent word to the inhabitants of Rhuddlan that they should not hold the fair ever again. But they need not have troubled themselves, Mr Elias had broken the back of the fair forever. It is said that at the end of his sermon he stated, 'It may be hinted by someone that this fair is an old custom, it will recover itself. I answer: If any one attempts to resurrect it again, he will be accursed before the Holy Trinity, Father, Son, and Holy Ghost.'

VISITS TO LONDON AND LIVERPOOL

In 1800 he visited London for the first time. He did so every two years for the remainder of his life, and his popularity in the city was as great as in Wales. It was not only the ignorant and the common people who gathered to hear him but authors, cultured men, clergymen of the Church of England, Nonconformist ministers of every kind, even men who had departed from the faith and who therefore held him to be in error. He preached every Sunday at seven in the morning to a full chapel and usually on another two occasions during the day. On Sunday nights the chapel would be overflowing with hundreds unable to gain access. Amongst his hearers were to be found men like Owain Myfyr, Dr William Owen Pugh, Howells, Long Acre, and Hughes, Clerkenwell. In one of his letters from London he wrote:

> Large congregations gather to hear the Word, so that many cannot gain entrance to the chapel. Glory be to God, I have not been left to myself to

> preach to them. It is an unspeakable blessing that God favours such a poor and unworthy creature with a measure of his presence and assistance. Alas! many of those who now come to hear are usually very careless of the sacred ordinance, yea, many of them are Deists and Socinians. O! that we might be faithful witnesses for God and his truth to them.

Some travelled many miles but would be present, on Sundays and in the week, as faithfully as the preacher himself.

The same popularity and desire to hear him was evident during his visits to Liverpool. He would there preach three times and sometimes four times on a Sunday. Every weekday he would preach at noon in Pall Mall Chapel. The service would last for an hour and the chapel would be full. The workers from the docks would hurry there in their dinner hour, eating their food on the way; the retailers would leave their shops, the traders their offices, in order to hear Mr Elias proclaim the word of life. The more he preached the greater would be the numbers attending, and very rarely did a service pass without an influence descending upon the crowd and overcoming all. His popularity is all the more remarkable when it is remembered that his ministry was so predominantly severe. He dwelt amongst the terrors of the eternal world; his main work was to hurl the thunderbolts of God's law into the midst of the careless and indifferent. He would often press his hearers to the brink of despair, though very rarely would he release them without opening to them a door of hope, and there was nothing that he feared more than making comfortable the seat of the ungodly.

One of his biographers relates how he heard him in December 1802. The previous month, that seraphic preacher, Robert Roberts, Clynnog, had been called home from his work and the occasion seemed to have affected John Elias greatly, filling his mind with the desire to save souls. In the service referred to he preached at Pall Mall on Isaiah 50:11, 'Behold, all ye that kindle a fire, that compass yourselves about with sparks: walk in the light of your fire, and in the sparks that ye have kindled. This shall ye have of mine hand: ye shall lie down in sorrow.' There was something terrifying in his countenance, his words fell upon the congregation as balls of fire, and a fear spread through the crowd as he described self-righteous and hypocritical religious people, after all their vain efforts over their fire and sparks, being made to lie down in a darkness of eternal woe; and their fire and sparks, that is, their hypocritical religious duties and achievements, instead of being a light to them as they approached the mountains of darkness, being rather the very cause of that outer darkness before them. This sermon was remembered in Liverpool for years. No wonder that Dr Owen Thomas would say of him that he was completely indescribable as a preacher and that there was something in him that produced a completely unique effect upon his hearers.

About the year 1800, Mr Elias was given a wonderful entrance into the treasures of the seventeenth chapter of John's Gospel – the prayer of the Lord Jesus before setting out for the garden of Gethsemane. He wrote:

> I received wonderful things from John chapter seventeen. I was given wonderful and delightful views respecting God's plan of salvation in his sovereign grace, the graciousness and stability of the plan of salvation! I now long for some of those manifestations. For more than a year I preached only from the 17th of John, except in a funeral or some special occasion. The Lord was very good to me; he gave me an open door to speak on the great subject of the gospel and the wonders of grace. I am amazed to this day at the goodness of God in this; he gave such amplitude to one of such limited knowledge and talents and advantages! I had neither time nor opportunity to write regular notes on what I was speaking: thus nothing has been preserved.

It is clear from his own testimony that a glory pertained to these views of the gospel given at this time, a glory beyond anything he received in later life. It is certainly a loss to the world that he had no leisure to write, and we can only regret that there was no one amongst his hearers with knowledge of shorthand so as to have recorded the glorious thoughts being expressed.

The period of persecution for the Methodists was over by the time John Elias began preaching. They had by this time become too numerous and strong to be harried by the mob and imprisoned by the gentry. But there was a remnant of the old spirit remaining and he experienced its sting more than once. He would never become agitated when attacked; he reasoned in a kindly way with the gentry, and one magistrate once said to him in an inn where they retired in order to inspect his licence, 'Stranger, there is nothing between myself and you, except that others cannot leave me alone. Good day to you.' A memorable event took place in 1809. It was the first afternoon of an Association at Beaumaris. Mr Charles of Bala had preached on Acts 26:18, and John Roberts, Llangwm, on Psalm 5:11. Mr Elias was lodging in the Bull Hotel and at nine o'clock in the evening, as was his custom at every Association, he was conducting family worship. He did so in the main parlour, which was full of people, with the window fully open so that those outside could hear. In the middle of his prayer one of the gentry, returning from hunting, discharged a shot from his gun into the room. All were frightened. Mr Elias opened his eyes and saw the room full of smoke, but the shot had been fired above their heads so that no one was hurt. Having been assured that all were unharmed, Mr

Elias continued his prayer and his first words were, 'O Lord, have mercy upon your enemies! Save your enemies!' Having finished the prayer he gave out a hymn to be sung, but at that point the landlord came into the room pleading with them to stop because the worship was infuriating some gentleman who was also lodging at the hotel. His wish was granted and a little later Mr Elias made a point of conversing with the offended party. This account was received from Mr Parry, Bangor, who was present on the occasion.

He was stopped from preaching at Llanidloes as late as 1819. He was speaking at the roadside in the middle of a saint's day wake that had not yet been driven from the town, and a great crowd of about five thousand, it is said, had gathered to hear him. After the Rev. Humphrey Gwalchmai had begun, Mr Elias took John 12:32 as a text, 'And I, if I be lifted up from the earth, will draw all men unto me.' The people listened to him quietly but when he had been speaking for about half an hour, having gained their rapt attention, a gentleman pushed forward to the wagon and called Mr Hugh Jones to him. He wanted Mr Elias to stop preaching. Mr Jones, who was a wealthy man, and a Methodist elder, sought to quieten him, and succeeded for a while. But the man then climbed on to the wagon and, laying his hand on Mr Elias's shoulder, ordered him to be silent. Many were frightened but Mr Elias merely asked him quietly for permission to end with prayer, which he was given. They therefore proceeded to the chapel, but hardly a quarter of the crowd could be accommodated. However he encouraged them not to be angry with the gentleman. Before leaving he went to speak with the man and understood that he was now ashamed of his actions, and, said Mr Elias, 'I am sure, having spoken to him, that he would now be willing for me to preach at his mansion.' He would speak also of an occasion when he was once stopped from preaching at Llanfair Caereinion.

Early in his career he was made a figure of scorn and misrepresentation by the Anglesey clergy. John Elias, Junior, in his memoirs of Llanfechell, described the Rev. Lewis Hughes, the vicar of the parish when Mr Elias first came to live there:

> My father, whenever he met him, would greet him respectfully; but for many years the vicar would take no notice of him, turning away as if he was nervous that the very breath of his Methodist neighbour would affect his speech in the church on a Sunday and cause him to preach like a Puritan.

But during his last illness, the vicar insisted that Mr Elias be sent for. Not only did he minister to the clergyman's soul, by reading to him from the Bible, praying with him, and directing him in the way of reconciliation, but he also ministered to his body. He would not take the doctor's medicines but requested that Mr Elias, who was very proficient in medicine, prepare his draughts for him. It must also be noted, however, that Mr Elias soon gained the approval of the local clergy, and that years before he died he was as highly regarded by them as he was by every other class of people.

During the years 1800 to 1809 his labours – involving wide reading, immense efforts towards gaining knowledge, intense study, frequent long journeys, the expenditure of such energy in the pulpit, and the extraordinary stirrings that would so often agitate his spirit when preaching to great congregations – proved almost too much for him. In August 1802, he set out for London in a weak state and with some complaint in his throat, so that his wife was very worried on his account. He ministered there for some ten weeks and then, with hardly any rest in between, he undertook another long journey through Merionethshire. In the summer of 1805 he was again poorly, his stomach troubling him and his voice weak. Thinking that a sea voyage would help him he took a passage in a ship sailing from Amlwch to Liverpool. On 23 July he wrote to his wife:

> I hope that seasickness has been of benefit to me; and I have been bathing every day except Sunday since I came here. I presently feel much strengthened; my stomach and voice are much improved.

He was so ill at this time that his friends in Liverpool thought that they would not see his face again. But for all his weakness, every day he preached at noon as usual, and usually every evening also, and that with overpowering might and influence. At the end of the same year he set out for London, preaching on the way at Llangollen, Rhos, Adwy'r Clawdd, Wrexham, etc. Having arrived in the capital he wrote:

> The work here is very great; a service every night apart from Saturday, and three services and a society on the Sabbath; yet, I am not tired in the work; The Lord is very good to me in it; he does not completely hide his face.

At Whitsun 1806, he was at the Liverpool yearly services. He regularly attended these; he was absent from them only four or five times in forty-three years. During this Whitsun period, the second Methodist chapel in the city was opened – namely, Bedford Street Chapel. The first, Pall Mall Chapel had been opened nineteen years before at Whitsun 1787. At these annual services Mr Elias preached at Pall Mall at six in the morning, for many years. He did so again now, and then proceeded to the new chapel where Mr Thomas Charles alone ministered. At two in the afternoon, Mr Elias preached, and another brother with him. A wonderful service was experienced in the night. The wine of heaven was poured out over the vessels, and the old brethren were jumping with joy. The old preacher, Mr Thomas Edwards, was leaping higher than any. He was a strong man, and about six foot tall, and was often very warm when preaching when compelled to break out in rejoicing; he was especially fervent. His leaping and praising at this time left an indelible impression upon the minds of some of the younger witnesses.

At the beginning of October 1806, Mr Elias went to London again at the request of the brethren at the Caernarvon Association. He had intended going to the Fishguard Association that month. The Rev. Ebenezer Morris had pressed him to come and his willingness to consent was all the readier in that Pembrokeshire was being shaken at the time by a powerful religious awakening. It was a great disappointment for him not to be able to visit them. He wrote home stating that the cause in London seemed to be flourishing; large numbers attending and signs that the Lord was dealing with many of them. He was in the capital on this occasion for some ten weeks. He preached every night and three times on the Sunday. He appears to have spoken on some seventy different texts. He travelled from London to Liverpool by Sunday, 22 December, where he stayed to preach until Christmas Day.

On Christmas morning he ministered at Pall Mall at six in the morning, and at Chester in the afternoon and evening. From there he went to the Llanrwst Association, and arrived back in Llanfechell at the beginning of January. On 13 February, he set out for the Rhuthun Association, preaching at many places on the way. He was back for the Monthly Meeting at Newborough on the 23rd. The day after was a day of general fasting and he delivered a solemn address on the occasion in three different chapels in the neighbourhood. On Sunday, 1 March, he preached four times – at Pantycolli, Llanrhuddlad, Cemaes, and Llanfechell. The following Wednesday he began a journey through Denbighshire and Flintshire; he reached Liverpool by the 14th and stayed there until the 18th before travelling to Manchester. He remained there until the following Monday, when he left for Chester, preaching there that same night.

We must restrain ourselves. We have recorded these itineraries in order to show the immense extent of his labours. His notes show that he preached ninety-five times between 13 February and 29 March, and travelled between six and seven hundred miles. Nothing similar had been accomplished by anyone in Wales other than Howell Harris, so that it is no surprise to find him at Llandrindod in the summer of 1808 and in the following summer, with his health weak and overcome by tiredness.

But because of the strength of his constitution and as the Lord had much work for him to do, he was restored on both occasions to his usual health – to strength of body and liveliness of spirit.

[1] The authors make considerable use in this chapter of two books: the *Memoir of the Rev. John Elias* by Edward Morgan, 1844; and *Some of the Great Preachers of Wales* by Owen Jones, 1885. The first work has been republished, together with letters and essays by John Elias, in *John Elias, Life and Letters* (Edinburgh: Banner of Truth, 1973, repr. 2004), and the second has been republished by Tentmaker Publications (Stoke-on-Trent, 1995).

42
JOHN ELIAS
(CONTINUED)

THOMAS CHARLES'S DEATH BRINGS JOHN ELIAS TO THE FORE

It is impossible for us, within reasonable bounds, to record all the history of Mr Elias's ministry; we must be satisfied with noting the main facts. We have already referred to the part he played in the argument over the ordination of ministers and need not repeat it. It was inevitable that he should be one of the eight men ordained in that first ordination service at Bala. It seems that he was the first to administer the ordinances amongst the Methodists of Liverpool. On a Sunday night, sometime before the end of 1811, he administered the Lord's Supper either in Pall Mall or in Bedford Street Chapel. Before the service he delivered a most effective address explaining the nature of the atoning sacrifice of the Saviour and the sufficiency to be found in it for the chiefest of sinners, and explaining also the nature of the sacred sacrament and the necessary qualifications for partaking of it. As he spoke a wonderful illumination descended upon his own spirit and upon the gathered communicants, so that there was not a dry eye in the place. If some previously still doubted the appropriateness of the Connexion in ordaining ministers, this disappeared forever that night. The following Monday he administered the ordinance of baptism. It could hardly have been said that this sacred ordinance had received its appropriate place amongst the Methodists previously; many viewed it purely as a ceremony involved in the naming of a child. But on this occasion Mr Elias explained its divine appointment, its nature and purpose, together with a description of who should receive baptism, and did so with such power and clarity that the people had a completely new view of the ordinance.

An important period in the history of the Rev. John Elias occurred immediately after the death of the Rev. Thomas Charles in 1814. The occasion brought him forward. All now acknowledged him as leader and he naturally assumed the chief seat amongst the Methodists, especially in the north. We do not mean to imply that his rule was completely dictatorial and that no one dared oppose him, rightly or wrongly. No, there were in the Connexion strong men such as Thomas Jones, Denbigh; Richard Jones, Wern; Mr Lloyd, Beaumaris; and others, who would be willing to disagree publicly with Mr Elias. And it is only fair to note that he, when convicted, would acknowledge his mistake and reveal a gentle and peaceable spirit. But very rarely did objections arise. His seriousness, his great zeal for purity in doctrine and behaviour and his unique ability at communicating his thoughts and influencing others, marked him out from amongst his brethren and claimed for him the foremost position. From now until the day of his death, the history of Methodism in Gwynedd is inseparably associated with his own history.

We have already described his gradual drift to a form of the heresy of Hyper-Calvinism; his sermon advocating an equivalent atonement; his conviction of his mistake by the arguments of the Rev. Thomas Jones, Denbigh; and the controversy and agitation that resulted. Mr Elias was some time escaping the slough in which he had been caught with respect to the nature of the atonement. In an essay on the doctrine of justification he made the following point:

> It is not appropriate to state that Christ's righteousness, as established for the whole Church, is put to the account of every believer; but rather that that which Christ did and suffered in his place is accounted to him. Whatever righteousness and law can demand of him, is accounted to him; he is justified from all those charges laid against him before the throne of God.

The thought here is confused and contains the essence of the idea of equivalent atonement; but Dr Owen Thomas notes that the idea taught by him here was not in any way acceptable to him in later years.[1] Though he did not completely agree with Mr Jones, Denbigh on the important topic of redemption, he never lost his respect for him, nor his faith in him, throughout the controversy. He wrote the following a little before he died:

> The Lord gave one very learned man to North Wales, the late Reverend Thomas Charles of Bala, who was as a Prince of God in our midst, a wise, thoughtful and careful leader. The late Reverend Thomas Jones of Denbigh also received an excellent education and was a learned man, laborious and very useful, although not ordained a minister of the Established Church. He and Mr Charles pulled together very peaceably under the yoke.

These words suggest that John Elias's respect for Mr Jones, Denbigh, was just as great as his respect for Mr Charles.

At no time did Mr Elias's leanings towards a higher Calvinism proceed as far as to stop him inviting all to Christ, nor to stop him placing all the responsibility for refusing the gospel upon the sinner. He thus wrote to his son, who was at school in Chester:

> Thy letter has too great a leaning to the Antinomian doctrine, in mistaking what is said about man's inability, and thereby tending to put the blame on God. Thou dost appear to think that thou hast nothing to do, except something wonderful should arrest thee, as happened to Saul in going to Damascus. Nothing to do but to remain in thy sins! And that the Almighty is to be blamed, that he does not call thee from them, and draw thee even against thy will! O! my dear son, beware of erring. Though man is dead in trespasses and sins, yet he is not dead as a stone or wood. Man is not without a soul and faculties, to act powerfully and quickly. But alas! Man's spiritual death and inability is his enmity against God, and his love to sin and evil! Romans 8:7,8. There is no inclination in his will to forsake sin, and to turn to the Lord. John 5:40. Our sin is our disgrace, and our inability is our shame. We ought to be ashamed, and to blush to confess, that we are unable to love God who is so delightful and glorious, and unable to hate sin which is so odious and abominable; unable to receive Christ who is so precious and excellent, and freely offered without money and price. The Lord, in saving sinners, deals with them as rational beings. He does not draw them as stones, or drive them as brute animals; but works in them as men, showing them the evil of sin, their deserts and misery, and that their ruin is entirely at their own door; then exhibiting Christ and complete salvation by him to them as lost sinners, until the soul is brought to desire, choose, and receive Christ, to cry out from the heart for salvation, saying, 'O! to be found in Christ!'

The tone of his sermons was exactly similar. They were full of exhortations for a sinner to leave his ways and of reminders that God held him responsible for his condemnation, should he not believe. Take for example his sermon at the Bala Association of 1836, with Proverbs 1:24 as a text, 'Because I have called, and you have refused; I have stretched out my hand, and no man regarded.' He laid great emphasis on regarding; he stressed that this was a duty that man was able to perform. He imagined a sinner excusing himself, 'I cannot repent.' He then answered him:

> Can you not bring yourself to regard God's goodness towards you, the innumerable mercies that you have received, and the great deliverances that you have experienced? 'I cannot believe.' Can you not bring yourself to regard the Bible, its witness to Christ and to your great need of him, and of the appropriateness in him to make up forever all your deficiencies? What is it that damns those who hear the gospel? Unbelief. What is the cause of unbelief? The enmity of heart towards God that manifests itself in its disregard. Why

> do they refuse the invitations of wisdom? 'Not regarding.' Here is the Lord himself having descended from heaven to earth, and having died in order to obtain a way of peace, extending his hand in the gospel, and desiring to make a covenant of peace with the rebel. Is the covenant performed? No. Why not? Listen to the Man with the outstretched arm explaining why not: 'I have stretched out my hand, and no man regarded. They disregarded all my counsel.' Why do those who are invited refuse to come to the wedding of the Son of the King? 'They made light of it.' [*Welsh*: 'They disregarded it.'] Was there not sufficient preparation for them? 'All things were ready.' 'They disregarded it.' Was the invitation ardent and sincere? Servant after servant had been sent to them to compel them. The King refused to accept their first refusal. 'They disregarded it.' Was there some deficiency in them that excused them? 'They would not come.' 'They disregarded it, and went their ways, one to his farm, another to his merchandise.' Their unwillingness revealed itself in their disregard, and their disregard strengthened their unwillingness.

A more compelling style of preaching the gospel could not be imagined, and it provides an undeniable proof that there was not the slightest tendency towards Antinomianism in the preaching or creed of the Rev. John Elias.

A DEATH, A SECOND MARRIAGE, AND AN ACCIDENT

About the beginning of the year 1828 he met with a severe providence in the death of his dear wife. He had been at the Mold Association during the last days of February and as Mrs Elias was not well he did not travel outside the county during March. At the same time he did not believe that her life was in any danger. On the last Sunday in March his engagement was in Holyhead. He did not believe that his wife was more ill than on other days, yet he wished to stay at home with her rather than go to his appointment. But she would not hear of it. Soon after he had started out her condition changed for the worse. The children pleaded that they be allowed to send for their father but she refused them absolutely, saying, 'What is my little affliction compared to the work that he has in hand?' When he returned he found her gravely ill, and she continued to deteriorate until the Wednesday, when she fell asleep in the Lord. He felt the blow deeply. The first thing he did after her death was to write a tribute to her in the family Bible. As we have said previously, Wales does not appreciate its debt to Mrs Elias for without her labour and care with the shop and the family he would never have been able to give himself to the work of the ministry as he did. Soon after burying his wife, he obeyed his doctor's instructions by undertaking a long journey through north and south Wales. He was present at Associations in Llanidloes, Aberystwyth, Liverpool, Manchester and Bala, and he was away for almost the whole of the remainder of the year. But he complained that, for all the kindness of his children and their care of him, it was deeply painful to have to return home to an empty house.

During the following year his main work, apart from his regular preaching, was to stir up the country – Anglesey in particular – to pay the debts on the chapels. Because of the extraordinary success of the gospel, much of it due to his own preaching, about forty chapels had been built in Anglesey alone, and a considerable burden of debt lay upon them. He felt the shame of this situation keenly, considering it an offence to God that the building of his house should incur a debt. He stirred up his brethren in the Monthly Meeting; he visited personally every chapel on the island, preaching and holding a society meeting, and urging every member to make every effort. He said:

> It is of the greatest inconsistency and shame to preach Christ as having paid every debt of his people in chapels that are weighed down by the heavy burden of debt. And I believe that I would preach much better in buildings free of debt than in those that are indebted in that we might expect more of God's presence with us.

He succeeded amazingly in his efforts and soon every chapel in his own county had cleared the last penny of their debts. He agitated and exhorted on this matter throughout Wales, in London, and in Liverpool, and with a considerable degree of success.

About the beginning of the year 1830 he married for a second time. He wrote in his autobiography:

> 10 February 1830, I married Lady Bulkeley, the widow of the late Sir John Bulkeley, Presaddfed. We went to Y Fron, near Llangefni, to reside, where we are to this day (22 April 1841). The tender Lord once again provided me with a helpmeet, a cheerful companion, a tender nurse, who is of much comfort to me in my troublesome days, and a great help to me in the Lord's work.

By now Mr Elias was a relatively wealthy man because, quite apart from what she had earned at her trade, his late wife had inherited her portion of her father's estate. He now freed himself of every worldly care, giving over the business to his children.

In June 1832 he met with a bad accident when travelling from Bronheulog to the Bala Association. The accident severely shook his constitution and left its mark upon him for the rest of his days. He had been at the Association on the previous day; he had delivered a very powerful address on the nature of the church at the ordination service and was announced to preach at ten o'clock on the Green on the last day. As he travelled to the meeting in a gig, together with Mr John Davies of Bronheulog and a Mr Smith, the mischief of two boys disturbed the horse causing it to bolt. The three men jumped out. Two of them escaped, not only without a scratch but without any damage to their clothes, but Mr Elias had landed on his head and was unconscious. He was carried back to Bronheulog and a doctor sent for but he was unconscious for some time. This sad accident cast its shadow over the Association. There was hardly an appetite to hear the famous preachers engaged. Between meetings, John Evans, New Inn, Ebenezer Richards, and nearly all the ministers came to Bronheulog to visit, and it is said that every minister and elder from Anglesey called at the house. He had intended to preach from the text in Ezekiel 10:13, 'O wheel!' and to speak of the mysterious turns of the wheel of providence. Instead, he had to be silent before it. He remained at Bronheulog for some time and could not preach again until the second Sunday of November. He then wrote:

> I spoke once last Sabbath (November 12th) and they told me that I spoke for an hour. I intend to attempt to preach once a Sabbath for a little yet, if I receive support from the Lord.

About the beginning of December he had strengthened sufficiently so as to travel to his engagements within the county, and early in the next year he took up again his itinerant preaching with the energy and commitment that so characterized him throughout his life.

During his long journeys up and down Wales, and to English towns, providence watched over him carefully and he was often delivered from dangers. About the spring of 1819 he was in London and he noted that he preached thirty-one times on this visit. He intended to leave the city on 26 April but because of some unknown circumstance he was kept there until the next day. On arriving later in Liverpool, he wrote:

> Mercy kept me from leaving at the 26th as I had intended, because that coach overturned on the way; some of the passengers fractured bones and they had to break their journey. I could have been one of them except for the care of a kind Father's providence over me.

There is an account of how he once was crossing the Menai Straits from Boldon, Anglesey. The horse that was with him on the boat was very nervous and Mr Elias asked the sailors not to raise the sail in case it frightened him. They obeyed for a time, but having rowed some distance from the land, they raised the sail. The horse took fright and jumped into the sea, pushing Mr Elias before him into the water. One of the men dived in after him, but Mr Elias was soon up and floating comfortably on his back. He was soon pulled back into the boat. Both he and the horse escaped with no more than a fright and a wetting. That night he preached at Caernarvon as powerfully as ever. Another time he was on his way to Criccieth and crossing a river. A heavy rainfall had swollen the river and he was pulled off his horse by the current. Providentially, he was carried towards some willow trees growing at the river edge and by holding on to the branches managed to reach the bank safely. It is perfectly true that Christ's servants are immortal until their work is done.

REMARKABLE SERVICES

To give an account of all of John Elias's powerful services would be impossible. There is hardly a neighbourhood from Holyhead to Cardiff that has not some tradition of him proclaiming the gospel as a prophet of God with the congregation transfixed before him in wonder and amazement. But we must refer to some of these occasions for which we have a record.

He had a remarkable meeting at a Bala Association in 1807. Indeed, this whole Association was remarkable throughout. This was the first time for the Rev. Ebenezer Richard to be at Bala and he preached from 2 Corinthians 10:4, 'For the weapons of our warfare are not carnal, but mighty through God to the pulling down of strongholds.' His melting strain of preaching was quite new to the north, and that morning his harp was in tune and his mild, gentle voice so softened the hearts of the congregation that they wept floods of tears, scarcely being aware that they were doing so. All realized that the weapons of warfare were powerfully at work in that meeting. This sermon was referred to in all the subsequent services. Mr Elias and Mr Evan Richardson were posted to speak at two. Mr Elias began about twenty past two, with his text from Ephesians 3:17–19, 'That ye, being rooted and grounded in love,' etc. He stood in the window of the old chapel so that he could be heard by the enormous crowd that filled the court, as well as by the large congregation packed into the chapel. As he began to deal with the love which passeth knowledge, some of the people in the chapel began to rejoice and shout. This was not acceptable to John Elias at that point, and with authority and great seriousness he commanded them to be quiet so that they did not frustrate those who had travelled far to hear. He was immediately obeyed and had perfect peace for the remainder of the sermon. It is said that this was one of the most glorious sermons that he ever preached, and that a powerful authority and illumination accompanied the truth. If the people were able to refrain from shouting, they were not able to refrain from tears; it could be seen in their faces that they were almost overcome by their feelings. Their bodies were woven into all shapes by the intensity of their inner convictions, as the preacher ascended higher and higher in his oratory and poured out upon them floods of living truths. Enjoying such views of the mysteries of incomparable love both preacher and congregation lost all sense of time, and it was four o'clock before the sermon ended. As he said 'Amen', Mr Richardson was on his feet, and the first words he said was, 'Let us pray.' As he began to address the throne, the dam broke. The feelings of the crowd that had been building up for an hour and a half overcame them completely. Thousands gave themselves up to unrestrained praising and rejoicing. They continued, quite oblivious of their physical needs, until the six o'clock meeting. Mr Elias was distressed at having taken up the time of his old schoolmaster and friend, but Mr Richardson was delighted, having appreciated the sermon as much as any.

His biography gives an account of a wonderful sermon delivered by him at Pall Mall Chapel, Liverpool, in 1809. His text was Ephesians 2:12, 'That at that time ye were without Christ':

> In this sermon he gave a most vivid picture of the lost condition of men without Christ. While he delineated that terrible state, the minds of the hearers were filled with awe. They beheld the ungodly without Christ, and they were afraid lest they themselves should be amongst the number. The preacher appeared to be in a terribly earnest mood. He was drawing no imaginary picture, but a picture that was real, there and then, in the chapel. And, with his tears falling down his cheeks, he shouted with a loud voice, 'To be without Christ! Oh! Oh! The dreadful condition of men without Christ! No tongue can ever describe, no mind can ever comprehend the terrible state of that man that is without Christ! He is naked, and without anything to put on; he is diseased, and without a physician; he is famished, but there is no bread for him; guilty, and no righteousness for him; vile, and no fountain to wash him; lost, and no Redeemer; damned, and no salvation for him.' After this pathetic strain, from the abundance of his own feelings, he wept, and put his face in his hands down on the Bible; and the people meanwhile were in floods of tears. After a short pause, he lifted up his head, his countenance beaming with the brightest and sweetest smile. 'Blessed be God! Every man that is without Christ here tonight need not be so any more. He can have Christ this very moment!' The congregation responded with a shout of gladness, 'Thanks be to God forever!'

This service was the beginning of eternal life for many, and scores came seeking membership in God's house as a consequence of it.

One of his most wonderful services occurred at two o'clock at the Pwllheli Association of 16 September 1831, when he spoke on Psalm 68:1, 'Let God arise and let his enemies be scattered.' Little of what he said was recorded but all in that meeting felt that God had arisen. It was a lifeless period for religion at the time and the effect of the sermon was as an earthquake suddenly shattering the silence. There was no breaking out into rejoicing but the truth was presented with such authority that hardly any one in the congregation was not convinced that there was something more than merely human in the gospel and that it would be vain to fight against it. The Rev. Lewis Jones of Bala said that he had never been in such a place or under such feelings, than in that service. A brother from Porthmadog said, 'John Elias preached that time at Pwllheli Association such that Caernarvonshire was shaking throughout, and it has never yet come to itself.' As a result of this sermon, many in Lleyn and Eifionydd were converted and the churches throughout the region were brought to feel for an ungodly world with a new intensity and compassion. The following week Mr Elias preached at Brynengan and a large crowd from Pwllheli came to hear him, though they had a distance of nine miles to walk. The influence that had begun in that remarkable sermon at Pwllheli seemed to have intensified. On 14 October, at Pontfechan, Llanystumdwy, on the Jubilee anniversary of the Sunday Schools, a powerful revival broke out. About fifty were added to that church in a very short time.

For a while it did not seem that the awakening would extend to the neighbouring regions. Before the end of the year however it became known that a cholera epidemic was raging in England and sweeping men and women away to another world in their thousands. This news greatly sobered believers and brought fear upon the careless. The revival spread throughout Caernarvonshire. Wednesday, 21 March 1832, was a remarkable day, the day set aside by the government for a season of fasting and submission. Every church and chapel was full. It was evident that heavenly powers were abroad; the fasting changed to rejoicing, the mourning into song. From now on, for months, all that was heard throughout Caernarvonshire was the sound of victory and rejoicing. Rarely did any service come to an end without some breaking out in praises, and about two thousand were added to the Methodist churches in that county alone. Humanly speaking, the beginning of the revival may be taken to be the sermon preached by Mr Elias at the Pwllheli Association. The reader might wish to know the order of preaching at that Association. On Wednesday night: Daniel Evans, Capel Drindod, and John Elias. On Thursday night: Richard Jones, Bala, and David Meyler, Fishguard. Friday morning: Rees Phillips, Llandovery, and Robert Evans, Llanidloes. At ten: Richard Davies, Llansadwrn, and Daniel Evans, Capel Drindod. At two: William Havard and John Elias. At six: Evan Griffiths, Meifod, and Robert Griffiths, Ruabon. On Saturday morning: John Peters, Trawsfynydd, and John Roberts, Llangwm.

An ever-to-be-remembered service occurred at the Bala Association of 1835. Owen Thomas's comment on it was that it was doubtful whether more wonderful effects had ever accompanied a sermon. God's terror filled the place and strong men fainted from fear. Mr Elias preached at ten on the main day, after the Rev. David Griffiths, Llantood. His text was Isaiah 6:9,10. 'Make the heart of this people fat.' Little of the sermon is known; its uniqueness arises perhaps not so much from the excellence of its contents as from the awful solemnity of the preacher and the overpowering influence that accompanied his words. Ungodly men and women were shouting from fear as if they had been stabbed with a knife; scores fainted, and Mr Robert Owen, Nefyn, turned to a young preacher at his side, his face as white as a sheet, saying, 'Dear brother, what shall we do?' John Williams, Llecheiddior, asked William Havard a similar question and was answered, 'Let us turn to the blood.' As he dealt with the words, 'Make their ears heavy,' and described the dangerous condition of those who will not hear, he used the illustration of an old man proceeding along the highway and unaware of a heavy carriage bearing quickly down upon him from behind:

> The horses are galloping up to him; the thunder of their feet on the ground is heard clear and far. Why does not that man turn aside? He is heavy of hearing. Cry out, then, 'Out of the way, man!' But he does not stir. The coach passes over him, and he is found dead on the road! So these men, who have deadened their senses by their sins, do not hear the heavy rumblings of the chariot of everlasting justice; and the chariot comes upon them at last and rolls over them, leaving them crushed under the wheels.

One witness said that his descriptions were so lively, and the picture so thrilling, that he could see the old man on the road and was aware of bracing himself to jump from where he was seated in order to run to save him. Before the end of the sermon, Mr Elias had been stirred to the very depths of his being.

At times he was addressing his congregation, at other times addressing God. At one point he looked up to heaven, half bending over the side of the pulpit, and with tears rolling down his cheeks he cried out in a voice full of anguish of soul, 'Almighty Lord, why didst thou give me this text? Thou knowest that I have been praying and entreating for another message, but another message thou wouldst not give me, other than, "Make the heart of this people fat." I would rather be a common hangman going from here to London, than that I should come here to the Green at Bala to make the heart of this people fat, their ears heavy, and their eyes blind.'

Mr William Evans, Tonyrefail, who was at the Association and was to preach at two o'clock, said that his words fell as balls of fire, and that the people fell in their scores as if they were being shot at from the Rhiwlas woods and were writhing on the ground in unspeakable anguish. He described it as one of the 'Woe! Woe!' services. Dr David Charles, the Principal of Trefeca College, who was also present, said, 'I do not believe that there was one dry eye in that vast congregation. The preachers were weeping and praying on the platform, many of the hearers had fallen as if dead, and impressions of dread and amazement were etched on every face. Mr Evan Richardson, when preaching that afternoon after Mr Evans, Tonyrefail, said, 'This pulpit is a painful place to me after the solemn charge delivered to the brethren yesterday (from Mr Roberts, Amlwch) and especially after that awesome sermon heard this morning. My whole frame was in terror, and I have not come to myself yet. I felt indeed as I listened, as if the earth shook for miles around me; I should be readier even now, if I consulted my own feelings, to ask you to turn this meeting into prayer. Still, we have fallen upon a very happy text, "The Lord is with you, while ye be with him."' It is the light of the last day alone that will reveal the extent of the influence of this sermon of John Elias's. Many were brought to consider their end and hundreds were added to the churches throughout the land.

The following account, received from the Rev. John Roberts, Tai Hen, describes something of the power that accompanied Mr Elias's preaching:

> Mr Elias's action in marrying Lady Bulkeley proved a great obstacle, not only to his late wife's family, but also to the majority of his friends in the ministry, and indeed to the Methodists of the county. Part of his offence was in marrying someone of the social standing of a lady, and that she was a member of the Church of England only made matters worse. Many of the leading brethren in the Monthly Meeting felt so bitter that they wished to put him under severe discipline, if they could see their way to do so. Mr Roberts, Amlwch, however, considered the whole matter a storm in a teacup. It is well that by now Mr Elias has regained his respect and high position in the eyes of all.
>
> However, the marriage resulted in bitter feelings for a season; and the coldness of his brethren and the harsh words heard now and then caused him to stay away from the Monthly Meeting for a while. At the time the Monthly Meeting for the county was held at Bethesda, Cemaes, his old neighbourhood, where there were a great many of his oldest and dearest friends, and where many of the greatest friends were deacons. He received fervent entreaties to attend the Monthly Meeting by letter from them. Having failed, two of them travelled all the way to Y Fron in Llangefni, where he lived, and they would

> not take no for an answer. Word came to the offended brethren and others that the friends from Cemaes had been successful and that Mr Elias would be at the Monthly Meeting. At that time, the Rev. Owen Jones, afterwards of Llandudno, a young man who had just begun to preach, happened to be travelling across the island from Beaumaris to Cemaes with the Rev. Richard Lloyd. Mr Jones afterwards related how Richard Lloyd spent the whole journey expressing his fears that the friends from Cemaes would place Mr Elias to preach in the Monthly Meeting and that they would do so on the first evening when all the fraternity would be there and would have to hear him. When Mr Elias was announced to preach after another brother on the first evening many were seen frowning and protesting, but others manifested great relief and happiness. When he was seen slowly ascending to the pulpit, some whispered, 'O king, live forever!' Others, with tears streaming down their cheeks could hardly restrain themselves from shouting out, 'My father, my father, the chariot of Israel and the horsemen thereof!' Once Mr Elias had begun to preach it was soon realized that the heavens were smiling upon him. Mr Owen Jones sat next to the Rev. Richard Lloyd, beneath the pulpit. Mr Prytherch stood in the middle of the 'big seat' weeping like a child. The whole congregation was bathed in tears with some here and there having broken out in rejoicing. Owen Jones looked sideways at his neighbour, to see how Richard Lloyd was responding, and saw that he also was completely overcome, with two streams of tears running down his face. This was too much for the young preacher to bear and he jumped up to join in the praising which by now had completely drowned the voice of the preacher. And it was a sight long remembered to see the brethren, Cadwaladr Williams, Richard Lloyd, John Prytherch, and others, fighting one another to shake hands and embrace John Elias almost before he had time to descend the pulpit stairs on that remarkable night. This put an end to all strife, and Mr Elias was restored to his throne. It proved also a great satisfaction and joy to all the Methodists of Anglesey.

We have inserted this interesting account here mainly as an example of the strange power that often accompanied Mr Elias's ministry.

A not dissimilar circumstance occurred at the Caernarvon Association of September 1830. Mr Elias was announced to preach in the open air at ten o'clock on the main day. The weather was fine while the first preacher spoke but before Mr Elias had even announced his text the rain poured down making it impossible for him to preach. It was announced that he would speak in Moriah Chapel, and the people ran there until the building was overflowing. At this time, John Elias, Junior, was greatly offended by his father because of his second marriage, but he had come to Caernarvon and could not keep himself from following the crowd to Moriah. He found a place in the gallery. Mr Elias's text was the barren fig tree. God's glory was soon felt to be filling the chapel; a terror ran through every heart as the preacher described the axe about to be laid to the root of the tree. But when he announced that there was hope of a reprieve, and described the Son of God in heaven interceding on its behalf, 'Let it alone this year also,' the people gave vent to their feelings and cried out, rejoicing, drowning the preacher's voice. The face of the younger John Elias in the gallery was a strange sight. At last, being completely beside himself, he shouted out loud, 'He is my father; yes, and my dear father also.' Clearly, not ill-feeling, nor anything else, could withstand Mr Elias when he was on his high places and God's blessing upon him.

A meeting of unknown date at a Bala Association is also remembered. The meetings had been lifeless throughout the Association. John Elias preached last, at two o'clock, from John 16:7, 'It is expedient for you that I go away: for if I go not away, the Comforter will not come unto you.' Though he spoke well and authoritatively, little influence accompanied his words. The crowd was large, about fifteen thousand in all, and seemed very unfeeling; and as the weather was fine and the heat fierce, many sat or half reclined wearily on the ground. Towards the end of the sermon it was clear that he was considerably distressed by the thought that the Association would end with no particular blessing and, looking seriously at the people, he said, 'The devil has been boasting for some time, telling me, "The people are my possession; they came here in my possession, and they shall leave here in my possession for all the efforts of you and your brethren." I must acknowledge that I can do nothing, however much I might wish to do. The crowd will be in his hand for all that we can do.' He said this in a complaining tone, full of anguish. But suddenly the cloud cleared from his face, and a joyful expression like a ray of sunlight shone in its place, and in a confident and challenging tone he cried, 'Yet, for all our weakness, and for all the strength of the chains that Satan has about the people, the Son of God said, "It is expedient for you that I go away: for if I go not away, the Comforter will not come to you." The words seemed to stir up his soul; he looked up to heaven, stretched out his right hand, and with all his strength shouted out the last part of his text, 'But if I depart, *I* will send *Him* unto you.' With these words it was as if an electric shock passed through the whole crowd; it was like a thunderbolt descending from a blue cloudless sky. The thousands that were lying and sitting sprang up and shouted for joy, so that little of the preacher's remaining words could be heard. The same thrill was felt by the preachers and elders on the platform and some, who had never been observed with a tear on their face, were found weeping uncontrollably. At the end of the service, the Rev. Simon Lloyd said to a friend by his side, 'I never saw such a clear evidence of divine power in my life.'

DIFFICULT SERVICES

There were times when he had difficult services, and Dr Owen Thomas notes that his hard services were very hard. Dr Thomas wrote of one such meeting at Bangor, a little before Whitsun 1835. The text was 'Make the heart of this people fat', and the sermon was the one that had produced such havoc in the Bala Association. Yet, for all the solemnity of the subject and the skill of delivery, and though the preacher made every effort to drive home the nails, the effect upon the hearers was negligible. No one manifested the least indication of feeling. It was Owen Thomas, at that time a young preacher, who had begun the service. Having returned home, his mother said to him, 'I am very sorry that it was you who began the service for John Elias tonight.' 'Why?' he asked. 'Well, in case someone thinks that it was your fault that he found it so hard.' When the elders asked Mr Elias when he would return, he promised at once that he would be with them the following Sunday, after the Bala Association. Owen Thomas relates the sequel:

> He came on Sunday night, 22 June 1835, and he had a never-to-be-forgotten service, the most powerful sermon that I ever heard from him. When I think of him, it is to that evening that my mind naturally runs. I have never heard anything like it, and I do not expect ever to hear anything like it. I remember sometime during the sermon turning almost unconsciously and looking at the gallery to see whether the pillars were in their place or not. His text was Hebrews 6:7,8. 'For the earth which drinketh in the rain that cometh oft upon it, and bringeth forth herbs meet for them by whom it is dressed, receiveth blessing from God; but that which beareth thorns and briars is rejected, and is nigh unto cursing; whose end is to be burned.' We could include what was said in the sermon here and we have no doubt that it would read well. But nothing that could be printed would give any indication, especially to those who had not themselves heard him, of the terrible place which the Tabernacle, Bangor, was that night. There were scores, if not hundreds, of men and women, some of them known for their ungodliness, crying out for mercy. He preached for an hour and twenty-five minutes, and was himself under such powerful influences that he could not preach again for nearly a month.

We heard of another similar occasion at an Association at Dolgellau. The Revs. William Roberts, Amlwch; John Jones, Talsarn; David Jones, Caernarvon; and Henry Rees, were there, all comparatively young men, and they had preached well. Somehow, Mr Elias had very little success. It might almost be thought that his glory had been eclipsed by the splendour of these bright stars that had appeared in the ministerial heavens. The elders realized that he felt disappointed and having conferred they visited him at his lodging that night and said, 'Mr Elias, the town is full of strangers and we feel it would be appropriate to have another service tomorrow morning before they disperse. Will you preach at seven in the morning?' He cheered up considerably, saying, 'I would be glad of the opportunity.' The crier was sent out with the announcement and at the appointed hour the chapel was overflowing. Mr Elias's text was Hebrews 9:28, 'So Christ was once offered to bear the sins of many; and unto them that look for him shall he appear the second time without sin unto salvation.' He depicted sin as a burden that pressed down upon its object, never to rise again; the angels that kept not their first estate sank under it into the bottomless pit, not able to free themselves from it; the Jewish sacrifices, upon which the sins of the nation were numbered, were pressed down to complete destruction; and even the scapegoat, to whom the transgressions of the sons of Israel were accounted, was driven so far into the desert that it could never reappear. He then portrayed the Lord Jesus upon Calvary with the sin of the world bearing upon him, being pressed out of sight by the awful load. But, unlike all others, he will reappear a second time. 'What will he be like? Is that load of sin still bearing upon him? No, thank God, he will appear *without sin;* WITHOUT SIN.' His descriptions were so vivid that the people believed that they could see Jesus coming on the clouds with all the glory of the victor, his person as glorious as the sun, and all connection with sin broken forever. The whole congregation rose up with one shout of joy. This meeting was the crowning glory of the Association. All went to their homes, Mr Elias amongst them, as ones who had found great spoil.

Other lifeless meetings that he experienced could be described. He was to preach one night at Crickhowell and when the miners of Beaufort, Ebbw Vale and Nant-y-glo heard, they gathered there in their hundreds without changing their clothes or washing, with their faces as black as soot. Mr William Morris, Cilgerran, began the service, and every word that distilled from his lips held his audience completely. But Mr Elias preached with no spark, and the people returned home deeply disappointed. Yet, on the following night, at Brecon, while speaking on 'the man on the white horse' he was on his high places, with the strongest growing pale in his presence. Dr Owen Thomas also writes of the first time that the Rev. John Jones, Talsarn, visited Llandovery. He and John Elias were to preach in a Monthly Meeting at two o'clock. The people had gathered to hear Mr Elias. Mr Jones was a stranger to them, many of them not having heard of him previously. John Jones had an effective service, greatly enjoyed by the congregation, but Mr Elias struggled. On the way home, many were to be heard praising John Elias, that he preached extraordinarily well, but asking,

'Who could the old man who preached after him have been?' It must be said however that these unsuccessful meetings were very rare; normally he would be as the angel flying into the midst of heaven, proclaiming gloriously the everlasting gospel.

JOHN ELIAS AT PRAYER

John Elias was as remarkable in his prayers as he was in his sermons. He practised a holy boldness before God; he would go to him with every kind of complaint, even comparatively small things, and would often receive wonderful and evident answers. This was typical of all the Methodist Fathers. John Wesley testified that he never prayed without receiving clear answers. He would take everything to God, even the lameness of a horse that was preventing him from arriving in time at a preaching engagement. Having prayed the horse's lameness improved and he was enabled to keep his engagement. Mr Elias did likewise. One morning he was called to the house of a neighbour. On arriving he found the household weeping and a two-month old baby on its mother's lap, seeming from all appearances to have died. 'Mr Elias,' said the father, 'she is warm, please pray to God for her.' He knelt on the floor and full of faith, prayed, 'If she is alive, O Lord, hear us on her behalf; be pleased to give her to her father and mother for a little while yet, if she is alive.' The little girl improved from that minute and lived a godly life to an age of sixty-six. A similar event occurred to him in Liverpool. A godly young girl had been in a fever. She had recovered in part but her mind had been left confused, and it was feared that she would be deranged for the rest of her life. At the beginning of a society meeting on a Whit Monday, Mr Elias offered a remarkable prayer on her behalf. He offered so many reasons and expressed such godly boldness before the great King that everyone present was struck with awe. From that day the girl got better and before long she fully recovered her senses.

He was sometimes answered in terrifying ways. In 1830 he was present at an Association in Manchester and on the same day a horse race was held at the edge of the town. Mr Elias was considerably agitated by such behaviour and at the beginning of the day he prayed earnestly for the Lord to put a stop to the enemy's presumption. All felt that there was something remarkable in the prayer; they were convinced that God would reveal his opposition to the event and one man commented to a friend nearby, 'Ahab had better harness his chariot and flee.' Mr Elias had hardly risen from his knees than the sky darkened to such an extent that all the gaslights in the town's shops had to be lit. It began to rain heavily by eleven and it poured incessantly until five the following day. Within half an hour of the rain beginning the crowds around the racecourse had gone and the races were never held that year. It is said that the shower was confined to the Manchester area.

Another time he was staying at Caernarvon for some days, and at the time a party of mountebanks were visiting the town and corrupting the place with their lewd plays. Mr Elias's righteous soul was disturbed by the ungodliness and licentiousness and at the end of a church meeting he prayed that the Lord, by some means, would put a stop to their activities. It was felt at the time that he had been granted evident access to the throne. The next day, the wagon in which the players were travelling overturned, and three of them were killed; two others fell from their tightrope and broke their necks. These events, particularly in their connection with Mr Elias's prayer, cast a fear throughout the town and neighbourhood. It is useless to try to explain these things by calling them strange coincidences; God's hand is evident in them, and in these days, just as in days of old, God hears prayer and his judgments are in the earth.

We will now proceed to describe the Rev. John Elias in various contexts, beginning with:

JOHN ELIAS IN HIS FAMILY

An important part of family life for John Elias was family worship. The shop would be closed twice during the day and the whole family gathered together; there would usually be a number of strangers present also, especially in the morning. One perhaps might have called being anxious over his condition and wanting guidance as to how to find assurance; another might be a messenger sent to obtain advice for a church that was in difficulties; and yet another might be there on behalf of someone ill in the neighbourhood, having come to obtain medicines. These would all arrive in the morning; firstly, in order to have the privilege of hearing Mr Elias reading and praying; and secondly, because they knew that once he had entered his study after breakfast, Mrs Elias would not call him down for anybody or anything. Mr Elias would read a complete chapter with the same care for an appropriate tone and emphasis, and the same effort to present the meaning clearly, as if he was beginning a public meeting at an Association. And the prayer would be a true wrestling with God. He would bring before the throne of grace the state of the world at that time, the specific condition of the church, some new aspects of sin and corruption that was paining his soul and damaging religion, and the cases of illness in the neighbourhood, mentioning them individually. In the family prayer he would present his own case, and the cases of all for whom he felt responsible, before the Hearer of prayer, and would plead with the Lord, and fill his mouth with arguments, in a most remarkable way. Thus:

> At another time a certain woman, a neighbour's wife, was extremely ill. Her case pressed much on Elias's mind in prayer. One morning he said to his wife, 'I have somehow missed Elizabeth in my prayer today, I fear she is not alive.' Just as he finished the expression, the husband of the wife was at the door, to inform them of her departure!

The family prayer at Mr Elias's house was the main event of the day, and it set the tone for the day. There would be a particular solemnity upon him when presenting the family to God's care on those mornings when he was departing on a journey. At the beginning of the century the land was shaking in fear of 'Boney', and terrified that he would invade the country with an army. Mr Elias shared in part in this fear and used sometimes to say when committing their cause to God, 'Who knows whether they might not be hiding in the clefts of the rocks by the time I return.'

He would rule his house well and was very careful to maintain home discipline, combining tenderness with severity. His son, Mr Elias, said:

> My father would never chastise for the first offence, but would give a strong warning. On the second offence, a surety would have to be found for me if I was to be spared. My surety would always be Margaret Williams.

This woman was a kind spinster who lived with her father in a house near the chapel. On these occasions a deed would be written out. Margaret would place her cross upon it; and it would be placed for safe-keeping in a desk with all due solemnity. Mr Elias, Junior, relates further of an occasion one dark and windy night when he was about ten years old, and riding a pony, when his father and mother passed, returning from the society and holding a lantern. The sudden light frightened the pony causing it to jump, and the boy said to it, *'Godacia ti,'* an expletive picked up from the local boys. He said:

> My father was very hurt on hearing me, he almost fainted on to the hedge, near to where the chapel is now. When I had cleaned and fed the horse, I went to the house where I saw a change in my dear father's face. Once I had gone to bed that night, my father came into my room with a whip, and he asked me seriously whether I knew I had been swearing. I said that I did not, and that was true for I knew nothing of the derivation of *'Godacia ti'*. He explained to me that it came from the English, 'God ache thee,' and was therefore an awful curse. "Well," said my father, "as you did not know what it was you said, I won't chastise you this time. It may be that I will have to look upon you as an ungodly man, but I am determined that I shall not see you a swearer and blasphemer, even if I have to lay you in your blood for a fortnight."

He said this in such seriousness that the boy was convinced he would carry out the threat.

The first time that John Elias, Junior, remembered being chastised by his father was when he absented himself from the day school that was held in the parish church. He spent the morning in the home of Margaret Williams who was always kind to him.

> When the children came out, I went in amongst them and was singing along with them. But my father had seen me coming from Margaret Williams's house. When I got home therefore, I had to stand before the judge and my sentence was to be thrown into prison. The prison was the small parlour, and my feet were to be in the chains of a sheep's fetters, and I was to stand thus at the bottom of the window. There was to be no bread or water in this prison, and it was therefore worse for me than if I had been in the county prison in Beaumaris. But little John Elias was not to be without food. Mary Jones of Bwlch came to the village and learnt somehow of the imprisonment, and in a house in the village she obtained some bread and butter, and I think also there was even some sugar scattered on the butter, and by opening the window she passed me the timely and pleasing gift. There was probably no clause in the rules of the small parlour that legislated against opening the window; it is difficult to lay down laws that have no loopholes at all in them.

Perhaps the parents shut their eyes to the feeding through the window, not wishing to be too hard on him at his young age, but by means of this punishment he learnt his lesson and never again played truant from school.

The younger John Elias adds:

> As for my mother, she also was severe in her rebukes. I would have to go to the loft and she would pray before administering punishment, but I do not remember saying 'Amen' to any of my mother's prayers at such times. But this was strange, my mother could never stay in the house when my father was disciplining us, nor could my father when my mother was disciplining.

John Elias was not only careful to keep his children from being corrupted by wicked practices, but also to nurture in them an inquisitive mind. He encouraged them to ask him for an explanation of difficult verses in the Bible, or of points of doctrine; he would write for them clear and easy explanations, appropriate to their age, making every effort to apply the truths to them practically. His son, John, would often place a question on the desk in his study; the next day, Mr Elias's answer would be found on the same place. When away from home he would write letters to his children. Many of them have been preserved and they are full of valuable advice, presented in the kindest and wisest way. The following is part of a letter he wrote when ministering in London, to his daughter when she was about fifteen:

> I know, my dear child, that thy dangers from the world, the flesh, and Satan, increase in proportion to thy advancement in age. O! pray much for grace – for godliness. I feel a pleasure in praying for thee. Thou art in the most advantageous position to look for every blessing – in the means of grace, in the church of God. O! ever abide there. Wait patiently there for the Lord. Think often of Jesus Christ, the Saviour of sinners, and the Saviour of children. He delights in having young disciples. He took children in his arms; he was pleased to be praised by children in the temple; he raised up from the dead the daughter of Jairus, when twelve years old; he saved the woman from Canaan's daughter; who knows but that he will save my daughter also! I think the Lord heard my prayers, and those of others for thee, when thy natural life was in the greatest danger. Who knows but that thou wast saved from that danger, in order to be saved into everlasting life!
>
> My dear Phoebe, endeavour to learn those things in thy youth, which will not be a disgrace to thee when advanced in age, if spared. Avoid every temper and habit which may be painful and disgraceful. Avoid a high proud carriage; it is abominable in the sight of God, and unbecoming before men. Beware of being impatient of instruction and correction – beware of an ungoverned dissatisfied revengeful temper – seek the meek and quiet spirit, which is in the sight of God of great price. 'The meekness of wisdom, which is gentle, easy to be entreated – the gentleness of Christ.' A lowly gentle temper is part of Christ's image; and 'after this manner the holy women of old adorned themselves'; and so the virtuous woman mentioned in Proverbs, has 'the law of kindness on her tongue' (31:26). The following things are accounted among the chief virtues of London ladies:
>
> Modesty: this gives the most pleasant air to our looks, gestures, and conversation, and has obtained such an esteem among the judicious, that it will cover many defects. But without modesty, wit and learning will not shine, beauty will be ungrateful, and even quality will be contemptible; nothing can atone for want of modesty.
>
> The other quality of a lady, is good temper. If we give indulgence to bad temper in youth, it will be extremely difficult to govern that temper, or to reform it, when grown to years of maturity; and it is certain that more evils arise from ill temper, than from what they call ill fortunes. Therefore the government of the temper is of the greatest importance; and much of the happiness of private life, and of families too, depends upon this. Nothing can be more pleasing than good temper. Therefore, my dear daughter, pray often and earnestly for grace to govern your temper.
>
> All ladies should endeavour to possess,
> An elegance of mind as well as dress.

> Be humble and submissive to thy dear mother – kind and agreeable to thy brother – pleasant to our servant girl. Don't tyrannize over her. My dear, do all in thy power to make thy poor mother happy, and to make our family an example of order and happiness. I hope thou wilt consider these things that thy poor father has sent in love to thy body and soul, and with a desire for thy happiness in time and eternity.

No better advice could be found for a young girl whose life was beginning to open up before her, and the affection of a father is felt as warmly as a circulation of the blood through every sentence. He would write often to his wife also when he was away, and these would not be short notes, merely noting his health, but long letters, containing descriptions of the state of religion in the regions through which he travelled, descriptions of his services, and important practical comments. His son wrote:

> At times, when my father was on his preaching journeys, it might become known abroad that my mother had received a letter from him giving an account of some Association or Meeting that he had attended. Many would ask to see or hear it and she, my dear mother, would therefore keep it in a pocket so as to answer her friends' requests.

Mr Elias's letter would therefore pass from one house to another; it was considered the next best thing to the Bible. As it was read in this way, passed from hand to hand, it would end up in pieces and, 'In this way,' according to the son, 'were lost many wonderful letters – letters that would have been worth keeping forever.' He remembered a sentence that was in one of his father's letters to his mother, 'My dear wife, I am amazed that such a poor worm as myself is sitting in a carriage, while my Master had only a donkey to ride.'

JOHN ELIAS IN HIS NEIGHBOURHOOD

The respect in which John Elias was held in Llanfechell and the neighbourhood, and indeed throughout Anglesey, was immeasurable. He was always called *Mr* Elias, as much behind his back as to his face, and he was the only Nonconformist minister honoured in this way for the title was generally reserved for clergymen and the nobility. He was the oracle of the locality; all in trouble turned to him. The people came from far and wide to him for legal advice, for medicines, for guidance when uncertain and for help when in trouble. For hundreds, his word carried the authority of law; his words were considered almost as the words of God. One man said that the inhabitants of Anglesey would not ask at any time what the Scriptures said but what John Elias said. This was, no doubt, an exaggeration, but it contained the truth that it was in the light of Mr Elias's interpretation of it that they, to a considerable degree, understood the Bible. There never was on the island, before or after, anyone else who possessed such a degree of spiritual influence. It was not only the poor and common people that looked up to him but the nobility of the island held him in great respect also. Whenever a stranger visited one of the noble families of Anglesey he would not dream of returning without having seen the 'Prophet', and to have shaken his hand was considered a privilege.

As an example of the respect felt towards him by the gentry, consider the following account. At midday, one Sunday, the late William Bulkeley Hughes, Esq., M.P., Plascoch, came to the chapel house at Llanfechell. A Methodist minister happened to be in the room to which the gentleman was brought and the two men conversed for some ten minutes. As he was rising to leave, Mr Hughes caught sight of a picture of John Elias that was hanging on the wall. In an instant he had removed his hat from his head and studied the picture in surprise. At last he said, 'Yes, that's him. One of the best of men I ever saw, and so also my father always said about him.' He added, 'I have in Plascoch a letter from him that I received at the time of my marriage, and I would not be parted from it for a hundred sovereigns.'

The idea of a pastor and a pastorate, at least in its present form, had not been conceived of at that time, but John Elias would conscientiously fulfil the work of a pastor for all the localities of the neighbourhood. According to the Rev. John Roberts, Tai-hen:

> As a rule, when Mr Elias would be at home in Llanfechell, he would go to three societies every week, namely, to Llanrhuddlad, where he and Mrs Elias were members, to Cemaes, and to Bethlehem. Llanfechell is in the middle, and he would have about two or three miles to travel to reach the other two places. After being all day in his study, concentrating on his studies and wrestling in prayer with God, he would be seen walking slowly to the church meeting or to the service where he was announced. He is dressed as carefully as if he were to appear before the Association field, and every action and gesture of his is gentlemanlike and dignified, and the gentleness and solemnity of a man of God is to be seen in his face. There would be no thought of anyone else beginning the society other than he; and such would be the feast of pleasure and blessing of hearing and seeing him as one having come, as it were, from God. The fragrance of myrrh was upon his dress, and before the end of the reading from God's word and of the prayer all would feel that their cup was full, and they were ready to share their thoughts, the one with the other. With a view to Mr Elias in these meetings, it would be hard to decide whether it was the kingly authority or the fatherly gentleness that was more evident.

> And at the end, no one was willing to leave without having the privilege of shaking hands with Mr Elias; this was not only considered a privilege but also a means of grace to their souls.

The movement of a blade reveals the direction of the wind, and the following fact, related by his son, reveals the position held by Mr Elias in the eyes of the public:

> Robert Edmonds, the local blacksmith, lived at Tan-y-fonwent. My father believed that he was the best man in Wales for shoeing his mare. When I was a boy, and taking the mare to his forge to be shod, the area around the forge would often be full of other people's horses. The minute that Robert Edmonds saw my face, he would know my message, knowing probably the journey that lay before my father. He would strike his hammer on the anvil as a sign that everyone's work was to stop, until the horse of the King's ambassador had received the necessary treatment.

John Elias preached often in the Llanfechell neighbourhood; there is hardly a house in the neighbourhood where he had not proclaimed the Word of life and his popularity was proverbial. When it was known that he would be preaching at home, there would be an excitement throughout the region. The people would say to one another, 'Mr Elias is to be here next Sunday, and the dust will be removed from every old pillion and saddle.' According to Mr Roberts Edwards, who lived in the chapel house at Llanfechell:

> Whenever he returned from a journey he had to preach in all the houses and chapels of the vicinity, and large gatherings would congregate to hear him in every place, as if he were a stranger. At these times he would have some of the most powerful meetings of his ministry. He would preach to the best of his ability always, whether he was in a poor house or on the Association field. Some of the texts he used in the houses around Llanfechell were: 'What shall one then answer the messengers of the nation?'(*Isa.* 14:32); 'It is good for a man that he bear the yoke in his youth' (*Lam.* 3:27); 'And what will ye do in the day of visitation?' (*Isa.* 10:3); 'To see thy power and thy glory, so as I have seen thee in the sanctuary' (*Psa.* 63:2); 'Judgment must begin at the house of God: and if it first begin at us, what shall the end be of them that obey not the gospel?' (1 *Pet.* 4:17). Mr Elias would always be sought to preach at weddings, watch nights, and all the funerals of the neighbourhood.

He would do all this for no payment. A man from the Llanrhuddlad area called John Jones came to him in great sadness, and asked him if he would preach at his wife's funeral.

'I will come immediately, John *bach*,' said Mr Elias.

'What will you need in order for you to come?'

'Only a crown,' was the answer.

The man did not profess religion at the time. Mr Elias came to the funeral and preached very effectively. At the end of the service, John Jones came to him and extending his hand, said:

'Here's the crown, Mr Elias.'

'No,' said he, 'that was not what I meant. I was referring to a much more costly crown. You keep the five shillings, John Jones.'

He would not hesitate to preach against the favourite sins of the various neighbourhoods, and he would do this so effectively that the transgressors imagined that someone had complained about them to him. According to his son:

> Herring fishing was one of the main employments of the people of Cemlyn in his time (Cemlyn was a rich neighbourhood, about three miles from Llanfechell); some of the sons of the local farms were to be found among the fishermen. William Owen would always be after my father to get him for a service there, before the boats set sail. My father promised to go. But somehow he heard that they used to set their nets on the Sabbath. And in the sermon he spoke severely against the desecration of the Sabbath, and the fishermen trembled before his thundering. William Owen was in a state, not knowing whether to go to the boat with the others, in that he was sure they would believe that it was he that had carried tales to my father. After the service he came up to him, and said, 'John Elias *annwyl*, what shall I do? You have spoken out against all our wicked deeds, and they will never believe that it was not me that told you.' However, this put an end to setting nets on the Sabbath in Cemlyn.

Whenever an important matter was under consideration, or a young man beginning with the work of the ministry in one of the churches near to Llanfechell, Mr Elias would without fail be the representative from the Monthly Meeting; and in this context he would often be the recipient of remarkable guidance. He was sent once to Bethlehem church to examine a young man who wished to begin preaching. This youth had an able mind and more extensive knowledge than most. All in the neighbourhood looked up to him as a man of knowledge and ability, but yet not without some doubt as to his character. The examination began, and the young giant, before Mr Elias and the whole church, hardly answered a single one of the questions asked of him. Every one was astonished. One of the elders, Mr John Owen, rose to defend him, saying, 'Don't be hard on him, Mr Elias; we all know as a church that he would normally easily answer all those questions that you asked him tonight, but that some darkness has come over him; fear of yourself perhaps.' 'Yes, John Owen *bach*', replied John Elias, 'what if it is a darkness from the Lord Jesus, the Head of the

Church?' His comment proved true. The young man turned his back on the church of God and on all means of grace, and wallowed in the vilest mires for many years.

He would be particularly careful over discipline. Said his son:

> My father was always called upon to perform that work when needed; and sometimes he was obliged to turn out of the church some respectable persons in the neighbourhood, and these greatly threatened to injure our business. As our trade was on a small scale, and very dependent, it would have been easy for a person of property to trample upon it and to crush it. However, my mother was much composed, trusting to the Lord; smilingly she would say, 'My beloved and tried head, being innocent, escaped out of the snare.' She was much afraid lest any toleration or connivance at sin in the powerful should be manifested, and the church of God sustain an injury thereby.

John Elias would demonstrate great courage, and deep conscientiousness on these occasions, as the following account shows. In a large church in Anglesey, having about three hundred members, three able young men who had received the benefits of education but were of a conceited nature, were causing trouble. They were not happy with the way the church was being run yet they would not leave it. They were thorns in the sides of the brethren of the church, who did not know what to do with them. At last the Monthly Meeting decided to send Mr Elias there. When the rebels heard this they decided to debate with him and beat him in argument, or at least cause him to lose his temper. The narrator of the account continues:

> When we understood that Mr Elias was there, leading a society, but not knowing the cause, we hastened to the chapel. He was in the middle of praying when we arrived. Though the prayer was earnest, serious, and very humble, we felt that there was to it a kind of indescribable severity that caused us to fear yet without knowing why. There were in it phrases like 'loving to have the preeminence', 'first and second admonition', 'being likeminded', 'withdrawing from those who walk disorderly', and similar words. At the close of the prayer, a silence that was almost painful settled over the congregation. Mr Elias began to speak to the church about church discipline, the necessity for it to be pure, honest, and determined. He then spoke to the transgressors – whom he knew well – respectfully, gently, and attractively, but with true majesty and authority and with complete self-possession. He spoke much of consecrating all learning, knowledge, and influence to the service of religion; for the need of repentance, faith, and love; and particularly of humility, self-denial, and of esteeming others better than ourselves. At this one of the three, the oldest, called on him to get to the point! A cloud came over Mr Elias's majestic face; fire shot out of his eyes so that a terror fell upon all present; but he did not lose his self-possession. His face changed again and he asked quite gently, yet

with dignity and authority, what was it they had to say. One of them began to argue with him; he responded prudently and magisterially, but before he finished his answer the second young man took him up; and when Mr Elias started a further answer, the third interrupted him. Elias stopped; he realized what was planned, that they intended to snare him and cause him to lose his temper rather than seeking to heal the wounds. He sat down and encouraged them to proceed. When the last had had his say he rose to his feet like a prince, his bearing manifesting great dignity and nobility, and with a voice of authority declared that it was evident to the whole church that the purpose of these men was to cause strife, and the Word of God commanded a withdrawal from all such, and he called on all who believed that this was the duty of the church to raise their right hand. The response was almost unanimous. He then pronounced the sentence of excommunication, with terrifying solemnity and authority, pronouncing, with his arm outstretched, 'Withdraw yourselves from these wicked men.' Such was the power accompanying his words that the people who were sitting next to the troublemakers scattered away from them, as if they were afraid lest the earth should swallow them up, and the three were left completely on their own. The three then slipped away quietly, 'and the door was shut'.

JOHN ELIAS ADMINISTERING THE SACRAMENTS

Mr Elias was always very happy administering the two sacraments that pertain to the Christian Church. Parents considered it a privilege for him to baptize their children. He rarely engaged in controversy on these occasions; he emphasized rather the important responsibilities with respect to both the parents and the church that were involved in the ordinance. But he could defend the principles involved if there was need for it. At one time there was a great awakening of the cause of religion in Anglesey, and men in their scores and hundreds were converted and joining the churches. Some Baptist brethren took advantage of this to confuse the minds of many of the converts, saying to them, 'Unless you are immersed you cannot be saved. You must be obedient and be baptized in the river, otherwise you will not be disciples of Christ.' One of them dared to approach Mr Elias, telling him that he came out of conscience before God to exhort him to be honest before the people and to baptize them by immersion according to the Word of the Lord, without which they could not be saved as they had not obeyed Christ's clear command. Mr Elias, in complete possession of himself, asked him two or three questions in reply, and he, not being able to answer them, then turned to condemning, threatening, and prophesying. Though he was not at all disturbed by the encounter, Mr Elias realized that he would have to strengthen the minds of the young converts on the subject of baptism at the first convenient opportunity. Soon afterwards, in a nearby town, he was to baptize one adult man and three babies. A larger than usual congregation had gathered as there was an expectation that Mr Elias would be outlining his principles. After a friend had begun the service, he began the baptismal service. He said:

> We who are here present are to commit individuals by baptism to the Lord. The occasion is unusual – the committing of an adult, together with others, to Christ by baptism. This places us in very similar circumstances to those of the apostles at the dawn of Christianity, when they were baptizing whole families and those of all ages. We are in similar circumstances also to those our missionaries often find themselves in, in pagan lands, when they baptize the converted, and committing parents and children, those of all ages, young and old, through the ordinance of baptism, to the Lord.

Having spoken very effectively on the purpose of baptism, and on the element used in baptism – pure water – and applied to those baptized in the name of the Trinity, he began to comment on the recipients of baptism. He began with the commandment recorded by the Evangelists, 'Go ye into all the world.' He then proceeded to show the similarity between Christian baptism and circumcision under the Old Dispensation. He said:

> The Lord never gave a promise to the people, in any age, without confirming it with an appropriate seal. A promise was given to Noah, and the rainbow was set in the cloud as a token to confirm it. He gave a promise to Abraham, and to his seed after him, and gave circumcision as a seal of his faithfulness. So also in the ordering of the new dispensation, under the gospel, baptism was ordained as a token, under seal, of his faithfulness to fulfil his promise to his people and to his children. As the children were part of God's Israel at that time, why should they not be part of God's Church now? On taking the kingdom away from the Jews, because they bore no fruit, their nature was not changed. When the branches were broken off, the trunk was not moved; and when they are returned, they shall be grafted back to the old root, their old olive tree. The Church is the same in its purpose, now as it was then. As the children were part of it then, so also must they be now, unless God himself has broken them away. Consider, who could break them away? Where is the chapter, where is the verse, where their excommunication is taught? Where, by commandment or example, is the least suggestion of such a thing? I cannot see it anywhere. And until that is shown us we do not dare deprive them of their due right in the Church presently, according to God's own decree.

As he spoke in this way the congregation was delighted, with smiles to be seen on many faces.

He then gave detailed comments on the appropriateness of sprinkling, referring to the promise, 'Then I will sprinkle clean water upon you,' (*Ezek.*

36:25). He showed that sprinkling as a symbol was exactly equivalent to the baptism of the Holy Spirit according to the scriptural depiction: 'Turn you at my reproof: behold, I will pour out my Spirit unto you,' (*Prov.* 1:23); 'Until the Spirit be poured upon us from on high' (*Isa.* 32:15); 'I will pour my Spirit upon thy seed,' (*Isa.* 44:3); etc.; and that it corresponded to the scriptural history at the time of the apostles, such as: 'He hath shed forth this, which you now see and hear' (*Acts* 2:33); etc. He then showed the appropriateness of sprinkling in terms of its correspondence to the gentle functions of gospel ministry; the harmless ease of its administration in every country, climate, season, and period. He then explained that a little water was as appropriate as a sign of baptism as was a little bread and a little wine in the Lord's Supper. He proceeded through every aspect of the question, in its various branches, with complete mastery; his phrases were like nails being secured in the minds of his hearers; they felt that the matter, as far as they were concerned, had been finally decided.

Then he turned to the adult believer and said, 'Rise up and be baptized,' and performed the ceremony. Afterwards the children were brought forward. When he took them in his arms, he appeared delighted; a happy smile on his face as if he were drawing pleasure and delight from the work. He recited the Saviour's words, 'Suffer little children to come unto me, and forbid them not; for of such is the kingdom of God.' Then, as one who has gained complete victory, he asked, 'If they were in the kingdom; if it pleased their heavenly Father to give them the kingdom, who are we to shut them out, or to keep from them any of the privileges of the kingdom; the kingdom that is not of this world?' After baptizing them, he prayed for them very effectively. This address brought about its intended effects; the minds of the converts were quietened, the excitement and arguments in the neighbourhood ceased, and the young disciples were relieved of the attacks of other teachers.

When administering the ordinance of the Lord's Supper, which he did more often than any other minister in Anglesey, his words would always be appropriate and often overpowering. Those participating would be brought to the middle of the floor, between the benches, while the other hearers would withdraw to the gallery, for no one would dream of absenting themselves before the close of the communion service; all felt bound to stay. He preferred it if all received the elements on their knees; he could not abide seated pews on the ground floor of the chapels. He chose always to have the floor clear so that benches might be brought and room made for the communicants in the rows between them. The usual method was for one of the elders to follow him, with the bread and wine, supplying him as he proceeded. We would be glad to give Gwalchmai's full account of a communion evening, but must be satisfied with the following *précis:*

> All have taken their place. There is a silence as of the grave over the whole chapel. The falling of a leaf would be heard in the complete silence that prevailed, other than an occasional soft groan escaping from the depths of a heart. The table has been prepared. Elias is sitting by the side, his elbow leaning on the side, his head in his hand, signs of tiredness to be seen in him after the energetic preaching. Everything about the table is plain, simple, and unadorned; yet, there is a kind of delightful beauty upon everything. There is here no crimson cloth edged with gold gimp fringe, and no 'I.H.S' in gilt, or any picture of the cross embroidered in silk; but what of that? There is a clean floor and a white cloth, as white as snow, spread over the table. It is true that there is no high flagon or decorated chalice; but for all that, the common black glass bottles look attractive on that clean white sheet. Though there are no choice cups sparkling in the light, yet the small china cups are very attractive. There are no gilt plates or silver baskets for the bread, yet, the plates that are there are clean and functional. Though there is no richness on display yet there might well be that which is a hundred times more precious, the sacrifices of God, namely, contrite hearts and broken spirits, which will never be despised by the King of heaven! There are no mediaeval carvings on table or chair to charm the feelings, but there is here a scribe who is instructed unto the kingdom of heaven to provide the service. He rises to his feet. As the people are kneeling, he appears above them all, and taller than usual . . . He begins his work. He calls the attention of the congregation to the table, and points towards the elements upon it.
>
> 'Now,' he says, 'we are to remember the Lord's death in obedience to his command, and out of respect to his wishes; do this in remembrance of me! I trust that we shall be found doing so, with clear signs of his approval.'
>
> Having spoken effectively on the nature of the sacrament, he proceeds to explain its institution by the Lord Jesus on the night he was betrayed.
>
> 'The Saviour chose the night in which he was betrayed to institute it because he was then, as it were, retiring from his public work. He had said, "I must work the works of him that sent me, while it is day: the night cometh, when no man can work." His night had by now come. The sun had set for the last time over his pure head for on the next day he was to be publicly delivered into the hands of his enemies to be crucified and killed. This was the night of his great suffering. His life was one of suffering, but by now all the streams of his sufferings on earth had merged together into one deep flood all around him. There was something notable in that comment of Pilate's about him, "Behold the man." He, poor fellow, saw only the man in him. Here is a call for us tonight in this supper to see him as if he were visible: "Behold the man," here. Behold also, "Immanuel, God with us."'

'Christ throughout his life had been a man of sorrows and acquainted with grief. The sadness of his friends, the weakness of his disciples, the hardness of his enemies, and the persecutions of the Jews, had forced many a groan from his breast from time to time; the tears of sympathy had run down his pure cheeks above Lazarus's grave, and above the city of Jerusalem; but by now, all the streams had converged, as a river in flood, from every direction, and from every world; his dark night had come! Hell was stirring under him; the earth seemed to have determined to reject him; and the heavens were beginning to darken above his head. His enemies had conspired together against him and were now thirsting for his blood. He himself had withdrawn to pray in the garden, in a still, quiet, peaceful place beside the brook Cedron; and Judas also knew the place, for Jesus often sought it out. There was some great haste upon everyone that night to accomplish their work. Judas was in haste. Jesus seeing the eagerness in him, told him, "That thou doest, do quickly." After reaching Gethsemane, he did not have the time to continue in prayer, for the crowd with their spears were near at hand. The soldiers were in haste to hold and bind him; in haste they led him through the streets and to the courts; in haste to condemn him and scourge him, to mock him and to crown him; in haste to drive him from this world!

'This is the object of our meditation this evening. "Behold the man!" Behold the one who was the brightness of his Father's glory and the express image of his person, condemned for sins of which he was not guilty. Behold the sentence of crucifixion pronounced upon the harmless and undefiled Lamb! Behold the one who holds the sceptre of the government of the world standing silent before the throne of a Roman governor! Behold him, who covers himself with light as with a garment, who stretches out the heavens like a curtain, with the soldiers sharing out his clothes and casting lots for his seamless coat. Behold the one who is crowned with glory and honour being crowned with thorns! No wonder that it was shouted out, "Behold the man!" Now, notice, how long did it take all these things to be accomplished? All in the night in which he was betrayed! These are some of the things that we are to remember, so that our hearts may be filled with true love towards him. What could have been filling his thoughts at this time? Has he forgotten everybody else under the immensity of his own sufferings? No, his love for his people is still at the focus of his heart! The High Priest carried the names of the twelve tribes of Israel upon his bosom to the Holiest of All; so also the names of his people were written on the heart of the Lord Jesus.'

By now the congregation were deeply moved. There was not a face, whether amongst the communicants or those looking on, that was not wet with tears. But it was quiet weeping; though the tears ran, and hearts were melting, a deep silence prevailed over all. As he distributes the elements, John Elias continues to speak; although the number of those who are to receive is great, and he is hurrying to supply them, he cannot cease from proclaiming the sufferings of the Son of God, and his words increasingly stir the feelings of the people. At one point he takes up the phrase, 'We show the Lord's death.'

'If the law comes in all its spirituality, and demands perfection, and we feel our guilt; what shall we do? Only show the Lord's death. What shall we do if our consciences condemn us? We shall show the Lord's death. If our enemy reminds us of our filthy garments, what shall we do? Only show the Lord's death. We will remind him of those before the throne, who have come out of the same great tribulation as ourselves, who have washed their robes and made them white in the blood of the Lamb! The blood of the covenant releases the prisoner from the chains of sin, from the bondage of corruption, and from the curse of the law. Our liberty has been won for us in blood! The blood has been sprinkled upon the law, and upon all the people.'

This was almost too much to bear; the people were suffused with tears, with one or two, here and there, having broken out into audible rejoicing. Mr Elias had returned to the table with the cup, after finishing his work. He takes hold of the next phrase, 'Till he come.'

'Is it not our great privilege that this pillar of remembrance has been raised on earth? How long is it to stand? "Till he come!" No matter how great the malice of the devil and his hordes towards it, the gates of hell shall not prevail against it. The King of Zion chooses that his subjects remember him in his blood! When the kings of this world win their victories, they must build great columns and adorn their pinnacles with brass images, but here is the Lord Jesus desiring to be portrayed before us as one crucified, and in his blood. John said of the glorious view that he had of him, "And I beheld a Lamb as it had been slain." For the strongest and noblest pillars erected by men, a few centuries of the storms of this world are enough to bring them down to their foundations; but here is a column, erected in a few short hours, that will stand until he comes in glory with his saints. There will be someone receiving the cup at the very instant when the voice of the archangel and the trump of God shall change him, in a moment, in the twinkling of an eye, and will carry him up in the clouds, to meet the Lord in the air, to remember him in that perfect land, the rest that awaiteth the people of God! The Mediator has established his kingdom upon blood; yes, even his own blood; not with the blood of another, but with his own blood he fulfilled all things. Much of the great city of Liverpool has been established in the blood of the poor Negroes, but the mediator established his kingdom in his own blood.'

'As we remember his death, we should remember the cause of it. The Messiah shall be cut off, but not for himself! For what cause, then? Because of your transgressions, sinner! "He was bruised for our iniquities."'

He then turned to the people and with overpowering vehemence, cried out:

'If it was sin that sharpened the thorns of the crown pressed upon his pure head until the blood flowed from the wounds, can we ever love sin again? If it was our sins that whetted the spear that pierced his side, so that blood and water flowed out, can we continue to live in sin?'

The congregation by now was on the point of bursting; only by a great effort were they able to contain themselves. After pausing for a moment, he said, in some excitement:

'Friends! With this view of Christ upon the cross at Calvary, bleeding because of our sins, I challenge anybody here to be able to live an ungodly life henceforth! Can the indifference of man withstand a view of the cross? Is there anyone here who will forget the One who loves him ever again? No, there is no one who will take one step from beneath the cross from tonight onwards. We should remember Judas's betrayal with disgust; we should remember his persecutors with a hatred of their wickedness; but we should remember that it was our sins that were his chief persecutors. We must look upon him whom we have pierced, until we mourn for him in pure repentance, and we fear lest we crucify to ourselves the Son of God afresh.'

The people could not restrain themselves further. They broke out throughout the building into loud cries; many a brother could not refrain from cheering and many of the older sisters were rejoicing gloriously. Mr Elias himself was overcome at this point. His broken feelings became too much for him; he took out his handkerchief and covered his face with it. After being silent for a minute and endeavouring to compose himself, he said, in a broken voice, 'Friends, I feel a greater debt tonight to love him than ever!' Before closing, he addressed the onlookers with great seriousness, and then prayed. He then gave out a hymn to sing. The familiar verses were sung with a new appreciation; the same lines were doubled and trebled, over and over again, for a long time. This communion service was sufficient for scores who had been in two minds to decide there and then to bow to Christ.

Before leaving Mr Elias in his association with his neighbourhood and with Anglesey, we might mention two facts as further indications of the general respect in which he was held. The first is that, without exception, he was placed to preach on the last night of any Association in his own county, and would often experience then the most powerful service of the Association. The second is that he was appointed to present an address on behalf of Anglesey to King George IV, when he was passing through the island on his way to Ireland in 1822. Mr Elias had received a word from the Lord Lieutenant of Anglesey expressing his pleasure at the arrangement and his desire for His Majesty to be introduced to the chief preacher of Wales. But as Mr Elias was engaged elsewhere at the time, in fact, in

London, and the brethren there were unwilling to release him, he failed to receive his audience with the King.

JOHN ELIAS IN HIS STUDY

When Mr Elias was frustrated by the old brethren of Caernarvonshire from furthering his desire for education and had to be satisfied with a few months at Evan Richardson's school, he vowed that the congregations of Wales would never be at a loss because of it, if effort and labour on his part could make up the deficiency. He kept his vow with the utmost conscientiousness. He gave himself to reading and to study, so that he became one of the most knowledgeable men in Wales.

He was not a scholar and could hardly have been called learned, in the usual sense of the word; he could not compose in the classical languages, nor understand them either without the help of dictionaries. But for general knowledge there was hardly his equal in the country. Mr Gwalchmai stated, in the funeral address that he gave for him, that very few of the college men, even those indeed who had received high degrees, could compete with Mr Elias in knowledge. He read thoroughly; he mastered every book he obtained. Mr Michael Roberts told Dr Owen Thomas that the first English book that John Elias read was Brown's *Compendious View of Natural and Revealed Religion*, and that he made it completely his own; that he had turned to every verse quoted in it, and studied the book in such detailed fashion that he almost memorised it all. And this was his usual practice with every book that he read from then until his death. He would consume them whole; absorbing them in his meditations as one digests food in the stomach, and their contents would become part of his mental constitution. He must have read considerably on his journeys as he rode, and in his lodgings, morning and evening. When at home, according to his son:

> My dear father would be in his library every minute that was possible; that room was his home. When kept from it by circumstances beyond his control he was as a man out of his element. He would often return to his library when we would be on our way to our beds, and he would often remain there until two or three in the morning. I often heard my dear mother calling him to bed, and he would say that he was coming; she would fall asleep again, and he would read and meditate.

When he was troubled by some matter over which he had to think long, he would find rest, not by relaxing from work, but by turning to some completely different branch of knowledge. His widow wrote:

> Some years ago I would attempt to get him to come out for a walk, for his health's sake, but I rarely succeeded; his answer would always be, 'Ah, my dearest, I do not have the time, my Master's work is great!'

He was very knowledgeable even in those areas of learning that are not directly connected with the pulpit. He had studied the political constitution of Great Britain thoroughly and was very familiar with its laws and judgments. He could provide legal advice for most circumstances that could be depended on as confidently as that of most solicitors.

Few doctors understood the human body as well as he. A young man recalled that he once lodged in the same house as Mr Elias. After supper they began conversing, amongst other things, on the human anatomy. Mr Elias began speaking on the wonders of God in the constitution of the human body, describing it as a living machine, made up of bones, veins, capillaries, and nerves, with the heart operating as a centre, and with each part collaborating perfectly with the others, until all were amazed. His description was so vivid that the young man could not get to sleep that night in amazement at himself. Mr Elias also studied thoroughly the various ailments that attacked the body and the medicines that were the best remedies for them. When he lived at Llanfechell, it was to him that all came for medical advice. A chemist from Liverpool knew of his prescriptions, and considered them proof of wide and detailed medical knowledge.

His knowledge of the geography of the world was remarkable; he knew of its rivers and mountains, and spoke of them as he would of the rivers and mountains of north Wales. His awareness of the inhabitants of the various countries, their morals, customs, religions, were almost as full and complete as those of his own country. This knowledge came clearly into view when he addressed the meetings of the Bible Society or the London Missionary Society. There is an account of an address he gave in a Bible meeting in Rhuthun. He depicted the world spinning on its axis, and the different countries coming into view, one by one. Vast China, with its three hundred million idol worshippers; Africa and its millions of black pagans; India, with its peoples throwing themselves under the wheels of the Juggernaut and their widows being burnt alive; Persia and Arabia, deceived by the false prophet; and Europe, part Roman Catholic, part Greek Orthodox, and part Protestant. For about an hour he described the world in this way, with such liveliness and detail as if he spent a lifetime travelling across the globe, so that one gentleman said to a friend as they left, 'I have never heard such an address at a Bible Society meeting before.' 'Amazing,' answered his friend. 'This man knows the history and geography of the whole world.' It is said that Mr Elias knew enough of astronomy as to discover a mistake in *Moore's Almanac* concerning the time of an eclipse. Indeed, so much is said of his knowledge in so many different branches that one would tend to view the reports as exaggerations, except that there is such decided evidence from so many witnesses, whose word cannot be doubted, that these reports are substantially true.

But the main branch of his studies was Theology and Biblical Studies. Dr Owen Thomas said that his knowledge of the Scriptures of the Old and New Testaments, with respect to the letter and the meaning, appeared inexhaustible. We have said that he could not read the classical languages, but he knew enough of Greek and Hebrew to be able to read them with dictionaries, and understand the arguments of commentators over the various words. Nearly every commentary published in English was to be found in his library, and when he was expounding his text it was easy to see that he had not only read them but compared them with one another, and formed his own judgment. His mind was enriched, more than any other in his day, by the works of divines of all ages, but in particular by those of the Puritans. In this way he was as a scribe instructed unto the kingdom of heaven.

When choosing a text he would take the utmost care to find out its true meaning. In an Association at Dolgellau once, when counselling young preachers, he said that whenever a preacher was reading his text, it was as if he had taken an oath before God that he would explain and expound the mind of God in that portion of the truth. He would never take a part of a sentence as a text, twisting the sense and misrepresenting the thought; he would, rather, select a complete phrase containing a clear reference to a duty or doctrine, so that he had a good foundation to his sermon. He would then read everything he could on that topic. But his sermon would never be a collection of the thoughts of others; not a posy of flowers collected from various fields, with nothing of his own in it except for the threads that bound them together. His mind, rather, was like a smelting furnace, in which the ideas of various authors would fuse with the rich ore of his own thoughts. His sermons also would not only be the product of deep meditation but the fruit of prayers. It is not too much to say that he never composed a sermon but with 'strong crying and tears.' He would consider the great truths of the gospel in his meditations until his feelings were kindled and his soul within him warmed. He would then take them again into God's presence, so that they might partake again of the divine fire; and so his sermons would be full of fiery coals, ready to be hurled into the midst of the ungodly. It was not enough for him to have a clear view of a truth and powerful, striking, and consistent thoughts to express. His main purpose was to have a message from God to sinners. Many days, yes, many nights, he spent in anguish of soul, wrestling with God for a message. His groans were sometimes heard in the room below his library and his tears were found in a pool beside his chair. He was once preparing a sermon for the Bala Association on the text, 'O wheel!' (*Ezek.* 10:13). At lunchtime, the maid came to call him. But there was no reply to her knocking. She heard the sound of weeping and groaning, as if someone's heart was breaking, but she could not get an answer. The faithful old maid, Nellie Hughes, became frightened, and opened the door, only to see, in her amazement, her master on his face on the floor with his books laid out beside him. The explanation of this mystery was that the verse was refusing to open out to him. He was seeking a sermon for Bala, and had found a text, but had failed to obtain a message. And what is truly mysterious is that it was while he was on his way to the main service, intending to speak on this verse, that the accident to which we have already referred took place, between Bronheulog and Bala, and he broke his arm.

Mr Elias, when preaching, would hurl out bullets, heated in the fires of the Divine Presence. Not only would he pray much when composing his sermons but also before delivering them, especially on special occasions. Scarcely would he allow himself to sleep the night before preaching to the Association. The night before one of the most remarkable services that he experienced at the Caernarvon Association he did not sleep at all, and went to the field without taking any breakfast. The old maidservant of the family said that there was something awe-inspiring in his countenance as he left the house. He lodged at the house of his sister-in-law who, like all his in-laws, was a zealous Churchwoman and too full of prejudice towards the Methodists to go to hear him. This woman said, on seeing his face as he passed her in the morning, 'He is certain to kill himself among the Roundheads.' According to Gwalchmai:

> His prayerful spirit brought all the objects of his meditation to a true clarity in his mind, strengthening his commitment to the work, purifying his sanctified taste, enlivening his fiery spirit, and bringing a solemn importance to all his labour. This is where the flint came into contact first with the steel, producing the spark that would kindle into a flame of fire, and would blaze up into consuming coals to be scattered over the vast congregation until every heart would melt under the heat.

JOHN ELIAS IN THE PULPIT

Notice him as he rises to his feet. He is a tall man, about five foot ten inches high, and slim of build. His face is not particularly handsome for the marks of smallpox are evident upon it. His forehead is high and his cheeks hollow. His hair, like his countenance, is dark; it is allowed to fall as it grows and is not parted in any direction; yet, so natural is it, it does not look unkempt. One feels that his face has been fitted by nature to manifest the feelings of his heart. But the glory of his countenance is his eyes; piercing and lively eyes, with a great soul looking out upon the world through them. His dress is remarkably neat with never a blemish upon it because of the high view he held of the dignity of the gospel. He does not follow the fashion of the age. He dresses like a Quaker, simply and tidily, but always with a very gentlemanlike appearance.

Note also his voice. It is not a strong, powerful voice, not a sound of thunder and of many waters, like Ebenezer Morris's voice. It is not a full, sweet, tuneful voice, like that of John Evans, Llwynffortun; nor is it a voice full of music and song, like that of John Jones, Talsarn. But it is clear, penetrating and completely steady, able to reach a congregation of ten thousand out of doors without any effort, and to speak to them for an hour and a half if there is need. Dr Owen Thomas said of him that his was one of the best, if not the best, speaking voice, that he had ever heard; but that it was completely lacking in that musicality which can charm a congregation on its own and was more fitted for the exciting and the terrible than for the gentle. He exercises complete control over it. He pronounces every word clearly and accurately, particularly the last syllable; in his greatest excitement and when under the strongest influence, the words are never allowed to run into one another. This is a lesson that he learnt from Mr Evan Richardson, who said to him one Monday morning in school:

'John *bach*, you were very much in error when preaching yesterday.'

'In what way, Mr Richardson?' he asked.

'Well, many times in the sermon, you called the Holy One of heaven and earth an "ugly Jesus" [*"Iesu hyll"*].'

It seems that at that time he added an *'yll'* sound when drawing breath at the end of every sentence whenever he became passionate in his sermon, but this was never heard again after that morning. His delivery was perfected by Mr Charles. When Mr Elias preached at the Caernarvon Association of 1836, Mr Morgan, Syston, and Christmas Evans were amongst his hearers. Mr Morgan mentioned admiringly the preacher's clear pronunciation, though he was getting old and had lost his teeth. 'Oh,' said Christmas Evans, 'he has learnt the art of controlling his voice.' When Mr Morgan afterwards met Mr Elias, he asked him if this was the case. John Elias confirmed that it was, and that it was to Mr Charles's tuition that he was indebted. The latter had taught him never to raise the pitch of his voice, nor to hurry his delivery, whatever the number of people listening to him, but to speak completely naturally.

An intense solemnity rests upon him in the pulpit when he faces the congregation; it is easy to see that he is aware of the urgency of his message and of his own awesome position as mediating between the quick and the dead. He takes hold of the Bible almost reverently; he takes out a linen handkerchief from his pocket and hides his face in it for a few minutes in fervent prayer to God. In his left hand there is a thin black book, with his forefinger acting as a bookmark. Before announcing his text, he takes one serious, leisurely view of his audience and then reads the verse slowly and solemnly, in a way that suggests to every hearer that there is so much more in the verse than he ever realized previously, and with a voice that reaches the furthest ranks of the crowd. With great skill he begins to explain the verse read, showing its connections and contexts, dealing separately with, and emphasizing the meanings of its individual words. He might perhaps refer to some different translations, to the customs and rites of the eastern world, to the interpretations and traditions of the Jews, and to the circumstances of Israel at the time and its relations with other nations. He might refer perhaps to the views of Ainsworth, Poole, Lightfoot, Lowth or Horsley; or perhaps Campbell, Macknight, Owen or Leigh. He adamantly refuses one exegesis, though many able men hold to it; he seems to hesitate between two other views, but then produces critical or interpretative, historical or theological reasons for the exegesis which he supports, so that all his hearers are quite certain that that is indeed the correct meaning, and the verse is henceforth completely familiar to them. By means of the exposition and the sermon that follows, the verse will be indelibly impressed forever upon their minds. He makes everything clear so that the verse remains with them as a path of light. When preaching on the vision of the dry bones in Ezekiel's prophecies, he was emphasizing the phrase, 'Bone to *his* bone' (*Ezek.* 37:7). 'Not bone to bone,' he said, 'but bone to *his* bone. This bone,' pointing out the tip of a finger of his left hand, 'to this bone,' moving down past the knuckle to the next bone. 'The bones of the hand to the bones of the wrist; the bones of the wrist to the bones of the arm; the bones of the arm to the bone of the shoulder.' And as he said this he pointed to those parts of the body being mentioned, painting such a vivid picture to the congregation that they could almost see the various bones coming together.

He had an extraordinary ability for making every word that he said stick in the mind, as if it had been graven with an iron pen and lead in the rock forever. The late Rev. David Charles Davies, M. A., said that he was once in a town in Denbighshire and was discussing a point of scriptural criticism with a fellow minister in the house where they lodged. They were interrupted by an old man of rustic appearance, who was also present.

'I also know some Greek,' he said.

'You know Greek?' said Mr Davies. 'How much Greek do you know?'

'I know,' said the old man, 'that *exagorazen* is the Greek word for the word *redeemed* in the verse in the third of Galatians.'

'You are correct,' said Mr Davies, 'but how did you come to know it?'

The old man described how John Elias had come to preach in one of the Associations in the north, and as he opened up his text he came across Galatians 3:13 and noted that *exagorazen* was the word used by Paul for 'fully redeemed'. Though he had only said the word once and that only in passing he had said it in such a way that it had lodged in the mind of this monoglot Welshman for tens of years afterwards.

If there was a metaphor or a historical reference in the text he would explain it in its details, making it live in the imagination. In the Caernarvon Association of 1836, when preaching on the words in James 1:21 on receiving the 'engrafted word', he explained the illustration of engrafting so effectively and with such appropriateness that one man said as he left the field, 'Whatever other benefits I have received in the Association, I know now how to graft trees.' We read of him preaching at an Association in Tredegar. His text was 1 Corinthians 15:3, 'For I delivered unto you first of all that which I also received, how that Christ died for our sins, according to the Scriptures.' He described the circumstances of the crucifixion – the nailing to the wood; the blood flowing from the holes of the nails; the awful darkness over all the land; the agonizing cry of the Saviour, 'My God, my God, why hast thou forsaken me?' – until the whole congregation were quite lost in the description. The portrait painted was so vivid that many on the field felt that they were seeing Jesus nailed to the tree with their natural eyes, and it would have been difficult, even impossible, to have convinced them otherwise, though their reason might tell them differently. At two o'clock, the Rev. Ebenezer Richard preached, and he said, 'My dear friends, I do not think I can preach, because my mind has been overcome by that sermon at ten o'clock this morning. I thought as I listened to the dear brother describe the crucifixion of the Son of God, that it was then, about two hours ago, that the event took place.'

It is doubtful whether there has ever been anyone in Wales so skilful as Mr Elias in placing his hearers so completely within the circumstances of any description painted by him. The late Rev. David Roberts, Cowbridge, spoke of a sermon of his at a Monthly Meeting in Glamorganshire. The next morning, two boys were talking together of the meetings and the preachers.

'Who,' said one, 'did you enjoy most?'

'Who?' said the other, 'Who else but John Elias.'

'Well yes, wasn't he good? He spoke excellently about Peter. *I could see Peter standing by the bridge there.'*

John Jones, Talsarn, used to describe how Mr Elias once preached in a local Association in Bangor on Ascension Thursday. He spoke in the open air near the Penrhyn Arms. His text was the passage relating Paul's judgment before Agrippa. He described Paul's defence of himself and so real was his portrayal of Paul's words, his voice, his gestures, the chains around his hands, that one sailor, listening on the field and standing next to Mr Jones, cried out, 'Fie, fie! Take those chains off the man's hands immediately.' A young preacher who had a high opinion of himself and his learning, once said to an old man who had been one of John Elias's hearers and a servant to Mr Elias's son:

'If John Elias were alive now, he would not be counted as much of a preacher.'

The old man became thoroughly agitated:

'Oh, indeed! You never heard him, my boy. Nobody who ever heard him would speak like that. His exposition of the text was better than most sermons, even before he had begun preaching. I heard him preaching of Paul before the Areopagus in such a way that I have been thoroughly familiar with the Areopagus ever since. Don't ever say that again about Mr Elias.'

Another story that demonstrates the ability John Elias possessed of painting a picture so that it came alive to his hearers relates to a Newport Association in Monmouthshire. The chairman of the Association was the Rev. David Charles, Carmarthen. In the private session, as they discussed the topic, namely, the omniscience of God, John Elias, for all his eloquence, had almost been cast in the shade by the glorious thoughts contributed by the chairman himself. In the public service in the open air, Mr Elias was the master of the congregation. His text was of the man riding on the white horse, Revelation 19:11. The vast crowd were held by his every word, and all were so caught up in the glory of Christ as a man of war that they had completely forgotten themselves. At one point, the preacher held his left arm curved before him, in the shape of a bow. He rested his right arm upon it, like an arrow. He aimed at the centre of the crowd, and gestured as if drawing the bow and releasing the arrow. So caught up by his words were the people standing in the direction along which he pointed, that they believed that a real arrow was being fired at them, that they threw themselves flat on their backs, so that a broad path opened up before him, from the edge of the platform to the back of the crowd. In this case they were not being overcome by the power of the word, but by the fear of an arrow.

The well-known Bangor doctor, Dr O. O. Roberts, has referred to the effect of Mr Elias upon him on one occasion. On returning home, after a day's hunting, Dr Roberts came upon a small chapel out in the country, not far from Llanrwst, in which a Monthly Meeting was being held. He could hear the voice of the preacher inside speaking in a fiery tone, and it was John Elias. His subject was the hand-writing on the wall in Belshazzar's feast. Dr Roberts continued:

> I stood there for a minute, intending to continue on my way home but, for all my attempts, I could not move an inch from the spot on which I stood. In a while I felt my gun fall from under my arm but I was too drained of strength to retrieve it. I forgot the dogs and everything else while he continued. I believed quite certainly that I was seeing with my own eyes the fingers of the hand, clearly before me, writing on the whitewashed wall of the chapel; and that I beheld the words, '*Mene, Mene, Tekel, Upharsin*', so distinctly was the event being portrayed before my mind. I was stood in the court in front of the chapel and feeling my hair standing on my head as straight as the quills of a porcupine. I had never heard anything like it before.

When forming the heads of his sermon, the divisions would generally be scriptural, that is, Mr Elias would use the particular words of the text and turn them into headings. He would handle the words very skilfully, comparing the various uses of them in Scripture. If the word 'hardness' (Welsh = '*caled*') was under discussion, he would trace the various connections of the word, such as 'hard-hearted', 'stiff-necked' (Welsh = '*gwar-galed*'), 'fierce countenance' (Welsh = '*wyneb-galed*'). Or if dealing with the word 'repentance', he would deal with 'repenting from', 'repenting for', 'repenting as', 'repenting towards', and 'repenting to'. He would proceed in this way until he had completed his first head, and a remarkable authority would accompany all he had to say. Everyone would be feeling: Well, that is now determined. Let it be thus, now and forevermore. On your life, beware from changing anything of it. He would then proceed to the second head, with the same result. Then, according to Dr Owen Thomas:

> Soon, a wonderful transformation would take place in him. His feelings would be fired, his eyes would flash, his voice would gain an almost unearthly tone, with a supernatural power about it. By now his outward appearance would be very different; he seems to be several inches taller than before. His body writhes in convulsion backwards and forwards by the upheaving power of the volcanic fire hid in his breast. At times he looks amazed, terror-stricken, and

> in dismay; he draws in his cheeks in a peculiar manner, compresses his lips; he seems to be gazing upon an awe-inspiring vision, and unable yet to grasp the meaning of it and to describe it properly. But after a pause, he stretches forth his hand, the forefinger of which plays as if it had an independent life of its own; the idea flashes forth like lightning; the crash of the thunder follows; the pattering rain falls; the people feel like Israel at the foot of Sinai; the shrieks of many are heard – like that man in Brynsiencyn, who on a similar occasion suddenly cried out, 'Oh! for Evan Richardson[2] from Caernarvon, or someone from somewhere, for five minutes, lest we die!'– and the sighing, the groaning and the weeping becomes general, and the terrors of God penetrate the place. But with that, however, there comes a change over the preacher, and the greatest love and tenderness beam in his countenance, his voice becomes full of pathos, and he declares the Gospel of redemption in all its riches – the Saviour who died that the guilty might live – and with such an unction that his hearers are convinced in their hearts that he himself had experienced it, so that hope dawns again upon the most despondent in the place; the black and threatening clouds are dispelled; the sky becomes clear, the sun rises, and the shadow of death itself is turned into the dawn of day. He closes by prayer, and gives out a hymn as appropriate to the subject of the sermon as if it had been composed purposely for the occasion, and all the people return to their homes under the deepest convictions, some of them saved to eternal life having passed through from death into life.

Though he writes in this way, Dr Thomas acknowledged that it was impossible to describe adequately the ministry of John Elias to those who had never heard him, and doubly impossible to describe those services when the power came upon him at its most extraordinary. His solemnity was intense. No sermon of his would ever include a light word or anything that would induce a smile; his soul was too full of the terrors of God to tolerate anything that bordered on levity. It was easy to believe he lived continually amongst the truths that he depicted. He spoke of hell as one who had been dangled above it; you would almost take an oath that he had seen the damned bound hand and foot and had heard the sound of their groans and the clink of their chains. He spoke of heaven as one who had entered beyond the veil and had seen the saints in their white robes, looking infinitely beautiful in the righteousness of their Redeemer, and had heard their praises rising to a glorious anthem. If he was describing the Judgment, you would imagine that his eyes were fixed upon the Judge sitting upon his great white throne, with heaven and earth fleeing from before him in fear. As it moves amongst these terrifying scenes, the soul of the preacher kindles within him, and in the heat of its flames he forms immensely powerful sentences. The late Dr Roberts, Mynyddgof, the father of Sir William Roberts, said:

> I heard him describing the image on a coin; he used the picture so as to explain how Satan's image had been impressed upon the soul of man, and his hearers turned pale before him. 'But,' he said, raising his voice, 'glory! Our God can re-mint Satan's coins.' [*'Fe fedr ein Duw ni ail-fintio ceiniogau'r cythraul.'*]

There are two other elements of Elias's oratory that we need to emphasize. The first is the use he made of his forefinger, described above by Dr Owen Thomas as seeming to have an independent life of its own. When the preacher's soul was excited, this finger would threaten in the most terrifying manner; it appeared to be a bodily representation of all the authority of the law of God; it moved unceasingly through the congregation, and every hearer felt that it was pointing towards him or her, and declaring in its own tongue, 'You are the guilty one; it is to you that this great truth applies.' The Rev. Michael Roberts said that John Elias's finger was one of the greatest influences upon him.

The other element to which we would refer was the awful silences that would occur in the midst of his oratory. These intense pauses were almost more eloquent than the torrent of words that had had been poured out before. If the lips were dumb, the muscles of the face spoke forth; the eyes flashed fire; the finger pointed. All knew that it was not because the preacher had no words to say that he was silent, but because he had too many; because his thoughts had so gathered within him that he could not give utterance to them, like water pouring into the neck of a bottle and hindering the flow. And soon the silence would be broken by a tearing thunderbolt, so awful in its sound that the most thoughtless would tremble with fear. Of these silences, *Eben Fardd* wrote:

And e'en the pauses in his speech	'Roedd hyd yn oed ei atal dywedyd
Were full of eloquence divine.	Yn gyfwng o huawdledd cu.

It could almost be said that in Mr Elias sacred oratory had been raised to perfection. The late Mr Henry Richard, M. P., said, as late as 1880, that in his day he had listened to most of the chief orators of Europe, but that he never heard anybody that approached John Elias. Mr Elias knew when to rein in his gifts as well as when to use them. One example of this occurred at an Association at Lampeter, Cardiganshire, in 1828; the second Association, we believe, held by the Methodists in that town. Mr Elias was to speak last, at ten o'clock, and his theme was the deity of the Lord Jesus Christ. Hundreds of Unitarians had come to the Association, being drawn by his fame as an orator, and they were full of rage as he preached on Christ as God. Towards the end of his sermon, in the full flow of his oratorical fluency, he referred directly to them. 'If you Unitarians are correct,' he said, ' then we are guilty of worshipping the creature; we are placing a worm, who has existed, as it were, only since yesterday, on a par with God; we shall be found guilty of idolatry in the Day of Judgment.' And as he said so, his face was working, the eyes flashing, and the finger pointing. 'But,' he added, 'if we are correct . . .' And with this, all expected a flood of condemnation to pour as an awful torrent upon the poor Unitarians; but he reined himself in, and all that he said was, 'If we are correct, then you Unitarians are wrong.' The Rev. Kilsby Jones, who was among the hearers, said that this restraint – a restraint of power – was the greatest example of oratorical skill that he had ever witnessed and was fully as effective as the most powerful speech. It did not moderate the fury of the Unitarians however. Some of them followed him to the house of the Rev. John Jones where he was lodging, threatening to attack him, and had it not been for the mediation of the Rev. Ebenezer Richard they would probably have carried out their threat.

We are tempted to include a description of him preaching in a chapel in Anglesey on a weekday evening. The Rev. Thomas Jones, Corwen, had preached before him and had had a very successful service, though he was then a relatively young man. He had gained complete mastery over his congregation. The crowd were all in tears and some were on the point of bursting into rejoicing, and he had sat down leaving his congregation enjoying the most pleasant feelings. It might almost have been announced, 'It will be in vain for anyone else to preach again this evening. We had better end the meeting now.' Indeed, some said this quietly at the time. But Mr Elias was not one to be so put down. He arose, slowly and modestly. He pointed to the gable wall window and asked, 'Would you be so good as to open that window?' He then repeated the request with respect to the rear wall window, as the air was very heavy. 'Would you be good enough to come forward from the doors; there is plenty of room in these pews.' The point in all this is to quieten the minds of the people and to gain their attention from what had been said in the previous sermon. He gives out a hymn, and listens to the singing in order to gauge the temperature of the meeting and to judge accordingly the best note on which to begin speaking. He reads his text clearly and simply: 'Many will say to me in that day, Lord, Lord, have we not prophesied in thy name? And in thy name have cast out devils? And in thy name done many wonderful works? And then will I profess unto them, I never knew you: depart from me ye that work iniquity.' The reading of the text throws a veil of solemnity over the congregation. He introduces and explains the various aspects of the text, so that the verses appear like a large storehouse, having its portals opened, and all the truth contained therein being exposed instantly, or at least within ten minutes or so, to the light of day, and to all the congregation. He divides the text expertly under various headings.

We have now passed through one phase of the sermon. He proceeds to reason with his hearers – illuminating, convicting, attracting; so that within twenty minutes he has gained their complete attention, and washed away all the excitement of the previous sermon and buried his poor predecessor from view. He shouts out, 'Listen now!' – a superfluous comment, if ever there was one; it would be an impossible task to distract anyone present from listening. His spirit has been fired by the truth as it is in Jesus. Conviction and expectation is seen in every face, and every ear is nailed to the door of his eloquence. He now seems like a general facing a mob with the sword of the Spirit in his hand, and supremely conscious that he is under the direct guidance of his Master. He seems like one determined to rescue some sinner from danger, were he never to preach again. In truth, not only does he seem conscious that the Captain of the host of the Lord is at his right hand but he seems to discern the feelings and situation of the congregation before him and to see that the edge of his sword is already touching the consciences of the people.

Ah! We have now passed the second phase. There is a change in his countenance. His voice has dropped into a gentler tone in the minor key. He begins to soothe, if not even melt, the crowd's feelings; but there is nothing yet of the rejoicing that was felt at the close of the first sermon. He returns to his reasoning mode, as if he had spotted someone who was not convinced. He is at his utmost stretch now. He speaks of the fruit of sin as one who has proved its bitterness himself. He speaks of repentance as one who has himself bled from its wounds. He pictures hell as one who has searched out all its grottoes with a lantern. He leads the people to the very edge of the pit of woe, until some are terrified of falling over the edge of the gallery of the chapel. Something like hopelessness has spread over the faces of all. The crowd would be despairing if they were released to go home in this state! It would have been better after all to have ended after the first sermon. He continues however, and shoots his fiery darts so rapidly and effectively that his hearers' hearts are pricked. A lively spirit is now at work throughout the congregation; there is a ferment throughout the place; they feel as if the ground has been shaken under their feet. All are still silent; there is nothing yet of the exalted feelings experienced in the first sermon, but there is something – something – that effect – what shall we call it? – that is a thousand times more effective than anything that preceded. The people's faces have lost their usual countenances; every line of their faces seems to have dropped. What, in truth, is this? Observing their pale faces, one imagines that they are secretly thinking, 'My sins are more than can be forgiven.' Ah! He now turns from the unbeliever to the backslider. His words fall as fire upon the heads of the people. His voice now has a hint of a crack in it; he almost breaks out in tears. What has now become of the congregation? Some are paralysed; some are amazed; some have collapsed. He shouts out, 'Now, let the redemption be brought into view! Would it have been honest of me to have shown you your hiding place before you had felt your danger?' The crowd are dumb once more. Some are retrieving their handkerchiefs to wipe their wet cheeks. A few old sisters are finding it too difficult to restrain their feelings. One, in the far corner, shouts out: 'Oh, my life!' Another, from another spot, unable to hold herself longer, cries out: 'Is there hope for one like me?' Another: 'Oh, my precious soul!' And another: 'What shall I do?' Strong men may be seen covering their faces, as they try to hide their feelings. And yet there is nothing of the general excitement present during the first sermon.

Now the preacher, from the midst of his reasoning, has been affected by a strong emotion. We have moved on to a further phase. He raises his voice and, as if he was running to the centre of the camp and raising the banner of the cross before all the people, with a penetrating cry, like the silver trumpet of the temple, he proclaims hope for the guilty and the opening of the prison doors to those who were bound. He calls upon all to come to the mercy seat. He pours forth myrrh over the rusted locks of the hearts of hardened sinners; he pours forth the oil of grace upon the wounds of those pierced. He opens a wide door of hope before the long-standing backslider, and he calls upon the prodigals to return to their Father's house. He is as a tender shepherd watching over his flock, driving his sheep before him into the fold. Relief at last has appeared; the door of mercy has been opened wide; the way to the refuge has been disclosed and is near at hand. He now stretches forth his long arm over the congregation as if he were untying the noose around the neck of an old sinner who had been standing over the drop, and the old man, jumping up in the midst of the crowd, shouts out, 'The snare is broken and I have escaped!' The whole congregation seems to fold under the weight of his ministry, just as a great oak tree falls to the ground before the mighty hurricane.

And now the scene changes again, and we have reached the last phase. His countenance brightens, and hope returns to his hearers' hearts. His applications of the doctrine to the people alternate with fervent prayers on their behalf – his fervency being sufficient to break the hardest heart! He is as if he had been lifted up to a third heaven, and speaks of the rest that awaits the people of God as if he had been resting there himself and has returned to bring the sense of glory back to earth to be presented to the heart of each individual in the congregation. Truly, here is the Day of Pentecost come to Wales! There were emotions created in these services that were long remembered in Anglesey – not even eternity would be sufficient to dislodge them from the memory.

JOHN ELIAS AT THE ASSOCIATIONS

We shall attempt to combine many different descriptions that have been given in order to convey as best we can the picture of John Elias at an Association. We shall provide later a description of him in the conferences; for now, we take it that the private meetings are over, the decisions have been made, and the time has come to begin the public meeting in the open air. The question on everyone's lips is whether John Elias has come. At last he is seen, striding towards the stage that has been raised. Perhaps the first sermon is only ordinary, but next comes one of the old giants of the south, and he preaches powerfully, producing strong feelings in the vast crowd.

Once he has finished, John Elias gets to his feet and approaches the desk. He looks over the vast throng, and then points with his finger to one or two spots where the people are not yet perfectly still. Then a pleasant smile appears on his face, and he begins to speak:

> I have a word or two to say before any one moves out of his place. It is not yet more than a quarter past seven o'clock, no one need hurry, and we have the long days of summer. I have understood a long while from your faces that you all feel tonight as if heaven were near. The servants of the Most High are in the hands of their Master. It is clear that they have already been clothed with power from on high. The trumpet call of the King is in our camp. We have seen and heard things that are almost incredible. We have heard the walls of Jericho crack; and we may reasonably hope to see them down in a ruinous heap before tomorrow night. And, surely, we shall see this, unless there be something in us, or in the behaviour of the people, or in the town, to grieve the Holy Spirit. Therefore, for the value of souls that are now in the labour of birth, I beseech you all to be on your guard. I would swear every man here present to be more sober than ever before. God forbid that any of us should be guilty of sending the heavenly dove away. For the love of souls, let not a single drunkard be seen on the streets tonight. May there be nothing in the conduct of any one, in or out, to offend the feelings of any magistrate or civil official, more than the preacher or ordinary believer. We expect the morals of this multitude to be without blemish tonight; if not, this is the last Association that shall ever come into this town!
>
> There are thousands of strangers to be entertained in the neighbourhood tonight; let every one go to the place where he is invited: it would not be

> much, this kind of weather, to go to a distance of three miles if necessary. Let every man be faithful and thankful for the hospitality he receives. And you that entertain the strangers, open your doors with a hearty welcome. 'Be not forgetful to entertain strangers.' Avoid trouble and expense: all we ask is a bed free from damp and safe, and a morsel of bread and a drop of water. Value this coming of strangers under your roofs. It is tonight, perhaps, that your hearths will be anointed for the first time with the tears of the saints; it is tonight, perhaps, that your roofs will be consecrated for the first time by the prayers of the faithful. Remember that some of the old pilgrims, by faith, entertained angels unawares, and that they feasted happily with them. Who knows but that you also tonight shall entertain good men in the invisible company of the angels of heaven! And you that make the arrangements, see that a man of prayer is sent to every house.
>
> Let all observe that family worship is to be held tonight in every family, exactly at nine o'clock. Heaven has already smiled upon us. An active intercourse has already been carried on by the angels between this field and the throne of God, and at nine o'clock we hope that Jacob's ladder will be full of angels ascending and descending, and that the prayers of this region for a compass of six miles will be so powerful that they will draw heaven down to earth, and lift earth so near heaven that the tabernacle of God will be with men, and that this Association will be the great subject of talk in the councils of heaven.

After such an address, every man and woman feared to do anything that would have offended God in any way.

Nine o'clock was the hour of prayer. Somehow, large numbers managed to find out in what house Mr Elias was staying, and at a quarter to nine the street opposite the house was full of people waiting to hear him read and pray. At nine, a window was opened and he gave out a hymn to be sung, read a psalm, and then knelt to pray. Any attempt to describe the prayer would be in vain. If Jacob ever wrestled with the angel, then Elias that night was wrestling in God's strength. He cried for a sign of God's blessing that night, before rising from his knees, as a first-fruit of a large harvest the next day. This prayer pierced the hearts of the ungodly as a flaming sword, turned every way, but it encouraged the souls of believers so that they imagined they were flying on angels' wings and being lifted off the ground. After praying, another verse was given out, and the singing was remarkable; such singing that the seraphim would have ceased their own praise that they might hear it. The effect of this prayer was great. Many were converted and proceeded to prove the sincerity of their faith by a lifetime of service to Christ.

The next day is the great day of the feast. The people may be seen pouring forth from all directions to the spot where the Association was being held

– some in carriages, some on horseback, but the majority on foot. People are to be seen everywhere – on the ridges of the nearby hills, scattered on all the roads, crossing the fields – all with their faces towards the same spot. By the starting time, ten o'clock, the crowd is immense, anything between ten thousand and twenty thousand. A relatively young man preaches first. He is a good speaker, handling his material well, and possessing obvious ministerial abilities. The people listen to him with great pleasure; the professors of religion in particular are being built up; a smile is seen on many faces and the occasional tear. Yet, not all commerce has been given up in the town; the occasional person is seen entering the lawyer's office, or turning into the shop, and many of the thoughtless youth are loitering in the streets. And if we were to look over the Association field we would see many half-hearted listeners either lying full length on the ground, or leaning on the surrounding hedges.

But as the first preacher comes to an end there is an evident change in the vast crowd. The town loiterers hurry up to the field; those lying on the surrounding banks hasten to join the congregation; all look towards the desk upon the stage where Mr Elias is to make his appearance. He comes into view with a serious look upon his face. It may be thought that he has resolved upon one great effort. Today, or never, to save the souls before him! His sermon may almost be seen in his face; his oratory is evident in the way he grasps the lapels of his coat, and uses his handkerchief. After singing a verse of a psalm, he reads his text, Ephesians 3:17–19. 'That ye, being rooted and grounded in love, may be able to comprehend with all saints what is the breadth, and length, and depth, and height; and to know the love of Christ, which passeth knowledge, that ye might be filled with all the fullness of God.' He reads the verses slowly in a sweet and penetrative voice; the reading is followed by a deep silence, and it is seen that a wave of concentration passes over the crowd to its furthest bounds, with all on their toes almost, in order to see and hear their favourite preacher.

Mr Elias takes about twenty minutes to comment on the various words, explaining the meaning of each one separately, and the particular meaning they bear in the sentence. He is almost like an engineer explaining the various parts of a machine, exhibiting each wheel and shaft, each pin and pinion, each crank and needle, and demonstrating how the various parts work together, and the teeth interlock. The explanation is so clear that all have understood it; all have appreciated the full meaning of each and every word; the verses have been indelibly impressed upon their minds, and the crowd smiles with pleasure.

While he has been expounding the Scriptures he has bound every ear to his words; he now proceeds to declare the majesty of God's love to a lost world:

> It is as if I perceive all the glory of the character of the great God expressed in three words, 'God is love.' All his attributes are nothing more than different manifestations of his love. What is his wisdom? His love, devising a plan to save a guilty sinner. What is his power? His love, executing the way of salvation. What is his truth? His love, fulfilling all that was needed to pardon the guilty. What is his holiness? His love, forbidding everything that is harmful for man's condition. What is his wrath? His love for order, which is as a fiery wall around us, keeping us from all evil.

These questions, together with their answers, stir his hearers; he addresses them, not only with his tongue, but with his eyes, his arms, his fingers, and his hands. It could almost be said that his whole head and body speak together, so that only with difficulty can the congregation restrain themselves. Indeed a cry has already broken out for mercy, for forgiveness, and for life.

He slows for a while, and encourages the crowd to control itself, in that he has not yet arrived at the heart of his message:

> And also it is too soon yet to start shouting; the seventh turn has not come. Israel were not to shout outside the walls of Jericho in ages past until they had seen the walls begin to crumble. Then it was that Joshua commanded them to shout. The walls of ungodliness have not yet begun to crumble here, though we expect great things before the end of this service, and indeed we almost imagine that we can already hear the old forts beginning to crack, and as soon as you see the old castles beginning to fall, then shout out the name of the Lord!

These were hardly the words for quietening the emotions of the listening thousands. The great crowd is on the brink of breaking out. Many are seen wiping their wet cheeks; others are straining every nerve to contain themselves so as to continue to hear the ministry.

Elias succeeds however in calming the throng and proceeds to describe the order of salvation, and the majesty of God's love in its immeasurable dimensions. At one point his own feelings begin to kindle and the fire of God burns in his soul. He grasps hold of the words of the text, 'To comprehend with all saints what is the breadth, and length, and depth, and height, etc.' In thrilling tones, he asks:

> What is the breadth of the way of salvation? Oh! It is too hard to say, but whatever it is, it is too broad for the thief on the cross to fall over its edge to hell! What is its length, then? It is impossible to say, but it is too long for Saul of Tarsus to fall off it to perdition!

At that, a man in the crowd shouts out, 'Thanks be to God! It is long enough for an old lost sinner like me, therefore!' The man's words pass in a moment through the congregation, like an electric charge. Mr Elias continues, though his feelings have almost overcome him:

> What is the depth of the gospel method of grace? It is too difficult to plumb its depths, but however deep it is, its foundations are too deep for one drop of damnation ever to touch that murderer Manasseh, once he had believed in Christ, though he had filled the streets of Jerusalem with the blood of the saints! What is the height of the plan of grace? It is impossible to say; but its tower is too high for any of the demons cast out of Mary Magdalen to climb over it so as to oppress her again!

By now it is impossible to hear a word because of the cries of the crowd. All are in tears. The preachers and the ministers on the stage are weeping like children. Elias ascends into even higher strains of oratory, dealing with the glorious metaphors of his text:

> What is the extent of salvation? It is as high as heaven; what can you do? It is deeper than hell; what can you know? Its measure is greater than earth, wider than the sea; what can mortal creatures bear? Its length reaches, as a golden chain, from the eternal purposes of God to the eternal glorification of the saints in heaven; its depth reaches to the lowermost pit of the Fall of Eden, its height reaches up to the throne of the Majesty on high.

The preacher's fluency surpasses all attempts at description and its effects are inconceivable. Before closing, his appeals to the people change into prayers on their behalf. There is a crack in his voice and a tenderness in his tone that melts the hearts of the hardest and most indifferent. The sermon ends with the congregation rejoicing generally and with an awareness that many have turned to God. As they depart from the field, there are many who seem not to know where they are going or what direction to take. The only conversation throughout the day is about 'the love! the salvation!' In one sense, this sermon ruins the whole of the remainder of the Association. A thunderous sermon is preached in the afternoon, but there is no lightning in it; and a tender sermon in the evening, but somehow it does not soften. There is no way to draw the minds of the people away from the morning's sermon. It is concluded that the occasion was the means for the conversion of many and the reviving of many churches.

We cannot avoid including part of another sermon of his in an Association as it is a typical example of his style of oratory and of the power of his imagination. His text was Isaiah 49:24, 'Shall the prey be taken from the mighty, or the lawful captive be delivered?' At the end of the sermon he asked, in a voice full of anxiety:

Satan, what do you say? Shall the prey be taken from the mighty?

'No! Never! Never! I will intensify the darkness of their minds, the hardness of their hearts, the power of their sins, and the strength of their chains, and my holds shall be made stronger. Never shall the prisoners be delivered. The feeble efforts of these preachers I scorn and despise.'

Gabriel, Gabriel, messenger of the Most High. What do you say? Shall the prey be taken from the mighty?

'Ah! I am afraid not. I have been hovering these two days over this vast assembly hearing the Word of God, expecting to see some chains broken, some prisoners liberated; but now the meetings are nearly over, the multitudes are on the point of separating. Ah! There is no sight of one being converted: and I cannot carry the tidings home of the repentance of a single sinner.'

He then turned to the preachers on the stage:

What think you, ministers of the living God? Shall the prey be taken from the mighty?

'Alas! Who hath believed our report, and to whom is the arm of the Lord revealed? We have laboured in vain and have spent our strength for nought. The Lord is as if he were hiding his face from us. Oh! We fear there is but little hope of the captives being delivered.'

Zion, shall the prey be taken from the mighty?

'Alas, the Lord hath forsaken me, and my God hath forgotten me. I am left alone, and am childless; so that my enemies say, "This is Zion, whom no man seeketh after!" Oh I am afraid none shall be delivered.'

Praying Christians, what do you think? Shall the prey be taken from the mighty?

'Lord God, Thou knowest. High is thy hand and strong is thy right hand. O that thou wouldest put forth thy strength and overcome! Let the sighing of the prisoner come before thee: according to the greatness of thy power, preserve thou those that are appointed to die. Though I am nearly weary in crying, yet I have a slender hope that the year of Jubilee is at hand.'

Then Elias looked up in a very serious manner, as if going to speak to the Almighty, and he humbly asked:

And what is the mind of the Lord respecting these captives?

'Thus saith the Lord, even the captives of the mighty shall be taken away, and the prey of the terrible shall be delivered.'

Blessed be God! There is now no doubt or hesitation respecting the liberty of the captives. It is positively declared, they shall be delivered, they shall be saved. Yea, the ransomed of the Lord shall return, and come to Zion, with songs and everlasting joy upon their heads.

JOHN ELIAS ON THE LECTURE STAGE

The Rev. John Elias was as complete a master of the lecture stage as he was of the pulpit. By his breadth of knowledge, the detail and clarity of his descriptions, his oratorical fluency, and his remarkable dramatic ability, he would carry an audience before him as if in the current of a river. He delivered ever-to-be-remembered addresses in relation to the London Missionary Society, the Bible Society, and the Temperance Society, and also from the Association stage. It would be easy to multiply examples, but we shall have to be satisfied with two.

The first is a speech delivered by him in a meeting arranged by the Bible Society at Bangor, when the Marquis of Anglesey, one of the heroes of Waterloo (he lost a leg at the battle), was in the chair. Many Churchmen viewed the Society with prejudice, considering it a Nonconformist institution intended to counteract the influence of the Society for the Propagation of Christian Knowledge. But as the Marquis was so highly respected (a memorial to him had recently been erected on the banks of the Menai Straits) they felt that they could not absent themselves from the meeting even though John Elias was engaged to speak. However, some clergymen approached the Marquis describing John Elias as an uneducated ranter and suggesting that it might be appropriate for His Lordship to request that he might be brief. The following is an account of the meeting as given by the Rev. W. Acworth, Vicar of Rothley, Leicestershire:

The great meeting took place; and the eye of the public was upon it. The neighbouring gentry were assembled, and all were anxiously listening for the noise of the carriage-wheels which would convey the noble Marquis, who at length arrived at precisely the time appointed, and immediately took the chair. He opened the proceedings by explaining in a few words the object of the Society, and said he fully approved of it. All went on in a pleasing manner.

At length the name of John Elias was pronounced as the next speaker; this changed the aspect of many; they immediately threw out the scornful lip, turned up the nose, and cast at Elias disdainful glances; the faces of some were even directed towards the door. But all this strange conduct was not sufficient to put him down: he came forward and addressed the chairman in a polite manner, who returned the compliment with a smile; he evidently saw something extraordinary in him at the first glance.

As Elias took a first view of the state of the Welsh before they had the Bible, it was soon seen that he was perfectly acquainted with the history of his country; especially when he gave an account of the Welsh translation of the Scriptures. When they heard him mention the names of William Salesbury, Dr William Morgan, Dr Richard Davies, Thomas Huet, Cantor of St David's; Dr Whitgift, Dr Hughes, Dr Bellot, Dr Gabriel Goodman, Dr David Powell, Vicar of Ruabon; Archdeacon Edmund Prys, Dr Richard Parry, and others, a sound attracted their ears which they did not expect; such names seemed to stir their hearts like sweet music. As he went on giving a statement of the different editions of the Welsh Bible, mentioning the names of Thomas Middleton, Rowland Heylin, Walter Cradock, Vavasor Powell, Thomas Gouge, Stephen Hughes, David Jones, Bishop Humphrey Lloyd, Moses Williams, and others, he gained their feelings, attention, and approbation; the frost had melted away imperceptibly; and, as he went on with his address, his good language, powerful words and persuasive eloquence overcame every contemptuous look. All persons listened with avidity; and as he led the assembly to view the present state of the Welsh, showing the necessity of some further attempt more effectual than any hitherto, however excellent, they were quite struck.

Then he moved to a higher elevation. He set forth the moral state of the country, as in warfare between light and darkness, holiness and sin, Christ and Belial; that the two large armies were drawing near, and that the truth must prevail. He showed that the happiness of the world depended on this great struggle; and that an example of the warfare and the victory had been seen lately at Waterloo. By this time the feelings of the people were completely at his command. He went forward to describe the late great struggle at Waterloo, showing that the happiness of nations, the progress of business, success of the arts, increase of knowledge, yea the prosperity of the gospel, turned on this important hour. But the hand of providence was seen visibly in it. Their captains were endowed with wisdom and power necessary for such a conquest. 'The Lord is a man of war; the Lord is his name.' Then he turned to describe one commander going forth to the field, the moment the scales were turned in their favour forever! He made use of the description given in the Book of Job of the war horse, and his rider, to set him forth. 'I imagine I see him,' said he, 'coming forth to the field on his white horse: which despiseth every fear and alarm; he paweth the valley, and rejoiceth in his strength; he mocketh at fear.' He set the horse forth as running in the midst of the trumpets, saying, 'Ah! Ah!' in contempt of them. 'He smelleth the battle afar off, the thunder of the captains and the shoutings.' But the great rider is all the time in perfect self-possession, in the midst of smoke and fire, directing and leading his armed men until he surrounded his enemy . . .

At this juncture the speaker was obliged to stop on account of the outbreak of the assembly, who were overwhelmed. But he soon resumed his address; and as he increased in warmth and power, he became more and more effective. 'Now I think I hear the shout of victory before it is gained; yes a conquest!

– but it will be at the sacrifice of one of the most illustrious of our nation! No, not the sacrifice of himself, but of one of his members! Then death advances throwing a ball, cutting off one of the brave captain's members – but what of that? Divine providence comes forward the same moment, calling on death as the angel did on Abraham formerly – 'Stay thy hand, so far shalt thou go, and no further. Touch not his life, go no further than taking off his limb. I shall need of his service hereafter, in a warfare of much higher nature than this – as a leader in the chair of the Bible Society – I shall have need of his service to dispense the Word of life to every country, language, people, and nation over the face of the whole world. The enemy is bound, but the word of God is not bound.'

By this time the whole assembly was altogether in a state of confusion; now silence prevailed, then whisperings and questionings. The English who did not understand the Welsh were more anxious than any, on observing the general thrill which passed over the assembly; asking – 'What was that?' – 'What did he say?' – 'What is the reason for this excitement?' Silk dresses were wetted with tears – the buckram softened and the starch dissolved. After a little silence and recovery of feeling, the noble chairman turned suddenly and with some anxiety to the friend by his side, and inquired what could be the cause of the great commotion? He, approaching his ear, said, 'It was an illusion to yourself, my Lord, and to the accident at Waterloo, when the interception of providence spared you to preside over this meeting.' The chairman was then seen searching in his haste for his pocket-handkerchief to wipe off the tears which ran down his face in drops as large as peas . . . All the thunders of the cannon at Waterloo produced no more effect on his feelings than on the rock – but now the speech of the Welshman turned the strong rock into a pool of water.

This was a notable event in Mr Elias's history. Many changed their opinions of him after this day. Before, there was no end to their prejudice against him and their disregard of him, but now they half-worshipped him. However, this speech gave fresh impulse to the Bible Society. The nobleman subsequently sent Elias an invitation to his house and table, but the friendship of the great was of no importance in his eyes, his duty was to fulfil the work of him who sent him while it was yet day, and so, very respectfully, he declined the invitation.

The second example referred to was an address at the Holyhead Association in October 1824, between the sermons of the Rev. Owen Jones of Gelli and the Rev. William Morris, Cilgerran. The Rev. Owen Thomas was present at this Association as a young boy, sitting at the top of the ladder by which the preachers and ministers climbed up on to the stage. Mr Elias began by warning the people against drunkenness, as a sin that at all times and in all places degrades men more than almost any other sin, but he emphasized in particular its heinousness at a religious conference; and he hoped that there was no one present who would take advantage of their meetings to bring down shame on their country, their religion, and themselves. He then continued:

> Are there any drunkards here? I am afraid there are. I beg of you, will you – at least today – control yourselves. If you have no respect for the Almighty, no respect for the laws of your land, no respect for yourselves, will you please – for our sakes today – behave soberly and decently. You are, by attending our meetings and by your drinking and disorderly conduct, undermining our character. Our enemies are not all dead. They are ready to use everything they can lay hold of as an occasion to destroy us. We have nothing but our character on which to fall back. We are not rich; we are not learned; we are not gifted; we have no high titles; we have no one of any high authority in our midst. But we have our character; we are unwilling to allow anybody to destroy our character. But the drunkards who are attending our Associations are undermining our character. What can we do with them, my brethren? And it is ourselves, poor Methodists, whom they follow.

Then with a quick impulse and a sudden start, he said:

> I feel inclined to put them all up for sale, by auction, to whomsoever will take them, that they might not disturb us any more.

Then at the top of his voice, with his arm outstretched, as if he held them in the palm of his hand, he shouted:

> Who will take them? Who will take them? Churchmen, will you take them?

> 'We? We, in our baptism have professed to renounce the devil and all his works. No; we cannot take them.'

Then, after a moment's silence:

> Independents, will you take them?

> 'What? We? We, ages ago, left the Church of England because of her corruptions. No; we will not take them.'

Another interval of silence:

> Baptists, will you take them?

> 'We? Certainly not. We dip all our people in water as a sign that we take those who have been cleansed. No; we will not have them.'

Silence again:

> Wesleyans, will you take them?

'What? We? Good works is a matter of life with us. We do not want them.'

Then he stretched forth his arm once again, as if holding the poor drunkards in his hand; and once again, at the top of his voice, he shouted:

> Who will take them? Who will take them? Who will take them?

Then suddenly, his whole nature became agitated. His eyes flashed as he turned his head aside, and in a low tone which could be heard by all, he said:

> Methinks I can hear the devil at my elbow saying, 'Knock them down to me! I will take them.'

Then, after thirty seconds of silence, he cried:

> I was going to say, Satan, that you could have them, but...

Looking upwards, he said in a loud, clear, yet gentle voice:

> ... I can hear Jesus saying, 'I will take them! I will take them! Unclean, to be washed; drunkards, to be sobered; in all their filth and degradation, I will take them, and cleanse them in mine own blood.'

By now the whole field was an extraordinary sight. The preachers on the stage were dumbstruck. The vast crowd was in a ferment, and the effects such that many had broken out into rejoicing. Dr Thomas says that the remainder of the service that morning was completely spoiled and, indeed, the remainder of the Association, until Elias again preached last, in the chapel, in the evening. His text was John 3:15, and he had one of the most remarkable meetings of his life. His imagination must have been very strong and remarkably quick, and the effects of his oratory incomparable.

JOHN ELIAS AS A LEADER OF HIS CONNEXION

We have already mentioned that he was the leader of the Methodist Connexion, in Gwynedd at least, from the death of Mr Charles until his own death. He did not push his way on to the throne; it came to him naturally as the fruit of his labour, his ability, and his influence. And all must acknowledge that he possessed in abundance the essential qualifications for leadership. He was always clear in his opinions; never double-minded in his thoughts so as to bring about inconsistency at times. He knew what he aimed for, and by what means he intended to gain it. We would not claim that he was always correct in his judgment; to do so would be to attribute infallibility to him; nor would we claim that he saw further and deeper than others of his fellow-ministers. But, rightly or wrongly, his views would be determined and unhesitating, and some of the main developments of the Connexion were carried forward by the sheer determination of his will. He, chiefly, was at the root of the production of a *Confession of Faith* for the denomination, as well as of the *Constitutional Deed.*

He had a discerning eye for recognizing and appreciating hopeful young men. This is one of the essentials in a leader. He was once engaged to preach at Beddgelert. Soon after he had reached the place he heard that Mr John Jones, Talsarn, who attended there, had been received as a member of the Monthly Meeting. He persuaded the elders to appoint him to preach with himself. Mr Jones had an extraordinary service. Afterwards, in the chapel house, when John Jones had departed for his home in Dolwyddelan, Mr Elias said, 'I felt, as I heard him pray, that there was something remarkable in him, but as soon as he began to preach, I saw at once that we had received a preacher from God. He is, in truth, an extraordinary young man, and I pray that heaven will protect him.'

When Mr John Jones went on his first journey to Anglesey, in the beginning of the year 1825, Mr Elias heard the announcer in Holyhead saying that John Jones of Caernarvonshire would preach there on the following Sunday at two and at six. Once he had finished speaking, Mr Elias got to his feet, 'I never usually say anything publicly about visiting preachers before they come to us. Indeed, I have deliberately not done so, so as not to raise expectations that are afterwards disappointed, and thereby cause the young men and the listeners more harm than good. But I believe that the man who was announced to be here the next Sabbath is such as to justify my breaking my almost invariable custom. There are many John Joneses in Caernarvonshire; many of these John Joneses are preachers; but it would be good for you to understand that the brother announced is no ordinary John Jones. I had the opportunity, nearly two years ago now, to hear him preaching one evening at Beddgelert. The young man, very modestly, did not wish to preach and considerable effort had to be made to secure his agreement. But I had heard mention of him previously and I was eager to hear him. I felt immediately that there was something new, powerful, and very valuable in his ability. He almost preached what little sermon I had prepared out of my mind. I never found it so hard to rise and preach as after him.' And then he closed his comments in his own effective manner, 'I am glad that the ground will hide me from the view of the preachers that the Lord is about to raise.'

The first time for him to hear the Rev. Henry Rees was at a Dolgellau Association, October 1822. Mr Rees's text was Nehemiah 3:5, 'And next unto them the Tekoites repaired; but their nobles put not their necks to the work of the Lord.' The meeting was a powerful one, and Mr Elias was immediately convinced that an able preacher had arisen. His son, Mr John Jones, Tre'rgof, described how he, and two or three of the young men of Llanfechell, questioned his father after he had returned from Dolgellau as to the success of the Association. 'Oh,' he replied, 'We had a remarkable Association. There was one young man there particularly, not much older than one of you, preaching very powerfully, and I am fairly sure that not one of you will know that the verse he spoke on is in the Bible, or if you do, that you will not know where to find it.' He then recited the text. 'And,' said the son, 'not one of us did know it.' After speaking of the sermon, Mr Elias said, 'That is the preacher for Wales.' Before leaving Dolgellau he had persuaded Mr Rees to take some engagements in Anglesey. Perhaps he remembered Ebenezer Morris meeting him and persuading him, when he was young, to take a journey through the south. Certainly, this gift for appreciating young, able preachers was an excellent qualification in Mr Elias for leadership.

He laid great stress on education for the ministry. Though he was frustrated by the older brethren of Caernarvonshire from going to school in Manchester, he laboured almost beyond his ability to make up for this deficiency and was a strong supporter of educating preachers throughout his life. It was he, in conjunction with Mr Charles, who first thought of establishing an academy to teach the young men aspiring to the pulpit. He found a young man from Llanrwst, called Owen Williams, of excellent ability and possessing a gift for teaching languages. He was noted also for his religion and godliness. By means of Mr Elias's efforts, Williams was sent to Cheshunt Academy near London in order that, when he returned, he might teach his fellow-preachers. In an address at an Anglesey Monthly Meeting on behalf of Bala College, the Rev. Henry Rees made the following comments:

> Do not think that it is only now that the desire has arisen for educating the minds of young preachers. I spoke to one who lodged with the late Mr Charles of Bala, who said that the idea weighed heavily on his mind, particularly after we began ordaining. He was very grieved that no plan could be carried out to enable the men to gain more knowledge. And who had more zeal for this cause than the late and dear Mr Elias? I know well of this myself. I remember how faithful he was in sending Mr Owen Williams from Llanrwst to London, in order to prepare him as an academic tutor amongst us. I remember hearing of him passing once through Shrewsbury on the way to London when Mr Williams was there, and as he mentioned to a certain family of Mr Williams's abilities and genius, he expressed a wish that the latter might stay in London until he had swallowed every drop of knowledge that was there. Part of this

> family was sympathetic to Methodism, and another part of it was decidely antagonistic, and one of the latter group noted, 'There is a Welshman's ambition, wanting him to stay in London until he swallows every drop of knowledge that is there!'

Unfortunately Owen Williams died before leaving London, and some said to John Elias that this was an indication of God's disapproval of the Connexion's intention. 'No,' he replied, 'but rather, God is proving us to see how much we can hold; our duty is to look for another, as soon as we can.'

He behaved similarly towards Mr Evan Rowland, Liverpool, a young man who had received every educational advantage from his youth and had been a student at Belfast College for two years. Mr Elias greatly desired that he would commit himself to the ministry and establish an academy for preachers of the Connexion. In 1827 he brought the matter before the Bala Association, arguing powerfully in its favour. He had every support from many of the leaders, but others determined to keep the Connexion from any such institution in that they feared that the young preachers would lose something of greater value than anything they could gain there. According to one brother:

> Some of our preachers are already rather dryly respectable. Their condition is rather similar to the state of the country at the moment. When we go looking for a carpenter to make gates in order to keep the animals from the wheat, there is none to be found. They have all become cabinet-makers; there is no one willing to condescend to do the coarse work needed on the farms. I am afraid that an academy would have the same effect on our young preachers.

For all the opposition however, a committee was appointed to further the campaign and circulars were printed. Somehow or other, nothing came of the effort at this time, and very soon afterwards Mr Evan Rowland died as a young man of only twenty-three years of age and of excellent character and witness. Yet, notwithstanding all these disappointments, Mr Elias continued with his goal of setting up an academy for the Connexion and when the Rev. Lewis Edwards, afterwards Dr Edwards, and the Rev. David Charles, afterwards Dr Charles, opened a school for preachers at Bala, there was no one so sympathetic to the establishment as he, and he continued a zealous supporter all his life.

His care for the cause of Christ was watchful and eager. He feared greatly that false doctrines or unworthy influences might gain an entrance. There were powerful revivals in parts of Caernarvonshire in the year 1819, and while speaking of these at Llangristiolus, the Sabbath morning before the Llangefni Association, Mrs Elias said, 'How happy we would be if we could have some of the fire from Caernarvonshire for the Association.' Mr Elias replied immediately, 'It would do us no good from there; we have to get it from heaven, and then its effect would be seen on the hard hearers of Anglesey.' In an Association once, when encouraging the preachers to depend upon heavenly aid, he said:

> A king once sent a messenger to a powerful warrior in order that he might look at his sword, for the warrior had performed many powerful exploits. The messenger was received, but was told, 'There is the sword, but tell the king that the sword will be of no benefit to him unless he has also the arm that wielded the sword.

Towards the end of his life he feared much that religion was declining in the land. In the Bala Association of 1836, he preached a very effective sermon from Psalm 77:5, 'I have considered the days of old, the years of ancient times.' Amongst other things, he said that many who were not familiar with better times might imagine that everything was well and that nothing more excellent was to be desired. He continued:

> On the establishment of the old temple we read that there were those who were so happy that they shouted aloud for joy, whilst there were others who wept with a loud voice. The young people, those who had not seen the first temple, felt cheerful, clapped their hands, rejoiced and were happy, shouting out, 'Ho! Our temple surpasses all others; behold the stones of the foundations. There will be fine walls and beautiful ornaments, everything of the best quality.' But now see an old priest pass by, with long hair and white beard, and his eyes are as fountains pouring out tears ceaselessly. Some of the young men ask him, 'Why are you weeping at such a time as this? Everything is well; we shall have an excellent temple.' 'Ah, boys!' says the priest, 'I remember the first temple, and this one shall never be like that.' 'But here are the stones, and here are the masons; and everything else that is needed shall be supplied; and there are thousands of gold and silver pieces given for the work.' 'Yes, dear boys, but where is the ark of the covenant? Where are the sacred tablets? Where is the golden pot that had the manna? Where are the cherubim? And more than all, where is the Shekinah? There was a glory in the old temple, where is that now? There is nothing for me but to weep, and you would weep too if you had seen the things that I have seen.'
>
> O Lord, is that how things are with us in Wales today? Are we happy enough with our large congregations, and orderly preaching, the fine singing, and the many and valuable outward ornaments? Is the glory evident? In the old days we saw glorious and terrible things on the Green in Bala; but have we not reason to fear, by now, that we are left to ourselves, and that our God is hiding?

Whether John Elias was exhibiting, in these words, something of that tendency so prevalent in older people for imagining that everything is getting worse, we do not know, but they show clearly that he was ever watchful, and faithfully warned his fellow countrymen in all honesty.

A minister with the Baptists related that one of the most powerful things that he had ever heard was an address by Mr Elias at a preachers' society that he was permitted to be present at during some Association. Mr Elias was pessimistic as to the condition of the ministry at the time, and he feared that the preaching might be ineffective. He said how he once lodged in a large house; the weather at the time was very hot. The door of his room was opened for him, and the first thing he saw at the far end of the room was a large, burning fire. The sight of the fire on such a hot day made him feel most uncomfortable so that he almost turned his back on the room. But he entered, and having done so, found that the fire was not warming the room at all. Intrigued by this mystery he approached the fire and found that it was only a picture of a fire. The form and colour of the embers and flames were there but no heat. And on looking even more closely, he saw that a spider had chosen the spot as a convenient place to trap and hold its victims, and that it was already wrapping its prey in amongst the flames. From this illustration Mr Elias painted an awful picture of ineffectual preaching and of religious gatherings without the Holy Spirit present, gatherings which Satan makes use of to net and trap his victims, gatherings that were causes of corruption and not means of dispelling corruption. He trembled in case his own preaching and that of his brethren who were present should become nothing but cold formalities, containing only a picture of that which was present in the ministry of the fathers. Of all God's watchers on the wall, none was more faithful than John Elias.

He possessed the courage of a lion in carrying out the convictions of his conscience. We will provide one example of this. A ship bound for Liverpool and carrying a cargo of cotton and tobacco was shipwrecked on the rocks near Holyhead. Much of this cargo was washed ashore, and as the inhabitants considered that the spoils of the sea were free for all they were not slow in taking advantage of the opportunity. In this, the professors of religion were no better than others. A complaint came to the Anglesey Monthly Meeting that most of their Holyhead members, if not all of them, had partaken of the illegal spoils. Mr Elias and a number of other brethren were sent to investigate the accusation, with full authority to take whatever measures they judged best. As a result, they found that more or less every member was guilty of the offence. Consequently, having demonstrated clearly and powerfully to them the sinfulness of their actions, he excommunicated the whole church, officers and members, commanding them to leave at once. There was no strength in them to disobey, and all departed. He made arrangements with other men to provide the ministry for a month. Amongst those who were thrown out were a Mr and Mrs Jones with whom he used to lodge when at Holyhead. But that night there was not a Methodist in Holyhead who would receive John Elias into his house. Having arrived home however, Mr Jones's conscience smote him and he sent his son-in-law back to look for John Elias. The young man found him sitting by himself in the chapel. He asked him where he intended to sleep that night. Mr Elias replied that he did not know. The man said that his father-in-law had sent him to bring Mr Elias back to his usual lodgings. At this, Mr Elias was greatly cheered, and having arrived at the house found his host behaving even more generously than usual, in that he believed that he had acted in a conscientious manner and so had gained a victory over his feelings. After about a month all were received back into fellowship, on confession of their fault and on expression of their repentance. This episode put an end to all spoiling of goods washed up by the sea.

John Elias was always of notably courteous behaviour. In the houses where he lodged he was always very grateful to his hosts. He would reward the ostler and all who served him. He could engage with the gentry, when he found himself in their company, without loss of self-respect and without causing offence. The Rev. William Evans, Tonyrefail, spoke of him on a journey through Glamorganshire, and staying at the home of a gentleman not connected with the Methodists, but a truly religious man. This man had followed him from meeting to meeting for some days. As he departed, the gentleman said to him, 'Mr Elias, I have been in your company for many days, and my soul has profited much from your prayers, sermons and conversations, and I wish to show you some small sign of my respect.' He then offered to him a handful of sovereigns, adding, 'Please do not be offended that I offer you these, and would you accept them kindly with the same spirit as that with which they are offered.' Mr Elias replied, 'With all due respect to you, sir, I cannot in any way accept such a sum; it would not be worthy of me as a minister of Jesus Christ. But in order to acknowledge your generosity and to show that I appreciate your feelings, I will take one pound, most gratefully.' Thus he did, and his refusal only increased the gentleman's respect for him.

At the same time we do not wish to present him in his capacity as a leader, or in any other capacity, as perfect. No, 'Elias was a man subject to like passions as we are,' and, just as his namesake, he was not lacking in weaknesses. One of these was that he was too ready to be deceived and misled by unworthy professors of religion who would bring to him accusations against some of their brethren. There were some from Flintshire who were often guilty of provoking his rage against the innocent. They would approach him, displaying much concern for purity of doctrine, and would pretend great grief because famous preachers, whom they named, were departing from the faith. He, as a consequence, would strongly attack those preachers in the private meetings of the Associations, doing so often when there was no cause whatsoever. Indeed, on the very day before his accident on the way to preach at the Bala Association, someone had brought to him some slander against his brethren and Mr Elias was intending to bring those men to account in the private meeting. Mr John Davies even considered the accident as a providential interposition in order to frustrate him. According to Mr Davies:

> There were two men from ——shire who had been with him the day before the accident occurred, telling him that many preachers from that county were departing from the doctrines of the Connexion. This worried him greatly. But in my opinion, our late friend was shamelessly deceived on this occasion again, as he had been many times before, by men who were attempting to raise themselves by belittling others.

Having been led to suspect his brethren, John Elias was not always fair in dealing with their opinions. Dr Owen Thomas refers to the 1835 Association at Bala. The Rev. John Jones, Talsarn, had experienced a powerful meeting in the afternoon when preaching from John 6:44. This was when he used the illustration of an admiral receiving a command from the government to bring the fleet back to England from somewhere in the Mediterranean. He said:

> No one expects the admiral and his men to carry the ships on their backs. No, what is expected is that they should use the appropriate means for getting the ships home: to raise the anchors; spread the sails; point the ships in the right direction and steer them correctly, depending on the wind and the sea to carry them to England. So, dear people, the Lord in the gospel calls upon you to repent, and to believe, and to live godly lives. He does not intend that you should do that in your own strength. No, what he expects is that you place yourselves in the most advantageous situation for his infinite powers to work upon you. Launch your vessel upon the sea of the Saviour's merit; raise the sail of prayer; steer carefully according to the directions of the word of truth, and anticipate with hope the heavenly breezes, and you will find yourself one day entering the fair haven. 'But,' says someone, 'what can I do? I cannot believe.' Can you not read? Open your Bible, bring your mind to bear upon the witness to the Lord Jesus, and ask for the illumination of the Holy Spirit. 'But I cannot pray.' Dear soul, can you not try? Can you not bend your knees? Are there not joints in those legs? Will they not bend? Dear people, make every

> effort for salvation. Do not go to hell on your own, whatever happens. Truly, I resolved many years ago that I would not go there if I could. I will direct myself often towards the Garden of Gethsemane; I will often go round about the hill of Calvary; every day of my life I will call upon the throne of grace. I may very well be on the road to hell having made every effort in this way to reach heaven. But blessed be God! It will not be the road to hell; we have every certainty that this is the road to heaven.

The vast congregation lay in his hand, and thousands of 'Amens' rose in response to his prayers that the Lord would stir up the people to strive to enter the kingdom of heaven. Mr Ebenezer Richard was listening, and was weeping like a child. Great shining drops ran down his cheeks and his warm 'Amen' was as loud as any.

But Mr Elias did not look as if he was enjoying these remarks; he seemed rather as if he did not know what to do with such doctrine. In the meeting for preachers and elders at eight o'clock in the next room, the topic being discussed was the saving work of the Holy Spirit. At some point, the Rev. John Jones was called upon to speak. He commented that God's Spirit worked consistently with the natural principles of the human mind. Whenever we wish to change someone's feelings towards something, the only way to do it is to change their thoughts of it; to so present the object to him as to make him revise his opinion of it. He added:

> In the same way does the Holy Spirit work in order to transform a sinner, and to bring him to think much of Jesus Christ; he shines with fresh light into the mind. The Spirit knows that there is such evil in sin that a man must only be brought to recognize it truly and he will hate it; that there is such danger in being in a state of sin that it need only be realized and it will produce anxiety to be rescued from it; that there is such appropriateness and worth and glory in the Son of God as Saviour, that it only needs a true sight of him to draw the heart after him, and to win the mind to trust in him.

As soon as John Jones had stopped speaking, Mr Elias was on his feet, and saying in some agitation:

> In heaven's name, dear brethren, let us avoid this ground. Our neighbours' houses are on fire, and some of the sparks are falling on our own roofs. Never imagine that any amount of light, however strong, falling upon the mind, will change the nature of the heart. For all I know, the light of an angel shines in Satan's mind, but he has the heart of a devil nevertheless.

He spoke strongly and powerfully; there was no great difference between his views and that of the preceding speaker except that they were considering matters from different perspectives but, if he had not lost his temper, Mr Elias was certainly speaking far too roughly and excitedly. His words produced a very unhappy effect upon the meeting. But before any could respond to him, Mr Ebenezer Richard stood up and said, with his customary authority:

> If we wish for God's Spirit to work amongst us we must be watchful over our own spirits. Every strife and excitement is very contrary to his nature and displeases him greatly. The dove takes fright very easily. Nothing grieves the heavenly dove more than quarrels, jealousies, controversies, and things that provoke these. Zeal is truly valuable, but it becomes completely valueless in heaven's eyes if we lose the correct spirit. 'Ye know not what manner of spirit ye are of,' said the Lord to his zealous disciples, who wished to command fire to come down from heaven to consume those who were unkind to him, 'even as Elias did'. Yes, he did, but not with your spirit. These disciples were becoming heated for their Master, and it was good to be so heated. Their warmth of feeling for him was not in any way being rebuked by him. But he frowned at that spirit within them that was directing their zeal. We also must be careful, even when we are defending the truth of the gospel, that we are not under the control of any spirit that would make our zeal unacceptable to our Master.

All felt the edge of his words, Mr Elias particularly so, and he was sufficiently godly and humble to receive the rebuke. The meeting ended completely peacefully. But the history illustrates that Mr Elias was not without his weaknesses as a leader of the Connexion.

Perhaps also he tended at times to be autocratic. He was surely acting beyond his authority when he wrote a letter to the church at Jewin Crescent, London, commanding them to excommunicate those members who had signed a petition in favour of the emancipation of Roman Catholics. At the same time it must be emphasized that this letter has been grossly misrepresented. Though Mr Elias very strongly opposed the granting of the full privileges of citizenship to Roman Catholics and considered the Emancipation Act as a step towards re-establishing Papal authority in Britain, it was not the petitioning on behalf of emancipation that was the offence of those for whom he demanded excommunication but the fact that they had done so in the name of the church, with the church itself having no knowledge of the matter. There were in the Jewin Crescent Church at the time a number of young men who were talented and who delighted in literature but who were rather wild in their views and their zeal for what they considered liberty often ran away with them. These young men met and in the name of the Calvinistic Methodist Church in London sent a petition in favour of emancipation for Roman Catholics. This was an issue that was agitating the whole country at the time. Protestants, on the whole, opposed the measure firmly, not so much because they suspected the fairness of the suggestion in and of itself but because they feared the consequences, and when it was made known that London Welsh Methodists had petitioned in favour there was considerable excitement. The matter came to the attention of Mr Elias through reading newspaper reports of House of Commons debates. He requested an immediate inquiry and having discovered that some members were guilty of deceit, having used the name of the church on a document of which the church itself had no knowledge, he demanded that those concerned should be thrown out. Different opinions may exist as to the appropriateness of excommunicating these young men, but that they were greatly at fault is evident. If Mr Elias's zeal led him astray in this matter, that is to be seen, not so much in the excommunication as in the fact that he demanded it, and therefore took upon himself an authority that resides in the Association or in the Monthly Meeting and not, according to the Methodist Constitution, in any individual minister.

It may well be that further weaknesses in Mr Elias as a leader of the Connexion could be discovered, but there is no point in merely adding examples. We have noted the above for the sake of historical accuracy and in case any should imagine that we are attempting to paint a picture of perfection. But let it first of all be acknowledged that he was an excellent leader: keenly discerning, quick in understanding, bold in spirit, great in zeal and commitment, ready to sacrifice everything for the sake of Christ. His weaknesses were merely spots on the sun's surface. They seem all the greater because of the brightness of his excellences.

JOHN ELIAS AS A NONCONFORMIST

At the beginning of his ministry Mr Elias had little respect for the Established Church. He perceived that many of its clergymen were immoral in their lives and careless of fulfilling their duties, and full of a spirit of persecution towards those who sought to correct the country's morals. Because of this he often condemned them publicly in the severest terms. It is said that at times this behaviour of his grieved Thomas Charles. After one Bala Association, where he had described the Church of England clergy as dumb dogs, etc., Mr Charles wrote him a strong letter rebuking him for the roughness of his language. There is no record of the nature of John Elias's reply, but knowing of his great respect for Mr Charles he probably received the rebuke in a Christian spirit. At the same time, he had hardly any contact with clergymen for many long years; they hated him and he condemned them.

But it must be noted that a complete transformation in attitude occurred in the last years of his life. His feelings towards the Church became more kindly, and its clergymen came to view him with a respect that bordered on worship. There were many reasons for this. The first is that he came into contact with many evangelical clergymen living moral lives and preaching with evident effect. He met them on the platforms of the Bible Society and on similar occasions. As a result he nurtured a hope that the Church would be leavened by these men and would again become a strong spiritual force. They in return looked for every opportunity to honour him, as they particularly admired his oratorical gifts and the passion of his zeal. But the main factor in this transformation was the passing of the Roman Catholic Emancipation Act in 1829. Mr Elias feared Popery more than anything. He had read of its cruelties and persecutions; of its work in keeping the Scriptures from the people, in selling indulgences, and in bringing saints to martyrdom. He believed that as a religion it was still the same and had not changed its nature in any way, and that the fires of Smithfield would burn again were the Roman Catholic Church to be given authority and opportunity. To give the full privileges of citizenship to Catholics seemed to him therefore to be a trespass against Christ, and a step towards setting up the Pope's authority in Britain once more. No wonder therefore that he was so aroused on seeing many Nonconformists supporting the Parliamentary measure. And somehow he was led to believe that the only effective barrier against Popery was the Established Church, and he considered that the way of ensuring the truth of the gospel in the country was by strengthening that Church. He received *The Record*, the Church of England newspaper, regularly and on the whole agreed with its contents. He formed a bright vision of an Established Church having repossessed its primitive condition, faithful to the gospel, with its bishops and clergy labouring energetically for the faith once delivered to the saints.

On his deathbed however this vision was shattered by the rise of Puseyism at Oxford. This caused him considerable anguish, because he could see his intended barrier against Popery in danger of itself becoming Papistical. He said, 'The Puseyites are sure to do mischief! God alone knows what the end of these things will be.' And had he lived to see the extreme ritualism of our day: the confessional having a place again within the walls of the Church, the preaching of Christ having disappeared and the burning of incense having taken its place, the administering clergy claiming that in the Holy Eucharist they are offering up the true body of the Lord, and many Churchmen anxious for closer intercourse with Rome and desiring that Anglican ordination be declared acceptable by the Pope; if Mr Elias, we say, had lived to see such things all his sympathy for the Church of England of necessity would have ceased and his Nonconformist zeal, most certainly, would have blazed forth. He was not a political statesman, but a minister of Christ, and he viewed all things from that standpoint.

THE LAST DAYS OF JOHN ELIAS

The last time for Mr Elias to visit the south was the occasion of the Aberystwyth Association of 1837, soon after the death of his dear friend, Ebenezer Richard. Cardiganshire was in deep mourning and he himself mourned the loss of his friend. One whole meeting was given over to discussing the passing of Mr Richard. Mr Elias commented then:

> A member very close to the heart has been broken off; there should be great grief and loss felt in Cardiganshire, for even we in Anglesey, at the tips of the fingers, as it were, feel the wound deeply. Nevertheless, do not despair, my brethren; though the bravest of the county has fallen there is no reason for the work to falter. But let none of you attempt to fill the place that he filled or to attempt to roll away the stone that he could have removed. Rather, go together to the work and you will then advance again and the presence of the Chief Shepherd will be with you.

Mr Elias was severely ill at the beginning of 1839 and confined to his house for about four months. He was suffering from an inflammation of one of his kidneys and his condition was considered dangerous, but he improved sufficiently to attend the Bala Association. He was ill again at the beginning of the next year, 1840, but strengthened with the coming of Spring. He preached with all his accustomed energy and was present at Associations at Llannerch-y-medd, Bala and Dolgellau. It is thought that it was while at Llanerch-y-medd that he caught the chill in his foot that was eventually to lead to his death. His last Association was at Dolgellau on 21–22 October. He travelled there in great concern as some had suggested to him that a departure from the faith was taking place amongst some of the younger preachers, and he said some severe and cutting things in the private meeting. But he was greatly relieved while at the Association. He heard the sermons of two of those who had been accused, namely, John Jones, Talsarn, and John Hughes, Liverpool, and the doctrines they preached warmed his heart. He said in the private society the next day:

> As long as the two truths that were preached last night and the previous night, namely, that Christ Jesus came into the world to save sinners, and that it is the Spirit of Christ who works in us every tendency towards goodness and holiness; as long as those two truths are kept alive in our experiences, and raised up in our ministries, we need not despair of our ultimate victory, though hell

> be against us. I feel that, after this Association at Dolgellau, I can descend into the valley with a mind at peace with respect to the great cause.

And, as we have noted, this was the last Association that he attended.

About the end of the year 1840 he began to feel pain in the thumb of his foot. He told a friend:

> I feel as healthy and as strong and as lively as I ever felt, but there is something in the thumb of my foot. And who knows? It may be that death has begun to work there.

He had spoken the truth. He was soon confined to the house and for a while suffered great pain. In a letter written in the beginning of March 1841, he noted:

> I do not know what will become of it [the illness]. But I am at peace; let the Lord do that which is good in his sight. If he leaves me long in pain, may he strengthen me to suffer in patience. I do not feel any great fear as I think of death; 'I know whom I have believed.' If I might, through being allowed to remain a little longer in the flesh, be of some usefulness to God's cause, I would be glad to recover for a little time further.

He did not have to wait long to know that there would be no recovery. One brother sought to persuade him that his thumb would improve again. 'No,' he said, 'it is death that is at work here.' On hearing this, his wife complained that she found such comments very discouraging. He answered her, 'See how great the kindness of the Lord is towards us, in sending death to begin its work in a foot, the most distant part from the seat of life, when he could have sent it to the head, or the heart, bringing about death at an instant. This way, the knot between us will be gradually untied, and I will be gradually removed from earth.'

He could not remain idle even when confined, and it was at this time that he wrote his *Autobiography*, which we have referred to and quoted frequently. Its last paragraph reads:

> I have written a brief account of my life from infancy till now (sixty-seven years of age), of the Lord's goodness towards me, and a review of his work amongst the Calvinistic Methodists. I have written this in my sick room, not knowing but that I am on the plains of Moab, on the brink of Jordan. I wrote a few lines now and then, in sorrow and through difficulty, considering myself as writing every line in the presence of God, and writing perhaps that which will be read when I shall be quiet in the grave. I have nothing to say of myself, but of my sinfulness, vileness, and great misery; but I would be happy to speak of God's goodness, mercy and grace towards me. 'This is the poor man that was raised out of the dust, and the needy man that was lifted out of the dunghill,

> and set with princes, even the princes of his people.' If any good has been done by my imperfect labour, God in his grace has performed it. To him belongs the glory; I was as nothing. This shall be seen in the day when God shall reveal all his secrets. If God took me to be an instrument in his hand, to bring some sinner or sinners to Christ, this is an unspeakable privilege. It will be a joy to me, 'in the day of Christ, that I have not run in vain, neither laboured in vain.' But if I had succeeded in bringing thousands to the Methodists, without coming to Christ, it would be vain and worthless before the throne of Christ! The work should be burned and the preacher sustain the loss.

His illness was painful as well as lingering, but his soul rejoiced in salvation. He said to the Rev. H. Griffiths, the Rector of Llanddrygan, who had come to visit him and with whom he was very friendly, 'I am as happy in my mind as a man could be, granted my pain. There is no cloud between my soul and God. The comforts I used to enjoy in the means of grace and in the ministry, still flow into my soul. Yes, they are sometimes stronger and livelier in their effects now than they have ever been.' By the beginning of June it was evident that he was sinking fast, and at about eleven o'clock on Tuesday night, 8 June 1841, quite quietly, without a sigh or a groan, he fell asleep in Jesus, one month into his sixty-seventh year.

In an incredibly short time, on considering that there was no telegraph in use at that period, the news travelled throughout Wales that Mr Elias had died, and it produced a sincere and general sadness. He was buried at Llanfaes, near Beaumaris, at his own request, as it was there that the remains of his old friend Mr Richard Lloyd rested. And this was the most remarkable funeral that had ever been seen in Anglesey, from the day that the island first raised its head out of the sea. The bodies of many noble men of great distinction and influence in their day have been laid in Anglesey's ground, but not one of their funeral days could be compared, in terms of the intensity of grief, the sense of loss, and the number of mourners, to that of Mr Elias. The burial took place on Tuesday, 15 June, and unfortunately the Bala Association was meeting on the same day. This prevented many of the leading ministers of the Connexion from being present at the funeral. The previous evening, the Rev. William Roberts, Amlwch, preached at Llangefni Chapel, from 2 Kings 2:11–14, to a large gathering of mourners. At the close a verse was given out, but the singing failed and all broke out in weeping. The next morning they set out for Llanfaes, a distance of about fourteen miles. The procession was large when departing from Llangefni, made up of clergymen, doctors, ministers of the gospel of all denominations, scores of carriages, many on horseback and thousands on foot. As it proceeded, the numbers swelled, and on approaching Beaumaris it contained at least ten thousand people. Very little work was done on Anglesey that day. Those who did not attend the funeral waited at the side of the road to see the procession pass. The people stood as those struck silent, and they wept many tears. At Llanfaes Church, the funeral service was read by the Rev. H. Griffiths, Llanddrygan, assisted by the Rev. H. Jones, the Rector of Llanfaes. Then, amidst signs of deepest distress, the remains of the Rev. John Elias were lowered into the grave. That night the Rev. John Ffoulkes, Abergele, preached at Beaumaris Chapel to a vast congregation, from Hebrews 13:7.

On Mr Elias's grave at Llanfaes was raised a handsome memorial bearing the following epitaph written by the Rev. Thomas Phillips, D.D., Henffordd:

In this sacred spot are deposited,
at his own request, the remains of
THE REVEREND JOHN ELIAS
Late of Llangefni in this county,
who, during the long period of forty-seven years,
laboured with singular diligence and success,
as a minister of the Gospel, in connection
with the Calvinistic Methodists.
He was a Christian of the highest order,
an 'Israelite indeed in whom was no guile.'
In the several relations of life, he was
upright, friendly, and affectionate.
Endowed with extraordinary graces and gifts,
he became, among his own countrymen,
the most attractive preacher of his day.
Institutions aiming at the promotion of religious or
charitable objects, found in him a powerful advocate.
But his highest distinction was the holy influence
diffused by his character and spirit, wherever he went.
Zealous for truth in doctrine, and purity in life,
he fought 'the good fight of faith,'
seeking not his own honour, but the good of souls,
and resting all his hope on the cross of Christ;
in this hope he finally triumphed over death,
and slept in Jesus, on the eighth day of June 1841;
in the sixty-eighth year of his age.

John Elias wrote very little for the press. He was a preacher, and it was to the great work of preaching the gospel that he consecrated his life; but certainly had he directed his mind towards literature he would have excelled as a writer, though not to the same degree as he excelled as a preacher. He wrote very able essays on Justification, and on Unequal Yoking, and an introduction to the sermons of Mr Hurrion. He possessed considerable poetic skills also, composing many sweet hymns, some of which are found in the latest collections, for example:

'The merit of the precious blood of God'	'Mae haeddiant mawr rhinweddol waed fy Nuw,'
'And was it for my sin That Jesus suffered so.'	'Ai am fy meiau i Dioddefodd Iesu mawr.'

We must now, reluctantly, part with the life of the Rev. John Elias, and in doing so we feel that the picture given of him is very poor compared to what he was in himself. Undoubtedly he was one of the most extraordinary men ever produced by Wales and, as an orator, the country has never seen his better. When we consider the obscurity from which he arose, the disadvantages under which he laboured, his exclusion from educational advantages, the heights to which he scaled, and the influence he wielded over his fellow countrymen, his history appears almost a miracle. Nature and grace combined in him to form a prince of the religious world. His name shall be a sweet savour in Wales for as long as respect for the preaching of the gospel and the influence of religion abide in the land.

[1] See the comment on this passage in Owen Thomas, *The Atonement Controversy in Welsh Theological Literature and Debate, 1707-1841* (Edinburgh: Banner of Truth, 2002), p. 317.

[2] A very sweet and evangelical preacher.

43

EBENEZER RICHARD, TREGARON

HENRY RICHARD, TRE-FIN

The Methodist Connexion in the south was never blessed with a more faithful and more useful minister in all the various parts of the work of the Lord than the Rev. Ebenezer Richard. He was a notable preacher; unique in his involvement with the Sunday Schools and as a catechist; and a brilliant organizer, the ablest in south Wales since the days of Howell Harris. In this last category we know of no one in the Connexion who could compare to him, apart from Howell Harris and Thomas Charles. He had a discerning eye, a determined will, unique abilities and never-ending energy. It was through his care and planning, more than that of any other man, that the Methodists took possession of the northern half of Cardiganshire, and it is still in their possession up to today. We are sorry that we do not have more of the history of this famous minister. Soon after his death a biography of him, written by his sons, was published but the book is comprised mainly of letters written by him and sent to him, so that to a large extent the history of his labours is lost. We must do the best we can with that which has survived.

He was the son of Henry Richard; his eldest child by his second wife, Hannah. Mr Richard had two sons by his first wife, namely John and William, both of whom lived all their lives in Pembrokeshire. Two other children were born to Hannah after the birth of Ebenezer, namely Thomas, who became famous throughout Wales as the Rev. Thomas Richard, Fishguard, and a girl called Mary. Henry Richard was something of an exhorter and a schoolmaster as well. He kept one of Madam Bevan's circulating schools in various places in the north and the south of the country. He had no abiding city for most of his life for various reasons: firstly, his work with the school moved him from place to place, keeping him from settling in any region; but also, he was too much of a Methodist to satisfy the local clergy who monitored Madam Bevan's schools. In those days all who were evangelical in belief, who sought to live godly lives, and who endeavoured to save the souls of their fellow-men were called Methodists.

His gifts as a preacher seem to have been limited but he was noted for his prayers. About the year 1767, he kept a school in the parish of Llanaber, not far from Barmouth. According to *Methodistiaeth Cymru* he was not preaching at this time but would pray wonderfully with the schoolchildren, would reprove severely all forms of immorality and lack of restraint, and would seek to lead the minds of the people towards eternal things. Such a man will not be tolerated long in any district and he was soon driven away rather than the neighbourhood be corrupted and all be brought to think of religion in the same way as himself. But they were too late: the leaven had already been added to the bread. The words of the schoolmaster, like seeds upon the ground, had already laid hold of one Robert Griffiths of Barmouth. The Lord dealt first with Mrs Griffiths, then with her son, Hugh, and lastly with Robert Griffiths himself, and this was the beginning of Methodism at Barmouth.

After moving from place to place with his school, Henry Richard finally settled at Tre-fin, Pembrokeshire. He spent the rest of his life in useful work, assisting Howell Davies, John Harries, Evan Harries his son, Jones Llan-gan, and others, in the work of the Lord in Pembrokeshire, and leaving the impression in the minds of all that though he might not be a great preacher he was eminently godly, and famous for his gift in prayer. He lived to a ripe old age but towards the end of 1812 his horse fell beneath him as he was travelling home from a preaching engagement, and he broke his knee. This injury eventually brought about his death, on 7 December 1812.

EBENEZER RICHARD'S EARLY YEARS AND CONVERSION

Ebenezer Richard was born at Tre-fin on 5 December 1781. He was therefore twelve years younger than Ebenezer Morris and David Evans, Aberaeron. He may well have had opportunity to hear Daniel Rowland and Williams, Pantycelyn, for he was close to nine years old when the first died, and approaching ten on the death of the second. But Howell Davies, the Apostle of Pembrokeshire, had been laid to rest eleven years before his birth. His brother states that Ebenezer was a timid and quiet child. He was never seen throwing himself into the play of the children of the neighbourhood, he preferred rather the company of his mother or his book. From a child he was religious; his mother, who was a very godly woman, took particular care to instruct him in the truths of the gospel and she would take him with her to the society at Tre-fin. It is said of him that at one Communion service at Tre-fin, when he was six years old, he stretched out his hand and took the bread. His mother noticed and stopped him from receiving the cup. After the service, she rebuked him, saying, 'My dear child, why ever did you do that?' He quietly asked back, 'Why did you do it?' 'I was remembering the death of God's Son,' she replied. 'That is what I was doing,' he answered, leaving his mother lost for a reply.

We know very little of his early days or of his education. As his father was a schoolmaster, he probably gave some early instruction to his sons and Ebenezer certainly took every advantage of this. He also, no doubt, was sent to the best schools in the region. It may be also that he spent some time in the Grammar School at Haverfordwest. The evidence for believing this is that the teaching at the time in the national schools was atrocious, whereas Ebenezer Richard was an excellent scholar. He could write English and Welsh accurately and grammatically, and he was almost certainly fluent in the classical languages or he would not have been appointed as tutor to the sons of a gentleman of some position. He was a rapid learner and very fond of books. As a youth, he loved to hear the gospel. At that time the itinerant ministry in Wales was at its height and when famous and popular preachers would visit Pembrokeshire he would follow them for days from place to place. When he was about fifteen years old he became ill with a dangerous disease. He was very near death at this time but God was kind to him, and to the churches of Wales. The next year the French landed at Fishguard. The history is so well known that we need not repeat it here but we may note that Tre-fin is within a few miles of the spot where they landed and that the occasion affected the young Ebenezer greatly. He wrote a poem on the event and it was published later that year.

A little while later he moved from his parents' home to keep a school at Brynhenllan, a place between Newport and Fishguard. The critical period of his spiritual life now arose. As has been mentioned, he was religious from childhood and had for some time been accepted as a member in the church. He was moral in his life, he received considerable pleasure in hearing the Word, he was careful in the meticulous fulfilling of his religious duties and was very acceptable to God's people. But he had not experienced any strong convictions; he had not, in the language of the believers of old, been led to Sinai to see the smoke ascending and the lightning flash, to hear the thunderings of the law, and to have his own soul held up as guilty before God so that he despaired of life. He greatly desired this and prayed earnestly to God for it. And his wish was granted. What means were used to stir up his soul is not known, but a great storm broke over him. For some time he wandered on the brink of despair; he felt that hell had opened its mouth to swallow him up and he could not find any door of hope. For a while he sought to establish a way of escape on the basis of the law, giving himself to fasting, to prayer, and to painful penances, day and night. To this end he separated from the company of his friends, spending most of his time on his own. But these things could not silence the roaring of his conscience and he did not dare present them to the Lord as works of righteousness. His spiritual distress was so great that he had to give up his work and return to his parents' home. But having been broken in the place of dragons he found the way of escape. He wrote as follows of the day, 1 July 1801:

> This night was the worst of my life, but I believe that in it a day began that will never end.

The word used to dispel the darkness from his mind was Hebrews 7:25, 'Wherefore he is able also to save them to the uttermost that come unto God by him, seeing he ever liveth to make intercession for them.' He believed afterwards that he had been guilty of presumption when praying for deep conviction, and he warned others from following his example. 'I did so,' he wrote, 'and was granted my request; but as a result I suffered pains and tortures that I would not wish a dog or snake to have to endure.'

HE BEGINS TO PREACH

Mr Richard returned to Brynhenllan a new man. We would not wish to have to decide whether or not he was a Christian before, but he had now passed through a deep crisis, a crisis that had made him a very different man. He was now full of desire to serve his Redeemer and the brethren encouraged him to take part in the services. He was willing to do so and there was such a freshness in his style, such appropriateness in his words, and such a passionate intensity in his spirit, that all were amazed. He was often asked to begin a service for visiting ministers, and often there would be more talk of the opening prayer than of the sermon that followed. In this way his evident qualifications for the ministry became apparent, and he was pressed by the elders of the church to preach. He hesitated to do so for some time; he was afraid of entering presumptuously upon such exalted work and of rushing in without being called, and it seems that he would have withstood every pressure except that he feared offending the Lord. He preached first at Dinas from Romans 8:34, 'It is Christ that died.' The divisions and sub-divisions of the sermon are still extant; there is nothing remarkable about them other than that they demonstrate a very Puritan-like style and a very scriptural content. It has been noted however that there was considerable blessing in the service; that a sweet influence fell upon the preacher's spirit and upon the spirits of the congregation.

He preached for some time before receiving permission from any religious court, other than that of the Dinas church. Within about a year his brother Thomas began to preach, and their cases were then brought before the Monthly Meeting. Mr Jones, Llan-gan, had by now moved to Pembrokeshire and he took the leading part in the examination. He questioned them severely and his countenance was strict and solemn but he was thoroughly satisfied with their replies, and he might well have had a previous opportunity of hearing them, because on leaving the meeting he said to a stranger present, 'These two boys preach like two angels.'

Mr Richard threw himself into the work of the gospel with great energy and determination. We have no information on the extent of his labours or any histories of remarkable meetings under his ministry but, because of the uniqueness of his gifts, he soon found himself in the front rank of Pembrokeshire preachers. He kept a journal but it consists mainly of notes on his spiritual condition and his experiences in the work, rather than an account of various religious meetings. We will include some quotations in order to show something of his frame of mind:

> 24 September 1805.
>
> I trust that I may, from experience, call the Lord Jehovah-Jireh, for he has wonderfully provided for his poor servant today, when I had feared that he had given me up. He brought me relief in his grace. I saw marvellous things from his word in Luke 14:23. Oh! for help not to grieve his dear Spirit, and to walk humbly before him.
>
> 12 November.
>
> Today was the Monthly Meeting of the county. Brother Evan Harries preached from Hebrews 1:3. And today I heard the startling news of the unexpected death of —. I see that in the midst of life we are in death, and I was struck by that word in Matthew 24:44. I sought to speak a little from it on the following day, at her funeral. Tonight, that is the 13th, was precious. Praise be to God. My meditation was upon his law; I felt his cause closer to me than anything else, and I longed that I might be able to do more for him in the world. To this end I found the throne of grace to be very precious.
>
> 24 November.
>
> Truly a Sabbath to my soul. Oh! for a soul to bless the Lord for his kindness to me, a worm, amongst my people today; in the morning, on Job 11:20; in the evening, on 1 Corinthians 10:4. I will never completely forget this Sabbath, for he fulfilled his gracious word to his poor servant; but I understood that I am never at any time in greater danger than when the Lord is pleased to reveal himself to my soul. O! make me watchful.

11 December.

The Monthly Meeting of the county met today at St David's. Mr Evan Harries and Mr Jones, Llan-gan, preached; the first from Revelation 6:2, and the second from Philippians 3:10. We had fresh cause to believe that the Lord has not departed from us and that his countenance is towards both the private and the public work.

1 January 1806.

I began a new year today. I met with the Loyal British Society today. I could not settle in my mind having been called to this present duty and after much darting back and forth I fixed on that part of God's Word, Luke 2:14, 'And on earth peace ...' I trust that the Lord helped me. I saw that he brings the blind by a way that they know not. I recall much of the state of my mind because I presumptuously promised to go to S. without bringing the matter before the Lord. Oh! that this would be a warning to me from henceforth. The pride of my heart was greatly excited by this matter, but the Lord saw fit to bring me low; to forgive me; and he made his face to shine, to some degree, upon my mind. What a wonderful God! I went to S— and A—; here again it is 'hitherto the Lord helped me'. Praise be to him!

19 March.

This is the day of our prayer-meeting. Alas! How unprepared and unqualified I am for the great work of seeking to draw near the Lord. I sought to meditate tonight, before beginning our meeting, on the fact that it is through the means of grace that the Lord restores and renews his people. Many people gathered, more than I have seen for many days. To God be all the thanks for this. The brethren were assisted in completing the public work gloriously. In private, many of us discoursed somewhat of our spiritual states. A degree of assistance was given to converse with two sisters, and at the end of the meeting we sang that hymn: *Dechrau canu, dechrau canmol.* In this part of the work, an extraordinary influence dawned upon us; many were loosed from their bonds, and we departed, though it was a very late hour of the night, in peace and cheerfulness. Thanks be to our God.

We cannot include more quotations but these should be sufficient to prove that Mr Richard, even at the age of twenty-four, was a man of keen observation and mature judgment, was wholly committed to the gospel, and was consistently watchful over his spiritual state. We would have been glad if he had noted a few more facts; a history of the Pembrokeshire Monthly Meeting over the period of the beginning of the ministries of the two Richard brothers, when Evan Harries and Jones Llan-gan were the main pillars, would have been more precious than lost gold. But we must be content with what we have. Between the lines we may read that it was a successful time for religion; that an evident unction accompanied the Monthly Meeting, that the Lord's countenance shone upon the preaching, upon the prayer-meetings, and upon the private societies. We are told that at times the bonds of many were loosed, and it is suggested that at times the rejoicing and singing of the saints were such that they failed to conclude their meetings until late into the night.

In 1806 Mr Richard moved to live at Cardigan. It seems that at the time he was very ill; all who saw him believed that he was in the throes of consumption and had not long to live. He visited Cardigan in order to consult a doctor. He told him that as long as he stayed for some time in the town and took his medicines regularly he should make a full recovery. He decided to stay and the doctor's prognosis proved correct. At this time Captain James Bowen, afterwards of Llwyngwair, lived at Cardigan. He was a godly man and a Methodist. He invited Mr Richard to his house as a tutor for his sons. Mr Richard agreed and spent the next three years here, being held in great respect. The religious environment within the home of this excellent family greatly appealed to him. During family worship Mr Richard would pray in Welsh and Captain Bowen in English after him, and often the heavenly dew would fall upon them around the altar. One Sabbath evening was long remembered when, after Mr Richard had returned from speaking for his Master and had knelt before the throne of grace, the Lord poured out the gracious rain upon him and upon those present to such an extent that they were caught up into the early hours of the morning in praising God. They doubled and trebled the words of the hymn:

Before them all, I'll raise my head, And cry out, 'Victory, by His blood'; Enter within my Father's house, And there for ever stay.	Caf godi 'mhen o dan eu traed, A gwaeddi concwest yn y gwaed, A mynd i mewn i dy fy Nhad, Ac aros yno byth.

A scene, surely, that was not often to be seen in the houses of the Welsh nobility.

EBENEZER RICHARD AND THE SUNDAY SCHOOLS

His coming to Cardigan proved of great blessing to the cause in the town and to all the neighbouring churches. The Rev. William Morris, Cilgerran, wrote as follows:

> Many here will never forget the time he lived at Cardigan. The Lord blessed his labours in a remarkable way, in calling many sinners from darkness to the glorious light of the gospel. Scores were added to the church here (Cilgerran) and to the churches of the district and many of these have passed to glory. The

Sunday School here, and throughout the region, benefited from his labours. How happy he was visiting the schools and examining the children. I often saw him and the children in tears together, so that the most hardened heart was compelled to weep along with them, and to confess that God was amongst them. He succeeded to a remarkable degree in raising the condition of the Sunday Schools to the order and success that they now present.

The reference to the Sabbath Schools leads us to one of the main elements of the life of Ebenezer Richard. It could almost be said that he was the Father of the Sunday Schools of south Wales. He possessed an unquenchable zeal on their behalf, a zeal that continued throughout his life. He used to boast that he was born in the same year that Sunday Schools were founded by Mr Robert Raikes. Most probably Sunday Schools had been begun in Cardiganshire before his arrival in the county, but they were not very lively nor well managed, and many of the older believers kept away from them, considering the work to be unworthy of the Sabbath. Mr Richard organized them thoroughly and breathed new life into their constitution. In this respect, what Mr Charles was to north Wales, Mr Richard proved to the south. And during his stay in Cardigan he began this work with an energy, commitment and perseverance that has never been excelled. To show his great interest in children and young people, we will quote an extract from his diary dated 28 February 1808:

At Capel Drindod, Eliza Griffiths, a four-year-old child, recited the first two Psalms accurately to me. At Clos-y-graig, on the afternoon of the same day, a fifteen-year-old girl, who was very ill and seemed in the last stages of consumption, saw me in order to recite a chapter that she had learned upon her bed. She did so, though suffering greatly from lack of breath – the 25th of Matthew, and fairly accurately. In Newcastle Emlyn, late the same day, when the service was over, crowds of children attached to the school followed me to the home of a friend, and having sung a little with their lovely small voices, two or three of the small boys asked me the following important questions:

1. How does the Holy Spirit apply to us the salvation purchased by Christ?

2. What are the effects of justification and sanctification?

3. Which comes first of justification and sanctification?

The Rev. Thomas Evans, Carmarthen, wrote to Mr Richard's sons with respect to his work among the Sunday Schools at this time in his life:

I think it was in New Inn that I first saw your father. He would come to us every month from Cardigan. No one else who came to us could compare with him in the way he would encourage, instruct and question the Sunday

School. The sincerity of his warmth towards us, the children of the School, was evident, and he put up with our darkness and ignorance (for at the time the Sunday Schools had only just begun in the land) with much gentleness, and we loved him almost as ourselves. I perfectly remember that the main points of his ministry, and what filled his mind as he catechized the schools, were the Person, Sacrifice, and Atonement of Christ. He would raise his strong and melodious voice on these great themes, until both he and we were in tears. Many times he said, years later, when we fellowshipped together and the conversation turned to reminiscences of the past, 'Here he is, I catechized him continually until he was in a sweat.' And he was correct. I often sweated while attempting to answer him.

In his work with the Sunday Schools he received every help from the Rev. Ebenezer Morris. The two co-operated perfectly in stirring up whole districts, planting schools, arranging festivals for reciting catechisms on various themes and for questioning the children, and teaching the importance of nurturing the young in God's Word. As an example of the interest they felt in the Sunday School, we include here the following letter from the Rev. Ebenezer Morris, when he was on a journey through Breconshire, to Mr Richard:

Brecon, 30 May 1808.

Dear Friend,

Providence opens a way for me to return home on Whit Saturday, convenient for me to come on Whit Monday to the meeting arranged at Blaenannerch for the children of the schools to meet. Would you please inform the places you think appropriate before the Sabbath. It would surely be good for ten or more schools to meet. If you could inform Twrgwyn and Penmorfa before I return, I would be grateful. You know best the other places to approach. Owen and I hope to begin the meeting at nine or ten in the morning; we can decide the time when we meet.

Your dear friend,

EBENEZER MORRIS

P.S. It would be good for two to preach after the examining; these will probably be myself and yourself. If you might see to speak on the benefit of catechizing, I will emphasize the value of early godliness. It would be good to announce it as a Children's Festival.

The 'Owen' referred to by Mr Morris was almost certainly Owen Enos, who often accompanied him on his journeys. It is easy to see from the letter that arrangements for the Sunday Schools had not been perfected in the south; that the bi-monthly and annual meetings had not yet been established but were clearly on the horizon. It is also evident that the two great motors, driving the vehicle onwards, were Mr Morris and Mr Richard. These two were the two greatest spiritual forces in Cardiganshire or, indeed, in south Wales, and the one supplemented the weakness of the other. Mr Morris was the more courageous, the more determined, and the more daring in his public ministry; no enemy could withstand him. But Mr Richard was the better organizer, the wiser in planning, and the more discerning in recognizing the signs of the times. Between the two of them the Sunday Schools were established on firm and unshakeable foundations.

In 1807, Mr Richard made his first visit to the north. So great was Captain Bowen's respect for him that he accompanied him the whole way, taking him in his own carriage. We know very little of the history of the journey but it made Mr Richard's name famous throughout Gwynedd, and from then on he was considered one of the giants of south Wales. It is said that a remarkable blessing was obtained at Devil's Bridge when the two were together at family worship. The influence upon the head of the household was such that he had to run out of the room, tears streaming down his cheeks, crying out, 'Oh! What shall I do? What shall I do?' They attended two Associations, those at Llanidloes and Bala. Mr Richard had a wonderful service at Bala. At ten in the morning he preached on 2 Corinthians 10:4, 'For the weapons of our warfare are not carnal.' When speaking of the value of the weapons, and encouraging his hearers to use them, the tears flowed from his eyes; yet they did not hinder his words but seemed to lubricate his speech, freeing the words, softening the voice, sweetening his tone. And if the preacher wept, the vast congregation followed suit so that Bala Green had never been so watered by the tears of God's saints. He overcame the vast gathering completely, as well as the preachers and clergymen on the platform, and his sermon was referred to in all the subsequent meetings. Up to the day of his death, Mr Richard was one of the elect preachers of the Bala Association and very rarely was he not in attendance.

HIS MARRIAGE AND REMOVAL TO TREGARON

On the first day of November 1809, Mr Richard married Miss Mary Williams of Tregaron. Mrs Richard was the grand-daughter, on her mother's side, of David Evan Jenkins, one of the earliest of the Methodist exhorters, a man notable for his godliness and his zeal for pure doctrine. She bore the image of her family, being committed to the service of religion. Because his wife's parents were elderly and failing, so that it was impossible for her to leave them, Mr Richard decided to move to Tregaron. This decision of his caused deep feeling in the south of the county; they would not by any means release their hold of him; they argued long with him, and having failed to persuade him personally, they took his case to the Monthly Meeting. Captain Bowen and one of the Cardigan Church elders travelled up to the Aberystwyth Monthly Meeting. There the matter was debated fully but the balance turned in favour of Tregaron. Colonel Lloyd, Bronwydd, was also at the meeting and he spoke up strongly, though in broken Welsh, for stopping Mr Richard from leaving Cardigan. Somehow, in his clumsiness with the language, he managed to quote the verse, 'For this cause shall a man leave his father and mother, and shall be joined unto his wife, and they two shall be one flesh.' Mr Williams, Lledrod, took the words from him and used them in argument against him. The old nobleman saw that he had made use of verses that did not serve his cause. Having failed at the Monthly Meeting, Captain Bowen attempted to get Mr Charles of Bala to write to Mr Richard. But Mr Charles was too wise to intervene, especially as he was ignorant of all the facts. He wrote a very sensible and spiritual letter to Captain Bowen suggesting to him that Providence might have important purposes to fulfil through the move. So determined and unyielding were the friends at Cardigan that Captain Bowen and the other elder made one more attempt: they travelled to Tregaron, hoping to influence Mrs Richard. But having arrived and seen her parents' condition they acquiesced in the arrangement and returned home reconciled to the situation.

Ebenezer Richard spent the rest of his life at Tregaron and undoubtedly he was God's gift to north Cardiganshire. He immediately took his place as a leader, not only of his own church, but of all the surrounding churches; all looked up to him as a prince with God; his word was law and unconditional obedience was paid to it. Amongst the preachers of that part of the county he was as a king amongst his host, with no one envying him nor anyone doubting his authority. He won this position by the uniqueness of his gifts, good sense, superior wisdom, an unusual ability for dealing with complex circumstances and, particularly, a complete commitment to the service of the Lord Jesus. He gave himself to the work, in all its parts, at once. As a result a new vigour entered the societies and the congregations; the Sunday Schools revived throughout the region, and new schools were planted in corners where they had been absent. In time, the school branches became religious causes. He would nurture them as a tender mother when they were weak, and they received every encouragement from him when they desired chapels. In this way he took possession of the land for Methodism and for Christianity. We truly do not believe that there is one part of Wales that is as thoroughly Methodist as the northern half of Cardiganshire. In the year in which he moved to Tregaron he was appointed secretary of the Monthly Meeting of the county and fulfilled this office up to the day of his death.

He was not long in his new home before he attacked the immorality of the region. One of the most fruitful forms of corruption was the wedding reception. The whole neighbourhood would gather at these weddings; strong drink would be sold, with the profits being given to the married couple. Those who drank most would, of course, be considered the best of their friends. Not only was the custom illegal, it also led to disgraceful immorality. The people would give themselves wholly to drunkenness, wantonness and lewdness, and very often savage fighting would result. As all of this was long established tradition, religious people would attend these receptions and though they did not take part in the drunkenness, debauchery and fighting, their very presence gave support to the custom. The Monthly Meeting was deeply concerned by this behaviour and it made many attempts to put a stop to the practice, at least amongst the Methodist membership. But so deeply-rooted had the tradition become in the region that every effort proved unsuccessful.

At last, on seeing this abomination of desolation daring to stand in the holy places and even receiving public support from some officers, fire was kindled in Mr Richard's soul and he resolved to lift up his voice for the Lord against such sin. He took the first opportunity afforded him in a church meeting at Tregaron. He stood up bravely, asking who it was who was on the Lord's side, and though only one elder supported him he proceeded, with the latter's help, to cleanse the house. Twelve members were found guilty and were all expelled in that same meeting. The next day his engagement was at Llangeitho and he proceeded there strong in faith, and with his soul burning in zeal within him for the glory of the Master. Two weddings, of the type described above, had occurred recently, and the church had acquiesced silently amidst such immorality, but he launched a formidable attack against the iniquity and the result was the excommunication of all members that had taken part in the irregularities. From now on all members of the Methodists were forbidden to attend such weddings, on pain of excommunication. Gradually, mainly through this condemnation by the Methodists, the practice withered and eventually disappeared. This stance taken by Mr Richard when only a young man of thirty years of age was proof of his unusual courage of heart and his zeal for the purity of God's people.

We have already given the history of the controversy over Ordination and the agitation it caused. As we noted, the main proponent in the south for ordination was the Rev. Ebenezer Morris, but Mr Richard and Mr Charles, Carmarthen, though they did not take such a public part in the affair, did much to ripen the opinions in the country towards such a step. Mr Richard, in private conversations particularly, would argue strongly on behalf of this development and the strength of his arguments convinced many. A proof of his brethren's respect for him was that once judgment had been sent forth to victory, he was among the first to be separated out to administer the sacraments, though he was the youngest of them all, not yet having reached thirty years of age. It seems that the Ordination Service at Llandeilo was notable for its great dignity and solemnity. One who was present wrote to Mr Richard's sons as follows:

> With respect to the first Ordination, though I was present, I have forgotten most of what occurred. But I remember three things perfectly: Firstly, that that Association was the most terrifying in which I have been present. Every one present was trembling; yes, many of the godliest, most fluent, and strongest in the Scriptures, could hardly answer, such was the sense of God's majesty. Secondly, Mr Charles's gracious manner in asking the questions. His face was handsome and serene; his words were tender and winning. As he began to question each one, he used the same words, namely, 'A.B., would you be so kind as to speak a word of your view on the being of God, etc.' Thirdly, on seeing many tremble and almost fail, I remember well that I was afraid for your father in case he broke down, as he was so much younger than the others. But he was given his favourite subject – the Deity of Christ – and when I heard that, all my burden fell away for I knew that this topic was dear to him and was as his A.B.C. to him. He expressed his mind upon it clearly, firmly, and to general satisfaction, and all my fears were unfounded.

His separation to administer the ordinances greatly increased Mr Richard's labours. It fell to him, or to Mr Williams, Lledrod, to serve all the churches of the northern part of the county. Often there was such unction upon his own spirit and such divine illumination upon the truths declared as he administered in the Communion that even the most prejudiced against the new dispensation became reconciled to it. In 1815, the first year for which we have his account, Mr Richard preached 343 times, administered the Lord's Supper 75 times, and baptized 21 children. This number of children appears small on first sight, in comparison with the number of the Communion services, but we must remember that the Methodists were much slower in separating from the priestly yoke as far as baptism was concerned than was the case with the ordinance of the Lord's Supper. For some reason – a reason of which we can give no account

– Methodists who were zealous in all other things would take their babies to clergymen to be baptized. And it has to be added, the clergymen would watch jealously over who it was who took their children to the chapels to be baptized by the minister, and would then take their revenge upon them by harming their business, or driving them from their farms, if this was within their power. Because he asked Mr Richard to baptize his baby, Mr David Jones, Dolaubach, a wise elder, respected throughout the county, was driven from his cottage. But the people's prejudices gradually disappeared and the persecution failed in its purpose, for we find that, six years later, that is in 1821, Mr Richard baptized 58 children, even though the number of Methodist ministers had greatly increased.

As described already, a great effort was made after the Ordination to persuade the most eminent of the Methodist ministers to receive Episcopal ordination. Mr Richard was amongst those approached. John Jones, Esq., Derry Ormond, who was related to his wife and had taken much interest in him, sent for him. Having arrived at the mansion and received every welcome, the nobleman told him that he, together with Mr Evans, the vicar of Llanbadarn Fawr, had decided to offer him a living in the Established Church. Such a post would ensure for him a much more comfortable life, and a position of much more status than he could hope for amongst the Methodists. Mr Jones also told him that he (Mr Jones) had given his word that he would persuade him to accept. Mr Richard answered at once, 'The thing is impossible, sir.' The nobleman was greatly surprised and asked him why. He answered:

> Firstly, for me to agree to your offer would go against my conscience, for I have separated from the Established Church on principle. Secondly, I judge that I might be more useful in the Lord's work where I am. And lastly, there is so much love and union between us as Methodist brethren that to tear myself from them would be too painful to my feelings.

Mr John Jones could not refute these reasons but he said, with some displeasure, that he considered him very foolish as far as his own good was concerned that he should refuse such an offer. Mr Richard continued a Nonconformist from principle throughout his life. Once, in a society meeting, reference was made to a preacher who had left his brethren and had joined the Established Church. Someone present said, 'As far as I'm concerned I cannot blame him, because he will have a much easier life, and the same opportunity to preach the gospel.' Mr Richard was immediately aroused and said with some severity, 'Oh no, if we do not have some degree of principle in these things we are worthless.' Another time, during his last visit to London, when he and Mrs Richard were passing through

Smithfield, he said, 'This is the place, Mary *fach*, where many believers of old were martyred.' 'Yes,' said a friend who was with them, 'but it is an easy time for us.' 'Yes,' replied Mr Richard, 'it is no doubt better, but there is still plenty of persecution. What do men mean by a Toleration Act? They still only tolerate us. Oh, fie! fie! Tolerating men to worship God according to their consciences.'

In the spring of 1811, the year of the Ordination, a strong religious revival broke out in Tregaron and the neighbouring churches, which subsequently spread as a flame throughout Wales. It may be that this was the most powerful visitation since the days of Daniel Rowland, and the country considered it as a sign of God's approval of the step taken by the Connexion. The thoughtless were overtaken by terror; the hearts of the most presumptuous and ungodly were filled with fear; a crying out for salvation was heard throughout all regions; and the old pilgrims of Zion were seen pulling down their harps from upon the willows and breaking out into singing and praise.

One of the most pre-eminent during this revival was Mr Richard. Unfortunately it is of only one of his powerful services at the time that we have a history. One Sabbath morning he preached at Llangeitho. The chapel was overflowing and as it was large and contained very few seats or benches, the congregation was immense. Mr Richard's text was Luke 16:23, 'And in hell he lift up his eyes.' It was a fearful sermon. An intense solemnity must have possessed the preacher's soul that he should see fit to choose such a text. Truly, it was a fearful place: threatenings and lightnings flashing, the thunderous curses of the law roaring forth against transgressors, men fainting with fright, and the ambassador of heaven in the pulpit as if he were declaring judgment in God's name. How the meeting ended we do not know, but surely the preacher opened wide a door of hope and directed the minds of the people towards Christ, such that the bonds of many were loosed. On one of the following days, Mr Williams, Lledrod, was at Llangeitho holding a society meeting, when thirty people in deep repentance sought a place in God's house. Of these, twenty-eight of them attributed their conviction to Mr Richard's sermon. As he examined the applicants on the means by which they had been brought to an awareness of their condition, and received the identical answer from so many of them, Mr Williams cried out in amazement, 'How could he have shot so many of you with the same discharge?' Indeed, it is said that many scores were added to the churches of the locality, as well as those received at Llangeitho, practically all of them having been convicted during that remarkable Sunday morning sermon.

SECRETARY OF THE SOUTH WALES ASSOCIATION

In 1814 he was appointed Secretary of the South Wales Association. It is said that the appointment was made on the suggestion of Mr Charles of Bala. No better person for the post could have been found. His love of order, the practical tendency of his mind, the early education that he had received, together with his acquaintance with all the attributes and workings of the Connexion, qualified him uniquely for the work. The Secretary, if he is an able man, is the life of every society, and from that time until the day of his death, Mr Richard was the main authority in the Association of the south. After the death of the Rev. Ebenezer Morris and with the long illness of Mr Charles, Carmarthen, it could almost be said that all the government of the Association lay upon the shoulders of Mr Richard and his able brother, Mr Thomas Richard. His contemporaries believed he was the perfect secretary. The Rev. William Morris, Cilgerran, said of him, in his funeral sermon:

> As the secretary to the Association he was unique. King David had Jehosophat as recorder and Zadok as secretary, but we believe that both of them together could not compare with our Ebenezer. Matters that were irregularly or badly debated, he would set out in order, and when he read out the minutes in the next Association all would feel that they had been sufficiently rewarded already for all the troubles of the journey to the Association. I hope that his words will be kept and entrusted to the press, so that their fragrance may diffuse throughout all the borders of the Welsh language.

His memoir states that about the year 1814 he consecrated much of his time and energy in calling the attention of the congregations to those two excellent societies, the Bible Society and the London Missionary Society. In this again we see him following in the footsteps of Mr Charles of Bala. Indeed, we are continually struck by the great similarity between the two men – a similarity of genius, of ability to discern the needs of the people, and of the completeness of commitment to those plans most appropriate for fulfilling the needs. Mr Richard would read the reports of these societies in great detail and familiarize himself with all their activities. He would then take a journey around the churches giving enthusiastic lectures on their behalf, describing the great good they accomplished, stimulating general sympathy towards them and collecting large sums of money for their treasuries. It is to Mr Richard's labours that we must attribute the strong allegiance to the Bible Society that still pertains in the north of Cardiganshire and the great efforts made, when considering the poverty of the region, in collecting on its behalf.

It is strange that Mr Richard did not minister to causes in London until the year 1818. We have no adequate explanation for this. It is hard to believe that he did not receive many pressing invitations before this time from the friends there. Perhaps the weight of his responsibilities and lack of time prevented him from accepting them. However, he found his way clear to visit in the spring of 1818. He kept a detailed journal of his activities during the stay. He was there for two months and as well as ministering to his fellow-countrymen he notes that he was present in twenty-six public meetings and heard twenty-six sermons in English.

In one sense, there is very little to Mr Richard's history. Or rather, his history, from the time of his coming to Tregaron, is the history of the Association in the south. In the first years, Mr Ebenezer Morris and Mr Charles, Carmarthen, had as much influence as himself, and were perhaps more forward in the Association, but even then, because of his great gifts, he was the main organizer. After the death of Mr Morris in 1825, and the removal through illness of Mr Charles in 1828, the leadership was completely in his hands, in unison with his brother, the Rev. Thomas Richard. Dr Owen Thomas states that it was such an effective leadership that no one dared rise up against it, while at the same time it was so tractable and courteous that it never verged on the tyrannical. Dr Lewis Edwards's testimony was identical. He claimed that the rule of the two Richards, as far as he witnessed it, was never foolish or oppressive, but consistently just, with the one exception, perhaps, that they had been heavy-handed in their treatment of Mr Rowlands, Coed-duon, afterwards Dr Rowlands of America, when he became bankrupt through being fooled by a deceiver. All the care of the churches lay upon the shoulders of the Rev. Ebenezer Richard. In his journal we find that in the twenty-two years from 1815 to 1836 he preached 6,859 times, that is about 312 times a year. During this time he travelled 60,000 miles and was present at about 700 public meetings: Monthly Meetings, Associations and Sunday School Festivals. As well as attending all the Associations of the south, which he was obliged to do as Secretary, he was also present at two or three of the northern Associations every year, preaching the gospel of the kingdom as he travelled to and fro. His labours must have been immense. The following is from a letter of his to the Rev. W. Morris, Cefncoedycymer, afterwards Pant-tywyll, where he is apologizing for not answering a letter:

> The one excuse that I have to offer for my discourteous behaviour towards you is that it was completely unintentional and was forced upon me by the oppressive law of necessity, as I was away from home most of the time preaching, and when I return, I am obliged to mend my nets and then sail out to sea again

> with the next tide. This is how I am thrown about from one Sunday to the next. The Sabbath is my hardest day of work, and some of the weekdays also are truly Sabbaths to my weary soul. Sometimes, when meditating, I almost wish I had two souls within the one body, at other times, when preaching, instructing, etc.; I would be glad to have two bodies for the one soul. But, after all, I am but a very unprofitable servant. The Master's work in the great world is not greatly advanced through me. O, the shame. And yet till now he has refrained from deleting my name from the registry, and I have not yet been drummed out of the regiment.

There were two matters at this time in the life of Mr Ebenezer Richard that, over and above his usual labours, gave him much concern and taxed his strength considerably. The first was the production of the *Cyffes Ffydd*, the *Confession of Faith*, of the Connexion, that was drawn up by a committee representing both the north and south Associations, meeting at the house of Mr Robert Davies, Great Darkgate Street, Aberystwyth. Mr Richard and the Rev. Humphrey Gwalchmai were joint secretaries of this committee. The other matter had to do with the Connexion's *Constitutional Deed*. For that *Deed* to become law it required the signatures of the trustees of all the chapels that had been built. The responsibility of collecting these signatures in the south was placed on Mr Richard and he spent most of the end of 1826 and the beginning of the following year at the work.

HIS CHARACTERISTICS AS A MAN AND AS A PREACHER

The portrait drawn of Mr Richard when he was at the height of his powers, that is when a little over forty years of age, provides a good likeness of the external man. He was a tall man, wide in the shoulders and of a large frame. His hair was as black as the raven until it began to grey quite early. He began to put on weight when young, and with this corpulence a heaviness came upon him and an accompanying sleepiness, so that he began to feel old before his time. His appearance within and without the pulpit was princely; not one of his contemporaries, with the exception of Ebenezer Morris, compared with him in terms of presence. Wherever he was, whether on a platform in an Association, in the pulpit, at a conference, or in an ordinary society meeting, it felt as if he filled the place. A moral courtesy and nobility marked him out at all times. He possessed a large heart, full of compassion, yet there was something about him that kept people from being too familiar with him; they would never dare to be presumptuous with him. Even in Tregaron, his home, he kept a distance between himself and others, though he behaved in a kindly and generous way to all. He would never be seen on the street except when on the way to the chapel or to visit the sick, but though he did not mix with people, his shrewdness and discernment were such that he recognized and understood all, not only as to external likeness, but also in terms of character. This was made evident on many specific occasions. In his family he was king. Yet an old long-serving maid declared that she had never seen a frown on his face.

HIS PRE-EMINENCE AS A PREACHER

Mr Richard belonged to the first rank of Welsh preachers. He possessed an excellent voice. Dr Owen Thomas said that his was the most melodious and melting voice that he ever heard. It was a loud, deep voice, not as penetrating as that of John Elias, and not so much like the sound of many waters as the voice of Ebenezer Morris, but it excelled both in its tenderness. The late Rev. David Howells, Swansea, was very similar to him in his manner of delivery and also, to some extent, in his voice; so much so that some of those who heard Mr Richard of old insisted that Mr Howells was imitating him, though, quite certainly, the likeness was only coincidental. Mr Howells's voice did not have the flexibility and tenderness of Mr Richard's, however, nor was his delivery as flowing. Mr Richard's gift was as a river, never would there be any ebb or deficiency about it. And his mastery of the language was such that he was never lost for words, nor even for appropriate words. In his latter years he rarely preached without weeping; great tears would stream from his eyes, but what was strange was that these tears would never hinder his preaching. They rather seemed to act as oil on his organs of speech, enabling him to speak all the more freely.

He was a diligent and constant student all his life. As was the case with many of the old preachers, he no doubt read and meditated much while on horseback. When at home, he would remain in his study from morning until night, never leaving it except for meals or for attending the means of grace. The working hours of Cardiganshire craftsmen at that time were unreasonably long, but the mother of Mr Daniel Davies, Ton, used to tell her son that no cobbler, carpenter or blacksmith were earlier or later in his workshop than was Mr Richard in his study. As was the case with Mr Elias, his meditations turned into prayers; he would take the thoughts received from books and meditation to God, spreading and presenting them before the Divine Presence, and pleading for blessing upon them. Often the maid, on entering his room unawares, would find him on his knees and with his chair wet with tears. In this way, his mind was full to overflowing with the truths of the gospel and his spirit immersed in its influence. Because of this, and because of the natural readiness of his gifts, he would have an abundance of material at his disposal whatever the subject on which he was called to speak. He was sometimes asked to discourse on specific and unfamiliar subjects completely without warning, but in each case he would deliver an address that seemed to have been particularly prepared for the occasion. But he would never presume to venture into the pulpit without a sermon prepared in detail. He was never tempted to complacency by his natural readiness but laboured hard at reading and thinking throughout his life.

His main characteristics as a preacher were his completeness and tenderness. He possessed an extensive understanding, a strong and lively imagination, a clear perception, and an unusual ability to melt a congregation and to draw them to his bosom. It is said that in his early days he was notably fiery, setting his hearers on fire also. He and his brother travelled much in those years and it was as if whole localities were being shaken by an earthquake when they passed through, so powerful would be their preaching. Often, great rejoicing would break out, and the two preachers would unite in the praising and singing until exhausted. But because of weakness, Mr Richard, Tregaron, had to slow down and change his style in the pulpit. Perhaps also the change in attitude of the times called for this. In his later years he would melt his hearers, and rarely would he fail to transform the hardest heart into a lake of water. According to Dr Owen Thomas: 'Then there would be such a sight: he weeping; the whole congregation weeping; and the whole place being one *"Bochim"* throughout.' Owen Elias, Esq., used to speak of the last time that Mr Richard was at Liverpool, when the older elders of the various churches would follow him from chapel to chapel all day, and our brother would note that two or three of the dear old men, the most feeling of them, would have their handkerchiefs ready beforehand in order to wipe their eyes, knowing that they would have to be used very soon. According to Mr John Elias, Tregof: 'His dear face! We might as well have begun weeping the moment we saw him, rather than wait, because it was inevitable, sooner or later, that we would all have to weep.'

Mr Richard hardly ever had a difficult or hard service, although some of his meetings would be more effective than others. Mr Elias at times would rise to the loftiest heights; he would be as an angel flying in the heavens; another time he would be as if chained to the ground, without as much as a breeze under his wing, but Mr Richard would invariably be effective and overcome his hearers. Often in the Associations, John Elias would be placed at ten in the morning and Ebenezer Richard last, at two; and when the evangelist of Anglesey would have had one of his powerful services, and the people stirred up to the point of madness, Mr Richard would be at an immense disadvantage when rising to speak after him. But his gift was so different and so amazingly melting, that Owen Thomas states that never once did he see him failing to achieve a victory over his congregation.

Dr Thomas gives the following history of the first time that he had the honour of hearing him, namely, at the Amlwch Association of 22–23 June, 1824:

> I was present at that Association, having gone there in my mother's care, and I hope I shall be excused for including some of my memories of her. The great attraction of the Association for my mother was that Mr Ebenezer Richard was expected, and I had heard her speak so much of him that I was also very eager to see and hear him. We had heard that he was engaged at Llannerch-y-medd on the Monday night before the Association, and so my mother decided to hear him there on the way to the Association... By the time we reached the chapel at Llannerch-y-medd the service had begun and someone was preaching freely and with some fire. We were ushered into some seats in front of the pulpit, but at once I was thrown into some tribulation. My mother had left me with the impression that Mr Richard was an unusually effective preacher, that he had a notably tender voice, and that he was a very fat man. This man now in the pulpit was a fairly fat man who had a gentle voice, but there was also a thin old man, in rather common clothing, standing close by him in the pulpit. I came to the conclusion that either Mr Richard was not as great a preacher as he was portrayed or that he had not kept his engagement and the thin old man had come in his place. Soon however the preacher said that it was time for him to close and to give way to the servant of the Lord. At that, a very fat man, a pulpit-ful of a man, came into sight, with thinning, black hair, and a very noble bearing. Before he gave out a hymn to sing, the thin old preacher, Mr Griffith Davies, asked the people to draw nearer to the front, away from the doors, and he encouraged those who could to jump into the empty pews in the gallery whose doors had been nailed up, 'because,' as he said, 'the people kept going into them without having paid for them.' The chapel appeared to be quite new. While I was pondering over such strange announcements, and at the sight of many leaping into the pews, Mr Richard gave out the hymn:
>
> Come, O fallen race of Adam, etc. Deuwch, hil syrthiedig Adda, etc.
>
> And the old precentor from Hafod-y-myn led the singing. The singing was warm and feeling, with perhaps too much of it to my mind, such was my desire to hear the preacher. His text was 2 Corinthians 9:15, 'Thanks be unto God for his unspeakable gift.' I do not remember much of the sermon except that he explained that the 'unspeakable gift' mentioned was Jesus Christ, the greatest gift ever given by God, and the reason for every other gift; and that he also spoke a great deal on the reasons why we should thank God for him.

> But I remember clearly how effectively he spoke. The preacher was weeping, the congregation was weeping, and the whole place being one *"Bochim"* throughout. Long before the end of the sermon, I was of exactly the same opinion as my dear mother with respect to the preacher, and he never lost his influence over me. All the tiredness of the walk from Holyhead disappeared while listening to him; and I looked forward with excitement to the feast that awaited us at Amlwch, when we would hear him again, together with all the other famous men expected there.

Dr Thomas was to hear Mr Richard at Amlwch, but he has not left a report of that service.

Many of Mr Richard's sermons were printed; there are three in the second volume of the *Cofadail Fethodistaidd* [*Methodists' Memorial*], of which two are written out almost fully. They clearly bear the mark of a master craftsman. They are full of attractive, discerning comments and overflowing with gospel. They suggest that Mr Richard's mind did not tend so much towards the doctrinal, though he was not in any way incapable of treating topics, but that his favourite work was to compel sinners to come to Christ and to show the sufficiency of Christ on their behalf. We might add that he was as popular in Tregaron and the neighbourhood as he was in the country generally. His people at home would not have it that any other man in Wales could compete with him, apart from John Elias and Ebenezer Morris.

MR RICHARD AS A LEADER

Mr Richard possessed all the qualities of leadership in abundance. The keenness of his perception, the practical bent of his mind, his adroitness when dealing with circumstances, his ability in managing men, the readiness of his preaching gifts, and his courage when required – these all qualified him uniquely as a leader. In the south he might not have been so evident, because of his work as Secretary, but behind the scenes he would be pulling all the wires. He knew perfectly who best to appoint so that various duties be fulfilled. At the Gwynedd Association his influence would be more manifest and his leadership more evident. More than once, when Mr Elias had become heated in temper and been misled by the bearers of tales, it would be Mr Richard who would lead the vessel into calmer waters and indirectly administer a gentle rebuke to the great man.

We have already referred to his work of mediation at the Bala Association of 1835 when Mr Elias attacked the Rev. John Jones, Talsarn, suggesting that he was departing from the faith. Matters might have become very disagreeable on that occasion had not Mr Richard stepped into the breach. As Mr Elias sat down, he stood up and said:

> If we are to know God's Spirit with us, and to stay with us, and to work through us and amongst us, nothing is more necessary than that we watch over our own spirits. We may understand what kind of Spirit he is by his fruits. 'The fruit of the Spirit is love, joy, peace, longsuffering, gentleness, goodness, faith, meekness, temperance.' Every strife and agitation is completely contrary to his nature, and greatly disturbs him. The dove is so easily disturbed. Nothing more wearies the Heavenly Dove than 'variance, emulations, strife,' and the feelings that cause them. You will drive him far away from you if anything of that nature comes in amongst you.

Mr Elias clearly felt the force of his words, and on the other hand, the Association felt that Mr Richard's indirect rebuke was sufficient. Peace was restored to the meeting and it continued to its close in an excellent spirit.

Dr Owen Thomas describes also a similar occasion in an Association at Caernarvon. It had been complained that religion was at a low ebb and many of the older brethren were tending to accuse the younger men of being unspiritual and deficient in those virtues that characterized the older preachers. Mr Elias spoke in this way:

> I must testify that the lukewarmness, worldliness, and unspiritual presumption of many believers, and even some preachers, in these days, troubles me greatly, particularly when they are compared with those whom I remember. I often think of those words of Micah, 'Woe is me! For I am as when they have gathered the summer fruits, and the grapegleanings of the vintage: there is no cluster to eat: my soul desired the firstripe fruit.' I long to live with those who are more holy; only a few think of religion and even they are very different from their fathers. Oh! 'the firstripe fruit!' – their deep repentance, their great humility, their strong faith, their fiery love, their holy conversations, their separateness from the world, their consecration to religion. It is impossible to remember them and to compare them with the formal, lukewarm, worldly believers of today, without feeling a deep longing after them. 'My soul desired the firstripe fruit!'

He spoke with deep feeling, and greatly affected the whole meeting. But Mr Richard felt that the pendulum had swung too far in one direction, and when called upon to speak, he said:

> I also am glad to remember the people of old, our dear fathers; and every reference to them touches the sweetest strings of my heart. As I heard just now such excellent words of them, I so longed for them that I could have wept. Oh! their fervent prayers! Oh! their great zeal! Oh! their hard work! Oh! their lively sermons! Oh! their warm, feeling listening! I have a longing for them at this moment. But theirs was not all goodness. The Master had a great deal of work forgiving them. And they did very well on the grounds of forgiveness. Yes, *on the grounds of forgiveness*, let it be remembered. Perhaps also the heavenly

Father tolerated more from them than he would be willing to pass by in us. We have had so many more advantages than they. Consider a small child in his mother's arms; because he does not get his own way, he slaps his mother's face with all the strength of his little arm; and his father laughs as he looks on at him. Had that boy been eighteen years old in doing such a thing he would have been turned out of the door. You have become youths; beware that you do not slap the mother, in case the father is wroth with you!

Dr Thomas added:

We do not ever remember hearing comments that produced such happy effects. They were the very best complement that could have been provided to the previous words, and were received so by the whole fraternity.

But of all Mr Richard's addresses, the most effective without doubt was the one he delivered at the Bala Association of 15–16 June 1836, the last Bala Association that he attended. Because of his freshness of approach his contributions were always eagerly awaited and when he stood up all eyes were upon him. He said:

Well, I suppose that you are probably saying to yourselves, 'Here is the cuckoo again; always singing the same song; one *cuckoo* after another, year after year. But though she might have the same tune, friends, the sound does not signify any evil, it only declares that summer is at hand. And it is to the work of the gospel that I want to invite you this year again. We have an Association to be held on the 6th and 7th of next month, July, in Twrgwyn, Cardiganshire – a consecrated spot, the old home of men of God, but a place where the Methodists have never before held an Association. It will be the first there, and I need appointments from my dear brethren from the north to honour the inauguration. I do not intend to be denied by you on this occasion. You must allow me to be importunate today because I am pleading with you to come to the place of my fathers' sepulchres. You may preach near to the spot where lie the dust of the valiant Dafydd Morris, and the famous Ebenezer Morris, those giants who cried out to the Welsh to awake from their sleep. Other than this, I do not wish to weary you further. I have risen to my feet at this time under the deepest feelings; there is an impression upon my mind that this will be the last time for ever that I will address you here at Bala. I have reached the year of my brothers [a reference to Mr Ebenezer Morris and Mr David Evans, Aberaeron, both of whom died in their fifty-sixth year] and something in me tells me it will be my year also, and before there will be another Association at Bala, I will have departed the field and be lying with my sword under my head.

As he spoke in this way, his large, beautiful eyes were streaming forth shining tears, and the whole fraternity was in tears with him. He failed to obtain a promise from Mr Elias but Mr Henry Rees agreed to his request.

HIS WORK WITH THE SUNDAY SCHOOL

Mr Richard excelled in the work of the Sunday School. To all intents and purposes he is to be considered the father of the Sunday School in south Wales. Though some schools may have been started in some places previously, they were feeble and disorganized, but he gave himself to breathe life into them and to bring all their operations under a common organisation. It was he who established the two-monthly meetings in the south. He composed detailed rules for the schools and these were universally adopted and are, to a large extent, still in force today. He laboured in season and out of season with this valuable work; he travelled a great deal to the School Festivals, and his presence at them would ensure a profitable meeting. We do not believe that there ever was in Wales a more able catechizer than he. The following is taken from an article in the June 1888 issue of the *Treasury* by Mr Daniel Davies, Ton:

> Though Mr Richard's influence as a preacher was great, it was no greater than his influence as a catechizer. Of the two, the influence accompanying his catechizing work was the stronger, or at least the more thrilling, than that accompanying his preaching, except for some very remarkable occasions. His labours in this field were the means of the conviction of very many. We had opportunity to know some of those who benefited in this way. One was the late Samuel Rowland, Tymawr near Llanddewi-brefi, a member of the family to which Rowland, Llangeitho, belonged. Mr Richard was catechizing on the topic of the Day of Judgment in a Sunday School Festival and though nearly every question that he asked could be answered with a straight 'yes' or 'no', the examiner had succeeded in portraying the great day so vividly, and to impress it so closely upon the minds of the hearers, that fear and terror had filled the hearts of many present. In the middle of the catechizing, Samuel Rowland gave out an agitated scream, as if someone had stabbed him, which caused some commotion in the congregation and we heard some who were present say that they never forgot the incident. At the time, Samuel Rowland was a strong young man who had begun to get into bad company, but from that day on he was a different man. He lived very many years after this event and his life was always a proof of the reality of the change worked in him in the School Festival.
>
> The most remarkable effects would often occur when Mr Richard catechized from his habit of asking a school to repeat, over and over again, a verse, or part of a verse, contained in the day's topic, or recited by someone in one of their answers. We heard of his once thrilling a congregation merely by reciting the name of the Redeemer. After asking who had been sent to redeem mankind, and the school replying, 'Jesus Christ', he began, in glorious tones, to praise the blessed name. He then invited them to recite the name again and again,

> and they did so, more warmly than the first time. 'Indeed,' he said, 'from listening to you reciting his name, one could conclude that you also loved this name, and that it would be good to hear you say it again.' So he asked them the same question again, and the school again replied, 'Jesus Christ'; and so they continued for some time; he, praising the name, and the school reciting it, until at last the whole congregation broke out in praises.
>
> Sometimes he would take up a verse and comment on it himself, and thereby produce the most sweeping effects. He once enlarged on those words, 'And when they had nothing to pay, he frankly forgave them both.'
>
> 'That is the history of many in this congregation,' he said, '"and when they had nothing to pay, he forgave them," and I believe that the great Forgiver will not be angry with the poor wretch before you for being so bold for once as to confess that such was the case for himself when his case was being discussed in the court above and he felt that prison awaited him; it turned out in the end that: "when he had nothing to pay, he forgave him." '
>
> Even as he began speaking he was under strong emotion, but as he continued, applying the verse to himself and repeating it, he placed his hands over his face and wept loudly, with the whole congregation weeping with him, so that the whole scene could most appropriately be described as a *Bochim* – a place of weeping.

The Rev Thomas Rowlands, Aberdare, once described how he was present at a Schools Festival at Llanddewibrefi in 1832, at the time of the last revival but one. The last three verses from Matthew 11 were included in the topic, 'Come unto me, all ye that labour and are heavy laden', etc. Mr Richard asked, 'Who is it who is calling?' and the school replied, 'Jesus Christ.' He then asked, 'Who is he calling? How many are there of them?' He then stood amazed that such a one was calling such people, and calling every one of them, and he asked again, 'What is he going to do with them?' The answers to all these questions were the relevant parts of the verses. When in response to the last questions and others that arose from it, they recited and re-recited the words, 'and I will give you rest,' the effects were extraordinary. And on reciting the following verse, 'And ye shall find rest unto your soul,' William Evans, Llanio Isaf, gave out a shout, 'Thanks be to God!' At that, general thanksgiving broke out throughout the congregation, so that it was impossible to proceed with the catechizing. With such scenes the Festival came to its close.

Often when he questioned a school he would hold on to one word or phrase of a verse, drawing the attention of all to it. The Rev. John Evans, Abermeurig, described Mr Richard catechizing Maesyffynnon school in a festival at Abermeurig. The subject here again was the judgment, the significant verse was, 'For we must all appear before the judgment seat of

Christ', and the words on to which he latched were 'we . . . all'. He asked, 'Who must appear?' 'We all.' 'Who?' 'We all.' 'Say it again.' 'We all.' 'Must all from Maesyffynnon School appear in judgment?' 'We must all.' The questioning and answering was strengthening and becoming warmer as the examining proceeded. After staying with the school for some time, he turned to the crowd. 'You vast congregation, you have all heard that all of Maesyffynnon's small school must appear before the judgment seat. Is this true of you?' The congregation replied, 'We must all.' After some further comment, he asked, 'And must you appear?' 'We must all.' 'Will everyone be willing to appear?' 'No, they will not.' 'Must they appear, who don't wish to?' 'We must all.' 'Will some be willing to appear?' 'Yes.' 'Who will they be?' Some answered, 'The saints,' and others, 'The godly.' But one person shouted from the middle of the crowd, 'They will be the friends of the Judge!' This answer passed as a thrill through the crowd; it was useless to question further. Some were shouting of 'boldness in the day of judgment'; some sang:

Before the bar we all must stand, etc.	O flaen y fainc rhaid sefyll, etc.;

while others rejoiced, 'Behold the God in whom we have hoped.' And thus the festival ended in the sound of singing and praising.

Mr Richard always encouraged the weak and less able as he catechized; he would receive irrelevant answers and turn them into acceptable answers. He and the remarkable Theophilus Jones, Tregaron, were once at a Schools Festival at Talley, Carmarthenshire. Theo Jones, as he was called, examined Cwmdu School on God, and asked for a clearer verse to prove his existence. At last a young boy stood up, reciting the verse, 'There was a man of the Pharisees, named Nicodemus.' The old preacher became agitated, saying, 'What kind of verse is that to prove the existence of God? Cwmdu School, that was a pitiful answer.' Mr Richard followed him in order to question another school, and he said, 'I am always happiest when in a School Festival, and I never felt happier than today. You are answering excellently. It would have been impossible to give a better answer than the one given by that little man to prove the point: 'There was a man.' What can more clearly prove that God is, than that man is? Well done, my boy, for giving us such a pertinent answer.' All smiled, while behind him Theo Jones groaned heavily, saying, 'Oh dear me! Oh dear me!'

He had a deep love for children. When travelling once to a Monthly Meeting at Llan-non, in the company of Mr David Jones, Dolaubach, he saw many of the children of Bethania Chapel playing on the road. He turned to them immediately and began to question them, and the children answered him with much delight. 'You have had a children's meeting, Mr

Richard,' said Mr Jones. 'Oh,' he answered, 'we must do what we can, in season and out of season.' He was very fond of Bethania. He was there to celebrate the Sunday Schools Jubilee Year in 1831 – a meeting long remembered by the older people. He was in the same place, soliciting promises for support for a second chapel, when he said, 'When men go to wash sheep, they usually throw the strongest lamb into the lake first, so that he might lead the others. I had better do the same thing, so I will ask for your name, John Davies, [a wealthy elder] first.'

MR RICHARD AS A CORRESPONDENT

Mr Richard was an excellent letter-writer. We have already mentioned his letter to a nobleman on behalf of the Llanddewibrefi church when they had been thrown out of their chapel at the time of the Ordination, asking him for a plot of land on which to build a new chapel. The letter came into the man's hands while he was at a rent-day dinner and it affected him so much that it brought tears to his eyes, though he was far from being a religious man. He turned to a number of clergymen with whom he was dining, and half-shouted at them, 'Why can't you write like this, you devils?'

Many of Mr Richard's letters are to be found in his *Life*. We would like to include them all here, but we must be satisfied with one only. It was sent to the Gwynedd Association at the request of the Cardiganshire Monthly Meeting, shortly after the deaths of the Revs. Ebenezer Morris and David Evans. It reads as follows:

> My dear and beloved Brethren,
>
> At the request of the Cardiganshire Monthly Meeting I direct these few lines to you, gathered as you are at your Quarterly Association, and to be received by you at the hands of our kind brother and faithful missionary, Mr John Morgans. He is a missionary in mourning, and represents a whole county of brethren in mourning. I do not have to tell you why we mourn. Long before now you have heard the sad news of the breach upon breach that our Heavenly Father has seen fit to make upon our ranks here; greater breaches than we have known since becoming a Body. To lose two such laborious, busy, useful and successful men within less than a week! Oh, who shall restore such a loss! To lose them in the midst of their labours, at mid-day, and to lose the latter before we had any fear of losing him, before any expectation of a turn, before imagining that any such thing was possible!
>
> They were our two wings by which we flew; our two staves upon which we leant; they were our two breasts upon which we suckled; our two eyes by which we saw; and our two arms by which we worked. But today, here we are without them. Without them, not for two months while they are in London, not for a month while in the north, and not for weeks in Bristol or some other

corner of the field, but without them forever on earth! Without their cheerful presence to comfort us, without their powerful sermons to enliven us, without their wise counsels to instruct us, and without their kindly rule to organize us. They were leaders amongst us after our own hearts, they were above all, careful for all, fatherly to all, without oppressing any, or paining any, or domineering any at any time. I must throw this pen from my hand; the tears darken my eyes, and their memory tears up my soul.

I can hardly stop asking you whether they are with you in Pwllheli? Is not my brother Roberts naming them as appointed to preach in the public meetings? Alas! Alas! Alas! I hear the answers of a hundred of you piercing my heart as spears: 'They are not, they are not. They were here in our bosom, they were here in the right hand of their Lord, they were here under a crown of unction, they were here often, and they were here lately – lately!' How lately? They were at your last Annual Association in Caernarvon; they came to you together and they there bade farewell to the churches of north Wales, as if they were wishing to indicate beforehand that they would lay down their arms together. O, how they glory today, having cast aside their weapons, ceased from their battles, finished their journeys, and thrown down the last of their burdens. They sing some heavenly hymns upon their harps and amongst the saints, where there are many mansions, all of them comfortable, peaceful and eternal.

My brethren, remember us, to pray for us; and if you should wish for opportunity to show love, sympathy, charity, and generosity towards us, turn towards poor Cardiganshire in its present distress . . . Do not let your great love for us, and your great sadness for us, allow you all to remain at home, but come over and help us, and quickly, and in great numbers; and comfort your brother by enriching him with your appointments.

I am, dear brethren, with sincere affection, on behalf of
the Cardiganshire Monthly Meeting,

EBENEZER RICHARD

HIS MISSIONARY SPIRIT

Mr Richard was full of a missionary spirit. There was no one to compare with him in this in the whole of Cardiganshire, nor indeed in the south, and this is why, as we have already mentioned, that the upper half of Cardiganshire is so fully possessed by the Methodists. His plan was to establish branches of the Sunday Schools wherever ten men were found who were too far away from any other branch. He used to say that this was the rule with respect to the Jewish synagogues wherever ten men could be found who would be consistently present. In every place within the circle of his influence he would require a large chapel, more than adequate for the congregation. This is what was done in Tregaron, though some were very unwilling for such a large building. He said that chapels ought to be as big as salvation, declaring in their own language, 'Yet there is room.'

HIS LAST ILLNESS AND DEATH

We cannot follow further the history of this servant of Jesus Christ. He was troubled in his last years by a heavy lethargy, causing unnatural sleep that he could hardly be awakened from. He suffered a serious attack of it in 1832, and again at the end of 1835. On these occasions he was bled profusely according to the custom in those days, but though the lancet benefited him for a while it no doubt harmed his constitution. About the end of 1836 he felt well and attended the Dolgellau Association in September and the Crickhowell Association in Breconshire on 25–26 October. But he was not so well at the beginning of the following year. In March he visited the churches of the lower half of Cardiganshire according to the appointment of the Monthly Meeting. But in the neighbourhood of Twrgwyn he felt himself weakening; he and his companion judged that it would not be wise for him to continue further and they returned to Tregaron. He was very weak but his mind was at perfect peace. He went to his bed and seemed to sleep easily and naturally. About six in the morning they had considerable difficulty in awakening him and giving him his medicine. He fell again into a heavy sleep. About two hours later, when he was again approached, it was found that he had greatly deteriorated and a change had come over him. Within about a quarter of an hour his spirit flew away to the land of eternal health. This was on Thursday morning, 9 March 1837, when he was a little over fifty-five years old. The following Tuesday his body was firstly taken to the chapel where the Rev. John Jones, Lampeter, preached from 2 Samuel 3:38, and Evan Evans, Aberffrwd, from 2 Timothy 1:10. Then, amidst a degree of grief that is not often seen, he was laid to rest in Tregaron cemetery. The following is carved on his gravestone:

THE REV. EBENEZER RICHARD

Who died 9th March 1837, aged 55 years.

This stone was raised by his family and friends, not to enumerate the virtues of the deceased, nor to announce their grief at his loss, for, 'The heart knoweth his own bitterness; and a stranger doth not intermeddle with his joy' (*Prov.* 14:10) but as a sign of their acknowledgement of God's grace in his faithful servant, whose praise is in all the churches. He was endowed abundantly with all the choice gifts that make beautiful a man, a Christian, and a minister of the Gospel.

His physical constitution was strong, and his appearance noble; and all the external ornaments of the man were a true portrayal of the princely excellences of the man within.

The wisdom and strength of his mind, the fortitude and correctness of his judgment, the liveliness of his imagination, the propriety of his emotions, together with the depth of his spiritual anointing, perfected him for the work of ministry, and gained for him a good degree in the church of God.

His talents were many, but his text was one: 'Christ Jesus and him crucified.' To exalt him, he faithfully consecrated all the powers of his mind throughout his life. The hearts of his many listeners would skip on hearing him speak of him, and his doctrine would drop upon them as the rain.

He was wise and zealous, like Paul, in planting; gentle and as the dew, like Apollos, in watering. To the sleepy and thoughtless conscience he was a 'son of thunder', and to the distressed soul he was a 'son of consolation'.

Amidst the youth of the Sabbath schools and the elders of the churches in the great Assembly, he reigned as a king amongst his host; his instructions were received as law and were respected as the wisdom of an oracle; 'unto him they gave ear, and waited, and kept silence at his counsel. After his words they spake not again; and his speech dropped upon them; they waited for him as for the rain.'

He rose up in place of his fathers (with the Calvinistic Methodists) to perfect their work, and to direct all that was wanting in the churches that they planted: and having finished his work he slept with them in the Lord, and was gathered to his people.

Also MARY RICHARD, dear wife of the aforementioned Rev. Ebenezer Richard, who died 14th February, 1865, aged 74.

John
Elias
ANGLESEY
Lla
Clynno
John
Eva
Robert
Jones
Gogledd Cymru
AGRh